ENGLISH WIZARD

(Descriptive & Objective)

For Competitive Examinations

ABOUT THE AUTHOR

A P Bhardwaj is a well known author and ELT expert based in Chandigarh. He has authored popular books on English, GK & CLAT with nationally and internationally recognised publishers. He is popular in Tricity as CLAT GURU & ENGLISH MASTER.

ENGLISH WIZARD

(Descriptive & Objective)

For Competitive Examinations

A P Bhardwaj

Title : English Wizard (Descriptive & Objective)

Language : English

Author's Name : A.P. Bhardwaj

Typeset Published by:

Career Launcher Infrastructure (P) Ltd.

A-45, Mohan Cooperative Industrial Area, Near Mohan Estate Metro Station, New Delhi - 110044

Marketed by :

G.K. Publications (P) Ltd.

Plot No. 9A, Sector-27A, Mathura Road, Faridabad, Haryana-121003

ISBN : 978-93-91061-04-3

Printer's Details : Made in India, New Delhi.

Dedicated
to
My Guruji

Master (Retd) Sh Megh Raj Sharma Ji

Govt Sr. Sec. school, Samrala (Ldh), Pb

A Teacher In A True Sense, A Man Of Word, A Humble, Simple & Profound Human Being, Absolutely Devoid Of Duality In Theory & Practice. May He Live Long!

ACKNOWLEDGEMENTS

At the outset, I must acknowledge the faith reposed by GKP-Career Launcher Infrastructure (P) Ltd that prompted me to translate my ideas and understanding of English into a high quality book titled ENGLISH WIZARD.

The monitoring of the project by Vinodji and working of Prakash Kannath are highly praise worthy.

From the conception of the idea of this book till it got converted into the concrete shape of an actual book, it could not have been possible without invaluable support of Sh R.C Tulli (XEN, RETD, PGI) . I owe him a lot for his inputs and multiple readings of my whole manuscript whole-heartedly.

None of my projects can be complete without steadfast support of my wife Upasana.

My daughter Anaadi who has always been my motivation is now matured enough at the age of 11 to provide me technical assistance in running and managing my laptop and desktop and saving my files and helping me search my files.

The blessings of near and dear ones always play a great role.

PREFACE

It is indeed a matter of immense pleasure to bring out my book, **'ENGLISH WIZARD' – DESCRIPTIVE & OBJECTIVE,'** for competitive examinations. The book is an outcome of my 20 years teaching and first hand experience of the problems faced by students regarding tests of English language. The material given in the book is tried, tested and trusted by thousands of students. So the quality, credibility and indispensability of the book go without saying.

As the title suggests, the book gives intensive and extensive coverage of textual content and practice questions. Clarity, conciseness, compactness, coherence and comprehensiveness have been the weaving threads running throughout the book. **The book is broadly divided into five parts:**

A – Vocabulary Building Booster

B – Elements of Grammar and Their Usage

C – Common Errors

D – Comprehension

E - Assess Your Actual Level

PART A: It starts with introducing students with 2500 essential words, their meanings and usage. It gradually unfolds the other variants of vocabulary building. Every chapter is followed by ample MCQs and practice exercises.

PART B: ELEMENTS OF GRAMMAR & ITS USAGE introduces students with the basics of grammar and enable them to check and enhance overall understanding of concepts.

PART C: COMMON ERRORS. Identifying common errors in a given set of sentences or a passage is one of the most important items in almost all the competitive examinations. However, it is a ticklish and taxing task indeed, and it requires a comprehensive knowledge of English language.

To enable the students to identify common errors, concepts of grammar and basic vocabulary have been outlined and explained extensively in Part A and Part B of the book. Having mastered Part A and Part B, students will find themselves in a comfortable position, while attempting the questions related to common errors.

In the chapter on COMMON ERRORS, earnest efforts have been made to provide sufficient sentences, where errors are most frequently and repetitively committed. The prominent areas, wherein errors are predominantly committed, have been identified and segregated under the topics as errors in the prepositions, nouns, pronouns, verbs, adverbs, adjectives etc. Having gone through the chapter on COMMON ERRORS, the students will be able to notice errors in the given sentences or passages quite easily and comfortably. After going through PARTS A, B & C, **PART D COMPREHENSION** will be an easy task.

PART E: 'ASSESS YOUR ACTUAL LEVEL & PROFICIENCY OF ENGLISH USAGE' has been framed with multiple purposes of assessing the level of understanding of words, their meanings, usage and proficiency in English language. The different chapters with different titles have been designed to check the mastery over usage from various angles. The tests of synonyms, antonyms, cloze tests, sentence completion, sentence sequencing or reordering of jumbled sentences and completing the paragraphs with appropriate words, are some of the prominent topics adapted herein under different chapters.

PART A of the book provides MCQs to check the retention of words and their variants. PART B, C & D of the book are prepared with a view to build a strong foundation in grammar, common errors and comprehension and check the same through various practice exercises. PART E, being the final part of the book, has been designed to check and enhance an overall and in depth understanding of the students. As the title suggests; **'English Wizard' – 'Descriptive & Objective,'** the book seeks to be a facilitator.

Sincere efforts have been made to make it a perfect **TWO-IN-ONE**, providing extensive and intensive coverage of the subject matter along with thousands of questions for practice. The breadth and depth of coverage, clarity and simplicity of usage, multiplicity and variety of practice exercises are some of the most prominent features of this book. The book has been made a concise, compact, complete, and comprehensive manual to act as a wizard for the students. Hence titled **ENGLISH WIZARD!**

This book ENGLISH WIZARD will be highly useful for:

- Banking , Insurance , Railways , Police, Defence and Postal Services Examinations
- SSC-CHSL-CGL, SSB , CTET and NTPC EXAMINATIONS
- States Subordinate and Allied Services Examinations
- States (Executive & Judicial) Services Examinations
- IIPM, Hotel Management & Law Entrances Examinations

Hope the students will like it and get benefited.

Constructive suggestions are welcome

A P Bhardwaj
Chandigarh
April, 2021

CONTENTS

PART – A : VOCABULARY BUILDING BOOSTER

PART – B : ELEMENTS OF GRAMMAR AND THEIR USAGE

PART C : COMMON ERRORS

PART D : COMPREHENSION

PART – E : ASSESS YOUR ACTUAL LEVEL & PROFICIENCY OF ENGLISH LANGUAGE

PART – A

VOCABULARY BUILDING BOOSTER

VOCABULARY BUILDING BOOSTER (VBB)

AN INTRODUCTION

The test of vocabulary is a very important and crucial segment in the English language papers in almost all competitive examinations. It can be very scoring as well as very damaging at the same time. **It requires a lot of effort, perseverance and finesse for scoring well in the vocabulary section.** Vocabulary building is not an easy, overnight task. Rather it is a long, tedious and rigorous process which one has to undergo. Reading, reading and reading is the only way out. But the first and foremost requirement is to know *what to read* and from *where to read.* **Exposure to high quality** words in good numbers from a good, reliable and authentic resource material is the first stepping stone towards a good vocabulary building.

PART A: VOCABULARY BUILDING BOOSTER (VBB) of this book is an outcome of my 20 years class tested teaching skills. **The quality of** the compiled material tried, tested and trusted by hundreds of students every year is a testimony to its authenticity and indispensability.

This **VBB** is a compilation of basic words, their ample variables and various other forms of words. This part of the book starts with an introduction of 2500 basic words which are basic and intrinsic to acquire the basic vocabulary. It gradually switches over to the variables of words provided in separate chapters under different headings. All the chapters are followed by either practice tests or MCQs in profuse numbers so as to enable the students to check their level of understanding and richness of their word bank.

The meanings, usage, examples and illustrations throughout this part have been framed to make the things clear, informative and interesting. Easy to understand approach, crystal clear presentation and strictly avoiding superficiality and superfluity, and eclectic choice and selection of words are the cornerstones of this part of the book.

The salient features put together will make the tedious task of vocabulary building easy and interesting. Having mastered this section of the book, the students will be enthused with a renewed confidence and develop a special proclivity and knack for vocabulary building. Attempting and solving vocabulary related questions will be a **cakewalk** after mastering the ***Part A*** of this book.

(2500) ESSENTIAL WORDS WITH MEANINGS & THEIR USAGE

To have a good command on any language, one needs to have a strong diction i.e. selection, retention and usage of specific, appropriate and context based words. It requires a **constant imbibing of high quality** words in good numbers with specific meanings and meaningful usage. Hence, the need and necessity of a **proficient** vocabulary is an obvious and imperative requirement. **Constant exposure to high quality words and their variables** through reading and re-reading is the only way out to **attain** and retain a **high** level of vocabulary and comprehension.

This Chapter **(Chapter 1)** will introduce students with 2500 basic words which are essential **and used frequently**. Without knowledge of these basic words, one just cannot be a good reader. Furthermore, without being a good reader, in the present era of cut throat competition, one just cannot imagine qualifying any English Language test in any competitive examination.

These 2500 basic words would provide a sound base to the students, introducing them to the realm of words and providing them **with the** stepping stones to lay a strong foundation for a rich vocabulary building. These words would enable the students to clear their basics and would help them to read, understand and retain them clearly and exactly and empower them to be better readers. The words in this chapter **have been carefully selected** and explained with clear cut meanings and the meaningful usage so as to clear the doubts, remove the fears and distill the worries of the students. **It will** enthuse the students with renewed confidence so as to enhance their reading skills and consequently **their level of** comprehension.

Almost all the competitive examinations have an English Language component which is meant to test the students' basic understanding of English language and comprehension which is just not possible without a knowledge and understanding of these basic words.

Having gone through these 2500 words, the students will find themselves as better readers and in a new mould and shape. Their reading skills will be sharpened and their vocabulary will stand enriched. In order to enable them to check their level of retention and understanding of words, practice exercises have been provided in the next chapter.

The study of these two chapters **(Chapter 1 and Chapter 2)** will not only be a word booster but a confidence booster too. Once the students go through these two chapters thoroughly, they will be able to switch over to **Chapter 3** containing 20,000 variables of these words as synonyms and antonyms. The 2500 words and their 20,000 variables have been selected and finalized after thorough examination of questions related to vocabulary in the various previous years' examinations. The students will be able to feel and understand the suitability and indispensability of these 2500 words and their 20,000 variables. It will be no less than a treasure trove to be cherished to hit the target with a bull's eye.

The students will find themselves fully equipped to understand and attempt any question related to vocabulary in any form e.g., to find contextual meaning, to match suitable synonyms and antonyms, to fix the correct usage, to do fill in the blanks with suitable words in a given paragraph, and to solve cloze tests etc.

So, all in all, Chapter 1 will be a great booster and would provide a good kick start to pick up the momentum and keep the tempo of English Language preparation for any competitive examination.

A	
1.	**Abandon (V)** desert; forsake Fair weather friends may often abandon us in adversity.
2.	**Abandonment (N)**
3.	**Abase (V)** lower oneself Do not abase yourself in others' eyes.
4.	**Abasement (N)**
5.	**Abduct (V)** take or lead a person by force They abducted the rich merchant and demanded a huge ransom.
6.	**Abduction (N)**
7.	**Abhor (V)** hate; hold in contempt I abhor this type of insulting behaviour.
8.	**Abhorrence (N)**
9.	**Abide by (V)** to accept; obey a decision One must abide by the rules of government.
10.	**Abiding (Adj.)**
11.	**Abject (Adj.)** unhappy; miserable; ashamed The painter died in abject poverty.
12.	**Abjectness (N)**
13.	**Abjure (V)** give up on oath; renounce Ashoka abjured violence after the battle of Kalinga and proclaimed Dharma.
14.	**Abjuration (N)**
15.	**Abominable (Adj.)** disgusting; contemptible Rape is an abominable and heinous crime.
16.	**Abominate (V)**
17.	**Abomination (N)**
18.	**Abortive (Adj.)** unsuccessful; unavailing The assassin made an abortive attempt to kill the minister.
19.	**Abrasive (Adj.)** impolite; coarse He is notorious for his abrasive behaviour.
20.	**Abrasiveness (N)**
21.	**Abreast (Adj.)** side by side; alongside A teacher must keep himself abreast of the latest updates about his subjects.
22.	**Abridged (Adj.)** short; brief Abridged edition of Oxford dictionary is a remarkable piece of work.
23.	**Abridgement (N)**
24.	**Abridge (V)**
25.	**Abrogate (V)** repeal; delete Certain obsolete laws need to be abrogated.
26.	**Abrogation (N)**
27.	**Abrupt (Adj.)** sudden; unexpected It rained and the match came to an abrupt end.
28.	**Abscond (V)** free from law; be at large The offender absconded after committing the offence.
29.	**Absolve (V)** free from blame; acquit He was absolved from the murder charge.
30.	**Absolution (N)**
31.	**Abstinence (N)** keeping away Doctors normally advise total abstinence from smoking and alcoholic drinks.
32.	**Abstruse (Adj.)** difficult to understand He writing is so abstruse that it is beyond the comprehension of a common reader.
33.	**Abysmal (Adj.)** complete; total His first attempts were an abysmal failure.
34.	**Acclaim (V)** applaud; welcome Arundhati Roy enjoys global acclaim.
35.	**Accolade (N)** praise; applause Sushil won accolades for winning the Olympic silver medal in wrestling.
36.	**Accomplice (N)** companion in wrongdoing He did not commit the crime but was certainly an accomplice.
37.	**Accord (N)** agreement India and Pakistan signed an accord.
38.	**Accost (V)** go up and speak He was accosted by a stranger in the street.
39.	**Accrue (V)** gather; pile up How much interest has accrued to my account?
40.	**Acme (N)** highest point His work is considered the acme of cinematic art.
41.	**Acumen (N)** sharpness of mind William Shakespeare and Einstein were men of great acumen.
42.	**Adamant (Adj.)** unmoved; unyielding The officer was very adamant on the issue.
43.	**Adroit (Adj.)** skillful; clever It was the adroit way to solve the problem.
44.	**Aegis (N)** under the protection of Under the aegis of Vajpayee government, nuclear tests were conducted.

45.	**Affable (Adj.)** friendly; courteous Anaadi is appreciated by all for her affable nature.
46.	**Affect (V)** influence; pretend Health can affect anyone irrespective of age.
47.	**Affectation (N)** pretense; not genuine He is very notorious among peer group for his affectations and snobbery.
48.	**Affinity (N)** love; affection There is no affinity between the two brothers.
49.	**Affliction (N)** suffering; pain; disease The old and poor have to endure their afflictions.
50.	**Afflict (V)** cause suffering
51.	**Affront (N)** insult; humiliation His speech brought affront to his own party.
52.	**Aggrandizement (N)** an increase in power, importance Politicians seek personal aggrandizement at any cost.
53.	**Aghast (Adj.)** shocked; traumatized Everyone was aghast at his rude behaviour.
54.	**Agility (N)** suppleness; resilience She moved with an agility that surprised him.
55.	**Agnostic (N)** one who says God may or may not be Khushwant Singh was an agnostic.
56.	**Agog (Adj.)** eager; excited The clamping of lockdown left everyone agog.
57.	**Alacrity (N)** promptness; readiness He responded with alacrity to my request for help.
58.	**Albeit (Conj.)** although; even if I give you all I have, albeit, it is not much.
59.	**Alchemy (N)** chemistry; magical power Good company is the best alchemy to transmute us.
60.	**Allay (V)** lessen; mitigate; alleviate The pain killer allayed his pain.
61.	**Alleviate (V)** lessen; mitigate We must help the poor to alleviate their misery.

62.	**Alibi (N)** excuse, plea The judge didn't accept his alibi of not being there at the time of committing the offence.
63.	**Alienate (V)** lose friends Your rudeness will alienate your friends
64.	**Allude (V)** refer to He alluded to a precedent settled by Hon'ble Supreme Court to prove his point.
65.	**Aloof (Adj.)** lost, alone He seemed sad and aloof in their company.
66.	**Altercation (N)** heated argument First they started the altercation and finally they come to blows.
67.	**Alternate (V)** happen by turns Sorrow and happiness alternate in life.
68.	**Amuck (Adv.)** wild The elephant ran amuck and felled many trees.
69.	**Anachronism (N)** being out of time The practice of 'Sati' is an anachronism nowadays.
70.	**Analogy (N)** likeness; parallel state We can draw an analogy between a big oak tree and an old man.
71.	**Anathema (N)** curse I find mathematics an anathema.
72.	**Anguish (N)** mental suffering She expressed her anguish at her unfaithful husband.
73.	**Animate (V)** make lively; make vivid He animated his speech with interesting jokes.
74.	**Anomalous (Adj.)** abnormal Friendship between a cat and a dog is quite anomalous.
75.	**Antecedent (Adj.)** background; prior happening His excellent academic antecedents won him the job.
76.	**Antediluvian (Adj.)** out of date; old fashioned The grandmother with her traditional dress and views seemed antediluvian to the young girls.
77.	**Apogee (N)** highest point; zenith; climax Joe Biden attained the apogee of his political career by becoming President of the US.
78.	**Apostasy (N)** turning away from one's faith Apostasy in the politics is the order of the day.

79. **Appall (V)** shock deeply; dismay greatly
The immoral ways and venal practices of politicians appall the ordinary man.

80. **Apparel (N)** uniform; dress
'For apparel often proclaims the man', said Shakespeare.

81. **Appease (V)** pacify
India's efforts to appease Pakistan was a disaster.

82. **Applaud (V)** give applause; show approval
The whole nation applauded Sushil Kumar for winning the Olympic medal.

83. **Applause (N)** loud approval; clapping
There was great applause when the speaker completed his speech.

84. **Apposite (Adj.)** germane; suitable
Your remarks are quite apposite to the case.

85. **Analogy (N)** likeness; parallel state
We can draw an analogy between a big oak tree and an old man.

86. **Anathema (N)** curse
I find mathematics an anathema.

87. **Anguish (N)** mental suffering
She expressed her anguish at her unfaithful husband.

88. **Animate (V)** make lively; make vivid
He animated his speech with interesting jokes.

89. **Anomalous (Adj.)** abnormal
Friendship between a cat and a dog is quite anomalous.

90. **Antecedent (Adj.)** background; prior happening
His excellent academic antecedents won him the job.

91. **Antediluvian (Adj.)** out of date; old fashioned
The grandmother with her traditional dress and views seemed antediluvian to the young girls.

92. **Apogee (N)** highest point; zenith; climax
Joe Biden attained the apogee of his political career by becoming President of the US.

93. **Apostasy (N)** turning away from one's faith
Apostasy in the politics is the order of the day.

94. **Appall (V)** shock deeply; dismay greatly
The immoral ways and venal practices of politicians appall the ordinary man.

95. **Apparel (N)** uniform; dress
'For apparel often proclaims the man', said Shakespeare.

96. **Appease (V)** pacify
India's efforts to appease Pakistan was a disaster.

97. **Applaud (V)** give applause; show approval
The whole nation applauded Sushil Kumar for winning the Olympic medal.

98. **Applause (N)** loud approval; clapping
There was great applause when the speaker completed his speech.

99. **Apposite (Adj.)** germane; suitable
Your remarks are quite apposite to the case.

100. **Appraise (V)** judge; evaluate
The judge appraised the attorney's arguments and dismissed the case.

101. **Apprehend (V)** arrest; understand
The murderer at large has finally been apprehended.

102. **Apprise (V)** inform; make known
Under Article 78 of Indian Constitution, Prime Minister of India is bound to apprise the President with everything he desires to be apprised of.

103. **Approbation (N)** praise; approval
The principal earned approbation from management for newly launched courses.

104. **Arbitrary (Adj.)** dictatorial; unjust
Saddam Hussein's arbitrary rule earned him world- wide notoriety.

105. **Arcane (Adj.)** secret; mysterious
A few religious conmen pretend to possess arcane power.

106. **Archaic (Adj.)** antiquated; outdated
Many customs, languages and devices are now rendered archaic.

107. **Arid (Adj.)** joyless; dry; lack of rainfall; parched
People earn piles of money and yet lead arid lives.

108.	**Arraign (V)** find fault The enraged wife arraigned her husband for his drinking spree.
109.	**Arrant (Adj.)** in the highest degree (in a bad sense) The teacher could not tolerate the arrant nonsense of spoiled brats.
110.	**Array (V)** arrange information; dress The little girl was arrayed like a queen.
111.	**Arrears (N)** money yet to be paid The government has yet to pay its employees arrears of increased allowances.
112.	**Arrogate (V)** to take powers Wherever political bosses are weak, bureaucrats attempt to arrogate powers.
113.	**Articulate (V)** communicate One must be able to articulate clearly to be successful in legal field.
114.	**Ascendancy (N)** sway; supremacy British ascendency was based on principle of Divide and Rule.
115.	**Asperse (V)** vilify; slander Don't try to asperse others' image for the sake of your ego satisfaction.
116.	**Asphyxia (N)** lack of air He strangulated his wife and she died of asphyxia.
117.	**Assail (V)** attack with words Verbally assailing each other has become order of the day in politics.
118.	**Assent (N)** agreement; approval Chief Minister gave his assent to inaugurate the function.
119.	**Asseverate (V)** aver; emphasize He asseverated that he would speak the truth, only truth, nothing else, but the truth.
120.	**Assiduous (Adj.)** continuous; persevering His assiduous efforts bore fruit.
121.	**Astound (V)** shock; amaze 9/11 attacks on USA astounded the whole world.
122.	**Astute (Adj.)** clever; shrewd; skillful He is too astute to be taken for a ride.
123.	**Asunder (Adv.)** tear apart It is an issue that can tear asunder the unity of the family.

124.	**Atone (V)** make amends; be penitent; seek forgiveness You must atone for misbehaviour with your teacher.
125.	**Atrocious (Adj.)** repugnant; distasteful; wicked The atrocious Act was soon repealed.
126.	**Atrocity (N)** cruelty Saddam Hussein paid with his life for the atrocities committed on his people.
127.	**Atrophy (N)** languish; waste away You must make use of your skills or they will atrophy with passage of time.
128.	**Attenuate (V)** erode; become weak Time is the biggest healer it attenuates all sorrows.
129.	**Attribute (N)** quality; trait; symbol Amitabh Bachchan is known for his unique attributes of acting.
130.	**Attribute (V)** bestow He attributed false motives to me.
131.	**Attrition (N)** rubbing off; wearing away; act of weakening Your bad deeds will lead to attrition of your reputation.
132.	**Attune (V)** harmonize We must learn to attune ourselves to our surroundings.
133.	**Augur (V)** forebide; foretell; indicate Terrorism does not augur well for world peace.
134.	**August (Adj.)** majestic; noble I was really glad to address the august gathering of students.
135.	**Austere (Adj.)** stark; ascetic; simple Mahavira advocated an austere life.
136.	**Avenue (N)** opportunity There are large avenues for employment in the retail sector.
137.	**Aver (V)** asseverate; emphasize He averred that he would follow the strenuous and difficult path of virtue.
138.	**Averse (Adj.)** against; opposite Mr. S.S. Virk was thoroughly averse to corruption.

139.	**Avert (V)** avoid; prevent The driver averted the accident with skill.
140.	**Avid (Adj.)** keen In order to be a good writer, you have to be an avid reader.
141.	**Awe (N)** fear; reverence Even his foes held the great General in awe.
142.	**Awe (V)** be afraid; be impressed The onlookers used to get awed with the charisma of Raja Ram Mohan Roy.
143.	**Awful (Adj.)** causing fear
144.	**Awesome (Adj.)** splendid The weather is really awesome today.
145.	**Awry (Adj.)** crooked; wrong; twisted He presented an awry picture of the incident.

B

146.	**Bawdy (Adj.)** obscene; indelicate I do not relish bawdy jokes.
147.	**Baffle (V)** confuse; bewilder The difficult question baffled the examinees.
148.	**Balderdash (N)** nonsense; meaningless Your speech is all balderdash, it makes no sense to me.
149.	**Beleaguer (V)** surround; hedged in The beleaguered king finally gave in.
150.	**Belittle (V)** disparage One must not belittle others.
151.	**Balmy (Adj.)** warm and pleasant The days are of scorching heat but the nights are balmy.
152.	**Barbaric (Adj.)** uncivilized The barbaric and heinous crime of Delhi gang rape of Damini had been censured by one and all.
153.	**Bard (N)** a great poet. Shakespeare is known as the bard of Avon.
154.	**Base (Adj.)** ignoble; mean Killing innocent civilians is a base act indeed.
155.	**Beatitude (N)** great joy; happiness The statue of Buddha oozes beatitude.
156.	**Beckon (V)** signal; call The sergeant beckoned the soldiers to stand in attention.
157.	**Become (V)** behove; beseem It does not become a boss to ill-treat his subordinates.
158.	**Bedevil (V)** spoil; smudge If you bedevil the investigation, the court will punish you for contempt of court.
159.	**Bedeck (V)** decorate; embellish The young bride was bedecked with D'damas jewellery.
160.	**Befall (V)** fall to one's lot, happen If anything bad should befall me, I leave all my possessions to my loving son.
161.	**Befit (V)** become; suit; beseem It does not befit a soldier to flee from the battlefield.
162.	**Befog (V)** muddle; confuse Some spiritual leaders befog the mind of their disciples through vague teachings.
163.	**Befriend (V)** aid; make friends I want to befriend good human beings.
164.	**Beget (V)** give birth to; generate Violence begets violence.
165.	**Begrudge (V)** envy; resent; be jealous One should not begrudge others' riches.
166.	**Beguile (V)** cheat Don't try to beguile your parents.
167.	**Behead (V)** decapitate; execute; kill In primitive times, the criminals were often beheaded.
168.	**Behest (N)** order; command He thanked the audience at the behest of the association.
169.	**Beholden (Adj.)** grateful; obliged I am really beholden to my teachers till the date.
170.	**Behove (V)** become; beseem It does not behove you to disobey your teachers.
171.	**Belabour (V)** batter; beat up The crowd caught hold of the pickpocket and belaboured him.
172.	**Belie (V)** fail to come up to expectations He belied our hopes.
173.	**Bellicose (Adj.)** ready for a fight; aggressive The bellicose tribals were up in arms.

174.	**Belligerent (Adj.)** jingoistic; aggressive; bellicose Religious fanatics are belligerent towards secular forces.
175.	**Bellow (V)** roar; shout The mighty wrestler bellowed at his opponent.
176.	**Bemoan (V)** fret; complain Don't bemoan your ill fate and get on with life.
177.	**Bemuse (V)** enjoy; pass time Let us bemuse ourselves with old songs.
178.	**Benediction (N)** blessing Education is the greatest benediction showered upon anyone.
179.	**Benefaction (N)** a good deed; charity Helping the needy is a benefaction.
180.	**Benefactor (N)** one who does good to others; kind helper Mother Teresa was a great benefactor.
181.	**Beneficence (N)** kindness; charity Mother Teresa is known for spreading message of beneficence.
182.	**Beneficiary (N)** one who receives a benefit All beneficiaries of the will were under suspicion.
183.	**Benighted (Adj.)** cursed We are benighted by our ignorance.
184.	**Benign (Adj.)** kind; gracious The benign old lady looked after the orphans.
185.	**Benignant (Adj.)** gracious; kind The benignant principal gave fee concession to the brilliant and poor children.
186.	**Benumb (V)** make numb; deprive of sensation The forest walkers were benumbed at the sight of the majestic lion.
187.	**Bequeath (V)** bestow; confer What are the legacies bequeathed to us by the British?
188.	**Bequest (N)** gift; donation The rich Sheikh made handsome bequests to his three wives.
189.	**Berate (V)** admonish; scold The father berated his son when he came to know about his habit of gambling.

190.	**Bereaved (Adj.)** one who suffers in someone's death; dispossessed The bereaved father was inconsolable.
191.	**Bereavement (N)**
192.	**Bereft (Adj.)** empty; unequipped He is bereft of all good sense.
193.	**Berserk (Adj.)** frenzied; one who goes into violent anger The mad man went berserk when he heard about the death of his son.
194.	**Beseech (V)** beg; ask earnestly Kasab beseeched mercy from President of India.
195.	**Beseem (V)** become; behove Sir, he said `It will not beseem me to wear the clothes of a king'.
196.	**Beset (V)** be afflicted with A poor man's life is beset with financial difficulties.
197.	**Besiege (V)** surround; lay siege The enemy besieged the city on all sides.
198.	**Besmirch (V)** give a bad name; discredit; disgrace Don't besmirch your family's good name with your unseemly ways.
199.	**Besotted (Adj.)** lovelorn; infatuated The besotted lover pained for his beloved.
200.	**Bête noire (N)** something disagreeable; bugbear The hotel's quality of food became its bête noire
201.	**Bevy (N)** crowd; group; flock A bevy of beautiful women enlivened the opening ceremony of Olympics.
202.	**Bewail (V)** wail; fret The widow of the officer bewailed over his death.
203.	**Bewilder (V)** puzzle; confuse Ravi tried to bewilder the audience but failed.
204.	**Bewitch (V)** spellbind; captivate Her affable outlook bewitched all and sundry.
205.	**Bewitching (Adj.)** captivating
206.	**Bias (N)** leaning; prejudice Judges must be free from bias.

207.	**Bicker (V)** quarrel; wrangle They bickered endlessly over the bill.
208.	**Bigot (Adj.)** a religious fanatic A bigot cannot think rationally and holistically.
209.	**Bizarre (Adj.)** unseemly; unpleasant The artists with their gaudy dress looked bizarre.
210.	**Blatant (Adj.)** loud; unbecoming The blatant display of riches at weddings is unfortunate.
211.	**Bludgeon (V)** beat badly The robbers bludgeoned him to death and fled with the plunder.
212.	**Blandishment (N)** coaxing; cajoling Her blandishments didn't move him at all.
213.	**Bohemian (Adj.)** unconventional; irregular; immoral He is a bohemian and does not live up to social norms.
214.	**Boisterous (Adj.)** noisy and full of energy Shashi Tharoor calls India as a boisterous democracy.
215.	**Bolster (V)** support; strengthen He bolstered his arguments with great skill, finesse and polemics.
216.	**Bondage (N)** slavery; thralldom We live in bondage to material things.
217.	**Bonhomie (N)** affability; friendliness The lifelong friends experienced bonhomie whenever they met.
218.	**Boorish (Adj.)** unpleasant and rude His boorish ways won him enemies but no friends.
219.	**Bounden (Adj.)** obligatory; compulsory; foremost It is our bounden duty to serve our parents.
220.	**Bountiful (Adj.)** rich and lavish It was a bountiful feast and we ate at our fill.
221.	**Bowdlerize (V)** expurgate; take out The obscene parts were bowdlerized from the book.
222.	**Brace (V)** be ready; encourage You must brace yourself for the next wave.

223.	**Bravado (V)** courage, brashness He behaved aggressively out of bravado.
224.	**Brave (V)** face; endure We must brave the ups and downs of life with confidence.
225.	**Breed (V)** give birth; beget; generate Parents' grooming breed good manners in their children.
226.	**Brew (V)** gather; generate With your unseemly ways, you are brewing trouble for yourself.
227.	**Bridle (V)** control; rein in Bridle your tongue.
228.	**Brittle (Adj.)** fragile; vulnerable; likely to break The feelings of youngsters are very brittle.
229.	**Bristle (V)** be angry; be full of; be excited The little town bristled with enthusiasm to receive the prime minister.
230.	**Browbeat (V)** frighten; threaten Academicians usually try to browbeat others with their pedantic display of knowledge.
231.	**Brunt (N)** the main force; immediate shock The villagers bore the brunt of the tsunami with patience.
232.	**Browse (V)** read at leisure; glance I prefer browsing books instead of going to the gym.
233.	**Bruise (N)** superficial injury He escaped with a few bruises in the accident.
234.	**Brusque (Adj.)** rough; unpolished His brusque ways won him enemies but no friends.
235.	**Brusqueness (N)**
236.	**Buccaneer (N)** an unscruplous adventurer The buccaneers terrorised the coastal village.
237.	**Budding (Adj.)** rising; emerging She is a budding IAS aspirant.
238.	**Buffer (N)** intervening territory Jammu and Kashmir is a buffer state between India and Pakistan.
239.	**Buffet (N)** batterings; attacks We must face with fortitude the buffets of fate.

240.	**Bulwark (N)** support Habeas corpus is the bulwark of personal freedom.
241.	**Buoyant (Adj.)** spirited; cheerful He seemed in a buoyant mood once he saw his result.
242.	**Bustle (N)** animation; excitement The town was agog and in great bustle on Diwali eve.
243.	**Buttress (V)** strengthen; support He buttressed his argument with helpful quotes.
244.	**Bygone (Adj.)** past; former Bygone is bygone once for all.

C

245.	**Cacophony (N)** discordant noise Real issues are lost in the cacophony of blame game.
246.	**Cajole (V)** coax; flatter to persuade The wife cajoled her husband to buy a diamond necklace on her birthday.
247.	**Calamity (N)** disaster; catastrophe Natural calamities come unbidden
248.	**Calamitous (Adj.)**
249.	**Calibre (N)** quality; ability He is an advocate of unparalleled calibre.
250.	**Callous (Adj.)** indifferent; hardened His callous attitude estranged his wife.
251.	**Callow (Adj.)** inexperienced; immature He was a callow youth but full of enthusiasm and energy.
252.	**Calm (N, Adj.)** quiet; peaceful He remained calm even in times of crisis.
253.	**Calumny (N)** disgrace; ignominy Calumny follows all our vices.
254.	**Calumniate (V)**
255.	**Camaraderie (N)** bonhomie; friendship Our peer group enjoyed great camaraderie during college days.
256.	**Camouflage (V)** hide She put up a cheerful face and camouflaged her sufferings.
257.	**Candid (Adj.)** frank; outspoken His candid views charmed the audience.
258.	**Candidness (N)**
259.	**Candour (N)** frankness; artlessness He had the candour to admit that he was in the wrong.
260.	**Canker (N)** an evil influence The canker of corruption pervades our system.
261.	**Canny (Adj.)** intelligent; shrewd Dhirubhai Ambani was a canny businessman who made good profits even during bad times.
262.	**Cannily (Adv.)**
263.	**Cantankerous (Adj.)** ill tempered Because of cantankerous attitude of his wife, nobody prefers to visit his house.
264.	**Cantankerousness (N)**
265.	**Capacious (Adj.)** spacious; roomy It was a capacious flat in DLF Colony.
266.	**Capitalize (V)** make full use of; take advantage of Neetu had many chances to progress but didn't capitalize on them.
267.	**Capitation (N)** tax; fee Many private medical colleges charge heavy capitation fee from student.
268.	**Caprice (N)** whim; caper He is given to caprice and is quite unpredictable.
269.	**Capsize (V)** overturn; upset The Titanic hit the iceberg and capsized.
270.	**Caption (N)** title; descriptive words; heading He hit upon a beautiful caption for the essay.
271.	**Captious (Adj.)** fault finder; complaining; peevish The referee didn't approve of his captious ways and showed him the red card.
272.	**Captiously (Adj.)**
273.	**Captivate (V)** charm; win over The maestro captivated the audience with his wizardry.
274.	**Captivating (Adj.)**
275.	**Caravan (N)** a group of travellers The caravan of tribals stopped at an oasis.
276.	**Cardinal (N, Adj.)** Chief; principal Corruption is the cardinal problem India is facing.

277.	**Caress (V)** love; a touch of affection Susheela started caressing her daughter when she cried out of fear.
278.	**Caricature (N, V)** ludicrous exaggeration President Bush is often caricatured as a war monger.
279.	**Carnage (N)** slaughter; killing a large number of people The carnage in Delhi riots was masterminded by political bosses.
280.	**Carnival (N)** festival; merry-go-rounds; fiesta Valentine Day is, nowadays, one of the greatest carnivals for youngsters.
281.	**Carte Blanche (N)** full freedom; full discretionary powers; a free hand The wife has the carte blanche to run the house.
282.	**Cascade (N, V)** waterfall; flow downwards The cascade of her dark curly hair bewitched the prince.
283.	**Casualty (N)** a person killed or injured There were hundreds of casualties in London and Delhi blasts.
284.	**Cataclysm (N)** sudden disaster; violent upheaval Earthquakes are horrendous natural cataclysms.
285.	**Catastrophe (N)** disaster; calamity Tsunamis and earthquakes are great catastrophes.
286.	**Catastrophic (Adj.)**
287.	**Cater (V)** meet demands Now-a-days, cricketers have to cater to the demand of a hectic schedule.
288.	**Catharsis (N)** release of purgation Comedies regale whereas tragedies bring about catharsis.
289.	**Catholic (Adj.)** broadminded Khushwant Singh had a catholic outlook.
290.	**Catholicism (N)**
291.	**Cattish (Adj.)** sly; clever Mahima is known among peer group for her cattish manipulations.
292.	**Cavalcade (N)** a procession of vehicles The prime minister's cavalcade passed through the streets.

293.	**Cavalier (Adj.)** casual; uncaring; nonchalant The patients were unhappy with the doctor's cavalier attitude.
294.	**Caveat (N)** warning in law; caution He was granted bail but with the caveat that he would not go abroad.
295.	**Cavil:** complain without much cause The mother-in-law caviled at everything that her daughter-in-law did.
296.	**Cede (V)** yield; forego territory or claim India will not cede Kashmir to Pakistan; come what may.
297.	**Celerity (N)** speed; quickness The courts must act with celerity because justice delayed means justice denied.
298.	**Celestial (Adj.)** divine; heavenly The celestial beauty of the artwork held the viewers in awe.
299.	**Celibacy (N)** abstinence from sex; state of being unmarried Celibacy is one of the cardinal rules of Jainism and is also the cause of its lopsided growth.
300.	**Celibate (N)**
301.	**Celibate (Adj.)**
302.	**Centrifugal (Adj.)** division; going away from the centre Religion, caste and language are centrifugal forces.
303.	**Centripetal (Adj.)** unifying; moving towards the centre Indian cinema has great centripetal force.
304.	**Cessation (N)** discontinuance; ceasing Following an agreement between commanders, there was a cessation of hostilities between two armies.
305.	**Chafe (V)** be angry; carp; complain People chafed at the late arrival of the train.
306.	**Chaotic (Adj.)** in complete confusion; disorderly There are too many rules but still traffic is chaotic.
307.	**Chaos (N)**
308.	**Charisma (N)** mysterious charm; unique attraction No other Indian actress has Madhubala's mystique and charisma.

309.	**Charlatan (N)** cheat; swindler One should be beware of charlatans.
310.	**Chaste (Adj.)** pure pristine Kashvi is a chaste lady.
311.	**Chasten (V)** scold; admonish The teacher chastened the truants.
312.	**Chastise (V)** admonish; reprimand The judge chastised the advocate.
313.	**Chastity (N)** abstinence from sex; virginity He took vows of chastity and joined the monastery.
314.	**Chauvinism (N)** blind enthusiasm for military glory Chauvinism is always detrimental in the long run.
315.	**Chauvinistic (Adj.)**
316.	**Chicanery (N)** dishonesty There is a lot of chicanery in the political system of this country.
317.	**Chide (V)** scold; admonish My father chided me for failing in maths.
318.	**Chivalrous (Adj.)** gallant; courteous to women The chivalrous young man rescued the damsel in distress.
319.	**Christen (V)** give a name; dedicate He christened his newly born daughter Asmita.
320.	**Chronic (Adj.)** inveterate; continuing for a long time He is a chronic litigant.
321.	**Chuckle (V)** laugh with satisfaction; laugh quietly The child chuckled as the mother caressed her.
322.	**Churlish (Adj.)** rude; bad-tempered It was churlish of him to disobey his teachers.
323.	**Circumlocution (N)** indirect reference; long-windedness Politicians are full of circumlocutions and seldom brief and to the point.
324.	**Circumscribe (V)** limit; hedge in The power of monarchy in Nepal has been vastly circumscribed.

325.	**Circumcise (V)** remove foreskin Muslim boys are circumcised when they enter their teen years.
326.	**Circumspect (Adj.)** cautious; careful He is a great trickster and fraud; you must be circumspect in dealing with him.
327.	**Circumspection (N)**
328.	**Circumvent (V)** bend rules The rules are rigorous but the lawyers know how to circumvent them.
329.	**Circumvention (N)**
330.	**Citadel;** stronghold USA is a citadel of real inclusive democracy.
331.	**Clairvoyance (N)** supernatural power of seeing distant objects; unusual insight; intuition; sagacity He had the clairvoyance to foresee and had even predicted the deadly earthquake.
332.	**Clairvoyant (N)**
333.	**Clandestine (Adj.)** furtive; secret; surreptitious The lovers had a clandestine rendezvous.
334.	**Claustrophobia (N)** fear of enclosed spaces A feeling of claustrophobia seized the cowboy in the big city.
335.	**Cleanse (V)** become clean; make clean; purify The room was cleansed before the arrival of the landlord.
336.	**Cleavage (N)** difference; schism Politicians are deft in creating cleavages based on castes, classes, regions and religions.
337.	**Clemency (N)** mercy; kindness Afzal's clemency petition was rejected.
338.	**Cloak (N, V)** an outer parchment; hide **(V)** Smiles can cloak evils and vices. **(N)** A cloak of darkness came over the forest.
339.	**Clog (V)** block; obstruct; obstruction Don't try to clog the court proceedings because it is an offence.
340.	**Cloying (Adj.)** too sweet; sentimental He sounded too glib and cloying to be sincere.

341.	**Clumsy (Adj.)** unskilled; ungainly; gawky; diffident Don't resort to clumsy methods of getting the things done.
342.	**Clumsiness (N)**
343.	**Clutter (V)** fill things in a disorderly manner; disorderly mess The mob cluttered the passage of police.
344.	**Coax (V)** flatter; persuade; cajole The child tried to coax the mother.
345.	**Cocky (Adj.)** overconfident; conceited He is very unpopular for his cocky conduct.
346.	**Coddle (V)** caress; fondle The lover was coddling his beloved.
347.	**Cogent (Adj.)** convincing; forceful The judge believed his argument to be cogent and granted relief.
348.	**Cogency (N)**
349.	**Cogitate (V)** contemplate; ponder He sat cogitating over present state of affairs.
350.	**Cognizance (N)** notice; knowledge The judge took cognizance of the matter.
351.	**Cohabit (V)** live together in sexual relationship They cohabited for 10 years and then separated.
352.	**Coherent (Adj.)** cohering; consistent The old man was not coherent and couldn't tell anything about his whereabouts.
353.	**Coherence (N)**
354.	**Cohorts (N)** cronies; minions The politician and his cohorts took out a victory procession.
355.	**Collate (V)** verify; compare and match He gathered facts and figures from different sources and collated them to reach a conclusion.
356.	**Collation (N)**
357.	**Collateral (Adj.)** parallel; concomitant Death and destruction are collateral damages of riots.
358.	**Combat (N, V)** contest; encounter It was a fierce combat between two great boxers. We must combat corruption in our body politics.
359.	**Combative (Adj.)**
360.	**Comely (Adj.)** attractive; charming The women from the upper hills appear so comely.
361.	**Comity (N)** understanding; friendship Hatred should give place to comity among nations to make this earth safer.
362.	**Commandeer (V)** seize; take over The pirate commandeered the luxury yacht.
363.	**Commemorate (V)** celebrate; to honour the memory A victory tower was raised to commemorate the great triumph.
364.	**Commemoration (N)**
365.	**Commensurate (Adj.)** adequate; corresponding The wages are not commensurate with the work.
366.	**Commingle (V)** join; mingle together The princes commingle with the commoners at the family functions.
367.	**Commiserate (V)** sympathise; condole The colleagues commiserated with Jha on the death of his father.
368.	**Commotion (N)** excitement; confusion There was a great commotion at the home of Yogita after she was found missing.
369.	**Communion (N)** rapport; company Ruskin Bond lives in great communion with nature.
370.	**Communiqué (N)** declaration; statement The talks reached at a deadlock and hence no communiqué was issued.
371.	**Compact (N, Adj.)** closely and neatly packed There is a compact cluster of houses in Shiwalik Hill colony.
372.	**Compendium (N)** brief but comprehensive summary A compendium was distributed before the start of his presentation.
373.	**Compere (N, V)** organize Karan Thapar comperes the *'Devil's Advocate'* on CNBC.
374.	**Complacency (N)** mild contentment Complacency is suicidal for success.

375.	**Complaisant (Adj.)** submissive; eager to please The complaisant subordinate was too eager to accept boss's suggestions.
376.	**Complaisance (N)**
377.	**Compliance (N)** consent; obedience The boss was unhappy with non-compliance of his orders.
378.	**Complicity (N)** collusion; participation in wrong doing The police interrogated the accused to find out the complicity of high ups.
379.	**Comply (V)** obey; fulfil The judge directed that his orders be immediately complied with.
380.	**Composure (N)** serenity; sang-froid; equanimity He displayed great composure in times of crisis.
381.	**Compound (V)** worsen; complicate; aggravate The Police-Politicians nexus was responsible for compounding Punjab problem.
382.	**Comprehension (N)** understanding; grip; intelligence He writes so obscure that it is beyond the comprehension of a common reader.
383.	**Compunction (N)** twinge; scruple; prick; remorse The rapist suffered from no compunction.
384.	**Concede (V)** agree; admit; allow He conceded to my request.
385.	**Conceit (N)** pride; hubris; arrogance Self-conceit is very dangerous.
386.	**Conciliation (N)** reconciliation We need to develop a policy of conciliation to improve Indo-Pak relations.
387.	**Conclave (N)** meeting; conference The *Hindustan Times* conclave was a great event.
388.	**Concomitant (N)** concurrent; accompanying; attendant things The concomitant riots were politically doctored after Indira Gandhi's assassination.
389.	**Concord (N)** agreement; harmony There is no extradition concord between India and Pakistan.
390.	**Concourse (N)** large flocking of people; a mammoth gathering A concourse attended Obama's oath ceremony as the 44th President of USA.
391.	**Conducive (Adj.)** helpful; inspiring We need to create conducive atmosphere for communal harmony.
392.	**Confabulate (V)** discuss; private chat The Prime Minister confabulated with his cabinet regarding various political issues.
393.	**Confer (V)** discuss; bestow; exchange views The Padma Shri award was conferred on Sachin Tendulkar by the President of India.
394.	**Confidant (N)** a close friend; a bosom friend My wife is my most trusted confidant; I share all my secrets with her.
395.	**Confide (V)** share secrets; repose trust He confides in me his entire secret plans.
396.	**Congenital (Adj.)** existing at birth He is a congenital liar and will not reform.
397.	**Conglomerate (N)** a large company; anything composed of heterogeneous elements Many small companies joined hands to form a large industrial conglomerate.
398.	**Congregation (N)** an assembly of religious people The congregation sang Vedic hymns in praise of God Indra.
399.	**Congregate (V)**
400.	**Conjecture (N)** imagination; estimate It was beyond my conjecture that he would qualify in IAS examination.
401.	**Conjugal (Adj.)** pertaining to the union of husband and wife The husband filed petition for restitution of conjugal rights against her aberrant wife.
402.	**Conjure (V)** invoke; concoct He conjured up a fake story but couldn't connive.
403.	**Connive (V)** conspire Both the friends connived to cheat in their exams.
404.	**Connoisseur (N)** a good judge; an expert Neetu is a connoisseur of art.
405.	**Conscientious (Adj.)** dutiful; honest He is a very conscientious fellow.

406.	**Consensus (N)** unanimity; common view All the decisions were taken with consensus.
407.	**Consonance (N)** harmony His ideas are in consonance with his writings.
408.	**Contention (N)** argument; plea; point of dispute The judge accepted his contention and granted him relief.
409.	**Constrain (V)** contain; compel; oblige I felt constrained after severing my relations with him.
410.	**Constrict (V)** restrict; tame Children shouldn't be undesirably constricted and restricted.
411.	**Construe (V)** understand; find out; infer; take it to be I construed from his letter that he was not in favour of the alliance.
412.	**Consummate (Adj., V)** skilful; first-rated He is a consummate liar.
413.	**Contaminate (V)** render impure; infect His corrupt attitude contaminated the whole atmosphere in the family.
414.	**Contamination (N)**
415.	**Contemplate (V)** think; consider We contemplated a change in our plans.
416.	**Contend (V)** compete; vie Don't contend with others, just contend with yourself.
417.	**Contentious (Adj.)** giving way to contention; disputatious; contested Kashmir has become a contentious issue.
418.	**Contiguous (Adj.)** adjoining; side by side India and Nepal are contiguous countries.
419.	**Contiguity (N)**
420.	**Continence (N)** control of passion; restraint One must exercise continence in food and drinks to maintain health.
421.	**Contraband (Adj.)** illegal goods Trade in contraband goods is called smuggling.
422.	**Contradict (V)** refute; prove false; deny The defence lawyer couldn't contradict the arguments of prosecution.
423.	**Contrition (N)** repentance; penitence The accused was filled with contrition once he was convicted.
424.	**Contrite (Adj.)**
425.	**Contrivance (N)** invention; device The story is filled with plot contrivances that do not fit the ending.
426.	**Contrive (V)**
427.	**Controvert (V)** refute; prove false He controverted the allegations against him.
428.	**Conundrum (N)** riddle; enigma; puzzle Palestine is still a political conundrum.
429.	**Convene (V)** organise; co-ordinate The Congress party convened an annual party meet.
430.	**Converge (V)** collect; assemble Lakhs of people converged at Delhi during Anna Hazare's fast for the Lok Pal Bill.
431.	**Convoke (V)** convene; call together The prime minister convoked a cabinet meeting to resolve deadlock of Anna's fast.
432.	**Copious (Adj.)** fertile; abundant; fecund; in good measure He has a copious vocabulary and seldom forgets any word.
433.	**Copiousness (N)**
434.	**Coquette (N)** a woman who attracts men; a flirt The coquette enticed many a young men with her flirtations gestures.
435.	**Cordon (N, V)** surround; lay siege The police cordoned off the city.
436.	**Corporeal (Adj.)** physical; material Man's corporeal needs are insatiable.
437.	**Corroborate (V)** confirm; testify The eyewitness corroborated the incident.
438.	**Corrosive (Adj.)** harmful; destructive Material pursuits have a corrosive effect on moral values.
	D
439.	**Daft (Adj.)** silly; foolish He gave a daft demonstration.
440.	**Daftly (Adv.)**
441.	**Dainty (Adj.)** charming; sweet Anaadi was looking dainty in her school dress.

442.	**Daintily (Adv.)**
443.	**Dandy (N)** a man who is excessively concerned about his dress and appearance Ken always wears gaudy dresses to look dandy.
444.	**Dauntless (Adj.)** intrepid; fearless The dauntless warrior fought to the last.
445.	**Dawdle (V)** waste time; move about aimlessly Right decision is the first step towards success; so don't dawdle.
446.	**Deadlock (N)** imbroglio; stalemate Lok Sabha and Rajya Sabha reached a deadlock over issue of Lok Pal Bill.
447.	**Debacle (N)** poor show; ignominious defeat The 2012 Punjab Assembly Elections proved to be a debacle for Congress.
448.	**Debar (V)** prohibit; disallow He was debarred from appearing in court for six months.
449.	**Debase (V)** become ignoble; touch the nadir; touch very low Don't debase yourself in front of others.
450.	**Debauched (Adj.)** immoral Avoid debauched characters.
451.	**Debauchery (N)**
452.	**Debilitate (V)** become weak; lose strength The scolding by parents debilitates the morale of children.
453.	**Debonair (Adj.)** courteous; gracious; cheerful; stylish The debonair young man truly looked like a hero in a movie.
454.	**Debris (N)** ruins; remains Certain people extricated from the debris after the earthquake were found alive.
455.	**Debunk (V)** severely criticize; denounce All nations should debunk terrorism.
456.	**Debut (N)** maiden appearance; the beginning of a profession *Shiva* was the debut movie of Ram Gopal Verma.
457.	**Decadence (N)** moral decay Materialistic pursuits and moral decadence go hand in hand.

458.	**Decadent (Adj.)**
459.	**Decimate (V)** devastate; destroy; raze The tsunami decimated many coastal towns.
460.	**Decimation (N)**
461.	**Decrepit (Adj.)** debilitated; feeble; infirm; weak Siddhartha, the Buddha decided to renounce the world at the sight of decrepit beggar, an old man, a sick man and a dead body.
462.	**Decrepitude (N)**
463.	**Decry (V)** strongly criticize; censure The opposition decried the policy of FDI announced by government.
464.	**Deface (V)** disfigure; vandalise The city walls are defaced with posters and handbills during elections.
465.	**Defacement (N)**
466.	**Defer (V)** put off to a future time; postpone The prime minister deferred his visit to Punjab.
467.	**Defile (V)** discredit; disgrace; desecrate He thought that condiments would defile the taste of the cooked chicken.
468.	**Deft (Adj.)** ingenious; clever; skillful Pradeep pleaded his case with deft arguments.
469.	**Deftness (N)**
470.	**Defunct (Adj.)** not extant; not existing any more Many old customs like the 'Sati' are defunct now.
471.	**Deify (V)** treat like a god; revere Indians are habitual to deify or deride.
472.	**Delectable (Adj.)** enjoyable; delightful I could not stop eating the delectable fish curry.
473.	**Delineate (V)** describe; depict Somerset Maugham beautifully delineated human nature in his novel ***'Human Bondage'***.
474.	**Delineation (N)**
475.	**Delinquent (Adj.)** socially unacceptable; unbecoming Mr Sharma was rusticated from the company for his delinquent ways.
476.	**Delinquency (N)**

477.	**Delirious (Adj.)** wild with excitement; very enthusiastic; very happy He is delirious with his sudden success.
478.	**Deleterious (Adj.)** harmful Scolding many a time leaves a very deleterious effect on children.
479.	**Deliverance (N)** salvation; freedom India attained deliverance from the foreign yoke in August 1947.
480.	**Delude (V)** cheat; swindle Youngsters of the day are deluded by the glitter and glamour of the corporate world.
481.	**Delusion (N)**
482.	**Deluge (N)** flood; abundance. He had a deluge of job offers.
483.	**Delve (V)** search; dive; go into Freud has delved deep into the unconscious mind.
484.	**Demagogue (N)** one who misleads people; rabble rouser The political demagogues lure the voters with false promises.
485.	**Demagogy (N)**
486.	**Demagogic (Adj.)**
487.	**Demagoguery (N)**
488.	**Demean (V)** degrade; debase Don't demean yourself by resorting to such unfair means of earning money.
489.	**Demeanor (N)** conduct; behaviour Bhagat Singh, Rajguru and Sukhdev went to the gallows with a brave demeanor.
490.	**Demur (N)** take expectation; hesitation He accepted my offer without any demur.
491.	**Demure (Adj.)** coy; modest; shy The bride looked demure and beautiful.
492.	**Denigrate (V)** belittle; disparage; devalue Aren't you denigrating my achievement out of pique?
493.	**Denounce (V)** censure; criticize The honest prime minister denounced the corrupt minister.
494.	**Deplete (V)** erode; dwindle Do not deplete your energy in running unnecessary errands.
495.	**Depletion (N)**

496.	**Deplore (V)** run down; disapprove The boss deplored the lack of punctuality in his subordinates.
497.	**Deport (V)** banish; expel from the country The spy was imprisoned and then deported to his native country.
498.	**Depose (V)** to testify under oath; remove from office He deposed before the court that he was innocent.
499.	**Depravity (N)** the state of vitiation; moral decline Addiction to drugs is sheer depravity.
500.	**Deprecate (V)** disapprove; belittle He was jealous of me and deprecated my plans.
501.	**Depreciate (V)** lessen; come down With rising prices, the value of money depreciates.
502.	**Depredation (N)** plunder The police must rein in the depredations of highway robbers.
503.	**Deprivation (N)** poverty; lack of resources The family passed through deprivation in the wake of business losses.
504.	**Derange (V)** make insane; be mentally unbalanced Her unsuccessful marriage has left her deranged.
505.	**Derelict (Adj.)** neglectful of duty; negligent He was found derelict in his duties and hence dismissed.
506.	**Deride (V)** mock; scoff; jeer Don't deride the hapless.
507.	**Derision (N)** ridicule; mockery
508.	**Derogatory (Adj.)** critical; belittling The derogatory speech by the chief minister was criticized by one and all.
509.	**Desecrate (V)** render impure; pollute Lack of love, reverence and trust desecrate a marriage.
510.	**Desideratum (N)** something wanted or needed; that which is desirable The happiness is the chief desideratum of human life which is not subject to just material fulfilment.

511.	**Despicable (Adj.)** detestable; hateful Forsaking one's parents in their old age is a most despicable act.
512.	**Despise (V)** hate; look down upon The rich must not despise the poor.
513.	**Despondent (Adj.)** morose; gloomy; unhappy He felt despondent at his failure to pass the IAS examination.
514.	**Despot (N)** dictator; tyrant Hitler is the most notorious despot known in the history.
515.	**Destitute (N, Adj.)** without means of subsistence; very poor Mother Teresa devoted her life to the service of the destitute.
516.	**Desultory (Adj.)** random; aimless Desultory efforts do not bear fruit.
517.	**Deter (V)** restrain from acting; discourage Difficulties can't deter a brave man.
518.	**Deterrent (N)** that which deters; something that discourages Capital punishment acts as a deterrent.
519.	**Detrimental (Adj.)** harmful Smoking is detrimental to health.
520.	**Deteriorate (V)** degenerate; grow worse; disintegrate Our society is deteriorating at a great pace.
521.	**Detract (V)** disparage; take away credit; devalue We should not detract the contributions of our freedom fighters.
522.	**Detriment (N)** loss; harm We must not pursue material goods to the detriment of our health.
523.	**Devious (Adj.)** askew; cunning; awry Some politicians resort to devious ways to gain and retain power.
524.	**Devise (V)** plan; think of You must devise some way out of this predicament.
525.	**Devoid (Adj.)** not possessing; empty He is devoid of common sense.
526.	**Devolve (V)** entrust; make one account for; render responsible After his father's death, all family responsibilities devolved on him.
527.	**Dexterity (N)** ingenuity; skill The Prime Minister is steering the country's economy with great integrity and dexterity.
528.	**Diabolic (Adj.)** devious; dangerous Pakistan's diabolic plans to usurp the Kargil heights were foiled by the great valour of Indian soldiers.
529.	**Dilettante (N)** dabbler in fine arts He is a bit of dilettante as far as wine is concerned.
530.	**Diffident (Adj.)** doubtful; confidence He felt diffident of his success.
531.	**Dilapidated (Adj.)** rickety; in a state of ill-repair The dilapidated house belies his false claims of royal background.
532.	**Diligent (Adj.)** painstaking; hardworking The intelligent and diligent are bound to succeed.
533.	**Dire (Adj.)** very troublesome; extreme; terrible One could never imagine the dire consequences Ravi faced in life because of his careless attitude.
534.	**Disaffection (N)** unfriendliness; hostility; disloyalty The disaffection among Shias, Sunnis and Kurds has jolted Iraq.
535.	**Disarm (V)** take away weapons; win over The rebels were captured and disarmed.
536.	**Disarray (N)** confusion; demoralization The leader's betrayal left his followers in disarray.
537.	**Disavow (V)** deny; disclaim He disavowed any share in the conspiracy.
538.	**Disband (V)** see through; find out I could not disband what the philosophers were discussing.
539.	**Discomfit (V)** confuse; disconcert The young teacher was discomfited by a flurry of questions.
540.	**Disconcert (V)** upset; distract; disappoint Traffic snarls disconcert the pedestrian.
541.	**Discard (V)** give up; omit We must discard bad habits and cultivate good ones.

542.	**Disconsolate (Adj.)** inconsolable; extremely unhappy The mother was disconsolate at the loss of her child.
543.	**Discreet (Adj.)** careful; tactful; wise The wife maintained a discreet silence at her husband's outburst.
544.	**Discreetly (Adv.)**
545.	**Discrepancy (N)** gap; schism There is huge discrepancy in the first and last statement of accounts.
546.	**Discretion (N)** individual judgment; prudence The higher authorities can use their discretion in important matters.
547.	**Discretionary (Adj.)**
548.	**Discrimination (N)** sifting; the power of making fine distinctions Many women still face the discrimination in Army.
549.	**Discriminating (Adj.)**
550.	**Discursive (Adj.)** random; digressive; not to the point His answers are always discursive and poor in quality that is why he could not qualify any exam.
551.	**Discursiveness (N)**
552.	**Disdain (N, V)** contempt; despise; scorn The newly rich and semi-literate people develop a strange disdain for the common man.
553.	**Disgruntled (Adj.)** frustrated; unhappy The youth are disgruntled with present education system.
554.	**Disgust (N)** disappointment The boss expressed his disgust at his lazy workers.
555.	**Disgusting (Adj.)**
556.	**Dishevelled (Adj.)** unkempt; unclean She came back dishevelled and unkempt after a long trek in the hills.
557.	**Disintegrate (V)** break away; scatter Joint family system is disintegrating in these days of globalization.
558.	**Disintegration (N)**

559.	**Disinterested (Adj.)** without a vested interest His façade of disinterest infuriated her.
560.	**Dislodge (V)** discourage; deter; displace Nothing could dislodge him from his resolve of marrying outside the caste.
561.	**Dismantle (V)** pull down; take apart The house was dismantled and constructed anew.
562.	**Dismember (V)** break apart; divide India was dismembered and Pakistan came into being in 1947.
563.	**Dismemberment (N)**
564.	**Disparity (N)** gap; inequality The disparity between the rich and the poor can be reduced but not bridged.
565.	**Dispel (V)** drive away; remove Knowledge dispels darkness and ignorance.
566.	**Dispensable (Adj.)** not necessary; not essential Most luxuries are not only dispensable but harmful as well.
567.	**Dispense (V)** administer; distribute A judge must dispense with justice only.
568.	**Dispense (with) (V)** do without We can easily dispense with luxuries.
569.	**Disseminate (V)** spread; scatter A real teacher disseminates knowledge and wisdom together.
570.	**Dissension (N)** quarrel; differences Social and political dissensions are inevitable in a pluralist society like India.
571.	**Dissent (N, V)** disagreement; disagree Debate, discussion and dissent are hallmarks of democracy. He dissented from the majority judgment.
572.	**Dissipate (V)** waste; destroy; expend Do not dissipate your energy in merry-go-rounds.
573.	**Dissipation (N)**
574.	**Dissuade (V)** deter by persuasion; advise against His father dissuaded him from going abroad.
575.	**Distort (V)** twist; give a wrong picture The soap operas on television present a distorted picture of reality.

576.	**Distortion (N)**
577.	**Distract (V)** divert; draw away one's attention The teacher was distracted by the noise outside the class room.
578.	**Distracted (Adj.)**
579.	**Distraction (N)**
580.	**Divulge (V)** tell facts; let out; betray secrets In a fit of drunkenness, he divulged the secrets.
581.	**Divulgence (N)**
582.	**Doctrine (N)** belief; theory; idea The doctrine that the king is God on earth no longer holds.
583.	**Dodder (V)** totter; walk with difficulty The frail old beggar doddered along with a stick and a begging bowl.
584.	**Dodge (V)** escape; cheat; trick The thief disguised himself as a beggar and dodged the police.
585.	**Dogged (Adj.)** determined; preserving Only dogged efforts bear fruit.
586.	**Doldrums (N)** depressed; unsteady Indian economy is in the doldrums.
587.	**Domineer (V)** rule over; dominate Rajesh's wife domineers over him.
588.	**Dormant (Adj.)** inactive; hibernating The cold-blooded reptiles lie dormant in winter.
589.	**Dotty (Adj.)** idiotic; idiot Watching television the whole day is a sure way to go dotty.
590.	**Drag (N, V)** burden; push; move The alcoholics are a drag on society.
591.	**Dubious (Adj.)** of poor quality; doubtful He has the dubious distinction of failing in all the subjects.
592.	**Dubiousness (N)**
593.	**Dubiously (Adv.)**
594.	**Duress (N)** compulsion; threat; coercion His confessed to his crime under duress.
595.	**Dwindle (V)** wane; deplete His resources dwindled as he played ducks and drakes with his money.

E	
596.	**Earnest (Adj.)** devoted; serious One has to make an earnest effort to qualify the IAS examination.
597.	**Ebullient (Adj.)** dashing; full of life She always behaves in an ebullient manner.
598.	**Éclat (N)** applause Aamir Khan earned worldwide éclat for his role in the movie Three Idiots.
599.	**Eclectic (Adj.)** broadminded; catholic The Mauryan rulers were highly eclectic in religious affairs.
600.	**Ecstasy (N)** great joy; bliss The state of Buddha seems to exude ecstasy.
601.	**Edict (N)** order; ordinance; proclamation; command Ashoka ruled and preached through edicts.
602.	**Educe (V)** develop; find out; bring forward The lawyer educed evidence and authority to prove his point.
603.	**Eerie (Adj.)** strange; weird; uncanny The eerie interiors of the house scared him.
604.	**Efface (V)** obliterate; rub off; erase You must efface the oily spots from your shirt.
605.	**Effacement (N)**
606.	**Effervescent (Adj.)** lively; animated; buoyant He seemed extremely effervescent.
607.	**Effervesce (V)**
608.	**Effervescence (N)**
609.	**Effete (Adj.)** worn out; exhausted; enfeebled Luxuries render us effete.
610.	**Efficacious (Adj.)** fruitful; effective His advice really proved efficacious.
611.	**Efficaciousness (N)**
612.	**Effluent (N)** liquid waste having chemicals or sewage The effluents from the factories pollute the rivers.
613.	**Effrontery (N)** brazenness; impudence He is very unpopular among friends for his effrontery.

614.	**Effulgent (Adj.)** glowing; radiant He was effulgent after seeing his exam result.
615.	**Effulgence (N)**
616.	**Effusive (Adj.)** expansive; inclined to talk The teacher was effusive in his praise of the student.
617.	**Effusiveness (N)**
618.	**Egalitarian (Adj.)** a person who believes in equality A casteless society will be truly egalitarian.
619.	**Egalitarianism (N)**
620.	**Egg (V)** incite; instigate The politicians egged the masses.
621.	**Ego (N)** self-importance; pride; hubris Inflated ego is the main reason of spoiling relationships.
622.	**Egoist (N)**
623.	**Egoistic (Adj.)**
624.	**Egregious (Adj.)** glaring; flagrant He is an egregious liar and no one believes him.
625.	**Elan (N)** joy and confidence Amitabh Bachchan conducts his shows with élan and authority.
626.	**Elate (V)** be happy; feel proud The parents felt elated at the success of their son.
627.	**Elated (Adj.)**
628.	**EI Dorado (N)** land of opportunity; promised land USA is the EI Dorado for fortune seekers.
629.	**Elementary (Adj.)** rudimentary; basic The fundamental rights are the elementary and intrinsic part of the constitution of India.
630.	**Elevate (V)** exalt; promote I hope that he will be elevated to a respectable position.
631.	**Elevation (N)**
632.	**Elusive (Adj.)** evasive; tending to escape His elusive replies irritated the judge.
633.	**Elusiveness (N)**
634.	**Emancipate (V)** be free; set free Raja Ram Mohan Roy emancipated women from many evils prevailing at that time.
635.	**Emancipation (N)**

636.	**Emasculate (V)** weaken; enfeeble Depressing thoughts emasculate the motivational level.
637.	**Emasculation (N)**
638.	**Embargo (N)** restrictions of trade India put embargo on Pakistan after the Mumbai attacks.
639.	**Embed (V)** inculcate; plant; fix firmly We must embed a value system in our children.
640.	**Embezzle (V)** misappropriate He was apprehended for embezzling public funds.
641.	**Embezzlement (N)**
642.	**Emblazon (V)** set a good example; achieve great success Surya emblazoned all the classmates with success in CLAT.
643.	**Emblem (N)** symbol; representative The three faced lion is the emblem of India.
644.	**Embody (V)** represent; symbolize Gandhiji embodies non-violence.
645.	**Embodiment (N)**
646.	**Embroil (V)** be mixed up in a quarrel; enmesh Arvind Kejriwal is embroiled in a number of controversies.
647.	**Empirical (Adj.)** based on observation Science believes in empirical evidence.
648.	**Empower (V)** bestow power Education and proprietary rights will empower women.
649.	**Empowerment (N)**
650.	**Emulate (V)** imitate with effort Let us emulate the principles laid by the founding fathers of India.
651.	**Emulation (N)**
652.	**Enamoured (Adj.)** charmed; fascinated; captivated The fans were enamoured by Sushmitha Sen's celestial beauty.
653.	**Encomiums (N)** praise; paeans Albert Einstein earned encomiums during and after his lifetime.
654.	**Encounter (N, V)** contest; competition The police officer was charged with the fake encounter.

655.	**Ensconce (V)** settle, sit securely He is well ensconced in his family business.
656.	**Encumber (V)** impede; hinder; burden India's growth is encumbered by her teeming millions.
657.	**Encumbrance (N)**
658.	**Enervate (V)** weaken; enfeeble The excessive physical activities enervate.
659.	**Enervating (Adj.)**
660.	**Enervation (N)**
661.	**Enfeeble (V)** weaken; famish Don't try to enfeeble his thoughts.
662.	**Enfeeblement (N)**
663.	**Enforce (V)** put into effect; implement These rules have not yet been enforced.
664.	**Enforceable (Adj.)**
665.	**Enforcement (N)**
666.	**Engrossed (Adj.)** occupied; busy She was engrossed in her studies oblivious of her surroundings.
667.	**Enjoin (V)** to prescribe a course of action; decree; order The court enjoined him not to leave the country.
668.	**Enkindle (V)** cultivate; excite; generate A good teacher can enkindle a student's interest for knowledge.
669.	**Enlighten (V)** instruct; make aware The teachers must enlighten the students.
670.	**Enlightenment (N)**
671.	**Enliven (V)** make things interesting; make lively; animate She enlivened the meeting with her wit and charm.
672.	**En-masse (Adv.)** in a body; in a group Brahamans left Jammu and Kashmir en-masse in 1990s.
673.	**Enmesh (V)** embroil; entangle The present day world is enmeshed in capitalistic allurements.
674.	**Ennui (N)** feeling of weariness or discontent; boredom A feeling of ennui made me disenchanted with usual routine.
675.	**Enormity (N)** base-ness; magnitude; seriousness The government could not gauge the enormity of the problem of corruption.
676.	**Enormous (Adj.)**
677.	**Enrage (V)** infuriate; make angry The terrorists 9/11 attack enraged the George Bush to hit back Afghanistan.
678.	**Enraged (Adj.)**
679.	**Enrapture (V)** captivate; fascinate Lata's melodies enrapture us.
680.	**Rapture (N)**
681.	**Enrich (V)** make rich; sharpen Great literature enriches our sensibilities.
682.	**Enrichment (N)**
683.	**En route (Adv.)** on the way; via The express train stops nowhere en route from Delhi to Mumbai.
684.	**Ensemble (N)** collection, mixture India is an exemplary ensemble of castes, classes, regions and religions.
685.	**Enshrine (V)** cherish as sacred, epitomize Rousseau's philosophy enshrines liberty, equality and fraternity.
686.	**Enshroud (V)** conceal; remain in mystery The death of Subash Chandra Bose is still enshrouded in mystery.
687.	**Ensue (V)** happen; follow Only death and destruction ensue after terrorism and insurgency.
688.	**Entail (V)** result into; become a necessary consequence The manager's scandal entailed a number of protests.
689.	**Entangle (V)** entrap; ensnare; embroil; enmesh Please don't entangle in your matrimonial disputes.
690.	**Entanglement (N)**
691.	**Enthral (V)** captivate; spellbind The circus artists enthralled the viewers with their acrobatics.
692.	**Entice (V)** snare; allure; inveigle Ajay was enticed by the glamour of the film industry.

693.	**Entity (N)** existence; being One should always strive to prove one's individual entity.
694.	**Entreat (V)** pray; supplicate; beseech; implore He entreated her to accept his proposal.
695.	**Entrench (V)** embed; settle Venal politicians are well entrenched in the Indian political system.
696.	**Entrenchment (N)**
697.	**Entrepreneur (N)** one who runs a business Azim Premji is an entrepreneur by nature.
698.	**Entrepreneurship (N)**
699.	**Entrust (V)** give in confidence; handover Ashoka entrusted his kingdom to his brothers.
700.	**Entrustment (N)**
701.	**Enunciate (V)** declare definitely; explain precisely The teachers should enunciate the theories to the students.
702.	**Enunciation (N)**
703.	**Envelop (V)** surround; encircle After sunset, darkness envelopes the surroundings.
704.	**Envelop (N)**
705.	**Envenom (V)** poison; embitter Greed envenoms relationships.
706.	**Envy (N)** ill will; jealously Plato said, 'Envy is the jaundice of soul'.
707.	**Envious (Adj.)**
708.	**Envisage (V)** envision; foresee One should have foresight to envisage one's own future.
709.	**Ephemeral (Adj.)** short lived; transient Life is an ephemeral journey.
710.	**Ephemerality (N)**
711.	**Epicure (N)** connoisseur of food and drinks; one who enjoys sensual delights An epicure enjoys the good things of life.
712.	**Epidemic (N)** a wide spread disease The influenza epidemic affected many people in the region.
713.	**Epitome (N)** idol; essence Obama is really the epitome of wit and wisdom.
714.	**Epitomize (V)**

715.	**Epoch (N)** a long period of time Buddha and Nanak were great harbingers of new epochs in their times.
716.	**Epochal (Adj.)**
717.	**Equanimity (N)** calmness; tranquility The brave do not buckle before misfortunes but face them with equanimity.
718.	**Equanimous (Adj.)**
719.	**Equipoise (N)** equilibrium; calm One must not lose equipoise in dire crises.
720.	**Equity (N)** fairness; justice The king treated all his subjects with equity.
721.	**Equivocal (Adj.)** questionable; dubious The courts do not accept equivocal replies.
722.	**Era (N)** a period of time We are passing through an era of competition where a mix of hard work and smart work is required.
723.	**Eradicate (V)** extirpate; root out It is the time to eradicate corruption from public life otherwise public will come to street for open protests.
724.	**Eradication (N)**
725.	**Erase (V)** efface; rub out Some unforgettable memories can never be erased.
726.	**Erasure (N)**
727.	**Erode (V)** destroy; eat into Corruption in public life erodes the vitals of society.
728.	**Erosion (N)**
729.	**Errant (Adj.)** deviating; erring Only an errant fool falls into bad company.
730.	**Erratic (Adj.)** fitful; irregular There were no rains this year and the electricity supplies had gone erratic.
731.	**Erroneous (Adj.)** mistaken; incorrect Following a wrong feedback, they reached erroneous conclusions.
732.	**Erudite (Adj.)** scholarly; learned Khushwant Singh was really an erudite person.
733.	**Erupt (V)** burst forth; break out A large number of public protests erupted with the death of a gang rape victim.

734.	**Eruption (N)**
735.	**Escapade (N)** elopement The entire city of Kotkapura was agog with Shruti's escapade and elopement.
736.	**Eschew (V)** avoid; abstain from; shun Eschew bad company and prosper.
737.	**Esoteric (Adj.)** difficult to understand Esoteric knowledge is possessed by a few select persons.
738.	**Espouse (V)** champion; support Mother Teresa espoused the cause of the destitute and she was honoured with Nobel Prize.
739.	**Espousal (N)**
740.	**Estranged (Adj.)** alienated The estranged wife wanted alimony from her husband.
741.	**Eternal (Adj.)** undying; immortal The Hindi word 'Anaadi' means eternal which is without beginning and without end.
742.	**Eternity (N)**
743.	**Ethereal (Adj.)** celestial Madhubala's beauty was ethereal.
744.	**Etiquette (N)** social manners; rules of behaviour I strongly feel that students nowadays lack in etiquette.
745.	**Euphoria (N)** excitement; a happy feeling There was great euphoria at BJP headquarters after U.P. elections.
746.	**Euphoric (Adj.)**
747.	**Euthanasia (N)** painless death; mercy killing Passive euthanasia is a legal reality now.
748.	**Evacuate (V)** shift people to safe place The floods inundated the town and the people had to be evacuated.
749.	**Evacuee (N)**
750.	**Evade (V)** shirk; be elusive Politicians equivocate and evade direct answers.
751.	**Evanescent (Adj.)** temporary; short-lived Life is an evanescent affair.
752.	**Evanescence (N)**
753.	**Evasive (Adj.)** unwilling; furtive He was evasive in his replies and never came out clean.

754.	**Eventual (Adj.)** in the end; final; ultimate Your snobbery will lead you to your eventual failure.
755.	**Eventuality (N)**
756.	**Evict (V)** vacate forcibly The police evicted the tenants after the court's eviction orders.
757.	**Eviction (N)**
758.	**Evident (Adj.)** obvious; apparent It is quite evident from the accident itself that he was wrong.
759.	**Evidence (N)**
760.	**Evince (V)** manifest; display interest She evinced no interest in her husband's peer groups get together.
761.	**Evoke (V)** kindle; bring forth He evoked great interest in the students.
762.	**Evocation (N)**
763.	**Evolve (V)** grow; become Man has gradually evolved since stone age.
764.	**Evolution (N)**
765.	**Exalt (V)** praise; glorify Bana Bhatt has exalted the glories of Harshvardhan in *Harshacharita*.
766.	**Exalted (Adj.)**
767.	**Exaltation (N)**
768.	**Exacerbate (V)** worsen; aggravate Harsh words only exacerbate strained relations.
769.	**Exasperate (V)** lose patience; become angry The son's lackadaisical attitude to studies exasperated the father.
770.	**Exasperation (N)**
771.	**Excel (V)** achieve excellence In order to excel, one must remember these words, 'Will, planning and perseverance lead to excellence'.
772.	**Excellence (N)**
773.	**Excerpt (N)** a passage taken out of a book; extract I have not read the whole book but only a few of its excerpts.
774.	**Exchequer (N)** treasury; public money The political gimmicks like 'Free atta dal' will exhaust the state exchequer.

775. **Excommunicate (V)** ostracize; shut out from society
Rapists should be excommunicated from the society.

776. **Excommunication (N)**

777. **Excoriate (V)** castigate; criticize severely
Vipin was excoriated by his father for failing in the examination.

778. **Excoriation (N)**

779. **Excruciating (Adj.)** very painful; torturous
During the operation, he experienced excruciating pain.

780. **Excruciate (V)**

781. **Excruciation (N)**

782. **Exculpate (V)** free from blame; acquit
The court exculpated him from the charge of rape.

783. **Exculpation (N)**

784. **Exculpatory (Adj.)**

785. **Excursion (N)** a short journey; jaunt
Our excursion to the hills on a toy train was exhilarating and vivifying.

786. **Execrable (Adj.)** contemptible; very bad
Rape is the worst, heinous and execrable offence.

787. **Execrate (V)**

788. **Execration (N)**

789. **Execution (N)** putting into effect; implementation
'This world is ill judged execution of well-conceived idea', said Thomas Hardy in his novel Tess of d' Urbervilles.

790. **Execute (V)**

791. **Executor (N)**

792. **Exert (V)** try; make an effort
In order to be successful, one needs to exert himself.

793. **Exertion (N)**

794. **Exhaustive (Adj.)** in great detail
Gurcharan Das's book India grows at *Night* is an exhaustive work on the sorry state of affairs prevailing in India.

795. **Exhaustion (N)**

796. **Exhilarate (V)** make lively; vivify
The November breeze exhilarates and rejuvenates all the tired souls.

797. **Exhort (V)** urge; enthuse; ask earnestly
The general exhorted his solders to crush the enemy or fall in the battlefield.

798. **Exhortation (N)**

799. **Exigency (N)** urgency; emergency
We must be prepared to face exigencies.

800. **Exigent (Adj.)**

801. **Existential (Adj.)** relating to the existing; pertaining to existence of an individual
The existential problems of death and disease made Siddhartha renounce the world and attain Buddhahood.

802. **Existentialism (N)**

803. **Exodus (N)** departure; mass migration
There was an exodus of Hindus from Jammu and Kashmir in the 1990s.

804. **Ex officio (Adj. Adv.)** by virtue of office
The deputy commissioner is an ex officio member of the city's Rotary Club.

805. **Exonerate (V)** free from blame; exculpate
The judge exonerated him from all charges.

806. **Exoneration (N)**

807. **Exorbitant (Adj.)** excessive; exaggerated
It is a style among a particular section of society to wear very exorbitant and branded clothes.

808. **Exorbitance (N)**

809. **Expedient (Adj.)** suitable; convenient
Narasimha Rao found it politically expedient to form a coalition government.

810. **Expediency (N)**

811. **Expound (V)** interpret; explain in detail
Osho expounded the most intricate philosophies in the simplest manner.

812. **Extempore (Adv.)** speak without preparation
His extempore speech earned him great applause.

813. **Extemporaneous (Adj.)**

814. **Extenuate (V)** take away guilty; justify
Nothing can extenuate the killing of innocent lives by terrorists.

815. **Extenuating (Adj.)**

816. **Extenuation (N)**

817. **Exterminate (V)** destroy totally; wipe out
George Bush wanted to exterminate Al-Qaida organization.

818.	**Extermination (N)**
819.	**Extinction (N)** cease to exist; nothingness The satisfactory reasons of extinction of dinosaur have not been found.
820.	**Extinct (Adj.)**
821.	**Extirpate (V)** uproot; destroy We must make concerted efforts to extirpate corruption from society.
822.	**Extirpation (N)**
823.	**Extol (V)** praise; glorify Extol the virtuous and expose the vicious.
824.	**Extort (V)** wrest by intimidation; obtain money by violence His luxurious lifestyle forced him to extort money from rich people.
825.	**Extortion (N)**
826.	**Extortioner (N)**
827.	**Extravagance (N)** profligacy; reckless spending His profligacy and extravagance led him to bankruptcy.
828.	**Extravagant (Adj.)**
829.	**Extricate (V)** retrieve; come out He extricates evidence even about the dead cases.
830.	**Extrication (N)**
831.	**Exuberance (N)** liveliness; buoyancy; ebullience Katrina Kaif's outlook is full of exuberance.
832.	**Exuberant (Adj.)**
833.	**Exude (V)** be full of; give out; emit Nikhil's daughter exudes celestial beauty.

F

834.	**Fabricate (V)** forge To fabricate evidence is an offence under Indian Penal Code.
835.	**Fabrication (N)**
836.	**Fabulous (Adj.)** magnificent; incredible *Rang De Basanti* is a fabulous movie.
837.	**Fallacious (Adj.)** untrue; misleading The judge held the lawyer's argument fallacious and dismissed the case.
838.	**Fallacy (N)**
839.	**Fallible (Adj.)** vulnerable; subject to error Human beings are fallible and that is why it is said, 'To err is human'.
840.	**Falsify (V)** prove untrue His hopes of clearing the IAS examination have been falsified.
841.	**Falter (V)** go astray You should not falter once you start your preparation for IAS.
842.	**Famished (Adj.)** weak; starving The poor children looked famished due to hunger.
843.	**Fascinate (V)** captivate; charm Glamorous world fascinates the mind of youngsters and take them away from realities of life.
844.	**Fascination (N)** harsh
845.	**Fatal (Adj.)** calamitous; deadly He had a fatal heart attack.
846.	**Fateful (Adj.)** very important; decisive Her decision to go abroad was indeed a fateful one.
847.	**Fathom (V)** find out; measure the depth It is quite impossible to fathom the mysteries of life.
848.	**Fatuous (Adj.)** silly; lacking intelligence His fatuous replies to my queries irked me.
849.	**Faze (V)** confuse; bewilder The stormy punches of mike Tyson fazed the opponent in the ring.
850.	**Feasible (Adj.)** plausible; that which can be done With your meagre funds, your grandiose plans are not feasible.
851.	**Feasibility (N)**
852.	**Feat (N)** a very creditable accomplishment Winning a gold medal at Olympics is a great feat indeed.
853.	**Feckless (Adj.)** unavailing; inefficient; ineffective; futile The feckless youngsters cannot hope for much in life.
854.	**Fecklessness (N)**
855.	**Fecund (Adj.)** copious; fertile In order to excel in today's cut-throat competition, one need to have a fecund word power at disposal.
856.	**Fecundity (N)**

857.	**Feeble (Adj.)** weak; emaciated Feeble-minded people fail to make a mark in life.
858.	**Feebleness (N)**
859.	**Feign (V)** affect; pretend He feigns innocence but in reality he is very shrewd.
860.	**Felony (N)** heinous crime Theft and murder are felonies indeed.
861.	**Ferment (N)** upheaval; excitement There was a great ferment after India won the world cup.
862.	**Ferocity (N)** fierceness; savageness The boxers fought with the ferocity.
863.	**Ferocious (Adj.)**
864.	**Fervent (Adj.)** ardent; enthusiastic He made fervent efforts to succeed but couldn't.
865.	**Fervid (Adj.)** passionate; emotional His fervid arguments in the court convinced the judge.
866.	**Fester (V)** become infested; rankle His insults still rankle and fester in my mind.
867.	**Festive (Adj.)** happy; joyous; merry Diwali and Dusshera are great festive occasions in India.
868.	**Festivities (N)** celebrations; merriment Diwali festivities last for a week.
869.	**Fetter (N)** constrain; shackle; confine It is high time that Indian women should be set free from fetters of orthodoxy, conservatism and clutches of ignorance.
870.	**Fettle (N)** shape condition I hope my letters will find you in fine fettle.
871.	**Fiasco (N)** disaster; complete failure The match was a great fiasco for India.
872.	**Fickle (Adj.)** inconstant; unsteady Fickle minded are not able to make any concrete decision.
873.	**Fiddle (V)** waste; destroy Time management is life management, so do not fiddle with time.
874.	**Fidelity (N)** loyalty The fidelity of dogs towards their masters is unquestionable.

875.	**Finesse (N)** skill; deftness Karan Thapar conducts the TV programme with great finesse.
876.	**Finicky (Adj.)** fussy; fastidious Nobody likes his finicky attitude.
877.	**Fissiparous (Adj.)** divisive; centrifugal Caste and creed are the most dangerous fissiparous forces fragmenting India.
878.	**Fissure (N)** cleft; schism; crack Caste fissures pose a great threat to the unity of India.
879.	**Fitful (Adj.)** not continuous He has a fitful and unsettling nature.
880.	**Fix (N)** riddle; difficulty I was in a fix and didn't know what to do.
881.	**Fizzle (out) (V)** end feebly All his grand plans fizzled out for want of money.
882.	**Flabbergast (V)** shock; amaze; stun The common man stands flabbergasted and flummoxed at the sorry state of affairs prevailing in India.
883.	**Flabbergasting (Adj.)**
884.	**Flagrant (Adj.)** shocking; obviously bad The flagrant violation of laws by spoiled brats is very common sight in India.
885.	**Flair (N)** skill; panache; bent; elan Rajesh has a flair for the English language.
886.	**Flamboyant (Adj.)** brilliant; sparkling Kapil Dev was a flamboyant cricketer.
887.	**Flamboyance (N)**
888.	**Flare (N, V)** flicker The flare in her eyes mesmerized him.
889.	**Flare (V)** bursting of passions An ordinary issue can be flared up by the media.
890.	**Flaunt (V)** display; show off He flaunts his riches to overawe his near and dear ones.
891.	**Flawless (Adj.)** impeccable; spotless Deepika Padukone's performance was flawless in *Padmavat*.
892.	**Flawlessness (N)**
893.	**Flicker (N, V)** wave to and fro; on and off The poet looked at the flicker of the stars.

894.	**Flippant (Adj.)** lacking respect; frivolously; shallow
895.	**Flounder (V)** hesitate; make mistakes He made a good beginning in his business but floundered later for want of resources.
896.	**Flummox (V)** disconcert; confound The people seem flummoxed in the wake of Covid-19.
897.	**Fluster (V)** confuse Don't try to fluster me.
898.	**Flux (N)** continuous change India is in a state of flux since the 1990s.
899.	**Foible (N)** slight defect of character We all have our individual foibles which we need to identify and rectify.
900.	**Forbear (V)** refrain; be patient We must forbear and not fly into a rage.
901.	**Forbearance (N)**
902.	**Forecast (N)** prediction; foretelling The weather forecasts often go awry.
903.	**Forego (V)** give up; renounce He decided to forego his share in the property.
904.	**Foremost (Adj.)** primary; chief It is our first foremost duty to serve our parents.
905.	**Foresight (N)** the ability to foresee; anticipation, farsightedness One should have foresight to plan one's future.
906.	**Foresighted (Adj.)**
907.	**Forestall (V)** prevent; pre-empt He had the foresight to anticipate the crisis and forestall it.
908.	**Foretell (V)** predict; prognosticate An astrologer foretold that greater things lie in store for me.
909.	**Forfeit (V)** lose; be deprived of His surety was forfeited because of poor performance in elections.
910.	**Forlorn (Adj.)** lonely; unhappy The jilted lover looked forlorn and despaired of life.
911.	**Forsake (V)** give up; renounce Do not forsake your principles for filthy worldly lucres.
912.	**Forswear (V)** reject; renounce Ashoka forswore violence after the battle of Kalinga.
913.	**Forte (N)** strong point Mathematics has never been my forte.
914.	**Fortitude (N)** patient courage; moral strength; endurance. Fortitude wins against all odds.
915.	**Foster (V)** sustain; encourage His mother fostered great values in him.
916.	**Founder (V)** sink; fail The project foundered for want of funds.
917.	**Frigid (Adj.)** cold; unfriendly The two boxers entered the ring and exchanged frigid smiles.
918.	**Frigidity (N)**
919.	**Frail (Adj.)** weak; lacking in strength He had a frail body but a strong determination.
920.	**Frantic (Adj.)** frenzied; wild with excitement We made a frantic effort to score a good rank in CLAT 2020.
921.	**Fray (N)** brawl; fight; skirmish The Badal brothers entered the political fray against each other in 2012 Assembly Elections.
922.	**Fret (V)** express annoyance; feed discontentment He frets when his mother-in-law comes home calling.
923.	**Frisk (V)** search The passengers were frisked before boarding the plane.
924.	**Fritter (V)** waste time or money Time is very precious, do not fritter it away.
925.	**Frivolous (Adj.)** silly; lacking seriousness Avoid frivolous people and frivolous talk.
926.	**Frivolousness (N)**
927.	**Frolic (V)** play about in a lively way The little ones frolic, the young ones struggle and the old ones contemplate.
928.	**Frolicsome (Adj.)**
929.	**Frugal (Adj.)** simple; austere; thrifty One must live a frugal life and have a sound thinking.
930.	**Frugality (N)**

931.	**Fugitive (N)** one who flees from law Amitabh Bachchan played a unique role in his movie *Fugitive*.
932.	**Fulminate (V)** protest loudly and bitterly; denounce She fulminated against her alcoholic husband.
933.	**Fulmination (N)**
934.	**Fulsome (Adj.)** insincere; cloying Politicians feed on fulsome paeans of their sycophants.
935.	**Fume (V)** boil with rage; be furious She fumed at her husband's betrayal.
936.	**Fumigate (V)** cleanse The doctor fumigated his clinic.
937.	**Furore (N)** anger; excitement There was great furore over Lok Pal Bill in the Parliament.
938.	**Furtive (Adj.)** sly; shifty; secret The lovers held a furtive rendezvous.
939.	**Futile (Adj.)** vain; pointless Without divine grace, our efforts go futile.
940.	**Futility (N)**
941.	**Fuzzy (Adj.)** blurred; indistinct Politicians give fuzzy answers to simple questions.

G

942.	**Gab (gift of) (N)** articulation; power of speech Pradeep Virk is blessed with gift of gab.
943.	**Gainsay (V)** challenge; call in question Nobody can gainsay the prime minister's unimpeachable integrity.
944.	**Galvanize (V)** energize; vivify; rejuvenate The Speaker has the knack to galvanize the motivational level of students.
945.	**Gambit (N)** a clever move; publicity stunt Free power to farmers is an election gambit.
946.	**Gamut (N)** entire range; the whole course The gamut of questions posed by the journalist bamboozled the minister.
947.	**Gape (V)** gawk; stare with an open mouth The young men gaped at the beauty queen as she walked the ramp.
948.	**Garb (N)** apparel; clothes; disguise He is a swindler in the garb of a friend.
949.	**Gargantuan (Adj.)** gigantic; enormous Writing a book is a gargantuan task.
950.	**Garish (Adj.)** showy; excessively ornate He always behaves in a garish and flamboyant manner.
951.	**Garner (V)** gather; acquire Politicians go from door to door to garner support.
952.	**Garnish (V)** add spice; embellish He has the wit and scholarliness to garnish his speech with delightful quotes.
953.	**Garrulous (Adj.)** excessively talkative; wordy The garrulous wife continued with her homilies till her husband fell asleep.
954.	**Garrulity (N)**
955.	**Gasp (V)** wonder; amaze Everyone in the colony was gasping to see her photo as a topper in the newspaper.
956.	**Gaudy (Adj.)** a little too colourful The film star with his bright red shirt and green trousers appeared gaudy.
957.	**Gaudiness (N)**
958.	**Gawk (N, V)** stare foolishly; gape The young men simply gawked as the stately woman walked past them.
959.	**Gawkiness (N)**
960.	**Genial (Adj.)** friendly; pleasant Her genial disposition makes her an ideal housewife.
961.	**Geniality (N)**
962.	**Genocide (N)** killing a large number of people of one race Hitler's attempt to exterminate the Jews was genocide indeed.
963.	**Germane (Adj.)** relevant; pertinent Your question is not germane to the topic under discussion.
964.	**Germinate (V)** grow; sprout Love and discipline germinate in an ideal household.
965.	**Germination (N)**
966.	**Gerrymander (V)** manipulate unfairly; falsify facts He gerrymandered facts and figures for political gains.

967.	**Gesture (N)** an action of goodwill The young man offered his seat to the old man as a gesture of goodwill.
968.	**Gibberish (N)** meaningless; nonsense He spoke in French which to me sounded gibberish.
969.	**Gibe (V)** a sly remark; sneer; ridicule Politicians gibe at each other in election rallies.
970.	**Giggle (V)** silly, spasmodic laughter The bashful girls giggled at the compliment.
971.	**Gimmick (N)** trick; device The author's sensational disclosures are only a sales gimmick.
972.	**Gird (up) (V)** prepare oneself; get ready for action Gird up your loins and pick up the gauntlet.
973.	**Gist (N)** essence; substance Truth and non-violence form the gist of Gandhiji's philosophy.
974.	**Glimmer (N)** faith; unsteady light; gleam; twinkle; shimmer Even a glimmer of hope can sustain a sinking patient.
975.	**Gloss (N)** sheen; superficial lustre Go for the substance and not the gloss.
976.	**Gloss over (V)** ignore A mother glosses over her son's flaws.
977.	**Glum (Adj.)** unhappy; morose The captain looked glum at the loss of toss.
978.	**Glut (N)** abundance There is a shortage of onions but a glut of potatoes in the market.
979.	**Glutton (N)** one with ravenous hunger He is a popular glutton in the school.
980.	**Gluttonous (Adj.)**
981.	**Goad (V)** incite; instigate; prompt The wife goaded the husband into buying a new car.
982.	**Gobble (V)** swallow; eat quickly The rich gobble all the gains and the poor wallow in misery.
983.	**Gore (N)** blood; shed blood The battlefield presented a macabre sight of mayhem and gore.

984.	**Gory (Adj.)** blood stained; ensanguined; fierce The scene of bomb blast with scattered body parts presented a gory sight.
985.	**Grandeur (N)** splendor; great beauty The grandeur of palace speaks volume of its' magnificence and glories.
986.	**Grandiloquence (N)** brilliance; scintillation The learned speaker befuddled the audience with his sheer grandiloquence.
987.	**Grandiose (Adj.)** grand; splendid The world book fair was a grandiose show.
988.	**Grapple (V)** face; fight; combat Learn to grapple with hardships of life.
989.	**Gratuitous (Adv.)** free; without fee Advice offered gratuitous is seldom acted upon.
990.	**Grill (V)** interrogate; investigate The police grilled the terrorist.
991.	**Grimace (N, V)** show disgust; express displeasure He bore insults with a grimace.
992.	**Grit (N)** piece of stone; courage Life is difficult; we need verve and grit to face it.
993.	**Gritty (Adj.)**
994.	**Grizzle (V)** complain; carp; fret Take the rough and the smooth in your stride without any grizzle.
995.	**Groan (N)** a deep articulated sound uttered in despair or anger; a painful cry Moaning and groaning never pay.
996.	**Groggy (Adj.)** dazed; staggering; intoxicated He felt groggy after a glass of beer.
997.	**Grogginess (N)**
998.	**Groove (N)** walk; mode; mood Come out of your groove of sloth, be up and doing.
999.	**Grope (V)** move about in ignorance Without good company, we always grope in the dark.
1000.	**Growl (V)** utter a deep guttural sound of anger or hostility; complain The boss growled at my coming late for work.
1001.	**Grubby (Adj.)** dirty; untidy; mired Wash your hands; they look so grubby with farm work.

1002.	**Gruesome (Adj.)** unpleasant; hateful; dreadful; shocking The site of bomb blast was a gruesome spectacle.
1003.	**Gruesomeness (N)**
1004.	**Gruff (Adj.)** rough; coarse; cheerless He appears gruff but he is a very amicable person.
1005.	**Grumpy (Adj.)** morose; peevish She bore patiently with her grumpy old mother-in-law.
1006.	**Grumpiness (N)**
	H
1007.	**Haggard (Adj.)** wasted; worn out The lovelorn knight looked haggard and tired.
1008.	**Halcyon (Adj.)** clam; tranquil; rich and prosperous The halcyon days of student life are lost in the humdrum of professional life.
1009.	**Hale (Adj.)** in good health; robust; vigorous The old farmer was hale and hearty.
1010.	**Hallow (V)** sanctify; consecrate Jallianwala Bagh at Amritsar is hallowed by the blood of martyrs who fell to General Dyer's bullets.
1011.	**Hallowed (Adj.)**
1012.	**Hallucination (N)** illusion; delusion Many youngsters suffer from hallucination of virtual reality
1013.	**Hallucinate (V)**
1014.	**Hamper (V)** impede; obstruct Procrastination robs you off opportunity and hampers your growth.
1015.	**Hapless (Adj.)** unlucky; helpless The hapless victims of the tsunami suffered great travails.
1016.	**Haplessness (N)**
1017.	**Harrowing (Adj.)** agonizing; distress The Indian prisoners in Pakistani jails have a harrowing time.
1018.	**Hiatus (N)** gap; difference Will the hiatus between the rich and the poor be ever bridged?
1019.	**Hibernate (V)** be dormant; stay inactive The reptiles like snakes and lizards hibernate in winter.
1020.	**Hibernation (N)**
1021.	**High time (N)** right time; time to act It is high time for you to start preparing for the final examination.
1022.	**Hocus-pocus (N)** nonsense; baseless Rajesh thinks that astrology is all hocus-pocus.
1023.	**Hoi polloi (N)** riff-riff; common people The blue-blooded people do not associate with the hoi polloi.
1024.	**Hone (V)** sharpen; keen; mend Keep honing your writing skills.
1025.	**Horrid (Ad.)** very unpleasant; ugly The worsening condition of Covid-19 looks horrid in Delhi.
1026.	**Horridness (N)**
1027.	**Hover (V)** suspend; hang in the air It is a great sight to watch the kites hover above the playground.
1028.	**Hotchpotch (N)** strange mixture His essay was a hotchpotch of borrowed ideas.
1029.	**Hubbub (N)** loud, confused noise I prefer the quiet countryside ambience to the hubbub of city life.
1030.	**Huddle (NV)** get together, things or people lying together The herd of cows huddled together as the lion roared.
1031.	**Hullaballoo (N)** uproar; loud noise In the wake of the police firing, there was a lot of hullabaloo in the city.
1032.	**Humbug (N)** fraud; deception The testing in the wake of spreading Covid-19 is made a humbug.
1033.	**Hurly-burly (N)** commotion; noise and excitement The king abdicated the throne to get away from the hurly-burly of a busy life.
1034.	**Hurtle (V)** rush violently; move with great speed Lightning struck the plane and it hurtled into the sea.
1035.	**Husband (V)** conserver; use frugally We must husband our scanty water resources.
1036.	**Hustings (N)** political goings on A quiet and clean person like Manmohan Singh cannot succeed at the Political hustings.

	I
1037.	**Icon (N)** picture; image; idol He is an icon for all sports lovers.
1038.	**Iconic (Adj.)** **Iconoclast (N)** person who attacks cherished benefits. The author was an iconoclast of her times
1039.	**Iconoclastic (Adj.)** **Idiosyncrasy (N)** peculiarity; uniqueness The personal idiosyncrasies affect one's decisions when one is in power.
1040.	**Idiosyncratic (Adj.)**
1041.	**Idol (N)** icon; image Idol worship is cardinal to Hinduism.
1042.	**Ignoble (Adj.)** base; very low Female foeticide is an ignoble practice prevalent in India.
1043.	**Ignominy (N)** shame; disgrace The ignominy of defeat in the final examination still rankles in my mind.
1044.	**Illusive (Adj.)** false; non-existent Youngsters nowadays live in an illusive world.
1045.	**Illustrious (Adj.)** brilliant and well known Dr Abdul Kalam is an illustrious son of India.
1046.	Imbecile (Adj.) very stupid No one likes him for his imbecile activities.
1047.	**Imbecility (N)**
1048.	**Imbibe (V)** learn; assimilate We must imbibe great lessons given by our forefathers.
1049.	**Imbroglio (N)** difficult situation The Kashmir imbroglio stands resolved after revocation of Article 370.
1050.	**Imbue (V)** impress; inculcate; fill We must try to imbue children with great ideas.
1051.	**Immaculate (Adj.)** spotless Anna Hazare has an immaculate background.
1052.	**Immemorial (Adj.)** beyond memory Since times immemorial, women are subjected to cruelty in India.
1053.	**Immense (Adj.)** vast; great; very huge It gives immense pleasure to motivate the youngsters.

1054.	**Immensity (N)**
1055.	**Immerse (V)** busy; absorbed He was immersed in his studies.
1056.	**Immersion (N)**
1057.	**Immigrate (V)** go and settle abroad Aryans immigrated to India in 1500 B.C.
1058.	**Immigration (N)**
1059.	**Imminent (Adj.)** about to happen; impending He did not disclose about his imminent visit to Chandigarh.
1060.	**Imminence (N)**
1061.	**Immolate (V)** burn; set to flames Some students immolated themselves after Mandal Commission recommendations.
1062.	**Immolation (N)**
1063.	**Immune (Adj.)** unaffected; exempt He has become immune to criticism by public.
1064.	**Immure (V)** shut in; confine Her brother was immured in a lunatic asylum.
1065.	**Impair (V)** damage; make worse Lack of exercise impairs our health.
1066.	**Impairment (N)**
1067.	**Impale (V)** fix upon; pierce; thrust He impaled the flower beds with little sticks to support the flowers.
1068.	**Impart (V)** tell; relate; communicate The parents must impart good lessons to their children.
1069.	**Impasse (N)** deadlock Farmers' protest has reached an impasse from where comeback is not possible.
1070.	**Impeach (V)** remove The President of India can be impeached by 2/3rd majority in both the Houses.
1071.	**Impeachment (N)**
1072.	**Impeccable (Adj.)** faultless; flawless Kanchan has an impeccable personality.
1073.	**Impede (V)** obstruct Complacency impedes growth.
1074.	**Impediment (N)**
1075.	**Impel (V)** goad; inspire Patriotism impels us to great and glorious acts.

1076.	**Impending (Adj.)** in the offing; about to happen His impending visit to Chandigarh was keenly looked forward by the staff.
1077.	**Impenetrable (Adj.)** difficult to understand; impermeable His personality is really impenetrable.
1078.	**Imperceptible (Adj.)** small and difficult to see; gradual; subtle Our body and mind undergo imperceptible changes every day.
1079.	**Imperil (V)** put in peril; endanger I cannot imperil your career for small profits.
1080.	**Peril (N)**
1081.	**Perilous (Adj.)**
1082.	**Imperious (Adj.)** domineering; bossy; dictatorial The imperious and callous attitude of boss was not appreciated by anyone.
1083.	**Imperiousness (N)**
1084.	**Imperishable (Adj.)** enduring; lasting Humans may come and go but nature is imperishable.
1085.	**Impermeable (Adj.)** impenetrable; inaccessible; impassable The Fort of Ranthambore was impermeable.
1086.	**Impersonate (V)** pretend to be somebody else; assume some other character He impersonated an IAS officer and was arrested.
1087.	**Impersonation (N)**
1088.	**Impervious (Adj.)** unaffected; not influenced He was obstinate and impervious to all good suggestions.
1089.	**Imperviousness (N)**
1090.	**Impetuous (Adj.)** rash; done in a hurry He took an impetuous decision to divorce his wife.
1091.	**Impetuosity (N)**
1092.	**Impetus (N)** stimulus; inspiration My motivational lecture gave impetus to his preparation during examinations.
1093.	**Impiety (N)** lacking in reverence; lacking in duty and respect Disobedience to elders is an act of impiety.
1094.	**Impious (Adj.)**
1095.	**Impinge (V)** encroach; infringe; collide She didn't allow her household duties to impinge on her studies.
1096.	**Impingement (N)**
1097.	**Impish (Adj.)** playful; naughty The teachers found the impish little boy too difficult to discipline.
1098.	**Impishness (N)**
1099.	**Implacable (Adj.)** bitter; not inclined to be pacified Will India and Pakistan remain implacable foes forever?
1100.	**Implicate (V)** show involvement; imply; infer The police tried to implicate the innocent man, but the court acquitted him.
1101.	**Implication (N)**
1102.	**Imply (V)** suggest indirectly; indicate If someone prefers silence, it doesn't imply 'cowardice'.
1103.	**Implode (V)** explode within; burst inwards The communist regime in Soviet Union imploded from within.
1104.	**Implore (V)** pray; request The students implored the teacher for extra class.
1105.	**Imploration (N)**
1106.	**Import (N)** significance; underlying meaning The full import of his statement has not yet dawned on us.
1107.	**Impolitic (Adj.)** undiplomatic; indiscreet It would be impolitic to argue with the boss.
1108.	**Importunate (Adj.)** insistent; pertinacious; vexing I don't believe in giving alms but the beggar was importunate.
1109.	**Impose (V)** thrust; obtrude We should not impose our failures and fractured dreams on our children.
1110.	**Imposition (N)**
1111.	**Impostor (N)** swindler; one who imposes himself fraudulently He was not the missing son but an impostor.

1112.	**Impoverish (V)** enfeeble; debase Intoxication impoverishes our will and impairs our health..
1113.	**Impoverishment (N)**
1114.	**Impregnable (Adj.)** not to be overcome; invincible; invulnerable The enemy attacked again and again but the fortress remained impregnable.
1115.	**Imprint (N)** impress; influence A few good books, movies, and TV programmes leave indelible imprints on our minds.
1116.	**Impromptu (Adj. Adv.)** extempore; without preparation He gave impromptu speech that captivated the imagination of audience.
1117.	**Impropriety (N)** inappropriateness; indelicacy Bawdy jokes in the presence of women amount to impropriety.
1118.	**Improper (Adj.)**
1119.	**Improvident (Adj.)** unwise; lacking foresight It is improvident to invest now in the share market.
1120.	**Improvidence (N)**
1121.	**Improvise (N)** innovate; devise Indians may not be the greatest of inventors but they are best at improvising.
1122.	**Improvisation (N)**
1123.	**Impudence (N)** rudeness; pertness He doesn't expect impudence from his wife.
1124.	**Impudent (Adj.)**
1125.	**Impugn (V)** challenge; question We have no reason to impugn the veracity of his statement.
1126.	**Impulse (N)** spontaneous impetus; He does not plan his movement but acts on impulse.
1127.	**Impulsive (Adj.)**
1128.	**Impute (V)** attribute; ascribe He imputed to me his selfish motives which I never entertained.
1129.	**Impunity (N)** without fear of punishment; exemption from punishment We cannot challenge the boss with impunity.

1130.	**Inaccessible (Adj.)** difficult to reach; distant; far away; not available The chief minister remains inaccessible even to his colleagues.
1131.	**Inaccessibility (N)**
1132.	**Inadvertent (Adj.)** unwittingly; unknowingly; inattentively The omission of the name from the list was inadvertent.
1133.	**Inadvertence (N)**
1134.	**Inane (Adj.)** stupid; silly The judge found his argument inane and turned down his plea.
1135.	**Inapt (Adj.)** inappropriate; out of place; unbecoming His remarks were quite inapt and had no bearing on the subject.
1136.	**Inaptness (N)**
1137.	**Inarticulate (Adj.)** inexpressive; incoherent The bashful boy wanted to propose to the girl but was inarticulate.
1138.	**Inarticulation (N)**
1139.	**Inauspicious (Adj.)** not auspicious; unfavourable It was an inauspicious start but a good completion of project.
1140.	**Inauspiciousness**
1141.	**Inborn (Adj.)** inherent; innate; native He has inborn leadership qualities.
1142.	**Incandescent (Adj.)** be in great anger The general was incandescent with rage at his soldiers' inability to take the fort.
1143.	**Incandescence (N)**
1144.	**Incapacitate (V)** render ineffective; disqualify, make unfit Ill health incapacitated him and he gave up politics.
1145.	**Incarnate (N)** personified Lord Krishna is called God incarnate.
1146.	**Incarnation (N)** **Incense (V)** instigate The politician tried to incense the public feelings.
1147.	**Inception (N)** beginning; start Since its inception, the company is growing by leaps and bounds.

1148.	**Incessant (Adj.)** continuous; unceasing The incessant rains have inundated many low-lying areas.
1149.	**Incessantly (Adv.)**
1150.	**Incipient (Adj.)** in the initial stages; beginning to appear The UPA failed to stop the Anna Hazare movement at an incipient stage.
1151.	**Incisive (Adj.)** sharp; penetrating His critique on the book is intelligent and incisive.
1152.	**Incisiveness (N)**
1153.	**Incite (V)** instigate; goad Antony incited the Romans against the conspirators.
1154.	**Inclement (Adj.)** hostile; not favourable This winter season was extremely inclement in Chandigarh.
1155.	**Incognito (Adv.)** in disguise; with a concealed identity He disguised as a rich man and left India incognito.
1156.	**Inconceivable (Adj.)** unthinkable; unimaginable; incredible It is inconceivable for a poor man to lead a life of comfort.
1157.	**Inconceivability (N)**
1158.	**Incongruous (Adj.)** out of place; inappropriate; unbecoming His remarks were quite incongruous.
1159.	**Incongruity (N)**
1160.	**Inconsolable (Adj.)** not consolable deeply grieved The poor were inconsolable as their houses caught fire.
1161.	**Incontestable (Adj.)** unquestionable; undoubted; unanimously agreed It is incontestable that Paulo Coelho is a great motivational writer of our times.
1162.	**Incontinence (N)** immoderation; lack of restraint He was notorious for his incontinence and profligacy.
1163.	**Incontinent (Adj.)**
1164.	**Incontrovertible (Adj.)** unquestionable; undoubted; irrefutable It is incontrovertible that Gandhiji played a great role in freedom movement.

1165.	**Incontrovertibility (N)**
1166.	**Incorporate (V)** include; adopt; embody; combine All the corrections/ modifications were incorporated in the new edition.
1167.	**Incorporation (N)**
1168.	**Incorrigible (Adj.)** beyond correction; beyond reform I am an incorrigible optimist.
1169.	**Incredible (Adj.)** unbelievable Neetu is very expert in weaving incredible cock and bull stories.
1170.	**Incredibility (N)**
1171.	**Incredulous (Adj.)** skeptical; disinclined to believe I remain incredulous to the stories of reincarnation.
1172.	**Incriminate (V)** charge with crime; condemn His testimony incriminated his friend.
1173.	**Incriminatory (Adv.)**
1174.	**Inculcate (V)** indoctrinate; inject; assimilate Parents must inculcate good values in children.
1175.	**Inculcation (N)**
1176.	**Incumbent (N)** one who holds an office, etc. The new incumbent has not yet taken over the charge of his office.
1177.	**Incumbent (Adv.)** obligatory; necessary It is incumbent on a father to provide basic needs for the family.
1178.	**Incumbency (N)**
1179.	Incur (V) invite censure; become liable I do not want to incur the wrath of my boss.
1180.	**Incursion (N)** raid; invasion; hostile entrance The troops foiled the enemy's incursion in our territory.
1181.	**Indebted (Adj.)** under obligation; grateful; obliged We are indebted to our parents for their love and care.
1182.	**Indefatigable (Adj.)** untiring; tireless He is a live example of indefatigable efforts.
1183.	**Indefatigability (N)**
1184.	**Indefeasible (Adj.)** not to be forfeited; not to be annulled The right to live with dignity is indefeasible and cannot be taken away.

1185.	**Indefeasibility (N)**
1186.	**Indelible (Adj.)** not to be deleted or erased; indestructible The words of few teachers leave indelible impression on students' minds.
1187.	**Indelicate (Adj.)** rough; crass; lacking propriety His speech was indelicate and unbecoming of gentleman.
1188.	**Indelicacy (N)** Indelicacy is too mild a term to convey the idea.
1189.	**Indeterminate (Adj.)** vague; uncertain The percentage of role of fate in one's success is rather indeterminate.
1190.	**Indict (V)** charge with crime; arraign The jury indicted him for embezzlement.
1191.	**Indifference (N)** lack of interest Public indifference towards public issues is the greatest reason for the sorry state of affairs in India.
1192.	**Indifferent (Adj.)**
1193.	**Indigenous (Adj.)** native; innate; inherent Litchi is an indigenous fruit of Bihar.
1194.	**Indigent (Adj.)** impoverished Mother Teresa took care of the poor and the indigent.
1195.	**Indigence (N)**
1196.	**Indignant (Adj.)** angry The manager used to be indignant if anybody came late.
1197.	**Indignity (N)** ignominy; humiliation; affront Pakistan still reels under the indignity of losing to India in 1971 war.
1198.	**Indiscreet (Adj.)** careless; imprudent It was indiscreet of the office to make public the Govt.'s secret policy to control terrorism.
1199.	**Indiscretion (N)**
1200.	**Indiscriminate (Adj.)** not careful; needless; choosing at random He is indiscriminate in spending money.
1201.	**Indispensable (Adj.)** absolutely necessary or requisite Nobody is indispensable in this world.

1202.	**Indispensability (N)**
1203.	**Indisputable (Adj.)** absolutely valid; undeniable It is indisputable that Narasimha Rao was the harbinger of policy of liberalization.
1204.	**Indisputability (N)**
1205.	**Indoctrinate (V)** instruct; inculcate Religious leaders indoctrinate their followers with their beliefs.
1206.	**Indoctrination (N)**
1207.	**Indolent (Adj.)** lazy; slothful An indolent person is not respected by society.
1208.	**Indolence (N)**
1209.	**Indomitable (Adj.)** unyielding; not to be overcome Gandhiji was an indomitable crusader for truth and non-violence.
1210.	**Indubitable (Adj.)** unquestionable; certain It is indubitable that Nehru was Gandhiji's blue-eyed boy.
1211.	**Induce (V)** persuade; urge Nothing could induce the grand old man to move away from his old mansion.
1212.	**Indulgent (Adj.)** tolerant; lenient The mother was harsh to her daughters but indulgent to her son.
1213.	**Indulgence (N)**
1214.	**Industrious (Adj.)** hardworking; diligent The industrious Lakshmi Mittal set up a great business empire.
1215.	**Industry (N)**
1216.	**Inebriated (Adj.)** drunk; intoxicated The inebriated young men created a ruckus outside the bar.
1217.	**Inebriation (N)**
1218.	**Inept (Adj.)** lacking in skill; inappropriate He is an inept painter.
1219.	**Ineradicable (Adj.)** not capable of being removed or rooted out Nepotism and corruption seem ineradicable in India.
1220.	**Inert (Adj.)** immobile; unmoving; lifeless The cold-blooded reptiles become inert in winter season.

1221.	**Inevitable (Adj.)** certain; unavoidable Sometime it becomes inevitable to face certain situations in life.
1222.	**Inevitability (N)**
1223.	**Inexorable (Adj.)** unyielding; unalterable Fate is inexorable and we can only submit to it.
1224.	**Infatuation (N)** foolish or all absorbing passion; unreasoning obsession The young boy had infatuation for his school mate.
1225.	**Infatuate (V)**
1226.	**Infer (V)** deduce; interpret; conclude We should not infer something wrong from someone's silence.
1227.	**Inference (N)**
1228.	**Infernal (Adj.)** hellish; fiendish; diabolical The massacre at Jallianwala Bagh was an infernal act.
1229.	**Infest (V)** haunt; overrun; abound Marshes and swamps are infested with deadly mosquitoes.
1230.	**Infested (Adj.)**
1231.	**Infidel (N)** unbeliever; Kafir The infidels are not respecters of holy places.
1232.	**Infidelity (N)**
1233.	**Influx (N)** act of flowing; an inflow The influx of terrorists can be checked if there is political will.
1234.	**Infraction (N)** breach; disobedience; transgression Jumping the red light is an infraction of traffic rules.
1235.	**Infringe (V)** violate; transgress; breach Don't infringe upon others' rights.
1236.	**Infringement (N)**
1237.	**Ingenious (Adj.)** skilled; clever; inventive Yash Raj Chopra was an ingenious director.
1238.	**Ingenuity (N)**
1239.	**Ingenuous (Adj.)** artless; innocent; honest She charms one and all with her ingenuous ways.
1240.	**Ingenuousness (N)**

1241.	**Inglorious (Adj.)** shameful; disgraceful The Indian cricket team is going through an inglorious phase.
1242.	**Ingratitude (N)** thanklessness Disrespecting your parents is height of ingratitude.
1243.	**Ingredient (N)** constituent; trait Hard work is the first and foremost ingredient of success.
1244.	**Inhere (V)** be a permanent part; exist inseparably The real powers in here in the Prime Minister of India whereas the President of India is only the de jure Head of the State.
1245.	**Inherent (Adj.)**
1246.	**Inhibit (V)** impede; obstruct Drinking inhibits your power of thinking rationally.
1247.	**Inhibition (N)**
1248.	**Inimical (Adj.)** hostile; opposed; harmful The boss was inimical to me and I was forced to resign.
1249.	**Inimitable (Adj.)** not to be imitated; unique He is a guitarist with inimitable skills.
1250.	**Iniquitous (Adj.)** unjust; wicked; sinful The gaping schism between the rich and the poor is iniquitous indeed.
1251.	**Iniquity (N)**
1252.	**Initiate (V)** to begin You should initiate anything with optimism.
1253.	**Initiation (N)**
1254.	**Injudicious (Adj.)** indiscreet; unwise One cannot afford to be injudicious while deciding the career options for children.
1255.	**Injunction (N)** order; admonition; a legal restriction In the wake of the High Court's injunction, his transfer was revoked.
1256.	**Injurious (Adj.)** harmful; hurtful Smoking and drinking are injurious to health.
1257.	**Inkling (N)** foreboding; foreknowledge; apprehension I had not even an iota of inkling that he will betray us.

1258.	**Inopportune (Adj.)** inappropriate; untimely; inauspicious The astrologers think that the time during solar eclipse is inopportune for beginning an enterprise.
1259.	**Inordinate (Adj.)** excessive; immoderate The house was ready, but incurred an inordinate amount of time and money.
1260.	**Inquisitive (Adj.)** keen; earnest Philosophers are as inquisitive as children are.
1261.	**Inquisitiveness (N)**
1262.	**Insatiable (Adj.)** unappeasable; not capable of being satisfied Nipun has an insatiable thirst for knowledge.
1263.	**Insatiate (Adj.)**
1264.	**Inscrutable (Adj.)** mysterious; difficult to know The ways of God to name a person and fame a person are really inscrutable.
1265.	**Insidious (Adj.)** beguiling; treacherous; deceitful Smoking, drinking and pollution are mankind's insidious enemies.
1266.	**Insidiousness (N)**
1267.	**Insinuate (V)** hint; imply He insinuated that I was acting against his interests.
1268.	**Insipid (Adj.)** dull; unanimated His insipid lecture exposed him.
1269.	**Insolence (N)** rudeness; impertinence Despite her talent Neetu's insolence cost him her job.
1270.	**Insolent (Adj.)**
1271.	**Insolvent (Adj.)** bankrupt; unable to pay debts His profligate ways soon rendered him insolvent.
1272.	**Insolvency (N)**
1273.	**Instigate (V)** incite; provoke His wife instigated him against his parents.
1274.	**Instigation (N)**
1275.	**Insurgent (N)** rebel; one who fights against the government The naxal insurgents launched land attacks on the police forces.
1276.	**Intrinsic (Adj.)** essential; basic Fundamental Rights are essential and intrinsic for the development of the individuals.

J

1277.	**Jargon (N)** vocabulary peculiar to a trade or group The speaker used academic jargon to try to bamboozle the audience.
1278.	**Jaundiced (Adj.)** prejudiced; biased Communal thinking makes our view point jaundiced and fanatic.
1279.	**Jeopardize (V)** endanger; hazard; imperil They tried to jeopardize the proceedings but failed.
1280.	**Jeopardy (N)**
1281.	**Jilt (V)** reject; cast aside His girl friend jilted him for another boy.
1282.	**Jocund (Adj.)** cheerful; jovial Wordsworth felt happy in the jocund company of daffodils.
1283.	**Jovial (Adj.)** Jocund; cheerful The jovial husband and jocund wife made a perfect couple.
1284.	**Joviality (N)**
1285.	**Jubilant (Adj.)** buoyant; delighted The fans were jubilant when India defeated Australia in the cricket series.
1286.	**Jubilation (N)**
1287.	**Junta (N)** a small group of rulers The military junta under leadership of Musharraf took over in Pakistan.
1288.	**Jury (N)** a body of persons sworn to administer justice The jury held him guilty with a unanimous verdict.
1289.	**Juvenile (Adj.)** immature; infantile Juvenile offenders are tried by juvenile courts.
1290.	**Juxtapose (V)** place side by side The hero and heroine were lying juxtaposing each other.
1291.	**Juxtaposition (N)**

K

1292.	**Keen (Adj.)** earnest; intense He has keen interest in mathematics.
1293.	**Keenness (N)**
1294.	**Kindle (V)** awaken; generate His motivational lecture kindled a new spirit in the youngsters.
1295.	**Knell (N)** peal or bell for funeral or death The death knell of communism has been sounded in most parts of the world.
1296.	**Knotty (Adj.)** difficult to solve; intricate; difficult It was a very knotty problem to be solved too easily.
1297.	**Kowtow (V)** follows obsequiously; bootlick Indians are addicted to kowtow and deify the English.
1298.	**Kudos (N)** praise; complements He deserves kudos for his writing skills.

L

1299.	**Laborious (Adj.)** hardworking; diligent Kanchan is a laborious girl.
1300.	**Lackadaisical (Adj.)** dull; lacking interest The bureaucrats in India have lackadaisical approach towards problems of a common man.
1301.	**Laconic (Adj.)** meaningful but brief; short His replies are always laconic but meaningful.
1302.	**Lacuna (N)** gap; something missing The Indian legal system has many lacunas.
1303.	**Laggard (N)** lazy; one who lags behind He is big laggard by nature.
1304.	**Lambaste (V)** denounce; criticize severely The oppositions always lambaste the ruling party.
1305.	**Lampoon (V)** ridicule; sharp satire We should not lampoon the needy.
1306.	**Languid (Adj.)** faint; lacking vigour His batting had a languid grace.
1307.	**Lascivious (Adj.)** lecherous; prurient, lewd, libidinous She didn't like his lascivious looks and kept him at a distance.
1308.	**Lax (Adj.)** lacking in severely; negligent; loose His lax attitude is reason of his bad reputation.
1309.	**Laxity (N)**
1310.	**Lechery (N)** lewdness; immortality His lechery rendered him unfit for the company.
1311.	**Lecherous (Adj.)**
1312.	**Legend (N)** a famous man; a celebrity Dilip Kumar remains a legend in the world of Indian cinema.
1313.	**Levy (V)** tax; impost The government levied new taxes on traders.
1314.	**Liable (Adj.)** responsible A master is liable for the acts of his servants which is called a vicarious liability.
1315.	**Liability (N)**
1316.	**Libertine (N)** rake; profligate; immoral The libertine is flush with money but lax in morals.
1317.	**Licentious (Adj.)** lewd; prurient His licentious ways have eroded his credibility among good people.
1318.	**Limp (Adj.)** walk listlessly; lacking firmness Since his leg was operated after accident, he still limps while walking.
1319.	**Limpid (Adj.)** clear; transparent He could see his reflection in the lake's limpid waters.
1320.	**Limpidity (N)**
1321.	**Lionize (V)** treat as a celebrity The crowds lionize the victors and boo the vanquished.
1322.	**Lionization (N)**
1323.	**Lineage (JN)** lineal descent; ancestry Balban claimed a royal lineage from the royal dynasty depicted by Firdausi in Shahnama.
1324.	**Listless (Adj.)** unenthusiastic; lifeless Listless efforts do not bear fruit.
1325.	**Listlessness (N)**
1326.	**Litter (V)** objects strewn or scattered around His room was littered with books.
1327.	**Lively (Adj.)** full of life; spirited Malayika is a lively and charming girl.
1328.	**Livid (Adj.)** very angry The boss was livid with rage at the clerk's insubordination.

1329.	**Loathe (V)** hate; abhor Don't loathe downtrodden and poor people.
1330.	**Longevity (N)** long life Healthy genes, simple life and balanced diet are the secrets of longevity.
1331.	**Loom (V)** appear; come into view threateningly A certain defeat looms large for our team.
1332.	**Loquacious (Adj.)** talkative Women are more loquacious than men.
1333.	**Loquaciousness (N)**
1334.	**Ludicrous (Adj.)** pointless; without substance The judge found the plea ludicrous and dismissed the case.
1335.	**Ludicrousness (N)**
1336.	**Lugubrious (Adj.)** sad; gloomy His lugubrious attitude made him unpopular among peer group.
1337.	**Luminous (Adj.)** radiating light The sky was luminous with stars.
1338.	**Luminosity (N)**
1339.	**Luscious (Adj.)** mouth watering Katrina Kaif is a luscious beauty.
1340.	**Lusty (Adj.)** full of lust His lusty looks earned him notoriety in the college.
1341.	**Luxuriant (Adj.)** lush; green; rich The woods are lovely, dark, deep and luxuriant.
1342.	**Luxuriance (N)**
1343.	**Luxuriate (V)** lead a life of luxury You can luxuriate in your retirement if you save money and health.
1344.	**Luxurious (Adj.)** full of comfort and riches The poor are famished and the rich lead a luxurious life.
1345.	**Lyrical (Adj.)** musical; poetic; spontaneous Javed Akhtar's book 'Tarkash' is a lyrical composition.

M

1346.	**Macabre (Adj.)** horrible; frightening; gruesome The Mumbai attacks were really a macabre act indeed.
1347.	**Machination (N)** conspiracy; intrigue; crafty plot Mahima is not liked because of her machinations.
1348.	**Magnanimous (Adj.)** large hearted; generous Micky is known for his magnanimous gestures.
1349.	**Magnanimity (N)**
1350.	**Magnify (V)** exaggerate; enlarge Politicians always try to magnify the things to galvanize the feelings of public.
1351.	**Magniloquent (Adj.)** grandiloquent; pompous; bombastic Dr Kumar is notorious for his magniloquent expressions.
1352.	**Magniloquence (N)**
1353.	**Magnum opus (N)** masterpiece Paulo Coelho's book *Alchemist* is his magnum opus.
1354.	**Maim (V)** mangle; cripple A bullet hit him in the leg and maimed him for life.
1355.	**Malaise (N)** sickness; uneasiness Corruption is the biggest malaise afflicting India.
1356.	**Malediction (N)** imprecation; curse; slander The poor people's malediction has no effects on authorities.
1357.	**Maleficent (Adj.)** malicious Stealing and playing dice are maleficent acts.
1358.	**Malevolent (Adj.)** wishing evil; vindictive Malevolent feelings do not pay.
1359.	**Malfeasance (N)** wrongdoing; contrary to law The district officer was charged with malfeasance and hence sacked.
1360.	**Malignant (Adj.)** disposed to cause harm or distress He suffered from a malignant tumor and was critical.
1361.	**Malignity (N)** malevolence; intense ill will He surged ahead in life despite the malignity of his business rivals.

1362.	**Maltreat (V)** ill-treat; abuse Power went into his head and he began to maltreat the poor relatives.
1363.	**Mangle (V)** maim; disfigure; spoil The collision with the truck mangled the car.
1364.	**Manoeuvre (V)** adroit move; smart strategy She is a vamp and always tries to manoeuvre and manipulate the customers.
1365.	**Manifest (V)** mirror; reflect; display Your character manifests in your day-to-day conduct.
1366.	**Maroon (V)** isolated as if on a desolate island The devastating tsunami marooned many islands.
1367.	**Maverick (N)** dissenter; one who follows his own path The mavericks make their own path and follow none.
1368.	**Mawkish (Adj.)** sentimental She made mawkish gestures to impress her boyfriend.
1369.	**Mawkishness (N)**
1370.	**Mayhem (N)** confusion and fear, terror After the Mumbai attacks, the Taj hotel was picture of mayhem.
1371.	**Maze (N)** zig-zag; serpentine path The maze of city traffic confounds men from the countryside.
1372.	**Meagre (Adj.)** inadequate; insufficient; scanty The widow managed the household with her meagre resources.
1373.	**Meagrely (Adv.)**
1374.	**Meagreness (N)**
1375.	**Meander (V)** maze around; move in a zigzag manner. The Kalka-Shimla toy train delightfully meanders through green valleys and high hills.
1376.	**Meek (Adj.)** humble; submissive Meek person cannot hope much in life.
1377.	**Meekness (N)**
1378.	**Melancholy (Adj.)** a gloomy state; depression He was in a state of melancholy after his wife's death.
1379.	**Melancholic (Adj.)**
1380.	**Mellifluous (Adj.)** sweet; melodious Lata's mellifluous voice renders everyone voiceless in front of her.
1381.	**Mellifluousness (N)**
1382.	**Mellow (Adj.)** mature; soften People mellow with age.
1383.	**Mellowness (N)**
1384.	**Menace (N)** threat; danger Population explosion is the greatest menace before our nation.
1385.	**Menacing (Adj.)**
1386.	**Menacingly (Adv.)**
1387.	**Mend (V)** repair; reform Mend your ways before you lose your friends.
1388.	**Mendacity (N)** untruth; falsity My rivals targeted me with scandal, malevolence and mendacity but could not scuttle my rise and growth.
1389.	**Mendacious (Adj.)**
1390.	**Mendicant (N)** beggar The mendicant monks were very gracious.
1391.	**Menial (Adj.)** domestic servant; servile; unskilled In foreign countries, menial jobs are not despised.
1392.	**Mentor (N)** master; guide; preceptor Gokhale was Gandhi's political mentor.
1393.	**Mercurial (Adj.)** volatile; sprightly; fickle; erratic His wife found his temperament too mercurial and divorced him.
1394.	**Meretricious (Adj.)** showy; tawdry The meretricious glitter and glamour at Punjabi weddings is appalling.
1395.	**Meretriciousness (N)**
1396.	**Mesmerize (V)** enchant; hypnotize; spellbind The onlookers were mesmerized by the maestro's wizardry.
1397.	**Metamorphose (V)** transform; bring out a complete change He totally metamorphosed into a new human being since he fell in love.
1398.	**Metamorphosis (N)**

1399.	**Meteoric (Adj.)** sudden; swift and brilliant Dhirubhai Ambani had a meteoric rise in his career with his diligence and entrepreneurial skills.
1400.	**Meticulous (Adj.)** extremely careful; impeccable Vipin is meticulous in his research.
1401.	**Meticulousness (N)**
1402.	**Mettle (N)** courage; substance; forte He kept his temper under control and showed his mettle in times of crisis.
1403.	**Mettlesome (Adj.)**
1404.	**Milieu (N)** ambience; social atmosphere Indian cultural milieu is really an exemplary one.
1405.	**Minion (N)** servile follower; subordinate The bureaucrats are the minions of politicians.
1406.	**Minutiae (N)** precise detail I learnt the salient points and ignored the minutiae of the new legislation.
1407.	**Mirage (N)** something illusory and without reality True love seems to be a mirage in today's world.
1408.	**Mire (N, V)** bog; marsh The wheels got stuck in the mire.
1409.	**Mirth (N)** joy; cheerfulness; jollity There was all around atmosphere of mirth, fun and frolic on occasion of Diwali.
1410.	**Misbegotten (Adj.)** ill conceived; illegitimate His misbegotten investment wrought his financial ruin.
1411.	**Miscarriage (N)** untimely expulsion of a foetus; mismanagement Justice delayed is also miscarriage of justice.
1412.	**Miscarry (V)**
1413.	**Mischance (N)** misfortune; mishap It was sheer mischance to be out of selection for final stage.
1414.	**Misconstrue (V)** misinterpret; misunderstand My words were misconstrued.

1415.	**Miscreant (N)** depraved; base; villain The miscreants resorted to looting during a prolonged blackout.
1416.	**Misdemeanour (N)** wrong doing; misbehavior Disobedience to one's parents is a misdemeanour.
1417.	**Miserly (Adj.)** parsimonious; penurious; niggardly The miserly old lady gave no alms to the poor beggar.
1418.	**Misgiving (N)** fear; apprehension He allayed her misgivings and assured her that all was well at home.
1419.	**Misgive (V)**
1420.	**Mishap (N)** unfortunate accident; mishap The plane flew in bad weather but landed without mishap.
1421.	**Mitigate (V)** lessen; make less severe The government has compensated the flood victims to mitigate the calamity.
1422.	**Mitigation (N)**
1423.	**Mock (V)** ridicule; assault; deride My rich cousins mock at my country ways.
1424.	**Modicum (N)** a small measure With a modicum of hard work and luck, you will pass the test.
1425.	**Mollify (V)** appease; pacify All the efforts to mollify Pakistan have gone waste.
1426.	**Momentary (Adj.)** lasting for a moment; very brief The pleasures of this world are momentary.
1427.	**Moment (N)**
1428.	**Momentous (Adj.)** of great importance; distinguished It would be a momentous occasion for India when she becomes a permanent member of the Security Council.
1429.	**Momentousness (N)**
1430.	**Momentum (N)** force; impetus As the exams came near, the students get momentum in their studies.
1431.	**Monstrous (Adj.)** ugly; hideous Politicians resort to monstrous ways for their own aggrandizement.

1432.	**Monstrosity (N)**
1433.	**Monumental (Adj.)** massive; imposing; of great importance Paulo Coelho's *Alchemist* is a monumental work.
1434.	**Moot (Adj.)** debatable; doubtful Whether he should have played that shot or not will remain the moot point forever.
1435.	**Morale (N)** confidence; zeal The regular scolding by parents leaves detrimental effects on the morale of children.
1436.	**Morass (N)** marsh; bog; a marshy ground. The statement is a morass of prevarications.
1437.	**Morbid (Adj.)** unwholesome; gloomy; diseased I have a morbid fear of driving since I met with an accident during my college days.
1438.	**Morbidity (N)**
1439.	**Mordant (Adj.)** caustic; sarcastic He outwitted his opponents with his mordant wit.
1440.	**Moribund (Adj.)** in a dying state; near death The joint family is almost a moribund institution.
1441.	**Morose (Adj.)** gloomy; sullen; ill-humored After his father's death, he was too morose to avoid his friend's marriage.
1442.	**Moroseness (N)**
1443.	**Mortal (Adj.)** subject to death; belonging to this world Man is a mortal being.
1444.	**Mortality (N)** conditions of death; death rate India has a high rate of child mortality.
1445.	**Motely (N)** mixed; varied India is a motely of castes, classes, languages, religions and regions.
1446.	**Muddle (V)** confuse; confound Don't try to muddle me.
1447.	**Muggy (Adj.)** humid and oppressive It was muggy day and we didn't go for a walk.
1448.	**Mull (V)** ponder; reflect The old man was mulling over the experiences of life.
1449.	**Mundane (Adj.)** ordinary; uninteresting; worldly The spiritual people do not take interest in mundane things.
1450.	**Mundaneness (N)**
1451.	**Munificence (N)** generosity; large-heartedness In a fit of munificence, he donated his estate to a charitable hospital.
1452.	**Munificent (Adj.)**
1453.	**Murky (Adj.)** gloomy; darkened It is necessary to bring him out of murky state of mind.
1454.	**Murkiness (N)**
1455.	**Murkily, (Adv.)**
1456.	**Muse (V)** ponder; mull; reflect The philosopher mused over his past life.
1457.	**Mushroom (V)** sprout in large numbers Educational institutes are mushrooming up in Chandigarh.
1458.	**Muster (V)** gather; measure up to You must muster courage to face the ups and downs in life.
1459.	**Mutable (Adj.)** subject to change Life is mutable and constantly in a state of flux.
1460.	**Mutability (N)**
1461.	**Mutilate (V)** maim; mangle; disfigure The car accident mutilated his arms and legs.
1462.	**Mutilation (N)**
1463.	**Muzzle (V)** stifle; restrain from free speech Politicians try to ruffle the feelings and muzzle the voices of the masses.
1464.	**Mystique (N)** the quality of being attractive and interesting Paulo Coelho's mystique as a writer will never vanish.

N

1465.	**Nadir (N)** lowest point Congress party is at nadir of its popularity.
1466.	**Nag (V)** pester; annoy There is no greater torture on earth than a wife who nags.
1467.	**Nausea (N)** sickness at the stomach A bus journey in the hills always gives him nausea.

1468.	**Nauseate (V)**
1469.	**Nauseating (Adj.)**
1470.	**Naïve (Adj.)** innocent; inexperienced in the ways of the world The rich heiress was naïve in the ways of the world and married a charlatan
1471.	**Naiveté (N)**
1472.	**Nap (N)** a short sleep An afternoon nap refreshed me.
1473.	**Nascent (Adj.)** beginning; unfolding The young girl's nascent love affair is yet to blossom.
1474.	**Nefarious (Adj.)** extremely wicked Nepotism is a nefarious practice indeed.
1475.	**Nepotism (N)** the act of favouring one's kin Nepotism is the bane of Indian society.
1476.	**Nettle (V)** annoy; irritate; irk Coming late to class nettled the tutor.
1477.	**Nettlesome (Adj.)**
1478.	**Nexus (Noun)** link; tie; binding The politicians-criminals-bureaucracy is the most fatal nexus in India.
1479.	**Niche (N)** suitable position He carved out a niche for himself in the Bollywood with sheer hard work.
1480.	**Nihilist (N)** one who reject everything A nihilist has no value system.
1481.	**Nincompoop (N)** fool; simpleton Naveen is virtually a nincompoop.
1482.	**Nonchalance (N)** indifference; casualness; carelessness He dealt with the crisis with nonchalance.
1483.	**Nonchalant (Adj.)**
1484.	**Nonentity (N)** of no importance; nonexistent His latest book is a tell tale of his journey from nonentity to celebrity.
1485.	**Nonplus (V)** perplex; puzzle The prosecution lawyer nonplussed the witness.
1486.	**Nostalgia (N)** homesickness; His nostalgia for his hometown was intense.
1487.	**Novelty (N)** the newness; freshness; originality His books lack novelty and variety.
1488.	**Novel (Adj.)**
1489.	**Novice (N)** inexperienced; beginner He is still a novice and has far to go.
1490.	**Noxious (N)** harmful; injurious Smoking and drinking are noxious habits.
1491.	**Noxiously (Adj.)**
1492.	**Noxiousness (N)**
1493.	**Nuance (N)** a subtle variation; shade; hue A novice takes time to learn the subtle nuances of his trade.
	O
1494.	**Oasis (N)** a green area in a desert; a pleasant refuge Books are great oasis of solitude.
1495.	**Obdurate (Adj.)** stubborn; mulish He was obdurate and did not fall in with his parents' wishes.
1496.	**Obduracy (N)**
1497.	**Obfuscate (V)** confuse; stupefy; bewilder With unnecessary and irrelevant details, he only obfuscated the issue.
1498.	**Obfuscation (N)**
1499.	**Obituary (N)** notice of death The obituary reads like a paean.
1500.	**Objurgate (V)** reproach; denounce His father objurgated him for his undesirable ways.
1501.	**Objurgation (N)**
1502.	**Obliterate (V)** erase; destroy We can relegate our memories but not obliterate them.
1503.	**Oblation (N)** offering to a God The poor beggar offered a handful of rice to the deity by way of an old oblation.
1504.	**Obliteration (N)**
1505.	**Oblivion (N)** forgetfulness; the state of being forgotten The stars of today are lost into oblivion with the passage of time.
1506.	**Oblivious (Adj.)**
1507.	**Obnoxious (Adj.)** offensive; odious His obnoxious manners estranged his wife.
1508.	**Obnoxiously (Adj.)**
1509.	**Obnoxiousness (N)**
1510.	**Obsequious (Adj.)** compliant She made an obsequious request.

1511.	**Obsequiousness (N)**
1512.	**Opportune (Adj.)** auspicious; in good time; timely Diwali is the most opportune time to begin a new enterprise.
1513.	**Oppress (V)** inflict misery Saddam Hussein was very notorious for oppressing the public.
1514.	**Oppression (N)**
1515.	**Opprobrium (N)** obloquy; disgrace; discredit He earns opprobrium for his snobbery and foppishness.
1516.	**Opprobrious (Adj.)** disgraceful; discreditable President Bush was unmoved by the opprobrious remarks about his Iraq policy.
1517.	**Opulence (N)** great riches; abundance Business tycoons lead life of opulence whereas public reel under abject poverty.
1518.	**Opulent (Adj.)**
1519.	**Opus (Magnum)** a writer's masterpiece The Alchemist is Paulo Coelho's magnum opus.
1520.	**Ordeal (N)** trouble; difficulty; crisis The earthquake victims are faced with a great ordeal.
1521.	**Ordinance (N)** a decree; a command; a public injunction The President of India has ordinance making power under Article 123.
1522.	**Orgy (N)** wild excess The terrorists went on an orgy of insensate killings.
1523.	**Orientate (V)** adjust; adapt; be in harmony I am yet to orientate myself in my new job.
1524.	**Orientation (N)**
1525.	**Ornate (Adj.)** highly adorned He entered the beautiful and ornate hotel.
1526.	**Ornately (Adv.)**
1527.	**Ornateness (N)**
1528.	**Ossify (V)** harden into bones; become rigid Her feelings got ossified when she was deserted by her husband.
1529.	**Ossification (N)**
1530.	**Ostentation (N)** pretentious show; pretension Mrs Sharma is being laughed at her for making an ostentation of her wealth.
1531.	**Ostentatious (Adj.)** pretentious The wedding was an ostentatious exhibition of pelf and power.
1532.	**Ostracize (V)** excommunicate; expel; rusticate The rapist should be ostracized from society.
1533.	**Ostracism (N)**
1534.	**Outcry (N)** protest; loud clamour There is a great outcry all over the country because of the issue of corruption.
1535.	**Outlandish (Adj.)** strange; bizarre; grotesque The foreign tourist finds the snake charmers, yogis and the caste system in India very outlandish.
1536.	**Outrageous (Adj.)** repugnant; revolting The offence of rape is the most outrageous offence.
1537.	**Outstanding (Adj.)** first rate; excellent He got outstanding grade in his essay competition.
1538.	**Overt (N)** direct; open He offered overt and covert support to me in elections.

P

1539.	**Panacea (N)** a remedy for all ills; cure-all Exercise and fresh air are a panacea for many ailments.
1540.	**Pandemonium (N)** uproar; tumult The parliament witnessed extremely bad scene of pandemonium, chaos and disorder on the issue of Lok Pal Bill.
1541.	**Panorama (N)** wide view; a comprehensive survey The old man recalled the panorama of his eventful life.
1542.	**Panoramic (Adj.)**
1543.	**Paradigm (N)** pattern; model; example There was a paradigm shift in his thinking once he came back from abroad.

1544.	**Paradox (N)** a truth which appears untrue; seemingly contradictory statement He is a man of paradoxes.
1545.	**Paragon (N)** ideal; example Gandhiji was a paragon of simple living.
1546.	**Paramount (Adj.)** supreme; foremost Inculcation of value system in the children is of paramount importance in the character building.
1547.	**Paramountcy (N)**
1548.	**Paraphernalia (N)** equipment; apparatus The entire government paraphernalia was activated to nab the offender.
1549.	**Pathetic (Adj.)** moving; evoking pity It was pathetic to see a former millionaire, struggling to make both ends meet.
1550.	**Pathos (N)**
1551.	**Paucity (N)** shortage; want I could not go for higher education due to paucity of funds.
1552.	**Pauper (N)** destitute; beggar The profligate prince soon turned into a pauper.
1553.	**Pejorative (Adj.)** disparaging; belittling Politicians are very skilled in making pejorative remarks against each other.
1554.	**Pell-mell (Adj.)** in a confused manner The crowd scattered pell-mell after the firing.
1555.	**Penetrate (V)** pierce; pass through There are wide gaps in the border through which the enemy penetrates.
1556.	**Penetration (N)**
1557.	**Penetrative (Adj.)** sharp; keen Einstein with his penetrative intellect solved many mysteries of the universe.
1558.	**Penitent (Adj.)** repentant; contrite The prodigal son was penitent and begged forgiveness of his father.
1559.	**Penitence (N)**
1560.	**Pensive (Adj.)** thoughtful He sat in a very pensive mood.
1561.	**Penury (N)** poverty; destitution Penury is the lot of millions of Indians.
1562.	**Penurious (Adj.)**

1563.	**Pep (N)** vigour; spirit; liveliness; animation The little ones are full of pep and zest for life.
1564.	**Perceptible (Adj.)** that which can be seen or felt Information technology has made a perceptible difference in the quality of life in India.
1565.	**Perceptibly (Adj.)**
1566.	**Perceptibility (N)**
1567.	**Perceptive (Adj.)** intelligent; keen; penetrative Freud's perceptive analysis of the different layers of human mind is enlightening.
1568.	**Perception (N)**
1569.	**Perchance (Adj.)** possibly; may be; by chance The patient perchance may respond to surgery.
1570.	**Perennial (Adj.)** enduring; continuous Hon'ble Justice Krishna Iyer is the perennial source of motivation for legal fraternity.
1571.	**Perfidy (N)** deceit; faithlessness; treachery His act of perfidy virtually broke her heart.
1572.	**Perfidious (Adj.)**
1573.	**Perfunctory (Adj.)** hasty; superficial; indifferent Your problem is grave, perfunctory efforts will not solve it.
1574.	**Perfunctorily (Adv.)**
1575.	**Perish (V)** die; decay; disappear *Work hard or perish* said Vivekananda.
1576.	**Pernicious (Adj.)** harmful; ruinous; injurious; hurtful Smoking and drinking are pernicious habits.
1577.	**Perniciously (Adv.)**
1578.	**Perniciousness (N)**
1579.	**Perpetrate (V)** commit a crime Hitler perpetrated unspeakable crimes on the Jews.
1580.	**Perpetration (N)**
1581.	**Perpetuate (V)** cause to continue The faulty system of distributive justice helps to perpetuate injustice & inequality.

1582.	**Perpetuation (N)**
1583.	**Perpetual (Adj.)**
1584.	**Perplex (V)** puzzle; bewilder; confuse The listeners perplexed the speaker.
1585.	**Persecute (V)** torture; punish The dictator persecuted the dissenters.
1586.	**Persecution (N)**
1587.	**Perspicacity (N)** keen intelligence; discernment Buddha had the perspicacity to understand that desire was mankind's arch enemy.
1588.	**Perspicacious (Adj.)**
1589.	**Pertinacious (Adj.)** determined; enduring Asma Jahangir of Lahore is a pertinacious champion of women's rights in Pakistan.
1590.	**Pertinacity (N)**
1591.	**Pertinent (Adj.)** applicable; relevant He always raises very pertinent questions.
1592.	**Pervade (V)** spread everywhere Death and destruction pervaded the earthquake site.
1593.	**Pervasive (Adj.)**
1594.	**Perversity (N)** willfulness; stubbornness The chief's pleasure in humiliating his subordinate is his perversity.
1595.	**Pester (V)** harass; trouble; annoy; bother The employees pestered the boss for money.
1596.	**Pestilence (N)** scourge; infectious disease; deadly epidemic The AIDS pestilence is spreading all over Africa.
1597.	**Petrify (V)** frighten The dictator's ruthless ways petrified the populace.
1598.	**Pettifogging (N)** pettiness; meanness; trivial The bureaucratic pettifogging is a common man's major problem.
1599.	**Phantasm (N)** illusion; apparition; specter The phantasm of his dead wife still haunts him.
1600.	**Phenomenal (Adj.)** truly impressive; extraordinary The success story of Amitabh Bachchan is truly phenomenal.
1601.	**Phenomenon (N)** strange happening; something difficult to explain He was witness to a strange phenomenon
1602.	**Philanderer (N)** a man who has sexual relations with many women; an insincere love A philanderer is not liked by truly good women.
1603.	**Pinnacle (N)** height; peak; summit He reached the pinnacle of glory and became the Chief Justice of India.
1604.	**Ponder (V)** mull; reflect The philosopher pondered over the mysteries of life and death.
1605.	**Ponderous (Adj.)**
1606.	**Pontificate (V)** lecture; instruct The teacher pontificated and the students dozed off.
1607.	**Pontifical (Adj.)**
1608.	**Populous (Adj.)** China and India are the most populous nations in the world.
1609.	**Portable (Adj.)** easy to carry This is a portable laptop to use.
1610.	**Portability (N)**
1611.	**Pragmatic (Adj.)** realistic; practical His approach to life is pragmatic.
1612.	**Prattle (V)** chatter; babble; talk a lot She prattled on about her skills to an impervious audience.
1613.	**Precarious (Adj.)** uncertain; insecure; dangerous The prices are rising and the economy is in a precarious condition.
1614.	**Precede (V)** come before; be more important He preceded me to the meeting.
1615.	**Precedent (N)** instance; example Keshav Nanda Bharti case is a landmark precedent.
1616.	**Precept (N)** instruction; commandment Practice is better than precept.
1617.	**Preceptor (N)** instructor; teacher; tutor The preceptor laid down stringent rules for his followers.

1618.	**Precocious (Adj.)** prematurely developed He is a precocious child.
1619.	**Predicament (N)** a difficult situation; a grave doubt The girl had to choose between her love and her parents, it was a grave predicament indeed.
1620.	**Predominance (N)** domination; supremacy The military predominance in Naxal areas continues.
1621.	**Predominant (Adj.)**
1622.	**Pre-eminent (Adj.)** superior; surpassing; truly excellent Paulo Coetho is a pre-eminent motivational writer.
1623.	**Premier (Adj.)** foremost; principal; leading Lahore and Karachi are Pakistan's premier cities.
1624.	**Premier (N)**
1625.	**Premise (N, V)** basis Compatibility is the essential premise of a successful marriage.
1626.	**Preponderant (Adj.)** superior in numbers; formidable India has a preponderant Hindu population yet it is a secular state.
1627.	**Preponderance (N)**
1628.	**Preposterous (Adj.)** untrue; outrageous; baseless America's claim that Iraq had weapons of mass destruction turned out to be preposterous.
1629.	**Presumption (N)** supposition, assumption It is a common presumption that the police are corrupt.
1630.	**Presumptuous (Adj.)** arrogant; overweening The father thought it was presumptuous of the son to demand his share in the property.
1631.	**Prevail (V)** win, triumph Truth always prevails.
1632.	**Prevaricate (V)** hide truth; mis-state; mis-represent The witness was trying to prevaricate with his evasive replies.
1633.	**Prevarication (N)**
1634.	**Primordial (Adj.)** existing since ages; original; elementary We are fast depleting earth of its primordial fossil fuels.
1635.	**Prior (Adj.)** previous; anterior; antecedent The guests arrived without prior notice.
1636.	**Pristine (Adj.)** virginal; untouched The pristine beauty of Aishwarya Rai Bachchan is without a parallel.
1637.	**Probable (N, Adj.)** likely to occur; very likely A solution to the Kashmir imbroglio does not seem probable.
1638.	**Probability (N)**
1639.	**Proceeds (N)** collected funds; income from sales The proceeds of the charity show will go to the earthquake victims.
1640.	**Proclivity (N)** inclination; bent of mind All political parties have a proclivity to cater to their vote banks at the expense of state exchequer.
1641.	**Procrastination (N)** postponement; delay Procrastination robs you off opportunity.
1642.	**Procrastinate (V)**
1643.	**Prod (V)** inspire; encourage The general prodded the soldiers into action with his pep talks.
1644.	**Prodigal (Adj.)** extravagant; reckless; wasteful The prodigal son lost all his money.
1645.	**Prodigality (N)**
1646.	**Prodigious (Adj.)** copious; fecund He has a prodigious vocabulary.
1647.	**Prodigy (N)** one who excels in some discipline; a young genius The little boy is a tennis prodigy who can one day win a grand slam.
1648.	**Profane (Adj.)** characterized by irreverence or contempt; showing lack of respect for holy things It is profane to enter a holy shrine with the shoes.
1649.	**Profanation (N)**

1650.	**Profess (V)** speak with emphasis; aver; asseverate He does not practise that which professor Saxena professes.
1651.	**Proffer (V)** offer; put forward a proposal for acceptance He proffered me a hand of friendship.
1652.	**Profligate (Adj.)** wasteful; immoral The profligate son fell on bad days and turned penitent.
1653.	**Profligacy (N)**
1654.	**Profound (Adj.)** deep; learned Nehru was a profound scholar of Indian history.
1655.	**Profundity (N)**
1656.	**Progenitors (N)** precursors; ancestors; forefathers Sher Shah Suri is called progenitor of Akbar in administrative reforms.
1657.	**Progeny (N)** offspring; descendants; scion The progeny of politicians enjoy power from cradle to grave.
1658.	**Prognosis (N)** forecast; prediction There was worldwide prognosis that Barrack Obama will be President of USA for 2nd time.
1659.	**Prognostication (N)** prediction; forecast Happily, his gloomy prognostications went awry.
1660.	**Progression (N)** a sequence of events; act of progressing Mankind's progression from Stone Age to computer age is amazing.
1661.	**Prohibit (V)** forbid; prevent The High Court prohibited the lower court from carrying on the proceedings.
1662.	**Prohibitive (Adj.)**
1663.	**Proletariat (N)** unpropertied class; working classes With disintegration of USSR, the dictatorship of the proletariat in communist countries has come to an end.
1664.	**Proliferate (V)** multiply; increase in numbers Love for money is proliferating in the present times.

1665.	**Promiscuous (Adj.)** permissive; licentious The Hindi serials on Indian TV are imparting legitimacy to promiscuous relationships.
1666.	**Promptitude (N)** promptness The government came to the rescue of the earthquake victims with great promptitude.
1667.	**Promulgate (V)** announce new law; issue a proclamation Under Article 123, the President of India can promulgate an ordinance when the parliament is not in session.
1668.	**Promulgation (N)**
1669.	**Propensity (N)** inclination; disposition His propensity for hard work is phenomenal.
1670.	**Prophesy (V)** predict; prognosticate The astrologer prophesied a happy married life for the couple.
1671.	**Prophecy (N)**
1672.	**Propitiate (V)** appease; placate He made an offering at the temple to propitiate the gods.
1673.	**Propitious (V)** favourable; well disposed; likely to bring good luck The omens are propitious, let us begin our enterprise.
1674.	**Proponent (N)** supporter; champion Nehru was a great proponent for democratic socialism.
1675.	**Propound (V)** put forward, support Gandhi propounded the doctrine of non-violence in politics.
1676.	**Prorogue (V)** defer; postpone; discontinue The members continued to misbehave and the speaker prorogued the House.
1677.	**Proscribe (V)** forbid; prohibit The doctor has proscribed tea and coffee for me.
1678.	**Prostrate (V. Adj.)** cast oneself face down on the ground; laying flat on the ground The devotee lay prostrate before the idol.
1679.	**Prowl (N)** move stealthily in search of prey The lion is on the prowl looking for a prey.
1680.	**Proximity (N)** nearness; closeness He flaunts his proximity with the high ups.
1681.	**Prudence (N)** wit; forethought She had the prudence to plan for her old age.

1682. Prudent (Adj.)

1683. Prune (V) cut-off vegetation; lop; trim
The shrubs have grown too luxuriant; they need to be pruned.

1684. Pry (V) peer; peep; interfere
Do not pry into my affairs.

1685. Pseudo (Adj.) false; counterfeit; bogus
Astrology at best is a pseudo-science.

1686. Psyche (N) mind; human soul or spirit
Childhood deprivations left a deep impression on his psyche.

1687. Psychiatric (Adj.) relating to mind.
She needs psychiatric help given her present state of mind.

Q

1688. Quack (N) a fraud; a charlatan
Majority of the politicians are charlatans and quacks.

1689. Quackery (N)

1690. Quagmire (N) mired, boggy ground
Indian economy is in quagmire after lockdown.

1691. Quail (V) fear; lose courage
The brave never quail in the face of difficulties.

1692. Qualm (N) pang of conscience; compunction
The venal practices of our politicians give them no qualms.

1693. Quandary (N) perplexity; uncertainty
He was in a state of quandary 'To be or not to be'.

1694. Quash (V) reject; declare invalid
The High Court Judge quashed the proceedings of the lower court.

1695. Quaver (V) quiver; shake
Her voice quavered as she recalled the earthquake scene.

1696. Quell (V) stifle; put down
Aurangzeb quelled all the rebellions and put the rebels to death.

1697. Quench (V) slake; come to an end
Do not let your insatiable thirst for knowledge ever be quenched.

1698. Quibble (V) prevaricate; evade
The judge told the lawyer to come to the main point and not quibble over unimportant details.

1699. Quicksand (N) difficult situation; mire
The NRI was sucked into the quicksand of his family problems.

1700. Quicksilver (Adj.) mercurial; unpredictable
The wife could not put up with her husband's quicksilver temperament.

1701. Quid pro quo (N) exchange of obligation; substitute
My support for him was a quid pro quo for his favours.

1702. Quiescent (Adj.) not moving; quiet
The snake lay quiescent in the winter sun.

1703. Quietude (N) peace and quiet
The quietude in the hills soothed my ruffled nerves.

1704. Quietus (Put) crush; put an end to; dampen
His poverty put a quietus on his soaring ambitions.

1705. Quirk (N) peculiarity; strange twist; idiosyncrasy
With a cruel quirk of fate, he came to ruin.

1706. Quiver (N) device for keeping arrows
He took out an arrow from the quiver and shot at the bird.

1707. Quiver (V) tremble; shake quaver
His body quivered with fear.

1708. Quixotic (Adj.) strange; peculiar; unusual
Poets are quixotic creatures with great imagination but little practicality.

R

1709. Radiate (V) emit; be full of
Mother Teresa radiates joy and compassion

1710. Radiation (N)

1711. Raffish (Adj.) attractive but gaudy; vulgar; tawdry
The village elders didn't quite approve of the city boy's raffish air.

1712. Rag (V) tease; teasing
The senior boys love to rag the new entrants.

1713. Ragging (N)

1714. Rage (N) craze; fury; violence
The collector left the office in rage after protest by employees.

1715. Raging (Adj.)

1716.	**Rake (N)** profligate; immoral person The young prince was a rake who was given to drugs.
1717.	**Rake (up) (V)** dig up; ransack It does not make for healthy relationship if we keep raking up the past.
1718.	**Ram (V)** collide; run into The driver fell asleep and rammed the truck into a tree.
1719.	**Ramble (V)** wander; saunter We rambled through the quiet countryside.
1720.	**Ramification (N)** consequence; result USA couldn't foresee the ramifications of an attack on Iraq.
1721.	**Ramify (V)**
1722.	**Rampage (N)** violence; agitation The mob went on a rampage after Delhi gang rape case.
1723.	**Rampant (Adj.)** pervasive; uncontrolled We must strive to eradicate the corruption rampant in all walks of life.
1724.	**Ramshackle (Adj.)** rickety; in a state of ill repair The ramshackled Indian system needs to be revamped and revitalized.
1725.	**Rancor (N)** bitterness; hatred; malice Let us not rake up the past and forget the rancor.
1726.	**Random (Adj.; Adv.)** irregular He made a random check in the office.
1727.	**Rankle (V)** stick like a thorn; fester The old rancor between the two brothers still rankles.
1728.	**Ransom (N)** payment for deliverance; money demanded for releasing a kidnapped person The kidnapper demanded a huge ransom for releasing the rich merchant.
1729.	**Rant (V)** rave; decry; declaim Ranting against fate does not bear any fruit.
1730.	**Rap (N)** scolding; knock; punishment My father gave me a rap on the knuckles for my sloth.
1731.	**Rapacious (Adj.)** greedy; predatory The venal and rapacious bureaucrats emptied the state coffers.

1732.	**Rapport (N)** relation; connection; understanding There is no rapport between the husband and the wife.
1733.	**Rapprochement (N)** conciliation; agreement; understanding Let us build bridges of rapprochement and move ahead.
1734.	**Rapture (N)** joy; delight The grandmother was in great raptures at the birth of her grandson.
1735.	**Rapturous (Adj.)**
1736.	**Rarity (N)** a rare thing; unusual Honesty is a biggest rarity nowadays.
1737.	**Rate (V)** judge Amitabh Bachchan is rated the best mega star of Bollywood.
1738.	**Ratify (V)** confirm; correct You have to ratify the actions of your son.
1739.	**Rattle (N. V.)** cacophony; harsh sound; unsettle; fray The rattle of crockery frays my nerves.
1740.	**Ravel (V)** complicate It is difficult to unravel the mysteries of life.
1741.	**Raucous (Adj.)** loud; impertinent Raucous laughter followed all his risqué jokes.
1742.	**Ravage (V)** damage; destroy Iraq has been badly ravaged following American occupation.
1743.	**Rave (V)** praise enthusiastically; shout I hope my article gets rave reviews.
1744.	**Ravenous (Adj.)** starving; greedy A trek through the hills gave us a ravenous appetite.
1745.	**Raze (V)** demolish; tear down; completely destroy The earthquake razed many a skyscraper.
1746.	**Razzmatazz (N)** noisy activity; high excitement The people of Delhi prefer its razzmatazz to the quiet life of countryside.
1747.	**Reactionary (Adj.)** orthodox; traditionalist The reactionaries love status quo and hate changes.

1748.	**Realm (N)** domain; kingdom The king put up a brave fight for the defence of his realm.
1749.	**Realtor (N)** a dealer in real estate The realtor helped me buy a good house.
1750.	**Realty (N)**
1751.	**Rebound (V)** recover; bounce back The politician had the resilience to rebound after his ignominious defeat.
1752.	**Rebuff (V)** refuse; reject She rebuffed his overtures of friendship.
1753.	**Rebuke (N, V)** scold; admonish I rebuked my friend for his betrayal.
1754.	**Rebut (V)** oppose by contrary proof; refute The defense counsel rebutted the prosecution charges with great ability.
1755.	**Rebuttal (N)**
1756.	**Recalcitrant (Adj.)** disobedient; rebellious The teacher found it difficult to discipline the recalcitrant boys.
1757.	**Recalcitrance (N)**
1758.	**Recant (V)** disavow; retract He had confessed to the murder but recanted soon afterwards.
1759.	**Recapitulate (V)** repeat the main points; summarize The news reader recapitulated the main points of the news bulletin.
1760.	**Recapitulation (N)**
1761.	**Recast (V)** change; remould We have to recast our programme because of bad weather.
1762.	**Recede (V)** retreat; withdraw The poet looked philosophically at the receding waves.
1763.	**Recession (N)** contraction in business The global economy is in a state of recession because of Covid-19.
1764.	**Recessive (Adj.)**
1765.	**Recidivist (Adj.)** one who relapses into crime The recidivist lapsed into crime despite punishments.
1766.	**Reciprocal (Adj.)** of mutual trust The two universities have a reciprocal treaty for the exchange of scholars.
1767.	**Reckon (V)** accept; consider We all reckon Gandhiji as the Father of Nation.
1768.	**Reckon (with)** keep in view; concede USA must reckon with China as a super power.
1769.	**Reclaim (V)** set right, rectify The king appointed the prince to reclaim the law and order situation.
1770.	**Recoil (V)** retreat in horror; shrink back Avni recoiled in horror at the sight of a lizard.
1771.	**Recollect (V)** recall; remember The old professor still recollects great lines from Shakespeare and the Bible.
1772.	**Recollection (N)**
1773.	**Recompense (N,V)** compensation; compensate No recompense has yet been paid to the flood victims.
1774.	**Reconnaissance (N)** detailed survey or examination; search for information. The helicopter flew over enemy positions for reconnaissance.
1775.	**Reconcile (V)** accept, befriend; acquiesce The two estranged friends have again reconciled with each other.
1776.	**Reconciliation (N)**
1777.	**Recondite (Adj.)** uncommon; obscure; abstruse Einstein's theory of relativity still remains a recondite concept for many.
1778.	**Recoup (V)** regain, recover We made good profits and recouped our earlier losses.
1779.	**Recreant (Adj.)** unfaithful; traitorous The recreant secretary betrayed her boss.
1780.	**Recrimination (N)** accusing in return; accusation and counter accusation Recriminations should yield to reconciliations.
1781.	**Recriminate (V)**
1782.	**Recriminatory (Adv.)**
1783.	**Recrudescence (N)** relapse; recurrence There is a recrudescence of violence after an interval of peace.

1784.	**Rectify (V)** reform; set right We must rectify the situation or it will get out of hands.
1785.	**Rectitude (N)** honesty; uprightness No one can impugn his rectitude.
1786.	**Recumbent (Adj.)** lying down, reclining The rich fat lady lay recumbent on her sofa.
1787.	**Recuperate (V)** recover from illness She is recuperating after a long illness.
1788.	**Redeem (V)** save; salvage; retrieve The prophets come to redeem us from our sinful ways.
1789.	**Redeemer (N)**
1790.	**Redemption (N)** salvation; freedom Gandhiji came from South Africa for redemption from slavery.
1791.	**Redolent (Adj.)** reminiscent The kitchen was redolent with the aroma of rich spices.
1792.	**Redoubtable (Adj.)** powerful; impressively strong Gandhiji was a redoubtable leader who fought for India's freedom.
1793.	**Redound (V)** help, espouse, aid Farmers' protest cannot redound credibility of Government.
1794.	**Redress (V)** compensate; remedy The government has enhanced the compensation to redress the injustice to earthquake victims.
1795.	**Redressal (N)**
1796.	**Redundant (Adj.)** surplus; superfluous Many industries closed down and their employees became redundant.
1797.	**Redundance (N)**
1798.	**Redundancy (N)**
1799.	**Refractory (Adj.)** stubborn; undisciplined The little boys were a refractory lot and much to the chagrin of their teacher.
1800.	**Refrain (N, V)** abstain He refrains from alcoholic drinks.
1801.	**Refulgent (Adj.)** brilliant; shining A refulgent sun added to the festivities of the day.
1802.	**Refulgence (N)**
1803.	**Regal (Adj.)** kingly; of a king or queen The queen's regal demeanor commanded awe and honour.
1804.	**Regale (V)** entertain; delight The actor regaled the audience with his skills.
1805.	**Regimen (N)** rules for food and exercise; mode or system of rules They followed a rigorous regimen to regain fitness.
1806.	**Regression (N)** sliding back; going backwards; retrogression; relapse After a nuclear holocaust, there would be a regression to our primeval days.
1807.	**Regress (V)**
1808.	**Rehabilitate (V)** join the main stream of life The drug addicts need to be detoxified and rehabilitated.
1809.	**Rehabilitation (N)**
1810.	**Rein (V)** check; bridle; control We must rein in our animal instincts or regress to stone age.
1811.	**Reins of power (N)** power; authority Akbar sent Bairam Khan on a Haj pilgrimage and assumed the reins of power.
1812.	**Reincarnate (V)** be given another body; be born again Bad people reincarnate as beasts.
1813.	**Reincarnation (N)**
1814.	**Reiterate (V)** repeat tediously Alexander Fleming reiterated that work, work, work, work, and work should be our motto.
1815.	**Reiteration (N)**
1816.	**Rejoinder (N)** formal reply; response The defence counsel gave a brilliant rejoinder to prosecution's allegations.
1817.	**Rejuvenate (V)** give new life; vivify; galvanize Clean water, fresh air and exercise will rejuvenate you.
1818.	**Rejuvenation (N)**
1819.	**Reek (V)** smell unpleasantly; suggest unpleasantly Her attitude reeks of arrogance.

1820. Rekindle (V) reignite; revive
His fortuitous meeting with his old friend rekindled his love.

1821. Relapse (N) backslide; slide back
The doctor warned him against a relapse of pneumonia.

1822. Relegate (V) appoint some one to a lower position; pushback
He was relegated to a lower rank on grounds of indiscipline.

1823. Relent (V) show mercy; soften
Portia urged Shylock to show mercy but he didn't relent.

1824. Reminisce (V) recall; recollect; call to memory
We reminisced about the school days in the meeting.

1825. Remiss (Adj.) at fault; careless
The teachers who remain absent are remiss in their duty.

1826. Remission (N) concession; pardon
He was granted a remission in fees on grounds of poverty.

1827. Remonstrate (V) argue; protest
The traders remonstrated with the government over new imposts.

1828. Remonstrance (N)

1829. Remorse (N) repentance; regret
The rapist and the murderer had no remorse for the heinous crime.

1830. Remorseful (Adj.)

1831. Remunerate (V) recompense; reward
His teaching services rendered during Covid-19 were duly remunerated.

1832. Remuneration (N)

1833. Renaissance (N) reawakening; revival
The migration of scholars from Constantinople to Europe resulted in an era of renaissance of arts and letters.

1834. Renaisant (Adj.)

1835. Rend (V) tear part; divide; pierce
The British succeeded in rending India into two halves.

1836. Rendition (N) rendering presentation; performance
Nusrat Fateh Ali Khan's rendition of Punjabi songs cannot be matched.

1837. Renounce (V) give up; forego
Buddha renounced the crown in search of greater and more lasting rewards.

1838. Renunciation (N)

1839. Repeal (V) Rescind; withdraw
The law could not be enforced and had to be repealed.

1840. Repercussions (N) outcome; consequences
We cannot escape the repercussions of our acts.

1841. Replenish (V) gather again; replace
You must take a break to recoup and replenish your energy.

1842. Replenishment (N)

1843. Replete (Adj.) well supplied; full of
The kitchen is replete with eatables.

1844. Repletion (N)

1845. Replica (N) a good copy; facisimile
He is a replica of his father in figure and features.

1846. Repository (N) storehouse
Some books are literally repository of knowledge.

1847. Reprehensible (Adj.) hateful; repugnant
Adultery is a reprehensible offence.

1848. Reprieve (N) pardon; respite; temporary relief
The president has given him a reprieve from the death sentence.

1849. Reprimand (V) official admonishment; scold
He was charged with dereliction of duty and reprimanded by boss.

1850. Reprisal (N) nemesis; relation
Our evil ways cannot escape divine reprisals.

1851. Reproach (V) blame; complain
His wife reproached him for his lack of giving alimony.

1852. Reprobate (N) an immoral man; rake
He is a notorious reprobate.

1853. Repudiate (V) deny; rebut
The guilty repudiated the allegations levelled against him.

1854. Repudiation (N)

1855. Repugnant (Adj.) disgusting; repellent
The corrupt practices of politicians are repugnant indeed.

1856.	**Repugnance (N)**
1857.	**Repulse (V)** push back; beat back The Pakistanis sneaked into the Kargil heights but were repulsed back by Indian army.
1858.	**Repulsion (N)**
1859.	**Repulsive (Adj.)** repellent; unpleasant The shanties were full of stench and looked very repulsive.
1860.	**Rescind (V)** cancel; withdraw Fearing fierce opposition, the government rescinded its decision to impose levies.
1861.	**Residuary (Adj.)** that which remains; reminder; residuum The residuary powers according to Constitution vest in the center government.
1862.	**Residue (N)** remainder; residuum After payment of taxes and debts, the residue of dead man's estate was distributed between his two sons.
1863.	**Resilience (N)** bouncing back; recovery The Indian democracy is known for its resilience &self-sufficiency.
1864.	**Resilient (Adj.)**
1865.	**Resolute (Adj.)** steadfast; firm; determined He overcame difficulties with resolute courage.
1866.	**Resolution (N)**
1867.	**Resonate (V)** echo; resound The stadium resonated with applause for the winner.
1868.	**Resonance (N)**
1869.	**Resolve (N)** determination; steadfastness His strong resolve helped him accomplish his mission in life.
1870.	**Resolve (V)** determine; settle He resolved to get the better of his foes.
1871.	**Resolution (N)**
1872.	**Resonant (Adj.)** deep; clear; continuous Mohammad Rafi's resonant voice was hallmark of his personality.
1873.	**Resonance (N)**
1874.	**Resort (V)** make use of; take recourse to We should always resort to fair means.
1875.	**Respite (N)** rest; relief We had to work the whole night with no respite.

1876.	**Resplendent (Adj.)** brilliant and glorious The beauty queen looked resplendent with her crown.
1877.	**Resplendence (N)**
1878.	**Restitution (V)** restoration; reparation She applied for the restitution of her conjugal rights in a court of law.
1879.	**Restive (Adj.)** uneasy; restless; impatient The newly married couple felt restive in others' company and preferred solitude.
1880.	**Resurface (V)** revive; resurrect He was lost in debts but resurfaced with his fortitude.
1881.	**Resurgent (Adj.)** on the move; progressing A resurgent India is emerging as a global power to reckon with.
1882.	**Resurgence (N)**
1883.	**Resurrection (N)** come back to life again; revival The coming of Joe Biden will herald resurrection of a dying democracy in the USA.
1884.	**Resuscitate (V)** help to breathe again; revive The drowning man was resuscitated by mouth-to-mouth respiration.
1885.	**Resuscitation (N)**
1886.	**Retaliation (N)** revenge; hitting back The soldiers killed the terrorist in retaliation
1887.	**Retard (V)** obstruct; put hurdles Procrastination retards all progress.
1888.	**Reticent (Adj.)** disinclined to speak; reserved She was quite reticent about her past life.
1889.	**Retinue (N)** a group of attendants; a train of companion The king was accompanied by a large retinue.
1890.	**Retort (V)** replay back in anger; retaliate He retorted back again, once recovered.
1891.	**Retreat (V)** withdraw; flee; go back The enemy had to retreat in the face of fierce retaliation.
1892.	**Retrench (V)** economize; cut expenses They retrenched by dispensing with their servant.
1893.	**Retribution (N)** nemesis; punishment Let the sinners beware of divine retribution.

1894.	**Retrieve (V)** recover; regain The football fell into a stream but a swimmer retrieved it.
1895.	**Retrieval (N)**
1896.	**Retroactive (Adj.)** retrospective; effective from a past date The ruling came into effect retroactively.
1897.	**Retrogressive (Adj.)** be against progress; moving backwards Opposition to modern technology is a retrogressive step.
1898.	**Retrogression (N)**
1899.	**Retrospection (N)** looking back on past; a survey of past events. You will appreciate my suggestion in retrospection.
1900.	**Retrospect (V)**
1901.	**Revamp (N)** renovate; redo; revise The building seems dilapidated, it needs a revamp.
1902.	**Revel (V)** make merry; delight in; enjoy An epicure revels in the good things of life.
1903.	**Revelry (N)**
1904.	**Reveller (N)**
1905.	**Reverberate (V)** echo; resound Applause and cheers reverberated the hall.
1906.	**Reverberation (N)**
1907.	**Revered (Adj.)** esteemed; respected Guru Nanak is the revered Guru of the Sikhs.
1908.	**Reverence (N)** great respect; esteem Devout Hindus hold Rama and Krishna in great reverence.
1909.	**Retaliation (N)** hit back in vengeance When the Akali government came into power they unleashed the politics of vendetta in retaliation against Congress.
1910.	**Revile (V)** assail; speak ill of; censure; castigate Political opponents revile one another.
1911.	**Revoke (V)** take back; rescind; cancel For fear of revolt, the king revoked his decree.
1912.	**Revocable (Adj.)**
1913.	**Revocation (N)**
1914.	**Revulsion (N)** repugnance; disgust The muck and scandals mongering of Bollywood fills me with revulsion.

1915.	**Rhetoric (N)** ability in the use of language; art and science of prose and verse The prosecution presented its case with much rhetoric but little logic.
1916.	**Rhetorical (Adj.)**
1917.	**Ribald (Adj.)** indelicate; obscene His ribald jokes didn't go well with women.
1918.	**Rickety (Adj.)** collapsing; in a state of ill repair The rickety buildings were the first to give way when the earthquake came calling.
1919.	**Riddle (N)** enigma; mystery The riddle of life is difficult to fathom.
1920.	**Ridicule (V)** deride; make fun of Do not ridicule the poor.
1921.	**Ridiculous (Adj.)** laughable; non-sensical The rationalists find the belief in astrology very ridiculous.
1922.	**Rife (Adj.)** prevalent; well spread; prevalence of an unpleasant thing Hooliganism is quite rife in the U.P.
1923.	**Rift (N)** quarrel difference of opinion; dissension There is a rift between the two brothers over property.
1924.	**Rig (V)** employ dishonest means; manipulate fraudulently The elections were rigged in favour of the ruling party.
1925.	**Rusticate (V)** expel He was rusticated from the school for indiscipline.
1926.	**Rustication (N)**

S

1927.	**Sabotage (N, V)** destroy; undermine; disturb The accused tried to sabotage the investigations.
1928.	**Sack (V)** dismiss from service The company sacked the accountant for embezzlement.
1929.	**Sacrilege (N)** desecration; profanation It is a sacrilege if you enter a Sikh temple without covering your head.
1930.	**Sacrosanct (Adj.)** sacred; inviolable Fundamental Rights are sacrosanct.
1931.	**Saddle (V)** encumber; burden I am saddled with my family affairs.

1932.	**Sadist (N)** one who seeks pleasure in inflicting pain A sadist delights in the misery of his neighbours.
1933.	**Saga (N)** narrative of heroic exploits; legend of valour The freedom movement witnessed a saga of valour and sacrifice.
1934.	**Sagacious (Adj.)** farsighted; sapient; wise The patriarch's sagacious advice to his family was to keep cool and take things in their stride.
1935.	**Sagacity (N)**
1936.	**Salacious (Adj.)** lustful; lecherous Salacious books sell like hot cakes whereas serious one gathers dust.
1937.	**Salaciousness (N)**
1938.	**Salient (Adj.)** prominent; conspicuous; important The blurb provided at the back cover of the book highlights salient features of the book.
1939.	**Salubrious (Adj.)** good for health; healthful We should prefer salubrious life style.
1940.	**Salubrity (N)**
1941.	**Salutary (Adj.)** healthful, wholesome The reprimand had a salutary effect on the recalcitrant employees.
1942.	**Salvage (V)** retrieve; save They could salvage neither men nor material from the debris.
1943.	**Salvation (N)** freedom from the cycle of birth and death; redemption The fools go for gold while the wise one work for salvation.
1944.	**Sanctimonious (Adj.)** excessively pious I was not quite impressed by his sanctimonious piety.
1945.	**Sangfroid (N)** cool demeanour in a crisis; quiet confidence The leader maintained his sangfroid in the grave crisis.
1946.	**Sanguinary (Adj.)** gory; bloody; blood thirsty The sanguinary boxers fought with the raw ferocity of wild animals.
1947.	**Sanguine (Adj.)** hopeful; optimistic; cheerful Let us forget the past and take a sanguine view of future.
1948.	**Sanguiness (N)**
1949.	**Sardonic (Adj.)** mocking scornful His sardonic remarks earned him bad name.
1950.	**Satiated (Adj.)** excessively satisfied; complacent I was quite satiated with functioning of judiciary.
1951.	**Satiety (N)** The state of being satiated; sufficiency Everybody wants more and yet more money, nobody reaches the point of satiety.
1952.	**Saunter (V)** wander aimlessly; stroll leisurely The tourists from Punjab saunter up and down the London markets; gawking and gaping at window shopping.
1953.	**Savant (N)** sapient; scholar The religious savant quoted the scriptures, chapters and verses, much to the amazement of the congregation.
1954.	**Saviour (N)** one who saves The Christians believe that Jesus Christ is mankind's saviour.
1955.	**Savour (V)** perceive by taste or smell; peculiar taste or odour I still savour my encounter with the great artist.
1956.	**Scamp (N)** rascal; rogue The teacher with her pedagogical skills managed the scamps well.
1957.	**Scapegoat (N)** One who is made to bear blame for others. It is the chief's doing, the poor secretary is only a scapegoat.
1958.	**Scathing (Adj.)** excoriating; searing The rationalists have launched a scathing campaign against superstitions.
1959.	**Scenario (N)** outline; view Samuel Huntington's scenario of a clash of civilizations is not untenable.
1960.	**Sceptic (N)** one who doubts; one who questions the validity of a thing She made it to the top and proved the sceptics wrong.
1961.	**Schism** division, differences It is difficult to heal the schism between broken hearts.

1962.	**Scintilla (N)** a small amount; very little quantity; speck There is yet a scintilla of hope that he would turn the corner.
1963.	**Scintillate (V)** sparkle; shine The beauty queen scintillated and sparkled with her wit and charm.
1964.	**Scintillation (N)**
1965.	**Scion (N)** descendant; a young member of a noble family The prince acted intrepidly, very much like the scion of an ancient family.
1966.	**Scrupulous (Adj.)** honest; conscientious The scrupulous accountant squared the accounts till the last penny.
1967.	**Scuffle (N)** scrimmage; struggle There was a scuffle for the ball in the penalty area.
1968.	**Scurrilous (Adj.)** abusive; coarse; derisive Political foes hurl scurrilous invectives at each other.
1969.	**Scurrility (N)**
1970.	**Scurvily (Adv.)**
1971.	**Scuttle (V)** checkmate; abandon The goalkeeper scuttled the move with a good anticipation.
1972.	**Seamy (Adj.)** unpleasant; unwholesome; disagreeable Betrayal and deprivation are seamy sides of life.
1973.	**Sear (V)** burn or scorch; wither; parch His wife's betrayal has seared his soul.
1974.	**Secession (N)** the act of seceding; breaking away from the mother country The Kashmiris fought for secession which the government did not allow.
1975.	**Secessionist (N)**
1976.	**Seclude (V)** withdraw into solitude; isolate; shut off The scholar secluded himself for months and produced a scholarly tome.
1977.	**Seclusion (N)**
1978.	**Secluded (Adj.)**
1979.	**Secrete (V)** discharge, release, generate The brand new Miss World secreted uninhibited joy.

1980.	**Secretion (N)**
1981.	**Sedative (N, Adj.)** tending to soothe The patient was kept under sedatives before and after the surgery.
1982.	**Sedentary (Adj.)** accustomed to sit or rest; not inclined to exercise Give up your sedentary habits and be up and doing.
1983.	**Sedition (N)** rebellion against the government The terrorists were charged with sedition.
1984.	**Seduce (V)** lead astray; entice A whore tried to seduce the onlookers.
1985.	**Seduction (N)**
1986.	**Sever (N)** cut; break off I would sever my relations with him.
1987.	**Shackle (V)** bind in chains; imprison His father died as he was shackled with responsibilities.
1988.	**Sham (N)** pretension The politicians' promises are no less than a sham.
1989.	**Shambles (N)** confusion and disorder The earthquake caused his life and house in shambles.
1990.	**Sheen (N)** shine; brightness; shiny quality There is more sheen than substance in what he says.
1991.	**Sheer (Adj.)** complete; thorough; absolute The Taj at Agra is an example of sheer beauty.
1992.	**Shimmer (N, V)** gleam faintly; shine softly The Taj shimmers on moonlit nights.
1993.	**Shrewd (Adj.)** sharp in practical matters; astute The shopkeepers are a shrewd race and do not rub people on the wrong side.
1994.	**Shrewdness (N)**
1995.	**Sluggish (Adj.)** indolent; lacking energy I felt sluggish after a heavy meal.
1996.	**Sluggishness (N)**
1997.	**Slumber (N)** sleep; doze; drowse After a long trek and a hearty meal I fell into a deep slumber.
1998.	**Slump (N)** steep fall in the prices; depression in business There is a slump in the prices following imports.

1999.	**Slush (N)** soft mud; foolish sentiment It rained heavily and we had to wade through slush and water.
2000.	**Sly (Adj.)** surreptitious; furtive The chief minister was ousted in a sly political coup.
2001.	**Smack (N, V)** hit with an open hand His suggestion smacks of chicanery.
2002.	**Smattering (N)** superficial knowledge He knows English well but has only a smattering knowledge of Hindi.
2003.	**Smirch (V)** stain; discredit; disgrace Do not associate with bad people; it will smirch your good name.
2004.	**Smite (V)** full of, absolutely involved He is smitten with remorse.
2005.	**Smog (N)** a combination of fog and smoke The London smog is injurious to the health of its citizenry.
2006.	**Smother (V)** stifle; choke; suppress The army in Pakistan smothers all democratic institutions.
2007.	**Smoulder (V)** burn slowly without flame; continue unnoticed. The rancour between them still smoulders.
2008.	**Smudge (V)** stain; smirch; blur Tears smudged her lipstick and mascara.
2009.	**Smug (Adj.)** complacent; self-satisfied Smug people hardly grow in life.
2010.	**Snaffle (V)** steal Somebody evidently liked my dainty pen and snaffled it.
2011.	**Snag (N)** difficulty; problem My computer had a snag to be fixed.
2012.	**Snap (V)** severe He might have conspired against me but I shall not snap ties.
2013.	**Snare (V)** trap; allure; attract Ordinary mortals are snared by the glitter and glamour of materialism.
2014.	**Snarl (V)** tangle; growl; speak in a harsh voice The boss snarls his subordinates into submission.
2015.	**Snarl (N)**

2016.	**Sneer (N)** derision, ridicule; contempt He persevered at the job, unmindful of cheers and sneers.
2017.	**Snicker (V)** snigger; laugh in a sly manner The audience snickered at my faux pas.
2018.	**Snicker (N)** ridicule; laugh disrespectfully His snickers at our simple ways left a bad taste.
2019.	**Snap (V)** cut with scissors The barber snipped through the little boy's luxuriant locks.
2020.	**Solicit (V)** make a request; supplicate We solicit your gracious presence at the inauguration.
2021.	**Solicitous (Adj.)**
2022.	**Solicitude (N)** anxiety; concern; anxious desire There is no lack of solicitude for those affected by Tsunami and Katrina.
2023.	**Solitary (Adj.)** alone; unattended; without companions The solitary reaper in the high hills bewitched William Wordsworth with her melancholy strains.
2024.	**Sombre (Adj.)** gloomy; depressing; dismal The school master's sombre look chilled the impish boys.
2025.	**Sophistication (N)** worldly wisdom; satisfactory performance The hostess with her gastronomical skills and sophistication of manners made it a happy affair.
2026.	**Sophistry (N)** clever argument The judge found his arguments mere sophistry nothing substantial
2027.	**Sordid (Adj.)** shabby; comfortless Covid-19 is the reason of present sordid state of affairs.
2028.	**Sore (N, Adj.)** unappealing; aggrieved The accident victims are still recovering from body sores.
2029.	**Soreness (N)**
2030.	**Sovereign (N, Adj.)** monarch; chief In the discharge of sovereign duties, one is not held guilty.

2031.	**Sozzled (Adj.)** besotted; very drunk He was sober when came but sozzled when he left the party.
2032.	**Spank (V)** punish; beat The teacher spanked the unruly boy.
2033.	**Spanking (Adj.)**
2034.	**Sparse (Adj.)** very few, scanty He has grandiose ideas but sparse resources to implement them.
2035.	**Sparseness (N)**
2036.	**Sparsity (N)**
2037.	**Spartan (Adj.)** rigorous; hard Siddhartha renounced his kingdom to lead a monk's spartan life.
2038.	**Spasmodic (Adj.)** fitful; sporadic; intermittent There is spasmodic firing at Siachen.
2039.	**Spat (N)** disagreement; slight quarrel The two lawyers had a spat in the courtroom and the judge had to intervene.
2040.	**Splendour (N)** magnificence; brightness The splendour of the Taj Mahal on a moonlit night is ineffable.
2041.	**Splendid (Adj.)**
2042.	**Splutter (V)** speak incoherently and rapidly His father spluttered angrily at his prodigality.
2043.	**Spontaneous (Adj.)** natural Poetry is a spontaneous overflow of powerful feelings.
2044.	**Spontaneity (N)**
2045.	**Sporadic (Adj.)** occasional; fitful; regular The sporadic eruption of fighting along the LOC is a regular feature.
2046.	**Spree (N)** a lively frolic Shopping spree is a regular feature during Indian festivities.
2047.	**Sprout (V)** grow; shoot forth It is the time of the year when trees sprout new leaves.
2048.	**Spruce (Adj. V)** neat and clean; well turned out The city was well spruced on the eve of Prime Minister's visit.
2049.	**Spurious (Adj.)** counterfeit; not genuine There is a big racket of spurious drugs in the market.

2050.	**Spuriousness (N)**
2051.	**Squander (V)** waste; fritter away Don't squander your scarce resources with your profligacy.
2052.	**Stagnant (Adj.)** not moving; stationary Mosquitoes breed in stagnant water.
2053.	**Stalwart (Adj.)** strong and stout The stalwart guard cut a fine figure.
2054.	**Startling (Adj.)**
2055.	**Startle (V)** alarm; agitate suddenly The earthquake tremors startled many a brave heart.
2056.	**Static (Adj.)** stationary; not dynamic Life is not a static but a dynamic process.
2057.	**Stature (N)** height; level of achievement Napoleon was short of stature but not short of genius.
2058.	**Staunch (Adj.)** firm and steadfast Osama Bin Laden was a staunch supporter of Jehad against Christianity.
2059.	**Staunch (V)**
2060.	**Steadfast (Adj.)** firm; enduring He is a steadfast supporter of his party since its inception.
2061.	**Stealth (N)** furtively The English posed as traders and by stealth came to rule India.
2062.	**Stem (V)** halt; put a stop India must stem her rising population numbers.
2063.	**Stern (Adj.)** strict; harsh; severe He was given a stern warning for his undisciplined ways.
2064.	**Stickler (N)** one who insists on rules; faithful to rules. The bureaucrat was a stickler for rules.
2065.	**Stifle (V)** gag; subdue; suppress The military rulers in Pakistan stifle democracy.
2066.	**Stigma (N)** discredit; stain He scored a magnificent century and erased the stigma of earlier failures.
2067.	**Stigmatize (V)**
2068.	**Stilted (Adj.)** inhibited; stiff; not spontaneous The starlet could make only stilted conversation in the company of established artists.

2069.	**Stimulant (N)** impetus; encouragement Tea and coffee are light stimulants.
2070.	**Stimulate (V)**
2071.	**Stimulus (N)**
2072.	**Stingy (Adj.)** niggardly How could there be any love between a stingy father and a prodigal son!
2073.	**Stint (N)** time span for an appointment His stint as the Chief Justice of India lasted only six months.
2074.	**Stipulate (V)** promise; agree by an arrangement It was stipulated that Antonio would pay Shylock a pound of his flesh if he didn't return the loan in time.
2075.	**Stipulation (N)**
2076.	**Stir (V)** move; wander Even the crows didn't stir out in this scorching heat.
2077.	**Stir (N)**
2078.	**Stocky (Adj.)** short and well-built The stocky Maradona was an unmatched footballer, but cocaine devastated him.
2079.	**Stodgy (Adj.)** heavy; dull; tedious The stodgy old professor was full of dull anecdotes.
2080.	**Stoic (N)** indifferent to pain and pleasure Sangfroid is innate in a stoic.
2081.	**Stoke (V)** kindle; generate Love begets love and hatred stokes hatred.
2082.	**Stolid (Adj.)** impassive; calm He was a stolid man who did not even show his emotions at his mother's death.
2083.	**Stolidness (N)**
2084.	**Stoop (V)** lower oneself; become humble; condescend A haughty wife estranges her husband, a humble one stoops to conquer him.
2085.	**Straddle (V)** sit or stand with legs widely separated; traverse The city houses straggled in all directions.
2086.	**Strand (N)** thread; hair; She had a few strands of white hair in her jet black locks.
2087.	**Strand (be stranded) (V)**

2088.	**Strapping (Adj.)** strong and impressive The strapping and lively lass stole the show.
2089.	**Stratagem (N)** trickery; deceit The conman's stratagem didn't work with me.
2090.	**Strategic (Adj.)** advantageous; well positioned The forces on the higher peaks have a strategic advantage.
2091.	**Straw (N)** week-kneed; lacking strength A man of straw wilts in a crisis.
2092.	**Stray (V, Adj.)** deviate; go astray; homeless He strayed from the straight and narrow path of virtue. The stray cattle should be confined to a pound.
2093.	**Streak (N, V)** move fast; long; thin She has a streak of grey hair in her otherwise jet black locks.
2094.	**Streets (ahead) (adj.)** be much ahead; superior He is streets ahead of me in the knowledge of English language.
2095.	**Street (man in the street) (N)** plebian; commoner The man in the street understands politics but not economics.
2096.	**Stricken (Adj.)** adversely affected; smitten Millions in Asia and Africa are stricken with poverty.
2097.	**Stricture (N)** adverse remark; criticism We cannot but pass strictures against criminals who have entered legislature.
2098.	**Stride (make) (V)** progress; march forward India has made great strides ever since trade restrictions eased.
2099.	**Strident (Adj.)** sharp; bitter; loud There was a strident criticism of imposition of president's rule in Bihar.
2100.	**Stridently (Adj.)**
2101.	**Strife (N)** quarrel; contention; conflict The strife over Kashmir between India and Pakistan has come to an end with revocation of Article 370.
2102.	**Stringent (Adj.)** severe; harsh; strict Traffic rules should be made stringent.
2103.	**Stringency (N)**

2104.	**Stroke (of luck) (N)** chance; happening; act It was a stroke of good luck when she married a noble man
2105.	**Stroke (V)**
2106.	**Stroke (N)** illness caused by fitful flow of blood She suffered a stroke and was paralysed in the left side.
2107.	**Stroll (N)** quiet walk; go for a walk The old lady has a daily stroll in the garden.
2108.	**Strut (V)** Walk with an upright posture and an imperious air Man is a but a poor player who frets and struts his hour on the stage and then is heard no more.
2109.	**Stubborn (Adj.)** wilful; intransigent; mulish The horse was stubborn and balked at the steep climb.
2110.	**Stubbornness (N)**
2111.	**Stubby (Adj.)** short and thick The rich fat lady with her stubby hands stroked her cat.
2112.	**Stultification (N)**
2113.	**Stultify (V)** render stupid; be dull Our mind stultifies unless we hone it with good reading.
2114.	**Stupefy (V)** benumb; lose one's ability to think The drug stupefied him.
2115.	**Stupefaction (N)**
2116.	**Stupor (N)** absence of sensibility Don't take too many drinks or you will sink in a stupor.
2117.	**Sturdy (Adj.)** vigorous; powerful He ran the marathon with sturdy strides.
2118.	**Sturdiness (N)**
2119.	**Stupendous (Adj.)** amazing; tremendous Lara's unbeaten innings of 400 runs is a stupendous performance.
2120.	**Stupendously (Adj.)**
2121.	**Subjugate (V)** subordinate; relegate; stifle He subjugated his personal ambitions at the altar of family responsibility.
2122.	**Subjugation (N)**
2123.	**Sublimate (V)** refine; purify; make nobler He undertook penance to sublimate the evil within.

2124.	**Sublimation (N)**
2125.	**Submissive (Adj.)** subdued; complaisant; tame Mansi was very submissive in the relationship.
2126.	**Submissiveness (N)**
2127.	**Suborn (V)** instruct The shrewd judge could see through that the witness was suborned.
2128.	**Subscribe (V)** agree with; make common cause I do not subscribe to your view even though I respect these.
2129.	**Subscribe (V)** pay a sum of money for a magazine, book, etc. Do you subscribe to the Reader's Digest?
2130.	**Subscribe (v)** make a donation He subscribes a large sum every month to a charity organization.
2131.	**Subsequent (Adj.)** afterwards; later on He failed in his first test but fared better in subsequent exams.
2132.	**Subsequently (Adv)**
2133.	**Subsistence (N)** existence; bare means to exist Millions in Africa and Asia live below subsistence level.
2134.	**Substance (N)** fibre; mettle; true ability A man of true substance prefers learning to earning.
2135.	**Substantial (Adj.)** in good measure; considerable Substantial numbers in poor countries live below subsistence level.
2136.	**Substantiate (V)** prove; support with facts She substantiated her views with strong evidence.
2137.	**Substantive (Adj.)** important; demanding immediate attention Nuclear disarmament and pollution control are substantive contemporary issues.
2138.	**Subsume (V)** include within; be classified together Air and water pollution, climatic changes, Tsunami, Katrina, Wilma et al. can be subsumed under the phenomenon of greenhouse effect.
2139.	**Subterfuge (N)** trickery; deception His illness is only a subterfuge to shirk work.

2140.	**Subversive (Adj.)** ruinous; destructive; undermining Military dictators believe that honest expression of opinion is a subversive activity.
2141.	**Subversiveness (N)**
2142.	**Subvert (V)** undermine; damage; corrode; overthrow Those who believe in a pan-Islamic regime subvert their own political system.
2143.	**Succinct (Adj.)** brief; concise; compressed The judge told the lawyer to leave out unnecessary details and be succinct.
2144.	**Succinctly (Adj.)**
2145.	**Succour (N)** help; aid Government is reaching succour to the hapless earthquake victims.
2146.	**Succumb (N)** die; give way; yield He succumbed to his injuries on the way to hospital.
2147.	**Sufferance (N)** Passive permission; tolerance; capacity to endure pain If a guest overstays he only does it on sufferance.
2148.	**Suffocate (V)** strangulate; choke; stifle; smother Enclosed arenas only suffocate spectators.
2149.	**Suffocation (N)**
2150.	**Suffrage (N)** right to vote and elect In many backward countries, there is no universal suffrage.
2151.	**Suffuse (v)** fill; spread all over The setting sun suffused the fields with a red glow.
2152.	**Suffusion (N)**
2153.	**Sultry (Adj.)** sweltering; oppressively hot; seductive It is a torture to play cricket on a sultry day.
2154.	**Sultriness (N)**
2155.	**Sumptuous (Adj.)** rich and impressive A sumptuous meal was served on Anaadi's birthday.
2156.	**Sumptuousness (N)**
2157.	**Supercilious (Adj.)** haughty; proud; arrogant She treats yokels with much superciliousness.
2158.	**Superciliousness (N)**
2159.	**Superciliously (Adj.)**

2160.	**Superfluous (Adj.)** unnecessary; not quite required My culinary skills appear superfluous to my wife.
2161.	**Superfluity (N)**
2162.	**Superimpose (V)** set over and above, join; add Shakespeare superimposed his genius on Plutarch's historical accounts and created works of wonder.
2163.	**Superimposition (N)**
2164.	**Supersede (v)** dispense with; replace; set aside The old statue was collapsing and superseded by a new one.
2165.	**Supersession (N)** setting aside; the state of being superseded The supersession of monarchy by republicanism is a happy augury.
2166.	**Supplication (N)** humble prayer; entreaty He remained unmoved by my supplications for mercy.
2167.	**Supplicate (V)**
2168.	**Surge (N)** wave; move forward There would be a great surge of pride when an Indian wins an Olympic gold medal or a tennis grand slam.
2169.	**Surly (Adj.)** ill tempered; peevish; unfriendly She was so surly and he radiated with joy, an ill-matched couple indeed.
2170.	**Surliness (N)**
2171.	**Surmise (V)** guess; conjecture I don't know for certain but I surmise he will propose to her.
2172.	**Surmount (V)** conquer; overcome If you persevere, you will surmount your difficulties.
2173.	**Surpass (V)** excel; exceed Shakespeare surpasses all other playwrights
2174.	**Surpassing (Adj.)**
2175.	**Surreptitious (Adj.)** furtive, on the sly Love and murder mystery cannot remain surreptitious but will be solved by the Police.
2176.	**Surreptitiously (Adj.)**

2177.	**Surrogate (Adj.)** representative; substitute The destitute at Mother Teresa's Home look upon her as their surrogate mother.
2178.	**Surveillance (N)** survey; close watch The terrorists have been released but are under surveillance.
2179.	**Survive (V)** escape; come through We survived the enemy attacks and lived to light another day.
2180.	**Susceptible (Adj.)** impressionable; vulnerable Most men are susceptible to greed and lust.
2181.	**Susceptibility (N)**
2182.	**Suspect (V)** doubt; estimate He suspects fidelity of his wife.
2183.	**Swaddle (V)** wrap a baby in a piece of clothe The nursing sister swaddled the new born in a warm blanket.
2184.	**Swagger (N, V)** boast; brag The supercilious rich lady swaggered out of the room.
2185.	**Swelter (V)** suffer from oppressive heat It was a hot night and there was no electricity, we really sweltered.
2186.	**Sweltering (Adj.)**
2187.	**Swerve (V)** deviate; stray A true solider never swerves from the path of duty.
2188.	**Swindle (V)** cheat; deceive The judge convicted the accused of swindling and cheating the innocent people.
2189.	**Swindler (N)**
2190.	**Sycophant (N)** boot licker; flatterer Powerful men are surrounded by sycophants
2191.	**Sycophancy (N)**
2192.	**Sycophantic (Adj.)**

T

2193.	**Tacit (Adj.)** unexpressed fact; understood but unsaid There was a tacit agreement between husband and wife, not to bring their marital discord in public.
2194.	**Tacitness (N)**
2195.	**Tacitly (Adj.)**
2196.	**Taciturn (Adj.)** quiet; reticent reserved The movie star seemed taciturn and entertained no query.
2197.	**Taciturnity (N)**
2198.	**Talisman (N)** an amulet; a charm Gandhiji gave a talisman for happy and prosperous life.
2199.	**Tamper (V)** meddle; interfere The clerk was dismissed for tampering with the office records.
2200.	**Tandem (N)** in close cooperation The partners worked in tandem and prospered.
2201.	**Tangible (Adj.)** obvious; that which can be felt India has made tangible progress since Independence.
2202.	**Tantalize (V)** give false hopes; tempt She tantalized him with a smile and ensnared him.
2203.	**Tantamount (V)** be equal to; amount to The accused's silence would tantamount to admission of guilt.
2204.	**Tantrum (N)** burst of ill temper; angry and rude behaviour He was thrown out of the job for throwing tantrums.
2205.	**Tariff (N)** impost; tax We must raise tariff on imports to protect our cottage industry.
2206.	**Tarnish (V)** bring a bad name; defame Give up your vices or you will tarnish your reputation.
2207.	**Tawdry (Adj.)** gaudy; showy and cheap The tawdry finery bought from roadside vendors does not last long.
2208.	**Tedium (N)** boredom; monotony I go for a walk in the woods to relieve the tedium of my office job.
2209.	**Temerity (N)** insolence; rudeness; rashness; recklessness The captain has the temerity to disagree with the general.
2210.	**Temperate (Adj.)** restrained; with limits He never gives way to excesses and remains temperate.

2211.	**Temperance (N)** restraint; moderation His temperance saves him from unhappy excesses.
2212.	**Tempestuous (Adj.)** stormy; passionate Their tempestuous love affair soon wore out and they parted ways.
2213.	**Tempest (N)**
2214.	**Temporal (Adj.)** worldly The Dalai Lama is a spiritual ruler not a temporal one.
2215.	**Temporize (V)** be indecisive; evasive He didn't dare refuse, so he temporized like a politician.
2216.	**Tenable (Adj.)** plausible The arguments did not sound tenable.
2217.	**Tenacious (Adj.)** pertinacious; holding fast; courageous He made tenacious efforts to win the race.
2218.	**Tenacity (N).**
2219.	**Tendentious (Adj.)** with a bias; controversial She raises tendentious issues and remains in the news.
2220.	**Tendentiousness (N)**
2221.	**Tenet (N)** principal belief; doctrine The chief tenets of Gandiji's philosophy are truth and nonviolence.
2222.	**Tenor (N)** drift; course They spoke in French but I could follow the tenor of the argument.
2223.	**Tentacles (N)** restrictions; limitations She cut loose from her family tentacles and went abroad.
2224.	**Tentative (Adj.)** provisional; not final We have held only tentative discussions and not reached any conclusions.
2225.	**Tenterhooks (N)** anxious expectancy; uneasy suspense The match was decided on the last ball and the spectators remained on tenterhooks.
2226.	**Tenuous (Adj.)** unsubstantial; vague They have maintained a tenuous relationship for keeping up appearances.
2227.	**Tenuousness (N)**
2228.	**Tepid (Adj.)** lukewarm; lifeless; unenthusiastic; dull It was not a great play and the applause at the end was tepid.
2229.	**Tepidness (N)**
2230.	**Throes (N)** trouble; agony Iraq is in great political throes following American occupation.
2231.	**Throng (V)** gather A mammoth crowd thronged the congregation.
2232.	**Thwart (N)** threat He felt thwarted by his own relatives in his new venture.
2233.	**Tiff (N)** petty quarrel; slight annoyance A warm embrace always followed the tiffs between Jim and Della.
2234.	**Tilt (V)** bend; inclination The earth is tilted on its axis.
2235.	**Tinge (V)** touch; colour The sunset tinged the fields with a red glow.
2236.	**Tirade (N)** denunciation; bitter speech His opponents let loose a flurry of tirades but he was unfazed.
2237.	**Titanic (Adj.)** enormous; colossal A titanic battle of attrition rages between the forces of good and evil.
2238.	**Titillate (V)** tickle; excite; tingle Movies which titillate rather than instruct do well on the box office.
2239.	**Titular (Adj.)** nominal; without real power. The queen is the de facto ruler; the king is only a titular head.
2240.	**Toil (V)** hard work; labour He toiled for his success.
2241.	**Topple (V)** oust; defeat The coup failed and the government was not toppled.
2242.	**Torment (N)** acute trouble; misery Flies and mosquitoes are a torment in summers.
2243.	**Tornado (N)** violent storm with circular winds The tornado uprooted trees and razed houses.
2244.	**Torpid (Adj.)** lifeless; with no energy The players felt torpid in the heat.
2245.	**Torpor (N)** lifelessness; sloth The travellers sank in a torpor in the wilting heat.
2246.	**Torrid (Adj.)** hot and dry; passionate The torrid Indian sun sent the tourists scurrying home.

2247.	**Torridity (N)**
2248.	**Tortuous (Adj.)** zigzag; serpentine; circuitous The tortuous Kalka–Simla rail track is marked with bridges and tunnels.
2249.	**Totalitarian (Adj.)** dictatorial; autocratic The totalitarian regime in Iraq came to an end with death of Saddam Hussain.
2250.	**Totalitarianism (N)**
2251.	**Totter (V)** be unstable; walk listless The monarchy is stable in England but tottering in Nepal.
2252.	**Tottering (Adj.)**
2253.	**Tour be force (N)** a skilful feat Two lives by Vikram Seth is a literary tour be force.
2254.	**Traduce (V)** speak ill of; slander She is a scandal monger and loves to traduce her friends.
2255.	**Traducer (N)**
2256.	**Trail (N, V)** left behind The earthquake left a trail of death and destruction.
2257.	**Trait (N)** characteristic Joie de vivre and sangfroid are common Punjabi traits.
2258.	**Trajectory (N)** flight; direction The batsman couldn't read the trajectory of the spinning ball and it bowled him.
2259.	**Trample (V)** crush under one's feet; domineer There was a stampede and many people were trampled underneath.
2260.	**Tranquil (Adj.)** peaceful; quiet The tranquil atmosphere of villages is more healthy than city life.
2261.	**Tranquility (N)**
2262.	**Transact (V)** go through (a deal); conduct business I can only transact a clean deal with clean people.
2263.	**Transaction (N)**
2264.	**Transcend (V)** rise above; go beyond Meditation makes one transcend space and time.

2265.	**Transcendent (Adj.)** ineffable; stupendous; remarkable Shakespeare was a poet and playwright of transcendent genius.
2266.	**Transcribe (V)** copy a speech or song in writing The clerk transcribed my speech from a cassette.
2267.	**Transfigure (V)** transform; be happy The mother was transfigured at reunion with her long lost son.
2268.	**Transfix (V)** fascinate; charm The Taj Mahal on moonlit nights transfixes lovers.
2269.	**Transfixing (Adj.)**
2270.	**Transfuse (V)** inject blood Blood was transfused to the accident victim.
2271.	**Transfusion (N)** supply; investment We need a large transfusion of cash to revive the dying project.
2272.	**Transgress (V)** violate; go beyond limits It is advisable not to transgress the traffic rules.
2273.	**Transgression (N)**
2274.	**Transient (Adj.)** short-lived; fleeting; ephemeral; transitory Life is a transient affair and we are all subject to decay.
2275.	**Transience (N)**
2276.	**Transitory (Adj.)**
2277.	**Transmigration (N)** going to another place; to be reborn after death Hindus believe in the transmigration of souls.
2278.	**Transmute (V)** bring about a metamorphosis; transform Good company transmutes sinners into saints.
2279.	**Transmutation (N)**
2280.	**Transpire (V)** occur; happen; take place Nobody knows what transpired at the conclave of archbishops.
2281.	**Trauma (N)** shock Many earthquake victims suffered no grievous injuries but suffered from shock and trauma.
2282.	**Traumatic (Adj.)**

2283.	**Travail (N)** pangs of childbirth; pain; anguish A man can only speculate about the travails of childbirth.
2284.	**Traverse (V)** covers; wander; go across Guru Nanak was an itinerant prophet who traversed long distances.
2285.	**Travesty (N)** a work of inferior quality; a mockery of justice Travesty of justice is the order of the day.
2286.	**Treacherous (Adj.)** deceptive; unreliable The weather is treacherous, take care of your health.
2287.	**Treachery (N)**
2288.	**Tread (V)** walk with heavy steps; hurt one's sensibilities Always try to tread path of virtue.
2289.	**Treadmill (N)** a tedious job; wearisome routine For the poor life is a treadmill.
2290.	**Treatise (N)** a large written document; an essay His treatise on China's economy and its political system has won him a Ph.D.
2291.	**Trenchant (Adj.)** sharp; harsh He is a trenchant critic of reckless exploitation of earth's resources.
2292.	**Trenchantly (Adj.)**
2293.	**Trenchancy (N)**
2294.	**Trepidation (N)** fear; perturbation He expressed his views with great candour and without trepidation.
2295.	**Trice (in a) (N)** in on time; at once He pays thrice who give in a trice.
2296.	**Trifle (N)** insignificant things Do not fall out over trifles
2297.	**Trifle (V)**
2298.	**Trinket (N)** anything trivial; an ornament of little value She accepted the trinket, he gave her on her birthday.
2299.	**Trite (Adj.)** unoriginal; banal The trite remarks by a non-serious tutor left the serious student disturbed.
2300.	**Trivial (Adj.)** insignificant; of no consequence Nehru was a great visionary who didn't heed the trivial details.

2301.	**Triviality (N)**
2302.	**Trounce (V)** rout; defeat badly India trounced Sri Lanka by 152 runs in the first ODI.
2303.	**Truant (N)** runaway; one who flees The school master was harsh on the truants.
2304.	**Truancy (N)**
2305.	**Truckle (V)** bow; fear I am my own master and trucked to no bullies.
2306.	**Truculent (Adj.)** aggressive; belligerent Indian wrestlers are truculent fighters.
2307.	**Trumpery (N)** showy ornament of small value; trinket The village girls adorned in trumpery flocked to the Sunday market.
2308.	**Trumpet (N)** self-praise; self-glorification The poet has delusions of grandeur and blows his own trumpet.
2309.	**Truncate (V)** divide; dismember; vivisect Gandhi and Jinnah couldn't reconcile and India was truncated in 1947.
2310.	**Tryst (N)** rendezvous; appointment; meeting '***Tryst with Destiny***' is a famous speech by Jawahar Lal Nehru.
2311.	**Tumult (N)** excitement; uproar There was much tumult in the market against new imposts.
2312.	**Tumultuous (Adj.)** full of applause or noise The victors receive a tumultuous welcome and the vanquished lick their wounds.
2313.	**Turbid (Adj.)** agitated; murky It rained heavily and the waters in the river turned turbid.
2314.	**Turbidity (N)**
2315.	**Turgid (Adj.)** swollen; distended; The river was inundated and its waters turned turgid.
2316.	**Turpitude (N)** base conduct; depravity He was sacked on ground of moral turpitude.
2317.	**Twiddle (V)** play or trifle idly; waste time; moving your thumb around After my retirement, I could either twiddle my thumbs or write this lexicon.

U

2318.	**Umpteen (Adj.)** time and again; very many times Umpteen times, the teacher told the boys to be attentive.
2319.	**Unabated (Adj.)** continuous; steadfast The old man's enthusiasm for life remained unabated.
2320.	**Unassuming (Adj.)** modest; humble Despite meteoric success, he remained unassuming.
2321.	**Unavailing (Adj.)** in vain; without profit; unsuccessful He tried hard to win back his estranged wife but it was unavailing.
2322.	**Unbecoming (Adj.)** undesirable; unhealthy It is unbecoming of a son not to take care of aged parents.
2323.	**Unbidden (Adj.)** of one's own wish; spontaneously The estranged wife came back to her husband unbidden.
2324.	**Unbounded (Adj.)** without limits; unrestrained His love for his daughter is unbounded.
2325.	**Unbridled (Adj.)** uncontrolled; unrestrained His lust for money is unbridled
2326.	**Unbroken (Adj.)** continuous; without a break; unceasing Milkha Singh's national record for 400 meters remained unbroken for many years.
2327.	**Uncalled (Adj.)** inappropriate; wrong; not in the right spirit His outburst against me was uncalled for.
2328.	**Uncanny (Adj.)** weird; inexplicable She had an uncanny feeling that someone was watching her.
2329.	**Unceasing (Adj.)** continuous; incessant There has been unceasing rain since morning.
2330.	**Unceremonious (Adj.)** without ritual; abrupt; hasty; rude The exit of Auditor General from the office was unceremonious and ignominious.
2331.	**Undaunted (Adj.)** fearless; intrepid He fought against heavy odds and remained undaunted.
2332.	**Underrate (V)** disparage; undervalue No society can prosper if it underrates the role of teachers.
2333.	**Undo (V)** unfasten; erase; cancel You must not moan and groan about the things which cannot be undone.
2334.	**Undoing (N)**
2335.	**Unearned (Adj.)** earned without efforts Don't hanker after unearned name and fame.
2336.	**Unearth (V)** find out; bring to light; unravel The police unearthed the murder mystery.
2337.	**Unfailing (Adj.)** continuous; steadfast She faces every crisis with unfailing tenacity.
2338.	**Unfaltering (Adj.)** unwavering; unfailing The popularity of Kejriwal is still unfaltering.
2339.	**Unfathomable (Adj.)** difficult to know or measure May God bless your with unfathomable success.
2340.	**Unfold (V)** make known; make intelligible The police unfolded the sequence of events which led to the murder.
2341.	**Unfounded (Adj.)** untrue; without basis His allegations were found to be false and unfounded.
2342.	**Unimpeachable (Adj.)** impeccable; above suspicion The integrity of a judge must be unimpeachable.
2343.	**Unimpeachability (N)**
2344.	**Unleash (V)** set free; let loose Saddam Hussein had unleashed a rein of terror on his countrymen.
2345.	**Unlettered (Adj.)** illiterate; uneducated He was unlettered and unfit for the office job.
2346.	**Unmitigated (Adj.)** disastrous; calamitous The earthquake brought death and destruction and was truly an unmitigated disaster.
2347.	**Unparalleled (Adj.)** unsurpassed; incomparable Yuvaraj Singh has unparalleled achievements in the game of cricket.

2348.	**Unparliamentary (Adj.)** rude; abusive; scurrilous Use of unparliamentary language on the TV channels is order of the day.
2349.	**Unprecedented (Adj.)** unparalleled, without an example Covid-19 is an unprecedented pandemic causing irreparable losses.
2350.	**Unravel (V)** solve; bring to light; unfold The murder mystery was unraveled and the killers were nabbed.
2351.	**Unremitting (Adj.)** continuous; incessant His unremitting efforts finally bore fruit.
2352.	**Unrivalled (Adj.)** peerless; unsurpassed Katrina Kaif is a woman of unrivalled beauty.
2353.	**Unruly (Adj.)** undisciplined; turbulent Much to the teacher's chagrin, it was a class of unruly boys.
2354.	**Unsavory (Adj.)** tasteless; insipid Nobody like his unsavory remarks.
2355.	**Unsavoriness (N)**
2356.	**Unscathed (Adj.)** unharmed; safe It was a serious accident but we came out unscathed.
2357.	**Unscrupulous (Adj.)** dishonest; immoral; disingenuous The ways of politicians are venal and unscrupulous.
2358.	**Unseemly (Adj.)** unsavoury; unbecoming; ill mannered Telling indelicate jokes with women around is unseemly.
2359.	**Usurp (V)** take by force; encroach; possess illegally Aurangzeb usurped the crown from his brothers through Machiavellian machinations.
2360.	**Unswerving (Adj.)** steadfast; firm The boss rewarded him with a promotion for his unswerving services.
2361.	**Untoward (Adj.)** unfortunate; unpleasant Nothing untoward happened in the market that day.
2362.	**Unutterable (Adj.)** unspeakable After wife's death, he was in unutterable grief.
2363.	**Unwieldy (Adj.)** difficult to carry; awkward; ungainly The unwieldy bags of little school students is an unhappy sight.
2364.	**Unwitting (Adj.)** unaware; oblivious She was an unwitting tool of her husband's nefarious activities.
2365.	**Upbraid (V)** scold; reproach; censure The school master would upbraid the truants.
2366.	**Upheaval (N)** an unhappy and violent change; great disturbance An earthquake is a natural upheaval and cannot be predicted accurately.
2367.	**Upkeep (N)** maintenance; upbringing The estranged couple separated but the wife took the responsibility for the upkeep of two little children.
2368.	**Uppishly (Adj.)** snobbish; conceited; awkward Nobody likes her uppishly ways.
2369.	**Uppity (N)**
2370.	**Uppishness (N)**
2371.	**Upright (Adj.)** straight; honest; truthful; righteous He was an upright officer who acted without fear or favour.
2372.	**Uprighteous (N)**
2373.	**Uproar (N)** noise; excitement; commotion Every time our cricket team loses, the country sways with an uproar.
2374.	**Uproot (V)** root out; extirpate; eliminate Let us pledge to uproot corruption from Indian public life.

V

2375.	**Vacillate (V)** waiver You must develop do or die spirit; if you vacillate you would not succeed.
2376.	**Vacillation (N)**
2377.	**Vagary (N)** shade; sudden change; colour Happiness and sorrow are vagaries of life.
2378.	**Vainglorious (Adj.)** vain; proud; conceited A humble man can never be vainglorious of his achievements.

2379.	**Valid (Adj.)** relevant; tenable The judge didn't find a valid point and turned down lawyer's plea.
2380.	**Validate (V)**
2381.	**Validity (N)**
2382.	**Valour (N)** courage; bravery He fought with great valour before falling in the battlefield.
2383.	**Valorous (Adj.)**
2384.	**Vandal (N)** one who delights in destroying beautiful thing The religious vandals destroyed idols.
2385.	**Vandalism (N)**
2386.	**Vanish (V)** lost He vanished in the crowd and was not traceable.
2387.	**Vanity (N)** arrogance; self-pride Vanity usually leads towards destruction.
2388.	**Vanquished (Adj.)** defeated; subdued He was vanquished but not cowed down.
2389.	**Vanquish (V)**
2390.	**Variance (N)** variety; variation My views are at variance with yours.
2391.	**Variegated (Adj.)** different; of various hues The variegated hues of flowers were a feast for the eyes at the rose festival.
2392.	**Variegation (N)**
2393.	**Veer (V)** lurch; turn; slide The car suddenly veered to the right and overturned.
2394.	**Vegetate (V)** live a passive life; be inactive Read good books, keep intelligent company lest you start vegetating.
2395.	**Vehement (Adj.)** zealot; ardent; passionate He was vehement in his denial of allegations against him.
2396.	**Vehemence (N)**
2397.	**Venal (Adj.)** corrupt; unscrupulous The venal ways of politician make politics a dirty game.
2398.	**Venality (N)**
2399.	**Vendetta (N)** a prolonged and bitter disagreement between two groups The political vendetta between the two parties finally exploded publicly.
2400.	**Veneer (N)** mask; superficial appearance The swindler cast off the veneer of friendship and came out in his true colours.
2401.	**Venerable (Adj.)** worthy of respect; veneration Our venerable grandfather is the family's patriarch.
2402.	**Veneration (N)**
2403.	**Venerate (V)** esteem; worship Most Hindus venerate Rama and Krishna as incarnations of God.
2404.	**Vengeance (N)** infliction of pain & revenge He sought vengeance for the murder of his children.
2405.	**Vengefully (Adj.)** vindictively; with a view to avenge We lost the first match but came back vengefully to claim the second.
2406.	**Vengeful (Adj.)**
2407.	**Venial (Adj.)** excusable; trifling Intemperate language is a venial act and ought to be forgiven and forgotten.
2408.	**Veniality (N)**
2409.	**Venom (N)** poison; spite; malice The political foes spewed venom against east other.
2410.	**Venomous (Adj.)**
2411.	**Vent (V)** pour; express; utter The boss vented his anger on the subordinates.
2412.	**Ventilate (V)** express or articulate a complaint or opinion Democracy gives us chances to ventilate our grievances/ minds.
2413.	**Ventilation (N)**
2414.	**Venturesome (Adj.)** daring; willing to take risk Mukesh Ambani is a venturesome businessman who has made it big in the world of business.
2415.	**Veracity (N)** truthfulness The defence lawyer had to prove veracity of facts beyond reasonable doubt.
2416.	**Verbatim (Adj.)** word for word; exactly the same words She has phenomenal memory who can produce everything verbatim whatever she crams.

2417.	**Verbose (Adj.)** wordy Academicians believe in verbose writing without meaning.
2418.	**Verbosity (N)**
2419.	**Verge (N)** brink; edge The lockdown had virtually driven the country on the verge of emergency.
2420.	**Verily (Adj.)** truly; really; indeed The USA is verily the most powerful nation in the world.
2421.	**Versed (Adj.)** learned; skilful; experienced She is well versed in her subject.
2422.	**Veteran (N)** a seasoned person; experienced The World War II veterans are still around with their delightful tales.
2423.	**Vex (V)** annoy; irk Unruly boys vexed the teacher.
2424.	**Vexation (N)**
2425.	**Vexatious (Adj.)**
2426.	**Vice (N)** a weakness of character; immoral habit Gambling and drinking are cardinal vices.
2427.	**Vicious (Adj.)** spiteful; depraved; immoral He has let loose a vicious campaign to smear my reputation.
2428.	**Viciousness (N)**
2429.	**Vicissitude (N)** ups and down The vicissitudes of life are actually the beauties of life.
2430.	**Vie (V)** compete; contend You should vie with others.
2431.	**Vigil (N)** wakefulness; watch Bureaucracy in India remains under vigil of politicians.
2432.	**Vigilant (Adj.)** watchful; circumspect Vigilant citizens are must for survival of democracy.
2433.	**Vigilance (N)**
2434.	Vindicate (V) uphold; justify Pradeep Virk vindicated his father's stand.
2435.	**Vindication (N)**
2436.	**Virtuoso (N)** exceptionally skilful; a connoisseur of arts Lata and Rafi are singing virtuosos.

2437.	**Virulent (Adj.)** deadly; trenchant AIDS is virulent disease and knows no remedy.
2438.	**Virulence (N)**
2439.	**Vital (Adj.)** life giving, important; necessary Hard work is vital for success.
2440.	**Vitality (N)**
2441.	**Vivid (Adj.)** fresh; bright; life like His vivid description and vitality of language make him an outstanding writer.
2442.	**Vividness (N)**
2443.	**Vivisect (V)** dissect; divide; dismember There was a clash of egos between leaders and the country was vivisected.
2444.	**Vivisection (N)**
2445.	**Vixen (N)** female fox She is a vixen, too clever for a guideless fellow like him.
2446.	**Vogue (N)** fashion; popular; current; acceptable Going to malls is a vogue nowadays.
2447.	**Voluptuous (Adj.)** sexually attractive; sensual Katrina Kaif is truly a voluptuous lady.
2448.	**Voracious (Adj.)** greedy; insatiable He is a voracious reader.
2449.	**Voracity (N)**
W	
2450.	**Waffle (N)** meaningless talk; nonsense The judge told the lawyer to stop waffling and come to the point.
2451.	**Wail (V)** lament; cry All the family members were wailing at the untimely demise of the young one.
2452.	**Waive (V)** relinquish; forgo Once you waive off your rights, you cannot reclaim them.
2453.	**Waiver (N)**
2454.	
2455.	**Wake (N)** the path; the course; the track In wake of soaring prices, government introduced new policy to check it.
2456.	**Wane (V)** decrease; grow less in size With the passing year, the popularity of the Bollywood stars wane.

2457.	**Wangle (V)** manage; accomplish There was a great rush but he wangled to get through.
2458.	**Want (N)** lack There is a want of common sense amongst the commoners.
2459.	**Wanton (Adj.)** heedless; reckless; unmindful of the consequences The wanton exploitation of earth's resources has led to the greenhouse effect.
2460.	**Wantonness (N)**
2461.	**Warp (V)** render awry; make askew; give a wrong twist Bad company warps the impressionistic minds of the youngsters.
2462.	**Wary (Adj.)** careful; cautious Be wary of bad company.
2463.	**Wastrel (N)** prodigal; profligate The son turned out to be a wastrel and brought the family to a financial precipice.
2464.	**Waver (V)** vacillate; be indecisive Do not waver at the last moment, once you have decided and resolved.
2465.	**Wax (V)** grow in size; praise The popularity of Amitabh Bachchan is waxing as he is ageing.
2466.	**Weal (N)** prosperity; happiness; well-being We should work for the common weal.
2467.	**Wean (V)** bring up Anaadi was weaned with love, care, and affection.
2468.	**Wee (N. Adj.)** a little; early I always prefer to write in the wee hours.
2469.	**Weft (N)** texture; fabric The woof and weft of life is a beauty to be enjoyed and celebrated.
2470.	**Weird (Adj.)** strange; eccentric Sometimes he exhibits very weird responses.
2471.	**Weirdness (N)**
2472.	**Welter (N)** mixture; medley The welter of ups and downs in life scares the common man.
2473.	**Wheedle (V)** coax; cajole; swindle The conman wheedled my hard-earned money out of me.

2474.	**Whirl (N, V)** turn around; spin; rotate The whirls of life never cease.
2475.	**Whoop (V)** cry; shout in excitement He whooped with delight when she consented to his proposal.
2476.	**Wield (V)** possess; exercise; make use of One who wields the purse, wields the power.
2477.	**Wilful (Adj.)** stubborn; adamant The wilful boy refused to obey the teacher.
2478.	**Wilfulness (N)**
2479.	**Wily (Adj.)** clever; cunning; crafty
2480.	**Winnow (V)** sift; to separate grain from chaff The farmers were winnowing the cotton crop.
2481.	**Wistful (Adj.)** full of longing; yearning In old age we all grow wistful about our youthful days.
2482.	**Wistfulness (N)**
2483.	**Wit (N)** understanding; intelligence He is known for wit and humour among his peer group.
2484.	**Witty (Adj.)**
2485.	**Wither (V)** shrivel; fade; decay Beauty withers away with time.
2486.	**Withstand (V)** hold firm; resist You must muster the courage to withstand the tough times in life.
2487.	**Wobble (V)** move unsteadily; move from side to side Dara Singh hit his opponent, who wobbled and fell down.
2488.	**Woe (N)** misery; suffering Weal and woe are colors of life.
2489.	**Wrath (N)** anger; ire The truants invite the teacher's wrath.
2490.	**Wreath (N)** flower garland; a circular band All the politicians put wreaths on their leader's dead body.
2491.	**Wrest (V)** snatch; take by force He wrested the title from last year's champion with a sterling performance.
2492.	**Wriggle (V)** twist and turn He faced the wriggles of life with great fortitude.

Y	
2493.	**Yearn (V)** long for He always yearned to be an IAS Officer.
2494.	**Yell (V)** shout with anger; cry The truculent wife yelled at her hapless husband and threatened to report against him.
2495.	**Yoke (N)** burden The yoke of daily needs leaves us with no time for leisure.
2496.	**Yore (N)** a long time back; long ago In the days of yore, people tramped on foot or rode bicycles.

Z	
2497.	**Zany (Adj.)** whimsical; ludicrous; comical Mr. Sharma is a zany fellow.
2498.	**Zenith (N)** highest point Amitabh Bachchan is at the zenith of his career.
2499.	**Zest (N)** gusto; passion The old man still retains his zest for living.
2500.	**Zigzag (Adj.)** circuitous; serpentine The hilly tracks run in a zigzag manner.

100 – PRACTICE TESTS
100 × 10 – Matching Words

This Chapter herein provides 100 practice sets containing 1000 words in the form of 100 tables. Each table contains 10 entries on the left side with their meanings as synonyms on the right side. So, these 1000 words would enable the students to check their range of words and their understanding. It will also help in retention of the 2500 basic words outlined and explained in detail in Chapter 1 with their meanings and usage.

Having gone through these 1000 words through 100 practice sets, the students would be able to make an actual evaluation of their level of understanding and proper estimation of their level of retention. This chapter would help the students to reflect and calibrate their efforts to boost their vocabulary and enhance the exactitude and accuracy in their attempts to solve any vocabulary-oriented questions in any competitive examination.

Having mastered Chapter 1 & 2, students will be able to switch over to Chapter 3 quite comfortably. Chapter 3 would further expose them to a vast repertoire of 20,000 variants of these basic words as synonyms and antonyms. Thorough reading and understanding of Chapter 1 and Chapter 2 would help them land safely in the realm of world of words provided in Chapter 3. Proper care and caution have been taken to make the vocabulary booster section highly useful for competitive examinations. All types of superficiality and superfluity have been avoided.

Match the words given on the left side of the tables with the words given on the right side of the tables which are exact variants/ synonyms nearest in meaning to the words given on the left side.

Match each word in the Left column with its meaning in the Right column.

TEST – 1

1.	Abate	a.	Step down from power
2.	Abdicate	b.	Hopeless
3.	Aberration	c.	Unsuccessful
4.	Abhor	d.	Exonerate
5.	Abject	e.	Complete
6.	Abnegate	f.	Subside
7.	Abortive	g.	Detest
8.	Abridge	h.	Shorten
9.	Absolute	i.	Deviation
10.	Absolve	j	Renounce

TEST – 2

1.	Abstinent	a.	Not easily understandable
2.	Abstract	b.	Temperate
3.	Abstruse	c.	Dreadful
4.	Abysmal	d.	Bitter
5.	Accolade	e.	Comply
6.	Accost	f.	Harsh
7.	Acerbic	g.	Mental sharpness
8.	Acquiesce	h.	Theoretical
9.	Acrimonious	i.	Honour
10.	Acumen	j	Greet

TEST – 3

1.	Astute	a.	Shrewd
2.	Adage	b.	Follower
3.	Adamant	c.	Awkward
4.	Address	d.	Warn
5.	Adherent	e.	Speak to
6.	Admonish	f.	Skillful
7.	Adroit	g.	Old saying
8.	Dexterous	h.	Admiration
9.	Gauche	i.	Unyielding
10.	Adulation	j.	Proficient

ANSWERS

	TEST – 1	TEST – 2	TEST – 3
1.	f	b	a
2.	a	h	g
3.	i	a	i
4.	g	c	e
5.	b	i	b
6.	j	j	d
7.	c	d	f
8.	h	e	f
9.	e	f	c
10.	d	g	h

TEST – 4

1.	Adulterate	a.	Opposed to
2.	Adverse	b.	Friendly
3.	Averse	c.	Rich
4.	Aesthetic	d.	Pretension
5.	Affable	e.	Artistic
6.	Affectation	f.	Contaminate
7.	Affinity	g.	Sympathy
8.	Affluent	h.	Unfavourable
9.	Agenda	i.	Program
10.	Agrarian	j.	Relating to agriculture

TEST – 5

1.	Aggregate	a.	Get together
2.	Congregate	b.	Unite
3.	Segregate	c.	Who doesn't believe in the existence of God
4.	Integrate	d.	Relieve
5.	Agnostic	e.	Keep apart
6.	Alacrity	f.	Combination of metals
7.	Allege	g.	Sum total
8.	Alleviate	h.	Distribute
9.	Allocate	i.	Accuse
10.	Alloy	j.	Keenness

TEST – 6

1.	Allusion	a.	Atmosphere
2.	Aloof	b.	Alone
3.	Altruism	c.	Unclear
4.	Ambience	d.	Generosity
5.	Ambiguous	e.	Indirect reference
6.	Ambivalent	f.	Undecided
7.	Assiduous	g.	Taxing
8.	Ascetic	h.	Hermit
9.	Avarice	i.	Greed
10.	Axiom	j.	Truth

TEST – 7

1.	Ameliorate	a.	Pleasantness
2.	Amenable	b.	Comparison
3.	Amenity	c.	Obedient
4.	Amiable	d.	Without moral feeling
5.	Amicable	e.	Loving
6.	Amnesty	f.	Improve
7.	Amoral	g.	Shapeless
8.	Amorous	h.	Politely friendly
9.	Amorphous	i.	Pardon
10.	Analogy	j.	Friendly

TEST – 8

1.	Anarchy	a.	Resentment
2.	Monarchy	b.	Racial oppression
3.	Anecdote	c.	Firm dislike
4.	Anguish	d.	Irregularity
5.	Animosity	e.	Prior
6.	Anomaly	f.	Agony
7.	Antecedent	g.	Tale
8.	Antipathy	h.	Government by king or queen
9.	Antithesis	i.	Lawlessness
10.	Apartheid	j.	Direct opposite

ANSWERS

	TEST – 4	TEST – 5	TEST – 6	TEST – 7	TEST – 8
1.	f	g	e	f	i
2.	h	a	b	c	h
3.	a	e	d	a	g
4.	e	b	a	j	f
5.	b	c	c	h	a
6.	d	j	f	i	d
7.	g	i	g	d	e
8.	c	d	h	e	c
9.	i	h	i	g	j
10.	j	f	j	b	b

TEST – 9

1.	Apathy	a.	Of dubious authenticity
2.	Aphorism	b.	Misunderstanding
3.	Apocalypse	c.	Increase in value
4.	Apocryphal	d.	Lack of interest
5.	Apotheosis	e.	Soothe
6.	Appease	f.	Prophetic revelation
7.	Appreciate	g.	Decrease in value
8.	Depreciate	h.	The perfect example
9.	Apprehensive	i.	Witty saying
10.	Misapprehension	j.	Worried

TEST – 10

1.	Approbation	a.	Misuse public money
2.	Appropriate	b.	Extremely old
3.	Misappropriate	c.	Take without permission
4.	Expropriate	d.	Weight opposing views
5.	Aptitude	e.	Mysterious
6.	Arbiter	f.	Approval
7.	Arbitrate	g.	Random
8.	Arbitrary	h.	Take property officially
9.	Arcane	i.	Judge
10.	Archaic	j.	Natural ability

TEST – 11

1.	Archetype	a.	Passionate
2.	Ardent	b.	Of noble birth
3.	Arduous	c.	Supremacy
4.	Aristocratic	d.	Hardworking
5.	Artful	e.	Difficult
6.	Artifice	f.	Trickery
7.	Ascendancy	g.	Hermitlike
8.	Ascetic	h.	Crafty
9.	Assiduous	i.	Original model
10.	Acme	k.	Zenith

TEST – 12

1.	Assimilate	a.	Shrewd
2.	Assuage	b.	Boldness
3.	Astute	c.	Favorable
4.	Attrition	d.	Grow
5.	Audacity	e.	Soothe
6.	Augment	f.	Extremely bossy
7.	Auspicious	g.	Absorb
8.	Austere	h.	Harsh
9.	Autocratic	i.	Gradual wearing away
10.	Acute	j.	Severe

TEST – 13

1.	Autonomous	a.	Greed
2.	Avarice	b.	Keen
3.	Avow	c.	Self-evident truth
4.	Avid	d.	Acting independently
5.	Awry	e.	Claim
6.	Axiom	f.	Twisted
7.	Agog	g.	Surprised
8.	Brevity	h.	Shortness
9.	Brazen	i.	Naked
10.	Bucolic	j.	Rustic

ANSWERS

	TEST – 9	TEST – 10	TEST – 11	TEST – 12	TEST – 13
1.	d	f	i	g	d
2.	i	c	a	e	a
3.	f	a	e	a	e
4.	a	h	b	i	b
5.	h	j	h	b	f
6.	e	i	f	d	c
7.	c	d	c	c	g
8.	g	g	g	h	h
9.	j	e	d	f	i
10.	b	b	j	j	j

TEST – 14

1.	Banal	a.	Make to seem little
2.	Bane	b.	Unoriginal
3.	Bastion	c.	Go over repeatedly
4.	Beget	d.	Stronghold
5.	Belabor	e.	Curse
6.	Beleaguer	f.	Give a false impression
7.	Belie	g.	Surround
8.	Belittle	h.	Give birth to
9.	Brazen	i.	Naked
10.	Bucolic	j.	Rustic

TEST – 15

1.	Belligerent	a.	Intending harm
2.	Bemused	b.	Donor
3.	Benefactor	c.	Not harmful
4.	Beneficiary	d.	Deadly
5.	Benevolent	e.	Confused
6.	Benign	f.	Generous
7.	Malignant	g.	Combative
8.	Malign	h.	Injure with lies
9.	Malevolent	i.	One who receive benefits
10.	Malefactor	j.	Evildoer

TEST – 16

1.	Bequest	a.	Left desolate
2.	Bequeath	b.	Something left in a will
3.	Bereft	c.	Harass
4.	beset	d.	Offensively noisy
5.	Blasphemy	e.	Leave in a will
6.	Blatant	f.	Irreverence
7.	Castigate	g.	Criticize severely
8.	Catalyst	h.	Agent
9.	Burgeon	i.	Flourish
10.	Burlesque	j.	Ludicrous imitation

TEST – 17

1.	Brevity	a.	Succinctness
2.	Blasphemy	b.	Irrelevance
3.	Belligerous	c.	Quarrelsome
4.	Bane	d.	Curse
5.	Awry	e.	Twisted
6.	Blatant	f.	Flagrant
7.	Agog	g.	Astounded
8.	Adulterous	h.	Pollute
9.	Averse	i.	Against
10.	Affluent	j.	Rich

TEST – 18

1.	Cacophony	a.	Truthfulness
2.	Cadence	b.	Harsh mixture of sounds
3.	Cajole	c.	Surrender
4.	Callow	d.	Distorted portrait
5.	Candor	e.	Unpredictable
6.	Capitalism	f.	Immature
7.	Capitulate	g.	Free enterprise
8.	Recapitulate	h.	Rhythm
9.	Capricious	i.	Summarize
10.	Caricature	j.	Persuade deceptively

ANSWERS

	TEST – 14	TEST – 15	TEST – 16	TEST – 17	TEST – 18
1.	b	g	b	a	b
2.	e	e	e	b	h
3.	d	b	a	c	j
4.	h	i	c	d	f
5.	c	f	f	e	a
6.	g	c	d	f	g
7.	f	d	g	g	c
8.	a	h	h	h	i
9.	i	a	i	i	e
10.	j	j	j	j	d

TEST – 19

1.	Categorical	a.	Unconditional
2.	Catharsis	b.	Relieving purification
3.	Catholic	c.	Abstinence from sex
4.	Caustic	d.	Brainy
5.	Celibacy	e.	Humiliation
6.	Censure	f.	Magical attractiveness
7.	Cerebral	g.	Corrosive
8.	Chagrin	h.	Condemn severely
9.	Charisma	i.	Universal
10.	Coherence	j.	Symmetry

TEST – 20

1.	Charlatan	a.	In order of occurrence
2.	Chasm	b.	Constant
3.	Chastise	c.	Hot-tempered
4.	Chicanery	d.	Punish
5.	Chimera	e.	Trickery
6.	Chivalrous	f.	List in time order
7.	Choleric	g.	Illusion
8.	Chronic	h.	Fraud
9.	Chronological	i.	Gallant
10.	Chronology	j.	Gap

TEST – 21

1.	Circuitous	a.	Cautious
2.	Circumlocution	b.	Secret
3.	Circumscribe	c.	Mercy
4.	Circumspect	d.	Polite
5.	Circumvent	e.	Roundabout
6.	Civil	f.	Frustrate
7.	Clandestine	g.	Overused saying
8.	Clemency	h.	Indirect expression
9.	Inclement	i.	Bad, as in weather
10.	Cliché	j.	Draw a line around

TEST – 22

1.	Coalesce	a.	Perceptive
2.	Coalition	b.	Unite
3.	Coerce	c.	Conversational
4.	Cogent	d.	Force someone to do something
5.	Cognitive	e.	Proportionate
6.	Cognizant	f.	Making sense
7.	Coherent	g.	Group with a purpose
8.	Colloquial	h.	Clear convincing
9.	Collusion	i.	Conspiracy
10.	Commensurate	j.	Conscious

TEST – 23

1.	Complacent	a.	Covering everything
2.	Complement	b.	Complete
3.	Complicity	c.	Consist of
4.	Comprehensive	d.	Make up
5.	Comprise	e.	Brief
6.	Compose	f.	Peace making
7.	Constitute	g.	Participation in wrongdoing
8.	Conciliatory	h.	Self-satisfied
9.	Concise	i.	Form
10.	Clique	j.	Exclusive group

ANSWERS

	TEST – 19	TEST – 20	TEST – 21	TEST – 22	TEST – 23
1.	a	h	e	b	h
2.	b	j	h	g	b
3.	i	d	j	d	g
4.	g	e	a	h	a
5.	c	g	f	a	c
6.	h	i	d	j	d
7.	d	c	b	f	i
8.	e	b	c	c	f
9.	f	a	i	i	e
10.	j	f	g	e	j

TEST – 24

1.	Concord	a.	Agreeably suitable
2.	Discord	b.	Innate
3.	Concurrent	c.	Harmony
4.	Condescend	d.	Flowing together
5.	Condone	e.	Promoting
6.	Conducive	f.	Patronize
7.	Confluence	g.	Overlook
8.	Congenial	h.	Happening at the same time
9.	Congenital	i.	Disharmony
10.	Contiguous	j.	Adjacent

TEST – 25

1.	Conjecture	a.	Incompatible
2.	Conjure	b.	Harmonious
3.	Connoisseur	c.	Make sacred
4.	Consecrate	d.	Unanimity
5.	Desecrate	e.	Entreat
6.	Consensus	f.	Treat irreverently
7.	Consonant	g.	Artistic expert
8.	Dissonant	h.	Guess
9.	Compelling	i.	Forceful
10.	Compendium	j.	Summary

TEST – 26

1.	Construe	a.	Repentant
2.	Consummate	b.	Interpret
3.	Contentious	c.	Perfect
4.	Contiguous	d.	Labored
5.	Contingent	e.	Dependent
6.	Contrite	f.	Abundant
7.	Contrived	g.	Adjoining
8.	Conventional	h.	Argumentative
9.	Convivial	i.	Festive
10.	Copious	j.	Common

TEST – 27

1.	Corollary	a.	Universal
2.	Corroborate	b.	Facial expression
3.	Cosmopolitan	c.	Envy
4.	Countenance	d.	Confirm
5.	Coup	e.	Solemn agreement
6.	Covenant	f.	Military take over
7.	Covert	g.	Natural consequence
8.	Covet	h.	Secret
9.	Charlatan	i.	Cheat
10.	Cacophony	j.	Echoing sounds

TEST – 28

1.	Credulous	a.	Related to cooking
2.	Credible	b.	Believable
3.	Incredible	c.	Believability
4.	Incredulous	d.	Worthy of praise
5.	Credence	e.	Gullible
6.	Creditable	f.	Unbelieving
7.	Criterion	g.	Unbelievable
8.	Cryptic	h.	Climax
9.	Culinary	i.	Standard
10.	Culminate	j.	Mysterious

ANSWERS

	TEST – 24	TEST – 25	TEST – 26	TEST – 27	TEST – 28
1.	c	h	b	g	e
2.	i	e	c	d	b
3.	h	g	h	a	g
4.	f	c	g	b	f
5.	g	f	e	f	c
6.	e	d	a	e	d
7.	d	b	d	h	i
8.	a	a	j	c	j
9.	b	i	i	i	a
10.	j	j	f	j	h

TEST – 29

1.	Culpable	a.	Free from guilt
2.	Exculpate	b.	Shorten
3.	Cursory	c.	Sceptic
4.	Curtail	d.	Casual
5.	Cynic	e.	Blameworthy
6.	Categorically	f.	Absolutely
7.	Chronic	g.	Acute
8.	Catalyst	h.	Stimulant
9.	Caricature	i.	Lampoon
10.	Cohesive	j.	Uniting

TEST – 30

1.	Daunt	a.	Conclude from evidence
2.	Dearth	b.	Lack
3.	Debacle	c.	Kill a large part of
4.	Debauchery	d.	Disrepute
5.	Debilitate	e.	Make fearful
6.	Decadent	f.	Decaying or decayed
7.	Decimate	g.	Proper
8.	Decorous	h.	Weaken
9.	Deduce	i.	Violent breakdown
10.	Defame	j.	Corruption

TEST – 31

1.	Deference	a.	Deteriorate
2.	Definitive	b.	Rabble Rouser
3.	Degenerate	c.	Describe accurately
4.	Deleterious	d.	Respect
5.	Delineate	e.	Conclusive
6.	Delude	f.	Wickedness
7.	Deluge	g.	Harmful
8.	Demagogue	h.	Inhabitant
9.	Denizen	i.	Deceive
10.	Depravity	j.	Flood

TEST – 32

1.	Derogatory	a.	Purposeless
2.	Desiccate	b.	Extremely depressed
3.	Despondent	c.	Amateur
4.	Despot	d.	Stay away from main subject
5.	Destitute	e.	Extremely poor
6.	Desultory	f.	Timid
7.	Dilettante	g.	Dry out
8.	digress	h.	Disapproving
9.	Didactic	i.	Absolute ruler
10.	Diffident	j.	Intended to teach

TEST – 33

1.	Discern	a.	Insight
2.	Discreet	b.	Belittle
3.	Discrete	c.	Not separated
4.	Indiscrete	d.	Not taking sides
5.	Discriminate	e.	Hate
6.	Disdain	f.	Prudent
7.	Disinterested	g.	Unconnected
8.	Disparage	h.	Differentiate
9.	Denigrate	i.	Humiliate
10.	dauntless	j.	Fearless

ANSWERS

	TEST – 29	TEST – 30	TEST – 31	TEST – 32	TEST – 33
1.	e	e	d	h	a
2.	a	b	e	g	f
3.	d	i	a	b	g
4.	b	j	g	i	c
5.	c	h	c	e	h
6.	f	f	i	a	e
7.	g	c	j	c	d
8.	h	g	b	d	b
9.	i	a	h	j	i
10.	j	d	f	f	j

TEST – 34

1.	Disparate	a.	Inharmonious
2.	Disseminate	b.	Dogmatic
3.	Dissipate	c.	Waste
4.	Dissolution	d.	Of the household
5.	Dissonant	e.	Firmly held system of ides
6.	Distend	f.	Pliable
7.	Distinguish	g.	Arrogantly assertive
8.	Docile	h.	Swell
9.	Doctrinaire	i.	Tell apart
10.	Dogmatic	j.	Incompatible

TEST – 35

1.	Dormant	a.	Uncertainty
2.	Dubiety	b.	Double-dealing
3.	Duplicity	c.	Inactive
4.	Dogma	d.	Hard belief
5.	Domestic	e.	Household
6.	Dilettante	f.	Amateur
7.	Demagogue	g.	Rabble-Rouse
8.	Deodorize	h.	Freshen
9.	Disinfectant	i.	Sanitizer
10.	Detergent	j.	Cleanser

TEST – 36

1.	Ebullient	a.	Pouring forth
2.	Eccentric	b.	Self-obsessed person
3.	Eclectic	c.	Extremely bad
4.	Edify	d.	Not conventional
5.	Efface	e.	Drawn from many sources
6.	Effusion	f.	Bubbling with excitement
7.	Egalitarian	g.	Erase
8.	Egocentric	h.	Selfish
9.	Egotist	i.	Enlighten
10.	Egregious	j.	Believing in social equality

TEST – 37

1.	Elicit	a.	Well known
2.	Elliptical	b.	Bring out
3.	Elusive	c.	Hard to pin down
4.	Emigrate	d.	Relying on experience
5.	Immigration	e.	Move from a country
6.	Eminent	f.	Move into a country
7.	Empirical	g.	Obscure
8.	Exult	h.	Rejoice
9.	Extrovert	i.	Outward person
10.	Erudition	j.	Learning

TEST – 38

1.	Emulate	a.	Cause to exist
2.	Encroach	b.	Mystery
3.	Endemic	c.	Remove voting rights
4.	Enervate	d.	Weaken
5.	Enfranchise	e.	Native
6.	Disfranchise	f.	Grant voting rights
7.	Engender	g.	Strive to equal
8.	Enigma	h.	Short-lived
9.	Enormity	i.	Vastness
10.	Ephemeral	j.	Trespass

ANSWERS

	TEST – 34	TEST – 35	TEST – 36	TEST – 37	TEST – 38
1.	j	c	f	b	g
2.	k	a	d	g	j
3.	c	b	e	c	e
4.	l	d	i	e	d
5.	a	e	g	f	f
6.	h	f	a	a	c
7.	i	g	j	d	a
8.	f	h	h	h	b
9.	b	i	b	i	i
10.	g	j	c	j	h

TEST – 39

1.	Epigram	a.	Brief summary
2.	Epigraph	b.	Fair
3.	Epitaph	c.	Composure
4.	Epithet	d.	Intentionally confusing
5.	Epitome	e.	Opt quotation
6.	Equanimity	f.	Say confusing things
7.	Equitable	g.	Inscription on a grave
8.	Equivocal	h.	Scholarly
9.	Equivocate	i.	Brief, witty saying
10.	Erudite	j.	Disparaging term

TEST – 40

1.	Esoteric	a.	Mysterious
2.	Espouse	b.	Make worse
3.	Ethereal	c.	Demanding
4.	Euphemism	d.	Glorify
5.	Evanescent	e.	Inoffensive expression
6.	Exacerbate	f.	Urge strongly
7.	Exacting	g.	Irritate
8.	Exalt	h.	Heavenly
9.	Exasperate	i.	Advocate
10.	Exhort	j.	Fleeting

TEST – 41

1.	Exigency	a.	Free from blame
2.	Existential	b.	Clearly expressed
3.	Exonerate	c.	Indirectly expressed
4.	Expatriate	d.	Having to do with existence
5.	Expedient	e.	Outgoing person
6.	Expedite	f.	Speed up
7.	Explicit	g.	Emergency
8.	Implicit	h.	Glorify
9.	Extol	i.	Immediately advantageous
10.	Extraneous	j.	Unnecessary

TEST – 42

1.	Fabrication	a.	Plants
2.	Facetious	b.	Foolish
3.	Facile	c.	Absurd
4.	Faction	d.	One who believes in fate
5.	Farcical	e.	Humorous
6.	Fastidious	f.	Animals
7.	Fatalist	g.	Superficially skillful
8.	Fatuous	h.	Group with a cause
9.	Fauna	i.	Concoction
10.	Flora	j.	Meticulous

TEST – 43

1.	Felicity	a.	Loyalty
2.	Fervor	b.	Zeal
3.	Fetter	c.	Restrain
4.	Fidelity	d.	Meaning what it says
5.	Figurative	e.	Glaringly bad
6.	Literal	f.	Show off
7.	Finesse	g.	Based on figures of speech
8.	Flagrant	h.	To disregard contemptuously
9.	Flaunt	i.	Skillful maneuvering
10.	Flout	j.	Happiness

ANSWERS

	TEST – 39	TEST – 40	TEST – 41	TEST – 42	TEST – 43
1.	i	a	g	i	j
2.	e	i	d	e	b
3.	g	h	a	g	c
4.	j	e	e	h	a
5.	a	j	i	c	g
6.	c	b	f	j	d
7.	b	c	b	d	i
8.	d	d	c	b	e
9.	f	g	h	f	f
10.	h	f	j	a	h

TEST – 44

1.	Forbear	a.	Economical
2.	Foment	b.	Incite
3.	Forego	c.	Move in confusion
4.	Forsake	d.	Do without
5.	Fortuitous	e.	Refrain from
6.	Founder	f.	Sink
7.	Flounder	g.	Secretive
8.	Frenetic	h.	Accidental
9.	Frugal	i.	Abandon
10.	Furtive	j.	Frantic

TEST – 45

1.	Futile	a.	Chatty
2.	Garrulous	b.	Surplus
3.	Genre	c.	Type
4.	Genteel	d.	Majestic
5.	Gesticulate	e.	Seriousness
6.	Glut	f.	Make gestures
7.	Grandiloquent	g.	Hopeless
8.	Grandiose	h.	Refined
9.	Gregarious	i.	Sociable
10.	Gravity	j.	Pompous

TEST – 46

1.	Hackneyed	a.	Leadership
2.	Hapless	b.	Unlucky
3.	Harbinger	c.	Uniform
4.	Hedonism	d.	Forerunner
5.	Hegemony	e.	Order
6.	Heresy	f.	Overused, trite
7.	Homogeneous	g.	Pursuit of pleasure
8.	Heyday	h.	Golden age
9.	Hiatus	i.	Break
10.	Hierarchy	j.	Strongly contrary belief

TEST – 47

1.	Iconoclast	a.	Peculiarity
2.	Ideology	b.	Naturally peaceful
3.	Idiosyncrasy	c.	Illegal
4.	Idyllic	d.	Flawless
5.	Ignominy	e.	Attacker of popular beliefs
6.	Illicit	f.	Just about to happen
7.	Imminent	g.	Fair
8.	Immutable	h.	System of social ideas
9.	Impartial	i.	Unchangeable
10.	Impeccable	j.	Deep disgrace

TEST – 48

1.	Impervious	a.	Begin
2.	Impetuous	b.	Execute
3.	Implement	c.	Powerless
4.	Impotent	d.	Impenetrable
5.	Impugn	e.	Silly
6.	Inane	f.	Attach the truth of
7.	Inaugurate	g.	Impulsive
8.	Gravity	h.	Seriousness
9.	Gregarious	i.	Sociable
10.	Genteel	j.	Refined

ANSWERS

	TEST – 44	TEST – 45	TEST – 46	TEST – 47	TEST – 48
1.	e	g	f	e	d
2.	b	a	b	h	g
3.	d	c	d	a	b
4.	i	h	g	b	c
5.	h	f	a	j	f
6.	f	b	j	c	e
7.	c	j	c	f	a
8.	j	d	h	i	h
9.	a	i	i	g	i
10.	g	e	e	d	j

TEST – 49

1.	Incandescent	a.	Increase
2.	Incantation	b.	Infuriate
3.	Incense	c.	Beginning
4.	Incessant	d.	Chant
5.	Incipient	e.	Not harmonious
6.	Incisive	f.	Incapable of being reformed
7.	Incongruous	g.	Apathetic
8.	Incorrigible	h.	Penetrating
9.	Increment	i.	Unceasing
10.	Indifferent	j.	Brilliant

TEST – 50

1.	Indigenous	a.	Native
2.	Indigent	b.	Inactive
3.	Indignant	c.	Lazy
4.	Indolent	d.	Inexpressible
5.	Indulgent	e.	Shamefully wicked
6.	Ineffable	f.	Poor
7.	Inept	g.	Relentless
8.	Inert	h.	Angry
9.	Inexorable	i.	Clumsy
10.	Infamous	j.	Lenient

TEST – 51

1.	Infer	a.	Stay order
2.	Imply	b.	Intensify
3.	Infinitesimal	c.	By birth
4.	Inflame	d.	Hint at
5.	Ingenuous	e.	Artless
6.	Inherent	f.	Inborn
7.	Injunction	g.	Conclude
8.	Innate	h.	Excessive
9.	Innocuous	i.	Harmless
10.	Inordinate	j.	Infinitely small

TEST – 52

1.	Insidious	a.	Hint
2.	Insinuate	b.	Uncontrollable
3.	Insipid	c.	Treacherous
4.	Insolent	d.	Essential
5.	Instigate	e.	Provoke
6.	Insular	f.	Like an island
7.	Insurgent	g.	Rebel
8.	Integral	h.	Dull
9.	Intractable	i.	Uncompromising
10.	Intransigent	j.	Arrogant

TEST – 53

1.	Intrinsic	a.	Irreversible
2.	Introspective	b.	Insulting speech
3.	Inundate	c.	Planned trip route
4.	Invective	d.	Flood
5.	Inveterate	e.	Inherent
6.	Irascible	f.	Reflective
7.	Ironic	g.	Meaning other than what's said
8.	Irrevocable	h.	Moving from place to place
9.	Itinerant	i.	Irritable
10.	Itinerary	j.	Habitual

ANSWERS

	TEST – 49	TEST – 50	TEST – 51	TEST – 52	TEST – 53
1.	j	a	g	c	e
2.	d	f	d	a	f
3.	b	h	j	h	d
4.	i	c	b	j	b
5.	c	j	e	e	j
6.	h	d	c	f	i
7.	e	i	a	g	g
8.	f	b	f	d	a
9.	a	g	i	b	h
10.	g	e	h	i	c

TEST – 54

1.	Judicious	a.	Sound judgement
2.	Juxtapose	b.	Praise
3.	Kinetic	c.	Brief
4.	Labyrinth	d.	Gargantuan
5.	Laconic	e.	Place side by side
6.	Lament	f.	Hidden/ Dormant
7.	Lampoon	g.	Mourn
8.	Languish	h.	Active
9.	Latent	i.	Become weak
10.	Laud	j.	Satirize

TEST – 55

1.	Libel	a.	Bright/ Resplended
2.	Slander	b.	Try in court
3.	Litigate	c.	Mournful
4.	Loquacious	d.	Easy to understand
5.	Lucid	e.	Written injurious falsehood
6.	Lugubrious	f.	Spoken injurious falsehood
7.	Luminous	g.	Talkative
8.	Legacy	h.	Bequest
9.	Lethargy	i.	Sluggishness
10.	Levity	j.	Vivacity

TEST – 56

1.	Machination	a.	Forgiving
2.	Macroeconomic	b.	Easy to shape
3.	Magnanimous	c.	Queasiness
4.	Magnate	d.	Command to do something
5.	Malaise	e.	Scheming evil activity
6.	malfeasance	f.	Dealing with economy
7.	Malinger	g.	Pretend to be sick
8.	Malleable	h.	Visible
9.	Mandate	i.	Business tycoon
10.	Manifest	j.	Impropriety

TEST – 57

1.	Maudlin	a.	Teacher
2.	Maverick	b.	Truism
3.	Maxim	c.	Lying
4.	mediate	d.	Arbitrate
5.	Mellifluous	e.	Sweetly flowing
6.	Mendacious	f.	Nonconformist
7.	Mendicant	g.	Emotionally unpredictable
8.	Mentor	h.	Beggar
9.	Mercenary	i.	Silly and sentimental
10.	Mercurial	j.	Hired soldier

TEST – 58

1.	Microcosm	a.	Miniature
2.	Milieu	b.	Moderate the effect of
3.	Minuscule	c.	Massive and unyielding
4.	Misanthropic	d.	Humiliate
5.	Mitigate	e.	Hating mankind
6.	Mollify	f.	Soften
7.	Monolithic	g.	Dying
8.	Moribund	h.	Very tiny
9.	Morose	i.	Gloomy
10.	Mortify	j.	Environment

ANSWERS

	TEST – 54	TEST – 55	TEST – 56	TEST – 57	TEST – 58
1.	a	e	e	i	a
2.	e	f	f	f	j
3.	h	b	a	b	h
4.	d	g	i	d	e
5.	c	d	c	e	b
6.	g	c	j	c	f
7.	j	a	g	h	c
8.	i	h	b	a	g
9.	f	i	d	j	i
10.	b	j	h	g	d

TEST – 59

1.	Narcissism	a.	Self love
2.	Nebulous	b.	In name only
3.	Nefarious	c.	New words
4.	Neologism	d.	Original
5.	Nepotism	e.	Evil
6.	Nihilism	f.	Absence of values
7.	Nominal	g.	Famous for something bad
8.	Nostalgia	h.	Vague
9.	Notorious	i.	Longing for the past
10.	Novel	j.	Favoritism

TEST – 60

1.	Obdurate	a.	Forgetfulness
2.	Obfuscate	b.	Hard to understand
3.	Oblique	c.	Stubborn
4.	Oblivion	d.	Insensitive
5.	Obscure	e.	Burdensome
6.	Obsequious	f.	Confuse
7.	Obtuse	g.	Indirect
8.	Officious	h.	Beseeching
9.	Onerous	i.	Intrusive
10.	Opaque	j.	Impossible to see through

TEST – 61

1.	Painstaking	a.	Obvious
2.	Palliate	b.	Model
3.	Palpable	c.	Alleviate
4.	Paltry	d.	Narrow in point of view
5.	Panacea	e.	Contradictory truth
6.	Paradigm	f.	Stingy
7.	Paradox	g.	Cure of everything
8.	Parochial	h.	Insignificant
9.	Parody	i.	Extremely careful
10.	Parsimonious	j.	Satirical imitation

TEST – 62

1.	Pliable	a.	Male head of a family
2.	Paternal	b.	Minor offense
3.	Pathology	c.	Imaginative
4.	Patriarch	d.	Scarcity
5.	Patrician	e.	Scholarly
6.	Patronize	f.	Science of diseases
7.	Paucity	g.	Treat as an inferior
8.	Peccadillo	h.	Fatherly
9.	Pedantic	i.	Flexible
10.	Pensive	j.	Aristocrat

TEST – 63

1.	Peremptory	a.	Outside edge of something
2.	Perennial	b.	Unenthusiastic
3.	Perfidy	c.	Penetrate
4.	Perfunctory	d.	Lying under oath
5.	Peripatetic	e.	Job-related privilege
6.	Periphery	f.	Continual
7.	Perjury	g.	Final
8.	Permeate	h.	Wandering
9.	Pernicious	i.	Evil
10.	Perquisite	j.	Treachery

ANSWERS

	TEST – 59	TEST – 60	TEST – 61	TEST – 62	TEST – 63
1.	a	c	i	i	g
2.	h	f	c	h	f
3.	e	g	a	f	j
4.	c	a	h	a	b
5.	j	b	g	j	h
6.	f	h	b	g	a
7.	b	d	e	d	d
8.	i	i	d	b	c
9.	g	e	j	e	i
10.	d	j	f	c	e

TEST – 64

1.	Pervade	a.	Love for mankind
2.	Petulant	b.	Spread throughout
3.	Philanthropy	c.	Pacify
4.	Philistine	d.	Ignorant
5.	Pious	e.	Low class
6.	Pivotal	f.	Expressing sadness
7.	Placate	g.	Reverent
8.	Plaintive	h.	Trite remark
9.	Platitude	i.	Rude
10.	Plebeian	j.	Crucial

TEST – 65

1.	Polarize	a.	Massive
2.	Polemic	b.	Rule to live by
3.	Ponderous	c.	Practical
4.	Portent	d.	Powerful refutation
5.	Portentous	e.	Axiom
6.	Postulate	f.	Taking concrete shape
7.	Pragmatic	g.	Cause opposing positions
8.	Precedent	h.	Ominous
9.	Precept	i.	Settled proposition
10.	Precipitate	j.	Omen

TEST – 66

1.	Preclude	a.	Outstanding
2.	Precursor	b.	Triumph
3.	Predilection	c.	Seize by prior right
4.	Preeminent	d.	Prevent
5.	Preempt	e.	Unspoiled
6.	Premise	f.	Natural preference
7.	Prepossess	g.	Preoccupy
8.	Prerogative	h.	Right or privilege
9.	Prevail	i.	Assumption
10.	Pristine	j.	Forerunner

TEST – 67

1.	Prodigious	a.	Declare
2.	Prodigy	b.	Irreverent
3.	Profane	c.	Working class
4.	Profess	d.	Flowing
5.	Proficient	e.	Extremely talented child
6.	Profligate	f.	Extraordinary
7.	Profound	g.	Spread rapidly
8.	Profuse	h.	Deep
9.	Proletariat	i.	Thoroughly competent
10.	Proliferate	j.	Extravagantly wasteful

TEST – 68

1.	Promulgate	a.	Natural inclination
2.	Propensity	b.	Good manners
3.	Propitious	c.	Advocate
4.	Proponent	d.	Prohibit
5.	Proprietary	e.	Proclaim
6.	Propriety	f.	Leading character
7.	Prosaic	g.	Constituting property
8.	Proscribe	h.	Convert
9.	Proselytize	i.	Dull
10.	Protagonist	j.	Favorable

ANSWERS

	TEST – 64	TEST – 65	TEST – 66	TEST – 67	TEST – 68
1.	b	g	d	f	e
2.	i	d	j	e	a
3.	a	a	f	b	j
4.	d	j	a	a	c
5.	g	h	c	i	g
6.	j	e	i	j	b
7.	c	c	g	h	i
8.	f	i	h	d	d
9.	h	b	b	c	h
10.	e	f	e	g	f

TEST – 69

1.	Provincial	a.	Commonly accepted
2.	Provisional	b.	Nearness
3.	Proximity	c.	Narrow in outlook
4.	Prudent	d.	Rumored
5.	Purported	e.	Careful
6.	Putative	f.	Conditional
7.	Cheating	g.	Trickery
8.	Protract	h.	Prolong
9.	Provident	i.	Judicious
10.	Prolific	j.	Productive

TEST – 70

1.	Qualify	a.	Having to do with quantity
2.	Qualitative	b.	Foolishly romantic
3.	Quantitative	c.	Complaining
4.	Querulous	d.	Modify or restrict
5.	Quixotic	e.	Having to do with quality
6.	Resolute	f.	Determined
7.	Ruminate	g.	Ponder
8.	Rustic	h.	Bucolic
9.	Stratum	i.	Strata
10.	Stricture	j.	Restraint

TEST – 71

1.	Ramification	a.	Hard to understand
2.	Rancor	b.	Criticize sharply
3.	Rapacious	c.	Consequence
4.	Rebuke	d.	Mutual
5.	Rebut	e.	Hermit
6.	Recalcitrant	f.	Bitter resentment
7.	Recant	g.	Stubborn
8.	Reciprocal	h.	Publicly deny
9.	Recluse	i.	Contradict
10.	Recondite	j.	Greedy

TEST – 72

1.	Recrimination	a.	Surrender
2.	Redolent	b.	Disown
3.	Redundant	c.	Rebirth
4.	Refute	d.	Argue against
5.	Reiterate	e.	Fragrant
6.	Relegate	f.	Banish
7.	Relinquish	g.	Say again
8.	Remonstrate	h.	Counteraccusation
9.	Renaissance	i.	Unnecessarily repetitive
10.	Renounce	j.	Prove to be false

TEST – 73

1.	Reparation	a.	Act of revenge
2.	Repercussion	b.	Reject
3.	Replenish	c.	Worthy of blame
4.	Replete	d.	Consequence
5.	Reprehensible	e.	Scold
6.	Reprisal	f.	Completely filled
7.	Reproach	g.	Paying back
8.	Reprove	h.	Necessary
9.	Repudiate	i.	Criticize mildly
10.	Requisite	j.	Fill again

ANSWERS

	TEST – 69	TEST – 70	TEST – 71	TEST – 72	TEST – 73
1.	c	d	c	h	g
2.	f	e	f	e	d
3.	b	a	j	i	j
4.	e	c	b	j	f
5.	d	b	i	g	c
6.	a	f	g	f	a
7.	g	g	h	a	e
8.	h	h	d	d	i
9.	i	i	e	c	b
10.	j	j	a	b	h

TEST – 74

1.	Respite	a.	Basic
2.	Reticent	b.	Honour
3.	Retract	c.	Vigorous
4.	Reverberate	d.	Withdraw
5.	Revere	e.	Speaking skills
6.	Rhetoric	f.	Taciturn
7.	Rigorous	g.	Scoundrel
8.	Robust	h.	Relief
9.	Rogue	i.	Echo
10.	Rudimentary	j.	Strict

TEST – 75

1.	Saccharine	a.	Blasphemy
2.	Sacrilege	b.	Wise
3.	Sacrosanct	c.	sweet
4.	Sagacious	d.	Pretending to be devout
5.	Sage	e.	Healthful
6.	Salient	f.	Mocking
7.	Salutary	g.	Cheerful
8.	Sanctimonious	h.	Sacred
9.	Sanguine	i.	Sticking out
10.	Sardonic	j.	Discerning

TEST – 76

1.	Scintillate	a.	Sparkle
2.	Scrupulous	b.	Having nothing to do with religion
3.	Scrutinize	c.	Treason
4.	Secular	d.	Having to do with the senses
5.	Sedition	e.	Set apart
6.	Sensory	f.	Strict
7.	Sensual	g.	Delighting the senses
8.	Sensuous	h.	Examine very carefully
9.	Sentient	i.	Devoted to pleasure
10.	Sequester	j.	Conscious

TEST – 77

1.	Serendipity	a.	Happenstance
2.	Servile	b.	Sleep-inducing
3.	Singular	c.	Eager and attentive
4.	Slavish	d.	Not bankrupt
5.	Sloth	e.	Submissive
6.	Sobriety	f.	Bankrupt
7.	Solicitous	g.	Laziness
8.	Solvent	h.	Pleasantness
9.	Insolvent	i.	Extremely subservient
10.	Soporific	j.	Unique

TEST – 78

1.	Sordid	a.	Deceptively plausible
2.	Staunch	b.	Stopping and starting
3.	Specious	c.	False
4.	Sporadic	d.	Inactivity
5.	Spurious	e.	Waste
6.	Squander	f.	Stationary
7.	Stagnation	g.	Firm
8.	Static	h.	Vile
9.	Steadfast	i.	Firmly committed
10.	Stigmatize	j.	Defame

ANSWERS

	TEST – 74	TEST – 75	TEST – 76	TEST – 77	TEST – 78
1.	h	c	a	a	h
2.	f	a	f	e	g
3.	d	h	h	j	a
4.	i	j	b	i	b
5.	b	b	c	g	c
6.	e	i	d	h	e
7.	j	e	i	c	d
8.	c	d	g	d	f
9.	g	g	j	f	i
10.	a	f	e	b	j

TEST – 79

1.	Strife	a.	Non obvious
2.	Stringent	b.	Awesome
3.	Stymie	c.	Brief and to the point
4.	Subjugate	d.	Thwart
5.	Sublime	e.	Subdue
6.	Subordinate	f.	Conflict
7.	Substantive	g.	Not respectful of authority
8.	Subtle	h.	Strict
9.	Subversive	i.	Lower in importance
10.	Succinct	j.	Having substance

TEST – 80

1.	Succumb	a.	Haughty
2.	Supercilious	b.	Yield
3.	Superficial	c.	flatterer
4.	Superfluous	d.	Substitute
5.	Surfeit	e.	Unnecessary
6.	Surreptitious	f.	On the surface only
7.	Surrogate	g.	Sneaky
8.	Sycophant	h.	Excess
9.	Stipulate	i.	Specify
10.	Stoic	j.	Indifferent to pleasure or pain

TEST – 81

1.	Tacit	a.	Persistent
2.	Taciturn	b.	Untalkative
3.	Tangential	c.	Boldness
4.	Tangible	d.	Equivalent to
5.	Tantamount	e.	Not deeply relevant
6.	Tautological	f.	Redundant
7.	Temerity	g.	Mild
8.	Temperate	h.	Defensible
9.	Tenable	i.	Implied
10.	Tenacious	j.	Touchable

TEST – 82

1.	Tenet	a.	Concise
2.	Tentative	b.	Go beyond
3.	Trepid	c.	Accusation
4.	Terse	d.	Fearless
5.	Transition	e.	Provisional
6.	Theology	f.	Not lasting long
7.	Torpor	g.	Standard
8.	Touchstone	h.	Principle
9.	Tirade	i.	Religious belief
10.	Transcend	j.	Sluggishness

TEST – 83

1.	Ubiquitous	a.	Oily
2.	Unconscionable	b.	Poised and sophisticated
3.	Unctuous	c.	Everywhere at once
4.	Uniform	d.	Pragmatic
5.	Unremitting	e.	Seize wrongfully
6.	Unwitting	f.	Unscrupulous
7.	Urbane	g.	An ideal society
8.	Usurp	h.	Unintentional
9.	Utilitarian	i.	Consistent
10.	Utopia	j.	Unceasing

ANSWERS

	TEST – 79	TEST – 80	TEST – 81	TEST – 82	TEST – 83
1.	f	b	i	h	c
2.	h	a	b	e	f
3.	d	f	e	d	a
4.	e	e	j	a	i
5.	b	h	d	f	j
6.	i	g	f	i	h
7.	j	d	c	j	b
8.	a	c	g	g	e
9.	g	i	h	c	d
10.	c	j	a	b	g

TEST – 84

1.	Vacillate	a.	Intense
2.	Vapid	b.	Be indecisive
3.	Vehement	c.	Corrupt
4.	Venal	d.	Wordy
5.	venerate	e.	Slang
6.	Veracity	f.	Dull
7.	Verbose	g.	Truthfulness
8.	Verisimilitude	h.	Revere
9.	Vernacular	i.	Last trace
10.	Vestige	j.	Similarity to reality

TEST – 85

1.	Vindicate	a.	Extremely poisonous
2.	Vindictive	b.	Masterful musician
3.	Virtuoso	c.	Dreamer
4.	Virulent	d.	Caustic
5.	Visionary	e.	Clear from suspicion
6.	Vitiate	f.	Noisy
7.	Vitriolic	g.	Shapeless
8.	Vocation	h.	Seeking revenge
9.	Vociferous	i.	Occupation
10.	Volatile	j.	Make impure

TEST – 86

1.	Foible	a.	Absurdly exaggerated
2.	Supercilious	b.	Skilful
3.	Neologism	c.	Unoriginal
4.	Banal	d.	Foolishly idealistic
5.	Grandiose	e.	Defensible
6.	Tenable	f.	Unlucky
7.	Recalcitrant	g.	Stubborn
8.	Adroit	h.	Minor character flaw
9.	Hapless	i.	New word or phrase
10.	Quixotic	j.	Shallow

TEST – 87

1.	Prodigy	a.	Brainy
2.	Vitiate	b.	Relating to land
3.	Belligerent	c.	Redundant
4.	Rebut	d.	Chatty
5.	Cerebral	e.	Flagrantly wicked
6.	Garrulous	f.	Combative
7.	Agrarian	g.	To contradict
8.	Flout	h.	Extremely talented child
9.	Nefarious	i.	To pollute
10.	Superflow	j.	To disregard contemptuously

TEST – 88

1.	Gregarious	a.	Humiliation
2.	Rebuke	b.	Corrosive
3.	Adulation	c.	Confused
4.	Caustic	d.	Skill
5.	Bemused	e.	Home sickness
6.	Glut	f.	Wild admiration
7.	Chagrin	g.	Abundant
8.	Nostalgia	h.	Sociable
9.	Finesse	i.	Criticize
10.	Profuse	j.	Surplus

ANSWERS

	TEST – 84	TEST – 85	TEST – 86	TEST – 87	TEST – 88
1.	b	e	h	h	h
2.	f	h	j	i	i
3.	a	b	i	f	f
4.	c	a	c	g	b
5.	h	c	a	a	c
6.	g	j	e	d	j
7.	d	d	g	b	a
8.	j	i	b	j	e
9.	e	f	f	e	d
10.	i	g	d	c	g

TEST – 89

1.	Decimate	a.	To make fearful
2.	Tenacious	b.	Extraordinary
3.	Bequest	c.	Reserved
4.	Daunt	d.	Something left in a will
5.	Prodigious	e.	Substitute
6.	Surrogate	f.	Persuade deceptively
7.	Abhor	g.	Persistent
8.	Virtuoso	h.	Masterful musician
9.	Cajole	i.	Massacre
10.	Taciturn	j.	Detest

TEST – 90

1.	Castigate	a.	Related to pigs
2.	Guile	b.	Free from guilt
3.	Debauchery	c.	Excessive love of self
4.	Narcissism	d.	Criticize severely
5.	Blasphemy	e.	Unsuccessful
6.	Exculpate	f.	To bring out
7.	Porcine	g.	Irreverence
8.	Elicit	h.	Rhythm
9.	Abortive	i.	Cunning
10.	Cadence	j.	Intemperance

TEST – 91

1.	Celibacy	a.	Drawn from many sources
2.	Alleviate	b.	Publicly deny
3.	Fetter	c.	Infamous
4.	Virulent	d.	Friendly
5.	Genteel	e.	Curse
6.	Recant	f.	Poisonous
7.	Affable	g.	Restrain
8.	Eclectic	h.	Relieve
9.	Notorious	i.	Aristocratic
10.	Bane	j.	Abstinence from sex

TEST – 92

1.	Assimilate	a.	Category
2.	Elusive	b.	Enlighten
3.	Noxious	c.	Productive
4.	Prolific	d.	Absorb
5.	Flaunt	e.	Resentment
6.	Edify	f.	Hard to pin down
7.	Affluent	g.	Strong hold
8.	Rancor	h.	Show off
9.	Genre	i.	Rich
10.	Bastion	j.	Harmful

TEST – 93

1.	Admonish	a.	Lack
2.	Curtail	b.	Implied
3.	Profane	c.	Excess
4.	Volition	d.	Caustic
5.	Surplus	e.	Warn
6.	Abetment	f.	Shorten
7.	Capricious	g.	Unpredictable
8.	Dearth	h.	Aiding
9.	Vitriolic	i.	Conscious choice
10.	Tacit	j.	Irreverent

ANSWERS

	TEST – 89	TEST – 90	TEST – 91	TEST – 92	TEST – 93
1.	i	d	j	d	e
2.	g	i	h	f	f
3.	d	j	g	j	j
4.	a	c	f	c	i
5.	b	g	i	h	c
6.	e	b	b	b	h
7.	j	a	d	i	g
8.	h	f	a	e	a
9.	f	e	c	a	d
10.	c	h	e	g	b

TEST – 94

1.	Temerity	a.	Noisy
2.	Censure	b.	Spread rapidly
3.	Adulterate	c.	Contaminate
4.	Eminent	d.	Condemn
5.	Flagrant	e.	Give birth to
6.	Vindicate	f.	Flatterer
7.	Belabor	g.	Boldness
8.	Vociferous	h.	Well-known
9.	Sycophant	i.	To justify
10.	Prostrate	j.	Glaringly bad

TEST – 95

1.	Gesticulate	a.	Thoroughly competent
2.	Proficient	b.	Exuberant
3.	Candor	c.	Approach someone
4.	Decadent	d.	Compelling attractiveness or charm
5.	Efface	e.	New
6.	Accost	f.	Make gestures
7.	Ebullient	g.	Erase
8.	Novel	h.	Hand to understand
9.	Charisma	i.	Truthfulness
10.	Abstruse	j.	Decaying or decayed

TEST – 96

1.	Catharsis	a.	Renounce
2.	Effusion	b.	Deep
3.	Abnegate	c.	Avaricious
4.	Proletariat	d.	Immature
5.	Bucolic	e.	Pouring forth
6.	Reclusive	f.	Charmingly rural
7.	Vindictive	g.	Relieving purification
8.	Rapacious	h.	Industrial working class
9.	Callow	i.	Revengeful
10.	Profound	j.	Hermit like

TEST – 97

1.	Catholic	a.	Pompous
2.	Profligate	b.	Believing in equality
3.	Ursine	c.	Forgive
4.	Abdicate	d.	Surrender
5.	Broach	e.	Related to bears
6.	Recondite	f.	Extravagantly wasteful
7.	Capitulate	g.	Open a subject
8.	Grandiloquent	h.	Step down from power
9.	Absolve	i.	Universal
10.	Egalitarian	j.	Hard to understand

TEST – 98

1.	Iconoclast	a.	Fill again
2.	Reprisal	b.	Luxurious
3.	Opulent	c.	Harmful
4.	Mellifluous	d.	Omnipresent
5.	Abstract	e.	Unspoiled
6.	Ubiquitous	f.	Sweet or musical
7.	Fastidious	g.	Finicky
8.	Deleterious	h.	Act at revenge
9.	Replenish	i.	Intangible
10.	Pristine	j.	Attacker of popular beliefs

ANSWERS

	TEST – 94	TEST – 95	TEST – 96	TEST – 97	TEST – 98
1.	g	f	g	i	j
2.	d	a	e	f	h
3.	c	i	a	e	b
4.	h	j	h	h	f
5.	j	g	f	g	i
6.	i	c	j	j	d
7.	e	b	i	d	g
8.	a	e	c	a	c
9.	f	d	d	c	a
10.	b	h	b	b	e

TEST – 99

1.	Exonerate	a.	Wickedness
2.	Mercurial	b.	Temperamental
3.	Precursor	c.	Bottomless
4.	Idyllic	d.	Unintentional
5.	Abysmal	e.	Harbinger
6.	Depravity	f.	Absolve
7.	Unwitting	g.	Deceive
8.	Delude	h.	Peaceful
9.	Fecund	i.	Defame
10.	Vilify	j.	Fertile

TEST – 100

1.	Replete	a.	Hard to understand
2.	Ostentatious	b.	Wastefully extravagant
3.	Idiosyncrasy	c.	Eccentricity
4.	Mercenary	d.	Foolish
5.	Prodigal	e.	Hired soldier
6.	Fatuous	f.	Completely filled
7.	Abstruse	g.	Insincere
8.	Unctuous	h.	To describe accurately
9.	Delineate	i.	Change in fortune
10.	Vicissitude	j.	Showing off

ANSWERS

	TEST – 99	TEST – 100
1.	f	f
2.	b	j
3.	e	c
4.	h	e
5.	c	b
6.	a	d
7.	d	a
8.	g	g
9.	j	h
10.	i	i

A Treasure Trove of 20,000 (Twenty Thousand) SYNONYMS & ANTONYMS

Synonyms

Synonyms are words that have the same, or almost the same, meaning as another word. You can say an *"easy task"* or a "*simple task*" because easy and simple are synonyms. You can say Hong Kong is a *"large city"* or a *"metropolis"* because *city* and *metropolis* are synonyms However, it is important to remember that not all pairs of words in the English language are so easily interchangeable. The slight but important differences in meaning between synonyms can make a big difference in your writing. For example, the words *boring* and *insipid* may have similar meanings, but the subtle differences between the two will affect the message your writing conveys. The word *insipid* evokes a scholarly and perhaps more pretentious message than *boring*. The English language is full of pairs of words that have subtle distinctions between them.

Antonyms

Antonyms are words that have the opposite meaning of a given word. The study of antonyms will not only help you choose the most appropriate word as you write; it will also sharpen your overall sense of language. Learning antonyms is an effective way to increase your vocabulary. Memorizing words in combination with or in relation to other words often helps us retain them.

Chapter 3 has approximately 1900 words as head words entries. Each head word entry has been provided with 10 plus variables as synonyms and antonyms. All of them put together cumulatively run into a sum total of more than 20,000 variants as synonyms and antonyms. This is the most detailed and elaborate chapter in the book after Chapter 1.

Having gone through Chapter 1, students would be able to read, retain and understand the basic, essential and indispensable words, without which one cannot even think of qualifying any competitive examination. This chapter would further help the students to develop and broaden their vocabulary, sharpen their reading skills and enrich their treasure trove.

These two chapters (Chapter 1 and Chapter 3) followed by practice exercises in the succeeding chapters would help the students to strengthen their base, broaden their range, sharpen their skills and enhance their performance. They will find it quite easy to solve any question related to vocabulary in any competitive examination.

	A
1.	**Abandon**
	Synonym: Verb: desert, reject, forsake, renounce ***Noun:*** gusto, dash, animation, verve
	Antonym: keep, claim, continue, maintain
2.	**Abandoned**
	Synonym: Adj: shameless, wild, loose, immoral, vacant, deserted, unoccupied
	Antonym: upright, moral, virtuous, chaste
3.	**Abandonment**
	Synonym: Noun: discontinuance, cessation, halt
	Antonym: continuation, prolongation
4.	**Abase**
	Synonym: Verb: humiliate, belittle, demean, lower, degrade, disgrace, disparage, debase
	Antonym: praise, appreciate, encourage, motivate
5.	**Abate**
	Synonym: Verb: subside, die down/away/ out, drop off/ away, lessen, diminish, moderate, decline, fade, dwindle, slacken
	Antonym: intensify, increase, accelerate, aggravate
6.	**Abatement**
	Synonym: Noun: subsiding, lessening, easing, decreasing, diminishing, moderation, decline, fade, dwindling, wane
	Antonym: intensification, acceleration

7.	**Abbreviate**
	Synonym: Verb: condense, shorten, contract, compress, reduce ***Noun:*** condensation, shortening, abridgment, compression, reduction
	Antonym: expansion, enlargement, extension, increase, lengthen, extend, expand, protract, prolong
8.	**Abdicate**
	Synonym: Verb: resign, renounce, relinquish, abandon, vacate, surrender
9.	**Aberration**
	Synonym: Noun: abnormality, irregularity, oddity, anomaly, deviation
10.	**Abhor**
	Synonym: Verb: loathe, detest, despise, hate, disdain, repulse
	Antonym: adore, love, admire, cherish
11.	**Abhorrence**
	Synonym: Noun: repugnance, aversion, detestation, disgust, hatred
	Antonym: approval, admiration, acceptance, endorsement
12.	**Abhorrent**
	Synonym: Adj: revolting, nauseating, abominable, detestable, repugnant, repulsive
	Antonym: admirable, commendable, laudable, praiseworthy
13.	**Abject**
	Synonym: Adj: wretched, hopeless, miserable, terrible, piteous, servile, cringing, grovelling
	Antonym: dignified, hopeful
14.	**Abnormal**
	Synonym: Adj: odd, unusual, unnatural, irregular, uncommon
	Antonym: normal, common, usual, simple, plain
15.	**Abnormality**
	Synonym: Noun: oddity, exception, irregularity, peculiarity, aberration
	Antonym: normal, common, ordinary, natural, usual
16.	**Abolish**
	Synonym: Verb: eliminate, negate, disallow, end, cancel, nullify, rescind, revoke
	Antonym: conserve, retain, establish, create, institute, continue

17	**Abolition**
	Synonym: Noun: termination, elimination, eradication, repeal
	Antonym: establishment, start, creation
18.	**Abominable**
	Synonym: Adj: awful, horrible, nasty, loathsome, despicable, deplorable
	Antonym: great, wonderful, commendable
19	**Abort**
	Synonym: Verb: cancel, terminate, abandon, halt, stop, cease
	Antonym: conclude, complete, finish, achieve
20.	**Abridge**
	Synonym: Verb: shorten, curtail, truncate, trim, condense, compress, reduce, summarize
	Antonym: lengthen, expand, increase, maximize
21.	**Abridged**
	Synonym: Adj: shortened, concise, condensed, reduced, curtailed, truncated, trimmed, summarized
	Antonym: lengthened, expanded
22.	**Abridgement**
	Synonym: Noun: summary, abstract, synopsis
	Antonym: expansion, enlargement
23.	**Abrupt**
	Synonym: Adj: sudden, immediate, instantaneous, quick, swift, rapid, unexpected, surprising, meteoric
	Antonym: gradual, unhurried
24.	**Absolute**
	Synonym: Adj: complete, conclusive, perfect, whole, total, full, unqualified, unlimited
	Antonym: restricted, partial, limited, incomplete, conditional
25.	**Absolutely**
	Synonym: Adj: definitely, doubtlessly, completely, entirely, wholly
	Antonym: possibly, probably, somewhat
26.	**Absolve**
	Synonym: Verb: exonerate, excuse, free, acquit, pardon, clear
	Antonym: charge, condemn, convict, punish

27. Abstain
Synonym: Verb: avoid, forgo, refrain, spurn, resist
Antonym: indulge, revel, overdo

28. Abstract
Synonym: Adj: hypothetical, theoretical, speculative, conceptual, ideal
Antonym: concrete, specific, practical, tangible, empirical

29. Abstruse
Synonym: Adj: obscure, arcane, esoteric, little known, difficult, hard, puzzling, perplexing, enigmatic, inscrutable, cryptic
Antonym: clear, obvious, precise, concise

30. Absurd
Synonym: Adj: senseless, insensible, foolish, ridiculous, preposterous, laughable, irrational, idiotic, ludicrous
Antonym: reasonable, sensible, rational

31. Absurdity
Synonym: Noun: foolishness, nonsense, craziness, silliness, idiocy, ridiculousness
Antonym: sense, wisdom, reality

32. Abundance
Synonym: Noun: profusion, sufficiency, ampleness, excess, surplus
Antonym: scarcity, lack deficiency, destitution

33. Abundant
Synonym: Adj: plentiful, ample, copious, rich, bountiful, bounteous
Antonym: scarce, rare, meagre, scant, insufficient

34. Abuse
Synonym: Verb: insult, malign, slander, scold, berate, reproach, misuse, exploit, mishandle, misapply, hurt, harm, injure, mistreat
Noun: misuse, mistreatment, cruelty, injury, harm, hurt, insult, scolding, berating, tirade
Antonym: praise, compliment, respect, honour, protect, praise

35. Abusive
Synonym: Adj: insulting, offensive, offending, rude, contemptuous
Antonym: respectful, complimentary, courteous, polite

36. Abysmal
Synonym: Adj: unfathomable, immeasurable, deep, bottomless, bad, awful, terrible, wretched, lousy
Antonym: shallow, measurable, fathomable, excellent, good, great

37. Abyss
Synonym: Noun: chasm, pit, emptiness, nothingness

38. Accelerate
Synonym: Verb: hasten, hurry, quicken, speed, expedite, rush
Antonym: decelerate, slow, delay, retard

39. Acclaim
Synonym: Noun: applause, honour, homage, praise, enthusiasm
Verb: commend, applaud, compliment
Antonym: condemnation, criticism, berate, denounce, criticize

40. Acclimatize
Synonym: Verb: adjust, adapt, attune, accustom, habituate, acculturate, reconcile, familiarize someone/oneself with

41. Accolade
Synonym: Noun: honour, commendation, applause, ovation, admiration, approbation
Antonym: criticism, cynosure

42. Accomplish
Synonym: Verb: achieve, attain, reach, realize, fulfil, complete, finish, perform
Antonym: fail, forsake, abort, attempt, neglect

43. Accomplished
Synonym: Adj: skilled, masterly, expert, gifted, brilliant, talented, polished, experienced, completed, established
Antonym: incompetent, amateurish, unproven, unestablished

44. Accomplishment
Synonym: Noun: achievement, attainment, triumph, victory, success, skill, gift, talent, expertness, proficiency
Antonym: failure, mishap, disappointment, lack, deficiency

45.	**Accumulate**
	Synonym: Verb: collect, gather, amass, assemble, stockpile, hoard
	Antonym: decrease, diminish, lessen, disperse, scatter
46.	**Accurate**
	Synonym: Adj: correct, precise, exact, right, faultless, reliable
	Antonym: inaccurate, inexact, loose
47.	**Accuse**
	Synonym: Verb: blame, charge, implicate, incriminate, indict, reproach
	Antonym: clear, acquit, absolve, exonerate
48.	**Acerbic**
	Synonym: Adj: sharp, sarcastic, sardonic, satirical, scathing, penetrating, piercing, acrimonious, harsh, vitriolic, virulent, venomous, spiteful, malicious, sour, acidic
	Antonym: mild, kind, sweet, smooth
49.	**Acme**
	Synonym: Noun: peak, pinnacle, zenith, highest point, crest, apex, apogee, climax
	Antonym: nadir, bottom, lowest point
50.	**Acquaint**
	Synonym: Verb: introduce, meet, present, inform, advise, notify, familiarize, divulge, reveal
	Antonym: withhold, conceal, hide, retain
51.	**Acquaintance**
	Synonym: Noun: familiarity, experience, awareness, knowledge, appreciation, colleague, associate, companion
	Antonym: unawareness, stranger
52.	**Acquire**
	Synonym: Verb: obtain, attain, get, gain, procure, secure, achieve, receive, realize
	Antonym: lose, forfeit, forgo, relinquish
53.	**Acquisition**
	Synonym: Noun: acquirement, attainment, obtainment, gain
54.	**Acquit**
	Synonym: Verb: excuse, forgive, exonerate, absolve, clear, exempt
	Antonym: condemn, sentence, convict

55.	**Acrid**
	Synonym: Adj: sharp, bitter, pungent, stinking, harsh, caustic
	Antonym: mild, sweet, kind, smooth
56.	**Actuate**
	Synonym: Verb: activate, trigger, initiate, initialize, energize, animate, motivate, stimulate, prompt, incite
57.	**Acute**
	Synonym: Adj: sharp, keen, penetrating, discerning, perceptive
58.	**Adapt**
	Synonym: Verb: adjust, accommodate, conform, reconcile, fit, change
59.	**Adaptable**
	Synonym: Adj: versatile, flexible, adjustable, accommodating, tractable
	Antonym: rigid, fixed, inflexible
60.	**Adaptation**
	Synonym: Noun: version, alteration, modification
61.	**Adamant**
	Synonym: Adj: unshakeable, inflexible, unwavering, uncompromising, resolute, determined, firm, rigid, steadfast, stubborn, unrelenting, unyielding, obdurate, inexorable
	Antonym: unsure, flexible, yielding
62.	**Addict**
	Synonym: Adj: dependent, obsessive, obsessional, devoted, dedicated, habitual
	Antonym: indifferent
63.	**Addiction**
	Synonym: Noun: dependency, craving, weakness, compulsion, enslavement
64.	**Adept**
	Synonym: Adj: skilled, expert, capable, proficient, competent, deft, dexterous
	Antonym: unskilled, bumbling, incompetent
65.	**Adhere**
	Synonym: Verb: cling, stick, hold, attach, fasten, follow, keep, be faithful, be loyal
66.	**Adherent**
	Synonym: Noun: follower, disciple, observer, devotee, believer, supporter
	Antonym: opponent, enemy, detractor

67.	**Adjacent**
	Synonym: Adj: next to, adjoining, touching, near, bordering, neighbouring
	Antonym: remote, distant, separate, removed
68.	**Adjourn**
	Synonym: Verb: defer, delay, postpone, suspend, to put off, postpone
	Antonym: convene, assemble, gather
69.	**Adjudicate**
	Synonym: Verb: judge, deem, determine, proclaim, hold, try, hear, examine, decide, settle, resolve
70.	**Adjudication**
	Synonym: Noun: arbitration, ruling, resolution, finding, verdict, conclusion
71.	**Adjudicator**
	Synonym: Noun: arbitrator, mediator, umpire
72.	**Adjust**
	Synonym: Verb: alter, adapt, regulate, set, change, order, repair, fix
73.	**Adjustment**
	Synonym: Noun: alignment, modification, ordering, fixing, regulating, accommodation, settlement, compromise, adapting
74.	**Administer**
	Synonym: Verb: govern, control, direct, manage, supervise, run, govern, control, provide, dispense, apply, give
75.	**Admire**
	Synonym: Verb: respect, esteem, value, revere, venerate, honour
	Antonym: dislike, detest, scorn, hate
76.	**Admonish**
	Synonym: Verb: warn, caution, advise, forewarn, scold, chastise, berate, rebuke
	Antonym: praise, commend, compliment
77.	**Ado**
	Synonym: Noun: fuss, difficulty, agitation, commotion, confusion, excitement, disturbance, hurly– burly, uproar
78.	**Adopt**
	Synonym: Verb: embrace, assume, appropriate, approve, agree accede, accept
	Antonym: abandon, give up

79.	**Adore**
	Synonym: Verb: worship, love, cherish, revere, venerate, idolize
	Antonym: abhor, hate, despise, dislike
80.	**Adorn**
	Synonym: Verb: decorate, embellish, ornament, beautify
	Antonym: divest, strip, mar, deface
81.	**Adroit**
	Synonym: Adj: skilful, adept, dexterous, nimble, skilled, expert, masterly, proficient, accomplished, talented, peerless
	Antonym: clumsy, incompetent, artless, unskilled
82.	**Adulation**
	Synonym: Noun: excessive praise, flattery, hero- worship, high regard, lionization, veneration, exaltation, magnification
	Antonym: denigration, vilification, disparagement
83.	**Adulterate**
	Synonym: Verb: make impure, degrade, debase, spoil, taint, defile, contaminate, pollute, foul, sully, tamper with, mix, lace, dilute, water down, thin out, weaken, corrupt, vitiate
	Antonym: refine, purify
84.	**Adverse**
	Synonym: Adj: unfavourable, hostile, contrary, difficult, hardship, misfortune, detrimental, hostile, destructive
	Antonym: beneficial, good, favourable
85.	**Afflict**
	Synonym: Verb: plague, trouble, distress, burden, torment, beset
86.	**Affluence**
	Synonym: Noun: wealth, prosperity, richness, plenty, riches
	Antonym: poverty, destitution
87.	**Affluent**
	Synonym: Adj: wealthy, prosperous, privileged
	Antonym: poor, impoverished, underprivileged
88.	**Affront**
	Synonym: Noun: insult, indignity, aspersion, outrage, insult

89.	**Aggravate**
	Synonym: Verb: worsen, inflame, compound, intensify, heighten, magnify
	Antonym: alleviate, improve, calm, conciliate
90.	**Agnostic**
	Synonym: Noun: sceptic, doubter, questioner, challenger, cynic, disbeliever, nonbeliever
	Antonym: believer, theist
91.	**Alacrity**
	Synonym: Noun: eagerness, willingness, readiness, enthusiasm, ardour, fervour, keenness, promptness, briskness
	Antonym: apathy, laziness, lethargy
92.	**Alarming**
	Synonym: Adj: frightening, startling, unnerving, shocking, perturbing, dismaying, harrowing, dreadful, monstrous
	Antonym: reassuring, peaceful, calm
93.	**Alibi**
	Synonym: Noun: excuse, story, explanation, plea, defence
94.	**Allegiance**
	Synonym: Noun: loyalty, faithfulness, fidelity, obedience, steadfastness, constancy, commitment
	Antonym: disloyalty, treachery,
95.	**Alleviate**
	Synonym: Verb: reduce, ease, relieve, diminish, lessen, weaken, soften, blunt, dilute, moderate, mitigate, modify, abate, pacify, placate, mollify, sweeten
	Antonym: aggravate, acerbate
96.	**Allude**
	Synonym: Verb: to refer indirectly, mention, suggest, hint, imply
97.	**Allure**
	Synonym: Verb: charm, attract, tempt, fascinate, captivate, enchant, draw ***Noun:*** attraction, lure, fascination, temptation, enticement, charm
	Antonym: repel, alienate, estrange
98.	**Alter**
	Synonym: Verb: change, make different, modify, vary, transform, revise, remake
	Antonym: maintain, continue, keep

99.	**Amalgamate**
	Synonym: Verb: unite, merge, combine, fuse, blend, mingle, coalesce, consolidate, intermix
	Antonym: separate, disintegrate
100.	**Amateur**
	Synonym: Noun: nonprofessional, novice, beginner, apprentice, hobbyist, dilettante
	Antonym: expert, professional, experienced
101.	**Amaze**
	Synonym: Verb: astonish, surprise, astound, bewilder, stun, impress, bamboozle
	Antonym: bore, tire, anticipate, expect
102.	**Ambiguity**
	Synonym: Noun: ambivalence, equivocation, obscurity, vagueness, uncertainty, enigma
	Antonym: unambiguousness, transparency
103.	**Ambit**
	Synonym: Noun: scope, extent, confines, limits, breadth, reach, sweep, purview, span, stretch, horizon
104.	**Ambition**
	Synonym: Noun: desire, will, determination, drive, energy, resolve, goal, end, aspiration, objective, purpose, dream
	Antonym: indifference, apathy, laziness
105.	**Ambivalent**
	Synonym: Adj: mixed, contradictory, wavering, indecisive, of two minds, on the fence
	Antonym: determined, steadfast, decisive, single-minded, certain, sure
106.	**Ameliorate**
	Synonym: Verb: improve, enhance, boost, refine
	Antonym: worsen, deteriorate
107.	**Amelioration**
	Synonym: Noun: improvement, betterment, enhancement, benefit, boost
	Antonym: worsening, deterioration
108.	**Amenable**
	Synonym: Adj: compliant, biddable, manageable, controllable, governable, persuadable, pliant, malleable
	Antonym: Uncooperative, stubborn

109.	**Amend**
	Synonym: Verb: correct, perfect, reform, revise, change, alter, modify
	Antonym: worsen, weaken, keep
110.	**Amiable**
	Synonym: Adj: friendly, agreeable, pleasant, congenial, gracious, sociable, amicable
	Antonym: unfriendly, disagreeable, unpleasant
111.	**Amicable**
	Synonym: Adj: peaceful, peaceable, friendly, cooperative, harmonious, civil
	Antonym: hostile, belligerent, unfriendly
112.	**Amoral**
	Synonym: Adj: unprincipled, unethical, unscrupulous
	Antonym: moral, principled
113.	**Amorous**
	Synonym: Adj: sexual, erotic, passionate, enamoured, lustful
	Antonym: unloving, cold
114.	**Amorphous**
	Synonym: Adj: shapeless, formless, unshaped, structureless, vague, nebulous, volatile
	Antonym: shaped, definite
115.	**Ample**
	Synonym: Adj: enough, sufficient, adequate, plenty, abundant, copious
	Antonym: insufficient, meager
116.	**Amplify**
	Synonym: Verb: enlarge, increase, extend, intensify, strengthen
	Antonym: reduce, decrease, diminish, lower
117.	**Amputate**
	Synonym: Verb: cut off, sever, remove, chop off, separate, detach, disconnect
118.	**Amuse**
	Synonym: Verb: entertain, please, occupy, interest, divert, charm, enliven, regale
	Antonym: bore, tire, depress
119.	**Anguish**
	Synonym: Noun: distress, agony, torment, misery, anxiety, despair, pain, suffering
	Antonym: comfort, solace, pleasure

120.	**Animate**
	Synonym: Verb: enliven, vitalize, energize, invigorate, revive, vivify, exhilarate, stimulate, galvanize, electrify
	Antonym: depress, inhibit, inanimate
121.	**Animated**
	Synonym: Adj: lively, spirited, high-spirited, energetic, full of life, excited, enthusiastic, vibrant, vivacious, buoyant, exuberant, zestful, passionate, fervent, ardent
	Antonym: lethargic, apathetic, lifeless
122.	**Animosity**
	Synonym: Noun: strong dislike, hatred, hostility, antipathy, antagonism, aversion, acrimony, bitterness, rancour, malice, spite, venom, grudges
	Antonym: goodwill, friendship
123.	**Annex**
	Synonym: Verb: add, attach, append, acquire, appropriate, connect, join *Noun:* addition, extension, supplement, wing, branch
	Antonym: detach, separate, disconnect
124.	**Annihilate**
	Synonym: Verb: demolish, destroy, exterminate, kill, eradicate, obliterate
125.	**Annoy**
	Synonym: Verb: irk, irritate, bother, vex, pester, disturb, harass, distract
	Antonym: comfort, soothe, please
126.	**Annul**
	Synonym: Verb: nullify, invalidate, repeal, rescind, revoke, set aside, cancel, abolish, abrogate
	Antonym: restore, enact
127.	**Antagonist**
	Synonym: Noun: opponent, adversary, rival, competitor, foe, enemy
	Antonym: friend, ally, partner
128.	**Antecedent**
	Synonym: Noun: ancestors, forefathers, predecessors, progenitors
	Antonym: descendent, later, subsequent
129.	**Anticipate**
	Synonym: Verb: expect, foresee, foretell, predict, forecast

130.	**Antipathy**
	Synonym: Noun: aversion, hatred, dislike, loathing, repugnance
	Antonym: liking, appeal, affection
131.	**Apathy**
	Synonym: Noun: indifference, unconcern, disinterest, passiveness, lethargy, coldness
	Antonym: enthusiasm, fervour, interest, concern
132.	**Apex**
	Synonym: Noun: highest point, peak, zenith, top, pinnacle, summit, climax
	Antonym: lowest point, bottom, nadir, abyss
133.	**Apparent**
	Synonym: Adj: plain, obvious, evident, clear, manifest, unmistakable
	Antonym: doubtful, uncertain, obscure
134.	**Appease**
	Synonym: Verb: placate, pacify, calm, soothe, ease, allay, quench
	Antonym: irritate, aggravate, provoke
135.	**Appreciate**
	Synonym: Verb: realize, understand, comprehend, recognize, perceive, value, esteem, prize, admire, honour, cherish
	Antonym: misunderstand, misjudge, dislike, scorn
136.	**Apprehend**
	Synonym: Verb: catch, capture, arrest, seize, take into custody
	Antonym: release, free
137.	**Appropriate**
	Synonym: Adj: suitable, proper, fitting, applicable, correct *Verb:* confiscate, seize, commander, steal, take, allocate, assign, allot, disburse, authorize
	Antonym: inappropriate, unfitting, unsuitable, return, relinquish, surrender, misappropriate
138.	**Arduous**
	Synonym: Adj: difficult, trying, exhausting, fatiguing, rigorous
	Antonym: easy, effortless, simple
139.	**Aroma**
	Synonym: Noun: fragrance, scent, smell, odour
	Antonym: stink, stench, reek

140.	**Arouse**
	Synonym: Noun: waken, rouse, stir, excite, stimulate
	Antonym: settle, stifle, repress
141.	**Arraign**
	Synonym: Verb: accuse, charge, indict, incriminate
	Antonym: acquit, exonerate, excuse
142.	**Arrogance**
	Synonym: Noun: haughtiness, presumptuousness, conceit, pride, ego, braggadocio, imperiousness
	Antonym: modest, humbleness, humility
143.	**Articulate**
	Synonym: Adj: eloquent, well-spoken, expressive, smooth-talking, facile, fluent
	Antonym: real, genuine, authentic
144.	**Ascend**
	Synonym: Verb: climb, mount, scale, rise, advance
	Antonym: descend, fall, drop
145.	**Ashamed**
	Synonym: Adj: embarrassed, feeling shame, guilt or remorse; humiliated, chagrined, mortified, uneasy
	Antonym: unashamed, proud, honoured
146.	**Assign**
	Synonym: Verb: distribute, dispense, give, allocate, allot, appoint, designate, name, nominate, delegate
147.	**Assimilate**
	Synonym: Verb: adapt, adjust, acclimatize, fit in, integrate, blend in
148.	**Assorted**
	Synonym: Adj: various, varied, mixed, miscellaneous, diverse
	Antonym: identical, uniform, similar
149.	**Assume**
	Synonym: Verb: presume, suppose, postulate, suspect, infer, adopt, embrace, acquire, take, undertake
	Antonym: renounce, abandon, relinquish
150.	**Assure**
	Synonym: Verb: reassure, promise, pledge, affirm
	Antonym: deny, refute, question

151.	**Astonish**
	Synonym: Verb: amaze, surprise, astound, startle, stun, dazzle
152.	**Astound**
	Synonym: Verb: astonish, amaze, surprise, startle, stun
153.	**Astray**
	Synonym: Adj: lost, adrift, off the mark, far afield, off course
	Antonym: on course, correct, in the right direction
154.	**Astute**
	Synonym: Adj: sharp, shrewd, keen, clever, canny
	Antonym: dumb, naïve, stupid, unintelligent
155.	**Asylum**
	Synonym: Noun: refuge, sanctuary, haven, shelter, protection, retreat
156.	**Atrocious**
	Synonym: Adj: horrible, terrible, dreadful, evil, cruel, brutal
	Antonym: good, kind, benevolent
157.	**Audacious**
	Synonym: Adj: bold, daring, fearless, intrepid, brave, unafraid, unflinching, courageous, valorous, heroic, dashing
	Antonym: timid, polite, humble, civil
158.	**Audacity**
	Synonym: Noun: courage, bravery, guts, fearlessness, nerve, daring
	Antonym: cowardice, fear, timidity, courtesy, politeness, deference
159.	**Augment**
	Synonym: Verb: increase, enlarge, extend, raise, expand, swell
	Antonym: decrease, lessen, diminish
160.	**Aura**
	Synonym: Noun: air, ambiance, emanation, vibe, atmosphere, mood
161.	**Auspices**
	Synonym: Adj: patronage, aegis, protection, backing, supervision, influence, control

162.	**Auspicious**
	Synonym: Adj: favourable, propitious, promising, full of promise, bright, rosy, good, optimistic, hopeful, encouraging, opportune, timely, well timed, lucky, fortunate, providential, felicitous, advantageous
	Antonym: inauspicious, unfavourable
163.	**Austere**
	Synonym: Adj: severe, rigid, strict, stern, harsh, stiff, formal
	Antonym: cheerful, friendly, lenient
164.	**Authentic**
	Synonym: Adj: genuine, real, true, actual, legitimate, pure
	Antonym: fake, imitation, unreal, false
165.	**Autonomy**
	Synonym: Noun: self-government, independence, self-rule, home rule, self-determination, self-sufficiency
166.	**Avert**
	Synonym: Verb: prevent, thwart, stop, turn away, halt, shunt, deter
	Antonym: cause, invite, bring about
167.	**Aversion**
	Synonym: Noun: dislike, distaste, abhorrence, hatred, loathing, antipathy, disgust, revulsion, repugnance
	Antonym: liking, inclination, desire
168.	**Avid**
	Synonym: Adj: eager, passionate, enthusiastic, fervent, zealous, ardent
	Antonym: unenthusiastic, apathetic
169.	**Avow**
	Synonym: Verb: assert, declare, state, maintain, aver, attest, swear, vow, confess
170.	**Awe**
	Synonym: Noun: wonder, wonderment, amazement, astonishment, admiration, reverence, veneration, respect, dread, terror, fear
	Antonym: contempt, indifference
171.	**Awful**
	Synonym: Adj: dreadful, terrible, horrible, appalling, bad, poor
	Antonym: delightful, wonderful, pleasant

172.	**Awkward**
	Synonym: Adj: clumsy, inept, ungraceful, uncoordinated, bungling, ungainly, embarrassing, disconcerting, difficult, ticklish, delicate, unwieldy, unmanageable, cumbersome, unhandy
	Antonym: graceful, coordinated, pleasant, comfortable, easy

B

173.	**Baffle**
	Synonym: Verb: confuse, puzzle, perplex, befuddle, bewilder, mix up
174.	**Bamboozle**
	Synonym: Verb: trick, deceive, hoodwink, fool, defraud, beguile, entrap
175.	**Banal**
	Synonym: Adj: not original or interesting, dull, trite, hackneyed, stereotyped, overused, overdone
	Antonym: original, pure
176.	**Barbarian**
	Synonym: Adj: an uncultured, brutish person, a lout ***Noun:*** outlandish, savage, vandal, brute, primitive
	Antonym: smart, sophisticated, cultured, civilized
177.	**Bawdy**
	Synonym: Adj: ribald, indecent, rude, titillating, obscene, vulgar, coarse, filthy, smutty, salacious, prurient, lascivious, licentious
	Antonym: clean, innocent, decent
178.	**Beauty**
	Synonym: Noun: appeal, attractiveness, prettiness, loveliness, charm, fairness
	Antonym: repulsiveness, ugliness
179.	**Beautiful**
	Synonym: Adj: attractive, pretty, handsome, appealing, charming, winsome, ravishing, gorgeous, stunning, graceful, elegant, decorative
	Antonym: ugly, repulsive, bad
180.	**Beautify**
	Synonym: Verb: adorn, embellish, enhance, decorate, ornament, prettify
	Antonym: spoil, uglify

181.	**Beckon**
	Synonym: Verb: motion, summon, signal, hail, call
182.	**Befuddled**
	Synonym: Adj: confused, muddled, bewildered, perplexed, stunned, stupefied, fuzzy, fuddled
	Antonym: clear, confident
183.	**Beholden**
	Synonym: Adj: indebted, obliged, obligated (duty-bound), grateful, thankful
184.	**Behove**
	Synonym: Verb: be incumbent on, obligatory for, be required of, be appropriate for, be expected of, be advisable for, befit, suit, be suitable of
185.	**Belated**
	Synonym: Adj: late, overdue, behindhand, behind time, not on time, behind schedule, delayed
	Antonym: early
186.	**Beleaguered**
	Synonym: Adj: besieged, under siege, blockaded, surrounded, encircled, hard-pressed
187.	**Belittle**
	Synonym: Verb: disparage, denigrate, deprecate, depreciate, downgrade, trivialize, scoff at, sneer at, laugh at, mock, ridicule, deride, scorn
	Antonym: praise, magnify, appreciate
188.	**Bellicose**
	Synonym: Adj: belligerent, hostile, antagonistic, combatative, quick-tempered, hot-tempered, ill-tempered, bad- tempered, irascible
	Antonym: peaceable, affable, amicable
189.	**Belligerent**
	Synonym: Adj: unfriendly, hostile, argumentative, quarrelsome, warlike
	Antonym: friendly, peaceable
190.	**Bemoan**
	Synonym: Verb: lament, bewail, deplore, complain about, mourn, wail over
	Antonym: applaud, praise, appreciate

191.	**Bemused**
	Synonym: Adj: bewildered, confused, puzzled, perplexed, baffled, mystified, stupefied, nonplussed, muddled, dumbfounded, unnerved, shaken, flummoxed, bamboozled
192.	**Benediction**
	Synonym: Noun: blessing, prayer, invocation, dedication, grace, thanksgiving
193.	**Benevolent**
	Synonym: Adj: kind, tender-hearted, compassionate, sympathetic, considerate, thoughtful, altruistic, charitable, philanthropic, generous, magnanimous
	Antonym: unkind, tight-fisted
194.	**Benign**
	Synonym: Adj: harmless, innocuous, curable, mild, favourable, helpful, kind, gentle, mild, merciful, compassionate, benevolent
	Antonym: harmful, dangerous, malignant, mean, cruel, vicious
195.	**Bequeath**
	Synonym: Verb: leave, hand down, entrust, grant, transfer, donate, bestow, confer
196.	**Berate**
	Synonym: Verb: rebuke, reprimand, reproach, chastise, chide, castigate
	Antonym: praise
197.	**Berserk**
	Synonym: Adj: destructively violent, wild, frenzied, crazy, insane, mad, maniacal
	Antonym: sane, calm, rational, cool
198.	**Beseech**
	Synonym: Verb: implore, beg, entreat, supplicate, pray
199.	**Besotted**
	Synonym: Adj: infatuated with, smitten with, passionate about, greatly enamoured, charmed by, captivated by, enchanted by, enthralled by, bewitched by
	Antonym: Indifferent
200.	**Bestial**
	Synonym: Adj: savage, brutish, brutal, depraved, degenerate, perverted, immoral, amoral
	Antonym: civilized, humane, moral

201.	**Betray**
	Synonym: Verb: deceive, trick, forsake, desert, abandon, disclose, reveal, expose, divulge, show
	Antonym: support, protect, guard, safeguard
202.	**Bigot**
	Synonym: Noun: chauvinist, fanatic, zealot, racist
203.	**Blasphemous**
	Synonym: Adj: sacrilegious, profane, irreligious, irreverent, impious, unholy
	Antonym: reverent
204.	**Blasphemy**
	Synonym: Noun: profanity, sacrilege, irreligiousness, irreverence
	Antonym: reverence
205.	**Blatant**
	Synonym: Adj: flagrant, glaring, unconcealed, shameless, unashamed, impudent, unblushing, brazen
	Antonym: inconspicuous, subtle
206.	**Bleak**
	Synonym: Adj: grim, dismal, disheartening, barren, desolate, bare, exposed
	Antonym: promising, bright, lush
207.	**Blemish**
	Synonym: Noun: flaw, imperfection, defect, blotch, discolouration, impurity ***Verb:*** mar, flaw, spoil, mark, spot
	Antonym: purity, perfection, flawlessness
208.	**Blizzard**
	Synonym: Noun: snowstorm, tempest, gale, storm
209.	**Blunt**
	Synonym: Adj: unsharpened, dull, edgeless, unpointed, frank, candid, tactless, abrupt, short, direct ***Verb:*** dull, deaden, numb, stifle, impair
	Antonym: sharp, pointed, edged, subtle, indirect, tactful, sharpen, excite
210.	**Blur**
	Synonym: Noun: smear, haze, blot, cloud, smudge ***Verb:*** obscure, shroud, confuse, smear

211.	**Boisterous**
	Synonym: Adj: noisy, rowdy, uproarious, tumultuous, unruly
	Antonym: calm, quiet, restrained, tranquil
212.	**Boomerang**
	Synonym: Verb: backfire, recoil, reverse, rebound, come back, bounce back, spring back, return
213.	**Brandish**
	Synonym: Verb: wave, wield, swing, flaunt, display ***Noun:*** show, exhibition, embellishment
214.	**Brevity**
	Synonym: Noun: shortness, quickness, briefness, conciseness, terseness
	Antonym: lengthiness, long-windedness, verbosity
215.	**Brisk**
	Synonym: Adj: lively, swift, quick, busy, energetic, sharp, exhilarating, nipping, crisp, keen, bracing
	Antonym: slow, sluggish, dead, stagnant
216.	**Brittle**
	Synonym: Adj: weak, breakable, fragile, crumbly, delicate
	Antonym: strong, unbreakable, sturdy, solid, durable, robust
217.	**Brutal**
	Synonym: Adj: barbaric, unmerciful, savage, cruel, mean, vicious, harsh, ruthless
	Antonym: kind, gentle, merciful, humane
218.	**Bully**
	Synonym: Noun: tormentor, oppressor, persecutor ***Verb:***: terrorize, scare, harass, threaten, horrify, petrify
	Antonym: charm, persuade, entice

C

219.	**Cacophony**
	Synonym: Noun: harsh, unpleasant, discordant sounds
220.	**Cajole**
	Synonym: Verb: persuade, coax, talk into

221.	**Calamity**
	Synonym: Noun: disaster, catastrophe, mishap, tribulation, misfortune
	Antonym: blessing, boon
222.	**Callous**
	Synonym: Adj: unsympathetic, uncaring, indifferent, insensitive, hard-hearted
	Antonym: tender, sympathetic, caring, soft
223.	**Camaraderie**
	Synonym: Noun: friendship, fellowship, sociability, fraternization
	Antonym: hostility, unfriendliness, coldness
224.	**Camouflage**
	Synonym: Noun: conceal, disguise, cover, mask
	Antonym: expose, reveal, show
225.	**Candid**
	Synonym: Adj: direct, frank, forthright, open, outspoken, unbiased
	Antonym: fake, untruthful, insincere, formal, rehearsed, planned
226.	**Candour**
	Synonym: Noun: frankness, openness, honesty, candidness, truthfulness
	Antonym: guardedness, evasiveness
227.	**Cantankerous**
	Synonym: Adj: bad-tempered, irascible, irritable, ill-natured, peevish, crabby, quarrelsome, crotchety
	Antonym: good-natured, affable
228.	**Capable**
	Synonym: Adj: able, skilful, competent, efficient, talented
	Antonym: incapable, unskilled, incompetent
229.	**Capacity**
	Synonym: Noun: size, dimensions, content, volume, range, measure, space, ability, competence, potential, aptitude
	Antonym: inability, incapacity, incompetence
230.	**Captivate**
	Synonym: Verb: enchant, dazzle, fascinate tantalize, enthral, charm, enchant, bewitch, fascinate, beguile
	Antonym: repel, bore

231.	**Captivating**
	Synonym: Adj: charming, enchanting, bewitching, fascinating, entrancing, alluring, charismatic, dazzling, seductive
	Antonym: repellent, boring
232.	**Capture**
	Synonym: Verb: catch, apprehend, seize, arrest, take captive, take into custody, imprison, detain
	Antonym: free, escape
233.	**Cardinal**
	Synonym: Adj: fundamental, basic, main, chief, primary, principal, premier, leading, paramount, pre-eminent, important, major, foremost
	Antonym: unimportant, insignificant
234.	**Caress**
	Synonym: Noun: stroke, touch, cuddle, embrace
235.	**Carnage**
	Synonym: Noun: massacre, great slaughter, bloodshed, bloodbath, butchery
236.	**Carnal**
	Synonym: Adj: sexual, sensual, erotic, lustful, lascivious, lecherous, lewd, prurient, physical, bodily
	Antonym: spiritual, platonic
237.	**Carnival**
	Synonym: Noun: festival, jubilee, amusement, jamboree
238.	**Cascade**
	Synonym: Noun: waterfall, fall, rapids ***Verb:*** plunge, fall, rush, surge
	Antonym: trickle, drip, leak
239.	**Casual**
	Synonym: Adj: informal, relaxed, nonchalant, carefree
	Antonym: formal, stiff, reserved
240.	**Cataclysm**
	Synonym: Noun: disaster, catastrophe, calamity, tragedy, devastation
	Antonym: salvation, godsend
241.	**Catalyst**
	Synonym: Noun: stimulus, activator, agitator, reactant, impetus

242.	**Catastrophe**
	Synonym: Noun: tragedy, misfortune, disaster, devastation, calamity, ruin
	Antonym: good fortune, blessing
243.	**Caustic**
	Synonym: Adj: corrosive, harsh, sarcastic, stinging, bitter, scathing, derisive, sardonic, scornful, acerbic, vitriolic, pungent, acrimonious
	Antonym: benign, soothing, kind
244.	**Cautious**
	Synonym: Adj: careful, watchful, attentive, alert, wary, vigilant, aware, guarded
	Antonym: rash, daring, careless, foolhardy
245.	**Cease**
	Synonym: Verb: stop, discontinue, spend, quit, terminate, halt, desist, conclude
	Antonym: continue, start, begin
246.	**Cede**
	Synonym: Verb: surrender, yield, give, grant
	Antonym: keep, retain, hold
247.	**Celestial**
	Synonym: Adj: astronomical, heavenly, universal
	Antonym: terrestrial, earthly, hellish, mundane
248.	**Censor**
	Synonym: Verb: ban, forbid, purge
	Antonym: allow, accept, approve
249.	**Censorship**
	Synonym: Noun: expurgation, sanitizing, removal, editing, deletion, cutting
	Antonym: freedom of speech and expression
250.	**Censure**
	Synonym: Noun: condemnation, criticism ***Verb:*** blame, criticize, reprimand, reproach
	Antonym: praise, approval, endorsement
251.	**Chaos**
	Synonym: Noun: disorder, confusion, disarray, mess, disorganization, jumble, upheaval, pandemonium
	Antonym: organization, harmony, order, calm

252.	**Chaotic**
	Synonym: Adj: out-of-control, wild, confused, disordered, turbulent, riotous
	Antonym: ordered, peaceful, within control
253.	**Characteristic**
	Synonym: Adj: typical, distinctive, marked, representative, particular, specific ***Noun:*** feature, mannerism, trait, attribute, distinction, peculiarity, quirk
	Antonym: uncharacteristic, atypical
254.	**Charisma**
	Synonym: Noun: magnetism, magnetic personality, dominance, charm, appeal, presence, power, authority
255.	**Charismatic**
	Synonym: Adj: powerful, charming, magnetic, hypnotic, dominant, authoritative
	Antonym: unappealing, dull, weak
256.	**Charitable**
	Synonym: Adj: giving, unselfish, generous, unsparing, humanitarian, nonprofit, lenient, tolerant, forgiving, kind, sympathetic
	Antonym: selfish, ungenerous, stingy, rigid
257.	**Charity**
	Synonym: Noun: aid, contribution, endowment, alms, benefaction, assistance, generosity, benevolence, philanthropy, altruism, humanity
	Antonym: stinginess, selfishness
258.	**Charlatan**
	Synonym: Noun: quack, sham, fraud, fake, humbug, impostor, pretender, hoodwinker, trickster, cheater, swindler, fraudster
259.	**Charm**
	Synonym: Noun: allure, appeal, captivation, pull, enchantment, attractiveness, magnetism, amulet, spell, chant, lucky ***Verb:*** delight, captivate, enthral, mesmerize, attract, bewitch, hypnotize
	Antonym: aversion, repulsion, revulsion, disgust, revolt, repel
260.	**Charming**
	Synonym: Adj: enchanting, captivating, delightful, pleasing, enjoyable, fascinating, bewitching
	Antonym: repulsive, disagreeable, nauseating, unpleasing
261.	**Chasm**
	Synonym: Noun: gorge, abyss, gulf, fissure, crevice
262.	**Chaste**
	Synonym: Noun: simple, unadorned ***Adj:*** pure, decent, wholesome, virginal, innocent, celibate, righteous, uncorrupted
	Antonym: unchaste, wanton, corrupt
263.	**Chastise**
	Synonym: Verb: punish, discipline, scold, berate
	Antonym: commend, compliment, reward
264.	**Chat**
	Synonym: Verb: talk, chatter, converse, gossip
265.	**Chatter**
	Synonym: Verb: babble, talk, jabber, gossip, prattle
266.	**Chauvinism**
	Synonym: Noun: bigotry, bias, prejudice, intolerance, jingoism
	Antonym: broad-mindedness, tolerance
267.	**Cheer**
	Synonym: Verb: shout, applaud, yell, encourage, acclaim, console, comfort, reassure, brighten, enliven
	Antonym: boo, hiss, discourage, demoralize
268.	**Cheerful**
	Synonym: Adj: merry, joyous, happy, bright, carefree, jolly, playful, delighted, gleeful
	Antonym: depressed, sad, cheerless
269.	**Cheerless**
	Synonym: Adj: bleak, gloomy, dismal, miserable
	Antonym: cheerful, bright, joyous
270.	**Chequered**
	Synonym: Adj: multicoloured, varied, irregular, erratic, inconstant, fluctuating, changeful, diverse, diversified, variegated
271.	**Cherish**
	Synonym: Verb: love, honour, revere, respect, nurture, adore, value
	Antonym: hate, detest, dislike
272.	**Chew**
	Synonym: Verb: crunch, munch, grind, gnaw, bite

273.	**Chicanery**
	Synonym: Noun: trickery, deception, deceit, duplicity, unscrupulousness, subterfuge, sophistry, swindling, duping, hoodwinking, intrigue
274.	**Chill**
	Synonym: Noun: coolness, bite, frostiness, nip, crispness, coldness, briskness
	Antonym: heat, warmth, balmy, hot
275.	**Chilly**
	Synonym: Adj: cold, frigid, cool, icy, frozen
	Antonym: warm, hot, balmy
276.	**Chivalrous**
	Synonym: Adj: gallant, honourable, courteous
	Antonym: rude, boorish, unmannerly
277.	**Chivalry**
	Synonym: Noun: gallantry, courtesy, graciousness
	Antonym: rudeness, boorishness
278.	**Choke**
	Synonym: Verb: strangle, smother, suffocate, drown, block, plug, obstruct, impede, clog
	Antonym: unclog, unplug
279.	**Chronic**
	Synonym: Adj: continual, endless, persistent, habitual, recurrent, established
	Antonym: infrequent, occasional, unusual
280.	**Churlish**
	Synonym: Adj: rude, ill-mannered, impolite, unmannerly, uncivil, ill-bred, boorish, oafish, loutish
	Antonym: polite
281.	**Circumstantial**
	Synonym: Adj: incidental, inconsequential, inconclusive, indirect, insignificant, speculative
	Antonym: central, significant, important
282.	**Civility**
	Synonym: Noun: politeness, courtesy, respect, consideration, tact, respectfulness
	Antonym: disrespect, impoliteness, rudeness
283.	**Civilized**
	Synonym: Adj: refined, cultured, urbane, educated, advanced, tamed, humanized
	Antonym: uncivilized, wild, untamed

284.	**Clairvoyant**
	Synonym: Adj: extrasensory, prescient, perceptive, having a sixth sense, telepathic
285.	**Clamour**
	Synonym: Noun: commotion, shouting, noise, uproar, disturbance, loudness
	Antonym: quiet, silence, peacefulness
286.	**Clandestine**
	Synonym: Adj: secret; furtive, covert, stealthy
287.	**Clemency**
	Synonym: Noun: forgiveness, pardon, mercy, kindness, charity
288.	**Cliché**
	Synonym: Noun: trite, banality, over-used expression, platitude
	Antonym: original, fresh line
289.	**Clout**
	Synonym: Noun: influence and power, dominance, pre-eminence
290.	**Clown**
	Synonym: Verb: joke, jest, play, fool, ridicule
291.	**Clue**
	Synonym: Noun: evidence, trace, hint, sign, suggestion, idea
292.	**Clumsy**
	Synonym: Adj: ugly awkward, ungainly, bumbling, uncoordinated
	Antonym: graceful, agile
293.	**Cluster**
	Synonym: Noun: group, clump, collection, band, gathering, pack, mass ***Verb:*** gather, mass, group, collect, assemble
	Antonym: scatter, disperse
294.	**Clutter**
	Synonym: Noun: jumble, mess, litter, disorder, hodgepodge, disarray
	Antonym: order, tidiness
295.	**Coalition**
	Synonym: Noun: alliance, confederacy, union, partnership, faction, league
296.	**Coarse**
	Synonym: Adj: rough, uneven, scraggly, gnarled, rugged, rude, uncivilized, impolite, crude, ill-mannered
	Antonym: soft, smooth, even, polite, mannered, refined

297.	**Coax**
	Synonym: Verb: persuade, urge, influence, charm, entice, cajole
	Antonym: force, intimidate, pressure
298.	**Coerce**
	Synonym: Verb: pressurage, force, intimidate, compel, frighten, harass
	Antonym: ask, request, coax
299.	**Coherent**
	Synonym: Adj: clear, intelligible, lucid, understandable, comprehensible
	Antonym: incoherent, unintelligible,
300.	**Coincide**
	Synonym: Verb: agree, concur, correspond, accord, match
	Antonym: disagree, differ, conflict
301.	**Coincidence**
	Synonym: Noun: accident, chance, fate, happening
	Antonym: plan, intent
302.	**Collaborate**
	Synonym: Verb: team-up, work-together, co-write, co-author, co-create, collude
303.	**Collapse**
	Synonym: Verb: sink, deflate, crumble, disintegrate, fall ***Noun:*** breakdown, downfall, failure, exhaustion, disintegration
304.	**Colossal**
	Synonym: Adj: huge, massive, enormous, gigantic, giant, mammoth, tremendous, mighty, stupendous, monumental
	Antonym: tiny, minute, small
305.	**Combat**
	Synonym: Noun: battle, fight, war, confrontation, conflict, dispute ***Verb:*** fight, battle, confront, attack, oppose, resist
	Antonym: peace, truce, harmony
306.	**Commend**
	Synonym: Verb: praise, applaud, honour, compliment, celebrate, approve
	Antonym: criticize, condemn, disapprove
307.	**Commendable**
	Synonym: Adj: praiseworthy, laudable, exemplary, excellent, admirable, meritorious
	Antonym: despicable, horrible, bad

308.	**Commotion**
	Synonym: Noun: uproar, frenzy, turmoil, disturbance, upheaval, fuss, hullabaloo
	Antonym: calm, peacefulness, quiet
309.	**Comical**
	Synonym: Adj: humorous, funny, amusing, witty
310.	**Compact**
	Synonym: Adj: small, compressed, packed ***Verb:*** pack, condense, press, stuff, cram, compress
	Antonym: large, loose, loosen, unpack, scatter
311.	**Compassion**
	Synonym: Noun: sympathy, tenderness, mercy, feeling, love, concern, caring, warmth
	Antonym: indifference, coldness, unconcern
312.	**Compassionate**
	Synonym: Adj: sympathetic, tender, kind, merciful, loving
	Antonym: uncompassionate, heartless
313.	**Compatible**
	Synonym: Adj: agreeable, cooperative, harmonious, compliant
	Antonym: incompatible, clashing, disagreeing
314.	**Complacent**
	Synonym: Adj: smug, self-satisfied, contented, self-assured, secure
	Antonym: insecure, uneasy, dissatisfied
315.	**Competent**
	Synonym: Adj: proficient, capable, efficient
316.	**Complex**
	Synonym: Adj: complicated, difficult, involved, perplexing, intricate
	Antonym: simple, straight
317.	**Complement**
	Synonym: Noun: addition, companion, accessory, supplement, totality, entirety ***Verb:*** supplement, complete, perfect, fulfil, satisfy
318.	**Complicate**
	Synonym: Verb: confuse, muddle, entangle
	Antonym: simplify, clarify, disentangle

319.	**Complicated**
	Synonym: Adj: complex, involved, intricate, elaborate
	Antonym: easy, simple, uninvolved
320.	**Compliment**
	Synonym: Noun: praise, acclaim, approval, commendation, congratulation
	Antonym: disapproval, insult, complaint, insult, condemnation
321.	**Complimentary**
	Synonym: Adj: praising, approving, flattering, admiring, favourable
	Antonym: uncomplimentary, unflattering, disapproving
322.	**Comply**
	Synonym: Verb: follow, conform, observe, obey, satisfy, fulfil, consent
	Antonym: disobey, evade, disregard, oppose
323.	**Composite**
	Synonym: Adj: combined, joined, blended, consolidated
324.	**Compound**
	Synonym: Verb: increase, augment, intensify, worsen, complicate, mix, blend, mingle, combine, devise, make ***Noun:*** combination, composite, blend, mixture, fusion
325.	**Comprehend**
	Synonym: Verb: understand, grasp, perceive, appreciate, discern, follow
	Antonym: misunderstand
326.	**Comprehensive**
	Synonym: Adj: complete, thorough, sweeping, broad, extensive, inclusive
	Antonym: partial, incomplete, specialized
327.	**Comrade**
	Synonym: Noun: friend, partner, associate, team-mate, companion, colleague
328.	**Conceal**
	Synonym: Verb: hide, camouflage, cover, mask, disguise, bury, clock, veil
	Antonym: reveal, expose, show
329.	**Concealment**
	Synonym: Noun: covering, masking, disguising, hiding, concealing
	Antonym: showing, disclosure, presentation

330.	**Concede**
	Synonym: Verb: accept, agree, grant, acknowledge, recognize, allow, surrender, relinquish, resign, yield, transfer
331.	**Concoct**
	Synonym: Verb: devise, formulate, create, fabricate
332.	**Concoction**
	Synonym: Noun: formulation, creation, invention, fabrication, compound
333.	**Concrete**
	Synonym: Adj: direct, actual, real, physical, solid, conclusive
	Antonym: vague, theoretical, obscure
334.	**Concur**
	Synonym: Verb: agree, assent, consent, approve
	Antonym: disagree, disapprove, reject
335.	**Condemn**
	Synonym: Verb: denounce, reproach, criticize, rebuke, accuse
	Antonym: applaud, admire, praise, acquit, free, excuse
336.	**Condemnation**
	Synonym: Noun: denunciation, reproach, criticism, rebuke, disapproval
	Antonym: praise, approval, acclaim
337.	**Condense**
	Synonym: Verb: compress, reduce, shorten, compact, consolidate, trim
	Antonym: expand, increase, enlarge
338.	**Condescending**
	Synonym: Adj: arrogant, supercilious, imperious, snobbish, patronizing, haughty
	Antonym: respectful, unpretentious
339.	**Condone**
	Synonym: Verb: pardon, forgive, excuse, disregard
	Antonym: criticize, condemn, disapprove
340.	**Confer**
	Synonym: Verb: converse, consult, deliberate, give, grant, bestow
	Antonym: revoke, withhold, deny

341.	**Confess**
	Synonym: Verb: admit, concede, acknowledge, own, disclose, reveal
	Antonym: hide, deny, withhold
342.	**Confession**
	Synonym: Noun: admission, acknowledgement, disclosure, assertion, revelation
	Antonym: denial, disclaimer, repudiation
343.	**Confident**
	Synonym: Adj: certain, assured, convinced, sure, optimistic, positive, self-assured, bold, daring, fearless, assertive
	Antonym: doubtful, uncertain, hesitant, anxious
344.	**Confidential**
	Synonym: Adj: private, secret, classified, restricted, undisclosed
	Antonym: open, circulated, public
345.	**Confine**
	Synonym: Verb: restrict, limit, hold, imprison, cage, constrain, enclose ***Noun:*** limit, margin, boundary, edge, border
	Antonym: free, loose, liberate
346.	**Confiscate**
	Synonym: Verb: take, seize, impound, claim, secure, possess
	Antonym: return, release, deliver
347.	**Confront**
	Synonym: Verb: meet, encounter, face, challenge, oppose, tackle, resist
	Antonym: avoid, flee, evade
348.	**Confrontation**
	Synonym: Noun: clash, showdown, challenge, defiance, conflict
349.	**Confuse**
	Synonym: Verb: bewilder, puzzle, baffle, perplex, mystify
	Antonym: clarify, enlighten, explain
350.	**Confusing**
	Synonym: Adj: puzzling, obscure, baffling, perplexing, disturbing
	Antonym: orderly, clear, simple

351.	**Confusion**
	Synonym: Noun: bewilderment, puzzlement, mystification, perplexity
	Antonym: clarification, enlightenment, explanation, orderliness, order
352.	**Congenial**
	Synonym: Adj: friendly, pleasant, cordial, sociable, agreeable, affable
	Antonym: unfriendly, standoffish, cold
353.	**Congested**
	Synonym: Adj: plugged, filled, jammed, choked, blocked, crowded, stuffed
	Antonym: empty, clear, uncrowded
354.	**Congregate**
	Synonym: Verb: gather, assemble, mass, meet, collect, group, swarm, cluster
	Antonym: separate, scatter, disband
355.	**Conjecture**
	Synonym: Noun: guesswork, guess, speculation, theorizing, supposition
356.	**Conscientious**
	Synonym: Adj: responsible, reliable, trustworthy, sincere, dependable, dedicated
	Antonym: unreliable, irresponsible, undependable
357.	**Conscious**
	Synonym: Adj: awake, aware, sensible, alert, aware, deliberate, wilful, intentional, planned, purposeful
	Antonym: unaware, unconscious
358.	**Consecutive**
	Synonym: Adj: successive, uninterrupted, continuous, unbroken, sequential
	Antonym: interrupted, broken, discontinuous
359.	**Consent**
	Synonym: Verb: agree, allow, accept, grant, approve, permit, sanction
	Antonym: disagree, disapprove, refuse
360.	**Consequence**
	Synonym: Noun: aftermath, outcome, result, upshot, development
	Antonym: source, cause, origin
361.	**Conservative**
	Synonym: Adj: right-wing, traditional, non-liberal, conventional, reactionary
	Antonym: liberal, progressive, radical

362.	**Conserve**
	Synonym: Verb: save, preserve, guard, maintain, protect, safeguard
	Antonym: waste, exhaust, consume
363.	**Considerable**
	Synonym: Adj: significant, noteworthy, great, major, impressive, substantial, sizable, extensive, massive
	Antonym: unimportant, trivial, minor, small, scant, meager
364.	**Considerate**
	Synonym: Adj: thoughtful, kind, sensitive, concerned, tactful
	Antonym: inconsiderate, thoughtless, unkind
365.	**Consideration**
	Synonym: Noun: reflection, regard, examination, deliberation, thoughtfulness, concern, regard
	Antonym: oversight, omission, discourtesy
366.	**Consolation**
	Synonym: Noun: relief, sympathy, comfort, condolence, support
	Antonym: discouragement, dismay, discomfort
367.	**Consolidate**
	Synonym: Verb: join, combine, unite, merge, concentrate
	Antonym: separate, divide, part
368.	**Conspicuous**
	Synonym: Adj: obvious, plain, visible, apparent, evident, noticeable, prominent
	Antonym: invisible, concealed, unnoticeable
369.	**Conspire**
	Synonym: Verb: plot, scheme, collude, collaborate, machinate
370.	**Conspiracy**
	Synonym: plot, scheme, intrigue, deception
371.	**Constant**
	Synonym: Adj: unchanging, fixed, even, regular, uniform, steady, continual, nonstop, unbroken, uninterrupted, endless
	Antonym: changing, irregular, uneven, infrequent, occasional, erratic
372.	**Constantly**
	Synonym: Adv: regularly, continually, frequently, habitually, continuously
	Antonym: occasionally, seldom, rarely

373.	**Consternation**
	Synonym: Noun: dismay, perturbation, anxiety, distress, stupefaction, trepidation
	Antonym: Satisfaction
374.	**Constrain**
	Synonym: Verb: restrain, restrict, confine, bind, detain, contain
	Antonym: free, release, loose
375.	**Constrict**
	Synonym: Verb: pinch, cramp, bind, squeeze, strangle, obstruct, block, clog, close, congest, choke
	Antonym: loosen, unbind, swell, unclog
376.	**Construct**
	Synonym: Verb: build, make, create, erect, assemble, form, produce
	Antonym: destroy, demolish, dismantle
377.	**Constructive**
	Synonym: Adj: useful, helpful, valuable, beneficial, practical, usable
	Antonym: destructive, harmful, worthless
378.	**Consume**
	Synonym: Verb: absorb, devour, drink, drain, use
	Antonym: produce, supply, save, restore
379.	**Consummate**
	Synonym: Adj: complete, perfect, accomplished, highest, supreme, masterful
	Antonym: imperfect, incomplete, amateurish
380.	**Consumption**
	Synonym: Noun: use, expenditure, depletion, usage, draining
	Antonym: conservation, production, saving
381.	**Contagious**
	Synonym: Adj: catching, transmittable, infectious, spreadable, transmissible
	Antonym: non-contagious, non-infectious
382.	**Contaminate**
	Synonym: Verb: pollute, poison, foul, spoil, taint, defile, corrupt
	Antonym: clean, cleanse, purify
383.	**Contamination**
	Synonym: Noun: adulteration, fouling, pollution, taint, infection, defilement

384.	**Contemplate**
	Synonym: Verb: ponder, consider, meditate, study, deliberate
385.	**Contemplation**
	Synonym: Noun: thought, reflection, deliberation
386.	**Contempt**
	Synonym: Noun: scorn, hatred, disrespect, revulsion, distaste, detestation, disregard
	Antonym: respect, admiration, affection
387.	**Contemptible**
	Synonym: Adj: shameful, low, mean, revolting, dishonourable, offensive
	Antonym: admirable, honourable, respectable, praiseworthy
388.	**Contend**
	Synonym: Verb: battle, fight, struggle, compete, wrestle, contest, claim, hold, maintain, assert, state, declare
	Antonym: surrender, quit, yield, reject, deny
389.	**Contentious**
	Synonym: Noun: quarrelsome, antagonistic, argumentative, combative, belligerent
	Antonym: agreeable, harmonious, peaceful
390.	**Contort**
	Synonym: Verb: twist, bend, distort, knot, deform
	Antonym: straighten, smooth, unbend
391.	**Contradict**
	Synonym: Verb: refute, deny, differ, counter, challenge, oppose, dispute
	Antonym: confirm, verify, support
392.	**Contradictory**
	Synonym: Adj: contrary, opposing, disagreeing, conflicting, different
	Antonym: similar, comparable, equivalent
393.	**Contrite**
	Synonym: Adj: remorseful, repentant, ashamed, regretful, apologetic
	Antonym: unapologetic, unremorseful
394.	**Contrition**
	Synonym: Noun: regret, sorrow, remorse, guilt, shame, repentance
	Antonym: self-righteousness, pride

395.	**Contrive**
	Synonym: Verb: invent, imagine, design, create, plan, improvise
396.	**Controversial**
	Synonym: Adj: delicate, questionable, debatable, arguable, doubtful
	Antonym: safe, certain, noncontroversial
397.	**Controversy**
	Synonym: Noun: debate, disagreement, dispute, argument, quarrel, strife, contention
	Antonym: agreement, harmony, accord
398.	**Conundrum**
	Synonym: Noun: problem, quandary, enigma, mystery
399.	**Convene**
	Synonym: Verb: assemble, gather, collect, meet, congregate, rally
	Antonym: disperse, disband, scatter
400.	**Conventional**
	Synonym: Adj: orthodox, traditional, conservative, conformist, old-fashioned, prosaic
	Antonym: unorthodox, unconventional, radical, bohemian, original
401.	**Converse**
	Synonym: Verb: talk, discuss, chat, speak, communicate, confer
402.	**Convert**
	Synonym: Verb: turn, change, alter, transform, modify, reshape ***Noun:*** disciple, follower, recruit, believer, proselyte
403	**Convince**
	Synonym: Verb: persuade, influence, impress, sway, satisfy, assure
404.	**Convulsion**
	Synonym: Noun: spasm, seizure, contraction, throe
405.	**Cope**
	Synonym: Verb: manage, survive, endure, handle
406.	**Copious**
	Synonym: Adj: abundant, rich, overflowing, plentiful, lavish
	Antonym: scant, light, sparse, scarce

407.	**Cordial**
	Synonym: Adj: friendly, warm, gracious, sociable, kindly, pleasant, cheerful
	Antonym: unfriendly, cold, reserved
408.	**Corroborate**
	Synonym: Verb: verify, validate, substantiate, confirm, document
	Antonym: invalidate, disprove, contradict
409.	**Corrode**
	Synonym: Verb: erode, deteriorate, disintegrate
410.	**Corrosion**
	Synonym: Noun: erosion, rust, decomposition, deterioration, breakdown, decay
411.	**Corrupt**
	Synonym: Adj: dishonest, immoral, crooked, dishonourable, wicked
	Antonym: honest, moral, honourable
412.	**Corruption**
	Synonym: Noun: immorality, dishonesty, fraud, graft, vice, wickedness
	Antonym: morality, goodness, honesty, integrity
413.	**Cosmopolitan**
	Synonym:Adj: worldly, urbane, sophisticated, cultured, cultivated, international
	Antonym: parochial, provincial, unsophisticated
414.	**Counterfeit**
	Synonym: Adj: pretended, false, fake, forged, imitation, bogus
	Antonym: genuine, original, authentic
415.	**Countermand**
	Synonym: Verb: revoke, rescind, reverse, undo, retract, override, scrap, overturn, overrule, cancel, annul, invalidate
	Antonym: uphold, validate
416.	**Courage**
	Synonym: Noun: bravery, valour, fearlessness, heroism
	Antonym: cowardice, timidity
417.	**Courageous**
	Synonym: Adj: daring, brave, bold, gallant, fearless, heroic, unafraid
	Antonym: cowardly, timid, fearful

418.	**Courteous**
	Synonym: Adj: polite, gracious, kindly, mannerly, thoughtful, considerate
	Antonym: discourteous, impolite, inconsiderate, rude
419.	**Courtship**
	Synonym: Noun: dating, wooing, pair bonding, wining and dining, romance, engagement
420.	**Courtesy**
	Synonym: Noun: politeness, gentility, graciousness, affability, urbanity
	Antonym: discourtesy, rudeness
421.	**Covert**
	Synonym: Adj: hidden, masked, disguised, secret, stealthy
	Antonym: overt, apparent, obvious
422.	**Covet**
	Synonym: Verb: desire, wish, long for, hunger for, crave, envy
	Antonym: reject, decline, spurn
423.	**Cowardice**
	Synonym: Noun: fearfulness, faintheartedness, spinelessness, fear, fright
	Antonym: bravery, courage, fearlessness
424.	**Cowardly**
	Synonym: Adj: timid, uncourageous, fearful, fainthearted, scared
	Antonym: brave, fearless, courageous, bold
425.	**Cower**
	Synonym: Verb: tremble, cringe, quail, quake
426.	**Coy**
	Synonym: Adj: modest, bashful, shy, shrinking, demure, blushing
	Antonym: boisterous, loud, assertive
427.	**Cozy**
	Synonym: Adj: snug, warm, comfortable, relaxing, sheltered, pleasant
	Antonym: cold, uncomfortable, unpleasant
428.	**Crack**
	Synonym: Verb: break, split, burst, snap, fracture, splint, snap, clap, pop, crackle, beat, slap

429.	**Craft**
	Synonym: Noun: ability, proficiency, skill, artistry, talent
	Antonym: inability, unskilfulness, incompetency
430.	**Crafty**
	Synonym: Adj: shifty, sly, deceitful, scheming, tricky, cunning, crooked
	Antonym: honest, straightforward, direct
431.	**Crash**
	Synonym: Verb: smash, bump, collide, hit, wreck, demolish, batter, destroy, break, shatter
432.	**Crass**
	Synonym: Adj: insensitive, rude, crude, tacky, uncouth, unrefined, vulgar
	Antonym: sensitive, polite, courteous
433.	**Crave**
	Synonym: Verb: desire, want, long for, hunger for, covet, need
	Antonym: dislike, reject, detest
434.	**Craving**
	Synonym: Noun: desire, need, longing, hunger, thirst, yearning
	Antonym: dislike, abhorrence, hate
435.	**Crawl**
	Synonym: Verb: creep, drag, squirm, wiggle, wriggle
	Antonym: walk, run
436.	**Crazy**
	Synonym: Adj: stupid, foolish, insane, mad, insensible, reckless, irrational, wild, infatuated, raving, excited, passionate, mad, strange, peculiar, bizarre, unusual, outrageous
	Antonym: sane, sensible, smart, indifferent, uninterested, unexcited, usual
437.	**Credence**
	Synonym: Noun: belief, trust, reliance
438.	**Credentials**
	Synonym: Noun: qualifications, certification, degrees, accreditation
439.	**Credibility**
	Synonym: Noun: reliability, integrity, character, trustworthiness, believability
	Antonym: dishonesty, lack of character

440.	**Credulous**
	Synonym: Adj: gullible, naive, impressionable, over-trusting, over-trustful, dupable, deceivable, innocent, ingenuous
	Antonym: worldly, suspicious
441.	**Cripple**
	Synonym: Verb: disable, weaken, damage, paralyse, stop, incapacitate
	Antonym: assist, encourage, strengthen
442.	**Cross**
	Synonym: Noun: blend, hybrid, combination, crossbreed, mixture
	Adj: opposed, opposing, contrary, opposite, counter, angry, mad, sullen, moody, touchy
	Antonym: agreeable, pleasant, amiable
443.	**Crude**
	Synonym: Adj: coarse, primitive, unfinished, unrefined, unpolished, rude, vulgar, uncivilized, tasteless, offensive, revolting, gross
	Antonym: refined, processed, finished, courteous, polite, elegant
444.	**Crumble**
	Synonym: Verb: collapse, fragment, disintegrate
445.	**Crumple**
	Synonym: Verb: crinkle, squash, rumple, crush, smash
446.	**Crusade**
	Synonym: Noun: campaign, drive, movement, action, struggle
447.	**Crusader**
	Synonym: Noun: campaigner, activist, champion, visionary, reformer
448.	**Crush**
	Synonym: Verb: smash, squash, pulverize, grind, squeeze, mash, destroy, overcome, quash, overwhelm, topple, demolish
449.	**Crucial**
	Synonym: Adj: critical, essential, important, urgent, grave, vital
	Antonym: unessential, trivial, unimportant
450.	**Cryptic**
	Synonym: Adj: secret, mysterious, hidden, perplexing, obscure
	Antonym: obvious, clear, apparent
451.	**Cuddle**
	Synonym: Verb: snuggle, embrace, hug, muzzle, caress

452.	**Culminate**
	Synonym: Verb: climax, conclude, finish, complete
	Antonym: begin, start, commence
453.	**Cultivate**
	Synonym: Verb: promote, encourage, support, foster, develop, improve
	Antonym: hinder, obstruct, discourage
454.	**Cultivation**
	Synonym: Noun: promotion, advancement, encouragement, fosterage, development
	Antonym: hindrance, obstruction, discouragement
455.	**Cumbersome**
	Synonym: Adj: burdensome, weighty, clumsy, tedious, tiring
	Antonym: manageable, easy, compact
456.	**Curiosity**
	Synonym: Noun: inquisitiveness, questioning, interest, novelty, wonder
	Antonym: indifference, disregard, unconcern
457.	**Curious**
	Synonym: Adj: inquisitive, searching, investigative, peculiar, unusual, weird, strange, odd, exotic, rare
458.	**Cursed**
	Synonym: Adj: jinxed, doomed, ill-fated, dammed
	Antonym: blessed, fortunate
459.	**Curt**
	Synonym: Adj: brusque, brief, short, abrupt
	Antonym: courteous, long-winded, polite
460.	**Curtail**
	Synonym: Verb: shorten, reduce, trim, cut, lessen, decrease, restrict
	Antonym: increase, extend, expand

D

461.	**Dangle**
	Synonym: Verb: hang, drag, trail, droop, swing, sag
462.	**Daunt**
	Synonym: Verb: thwart, deter, intimidate, frighten, dishearten
	Antonym: encourage, rouse, stir
463.	**Daunting**
	Synonym: Adj: intimidating, discouraging, frightening, dispiriting, disheartening, scary
	Antonym: encouraging, heartening
464.	**Dawdle**
	Synonym: Verb: idle, dally, fiddle
	Antonym: hurry, rush, hustle
465.	**Deadlock**
	Synonym: Noun: gridlock, stalemate, impasse, standstill
466.	**Deadly**
	Synonym: Adj: poisonous, lethal, toxic, harmful, dangerous, hazardous
	Antonym: safe, harmless, innocuous
467.	**Dearth**
	Synonym: Noun: lack, scarcity, scarceness, shortage, deficiency, insufficiency, inadequacy, scantiness, rareness
	Antonym: abundance, surfeit
468.	**Debatable**
	Synonym: Adj: disputable, contestable, unsettled, controversial, undecided, moot
469.	**Debauch**
	Synonym: Adj: debauched, dissolute, degenerate, depraved, shameless, sinful, lascivious, promiscuous
	Antonym: wholesome, clean-living
470.	**Debauchery**
	Synonym: Noun: dissipation, degeneracy, turpitude, depravity, perversion, wickedness, sinfulness, impropriety, lewdness
	Antonym: morality, clean-living
471.	**Debility**
	Synonym: Noun: infirmity, handicap, weakness, frailty
472.	**Debilitate**
	Synonym: Verb: weaken, enfeeble, enervate, devitalize, exhaust, incapacitate, cripple, disable
	Antonym: strengthen, invigorate
473.	**Debilitating**
	Synonym: Adj: weakening, enfeebling, enervating, devitalizing, draining, crippling, paralysing
	Antonym: restorative, energizing

474.	**Debonair**
	Synonym: Adj: suave, sophisticated, cultured, polished, genteel, refined, carefree, charming, cheerful
	Antonym: unsophisticated, crude, unrefined
475.	**Debris**
	Synonym: Noun: trash, wreckage, waste, rubble, garbage
476.	**Debunk**
	Synonym: Verb: disprove, expose, refute, hold up, ridicule, deflate
	Antonym: prove, confirm, substantiate
477.	**Decay**
	Synonym: Verb: deteriorate, rot, decompose, disintegrate, decline
478.	**Deceive**
	Synonym: Verb: fool, mislead, trick, delude, dupe
479.	**Deception**
	Synonym: Noun: dishonesty, trickery, fraud, subterfuge
	Antonym: honesty, truthfulness, credibility
480.	**Deceit**
	Synonym: Noun: deception, dishonesty, trickery, cheating, cunning, fraud
	Antonym: honesty, truthfulness, sincerity
481.	**Decipher**
	Synonym: Verb: solve, figure out, decode, understand, crack
482.	**Decorum**
	Synonym: Noun: propriety, decency, etiquette, civility, protocol, demeanour
	Antonym: impropriety, bad manners, rudeness
483.	**Decorous**
	Synonym: Adj: proper, seemly, decent, becoming, befitting, appropriate, suitable, fitting
	Antonym: indecorous, unseemly, immodest
484	**Decrepit**
	Synonym: Adj: feeble, infirm, weak, weakened, debilitated, crippled, dilapidated, deteriorated, rickety, run-down
	Antonym: strong, fit

485.	**Deduce**
	Synonym: Verb: infer, conclude, reason, interpret, assume, analyse
486.	**Defame**
	Synonym: Verb: malign, smear, traduce
487.	**Defer**
	Synonym: Verb: delay, postpone, suspend, table
488.	**Deference**
	Synonym: Noun: respect, respectfulness, esteem, reverence, veneration
	Antonym: disrespect
489.	**Deferential**
	Synonym: Adj: obsequious, humble, respectful, reverent, reverential, obedient, submissive, subservient
	Antonym: arrogant, impolite
490.	**Defiant**
	Synonym: Adj: rebellious, recalcitrant, unruly, stubborn, obdurate, arrogant
	Antonym: obedient, submissive, agreeable
491.	**Deficient**
	Synonym: Adj: lacking, incomplete, wanting, insufficient, short
	Antonym: complete, sufficient, adequate
492.	**Deficit**
	Synonym: Noun: shortage, shortfall, insufficiency, deficiency
493.	**Deformity**
	Synonym: Noun: malformation, disfigurement, abnormality, contortion, imperfection, flaw
494.	**Deflate**
	Synonym: Verb: let down, subdue, go down, reduce, depreciate
	Antonym: blow up, expand, aggrandize, inflate
495.	**Deft**
	Synonym: Adj: skilful, adroit, able, skilled, expert, efficient, dexterous
	Antonym: clumsy, awkward, inept, unskilled
496.	**Defy**
	Synonym: Verb: disobey, resist, elude, escape, foil
	Antonym: obey, surrender

497.	**Degenerate**
	Synonym: Adj: debase, degraded, corrupt, vitiated, decadent, dissolute, debauched, depraved, pervert ***Verb:*** deteriorate, decline, sink, slide, worsen
	Antonym: improve, regenerate
498.	**Degrade**
	Synonym: Verb: humiliate, shame, dishonour, debase, reduce, demean, lower
499.	**Deify**
	Synonym: Verb: exalt, worship, revere, idolize, venerate, adore
	Antonym: denigrate, abuse, criticize
500.	**Dejected**
	Synonym: Adj: depressed, unhappy, sorrowful, disheartened, downcast, despondent, despicable
	Antonym: happy, joyous, cheerful
501.	**Delegate**
	Synonym: ***Verb:*** assign, relegate, name, designate ***Noun:*** representative, spokesperson, diplomat, envoy, ambassador
502.	**Delete**
	Synonym: Verb: erase, eradicate, cancel, remove, cut, omit, obliterate, repeal
	Antonym: insert, add, include
503.	**Deleterious**
	Synonym: Adj: damaging, harmful, destructive, hurtful, injurious, pernicious
	Antonym: beneficial, advantageous Helpful
504.	**Deliberate**
	Synonym: Verb: examine, consider, weigh, ponder, study ***Adj:*** intentional, planned, thoughtful, calculated, prearranged, pre-mediated
	Antonym: spontaneous, hasty, rash
505.	**Deliberately**
	Synonym: Adj: intentionally, purposefully, wilfully, thoughtfully, wittingly
	Antonym: unintentionally, unwittingly
506.	**Delicacy**
	Synonym: Noun: fragility, flimsiness, slightness, frailness, finesse, sensitivity, consideration, gentleness
	Antonym: coarseness, roughness, bluntness, insensitivity

507.	**Delicate**
	Synonym: Adj: fragile, frail, flimsy, fine, slight, small, tactful, sensitive, considerate, careful, diplomatic
	Antonym: rough, coarse, sturdy, easy, safe, inconsiderate, insensitive, careless
508.	**Delicious**
	Synonym: Adj: appetizing, rich, luscious, tasty, savoury, pleasing, delightful
	Antonym: sickening, unpleasant, terrible
509.	**Delinquent**
	Synonym: Noun: criminal, lawbreaker, hoodlum, miscreant, felon ***Adj:*** lax, slack, irresponsible, negligent, derelict
	Antonym: law abider, responsible, conscientious
510.	**Delirious**
	Synonym: Adj: confused, muddled, incoherent, bewildered, hallucinating
	Antonym: lucid, rational, clear-thinking
511.	**Delude**
	Synonym: Verb: deceive, mislead, fool, dupe, trick
512.	**Delusion**
	Synonym: Noun: illusion, misbelief, misconception, fantasy, hallucination
	Antonym: fact, reality, actuality
513.	**Demagogue**
	Synonym: Noun: rabble-rouser, agitator, troublemaker
514.	**Demean**
	Synonym: Verb: cheapen, lower someone's dignity, abase, humiliate, disgrace, dishonour, vilify, denigrate
	Antonym: dignify, exalt
515.	**Demeaning**
	Synonym: Adj: degrading, humiliating, shaming, lowering, undignified
	Antonym: ennobling
516.	**Demolish**
	Synonym: Verb: wreck, ruin, destroy, break, devastate, pulverize, annihilate
	Antonym: build, restore, create

517.	**Demonstrate**
	Synonym: Verb: protest, march, rally, picket, strike, show, display, exhibit, illustrate, describe
518.	**Demoralize**
	Synonym: Verb: dishearten, deflate, depress, discourage, dispirit, crush
	Antonym: encourage, hearten, charge
519.	**Demote**
	Synonym: Verb: lower, downgrade, reduce, degrade, displace
	Antonym: elevate, raise
520.	**Demur**
	Synonym: Adj: modest, unassuming, meek, mild, timid, ladylike
	Antonym: brazen, shameless
521.	**Denigrate**
	Synonym: Verb: criticize, put down, defame, belittle, vilify, malign
	Antonym: praise, compliment, flatter
522.	**Denounce**
	Synonym: Verb: condemn, criticize, censure, castigate, decry, revile, vilify, besmirch
	Antonym: praise
523.	**Dense**
	Synonym: Adj: crowded, crammed, jammed together, compressed, compact
	Antonym: sparse
524.	**Deodorize**
	Synonym: Verb: freshen, sweeten, purify, disinfect, sanitize, sterilize, fumigate, aerate, air, ventilate, depollute
525.	**Depart**
	Synonym: Verb: leave, exit, withdraw, go, embark
	Antonym: arrive, enter, appear
526.	**Dependable**
	Synonym: Adj: trustworthy, trusty, reliable, responsible, faithful, conscientious
	Antonym: undependable, unreliable, untrustworthy
527.	**Depict**
	Synonym: Verb: describe, portray, picture, characterize, represent

528.	**Deplete**
	Synonym: Verb: drain, exhaust, empty, consume, weaken, reduce, diminish
	Antonym: restore, replenish, increase
529.	**Deplorable**
	Synonym: Adj: wretched, miserable, pathetic, regrettable, contemptible, shameful
	Antonym: acceptable, good, agreeable
530.	**Depraved**
	Synonym: Adj: evil, wicked, immoral, corrupt, vile, base, foul
	Antonym: good, moral, virtuous
531.	**Depreciate**
	Synonym: Verb: lower, reduce, devalue, deflate, cut, decrease, diminish
	Antonym: increase, raise, boost
532.	**Deprivation**
	Synonym: Noun: poverty, impoverishment, hardship, destitution, distress
	Antonym: wealth, possession
533.	**Deprived**
	Synonym: Adj: disadvantaged, underprivileged, impoverished, destitute, needy, distressed, forlorn
	Antonym: fortunate, wealthy
534.	**Derelict**
	Synonym: Adj: abandoned, deserted, discarded, forsaken, forlorn, negligent, slack, lax, delinquent, loose, lazy
535.	**Derision**
	Synonym: Noun: ridicule, disrespect, contempt, disdain, disparagement, scorn
536.	**Derogatory**
	Synonym: Adj: disparaging, denigratory, belittling, depreciative, disrespectful, demeaning, discrediting
	Antonym: complimentary, flattering, respectful
537.	**Desecrate**
	Synonym: Verb: violate, spoil, profane, dishonour, disrespect, debase
	Antonym: honour, respect, worship
538.	**Desirable**
	Synonym: Adj: attractive, inviting, agreeable, valuable, worthy, excellent
	Antonym: undesirable, unattractive, repulsive

539.	**Desist**
	Synonym: Verb: abstain, refrain, forbear, back, stop
	Antonym: continue, persist in
540.	**Desolate**
	Synonym: Adj: barren, grim, waste, sterile, deserted, uninhabited, unoccupied, forsaken, godforsaken, abandoned, miserable, sad, unhappy, melancholy, gloomy, despondent, depressed
	Antonym: fertile, populous, joyful
541.	**Despair**
	Synonym: Noun: hopelessness, desperation, dejection, despondency
	Antonym: hope, joy
542.	**Desperado**
	Synonym: Noun: outlaw, criminal, gunman, thug, bandit
543.	**Desperate**
	Synonym: Adj: frantic, hasty, wild, risky, reckless, hopeless, despairing, wretched, depressed
	Antonym: cautious, careful, happy, hopeful, optimistic
544.	**Despicable**
	Synonym: Adj: detestable, disgraceful, contemptible, loathsome
	Antonym: commendable, admirable, laudable
545.	**Despise**
	Synonym: Verb: detest, hate, loathe, scorn, dislike, abhor, disdain
	Antonym: like, admire, respect
546.	**Despotism**
	Synonym: Noun: tyranny, dictatorship, totalitarianism, authoritarianism, absolutism, oppression, repression, suppression, autocracy, monocracy, autarchy
	Antonym: democracy
547.	**Destined**
	Synonym: Adj: fated, ordained, pre-ordained, pre-destined, pre-determined, certain, sure, bound, guaranteed
548.	**Destitute**
	Synonym: Adj: poor, impoverished, penniless, needy
	Antonym: rich, affluent, wealthy
549.	**Destruction**
	Synonym: Noun: ruination, devastation, wrecking, razing, demolition, levelling
	Antonym: preservation, conservation
550.	**Desultory**
	Synonym: Adj: casual, cursory, superficial, perfunctory, random, aimless, unmethodical, unsystematic
	Antonym: keen, systematic, lasting
551.	**Detach**
	Synonym: Verb: disconnect, unfasten, separate, free, loosen
	Antonym: attach, fix, secure
552.	**Detention**
	Synonym: Noun: restraint, delaying, retention
	Antonym: freedom, liberation, release
553.	**Deter**
	Synonym: Verb: discourage, prevent, stop, thwart, block, hinder
	Antonym: encourage, reassure, stimulate
554.	**Deteriorate**
	Synonym: Verb: degrade, fall-apart, decay, crumble, rot, degenerate, corrode
	Antonym: strengthen, grow, harden
555.	**Deterrent**
	Synonym: Noun: check, roadblock, impediment, stumbling block, hurdle, obstacle, embargo
556.	**Detest**
	Synonym: Verb: hate, dislike, despise, loathe, abhor, disdain
	Antonym: love, like, adore
557.	**Detrimental**
	Synonym: Adj: damaging, harmful, destructive, injurious, deleterious, pernicious
	Antonym: helpful, healthy, beneficial
558.	**Devastate**
	Synonym: Verb: ravage, waste, ruin, destroy, despoil, raze
559.	**Devastation**
	Synonym: Noun: destruction, ruin, annihilation, wreckage, demolition, fallout
560.	**Deviant**
	Synonym: abnormal, anomalous, unusual, weird, unorthodox, irregular
	Antonym: normal, usual, regular

561.	**Devilish**
	Synonym: Adj: diabolical, fiendish, satanic, demonic, wicked, evil, sinful, nefarious, monstrous, dreadful, ghastly, difficult, troublesome, problematic, impossible, messy
	Antonym: angelic, saintly, good
562.	**Devilry**
	Synonym: Noun: wickedness, evil, iniquity, devilishness, fiendishness, mischief, misconduct
563.	**Devious**
	Synonym: Adj: underhand, sneaky, tricky, scheming, calculating, deceitful
	Antonym: honest, straightforward
564.	**Devoid**
	Synonym: Adj: lacking, without, free from/or, vacant of, void of, bereft of, drained of, deprived of, depleted of
565.	**Devolve**
	Synonym: Verb: delegate, pass (down/on), hand down/over/on, depute, assign, consign, bestow
	Antonym: centralize, retain
566.	**Devout**
	Synonym: Adj: pious, devoted, dedicated, committed, firm, steadfast, resolute, fervent, intense, vehement, pledged
	Antonym: insincere, lapsed, apathetic
567.	**Dexterity**
	Synonym: Noun: skill, agility, facility, proficiency, adroitness
	Antonym: clumsiness, awkwardness, ineptitude
568.	**Dichotomy**
	Synonym: Noun: division, separation, split, gulf, chasm, polarity
569.	**Diffident**
	Synonym: Adj: shy, bashful, modest, self-effacing, unassuming, introverted, reserved, hesitant, nervous, reluctant
	Antonym: confident, conceited
570.	**Dilapidated**
	Synonym: Adj: broken-down, decaying, crumbling, deteriorated, falling apart
	Antonym: sound, solid, new

571.	**Dilemma**
	Synonym: Noun: quandary, fix, predicament, stalemate, perplexity
572.	**Dilettante**
	Synonym: Noun: dabbler, tinkerer, trifler, nonprofessional, laymen, amateur
	Antonym: Professional
573.	**Diligence**
	Synonym: Noun: persistence, perseverance, earnestness, exertion, application
574.	**Dilly-dally**
	Synonym: Verb: linger, procrastinate, dither, falter, vacillate, waver, fluctuate
	Antonym: hurry, focus
575.	**Diminish**
	Synonym: Verb: lessen, reduce, decrease, recede, shrink, lower, dwindle, subside
	Antonym: increase, magnify, enlarge
576.	**Diminutive**
	Synonym: Adj: tiny, small, little, minuscule, pygmy, Lilliputian
	Antonym: enormous, huge, gargantuan
577.	**Dingy**
	Synonym: Adj: shabby, dirty, seedy, run-down, grimy, drab, gloomy
	Antonym: luxurious, shiny, clean
578.	**Dire**
	Synonym: Adj: grievous, awful, alarming, terrible, horrible, fearsome
579.	**Disaster**
	Synonym: Noun: catastrophe, tragedy, misfortune, calamity, accident, mishap
	Antonym: fortune, blessing, blessedness
580.	**Disastrous**
	Synonym: Adj: calamitous, ruinous, catastrophic, devastating, tragic, fatal
	Antonym: fortunate, beneficial, helpful
581.	**Discard**
	Synonym: Verb: dispose of, throw away, throw out, get rid of, reject
	Antonym: keep, acquire
582.	**Discreet**
	Synonym: Adj: careful, circumspect, cautious, wary, guarded, tactful
	Antonym: Obtrusive

583.	**Discrepancy**
	Synonym: Noun: inconsistency, conflict, disparity, error, incongruity, disagreement
	Antonym: match, consistency, agreement
584.	**Discrimination**
	Synonym: Verb: bigotry, prejudice, bias, intolerance, racism
585.	**Disdain**
	Synonym: Verb: loathe, despise, hate, abhor, spurn, hold in contempt
	Antonym: like, admire, respect
586.	**Disfigure**
	Synonym: Verb: deface, deform, damage, scar, blemish, flaw
587.	**Disgrace**
	Synonym: Noun: dishonour, shame, embarrassment, humiliation, stain, taint
	Antonym: honour, glory, credit, distinction
588.	**Disguise**
	Synonym: Verb: camouflage, mask, conceal, veil, cloak, cover
	Antonym: uncover, reveal, disclose
589.	**Disgust**
	Synonym: Verb: sicken, revolt, shock, nauseate, repel, appal, loathe
	Antonym: please, delight
590.	**Disheveled**
	Synonym: Adj: messy, sloppy, ruffled, unkempt, tousled, disorderly
	Antonym: neat, tidy
591.	**Disintegrate**
	Synonym: Verb: shatter, crumble, decompose, fragment, decay
592.	**Dismal**
	Synonym: Adj: bleak, gloomy, cheerless, dreary, sombre, depressing
	Antonym: cheerful, sunny, bright
593.	**Dismantle**
	Synonym: Verb: disassemble, tear down, remove, raze, strip, fell
	Antonym: build, assemble, construct
594.	**Dismay**
	Synonym: Verb: dishearten, distress, alarm, discourage, frighten, appal
	Antonym: encourage, hearten, relieve, encouragement, assurance

595.	**Disown**
	Synonym: Verb: reject, spurn, throw out, disclaim, repudiate, forsake
	Antonym: adopt, claim, own
596.	**Disparage**
	Synonym: Verb: criticize, put down, belittle, malign, ridicule, defame
	Antonym: compliment, praise, commend
597.	**Dispel**
	Synonym: Verb: scatter, disperse, banish, repel, dismiss, remove, expel
598.	**Dispense**
	Synonym: Verb: distribute, give, furnish, supply, allot, administer, forgo, abstain, cancel, waive, relinquish, release
599.	**Disperse**
	Synonym: Verb: scatter, disband, dissolve, separate, spread
	Antonym: assemble, gather, collect
600.	**Dissect**
	Synonym: Verb: analyse, examine, study, scrutinize, inspect, explore
601.	**Disseminate**
	Synonym: Verb: distribute, disperse, broadcast, scatter, spread, circulate
	Antonym: gather, collect
602.	**Dissent**
	Synonym: Verb: disagree, oppose, object, differ, protest
	Antonym: agree, consent, concur
603.	**Distress**
	Synonym: Verb: upset, disturb, worry, trouble, sadden, depress ***Noun:*** agony, sorrow, anguish, misery, sadness, depression
	Antonym: comfort, console, relieve, relief, solace, comfort
604.	**Distrust**
	Synonym: Noun: mistrust, suspicion, disbelief, misgiving, scepticism, wariness
	Antonym: trust, faith, belief
605.	**Distorted**
	Synonym: Adj: twisted, contorted, buckled, deformed, misshaped, disfigured, crooked
	Antonym: straight

606.	**Diverge**
	Synonym: Verb: separate, divide, split, fork, swerve, part
	Antonym: merge, join, unite
607.	**Diverse**
	Synonym: Adj: varied, assorted, diversified, unlike, mixed
	Antonym: identical, similar, same
608.	**Diversify**
	Synonym: Verb: mix, spread out, branch out, expand, vary, broaden
	Antonym: limit, reduce, concentrate
609.	**Divert**
	Synonym: Verb: deflect, shift, sidetrack, swerve, shunt
610.	**Divulge**
	Synonym: Verb: tell, reveal, bare, expose, disclose, release
	Antonym: hide, conceal, cloak
611.	**Dizzy**
	Synonym: light-headed, reeling, off balance, unsteady, vertiginous, wobbly
	Antonym: steady, balanced, clear-headed
612.	**Docile**
	Synonym: Adj: gentle, passive, subdued, agreeable, tame, obedient
	Antonym: unruly, rebellious, wild
613.	**Dogged**
	Synonym: Adj: tenacious, persistent, persevering, determined, stubborn, relentless
	Antonym: irresolute, half-hearted
614.	**Dogma**
	Synonym: Noun: belief, doctrine, views, convictions, gospel, canon
615.	**Doldrums**
	Synonym: Noun: depression, lassitude, malaise, listlessness, blues
616.	**Doleful**
	Synonym: Adj: mournful, dismal, gloomy, morose, melancholy
	Antonym: cheerful
617.	**Domain**
	Synonym: Noun: territory, area, region, zone, realm, empire, scope

618.	**Dominant**
	Synonym: Adj: strongest, prominent, prime, controlling, principal
	Antonym: weakest, subordinate, inferior
619.	**Domineer**
	Synonym: Verb: browbeat, bully, intimidate, pressurize, overbear
620.	**Domineering**
	Synonym: Adj: overbearing, authoritarian, imperious, high-handed, high and mighty, autocratic, bossy, arrogant, haughty, masterful
	Antonym: meek
621.	**Doom**
	Synonym: Noun: destiny, lot, fate, dearth, extinction, ruin ***Verb:*** fate, destiny, ordain
622.	**Dormant**
	Synonym: Adj: inactive, sleeping, lethargic, sluggish, passive, latent
	Antonym: active, wakeful, alert
623.	**Dowdy**
	Synonym: Adj: unfashionable, dull, outmoded, out-of-style, inelegant, ill-dressed, shabby, untidy
	Antonym: fashionable, savvy, sassy
624.	**Drastic**
	Synonym: Adj: extreme, serious, forceful, far- reaching, momentous, substantial, severe, rigorous, draconian
	Antonym: mild, moderate
625.	**Dreadful**
	Synonym: Adj: fearful, frightful, ghastly, horrible, awful, offensive
626.	**Dreary**
	Synonym: Adj: uninteresting, tedious, wearisome, dismal, cheerless, bleak
	Antonym: interesting, exciting, cheerful
627.	**Drift**
	Synonym: Verb: wander, tramp, ramble, amble, meander
628.	**Dubious**
	Synonym: Adj: questionable, debatable, doubtful, uncertain, unclear
	Antonym: certain, sure, definite
629.	**Dumbfound**
	Synonym: Verb: astonish, stun, flabbergast, stupefy, render speechless

630.	**Duplicity**
	Synonym: Noun: double-dealing, deception, backstabbing, dishonesty, disloyalty, artifice
	Antonym: loyalty, honesty, faithfulness
631.	**Dwindle**
	Synonym: Verb: diminish, decrease, reduce, fade, wither, ebb, shrink, disappear
	Antonym: increase, flourish, grow, thrive
632.	**Dysfunctional**
	Synonym: Adj: maladjusted, troubled, abnormal, impaired, sick, unhealthy
	Antonym: functional, normal, healthy

E

633.	**Earnest**
	Synonym: Adj: serious, steady, intense, committed, dedicated, assiduous, devout, heartfelt, wholehearted, sincere, fervent, ardent
	Antonym: frivolous, apathetic, half-hearted
634.	**Ebullient**
	Synonym: Adj: exuberant, buoyant, cheerful, joyful, exhilarated, elated, jubilant, animated, effervescent, vivacious
	Antonym: depressed, gloomy, dejected
635.	**Eccentric**
	Synonym: Adj: odd, peculiar, weird, queer, strange, bizarre
636.	**Eccentricity**
	Synonym: Noun: peculiarity, oddness, quirk, idiosyncrasy, abnormality, weirdness
637.	**Echelon**
	Synonym: Noun: level, rank, grade, rung, stratum, position, order, sector
638.	**Eclectic**
	Synonym: Adj: selective, discriminating, discerning
	Antonym: dogmatic
639.	**Ecstasy**
	Synonym: Noun: pleasure, delight, rapture, joy, bliss, elation
	Antonym: misery, suffering, torment
640.	**Ecstatic**
	Synonym: Adj: delighted, overjoyed, happy, elated, joyful
	Antonym: gloomy, despondent, unhappy

641.	**Efface**
	Synonym: Verb: erase, eradicate, expunge, blot out, rub out, wipe, eliminate, delete
	Antonym: preserve, make one's presence felt
642.	**Effervescence**
	Synonym: Noun: sparkle, vivacity, liveliness, animation, exuberance, buoyancy
	Antonym: depression
643.	**Efficacious**
	Synonym: Adj: effective, constructive, fruitful, potent, powerful, useful
	Antonym: inefficacious, ineffective
644.	**Efficient**
	Synonym: Adj: effective, competent, productive, capable, practical
	Antonym: ineffective, inefficient
645.	**Effusive**
	Synonym: Adj: gushing, unrestrained, unreserved, extravagant, demonstrative, lavish
	Antonym: restrained, reserved, limited
646.	**Egregious**
	Synonym: Adj: shocking, appalling, horrific, awful, dreadful, frightful, abominable, abhorrent, outrageous, harrowing, unspeakable, glaring, blatant, scandalous, unforgivable, unpardonable, intolerable
	Antonym: marvelous, wonderful
647.	**Elated**
	Synonym: Adj: delighted, excited, happy, overjoyed, joyful, cheerful
	Antonym: sad, unhappy, gloomy morose
648.	**Elegant**
	Synonym: Adj: tasteful; refined; dignified ***Noun:*** richness, grandeur, grace, dignity, refinement
	Antonym: tastelessness, plainness, crudeness
649.	**Elephantine**
	Synonym: Adj: enormous, huge, great, massive, giant, immense, tremendous, colossal, mammoth, gargantuan, titanic
	Antonym: small, little, tiny
650.	**Elevate**
	Synonym: Verb: raise, promote, upgrade, improve, advance, exalt, aggrandize, maximize
	Antonym: lower, demote, degrade

651.	**Eliminate**
	Synonym: Verb: remove, omit, exclude, expel, erase, drop, cancel
	Antonym: include, admit, obtain
652.	**Eloquent**
	Synonym: Adj: persuasive, expressive, articulate, fluent, poetic, impassioned
	Antonym: dull, ordinary, weak
653.	**Elude**
	Synonym: Verb: avoid, dodge, escape, evade, shun
	Antonym: encounter, face, chase
654.	**Elusive**
	Synonym: Adj: evasive, illusory, fleeting, slippery, tricky, baffling, puzzling, mysterious, confusing, deceptive
655.	**Emancipation**
	Synonym: Noun: freeing, liberation, release, unchaining, unfettering, unshackling, untying, unyoking, unbridling
	Antonym: enslavement, slavery
656.	**Emasculate**
	Synonym: Verb: weaken, debilitate, enfeeble, enervate, dilute, castrate, sterilize
	Antonym: strengthen
657.	**Embargo**
	Synonym: Noun: ban, prohibition, proscription, blockage, stoppage, restriction
658.	**Embarrass**
	Synonym: Verb: shame, humiliate, upset, discomfort, humble
659.	**Embellish**
	Synonym: Verb: adorn, decorate, garnish, enhance, enrich, elaborate
660.	**Embezzle**
	Synonym: Verb: steal, defraud, swindle, cheat, pilfer, rob, misuse
661.	**Embrace**
	Synonym: Verb: hug, hold, clasp, caress, enfold, grasp, include, cover, enclose, contain, involve, encompass
	Antonym: exclude, omit, ignore, neglect
662.	**Empathy**
	Synonym: Noun: understanding, appreciation, affinity, communion, sympathy, rapport

663.	**Emphasis**
	Synonym: Noun: stress, weight, accent, force, importance, attention
664.	**Emphasize**
	Synonym: Verb: stress, accent, highlight, spotlight, press
	Antonym: minimize, underplay, understate
665.	**Emphatic**
	Synonym: Adj: strong, definite, powerful, forceful, decisive, assertive
	Antonym: weak, hesitant, indecisive
666.	**Enamoured**
	Synonym: Adj: infatuated, besotted with, smitten with, captivated by, charmed by, entranced by, enraptured by
	Antonym: indifferent to
667.	**Enchant**
	Synonym: Verb: bewitch, charm, conjure, delight, please, fascinate, enthral, captivate
	Antonym: release, exorcise, free, bore, tire, repel
668.	**Enchanting**
	Synonym: Adj: charming, fascinating, captivating, intriguing, alluring
669.	**Endearing**
	Synonym: Adj: lovable, adorable, dear, sweet, charming, winning
	Antonym: repulsive, disgusting, sickening
670.	**Endeavour**
	Synonym: Verb: attempt, try, undertake, strive, aim, venture, seek
671.	**Endowment**
	Synonym: Noun: gift, funding, contribution, donation, grant
672.	**Endurance**
	Synonym: Noun: stamina, durability, persistence, fortitude, hardiness, tolerance
	Antonym: weakness, weariness, frailty
673.	**Endure**
	Synonym: Verb: last, continue, remain, persist, hold, stay prevail, suffer, experience, bear, tolerate, withstand, sustain
	Antonym: fail, decay, perish, escape, succumb

674.	**Enervate**
	Synonym: Verb: exhaust, tire, fatigue, weary, devitalize, enfeeble, debilitate, prostrate
	Antonym: invigorate, vivify, animate
675.	**Engaging**
	Synonym: Adj: charming, captivating, enchanting, pleasing, likable, delightful
	Antonym: unlikable, unpleasant, dull
676.	**Engross**
	Synonym: Verb: involve, immerse, absorb, occupy, preoccupy, engage
	Antonym: bore, tire, weary
677.	**Enigma**
	Synonym: Noun: puzzle, riddle, mystery, secret, problem, question
678.	**Ennui**
	Synonym: Noun: boredom, tedium, listlessness, lethargy, languor, weariness
	Antonym: animation, contentment
679.	**Enormous**
	Synonym: Adj: huge, giant, immense, gigantic, colossal, tremendous, mammoth
	Antonym: tiny, small, slight
680.	**Entangle**
	Synonym: Verb: catch, trap, involve, ravel, ensnarl
	Antonym: disentangle, free, extricate
681.	**Enthral**
	Synonym: Verb: captivate, charm, enchant, bewitch, fascinate, delight, ensnare, dazzle
	Antonym: bore, repel, disenchant
682.	**Entice**
	Synonym: Verb: attract, allure, insight, stimulate
	Antonym: discourage, dissuade, frighten
683.	**Entity**
	Synonym: Noun: being, body, creature, individual, organism, person, object, article, thing
	Antonym: nonentity, non-existence
684.	**Enunciate**
	Synonym: Verb: pronounce, articulate, speak
685.	**Envious**
	Synonym: Adj: jealous, covetous, desirous, yearning, resentful

686.	**Envy**
	Synonym: Verb: covet, desire, want, crave, resent, begrudge ***Noun:*** jealousy, resentment, spite, grudging, malice
687.	**Ephemeral**
	Synonym: Adj: transitory, transient, fleeting, passing, short-lived, momentary, brief, short, cursory, impermanent
	Antonym: long-lived, permanent
688.	**Epidemic**
	Synonym: Noun: outbreak, widespread illness/ disease, eruption, upsurge, upswing, mushrooming
	Antonym: limited, local
689.	**Epitome**
	Synonym: Noun: personification, embodiment, paragon, exemplar, model
	Antonym: complete version, full text
690.	**Equanimity**
	Synonym: Noun: composure, calmness, self-control, presence of mind, serenity, tranquility, imperturbability, equilibrium
	Antonym: anxiety
691.	**Equitable**
	Synonym: Adj: fair, even, just, impartial, objective, unbiased, reasonable
	Antonym: uneven, unfair, unjustice
692.	**Equivocal**
	Synonym: Adj: ambiguous, indefinite, indeterminate, imprecise, inexact, cryptic, enigmatic, ambivalent, roundabout, circumlocutory, equivocating, prevaricating
	Antonym: unequivocal, definite
693.	**Equivocate**
	Synonym: Verb: evade, sidestep, mince words, beat around the bush, hedge, waffle
694.	**Eradicate**
	Synonym: Verb: erase, eliminate, remove, destroy, exterminate, demolish
	Antonym: create, establish, generate
695.	**Erosion**
	Synonym: Noun: wear off, deterioration, wasting, corrosion, disintegration, weathering

696.	**Erotic**
	Synonym: Adj: sexually arousing, exciting, stimulating, titillating, libidinous, lustful, sensual, seductive
697.	**Erratic**
	Synonym: Adj: irregular, unpredictable, unsteady, uneven, odd, eccentric
	Antonym: regular, normal, constant
698.	**Erroneous**
	Synonym: Adj: wrong, incorrect, false, mistaken, inaccurate
	Antonym: right, correct, true, accurate
699.	**Erudite**
	Synonym: Adj: learned, scholarly, well educated, lettered, sagacious, cerebral, pedant
	Antonym: ignorant, ill-educated
700.	**Erudition**
	Synonym: Noun: learning, scholarliness, enlightenment, understanding
	Antonym: ignorance
701.	**Erupt**
	Synonym: Verb: burst, explode, expel, eject, spew, gush, discharge
702.	**Eruption**
	Synonym: Noun: upheaval, cataclysm, blast, ejection, explosion, surge
703.	**Escalate**
	Synonym: Verb: increase rapidly, soar, shoot up, surge, grow, zoom, boom
	Antonym: plunge, shrink
704.	**Escalation**
	Synonym: Noun: rapid increase, rise, hike, upsurge, spiralling, intensification, aggravation, enlargement, magnification, amplification, augmentation, expansion
	Antonym: relaxation
705.	**Esoteric**
	Synonym: Adj: arcane, incomprehensible, abstruse, obscure, mysterious
	Antonym: obvious, comprehensible, simple
706.	**Esteem**
	Synonym: Noun: respect, admiration, honour, reverence, regard
	Antonym: contempt, disdain, ridicule

707.	**Estrange**
	Synonym: Verb: alienate, turn away, distance, severe, sow dissension
	Antonym: attract, unite, close, intimate, friendly
708.	**Eternity**
	Synonym: Noun: infinity, forever, timelessness, immortality, perpetuity
709.	**Ethereal**
	Synonym: Adj: delicate, exquisite, elegant, graceful, celestial, heavenly, unearthly, paradisiacal, elysian
	Antonym: tangible, substantial, earthly
710.	**Ethical**
	Synonym: moral, virtuous, upright, honourable
711.	**Ethos**
	Synonym: Noun: the distinctive character, spirit and attitudes of a culture, people, movement, era, etc.
712.	**Etiquette**
	Synonym: Noun: manners, conduct, behaviour, customs, decorum, protocol, courtesy
713.	**Eulogy**
	Synonym: Noun: accolade, testimonial, commendations, acclaim
714.	**Euphonious**
	Synonym: Adj: pleasant-sounding, sweet-sounding, mellow, mellifluous, rhythmical, soothing, harmonious, melodious, symphonious
	Antonym: cacophonous
715.	**Euphoria**
	Synonym: Noun: joy, happiness, ecstasy, elation, rapture, bliss
	Antonym: misery, depression, despondency
716.	**Euphoric**
	Synonym: Adj: elated, joyful, delighted, gleeful, excited, exhilarated, jubilant, ecstatic, enraptured, on cloud nine, on top of the world, over the moon
	Antonym: miserable
717.	**Everlasting**
	Synonym: Adj: eternal, never-ending, perpetual, immutable, abiding, enduring, timeless, perennial
	Antonym: transient, temporary

718.	**Evince**
	Synonym: Verb: reveal, show, make, manifest, indicate, exhibit, demonstrate
	Antonym: conceal
719.	**Exaggerate**
	Synonym: Verb: overstate, magnify, aggrandize, amplify
	Antonym: play down, understate
720.	**Evoke**
	Synonym: Verb: summon, awaken, invoke, provoke, arouse, induce
	Antonym: suppress, prevent, repress
721.	**Exacerbate**
	Synonym: Verb: aggravate, worsen, intensify, inflame, provoke
	Antonym: diminish, soften, mitigate
722.	**Exacting**
	Synonym: Adj: demanding, meticulous, painstaking, strict
	Antonym: undemanding, imprecise, sloppy
723.	**Exalted**
	Synonym: Adj: revered, glorified, honourable, noble, dignified, lordly, high, grand
	Antonym: lowly, common, humble, low
724.	**Exasperate**
	Synonym: Verb: annoy, irritate, bother, irk, provoke, anger, infuriate
	Antonym: calm, tranquilize, soothe
725.	**Exasperating**
	Synonym: Adj: infuriating, annoying, irritating, maddening, antagonizing, provoking
	Antonym: pleasing, delightful
726.	**Exasperation**
	Synonym: Noun: irritation, annoyance, vexation, anger, fury, rage, wrath, resentment, disgruntlement, disgust, discontent
	Antonym: pleasure, delight
727.	**Exclusive**
	Synonym: Adj: select, high-class, elite, elegant, special, premier, sole
	Antonym: open, partial, inclusive of
728.	**Excessive**
	Synonym: Adj: extreme, unreasonable, overdone, undue, excess
	Antonym: deficient, conservative, insufficient

729.	**Excruciating**
	Synonym: Adj: painful; agonizing, terrible; irritating, unbearable, unendurable, torturous, insufferable
	Antonym: delightful, soothing, anaesthetizing
730.	**Exempt**
	Synonym: Adj: immune, excused, free, released, spared
	Antonym: responsible, liable, subject
731.	**Exemplary**
	Synonym: model, ideal, prototypical, classic, quintessential, superb
	Antonym: terrible, substandard, awful
732.	**Exemplify**
	Synonym: Verb: embody, depict, represent, typify
733.	**Exhaustion**
	Synonym: Noun: fatigue, weariness, tiredness, draining, depletion
	Antonym: strength, energy, replenishment
734.	**Exhaustive**
	Synonym: Adj: thorough, complete, extensive, full, total, profound
	Antonym: incomplete, partial, superficial
735.	**Exhilarate**
	Synonym: Verb: stimulate, excite, energize, invigorate, cheer, delight
	Antonym: sadden, depress, dishearten
736.	**Exodus**
	Synonym: Noun: flight, exit, departure, withdrawal, migration, emigration
	Antonym: return, influx, immigration
737.	**Exonerate**
	Synonym: Verb: absolve, discharge, relieve, liberate, excuse, exempt
	Antonym: charge, convict
738.	**Exorbitant**
	Synonym: Verb: unreasonable, excessive, overpriced, extreme, enormous
	Antonym: reasonable, modest, fair, just
739.	**Exorcism**
	Synonym: Noun: purging, expulsion, casting out, banishment

740.	**Exotic**
	Synonym: Adj: foreign, strange, unfamiliar, unusual, unique, different
	Antonym: familiar, normal, ordinary
741.	**Expedient**
	Synonym: Adj: useful, helpful, practical, profitable, beneficial, worthwhile
	Antonym: futile, ineffective, useless
742.	**Expedite**
	Synonym: Verb: speed up, hasten, grease the wheels, facilitate, accelerate, rush
	Antonym: slow, bog down, stop
743.	**Expel**
	Synonym: Verb: discharge, eject, oust, banish, exile, remove
	Antonym: admit, accept, invite
744.	**Explicit**
	Synonym: Adj: clear, graphic, unambiguous, frank, express, specific, straightforward
	Antonym: unclear, ambiguous, indirect
745.	**Explore**
	Synonym: Verb: examine, probe research, pry, search, traverse, survey, scout
746.	**Exquisite**
	Synonym: Adj: delicate, elegant, beautiful, precious, perfect, lovely
	Antonym: ugly, common, plain
747.	**Extenuate**
	Synonym: Verb: excuse, mitigate, palliate, soften, reduce, temper, weaken, diminish, lessen, moderate
	Antonym: Aggravate
748.	**Extenuating**
	Synonym: Adj: mitigating, vindicating, moderating, qualifying, softening, tempering, diminishing, lessening
	Antonym: aggravating
749.	**Exterminate**
	Synonym: Verb: destroy, kill, murder, eliminate, slaughter, massacre
	Antonym: save, conserve, create

750.	**Extinct**
	Synonym: Adj: vanished, dead, lost, deceased, departed
	Antonym: living, thriving, flourishing
751.	**Extinguish**
	Synonym: Verb: put out, quench, smother, douse, suffocate, destroy, demolish, eliminate, erase, crush
	Antonym: light, start, ignite, heighten, foster
752.	**Extol**
	Synonym: Verb: praise, acclaim, honour, laud, applaud, glorify, celebrate
	Antonym: disparage, condemn, vilify
753.	**Extort**
	Synonym: Verb: blackmail, exact, extract, force, coerce, cheat, fleece
754.	**Extraneous**
	Synonym: Adj: unrelated; irrelevant, extra, unnecessary, inessential, superfluous, needless, irrelevant
	Antonym: essential, necessary, needed
755.	**Extraordinary**
	Synonym: Adj: unusual, uncommon, rare, exceptional, unique, amazing
	Antonym: usual, common, normal, average
756.	**Extravagant**
	Synonym: Adj: lavish, wasteful, excessive, exorbitant, spendthrift, wild
	Antonym: thrifty, frugal, economical
757.	**Extremist**
	Synonym: Noun: radical, zealot, fanatic, revolutionist, hard liner
	Antonym: moderate, centrist
758.	**Extrovert**
	Synonym: Noun: gregarious, sociable
	Antonym: introvert, lone, hermit
759.	**Exuberance**
	Synonym: Noun: enthusiasm, vitality, exhilaration, eagerness, excitement
	Antonym: despair, dejection, depression
760.	**Exuberant**
	Synonym: Adj: spirited, exciting, lively, zestful, enthusiastic
	Antonym: lethargic, dispirited, solemn

	F
761.	**Fabulous**
	Synonym: Adj: marvellous, amazing, incredible, remarkable, fantastic
	Antonym: ordinary, routine, common
762	**Fallacious**
	Synonym: Adj: untrue, false, erroneous, incorrect, wrong, mistaken
	Antonym: true, correct, right
763.	**Fallible**
	Synonym: Adj: imperfect, prone to error, faulty, defective, errand
	Antonym: infallible, perfect, inerrant
764.	**Fanatic**
	Synonym: Noun: zealot, extremist, partisan, freak ***Adj:*** fanatical, extremist, zealous, fervent, enthusiastic
765.	**Fanaticism**
	Synonym: Noun: zeal, dogma, single-mindedness
766.	**Farce**
	Synonym: Noun: mockery, nonsense, travesty, burlesque, satire
767.	**Farfetched**
	Synonym: Adj: unbelievable, incredible, improbable, unlikely, implausible
	Antonym: believable, credible, plausible
768.	**Fascinate**
	Synonym: Verb: enrapture, charm, enchant, captivate, delight
	Antonym: bore, disenchant
769.	**Fascinating**
	Synonym: Adj: enthralling, captivating, engrossing, absorbing, interesting
	Antonym: boring, uninteresting, dull
770.	**Fastidious**
	Synonym: Adj: scrupulous, painstaking, meticulous, assiduous, perfectionist, overcritical
	Antonym: easy-going, sloppy
771.	**Fathom**
	Synonym: Verb: understand, comprehend, work out, follow, perceive, penetrate, measure

772.	**Fathomless**
	Synonym: Adj: enigmatic, mysterious, impenetrable, profound, unfathomable, immeasurable, endless, infinite
	Antonym: shallow
773.	**Fatigue**
	Synonym: Noun: weariness tiredness, exhaustion
	Antonym: strength, vigour, vitality
774.	**Fatuous**
	Synonym: Adj: silly, foolish or stupid
775.	**Faze**
	Synonym: Verb: bother, disturb, discompose, perturb, upset, unnerve
776.	**Feasible**
	Synonym: Adj: possible, practical, achievable, attainable, reasonable
	Antonym: Impractical, impossible
777.	**Fecund**
	Synonym: Adj: fertile, fruitful, productive, high-yielding, prolific, proliferating, propagative, generative
	Antonym: barren
778.	**Feeble**
	Synonym: Adj: weak, faint, unconvincing, lacking force, not effective, frail, fragile, infirm, impotent, enfeebled, enervated, debilitated, tottering, tottery, ineffective, ineffectual, unconvincing, implausible, unsatisfactory, flimsy, insubstantial, futile, faint-hearted, spiritless, lily-livered, chicken- livered, pigeon-hearted
	Antonym: strong, vigorous, effective
779.	**Felicity**
	Synonym: Noun: happiness, joy, joyfulness, euphoria, delight, gaiety, eloquence, aptness
	Antonym: unhappiness, inappropriateness
780.	**Felonious**
	Synonym: Adj: criminal, evil, wicked, illegal, unlawful, larcenous
	Antonym: moral, good, angelic
781.	**Ferocious**
	Synonym: Adj: fierce, savage, cruel, dangerous, violent, bloody, ruthless, intense, extreme, strong, severe, acute
	Antonym: tame, gentle, mild

782.	**Ferocity**
	Synonym: Noun: savagery, brutality, fierceness, aggression, ruthlessness, intensity, severity, extremity
	Antonym: gentleness
783.	**Fervent**
	Synonym: Adj: ardent, zealous, passionate, enthusiastic, intense, heated
	Antonym: dispassionate, apathetic, cool
784.	**Fervour**
	Synonym: Noun: intensity, passion, enthusiasm, zeal, ardour, spirit
	Antonym: apathy, indifference, coolness
785.	**Fiasco**
	Synonym: Noun: mess, disaster, ruin, defeat, failure
	Antonym: victory, success, triumph
786.	**Fickle**
	Synonym: Adj: unpredictable, changeable, capricious, erratic, whimsical, variable, unpredictable
	Antonym: stable, constant, reliable
787.	**Fictitious**
	Synonym: Adj: imaginary, made-up, untrue, created, fabricated
	Antonym: true, factual, real
788.	**Fidelity**
	Synonym: Adj: faithfulness, loyalty, integrity, reliability
	Antonym: infidelity, disloyalty, unfaithfulness
789.	**Fierce**
	Synonym: Adj: violent, savage, ferocious, furious, wild, powerful
	Antonym: gentle, moderate, tame
790.	**Figurative**
	Synonym: Adj: metaphorical, symbolic, emblematic, representative, illustrative
	Antonym: literal, exact
791.	**Filthy**
	Synonym: Adj: dirty, foul, grimy, soiled, muddy
	Antonym: clean, washed, cleansed
792.	**Finesse**
	Synonym: Noun: skill, adroitness, artfulness, savvy, knack, expertise
	Antonym: incompetence, clumsiness

793.	**Finicky**
	Synonym: Adj: fussy, picky, discriminating, choosy, particular, fastidious
	Antonym: easy-to-please, undiscriminating
794.	**Fissure**
	Synonym: Noun: opening, crevice, cleft, hole, chasm
795.	**Flabbergasted**
	Synonym: Adj: astonished, amazed, astounded, bamboozled
796.	**Flagrant**
	Synonym: Adj: outrageous, blatant, glaring, obvious, overt, conspicuous, naked, barefaced
	Antonym: unobstrusive, slight
797.	**Flamboyant**
	Synonym: Adj: showy, flashy, garish, ostentatious
	Antonym: dull, reserved, understated
798.	**Flaunt**
	Synonym: display, show-off, vaunt, advertise
	Antonym: strut, conceal, hide
799.	**Flaw**
	Synonym: Noun: defect, blemish, fault, imperfection, deficiency, shortcoming, limitation, shortfall, lack, want, deformity
	Antonym: perfect, flawless, stainless
800.	**Flicker**
	Synonym: Verb: flutter, flash, blink, twinkle, waver
801.	**Flimsy**
	Synonym: Adj: frail, fragile, delicate, feeble, weak, unsubstantial
	Antonym: solid, strong, substantial
802.	**Flippant**
	Synonym: Adj: disrespectful, irreverent, insolent, rude, fresh, sassy
	Antonym: respectful, reverent, polite
803.	**Flirtatious**
	Synonym: Adj: teasing, enticing, inviting, tantalizing, coquettish, provocative
804.	**Flounder**
	Synonym: Verb: wallow, struggle, tumble, lurch, falter, waver

805.	**Flourish**
	Synonym: Verb: grow, succeed, prosper, thrive, develop, bloom
	Antonym: decline, fail, wither
806.	**Fluctuate**
	Synonym: Verb: waver, vacillate, vary, sway, oscillate, wobble
	Antonym: stabilize, settle, persist
807.	**Flummox**
	Synonym: Verb: bewilder, baffle, bemuse, perplex, puzzle, confuse, confound, nonplus, bamboozle, discombobulate
808.	**Flummoxed**
	Synonym: Adj: baffled, bewildered, mystified, bemused, perplexed, puzzled, confused, confounded, nonplussed, bamboozled
809.	**Fluster**
	Synonym: Verb: make nervous, unnerve, agitate, ruffle, upset, disturb, alarm, perturb, confuse
	Antonym: calm, pacify, please
810.	**Flutter**
	Synonym: Noun: wave, rush, surge, flash, tremble, quiver, shake, shaking, shudder, fluster, flurry, bustle, panic
811.	**Flux**
	Synonym: Noun: flow, movement, changeability, variability, inconstancy, fluidity, instability, fluctuation, variation, shift, alteration, swing, movement, oscillation, alternation, rise and fall, rising and falling see-sawing, yo-yoing
	Antonym: stability, constancy
812.	**Foil**
	Synonym: Verb: thwart, frustrate, hinder, prevent, baffle
	Antonym: aid, abet, support
813.	**Forbidden**
	Synonym: Adj: prohibited, outlawed, illegal, taboo, proscribed
	Antonym: allowed, permitted
814.	**Foreboding**
	Synonym: Noun: premonition, apprehension, dread, intuition, misgiving

815.	**Forecast**
	Synonym: Noun: prediction, prophecy, prognosis, foretelling
816.	**Foresee**
	Synonym: Verb: anticipate, envision, predict, foretell
817.	**Forfeit**
	Synonym: Verb: lose, renounce, relinquish, sacrifice, yield
	Antonym: keep, retain
818.	**Forgery**
	Synonym: Noun: fake, fraud, counterfeit, sham, imitation, copy
819.	**Forlorn**
	Synonym: Adj: forsaken; pitiful, unhappy
820.	**Formidable**
	Synonym: Adj: awesome, impressive, intimidating, bold, forbidding, difficult
	Antonym: weak, insignificant, easy
821.	**Fornication**
	Synonym: Noun: extramarital relations, adultery, infidelity, unfaithfulness, cuckoldry
822.	**Forsake**
	Synonym: Verb: renounce, forswear, abandon, desert, leave, quit
823.	**Fortitude**
	Synonym: Noun: courage, bravery, valour, resolution, determination
	Antonym: cowardice, weakness, timidity
824.	**Fortuitous**
	Synonym: Adj: unexpected, unanticipated, unpredictable, unforeseen, incidental, random, unplanned
	Antonym: predictable
825.	**Founder**
	Synonym: Verb: sink, swamp, submerge, wallow
826.	**Fractious**
	Synonym: Adj: cross, irritable, peevish
827.	**Fragile**
	Synonym: Adj: breakable, delicate, weak, brittle, frail, feeble
	Antonym: strong, sturdy, unbreakable

828.	**Fragment**
	Synonym: Noun: portion, part, piece, section, segment
829.	**Fragrance**
	Synonym: Noun: aroma, scent, smell, odour, perfume
	Antonym: stink, reek, stench
830.	**Fragrant**
	Synonym: Adj: aromatic, sweet-smelling, ambrosial, perfumed, sweet
831.	**Frail**
	Synonym: Adj: fragile, delicate, weak, feeble brittle, breakable
	Antonym: strong, sturdy, tough
832.	**Frailty**
	Synonym: Noun: weakness, vulnerability, debility infirmity, Achilles heel
	Antonym: strength, power, vigor
833.	**Frank**
	Synonym: Adj: honest, straightforward, forthright, candid, explicit, blunt
	Antonym: dishonest, euphemistic, insincere
834.	**Frantic**
	Synonym: Adj: frenzied, excited, agitated, frenetic
	Antonym: composed, calm, serene
835.	**Fray**
	Synonym: Noun: fight, brawl, scuffle, tussle, row, battle
836.	**Freak**
	Synonym: Adj: odd, unusual, abnormal, strange, unexpected, weird ***Noun:*** abnormality, oddity, curiosity, deviation, anomaly, monstrosity
	Antonym: normal, ordinary, expected
837.	**Frenetic**
	Synonym: Adj: frantic, wild, frenzied, feverish, intense, furious, turbulent, tumultuous
	Antonym: calm
838.	**Frenzy**
	Synonym: Noun: furore, turmoil, rage, rush, agitation
839.	**Fritter**
	Synonym: Verb: squander, waste, misuse, misspend, dissipate
	Antonym: save, spend wisely

840.	**Frighten**
	Synonym: Verb: scare, terrify, shock, alarm, terrorize, horrify, petrify
841.	**Frightening**
	Synonym: Adj: terrifying, scary, fearful, alarming, intimidating, horrifying
	Antonym: calming, reassuring, encouraging
842.	**Frigid**
	Synonym: Adj: icy, freezing, cold, chilly, piercing, biting
	Antonym: warm, hot, temperate
843.	**Fringe**
	Synonym: Noun: border, margin, edge, rim, periphery, limit
	Antonym: centre, core, heart
844.	**Frisky**
	Synonym: Adj: playful, frolicsome, coltish, kittenish, lively, active
	Antonym: lifeless, dead, slothful
845.	**Frivolous**
	Synonym: Adj: silly, foolish, senseless, trivial, petty, unimportant
	Antonym: serious, sensible, important
846.	**Frown**
	Synonym: Verb: scowl, glower, pout, glare
	Antonym: smile
847.	**Frugal**
	Synonym: Adj: economical, thrifty, meagre, stingy, penny-pinching, parsimonious, scrimping
	Antonym: extravagant, lavish, profligate
848.	**Frustrate**
	Synonym: Verb: thwart, foil, spoil, disappoint, obstruct, impede, hamper, hinder
	Antonym: help, facilitate, please
849.	**Frustration**
	Synonym: Noun: exasperation, annoyance, anger, vexation, irritation, bitterness, resentment, disappointment
	Antonym: satisfaction, success, promotion
850.	**Fulsome**
	Synonym: Adj: enthusiastic, excessive, overdone, inordinate, flattering, effusive, cloying

851.	**Fumble**
	Synonym: Verb: mishandle, mismanage, muff, bumble, botch
852.	**Furious**
	Synonym: Adj: angry, irate, mad, incensed, furiated, wrathful
	Antonym: pleased, gratified, happy, mild, tame, calm
853.	**Furore**
	Synonym: Noun: uproar, rage, outrage, outburst, ruckus
854.	**Furtive**
	Synonym: Adj: secret, sly, covert, clandestine, hidden, concealed
	Antonym: open, direct, unconcealed
855.	**Fusion**
	Synonym: union, blend, merger, integration, melding
	Antonym: split, division
856.	**Fussy**
	Synonym: Adj: picky, discriminating, fastidious, finicky, particular
	Antonym: easy to please, unparticular, undiscriminating
857.	**Futuristic**
	Synonym: Adj: innovative, cutting-edge, modern, ultramodern, visionary, groundbreaking
	Antonym: old fashioned, antiquated, outmoded

G

858.	**Gag**
	Synonym: Verb: choke, silence, muzzle, mute, muffle, stifle
859.	**Gainsay**
	Synonym: Verb: deny, dispute, disagree with, dissent from, contradict, repudiate, contest, counter
	Antonym: confirm
860.	**Gala**
	Synonym: Noun: fete, fair, celebration, jubilee, party, festival, pageant, jamboree
861.	**Galore**
	Synonym: Adj: aplenty, in abundance, in profusion, in great quantity, in large numbers
	Antonym: in short supply
862.	**Galvanize**
	Synonym: Verb: stimulate, spur, jolt, energize, inspire, electrify, arouse
863.	**Garbled**
	Synonym: Adj: distorted, jumbled, confused, warped, twisted
	Antonym: clear, straight, understandable
864.	**Gargantuan**
	Synonym: Adj: gigantic, massive, huge, towering, colossal, immense
	Antonym: tiny, miniature, microscopic
865.	**Garrulous**
	Synonym: Adj: talkative, loquacious, wordy
866.	**Gauche**
	Synonym: Adj: tactless, ill-mannered, boorish, crude, graceless, unsophisticated
	Antonym: tactful, refined, sophisticated
867.	**Gaudy**
	Synonym: Adj: loud, flashy, garish, vulgar, tawdry, tasteless
	Antonym: tasteful, subtle, quiet
868.	**Gawk**
	Synonym: Verb: gape, ogle, stare, gaze, look
869.	**Generous**
	Synonym: Adj: charitable, unselfish, kindly, considerate, thoughtful
	Antonym: mean, selfish, miserly
870.	**Genesis**
	Synonym: Noun: a beginning, creation or origin, birth, origin, inception, start, beginning, creation
	Antonym: death, end, close
871.	**Genial**
	Synonym: Adj: friendly, agreeable, cordial, pleasant, cheerful, comfortable
872.	**Genuine**
	Synonym: real, true, actual, factual, authentic
	Antonym: false, phoney, fake, counterfeit
873.	**Genre**
	Synonym: Noun: category, type, kind, class, style, sort
874.	**Genteel**
	Synonym: Adj: refined, cultured, polite, civil, gentlemanly, ladylike
	Antonym: rough, unrefined, uncultured

875.	**Germinate**
	Synonym: Verb: grow, generate, sprout, develop
876.	**Gesture**
	Synonym: Noun: sign, movement, signal, motion, indication
877.	**Ghastly**
	Synonym: Adj: horrible, gruesome, hideous, terrible, dreadful, frightful
	Antonym: beautiful, attractive, lovely
878.	**Giddy**
	Synonym: Adj: dizzy, light-headed, unsteady
879.	**Giggle**
	Synonym: Verb: laugh, chuckle, titter, chortle, snicker, tee-hee
880.	**Gigantic**
	Synonym: Adj: giant, huge, enormous, monstrous, immense, colossal, titanic
	Antonym: small, tiny, little
881.	**Gimmick**
	Synonym: Noun: stunt, scheme, trick, angle, ruse
882.	**Gist**
	Synonym: Noun: essence, point, heart, sum
883.	**Glamorous**
	Synonym: Adj: attractive, exciting, alluring, enchanting, charming
	Antonym: dull, ordinary, tedious
884.	**Glare**
	Synonym: Verb: stare, scowl, glower, frown, scrutinize, shine, flare, blaze, flash, dazzle ***Noun:*** light, shine, brightness, glimmer, flash, brilliance, stare, scowl, frown, glower, look
885.	**Glaring**
	Synonym: Adj: flagrant, obvious, conspicuous, blatant
	Antonym: unobvious, inconspicuous, hidden
886.	**Gleam**
	Synonym: Noun: glimmer, shine, radiance, sparkle, reflection, glow
887.	**Glee**
	Synonym: Noun: great joy, merriment, joyfulness, gladness, ecstasy
	Antonym: sadness, sorrow, dejection

888.	**Glib**
	Synonym: Adj: facile, offhanded, shallow, superficial, quick, silver tongued
889.	**Glimmer**
	Synonym: Noun: gleam, twinkling, glimmering, shimmer, flicker, flash, hint ***Verb:*** twinkle, flicker, shine, sparkle
890.	**Glimpse**
	Synonym: Verb: observe, witness, view, sight, spot ***Noun:*** glance, peek, look, view, peep
891.	**Gloat**
	Synonym: Verb: bask, brag, revel, triumph, delight
	Antonym: despair, regret, envy, grudge
892.	**Gloom**
	Synonym: Noun: sadness, unhappiness, misery, despair, dejection, dimness, darkness, murkiness
	Antonym: happiness, cheer, delight
893.	**Gloomy**
	Synonym: Adj: sad, unhappy, depressed, miserable, downcast, dismal, cheerless, dreary, dark, murky, overcast, shadowy, dim, dull
	Antonym: happy, cheerful, gay, bright
894.	**Glorify**
	Synonym: Verb: celebrate, exalt, honour, venerate, idolize, revere, adore
	Antonym: disparage, disrespect, dishonor
895.	**Glorious**
	Synonym: Adj: wonderful, splendid, marvellous, gorgeous, superb, beautiful
	Antonym: awful, terrible, horrible
896.	**Glossy**
	Synonym: Adj: shiny, shimmering, glowing, lustrous, glassy, gleaming
	Antonym: dark, dusky, dull
897.	**Goad**
	Synonym: Verb: urge, push, prod, incite, spur, provoke, exhort
898.	**Goody-goody**
	Synonym: Adj: prudish, prissy, uptight, puritan, moral
	Antonym: devilish, wild, immoral

899.	**Goofy**
	Synonym: Adj: silly, foolish, childish
	Antonym: serious, uptight
900.	**Gorgeous**
	Synonym: Adj: beautiful, pretty, lovely, attractive, stunning, glorious, splendid
	Antonym: ugly, drab, plain
901.	**Grace**
	Synonym: Noun: charm, elegance, gracefulness, refinement, mercy, charity, pardon, forgiveness, leniency ***Verb:*** honour, dignify, glorify, exalt, favour, adorn, embellish, enrich, beautify, ornament, decorate
	Antonym: clumsiness, crudeness, coarseness, cruelty, harshness, disfavour, dishonour, shame, insult
902.	**Graceful**
	Synonym: Adj: elegant, lovely, beautiful, cordial, genial
	Antonym: clumsy, awkward, graceless
903.	**Gracious**
	Synonym: Adj: kind, courteous, polite, friendly, cordial, genial
	Antonym: haughty, unkind, cool
904.	**Gradual**
	Synonym: Adj: slow, moderate, steady, measured
	Antonym: sudden, instant, abrupt
905.	**Grand**
	Synonym: Adj: royal, majestic, impressive, magnificent, total, complete, full, comprehensive, wonderful, great, superb, marvellous
	Antonym: mediocre, inferior, unimpressive, partial, incomplete, fractional, bad, awful, terrible
906.	**Grandeur**
	Synonym: Noun: splendour, majesty, glory, magnificence, resplendence
	Antonym: plainness, squalor, commonness
907.	**Grandiose**
	Synonym: Adj: great, grand, magnificent, impressive, theatrical, pompous
	Antonym: understated, subdued, modest

908.	**Grapple**
	Synonym: Verb: contend, struggle, battle, cope
909.	**Grasp**
	Synonym: Verb: seize, grab, clutch, grip, catch, hold, understand, perceive, comprehend, see, follow ***Noun:*** hold, reach, possession, grip, clasp, understanding, perception, knowledge, sense
	Antonym: release, free, loose, misunderstand, confuse, misjudge
910.	**Gratify**
	Synonym: Verb: please, satisfy, delight, content
	Antonym: disappoint, displease, dissatisfy
911.	**Gratitude**
	Synonym: Noun: thankfulness, appreciation, gratefulness
	Antonym: ingratitude, ungratefulness
912.	**Gratuitous**
	Synonym: Adj: unnecessary, unjustified, needless, inessential, superfluous
	Antonym: necessary, justified, needed
913.	**Gravity**
	Synonym: Noun: seriousness, weight, importance, magnitude, significance, enormity
	Antonym: insignificance, triviality
914.	**Gregarious**
	Synonym: Adj: friendly, social, personable, outgoing, extroverted, affable
	Antonym: aloof, reserved, shy
915.	**Grief**
	Synonym: Noun: sorrow, sadness, distress, misery, agony, anguish, despair
	Antonym: happiness, joy, bliss
916.	**Grievance**
	Synonym: Noun: complaint, wrong, objection, problem
917.	**Grieve**
	Synonym: Verb: mourn, weep, lament, bemoan, deplore, distress, sorrow, sadden, depress, dishearten
	Antonym: praise, celebrate, rejoice, delight, comfort, please

918.	**Grievous**
	Synonym: Adj: dreadful, horrible, shameful, painful, unfortunate, tragic
	Antonym: pleasant, happy, joyous
919.	**Grill**
	Synonym: Verb: interrogate, examine, question, quiz, barbecue, broil, cook, sear, fry
920.	**Grim**
	Synonym: Adj: severe, harsh, stern, cold, hard, forbidding, ghastly, sinister, horrible, terrible, grisly, gruesome
	Antonym: kind, merciful, gentle, pleasing, pleasant, cheerful
921.	**Grimy**
	Synonym: Adj: filthy, dirty, dingy, smudged, grubby, sooty, muddy
	Antonym: clean, sparkling, immaculate
922.	**Grind**
	Synonym: Verb: sharpen, whet, smooth, polish, file, crush, crumble, pulverize, crunch, pound
923.	**Grisly**
	Synonym: Adj: gruesome, grim, shocking, hideous, horrid, horrible, frightful
	Antonym: pleasant, handsome, pretty
924.	**Groan**
	Synonym: Verb: moan, complain, sob, mumble, grumble, whimper ***Noun:*** whine, wail, moan, whimper, cry
925.	**Grotesque**
	Synonym: Adj: bizarre, queer, weird, strange, freakish, fantastic, unnatural
	Antonym: normal, ordinary, routine
926.	**Growl**
	Synonym: Verb: snarl, rumble, grumble, gnarl
927.	**Grubby**
	Synonym: Adj: dirty, grimy, filthy, mud-stained
	Antonym: clean, sparkling, immaculate
928.	**Grudge**
	Synonym: Noun: resentment, bitterness, spite, malice, ill will ***Verb:*** begrudge, resent, envy, refuse, deny
	Antonym: liking, good-will, friendliness, allow, accept, celebrate

929.	**Gruelling**
	Synonym: Adj: demanding, punishing, difficult, hard, strenuous, tiring, exhausting, taxing, trying
	Antonym: easy, light, effortless
930.	**Gruesome**
	Synonym: Adj: frightful, horrific, grisly, ugly, hideous, horrible, horrid, frightening, scary, repulsive
	Antonym: beautiful, handsome, pleasing
931.	**Grumble**
	Synonym: Verb: complain, gripe, fuss, protest, growl, mutter, grouch
	Antonym: praise, compliment, applaud
932.	**Gullible**
	Synonym: Adj: naive, innocent, trustful, trusting, unsuspecting, easy, credulous
	Antonym: sceptical, suspicious

H

933.	**Hackneyed**
	Synonym: Adj: trite, clichéd, unoriginal, banal
	Antonym: original, fresh, imaginative
934.	**Haggard**
	Synonym: Adj: weary, worn, gaunt, drawn, pale, fatigued, tried
	Antonym: refreshed, energetic, robust
935.	**Haggle**
	Synonym: Verb: argue, quarrel, bicker, dispute, disagree
936.	**Hallmark**
	Synonym: Noun: characteristic, sign, indicator, symbol, stamp, badge
937.	**Hallowed**
	Antonym: profane, secular, unholy, unsanctified
938.	**Hallucination**
	Synonym: Noun: delusion, illusion, mirage, vision, fantasy, dream
939.	**Hamper**
	Synonym: Verb: hinder, obstruct, impede, prevent, restrain, thwart, inhibit
	Antonym: aid, assist, promote, help

940.	**Handicap**
	Synonym: Noun: disability, defect, impairment, disadvantage, impediment, hindrance, obstacle, barrier, bar, encumbrance, drawback, stumbling, difficulty, shortcoming, obstruction, constrain, restriction
	Antonym: benefit, advantage
941.	**Hanker**
	Synonym: Verb: yearn, long, have a longing, crave, desire, thirst, lust, be desperate
	Antonym: be averse
942.	**Hanky-Panky**
	Synonym: Noun: goings-on, mischief, chicanery, subterfuge, trickery, machinations
	Antonym: good behaviour, fidelity
943.	**Haphazard**
	Synonym: Adj: random, unplanned, unsystematic, unmethodical, disorganized, disorderly, irregular, chaotic
	Antonym: methodical, systematic
944.	**Hapless**
	Synonym: Adj: unlucky, unfortunate, star-crossed, jinxed, woeful, cursed
	Antonym: lucky, fortunate, blessed
945.	**Harass**
	Synonym: Verb: pester, plague, torment, bother, annoy, exasperate, disturb, trouble, provoke
	Antonym: leave in peace
946.	**Harbinger**
	Synonym: Noun: forerunner, signal, portent, omen
947.	**Harlot**
	Synonym: Noun: prostitute, whore, call girl
948.	**Harness**
	Synonym: Verb: control, exploit, utilize, render useful, make productive, channel, mobilize, capitalize on
949.	**Harrowing**
	Synonym: Adj: alarming, terrifying, scary, upsetting, traumatic
950.	**Hassle**
	Synonym: Noun: quarrel, dispute, fight, argument, squabble, struggle *Verb:* harass, harry, bother, argue, fight

951.	**Hatch**
	Synonym: Verb: concoct, devise, plan, create, produce, invent, generate, breed, incubate, brood, produce
952.	**Haughty**
	Synonym: Adj: proud, arrogant, prideful, conceited, vain, pompous
	Antonym: Humble, modest, simple
953.	**Haunt**
	Synonym: Verb: obsess, plague, torment, distress, frighten, terrorize *Noun:* hideaway, hangout, rendezvous, spot, place
954.	**Haunting**
	Synonym: Adj: unforgettable, upsetting, disturbing, distressing, hypnotic, horrifying, terrifying, petrifying
955.	**Havoc**
	Synonym: Noun: ruin, disaster, destruction, chaos, disorder, devastation
	Antonym: peace, calm, order, serenity
956.	**Hazard**
	Synonym: Noun: danger, risk, peril, threat *Verb:* venture, risk, guess, gamble, dare, offer, attempt
957.	**Hazardous**
	Synonym: Adj: dangerous, perilous, risky, unsafe
	Antonym: safe, reliable, secure
958.	**Hazy**
	Synonym: Adj: foggy, cloudy, misty, murky, overcast, dim, obscure, faint, uncertain, muddled, vague
	Antonym: sunny, clear, bright, certain, clear
959.	**Hearsay**
	Synonym: Noun: rumour, talk, gossip, second-hand information, scuttlebutt
960.	**Hectic**
	Synonym: Adj: very busy, rushed, frantic, wild, mad, excited, chaotic, feverish
	Antonym: quiet, calm, slow, peaceful
961	**Hefty**
	Synonym: Adj: vigorous, strong, weighty, massive, large, ample, powerful
	Antonym: light, small, insignificant

962.	**Heinous**
	Synonym: Adj: evil, abominable, wicked, despicable, monstrous, revolting
	Antonym: angelic, saintly, moral
963.	**Hellish**
	Antonym: infernal, satanic, evil, wicked, cruel, diabolical
964.	**Helter-Skelter**
	Synonym: Adj: disordered, disorderly, chaotic, muddled, jumbled, haphazard disorganized, shambles, at sixes and sevens, out of order
	Antonym: moderately, orderly
965.	**Herald**
	Synonym: Noun: messenger, forerunner, carrier ***Verb:*** announce, proclaim, broadcast
966.	**Herculean**
	Synonym:Adj: arduous, laborious, onerous, strenuous, formidable, burdensome, hard, tough, huge, heavy, massive, uphill, demanding, exhausting, taxing, exacting
	Antonym: easy, comfortable
967.	**Heresy**
	Synonym: Noun: dissension, unorthodoxy, apostasy, blasphemy, nonconformity
	Antonym: conformity, agreement, orthodoxy
968.	**Heretic**
	Synonym: Noun: disbeliever, dissenter, nonconformist, renegade, infidel
	Antonym: believer, loyalist, traditionalist
969.	**Hiatus**
	Synonym: Noun: break, interim, gap, interruption
970.	**Hideous**
	Synonym: Adj: ugly, repulsive, ghastly, horrible, terrifying, gruesome
	Antonym: beautiful, attractive, pleasing
971.	**Hilarious**
	Synonym: Adj: funny, delirious, hysterical, riotous, laughable, uproarious
	Antonym: sad, solemn, depressing
972.	**Hoax**
	Synonym: ***Noun:*** fraud, deception, deceit, sham ***Verb:*** deceive, trick, fool, dupe, swindle
	Antonym: truth, actuality, fact
973.	**Hoarse**
	Synonym: Adj: harsh, rough, grating, scratchy, cracked, coarse
	Antonym: clear, smooth
974.	**Hobble**
	Synonym: Verb: limp, falter, stagger, shuffle, totter
975.	**Holistic**
	Synonym: Adj: whole, integrated, comprehensive, complete, systemic, integral
	Antonym: partial, individual, divided
976.	**Holocaust**
	Synonym: Noun: annihilation, genocide, extermination, massacre, mass killing, devastation, destruction
977.	**Hoodwink**
	Synonym: Verb: deceive, trick, mislead
978.	**Horrible**
	Synonym: Adj: terrible, awful, gruesome, dreadful, horrid, frightful, hideous
	Antonym: delightful, wonderful, good, nice
979.	**Horrify**
	Synonym: Verb: shock, dismay, scare, revolt, petrify, appal, frighten, horrify
980.	**Horror**
	Synonym: Noun: terror, dread, fear, fright, panic, dismay, alarm, repulsion, cruelty, atrocity, outrage, torment
	Antonym: good, kindness, happiness
981.	**Hostile**
	Synonym: Adj: unfriendly, opposing, aggressive, warlike, belligerent, unfavourable
	Antonym: friendly, agreeable, peaceful
982.	**Hostility**
	Synonym: Noun: ill will, unfriendliness, malevolence, enmity, antagonism
	Antonym: friendliness, warmth, goodwill
983.	**Hover**
	Synonym: Verb: float, drift, hang, flutter, loiter, linger, loom, vacillate, waver, falter
984.	**Howl**
	Synonym: Verb: yell, yowl, cry, wail, screech, shriek, bellow, bay
985.	**Hubbub**
	Synonym: Noun: commotion, fuss, hullabaloo, clamour, uproar, noise
	Antonym: stillness, inactivity, silence

986.	**Huddle**
	Synonym: Verb: bunch, crowd, mass, cram, cluster, snuggle, gather ***Noun:*** mass, heap, pile, jumble, mess, clump, bunch
	Antonym: separate, divide, scatter, disperse
987.	**Humbug**
	Synonym: Noun: hypocrisy, posturing, sham, deceit, deception, imposture, pretence, trickery, hypocrite, charlatan ***Verb:*** deceive, trick, delude, mislead, fool, hoodwink, dupe, hoax
988.	**Humdrum**
	Synonym: Adj: dull, boring, routine, monotonous
989.	**Humiliate**
	Synonym: Verb: shame, embarrass, disgrace, degrade, dishonour, humble, demean
	Antonym: honour, exalt, dignify, elevate
990.	**Humiliation**
	Synonym: Noun: shame, embarrassment, dishonour, degradation, lowering
	Antonym: honour, prestige, pride, exaltation
991.	**Humility**
	Synonym: Noun: modesty, humbleness, meekness, unpretentiousness, lowliness
	Antonym: conceit, pride, arrogance
992.	**Hurdle**
	Synonym: Noun: barrier, obstacle, obstruction, barricade, hazard, block ***Verb:*** jump, leap, scale, bound, spring
993.	**Hustle**
	Synonym: Verb: hurry, hasten, speed, rush, dash, scurry ***Noun:*** hurry, fuss, turmoil, stir, flurry
	Antonym: linger, dawdle, loiter, rest
994.	**Hybrid**
	Synonym: Noun: cross, mixed breed, composite, crossbreed, mix
995.	**Hypocritical**
	Synonym: Adj: false, deceptive, insincere, deceitful, dishonest
	Antonym: sincere, honest, honourable
996.	**Hypothetical**
	Synonym: Adj: theoretical, unproven, guessed, conjectural, supposed, imaginary
	Antonym: factual, actual, true
997.	**Hysterical**
	Synonym: Adj: uncontrollable, frenzied, panicky, emotional, wild, raving, funny, hilarious, laughable, comical, absurd
	Antonym: controlled, calm, composed, serious, sad, solemn, sombre

I

998.	**Ideal**
	Synonym: Adj: perfect, flawless, faultless, exemplary, classic, model, ultimate
999.	**Idiot**
	Synonym: Noun: nincompoop, dunce, imbecile, moron, simpleton, clod, dimwit, dumbo, foolish, stupid, senseless
1000.	**Idiotic**
	Synonym: Adj: stupid, silly, foolish, foolhardy, senseless, nonsensical, inane
	Antonym: sensible, wise, sane
1001.	**Ignoble**
	Synonym: Adj: dishonourable, unworthy, shameful, contemptible, despicable, abject, low, sordid, degraded, corrupt, mean, shameful, contemptible
	Antonym: honourable, worthy
1002.	**Illegal**
	Synonym: Adj: unlawful, illicit, criminal, banned, unauthorized, forbidden, prohibited
	Antonym: legal, permitted, lawful
1003.	**Illegible**
	Synonym: Adj: unreadable, obscure, unintelligible, unclear, indistinct
	Antonym: readable, clear, legible
1004.	**Illogical**
	Synonym: Adj: ludicrous, unsound, absurd, unreasonable, inconsistent, preposterous, ridiculous
	Antonym: logical, sensible, reasonable
1005.	**Illusion**
	Synonym: Noun: mirage, delusion, phantom, fallacy, misbelief, fantasy, misconception, dream
	Antonym: reality, actuality, fact, truth, certainty, probability

1006.	**Illustrious**
	Synonym: Adj: famous, distinguished, renowned, splendid, glorious, celebrated, famous, noted, prominent
	Antonym: obscure, undistinguished, lowly
1007.	**Imbecile**
	Synonym: Noun: stupid, silly, dumb, fool, moron, dolt, idiot, simpleton, blockhead
1008.	**Imbibe**
	Synonym: Verb: assimilate, absorb, soak up, take in, digest, ingest, acquire, grasp, gain, pick up
1009.	**Imbroglio**
	Synonym: Noun: problem, difficulty, predicament, trouble, confusion, muddle, mess, quandary, dilemma
1010.	**Imitation**
	Synonym: Noun: copy, simulation, reproduction, duplication, counterfeit, replica ***Adj:*** artificial, phoney, simulated, fake, false, copied
	Antonym: original, real, authentic
1011.	**Immaculate**
	Synonym: Adj: pure, spotless, clean, unstained, unblemished, perfect, flawless
	Antonym: impure, flawed
1012.	**Immense**
	Synonym: Adj: large, enormous, great, vast, huge, gigantic, colossal
	Antonym: small, little, tiny
1013.	**Immerse**
	Synonym: Verb: submerge, dunk, dip, plunge, soak, drench, absorb, engross, involve, engage, occupy
1014.	**Imminent**
	Synonym: Adj: near, approaching, immediate, impending, forthcoming
	Antonym: distant, remote, unlikely
1015.	**Immoral**
	Synonym: Adj: wrongful, unethical, sinful, evil, corrupt, wicked, bad
	Antonym: moral, good, ethical
1016.	**Immortal**
	Synonym: Adj: living for ever, everlasting, enduring, eternal, undying, deathless, endless, imperishable
	Antonym: mortal, temporary, perishable
1017.	**Immune**
	Synonym: Adj: invulnerable, resistant, safe, unaffected, protected, spared
	Antonym: susceptible, vulnerable
1018.	**Immunity**
	Synonym: Noun: resistance, protection, defence, exemption, impunity, exception
	Antonym: susceptibility, vulnerability
1019.	**Impartial**
	Synonym: Adj: fair, neutral, objective, unbiased, even-handed, unprejudiced
	Antonym: partial, biased, prejudiced
1020.	**Impasse**
	Synonym: Noun: dead-end, roadblock, deadlock, bottleneck, stalemate, standstill
	Antonym: passage, clearance, clearing
1021.	**Impatient**
	Synonym: Adj: restless, anxious, fidgety, jumpy, eager, hurried
	Antonym: patient, composed, unhurried
1022.	**Impeach**
	Synonym: Verb: charge, indict, incriminate, discredit
1023.	**Impeccable**
	Synonym: Adj: faultless, flawless, perfect, unblemished, spotless, immaculate
	Antonym: faulty, imperfect, flawed, defective
1024.	**Impede**
	Synonym: Verb: delay, sow, hinder, inhibit, block, thwart, obstruct
	Antonym: assist, further, support
1025.	**Imperative**
	Synonym: Adj: vital, important, essential, mandatory, compulsive, required, essential, urgent, necessary
	Antonym: unimportant, optional, unnecessary
1026.	**Imperial**
	Synonym: Adj: royal, majestic, lordly, regal, grand
1027.	**Imperil**
	Synonym: Verb: endanger, risk, jeopardize, hazard
	Antonym: protect, preserve, safeguard

1028.	**Impetuous**
	Synonym: Adj: rash, impulsive, headlong, reckless, careless
	Antonym: careful, thoughtful, cautious
1029.	**Impetus**
	Synonym: Noun: acceleration, momentum, propulsion, impulsion, driving force, stimulus, inducement, boost
1030.	**Implacable**
	Synonym: Adj: unappeasable, unpacifiable, unmollifiable, unforgiving, inexorable, inflexible, unyielding, unbending
	Antonym: appeased, reconciled, pacified
1031.	**Implant**
	Synonym: Verb: instil; establish firmly, to insert, immerse
1032.	**Implausible**
	Synonym: unlikely, improbable, doubtful, unconvincing, far-fetched, unrealistic, incredible, unbelievable, unimaginable, inconceivable, fanciful
	Antonym: plausible, convincing
1033.	**Implicate**
	Synonym: Verb: connect, associate, involve, include, entangle, embroil
	Antonym: exclude, eliminate, acquit
1034.	**Implicit**
	Synonym: Adj: implied, suggested, understood, inferred, tacit, unexpressed
	Antonym: explicit, spoken
1035.	**Implore**
	Synonym: Verb: beg, plead, beseech, entreat, urge
1036.	**Imply**
	Synonym: Verb: suggest, hint, indicate, signify, mean, denote
1037.	**Impolite**
	Synonym: Adj: rude, discourteous, disrespectful, uncivil, inconsiderate
	Antonym: polite, mannerly, civil
1038.	**Imposing**
	Synonym: Adj: grand, majestic, striking, stately, impressive
	Antonym: ordinary, unimpressive, unimposing

1039.	**Imposter**
	Synonym: Noun: imitator, impersonator, fraud, deceiver, pretender, phoney, cheat
1040.	**Impotent**
	Synonym: Adj: powerless, weak, helpless, ineffectual, inadequate, unproductive, incapable
	Antonym: potent, powerful, effective
1041.	**Impoverish**
	Synonym: Verb: weaken, exhaust, drain, diminish, enervate
	Antonym: strengthen, enrich
1042.	**Impregnable**
	Synonym: Adj: invulnerable, impenetrable, unassailable, inviolable, unbeatable, undefeatable, unshakeable, invincible, indomitable, unconquerable
	Antonym: vulnerable, flawed, beatable
1043.	**Impregnate**
	Synonym: Verb: infuse, drench, suffuse, imbue, saturate, permeate, soak
1044.	**Impressive**
	Synonym: Adj: imposing, striking, awesome, majestic, stirring, inspiring, grand, grandiose
	Antonym: ordinary, routine, unimpressive
1045.	**Improbable**
	Synonym: Adj: unlikely, doubtful, questionable, implausible, dubious
	Antonym: likely, certain, possible, plausible
1046.	**Impromptu**
	Synonym: Adj: impulsive, unrehearsed, unprepared, spontaneous, improvised
	Antonym: planned, rehearsed, prepared
1047.	**Improvident**
	Synonym: Adj: spendthrift, thriftless, unthrifty, wasteful, prodigal, profligate, extravagant, squandering, uneconomical, free-spending, lavish, immoderate, excessive, shiftless, feckless, imprudent, irresponsible, incautious, careless, reckless, rash, impetuous, hasty, thoughtless
	Antonym: thrifty, cautious

1048.	**Imprudent**
	Synonym: Adj: unwise, unadvisable, incautious, thoughtless, careless, rash, foolish
	Antonym: cautious, thoughtful, careful
1049.	**Impudent**
	Synonym: Adj: insolent, offensive, rude, disrespectful, impertinent, fresh
	Antonym: respectful, polite, reverent
1050.	**Impulsive**
	Synonym: Adj: impromptu, rash, abrupt, spontaneous, sudden, unplanned
	Antonym: planned, cautious, deliberate
1051.	**Impunity**
	Synonym: Noun: immunity, freedom, exemption, exception, license, privilege
	Antonym: liability, punishment, consequence
1052.	**Inadvertent**
	Synonym: Adj: accidental, unintentional, unplanned, unwitting, involuntary, undeliberate
	Antonym: intentional, designed, deliberate
1053.	**Inane**
	Synonym: Adj: silly, senseless, foolish, ridiculous, empty, stupid, absurd
	Antonym: sensible, reasonable, intelligent
1054.	**Inanimate**
	Synonym: Adj: lifeless, dead, inert, inorganic
	Antonym: alive, living, animate
1055.	**Inappropriate**
	Synonym: Adj: improper, unfit, unsuitable, wrong, unseemly
	Antonym: appropriate, proper, suitable
1056.	**Inarticulate**
	Synonym: Adj: not articulate; unable to speak or express yourself clearly, not spoken or expressed in words
1057.	**Incense**
	Synonym: Verb: anger, irritate, enrage, infuriate, inflame, provoke
	Antonym: cheer, calm, soothe
1058.	**Incidental**
	Synonym: Adj: secondary, subordinate, minor, unimportant, trivial, casual
	Antonym: major, primary, dominant

1059.	**Incisive**
	Synonym: Adj: sharp, penetrating, piercing, trenchant
	Antonym: dull, superficial, shallow
1060.	**Incite**
	Synonym: Verb: rouse, arouse, induce, urge, provoke, instigate, encourage
	Antonym: dissuade, restrain, discourage
1061.	**Incoherent**
	Synonym: Adj: unintelligible, incomprehensible, indistinct, confused, muddled
	Antonym: coherent, clear, intelligible
1062.	**Incompatible**
	Synonym: Adj: mismatched, opposite, contradictory, clashing, antagonistic, contrary
	Antonym: compatible, suited, matching
1063.	**Incompetent**
	Synonym: Adj: incapable, unfit, ineffective, inefficient, inept, unqualified
	Antonym: competent, able, fit, effective
1064.	**Incomprehensible**
	Synonym: Adj: unintelligible, inscrutable, baffling, mysterious, unexplainable
	Antonym: comprehensible, understandable
1065.	**Inconceivable**
	Synonym: Adj: unbelievable, unthinkable, incredible, unlikely, unimaginable
	Antonym: believable, plausible, likely
1066.	**Inconclusive**
	Synonym: Adj: unclear, unresolved, indefinite, open, debatable
	Antonym: conclusive, clear, definite
1067.	**Inconsiderate**
	Synonym: Adj: selfish, thoughtless, unthinking, tactless, negligent
	Antonym: considerate, thoughtful, kind
1068.	**Inconsistent**
	Synonym: Adj: contradictory, illogical, contrary, incompatible, conflicting, erratic, fickle, changeable, uncertain, unstable
	Antonym: consistent, logical, uniform, stable, unchanging, steady

1069.	**Inconspicuous**
	Synonym: Adj: indistinct, obscure, unapparent, unnoticeable, muted, dim
	Antonym: obvious, conspicuous, clear
1070.	**Incredible**
	Synonym: Adj: unbelievable, extraordinary, unimaginable, amazing, fantastic
	Antonym: credible, ordinary, believable
1071.	**Incredulous**
	Synonym: Adj: disbelieving, sceptical, distrusting, dubious, unconvinced, doubting, questioning
	Antonym: credulous, believing, trusting
1072.	**Incriminate**
	Synonym: Verb: accuse, charge, blame, implicate
1073.	**Indecent**
	Synonym: Adj: immodest, improper, immoral, offensive, obscene, shameful
	Antonym: decent, tasteful, proper
1074.	**Indelible**
	Synonym: Adj: lasting, permanent, fixed, indestructible, unforgettable
	Antonym: temporary, erasable, forgettable
1075.	**Indigenous**
	Synonym: Adj: native, aboriginal, original, natural, endemic, homegrown
	Antonym: foreign, alien
1076.	**Indigent**
	Synonym: Adj: impoverished, poor, destitute, needy, poverty-stricken
	Antonym: wealthy, rich, affluent
1077.	**Indignant**
	Synonym: Adj: angry, irate, incensed, mad, offended, wrathful
	Antonym: serene, pleased, calm
1078.	**Indict**
	Synonym: Verb: accuse, charge, arraign, incriminate, impute
1079.	**Indictment**
	Synonym: Noun: charge, accusation, arraignment, incrimination

1080.	**Indiscreet**
	Synonym: Adj: careless, incautious, rash, reckless, foolish, thoughtless
	Antonym: discreet, careful, prudent
1081.	**Indispensable**
	Synonym: Adj: essential, necessary, required, needed, vital, basic
	Antonym: dispensable, disposable, unnecessary
1082.	**Indoctrinate**
	Synonym: Verb: instruct, imbue, teach, enlighten, train, brainwash, program
1083.	**Indomitable**
	Synonym: Adj: invincible, unconquerable, unbeatable, dominant, staunch
	Antonym: beatable, weak, defeatable
1084.	**Induce**
	Synonym: Verb: cause, prompt, influence, persuade, impel, inspire, urge
	Antonym: dissuade, discourage, hinder
1085.	**Indulge**
	Synonym: Verb: satisfy, gratify, humor, favour, pamper, spoil, placate
1086.	***Antonym:*** deny, forbid, thwart, abstain
	Indulgence
	Synonym: Noun: luxury, excess, privilege, allowance, satisfaction, understanding, tolerance, patience, forgiveness, leniency
	Antonym: denial, repression. Intolerance, impatience
1087.	**Industrious**
	Synonym: Adj: hardworking, persistent, diligent, productive, active, tireless
	Antonym: lazy, sluggish, slothful
1088.	**Inefficient**
	Synonym: Adj: ineffective, inadequate, incapable, unsuccessful, incompetent, unable
	Antonym: efficient, successful, able
1089.	**Inept**
	Synonym: Adj: clumsy, unskilled or incompetent, bumbling, untrained, maladroit
	Antonym: competent, skilled, expert
1090.	**Inert**
	Synonym: Adj: unmoving, fixed, motionless, static, inactive, immobile, passive
	Antonym: active, moving, mobile

1091.	**Inertia**
	Synonym: Noun: inactivity, lifelessness, immobility, passivity, paralysis
	Antonym: motion, activity, movement
1092.	**Inevitable**
	Synonym: Adj: certain, sure, destined, unavoidable, inescapable, fated
	Antonym: unsure, uncertain, doubtful
1093.	**Inexorable**
	Synonym: Adj: unstoppable, unceasing, relentless
1094.	**Infallible**
	Synonym: Adj: perfect, faultless, flawless, unfailing, unerring, reliable
	Antonym: faulty, imperfect, fallible
1095.	**Infatuated**
	Synonym: Adj: smitten, enamoured, bewitched, enchanted, beguiled, enraptured
	Antonym: repulsed, repelled, disgusted
1096.	**Infamy**
	Synonym: Noun: disrepute, notoriety, ignominy, villainy
	Antonym: repute, honour
1097.	**Infinite**
	Synonym: Adj: endless, limitless, unlimited, boundless, immense, enormous
	Antonym: limited, finite, restricted
1098.	**Inflate**
	Synonym: Verb: expand, distend, blow up, swell, enlarge
	Antonym: deflate, collapse
1099.	**Inflict**
	Synonym: Verb: impose, wreak, perpetrate, apply, subject, give
1100.	**Influential**
	Synonym: Adj: effective, powerful, persuasive, potent, forceful, inspiring
	Antonym: ineffective, impotent, powerless
1101.	**Infuriate**
	Synonym: Verb: enrage, outrage, inflame, madden, anger, incense
	Antonym: please, delight, satisfy
1102.	**Ingenious**
	Synonym: Adj: clever, imaginative, inventive, skilful, resourceful, creative
	Antonym: unoriginal, ordinary, unimaginative

1103.	**Ingenuity**
	Synonym: Noun: inventiveness, creativity, imagination, cleverness, resourcefulness, intelligence
1104.	**Ingredient**
	Synonym: Noun: element, particle, part, factor, item, piece, aspect, feature
1105.	**Inherent**
	Synonym: Adj: essential, natural, inborn, inbred, ingrained, innate, elemental
	Antonym: alien, superficial, artificial
1106.	**Inhibition**
	Synonym: Noun: shyness, reserve, reticence, self-consciousness, withdrawal, bashfulness
	Antonym: spontaneity, freedom, abandon
1107.	**Innate**
	Synonym: Adj: natural, instinctive, inborn, inbred, inherent
	Antonym: learned, acquired, cultivated
1108.	**Innumerable**
	Synonym: Adj: countless, many, limitless, unlimited, infinite, numerous
	Antonym: limited, few, countable
1109.	**Insane**
	Synonym: Adj: crazy, mad, lunatic, unbalanced, deranged, psychotic, senseless, foolish, silly, stupid, dumb, idiotic, moronic, absurd
	Antonym: sane, sound, rational, wise, reasonable, sensible
1110.	**Insanity**
	Synonym: Noun: mental illness, craziness, psychosis, derangement, dementia, lunacy
	Antonym: sanity, mental health, stability
1111.	**Insatiable**
	Synonym: Adj: limitless, unsatisfiable, unquenchable, uncontrolled, demanding
	Antonym: limited, satisfied, controlled
1112.	**Insidious**
	Synonym: Adj: stealthy, sneaky, treacherous, covert, surreptitious, dangerous, perilous
	Antonym: overt, open

1113.	**Insipid**
	Synonym: Adj: dull, tasteless, bland, shallow, flavourless, vapid
	Antonym: flavourful, rich, interesting
1114.	**Insolent**
	Synonym: Adj: insulting, disrespectful, rude, surly, arrogant, defiant
	Antonym: polite, courteous, respectful
1115.	**Instigate**
	Synonym: Verb: goad, foment, incite, prompt, spark, spur
	Antonym: end, discourage, quell
1116.	**Instil**
	Synonym: Verb: implant, imbue, infuse, impart, inject, inculcate
	Antonym: remove, take out, expunge
1117.	**Instinct**
	Synonym: Noun: tendency, aptitude, feeling, intuition, impulse, capacity
1118.	**Instinctive**
	Synonym: Adj: innate, natural, involuntary, intuitive, inherent
	Antonym: acquired, learned, artificial
1119.	**Insurgent**
	Synonym: Noun: rebel, revolutionary, dissident, mutineer, anarchist
	Antonym: loyalist, loyal, obedient, patriotic
1120.	**Insurrection**
	Synonym: Noun: revolution, mutiny, rebellion, coup, revolt, uprising
	Antonym: submission, obedience
1121.	**Intangible**
	Synonym: Adj: imperceptible, impalpable, invisible, untouchable, immaterial, elusive
	Antonym: segregate, separate, part, divide
1122.	**Intense**
	Synonym: Adj: extreme, severe, great, powerful, strong, acute
	Antonym: weak, mild, moderate
1123.	**Intensify**
	Synonym: Verb: increase, strengthen, magnify, reinforce, concentrate, amplify
	Antonym: reduce, diminish, lessen

1124.	**Intensity**
	Synonym: Noun: strength, power, force, magnitude, concentration, volume
1125.	**Intermittent**
	Synonym: Adj: recurrent, spasmodic, occasional, periodic, irregular, alternating
	Antonym: steady, continuous
1126.	**Interpret**
	Synonym: Verb: explain, define, construe, clarify, illustrate, translate, paraphrase, decipher, reword, restate
1127.	**Intervene**
	Synonym: Verb: interfere, mediate, intrude, interrupt, intercede
1128.	**Intimidate**
	Synonym: Verb: scare, frighten, threaten, menace, dismay, alarm, terrify, terrorize
1129.	**Intimacy**
	Synonym: Noun: closeness, caring, fondness, familiarity, friendship
	Antonym: indifference, aloofness
1130.	**Intolerable**
	Synonym: Adj: unbearable, unendurable, insufferable, excessive, unreasonable
	Antonym: tolerable, bearable, comfortable, endurable
1131.	**Intolerant**
	Synonym: Adj: biased, prejudiced, bigoted, disdainful, hostile, resentful
	Antonym: tolerant, fair, accepting
1132.	**Intoxicated**
	Synonym: Adj: drunk, drunken, tipsy, inebriated, enthralled, enchanted, excited, elated, moved
	Antonym: sober, dry, straight, bored, unmoved
1133.	**Intrepid**
	Synonym: Adj: fearless, bold, brave, heroic, valiant, courageous, daring
	Antonym: cowardly, frightened, meek, timid
1134.	**Intricate**
	Synonym: Adj: complex, complicated, elaborate, involved, detailed
	Antonym: simple, uncomplicated, plain

1135.	**Intrigue**
	Synonym: Verb: fascinate, interest, captivate, excite, enthral, charm ***Noun:*** scheme, plot, conspiracy, espionage, ruse
	Antonym: bore, tire, weary
1136.	**Intrinsic**
	Synonym: Adj: inherent, innate, inner, natural, internal, basic
	Antonym: extrinsic, external, unnatural
1137.	**Intrude**
	Synonym: Verb: trespass, encroach, infringe, intervene, impose, invade, interfere
1138.	**Invigorating**
	Synonym: Adj: refreshing, stimulating, bracing, vitalizing, energizing
	Antonym: weakening, enervating, tiring
1139.	**Invincible**
	Synonym: Adj: invulnerable, unbeatable, unconquerable, untouchable, secure
	Antonym: beatable, vulnerable, weak
1140.	**Invisible**
	Synonym: Adj: imperceptible, impalpable, imperceivable, transparent, indiscernible, concealed
1141.	**Invoke**
	Synonym: Verb: summon, address, entreat, beseech, call, beg
1142.	**Irate**
	Synonym: Adj: angry, enraged, mad, angered, wrathful, infuriated, incensed
	Antonym: pleased, happy, glad
1143.	**Irk**
	Synonym: Verb: irritate, annoy, vex, bother, trouble, peeve, provoke
	Antonym: cheer, delight, satisfy
1144.	**Ironic**
	Synonym: Adj: sarcastic, biting, cutting, cynical, caustic, satiric, strange, inconsistent, weird, contradictory, curious, odd
	Antonym: tactful, inoffensive, consistent, understandable
1145.	**Irreverent**
	Synonym: Adj: disrespectful, profane, impious, irreligious, uncivil, flippant
	Antonym: reverent, respectful, pious

1146.	**Irreversible**
	Synonym: Adj: not reversible; irrevocable, solitary, separate, on its own
J	
1147.	**Jealous**
	Synonym: Adj: envious, covetous, desirous, resentful, grudging
	Antonym: admiring, proud
1148.	**Jeopardize**
	Synonym: Verb: risk, imperil, endanger, menace
	Antonym: save, protect, defend
1149.	**Jeopardy**
	Synonym: Noun: risk, danger, peril, threat, vulnerability
	Antonym: safety, security
1150.	**Jitters**
	Synonym: Noun: nervousness, anxiety, tension, fretfulness
	Antonym: calmness, serenity
1151.	**Jovial**
	Synonym: Adj: cheerful, jolly, merry, joyful, joyous
	Antonym: sad, depressed, melancholy, gloomy
1152.	**Jubilant**
	Synonym: Adj: ecstatic, elated, exhilarated, thrilled, excited
	Antonym: disappointed, dejected, despondent
1153.	**Jumble**
	Synonym: Verb: disorder, disorganize, disarrange, unsettle, mix
	Antonym: order, organize, arrange
1154.	**Judgmental**
	Synonym: Adj: critical, faultfinding, self-righteous, holier-than-thou, censorious
	Antonym: non-judgmental, accepting
1155.	**Judicious**
	Synonym: Adj: prudent, wise, thoughtful, sensible, mindful, careful
	Antonym: injudicious, careless, senseless
1156.	**Juggle**
	Synonym: Verb: manoeuvre, manipulate, fake, alter, tamper, modify

K

1157.	**Kindle**
	Synonym: Verb: ignite, light, fire, torch, burn, arouse, excite, stir, provoke
	Antonym: extinguish, quench, smoother
1158.	**Knack**
	Synonym: Noun: skill, talent, aptitude, gift, ability
1159.	**Kudos**
	Synonym: Noun: praise; honour; acclaim, credit, esteem, applause, glory
	Antonym: criticism, dishonor, discredit

L

1160.	**Laborious**
	Synonym: Adj: strenuous, difficult, burden- some, hard, arduous, tiresome
	Antonym: light, easy, simple, effortless
1161.	**Labyrinth**
	Synonym: Noun: maze, network, complex, entanglement, tangle, web
1162.	**Lackadaisical**
	Synonym: Adj: disinterested, indifferent, listless, languid, unmotivated, spiritless
	Antonym: enthusiastic, interested, spirited
1163.	**Lament**
	Synonym: Verb: moan, weep, wail, mourn, cry, grieve, deplore
	Antonym: celebrate, cheer, enjoy
1164.	**Languish**
	Synonym: Verb: sicken, weaken, fade, wither, decline, deteriorate
	Antonym: flourish, revive, recover, thrive
1165.	**Lascivious**
	Synonym: Adj: indecent, improper, immoral, obscene, vulgar
	Antonym: moral, decent, proper
1166.	**Latch**
	Synonym: Verb: lock, bolt, fasten, secure, close
	Antonym: open, unlock, unlatch
1167.	**Latent**
	Synonym: Adj: dormant, hidden, inactive, inert, sleeping, unrealized
	Antonym: realized, developed, active
1168.	**Lavish**
	Synonym: Verb: squander, waste, shower, bestow, overindulge ***Adj:*** liberal, extravagant, abundant, bountiful, generous, plentiful
	Antonym: save, retain, withhold, scanty, economical, stingy
1169.	**Lenient**
	Synonym: Adj: merciful, kind, tolerant, gentle, lax, forgiving, sparing
	Antonym: strict, harsh, stern, severe
1170.	**Lethal**
	Synonym: Adj: fatal, deadly, dangerous, destructive, mortal, killing
	Antonym: safe, harmless, beneficial
1171.	**Lethargic**
	Synonym: Adj: listless, tired, slothful, languid, sluggish, fatigued
	Antonym: energetic, lively, active
1172.	**Linger**
	Synonym: Verb: stay, remain, idle, tarry, persist, loiter, delay, dawdle
	Antonym: depart, disappear, hasten
1173.	**Loathe**
	Synonym: Verb: hate, detest, despise, abhor, scorn, abominate, repulse
	Antonym: love, like, adore, relish
1174.	**Loathsome**
	Synonym: Adj: abominable, repulsive, repellent, foul, disgusting, despicable
	Antonym: lovable, adorable, delightful
1175.	**Lofty**
	Synonym: Adj: haughty, proud, exalted, lordly, arrogant, snobbish, towering, high, tall, elevated, soaring
	Antonym: modest, humble, unassuming, short, low, stunted
1176.	**Lopsided**
	Synonym: Adj: uneven, unbalanced, slanted, distorted, unequal, disproportionate
	Antonym: even, balanced, equal
1177.	**Loquacious**
	Synonym: Adj: talkative, gabby, chatty, garrulous
	Antonym: taciturn, reserved, quiet

1178.	**Lucid**
	Synonym: Adj: clear, understandable, accurate, sensible, rational, intelligible, transparent, translucent, clear, light, bright
	Antonym: vague, confused, unclear, dim, dark, murky, gloomy
1179.	**Lucrative**
	Synonym: Adj: money-making, profitable, prosperous, rewarding, wealth- producing, remunerative
	Antonym: unprofitable, money-losing, expensive
1180.	**Ludicrous**
	Synonym: Adj: silly, ridiculous, absurd, crazy
	Antonym: serious, sensible, solemn
1181.	**Lukewarm**
	Synonym: Adj: warm, tepid, mild, temperate, indifferent, half-hearted, unenthusiastic, cool
	Antonym: burning, excited
1182.	**Lull**
	Synonym: Noun: calmness, pause, stillness, hush, quiet, break, interval *Verb:* calm, quiet, hush, soothe, pacify, still
	Antonym: continuation, turbulence, excite, rouse, agitate
1183.	**Lurid**
	Synonym: Adj: shocking, startling, sensational, gruesome, grisly, grim, horrid
	Antonym: mild, light-hearted, tame, cheerful
1184.	**Luscious**
	Synonym: Adj: delicious, succulent, delightful, tasty, delectable, savoury
	Antonym: flavourless, nauseating, tasteless

M

1185.	**Macabre**
	Synonym: Adj: gruesome, deadly, horrifying, morbid, ghastly, grisly
1186.	**Machismo**
	Synonym: Noun: maleness, masculinity, strength, virility, fierceness, potency
	Antonym: femininity, weakness, impotence
1187.	**Macho**
	Synonym: Adj: masculine, virile, male, tough, strong, dominant, fierce
	Antonym: feminine, effeminate, weak
1188.	**Magnificent**
	Synonym: Adj: fantastic, impressive, superb, extraordinary, wonderful
	Antonym: poor, ordinary, terrible
1189.	**Magnify**
	Synonym: Verb: enlarge, increase, exaggerate, dramatize, inflate
	Antonym: reduce, diminish, minimize
1190.	**Magnitude**
	Synonym: Noun: degree, importance, intensity, significance, weight
1191.	**Majestic**
	Synonym: Adj: awesome, impressive, grand, elegant, stately, magnificent, imposing, grandiloquent
	Antonym: puny, undistinguished, humble
1192.	**Malaise**
	Synonym: Noun: unease, depression, discomfort, lassitude, sickness, angst
	Antonym: health, vigor, vitality
1193.	**Malevolent**
	Synonym: Adj: malicious, cruel, mean, hateful, vicious, vindictive, hostile
	Antonym: kind, compassionate, nice
1194.	**Malicious**
	Synonym: Adj: vicious, slanderous, hateful, spiteful, nasty, mean
	Antonym: nice, kind, friendly
1195.	**Malignant**
	Synonym: Adj: fatal, lethal, deadly, cancerous
	Antonym: good, healthy, benign
1196.	**Mammoth**
	Synonym: Adj: huge, enormous, gigantic, colossal, monstrous, oversized, immense, gargantuan
	Antonym: tiny, little, small, undersized
1197.	**Maniac**
	Synonym: Noun: psychopath, psychotic, sociopath, lunatic, (slang) nut, madman
1198.	**Manifest**
	Synonym: Adj: evident, obvious, plain, apparent, clear, unmistakable
	Antonym: concealed, masked, hidden

1199.	**Manipulate**
	Synonym: Verb: mould, shape, work, steer, manoeuvre, guide
1200.	**Manoeuvre**
	Synonym: Verb: contrive, plot, scheme, conspire, move, direct, deploy, manipulate, steer
1201.	**Mangle**
	Synonym: Verb: damage, mutilate, twist, ruin, maul, tear
1202.	**Marauder**
	Synonym: Noun: raider, plunderer, attacker
1203.	**Maroon**
	Synonym: Verb: abandon, leave behind, desert, put, ashore, forsake
1204.	**Marvellous**
	Synonym: Adj: terrific, fabulous, great, fantastic, wondrous, exceptional, superb
	Antonym: terrible, bad, horrible, awful
1205.	**Massacre**
	Synonym: Noun: slaughter, killing, annihilation, execution, extermination
1206.	**Mayhem**
	Synonym: Noun: chaos, confusion, havoc, pandemonium, disorder, violence
	Antonym: peace, tranquility, inactivity
1207.	**Meagre**
	Synonym: Adj: skimpy, sparse, inadequate, scarce, slender, insufficient, slight
	Antonym: large, plentiful, abundant
1208.	**Meddle**
	Synonym: Verb: interfere, intrude, pry, snoop, intervene
1209.	**Meddlesome**
	Synonym: Adj: interfering, officious, obtrusive, noisy, intrusive
1210.	**Meek**
	Synonym: Adj: unassertive, mild, gentle, docile, submissive, passive, shy, unassuming, weak, timid
	Antonym: bold, assertive, aggressive
1211.	**Melancholy**
	Synonym: Adj: sad, depressed, downcast, dejected, gloomy, forlorn
	Antonym: happy, glad, cheerful

1212.	**Mellow**
	Synonym: Adj: gentle, mild, light, delicate, moderate
	Verb: soften, improve, mature, season, develop
	Antonym: harsh, sharp, harden
1213.	**Melodious**
	Synonym: Adj: melodic, musical, tuneful, euphonic, symphonic, mellifluous
	Antonym: discordant, cacophonous
1214.	**Menace**
	Synonym: Noun: danger, threat, risk, hazard, peril
	Antonym: blessing, friend, boon, guard, help, aid
1215.	**Mend**
	Synonym: Verb: repair, patch, heal, restore, stitch
1216.	**Menial**
	Synonym: Adj: lowly, humble, degrading, servile, base
	Antonym: elevated, dignified, stately
1217.	**Mentor**
	Synonym: Noun: teacher, guide, instructor, guru, adviser
	Antonym: student, learner, novice, apprentice
1218.	**Merge**
	Synonym: Verb: converge, combine, fuse, join, unite
	Antonym: diverge, split, separate
1219.	**Merger**
	Synonym: Noun: alliance, union, consolidation, incorporation, fusion
1220.	**Metamorphosis**
	Synonym: Noun: transformation, transmogrification, rebirth, transmutation, sublimation
1221.	**Metaphysical**
	Synonym: Adj: supernatural, immaterial, spiritual, impalpable, unearthly, mystical
	Antonym: physical, earthly, mundane
1222.	**Meticulous**
	Synonym: Adj: careful, painstaking, exact, fastidious, particular
	Antonym: careless, sloppy, slack

1223.	**Mimic**
	Synonym: Verb: impersonate, copy, echo, reproduce, imitate, mirror
1224.	**Mind-boggling**
	Synonym: Adj: astonishing, stunning, overwhelming, staggering, mind- blowing, unbelievable
1225.	**Mingle**
	Synonym: Verb: mix, socialize, circulate, merge, blend
	Antonym: separate, scatter, disperse
1226.	**Mirth**
	Synonym: Noun: happiness, cheerfulness, joyfulness, amusement, merriment, gaiety
	Antonym: sadness, melancholy, depression
1227.	**Miraculous**
	Synonym: Adj: wondrous, magical, extraordinary, unbelievable, amazing
	Antonym: ordinary, natural, common
1228.	**Miscellaneous**
	Synonym: Adj: varied, various, mixed, assorted, diverse
	Antonym: uniform, identical, similar
1229.	**Mischievous**
	Synonym: Adj: playful, prankish, impish, teasing, exasperating
1230.	**Misdemeanour**
	Synonym: Noun: offence, misdeed, violation, indiscretion, misconduct, wrongdoing
1231.	**Miserable**
	Synonym: Adj: unhappy, depressed, sad, dejected, despondent, forlorn, unpleasant, joyless, troublesome, wretched, pitiful
	Antonym: happy, joyous, cheerful, comfortable, untroubled
1232.	**Mitigate**
	Synonym: Verb: lessen, soften, diminish, lighten, alleviate, moderate
	Antonym: increase, worsen, deepen
1233.	**Moan**
	Synonym: Noun: groan, wail, sob, keen, whimper ***Verb:*** groan, wail, sob, keen, whimper, cry

1234.	**Mob**
	Synonym: ***Noun:*** crowd, gathering, horde, throng, swarm, group, pack, host ***Verb:*** crowd, swarm, deluge, inundate, attack
1235.	**Mock**
	Synonym: Verb: ridiculous, insult, abuse, jeer, taunt, tease, deride
	Antonym: praise, compliment, admire
1236.	**Mockery**
	Synonym: Noun: ridicule, insulting, jeering, taunting, teasing, scorn, sham, joke, laughingstock, absurdity, farce
	Antonym: praise, respect, approval
1237.	**Modest**
	Synonym: Adj: shy, humble, unassuming, bashful, blushing, unpretentious, limited, moderate, adequate, small, passable
	Antonym: immodest, proud, arrogant, grand, generous, impressive
1238.	**Modesty**
	Synonym: Noun: humbleness, humility, diffidence, bashfulness, shyness, decency, reserve, propriety, decorum, discretion
	Antonym: boastfulness, arrogance, vanity, immodesty, showiness
1239.	**Molest**
	Synonym: Verb: abuse, harass, assault, torment, annoy, plague
1240.	**Mollify**
	Synonym: Verb: soothe, appease, soften, calm, mellow, pacify
	Antonym: intensify, inflame, aggravate
1241.	**Momentous**
	Synonym: Adj: important, major, significant, memorable, eventful
	Antonym: insignificant, unimportant, trivial
1242.	**Monster**
	Synonym: Noun: ogre, brute, fiend, beast, demon
1243.	**Monstrous**
	Synonym: Adj: horrible, terrifying, frightful, gruesome, evil, foul, vile, diabolical, huge, enormous, gigantic, immense, mammoth
	Antonym: pleasing, kindly, gentle, small, tiny, minute

1244.	**Monotonous**
	Synonym: Adj: unchanging, unvarying, dull, boring, tedious, dreary, routine
	Antonym: exciting, invigorating, changing
1245.	**Morbid**
	Synonym: Adj: unwholesome, sickly, unsound, unhealthy, grim, gruesome, macabre
	Antonym: wholesome, sound, healthy
1246.	**Moron**
	Synonym: Noun: idiot, imbecile, ignoramus, dope, nitwit, dullard
	Antonym: genius, savant, scholar
1247.	**Morose**
	Synonym: Adj: sullen, sulky, grim, gloomy, sombre, depressed
	Antonym: cheerful, joyful, happy
1248.	**Moot**
	Synonym: Adj: debatable, unsettled, open for discussion, unresolved, arguable, controversial
	Antonym: resolved, determined, indisputable
1249.	**Morsel**
	Synonym: Noun: bite, mouthful, scrap, crumb, shred, pinch, bit
1250.	**Muddled**
	Synonym: confused, bewildered, befuddled, mixed-up, lost, disoriented
	Antonym: clear, lucid, sharp
1251.	**Mudslinging**
	Synonym: Noun: defamation, slander, name-calling, smear campaign, insulting
1252.	**Muffle**
	Synonym: Verb: dampen, mute, quiet, hush, silence, cloak, shroud
	Antonym: heighten, intensify, amplify
1253.	**Multitude**
	Synonym: Noun: crowd, gathering swarm, mass, pack, assembly, throng, horde
1254.	**Mutilate**
	Synonym: Verb: disfigure, mangle, maul, maim, butcher, deform
1255.	**Myriad**
	Synonym: Noun: assortment, array, host, crowd, swarm, abundance, torrent
	Antonym: few, limited

	N
1256.	**Nag**
	Synonym: Verb: pester, harass, annoy, bother, irritate, torment, badger
	Antonym: Appease, soothe
1257.	**Naïve**
	Synonym: Adj: innocent, simple, unworldly, unsophisticated, unaffected
	Antonym: sophisticated, experienced
1258.	**Narcissistic**
	Synonym: Adj: egotistical, conceited, self-infatuated, egocentric, self- absorbed, in love with oneself, self-loving, self-admiring, self-obsessed, self-centred, self-regarding, egomaniac
	Antonym: modest, self-effacing
1259.	**Nasty**
	Synonym: Adj: unpleasant, disagreeable, disgusting, distasteful, terrible, awful, mean, cruel, vicious, hateful, vile, beastly
	Antonym: enjoyable, pleasant, nice, sweet
1260.	**Nemesis**
	Synonym: Noun: retribution, vengeance, vindication, punishment
1261.	**Niche**
	Synonym: Noun: corner, nook, recess, hollow, cavity, hole, position, place, purpose, slot
1262.	**Nimble**
	Synonym: Adj: agile, speedy, active, lively, quick, swift, alert
	Antonym: slow, awkward, clumsy
1263.	**Nitty-gritty**
	Synonym: Noun: basics, essentials, essence, fundamentals, substance, quintessence, crux, nucleus
1264.	**Nonchalant**
	Synonym: Adj: casually, unconcerned, indifferent, uninvolved, calm, cool, easygoing, composed
	Antonym: anxious, concerned, disturbed
1265.	**Nonconformist**
	Synonym: Noun: individualist, eccentric, freethinker, dissenter, rebel, original
	Antonym: conformist, follower, orthodox

1266.	**Nonpareil**
	Synonym: Adj: incomparable, matchless, unparalleled, unequalled, without equal, peerless, unmatched, beyond comparison, unsurpassed, unsurpassable, unbeatable, inimitable, unique
	Antonym: mediocre, average, common
1267.	**Nonsense**
	Synonym: Noun: rubbish, balderdash, claptrap, ridiculousness, stupidity, absurdity, ludicrousness
	Antonym: sense, wisdom
1268.	**Nostalgia**
	Synonym: Noun: longing, wistfulness, remembrance
1269.	**Notoriety**
	Synonym: Noun: infamy, scandal, disrepute, disgrace, dishonour, shame
	Antonym: honour, esteem, standing
1270.	**Notorious**
	Synonym: Adj: infamous, scandalous
	Antonym: renowned, celebrated
1271.	**Notwithstanding**
	Synonym: Adv: nevertheless, nonetheless, even so, in spite of this/that, despite this/that, after everything, however, still, yet, at all events *Conj:* although, in spite of the fact that, despite the fact that, even though, though, for all that
1272.	**Nourish**
	Synonym: Verb: nurture, feed, support, supply, sustain, strengthen
	Antonym: starve, deprive
1273.	**Novice**
	Synonym: Noun: beginner, starter, learner, apprentice, trainee, newcomer, rookie
	Antonym: master, expert, veteran
1274.	**Noxious**
	Synonym: Adj: toxic, harmful, poisonous, injurious, damaging, foul, lethal
	Antonym: safe, harmless, healthful
1275.	**Nurture**
	Synonym: Verb: nourish, feed, nurse, strengthen, sustain, raise, rear, develop, foster

O	
1276.	**Obdurate**
	Synonym: Adj: hardhearted, stubborn, unyielding
1277.	**Obliterate**
	Synonym: Verb: destroy, annihilate, raze, level, ruin, crush, erase, remove, delete
	Antonym: build, restore, create, preserve
1278.	**Oblivious**
	Synonym: Adj: unaware, unobservant, unmindful, heedless, neglectful
	Antonym: aware, mindful, conscious, heedful
1279.	**Obnoxious**
	Synonym: Adj: annoying, offensive, objectionable, unpleasant, disagreeable, repulsive
	Antonym: pleasant, agreeable, congenial
1280.	**Obsessed**
	Synonym: Adj: fixated, driven, preoccupied, crazed, possessed, consumed, gripped
1281.	**Obsession**
	Synonym: Noun: passion, compulsion, mania, fixation, preoccupation
1282.	**Obsolete**
	Synonym: Adj: old-fashioned, outdated, outmoded, extinct, antiquated
	Antonym: current, fashionable, new, modern
1283.	**Obstinate**
	Synonym: Adj: stubborn, headstrong, inflexible, unyielding, determined
	Antonym: flexible, pliable, yielding
1284.	**Obstruction**
	Synonym: Noun: obstacle, barrier, block, impediment, interference, barricade, bar
	Antonym: freeing, clearing, aid, opening
1285.	**Obtrusive**
	Synonym: Adj: interfering, intruding, pushy, meddlesome
	Antonym: reserved, patient, unassuming
1286.	**Obvious**
	Synonym: Adj: plain, clear, unmistakable, evident, visible, apparent, distinct
	Antonym: indistinct, obscure, subtle, hidden

1287.	**Occult**
	Synonym: Adj: supernatural, mystical, paranormal, secret, obscure, esoteric, arcane, otherworldly
1288.	**Oddity**
	Synonym: Noun: abnormality, irregularity, peculiarity, anomaly, quirk
1289.	**Offend**
	Synonym: Verb: displease, annoy, irritate, anger, provoke, upset, disturb
	Antonym: please, delight, charm
1290.	**Offensive**
	Synonym: Adj: insulting, obnoxious, rude, repugnant, revolting, sickening, nasty
	Antonym: pleasing, respectful
1291.	**Onerous**
	Synonym: Adj: burdensome, weighty, arduous, strenuous, uphill, difficult, severe, formidable, Herculean, taxing
	Antonym: easy, effortless
1292.	**Opaque**
	Synonym: Adj: impenetrable, impervious, nontransparent, murky, unclear, abstruse
	Antonym: clear, transparent, lucid
1293.	**Opprobrium**
	Synonym: vilification, vituperation, condemnation, criticism, censure, castigation, denunciation, denigration, disparagement, derogation, slander, disgrace, shame, dishonour, discredit, stigma, humiliation, ignominy
	Antonym: praise, honour
1294.	**Oppress**
	Synonym: Verb: subdue, tyrannize, keep down, crush, subjugate, depress, stifle, dominate
	Antonym: liberate, emancipate, free
1295.	**Oppression**
	Synonym: Noun: tyranny, subjugation, domination, control, abuse, subjection, force
	Antonym: freedom, liberation, emancipation
1296.	**Oppressive**
	Synonym: Adj: tyrannical, cruel, brutal, harsh, repressive, burdensome, trying, depressing, overpowering, discouraging, difficult, exacting
	Antonym: liberating, humane, just, heartening, encouraging

1297.	**Oscillate**
	Synonym: Verb: alternate, swing, vibrate, pulsate, flicker, waver, sway
1298.	**Ostentatious**
	Synonym: Adj: flaunting, pretentious, pompous, boastful, flashy, showy
	Antonym: modest, simple, reserved
1299.	**Ostracism**
	Synonym: Noun: banishment, exile, expulsion, rejection, shunning
	Antonym: inclusion, acceptance, welcoming
1300.	**Ostracize**
	Synonym: Verb: banish, exile, exclude, reject, shun, excommunicate
	Antonym: include, welcome, accept
1301.	**Outburst**
	Synonym: Noun: outbreak, explosion, eruption, outpouring, flood, rush, torrent
	Antonym: control, restraint, repression
1302.	**Outcry**
	Synonym: Noun: cry, uproar, scream, clamour, tumult, shout, outburst
	Antonym: murmur, whispering, calm
1303.	**Outlandish**
	Synonym: Adj: wild, weird, unusual, odd, offbeat, alien, strange, freakish, bizarre
1304.	**Outmoded**
	Synonym: Adj: old-fashioned, outdated, antiquated, obsolete
	Antonym: new, modern, cutting-edge
1305.	**Outrageous**
	Synonym: Adj: atrocious, brutal, vicious, evil, fiendish, monstrous, inhumane, shocking, disgraceful, shameful, offensive, horrible, awful, excessive, unreasonable
	Antonym: humane, beneficial, kind, decent, acceptable, proper, reasonable
1306.	**Outstanding**
	Synonym: Adj: remarkable, exceptional, excellent, prominent, foremost
	Antonym: ordinary, common, average
1307.	**Overbearing**
	Synonym: Adj: domineering, oppressive, overpowering, overwhelming
	Antonym: casual, subdued, timid

1308.	**Overthrow**
	Synonym: Verb: conquer, overpower, destroy, vanquish, defeat, overturn, upset
	Antonym: restore, support, uphold, preservation, protection
1309.	**Overwhelm**
	Synonym: Verb: overpower, overcome, devastate, shatter, defeat, beat, crush

P

1310.	**Painstaking**
	Synonym: Adj: exacting, careful, meticulous, thorough, diligent
	Antonym: careless, haphazard
1311.	**Palatable**
	Synonym: Adj: tasteful, delicious, enjoyable, savoury, pleasant, appetizing
	Antonym: distasteful, repugnant
1312.	**Pale**
	Synonym: Adj: colourless, pallid, sickly, anaemic
	Antonym: bright, vivid
1313.	**Palpable**
	Synonym: Adj: perceptible, touchable, tangible, perceivable, physical
1314.	**Paltry**
	Synonym: Adj: small, insignificant, trivial, trifling, meagre, petty, worthless
	Antonym: important, significant, major, worthy
1315.	**Pamper**
	Synonym: Verb: favour, indulge, coddle
	Antonym: neglect, ignore, mistreat
1316.	**Panacea**
	Synonym: Noun: cure-all, catholicon, fix-all, remedy, elixir
1317.	**Pandemonium**
	Synonym: Noun: bedlam, chaos, mayhem, uproar, havoc, turmoil, tumult, commotion, confusion, disorder, anarchy, furore, frenzy
	Antonym: silence, peace
1318.	**Panic**
	Synonym: Noun: terror, fear, alarm, fright, hysteria, dread, frenzy, scare
	Antonym: calm, composure

1319.	**Parable**
	Synonym: Noun: fable, allegory, lesson, moral tale
1320.	**Paradigm**
	Synonym: Noun: model, example, ideal, standard, pattern
1321.	**Paradox**
	Synonym: Noun: inconsistency, contradiction, enigma, mystery
1322.	**Paramount**
	Synonym: Adj: supreme, superior, dominant, principal, foremost, pre-eminent
	Antonym: least, secondary, minor
1323.	**Paraphernalia**
	Synonym: Noun: equipment, effects, gear, things, stuff, accoutrements
1324.	**Parochial**
	Synonym: Adj: provincial, local, regional, limited, narrow, insular
	Antonym: cosmopolitan, worldly, broad
1325.	**Partial**
	Synonym: Adj: incomplete, part, limited, unfinished, fragmentary, fractional, biased, prejudiced, one-sided, partisan, unfair, unjust, unbalanced
	Antonym: all, whole, complete, fair, impartial, balanced, just
1326.	**Partisan**
	Synonym: Adj: partial, biased, one-sided, sectarian, prejudiced
	Antonym: unbiased, bipartisan, open-minded
1327.	**Passable**
	Synonym: Adj: acceptable, allowable, adequate, tolerable, fair, satisfactory, clear, navigable, unobstructed
	Antonym: unacceptable, inadequate, unsatisfactory, impassable, obstructed, closed
1328.	**Passive**
	Synonym: Adj: inactive, quiet, submissive, apathetic, resigned, non-resistant
	Antonym: active, assertive, aggressive
1329.	**Pastime**
	Synonym: Noun: entertainment, amusement, recreation, enjoyment, diversion

1330.	**Pathetic**
	Synonym: Adj: pitiful, sad, touching, pitiable
	Antonym: laughable, amusing
1331.	**Peculiar**
	Synonym: Adj: odd, unusual, strange, distinctive, abnormal, queer, unique
	Antonym: common, usual, ordinary, general
1332.	**Peculiarity**
	Synonym: Noun: feature, particularity, trait, oddity, uniqueness, characteristic
1333.	**Pedant**
	Synonym: Noun: dogmatist, formalist, doctrinaire, quibbler, hair-splitter, sophist
1334.	**Peer**
	Synonym: *Verb:* examine, stare, gaze, look, pry *Noun:* equal, counterpart, match, colleague
1335.	**Peerless**
	Synonym: Adj: unrivalled, unmatched, superior, incomparable, best, greatest, matchless, inimitable, beyond compare, unparalleled, unequalled, without equal, second to none, unsurpassed, unsurpassable, nonparallel
	Antonym: second-rate, inferior
1336.	**Peevish**
	Synonym: Adj: irritable, ill-tempered, grouchy, moody, touchy, crabby
	Antonym: cheerful, contented, happy
1337.	**Pejorative**
	Synonym: Adj: disparaging, negating, deprecatory, belittling, degrading, uncomplimentary
	Antonym: complimentary, reverent, flattering
1338.	**Pell-mell**
	Synonym: Adv: helter-skelter, disorder, confusion, disarray, disorganized manner
1339.	**Pensive**
	Synonym: Adj: reflective, meditative, absorbed, thoughtful, dreamy, melancholy
	Antonym: happy, carefree, frivolous
1340.	**Perceptible**
	Synonym: Adj: perceivable, palpable, discernible, observable, apparent, conspicuous
	Antonym: imperceptible, invisible, impalpable

1341.	**Perennial**
	Synonym: Adj: returning, perpetual, recurrent, everlasting, enduring, continuous
	Antonym: short-lived, temporary
1342.	**Perfidious**
	Synonym: Adj: disloyal, treacherous, deceitful, disloyal, faithless, unfaithful, traitorous, treasonous
	Antonym: faithful, loyal
1343.	**Perfidy**
	Synonym: Noun: treachery, duplicity, deceit, perfidiousness, deceitfulness, disloyalty, infidelity, faithlessness, unfaithfulness, betrayal, treason, falseness, falsity, double-dealing, dishonesty
	Antonym: faithfulness, loyalty
1344.	**Peril**
	Synonym: Noun: danger, risk, hazard, jeopardy, threat, pitfall
	Antonym: safety, security
1345.	**Perilous**
	Synonym: Adj: dangerous, hazardous, threatening, precarious, chancy, risky
	Antonym: safe, secure, harmless
1346.	**Perjury**
	Synonym: Noun: lying, dishonesty, deception, falsification, false testimony, prevarication
1347.	**Permeate**
	Synonym: Verb: pervade, fill, spread, penetrate, saturate, suffuse
1348.	**Pernicious**
	Synonym: Adj: harmful, damaging, destructive, injurious, detrimental, deleterious, dangerous, adverse, malignant, noxious, poisonous, cancerous, ruinous, deadly, lethal, fatal
	Antonym: beneficial, benign, favourable
1349.	**Perpetrate**
	Synonym: Verb: commit, perform, execute, accomplish, inflict, wreak
1350.	**Perpetual**
	Synonym: Adj: everlasting, permanent, eternal, continuing, endless, continual, constant, ceaseless
	Antonym: temporary, inconstant, transitory

1351.	**Perplex**
	Synonym: Verb: confuse, puzzle, bewilder, confound, baffle, mystify
	Antonym: enlighten, assure
1352.	**Persecute**
	Synonym: Verb: harass, oppress, torment, abuse, maltreat, hound, victimize, badger, bully
	Antonym: support, uphold, favour, accommodate
1353.	**Persevere**
	Synonym: Verb: persist, continue, strive, endure, pursue
	Antonym: stop, falter, discontinue
1354.	**Perseverance**
	Synonym: Noun: persistence, diligence, steadfastness, doggedness, dedication, drive, tenacity
1355.	**Persistent**
	Synonym: Adj: determined, constant, stubborn, relentless, tireless, unceasing
	Antonym: inconstant, wavering, changeable
1356.	**Personify**
	Synonym: Verb: represent, embody, exemplify, symbolize, epitomize, typify
1357.	**Perspicacious**
	Synonym: Adj: discerning, shrewd, perceptive, astute, penetrating, observant, percipient, sharp-witted, sharp, quick, quick-witted, keen-witted, clear-sighted, sharp-sighted, clear- eyed, far-sighted, far-seeing, canny, intelligent, insightful, judicious, wise, sagacious, intuitive
	Antonym: inattentive, dull, stupid
1358.	**Persuade**
	Synonym: Verb: convince, induce, urge, influence, coax, prompt, sway, entice
	Antonym: discourage, dissuade
1359.	**Pertinent**
	Synonym: Adj: relevant, germane, applicable, related, connected, pertaining
	Antonym: impertinent, irrelevant, immaterial
1360.	**Perturb**
	Synonym: Verb: disturb, worry, trouble, upset, disquiet, fluster, unsettle
	Antonym: calm, quiet, soothe, compose

1361.	**Peruse**
	Synonym: Verb: examine, read, review, scrutinize, study, scan, observe
1362.	**Pervade**
	Synonym: Verb: permeate, saturate, penetrate, suffuse, imbue, spread
1363.	**Perverse**
	Synonym: Adj: stubborn, obstinate, unreasonable, headstrong
	Antonym: agreeable, reasonable, proper
1364.	**Perverted**
	Synonym: Adj: distorted, corrupt, warped, depraved, sick, immoral, deviant, impaired
	Antonym: normal, balanced, sound, healthy
1365.	**Pester**
	Synonym: Verb: bother, annoy, harass, irritate, torment, disturb, badger, trouble
1366.	**Pestilence**
	Synonym: Noun: plague, pest, epidemic, scourge, disease, curse
1367.	**Petrify**
	Synonym: Verb: stun, paralyse, daze, numb, transfix, immobilize, shock, fossilize, solidify, harden, mineralize, calcify
	Antonym: soften, liquefy
1368.	**Petty**
	Synonym: Adj: small, trivial, little, unimportant, insignificant, minor, trifling, paltry, mean
	Antonym: major, important, vital
1369.	**Petulant**
	Synonym: Adj: irritable, moody, grouchy, crabby, touchy, peevish, ill-tempered
	Antonym: cheerful, light-hearted, good-humoured
1370.	**Phenomenal**
	Synonym: Adj: extraordinary, miraculous, remarkable, amazing, fantastic
	Antonym: ordinary, routine, unexceptional
1371.	**Pilfer**
	Synonym: Verb: steal, rob, plunder, thieve, swipe, lift, take, snatch
1372.	**Pillage**
	Synonym: Noun: theft, plundering, destruction, devastation, robbery

1373.	**Pinnacle**
	Synonym: Noun: top, summit, apex, peak, zenith, crest, climax
	Antonym: bottom, low, nadir
1374.	**Pioneer**
	Synonym: Noun: settler, explorer, pathfinder, frontiersman, originator, innovator, founder, developer, forerunner ***Verb:*** lead, start, initiate, develop, establish, originate
	Antonym: descendant, successor, follower, disciple, follow, continue, succeed
1375.	**Piteous**
	Synonym: Adj: sad, pitiful, sorrowful, touching, heartbreaking, distressing, pathetic, poignant
	Antonym: heartwarming, cheerful, delightful
1376.	**Placate**
	Synonym: Verb: calm, soothe, appease, pacify, quiet, satisfy
	Antonym: anger, displease, dissatisfy
1377.	**Placid**
	Synonym: Adj: calm, serene, tranquil, peaceful, quiet, untroubled
	Antonym: agitated, temperamental, turbulent
1378.	**Plagiarism**
	Synonym: Noun: copying, imitation, cribbing, stealing, infringement, counterfeiting
1379.	**Platonic**
	Synonym: Adj: nonphysical, emotional, ideal, spiritual, celibate, intellectual
	Antonym: physical, sexual, lustful
1380.	**Plausible**
	Synonym: Adj: believable, likely, credible, reasonable, feasible, possible
	Antonym: unbelievable, unlikely, implausible
1381.	**Plethora**
	Synonym: Noun: overabundance, excess, profusion, overflow, surplus, deluge
	Antonym: scarcity, paucity, dearth
1382.	**Pliable**
	Synonym: Adj: flexible, pliant, elastic, supple, malleable
	Antonym: hard, rigid, unyielding

1383.	**Plunder**
	Synonym: Verb: rob, loot, pillage, ransack, raid, ravage, steal
1384.	**Plunge**
	Synonym: Verb: immerse, dip, submerge, dunk, sink, douse, dive, jump, splash, fall, plummet, descend
	Noun: fall, dive, jump, drop, leap, descent
1385.	**Poignant**
	Synonym: Noun: touching, soul-stirring, moving, heartrending, emotional, sad
1386.	**Poke**
	Synonym: Verb: prod, jab, push, hit, shove, nudge, stab
	Noun: punch, jab, thrust, hit
1387.	**Polarize**
	Synonym: Verb: contradict, take sides, oppose, conflict, diverge, differ
	Antonym: agree, come together, ally
1388.	**Pompous**
	Synonym: Adj: boastful, pretentious, arrogant, self-important, grandiose, vain, overbearing
	Antonym: humble, modest, unassuming
1389.	**Ponder**
	Synonym: Verb: consider, study, think, examine, reflect, deliberate, contemplate
1390.	**Ponderous**
	Synonym: Adj: cumbersome, unwieldy, bulky, massive, heavy, awkward
1391.	**Pragmatic**
	Synonym: Adj: practical, real, actual, real-world, workable, utilitarian
	Antonym: unrealistic, idealistic, theoretical
1392.	**Precarious**
	Synonym: Adj: hazardous, risky, perilous, treacherous, uncertain, unstable, unreliable, insecure
	Antonym: safe, steady, dependable, certain
1393.	**Precedence**
	Synonym: Noun: priority, pre-eminence, supremacy, importance, superiority
	Antonym: second place, inferiority

1394.	**Precedent**
	Synonym: Noun: model, example, prior instance, exemplar, classic case, antecedent
1395.	**Precept**
	Synonym: Noun: law, rule, principle, guideline, commandment, maxim
1396.	**Precise**
	Synonym: Adj: exact, specific, definite, explicit, correct, accurate, inflexible, rigid, strict, unbending
	Antonym: approximate, vague, ambiguous, informal, casual
1397.	**Precision**
	Synonym: Noun: accuracy, exactness, correctness
	Antonym: inaccuracy, vagueness
1398.	**Preclude**
	Synonym: Verb: prevent, stop, hinder, forestall, thwart, foil
	Antonym: help, enable, allow, permit
1399.	**Precocious**
	Synonym: Adj: advanced, premature, bright, mature, gifted, early-blooming
	Antonym: late-blooming, immature, behind
1400.	**Predator**
	Synonym: Noun: hunter, carnivore, meat-eater, killer, stalker, prowler
1401.	**Predicament**
	Synonym: Noun: dilemma, fix, mess, crisis, difficulty
1402.	**Predominant**
	Synonym: Adj: dominant, important, prevailing, primary, supreme, major, main
	Antonym: secondary, minor, lesser, subordinate
1403.	**Preeminent**
	Synonym: Adj: superior, foremost, dominant, incomparable, peerless, unsurpassed
	Antonym: inferior, minor, unimportant
1404.	**Preempt**
	Synonym: Verb: appropriate, usurp, seize, assume, take over, bump
1405.	**Prejudice**
	Synonym: Noun: bias, intolerance, partiality, unfairness, preconception, prejudgment, bigotry
	Antonym: objectivity, open-mindedness

1406.	**Preliminary**
	Synonym: Adj: opening, introductory, beginning, preparatory, starting
	Antonym: final, concluding, ending
1407.	**Premonition**
	Synonym: Noun: foreboding, intuition, gut feeling, hunch, apprehension, suspicion
1408.	**Preposterous**
	Synonym: Adj: silly, ridiculous, unreasonable, outrageous, absurd, foolish, crazy
1409.	**Presumptuous**
	Synonym: Adj: overconfident, arrogant, forward, nervy, audacious, pompous
	Antonym: unassuming, humble, modest
1410.	**Pretentious**
	Synonym: Adj: pompous, self-important, showy, gaudy, affected, smug
	Antonym: modest, unassuming, simple
1411.	**Prevail**
	Synonym: Verb: win, overcome, beat, dominate, conquer, succeed
	Antonym: lose, fail, flop
1412.	**Prevailing**
	Synonym: Adj: reigning, superior, dominating, dominant, predominant, preponderant
	Antonym: failing, outmoded, inferior
1413.	**Prim**
	Synonym: Adj: proper, prudish, upright, correct, straightlaced, stiff
	Antonym: wild, casual, unrefined
1414.	**Pristine**
	Synonym: Adj: untouched, clean, uncontaminated, unpolluted, unspoiled, pure
	Antonym: spoiled, contaminated, sullied
1415.	**Probable**
	Synonym: Adj: likely, believable, credible, presumable, feasible, reasonable, expected, promising, presumed
	Antonym: unlikely, improbable unreasonable
1416.	**Prodigal**
	Synonym: Adj: wasteful, extravagant, spendthrift, lavish, excessive, immoderate
	Antonym: thrifty, frugal, moderate

1417. Prodigious

Synonym: Adj: enormous, stupendous, extraordinary, monumental, Herculean, impressive, phenomenal

Antonym: tiny, insignificant, trivial

1418. Profane

Synonym: Adj: wicked, sinful, obscene, blasphemous, worldly, secular
Verb: debase, desecrate, abuse, offend, revile, violate, blaspheme

Antonym: reverent, pious, respect

1419. Profound

Synonym: Adj: deep, penetrating, thoughtful, wise, intellectual, insightful, learned, serious, thorough, severe, deep, total, exhaustive, intense

Antonym: shallow, stupid, meaningless, silly, slight, superficial

1420. Profuse

Synonym: Adj: free-flowing, abundant, copious, plentiful, excessive, lavish

Antonym: sparse, meagre, limited

1421. Profusion

Synonym: Noun: outpouring, overflow, abundance, deluge, flood, plethora, excess

Antonym: dearth, scarcity

1422. Proliferate

Synonym: Verb: grow, mushroom, expand, spread, multiply, increase

Antonym: decrease, die out, recede

1423. Prolific

Synonym: Adj: productive, fertile, fruitful, creative

Antonym: unproductive, unfruitful

1424. Prolong

Synonym: Verb: extend, lengthen, stretch, continue, delay, draw out

Antonym: abbreviate, shorten, limit, curtail

1425. Prompt

Synonym: Adj: quick, immediate, done without delay

1426. Promptly

Synonym: Adv: immediately, at once, instantly, now, quickly

Antonym: slowly, eventually

1427. Promulgate

Synonym: Verb: proclaim, publicize, publish, state, announce communicate, broadcast

1428. Propensity

Synonym: Noun: inclination, tendency, penchant, proclivity, bent, predilection

1429. Prophecy

Synonym: Noun: prediction, forecast, divination, revelation, foretelling

1430. Prophesy

Synonym: Verb: predict, forecast, foretell, divine, forewarn, soothsay

1431. Propitious

Synonym: Adj: favourable, auspicious, fortunate, opportune, timely, advantageous

Antonym: unfavourable, unfortunate, untimely

1432. Proponent

Synonym: Noun: advocate, supporter, backer, champion, exponent, defender

Antonym: opponent, foe, detractor

1433. Propriety

Synonym: Noun: manners, properness, decorum, etiquette, politeness, appropriateness

Antonym: impropriety, rudeness

1434. Propulsion

Synonym: Noun: thrust, force, power, energy, push, drive

1435. Prosaic

Synonym: Adj: dull, boring, monotonous, humdrum, unimaginative

Antonym: interesting, imaginative, exciting

1436. Proscribe

Synonym: Verb: ban, prohibit, outlaw, forbid, condemn, boycott

Antonym: allow, permit, accept

1437. Prospective

Synonym: Adj: future, proposed, coming, expected, impending, eventual, anticipated, planned

1438. Prosperous

Synonym: Adj: profitable, flourishing, successful, thriving, booming, lucrative

Antonym: unprofitable, failing, bankrupt

1439.	**Prosperity**
	Synonym: Noun: success, wealth, fortune, affluence, riches, abundance
1440.	**Prostrate**
	Synonym: Adj: prone, recumbent, horizontal, flat, lying down
	Antonym: upright, standing, erect
1441.	**Protagonist**
	Synonym: Noun: principal, lead, hero, heroine, exponent, central figure
1442.	**Provoke**
	Synonym: Verb: annoy, irritate, bother, irk, enrage, anger, aggravate, vex, cause, prompt, incite, kindle, arouse, produce, awaken
1443.	**Provocation**
	Synonym: Noun: incitement, spark, instigation, inducement, stimulus
1444.	**Provocative**
	Synonym: Adj: provoking, stimulating, aggravating, exciting, arousing, instigating
	Antonym: inane, dull, uninteresting
1445.	**Prowess**
	Synonym: Noun: strength, skill, courage, bravery, heroism, valour, might, power
	Antonym: weakness, cowardice, fear, incompetence
1446.	**Prudent**
	Synonym: Adj: cautious, discreet, careful, sensible, levelheaded, thoughtful, wise, cool, frugal, thrifty, economical, sparing, saving
	Antonym: reckless, rash, careless, foolish, wasteful, extravagant
1447.	**Prudish**
	Synonym: Adj: prim, prissy, formal, puritanical
	Antonym: casual, tolerant, natural, free
1448.	**Pugnacious**
	Synonym: Adj: fond of fighting, aggressive, hostile, antagonistic, combative, contentious, belligerent, bellicose
	Antonym: peaceful, pacifistic, passive
1449.	**Pulverize**
	Synonym: Verb: grind, demolish, atomize, shatter, crumble, crush, smash
1450.	**Pungent**
	Synonym: Adj: sharp-tasting, spicy, strong, flavourful, peppery, seasoned, zesty, biting, sharp, caustic, piercing, pointed, sarcastic
	Antonym: bland, mild, tasteless, dull, inane
1451.	**Punitive**
	Synonym: Adj: punishing, penalizing, penal, disciplinary, corrective, harsh
1452.	**Purge**
	Synonym: Verb: clear, expel, dump, remove, clean, cleanse, eliminate
1453.	**Putrid**
	Synonym: Adj: rotten, spoiled, decayed, decomposed, rancid, bad, foul
	Antonym: fresh, healthy, unspoiled
1454.	**Puzzle**
	Synonym: Noun: mystery, problem, dilemma, riddle, enigma, paradox ***Verb:*** confuse, confound, bewilder, perplex, baffle, mystify, bemuse
1455.	**Puzzling**
	Synonym: Adj: perplexing, bewildering, baffling, confounding, mysterious, mystifying

Q

1456.	**Quagmire**
	Synonym: Noun: bog, marsh, morass, swamp, predicament, quandary, mess, plight, entanglement
1457.	**Quake**
	Synonym: Verb: shake, tremble, quiver, shiver, shudder, sway, rock, wobble, move, heave, convulse
1458.	**Quail**
	Synonym: Verb: cower, cringe, flinch, tremble, shudder, shake
1459.	**Quandary**
	Synonym: Noun: dilemma, plight, predicament, perplexity, difficult situation, awkward situation, trouble, muddle, mix-up, confusion
1460.	**Quaver**
	Synonym: Verb: tremble, shake, quiver, shiver, shudder
1461.	**Queer**
	Synonym: Adj: strange, uncommon, odd, unusual, peculiar, weird
	Antonym: normal, conventional, usual
1462.	**Quell**
	Synonym: Verb: to put an end to, suppress, extinguish, silence, subdue, stifle
	Antonym: incite, arouse, encourage

1463.	**Quench**
	Synonym: Verb: allay, satiate, satisfy, extinguish, suppress
1464.	**Quest**
	Synonym: Noun: search, hunt, pursuit, pilgrimage, journey
1465.	**Quirk**
	Synonym: Noun: idiosyncrasy, peculiarity, mannerism, trait
1466.	**Quiver**
	Synonym: Verb: shake, tremble, shiver, quake, vibrate

R

1467.	**Rambunctious**
	Synonym: Adj: noisy, raucous, wild, unruly, unrestrained, boisterous
	Antonym: quiet, restrained, subdued
1468.	**Ramification**
	Synonym: Noun: result, consequence, fallout, repercussion, complication, upshot, effect
1469.	**Rampage**
	Synonym: Verb: rage, rant, rave, storm
1470.	**Rampant**
	Synonym: Adj: widespread, epidemic, uncontrolled, unrestrained, raging, unchecked
	Antonym: controlled, contained
1471.	**Ramshackle**
	Synonym: Adj: broken-down, rickety, decrepit, crumbling, dilapidated
	Antonym: sound, solid, luxurious
1472.	**Rancid**
	Synonym: Adj: stagnating, stinking, rotten, spoiled, repugnant, reeking, fetid, putrid
	Antonym: fresh, sweet-smelling, aromatic
1473.	**Rancour**
	Synonym: Noun: ill will, hatred, animosity, malevolence, malice, enmity
	Antonym: goodwill, friendship, love
1474.	**Random**
	Synonym: Adj: unplanned, undesigned, haphazard, accidental
	Antonym: planned, ordered, predetermined
1475.	**Ransack**
	Synonym: Verb: rummage, plunder, rob, pillage, loot, sack
	Antonym: return, repair, restore
1476.	**Rapport**
	Synonym: Noun: affinity, compatibility, closeness, friendliness, harmony, understanding
	Antonym: alienation, hostility, difference
1477.	**Rapture**
	Synonym: Noun: delight, ecstasy, joy, elation
	Antonym: sorrow, distress, misery
1478.	**Ratify**
	Synonym: Verb: confirm, certify, verify, uphold, authorize, sanction, validate
	Antonym: invalidate, veto, oppose
1479.	**Rationale**
	Synonym: Noun: reasoning, argument, grounds, justification, explanation
1480.	**Raucous**
	Synonym: Adj: loud, boisterous, riotous, uproarious, vociferous
	Antonym: still, silent, quiet
1481.	**Raunchy**
	Synonym: Adj: obscene, vulgar, lewd, dirty, explicit, pornographic
	Antonym: wholesome, clean
1482.	**Rave**
	Synonym: Verb: roar, rage, vociferate, rant, thunder, fume, explode
1483.	**Ravenous**
	Synonym: Adj: starving, hungry, famished, plundering, predatory, greedy, piratical, insatiable
	Antonym: satiated, charitable
1484.	**Ravishing**
	Synonym: Adj: captivating, enchanting, bewitching, fascinating, beautiful, seductive
	Antonym: repulsive, revolting, disgusting
1485.	**Razzle-dazzle**
	Synonym: Noun: razzmatazz, glamorous entertainment, noisy or showy fuss

1486.	**Raze**
	Synonym: Verb: destroy, demolish, topple, crush, smash, ruin, wreck, annihilate
	Antonym: build, repair, restore
1487.	**Realm**
	Synonym: Noun: domain, kingdom, sphere, region, province
1488.	**Reasonable**
	Synonym: Adj: sensible, practical, logical, wise, intelligent, fair, just, moderate
	Antonym: unreasonable, impractical, unintelligent, unfair, unjust
1489.	**Rebellious**
	Synonym: Adj: defiant, nonconforming, revolutionary, ungovernable, mutinous, resistant
	Antonym: conforming, obedient, passive
1490.	**Rebound**
	Synonym: Verb: bounce back, return, recoil, recover, boomerang
1491.	**Rebuke**
	Synonym: Noun: reprimand, scolding, reproach, chiding
	Antonym: praise, approve, praise
1492.	**Rebuttal**
	Synonym: Noun: refutation, retort, contra-diction, argument, opposition, invalidation
	Antonym: support, agreement, validation
1493.	**Recalcitrant**
	Synonym: Adj: disobedient, defiant, rebellious, resistant, contrary, insubordinate
	Antonym: obedient, agreeable, submissive
1494.	**Recapitulate**
	Synonym: Verb: recap, recount, repeat, rehash, restate, review
1495.	**Recede**
	Synonym: Verb: retreat, dwindle, diminish, regress, leave, subside
	Antonym: emerge, advance, increase
1496.	**Recession**
	Synonym: Noun: decline, inflation, slump, slowdown, crisis, indentation
	Antonym: improvement, recovery, upturn

1497.	**Reciprocate**
	Synonym: Verb: interchange, share, trade, swap
1498.	**Reckless**
	Synonym: Adj: wild, rash, thoughtless, careless, unthinking, irresponsible
	Antonym: thoughtful, careful, responsible
1499.	**Reckoning**
	Synonym: Noun: computation, counting, calculation, tally, totalling
1500.	**Recoil**
	Synonym: Verb: react, bridle, jump, withdraw, cringe, flinch
1501.	**Reconnaissance**
	Synonym: Noun: survey, scouting, observation, look-see, mission, reconnoiter
1502.	**Rectify**
	Synonym: Verb: correct, fix, mend, right, amend
1503.	**Rectitude**
	Synonym: Noun: moral correctness, uprightness, righteousness, goodness, virtue, morality, honour, integrity, probity, honesty
	Antonym: infamy, dishonesty
1504.	**Recuperate**
	Synonym: Verb: recover, get well, heal, mend, convalesce, rally, get better
1505.	**Recure**
	Synonym: Verb: reappear, return, repeat, continue
1506.	**Redeem**
	Synonym: Verb: retrieve, recover, regain, rescue, exchange, cash, deliver, free, liberate, absolve, acquit
	Antonym: lose, abandon
1507.	**Redundant**
	Synonym: Adj: repetitive, unnecessary, wordy
	Antonym: necessary, vital
1508.	**Reek**
	Synonym: Verb: stink, smell, fume, stench, emit odours, pollute
1509.	**Refinement**
	Synonym: Noun: polish, cultivation, perfection, graciousness, gentility, taste
	Antonym: coarseness, roughness, crudeness

1510.	Refurbish
	Synonym: Verb: restore, fix up, renovate, rejuvenate, renew, recondition
1511.	Regress
	Synonym: Verb: revert, reverse, go back, backslide, retreat, degenerate
	Antonym: progress, advance, go forward
1512.	Rejuvenate
	Synonym: Verb: renew, revive, revitalize, refurbish, restore, refresh, invigorate
	Antonym: exhaust, drain, sap
1513.	Relentless
	Synonym: Adj: tireless, harsh, ruthless, unyielding, unmerciful, hard
	Antonym: yielding, gentle, considerate, merciful
1514.	Relinquish
	Synonym: Verb: surrender, abandon, renounce, discard, release, forsake
	Antonym: keep, maintain, retain
1515.	Relish
	Synonym: Verb: enjoy, like, love, adore, savor, appreciate
1516.	Reluctant
	Synonym: Adj: unwilling, resistant, opposed, hesitant, slow
	Antonym: willing, enthusiastic, eager
1517.	Remnant
	Synonym: Noun: remainder, trace, remains, record, residue, leftover
1518.	Remote
	Synonym: Adj: faraway, distant, isolated, solitary, secluded, slim, faint, unlikely, imp-robable, withdrawn, detached, distant, disinterested
	Antonym: close, nearby, likely, probable, interested, involved, animated
1519.	Renaissance
	Synonym: Noun: rebirth, resurgence, revival, renewal, regeneration, reawakening
1520.	Rendezvous
	Synonym: Noun: date, meeting, encounter, appointment, meeting place
1521.	Rendition
	Synonym: Noun: interpretation, rendering, presentation, arrangement, performance, depiction

1522.	Renegade
	Synonym: Noun: fugitive, outlaw, deserter, traitor, rebel *Adj:* traitorous, disloyal, mutinous, treacherous, unfaithful
	Antonym: loyalist, follower, loyal, faithful, renounce
1523.	Repercussion
	Synonym: Noun: consequence, result, fallout, backlash, reaction, impact
1524.	Replenish
	Synonym: Verb: refill, restock, restore, replace
	Antonym: empty, drain
1525.	Replete
	Synonym: Noun: full, filled, abounding, overflowing, loaded, plentiful, crammed, packed
	Antonym: empty, bare, scant
1526.	Replica
	Synonym: Noun: model, reproduction, imitation, duplicate
1527.	Reprehensible
	Synonym: Adj: reproachable, shameful, heinous, unforgivable, blameworthy
	Antonym: virtuous, honourable, praiseworthy
1528.	Reprimand
	Synonym: Noun: rebuke, censure, admon-ishment, reproach, scolding, chastisement
	Antonym: approval, praise
1529.	Repudiate
	Synonym: Verb: reject, disavow, spurn, cast off, disapprove
	Antonym: accept, approve, support
1530.	Repugnant
	Synonym: Adj: disgusting, distasteful, repulsive, repellent, revolting, offensive, sickening
	Antonym: Honourable, praiseworthy, appealing
1531.	Repulsive
	Synonym: Adj: sickening, disgusting, revolting, offensive, disagreeable
	Antonym: pleasing, attractive, agreeable

1532.	**Requisition**
	Synonym: Noun: request, call, summons, command
	Antonym: refusal, refuse, reject
1533.	**Rescind**
	Synonym: Verb: repeal, revoke, recall, annul, reverse, cancel
	Antonym: implement, uphold, confirm
1534.	**Resentment**
	Synonym: Noun: bitterness, jealousy, displeasure, soreness, malice, anger, envy
	Antonym: pleasure, cheerfulness, friendliness
1535.	**Resilient**
	Synonym: Adj: flexible, elastic, pliable
	Antonym: inflexible, rigid, repressible
1536.	**Restitution**
	Synonym: Noun: reparation, amends, redress, recompense, remuneration, compensation
1537.	**Restoration**
	Synonym: Noun: repair, reconstruction, revival, recovery
1538.	**Restraint**
	Synonym: Noun: bonds, handcuffs, gag, ties, self-control, moderation, reserve, poise
1539.	**Restriction**
	Synonym: Noun: limitation, curb, regulation, constraint
1540.	**Resume**
	Synonym: Verb: continue, restart, proceed, re-establish
	Antonym: discontinue, halt, stop
1541.	**Resurgence**
	Synonym: Noun: rebirth, renaissance, regeneration, revival, resurrection, renewal
	Antonym: death, decline, decrease
1542.	**Resurrection**
	Synonym: Noun: rebirth, regeneration, revival, renewal, restoration
1543.	**Resuscitate**
	Synonym: Verb: revive, revitalize, breathe life into, bring back from the dead
1544.	**Retaliate**
	Synonym: Verb: avenge, pay back, reciprocate, take revenge, settle

1545.	**Retard**
	Synonym: Verb: check, curb, block, slow, halt
	Antonym: advance, encourage
1546.	**Reticence**
	Synonym: Noun: quietness, shyness, reserve, restraint
	Antonym: loudness, sociability
1547.	**Reticent**
	Synonym: Adj: quiet, silent, withdrawn, subdued, unsociable, untalkative, taciturn
	Antonym: noisy, talkative, sociable
1548.	**Retort**
	Synonym: Noun: answer, reply comeback, rebuttal
1549.	**Retribution**
	Synonym: Noun: revenge, payback, retaliation, punishment, comeuppance, reprisal
1550.	**Retrieve**
	Synonym: Verb: recover, reclaim, regain, rescue, fetch
1551.	**Reverberate**
	Synonym: Verb: resonate, vibrate, echo, resound, ring, rebound
1552.	**Reverence**
	Synonym: Noun: respect, veneration, idolization, adoration, exaltation, deference
	Antonym: disrespect, irreverence, contempt
1553.	**Revile**
	Synonym: Verb: scold, vituperate, vilify, disparage, lambaste, denigrate
	Antonym: praise, compliment, commend
1554.	**Revival**
	Synonym: Noun: rebirth, renaissance, resurgence, return, reawakening, restoration
1555.	**Rhetoric**
	Synonym: Noun: eloquence, discourse, expressiveness, fluency, grandiloquence, oration, oratory
1556.	**Rhythm**
	Synonym: Noun: pulsation, movement, throb, beat
1557.	**Ridicule**
	Synonym: Noun: sarcasm, mockery, teasing, scorn, sneering
	Antonym: praise, approval, commend, applaud

1558.	**Ridiculous**
	Synonym: Adj: foolish, idiotic, silly, comical, laughable, ludicrous, stupid
1559.	**Riffraff**
	Synonym: Noun: commoners, lower class, hoi polloi, scum, dregs
	Antonym: noble, upper, class, elite, royal class, blue blooded
1560.	**Righteous**
	Synonym: Adj: virtuous, upright, moral, guiltless, angelic, saintly, good
	Antonym: immoral, bad, sinful
1561.	**Rigorous**
	Synonym: Adj: tough, stern, demanding, challenging, severe, exacting, excruciating
	Antonym: easy, undemanding
5162.	**Rivalry**
	Synonym: Noun: contest, struggle, opposition, competition
	Antonym: cooperation, alliance, teamwork
1563.	**Roar**
	Synonym: Verb: howl, thunder, yell, growl
1564.	**Roast**
	Synonym: Verb: bake, cook, broil, brown, barbecue, sear, grill
1565.	**Robust**
	Synonym: Adj: strong, healthy, sturdy, brawny, stalwart, powerful
	Antonym: scrawny, weak, sickly, skinny
1566.	**Rowdy**
	Synonym: Adj: wild, unruly, boisterous, rough, rambunctious, trouble-making
	Antonym: behaved, polite, mild-mannered
1567.	**Rubbish**
	Synonym: Noun: trash, garbage, waste, refuse, nonsense, babble, gibberish
1568.	**Rudimentary**
	Synonym: Adj: basic, elementary, elemental, fundamental
	Antonym: advanced, complete, finished
1569.	**Ruffle**
	Synonym: Verb: disturb, upset, disorder, jumble, stir, perturb
	Antonym: settle, smooth, calm

1570.	**Rugged**
	Synonym: Adj: uneven, rocky, tough, sturdy, robust, harsh, stern, severe, solid
	Antonym: soft, frail, cultivated
1571.	**Rumble**
	Synonym: Noun: thunder, roar, booming, roll, growl
1572.	**Ruminate**
	Synonym: Verb: think, contemplate, meditate, deliberate, consider, ponder, muse
1573.	**Rupture**
	Synonym: Noun: break, split, crack, fissure, rent ***Verb:*** burst, split, crack, break, divide
	Antonym: repair, mend, heal, unite
1574.	**Ruthless**
	Synonym: Adj: unmerciful, heartless, cold, brutal, unfeeling, callous, brutal
	Antonym: merciful, compassionate, kind

S

1575.	**Sabotage**
	Synonym: Noun: destruction, undermining, demolition, wrecking
1576.	**Sacrilege**
	Synonym: Noun: violation, desecration, profanation, disrespect, irreverence, blasphemy
	Antonym: reverence, respect
1577.	**Sacrilegious**
	Synonym: Adj: disrespectful, irreverent, blasphemous, impious, profane, unholy
	Antonym: reverent, respectful, pious
1578.	**Sacrosanct**
	Synonym: Adj: sacred, holy, hallowed, consecrated, divine, venerated
	Antonym: unholy, impious, profane
1579.	**Sagacious**
	Synonym: Adj: clever, wise, sane, knowing, smart, knowledgeable
	Antonym: stupid, dumb, ignorant
1580.	**Salacious**
	Synonym: Adj: indecent, obscene, sexual, pornographic, improper, erotic, vulgar, lustful, lewd, sensual

1581.	**Salubrious**
	Synonym: Adj: healthy, healthful, beneficial, wholesome, pleasant, nice, fashionable, luxurious, fancy
	Antonym: unhealthy, unpleasant
1582.	**Salutary**
	Synonym: Adj: good, beneficial, advantageous, helpful, valuable, relevant, healthy
	Antonym: irrelevant, unhealthy, unwholesome
1583.	**Sarcasm**
	Synonym: Noun: snideness, jeering, put-downs, mockery, ridicule
1584.	**Sarcastic**
	Synonym: Adj: insulting, mocking, sneering, scornful, bitter
	Antonym: pleasant, flattering, agreeable
1585.	**Sardonic**
	Synonym: Adj: sarcastic, nasty, snide, bitter, mocking, contemptuous
	Antonym: sweet, complimentary, nice
1586.	**Savage**
	Synonym: Adj: fierce, vicious, merciless, ruthless, cruel, wild, brute
	Antonym: gentle, timid, tender
1587.	**Savagery**
	Synonym: Noun: brutality, barbarism, cruelty, viciousness, monstrosity
1588.	**Scandalous**
	Synonym: Adj: disgraceful, shocking, odious, improper, sinful, outrageous
1589.	**Scanty**
	Synonym: Adj: meagre, skimpy, insufficient, sparse, inadequate
	Antonym: abundant, sufficient
1590.	**Scarce**
	Synonym: Adj: rare, unusual, uncommon, infrequent
	Antonym: usual, common
1591.	**Scarcely**
	Synonym: Adv: barely, hardly, slightly, only, just
1592.	**Scarcity**
	Synonym: Noun: rarity, want, need, shortage, insufficiency
	Antonym: sufficient, enough

1593.	**Scathing**
	Synonym: Adj: searing, acidic, biting, sharp, vitriolic, bitter, pungent
	Antonym: mild, gentle, soft
1594.	**Scatter**
	Synonym: Verb: spread, disperse, sprinkle, strew
	Antonym: collect, group, unite
1595.	**Scintillating**
	Synonym: Adj: sparkling, glittering, glinting, shimmering, shining, gleaming
	Antonym: lacklustre, dull, boring
1596.	**Scoundrel**
	Synonym: Noun: rogue, villain, knave, rascal, swindler, charlatan
1597.	**Scramble**
	Synonym: Verb: race, rush, scurry, hurry, clamber, struggle, mix, disorder, jumble, shuffle
	Antonym: order, arrange
1598.	**Scrupulous**
	Synonym: Adj: principled, upright, moral, ethical
	Antonym: unscrupulous, unprincipled, immoral
1599.	**Scuffle**
	Synonym: Noun: struggle, tussle, scrap, fight, fray
1600.	**Secession**
	Synonym: Noun: withdrawal, defection, disaffiliation, expatriation, separation, breakup
	Antonym: merger, joining
1601.	**Secluded**
	Synonym: Adj: hidden, isolated, remote, unvisited, lonely
	Antonym: public, open, visited
1602.	**Seclusion**
	Synonym: Noun: isolation, solitude, privacy, retreat, segregation
1603.	**Sedate**
	Synonym: Adj: calm, quiet, still, unexcited, composed, serious
	Antonym: agitated, excited, loud

1604.	**Sedative**
	Synonym: Adj: calming, soothing, relaxing, numbing, tranquilizing
	Antonym: arousing, stimulating, stimulant
1605.	**Sedentary**
	Synonym: Adj: inactive, stationary, idle, unmoving, motionless, vegetative
	Antonym: active, busy, on-the-go
1606.	**Sedition**
	Synonym: Noun: insurrection, treason, incitement, rebellion, rabble-rousing, subversion
1607.	**Seduce**
	Synonym: Verb: tempt, snare, lure, trap, attract
	Antonym: repel, repulse, disgust
1608.	**Seduction**
	Synonym: Noun: enticement, allurement, temptation, persuasion, attraction
1609.	**Seductive**
	Synonym: Adj: enticing, alluring, tempting, persuasive, tantalizing, beguiling, attractive, flirtatious
	Antonym: repulsive, repellent, repugnant
1610.	**Segregate**
	Synonym: Verb: separate, divide, isolate, dissociate, split up, insulate
	Antonym: join, combine, desegregate
1611.	**Segregation**
	Synonym: Noun: separation, division, isolation, dissociation, split, insulation
	Antonym: integration, joining
1612.	**Seminal**
	Synonym: Adj: influential, originating, basic, germinal, developmental, pioneering
1613.	**Senile**
	Synonym: Adj: demented, mentally deficient, disoriented, confused, feeble-minded, doddering
	Antonym: sharp, lucid, clear-headed
1614.	**Sensual**
	Synonym: Adj: sensory, physical, stimulating, arousing, exciting, lustful
	Antonym: cerebral, spiritual, intellectual

1615.	**Serendipity**
	Synonym: Noun: good fortune, happenstance, chance, fluke, fortuity, luck
	Antonym: misfortune, bad luck
1616.	**Serene**
	Synonym: Adj: calm, quiet, peaceful, restful, unexcited
	Antonym: excited, agitated, stormy
1617.	**Serenity**
	Synonym: Noun: peacefulness, calmness, restfulness, tranquility
	Antonym: excitement, anxiety, agitation
1618.	**Servile**
	Synonym: Adj: slavish, submissive, subservient, grovelling, fawning
	Antonym: domineering, bossy
1619.	**Shabby**
	Synonym: Adj: worn, ragged, tattered, scruff
	Antonym: fine, new, neat
1620.	**Shackle**
	Synonym: Verb: chain, manacle, bond, handcuff
	Antonym: free, unchain, aid
1621.	**Shatter**
	Synonym: Verb: break, burst, smash, fragment, splinter, devastate, crush, dumbfound, overwhelm, destroy
	Antonym: uplift, reinforce
1622.	**Shirk**
	Synonym: Verb: avoid, dodge, escape, evade, ignore
	Antonym: fulfil, accomplish, do
1623.	**Shiver**
	Synonym: Verb: tremble, shake, quiver, shudder, quake, waver
1624.	**Shrink**
	Synonym: Verb: retreat, retire, withdraw, cringe, cower, reduce, constrict, shrivel, shorten, decrease
	Antonym: confront, face, increase, expand, lengthen
1625.	**Shudder**
	Synonym: Verb: shiver, tremble, shake, quake, convulse, quiver, waver

1626.	**Shuffle**
	Synonym: Verb: drag, hobble, scrape, limp, shamble, mix, intermix, jumble, rearrange, disorder
	Antonym: order, arrange
1627.	**Significant**
	Synonym: Adj: important, noteworthy, notable, outstanding, important, serious, crucial, particular, meaningful
	Antonym: insignificant, minor, meaningless
1628.	**Silly**
	Synonym: Adj: foolish; senseless, stupid, reckless, rash, imprudent, irresponsible, mad, erratic, childish, unwise, mindless
1629.	**Simpleton**
	Synonym: Noun: ignoramus, dunce, moron, imbecile, fool, dolt
	Antonym: genius, intellectual, scholar
1630.	**Sinister**
	Synonym: Adj: evil, dangerous, wicked, frightening, treacherous
	Antonym: harmless, safe
1631.	**Sceptic**
	Synonym: Noun: doubter, nonbeliever, questioner, cynic, Doubting Thomas, scoffer
	Antonym: believer
1632.	**Sceptical**
	Synonym: Adj: doubting, unbelieving, questioning, cynical, distrusting, unconvinced
	Antonym: believing, naïve, gullible
1633.	**Scepticism**
	Synonym: Noun: doubt, disbelief, questioning, cynicism, distrust, mistrust
1634.	**Skirmish**
	Synonym: Noun: battle, fight, clash, engagement, conflict
1635.	**Smoulder**
	Synonym: Verb: fume, smoke, simmer, sizzle, fester
1636.	**Smug**
	Synonym: Adj: complacent, self-satisfied, cocky, pompous, self-righteous
1637.	**Solicit**
	Synonym: Verb: request, seek, plead, beseech, beg

1638.	**Solicitous**
	Synonym: Adj: concerned, caring, attentive, worried, motherly, apprehensive
	Antonym: uncaring, indifferent, apathetic
1639.	**Solidarity**
	Synonym: Noun: unity, unification, union, consensus, oneness, alliance, unanimity
	Antonym: division, dissension, individuality
1640.	**Solitary**
	Synonym: Adj: isolated, secluded, reclusive, individual, single
	Antonym: united, integrated, concerted
1641.	**Solitude**
	Synonym: Noun: aloneness, seclusion, loneliness, reclusion, isolation, remoteness
1642.	**Sombre**
	Synonym: Adj: grim, serious, gloomy, solemn, mournful
	Antonym: joyful, happy, gleeful
1643.	**Soothe**
	Synonym: Verb: relieve, ease, calm, relax, quiet
	Antonym: irritate, upset, agitate
1644.	**Soothing**
	Synonym: Adj: calming, relaxing, tranquil-izing, mollifying, comforting, softening
	Antonym: irritating, intensifying, aggravating
1645.	**Sophisticated**
	Synonym: Adj: worldly, urbane, experienced, refined, cosmopolitan, complex, complicated, high-tech, intricate
	Antonym: naive, unsophisticated, simple
1646.	**Sordid**
	Synonym: Adj: dirty, filthy, squalid, despicable, degraded, selfish, vulgar, corrupt, unclean, foul
	Antonym: clean, upstanding, moral
1647.	**Sore**
	Synonym: Adj: painful, aching, sensitive, hurt, angry, resentful, aggrieved
1648.	**Specious**
	Synonym: Adj: misleading, fallacious, hollow, deceptive, invalid, unsound
	Antonym: valid, accurate, true

1649.	**Splendid**
	Synonym: Adj: magnificent, brilliant, remarkable, excellent, beautiful
	Antonym: poor, unremarkable, dreadful, awful
1650.	**Splendour**
	Synonym: Noun: magnificence, brilliance, beauty, nobility, glory
	Antonym: dullness, drabness, plainness
1651.	**Spontaneous**
	Synonym: Adj: impulsive, unplanned, unhesitating, automatic, natural
	Antonym: planned, deliberate, calculated
1652.	**Spurious**
	Synonym: Adj: false, fake, unauthentic, bogus, fraudulent, sham, adulterated
	Antonym: real, authentic, genuine
1653.	**Squabble**
	Synonym: Verb: argue, fight, wrangle, quarrel, disagree, scrap, quibble
	Antonym: agree, concur
1654.	**Stagger**
	Synonym: Verb: stumble, reel, lurch, sway, totter, stun, shock, startle, jolt, alternate, fluctuate, zigzag, overlap
1655.	**Stagnant**
	Synonym: Adj: motionless, stationary, inactive, stale
	Antonym: moving, running, fresh, unpolluted
1656.	**Stagnate**
	Synonym: Verb: stop, pause, idle, decline, fester, rot
	Antonym: grow, flow, flourish, expand
1657.	**Stalemate**
	Synonym: Noun: deadlock, draw, standstill, standoff, checkmate
	Antonym: decision, resolution
1658.	**Stampede**
	Synonym: Noun: rush, flight, rout, scattering
1659.	**Static**
	Synonym: Adj: changeless, stationary, unvarying, stagnant, fixed
	Antonym: changing, moving, dynamic

1660.	**Staunch**
	Synonym: Adj: dedicated, loyal, devoted, firm, steadfast, solid, unfaithful, shaky
	Antonym: hesitant, uncommitted
1661.	**Steadfast**
	Synonym: Adj: constant, steady, unwavering, fixed, firm, stalwart, resolute
	Antonym: unsteady, wavering
1662.	**Sterile**
	Synonym: Adj: unproductive, impotent, unfruitful, fallow, barren, clean, disinfected
	Antonym: productive, fruitful, potent, infected, unclean
1663.	**Stern**
	Synonym: Adj: severe; strict; uncompromising, serious, grim, authoritarian, etc.
	Antonym: lenient, democratic
1664.	**Stifle**
	Synonym: Verb: smother, choke, strangle, suppress, restrain
	Antonym: encourage, free, release
1665.	**Stigma**
	Synonym: Noun: disgrace, shame, dishonour, blemish, taint
	Antonym: honour, glory, acclaim
1666	**Stimulating**
	Synonym: Adj: arousing, exciting, enlivening, exhilarating, inciting, enticing
	Antonym: dreary, boring, dull
1667.	**Stringent**
	Synonym: Adj: rigorous, strict, rigid, severe, tight, demanding, exacting
1668.	**Stupefy**
	Synonym: Verb: stun, daze, dumbfound, astonish, confuse, bamboozle, terrify, petrify
1669.	**Stupendous**
	Synonym: Adj: great, amazing wonderful, huge, gigantic, gargantuan, astounding, fabulous
	Antonym: trivial, insignificant, inconsequential
1670.	**Stunning**
	Synonym: Adj: awesome, dazzling, electrifying, astonishing, striking, brilliant, magnifying
	Antonym: dull, unimpressive, unremarkable

1671.	**Subjective**
	Synonym: Adj: personal, individual, biased, non-objective
	Antonym: objective, impersonal, empirical, practical
1672.	**Subjugate**
	Synonym: Verb: enslave, dominate, control, conquer, subject
	Antonym: empower, free, liberate
1673.	**Sublime**
	Synonym: Adj: majestic, lofty, elevated, transcendent, divine, holy
	Antonym: low, ordinary
1674.	**Subsequent**
	Synonym: Adj: next, following, ensuing, successive, succeeding
	Antonym: previous, earlier
1675.	**Subservient**
	Synonym: Adj: submissive, servile, subordinate, compliant
	Antonym: dominant, rebellious, controlling
1676.	**Substantial**
	Synonym: Adj: great, large, sizable, considerable, significant
	Antonym: small, tiny, insignificant
1677.	**Subterfuge**
	Synonym: Noun: deception, trick, machination, device, scheme
1678.	**Subversive**
	Synonym: Adj: rebellious, insurrectionary, undermining, revolutionary, treasonous, destructive
	Antonym: constructive, patriotic, loyal
1679.	**Succinct**
	Synonym: Adj: concise, to-the-point, pithy, condensed, short, brief
1680.	**Subtle**
	Synonym: Adj: delicate, fine, hardly noticeable, difficult to define or explain, acute, penetrating, ingenious, cunning
1681.	**Sultry**
	Synonym: Adj: hot, humid, torrid, sweltering, steamy, muggy
	Antonym: cold, freezing, frigid

1682.	**Sumptuous**
	Synonym: Adj: magnificent, extravagant, splendid
1683.	**Superficial**
	Synonym: Adj: shallow, surface, skin-deep, external
	Antonym: deep, internal
1684.	**Superfluous**
	Synonym: Adj: extraneous, unnecessary, excess, inessential, expendable, surplus
	Antonym: necessary, essential, needed
1685.	**Supersede**
	Synonym: Verb: replace, succeed, supplant, outmode, take the place of, override
1686.	**Superstitious**
	Synonym: Adj: fearful, irrational, delusional, neurotic, apprehensive

T

1687.	**Tacit**
	Synonym: Adj: silent, uncommunicative, implied, acknowledged, unspoken, unstated
1688.	**Taciturn**
	Synonym: Adj: quiet, uncommunicative, reticent, withdrawn, reserved, mute, silent
	Antonym: loquacious, talkative, voluble
1689.	**Tactful**
	Synonym: Adj: considerate, sensitive, thoughtful, delicate, diplomatic, discrete
	Antonym: tactless, untactful, blunt, indiscrete, indelicate, clumsy, thoughtless, insensitive
1690.	**Tactic**
	Synonym: Noun: stratagem, plan, strategy, policy, scheme, course, approach, method, system
1691.	**Tactless**
	Synonym: Adj: impolite, inconsiderate, insensitive, thoughtless, rude, untactful, tasteless, undiplomatic
	Antonym: tactful, considerate, thoughtful
1692.	**Tamper**
	Synonym: Verb: interfere, intrude, meddle, change, alter, mess

1693.	**Tangible**
	Synonym: Adj: substantial, solid, obvious, concrete, real, physical, material
	Antonym: intangible, vague, imaginary
1694.	**Tantalize**
	Synonym: Verb: entice, lure, seduce, tempt, titillate
	Antonym: repel, sicken
1695.	**Tantamount**
	Synonym: Adj: equal, equivalent, like, comparable, as good as, the same
	Antonym: unlike, different, opposite
1696.	**Tarnish**
	Synonym: Verb: darken, discolour, corrode, stain, taint, besmear, defile, disgrace, darken, blemish
	Antonym: brighten, shine, sparkle, gleam, enhance, heighten, improve, strengthen
1697.	**Tattered**
	Synonym: Adj: ragged, frazzled, frayed, torn, shabby, shoddy
	Antonym: Vigorous, robust, strong
1698.	**Taxing**
	Synonym: Adj: tiring, exhausting, draining, strenuous, demanding, sapping
	Antonym: invigorating, energizing, refreshing
1699.	**Tedious**
	Synonym: Adj: dreary, irksome, weary, tiresome, boring, monotonous, uninteresting, routine
	Antonym: interesting, exciting, challenging, stimulating
1700.	**Teeming**
	Synonym: Adj: overflowing, overrun, swarming, bristling, dense, thick
	Antonym: empty, unoccupied, vacant
1701.	**Teeter**
	Synonym: Verb: wobble, sway, stagger, lurch, weave
1702.	**Temperity**
	Synonym: Noun: foolhardiness, recklessness, carelessness, gall, indiscretion
	Antonym: prudence, caution

1703.	**Temperamental**
	Synonym: Adj: moody, irritable, excitable, capricious, volatile, passionate, emotional
	Antonym: serene, steady, calm, stable, unexcitable
1704.	**Tempestuous**
	Synonym: Adj: stormy, wild, tumultuous, blustery, raging, violent, feverish
	Antonym: calm, tranquil, serene
1705.	**Tempt**
	Synonym: Verb: attract, entice, induce, invite, lure, lead on, seduce, tantalize
	Antonym: discourage, dissuade, repel, repulse
1706.	**Temptation**
	Synonym: Noun: attraction, enticement, lure, allurement, pull, draw
1707.	**Tempting**
	Synonym: Adj: attractive, alluring, enticing, inviting, provocative, appetizing, tantalizing
	Antonym: unattractive, uninviting, repulsive
1708.	**Tenacious**
	Synonym: Adj: determined, stubborn, obstinate, persistent, strong, firm, clinging, unyielding
	Antonym: lax, slack, loose, yielding
1709.	**Tenacity**
	Synonym: Noun: perseverance, persistence, resolve, doggedness, endurance
1710.	**Tentative**
	Synonym: Adj: conditional, unconfirmed, contingent, provisional, indefinite, temporary
	Antonym: confirmed, definite, settled, final
1711.	**Terrible**
	Synonym: Adj: horrible, horrid, horrifying, alarming, awful, dreadful, fearful, frightful
	Antonym: pleasant, mild, harmless
1712.	**Terrific**
	Synonym: Adj: great, superb, magnificent, wonderful, marvellous, awesome, extraordinary, splendid
	Antonym: mediocre, poor, bad, unpleasant, minor, moderate, slight

1713.	**Terrify**
	Synonym: Verb: frighten, scare, alarm, terrorize, horrify, petrify, appal, dismay
	Antonym: reassure, comfort, soothe, calm
1714.	**Terse**
	Synonym: Adj: brief, concise, short, curt, succinct, crisp
	Antonym: lengthy, long, wordy, verbose
1715.	**Thrash**
	Synonym: Verb: flog, whip, beat, trounce, punish, defeat, conquer, vanquish
1716.	**Threshold**
	Synonym: Noun: entrance, entranceway, doorsill, doorway, gateway, verge, beginning, outset, start, edge, brink, opening, dawn
	Antonym: end, close, conclusion, finish, twilight
1717.	**Thrifty**
	Synonym: Adj: economical, economizing, saving, frugal, sparing, conserving, careful
	Antonym: uneconomical, extravagant, prodigal
1718.	**Thrive**
	Synonym: Verb: prosper, flourish, bloom, advance, progress, succeed, increase, grow
	Antonym: stagnate, thrive, languish, wither, wane, fail, die
1719.	**Thriving**
	Synonym: Adj: flourishing, blooming, prospering, prosperous, successful
	Antonym: failing, dying, withering
1720.	**Throng**
	Synonym: Verb: crowd, jam, swarm, teem, press, push, gather, assemble
1721.	**Thwart**
	Synonym: Verb: frustrate, obstruct, oppose, hinder, foil, prevent, bar, stop, defeat
	Antonym: assist, support, help, encourage, abet
1722.	**Tickle**
	Synonym: Verb: please, delight, amuse, excite, interest, fascinate, cheer, caress, stroke brush, tingle, twitch
	Antonym: irritate, annoy, bother

1723.	**Ticklish**
	Synonym: Adj: delicate, difficult, intricate, awkward, sensitive, tough, complicated
	Antonym: easy, simple, uncomplicated
1724.	**Tilt**
	Synonym: Noun: incline, slope, slant, lean
1725.	**Timid**
	Synonym: Adj: shy, bashful, diffident, unassertive, hesitant, cautious, unassuming, afraid, apprehensive, fearful
	Antonym: Fearless, bold, assertive, confident
1726.	**Titillate**
	Synonym: Verb: arouse, tantalize, excite, stimulate
	Antonym: bore, put to sleep
1727.	**Topple**
	Synonym: Verb: overturn, overthrow, upset, fall, drop, collapse
1728.	**Torment**
	Synonym: Verb: tease, annoy, agonize, distress, torture, plague, annoy, provoke
	Antonym: comfort, soothe, ease, relieve
1729.	**Torrent**
	Synonym: Noun: deluge, flood, downpour, inundation, rain, stream, outburst, outpouring
1730.	**Torrid**
	Synonym: Adj: hot, sweltering, blistering, sultry, scorching, blazing, passionate, lustful
	Antonym: cold, frigid, icy
1731.	**Torturous**
	Synonym: Adj: excruciating, agonizing, tormenting, torturing, painful, anguished, distressful
	Antonym: painless, pleasant, comforting
1732.	**Totter**
	Synonym: Verb:: reel, falter, stagger, wobble, sway, falter, shake, flounder
1733.	**Traitorous**
	Synonym: Adj: treacherous, treasonous, two- faced, double-crossing, backstabbing
	Antonym: loyal, devoted, faithful
1734.	**Tranquility**
	Synonym: Noun: peacefulness, serenity, calmness, stillness, peace, quiet, restfulness
	Antonym: commotion, disturbance, disorder

1735.	**Transcendental**
	Synonym: Adj: unsurpassed, extraordinary, supreme, incomparable, unrivalled, topping, supernatural, spiritual, mystical, otherwordly, metaphysical
	Antonym: ordinary, earthly, worldly, mundane
1736.	**Transgress**
	Synonym: Verb: violate, break the law, overstep one's bounds, disobey, infringe
1737.	**Transgression**
	Synonym: Noun: sin, violation, crime, offence, felony, wrong, infraction
1738.	**Transient**
	Synonym: Adj: temporary, brief, passing, Ephemeral, fleeting, momentary, short-lived
	Antonym: permanent, enduring, lasting, perpetual
1739.	**Trash**
	Synonym: Noun: garbage, junk, waste, rubbish, refuse, litter, debris, nonsense, drivel, inanity, gibberish
	Antonym: treasure, valuables, sense, substance
1740.	**Trauma**
	Synonym: Noun: shock, upset, ordeal, jolt, stress, wound, injury
1741.	**Traumatic**
	Synonym: Adj: shocking, upsetting, injurious, hurtful, stressful, wounding, scarring
	Antonym: soothing, tranquilizing, comforting
1742.	**Traumatize**
	Synonym: Verb: shock, upset, injure, hurt, stress, wound, scar
	Antonym: soothe, comfort, tranquilize
1743.	**Travesty**
	Synonym: Noun: gross imitation, farce, caricature, burlesque, parody, mockery, joke
1744.	**Treacherous**
	Synonym: Adj: dangerous, unsafe, hazardous, precarious, perilous, risky, undependable, traitorous, disloyal, treasonous, unfaithful, deceitful
	Antonym: safe, reliable, sound, loyal, faithful, dependable

1745.	**Treachery**
	Synonym: Noun: betrayal, perfidy, treason, disloyalty, backstabbing, double-cross
	Antonym: loyalty, faithfulness, fidelity
1746.	**Tread**
	Synonym: Verb: walk, step, tramp, stamp, trample ***Noun:*** footstep, step, football, walk, plod
1747.	**Treason**
	Synonym: Noun: disloyalty, betrayal, treachery, subversion, sedition, conspiracy
	Antonym: loyalty, allegiance, patriotism
1748.	**Treasonous**
	Synonym: Adj: betraying, disloyal, back-stabbing, duplicitous, double- crossing, unfaithful
	Antonym: loyal, faithful, true
1749.	**Tremble**
	Synonym: Verb: shake, quake, quiver, shiver, shudder, throb, pulsate
1750.	**Tremendous**
	Synonym: Adj: huge, gigantic, enormous, immense, vast, great, mammoth, large, wonderful, marvellous, exceptional, remarkable, extraordinary, fabulous, excellent
	Antonym: small, tiny, little, ordinary, average, mediocre
1751.	**Trepidation**
	Synonym: Noun: fear, apprehension, anxiety, nervousness, fright, uneasiness, misgiving
	Antonym: fearlessness, confidence, composure
1752.	**Tribulation**
	Synonym: Noun: suffering, misery, affliction, distress, hardship, adversity, woe
1753.	**Trickle**
	Synonym: Verb: seep, leak, ooze, drop, drip, dribble
	Antonym: gush, flood, stream, pour, spurt, stream
1754.	**Trifling**
	Synonym: Adj: trivial, petty, unimportant, insignificant, inconsequential, slight, negligible, small
	Antonym: important, significant, considerable, large

1755.	**Trite**
	Synonym: Adj: ordinary, routine, common, stale, dull, banal, overused
	Antonym: fresh, original, new, unique
1756.	**Triumph**
	Synonym: Noun: victory, success, conquest, win, mastery
	Antonym: defeat, failure, lose
1757.	**Triumphant**
	Synonym: Adj: victorious, winning, conquering, triumphal, joyful, exultant
	Antonym: defeated, unsuccessful, humbled
1758.	**Trivial**
	Synonym: Adj: unimportant, insignificant, petty, slight, trifling, meaningless, worthless
	Antonym: significant, important, serious, substantial
1759.	**Troublesome**
	Synonym: Adj: annoying, irritating, disturbing, upsetting, exasperating, bothersome, worrisome
	Antonym: calming, soothing, innocuous
1760.	**Tumbledown**
	Synonym: Adj: dilapidated, broken-down, ramshackle, rickety, decrepit
	Antonym: sturdy, stable, sound
1761.	**Tumult**
	Synonym: Noun: commotion, disturbance, uproar, furore, clamour, ferment, turmoil
	Antonym: peace, quiet, serenity, tranquility
1762.	**Tumultuous**
	Synonym: Adj: wild, turbulent, stormy, uproarious, tempestuous, clamorous
	Antonym: calm, tranquil, serene
1763.	**Turbulence**
	Synonym: Noun: agitation, instability, disturbance, turmoil
	Antonym: calm, stillness
1764.	**Turbulent**
	Synonym: Adj: tumultuous, disturbed, agitated, wild, raging, stormy
	Antonym: calm, quiet, placid, orderly

1765.	**Turmoil**
	Synonym: Noun: tumult, pandemonium, chaos, uproar, commotion, ferment
	Antonym: order, peace, quiet, tranquility
1766.	**Tutelage**
	Synonym: Noun: instruction, teaching, coaching, guidance, direction, training
1767.	**Tyrannical**
	Synonym: Adj: dictatorial, autocratic, despotic, authoritarian, totalitarian, oppressive
	Antonym: democratic, liberal
1768.	**Tyranny**
	Synonym: Noun: despotism, dictatorship, oppression, repression, severity, cruelty
	Antonym: benevolence, humanity, kindness
1769.	**Tyrant**
	Synonym: Noun: dictator, despot, autocrat, totalitarian, oppressor

U

1770.	**Unabridged**
	Synonym: Adj: uncut, complete, full, entire, whole, total
	Antonym: abridged, shortened, condensed, truncated, trimmed, curtailed
1771.	**Unanimity**
	Synonym: Noun: accord, agreement, unity, conformity, consent
	Antonym: disagreement, discord
1772.	**Unassuming**
	Synonym: Adj: modest, humble, reserved, retiring, unpretentious, simple, plain
	Antonym: arrogant, pretentious, assuming
1773.	**Undermine**
	Synonym: Verb: weaken, undercut, erode, subvert, impair, debilitate
	Antonym: support, bolster, buttress
1774.	**Undertaking**
	Synonym: Noun: project, task, job, enterprise, endeavour, venture
1775.	**Unduly**
	Synonym: Adv: excessively, extremely, overly, inordinately, unnecessarily, unusually
	Antonym: properly, appropriately, reasonably

1776.	**Unequivocal**
	Synonym: Adj: unambiguous, concrete, plain, clear, unmistakable, definite
	Antonym: ambiguous, equivocal, unclear
1777.	**Uneven**
	Synonym: Adj: irregular, rough, jagged, lopsided, unbalanced, coarse, unlevelled, unequal, disparate, different, unlike, dissimilar
	Antonym: smooth, level, straight, even, equal, balanced
1778.	**Unkempt**
	Synonym: Adj: slovenly, disheveled, sloppy, careless, neglected
	Antonym: neat, tidy, well-groomed
1779.	**Unlike**
	Synonym: Adj: different, dissimilar, unrelated, opposite, heterogeneous
	Antonym: like, similar, identical, homogeneous
1780.	**Unprecedented**
	Synonym: unique, novel, singular, extraordinary, unparalleled, original
	Antonym: precedented, usual, ordinary
1781.	**Unscrupulous**
	Synonym: Adj: dishonest, unprincipled, unethical, immoral, conscienceless, deceitful, devious, ignoble, degenerate, venal
	Antonym: ethical, honest
1782.	**Untoward**
	Synonym: Adj: unfortunate, unexpected, unforeseen, unpredictable, surprising, unusual, untimely
	Antonym: expected, timely, appropriate
1783.	**Unyielding**
	Synonym: Adj: inflexible, resolute, persistent, obstinate, stubborn, firm, rigid
	Antonym: yielding, flexible, adaptable
1784.	**Upcoming**
	Synonym: Adj: forthcoming, approaching, coming, nearing, imminent
	Antonym: distant, remote
1785.	**Upheaval**
	Synonym: Noun: eruption, explosion, blowup, catastrophe, disruption, disturbance
1786.	**Uppity**
	Synonym: Adj: presumptuous, arrogant, haughty, conceited, snobbish
	Antonym: down-to-earth, humble, modest
1787.	**Upright**
	Synonym: Adj: vertical, perpendicular, erect, raised, honest, just, virtuous, honourable, moral, trustworthy
	Antonym: horizontal, prone, dishonest, corrupt, unethical
1788.	**Uprising**
	Synonym: Noun: revolt, rebellion, revolution, insurrection, mutiny, outbreak, upheaval
1789.	**Uproar**
	Synonym: Noun: commotion, turmoil, tumult, clamour, furore, stir, noise, disturbance
	Antonym: serenity, tranquillity, peace, calm
1790.	**Urge**
	Synonym: Verb: plead, beg, implore, beseech, entreat, advise, force, drive, push, press, prod, impel ***Noun:*** impulse, yearning, longing, desire
	Antonym: discourage, dissuade, caution, restrain, prevent, distaste, repugnance, aversion
1791.	**Usurp**
	Synonym: Verb: seize, steal, grab, preempt, appropriate, assume
	Antonym: surrender, yield, relinquish
1792.	**Utilize**
	Synonym: Verb: use, employ, exploit, handle, apply
1793.	**Utter**
	Synonym: Adj: complete, total, entire, absolute, extreme, thorough, unqualified ***Verb:*** speak, say, articulate, express, pronounce talk
	Antonym: incomplete, partial, limited

V

1794.	**Vacillate**
	Synonym: Verb: oscillate, swing, go back and forth, waver, equivocate, shilly–shally
	Antonym: commit, be decisive

1795.	**Vacuous**
	Synonym: Adj: empty, vacant, blank, stupid, dumb, empty-headed
	Antonym: intelligent, bright, comprehending
1796.	**Vagabond**
	Synonym: Noun: vagrant, rover, wanderer, tramp, transient, drifter
1797.	**Valediction**
	Synonym: Noun: a formal word for farewell or goodbye, adieu, leave-taking, parting, send-off
	Antonym: salutation, welcome
1798.	**Valiant**
	Synonym: Adj: brave, fearless, courageous, valorous, intrepid, heroic, stout-hearted, lionhearted, stalwart, staunch, indomitable, resolute, steadfast, firm
	Antonym: cowardly, irresolute
1799.	**Validate**
	Synonym: Verb: substantiate, authenticate, certify, prove, verify, corroborate
	Antonym: invalidate, disprove, challenge
1800.	**Vandalism**
	Synonym: Noun: destruction, defacement, mutilation, sabotage, mischief
1801.	**Vanity**
	Synonym: Noun: self-admiration, conceit, excessive pride
1802.	**Vanquish**
	Synonym: Verb: conquer, defeat, overcome, trounce, annihilate, triumph, subdue, beat, eliminate, master, subjugate
	Antonym: lose, surrender, yield, submit
1803.	**Vanguard**
	Synonym: Noun: front, advance guard, cutting edge, trailblazers, forerunners, pioneers
	Antonym: rear, back, followers
1804.	**Vapid**
	Synonym: Adj: dull, insipid, uninteresting
1805.	**Variegated**
	Synonym: Adj: varicoloured, mottled, streaked, polychromatic
	Antonym: monochromatic, uniform
1806.	**Vehemence**
	Synonym: Noun: passion, fierceness, fervour, ardour, zeal, fire
	Antonym: apathy, indifference
1807.	**Vehement**
	Synonym: Adj: passionate, enthusiastic, ardent, fervent, zealous, forceful, eager
	Antonym: indifferent, unconcerned, apathetic
1808.	**Vendetta**
	Synonym: Noun: feud, quarrel, fight, bad blood, vengeance, blood feud, retaliation
1809.	**Venerable**
	Synonym: Adj: honoured, revered, respected, respectable, dignified, worthy
	Antonym: dishonourable, undeserving, unworthy
1810.	**Vengeance**
	Synonym: Noun: revenge, retaliation, reprisal, retribution, avenging
	Antonym: friendship, camaraderie
1811.	**Veracity**
	Synonym: Noun: truthfulness, accuracy, honesty, credibility, authenticity, reality, integrity
	Antonym: deception, inaccuracy, dishonesty
1812.	**Verve**
	Synonym: Noun: vitality; vigour; enthusiasm
1813.	**Vestige**
	Synonym: Noun: trace, hint, suggestion, remnant, remains, evidence
1814.	**Veteran**
	Synonym: Adj:: experienced, practiced, seasoned, skilled, proficient, expert
	Antonym: novice, beginner, recruit, inexperienced, unpracticed
1815.	**Viable**
	Synonym: Adj: workable, practical, doable, feasible, possible
	Antonym: unworkable, impractical, fanciful
1816.	**Vex**
	Synonym: Verb: annoy, bother, irritate, trouble, distress, provoke, worry

1817.	**Vicarious**
	Synonym: Adj: indirect, imagined, second-hand, secondary, surrogate, sympathetic
	Antonym: direct, firsthand, personal
1818.	**Vicious**
	Synonym: Adj: savage, dangerous, ferocious, fierce, violent, depraved, wicked, evil, vile, terrible, spiteful, malicious, hateful, hurtful, cruel
	Antonym: tamed, gentle, friendly, moral, decent, virtuous, kind, good- natured, complimentary
1819.	**Vicissitudes**
	Synonym: Noun: changes, shifts, ups and downs, reversals, variations, peaks and valleys, fluctuations
1820.	**Vigil**
	Synonym: Noun: watch, monitoring, observation, surveillance
1821.	**Vigorous**
	Synonym: Adj: energetic, active, robust, dynamic, strong, forceful, lively
	Antonym: lethargic, unenergetic, feeble, weak
1822.	**Vigour**
	Synonym: Noun: energy, vitality animation, fervour, strength, force, might
	Antonym: indifference, apathy, weakness
1823.	**Vilify**
	Synonym: Verb: defame, denounce, slander, smear, criticize, denigrate, vilify
	Antonym: honour, praise, commend
1824.	**Vindicate**
	Synonym: Verb: clear, exonerate, acquit, absolve, exculpate
	Antonym: implicate, damn, convict
1825.	**Vindictive**
	Synonym: Adj: spiteful, revengeful, vengeful, malicious, bitter
	Antonym: forgiving, charitable
1826.	**Vintage**
	Synonym: Adj: superior, supreme, best, classic, select, prime
	Antonym: inferior, poor, second-rate

1827.	**Virile**
	Synonym: Adj: potent, manly, macho, strong, masculine, powerful
	Antonym: weak, impotent, effeminate
1828.	**Virility**
	Synonym: Noun: potency, manliness, strength, masculinity, power, vigor
	Antonym: impotence, weakness, femininity
1829.	**Virtuoso**
	Synonym: Noun: master, expert, professional, ace, superstar, savant, artist
	Antonym: amateur, bumbler, neophyte
1830.	**Virtuous**
	Synonym: Adj: moral, good, righteous, honourable, ethical, principled
	Antonym: immoral, bad, sinful
1831.	**Virulent**
	Synonym: Adj: infectious, contagious, poisonous, toxic, noxious, deadly
	Antonym: harmless, benign, mild
1832.	**Vitriolic**
	Synonym: Adj: caustic, scathing, bitter, venomous, acidic, biting, nasty
	Antonym: sweet, soothing, nice
1833.	**Vivacious**
	Synonym: Adj: lively, animated, bubbly, vital, effervescent, ebullient
	Antonym: lifeless, dead, dull
1834.	**Vivid**
	Synonym: Adj: keen, sharp, intense, strong, acute, clear, bright, brilliant, loud, colourful, shiny
	Antonym: average, routine, dull, drab, colourless
1835.	**Vociferous**
	Synonym: Adj: loud, vehement, clamorous, uproarious, vocal, thunderous, noisy
	Antonym: quiet, reserved, mousy
1836.	**Volatile**
	Synonym: Adj: unstable, changeable, capricious, inconstant, explosive, inflammable, incendiary
	Antonym: stable, steady, predictable

1837.	**Volition**
	Synonym: Noun: choice, will, desire, willingness, determination
1838.	**Voracious**
	Synonym: Adj: ravenous, hungry, starved, greedy, insatiable, gluttonous
1839.	**Vulgar**
	Synonym: Adj: coarse, crude, rude, impolite, unrefined, tasteless, indecent
	Antonym: polite, refined, tasteful
1840.	**Vulnerable**
	Synonym: Adj: defenceless, susceptible, unguarded, unprotected, exposed
	Antonym: protected, guarded, invincible
1841.	**Volatile**
	Synonym: Adj: quick to evaporate; likely to explode, changeable, unpredictable, fickle, unstable; short-lived
	Antonym: concrete, stable, tangible, long lasting

W

1842.	**Wail**
	Synonym: Verb: moan, weep, cry, whine, howl, roar
1843.	**Waffle**
	Synonym: Verb: equivocate, hedge, sidestep, evade, dodge, hem and haw
1844.	**Waive**
	Synonym: Verb: relinquish, renounce, drop, forgo, resign, yield
	Antonym: demand, require, claim
1845.	**Wane**
	Synonym: Verb: decrease, lessen, ebb, reduce, weaken, decline, fade
	Antonym: grow, increase, wax
1846.	**Wanton**
	Synonym: Adj: vicious, wicked, evil, cruel, promiscuous, immoral, immodest, indecent, unchaste, unvirtuous, lustful, lecherous, lascivious, frisky, impetuous, rash, reckless
1847.	**Weary**
	Synonym: Adj: tired, tedious, exhausted, fatigued, drained, boring, dull
	Antonym: refreshed, revived, energetic, refreshing, interesting, exciting
1848.	**Weird**
	Synonym: Adj: unnatural, strange, abnormal, unusual, bizarre, offbeat, quirky, outlandish, eccentric, unconventional, surreal, crazy, absurd, peculiar, odd, queer, strange
	Antonym: normal, ordinary, conventional
1849.	**Welter**
	Synonym: Noun: confusion, jumble, tangle, clutter, mess, hotchpotch, mishmash, flurry
1850.	**Whore**
	Synonym: Noun: prostitute, strumpet, harlot
1851.	**Whet**
	Synonym: Verb: sharpen, excite, stimulate, arouse, entice
	Antonym: satisfy, stifle, deaden
1852.	**Whimsical**
	Synonym: Adj: erratic, unpredictable, capricious, uncertain, eccentric, impulsive
	Antonym: planned, predictable, thoughtful
1853.	**Whirl**
	Synonym: Noun: turn, spin, revolution, rotation, twirl, bustle, rush, flurry, tumult, uproar
1854.	**Wholesome**
	Synonym: Adj: healthy, healthful, nutritious, nourishing, moral, virtuous, decent, pure, clean
	Antonym: unwholesome, unhealthy, harmful, immoral, sinful
1855.	**Wicked**
	Synonym: Adj: immoral, bad, sinful, evil, vile, foul
	Antonym: moral, good, noble
1856.	**Wield**
	Synonym: Verb: command, exercise, manage, handle, exert

1857.	**Wilful**
	Synonym: Adj: deliberate, purposeful, intentional, planned, premeditated, voluntary
	Antonym: involuntary, coerced, unplanned
1858.	**Winsome**
	Synonym: Adj: attractive, charming, appealing, engaging, pretty, sweet, endearing, captivating, fetching, bewitching
	Antonym: ugly, repulsive, repugnant
1859.	**Wishy-washy**
	Synonym: Adj: indecisive, irresolute, spineless, weak, vacillating, equivocating
	Antonym: decisive, resolute, firm
1860.	**Wistful**
	Synonym: Adj: thoughtful, regretful, nostalgic, yearning, longing, pensive, sad, wishful, heartsick, troubled
1861.	**Wither**
	Synonym: Verb: wilt, shrivel or dry up, diminish, dwindle, shrink, fade, weaken, languish, evaporate, melt away, disappear, decay, atrophy
	Antonym: grow, thrive, flourish, prosper, progress
1862.	**Withhold**
	Synonym: Verb: hold, keep, retain, repress, suppress
	Antonym: give, provide, reveal
1863.	**Withstand**
	Synonym: Verb: oppose, resist, defy, endure, confront, brave
	Antonym: yield, capitulate, surrender to
1864.	**Witty**
	Synonym: Adj: humorous, funny, amusing, entertaining
	Antonym: dull, witless, humourless
1865.	**Wizard**
	Synonym: Noun: mage, magician, sorcerer, conjuror, expert, genius, prodigy, master
	Antonym: duffer, amateur, imbecile
1866.	**Wobble**
	Synonym: Verb: sway, stagger, totter, shake, quake

1867.	**Worrisome**
	Synonym: Adj: troubling, distressing, disquieting, disturbing, bothersome, unnerving
	Antonym: reassuring, comforting, encouraging
1868.	**Wretched**
	Synonym: Adj: distressed, miserable, forlorn, depressed, unhappy, despicable, contemptible, dreadful, horrid, terrible
	Antonym: happy, cheerful, admirable, wonderful
1869.	**Wry**
	Synonym: Adj: twisted, crooked, slanted, contorted, distorted
	Antonym: straight, direct, normal
1870.	**Wrangle**
	Synonym: Noun: argument, quarrel, dispute, disagreement, squabble, altercation, tussle, brawl, clash
	Antonym: agreement, agree
1871.	**Wreak**
	Synonym: Verb: inflict, unleash, commit, exercise, work
X	
1872.	**Xerox**
	Synonym: Noun:: photocopy, copy, duplicate, reproduction, facsimile, reproduce
Y	
1873.	**Yearn**
	Synonym: Verb: to long for; to want very much, especially something you can't, have, long, crave, desire, want, have/feel a longing, covet, lust, thirst, hanker after, dream of, ache, hunger
	Antonym: dread, fear, abhor, hate, loathe, despise
1874.	**Yearning**
	Synonym: Noun: craving, desire, longing, wish, inclination, hunger, thirst
1875.	**Yell**
	Synonym: Verb: shout, scream, holler, bellow, howl, shriek, cry ***Noun:*** call, shout, cry, holler

Z

1876.	**Zany**
	Synonym: Adj: ludicrous, clownish, foolish, absurd, funny, comical, silly *Noun:* jester, joker, clown, fool, comic, buffoon
1877.	**Zeal**
	Synonym: Noun: enthusiasm, eagerness, passion, zealousness, ardour, fervour, keenness, gusto, vigour, verve, zest, devotion
	Antonym: indifference, apathy, unconcern, disinterest
1878.	**Zealot**
	Synonym: Noun: enthusiast, fanatic, devotee, addict, disciple, follower
1879.	**Zealous**
	Synonym: Adj: enthusiastic, ardent, fervent, eager, obsessed, fanatic, devoted
	Antonym: apathetic, uninterested, unenthusiastic, passionless
1880.	**Zenith**
	Synonym: Noun: peak, top, high point, crest, climax, culmination, pinnacle, apex, apogee, summit
	Antonym: Abyss, low point, bottom, nadir, depths
1881.	**Zest**
	Synonym: Noun: gusto, ardour, fervour, passion, zeal, delight, enthusiasm, eagerness, thrill, pleasure
	Antonym: distaste, dislike, aversion, apathy
1882.	**Zestful**
	Synonym: Adj: exciting, thrilling, delightful, stimulating, enjoyable
	Antonym: boring, dull, unexciting, un-enjoyable
1883.	**Zoom**
	Synonym: Verb: race, flash, streak, fly, whiz, zip, speed, climb, soar, rise, ascend, escalate, advance
	Antonym: plummet, drop, fall, decrease, minimize, zoomout, descend

SYNONYMS
Alphabetically Arranged MCQs

DIRECTIONS: ***Given below are some words arranged alphabetically. Each word is followed by four options. You have to find out the word which is nearest in meaning to the given word. NOTA means 'None Of The Above' from the given options.***

A

1. *Absolute*
(a) reasonable (b) narrow
(c) limitless (d) reliable

2. *Abandon*
(a) neglect (b) condense
(c) discontinue (d) abscond

3. *Affable*
(a) helpful (b) neutral
(c) friendly (d) cheerfull

4. *Abash*
(a) acuit (b) confuse
(c) blush (d) condemn

5. *Accomplice*
(a) friend (b) abettor
(c) criminal (d) thief

6. *Allegiance*
(a) disaffection (b) satisfactory
(c) loyalty (d) enemity

7. *Amicable*
(a) poisonous (b) friendly
(c) satisfying (d) heartening

8. *Apogee*
(a) middle (b) bottom
(c) climax (d) beginning

9. *Adversity*
(a) failure (b) helplessness
(c) crisis (d) misfortune

10. *Acumen*
(a) beauty (b) appearance
(c) insight (d) skill

11. *Abstain*
(a) influence (b) refrain
(c) retain (d) retard

12. *Abase*
(a) low (b) peaceful
(c) humble (d) cruel

13. *Abet*
(a) force (b) discourage
(c) assist (d) neglect

14. *Abridge*
(a) desire (b) condense
(c) graceful (d) disconnect

15. *Admonish*
(a) appeal (b) support
(c) warn (d) praise

16. *Accolade*
(a) applause (b) award
(c) affection (d) arrival

17. *Antique*
(a) old (b) rare
(c) modern (d) uniue

18. *Ascend*
(a) leap (b) mount
(c) deviate (d) grow

19. *Adept*

(a) profesional (b) proficient
(c) sufficient (d) intelligent

20. *Admonition*

(a) award (b) amazement
(c) pardon (d) warning

21. *Applaud*

(a) pray (b) flatter
(c) reuest (d) praise

22. *Appraisal*

(a) invedtigation (b) estimation
(c) praise (d) approval

23. *Anxiety*

(a) worry (b) comfort
(c) faith (d) reassurance

24. *Accord*

(a) agreement (b) disagreement
(c) dispute (d) disparity

25. *Aromatic*

(a) stinking (b) sentimental
(c) fragrant (d) crippled

26. *Ambit*

(a) eviction (b) scope
(c) restriction (d) barrier

27. *Adjourn*

(a) postpone (b) avoid
(c) complain (d) suppress

28. *Accentuated*

(a) mitigated (b) projected
(c) exhibited (d) sharpened

29. *Acute*

(a) rice (b) accidental
(c) severe (d) curious

30. *Abscond*

(a) flee (b) manage
(c) avoid (d) turn

31. *Albeit*

(a) although (b) further more
(c) because (d) not only

32. *Amalgamate*

(a) try (b) collect
(c) mix (d) hate

33. *Assay*

(a) attack (b) accept
(c) case (d) evaluate

34. *Acrid*

(a) unripe (b) pungent
(c) bitter (d) dirty

35. *Adage*

(a) order (b) request
(c) proverb (d) mystery

36. *Abominable*

(a) odd (b) weird
(c) fine (d) awful

37. *Abstemious*

(a) moderate (b) proud
(c) excessive (d) rustic

38. *Abomination*

(a) revulsion (b) disgust
(c) criticism (d) attack

39. *Alacrity*

(a) eagerly (b) suspicion
(c) unhesitatingly (d) unwillingly

40. *Augur*

(a) heal (b) hurt
(c) signify (d) reform

41. *Assuage*

(a) rub (b) prohibit
(c) ease (d) enlarge

42. *Addle*

(a) soar (b) strike
(c) stop (d) confuse

43. *Animosity*

(a) vanity (b) hostility
(c) indifference (d) treason

44. *Abrupt*

(a) pure (b) alert
(c) sudden (d) quick

45. *Abstruse*

(a) abstract (b) profound
(c) perfect (d) ignorant

46. *Altercation*

(a) drastic change (b) angry dispute
(c) noisy dialogue (d) loud explosion

47. *Anomaly*

(a) abnormality (b) ignorance
(c) accident (d) rarity

48. *Aphorism*

(a) wise saying (b) digression
(c) casual remark (d) repetition

49. *Abrade*

(a) twist (b) wear off
(c) attach (d) scold

50. *Abstruse*

(a) missing (b) sprawling
(c) obscure (d) stupid

51. *Abnegation*

(a) association (b) renunciation
(c) affirmation (d) indignation

B

52. *Barbarian*

(a) ruffian (b) impolite
(c) partiality (d) distortion

53. *Biased*

(a) careful (b) partial
(c) expert (d) unskilled

54. *Brutal*

(a) humane (b) adamant
(c) ruthless (d) criminal

55. *Boisterous*

(a) boiling (b) hot
(c) noisy (d) dangerous

56. *Berserk*

(a) clever (b) morose
(c) cheerful (d) wild

57. *Benefactor*

(a) guardian (b) saint
(c) do-gooder (d) friend

58. *Baffle*

(a) puzzle (b) tease
(c) hoodwink (d) trick

59. *Belligerent*

(a) pacifist (b) generous
(c) aggressive (d) reasonable

60. *Bifurcated*

(a) reduced (b) stabbed
(c) ploughed (d) sagregated

61. *Bewail*

(a) tear apart (b) envy
(c) lament (d) accuse

62. *Balmy*

(a) soothing (b) fruitful
(c) modest (d) tempestuous

63. *Blithe*

(a) other worldly (b) giddy
(c) graceful (d) joyous

64. *Befuddled*

(a) wounded (b) crowded
(c) enlightened (d) confused

65. *Besiege*

(a) acuire (b) attack
(c) seize (d) surround

66. *Bandit*

(a) convict (b) robber
(c) thief (d) cut-throat

67. *Bankrupt*

(a) insolvent (b) debtor
(c) creditor (d) solvent

68. *Bane*

(a) acuse (b) curse
(c) reject (d) abolish

69. *Barter*

(a) return (b) exchange
(c) borrow (d) buy

70. ***Bucolic***
(a) angry (b) revengeful
(c) rustic (d) imaginative

71. ***Bizarre***
(a) joyful (b) colourful
(c) grotesque (d) hearty

72. ***Brutal***
(a) humane (b) adamant
(c) ruthless (d) criminal

73. ***Burlesue***
(a) irritate (b) insult
(c) annoy (d) mock

74. ***Bumptious***
(a) ill-tempered
(b) colliding
(c) brashly self-assertive
(d) illiterate

75. ***Baleful***
(a) overflowing (b) pernicious
(c) unethical (d) NOTA

76. ***Bemused***
(a) enchanted (b) entertained
(c) lost in thought (d) ridiculous

C

77. ***Connoisseur***
(a) delinuent (b) interpreter
(c) expert judge (d) Ignorant

78. ***Callous***
(a) large (b) hardened
(c) thick (d) dangerous

79. ***Colossal***
(a) dangerous (b) gigantic
(c) fatal (d) honourable

80. ***Conciseness***
(a) correctness (b) frankness
(c) brevity (d) refines

81. ***Candid***
(a) sweet (b) pleasing
(c) frank (d) dishonest

82. ***Cowardice***
(a) timidity (b) gallantry
(c) criminal (d) humanity

83. ***Compendium***
(a) glossary (b) reference
(c) index (d) summary

84. ***Concise***
(a) small (b) strong
(c) solid (d) brief

85. ***Coterie***
(a) institution (b) group
(c) mob (d) family

86. ***Corroborate***
(a) verify (b) refute
(c) disprove (d) disapprove

87. ***Chimerical***
(a) imaginary (b) uncertain
(c) short-lived (d) erratic

88. ***Conundrum***
(a) discussion (b) expanation
(c) solution (d) imbroligio

89. ***Castigate***
(a) deligate (b) evaluate
(c) reprimand (d) enforce

90. ***Concealed***
(a) disclosed (b) opened
(c) camouflaged (d) released

91. ***Caveat***
(a) dispute (b) challenge
(c) advice (d) warning

92. ***Condemn***
(a) blame (b) underrate
(c) hate (d) avoid

93. ***Congregation***
(a) combination (b) meeting
(c) assembly (d) collection

94. *Colossus*
(a) huge (b) towering
(c) lofty (d) tall

95. *Cantankerous*
(a) rash (b) sisrespectful
(c) noisy (d) quarrelsome

96. *Consequence*
(a) manner (b) result
(c) cause (d) order

97. *Clairvoyance*
(a) foretelling (b) recklessness
(c) astrology (d) none of these

98. *Culpable*
(a) correct (b) guilty
(c) right (d) innocent

99. *Chivalry*
(a) bravery (b) cowardice
(c) joviality (d) gleefulness

100. *Crass*
(a) spiritless (b) wicked
(c) insensitive (d) rustic

101. *Catapult*
(a) restrain (b) control
(c) contain (d) shoot

102. *Console*
(a) solace (b) sympathise
(c) pacify (d) courage

103. *Convivial*
(a) aloof (b) shy
(c) jovial (d) lively

104. *Construe*
(a) meaning (b) interpret
(c) narration (d) confuse

105. *Callous*
(a) hard (b) cruel
(c) big (d) mighty

106. *Censure*
(a) condemn (b) blame
(c) pin point (d) charge

107. *Careen*
(a) secure (b) sway
(c) decay (d) fondle

108. *Cherubic*
(a) mischievous (b) expensive
(c) rustic (d) angelic

109. *Consternation*
(a) group of star
(b) humble service
(c) large display
(d) great amazement/ terror

110. *Cumbersome*
(a) taxing (b) sorrowful
(c) unwieldy (d) laborious

111. *Complicity*
(a) deceit (b) variety
(c) connaivance (d) relief from debt

112. *Categorically*
(a) purposefully (b) introductorily
(c) unequivocally (d) relatively

113. *Confabulate*
(a) embroider on (b) private chat
(c) muddle (d) put an end to

D

114. *Deride*
(a) mock (b) confuse
(c) shout (d) snarl

115. *Deify*
(a) challenge (b) face
(c) worship (d) flatter

116. *Delusion*
(a) actuality (b) illusion
(c) clarity (d) emulating

117. *Decry*
(a) deviate (b) despoil
(c) demure (d) disparage

118. *Doleful*
(a) bright (b) mournful
(c) colourful (d) jovial

119. *Delegate*
(a) officer (b) participant
(c) member (d) representative

120. *Deplete*
(a) exhaust (b) vanish
(c) finish (d) destroy

121. *Docile*
(a) gentle (b) vague
(c) stubborn (d) stupid

122. *Denounce*
(a) support (b) sustain
(c) maintain (d) condemn

123. *Disrupt*
(a) join (b) disturb
(c) refuse (d) deny

124. *Dodge*
(a) avoid (b) thwarft
(c) frustrate (d) confuse

125. *Domain*
(a) area (b) main
(c) marketing (d) fielding

126. *Dynamic*
(a) active (b) robust
(c) forceful (d) vigorous

127. *Delirious*
(a) happy (b) content
(c) amused (d) deranged

128. *Dilettante*
(a) expert (b) adventure
(c) specialist (d) amateur

129. *Delectable*
(a) desirable (b) attractive
(c) delicate (d) delightful

130. *Dominion*
(a) recreation (b) separation
(c) issue (d) realm

131. *Desultory*
(a) regualr (b) obedient
(c) abandoned (d) punctual

132. *Drowsy*
(a) soothing (b) energetic
(c) exhausted (d) sleepy

133. *Disparage*
(a) discourage (b) compare
(c) separate (d) belittle

134. *Diligent*
(a) modest (b) spare
(c) intelligent (d) industrious

135. *Deference*
(a) obligation (b) respect
(c) postponement (d) pride

136. *Dilemma*
(a) hard (b) severe
(c) difficult choice (d) scarcity

137. *Derisive*
(a) mocking (b) copied
(c) limited (d) borrowed

138. *Derogatory*
(a) questionab (b) inquisitive
(c) humble (d) depreciating

139. *Diurnal*
(a) news account (b) solar
(c) daily (d) everlasting

140. *Dolorous*
(a) sorrowful (b) financial
(c) sacred (d) parsimonious

141. *Debauch*
(a) corrupt (b) open a bottle
(c) branch off (d) cheapen

142. *Debilitate*
(a) attack
(b) weaken
(c) become accustomed
(d) overwhelm

143. *Decadent*
(a) aristocratic
(b) subtle
(c) occurring every ten years
(d) deteriorating

144. ***Demise***
(a) false statement (b) death
(c) message (d) stage set

145. ***Depredation***
(a) disapproval (b) decrease in value
(c) warding off (d) plundering

146. ***Denigrate***
(a) deny (b) defame
(c) ridicule (d) irritate

E

147. ***Ephemeral***
(a) short-living (b) mythical
(c) unreal (d) artificial

148. ***Extempore***
(a) praise worth (b) impromptu
(c) extraordinary (d) essential

149. ***Ecstatic***
(a) animated (b) enraptured
(c) bewildered (d) fitful

150. ***Equivocal***
(a) ambiguous (b) uarrelsome
(c) reasonable (d) feasible

151. ***Estrange***
(a) endanger (b) alienate
(c) miscalculate (d) puzzling

152. ***Excruciate***
(a) torture (b) extract
(c) imprison (d) refine

153. ***Enthusiastic***
(a) angry (b) excited
(c) noisy (d) violent

154. ***Echelon***
(a) rank (b) opponent
(c) follower (d) identity

155. ***Exude***
(a) ooze (b) wither
(c) overflow (d) evaporate

156. ***Enigmatic***
(a) pithy (b) puzzling
(c) complicated (d) illusive

157. ***Erotic***
(a) attractive (b) beautiful
(c) sensuous (d) sexual

158. ***Exceedingly***
(a) politely (b) extremely
(c) freely (d) outwardly

159. ***Effete***
(a) affected (b) injured
(c) feeble (d) sick

160. ***Enigma***
(a) puzzle (b) elusive
(c) praise (d) clear

161. ***Extravaganza***
(a) profligacy (b) spectacular show
(c) over reaching (d) falsification

162. ***Enthuse***
(a) pester (b) provoke
(c) excite (d) annoy

163. ***Ebullient***
(a) exorbitant (b) exuberant
(c) obscure (d) still

164. ***Edify***
(a) consume (b) satisfy
(c) instruct (d) amuse

165. ***Entice***
(a) cheat (b) lure
(c) flight (d) love

166. ***Emancipate***
(a) set free (b) exist
(c) correct morally (d) restrain

167. ***Elan***
(a) flair (b) spiritual
(c) inspiration (d) boredom

168. ***Empirical***
(a) spiritual (b) practical
(c) theoretical (d) royal

169. *Erudite*
(a) scholar (b) strong
(c) courteous (d) precious

170. *Encumbrance*
(a) disturbance (b) liability
(c) distraction (d) hindrance

171. *Enthral*
(a) annoy (b) glorify
(c) charm (d) persuade

172. *Explicit*
(a) clear (b) exciting
(c) precise (d) refined

173. *Epoch*
(a) turning point (b) time point
(c) neutral (d) ancient

174. *Equivocal*
(a) tought (b) uncertain
(c) hard (d) mistrust

175. *Enigma*
(a) riddle (b) dilemma
(c) fiddle (d) NOTA

176. *Eradicate*
(a) remove (b) evaporate
(c) eliminate (d) complete

177. *Enervate*
(a) calm down (b) weaken
(c) pep up (d) lure on

178. *Exorcise*
(a) expel an evil spirit (b) impress
(c) train thoroughly (d) torture

179. *Escheat*
(a) confiscate (b) swindle
(c) avoid (d) chew thoroughly

180. *Exordium*
(a) beginning of a speech
(b) plea
(c) essence
(d) final appeal

181. *Empirical*
(a) relating to a market
(b) based upon experience
(c) ruling despotically
(d) expansionist

F

182. *Fraternise*
(a) associate (b) organise
(c) expel (d) cheat

183. *Forsake*
(a) forgive (b) punish
(c) abandon (d) benefit

184. *Fatigue*
(a) tension (b) drowsiness
(c) tireness (d) sweating

185. *Forlorn*
(a) uncared (b) funny
(c) fearful (d) fortunate

186. *Fickle*
(a) nervous (b) changeable
(c) poor (d) constant

187. *Fiddle*
(a) frown (b) discard
(c) examine (d) trifle

188. *Foreigner*
(a) alien (b) native
(c) local (d) national

189. *Feign*
(a) hesitate (b) pretend
(c) deserve (d) attend

190. *Fragment*
(a) scrap (b) crumble
(c) dissection (d) cut

191. *Foment*
(a) pacify (b) incite
(c) rectify (d) restrict

192. *Foster*
(a) encourage (b) fabricate
(c) foment (d) nurture

193. *Filthy*
(a) healthy (b) ugly
(c) dirty (d) angry

194. *Flak*
(a) adventure (b) advice
(c) criticism (d) praise

195. *Forthright*
(a) straight forward (b) open
(c) frank (d) typical

196. *Fiasco*
(a) failure (b) hope
(c) strength (d) success

197. *Flippancy*
(a) levity (b) dexterity
(c) eaviness (d) clumsiness

198. *Fecundity*
(a) validity (b) poverty
(c) fertility (d) depth

G

199. *Gratify*
(a) pacify (b) indulge
(c) frank (d) appreciate

200. *Genesis*
(a) relevant (b) beginning
(c) style (d) movement

201. *Gist*
(a) contribution (b) substance
(c) prestige (d) accessory

202. *Glorious*
(a) delightful (b) painful
(c) cowardly (d) humiliating

203. *Gainsay*
(a) advantage (b) proposal
(c) contradict (d) suggestion

204. *Gregarious*
(a) pugnacious (b) turbulent
(c) sociable (d) sociable

205. *Glib*
(a) tough (b) smooth
(c) rough (d) rouge

206. *Grandiloquent*
(a) generous (b) domineering
(c) pompous (d) genuine

H

207. *Haggle*
(a) bargain (b) reject
(c) postpone (d) accept

208. *Hinder*
(a) obstruct (b) challenge
(c) damage (d) ruin

209. *Humbug*
(a) desire (b) craving
(c) illusion (d) deceit

210. *Handsome*
(a) polite (b) noble
(c) gentle (d) good looking

211. *Hassle*
(a) greed (b) jealousy
(c) gossip (d) wrangle

212. *Hoodlum*
(a) devotee (b) criminal
(c) pioneer (d) scholar

213. *Hanker*
(a) renounce (b) denounce
(c) desire (d) run after

214. *Hood-wink*
(a) collide (b) deceive
(c) prefer (d) stab

215. *Helm*
(a) corner (b) handle
(c) head (d) edge

216. *Hegemony*
(a) domination (b) materialism
(c) subordination (d) booty

217. ***Hiatus***
(a) contempt (b) narrow
(c) tight (d) gap

218. ***Hallowed***
(a) holy (b) reverend
(c) sacred (d) respected

219. ***Harass***
(a) grieve (b) injure
(c) excite (d) annoy

220. ***Harbinger***
(a) pilot (b) forerunner
(c) steward (d) messenger

221. ***Heterogeneous***
(a) similar parts (b) unlike elements
(c) smooth surfaces (d) complex problems

222. ***Hybrid***
(a) of mixed origin (b) spirited
(c) well-mannered (d) poor

223. ***Histrionic***
(a) theatrical (b) informed
(c) famous (d) microscopic

I

224. ***Icon***
(a) monument (b) memorial
(c) painting (d) statue

225. ***Indict***
(a) accuse (b) condemn
(c) allege (d) reprimand

226. ***Imposter***
(a) imposer (b) lazy
(c) cheat (d) painful

227. ***Innate***
(a) uniue (b) important
(c) inborn (d) essential

228. ***Indigence***
(a) poverty (b) prosperity
(c) suffering (d) scarcity

229. ***Incite***
(a) discourage (b) encourage
(c) internal (d) crime

230. ***Impertinent***
(a) impudent (b) sceptical
(c) thoughtless (d) irritable

231. ***Impediment***
(a) passage (b) obstruction
(c) fateful (d) destruction

232. ***Indomitable***
(a) inactive (b) authoritative
(c) rebellious (d) unconquerable

233. ***Indolence***
(a) leniency (b) relaxation
(c) laziness (d) stagnation

234. ***Innocent***
(a) guilty (b) clean
(c) deadly (d) sinful

235. ***Ingenuous***
(a) active (b) skilful
(c) smart (d) none of these

236. ***Insidious***
(a) slow (b) pessimistic
(c) treacherous (d) patriotic

237. ***Improvident***
(a) thriftiness (b) incautious
(c) unhappy (d) shabby

238. ***Incensed***
(a) inspired (b) encouraged
(c) incited (d) affected

239. ***Inconsistent***
(a) unrestrained (b) restless
(c) inconstant (d) uncertain

240. ***Infirm***
(a) dull (b) sickly
(c) slim (d) unyielding

241. ***Inexplicable***
(a) unconnected (b) chaotic
(c) unaccountable (d) confusing

242. *Irk*
(a) bore (b) insult
(c) urge (d) annoy

243. *Industrious*
(a) intelligent (b) hard-working
(c) clever (d) reserved

244. *Insolvent*
(a) penniless (b) bankrupt
(c) roke (d) poor

245. *Ironic*
(a) sarcastic (b) inflexible
(c) bitter (d) good natured

246. *Impeccable*
(a) fussy (b) precise
(c) having integrity (d) faultless

247. *Intimidate*
(a) hint (b) harass
(c) bluff (d) frighten

248. *Insipid*
(a) flat (b) lucid
(c) wily (d) witty

249. *Immanent*
(a) impending (b) inherent
(c) urgent (d) soon

250. *Internecine*
(a) deadly (b) foolhardy
(c) stealthy (d) international

251. *Imbroglio*
(a) difficulty (b) impossibility
(c) confrontation (d) stalemate

252. *Impasse*
(a) confrontation (b) stalemate
(c) difficulty (d) impossibility

253. *Immaculate*
(a) shining (b) dirty
(c) clean (d) spotless

254. *Interim*
(a) temporary (b) internal
(c) interval (d) timely

255. *Imprecation*
(a) oath (b) blessing
(c) bliss (d) abuse

256. *Inordinate*
(a) subordinate (b) inanimate
(c) excessive (d) extraordinary

257. *Inevitable*
(a) fixed (b) unavoidable
(c) expected (d) probable

258. *Insidious*
(a) slow (b) treacherous
(c) pessimistic (d) unfortunate

259. *Iota*
(a) little (b) scintilla
(c) uncountable (d) dole

260. *Intrinsic*
(a) shy (b) inherent
(c) talkative (d) aloof

261. *Intrepid*
(a hopeless (b) fearless
(c) bold (d) strong

262. *Insolent*
(a) arrogant (b) lethargic
(c) rude (d) helpful

263. *Infrequent*
(a) never (b) usual
(c) rare (d) sometimes

264. *Infernal*
(a) hateful (b) exciting
(c) devilish (d) damaging

265. *Indict*
(a) accuse (b) condemn
(c) allege (d) reprimand

266. *Idiosyncray*
(a) personality (b) lack of intelligence
(c) absolute rule (d) characteristic

267. *Impinge*
(a) paint (b) constrict
(c) steal (d) encroach

268. *Incisive*
(a) penetrating (b) short
(c) compendious (d) assured

269. *Insinuate*
(a) spy upon (b) suggest slyly
(c) set free (d) indicate

270. *Immutable*
(a) debatable (b) unalterable
(c) impractical (d) not susceptible

271. *Inscrutable*
(a) mad (b) malicious
(c) misleading (d) unfathomable

272. *Imponderable*
(a) incapable (b) very small
(c) unthinkable (d) tremendous

273. *Ineffable*
(a) speechless (b) feminine
(c) rude (d) indescribable

274. *Inuendo*
(a) investigation (b) insinuation
(c) injustice (d) hinting

275. *Immanent*
(a) inherent (b) decisive
(c) impending (d) prominent

J

276. *Juvenile*
(a) hidden (b) young
(c) humorous (d) tedious

277. *Jovial*
(a) smart (b) funny
(c) triumphant (d) merry

278. *Jeer*
(a) clean (b) deride
(c) pulsate (d) hear

279. *Jocular*
(a) merry (b) jolting
(c) craving (d) imperial

280. *Jubilant*
(a) disturbed (b) scared
(c) gloomy (d) exultant

281. *Jingoistic*
(a) dashing (b) victorious
(c) compromise (d) patriotic

282. *Jocose*
(a) trite (b) playful
(c) useless (d) illusory

K

283. *Knavery*
(a) stupidity (b) heroism
(c) cowardice (d) dishonesty

284. *Kindle*
(a) set on fire (b) light
(c) conserve (d) preserve

285. *Knack*
(a) own (b) skill
(c) job (d) quality

286. *Kowtow*
(a) blockhead (b) illuminate
(c) practise (d) flatter

L

287. *Lethal*
(a) deadly (b) sluggish
(c) uncivilised (d) smooth

288. *Ludicrous*
(a) simple (b) dismal
(c) clear (d) absurd

289. *Loquacious*
(a) uiet (b) talkative
(c) secretive (d) sad

290. *Levitate*
(a) evaporate (b) fall
(c) rise (d) subsidize

291. *Lurid*
(a) sensational (b) old
(c) showy (d) pale

292. *Latent*
(a) hard (b) concealed
(c) visible (d) display

293. *Lenient*
(a) cruel (b) rough
(c) kind (d) harsh

294. *Lethargy*
(a) dynamism (b) laziness
(c) cool headed (d) lavish

295. *Loquacious*
(a) verbose (b) taciturn
(c) rational (d) alluring

296. *Loath*
(a) tired (b) unwilling
(c) sickly (d) latest

297. *Licentious*
(a) gay (b) immoral
(c) generous (d) hungry

298. *Lamentable*
(a) remorseful (b) deploralbe
(c) scornful (d) contemptible

299. *Lugubrious*
(a) sleek (b) consolatory
(c) mournful (d) deceitful

300. *Lascivious*
(a) fragrant (b) foul
(c) naughty (d) lustful

301. *Languish*
(a) destroy (b) decay
(c) lack vigour (d) imprisonment

302. *Livid*
(a) discolored (b) sensational
(c) bilious (d) smarting

303. *Libidinous*
(a) lustful (b) disagreeable
(c) discolored (d) headstrong

M

304. *Moribund*
(a) stagnant (b) superfluous
(c) dying (d) gloomy

305. *Massacre*
(a) murder (b) assassinate
(c) stab (d) slaughter

306. *Mollify*
(a) chastise (b) testify
(c) rebuke (d) appease

307. *Morose*
(a) cam (b) disappointe
(c) gloomy (d) diseased

308. *Machination*
(a) labour saving (b) evil plot
(c) factory work (d) engine part

309. *Malaise*
(a) stagnation (b) spite
(c) curse (d) sickness

310. *Mystical*
(a) imaginary (b) vague
(c) prophetic (d) spiritually

311. *Muffle*
(a) soften (b) soften
(c) wrap (d) hasten

312. *Masticate*
(a) swallow (b) organize
(c) meander (d) reduce

313. *Macabre*
(a) innocent (b) tarried
(c) gruesome (d) pleasing

314. *Marvellous*
(a) pleasing (b) wonderful
(c) charming (d) attractive

315. *Morbid*
(a) angry (b) diseased
(c) irritated (d) dying

316. *Mellifluous*
(a) sweet (b) stale
(c) tasteful (d) stupid

317. *Malign*
(a) depriciate (b) deviate
(c) perforate (d) assign

318. *Moot*
(a) unexpected (b) obseuious
(c) controversial (d) invisible

319. *Moronic*
(a) imbecile (b) invective
(c) abusive (d) sharp

320. *Magnanimous*
(a) kind (b) generous
(c) loyal (d) loving

321. *Myopic*
(a) astigmatic (b) short-sighted
(c) cross-eyed (d) blind

322. *Magnifying*
(a) enlarging (b) discriminating
(c) reducing (d) denying

323. *Modish*
(a) adorned (b) sentimental
(c) stylish (d) vacillating

324. *Maverick*
(a) novice (b) reformer
(c) wonderful (d) unorthodox

325. *Malady*
(a) ill will (b) ill luck
(c) ill feeling (d) illness

326. *Mundane*
(a) luxurious (b) worldly
(c) spiritual (d) global

327. *Magniloquent*
(a) tactful (b) amusing
(c) humorous (d) boastful

328. *Mutation*
(a) variation (b) display
(c) sverance (d) silence

329. *Mordant*
(a) festering (b) sarcastic
(c) depressed (d) mild

330. *Monotonous*
(a) uniform (b) equal
(c) same (d) dull

331. *Maim*
(a) copy (b) imitate
(c) disfigure (d) severe

332. *Manifesto*
(a) cargo list (b) secret treaty
(c) revolutionary plot (d) public declaration

333. *Motley*
(a) of various color (b) undistinguished
(c) dirty (d) abundant

334. *Mayhem*
(a) depth (b) measurement
(c) havoc (d) murder

335. *Meticulous*
(a) lying (b) painstaking
(c) irascible (d) tawdry

336. *Mollification*
(a) magnification (b) pacification
(c) amplification (d) NOTA

337. *Malleable*
(a) permeable (b) pliant
(c) stringy (d) punctureproof

338. *Miasma*
(a) stench (b) aroma
(c) sweetness (d) NOTA

339. *Mordant*
(a) trenchant (b) festering
(c) sweet (d) fragrant

N

340. *Nepotism*
(a) favouritism (b) carelessness
(c) inefficiency (d) corruption

341. *Nostalgic*
(a) soothing (b) homesick
(c) diseased (d) indolent

342. ***Naive***

(a) natural (b) novice
(c) credulous (d) primitives

343. ***Niggard***

(a) cunning (b) miser
(c) shrewd (d) clover

O

344. ***Obfuscate***

(a) push (b) compete
(c) confuse (d) remove

345. ***Onerous***

(a) awesome (b) dutiful
(c) difficult (d) burdensome

346. ***Omnipotent***

(a) all knowing (b) all powerful
(c) everlasting (d) all merciful

347. ***Ostensibly***

(a) actually (b) conspicuously
(c) apparently (d) uietly

348. ***Ostentation***

(a) protruding (b) wealthy
(c) decorative (d) showy

349. ***Ostracize***

(a) fearful (b) fortunate
(c) uncared (d) cut off

350. ***Ostensible***

(a) apparent (b) elaborate
(c) traditional (d) showy

351. ***Optimistic***

(a) optician (b) favourable
(c) wishful (d) hopeful

352. ***Obdurate***

(a) adamant (b) helpful
(c) simple (d) flexible

353. ***Ostentatious***

(a) showy (b) noisy
(c) wealthy (d) talkative

354. ***Ogle***

(a) look (b) stare
(c) peep (d) see

355. ***Overtures***

(a) glimpses (b) promises
(c) rewards (d) offers

356. ***Overweening***

(a) crushing (b) arrogant
(c) pampering (d) massive

P

357. ***Placid***

(a) calm (b) dull
(c) enjoyable (d) clear

358. ***Prolific***

(a) fertile (b) destroy
(c) modest (d) pretty

359. ***Placate***

(a) appease (b) amuse
(c) pity (d) embroil

360. ***Prohibit***

(a) banish (b) punish
(c) forbid (d) exhibit

361. ***Penchant***

(a) disability (b) dislike
(c) like (d) eagerness

362. ***Pertinacius***

(a) determined (b) delicate
(c) defensive (d) humble

363. ***Pilferage***

(a) steal (b) snatch
(c) destroy (d) damage

364. ***Prudent***

(a) skilled (b) experienced
(c) cautious (d) wise

365. ***Parochial***

(a) gloomy (b) reluctant
(c) troublesome (d) narrow-minded

366. *Prevaricate*
(a) anticipate (b) lie
(c) delay (d) authenticate

367. *Penitence*
(a) retribution (b) submission
(c) confinement (d) repentance

368. *Profound*
(a) fathomless (b) scanty
(c) scary (d) shallow

369. *Prerogative*
(a) command (b) privilege
(c) request (d) desire

370. *Paramour*
(a) fival (b) lover
(c) companion (d) friend

371. *Precarious*
(a) critical (b) cautious
(c) perilous (d) brittle

372. *Paramount*
(a) urgent (b) suprme
(c) valuable (d) prestigious

373. *Perilous*
(a) tempting (b) obsolete
(c) dangerous (d) concrete

374. *Preposterous*
(a) formal (b) judicious
(c) ridiculous (d) ceremonious

375. *Pristine*
(a) traditional (b) expensive
(c) original (d) meritorious

376. *Prowess*
(a) eagerness (b) keenness
(c) understanding (d) bravery

377. *Prattle*
(a) chatter (b) construct
(c) meditate (d) loiter

378. *Proliferate*
(a) generate (b) proclaim
(c) support (d) assust

379. *Pettifogging*
(a) stable (b) unimportant
(c) strong (d) lenient

380. *Paradigm*
(a) theme (b) example
(c) proof (d) paragon

381. *Prune*
(a) lend (b) reduce
(c) expand (d) prolong

382. *Promulgate*
(a) proclaim (b) inform
(c) promote (d) enforce

383. *Paparazzo*
(a) actor (b) director
(c) dancer (d) photographer

384. *Proscribe*
(a) banish (b) prohibit
(c) allow (d) accept

385. *Palpable*
(a) subtle (b) persuasive
(c) excited (d) obvious

386. *Parsimonios*
(a) stingy (b) hypocritical
(c) stiff (d) miserly

387. *Pragmatic*
(a) perplexing (b) ideal
(c) practical (d) experienced

388. *Perfidy*
(a) confidence (b) treachery
(c) obstinacy (d) insolence

389. *Peruse*
(a) exhaust (b) change
(c) analyze (d) condense

390. *Platitudinous*
(a) banal (b) level
(c) boastful (d) oratorical

391. *Pertinacious*
(a) stubbornly (b) related
(c) bold (d) unabashed

392. *Polemic*

(a) eloquent (b) awkward
(c) scatthing (d) disparaging

393. *Predatory*

(a) plundering (b) anticipating
(c) powerful (d) carnivorous

394. *Predilection*

(a) forecast (b) preference
(c) remembrance (d) gratification

395. *Preempt*

(a) vacate (b) substitute
(c) prevent (d) place a bet

396. *Protagonist*

(a) opponent (b) proponent
(c) rebel (d) wrestler

397. *Paucity*

(a) costliness (b) short rest
(c) scantiness (d) misuse

398. *Prodigality*

(a) lavishness (b) stimulus
(c) sinfulness (d) negligence

Q

399. *Quack*

(a) pyromaniac (b) charlatan
(c) dilemma (d) victim

400. *Quell*

(a) kill (b) destroy
(c) overwhelm (d) overthrow

401. *Quibble*

(a) discuss (b) deliberate
(c) argue (d) haggle

402. *Quizzical*

(a) puzzling (b) queer
(c) ill-tempered (d) antiquated

403. *Quagmire*

(a) large clam (b) bog
(c) underbrush (d) gradual rise

R

404. *Ribald*

(a) refined (b) indifferent
(c) vulgar (d) attractive

405. *Reiterate*

(a) reassess (b) rewrite
(c) repeat (d) stutter

406. *Replenish*

(a) refill (b) supply
(c) provide (d) restore

407. *Reverberate*

(a) resonate (b) accelerate
(c) revitalize (d) gibberish

408. *Reticence*

(a) generosity (b) frankness
(c) sincerity (d) taciturnity

409. *Robust*

(a) wear (b) useless
(c) forceful (d) stupid

410. *Reluctant*

(a) inclined (b) ready
(c) hesitating (d) willing

411. *Reckless*

(a) courageous (b) daring
(c) bold (d) rash

412. *Repercussion*

(a) remuneration (b) consequence
(c) reaction (d) recollection

413. *Retrograde*

(a) pushback (b) backward
(c) go back (d) draw

414. *Reverberations*

(a) repetition (b) reverse
(c) echo (d) imitate

415. *Resilient*

(a) rigid (b) flexible
(c) convenient (d) hard

416. *Rakish*

(a) illegitimate (b) illegal
(c) immoral (d) henous

417. *Retribution*
(a) contempt (b) revenge
(c) punishment (d) discount

418. *Replica*
(a) mythical creature (b) answer
(c) duplicate (d) public building

419. *Recluse*
(a) miser (b) aged person
(c) woman-hater (d) hermit

420. *Recrudescene*
(a) rawness (b) revival
(c) refinement (d) lack of manners

S

421. *Savvy*
(a) deformed (b) understanding
(c) disatisfied (d) NOTA

422. *Serene*
(a) calm (b) meak
(c) solemn (d) delicate

423. *Sanguine*
(a) hopeful (b) modest
(c) clever (d) proud

424. *Stamina*
(a) endurance (b) intensity
(c) eagerness (d) energy

425. *Stubborn*
(a) willing (b) pliable
(c) easy (d) obstinate

426. *Stalemate*
(a) deadly (b) dead-end
(c) diffusion (d) dead-drunk

427. *Slander*
(a) circular (b) spherical
(c) fragile (d) defame

428. *Stringent*
(a) causing to shrink (b) strict
(c) stringy (d) tense

429. *Shrewd*
(a) naive (b) clever
(c) raw (d) youthful

430. *Serenity*
(a) agitation (b) protest
(c) stir (d) calmness

431. *Sustain*
(a) support (b) review
(c) believe (d) survive

432. *Succour*
(a) search (b) flow
(c) raise (d) support

433. *Severe*
(a) rigid (b) aggressive
(c) offensive (d) accute

434. *Stridency*
(a) fippancy (b) stress
(c) consistency (d) harshness

435. *Simon-pure*
(a) false (b) genuine
(c) holy (d) artificial

436. *Surreptitious*
(a) mysterious (b) abstract
(c) secretive (d) secret

437. *Scintillating*
(a) touching (b) warming
(c) gutterubg (d) smouldering

438. *Sycophant*
(a) flatterer (b) follower
(c) admirer (d) suppliant

439. *Salacity*
(a) depression (b) recession
(c) bliss (d) indecency

440. *Surreal*
(a) unreal (b) reality
(c) bizarre (d) precise

441. *Stringent*
(a) tough (b) principled
(c) strict (d) harmful

442. *Sultry*
(a) foul (b) bad
(c) hot (d) oppressive

443. *Spasmodic*
(a) intestinal (b) internal
(c) intermittent (d) gradual

444. *Solicit*
(a) request (b) beseech
(c) demand (d) expectation

445. *Stalemate*
(a) deadlock (b) stoppage
(c) blockade (d) postpone

446. *Sagacity*
(a) morality (b) knowledge
(c) wisdom (d) sanctity

447. *Salacious*
(a) briny (b) purchasable
(c) obscene (d) flavored

448. *Savant*
(a) cleansing agent (b) learned person
(c) young student (d) french courtier

449. *Sanguinary*
(a) hopeful (b) unlimited
(c) unnecessary (d) bloody

450. *Salubrious*
(a) flavored (b) healthy
(c) lewd (d) pathetic

T

451. *Terrific*
(a) tragic (b) terrible
(c) big (d) excellent

452. *Tete a tete*
(a) delightful (b) penetrating
(c) piercing (d) conversation

453. *Triumph*
(a) gain (b) victory
(c) excitement (d) joy

454. *Tedious*
(a) lengthy (b) tiresome
(c) saint (d) widower

455. *Temperate*
(a) cool (b) moderate
(c) favourable (d) dangerous

456. *Twain*
(a) discarded (b) worthless
(c) couple (d) strong

457. *Trivial*
(a) economical (b) uneconomical
(c) friviolous (d) commonplace

458. *Testify*
(a) witness (b) describe
(c) recognise (d) appreciate

459. *Tentative*
(a) final (b) provisional
(c) current (d) unreliable

460. *Tenacious*
(a) bold (b) poisonous
(c) uncomfortable (d) piercing

461. *Taciturnity*
(a) silence (b) violence
(c) insolence (d) prudence

462. *Truncate*
(a) cut off (b) end swiftly
(c) act cruelly (d) cancel

463. *Tutelage*
(a) rejection (b) perfection
(c) protection (d) dejection

464. *Teeter*
(a) hesitate (b) descend
(c) pretend (d) toddle

465. *Tranquil*
(a) sedate (b) calm
(c) quite (d) dull

466. *Tycoon*
(a) leader (b) ruler
(c) prophet (d) magnate

467. *Tantamount*
(a) equivalent (b) gigantic
(c) superior (d) far-removed

468. *Talisman*
(a) charm/ formula (b) juror
(c) informer (d) lecturer

469. *Transcend*
(a) move (b) degrade
(c) surpass (d) delay

470. *Tonsure*
(a) baldness (b) furry
(c) hairy (d) NOTA

471. *Transmogrify*
(a) transmute (b) haunt
(c) pierce (d) terrify

472. *Traumatic*
(a) dreamy (b) magic
(c) emphatic (d) turbulent

U

473. *Undaunted*
(a) careless (b) unafraid
(c) worthless (d) prudent

474. *Unanimously*
(a) friendly (b) forcefully
(c) unuestionably (d) democratically

475. *Ulterior*
(a) revealed (b) undisclosed
(c) extreme (d) decisive

476. *Upbraid*
(a) plait (b) reproach
(c) elevate (d) foster

477. *Unconscionable*
(a) unmindful
(b) excessive
(c) unmangeable
(d) distasteful

V

478. *Venality*
(a) hope (b) sacrifice
(c) respect (d) corruption

479. *Votary*
(a) devotee (b) conscious
(c) religious (d) amiable

480. *Virginity*
(a) decency (b) maidenhood
(c) beauty (d) attractiveness

481. *Venture*
(a) entrust (b) risk
(c) travel (d) adventure

482. *Venerate*
(a) defame (b) abuse
(c) respect (d) accuse

483. *Vendetta*
(a) revenge (b) proposal
(c) compromise (d) feud

484. *Vituperate*
(a) encourage (b) pretend
(c) appraise (d) vilify

485. *Vilify*
(a) deceive (b) desert
(c) deprive (d) defame

486. *Vindicate*
(a) approve (b) justify
(c) express (d) exonerate

487. *Virile*
(a) childish (b) womanly
(c) manly (d) brave

488. *Voracious*
(a) voluptuous
(b) victorious
(c) hungry
(d) vild

W

489. ***Wary***
(a) cautious (b) accurate
(c) quick (d) practical

490. ***Waive***
(a) restrict (b) relax
(c) permit (d) admit

491. ***Wry***
(a) sad (b) twisted
(c) smiling (d) undeserved

492. ***Worthless***
(a) cheap (b) valuable
(c) invalid (d) variable

493. ***Wither***
(a) dry up (b) shrivell
(c) destroy (d) die

494. ***Whim***
(a) thought (b) dream
(c) fit (d) fantasy

495. ***Wallow***
(a) fantasy (b) suffer
(c) luxuriate (d) comfort

496. ***Wrath***
(a) jealousy (b) hatreed
(c) anger (d) violence

Z

497. ***Zenith***
(a) sharp (b) bright
(c) bravery (d) climax

498. ***Zany***
(a) thief (b) magician
(c) clown (d) pet

499. ***Zeal***
(a) ardour (b) apathy
(c) indifference (d) NOTA

500. ***Zealot***
(a) fanatic (b) moderate
(c) liberal (d) feminist

ANSWERS

1. (c)	**2.** (c)	**3.** (c)	**4.** (b)	**5.** (b)	**6.** (c)	**7.** (b)	**8.** (c)	**9.** (d)	**10.** (d)
11. (b)	**12.** (c)	**13.** (c)	**14.** (b)	**15.** (c)	**16.** (a)	**17.** (a)	**18.** (b)	**19.** (b)	**20.** (d)
21. (d)	**22.** (b)	**23.** (a)	**24.** (a)	**25.** (c)	**26.** (b)	**27.** (a)	**28.** (d)	**29.** (c)	**30.** (a)
31. (a)	**32.** (c)	**33.** (a)	**34.** (b)	**35.** (c)	**36.** (d)	**37.** (a)	**38.** (a)	**39.** (a)	**40.** (a)
41. (c)	**42.** (d)	**43.** (b)	**44.** (c)	**45.** (a)	**46.** (c)	**47.** (a)	**48.** (a)	**49.** (b)	**50.** (c)
51. (b)	**52.** (a)	**53.** (b)	**54.** (c)	**55.** (c)	**56.** (d)	**57.** (c)	**58.** (a)	**59.** (c)	**60.** (d)
61. (c)	**62.** (a)	**63.** (d)	**64.** (d)	**65.** (c)	**66.** (b)	**67.** (a)	**68.** (b)	**69.** (b)	**70.** (c)
71. (c)	**72.** (c)	**73.** (d)	**74.** (c)	**75.** (b)	**76.** (c)	**77.** (c)	**78.** (b)	**79.** (b)	**80.** (c)
81. (c)	**82.** (a)	**83.** (d)	**84.** (d)	**85.** (b)	**86.** (a)	**87.** (a)	**88.** (d)	**89.** (c)	**90.** (c)
91. (d)	**92.** (a)	**93.** (c)	**94.** (a)	**95.** (d)	**96.** (b)	**97.** (a)	**98.** (b)	**99.** (a)	**100.** (d)
101. (d)	**102.** (b)	**103.** (c)	**104.** (b)	**105.** (a)	**106.** (a)	**107.** (d)	**108.** (d)	**109.** (d)	**110.** (a)
111. (c)	**112.** (c)	**113.** (b)	**114.** (a)	**115.** (c)	**116.** (b)	**117.** (d)	**118.** (b)	**119.** (b)	**120.** (a)
121. (a)	**122.** (d)	**123.** (b)	**124.** (b)	**125.** (a)	**126.** (d)	**127.** (d)	**128.** (d)	**129.** (d)	**130.** (d)
131. (c)	**132.** (b)	**133.** (d)	**134.** (d)	**135.** (b)	**136.** (c)	**137.** (a)	**138.** (d)	**139.** (c)	**140.** (a)
141. (a)	**142.** (b)	**143.** (d)	**144.** (b)	**145.** (d)	**146.** (c)	**147.** (a)	**148.** (b)	**149.** (b)	**150.** (a)

151. (b)	**152.** (a)	**153.** (b)	**154.** (a)	**155.** (a)	**156.** (b)	**157.** (d)	**158.** (b)	**159.** (c)	**160.** (a)
161. (b)	**162.** (c)	**163.** (b)	**164.** (c)	**165.** (b)	**166.** (a)	**167.** (a)	**168.** (b)	**169.** (a)	**170.** (b)
171. (c)	**172.** (a)	**173.** (b)	**174.** (b)	**175.** (a)	**176.** (c)	**177.** (b)	**178.** (a)	**179.** (a)	**180.** (a)
181. (b)	**182.** (a)	**183.** (c)	**184.** (c)	**185.** (a)	**186.** (b)	**187.** (d)	**188.** (a)	**189.** (b)	**190.** (a)
191. (b)	**192.** (d)	**193.** (b)	**194.** (c)	**195.** (a)	**196.** (a)	**197.** (a)	**198.** (c)	**199.** (a)	**200.** (b)
201. (b)	**202.** (a)	**203.** (c)	**204.** (c)	**205.** (b)	**206.** (c)	**207.** (a)	**208.** (a)	**209.** (d)	**210.** (d)
211. (d)	**212.** (b)	**213.** (d)	**214.** (b)	**215.** (c)	**216.** (a)	**217.** (d)	**218.** (a)	**219.** (d)	**220.** (b)
221. (b)	**222.** (a)	**223.** (a)	**224.** (d)	**225.** (a)	**226.** (c)	**227.** (c)	**228.** (a)	**229.** (b)	**230.** (a)
231. (b)	**232.** (d)	**233.** (c)	**234.** (b)	**235.** (b)	**236.** (d)	**237.** (a)	**238.** (c)	**239.** (c)	**240.** (b)
241. (c)	**242.** (b)	**243.** (b)	**244.** (b)	**245.** (a)	**246.** (d)	**247.** (d)	**248.** (c)	**249.** (a)	**250.** (a)
251. (a)	**252.** (b)	**253.** (d)	**254.** (a)	**255.** (d)	**256.** (c)	**257.** (b)	**258.** (b)	**259.** (b)	**260.** (b)
261. (c)	**262.** (b)	**263.** (c)	**264.** (c)	**265.** (a)	**266.** (d)	**267.** (d)	**268.** (a)	**269.** (d)	**270.** (b)
271. (d)	**272.** (c)	**273.** (d)	**274.** (b)	**275.** (c)	**276.** (b)	**277.** (d)	**278.** (b)	**279.** (a)	**280.** (d)
281. (d)	**282.** (b)	**283.** (d)	**284.** (a)	**285.** (b)	**286.** (d)	**287.** (a)	**288.** (d)	**289.** (b)	**290.** (c)
291. (c)	**292.** (b)	**293.** (c)	**294.** (b)	**295.** (a)	**296.** (c)	**297.** (b)	**298.** (a)	**299.** (c)	**300.** (d)
301. (d)	**302.** (b)	**303.** (a)	**304.** (d)	**305.** (a)	**306.** (d)	**307.** (c)	**308.** (b)	**309.** (d)	**310.** (d)
311. (b)	**312.** (a)	**313.** (c)	**314.** (b)	**315.** (b)	**316.** (a)	**317.** (a)	**318.** (c)	**319.** (a)	**320.** (b)
321. (b)	**322.** (a)	**323.** (c)	**324.** (d)	**325.** (d)	**326.** (b)	**327.** (d)	**328.** (a)	**329.** (c)	**330.** (a)
331. (c)	**332.** (d)	**333.** (a)	**334.** (c)	**335.** (b)	**336.** (b)	**337.** (a)	**338.** (a)	**339.** (a)	**340.** (a)
341. (b)	**342.** (b)	**343.** (b)	**344.** (c)	**345.** (d)	**346.** (b)	**347.** (c)	**348.** (d)	**349.** (d)	**350.** (d)
351. (d)	**352.** (a)	**353.** (a)	**354.** (b)	**355.** (d)	**356.** (b)	**357.** (a)	**358.** (a)	**359.** (a)	**360.** (c)
361. (c)	**362.** (a)	**363.** (a)	**364.** (d)	**365.** (d)	**366.** (c)	**367.** (d)	**368.** (a)	**369.** (b)	**370.** (b)
371. (a)	**372.** (b)	**373.** (c)	**374.** (c)	**375.** (c)	**376.** (d)	**377.** (a)	**378.** (a)	**379.** (b)	**380.** (b)
381. (b)	**382.** (a)	**383.** (d)	**384.** (b)	**385.** (b)	**386.** (d)	**387.** (c)	**388.** (b)	**389.** (c)	**390.** (a)
391. (a)	**392.** (c)	**393.** (a)	**394.** (b)	**395.** (c)	**396.** (b)	**397.** (c)	**398.** (a)	**399.** (b)	**400.** (b)
401. (c)	**402.** (a)	**403.** (b)	**404.** (c)	**405.** (c)	**406.** (a)	**407.** (a)	**408.** (d)	**409.** (c)	**410.** (c)
411. (d)	**412.** (b)	**413.** (c)	**414.** (c)	**415.** (b)	**416.** (c)	**417.** (b)	**418.** (c)	**419.** (d)	**420.** (b)
421. (b)	**422.** (a)	**423.** (a)	**424.** (a)	**425.** (d)	**426.** (b)	**427.** (d)	**428.** (b)	**429.** (b)	**430.** (d)
431. (d)	**432.** (d)	**433.** (d)	**434.** (d)	**435.** (c)	**436.** (a)	**437.** (d)	**438.** (a)	**439.** (d)	**440.** (a)
441. (c)	**442.** (c)	**443.** (c)	**444.** (a)	**445.** (a)	**446.** (c)	**447.** (c)	**448.** (b)	**449.** (a)	**450.** (b)
451. (b)	**452.** (d)	**453.** (b)	**454.** (b)	**455.** (b)	**456.** (c)	**457.** (c)	**458.** (a)	**459.** (b)	**460.** (a)
461. (a)	**462.** (a)	**463.** (c)	**464.** (d)	**465.** (b)	**466.** (d)	**467.** (a)	**468.** (a)	**469.** (c)	**470.** (a)
471. (a)	**472.** (d)	**473.** (b)	**474.** (d)	**475.** (b)	**476.** (b)	**477.** (a)	**478.** (d)	**479.** (a)	**480.** (b)
481. (d)	**482.** (c)	**483.** (d)	**484.** (d)	**485.** (d)	**486.** (b)	**487.** (a)	**488.** (c)	**489.** (a)	**490.** (b)
491. (b)	**492.** (a)	**493.** (a)	**494.** (d)	**495.** (d)	**496.** (c)	**497.** (d)	**498.** (c)	**499.** (a)	**500.** (a)

ANTONYMS
Alphabetically Arranged MCQs

DIRECTIONS: ***Given below are some words arranged alphabetically. Each word is followed by four options. You have to find out the word which is exactly opposite in meaning to the given word. NOTA means `None Of The Above' from the given options.***

A

1. *Autonomy*
(a) freedom
(b) dependence
(c) authority
(d) independence

2. *Abhorrence*
(a) aversion (a) liking
(c) appreciation (d) fear

3. *Audacious*
(a) timid (b) vulgar
(c) low (d) unpractised

4. *Absolute*
(a) scarce (b) limited
(c) faulty (d) eficient

5. *Acute*
(a) sharp (b) critical
(c) dull (d) sensitive

6. *Antipathy*
(a) obedience (b) admiration
(c) agreement (d) fondness

7. *Apposite*
(a) inappropriate (b) intemperate
(c) inconsistent (d) irregular

8. *Amplify*
(a) mummify (b) shock
(c) curtail (d) embalm

9. *Acumen*
(a) intelligence (b) imbecility
(c) potentiality (d) unfamiliarity

10. *Adversity*
(a) enmity (b) severity
(c) prosperity (d) calamity

11. *Auspicious*
(a) spicy (b) unfavourable
(c) clever (d) cunning

12. *Adherent*
(a) rival (b) alien
(c) detractor (d) enemy

13. *Amicable*
(a) friendly (b) shy
(c) hostile (d) crazy

14. *Applaud*
(a) request (b) criticise
(c) pray (d) flatter

15. *Abundant*
(a) long (b) heavy
(c) scarce (d) excessive

16. *Adroit*
(a) deterred (b) skillful
(c) foolish (d) unskilled

17. *Appease*
(a) sympathise (b) irritate
(c) peaceful (d) apart

18. *Absurd*
(a) awkward (b) unreasonable
(c) reasonable (d) worthless

19. *Ancient*
(a) latent (b) raw
(c) recent (d) historical

20. ***Acquittal***
(a) warrant (b) condemnation
(c) conviction (d) castigation

21. ***Affluent***
(a) talkative (b) poor
(c) prosperous (d) close

22. ***Agony***
(a) pleasure (b) bliss
(c) ecstasy (d) fear

23. ***Aberration***
(a) typicalbehaviour (b) correct manners
(c) straight aim (d) full truthfulness

24. ***Ameliorate***
(a) increase (b) deteriorate
(c) clasp (d) dissemble

25. ***Artificial***
(a) solid (b) truthful
(c) authentic (d) natural

26. ***Abominate***
(a) praise (b) attract
(c) like (d) adorn

27. ***Adamant***
(a) reluctant (b) yielding
(c) burly (d) unwanted

28. ***Abusive***
(a) wretched (b) decent
(c) complimentary (d) respectful

29. ***Averse***
(a) willing (b) unwilling
(c) refusal (d) rejection

30. ***Agile***
(a) undeft (b) lazy
(c) clumsy (d) lethargic

31. ***Arduous***
(a) ordinary (b) easy
(c) expected (d) NOTA

32. ***Abridge***
(a) expand (b) increase
(c) lengthen (d) continue

B

33. ***Bliss***
(a) anguish (b) sorrow
(c) agony (d) suffering

34. ***Blatant***
(a) noisy (b) quiet
(c) barren (d) slow

35. ***Boost***
(a) hinder (b) obstruct
(c) discourage (d) rebuke

36. ***Base***
(a) roof (b) height
(c) top (d) climax

37. ***Bridge***
(a) divide (b) bind
(c) release (d) open

38. ***Beautiful***
(a) ugly (b) dark
(c) rough (d) dirty

39. ***Bashful***
(a) daring (b) boastful
(c) upright (d) confident

40. ***Beseech***
(a) bully (b) solicit
(c) demand (d) dismiss

41. ***Boorish***
(a) handsome (b) happy
(c) quite (d) genteel

42. ***Benign***
(a) gracious (b) sinister
(c) novel (d) humane

43. ***Blemish***
(a) preserve (b) purify
(c) defect (d) tarnish

44. ***Bizarre***
(a) soft (b) usual
(c) gentle (d) same

45. ***Brazen***
(a) respectful (b) innocent
(c) delicious (d) helpful

46. *Benevolence*
(a) contempt (b) malevolence
(c) hatred (d) derision

47. *Balmy*
(a) hard (b) genuine
(c) mild (d) fragrant

48. *Brutality*
(a) criminal (b) humanity
(c) adamant (d) without fear

49. *Biosterous*
(a) calm (b) comfortable
(c) good (d) happy

50 *Blithe*
(a) soft (b) aloof
(c) cheerless (d) gloomy

51. *Brief*
(a) short (b) abridged
(c) concise (d) detailed

52. *Baffle*
(a) elaborate (b) clarify
(c) explain (d) in order

C

53. *Condense*
(a) lengthen (b) expand
(c) distribute (d) interpret

54. *Comply*
(a) accept (b) agree
(c) disagree (d) consent

55. *Commodious*
(a) limited (b) expensive
(c) numerous (d) leisurely

56. *Cajole*
(a) dissuade (b) detract
(c) disclose (d) confide

57. *Carnal*
(a) sensuous (b) spiritual
(c) visionary (d) imaginary

58. *Conspicuous*
(a) indifferent (b) harmless
(c) insignificant (d) unknown

59. *Criticise*
(a) judge (b) appreciate
(c) flatter (d) analyse

60. *Catholic*
(a) rough (b) orthodox
(c) open (d) NOTA

61. *Chide*
(a) praise (b) fear
(c) criticise (d) flatter

62. *Crass*
(a) gross (b) refined
(c) coarse (d) dense

63. *Culpable*
(a) irresponsible (b) careless
(c) blameless (d) defendable

64. *Covert*
(a) clandestine (b) overt
(c) virtuous (d) wide

65. *Considerate*
(a) harsh (b) infuriated
(c) opposed (d) indifferent

66. *Coarse*
(a) beautiful (b) soft
(c) fine (d) attractive

67. *Callous*
(a) confident (b) sentimental
(c) sensitive (d) capable

68. *Concealment*
(a) identification (b) broadness
(c) evidence (d) indication

69. *Consistency*
(a) stability
(b) harmony
(c) defective
(d) inconsistency

70. *Capacious*

(a) changeable (b) foolish
(c) caring (d) limited

71. *Culminate*

(a) frustrate (b) fail
(c) abort (d) defeat

72. *Chaos*

(a) symmetric (b) inexperienced
(c) disturb (d) mould

73. *Clandestine*

(a) above ground (b) public
(c) outside (d) burnt out

74. *Cognisance*

(a) idiom (b) ignorance
(c) obeyance (d) anecdote

75. *Clumsy*

(a) mercy (b) dull
(c) bright (d) dexterous

76. *Cohesion*

(a) disintegration (b) anomaly
(c) disunity (d) internal

77. *Cozy*

(a) honestly (b) cold
(c) treacherous (d) falsehood

78. *Circumscribed*

(a) unrestricted (b) unconfined
(c) open (d) free

79. *Crafty*

(a) simple (b) artless
(c) ingeneous (d) improper

80. *Confiscate*

(a) release (b) allow
(c) use (d) confer

81. *Competent*

(a) intelligent (b) deligent
(c) inefficient (d) deficit

D

82. *Dissent*

(a) agreement (b) dispute
(c) disunity (d) controversy

83. *Dissuade*

(a) incite (b) persuade
(c) advise (d) instigate

84. *Delete*

(a) impound (b) insert
(c) inspire (d) injure

85. *Despondency*

(a) humility (b) cheerlessness
(c) cheerfulness (d) NOTA

86. *Degenerate*

(a) create (b) progress
(c) restore (d) reproduce

87. *Deliberate*

(a) premeditated (b) sparking
(c) methodical (d) impulsive

88. *Debauchee*

(a) moralist (b) thinker
(c) schemer (d) dreamer

89. *Dreary*

(a) plenty (b) monotonous
(c) unhappy (d) cheerful

90. *Depraved*

(a) great (b) enhanced
(c) moral (d) prosperous

91. *Dauntless*

(a) courageous (b) thoughtful
(c) weak (d) NOTA

92. *Deplete*

(a) refund (b) replenish
(c) fulfil (d) recover

93. *Deviate*

(a) follow (b) locate
(c) break (d) concentrate

94. *Deficit*
(a) superfluous (b) surplus
(c) explicit (d) implicit

95. *Debilitating*
(a) strengthening (b) enfeebling
(c) occupying (d) inhabiting

96. *Dainty*
(a) splendid (b) aggressive
(c) vigorous (d) towering

97. *Disdain*
(a) depreciate (b) admiration
(c) penitence (d) contempt

98. *Debacle*
(a) regain (b) solution
(c) rise (d) movement

99. *Doleful*
(a) poor (b) happy
(c) rich (d) steady

100. *Diabolic*
(a) patient (b) generous
(c) kind (d) simple

101. *Discrepancy*
(a) variance (b) inappropriate
(c) consistency (d) inconsistency

102. *Denounce*
(a) defend (b) gather
(c) fight (d) rally

103. *Debonair*
(a) worried (b) pensive
(c) grim (d) serious

104. *Disperse*
(a) collect (b) considerate
(c) clever (d) cunning

105. *Dissipate*
(a) sustain (b) conserve
(c) preserve (d) maintain

106. *Dormant*
(a) active (b) modern
(c) permanent (d) transient

107. *Defection*
(a) resignation (b) invitation
(c) joining (d) co–operation

108. *Dusky*
(a) visible (b) fair
(c) obscure (d) shadowy

109. *Dither*
(a) cry (b) refer
(c) decide (d) defer

110. *Derogatory*
(a) immediate (b) praising
(c) opinionated (d) roguish

111. *Disastrous*
(a) constructive (b) demolishing
(c) positive (d) none

112. *Deletreious*
(a) impulsive (b) salubrious
(c) pathetic (d) inclusive

113. *Disdain*
(a) depreciate (b) admiration
(c) penitence (d) contempt

114. *Diverge*
(a) repulse (b) converge
(c) resurge (d) constrict

115. *Disperse*
(a) collect (b) assemble
(c) hoard (d) save

116. *Defiance*
(a) dismay (b) suspicion
(c) obedience (d) anxiety

117. *Discrete*
(a) loud (b) combined
(c) loose (d) circle

118. *Diminish*
(a) decrease (b) increase
(c) lower (d) rise

119. *Desecrate*
(a) manage (b) build
(c) consecrate (d) concentrate

E

120. *Endow*
(a) borrow (b) steal
(c) snatch (d) extort

121. *Exhibit*
(a) conceal (b) prevent
(c) withdraw (d) concede

122. *Enough*
(a) inadequate (b) scarce
(c) deficit (d) less

123. *Erudite*
(a) professional (b) immature
(c) unimaginative (d) ignorant

124. *Escalate*
(a) lessen (b) subside
(c) reduce (d) fashionable

125. *Evacuate*
(a) admit (b) emerge
(c) abandon (d) invade

126. *Eclipse*
(a) shine (b) enlarge
(c) goggle (d) gleam

127. *Embrace*
(a) suspect (b) harm
(c) reject (d) hurt

128. *Exonerate*
(a) compel (b) accuse
(c) imprison (d) boldness

129. *Extension*
(a) condensation (b) subtraction
(c) deletion (d) weakening

130. *Execrable*
(a) importable (b) acceptable
(c) desirable (d) irritable

131. *Euphonious*
(a) strident (b) lethargic
(c) literary (d) musical

132. *Exterior*
(a) internal (b) inner
(c) interior (d) inward

133. *Exodus*
(a) restoration (b) return
(c) home–coming (d) influx

134. *Edification*
(a) lamentation (b) annotation
(c) corruption (d) segregation

135. *Exasperate*
(a) belittle (b) annoy
(c) please (d) tarnish

136. *Exotic*
(a) poor (b) inexpensive
(c) ugly (d) conventional

137. *Explicit*
(a) inspiring (b) plain
(c) invigorating (d) implied

138. *Exalt*
(a) depreciate (b) ennoble
(c) glorify (d) simplify

139. *Encourage*
(a) warn (b) discourage
(c) dampen (d) disapprove

140. *Erratic*
(a) reliable (b) right
(c) punctual (d) free

141. *Engulfed*
(a) encircled (b) groped
(c) disfigured (d) detached

142. *Epilogue*
(a) conversation (b) dialogue
(c) dramatic (d) prologue

143. *Execrate*
(a) care (b) praise
(c) love (d) bless

144. *Extravagant*
(a) miserly (b) uneconomical
(c) mean (d) narrow-minded

145. *Equanimity*
(a) excitement (b) duplicity
(c) dubiousness (d) resentment

146. ***Extirpate***
(a) preserve (b) inseminate
(c) ingratiate (d) enter

147. ***Exggegrate***
(a) minimise (b) maximise
(c) cessation (d) difficult

148. ***Eloquent***
(a) inarticulate (b) clear
(c) lucid (d) coherent

149. ***Enervate***
(a) debilitate (b) fortify
(c) introduce (d) conclude

150. ***Eschew***
(a) traduce (b) invite
(c) use (d) emanate

151. ***Effulgence***
(a) murky (b) harshness
(c) mercenary (d) quiet

152. ***Ensemble***
(a) complement (b) cacophony
(c) coordination (d) solo

153. ***Ethereal***
(a) heavenly (b) earthly
(c) lifelike (d) affectionate

F

154. ***Fecund***
(a) barren (b) solid
(c) unploughed (d) hard

155. ***Facsimile***
(a) reproduction (b) sincere
(c) original (d) engineered

156. ***Frailty***
(a) emaciation (b) strength
(c) health (d) boldness

157. ***Furtive***
(a) straight (b) obvious
(c) unambiguous (d) open

158. ***Frantic***
(a) calm (b) hopeful
(c) active (d) bitter

159. ***Fickle***
(a) diseased (b) fast
(c) constant (d) quick

160. ***Frugal***
(a) gaudy (b) generous
(c) extravagant (d) charitable

161. ***Fraction***
(a) ignition (b) acceleration
(c) mummification (d) NOTA

162. ***Factitious***
(a) bogus (d) fake
(c) spurious (d) genuine

163. ***Forbidden***
(a) allowed (b) prohibited
(c) agreed (d) forsaken

164. ***Frail***
(a) vigorous (b) sturdy
(c) hardy (d) strong

165. ***Forbid***
(a) provoke (b) appreciate
(c) celebrate (d) permit

166. ***Fluctuate***
(a) strong (b) sturdy
(c) slow (d) steady

167. ***Furious***
(a) mild (b) restrained
(c) ticklish (d) disjointed

168. ***Fallacious***
(a) true (b) faulty
(c) wrong (d) dirty

169. ***Forlorn***
(a) elated (b) gloomy
(c) joyless (d) credible

170. ***Frugality***
(a) showy (b) exhibition
(c) extravagance (d) visage

171. *Fierce*
(a) wild (b) docile
(c) calm (d) timid

172. *Fabricate*
(a) damage (b) destroy
(c) disintegrate (d) implicate

173. *Filthy*
(a) stainless (b) shining
(c) sterilized (d) clean

G

174. *Gorgeous*
(a) desperate (b) plain
(c) fashionable (d) sumptuous

175. *Glut*
(a) dearth (b) limit
(c) drain (d) supply

176. *Gruesome*
(a) pleasant (b) rude
(c) fresh (d) clear

177. *Gigantic*
(a) huge (b) small
(c) dangerous (d) fantastic

178. *Glamour*
(a) silence (b) incubate
(c) murmur (d) whisper

179. *Gusto*
(a) sadness (b) distaste
(c) discolour (d) gloom

180. *Gratitude*
(a) wretched (b) ingratitude
(c) unfaithfulness (d) wickedness

H

181. *Hoard*
(a) deposit (b) supply
(c) satisfy (d) accumulate

182. *Humble*
(a) dominant (b) proud
(c) despotic (d) pompous

183. *Hide*
(a) search (b) show
(c) shine (d) NOTA

184. *Haughty*
(a) pitiable (b) scared
(c) humble (d) cowardly

185. *Hawk*
(a) peaceful (b) pigeon
(c) fighter (d) dove

186. *Homely*
(a) rough (b) outgoing
(c) smooth (d) beautiful

187. *Hostile*
(a) friendly (b) sudden
(c) costly (d) unfair

188. *Homogeneous*
(a) heterogeneous (b) consciousness
(c) variegated (d) loquacious

189. *Hesitant*
(a) proud (b) confident
(c) shy (d) reluctant
(e) tacit

190. *Hapless*
(a) lucky (b) kind
(c) helpful (d) futile

191. *Hamper*
(a) open (b) release
(c) hold (d) hasten

I

192. *Insipid*
(a) nervous (b) pungent
(c) saucy (d) sour

193. *Infalible*
(a) dubious (b) mistaking
(c) erring (d) unreliable

194. *Impeccable*
(a) good (b) sound
(c) faulty (d) candid

195. *Impervious*
(a) penetrable (b) hidden
(c) tolerable (d) gentle

196. *Impropriety*
(a) decorum (b) purity
(c) ideal (d) conformity

197. *Intrude*
(a) withhold (b) withdraw
(c) accept (d) surrender

198. *Indulge*
(a) avoid (b) abstain
(c) forego (d) neglect

199. *Impound*
(a) generate (b) strengthen
(c) stimulate (d) release

200. *Ignore*
(a) support (b) favour
(c) redress (d) accept

201. *Innocent*
(a) sinful (b) guilty
(c) deadly (d) corruption

202. *Illegible*
(a) clear (b) imitable
(c) clean (d) readable

203. *Inimical*
(a) related (b) friendly
(c) neutral (d) cheerful

204. *Immediate*
(a) delayed (b) gradual
(c) leisurely (d) slow

205. *Illustrious*
(a) uneducated (b) uncivilized
(c) unintelligent (d) unknown

206. *Innocence*
(a) crime (b) mischief
(c) guilt (d) sin

207. *Intransigent*
(a) ever–ready (b) faithful
(c) flexible (d) obedient

208. *Insolent*
(a) sullen (b) rich
(c) determined (d) affable

209. *Illusory*
(a) nimble (b) realistic
(c) powerful (d) underrated

210. *Inadequate*
(a) glossy (b) rapid
(c) aspiring (d) sufficient

211. *Intrude*
(a) to tear away (b) keep away
(c) force (d) compelled

212. *Implicate*
(a) involve (b) exonerate
(c) corrupt (d) accuse

213. *Implode*
(a) extract (b) explode
(c) burst (d) erupt

214. *Impede*
(a) demote (b) promote
(c) eclipse (d) NOTA

215. *Illicit*
(a) lawful (b) delusive
(c) legitimate (d) NOTA

216. *Inclement*
(a) pleasant (b) bad
(c) beautiful (d) NOTA

217. *Impudent*
(a) discourteous (b) courteous
(c) kind (d) helpful

218. *Inveterate*
(a) stupid (b) uneducated
(c) ignorant (d) inexperienced

219. *Indolent*
(a) desirable
(b) adequate
(c) energetic
(d) consistent

J

220. *Judicious*
(a) unequal (b) unlawful
(c) impure (d) indiscreet

221. *Jeer*
(a) mourn (b) praise
(c) mock (d) sneer

222. *Jettision*
(a) rejoice (b) surrender
(c) accept (d) defend

223. *Jittery*
(a) relax (b) tense
(c) bold (d) shaky

224. *Jocose*
(a) dull (b) humorous
(c) playful (d) diseased

225. *Justify*
(a) accuse (b) infuriate
(c) absolve (d) vindicate

226. *Jubilant*
(a) scared (b) disturbed
(c) gloomy (d) quiet

227. *Juxtapositions*
(a) unity (b) opposition
(c) separation (d) difference

K

228. *Knowledge*
(a) ignorance (b) illiteracy
(c) foolishness (d) backwardness

229. *Knack*
(a) dullness (b) rested
(c) talent (d) dexterity

230. *Keen*
(a) dull (b) progue
(c) ardent (d) shrewd

231. *Kindle*
(a) ignite (b) encourage
(c) ignore (d) merciless

L

232. *Luscious*
(a) dry (b) sour
(c) ugly (d) stale

233. *Laconic*
(a) prolix (b) profligate
(c) prolific (d) bucolic

234. *Languid*
(a) smart (b) energetic
(c) fast (d) ferocious

235. *Lethal*
(a) safe (b) playful
(c) virulent (d) forgiving

236. *Lofty*
(a) assessed (b) debased
(c) general (d) intrusive

237. *Livid*
(a) faded (b) shining
(c) undiscoloured (d) polished

M

238. *Magnify*
(a) induce (b) diminish
(c) destroy (d) shrink

239. *Malicious*
(a) boastful (b) indifferent
(c) kind (d) generous

240. *Meticulous*
(a) slovenly (b) meretricious
(c) shaggy (d) mutual

241. *Mundane*
(a) extraordinary (b) superb
(c) heavenly (d) excellent

242. *Musty*
(a) fresh (b) expensive
(c) clean (d) fine

243. *Marvellous*
(a) pleasing (b) charming
(c) attractive (d) shabby

244. *Mendacious*
(a) broken (b) efficacious
(c) truthful (d) destructive

245. *Morbid*
(a) healthy (b) clever
(c) upright (d) sickly

246. *Magnanimous*
(a) selfish (b) naïve
(c) generous (d) small

247. *Mammoth*
(a) dull (b) weak
(c) tiny (d) bright

248. *Mawkish*
(a) sentimental (b) intelligent
(c) certain (d) carefree

N

249. *Naive*
(a) cunning (b) wealthy
(c) sophisticated (d) complicated

250. *Nadir*
(a) progress (b) liberty
(c) zenith (d) modernity

O

251. *Obsolete*
(a) conductive (b) rare
(c) useless (d) recent

252. *Obstinate*
(a) agreeing (b) accepting
(c) yielding (d) accommodating

253. *Overweening*
(a) humble (b) sedate
(c) miserly (d) clever

254. *Onerous*
(a) rough (b) burdensome
(c) easy (d) tough

255. *Obfuscate*
(a) simplify (b) explain
(c) describe (d) clarify

256. *Ostentatious*
(a) awkward (b) bankrupt
(c) ignorant (d) unpretentious

257. *Outmoded*
(a) polished (b) practicable
(c) stylish (d) fashionable

P

258. *Precarious*
(a) dangerous (b) safe
(c) cautious (d) easy

259. *Profane*
(a) arrogant (b) benign
(c) respectful (d) pious

260. *Paucity*
(a) surplus (b) scarcity
(c) presence (d) richness
(e) want

261. *Pretentious*
(a) deranged (b) small
(c) depressing (d) humble

262. *Parsimonious*
(a) generous (b) frugal
(c) crude (d) stingy

263. *Prim*
(a) rash (b) extravagant
(c) foul (d) shameful

264. *Pertinent*
(a) indifferent (b) detached
(c) determined (d) irrelevant

265. *Prevent*
(a) excite (b) support
(c) invite (d) incite

266. *Predilection*
(a) denial (b) concealment
(c) aversion (d) attraction

267. *Persistent*
(a) wavering (b) obstinate
(c) enduring (d) steady

268. ***Provocation***

(a) destruction (b) peace
(c) pacification (d) vocation

269. ***Pompous***

(a) feeble (b) normal
(c) humble (d) mild

270. ***Persuasive***

(a) demoralizing (b) false
(c) discouraging (d) unconvincing

271. ***Paltry***

(a) strong (b) worthy
(c) mean (d) bitter

272. ***Putrid***

(a) fresh (b) fragrant
(c) sweet (d) agreeable

273. ***Passionate***

(a) calm (b) arrogant
(c) sure (d) fervent

274. ***Preposterous***

(a) complaisant (b) conceited
(c) apologetic (d) credible

275. ***Pungent***

(a) clear (b) turbid
(c) sharp (d) harmless

276. ***Piquant***

(a) spicy (b) tasty
(c) pungent (d) insipid

277. ***Partisan***

(a) supporter (b) follower
(c) devotee (d) unbiased

278. ***Perpetual***

(a) just (b) discontinue
(c) momentary (d) ordinary

R

279. ***Recede***

(a) rush (b) advance
(c) approacforward (d) none of these

280. ***Retrieve***

(a) respond (b) dismiss
(c) foil (d) abandon

281. ***Ruthless***

(a) mindful (b) compassionate
(c) majestice (d) merciful

282. ***Respite***

(a) tension (b) exertion
(c) regularity (d) delay

283. ***Reject***

(a) agree (b) accept
(c) embrace (d) adopt

284. ***Robust***

(a) thin (b) emaciated
(c) light (d) strong

285. ***Relinquish***

(a) withdraw (b) attack
(c) assume (d) conquer

286. ***Requisite***

(a) dispensable (b) random
(c) inappropriate (d) chaotic

287. ***Reluctant***

(a) inclined (b) worried
(c) willing (d) ready

288. ***Remorseful***

(a) ingrateful (b) unrepentent
(c) wretched (d) arrogant

289. ***Repugnant***

(a) inoffensive (b) loving
(c) caring (d) pleasing

290. ***Ramshackle***

(a) study (b) ruinous
(c) dilapidated (d) NOTA

291. ***Ruthless***

(a) mindful (b) compassionate
(c) majestic (d) merciful

S

292. *Superficial*
(a) artificial (b) deep
(c) shallow (d) real

293. *Seldom*
(a) rarely (b) daily
(c) often (d) never

294. *Smooth*
(a) ugly (b) awkward
(c) hard (d) rough

295. *Synthetic*
(a) cosmetic (b) plastic
(c) affable (d) natural

296. *Shallow*
(a) high (b) hidden
(c) deep (d) hallow

297. *Sordid*
(a) miserly (b) generous
(c) hopeful (d) open

298. *Shrewd*
(a) turbid (b) naive
(c) muffled (d) mundane

299. *Sluggish*
(a) quick (b) sharp
(c) alert (d) vigilant

300. *Strenuous*
(a) unfaltering (b) irresolute
(c) unwavering (d) lazy

301. *Setback*
(a) bonus (b) misfortune
(c) shock (d) upset

302. *Scold*
(a) enamour (b) rebuke
(c) criticise (d) praise

303. *Segregation*
(a) appreciation (b) alteration
(c) integration (d) NOTA

304. *Succumb*
(a) curb (b) resist
(c) injure (d) shoot

305. *Significant*
(a) distinct (b) extreme
(c) alive (d) unimportant

306. *Subjugate*
(a) enrich (b) liberate
(c) enslave (d) free

307. *Sancitity*
(a) sacred (b) sophisticacy
(c) unlawfulness (d) eagerness

308. *Serene*
(a) jovial (b) moving
(c) agitated (d) nervous

309. *Sagacious*
(a) casual (b) cunning
(c) foolish (d) false

310. *Strident*
(a) stable (b) pleasant
(c) musical (d) melodious

T

311. *Tragedy*
(a) humorous (b) comedy
(c) romance (d) calamity

312. *Transparent*
(a) coloured (b) childlike
(c) opaque (d) imminent

313. *Terrible*
(a) horrible (b) awesome
(c) delightful (d) hideous

314. *Tragic*
(a) funny (b) comic
(c) light (d) humorous

315. *Terse*
(a) concise (b) detailed
(c) expressive (d) descriptive

316. *Timid*

(a) fearful (b) tasteless
(c) bold (d) busy

317. *Tranquil*

(a) peaceful (b) disturbed
(c) painful (d) punishing

318. *Timidity*

(a) gallantry (b) fearing
(c) weakness (d) guilty

319. *Taciturn*

(a) dubious (b) garrulous
(c) strategic (d) pleasant

U

320. *Unsullied*

(a) untrained (b) trained
(c) spotless (d) NOTA

V

321. *Validate*

(a) legalise (b) spurious
(c) authenticate (d) disprove

322. *Violent*

(a) tame (b) humble
(c) gentle (d) harmless

323. *Virtue*

(a) vice (b) fraud
(c) wickedness (d) crime

324. *Vulgar*

(a) refined (b) cheerful
(c) jolly (d) relevant

325. *Vanquish*

(a) surrender (b) debase
(c) destroy (d) ruin

326. *Voluntary*

(a) ordered (b) alternative
(c) compulsory (d) essential

327. *Vigour*

(a) failure (b) negligence
(c) frailty (d) healthy

328. *Virtuous*

(a) scandalous (b) vicious
(c) wicked (d) corrupt

329. *Virulent*

(a) harmless (b) malignant
(c) hostile (d) vicious

330. *Vanity*

(a) modesty (b) kindness
(c) compassion (d) moderation

331. *Vivacious*

(a) quarrelsome (b) sober
(c) notorious (d) sluggish

332. *Vital*

(a) peripheral (b) dead
(c) outer (d) unimportant

333. *Villify*

(a) flattery (b) pray
(c) admonish (d) worship

334. *Vindictive*

(a) praise (b) forgiving
(c) useless (d) piercing

335. *Vociferous*

(a) laudable (b) quiet
(c) dangerous (d) powerful

336. *Vague*

(a) foggy (b) cloudy
(c) clear (d) rare

337. *Vomit*

(a) swallow (b) ingest
(c) deplore (d) endure

338. *Vie*

(a) guard (b) maintain
(c) discover (d) yield

339. ***Validate***
(a) legalise (b) avoid
(c) disprove (d) diswallow

340. ***Verbose***
(a) compact (b) brief
(c) concise (d) NOTA

341. ***Voluminous***
(a) long (b) sleek
(c) belittle (d) loud

342. ***Valubale***
(a) inferior (b) invalubale
(c) lowly (d) worthless

W

343. ***Wrath***
(a) unangry (b) peace
(c) delight (d) choler

344. ***Wane***
(a) swell (b) prosper
(c) wax (d) widen

345. ***Wonder***
(a) expectation (b) surprise
(c) possibility (d) probability

346. ***Wicked***
(a) sober (b) helpful
(c) conscientious (d) faithful

347. ***Within***
(a) without (b) past
(c) over (d) beyond

348. ***Woeful***
(a) smiling (b) cheerful
(c) demanding (d) lively

349. ***Wreck***
(a) work (b) build
(c) restore (d) relieve

Z

350. ***Zany***
(a) cautious (b) calculating
(c) cunning (d) sane

351. ***Zest***
(a) restive (b) callous
(c) indifference (d) distate

352. ***Zeal***
(a) lithe (b) apathy
(c) verbatim (d) NOTA

ANSWERS

1. (b)	**2.** (b)	**3.** (a)	**4.** (b)	**5.** (c)	**6.** (b)	**7.** (a)	**8.** (c)	**9.** (b)	**10.** (c)
11. (b)	**12.** (c)	**13.** (c)	**14.** (b)	**15.** (c)	**16.** (d)	**17.** (b)	**18.** (c)	**19.** (c)	**20.** (c)
21. (b)	**22.** (b)	**23.** (b)	**24.** (b)	**25.** (d)	**26.** (c)	**27.** (b)	**28.** (d)	**29.** (a)	**30.** (b)
31. (b)	**32.** (a)	**33.** (c)	**34.** (b)	**35.** (c)	**36.** (c)	**37.** (a)	**38.** (a)	**39.** (c)	**40.** (a)
41. (d)	**42.** (b)	**43.** (b)	**44.** (b)	**45.** (a)	**46.** (b)	**47.** (a)	**48.** (b)	**49.** (a)	**50.** (d)
51. (d)	**52.** (b)	**53.** (b)	**54.** (c)	**55.** (a)	**56.** (b)	**57.** (b)	**58.** (d)	**59.** (b)	**60.** (b)
61. (a)	**62.** (b)	**63.** (c)	**64.** (b)	**65.** (d)	**66.** (b)	**67.** (c)	**68.** (a)	**69.** (d)	**70.** (c)
71. (a)	**72.** (a)	**73.** (b)	**74.** (b)	**75.** (c)	**76.** (a)	**77.** (b)	**78.** (a)	**79.** (b)	**80.** (a)
81. (c)	**82.** (a)	**83.** (b)	**84.** (b)	**85.** (c)	**86.** (b)	**87.** (d)	**88.** (a)	**89.** (d)	**90.** (c)
91. (a)	**92.** (b)	**93.** (d)	**94.** (b)	**95.** (a)	**96.** (c)	**97.** (b)	**98.** (b)	**99.** (b)	**100.** (c)

101. (c) **102.** (a) **103.** (d) **104.** (a) **105.** (b) **106.** (a) **107.** (c) **108.** (b) **109.** (c) **110.** (b)
111. (a) **112.** (b) **113.** (b) **114.** (b) **115.** (b) **116.** (c) **117.** (c) **118.** (b) **119.** (c) **120.** (c)
121. (a) **122.** (a) **123.** (d) **124.** (b) **125.** (d) **126.** (b) **127.** (c) **128.** (b) **129.** (a) **130.** (b)
131. (b) **132.** (c) **133.** (c) **134.** (a) **135.** (c) **136.** (d) **137.** (d) **138.** (a) **139.** (b) **140.** (c)
141. (d) **142.** (d) **143.** (b) **144.** (a) **145.** (c) **146.** (a) **147.** (a) **148.** (a) **149.** (a) **150.** (b)
151. (a) **152.** (d) **153.** (b) **154.** (a) **155.** (b) **156.** (b) **157.** (d) **158.** (a) **159.** (c) **160.** (c)
161. (d) **162.** (d) **163.** (a) **164.** (d) **165.** (d) **166.** (d) **167.** (a) **168.** (a) **169.** (a) **170.** (c)
171. (c) **172.** (b) **173.** (d) **174.** (b) **175.** (b) **176.** (a) **177.** (b) **178.** (a) **179.** (d) **180.** (b)
181. (b) **182.** (b) **183.** (a) **184.** (c) **185.** (a) **186.** (b) **187.** (a) **188.** (a) **189.** (b) **190.** (a)
191. (b) **192.** (c) **193.** (c) **194.** (c) **195.** (a) **196.** (a) **197.** (d) **198.** (b) **199.** (d) **200.** (a)
201. (b) **202.** (d) **203.** (b) **204.** (a) **205.** (d) **206.** (c) **207.** (b) **208.** (d) **209.** (b) **210.** (d)
211. (b) **212.** (b) **213.** (b) **214.** (b) **215.** (a) **216.** (a) **217.** (b) **218.** (b) **219.** (c) **220.** (d)
221. (b) **222.** (b) **223.** (a) **224.** (a) **225.** (a) **226.** (c) **227.** (c) **228.** (a) **229.** (a) **230.** (a)
231. (c) **232.** (d) **233.** (c) **234.** (b) **235.** (a) **236.** (b) **237.** (a) **238.** (b) **239.** (a) **240.** (a)
241. (c) **242.** (a) **243.** (d) **244.** (c) **245.** (a) **246.** (a) **247.** (c) **248.** (a) **249.** (c) **250.** (c)
251. (d) **252.** (c) **253.** (a) **254.** (c) **255.** (a) **256.** (d) **257.** (d) **258.** (b) **259.** (d) **260.** (a)
261. (d) **262.** (b) **263.** (b) **264.** (d) **265.** (b) **266.** (c) **267.** (a) **268.** (c) **269.** (c) **270.** (d)
271. (b) **272.** (a) **273.** (a) **274.** (a) **275.** (a) **276.** (d) **277.** (c) **278.** (b) **279.** (b) **280.** (a)
281. (b) **282.** (d) **283.** (b) **284.** (a) **285.** (d) **286.** (c) **287.** (c) **288.** (b) **289.** (d) **290.** (a)
291. (b) **292.** (b) **293.** (c) **294.** (d) **295.** (d) **296.** (c) **297.** (b) **298.** (b) **299.** (c) **300.** (d)
301. (a) **302.** (d) **303.** (c) **304.** (b) **305.** (d) **306.** (b) **307.** (c) **308.** (c) **309.** (c) **310.** (d)
311. (b) **312.** (c) **313.** (c) **314.** (b) **315.** (b) **316.** (c) **317.** (b) **318.** (a) **319.** (b) **320.** (b)
321. (d) **322.** (c) **323.** (a) **324.** (a) **325.** (a) **326.** (c) **327.** (c) **328.** (b) **329.** (a) **330.** (a)
331. (d) **332.** (d) **333.** (d) **334.** (b) **335.** (b) **336.** (c) **337.** (a) **338.** (d) **339.** (c) **340.** (b)
341. (b) **342.** (b) **343.** (c) **344.** (c) **345.** (d) **346.** (d) **347.** (a) **348.** (b) **349.** (b) **350.** (d)
351. (c) **352.** (b)

WORD SUBSTITUTIONS

INTRODUCTION

Shakespeare said, 'Brevity is the soul of wit' which emphasize how one must be brief and also at the same time lucid, clear, exact and accurate in one's expression. A verbose style reveals a confused mind.

The study of this chapter will help the young students to be brief and clear in their expression. It will help them develop a habit of clear thinking and clear expression.

A		
1.	To give up the throne or any other office of dignity	**Abdicate**
2.	Washing of the hands or the body as an act of religion	**Ablution**
3.	Termination of pregnancy	**Abortion**
4.	To increase the speed	**Accelerate**
5.	Setting a person free after declaring him innocent	**Acquittal**
6.	Period of life between childhood and maturity	**Adolescence**
7.	Concerned with beauty	**Aesthetic**
8.	A written declaration that has been made on oath in the presence of a magistrate	**Affidavit**
9.	A list of things to be done or discussed at a meeting	**Agenda**
10.	A person who believes that nothing can be known about God	**Agnostic**
11.	A person who belongs to another country	**Alien**
12.	Allowance due to a wife from her husband on separation	**Alimony**
13.	A mixture of different metals	**Alloy**
14.	A person who does something only for pleasure and not for money	**Amateur**
15.	That which has more than one meaning	**Ambiguous**
16.	A van for carrying patients	**Ambulance**
17.	Lack of enough blood that causes paleness	**Anemia**
18.	Lack for government, law and order	**Anarchy**
19.	Parents of the parents	**Ancestors**
20.	A tank meant for water plants or fish	**Aquarium**
21.	An animal able to live both on land and in water	**Amphibian**
22.	Belonging to times long past	**Ancient**
23.	A real incident of private life	**Anecdote**
24.	A day of celebration coming after a year	**Anniversary**
25.	Happening every year	**Annual**
26.	Deviation from a rule	**Anomaly**
27.	Without the name of the writer or author	**Anonymous**
28.	A collection of poems, etc.	**Anthology**
29.	A medicine used against poison	**Antidote**
30.	That which prevents the growth of germs in a wound	**Antiseptic**
31.	Praise expressed by clapping the hands	**Applause**
32.	One bound to another to learn a trade or art	**Apprentice**
33.	Of animals living in water	**Aquatic**

34.	A person appointed by two parties to settle a dispute	**Arbitrator**
35.	A place where ammunition and weapons are stored	**Arsenal**
36.	To understand completely or absorb food completely	**Assimilate**
37.	A government by persons of the highest social rank	**Aristocracy**
38.	Money that remains unpaid	**Arrears**
39.	A traveller through outer space	**Astronaut**
40.	One who leads a hard life of self-discipline for religious reasons	**Ascetic**
41.	One who believes that there is no God	**Atheist**
42.	A word opposite in meaning to another	**Antonym**
43.	That which can be heard	**Audible**
44.	Life story of a person written by himself	**Autobiography**
45.	Government by one man having unlimited power	**Autocracy**
46.	Too much greed for money	**Avarice**
47.	A place for keeping birds	**Aviary**
48.	Flying in aircraft	**Aviation**
	B	
49.	An unmarried man	**Bachelor**
50.	One who talks ill of others in their absence	**Backbiter**
51.	A place where bread and cakes are made	**Bakery**
52.	Having no hair on the head	**Bald**
53.	A song or poem that tells an old story	**Ballad**
54.	One who cannot pay his debts	**Bankrupt**
55.	Land which cannot grow anything	**Barren**
56.	A child born of parents not married	**Bastard**
57.	One who gives help or benefit to another	**Benefactor**
58.	A list of books by one author or on one subject	**Bibliography**
59.	Having two husbands or wives at a time	**Bigamy**
60.	Breaking into the house for stealing	**Burglary**
61.	A factory for manufacturing beer	**Brewery**
62.	A building for soldiers to live in	**Barracks**
63.	Life story of a person	**Biography**
64.	A blind follower of a religion or party	**Bigot**
65.	Well versed in two languages	**Bilingual**
66.	Insulting God and sacred things	**Blasphemy**
67.	Which can be easily broken	**Brittle**
68.	A bunch of flowers	**Bouquet**
69.	Place where women sell their body	**Brothel**
70.	A government by officials	**Bureaucracy**
	C	
71.	A table of the days, week and months of a year	**Calendar**
72.	Not caring for the suffering of others	**Callous**
73.	One who eats human flesh	**Cannibal**
74.	A systematic list of books in a library	**Catalogue**
75.	Soldiers who fight on horseback	**Cavalry**
76.	One who has taken an oath not to marry	**Celibate**
77.	Area of land where the dead are buried	**Cemetery**
78.	Pertaining to a hundred years	**Centenary**
79.	One who is hundred years old	**Centenarian**
80.	A period of hundred years	**Century**
81.	Union of political parties for a special purpose	**Coalition**
82.	Two or more things happening together by chance	**Coincidence**

83.	Persons working together	**Colleagues**
84.	A play full of fun and laughter	**Comedy**
85.	A place where two rivers meet	**Confluence**
86.	A device or drug which prevents pregnancy	**Contraceptive**
87.	Persons living at the same time	**Contemporaries**
88.	That which can be corrected	**Corrigible**
89.	Which can be understood fully	**Comprehensible**
90.	A disease present from birth	**Congenital**
91.	A person or party opposed to change	**Conservative**
92.	A person held guilty and punished by court	**Convict**
93.	One who loves all countries of the world	**Cosmopolitan**
94.	Which can be believed	**Credible**
95.	A nursery where babies are looked after while their mothers are at work	**Crèche**
96.	Place or building where nuns live and work	**Convent**
97.	A small piece of machinery used for arithmetical calculations	**Calculator**
98.	The art of beautiful handwriting	**Calligraphy**
99.	A picture drawn to make people laugh	**Caricature**
100.	One who believes things very easily	**Credulous**
101.	Pertaining to cooking or the kitchen	**Culinary**
102.	A person or thing that attracts everyone's attention	**Cynosure**
	D	
103.	One who pays too much attention to dress	**Dandy**
104.	A period of 10 years	**Decade**
105.	Attack on the good reputation of a person	**Defamation**
106.	Government of the people, by the people and for the people	**Democracy**
107.	A person held or detained by law	**Detenue**
108.	To lower the worth or value of a thing	**Depreciate**
109.	To give one's authority to others	**Delegate**
110.	A group of representatives	**Delegation**
111.	One who drinks too much alcohol	**Drunkard**
112.	A song sung by two persons	**Duet**
113.	Government by one man	**Dictatorship**
114.	Money or gifts given to a girl in her marriage	**Dowry**
115.	To challenge authority	**Defy**
116.	A place of permanent residence	**Domicile**
117.	To spoil the holiness of a sacred place or thing	**Desecrate**
118.	The art practiced by statesmen	**Diplomacy**
119.	A cruel ruler with unlimited power	**Despot**
120.	To go from bad to worse	**Deteriorate**
121.	To find the nature of a disease	**Diagnose**
122.	A language which is used by a particular region or class	**Dialect**
123.	Likely to last long	**Durable**
124	A man small in size	**Dwarf**
	E	
125.	One having strange habits	**Eccentric**
126.	Fit to be eaten	**Edible**
127.	A person who talks or thinks too much of himself	**Egoist**
128.	To describe in detail	**Elaborate**
129.	Fit to be chosen	**Eligible**
130.	A book giving information about every branch of knowledge	**Encyclopedia**
131.	One who believes in 'eat, drink and be merry'	**Epicurean**

132.	A disease which spreads among many people	**Epidemic**
133.	Words written on the grave of a person	**Epitaph**
134.	Imaginary line through the centre of the earth	**Equator**
135.	When day and night are of equal length	**Equinox**
136.	Anything having more than one meaning	Equivocal
137.	To completely destroy something	**Eradicate**
138.	Dealing with sexual desire	**Erotic**
139.	A man who behaves like a woman	**Effeminate**
140.	Something confusing and difficult to understand	**Enigma**
141.	To free a person from all blame	**Exonerate**
142.	An intense feeling of happiness and spiritual upliftment	**Ecstasy**
143.	A medicine that produces the desired effect	**Efficacious**
144.	That which can be explained	**Explicable**
145.	A person taking an examination	**Examinee**
146.	To turn out a person from society	**Ex-communicate**
147.	To atone for one's sins	**Expiate**
148.	Misappropriation of money	**Embezzlement**
149.	To run away with a lover in order to get married secretly	**Elope**
150.	A person who secretly listens to the conversation of others	**Eavesdropper**
151.	Practice of getting secret information	**Espionage**
152.	Rules of formal behaviour in society	**Etiquette**
153.	To make a mountain of a mole hill	**Exaggerate**
154.	To dig the earth to find something	**Excavate**
155.	To send goods to another country for sale	**Export**

156.	Speech delivered without previous thought or preparation	**Extempore**
157.	No longer in existence	**Extinct**
158.	In the habit of wasting money	**Extravagant**
159.	A person who takes interest in things around him	**Extrovert**
	F	
160.	To make something easy	**Facilitate**
161.	Liable to make mistakes	**Fallible**
162.	Which results or ends in death	**Fatal**
163.	One who believes in fate	**Fatalist**
164.	One who has too much religious enthusiasm	**Fanatic**
165.	Difficult to please	**Fastidious**
166.	That can be done	**Feasible**
167.	One who supports the cause of women	**Feminist**
168.	State of complete disappointment	**Frustration**
169.	A period of two weeks	**Fortnight**
170.	Which can be changed or molded	**Flexible**
171.	Used for finding out about a crime	**Forensic**
172.	Copying signature, etc. in order to deceive	**Forgery**
173.	Killing one's brother	**Fratricide**
	G	
174.	A person having extraordinary mental powers	**Genius**
175.	Mass murder of a race or community	**Genocide**
176.	Medicine which kills germs	**Germicide**
177.	A person who eats too much	**Glutton**
178.	A woman employed to teach young children in a private family	**Governess**
179.	Money given to an employee on retirement	**Gratuity**
180.	Animals living on grass	**Graminivorous**
181.	A storehouse of grain	**Granary**

182.	Animals living in groups	Gregarious
183.	A place for keeping cars	Garage
184.	A room or hall with apparatus for physical training and exercises	Gymnasium
185.	One who talks too much	Garrulous
186.	Make-up room behind the stage	Green room
187.	Rubbish or left over useless things	Garbage
188.	A list of explanations of rare and technical words	Glossary
189.	One who can be easily cheated or deceived	Gullible
	H	
190.	The art of cultivating gardens	Horticulture
191.	Sleep-like state of animals for the whole of winter	Hibernation
192.	A number of cattle driven together	Herd
193.	A person living alone	Hermit
194.	Killing of a human being	Homicide
195.	(A job, title, rank, or degree (position) etc.) for which no money is paid	Honorary
196.	Meeting point of the earth and sky	Horizon
197.	Entertaining guests kindly	Hospitable
198.	One who works for the welfare of all human beings	Humanitarian
199.	Dishonest and deceiving behaviour	Humbug
200.	One who makes a false show of virtue or goodness	Hypocrite
	I	
201.	One who knows nothing	Ignorant
202.	Against law	Illegal
203.	Difficult or impossible to read	Illegible
204.	Unable to read or write	Illiterate
205.	Forbidden by law	Illicit
206.	Existing only in the mind	Imaginary
207.	Going back beyond the reach of memory	Immemorial

208.	Likely to happen soon	Imminent
209.	Not favouring anyone	Impartial
210.	Not showing proper respect	Impertinent
211.	Not allowing anything to enter or pass through	Impervious
212.	Which cannot be put into practice	Impracticable
213.	Which cannot be met or approached	Inaccessible
214.	Which cannot be calculated	Incalculable
215.	Which cannot be heard	Inaudible
216.	Having no life	Inanimate
217.	Something which encourages one to do something	Incentive
218.	In an early stage	Incipient
219.	Someone who cannot be corrected	Incorrigible
220.	That which cannot be corrupted	Incorruptible
221.	Something extraordinary nto easily believable	Incredible
222.	Which cannot be cured	Incurable
223.	(One) who does not get tired	Indefatigable
224.	Which cannot be rubbed off	Indelible
225.	Which cannot be described	Indescribable
226.	Which cannot be destroyed	Indestructible
227.	Which cannot be digested	Indigestible
228.	Without which we cannot do	Indispensable
229.	Working very hard	Industrious
230.	Not fit to be eaten	Inedible
231.	Not fit to be chosen	Ineligible
232.	Without power to move or act	Inert
233.	Which cannot be avoided	Inevitable
234.	Which cannot be excused	Inexcusable
235.	Which cannot be explained	Inexplicable
236.	Which cannot be expressed in words	Inexpressible
237.	One who cannot make mistakes	Infallible
238.	(Disease) which spreads through the air	Infectious

239.	Which catches fire very easily	**Inflammable**
240.	Which cannot be copied or imitated	**Inimitable**
241.	Too large in number	**Innumerable**
242.	Eager to know or learn	**Inquisitive**
243.	Which cannot be satisfied	**Insatiable**
244.	Which cannot be known	**Inscrutable**
245.	Doing harm secretly	**Insidious**
246.	One who cannot pay debts	**Insolvent**
247.	Which cannot be touched	**Intangible**
248.	Which can be easily understood	**Intelligible**
249.	Done on purpose	**Intentional**
250.	One who immediately translates words spoken in another language	**Interpreter**
251.	Which cannot be tolerated	**Intolerable**
252.	Which cannot be defeated	**Invincible**
253.	Which cannot be seen	**Invisible**
254.	Not to the point	**Irrelevant**
255.	Which cannot be repaired	**Irreparable**
256.	Which cannot be resisted	**Irresistible**
257.	(A step or decision) from where there is no going back	**Irrevocable**
258.	One who is easily annoyed	**Irritable**
J		
259.	One who is wise	**Judicious**
260.	A station where railway lines meet or diverge	**Junction**
261.	Concerning a court of justice	**Judicial**
262.	A technical language or vocabulary used by a particular group of people	**Jargon**
L		
263.	A common man without professional knowledge	**Layman**
264.	A book in which accounts are kept	**Ledger**
265.	Anything that a person gets after the death of another	**Legacy**
266.	Connected with law	**Legal**
267.	A law-making body	**Legislature**
268.	A person who compiles a dictionary	**Lexicographer**
269.	A person who leads an immoral life with women	**Libertine**
270.	A person skilled in languages	**Linguist**
271.	Word for word translation	**Literal**
272.	Fighting cases in a court of law	**Litigation**
273.	Ability to read and write	**Literacy**
274.	One who is able to read and write	**Literate**
275.	Way in which one earns money	**Livelihood**
276.	A place where clothes are washed and ironed	**Laundry**
277.	A railway engine	**Locomotive**
278.	Handwriting which can be read	**Legible**
279.	A liquid that is neither hot nor cold	**Lukewarm**
280.	Song for sending a baby to sleep	**Lullaby**
M		
281.	A speech made for the first time	**Maiden speech**
282.	Animals that feed their young ones with milk from the breast	**Mammals**
283.	Order from a superior given with authority	**Mandate**
284.	Care of the hands and fingernails	**Manicure**
285.	A declaration of principles and policies by a party	**Manifesto**
286.	(Labour) done with the hands	**Manual**
287.	A long distance race	**Marathon**
288.	Belonging to the sea or ocean	**Marine**
289.	Something written by hand	**Manuscript**
290.	A person who is strict about discipline	**Martinet**

291.	A person who lays down his life for a great cause	**Martyr**
292.	Cruel killing of a large number of defenseless people	**Massacre**
293.	A show held in the afternoon	**Matinee**
294.	A woman as head of a family or tribe	**Matriarch**
295.	Killing of one's own mother	**Matricide**
296.	Which has no match or equal	**Matchless**
297.	Neither very good nor very bad	**Mediocre**
298.	Pertaining to trade and merchants	**Mercantile**
299.	Working only for money	**Mercenary**
300.	Goods bought and sold for gain	**Merchandise**
301.	Deserving praise, honour or reward	**Meritorious**
302.	An important city of a country	**Metropolis**
303.	An instrument which makes small things look bigger	**Microscope**
304.	(Birds) which come and go with seasons	**Migratory**
305.	A person who has ten lakhs or more rupees	**Millionaire**
306.	A small copy or model of anything	**Miniature**
307.	To reduce the importance of something	**Minimize**
308.	Place where coins are made	**Mint**
309.	An act or event which causes wonder	**Miracle**
310.	The illusion of sand seeming water in a desert	**Mirage**
311.	One who hates mankind	**Misanthrope**
312.	Wrong use of a name or word	**Misnomer**
313.	A hater of women	**Misogynist**
314.	Of the present or recent times	**Modern**
315.	Marriage with one person at a time	**Monogamy**
316.	The sole right to supply something	**Monopoly**
317.	Dull because of repetition	**Monotonous**
318.	A building or statue which keeps alive the memory of a person	**Monument**
319.	A place where dead bodies are kept	**Mortuary**
320.	A preserved dead body	**Mummy**
321.	A place where curious things of art, science and history are kept	**Museum**
322.	Open rebellion of soldiers against lawful authority	**Mutiny**
323.	An imaginary story or belief	**Myth**
	N	
324.	A person with the same name as another	**Namesake**
325.	A drug that causes sleep	**Narcotic**
326.	Not fit to be considered	**Negligible**
327.	To settle by discussion	**Negotiate**
328.	Giving special favours to one's relatives	**Nepotism**
329.	Helping neither side in a war or quarrel	**Neutral**
330.	A name given to a person to tease him	**Nickname**
331.	Belief in nothing	**Nihilism**
332.	Happening or done at night	**Nocturnal**
333.	Widely known for something bad	**Notorious**
334.	One who is new in something	**Novice**
335.	A person or thing that causes trouble	**Nuisance**
336.	Having high food value	**Nutritious**
	O	
337.	A printed notice about somebody's death	**Obituary**
338.	No longer in use or fashion	**Obsolete**

339.	Happening from time to time	Occasional
340.	A figure with eight sides and angles	Octagon
341.	A person in his eighties	Octogenarian
342.	An eight-footed animal	Octopod
343.	Government by a small group of persons	Oligarchy
344.	Having all power	Omnipotent
345.	Present everywhere	Omnipresent
346.	Knowing everything	Omniscient
347.	One who eats everything	Omnivorous
348.	Through which light cannot pass	Opaque
349.	Of the eyes	Optical
350.	One who makes or sells glasses, etc. for the eyes	Optician
351.	One who looks upon the bright side of things	Optimist
352.	One who is expert in making speeches	Orator
353.	A trial or test which is as hard as passing through fire	Ordeal
354.	A child whose parents have died	Orphan
355.	A house for orphans	Orphanage
356.	Believing in old accepted ideas	Orthodox
357.	To banish or shut out a person from society	Ostracize
358.	Borders or outlying parts of a town or city	Outskirts
359.	A warm and enthusiastic welcome	Ovation
360.	To repair or improve a machine system, etc.	Overhaul
361.	To hear something without the knowledge of the speaker	Overhear
P		
362.	One who loves peace and hates war	Pacifist
363.	One who tells the future by reading the palm of a person	Palmist
364.	A remedy for all diseases or troubles	Panacea
365.	Sudden fear which spreads like wild fire	Panic
366.	Something like an umbrella used for jumping from an aircraft	Parachute
367.	A statement which seems false but is really true	Paradox
368.	One who lives or depends on others	Parasite
369.	Murderer of one's father	Patricide
370.	Property inherited from forefathers	Patrimony
371.	One who gives help or support	Patron
372.	One who is extremely poor and helpless	Pauper
373.	One who walks on foot	Pedestrian
374.	Without money	Penniless
375.	One who looks on the dark side of things	Pessimist
376.	Systematic study of a language or languages	Philology
377.	One who loves and helps mankind	Philanthropist
378.	Natural constitution of a person	Physique
379.	One who journeys to a holy place	Pilgrim
380.	A person who loves his country and serves it devotedly	Patriot
381.	A writer who takes and uses the words and ideas of others	Plagiarist
382.	A wife having many husbands at a time	Polyandry
383.	A husband having many wives at a time	Polygamy
384.	Dealing with many arts or trades	Polytechnic
385.	Loved and liked by the people	Popular
386.	A city full of people	Populous

387.	Which can be carried about easily	**Portable**
388.	Coming generations	**Posterity**
389.	Happening after one's death	**Posthumous**
390.	Medical examination after death	**Post-mortem**
391.	An incident which serves as an example in future	**Precedent**
392.	A person having the mind developed at an early age	**Precocious**
393.	One who has been before another in any office or position	**Predecessor**
394.	A sign or feeling of what is going to happen	**Premonition**
395.	Belonging to the earliest times	**Primitive**
396.	A right enjoyed only by a few	**Privilege**
397.	Forbidding something by law or the act of officially stopping something by law	**prohibition**
398.	One inspired by God to warn and teach mankind	**Prophet**
399.	A woman having sex for money	**Prostitute**
400.	A fictitious name used by an author	**Pseudonym**
401.	The science of the mind	**Psychology**
402.	A pile of wood for burning the dead	**Pyre**
	Q	
403.	A doctor who has no knowledge of medicine	**Quack**
404.	A figure with four sides and angles	**Quadrangle**
405.	A four-legged animal	**Quadruped**
406.	Four babies born together at the same time to the same mother	**Quadruplet**
407.	Place from where we get stone, sand, etc.	**Quarry**
408.	Once after every three months	**Quarterly**
409.	A line of people waiting for their turn	**Queue**
410.	A general knowledge test	**Quiz**
411.	The numbers required at a meeting to start business	**Quorum**
	R	
412.	Able to reason and think	**Rational**
413.	A formula to prepare some dish or medicine	**Recipe**
414.	Given and received in return	**Reciprocal**
415.	Official rules that delay because of formality	**Red tape**
416.	The murder of a king	**Regicide**
417.	To make or become young again	**Rejuvenate**
418.	A token of memory preserved after the death of a saint	**Relic**
419.	Recalling of past experiences	**Reminiscence**
420.	Payment for work	**Remuneration**
421.	A place appointed for meeting	**Rendezvous**
422.	Which can be repaired	**Reparable**
423.	Sending or bringing back somebody to his own country	**Repatriation**
424.	An animal that creeps or crawls	**Reptile**
425.	A place where water is kept and stored	**Reservoir**
426.	Tit for tat	**Retaliation**
427.	Speaking very little	**Reticent**
428.	With reference to the past	**Retrospective**
429.	Which can be turned inside out	**Reversible**
430.	A style which aims at impressing and persuading people	**Rhetorical**
431.	Similar sound at the end of two or more lines of poetry	**Rhyme**
432.	A leader of undesirable persons	**Ring leader**
433.	Persons trying for the same prize	**Rivals**
434.	A string of beads for prayer	**Rosary**
435.	A report which is not based on truth	**Rumour**

S		
436.	Fit for sale	**Saleable**
437.	A hospital where patients suffering long from illness are treated	**Sanatorium**
438.	Which can be satisfied	**Satiable**
439.	A platform for construction or hanging criminals	**Scaffold**
440.	A device to frighten away birds	**Scare-crow**
441.	A sacred book of religion	**Scripture**
442.	An artist who makes statues of stone	**Sculptor**
443.	Having nothing to do with any religion	**Secular**
444.	To put apart from the rest	**Segregate**
445.	A group of students who study and discuss a problem with the help of teacher	**Seminar**
446.	Showing disrespect to something holy and sacred	**Sacrilege**
447.	One who watches a game or show	**Spectator**
448.	One who takes over after another in office or employment	**Successor**
449.	Speaking to oneself when one is alone	**Soliloquy**
450.	A doctor who performs operations	**Surgeon**
451.	The bony framework of the body	**Skeleton**
452.	Medicine which calms the nerves	**Sedative**
453.	The rod of authority of a king	**Scepter**
454.	Appealing to the senses	**Sensuous**
455.	Easily moved by tender feelings	**Sentimental**
456.	Which can be separated	**Separable**
457.	A person in his sixties	**Sexagenarian**
458.	Sleep enjoyed in the afternoon	**Siesta**
459.	One who signs a document or agreement	**Signatory**
460.	Comparison of one thing to another	**Simile**
461.	At the same time	**Simultaneous**
462.	A job with salary but without much work	**Sinecure**
463.	A partner in business who does not work	**Sleeping partner**
464.	To burn slowly without flame	**Smolder**
465.	One who makes a show of superiority	**Snob**
466.	Which gets dissolved easily	**Soluble**
467.	One who walks in sleep	**Somnambulist**
468.	An old unmarried woman	**Spinster**
469.	Sharp or pointed pieces of a bomb, etc.	**Splinters**
470.	One who speaks for others	**Spokesman**
471.	One who spends a lot of money	**Spendthrift**
472.	Enclosed area meant for games	**Stadium**
473.	Not in motion	**Stationary**
474.	A mark of shame	**Stigma**
475.	One who accepts pain and pleasure equally	**Stoic**
476.	To kill by pressing the throat	**Strangle**
477.	A person or thing that takes the place of another	**Substitute**
478.	Killing one's own self	**Suicide**
479.	More than is needed	**Superfluous**
480.	Highest in authority	**Supreme**
481.	Anything that remains after satisfying the needs	**Surplus**
482.	A person who remains alive after some event	**Survivor**
483.	Last work before death	**Swan-song**
484.	One who flatters important people for gain	**Sycophant**
485.	A word or a part of a word which contains single vowel sound can be produced by one chest-pulse	**Syllable**
486.	Summary of a course of studies	**Syllabus**
487.	Words similar in meaning	**Synonyms**

T		
488.	Something that is forbidden in society or religion	Taboo
489.	One who does not drink alcohol	Teetotaler
490.	Communication between minds	Telepathy
491.	An instrument which makes distant objects look nearer and larger	Telescope
492.	One who pays rent for the land, building or house occupied by him	Tenant
493.	Made or done as a trial	Tentative
494.	Station beyond which a train or bus does not go	Terminus
495.	One who believes in the existence of God	Theist
496.	A government by men of religion	Theocracy
497.	One who flatters others for gain	Toady
498.	Medicine which gives energy and strength	Tonic
499.	A play or story with a sad ending	Tragedy
500.	One who betrays one's country, friends, etc.	Traitor
501.	Lasting for a short time	Transient or Transitory
502.	The soul leaving one body and entering another	Transmigration
503.	Through which light can pass	Transparent
504.	To pass through another's land without permission	Trespass
505.	A flag of three colors as that of India	Tricolor
506.	A thing of no importance	Trifle
507.	An issue of no importance	Trivial
508.	Three children born at a time	Triplets
509.	A child who runs away from school	Truant
510.	One who changes his party or principles	Turncoat
511.	A cruel or unjust ruler	Tyrant

U		
512.	With one voice	Unanimous
513.	Which cannot be avoided	Unavoidable
514.	Being the only one of its kind	Unique
515.	Found everywhere or concerning all	Universal
516.	Never done or known before	Unprecedented
517.	Which cannot be understood	Unintelligible
518.	Who does not mix in society	Unsociable
519.	One who has suddenly risen from a low position to a high position	Upstart
520.	Which needs quick or prompt action	Urgent
521.	Imaginary perfect, social and political system	Utopia

V		
522.	One in the habit of wandering	Vagabond
523.	In the nature of farewell	Valedictory
524.	One who eats only vegetables	Vegetarian
525.	Deserving respect because of age	Venerable
526.	Using more words than necessary	Verbose
527.	Expert in many things	Versatile
528.	One having long experience in a field	Veteran
529.	A person who offers his services of his own free will	Volunteer
530.	A person who destroys works of art	Vandal
531.	To prove the truth or justice of something	Vindicate
532.	Concerned with the diseases of animals	Veterinary
533.	The right to reject a decision	Veto
534.	A wicked man	Villain

535.	Having a desire for revenge	**Vindictive**
536.	A person who never had sex	**Virgin**
537.	Having manly qualities of strength, etc.	**Virile**
538.	Which can be seen	**Visible**
539.	An oral test	**Viva-voce**
540.	Concerned with the voice	**Vocal**
541.	A stretch of land surrounded by hills	**Valley**
542.	A sea journey in a ship	**Voyage**
543.	Which can be wounded or injured	**Vulnerable**
W		
544.	A place for keeping clothes	**Wardrobe**
545.	Hair on the sides of a man's face	**Whickers**
546.	A wife whose husband has died	**Widow**
547.	A husband whose wife has died	**Widower**
548.	A woman with magical powers	**Witch**
549.	A man with magical powers	**Wizard**
Y		
550.	The yellow part of an egg	**Yolk**
Z		
551.	The highest point in the sky	**Zenith**
552.	A path which turns right and left	**Zigzag**
553.	A place where birds and animals are kept	**Zoo**
554.	One who studies animals and their behaviors	**Zoologist**
555.	The science of animal life	**Zoology**

ONE WORD SUBSTITUTION MCQs

Each sentence is followed by four options. You have to find out the correct one word substitution for the given sentences.

1. A man who diagnoses sick people is called
   (a) operator (b) surgeon
   (c) physician (d) physiotherapist
2. A book containing summarized information on all branches of knowledge is known as
   (a) dictionary (b) microscope
   (c) periscope (d) encyclopedia
3. An instrument for viewing objects at a distance is
   (a) telescope (b) microscope
   (c) periscope (d) kaleidoscope
4. A hater of learning and knowledge is called
   (a) illiterate (b) bibliophile
   (c) misologist (d) misogynist
5. A person who does not believe in any religion is known as
   (a) atheist (b) philatelist
   (c) pagan (d) rationalist
6. A person who looks at the dark side of everything is called
   (a) sadist (b) blind
   (c) pessimist (d) optimist
7. A man of lax moral is
   (a) pirate (b) ruffian
   (c) vagabond (d) licentious
8. Animals who eat flesh of another animal are
   (a) man-eater (b) beast
   (c) carnivorous (d) cannibal
9. A government by the nobles is
   (a) aristocracy (b) democracy
   (c) bureaucracy (d) autocracy
10. Animals that can live on land and water are
    (a) aquatic (b) amphibians
    (c) reptiles (d) gregarious
11. Anything written in a letter after it is signed is called
    (a) postdiction (b) posterity
    (c) corrigendum (d) postscript
12. A woman having several husbands at the same time is practice of
    (a) polygamy (b) polyandry
    (c) polysexual (d) polyglot
13. A person who has no money to pay off his debts is called
    (a) insolvent (b) debtor
    (c) pauper (d) beggar
14. A person who hates women is
    (a) intolerant (b) misogamist
    (c) bigamist (d) gullible
15. A sleeping room for many persons
    (a) boarding (b) hostel
    (c) dormitory (d) dwelling
16. A process involving too much official formality is
    (a) red–tapism (b) bureaucracy
    (c) diplomacy (d) nepotism
17. A large scale departure of people from a territory is known as
    (a) migration (b) immigration
    (c) exodus (d) aberration

18. A post without remuneration is
(a) involuntary (b) voluntary
(c) sinecure (d) honorary

19. A disease that spreads by means of germs carried in atmosphere is
(a) infectious (b) epidemic
(c) contagious (d) endemic

20. A government run by a dictator is called
(a) autocracy (b) democracy
(c) theocracy (d) oligarchy

21. A speech delivered without preparation is
(a) straightforward (b) extempore
(c) verbose (d) maiden

22. A person who believes that pleasure is the chief good is called
(a) sensual (b) stoic
(c) hedonist (d) epicure

23. A speech made by someone for the first time
(a) spontaneous (b) extempore
(c) maiden speech (d) sermon

24. A physician who specializes in diseases of skin
(a) obstetrician (b) dermatologist
(c) cardiologist (d) none of these

25. A person who is fond of sensuous enjoyment
(a) epicure (b) witty
(c) hedonist (d) humorous

26. A disease that affects a large number of people in an area at the same time
(a) endemic (b) epidemic
(c) infectious (d) contagious

27. A religious discourse is called
(a) preach (b) stanza
(c) sanctorum (d) sermon

28. A place that provides refuge
(a) asylum (b) sanatorium
(c) shelter (d) orphanage

29. A large dark grey cloud that brings rain or snow
(a) nimbus (b) blizzard
(c) hail (d) fog

30. A person who makes love without being serious is known as
(a) romeo (b) consort
(c) goon (d) philanderer

31. A child of unusual or remarkable talent
(a) prodigy (b) scholar
(c) diligent (d) stupid

32. A disease which ends in death
(a) cancerous (b) contagious
(c) incurable (d) lethal

33. A person who does not believe in the existence of God
(a) theist (b) heretic
(c) atheist (d) fanatic

34. A person who tries to deceive people by claiming to be someone else's identity
(a) trickster (b) impostor
(c) magician (d) mountebank

35. A place for sick people who need long periods for recovery
(a) clinic (b) hospital
(c) sanatorium (d) asylum

36. A sudden rush of wind
(a) gust (b) gale
(c) storm (d) typhoon

37. A person who eats too much
(a) glutton (b) reveller
(c) sensualist (d) omnivore

38. A person who is reserved in talks
(a) silent (b) reticent
(c) garrulous (d) mendicant

39. A short stay at a place
(a) interlude (b) refuge
(c) sojourn (d) asylum

40. A general pardon granted by the government to political offenders
(a) pardon (b) excuse
(c) honesty (d) amnesty

41. A person who is out to destroy government
(a) anarchist (b) destroyer
(c) atheist (d) theist

42. A person who looks on the bright side of things
(a) atheist (b) optimist
(c) cynic (d) agnostic

43. A Government that is carried on through officers
(a) bureaucracy (b) officiousness
(c) class–one (d) dictatorship

44. A woman whose husband is dead
(a) widow (b) virgin
(c) spinster (d) wedlock

45. A man of odd habits
(a) cynical (b) eccentric
(c) moody (d) introvert

46. A statement that is absolutely clear
(a) clean (b) confused
(c) ambiguous (d) unequivocal

47. Animals living on land and in water are known as
(a) ambivalent (b) ambiguous
(c) amphibian (d) amorphous

48. A political leader who tries to stir people is called
(a) martinet (b) statesman
(c) demagogue (d) dictator

49. A man who pays too much attention to his clothes and personal appearance
(a) duffer (b) snob
(c) licentious (d) dandy

50. A person very hard to please
(a) obstinate (b) unconquerable
(c) fastidious (d) invincible

51. A funny imitation of a poem
(a) dialogue (b) sonnet
(c) caricature (d) parody

52. A person without manners or polish
(a) boorish (b) rude
(c) dandy (d) dude

53. A speech by an actor at the end of a play
(a) prologue (b) epilogue
(c) monologue (d) duologue

54. Act of taking one's own life
(a) homicide (b) suicide
(c) immolation (d) slaughter

55. A person who brings goods illegally into the country
(a) importer (b) esporter
(c) imposter (d) smuggler

56. A man who dances to the tunes of his wife
(a) chum (b) effeminate
(c) slave (d) henpecked

57. A person who has just started learning
(a) accomplice (b) forman
(c) apprentice (d) novice

58. A woman of lax moral
(a) concubine (b) prostitute
(c) hostess (d) NOTA

59. A slow-witted and incompetent person
(a) duffer (b) commoner
(c) simple (d) simpleton

60. A person's first speech
(a) opener (b) maiden
(c) extempore (d) preface

61. Virus is a biological entity which lives on another organism is called
(a) symbiotic
(b) dependent
(c) plebiscite
(d) parasite

62. An old unmarried woman
(a) bachelor (b) virgin
(c) matron (d) spinster

63. A written declaration made on oath in the presence of a magistrate
(a) dossier (b) voucher
(c) document (d) affidavit

64. A physician who delivers babies
(a) psychiatrist (b) paediatrician
(c) obstetrician (d) gynaecologist

65. A man who is having the qualities of woman
(a) epicurean (b) loquacious
(c) celibate (d) effeminate

66. A word no longer in use
(a) primitive (b) exotic
(c) ancient (d) obsolete

67. A person 70 to 79 years old
(a) centenarian (b) septuagenarian
(c) nonagenarian (d) octogenarian

68. A person who sneaks into a country
(a) invader (b) infiltrator
(c) aggressor (d) sniper

69. A person who readily believes others
(a) sensible (b) credible
(c) sensitive (d) credulous

70. A paper written in one's own handwriting
(a) parchment (b) manuscript
(c) transcript (d) scroll

71. A small named group of fixed stars
(a) constellation (b) cluster
(c) couster (d) galaxy

72. Voluntarily giving up throne by king in favour of his son
(a) accession
(b) abdication
(c) rejuvenation
(d) resurrection

73. A person who wishes to throw over all establishments
(a) terrorist (b) hooligan
(c) anarchist (d) rebel

74. A person interested in reading books
(a) scholar (b) student
(c) book-keeper (d) book worm

75. Unreasoning enthusiasm for the glorification of one's country
(a) chauvinism (b) communism
(c) patriotism (d) imperialism

76. A person who collects coins
(a) numismatist (b) narcissist
(c) fatalist (d) philatelist

77. A school for infants and young children
(a) infantile (b) school
(c) kindergarten (d) nursery

78. A ride on someone else's back or shoulders
(a) kickback (b) piggyback
(c) cuddle (d) hunchback

79. A cure for all diseases
(a) panacea (b) excorcism
(c) antibiotic (d) incantation

80. A short walk for pleasure or exercise
(a) gallop (b) jog
(c) promenade (d) stroll

81. A person who is more interested in himself rather than anything that is going on around him
(a) introvert (b) egotist
(c) eccentric (d) extrovert

82. A sea abounding in islands
(a) ocean (b) strait
(c) gulf (d) archipelago

83. A song sung at a burial
(a) dirge (b) elegy
(c) ballad (d) ode

84. A soldier who fights for sake of money cannot be branded as courageous and patriotic
(a) mercenary (b) sinecure
(c) equestrian (d) honorary

85. A careful preservation and protection of wildlife is the need of the hour.
(a) conservation (b) embarkment
(c) enhancement (d) management
(e) promotion

86. Both Buddha and Mahavira lived at the same time
(a) coincident (b) simultaneous
(c) synchronised (d) contemporary

87. Custom of having many wives
(a) matrimony (b) monogamy
(c) bigamy (d) polygamy

88. Cessation of arms before a formal treaty is signed during war
(a) truce (b) stalemate
(c) cessation (d) retreat

89. Child bereaved of one or both the parents
(a) lout (b) desolate
(c) orphan (d) destitute

90. Contempt of god is called
(a) agnosticism (b) blasphemy
(c) nihilism (d) athesim

91. Changing one's mind too quickly
(a) vacillation (b) adaptability
(c) instability (d) versatility

92. Clumsy or ill-bred fellow
(a) dandy (b) boor
(c) dude (d) rural

93. Code of diplomatic etiquette and precedence is called
(a) hierarchy
(b) formalism
(c) statesmanship
(d) protocol

94. Destruction of unborn baby in mother's womb is known as
(a) foeticide (b) infanticide
(c) abortion (d) regicide

95. Deriving pleasure from inflicting pain on others is called
(a) masochism (b) sadism
(c) malevolence (d) bigotry

96. Elimination of a racial group by killing is called
(a) homicide (b) regicide
(c) genocide (d) patricide

97. Government by a single person is known as
(a) autocracy (b) plutocracy
(c) aristocracy (d) monarchy

98. Government by the representatives of the people is called
(a) socialism (b) autocracy
(c) democracy (d) diplomacy

99. Habit of secretly listening to private conversation is
(a) spying (b) spelling
(c) condign (d) murmering

100. Handwriting that cannot be read
(a) illegible (b) unreadable
(c) dim (d) dull

101. His father is a doctor who treats children and infants
(a) podiatrist (b) dermatologist
(c) pediatrician (d) gynecologist

102. Incapable of being explained
(a) nondescript (b) untold
(c) unexplained (d) inexplicable

103. Indifference to pleasure or pain
(a) patience (b) ducility
(c) reticence (d) stoicism

104. Incapable of being explained or accounted for
(a) inexplicit (b) incredible
(c) inexpressible (d) inexplicable

105. Incapable of being wounded
(a) infallible (b) invulnerable
(c) impregnable (d) invincible

106. Joint sovereignty exercised over a country by two or more countries is known as
(a) pandemonium (b) condominium
(c) entente (d) colonialism

107. Killing of human being is called
(a) murder (b) suicide
(c) homicide (d) assassination

108. Killing of one's own brother is
(a) murder (b) matricide
(c) fratricide (d) genocide

109. Life history of a person written by another is known as
(a) biography (b) autobiography
(c) memoir (d) bibliography

110. Likely to break apart easily
(a) hard (b) thin
(c) brittle (d) harsh

111. Lack of enough blood
(a) allergy (b) amnesia
(c) insomnia (d) anaemia

112. Land so surrounded by water as to be almost an island
(a) lagoon (b) archipelago
(c) isthmus (d) peninsula

113. Mania for stealing articles
(a) hypomania (b) logomania
(c) nymphomania (d) kleptomania

114. Man whose wife has been unfaithful to him is called
(a) cuckold (b) dandy
(c) bastard (d) concubine

115. Murder of a new-born child
(a) infanticide (b) homicide
(c) regicide (d) fratricide

116. Murder of a king
(a) homicide (b) matricide
(c) regicide (d) genocide

117. Using of new words
(a) malaproism (b) coinage
(c) vocabulary (d) neologism

118. One who eats everything
(a) carnivorous (b) gourmet
(c) omnivorous (d) omnipotent

119. Murder of one's mother
(a) genocide (b) gamicide
(c) matricide (d) patricide

120. One who loves all and sundry
(a) altruist (b) optimist
(c) philanthropist (d) humanist

121. Official misconduct
(a) malefactor (b) malfeasance
(c) maltreatment (d) maladministration

122. One who is interested in the welfare of women
(a) feminist (b) feminine
(c) flamboyant (d) effeminate

123. One who takes delight in excessive cruelty
(a) sadist (b) anarchist
(c) nihilist (d) sophist

124. One who deserts his religion is called
(a) turn-coat (b) deserter
(c) apostate (d) fanatic

125. One who feels at home in every country
(a) metropolitan (b) cosmopolitan
(c) citizen (d) denizen

126. One who totally abstains from alcoholic drinks
(a) edant (b) teetotaller
(c) samaritan (d) puritan

127. One who is honourably discharged from service
(a) sinecure (b) emeritue
(c) retired (d) honorary

128. One who talks very little is called
(a) stoic (b) reticent
(c) mute (d) phlegmatic

129. One who loves books is called
(a) bibliophagist (b) bibliophobe
(c) bibliographer (d) bibliophile

130. One knowing everything
(a) omniscient (b) learned
(c) omnipresent (d) omnipotent

131. One who is neither intelligent nor dull
(a) commoner (b) tolerable
(c) diligent (d) mediocre

132. One who eats human flesh
(a) cannibal (b) beast
(c) carnivorous (d) savage

133. One who sacrifices his life for a cause is a
(a) martyr (b) soldier
(c) patriot (d) revolutionary

134. One who cannot be corrected is
(a) hardened (b) incurable
(c) invulnerable (d) incorrigible

135. One who does not know how to save money
(a) lavish (b) reckless
(c) spendthrift (d) careless

136. One who talks continuously is
(a) loquacious (b) impecunious
(c) avaricious (d) voracious

137. One who can use either of his hands with ease is called
(a) ambidextrous (b) gluttonous
(c) expert (d) amateur

138. One who speaks or understands many languages
(a) grammarian (b) scholar
(c) polyglot (d) linguist

139. One who possesses many talents
(a) exceptional (b) versatile
(c) nubile (d) gifted

140. One who believes that everything is predestined
(a) fatalist (b) pessimist
(c) astrologer (d) palmist

141. One who resides in a country of which he is not a citizen
(a) foreigner (b) alien
(c) prodigal (d) native

142. Practice of a married woman having extra marital relationship is
(a) adultery (b) polygamy
(c) puberty (d) lechery

143. Person who brings an action at law is called
(a) deponent (b) defendant
(c) litigant (d) plaintiff

144. Paying back injury with injury is called
(a) subjugation (b) vendetta
(c) reprisal (d) repression

145. Person who believes that god is everything and everything is god.
(a) pantheist (b) agnostic
(c) pantechnicon (d) theist

146. Perceptible to the ear
(a) audible (b) laudable
(c) praiseable (d) adorable

147. People working in the same department or office are known as
(a) fellows (b) colleagues
(c) mates (d) companions

148. Place where birds are kept
(a) apiary (b) zoo
(c) aviary (d) armoury

149. Person who has long experience
(a) veteran (b) stalwart
(c) vedantic (d) itinerant

150. Plain or self-evident truth
(a) truism (b) proverb
(c) formula (d) percept

151. People in a riot are called
(a) mob (b) crowd
(c) congregation (d) rabble

152. Policy of a political party is called
(a) report (b) manifesto
(c) circular (d) agenda

153. Rainfall at irregular intervals or occasionally is called
(a) irregular (b) sporadic
(c) accidental (d) temporary

154. Relationship by blood or birth is relationship by
(a) consanguinity (b) parentage
(c) nepotism (d) affiliation

155. Run away from home with lover
(a) vanquish (b) abscond
(c) elope (d) asylum

156. Ravi impressed everyone with his persuasive and fluent speech.
(a) eloquence (b) discourse
(c) lecture (d) expression

157. Strong and settled dislike between two
(a) animosity (b) antipathy
(c) hatred (d) apathy

158. Something that becomes outdated
(a) old (b) ancient
(c) obsolete (d) useless

159. Study of mankind
(a) philology
(b) pathology
(c) anthropology
(d) physiology

160. Study of statistics of births, deaths, diseases to show the state of community is called
(a) anthropology (b) geography
(c) demography (d) topography

161. Something shining brilliant and magnificent is called
(a) resplendent (b) cheerful
(c) grandiose (d) joyful

162. Something which is not thorough or profound
(a) superstitious (b) superficial
(c) supernatural (d) superfluous

163. Story told to illustrate a moral or spiritual truth is called
(a) paragon (b) paradigm
(c) parable (d) didactic

164. The state of complete continence on the part of a woman
(a) celibacy (b) virginity
(c) unmarried (d) spinster

165. The policy of extending a country's empire and influence is known as
(a) internationalism (b) communism
(c) capitalism (d) imperialism

166. The study of ancient societies is called
(a) anthropology (b) archaeology
(c) history (d) ethnology

167. To send an unwanted person out of the country
(a) deport (b) exclude
(c) expatriate (d) ostracise

168. To killing for political reasons is called
(a) homicide (b) murder
(c) assassination (d) genocide

169. The cessation of warfare before a treaty is signed
(a) amnesty (b) affidavit
(c) agreement (d) armistice

170. Teetotaler means
(a) one who abstains from theft
(b) one who abstains from meat
(c) one who abstains from taking wine
(d) one who abstains from taking malice

171. Through which light cannot pass
(a) dark (b) dull
(c) opaque (d) obscure

172. To talk much without coming to the point
(a) circumlocution (b) loquacity
(c) garulousness (d) verosity

173. The state of being unmarried
(a) single (b) celibacy
(c) lonely (d) aloofness

174. That which can be interpreted in any way
(a) amphibious (b) ambient
(c) ambiguous (d) ambivalent

175. To do away with a rule/ law
(a) erase (b) cancel
(c) repeal (d) obliterate

176. The list of courses at a meal or of dishes that can be served in a restaurant
(a) menu (b) agenda
(c) catalogue (d) biodata

177. The place where bricks are baked
(a) cemetery (b) mint
(c) mint (d) foundry

178. The act of violating the sanctity of church is
(a) sedation (b) heresy
(c) sacrilege (d) desecration

179. To atone for one's sins is known as
(a) expiate (b) apologise
(c) propitiate (d) ingratiate

180. That which can be carried
(a) portable (b) handy
(c) bearable (d) pootable

181. To remove the skin of a potato or an orange
(a) remove (b) rinse
(c) peel (d) scrub

182. To surround with armed forces
(a) attack (b) seize
(c) besiege (d) cease

183. To move along with quick, short twistings
(a) wriggle (b) swagger
(c) crawl (d) stumble

184. That which cannot be done without
(a) indispensable (b) irrevocable
(c) impossible (d) impracticable

185. That which cannot be rectified or made good
(a) irreconcilable (b) irreparable
(c) irreplaceable (d) irrevocable

186. Feeling of self importance is known as
(a) insanity (b) paroxysm
(c) braggart (d) megalomania

187. That which is perceptible by touch
(a) contagious (b) tangible
(c) contingent (d) tenacious

188. That which cannot be understood
(a) unknown (b) illegible
(c) undecipherable (d) incomprehensible

189. Tuberculosis is a disease which spreads by contact.
(a) fatal (b) infectious
(c) contagious (d) contiguous

190. The committee insisted on a total check on all social evils and he was the one who heralded the revolution.
(a) renegade
(b) harbinger
(c) apostle
(d) apostate

ANSWERS

1. (c)	**2.** (d)	**3.** (a)	**4.** (c)	**5.** (c)	**6.** (c)	**7.** (d)	**8.** (d)	**9.** (a)	**10.** (b)
11. (d)	**12.** (b)	**13.** (a)	**14.** (b)	**15.** (c)	**16.** (a)	**17.** (c)	**18.** (d)	**19.** (a)	**20.** (a)
21. (b)	**22.** (c)	**23.** (c)	**24.** (b)	**25.** (a)	**26.** (b)	**27.** (d)	**28.** (a)	**29.** (a)	**30.** (d)
31. (a)	**32.** (d)	**33.** (c)	**34.** (b)	**35.** (d)	**36.** (a)	**37.** (a)	**38.** (b)	**39.** (c)	**40.** (d)
41. (a)	**42.** (b)	**43.** (a)	**44.** (a)	**45.** (b)	**46.** (d)	**47.** (c)	**48.** (c)	**49.** (d)	**50.** (a)
51. (c)	**52.** (a)	**53.** (b)	**54.** (b)	**55.** (d)	**56.** (d)	**57.** (d)	**58.** (b)	**59.** (a)	**60.** (b)
61. (d)	**62.** (d)	**63.** (d)	**64.** (d)	**65.** (d)	**66.** (d)	**67.** (b)	**68.** (b)	**69.** (d)	**70.** (b)
71. (a)	**72.** (b)	**73.** (c)	**74.** (d)	**75.** (a)	**76.** (a)	**77.** (c)	**78.** (b)	**79.** (a)	**80.** (d)
81. (b)	**82.** (d)	**83.** (a)	**84.** (a)	**85.** (a)	**86.** (d)	**87.** (d)	**88.** (a)	**89.** (c)	**90.** (b)
91. (a)	**92.** (b)	**93.** (d)	**94.** (a)	**95.** (b)	**96.** (c)	**97.** (d)	**98.** (c)	**99.** (a)	**100.** (a)
101. (c)	**102.** (d)	**103.** (d)	**104.** (d)	**105.** (b)	**106.** (b)	**107.** (c)	**108.** (c)	**109.** (a)	**110.** (c)
111. (d)	**112.** (d)	**113.** (d)	**114.** (a)	**115.** (a)	**116.** (c)	**117.** (d)	**118.** (c)	**119.** (c)	**120.** (c)
121. (b)	**122.** (a)	**123.** (a)	**124.** (c)	**125.** (b)	**126.** (b)	**127.** (c)	**128.** (b)	**129.** (d)	**130.** (a)
131. (d)	**132.** (a)	**133.** (a)	**134.** (d)	**135.** (c)	**136.** (a)	**137.** (a)	**138.** (c)	**139.** (b)	**140.** (a)
141. (b)	**142.** (a)	**143.** (d)	**144.** (b)	**145.** (a)	**146.** (a)	**147.** (b)	**148.** (c)	**149.** (a)	**150.** (a)
151. (a)	**152.** (b)	**153.** (b)	**154.** (a)	**155.** (c)	**156.** (a)	**157.** (a)	**158.** (c)	**159.** (c)	**160.** (c)
161. (a)	**162.** (b)	**163.** (c)	**164.** (a)	**165.** (d)	**166.** (a)	**167.** (c)	**168.** (c)	**169.** (d)	**170.** (c)
171. (c)	**172.** (a)	**173.** (a)	**174.** (c)	**175.** (c)	**176.** (a)	**177.** (d)	**178.** (c)	**179.** (a)	**180.** (a)
181. (c)	**182.** (c)	**183.** (d)	**184.** (a)	**185.** (b)	**186.** (d)	**187.** (b)	**188.** (d)	**189.** (c)	**190.** (b)

525 IDIOMS
A – Z Alphabetically Arranged, With Meaning and Usage

INTRODUCTION

Idioms appear in every language, and English has thousands of them. They are often confusing because the meaning of the whole group of words taken together has little, often nothing, to do with the meanings of the words taken one by one.

For instance, to "let the cat out of the bag" means to reveal a secret. Today the phrase has nothing to do with a cat or a bag, but hundreds of years ago it actually did.

In order to understand a language, you must know what the idioms in that language mean. If you try to figure out the meaning of an idiom literally, word by word, you will get befuddled. You have to know its "intended" meaning.

Idioms come from all different sources, from the Bible to horse racing, from ancient fables to modern slang. Sometimes famous authors and storytellers such as Homer, Aesop, Geoffrey Chaucer, or William Shakespeare made them up to add spark to their writings. The authors were popular, so the expression they created became popular. Often however, we don't know the name of the first author or speaker who used a particular expression.

In all the competitive examinations, test of knowledge of idioms is one of the essential ingredients of English language section. So, in order to help the students to learn the most relevant idioms, this chapter has been compiled to apprise the students with 525 idioms.

These idioms have been culled and finalized after a thorough and eclectic search. The students would find them highly useful for their competitive exams, and in their day-to-day usage for making their writing skills ornamental and consequently impressive & rewarding. The idioms asked in various previous examinations have been examined before finalizing these 525 most relevant idioms. These would really serve the purpose of the students.

	A
1.	**Ace up your sleeve**
	Meaning: a surprise or secret advantage; especially something tricky that is kept hidden until needed I do not know how Anaadi is going to get her mom to buy her a cycle, but I'm sure she has an ***ace up her sleeve.***
2.	**Achilles' heel**
	Meaning: the one's weakness; fault; flaw; or vulnerable spot in one's otherwise strong character I am good in Mathematics and Science, but English is my ***Achilles' heel.***
3.	**Add fuel to the fire**
	Meaning: to make a bad situation worse; to do or say something that causes more trouble, makes someone angrier I was already angry with you, and when you forgot to pick me up, that really ***added fuel to the fire.***
4.	**Air your dirty laundry in public**
	Meaning: to talk about your private disagreements or embarrassing matters in public, usually while quarreling My neighbors fight a lot and ***air their dirty laundry in public.***
5.	**Albatross around your neck**
	Meaning: a very difficult burden that you cannot get rid of or a reminder of something you did that was wrong Everywhere I go, my mother compels me to take my nagging sister along. She is an ***albatross around my neck.***
6.	**All ears**
	Meaning: eager to listen; sharply attentive; curious Good students give ***all ears*** to their teachers in the class.

7.	**All that glitters is not gold**
	Meaning: something that seems attractive and valuable at first might turn out to be worthless Normally the goods bought online turn out to be ***all that glitters is not gold.***
8.	**Ants in your pants**
	Meaning: extreme restlessness; overactivity You never sit still. You must have ***ants in your pants.***
9.	**Apple of your eye**
	Meaning: a person or thing that is greatly loved, treasured, and adored My youngest sister is the ***apple of my eye.***
10.	**As the crow flies**
	Meaning: by the shortest and most direct route; measured in a straight, direct line between two places We live at a stone's through from my daughter's school ***as the crow flies.***
11.	**Asleep at the switch**
	Meaning: not attending to one's job or failing to react quickly; not being alert Ravi lost his job because he was ***asleep at the switch.***
12.	**At the drop of a hat**
	Meaning: right away; at once; without delay; willing at any moment The children are all ready to switch on their TVs ***at the drop of a hat.***
13.	**At the end of your rope**
	Meaning: at the limit of your ability, endurance, or patience to do something I have tried everything, but nothing has worked. I am at ***the end of my rope.***
14.	**Axe to grind**
	Meaning: something to gain for yourself for a selfish reason; flattery or trickery used to get a favour from another person Nowadays relationships are nothing but opportunities where everyone has one's ***axe to grind.***

B	
15.	**Babe in the woods**
	Meaning: a person who is inexperienced; a naive, trusting person Sameer thinks so much of himself as very shrewd person, but he is actually **a babe in the woods**.
16.	**Back to square one**
	Meaning: return to the beginning because of a failure to accomplish the desired result N.K. Sharma's plans are always making castles in the air, that is why he is always ***back to square one.***
17.	**Backseat driver**
	Meaning: a bossy person who tells another person what to do; a person who gives unwanted advice and directions In Indian folk jokes, the wife is referred to as the ***backseat driver.***
18.	**Bark is worse than your bite**
	Meaning: the way a person sounds is much more frightening than the way she or he acts; the threat is often worse than the action taken The new director yells a lot, but her ***bark is worse than her bite.***
19.	**Bark up the wrong tree**
	Meaning: to direct your attention or efforts towards the wrong person or thing; to have the wrong idea about something Avni's father wants to make her an IAS officer, but was ***barking up the wrong tree*** because she wanted to be a doctor.
20.	**Batten down the hatches**
	Meaning: to get ready for trouble; prepare for any emergency In the present time of Covid-19 pandemic, everyone ***battens down the hatches.***
21.	**Beat a dead horse**
	Meaning: to pursue a useless goal; to continue fighting a battle that has been lost; to keep arguing a point that has already been decided. He tried to convince his sister, but he was ***beating a dead horse.***

22. Beat around the bush

Meaning: to avoid answering a question; to approach something carefully or in a roundabout way

The politicians normally do not come to the point, they keep ***beating around the bush.***

23. Beat the band

Meaning: with much noise; excitement, or commotion; very much, very fast; outdoing all others

On his selection in the civil services, his entire family was ***beating the band.***

24. Beat your swords into ploughshare

Meaning: to stop fighting and turn your attention toward peaceful activities

It is advisable for Pakistan to shun the path of terrorism and ***beat its swords into ploughshare.***

25. Beauty is in the eye of the beholder

Meaning: there is no standard for beauty, so what one person likes or sees in someone or something is not necessarily what others see; different people have different opinions

Only a beautiful mind can appreciate others' beauty because ***beauty is in the eye of the beholder.***

26 Bed of roses

Meaning: a wonderful, pleasant situation or position; an easy, comfortable life

The position of a leader is not a ***bed of roses*** but a responsibility toward public.

27. Bee in your bonnet

Meaning: a crazy idea; an obsession with an idea

Mr. Saxena always weaves fanciful and chimerical ideas; he always has a ***bee in his bonnet.'***

28. Beggars cannot be choosers

Meaning: needy people have to take whatever they can get and cannot be concerned about the quality if they cannot afford to buy it for themselves

One with limited resources should not raise eyebrows at whatever they are offered because ***beggars cannot be choosers.***

29. Bells and whistles

Meaning: impressive accessories, especially flashy, high-technology features, and frills, which may sometimes be more decorative than necessary

Our teacher says we are getting a new computer with all the latest ***bells and whistles:*** CD-burner, stereo speakers, color printer, and full multimedia.

30. Below the belt

Meaning: cruel, unfair, hurtful; against the rules of sportsmanship

Normally incompetent players resort to clumsy ways of hitting ***below the belt.***

31. Better half

Meaning: either partner in marriage

I am not making a decision until I check with my ***better half.***

32. Better safe than sorry

Meaning: be careful; avoid risks and possible injury that you will regret.

The mother told daughter to put on her seat belt, even for a short drive. ***"Better safe than sorry,"*** she said.

33. Between a rock and a hard place

Meaning: being in a very tight spot and faced with a difficult decision

For a soldier, looking after the family& fighting for the country is always like a choice between ***a rock and hard place.***

34. Between the devil and the deep blue sea

Meaning: between two great dangers and not knowing what to do; in a very difficult position

Leaving my present assignment of teaching and joining new assignment was like choosing between the ***devil and the deep blue sea.***

35. Beware of Greeks bearing gifts

Meaning: be suspicious of presents from certain people who are just looking for something from you; be on guard against treachery in the disguise of a gift

Nowadays presenting gifts on festivals have become opportunities of getting undue favours. ***Beware of Greeks bearing gifts.***

36. Bird in the hand is worth two in the bush

Meaning: what you already have is better than what you might or might not get in the future; a guarantee is worth more than a promise

Take this job now because you do not know if you will get another one. Remember that a *bird in the hand is worth two in the bush.*

37. Birds of a feather flock together

Meaning: people who have things in common, such as interests and ideas, usually hang out together; people who are alike often become friends

Everyone at that table plays soccer; I guess that *birds of a feather flock together.*

38. Bread and butter

Meaning: basic necessaries of life

Making daily bread and butter is the man focus of a common man's life

39. By and by

Meaning: after a time

By and by, you will come to know everything.

40. Bite off more than you can chew

Meaning: to take on a task that is more than you can accomplish; or too ambitious by taking on more jobs or responsibilities than you can deal with at one time

You cannot accomplish so many tasks at the same time, don't *bite off more than you can chew.*

41. Bite the bullet

Meaning: prepare for an unpleasant experience; brace yourself to endure with courage something painful but necessary

The principal wants to see you in her office. Get ready to *bite the bullet.*

42. Bite the dust

Meaning: to die; to fall in defeat; to fail to succeed

Indian Army compelled Pakistan Army to *bite the dust* in the battle of 1971.

43. Bite the hand that feeds you

Meaning: to turn against someone who helps you; to do harm to someone who does good things for you

He is a chronic wrong doer; he always *bites the hand that feeds him.*

44. Bite your tongue

Meaning: take back or be ashamed of what you have said.

For his wrong doings, he had to *bite his tongue.*

45. Black sheep of the family

Meaning: the most unsuccessful, least admirable member of a family or similar group; a disgraced person

Subash is the *black sheep of the family* who always causes trouble.

46. Bleeding heart

Meaning: an extremely softhearted person who feels compassion or pity towards all people,

Bhagat Puran Singh had a *bleeding heart* for poor, needy and helpless people.

47. Blessing in disguise

Meaning: something that at first seems bad but turns out to be good.

Online coaching proves a *blessing in disguise* in the wake of Covid-19.

48. Blind as a bat

Meaning: totally blind

When the heavy fog rolled in, she was as *blind as a bat* because she could not see an inch in front of her.

49. Blind leading the blind

Meaning: the uninformed attempting to inform others

When an ill-informed teaches the ignorant, it is just like the *blind leading the blind.*

50. Blood is thicker than water

Meaning: one can expect more kindness from a family member than from a stranger

Blood is thicker than water that is why family is the first and last choice for everyone.

51. Blow your own horn

Meaning: to praise yourself; to call attention to your own merits (intelligence, skills, success, or abilities); to brag about yourself

Incapable and incompetent people keep *blowing their own horn.*

52. Blue blood

Meaning: of high or noble birth; an aristocrat; from the upper class of society

The *blue-blooded* people do not prefer to mix up with commoners.

53.	**Bolt from the blue**
	Meaning: something sudden, unexpected, and shocking His father's untimely demise came as a bolt from the blue.
54.	**Born with a silver spoon in your mouth**
	Meaning: born to wealth, comfort, and privilege Jawaharlal Nehru was ***born with a silver spoon in his mouth.***
55.	**Born yesterday**
	Meaning: inexperienced and easily fooled; not alert to trickery Ramesh is naive; just seems to have ***born yesterday.***
56.	**Bottom line**
	Meaning: the most crucial fact; the net result The bottom line of the stuck farmers' demand is the repeal of the three farming laws.
57.	**Break a leg**
	Meaning: good luck; do a great job in the show Amrita ***broke the leg*** and stole the show at the annual function of the school.
58.	**Break the ice**
	Meaning: to start conversation Kapil was very shy when he met Savita. He did not know how to ***break the ice.***
59.	**Breath of fresh air**
	Meaning: someone or something new, stimulating, invigorating, and refreshing The Hindi movie *Manto* was a ***breath of fresh air*** for movie lovers.
60.	**Bright-eyed and bushy-tailed**
	Meaning: healthy, fit, bright, and lively After her morning walk, she always looks ***bright-eyed and bushy tailed.***
61.	**Bring down the house**
	Meaning: to get an audience to clap enthusiastically or laugh loudly Kapil Sharma's stellar performance ***brought down the house.***
62.	**Bring home the bacon**
	Meaning: to support a family by working; to earn a living He is struggling hard to ***bring home the bacon*** for old parents.
63.	**Bug off**
	Meaning: to leave someone alone; go away; stop annoying someone Sita earnestly requested her sister to ***bug off*** for a moment.
64.	**Bug someone**
	Meaning: to irritate, annoy, and bother someone a lot I wish you would just stop ***bugging me*** and leave me in peace!
65.	**Bull in a china shop**
	Meaning: a clumsy person who deals too roughly with a delicate situation; a tactless person who says or does something that angers people or upsets their plans Inviting a wrestler as a jury member at dance show is just like a ***bull in a china shop.***
66.	**Burn the candle at both ends**
	Meaning: to overwork yourself mentally or physically and until you're exhausted He is ***burning candle at both ends*** to qualify IAS in his first attempt.
67.	**Burn the midnight oil**
	Meaning: to stay up very late at night studying or working One has to ***burn the midnight oil,*** to qualify for the IIT examination.
68.	**Burn your bridges behind you**
	Meaning: to make a decision you cannot change; to commit yourself to a course of action If you drop out of school now, you will be ***burning your bridges behind you.***
69.	**Bury the hatchet**
	Meaning: to settle an argument; end a war; make peace; become friends after being enemies Stop fighting and ***bury the hatchet.***

70.	**Bury your head in the sand**
	Meaning: to ignore danger by pretending you do not see it; to hide from obvious signs of danger You are ***burying your head in the sand*** if you think that smoking isn't bad for your health.
71.	**Busy as a beaver**
	Meaning: working very hard; extremely industrious Amit is as ***busy as a beaver,*** to navigate through tough times of Covid-19 pandemic.
72.	**Butter someone up**
	Meaning: to flatter someone; to try to get a favor by praising someone Maybe if you ***butter up*** the math teacher, she will raise your final grade.
73.	**Butterflies in the stomach**
	Meaning: a fluttery feeling in the stomach, usually caused by nervousness During my first public speech to an august gathering, there were ***butterflies in the stomach.***
74.	**Button your lip**
	Meaning: to stop talking; be quiet The teacher asked all students to ***button their lips.***
75.	**Buy a pig in a poke**
	Meaning: to buy something without seeing or examining it Without bare knowledge of computer, buying a secondhand computer will be like ***buying a pig in a poke.***
76.	**By hook or by crook**
	Meaning: by any means possible (legal or not) He is crazy to win the match ***by hook or by crook.***
77.	**By the book**
	Meaning: exactly according to the rules; precisely as instructed The law-abiding citizens prefer to go ***by the book.***
78.	**By the skin of your teeth**
	Meaning: just barely; by the narrowest of margins He needed only 400 marks to qualify NEET Examination, but by securing 399 marks he lost it ***by the skin of his teeth.***

C

79.	**Call it a day**
	Meaning: to stop work for the day; to bring a project to an end for the time being You have been working on that history report since before breakfast. Why don't you ***call it a day?***
80.	**Call the shots**
	Meaning: to make the decision; to be in charge; to give orders He is a henpecked husband, so his wife ***calls the shots.***
81.	**Call you on the carpet**
	Meaning: to call a person before an authority for a scolding The principle ***called*** the erring teacher ***on the carpet*** to make her realize what wrong she had done.
82.	**Call your bluff**
	Meaning: to demand that someone prove a claim; to challenge, someone to carry out a threat The Taxila House was bragging of winning the final trophy, but Nalanda ***called that bluff.***
83.	**Calm before the storm**
	Meaning: a period of unusual peace before a disturbance or crisis; an unnatural or false calm before a storm The meeting may be peaceful now, but this is only the ***calm before the storm.***
84.	**Cannot fight city hall**
	Meaning: an ordinary person cannot win a struggle against an administrative system A commoner who has to slog to make both ends meet ***cannot fight the city hall.***
85.	**Cannot get blood from a stone**
	Meaning: you cannot ask for or do the impossible Do not expect any favours from the Sharma family because you ***can't get blood from a stone.***
86.	**Cannot hold a candle to**
	Meaning: to be second-rate in a certain skill; to be greatly inferior; to be not good as someone else When it comes to question of topping the class, Atul ***cannot hold a candle to*** anyone else.

87.	**Cannot see the forest for the trees**
	Meaning: to overlook the overall situation because of a focus on small details My teacher catches all my grammar mistakes, but he misses my brilliant writing. He ***cannot see the forest for the trees.***
88.	**Carry coals to Newcastle**
	Meaning: to bring something to a place where it is already plentiful Taking flowers to the florist's daughter is like ***carrying coals to Newcastle.***
89.	**Carry the ball**
	Meaning: to be in charge or be responsible; to make sure that a job gets done right Mrs. Sharma heads her company; she will ***carry the ball*** during the annual function.
90.	**Carry the weight of the world on your shoulders**
	Meaning: to be burdened by all the problems in the world Some people unnecessarily ***carry the weight of the world on their shoulders*** instead of focusing on their own lives.
91.	**Carved in stone**
	Meaning: permanent and unalterable The teacher's rule about no cell phones in class is ***carved in stone.*** Do not even think about making a call here.
92.	**Cast pearls before swine**
	Meaning: to waste something good or valuable on someone who won't appreciate or understand it Your investment in your pastime friends is just like ***casting pearls before swine.***
93.	**Cast the first stone**
	Meaning: to be the first to attack, blame, or criticize someone Do not criticize. You have done it yourself, so you shouldn't ***caste the first stone.***
94.	**Cat got your tongue**
	Meaning: is there a reason that you are not speaking? Why don't you answer me? ***Cat got your tongue.***

95.	**Cat that swallowed the canary**
	Meaning: very self-satisfied Once after the final selection of Ravi in the defense services, he seemed like the ***cat that swallowed canary.***
96.	**Catch more flies with honey than with vinegar**
	Meaning: more can be accomplished by being pleasant than by being disagreeable Ask her nicely. Remember, you can ***catch more flies with honey than with vinegar.***
97.	**Catch someone red-handed**
	Meaning: to catch someone in the act of doing something wrong Kasab was ***caught red-handed*** on the spot during te attack on Taj Hotel in Mumbai in 2011.
98.	**Catch you later**
	Meaning: good-bye; I'll see or speak to you at another time Leaving for home, Suresh asked Rajesh to ***catch him later.***
99.	**Champing at the bit**
	Meaning: to be impatient to start; to be ready and enthusiastic to do something Anaadi was champing at the bit to play with her friends after announcement of her school results.
100.	**Chew someone out**
	Meaning: to scold severely or roughly; to bawl someone out Leena's mother-in-law ***chewed her out*** publicly in the colony.
101.	**Chew the fat**
	Meaning: to have a friendly, informal talk; to chat in a relaxed way The old friends ***chewed the fat*** till midnight.
102.	**Chew up the scenery**
	Meaning: to overact; to exaggerate your emotions Veena is a great artist extremely expert in ***chewing the scenery*** before other.
103.	**Chew your cud**
	Meaning: to think deeply to oneself; to turn a matter over and over in your mind Some people have habit of ***chewing the cud.***

104.	**Chicken feed**
	Meaning: a very small or insignificant amount of money During Covid-19, there was heavy salary cuts in the private sector and the employees were paid only ***chicken feed.***
105.	**Chickens come home to roost**
	Meaning: bad words or actions come back to haunt a person; evil acts will return to plague the doer You better be careful what you say when you're happy. ***Chickens come home to roost.***
106.	**Chill out**
	Meaning: relax, calm down After almost one year's excruciating torture of Corona, people may ***chill out*** in New Year 2021.
107.	**Chip off the old block**
	Meaning: a child who resembles a parent in behaviour, looks, or abilities My wife is the exact replica of her mother. She is really ***chip off the old block.***
108.	**Chip on your shoulder**
	Meaning: to be quarrelsome, aggressive, or crude; to be ready to fight Avoid him today because he has a real ***chip on his shoulders.***
109.	**Chips are down**
	Meaning: the situation is urgent and has to be dealt with now Girls, the ***chips are down.*** If we do not win this game, we are out of the playoffs.
110.	**Clam up**
	Meaning: to refuse to talk; to become silent When the teacher asked who had broken the windowpanes, all students ***clammed up.***
111.	**Clean as a whistle**
	Meaning: completely free from dirt; perfectly neat The science lab is as ***clean as a whistle.***
112.	**Clean bill of health**
	Meaning: declaration of satisfaction, healthy condition, or proven innocence The gas station that inspected Dad's old car gave it a ***clean bill of health.***

113.	**Clear as a bell**
	Meaning: easily and clearly understood with no confusion whatsoever The principle's message was ***clear as a bell*** to all the late comers.
114.	**Clear the decks**
	Meaning: to get all of the minor details out of the way in order to focus on a major project Before we can build our model for the science fair, we have to ***clear the decks*** of other homework.
115.	**Climb the walls**
	Meaning: to be frustrated or anxious during a challenging situation; to be unable to endure The assembly was so dull that all the kids were ***climbing the walls.***
116.	**Clip your wings**
	Meaning: to end a person's privileges; to take away someone's power or freedom to do something It is said that Raja's favours are not permanent, he can ***clip anyone's wings*** anytime.
117.	**Cloak-and-dagger**
	Meaning: concerning or involving spies, secret agents, intrigue, and mystery; involving plotting and scheming ***Cloak-and-dagger*** stories were the most favourite area of Sunita.
118.	**Close shave**
	Meaning: a very narrow escape from danger During head-on-collision Raju had a ***close shave*** with the grace of God.
119.	**Cold feet**
	Meaning: a fear of doing something; a loss of nerve or confidence Waiting for the first result, she had ***cold feet.***
120.	**Cold shoulder**
	Meaning: unfriendly treatment of a person by ignoring him or her Though William met his old friend with warmth but his friend gave him the ***cold shoulder.***

121. Cold turkey

Meaning: the sudden stopping of any habit (smoking or drugs)

I stopped*cold turkey* on my smoking habit.

122. Come apart at the seams

Meaning: to become so upset that all self-control is gone

If anyone tires to check the family antecedents of Parvesh, he*comes apart at the seams.*

123. Come out of your shell

Meaning: to stop being so shy; to become more friendly

In the present times, one cannot excel being introvert, one has to*come out of his shell.*

124. Come up smelling like a rose

Meaning: to get out of a possibly embarrassing or disgraceful situation without hurting your reputation, and maybe even improving it

Even though my sister forgot to do her chores last week, she still*came up smelling like a rose.*

125. Cook your goose

Meaning: to wreck someone's plans; to ruin someone's project; to spoil someone's happiness

Milkha Singh's opponents tried to*cook his goose* but could not succeed.

126. Cooking with gas

Meaning: performing with skill, energy, enthusiasm, and excellence

Yesterday, he did not score a single point. But in tonight's game, he was really*cooking with gas.*

127. Cool as a cucumber

Meaning: very calm, not nervous, or emotional

Ravish Kumar was as*cool as a cucumber* when he got the Magsaysay Award from the President of the Philippines.

128. Cool your heels

Meaning: to be kept waiting for a long time, usually by someone in power or authority

The officer made the delegates to*cool their heels* before meeting them.

129. Cost an arm and a leg

Meaning: very expensive; high-priced, though possibly not worth the cost

Though it may*cost an arm and a leg* for a commoner to go abroad, but nowadays it is a status symbol.

130. Couch potato

Meaning: a person who spends a lot of time watching television

He will not come out to play because he is a *couch potato.*

131. Cream of the crop

Meaning: the best person or thing of all; the top choice; the best part

Among all the chefs at hotel Taj Mumbai, Mr. Saxena is*cream of the crop.*

132. Crocodile tears

Meaning: fake tears; false grief

I begged and cried to go to the party, but Dad said I was crying*crocodile tears.*

133. Cross the bridge when you come to it

Meaning: don't predict problems until they actually happen; don't worry about future events now; don't deal with a difficulty until you have to

The optimists *cross the bridge when they come to it* and the pessimist keep moaning and groaning.

134. Cry over spilled milk

Meaning: to cry or complain about an event that has already taken place and can't be changed

It is no use to*cry over spilled milk.*

135. Cry wolf

Meaning: to give a false alarm of danger; to warn of a peril that you know is not real

Don't worry if my little brother starts screaming that there's a ghost in his room. He always*cries wolf.*

136. Cut off your nose to spite your face

Meaning: to injure yourself out of anger toward another; to make a situation worse for yourself when angry with someone

Out of anger some people*cut off their nose to spit their face.*

137.	**Cut the mustard**
	Meaning: to be able to handle a job or fulfill the requirements He was forty and many people thought he was too old to ***cut the mustard,*** but he handled it skillfully.
138.	**Cut to the quick**
	Meaning: to hurt someone's feelings very deeply; to be extremely unkind or nasty The teacher was ***cut to the quick*** when the parents unnecessarily complained against him.
139.	**Cut your eyeteeth on something**
	Meaning: to acquire wisdom; to gain valuable experience, often at a young age The life's ups and downs enables ***everyone to cut one's eyeteeth on something.***
140.	**Cutting edge**
	Meaning: the forefront, the most advanced or important position, usually in science and technology Nipun always had a ***cutting edge*** over others in the pre-board examination.

D

141.	**Dark-horse candidate**
	Meaning: a contestant about whom little is known and who wins unexpectedly Everyone was surprised when Tejasvi Yadav came out victorious with his party as a single largest Party in Bihar elections because he was a dark horse candidate.
142.	**Dead as a doornail**
	Meaning: totally dead or hopeless; without a chance of success Congress party in the present times seems ***dead as a doornail,*** but it needs to be reorganized to rejuvenate.
143.	**Dead duck**
	Meaning: a person who is ruined When Ravi lost all the money in the share market, he was as a ***dead duck.***
144.	**Diamond in the rough**
	Meaning: someone or something that doesn't look so good now, but that has great merit and the potential to be beautiful Nowadays, the simple and innocent people are mistakenly considered as ***diamond in the rough.***
145.	**Do or die**
	Meaning: to succeed or fail completely Gandhiji gave the slogan of ***"Do or Die"*** during Quit India Movement.
146.	**Dog days of summer**
	Meaning: the hottest and most humid days of summer Sales of air conditioners are usually highest during the ***dog days of summer.***
147.	**Dog-eat-dog world**
	Meaning: a way of life marked by fierce competition in which people compete ruthlessly for survival or success In the era of fierce and cutthroat competition, present day world is no less than ***dog-eat-dog world.***
148.	**Dog's life**
	Meaning: a bleak, terrible existence without much happiness or freedom Covid-19 has totally rendered poor people's life worse than ***dog's life.***
149.	**Do not count your chickens before they hatch**
	Meaning: do not count on profits before you earn them or have them in hand It is advisable that one should ***not count one's chicken before they hatch.***
150.	**Do not look a gift horse in the mouth**
	Meaning: don't complain if a gift is not perfect; take what you've been given without criticism or emphasis on its worth When Mona complained about her present, her dad told her ***not to look a gift horse in the mouth.***

151.	**Do not take any wooden nickels**
	Meaning: do not let anyone cheat your or take advance of you One should learn the ways of society with passage of time so as ***not to take any wooden nickels.***
152.	**Dose of one's own medicine**
	Meaning: the same or a similar bad thing done back to the person who did it first Indians believe in theory of karma, according to which one gets a ***dose of one's own medicine,*** if he puts others in troubles.
153.	**Dot your I's and cross your t's**
	Meaning: to take great care over details Before taking final decision of starting a new project ***dot your I's and cross your t's.***
154.	**Down in the dumps**
	Meaning: sad and depressed When Geeta could not figure in final merit list of IAS, she was ***down in the dumps.***
155.	**Down the drain**
	Meaning: lost forever; wasted During Covid-19 pandemic, the business of the number of people went ***down the drain.***
156.	**Down the hatch**
	Meaning: swallow a drink in one gulp Grandma handed me a glass of smelly medicine and said, ***"Down the hatch."***
157.	**Down-to-earth**
	Meaning: practical; sensible; realistic Even though Lokesh's parents are millionaires, they do not act snobbishly, they are really quite ***down-to-earth.***
158.	**Down-to-the-wire**
	Meaning: running out of time; at the very last minute I cannot talk to you now. I am ***down-to-the-wire*** on this research report.
159.	**Draw the line at**
	Meaning: to set a specific limit, especially about behaviour My parents give me a lot of freedom, but they ***draw the line at*** letting me stay out late on school nights.
160.	**Dressed to the nines**
	Meaning: wearing fashionable clothing; dressed to attract attention Indians are normally ***dressed to nines*** at weddings.
161.	**Drive a hard bargain**
	Meaning: to buy or sell at a good price Real Estate property dealers are smart enough to ***drive a hard bargain.***
162.	**Drive you crazy**
	Meaning: to make someone uncontrolled I can't help stopping myself when I see any book of Paulo Coelho, it literally ***drives me crazy.***
163.	**Drop in the bucket**
	Meaning: a very small, insignificant amount Because of Covid-19, majority of the people are left with a ***drop in their buckets.***
164.	**Drop you like a hot potato**
	Meaning: to get rid of something or somebody as quickly as possible The father advised his son to ***drop his*** bad friend ***like a hot potato.***
165.	**Dull as dishwater**
	Meaning: not inspiring; uninteresting Programs on that channel are as ***dull as dishwater.***
166.	**Dyed-in-the-wool**
	Meaning: complete, permanent, stubborn A number of people are ***dyed-in-the-wool*** BPJ voters, who do not wavier or falter.

E

167.	**Early bird catches the worm**
	Meaning: a person who gets up early and starts a project ahead of others has the best chance of accomplishing his or her goal Jaskaran slept overnight in front of the stadium in order to get tickets. The ***early bird catches the worm.***
168.	**Easy as pie**
	Meaning: not difficult; requiring practically no effort Nowadays scoring more than 90% in boards is as ***easy as pie.***

169. Easy as rolling off a log

Meaning: very, very easy; requiring little or no effort

Anaadi made me realize that running online classes is as *easy as rolling off a log.*

170. Easy come, easy go

Meaning: something that is easily obtained, as money, can be lost or parted with just as easily

It is commonly said that ill gotten money goes like *easy come, easy go.*

171. Eat crow

Meaning: to be forced to do something very disagreeable; to acknowledge a mistake or defeat

I made Arun admit that he was wrong, and now he has to *eat crow.*

172. Eat humble pie

Meaning: to be apologetic or suffer humiliation; to act humble or admit guilt

When he finds out how wrong he has been, he will *eat humble pie.*

173. Eat out of your hand

Meaning: to be very cooperative or submissive

Abhimanyu *eats out of your hand* once you assign him any job.

174. Eat you out of house and home

Meaning: to be so expensive to feed and keep that the person paying cannot afford it

Mandy grew four inches, he is *eating his* parents *out of house and home.*

175. Eat your hat

Meaning: a statement made when you are positive that something will happen

Mr. Sharma was always boastful of his children, but he had to *eat his hat* when they finally failed in all the exams.

176. Eat your heart out

Meaning: to feel extremely unhappy about a hopeless situation; to make yourself sick with grief and worry

After Serena lost the plane tickets, she *ate her heart out* over the mistake.

177. Eat your words

Meaning: to have to take back what you said; to admit humbly that you were wrong

Mr. Kaushal had predicted that Chandan can never be selected in IAS, but when selected, he had to eat his words.

178. Egg on your face

Meaning: to be very embarrassed or humiliated for something foolish that you did or said

The farmers laws passed by government may be *egg on government's face.*

179. Elbow grease

Meaning: hard, energetic manual labor

Put a little *elbow grease* into hat job. Polish that car until it shines!

180. Eleventh hour

Meaning: at the latest possible time, just before the absolute deadline

Prof. Jaiswal is habitual to complete everything at the *eleventh hour.*

181. Every cloud has a silver lining

Meaning: there is something good in every bad situation

When the night is deep, dead & dark, it means dawn is about to break as *every cloud has a silver lining.*

182. Every Tom, Dick, and Harry

Meaning: every person possible, especially very ordinary people

One cannot satisfy *every Tom, Dick and Harry* rather one should focus on one's own life.

183. Eye for an eye and a tooth for a tooth

Meaning: revenge or punishment exactly like the original crime or offense

In the ancient times the philosophy of *eye for an eye and a tooth for a tooth* was the most acceptable philosophy.

184. Eyes in the back of your head

Meaning: ability to sense what is happening outside of one's field of vision; ability to know what happens when one's back is turned

My teacher always knows when we are passing notes. He must have *eyes in the back of his head.*

F

185.	**Face the music**
	Meaning: to endure the consequence of one's actions I was caught cheating and now I have to ***face the music.***
186.	**Fair-weather friend**
	Meaning: a person who is a faithful friend only when everything is going well but who deserts you in times of difficulty One must remain beware of one's ***fair-weather friends.***
187.	**Fat cat**
	Meaning: a wealthy person; a rich benefactor The ***fat cats*** must contribute towards funds for victims of earthquake.
188.	**Feast or famine**
	Meaning: great success or total failure; either too much or too little of something Covid-19 made business feast ***or famine*** because grocery and pharmaceutical sector flourished manifold, whereas many others lost.
189.	**Feather in your cap**
	Meaning: a great achievement or special honor A new book of Bhardwaj is a ***feather in his cap.***
190.	**Feather your nest**
	Meaning: to be more interested in taking care of yourself The bureaucracy in India is more interested in ***feathering its own nest.***
191.	**Feel your oats**
	Meaning: to be in high spirits, energetic; to act in a proud way The whole class was celebrating the farewell party and all the classmates were ***feeling their oats.***
192.	**Feet of clay**
	Meaning: a hidden fault of character; a weak point If one is able to fix his ***feet of clay,*** one can rectify it.
193.	**Fiddle while Rome burns**
	Meaning: do nothing or busy yourself with unimportant matters instead of acting in an urgent situation The government ***fiddled while Rome burned,*** doing nothing to control the Covid-19 pandemic.
194.	**Field day**
	Meaning: to have unlimited opportunities; to have it all your own way Anaadi had a ***field day*** on her birthday to get all the toys of her choice.
195.	**Fifth wheel**
	Meaning: extra person The office of Comptroller and Auditor-General is known as ***fifth wheel*** of the coach.
196.	**Fight tooth and nail**
	Meaning: to fight fiercely, furiously, and ferociously Alauddin Khilji had to fight tooth and nail to win over Padmavati of Chittor.
197.	**Fill the bill**
	Meaning: to be very competent, effective Rajesh as the accountant in office ***fills the bill.***
198.	**Finger in every pie**
	Meaning: to have a part in something; to be involved in many matters, businesses, or activities Mrs. Lokhande has her ***finger in every pie*** when it comes to music, dance, and theater.
199.	**Fish out of water**
	Meaning: a person who is out of his or her usual place Getting into police force, Deepak was feeling like a ***fish out of water.***
200.	**Fit as a fiddle**
	Meaning: in good health; in fine shape Mr. Bhushan is nearly ninety, but he is still ***fit as a fiddle.***
201.	**Fit like a glove**
	Meaning: to fit a person or thing perfectly; to be exactly right These new curtains match your bedspread perfectly. They ***fit*** your bedroom ***like a glove.***

202.	**Fix your wagon**
	Meaning: to get even with or punish someone; to thwart or frustrate another or cause his or her failure in something
	Mr. Singh was found derelict of his duty and now his superiors would fix ***his wagon.***
203.	**Flash in the pan**
	Meaning: a temporary success which yields no long-term results
	Thought initially the team of Punjab exhibited a great performance, but it was just ***flash in the pan.***
204.	**Flotsam and jetsam**
	Meaning: a collection of mostly worthless and useless objects; rubbish and refuse
	I am cleaning out my room of all ***flotsam and jetsam.***
205.	**Fly-by-night**
	Meaning: selling for quick profit, then disappearing; a swindler or unreliable person
	The store from where I bought that defective computer was a ***fly-by-night*** operation.
206.	**Fly by the seat of your pants**
	Meaning: to do something by instinct and feel without any earlier experience or instruction
	Though I took chance to write a book on Legal Aptitude when I had no earlier experience, but I ***flew by the seat of my pants.***
207.	**Fly in the ointment**
	Meaning: a small annoyance that spoils an otherwise pleasant situation
	The food, the music, and the decorations were prefect, but her camera broke. That was the ***fly in the ointment.***
208.	**Fly off the handle.**
	Meaning: to lose your temper; to become furiously angry
	When he saw the report card of his son, he ***flew off the handle.***
209.	**Fly the coop**
	Meaning: to escape; to leave suddenly and secretly
	I tried to chain my dog, when I was looking for the chain, he ***flew the coop.***
210.	**Foam at the mouth**
	Meaning: to be uncontrollably furious, like a mad dog
	When the father found the son sleeping just before the exam, he was ***foaming at the mouth.***
211.	**Follow your nose**
	Meaning: to go straight ahead in the same direction
	When he asked me the way to the cafeteria, I told him to ***follow his nose.***
212.	**Food for thought**
	Meaning: an interesting idea worth thinking about carefully
	The column "Inner voice", in Hindustan Times daily literally provides ***food for thought.***
213.	**Footloose and fancy-free**
	Meaning: not attached to anyone; not involved with anyone romantically; free
	Nowadays the people are losing sensitivity and sensibility and they are just ***footloose and fancy-free.***
214.	**For the birds**
	Meaning: worthless; useless; stupid
	That movie was ***for the birds.*** I am sorry I wasted my money on it.
215.	**Forty winks**
	Meaning: a short nap
	I just need ***forty winks*** and I will be able to work all night.
216.	**Four corners of the earth**
	Meaning: from all over the planet; all parts of a place
	The death of soccer Venezuelan legend Maradona was mourned by all from the ***four corners of the earth.***
217.	**From soup to nuts**
	Meaning: the whole things from beginning to end
	I want to listen your life history ***from soup to nuts.***
218.	**From the word go**
	Meaning: from the very beginning
	Her mother did not like her boyfriend ***from the word go.***

219.	**Full of beans**
	Meaning: lively, happy and energetic, high-spirited After final exams, some of us were exhausted and others were ***full of beans.***
220.	**Full of hot air**
	Meaning: being foolish and talking nonsense; pompous; vain I do not believe a word he says. He is ***full of hot air.***
221.	**Full steam ahead**
	Meaning: proceed with all possible speed and power The captain of the team shouted, ***"Full steam ahead!"*** to get his tired players out onto the field.

G

222.	**Get a handle on something**
	Meaning: to start to overcome a difficult problem or situation Nipun had a lot of trouble with geometry, but I think he is ***getting a handle on it.***
223.	**Get a kick out of something**
	Meaning: to enjoy doing something; to get a thrill our of something My grandmother really ***gets a kick out of*** playing these video games with me.
224.	**Get away with murder**
	Meaning: to do something bad, wrong, or illegal and not get caught or punished Most of the accused, most of the time think that they will ***get away with murder.***
225.	**Get in on the ground floor**
	Meaning: to be part of some big or important project or business at its start Shukla Ji ***got in on the ground floor*** with Aadhar Card project of Govt. of India.
226.	**Get into the swing of things**
	Meaning: to become accustomed to routine activities Once the Covid-19 pandemic will be over, the people will ***get into the swings of things.***
227.	**Get off the hook**
	Meaning: to free yourself or someone from a distasteful obligation; to get out of trouble; to evade a punishment Though he carried on all the responsibilities of family after his father's death, but now he wants to ***get off the hook.***
228.	**Get out of my face**
	Meaning: stop standing in front of me in a provocative manner, arguing with me You would better ***get out of my face*** right now or you will be sorry!
229.	**Get real**
	Meaning: face reality; stop fantasizing Mr. Digvijay must ***get real*** feel of the divorce proceeding, instead of flying in the air.
230.	**Get something off your chest**
	Meaning: to make known something that is bothersome, but kept secret for a time Something is bothering me, and I want to ***get it off my chest.*** Please do not smoke here.
231.	**Get the green light**
	Meaning: get permission to go ahead with a project Mrs. Nischint Kaur hoped to ***get the green light*** from the principal to redesign her science lab.
232.	**Get the lead out of your feet**
	Meaning: to get busy; to move or work more quickly The Captain encourages the team to ***get the lead out of its feet.***
233.	**Get the sack**
	Meaning: to be fired A number of employees in the private sector ***got the sack*** because of Covid-19.
234.	**Get this show on the road**
	Meaning: get going; move forward; get the work started; do it Every morning, Dad shouts, "Let us ***get this show on the road.*** You do not want to be late for school."

235.	**Get to the bottom of something**
	Meaning: to find out the real cause of something The police left no stone unturned to ***get to the bottom of*** crime .
236.	**Get under your skin**
	Meaning: to bother or upset someone It really ***gets under my skin*** when my parents clean up my room.
237.	**Get-up-and-go**
	Meaning: energy and motivation; pep; enthusiasm; ambition Since Grandmother joined that health club, she has had a lot more ***get-up-and-go.***
238.	**Get up on the wrong side of the bed**
	Meaning: to awake a bad temper or mood, feeling cross or grouchy It is advisable to start the day afresh and not ***get up on the wrong side of the bed.***
239.	**Get your feet wet**
	Meaning: to have a first experience in something; to begin to do something for the first time Mansi had never been in a play, but she took a small part just to ***get her feet wet.***
240.	**Get your goat**
	Meaning: to annoy very badly; to make a person angry It really ***got his goat*** when he cooked for three hours and no one ate the meal.
241.	**Gift of gab**
	Meaning: skill in talking, especially in an interesting and colorful way A good politician makes best time of his ***gift of the gab.***
242.	**Gild the lily**
	Meaning: to spoil something that is already beautiful by adding something extra Anamika really doesn't need all that makeup. That is like ***gilding the lily.***
243.	**Give me five**
	Meaning: to slap a person's hand as a hearty greeting or a sign of solid agreement My little cousin always yells, ***"Give me five!"***

244.	**Give someone the shift off your back**
	Meaning: to be extremely generous Mr. Rajesh would ***give you the shift off his back*** if you needed it.
245.	**Give someone the third degree**
	Meaning: use mental or physical pressure to get information or a confession from someone The teacher ***gave the third degree*** to every student to find out who had glued his briefcase shut.
246.	**Give up the ghost**
	Meaning: to die; to stop running His computer ***gave up the ghost*** when he was taking online classes.
247.	**Give your eyeteeth for something**
	Meaning: to want something very badly I'd ***give my eyeteeth*** to own a book like the books by Abdul Kalam.
248.	**Go against the grain**
	Meaning: to say or to do something in an unconventional way that annoys people He really ***goes against her grain*** when he says that a woman cannot be president.
249.	**Go along for the ride**
	Meaning: to watch but not take part in an activity; to keep someone company Aman swore that she did not trash any lawns. She just ***went along for the ride.***
250.	**Go bananas**
	Meaning: to be or go crazy Your brother has ***gone bananas*** for Hindi movies.
251.	**Go fly a kite**
	Meaning: go away; leave; stop bothering me When he asked for her help, she told him to ***go fly a kite.***
252.	**Go for broke**
	Meaning: to risk everything on one big goal or effort; to try as hard as possible Instead of applying for separate law entrance, he ***went for broke*** and applied only for CLAT.
253.	**Go over like a lead balloon**
	Meaning: to fail miserably I asked to go to Antarctica for vacation, but my idea ***went over like a lead balloon.***

254.	**Go over with a fine-tooth comb**
	Meaning: to search with great care or attention
	She went ***over the lawn with a fine-tooth comb,*** but she could not find her contact lens.
255.	**Go to bat for someone**
	Meaning: to help someone out; to defend someone
	Ravi ***went to bat for his friend*** Chander when he defended him in front of the investigating agencies.
256.	**Go to the dogs**
	Meaning: to decline in looks or health; to be ruined or destroyed; to ruin oneself
	Because of addiction to drugs, the star of yesteryears has ***gone to the dogs.***
257.	**Gone to pot**
	Meaning: become ruined; to get worse and worse
	This was once a beautiful park, but now it has all ***gone to pot.***
258.	**Goody Two-shoes**
	Meaning: a person who thinks he or she is perfect and tries to be
	Mona is such a ***Goody Two-shoes*** that everyone hates her for her vain display.
259.	**Grease someone's palm**
	Meaning: to bribe someone
	In government office, one has to ***grease the concerned officer's palm*** to get the things done in time.
260.	**Greek to me**
	Meaning: too difficult to understand; unknown
	Taking online classes was literally ***Greek to me.***
261.	**Green thumb**
	Meaning: having a special talent for making flowers and green plants grow well
	My uncle has a ***green thumb.*** You should see his roses.
262.	**Green with envy**
	Meaning: extremely jealous
	Mrs. Sharma is ***green with envy*** at anyone's success.

263.	**Grit your teeth**
	Meaning: to not show one's feelings; to put up with difficulty; to bear pain
	In the present times of selfishness, one has to ***grit one's teeth*** to avoid unnecessary mockery.

H

264.	**Handle with kid gloves**
	Meaning: to treat gently and carefully
	Handle the kid's problems ***with kid gloves.***
265.	**Hand-to-mouth existence**
	Meaning: to spend your salary as fast as it's earned without saving any for the future
	He lives a ***hand-to-mouth existence*** doing odd jobs around town.
266.	**Handwriting on the wall**
	Meaning: a sign that something bad is going to happen; a warning of danger
	The Covid-19 damages are clearly ***handwriting on the wall.***
267.	**Hanging by a thread**
	Meaning: to be in a dangerous or unsafe position
	The jobs of many in private sector are ***hanging by a thread*** in the wake of Covid-19.
268.	**Hat in hand**
	Meaning: to beg or plead for a favor or a pardon
	Hat in hand, I went to the judge pleading for mercy.
269.	**Have a bone to pick with you**
	Meaning: to have an argument or unpleasant matter to settle with someone
	My new boss said she ***had a bone to pick with me*** and called me into her office.
270.	**Have a screw loose**
	Meaning: to behave or look in a strange or foolish manner; to be odd and not ordinary
	The substitute English teacher must ***have a screw loose.***
271.	**Have your cake and eat it too**
	Meaning: to spend or use something up but still have it
	You can either go to a movie or get pizza, but you cannot ***have your cake and eat it too.***

272.	**Have your heart in your mouth**
	Meaning: to be extremely frightened about something
	My ***heart was in my mouth*** when I reached the top of the roller coaster.
273.	**Head and shoulders above someone**
	Meaning: far superior; much better than
	She is ***head and shoulders above*** all the classmates in English language.
274.	**Head honcho**
	Meaning: the person in charge; the chief, boss, leader
	Do what the ***head honcho*** tells you if you want to keep your job.
275.	**Head in the clouds**
	Meaning: absentminded; daydreaming; lost in thought
	My report card said that I should pay more attention in class and avoid my head in the clouds.
276.	**Head over heels in love**
	Meaning: completely and helplessly in love
	He fell ***head over heels in love*** with the Science teacher.
277.	**Hear a pin drop**
	Meaning: so silent you can hear very soft things happening; without sound; noiseless
	At the break of the dawn, you can ***hear a pin drop,*** even ticking of a clock.
278.	**Heart of gold**
	Meaning: an extremely kind, generous, humane, and forgiving nature
	Upasna has a ***heart of gold,*** and everyone loves her for it.
279.	**Heart's in the right place**
	Meaning: to be well-meaning and kindhearted; to have good intentions even though mistakes occur
	Atul messes up sometimes, but his ***heart's in the right place.***
280.	**High horse**
	Meaning: acting superior and arrogant as if you were better than other people
	Neetu always runs his ***high horse*** without being aware of his ground reality.
281.	**Highway robbery**
	Meaning: an extremely high price or charge for something
	Shopping at malls is no less than a ***highway robbery.***
282.	**Hit below the belt**
	Meaning: to use unfair tactics or be unsportsmanlike
	He ***hit below the belt*** to top in the exam.
283.	**Hit the jackpot**
	Meaning: to be very lucky; to achieve amazing success
	Today I ***hit the jackpot;*** I got the highest grade in the spelling test.
284.	**Hit the nail right on the head**
	Meaning: to be exactly correct about a description or come to the right conclusion
	She really hit the nail right on the head, when she instantly identified the accused in identification parade.
285.	**Hit the road**
	Meaning: to begin a journey, to leave
	The car rallyists ***hit the road*** early in the morning.
286.	**Hit the roof**
	Meaning: to lose your temper suddenly; to become violently angry
	On seeing the report card, Arnav's father ***hit the roof.***
287.	**Hit the spot**
	Meaning: to fully satisfy and refresh, especially with food or drink
	After than long hike through the desert, a cold drink ***hit the spot.***
288.	**Hitch your wagon to a star**
	Meaning: to aim high; to try to reach the highest level; to follow a great ambition
	Dr. APJ Abdul Kalam always advised youngsters to ***hitch their wagon to a star.***
289.	**Hold the fort**
	Meaning: to temporarily be responsible for watching over a place
	Our teacher was late, so the teacher next door ***held the fort*** in our room until he showed up.

290.	**Hold your horses**
	Meaning: slow down; wait a minute; be patient ***Hold your horses,*** why are you walking so fast?
291.	**Horse of a different color**
	Meaning: a different matter altogether Making arrangements for English class was a ***horse of a different color*** than that of a hobby class.
292.	**Hot under the collar**
	Meaning: very angry; upset Better say good night. My father is starting to get ***hot under the collar.***
	I
293.	**If the shoe fits, wear it**
	Meaning: if a remark applies to you, you should admit that it is true Some students never clean up after art class. I am not mentioning names, but ***if the shoe fits, wear it.***
294.	**Ignorance is bliss**
	Meaning: it is better not to know bad news sometimes, especially if you're happy Sometimes it causes losses to be wise and in that situation, ***ignorance is bliss.***
295.	**In a nutshell**
	Meaning: in very few words; briefly; clearly and to the point ***In a nutshell,*** tell me what the show was about.
296.	**In hot water**
	Meaning: in serious trouble or in an embarrassing situation with someone of authority The officer was ***in hot water*** for disobeying the orders of the court.
297.	**In one ear and out the other**
	Meaning: not listening to what is being said, not attentive In case of majority of the children, the parents' advice goes ***in one ear and out the other.***
298.	**In the bag**
	Meaning: absolutely certain to be won, gotten, or achieved; sure, definite Our soccer team had the championship ***in the bag*** when the other team's best player got sick.

299.	**In the catbird seat**
	Meaning: in a position of advance or superiority The students with good family background are always in the catbird seat.
300.	**In the driver's seat**
	Meaning: in control; in the position of authority Mrs. Saxena is always ***in the driver's seat*** as Mr. Sharma is a henpecked husband.
301.	**In the lap of luxury**
	Meaning: surrounded by luxuries; having the most lavish things that money can buy Pradeep lives ***in the lap of luxury*** in his mansion in Sector 2, Chandigarh.
302.	**In the limelight**
	Meaning: at the center of attention Kangana Ranaut was ***in the limelight*** after the death of Sushant Singh Rajput.
303.	**In the nick of time**
	Meaning: just at the exact right time; at the precise moment required Though he seemed late, but he reached just ***in the nick of time*** before the program started.
304.	**In the pink**
	Meaning: in excellent health physically and emotionally I was pleased to see that Mr. Singh ***in the pink.***
305.	**In the same boat**
	Meaning: in the same bad situation; sharing the same problem or difficulty In the present times of lockdown, most of the people are sailing ***in the same boat.***
	J
306.	**Jack-of-all-trades**
	Meaning: a person who can do different kinds of jobs It is advised to be master of few and ***jack-of-all-trades.***
307.	**Jet set**
	Meaning: the wealthy, fashionable, and famous people who travel frequently The ***jet set*** section of the society do not mix up with riff-raff and bob-tail.

308.	**Johnny-come-lately**
	Meaning: someone who is new to a place or group; an inexperienced person The older teachers in the math department call the new teacher a *Johnny-come-lately.*
309.	**Jump down your throat**
	Meaning: to talk or scream at someone in a sudden, angry way The father jumped down his throat at the children making noise.
310.	**Jump off the deep end**
	Meaning: to act emotionally without carefully thinking about the end result Inter-caste marriage in India even today is no less than *jumping off the deep end.*
311.	**Jump on the bandwagon**
	Meaning: to become part of the newest activity because many other people are Last year nobody liked my idea of a school carnival. Now everyone wants to *jump on the bandwagon.*
312.	**Jump the gun**
	Meaning: to act prematurely or hastily I could not wait to give my mother her Mother's Day gift, so I *jumped the gun* and gave it to her a week early.
313.	**Just deserts**
	Meaning: the punishment a person deserves The rape accused need to be given the *just deserts.*
K	
314.	**Keep a stiff upper lip**
	Meaning: to be brave and not show emotion in a time of trouble Even undergoing the worst and toughest times of her life, she *keeps a stiff upper lip.*
315.	**Keep a straight face**
	Meaning: to keep from laughing It is very difficult to *keep the straight face* after watching clownish behaviour of Mrs. Poonam.
316.	**Keep body and soul together**
	Meaning: to keep alive; to have just enough to survive He got a job that paid so little, he was barely able to *keep body and soul together.*

317.	**Keep something under your hat**
	Meaning: to keep something secret The Chandigarhians are so introvert that they *keep everything under their hats.*
318.	**Keep the wolf from the door**
	Meaning: to keep away from suffering poverty or starvation He got two extra jobs just to *keep the wolf from the door.*
319.	**Keep your ear to the ground**
	Meaning: know what is going on; pay attention and be well informed Mr. Mittal always *keeps his ear to the ground* and knows who is who and what is what.
320.	**Keep your fingers crossed**
	Meaning: to wish for good luck and success for someone or something Before the final results all the candidates were *keeping their fingers crossed.*
321.	**Keep your head above water**
	Meaning: to earn enough to stay out of debt and avoid financial ruin Business is in doldrums because of Covid-19, and Dad is barely *keeping his head above water.*
322.	**Kick up your heels**
	Meaning: to celebrate and have a wonderful time After the good results, the successful candidates kept *kicking up their heels* the whole night.
323.	**Kill the goose that lays the golden eggs**
	Meaning: to spoil or destroy something good out of stupidity, greed, or impatience Sometimes people out of sheer greed *kill the goose that lays the golden eggs.*
324.	**Kill two birds with one stone**
	Meaning: to do two things by one action; to get two results with just one effort Anaadi prepared her English language with twin purpose of school examination as well as English Olympiad *killing two birds with one stone.*

325.	**Knock your socks off**
	Meaning: thrill, amaze, delight, overwhelm, startle, excite, shock At Indian Idol music talent hunt show, Kamakshi ***knocked the jury with their socks off.***
	L
326.	**Lame duck**
	Meaning: an elected official in the last days of his or her time on the job After defeat in US 2020 Presidential Elections, Donald Trump was a ***lame duck*** for the remainder of his term.
327.	**Laugh out of the other side of your mouth**
	Meaning: to be made to feel sorrow, to cry at a change in luck after experiencing some happiness Once the news gets out the Donald Trump bought votes to win the election, he'll be ***laughing out of the other wide of his mouth.***
328.	**Lay an egg**
	Meaning: to give an embarrassing performance She really ***laid an egg*** at the talent show with clumsy performance.
329.	**Lay your cards on the table**
	Meaning: to reveal all the facts openly and honestly; to reveal one's purpose and plans The mayor ***laid his cards on the table*** about beautification project.
330.	**Lead you by the nose**
	Meaning: to dominate or control someone Everyone knows that Mr. Sharma is a henpecked husband, his wife ***lead him by the nose.***
331.	**Leave no stone unturned**
	Meaning: to make all possible efforts to carry out a task She vowed that she would ***leave no stone unturned*** in finding out who let the air out of her car's tires.
332.	**Leave someone holding the bag**
	Meaning: to force someone to take blame when it should be shared When the teacher demanded to know who wrote the joke on the blackboard, Arnav was ***left holding the bag.***

333.	**Left out in the cold**
	Meaning: to not tell someone something; to exclude someone from a place or activity Ravi told everyone else about the party, but he ***left me out in the cold.***
334.	**Lend an ear**
	Meaning: to listen and pay attention to Good students always ***lend their ears*** to their teachers.
335.	**Let sleeping dogs lie**
	Meaning: to not make someone angry by stirring up trouble Do not remind the director that you missed two rehearsals. Better to ***let sleeping dogs lie.***
336.	**Let the cat out of the bag**
	Meaning: to give away a secret Ravi's younger brother ***let the cat out of the bag*** about surprise party.
337.	**Life in the fast lane**
	Meaning: a fast, busy way of life In the present age of fast foods, the youngsters are leading their ***lives in the fast lane.***
338.	**Light at the end of the tunnel**
	Meaning: a long-searched-for answer, goal, or success After 10 years' long legal battle, the victim finally saw the ***light at the end of the tunnel.***
339.	**Like a bump on a log**
	Meaning: inactive and not responding Do not just sit there ***like a bump on a log.*** Help the people in distress because of Covid-19.
340.	**Like it or lump it**
	Meaning: whether you like it or not; certain to happen Covid-19 is a grim reality. We ***like it or lump it*** but we need to take precautions.
341.	**Like pulling teeth**
	Meaning: something very hard to do Asking Sameer to follow a disciplined routine is ***like pulling teeth.***
342.	**Like two peas in a pod**
	Meaning: identical; alike in looks and behaviour Anaadi and Upasna are ***like two peas in a pod.***

343.	**Lock, stock and barrel**
	Meaning: the whole of something; all the parts of a thing; everything
	The company was sold – ***lock, stock, and barrel.***
344.	**Long in the tooth**
	Meaning: old; aged; elderly
	Mr. & Mrs. Dhawan are a quite ***long in the tooth.***
345.	**Look down your nose at someone**
	Meaning: to think of and treat people as if they were lower in quality or ability
	The newly rich class ***look down their nose at the poor people.***
346.	**Loose cannon**
	Meaning: a person who is unpredictable and sometimes out of control
	He got fired because he was a ***loose cannon*** and caused everybody a lot of trouble.
347.	**Lose your shirt**
	Meaning: to lose everything; especially money
	Mr. Mahajan ***lost his shirt*** in share market.
348.	**Lower the boom**
	Meaning: to scold or punish strictly; to make someone follow the rules
	Sometimes the parents unnecessarily ***lower the boom*** on their children.

M

349.	**Mad as a hatter**
	Meaning: completely crazy, strange, eccentric
	Chaudhary is as ***mad as a hatter,*** but he is my first friend. It is a reality.
350.	**Mad as a wet hen**
	Meaning: very upset; extremely angry; ready to fight
	When Avni realized that her brother had eaten all the cookies, she was as ***mad as a wet hen.***
351.	**Make a mountain out of a molehill**
	Meaning: to turn a small, unimportant issue into a big, important one; to exaggerate
	Some people are in the habit of ***making a mountain out of a molehill.***
352.	**Make ends meet**
	Meaning: to earn just enough to live within one's income
	With 50 percent salary cut because of Covid-19, the salaried class find it difficult to ***make ends meet.***
353.	**Make hay while the sun shines**
	Meaning: to make the best of a limited opportunity
	For some people Covid-19 proved a blessing in disguise, they ***made hay while the sun shone.***
354.	**Make heads or tails out of something**
	Meaning: to understand how something works; to figure something out
	We are not able to ***make heads or tails out of the instructions*** for assembling the new weather-forecasting machine.
355.	**Make no bones about something**
	Meaning: to speak directly, plainly, honestly, and without hesitation or doubt
	The substitute teacher ***made no bones about colourful hats worn*** in class.
356.	**Make your mouth water**
	Meaning: to look so attractive and desirable that it makes you want to have it very much; to want to eat or drink something that looks or smells delicious
	The egg paranthas ***made my mouth water.***
357.	**March to the beat of a different drummer**
	Meaning: be an individual; do your own thing; don't do what everybody else does; be original and creative
	Arnav never imitates others, he ***marched to the beat of a different drummer.***
358.	**Mess with someone**
	Meaning: to annoy, argue with, hassle, or otherwise anger and irritate a person
	Do not even think of ***messing with the new teacher.*** She is tough.
359.	**Midas touch**
	Meaning: to make a lot of money at whatever you do
	Dhirubhai Ambani is said to have a ***Midas touch.***

360.	**Mince words**
	Meaning: not to come right to the point; to be less than 100% honest
	Please don't ***mince words.*** Tell me exactly what do you think of me.
361.	**Mind over matter**
	Meaning: the power of your mind is stronger than the body
	Mind over matter is centuries old established philosophy.
362.	**Mind your p's and q's**
	Meaning: to be extremely exact; be careful not to say or do anything wrong
	Please try to ***mind your p's and q's*** when the Prime Minister visits the school.
363.	**Money burns a hole in your pocket**
	Meaning: cannot stop yourself from spending whatever money you have
	He is a pathological spendthrift who can't save a single penny, ***money burns a hole in his pocket.***
364.	**Monkey business**
	Meaning: silliness or fooling around; dishonest or illegal activities; idiotic pranks
	No more ***monkey business!*** Settle down.
365.	**More than meets the eye**
	Meaning: there are hidden facts that can't be seen or understood right away
	The police could easily make out that there was ***more than meets the eye.***

N

366.	**Needle in a haystack**
	Meaning: something hard or impossible to find; anything hopeless (in a search)
	Without any clue about offence or offender, the police felt like finding a ***needle in a haystack.***
367.	**Nickel-and-dime**
	Meaning: unimportant, small-time, trivial, petty
	He said he worked for a big corporation, but it was really only a ***nickel-and-dime*** company.
368.	**Nitty-gritty**
	Meaning: the specific heart of the matter; the practical details; the fundamental core of something
	A Judge must look into the ***nitty-gritty*** of every case.
369.	**Nose out of joint**
	Meaning: angry, jealous, or annoyed at someone
	When Mannat could not win in Olympiad, her ***nose was out of joint*** for a week.
370.	**Not your cup of tea**
	Meaning: not what one likes or prefers; not suitable; not to your taste
	He advised me to join a MNC and I told him that it was ***not my cup of tea.***
371.	**Nothing new under the sun**
	Meaning: everything is just a little different but pretty much the same as an earlier invention
	This expensive pasta is really just macaroni. There's ***nothing new under the sun.***
372.	**Nothing to sneeze at**
	Meaning: not small or unimportant; something to be taken seriously
	He won the silver medal, not the gold, but that is still ***nothing to sneeze at.***
373.	**Nothing ventured, nothing gained**
	Meaning: if you don't try to do something, you'll never accomplish it
	Keep trying because if you stop trying, ***nothing ventured, nothing gained.***

O

374.	**Off your rocker**
	Meaning: crazy; silly; foolish; not thinking correctly
	The Head in the company is ***off his rocker,*** nobody likes his ways.
375.	**Old hat**
	Meaning: out-of-date; not new; too familiar; uninteresting
	Let us try a new place for our next vacation. Shimla is so ***old hat.***

376.	**On cloud nine**
	Meaning: blissfully happy; joyous Anaadi was ***on cloud nine*** when she won the scholar's badge.
377.	**On pins and needles**
	Meaning: waiting anxiously for something; extremely nervous I was ***on pins and needles*** until I got the phone call that the plane had landed safely.
378.	**On tenterhooks**
	Meaning: uncertain, anxious, very tense; in painful suspense about how something will turn out The police was ***on tenterhooks*** to nab the offender.
379.	**On the ball**
	Meaning: alert; effective; skillful; knowledgeable Those who are selected for the hot seat in KBC program, always prefer their friends ***on the ball*** to be consulted.
380.	**On the horns of a dilemma**
	Meaning: having to choose between two unavoidable options Having selected for P.O. in bank and Inspector in Police, he was ***on the horns of a dilemma, what to join and what to leave.***
381.	**On the hot seat**
	Meaning: in a difficult or uncomfortable position When Akshay was found absent from duty, he was really ***on the hot seat.***
382.	**On the rocks**
	Meaning: financially ruined or wrecked; near disaster; finished I need a loan because of my dog-walking business is ***on the rocks.***
383.	**On the ropes**
	Meaning: almost failing; on the verge of collapse; nearly ruined Because of Covid-19 pandemic, a number of businessmen are ***on the ropes.***
384.	**On the spur of the moment**
	Meaning: suddenly; acting without thinking about it first, impulsively He took an immediate decision ***on the spur of the moment*** to take accident victims to the hospitals.
385.	**On the tip of your tongue**
	Meaning: temporarily forgotten but at the point where one can almost say it The name of the song was ***on the tip of her tongue,*** but she could not remember it fast enough to win the contest.
386.	**On the warpath**
	Meaning: in a very angry mood; infuriated Mr. Sharma is ***on the warpath*** because his car broke down again.
387.	**On top of the world**
	Meaning: feeling extremely happy When my first book got published, I was ***on top of the world.***
388.	**Once in a blue moon**
	Meaning: almost never; very seldom; hardly ever The teacher is tough, but ***once in a blue moon*** she does not give us homework.
389.	**One good turn deserves another**
	Meaning: one good deed should be paid back with another One must always recognize others' contributions. ***One good turn deserves another.***
390.	**Open a can of worms**
	Meaning: to cause trouble; to set unpleasant events in motion If you mention my report card to my mother, you will ***open a can of worms.***
391.	**Other side of the coin**
	Meaning: opposite side or point of view He conducts in public decently but in his private life, you can see the ***other side of the coin.***
392.	**Out of sight, out of mind**
	Meaning: if you do not see something for a long time, you'll eventually stop thinking about it It is the prevalent practice that one you go away from someone it means ***out of sight, out of mind.***

393.	**Out of the frying pan and into the fire**
	Meaning: from a bad situation into one that is worse The thief escaped from the dog and ran into a policeman landing himself *out of frying pan into the fire.*

P

394.	**Penny-wise and pound-foolish**
	Meaning: careful in small matters but carless about important things; saving small amounts of money while wasting large amounts Mrs. Sharma makes cut on her health expenses but wastes too much money on unnecessary things. It is like *penny-wise and pound-foolish.*
395.	**People who live in glass houses should not throw stones**
	Meaning: you should not criticize others if you are just as bad as they are He complained about her driving, but he has already had two accidents. *People who live in glass houses should not throw stones*
396.	**Piece of cake**
	Meaning: an especially easy and pleasant task Writing an essay on any topic is just a *piece of cake* for Rajesh.
397.	**Play cat and mouse**
	Meaning: to tease or fool someone She *plays cat and mouse* with her little brother, pretending to hand him a lollipop, then taking it away when he reaches for it.
398.	**Play fast and loose**
	Meaning: to do whatever pleases you without caring about what will happen to others Promising help and dodging at a critical moment is not good. You should not *play fast and loose* with your friends.
399.	**Play second fiddle**
	Meaning: to be a follower; to be in an inferior position The employees habitual of flattery always *play second fiddle* to the bosses.
400.	**Play with fire**
	Meaning: to take an unnecessary and dangerous risk; to court danger Openly intimidating your neighbor in front of all was no less than *playing with fire.*
401.	**Point of no return**
	Meaning: the position or time after which it is impossible to go back, change your mind, or do something different We cannot cancel the show now. We have reserved the theater and sold tickets. We have reached the *point of no return.*
402.	**Poor as a church mouse**
	Meaning: very poor; poverty-stricken The Sharmas used to be wealthy, but after the stock market crash, they were as *poor as a church mouse.*
403.	**Pour oil on troubled waters**
	Meaning: to calm an angry quarrel My brothers were having a terrible fight in the car, but my mother *poured oil in troubled waters* by saying they were both right.
404.	**Power behind the throne**
	Meaning: the actual, but unrecognized, person in charge Gandhi family runs the Congress Party though Sonia Gandhi's not the President, but she is the real *power behind the throne.*
405.	**Pull a rabbit out of a hat**
	Meaning: to produce something that is needed as if by magic; to unexpectedly find a solution to a problem We were very hungry, and suddenly Mr. Jindal took some cookies out of his pocket. It was like *pulling a rabbit out of a hat.*
406.	**Pull no punches**
	Meaning: to hit as hard as possible; to attack with full force; to be perfectly honest; to not hold back Tell me what you thought of my acting. Do not *pull any punches.*
407.	**Pull out all the stops**
	Meaning: to do everything possible to succeed; to do something as enthusiastically as you can He *pulled out all the stops* to persuade parents for love marriage.

408.	**Pull strings**
	Meaning: to exert behind-the-scenes influence; to secretly control others from a distance as if they were puppets The Party President ***pulls strings*** of all party workers after election defeat.
409.	**Pull the wool over your eyes.**
	Meaning: to fool, deceive, or trick someone He was ***pulling the wool over the eyes*** of his parents and instead of focusing on studies he was just watching movies.
410.	**Pull your leg**
	Meaning: to tease or fool someone; to jokingly try to lie to somebody Oh, do not get so annoyed at them for teasing you. They are just ***pulling your leg.***
411.	**Pull yourself together**
	Meaning: to regain control over one's emotions and become calm after being very upset Calm down, ***pull yourself together,*** and plan a new trip.
412.	**Put all your eggs into one basket**
	Meaning: to risk everything you have at once on a single idea or plan; to commit all your resources at one time One should apply for different jobs instead of trying only for Civil Services just like ***putting all your eggs into one basket.***
413.	**Put the cart before the horse**
	Meaning: do things in backward or reverse order If you pull your shoes on before your socks, you were ***putting the cart before the horse.***
414.	**Put your best foot forward**
	Meaning: to make the best attempt possible; to do your best to make the greatest impression you can When you go in for your interview, try to ***put your best foot forward.***

Q

415.	**Quiet as a mouse**
	Meaning: silent or still; making very little noise; saying nothing; hushed, subdued ***Quiet as a mouse,*** she slipped back into her dormitory after hours.

R

416.	**Rain on your parade**
	Meaning: to spoil someone's day, performance, special occasion, celebration, plans Heavy rains spoiled the marriage celebrations and it ***rained on his parade.***
417.	**Raining cats and dogs**
	Meaning: to rain very heavily; to pour It is ***raining cats and dogs,*** and our picnic is ruined.
418.	**Rat race**
	Meaning: a fierce, unending, stressful competition in business or society All Indian youngsters, without evaluating their potentials run ***rat race*** of Civil Services preparations.
419.	**Rats abandoning a sinking ship**
	Meaning: disloyal people who desert a failing enterprise before it is too late Like ***rats abandoning a sinking ship,*** they switched to the other candidate when theirs began to lose.
420.	**Read between the lines**
	Meaning: to discern the true, hidden meaning or fact in any document or action The spiritual mystic show always advised to ***read between the lines.***
421.	**Red-carpet treatment**
	Meaning: great respect and hospitality given to someone important; special treatment The Booker Prize winner is given ***red-carpet treatment.***
422.	**Red-letter day**
	Meaning: a day remembered as especially happy and significant 15 August, 1947 is a ***red-letter day*** in the Indian history.
423.	**Red tape**
	Meaning: excessive formality and time-consuming, rigid adherence to rules and regulations ***Red-tapism*** is the most serious malady afflicting Indian bureaucracy.

424.	**Ring a bell**
	Meaning: to sound familiar; to call something to mind; to stir a vague memory I do not remember her face, but her name ***rings a bell.***
425.	**Roll with the punches**
	Meaning: to adjust to a difficult situation Try not to be too discouraged with your new job. Just ***roll with the punches*** a while.
426.	**Rolling stone gathers no moss**
	Meaning: a person who is always on the move or who changes jobs often will not be able to save or keep much He has changed 5 jobs in 2 years which goes against his credentials as a ***rolling stone gathers no moss.***
427.	**Rome was not built in a day**
	Meaning: a difficult or important goal or task cannot be achieved quickly or all at once Writing a book for IAS Examination is not an overnight job as ***Rome was not built in a day.***
428.	**Rotten apple spoils the barrel**
	Meaning: one bad person or thing may spoil an entire group A tiny group of kids starts fights in our school, and people think that one ***rotten apple spoils the barrel.***
429.	**Round peg in a square hole**
	Meaning: a person whose abilities, character, or personality are not suited to his or her position Though Sunita opted for Science on her parent's insistence but it is as she is ***round peg in a square hole.***
430.	**Rub the wrong way**
	Meaning: to annoy and irritate someone; to handle someone insensitivity Repeated reminders to the bosses for promotion proved as rubbing the wrong way.
431.	**Rule with an iron hand**
	Meaning: to be a strict, stern, something harsh ruler Sardar Patel could make unification of princely Indian states because he ***ruled with an iron hand.***
432.	**Run off at the mouth**
	Meaning: to talk too much; to talk nonstop Ravi keeps ***running off at the mouth*** about University Faculty.

S

433.	**Salt of the earth**
	Meaning: a person or group considered to be the finest, most admirable, and noble The martyrs like Bhagat Singh and Subhash Chander Bose are considered ***salt of the earth.***
434.	**Same old song and dance**
	Meaning: dull, nonsense that has been said many times before; a lie or excuse that's been told before Mr. Saxena keeps blowing the same trumpet like the ***same old song and dance.***
435.	**Save for a rainy day**
	Meaning: to save for a time of need; to put something away for the future It is advisable to make savings so as to ***save some money for a rainy day.***
436.	**Scarce as hen's teeth**
	Meaning: very, very rare or totally nonexistent During the holidays, seats on any flight were as ***scarce as hen's teeth.***
437.	**School of hard knocks**
	Meaning: challenging experiences that can teach you a lot Mrs. Suri never went to college, but she learned how to be successful in the ***school of hard knocks.***
438.	**Scratch the surface**
	Meaning: to just begin to deal with a problem; to deal with only a very small part of a subject Scientists have only ***scratched the surface*** in finding the vaccine for Covid-19.
439.	**See eye to eye**
	Meaning: to agree fully; to have the same opinion My parents and I do not always ***see eye to eye*** about my allowance.

440.	**Sell like hotcakes**
	Meaning: to sell quickly, effortlessly, and in quantity My book LA/ LR is ***selling like hotcakes*** for the last 10 years.
441.	**Set your teeth on edge**
	Meaning: to cause annoyance or discomfort to someone When I watch any Indian media channel except NDTV, it sets my teeth on edge
442.	**Settle an old score**
	Meaning: to get back at; to get revenge for past wrongs The Ruling Parties in Power always try to ***settle an old score*** with opponents.
443.	**Shape up or ship out**
	Meaning: to correct your behaviour, improve your performance Neetu has been asked to be regular and punctual to ***shape up or ship out.***
444.	**Shoe is on the other foot**
	Meaning: the situation is now the opposite of what it once was; places are reversed Once your drove right by me in the rain and did not stop. Now the ***shoe is on the other foot,*** I would be driving, you were walking.
445.	**Shoot from the hip**
	Meaning: to speak or act without first thinking about the consequences Mr. Singh is known for his impulsive behaviour, he just ***shoots from the hip*** and lands himself into a trouble.
446.	**Shot in the arm**
	Meaning: something that lifts your spirits, energy, and confidence Mr. Sharma was feeling pretty low in the hospital, but your letter really gave him a ***shot in the arm.***
447.	**Show must go on**
	Meaning: the proceedings must continue regardless of any catastrophe or difficulty; nothing can stop what has been planned The bride had planned a wedding outdoors, and even when it rained, she insisted that the ***show must go on.***
448.	**Show your true colors**
	Meaning: to reveal what you are really like Fair weather friends ***show their true colors*** in bad times.
449.	**Sight for sore eyes**
	Meaning: a most welcome, unexpected sight; a pleasant surprise After prolonged illness, when the reports of gradual recovery came, Mr. Sharma saw a ***sight for the sore eyes.***
450.	**Sink or swim**
	Meaning: to fall or succeed by one's own efforts without anyone's help or interference Once I had taken the risk to run the institute, it was ***sink or swim*** situation.
451.	**Sitting pretty**
	Meaning: to be in a lucky, superior, or advantageous position Indian hockey team had scored four goals in the first half, so it was ***sitting pretty.***
452.	**Six of one and a half dozen of the other**
	Meaning: one and the same thing; nothing to choose between; equal I do not care if we eat veg or non-veg food. To me, it is ***six of one and a half dozen of the other.***
453.	**Skeleton in your closet**
	Meaning: a shameful and shocking secret that people try to keep hidden Everyone has bright and dark facets of life, but people prefer to keep dark as ***skeleton in the closet.***
454.	**Sky is the limit**
	Meaning: there is no limit to what you can spend or how far you can go or what you can achieve In the field of journalism, ***sky is the limit.***
455.	**Slow on the draw**
	Meaning: slow to understand or figure something out; slow to respond or react; not alert; not a deep thinker Some of Albert Einstein's teachers thought he was a little ***slow on the draw.***

456.	**Smell a rat**
	Meaning: to be suspicious; to feel that something is wrong Although everything looked all right, the investigator *smelled a rat.*
457.	**Smell like a rose**
	Meaning: to look good in a bad situation; to avoid a damaged reputation when involved with corruption; to appear pure and innocent Though the officer was caught red-handed while taking bribe, but he came *smelling like a rose.*
458.	**Snake in the grass**
	Meaning: an unfaithful, untrustworthy, underhanded, and deceitful person; a traitor Beware of opportunists, they are *snake in the grass.*
459.	**Snug as a bug in a rug**
	Meaning: cozy and comfortable; safe and secure Granma tucked her in, as *snug as a bug in a rug,* shut off the lights, and tiptoed out of the room.
460.	**Sow your wild oats**
	Meaning: to behave wildly and foolishly, especially when young Can you believe that our quiet, dignified grandfather *sowed his wild oats* when he was just out of college?
461.	**Spare the rod and spoil the child**
	Meaning: to physically punish children when they misbehave so they will learn to behave properly in the future *"Spare the rod and spoil the child",* practice is quiet imperative to make the children behave properly.
462.	**Spick-and-span**
	Meaning: extremely clean, tidy, neat Mr. Balwant Chaudhary always had *spick-and-span* surroundings and lived life in the same style.
463.	**Spill the beans**
	Meaning: to give away a secret to someone who is not supposed to know it He was afraid that his wife would *spill the beans.*

464.	**Spitting image**
	Meaning: a perfect resemblance; an exact likeness He must be Aarav's father. He is the *spitting image* of Aarav
465.	**Stick-in-the-mud**
	Meaning: a person with old-fashioned ideas who avoids anything new, ignores progress, and fights change Mr. Wilson is still stuck up in old duddy fuddy ideas. He is just *stick-in-the-mud.*
466.	**Stick to your guns**
	Meaning: to stand firm and hold to one's position in the face of opposition; to stand up for your rights no matter what trouble you get into In the sharp opposition of new farmers' laws, the entire farmers' community *stuck to its guns.*
467.	**Stick your neck out**
	Meaning: to take a bold or dangerous risk; to expose yourself to criticism You should not have to be the only one to complaint. Why should you *stick your neck out?*
468.	**Still waters run deep**
	Meaning: somebody can be more knowledgeable or emotional than he or she first appears to be; a silent person may be intelligent Arnav was a quiet student, but he was very brilliant. *Still waters run deep.*
469.	**Stir up a hornet's nest**
	Meaning: to make many people furious; to cause trouble The new farmers laws have *stirred up a hornet's nest* all over India.
470.	**Straight from the horse's mouth**
	Meaning: directly from the person or place that is the most reliable source or the best authority I got it *straight from the horse's mouth* that there is going to be a surgical strike against Pakistan.

471. Straight from the shoulder

Meaning: frankly, honestly

This is ***straight from the shoulder:*** I do not want to share room with you because you smoke.

472. Strike a happy medium

Meaning: to find a compromise to a problem; to find a sensible solution midway between two opposite desires

In order to pacify the agitating farmers, the government has to ***strike a happy medium.***

473. Strike while the iron is hot

Meaning: to act at the most favourable time or moment to get the best results; to take advantage of favourable conditions

One must have patience to think for the best opportunity and must ***strike while the iron is hot.***

474. Stuffed shirt

Meaning: a self-important person who shows a lot of phony dignity

The chairman of the board is such a ***stuffed shirt.***

475. Swallow hook, line, and sinker

Meaning: to believe a story completely without questioning it; to be very gullible

I told him a ghost story, and he ***swallowed it hook, line, and sinker.***

476. Swan song

Meaning: the final, farewell performance of an actor or singer; one's last words or actions

The Hindi movie Chichore was the ***swan song*** of Sushant Singh Rajput.

477. Sweep under the rug

Meaning: to hide or ignore unpleasant matters

Her parents found out about her failing grades, even though she tried to ***sweep them under the rug.***

478. Sweep you off your feet

Meaning: to make a favourable impression; to effect with strong emotion or enthusiasm; to overcome someone with feelings of love or happiness so strong that he or she can't resist you

Being the topper of IAS 2020, Kanchan Singla ***swept everyone off his/ her feet.***

T

479. Take off your hat to someone

Meaning: to admire or praise someone for a notable accomplishment

Even with her arm in a sling, she cooked a marvelous meal. I have to ***take my hat off to her.***

480. Take someone under your wing

Meaning: to help, guide, or protect someone

Looking at deteriorating results, the father ***took son under his wing*** for final Boards Examination.

481. Take the bitter with the sweet

Meaning: to accept the bad things that happen along with the good

Life in sum total of good and bad happenings, it is better to learn to ***take the bitter with the sweet.***

482. Take the bull by the horns

Meaning: to act bravely in a troublesome situation

Covid-19 pandemic is a grim reality, but everyone has to ***take the bull by horns.***

483. Take with a grain of salt

Meaning: to not believe completely; to be doubtful

Happy Singh tends to exaggerate. ***Take*** what he says ***with a grain of salt.***

484. Talk through your hat

Meaning: to talk nonsense

Do not let what Micky said upset you. He is just ***talking through his hat.***

485. Throw caution to the wind

Meaning: to take a huge risk; to act recklessly and hastily

Many people are ***throwing cautions to the wind*** without wearing mask and not maintaining social distance inspite of Covid-19 prevalence.

486. Throw cold water on something

Meaning: to say or do something discouraging; to dampen one's enthusiasm for something

Rekha's father refused her to take part in dance competition and ***threw cold water on her plans.***

487.	**Throw your hat into the ring**
	Meaning: to announce one's candidacy for election to office; to issue a challenge Dayal Partap ***threw his hat into the ring*** today. He is running for post of President High Court Bar Association
488.	**Tickle your funny bone**
	Meaning: to make you laugh; to amuse somebody Kapil Sharma show literally ***tickles everyone's funny bone.***
489.	**Tighten your belt**
	Meaning: to live on less money; to make sacrifices and lower one's standard of living Everyone is constrained to ***tighten his/ her belt*** because of shrinking sources of income in the Covid-19 times.
490.	**Till the cows come home**
	Meaning: for a long, long time I'll stand here ***till the cows come home*** unless you pay me back the money, I lent you.
491.	**Tip of the iceberg**
	Meaning: just a small part of a larger problem or a worse situation In Chemistry, learning the symbols for the elements is just the ***tip of the iceberg.***
492.	**Toe the line**
	Meaning: do what you are supposed to do; obey all rules and orders All the employees were supposed to ***toe the line*** and follow all the regulations of the company or he was out of a job.
493.	**Too many cooks spoil the broth**
	Meaning: a project is set back rather than helped by too many organizers; the more people who work on one project, the worse it will turn out The decorations look terrible because the committee could not agree on anything. ***Too many cooks spoil the broth.***
494.	**Top banana**
	Meaning: the leading comedian in a variety show; a boss Kapil Sharma has been a ***top banana*** in Indian comedian shows.

495.	**Tough nut to crack**
	Meaning: something very complicated to understand or to do; an extremely tough or thorny problem to solve Mr. Sharma never seeks help of anyone and never open up his heart; he is a ***tough nut to crack.***
496.	**True-blue**
	Meaning: very loyal, dependable, and faithful Ahmed Patel, who expired recently, was a ***true-blue*** supporter of Congress.
497.	**Turn over a new leaf**
	Meaning: to correct one's behaviour or attitude; to begin anew; to make a fresh start If you have not been feeling fit, maybe it is time to ***turn over a new leaf*** and start exercising.
498.	**Turn the tables**
	Meaning: to reverse the situation; to make the opposite happen Our school football team ***tuned the tables*** at the last moment and won the match.

U

499.	**Under the table**
	Meaning: in secret, dishonestly; not out in the open Bribe ***under the table*** is a norm in India – nobody minds.
500.	**Up a creek without a paddle**
	Meaning: in deep trouble and unable to do anything about it; in serious trouble Ravi lost his notes just one day before exams, he is ***up a creek without a paddle.***
501.	**Up against the wall**
	Meaning: in big trouble; in a difficult or desperate situation The Covid-19 pandemic has left the large number of employees ***up against the wall.***
502.	**Upper crust**
	Meaning: high society; social or financial elite; important people The poor student fell hopelessly in love with a girl from the ***upper crust.***

503.	**Upset the applecart**
	Meaning: to spoil or interfere with a plan; to obstruct progress; to mess everything up by surprise or accident The elder sister *upset the applecart* when she came to know about younger sister trip to Agra.
504	**Walking on air**
	Meaning: to be exuberantly happy, excited, and joyful When she found out that she was having a baby, she left the doctor's clinic *walking on air.*
505.	**Walk on eggs**
	Meaning: to be very cautious; to proceed warily Ashima was *walking on eggs* when she tried to return the necklace she had borrowed without asking.
506.	**Wash your hands of something**
	Meaning: to withdraw from something; to end one's association or responsibility for something; to disavow, disclaim, or disown I am tired of arguing with my lab partners, so I am *washing my hands of the science project.*
507.	**Water over the dam**
	Meaning: Something that is past and cannot be changed Lost your ring last week? It's *water over the dam now.*
508.	**Wear your heart on your sleeve**
	Meaning: to show one's emotions and feelings openly A weak personality person *wears his heart on his sleeves.*
509.	**Wet behind the ears**
	Meaning: young, inexperienced, and immature The big companies prefer the experienced people but they don't engage those who are *wet behind the ears.*
510.	**Wet blanket**
	Meaning: a person who spoils other people's fun by being depressing, dull, sour, nagging, or humorless I never prefer to invite Mr. Singh in any gathering because he is a *wet blanket.*
511.	**What's good for the goose is good for the gander**
	Meaning: a rule or method of treatment that applies to one person or group must also apply to others, especially your mate If the girls team cannot travel to the championship, neither should the boys team. *What's good for the goose is good for the gander.*
512.	**Wheel and deal**
	Meaning: to skillfully and aggressively make big plans with important business, usually to earn a lot of money Sasha's uncle is an international businessman who *wheels and deals* all over the world.
513.	**When the cat's away, the mice will play**
	Meaning: when the person in charge is absent, people will usually do as they please and take advantage of the freedom It is a joke here in India about husband- wife relationship that in the absence of wife, the husband is free as when the cat is away, the mice will play.
514.	**Where there's smoke, there's fire**
	Meaning: there is always a basis for a rumor, no matter how untrue it appears There cannot be smoke without fire meaning there by rumours also have background.
515.	**Which way the wind blows**
	Meaning: the direction in which something is going or may go; how matters stand Before privatizing the electricity, Chandigarh Corporation Mayor just wanted to know *which way the wind blows.*
516.	**White elephant**
	Meaning: any possession that is useless, unwanted, or costs a lot of money to keep He is good for nothing just like a *white elephant* and an unnecessary burden on the family.
517.	**Wild-goose chase**
	Meaning: a useless or hopeless search, especially because something does not exist or cannot be found It is a *wild-goose chase* trying to discover from whom you got infected with Covid-19.

518.	**With flying colors**
	Meaning: with ease and great success; in triumph As expected, Nippun passed his tests ***with flying colours.***
519.	**Without batting an eyelash**
	Meaning: without showing emotion or interest; impassive Ranveer Kapoor accepted the award ***without batting an eyelash.***
520.	**Wolf in sheep's clothing**
	Meaning: somebody who appears to be harmless but is really dangerous The new landlord acts friendly, but he might be a ***wolf in sheep's clothing.***
521.	**Word of mouth**
	Meaning: by one person telling another; by speaking, rather than writing The movie got bad reviews, but it became popular by ***word by mouth.***
522.	**Worth your salt**
	Meaning: deserving the pay or reward that you get In order to get a raise, you have to prove that you are ***worth your salt.***
523.	**Wrong side of the tracks**
	Meaning: from a less socially desirable part of town; the poor, unfashionable Mukesh's father was upset when he started dating a girl from the ***wrong side of the tracks.***

Y

524.	**You can lead a horse to water but you can't make him drink**
	Meaning: you can encourage, but not force, someone to do something You can guide someone to do something worthwhile but cannot make it happen as ***you can lead a horse to water but you can't make him drink.***
525.	**You can't teach an old dog new tricks**
	Meaning: people who find it difficult or impossible to change their ways or adjust to new ideas The old generations find it difficult to develop taste for junk food. ***You cannot teach an old dog new tricks.***

IDIOMS AND PHRASES MCQs

CATEGORY – ONE

DIRECTIONS: ***Every idiom/ phrase provided in bold & italics is followed by four options. You have to find out the correct option from the given ones. NOTA means None Of The Above given answers.***

1. ***All agog***

(a) restless (b) everybody

(c) almighty (d) all ready

2. ***A snake in the grass***

(a) unreliable person

(b) secret or hidden enemy

(c) unforeseen happening

(d) unrecognisable danger

3. ***A tall order***

(a) a big problem

(b) a task difficult to perform

(c) a big demand

(d) untenable claim

4. ***All and sundry***

(a) all of a sudden

(b) greater share

(c) everyone without distinction

(d) completion of work

5. ***A storm in a teacup***

(a) a danger signal

(b) a great noise

(c) much excitement over something trivial

(d) unexpected event

6. ***Adam's ale***

(a) water (b) grace

(c) wine (d) pleasure

7. ***A jaundiced eye***

(a) angry (b) jealousy

(c) prejudice (d) a generous view

8. ***A bull in a china shop***

(a) a person who becomes too excited where no excitement is warranted

(b) a person who is very ugly but loves the beautiful things of life

(c) a person who is rough and clumsy where skill and care are required

(d) a person who takes a sadistic delight in harming innocent people

9. ***At one's back and call***

(a) to be in an advantageous position

(b) enjoying oneself without caring for others

(c) to be always at one's service

(d) to be under one's subjugation

10. ***By fair means or foul***

(a) in any way, honest or dishonest

(b) without difficulty

(c) having been instigated

(d) without using common sense

11. ***By the rule of thumb***

(a) by cheating and deception

(b) by the use of force

(c) by practical experience which is rather rough

(d) by the use of trickery

12. ***Castles in the air***

(a) perfect plans (b) visionary projects

(c) fanciful schemes (d) romantic designs

(e) ideal projects

13. ***Don't stick your neck out***
(a) move
(b) invite trouble unnecessarily
(c) interfere
(d) look outside

14. ***Do not add fuel to the fire***
(a) aggravate trouble (b) create problem
(c) calm down (d) harass

15. ***Hush money***
(a) easy money
(b) money overdue
(c) bribe paid to secure silence
(d) money earned by wrong means

16. ***In a jiffy***
(a) in a hurry (b) in a moment
(c) in a funny mood (d) immediately

17. ***Leave one to sink or swim***
(a) to put one in difficulty
(b) to be in a dilemma
(c) not to help one
(d) to leave to one's fate

18. ***Pin–money***
(a) money paid for compensation
(b) bribery
(c) allowance made to a lady for her expenses
(d) alimony

19. ***Spick and span***
(a) a ready–made thing
(b) neat and clean
(c) garrulous
(d) outspoken

20. Seema is a little ***hard of hearing***
(a) deaf (b) inaudible
(c) insensitive (d) disinterested

21. ***To turn over a new leaf***
(a) to change the old habits and adopt new ones
(b) to cover up one's faults by wearing new marks
(c) to change completely one's course of action
(d) to shift attention to new problems after having studied the old ones thoroughly

22. ***To frame a person***
(a) to make one appear guilty
(b) a narrow escape
(c) to befool someone
(d) to praise someone

23. ***To cross swords***
(a) to defend (b) to fight
(c) to rob (d) to kill

24. ***To give up the ghost***
(a) to become rational (b) to suffer
(c) to fight evil forces (d) to die

25. ***Hobson's choice***
(a) feeling of strength
(b) feeling of insecurity
(c) excellent choice
(d) accept or leave the offer

26. ***To be at loggerheads***
(a) to face stiff opposition
(b) to have tough encounter
(c) to tax one's mind and body
(d) to be at enmity or strife

27. ***To talk through one's hat***
(a) to talk wisdom (b) to speak fluently
(c) to speak at random (d) to talk nonsense

28. ***To snap one's fingers***
(a) to accept immediately
(b) to be anxious
(c) to become contemptuous of
(d) to speak abruptly

29. ***To lose one's head***
(a) to become nervous
(b) to become confused and over excited
(c) to lose the balance
(d) to go mad

30. ***To smell a rat***
(a) to misunderstand
(b) to suspect a trick or deceit
(c) to see hidden meaning
(d) none of these

31. *To hit below the belt*

(a) to harm unfairly

(b) to work confidentially

(c) to hit the correct mark

(d) to harm unfairly

32. *To get cold feet*

(a) to fall sick

(b) to run for life

(c) to become discourteous

(d) to be afraid

33. *To take a leap in the dark*

(a) to do a task secretly

(b) to run for life

(c) to do a hazardous thing without any idea of the result

(d) to be afraid

34. *To be at daggers drawn*

(a) to threaten one

(b) to be frightened

(c) to be bitter enemy

(d) to be ready to face danger

35. *To turn up one's nose at a thing*

(a) to treat it with contemptuous dislike or disgust

(b) to show eagerness to have something

(c) to start to grapple with it

(d) to show indifference

36. *To save one's face*

(a) to oppose (b) to hide oneself

(c) to say plainly (d) to evade disgrace

37. *To throw dust in one's eyes*

(a) to harm someone (b) to show false things

(c) to deceive (d) to make blind

38. *To be rolling in money*

(a) borrowing money liberally

(b) wasting a lot of money

(c) spending more than his income

(d) very rich

39. *To get into hot waters*

(a) to get into trouble

(b) to be impatient

(c) to be in a confused state of mind

(d) to suffer a huge financial loss

40. *To read between the lines*

(a) to suspect

(b) to concentrate

(c) to grasp the hidden meaning

(d) to read carefully

41. *To be lost in the cloud*

(a) to be concealed from view

(b) to be perplexed

(c) to find oneself in a very uncomfortable position

(d) to meet with one's death

42. *To turn the tables*

(a) to change completely the position of disadvantage

(b) to create chaos

(c) to change the sorry scheme

(d) to oppose

(e) to defeat

43. *To keep the ball rolling*

(a) to work constantly

(b) to make the best use of

(c) to earn more and more

(d) to keep the conversation going

44. *To play fast and loose*

(a) to be winning sometimes and losing at other times

(b) to play with someone's feelings

(c) to play tricks

(d) to beguile others

45. *To give currency*

(a) to misinterpret

(b) to bestow importance

(c) to originate

(d) to make publicly known

46. ***To lose face***

(a) to be helpless (b) to look angry

(c) to look vacant (d) to be humiliated

47. ***To bite one's lips***

(a) to have double (b) to be angry

(c) to laugh at others (d) to feel sorry

48. ***To blow hot and cold***

(a) to be untrustworthy

(b) changing weather

(c) to be rich and poor frequently

(d) to be inconsistent

49. ***To set the people by ears***

(a) to insult and disgrace the people

(b) to box the people

(c) to excite people to a quarrel

(d) to punish heavily

50. ***To hit the jackpot***

(a) to inherit money

(b) to gamble

(c) to become bankrupt

(d) to make money unexpectedly

51. ***To fight to the bitter end***

(a) to die fighting

(b) to drink little

(c) to carry on a contest regardless of consequences

(d) to fight to the last point of enemy position

52. ***To give a false colouring***

(a) to be dishonest

(b) to misrepresent

(c) to conceal the facts

(d) to submit the false report

53. ***To see eye to eye with***

(a) to stare fixedly (b) to agree

(c) to take revenge (d) to be angry

54. ***To be in two minds***

(a) to work on somebody else's advice

(b) to be dominated by someone else

(c) to be in a critical state

(d) to be uncertain

55. ***To show the white feather***

(a) to show arrogance

(b) to show signs of cowardice

(c) to become polite

(d) to seek peace

56. ***To take the wind out of another's sails***

(a) to defeat the motives of another

(b) to manouevre to mislead another on the high seas

(c) to anticipate another and to gain advantage over him

(d) to cause harm to another

57. ***To carry the coal to newcastle***

(a) to do unnecessary things

(b) to work hard

(c) to do menial jobs

(d) to finish a job

58. ***To turn the cover***

(a) to pass the crises

(b) to take a new way of life

(c) to hide the reality

(d) to work hard

59. ***The pros and cons***

(a) good and evil

(b) for and against a thing

(c) former and latter

(d) foul and fair

60. ***To hit the nail on the head***

(a) to guess right

(b) to hit the target

(c) to settle the old score

(d) to catch someone nappping

61. ***To run amuck***

(a) to feel exhausted

(b) to run a race

(c) to run to somebody's help

(d) to run about in frenzy

62. ***To be at one's finger's end***

(a) to be highly perplexed

(b) to be completely conversant with

(c) to count things

(d) to be hopeless

63. *To be as old as the hills*

(a) to be wise and learned
(b) not being worth the age
(c) to be very ancient
(d) to be old but foolish

64. *To show one's teeth*

(a) to adopt a threatening attitude
(b) to ridicule
(c) to be humble
(d) to face difficulties

65. *To pour oil in troubled water*

(a) to instigate
(b) to foment trouble
(c) to calm a quarrel with soothing words
(d) to add to the trouble

66. *To play on a fiddle*

(a) to be busy over trifles
(b) to play upon a musical instrument
(c) to be busy over important matter
(d) to play an important role

67. *To mind one's P's and Q's*

(a) to be careful of one's accounts
(b) to be cautious
(c) to be careful of one's personality
(d) to be careful about one's language

68. *To break the ice*

(a) to end the hostility
(b) to start a conversation
(c) to end up partnership
(d) to start quarreling

69. *To pull one's socks up*

(a) to depart (b) to prepare
(c) to get ready (d) to try–hard

70. *To rule the roost*

(a) to advance in harmony
(b) to preserve oneself from harm
(c) to move forward on the same path
(d) to domineer over others with whom one is associated

71. *To keep somebody at bay*

(a) to make someone a close friend
(b) to keep at distance
(c) to keep someone in bad condition
(d) to face the challenge

72. *To cock a snook at somebody*

(a) to make a rude gesture
(b) to ridicule someone
(c) to help somebody secretly
(d) to deceive somebody

73. *Ad hock*

(a) for the special purpose
(b) arranged systematically
(c) arranged in order
(d) none of these

74. *Raining cats and dogs*

(a) heavily (b) drizzling
(c) scatteredly (d) thinly

75. *To look down one's nose*

(a) to show anger
(b) to retaliate
(c) to insult in the presence of others
(d) to regard with contempt

76. *Sought after*

(a) highly paid (b) pursued by
(c) in great demand (d) with great talent

77. *To set the Thames on fire*

(a) do a heroic deed
(b) do something to suit one's own purpose
(c) to turn someone alive
(d) destroy with fire

78. *Wet blanket*

(a) good companion (b) warm and friendly
(c) who kills joy (d) helpful

79. *To bury the hatchet*

(a) to obtain money
(b) to make friends
(c) to keep a secret
(d) to make peace

80. ***To win laurels***

(a) to be victorious in a game
(b) to memorize
(c) to be disappointed
(d) to earn great prestige/ honour

81. ***To put two and two together***

(a) to mix several things
(b) to make an arithmetical calculation
(c) to keep people in pairs
(d) to deduce from given facts

82. ***To beat about the bush***

(a) to cut down trees
(b) to plant more trees
(c) to hurt someone
(d) not to come to the point

83. ***Watch his step***

(a) behave with caution
(b) observe the threshold
(c) walk carefully
(d) watch his friends

84. ***A bird's eye view***

(a) a beautiful view (b) a narrow view
(c) an overview (d) an ugly view

85. ***To be in hot water***

(a) to be in trouble (b) to bath in hot water
(c) to jump into a pool (d) to commit suicide

86. ***To keep in abeyance***

(a) in a state of permanence
(b) in a state of emergency
(c) in a state of suspension
(d) in a state of revision

87. ***To be in a fix***

(a) in pain (b) in distress
(c) depressed (d) in a difficult situation

88. ***To grease the palm***

(a) to rub oil on the hand
(b) to lubricate the machine parts
(c) to bribe
(d) to cut the tree
(d) made people relaxed and comfortable

89. ***Sit on the fence***

(a) to be in a tricky situation
(b) to be relaxed and comfortable
(c) avoid making a decision or choice
(d) to be defeated and dejected

90. ***A sacred cow***

(a) a person never to be criticized
(b) a saintly person
(c) a helpful person
(d) a very religious person

91. ***At one's wit's end***

(a) to be very witty
(b) to confuse others
(c) to be completely confused
(d) to minimize expenses

92. ***Have a finger in every pie***

(a) to be greed (b) to be meddlesome
(c) to be efficient (d) to be quarrelsome

93. ***The jury is out***

(a) no decision has been reached
(b) a jury member is absent
(c) the entire jury decided to stay out of the proceedings
(d) the jury has taken a break between hearings

94. ***Took to her heels***

(a) bent down
(b) ran off
(c) kicked off her shoes
(d) rubbed her heels

95. ***Plain sailing***

(a) was very easy (b) was complicated
(c) was competitive (d) was uncomfortable

96. ***A bolt from the blue***

(a) struck by thunder (b) a piece of bad luck
(c) a flash of lighting (d) a complete surprise

97. ***Gift of the gab***

(a) lucky
(b) a big surprise
(c) an honest person
(d) persuasive way of speaking

98. *A wild goose chase*
(a) run after a bird (b) a fruitful search
(c) long pursuit (d) a fruitless pursuit

99. *A close fisted person*
(a) a powerful person (b) a miser
(c) a close friend (d) a cowardly person

100. *To feather one's nest*
(a) to harbour ill feelings
(b) to build one's house
(c) to enrich oneself when opportunity occurs
(d) to get something in abundance

101. *A close shave*
(a) a narrow escape from danger
(b) stubble
(c) very short hair
(d) hairless skin

102. *To keep up one's appearances*
(a) to make public appearances now and then
(b) to maintain one's look and appearance
(c) to keep up an outward show of prosperity
(d) to make it appear that one is not concerned

103. *To call a spade a spade*
(a) to be biased (b) to be impartial
(c) to be frank (d) to be a hypocrite

104. *A shot in the dark*
(a) be very violent
(b) an attempt to guess something
(c) to love to go out on adventures
(d) be able to work very quickly

105. *In a nut shell*
(a) writing (b) briefly
(c) angrily (d) casually

106. *From the bottom of my heart*
(a) totally (b) wholly
(c) sincerely (d) casually

107. *A hard nut to crack*
(a) a foolish search (b) a difficult problem
(c) an easy question (d) an expensive thing

108. *To cut one short*
(a) to insult one (b) to criticize one
(c) to interrupt one (d) to love one

109. *To fight tooth and nail*
(a) to fight heroically
(b) to fight like a brute
(c) to make every possible effort to win
(d) to fight a losing battle

110. *To make castles in the air*
(a) to do day-dreaming
(b) to be boastful
(c) to be conceited
(d) to be too ambitious

111. *Turn the tide*
(a) save (b) reverse a situation
(c) touch (d) spare

112. *Let the cat out of the bag*
(a) to leak out the secrets
(b) to release the cat
(c) to help the cat
(d) to kill the cat

113. *To make both ends meet*
(a) to unite
(b) to reconcile
(c) to mix
(d) to live within one's means

114. *To bell the cat*
(a) to run after the cat
(b) to avoid an encounter
(c) to run away in fear
(d) to lead and face danger

115. *Cock and bull stories*
(a) stories of birds and animals
(b) unbelievable stories
(c) stories dealing with fight
(d) stories of adventures

116. *Turn down*
(a) accept (b) reject
(c) twist (d) weave

117. *Stem the tide*
(a) save (b) stop
(c) touch (d) spare

118. ***To read between the lines***

(a) to read loudly
(b) to understand the hidden meaning of the word
(c) to do some important work
(d) to escape from reality

119. ***Feathering one's nest***

(a) enriching oneself at the expense of the public
(b) buying insurance in time
(c) taking adequate precaution against danger
(d) making a new home

120. ***Throw cold water***

(a) encourage (b) discourage
(c) attack (d) drench

121. ***Under a cloud***

(a) sheltered from the sun
(b) under suspicion
(c) out in the open
(d) get wet

122. ***Get the sack***

(a) look for a sack (b) find a sack
(c) get a call back (d) be dismissed

123. ***Die hard***

(a) unwilling to change (b) ready to change
(c) egoist (d) arrogant

124. ***At the eleventh hour***

(a) at eleven o' clock
(b) at the wrong time
(c) at the last possible moment
(d) at the initial moment

125. ***To catch a tartar***

(a) to deal with a person who is more than one's match
(b) to catch a dangerous person
(c) to trap a wanted criminal with great difficulty
(d) to meet with disaster

126. ***Kith and kin***

(a) relatives (b) neighbours
(c) villagers (d) friends

127. ***To explore every avenue***

(a) to search all streets
(b) to scout the wilderness
(c) to find adventure
(d) to try every opportunity

128. ***To shed crocodile tears***

(a) to weep profusely
(b) to pretend grief
(c) to grieve seriously (d) to mock at something

129. ***A red letter day***

(a) a dangerous day in one's life
(b) a sorrowful day in one's life
(c) an important or joyful occasion in one's life
(d) both a dangerous and a sorrowful day in one's life

130. ***Hand in glove***

(a) very difficult (b) open enemy
(c) very intimate (d) very rude

131. ***To break the ice***

(a) to shatter peace (b) to cause harm
(c) to break free (d) to initiate something

132. ***In apple pie order***

(a) last in the sequence
(b) by government order
(c) everything in its place
(d) neatly demolished

133. ***By leaps and bounds***

(a) in calculated ways (b) rapidly and speadily
(c) as proposed (d) very slowly

134. ***Wet behind the ears***

(a) skillful
(b) young and rich with experience
(c) young and without much experience
(d) hearing impaired

135. ***Carry out***

(a) bring
(b) continue
(c) complete something
(d) to take in

136. ***To cut the Gordian knot***
(a) to perform a difficult task
(b) to cut a piece of cloth
(c) to perform an easy task
(d) to do a job perfunctorily

137. ***Out of sorts***
(a) not rich (b) out of reach
(c) out of sight (d) not well

138. ***A golden mean***
(a) comfortable and easy work
(b) middle course between two extremes
(c) a sudden sad event
(d) a subject of contention

139. ***A Herculean task***
(a) an easy puzzle (b) a good contest
(c) a difficult thing (d) a hurried job

140. ***All at sea***
(a) very proud (b) overjoyed
(c) in great loss (d) excited

141. ***To cry wolf***
(a) to listen eagerly (b) to give false alarm
(c) to turn pale (d) to keep off starvation

142. ***To be above board***
(a) to have a good height
(b) to be honest in any business deal
(c) to have no doubts
(d) to try to be beautiful

143. ***The pros and cons***
(a) arguments in favour and against
(b) the summary
(c) the merits
(d) the demerits

144. ***Ins and outs***
(a) both sides (b) complete details
(c) inside information (d) full history

145. ***Between the devil and the deep sea***
(a) to be in a dilemma
(b) to be in a temper
(c) to choose correctly
(d) to live dangerously

146. ***To take to heels***
(a) to run away (b) to jump out
(c) to hurry (d) to take out

147. ***At sixes and sevens***
(a) in disorder (b) at a certain point
(c) very few (d) altogether thirteen

148. ***To feel like a fish out of water***
(a) disgusted (b) knowingly
(c) disappointed (d) homeless

149. ***To take to one's heels***
(a) to measure up to one's standard
(b) to shake in one's shoes
(c) to run away
(d) to run slowly

150. ***To call it a day***
(a) to concluded proceedings
(b) to initiate proceedings
(c) to work through the day
(d) to call somebody

151. ***To face the music***
(a) to enjoy a musical recital
(b) to bear the consequences
(c) to live in a pleasant atmosphere
(d) to have a difficult time

152. ***To strain every nerve***
(a) to make utmost efforts
(b) to feel weak and tired
(c) to be diligent workers
(d) to be methodical in work

153. ***With open arms***
(a) with free arms (b) with warmth
(c) with restraint (d) with gratitude

154. ***At the eleventh hour***
(a) too late (b) too early
(c) immediately (d) at the last moment

155. ***To throw dust in one's eyes***
(a) to deceive (b) to show false things
(c) to make blind (d) to harm someone

156. *To have an axe to grind*
(a) a private end to serve
(b) to fail to arouse interest
(c) to have no result
(d) to work for both sides

157. *To drive home*
(a) to find one's root
(b) to return to place of rest
(c) back to original position
(d) to emphasise

158. *A storm in a tea cup*
(a) useless work
(b) stampede
(c) rare achievement
(d) much ado about nothing

159. *A white elephant*
(a) a very huge item
(b) a costly and useless possession
(c) a very expensive investment
(d) a useful material

160. *On the cards*
(a) impossible (b) shocking
(c) evident (d) due

161. *By hook or by crook*
(a) by compromising or other responsibilities
(b) by impressing the interviewer
(c) by any means, right or wrong
(d) by becoming a specialist in the field

162. *To give the cold shoulder*
(a) to run shoulder
(b) to give unfriendly response
(c) to take notice of
(d) to give a cold shower

163. *Bad blood*
(a) war
(b) ill feeling
(c) threatening attitude
(d) in an infected state of being

CATEGORY – TWO

DIRECTIONS: ***Every idiom/ phrase provided in bold, italics & underlined is followed by four options. You have to find out the exact option from the given options.***

1. At a party, he is always in ***high spirits***
(a) drunk (b) talkative
(c) uncontrollable (d) cheerful

2. A movement for the world ***unity is in the offing***.
(a) at the end (b) about to start
(c) one decline (d) in the air

3. At Christmas, even the elderly fathers ***paint the town red***
(a) have a lovely time (b) indulge in rioting
(c) paint the houses red (d) spill red wine

4. Akshay can ***turn his hand*** to anything
(a) take advantage of (b) refuse to do
(c) find fault with (d) adapt himself to

5. As our army attack, the enemy retreated ***pell–mell***
(a) in a disorderly manner
(b) hurriedly
(c) without the least thought
(d) in a heap

6. A hen pecked husband ***plays second fiddle to his wife***
(a) humours
(b) pleases
(c) plays a subordinate role to
(d) fondles with

7. All his schemes to murder the king ***ended in smoke***
(a) were discarded
(b) fructified gradually
(c) were partially carried out
(d) came to nothing

8. At the ***eleventh hour***, Mridul arrived and saved him from the crisis
(a) at the last minute
(b) one hour before twelve
(c) when in trouble
(d) right at the end

9. Being an introvert, he will only *eat his heart out*
(a) suffer silently (b) eat too much
(c) keep brooding (d) invite trouble

10. By putting on the mimic act, Deepak *stole some of the thunder of peter's speech*
(a) filched something
(b) made unimpressive
(c) detracted the listeners from
(d) made a lot of noise

11. By doing these errands he is merely trying to *curry favour* with his boss
(a) gain favour (b) earn goodwill
(c) gain influence (d) expect promotion

12. Chandu used very ugly words against his kind uncle; he *threw down the gauntlet* before him
(a) he showed his readiness to leave the place
(b) he abuse and insulted him
(c) he put several conditions for negotiation
(d) he behaved as if he was very great and important person

13. Caesar was *done to death* by the conspirators
(a) eliminated (b) murdered
(c) removed (d) attacked

14. Dowry is a *burning question* of the day
(a) an irrelevant problem
(b) a relevant problem
(c) a widely debated issue
(d) a dying issue

15. Discipline is *on the wane* in schools and colleges these days
(a) spreading (b) increasing
(c) spiralling (d) declining

16. Don't *thrust your nose* in to my affairs
(a) advise me about
(b) be in opposition to
(c) meddle officiously in
(d) deal with

17. Dishonesty is *at a premium* in almost all spheres of public life
(a) encouraged (b) prevalent
(c) valued highly (d) practised openly

18. Do you know why I avoid this man? He has *a bee in bonnet*
(a) is over confident
(b) is crazy
(c) self possessed or self obsessed
(d) is ambitious

19. Eloquent lamentations regarding the fate of the flora and fauna are certain to be rendered a *cry in the wilderness*
(a) a cry with a laughter
(b) a cry in vain
(c) a laughter having no end
(d) an unpleasant situation

20. His voice gets *on my nerves*
(a) makes me sad (b) irritates me
(c) makes me ill (d) pierces my eardrums

21. He works by *fits and starts*
(a) irregularly (b) consistently
(c) enthusiastically (d) in high spirits

22. He *threw cold water* over the project that the secretary had prepared
(a) discouraged (b) encouraged
(c) rejected (d) cleared

23. He is a plain, simple and sincere man. He will always *call a spade a spade*
(a) be outspoken in language
(b) say something to be taken seriously
(c) avoid controversial situations
(d) find meaning or purpose in your action
(e) desist from making controversial statement

24. He is *at loggerheads* with his assistants about the management of the concern
(a) undecided (b) differing strongly
(c) in agreement (d) in confusion

25. He is in the habit of *fishing in troubled waters*
(a) aggravating the situation
(b) putting others in trouble
(c) taking advantage of troubled conditions for personal profit
(d) indulging in evil conspirancies

26. Harassed by repeated acts of injustice, he decided to ***put his foot down***
(a) accept the proposal unconditionally
(b) withdraw
(c) not to yield
(d) resign

27. His father advised him to be ***fair and square*** in his dealings lest he should fall into trouble.
(a) careful (b) considerate
(c) polite (d) upright

28. He has made his ***mark in politics***
(a) distinguish himself (b) attained notoriety
(c) ruined his wealth (d) acquired wealth

29. He ***rides the high horse*** because of his high connection.
(a) talks flatteringly (b) is famous
(c) is prosperous (d) puts on airs

30. He is a person ***after my own heart***
(a) a happy–go–lucky fellow
(b) an object of mockery
(c) exactly to one's own liking
(d) an emotional man

31. He felt ***ill at ease*** after receiving the letter from his son
(a) embarrassed (b) disturbed
(c) sick (d) relieved

32. His hard–earned money has ***gone down the drain***
(a) has been collected (b) has been wasted
(c) has been looted (d) has been spent

33. His best jokes ***fell flat***
(a) became completely unnerved
(b) were not paid attention to
(c) faced total failure
(d) had no effect

34. Having sold off his factory, Mr. Roy is now a gentleman ***at large***
(a) respected by everybody
(b) living comfortably
(c) held in high esteem
(d) has no serious occupation

35. He always says that he will help. But when if ***comes to the crunch***, he does nothing
(a) confused situation
(b) decisive moment
(c) troublesome moment
(d) difficult time

36. He will win this election ***hands down***
(a) win with narrow margin
(b) win easily
(c) scrape through
(d) win with a big margin

37. He has been working ***on and off*** for several years on this research project
(a) rarely (b) at intervals
(c) painstakingly (d) continuously

38. He was a king who ruled his subjects with ***a high hand***
(a) democratically (b) oppressively
(c) sympathetically (d) conveniently
(e) kindly

39. He got hold of the wrong ***end of the stick***
(a) fixed wrong priorities
(b) committed a blunder
(c) felt uneasy
(d) misjudged a situation

40. He was ***cool as a cucumber***
(a) dead
(b) nervous
(c) calm and composed
(d) fainted

41. He ***took to heart*** the death of his wife as he was very much attached to her
(a) was deeply affected by
(b) was shocked by
(c) was condoled
(d) was ruined by

42. He always ***cuts both ends***
(a) behaves dishonestly
(b) works for both sides
(c) creates discord among friends
(d) argues in support of both sides of the issue

43. He is temporarily in charge of the company and is trying to ***feather his nest***

(a) act for his own future benefits

(b) raise the image of the company

(c) practice his own brand of management philosophy

(d) bring order and discipline in the company

44. He left his friend ***in lurch***

(a) left temporarily

(b) left forever

(c) left when he was needing help

(d) left to his fate

45. He has accomplished ***a herculean task***

(a) impossible job

(b) allotted work

(c) incomplete work

(d) work requiring great effort

46. His phenomenal success shows that he has got ***the midas touch***

(a) super human qualities

(b) fabulous wealth

(c) ability to succeed in all projects

(d) tremendous acquaintances and resources

47. He is on the ***wrong side of fifty***

(a) a sinner (b) not yet fifty

(c) old and haggard (d) over fifty years old

48. He was undecided. He let the ***grass grow under his feet***

(a) stayed out (b) moved away

(c) sat unmoving (d) loitered around

49. He cannot make ***both ends meet.***

(a) earn enough (b) manage the business

(c) control affairs (d) work hard

50. He ***made light*** of his father's advice

(a) rejected (b) followed readily

(c) disregarded (d) treated lightly

51. He believes in the policy of ***making hay while the sun shines***

(a) helping those who help him

(b) giving bribes to get his work done

(c) seeking advice from one and all

(d) making the best use of a favourable situation

52. He gave his erring son ***a piece of his mind***

(a) encouraged him (b) advised him

(c) suggested anew (d) scolded him

53. His boss was always ***breathing down his neck***

(a) shouting loudly at him

(b) abusing and ill–treating him

(c) giving him strenuous work

(d) watching all his actions closely

54. His ***oily tongue*** has won him promotion

(a) word power (b) fluency in speech

(c) soft speech (d) flattery

55. He had to ***eat a humble pie*** owing to his misdeeds

(a) be humiliated (b) feel downtrodden

(c) accept abuses (d) apologise humbly

56. He managed to secure the job through ***back stair influence***

(a) strong recommendation

(b) sheer merit

(c) underhand means

(d) hard effort

57. He is really ***worth his salt***

(a) of value (b) loyal

(c) untrustworthy (d) affectionate

58. He ***blew out all the candles at one go***

(a) simultaneously (b) suddenly

(c) at one attempt (d) at once

59. He finds no difficulty in ***keeping the wolf away*** from the door

(a) keeping off starvation

(b) guarding against wild animals

(c) guarding himself against enemies

(d) keeping aloof from disputed matters

60. He knows what side his ***bread is buttered***

(a) knows how to flatter

(b) knows the art of cooking

(c) knows where his advantage lies

(d) knows how to accomplish a task

61. His promotion is ***on the cards.***

(a) certain (b) due

(c) probable (d) evident

62. He resigned the post of his ***own accord***
(a) voluntarily and willingly
(b) according to his judgement
(c) according to his convenience
(d) which he liked

63. He ***faced the music*** for reaching home late
(a) faced reprimand
(b) faced punishment
(c) faced pleasure
(d) faced entertainment

64. He has too many ***irons in the fire***
(a) is very selfish and greedy
(b) wants to grab everything
(c) is engaged in too many enterprises simultaneously
(d) pokes his nose in every affair

65. He is disliked because of his habit of ***making a mountain of a mole hill***
(a) taking undue advantage of a favourable opportunity
(b) giving great importance to trifles
(c) boasting
(d) exaggerating

66. His ***prodigal son*** was a constant source of trouble to him
(a) extravagant (b) given into bad habits
(c) step–son (d) poor and miserly

67. He was ***carried off his feet*** when he was declared to have won the prize
(a) was dizzy
(b) became delirious
(c) was wild with excitement
(d) danced on his toes

68. He has ***turned the tables*** on his enemy
(a) hit
(b) behaved hospitably towards
(c) changed possible defeat into victory
(d) created obstacle for

69. I won't mind even if he ***goes to dogs***
(a) is insulted (b) goes mad
(c) becomes brutal (d) is ruined

70. In parliament, every member can have the ***floor with the permission*** of the speaker
(a) speak against his own party
(b) leave the house
(c) make a speech
(d) raise an issue

71. I did not mind what he was saying, he was only ***talking through his hat***
(a) talking ignorantly (b) talking insultingly
(c) talking nonsense (d) talking irresponsibly

72. If you pass this difficult examination. It will be a ***feather in your cap***
(a) you will get a scholarship for higher studies
(b) you will get a very good job
(c) it will be one more achievement
(d) your parents will be very happy

73. In the Armed Forces, it is considered a great privilege ***to die in harness.***
(a) die with honour
(b) die on a horse back
(c) die while still working
(d) die in the battle field

74. If you ***rub him the wrong way***, he is bound to react
(a) annoy (b) abuse
(c) flatter (d) encourage

75. I am afraid the two brothers are at ***cross purposes***
(a) are working against each other
(b) quarrel with each other
(c) are misunderstanding each other
(d) dislike each other

76. It will be wise on your part to ***let the bygones be bygones***
(a) recollect the past (b) resist the past
(c) revive the past (d) ignore the past

77. I am afraid he is ***burning the candle*** at both ends.
(a) working hard
(b) utting in sustained effort
(c) overtaxing his energies
(d) working at night also

78. In the organised society of today individual or nation cannot ***plough a lonely furrow***
(a) survive in isolation
(b) remain unaffected
(c) remain non–aligned
(d) do without the help of others

79. It has been ***raining cats and dogs.***
(a) endlessly (b) incessantly
(c) continuously (d) heavily

80. It requires unparalleled courage to set the ***Thames on fire***
(a) do something extraordinary or brilliant
(b) do a heroic deed
(c) wreak evil on something
(d) destroy with fire

81. It is Rashmi who ***wears the trousers*** in their house
(a) is dominant
(b) dresses glamorously
(c) makes all the decisions
(d) earns a living

82. In modern democratic societies ***lynch law*** seems to have become a common feature in almost all the spheres of life
(a) law of the underworld
(b) law of the parliament
(c) law of the constitution
(d) law of the mob

83. It is difficult for me to believe you, so please put down everything in ***black and white***
(a) sequentially, as it happened
(b) in detail
(c) what you saw
(d) in written form

84. If we give them this concession it will be the ***thin end of the wedge***
(a) the beginning of further concessions
(b) a compromise on principles
(c) inadequate for their needs
(d) the least we could do for them

85. It was such a strange affair that i could not make ***head or tail*** of it
(a) remember it (b) face it
(c) believe it (d) understand it

86. I saw him make a ***wry face***
(a) abuse
(b) feel sick
(c) show disappointment
(d) cry with pain

87. I have been betrayed by my own ***flesh and blood***
(a) children (b) relatives
(c) acquaintances (d) friends

88. It has been the first time in this office that a clerk ***wiped the nose of the boss***
(a) cheated
(b) abused
(c) complained against
(d) slapped

89. In life, we have to take the ***rough with the smooth***
(a) accept unpleasant as well as pleasant things
(b) make unpleasant things better
(c) use pleasant words to make things smooth
(d) be tough in order to be successful

90. It was discovered that the young man was over ***head and ears*** in love with her
(a) completely (b) secretly
(c) sufficiently (d) openly

91. It is ***high time*** that India did something about the population problem
(a) appropriate time (b) auspicious moment
(c) already late (d) desired occasion

92. ***I berated*** my assistant soundly for his slackness
(a) dismissed (b) suspended
(c) criticised (d) censured strongly

93. If you give Ashish all your money, you are likely to ***burn your fingers***
(a) suffer (b) be happy
(c) be unhappy (d) be unhappy

94. I did not know that he was ***pulling my leg*** all the time
(a) defaming me (b) befooling me
(c) complimenting me (d) degrading me

95. Kunika was ***cocksure*** that she was able to do the job as desired
(a) least worried (b) doubtful
(c) perfectly confident (d) not able to imagine

96. Kishan is a ***chicken–hearted*** fellow

(a) hold (b) weak
(c) cowardly (d) kind hearted

97. Let us admit that we could not ***heap coals of fire*** on his head.

(a) put him to shame
(b) agitate him
(c) make him feel sorry
(d) incite him to a fight

98. Lord Clive ***won his laurels*** in the battle of plassey

(a) overpowered his enemies
(b) fought bravely
(c) defeated his enemies
(d) acquired distinction

99. Mrs. Khanna has been in the ***blues for the last*** several weeks

(a) depressed (b) unwell
(c) lonely (d) penniless

100. Manoj always ***keeps himself to himself***

(a) is unsociable (b) is selfish
(c) is too busy (d) does not take sides

101. My father strained ***every nerve to enable*** me to get settled in life

(a) tried all tricks
(b) worked very hard
(c) bribed several persons
(d) spent a huge amount

102. My aunt was ***in a flutter*** last night

(a) in a jovial mood
(b) frightened
(c) in a state of nervous excitement
(d) very angry

103. None of this ***hanky-panky***; please talk straight

(a) diversification (b) indifference
(c) obsession (d) jugglery

104. Our school is within a ***stone's throw*** of the railway station

(a) within a definite circumference
(b) within a certain radius
(c) very far off
(d) at a short distance

105. One should be prepared to get a ***bolt from the blue*** in life, but should not get unnerved by them

(a) unexpected loss (b) sad experience
(c) depreciation (d) sudden shock

106. One should not indulge ***in tall talks***

(a) ideal talk (b) flattering
(c) irrelevant talk (d) boasting

107. Please do not indulge in ***double dealing***

(a) two standards (b) dealing improperly
(c) two jobs (d) deception

108. Rahul fought ***tooth and nail*** to save his company

(a) with strength and fury
(b) with weapons
(c) as best as he could
(d) using unfair means

109. Rajeev achieved success by resorting to a ***hole and corner*** method

(a) underhand (b) obscure
(c) clever (d) usual

110. Rajesh and Vikas have remained friends through ***thick and thin***

(a) through days of struggle
(b) inspite of all difficulties
(c) through happy days
(d) always

111. Sumit had to look ***high and low*** before he could find his scooter key

(a) always (b) nowhere
(c) somewhere (d) everywhere

112. She rejected his proposal of marriage ***point–blank***

(a) pointedly (b) directly
(c) briefly (d) abruptly

113. Some people have a habit of wearing their ***heart on their sleeve***

(a) wasting their time on unnecessary details
(b) avoiding being friendly with others
(c) saying something which is not to be taken
(d) exposing their innermost feelings to others

114. She was received by her friends with ***open arms***

(a) warmly (b) casually
(c) coldly (d) indifferently

115. Some of us are really in a ***catch–22*** situation

(a) hopeful (b) absurd
(c) depressive (d) dangerous

116. She exhibited remarkable ***sang froid*** during the crisis

(a) composure (b) temper
(c) anger (d) irritation

117. Some people now wonder whether we just ***pay lip service*** or genuinely subscribe to democracy

(a) remain indifferent
(b) pay oral tribute
(c) show only outward respect
(d) attach no value

118. There was opposition to the new policy by the ***rank and file*** of the government.

(a) the majority
(b) the ordinary members
(c) the cabinet members
(d) the official machinery

119. The parliamentary inquiry into the bofors deal has not ***brought to light*** any startling facts

(a) probed (b) proved
(c) highlighted (d) disclosed

120. To all ***intents and purposes*** he is a good man

(a) above all
(b) practically
(c) to censure someone in strong terms
(d) in practice
(e) finally

121. I am ambitious too and never want to ***rest on my laurels***

(a) be satisfied (b) be good
(c) be dissatisfied (d) be complacent

122. The casting vote of the chairman ***clinched the issue***

(a) finished (b) closed
(c) started (d) decided

123. The aroma from the kitchen makes my ***mouth water***

(a) stimulates my appetite
(b) makes me sick
(c) makes me giddy
(d) makes me vomit

124. This place affords ***a bird's eye view*** of the green valley below

(a) narrow view (b) beautiful view
(c) ugly view (d) general view

125. The doctor says the patient has ***turned the corner***

(a) died
(b) completely recovered
(c) become worse
(d) passed the crisis

126. The robbery was committed ***in the wee hours*** of the day

(a) in the evening (b) at noontime
(c) after midnight (d) at dawn

127. The popularity of the yester years superstar is ***on the wane***

(a) growing less (b) at rock – bottom
(c) at its peak (d) growing more

128. The young heir to his father's huge estate made ***ducks and drakes*** of his patrimony

(a) invested wisely (b) squandered lavishly
(c) made best use of (d) took stock of

129. There is no ***love lost*** between the two neighbours

(a) cool indifference
(b) close friendship
(c) intense dislike
(d) a love–hate relationship

130. The company has been handed over to new masters ***lock, stock and barrel***

(a) completely (b) financially
(c) administratively (d) partially

131. The sailor found himself between ***the devil and the deep sea***

(a) confronting two opportunities
(b) lost in the deep ocean
(c) facing two challenges
(d) facing two equally bad alternatives

132. The sight of the accident ***made my flesh creep***
(a) confused me (b) worried me
(c) drew my attention (d) frightened me

133. The sworn enemies have decided to ***bury the hatchet***
(a) to make peace (b) to help each other
(c) to become partners (d) to avoid each other

134. The politician was able to sway the mob with his ***gift of the gab***
(a) abundance of promises
(b) fluency of speech
(c) political foresight
(d) flattering words

135. The detective left ***no stone unturned*** to trace the culprit
(a) took no pains
(b) did very irrelevant things
(c) resorted to illegitimate practices
(d) used all available means

136. They sold their house because it was a real ***white elephant***
(a) a useless one (b) an expensive one
(c) a rare find (d) a big one

137. The captors of the kidnapped kept his family ***on tenterhooks***
(a) on constant move (b) in excited wait
(c) in anxious suspense (d) in seething anger

138. There is no ***hard and fast*** rule regarding this subject
(a) rule that cannot be broken or modified
(b) rule that is difficult
(c) rule that can be broken or modified
(d) rule that is fast–changing

139. The question of abolition of private property is still a ***moot point***
(a) not clear (b) unknown
(c) uncertain (d) undecided

140. Your words can't ***throw cold water*** on my plans to start a business.
(a) to discourage
(b) to make someone calm
(c) to listen
(d) to get a loss

141. An athlete must be ***as fit as a fiddle*** to remain competitive.
(a) very weak (b) free from illness
(c) ready to compete (d) strong and healthy

142. He took ***a leap in the dark*** with his latest investment in stocks.
(a) an adventure
(b) jump from a high place
(c) a daring step whose consequences are unpredictable
(d) a thoughtless action

143. There is a lot of work to do, so ***roll up your sleeves*** and get busy.
(a) speed up
(b) to prepare oneself for work
(c) in corporate
(d) decrease

144. I'll bet you ***dollar to doughnuts*** she won't accept his marriage proposal
(a) most probably
(b) almost certainly
(c) not at all
(d) considerably

145. You may become successful in your business someday. ***Every dog has his day.***
(a) sooner or later, everyone has his share of good fortune
(b) will get a contract of worth in future
(c) will be successful in establishing business
(d) sooner or later one will get the result of hard work

146. The politician was in the ***eye of the storm*** because of the accounting scandal.
(a) to trap wanted criminal with great difficulty
(b) to catch a dangerous person
(c) the center of a problem
(d) to meet with disaster

147. A good student has ***an eagle eye*** for his errors.
(a) an ignoring way
(b) an eye for detail
(c) slow and ignorant to discover
(d) quick to discover

148. Finding a violin in my attic I started ***flogging the dead horse.***
(a) to weep for something lost
(b) to enjoy even if something lost
(c) to revive interest in old matters
(d) to forget old matters

149. Look at that painting. It is really ***a feast for the eyes.***
(a) reality
(b) very beautiful thing or person
(c) a dream
(d) something ugly

150. Seeing the invasion, the army ***grid up the lions.***
(a) to get ready to protect
(b) to prepare for hard work
(c) to get ready for attack
(d) none of above

151. If you ***grease the palm,*** your work will be done easily.
(a) to break promise (b) to break trust
(c) to help (d) to bribe

152. One should ***give a wide berth*** to the evil persons.
(a) to welcome (b) to applaud
(c) to motivate (d) to avoid

153. The robber disappeared from the bank ***in the blink of an eye.***
(a) very easily (b) in an instant
(c) with closed eyes (d) open eyes

154. My mother always keeps my room ***spick and span.***
(a) in order (b) disorder
(c) all qualities (d) no quality

155. She was unemployed and homeless, but somehow managed to ***keep body and soul together.***
(a) stay fit and fine
(b) remain outstanding in work
(c) managed to be competitive
(d) manage to survive

156. A ***lion's share*** is always desired in the business.
(a) a non-uniform distribution
(b) a disproportionate distribution
(c) small part in a distribution
(d) large part in a distribution

157. Major newspapers predict a ***landslide victory*** for the BJP.
(a) by an overwhelming majority
(b) not a considerable victory
(c) a victory with difficulty
(d) an unexpected victory

158. These days student try to ***mince matters*** from their parents.
(a) make use of opportunity
(b) hide the truth of and pretend
(c) to be calm when matter gets worst
(d) to make matter worst

159. Communal riots is something to ***set people by ears.***
(a) to incite people
(b) to listen carefully
(c) to given long speech
(d) to abuse

160. His condescending attitude ***made my blood boil.***
(a) made me angry (b) insulted me
(c) abused me (d) ignored me

161. I would move ***heaven and Earth*** to get into politics.
(a) struggle (b) do one's utmost
(c) fight with others (d) destroy everything

162. By changing her job to an unknown company she ***jumped from the frying pan into the fire.***
(a) to enter in a comfortable situation
(b) from bad situations to worse
(c) in a dangerous situation
(d) difficult to please

163. Employers don't like those employees who ***play truant.***
(a) to be happy
(b) to be away from home
(c) to be absent from duty without permission
(d) to be sad

164. There is no use ***paying lip service*** when you don't do it from heart.
(a) false appreciation (b) pretend to regard
(c) true relation (d) false commitment

ANSWERS

CATEGORY – ONE

1. (a) 2. (a) 3. (d) 4. (c) 5. (c) 6. (a) 7. (c) 8. (c) 9. (c) 10. (a)
11. (b) 12. (c) 13. (c) 14. (a) 15. (c) 16. (a) 17. (d) 18. (d) 19. (b) 20. (a)
21. (c) 22. (a) 23. (b) 24. (b) 25. (d) 26. (a) 27. (d) 28. (b) 29. (c) 30. (b)
31. (d) 32. (d) 33. (c) 34. (c) 35. (a) 36. (d) 37. (c) 38. (d) 39. (a) 40. (c)
41. (c) 42. (a) 43. (d) 44. (d) 45. (d) 46. (d) 47. (d) 48. (d) 49. (a) 50. (d)
51. (d) 52. (b) 53. (c) 54. (d) 55. (b) 56. (c) 57. (a) 58. (b) 59. (a) 60. (a)
61. (d) 62. (b) 63. (c) 64. (b) 65. (b) 66. (a) 67. (d) 68. (b) 69. (c) 70. (d)
71. (b) 72. (b) 73. (a) 74. (a) 75. (d) 76. (c) 77. (a) 78. (c) 79. (d) 80. (d)
81. (d) 82. (d) 83. (c) 84. (c) 85. (a) 86. (c) 87. (d) 88. (c) 89. (c) 90. (a)
91. (c) 92. (b) 93. (a) 94. (b) 95. (a) 96. (d) 97. (d) 98. (d) 99. (b) 100. (c)
101. (a) 102. (c) 103. (c) 104. (b) 105. (b) 106. (c) 107. (b) 108. (c) 109. (a) 110. (a)
111. (b) 112. (a) 113. (d) 114. (d) 115. (b) 116. (b) 117. (b) 118. (b) 119. (a) 120. (b)
121. (b) 122. (d) 123. (a) 124. (c) 125. (a) 126. (a) 127. (d) 128. (b) 129. (c) 130. (c)
131. (d) 132. (c) 133. (b) 134. (d) 135. (c) 136. (a) 137. (d) 138. (b) 139. (c) 140. (c)
141. (b) 142. (b) 143. (a) 144. (b) 145. (a) 146. (a) 147. (a) 148. (c) 149. (c) 150. (a)
151. (b) 152. (a) 153. (b) 154. (d) 155. (a) 156. (a) 157. (d) 158. (d) 159. (b) 160. (d)
161. (c) 162. (b) 163. (b)

CATEGORY – TWO

1. (d) 2. (b) 3. (a) 4. (d) 5. (a) 6. (c) 7. (d) 8. (a) 9. (a) 10. (c)
11. (a) 12. (d) 13. (d) 14. (c) 15. (d) 16. (c) 17. (b) 18. (c) 19. (d) 20. (b)
21. (a) 22. (c) 23. (a) 24. (b) 25. (c) 26. (d) 27. (d) 28. (a) 29. (d) 30. (c)
31. (b) 32. (b) 33. (b) 34. (d) 35. (c) 36. (b) 37. (a) 38. (b) 39. (d) 40. (c)
41. (a) 42. (a) 43. (a) 44. (c) 45. (d) 46. (c) 47. (d) 48. (c) 49. (a) 50. (d)
51. (d) 52. (b) 53. (b) 54. (d) 55. (a) 56. (c) 57. (b) 58. (d) 59. (c) 60. (c)
61. (b) 62. (a) 63. (a) 64. (c) 65. (b) 66. (a) 67. (c) 68. (c) 69. (d) 70. (d)
71. (c) 72. (c) 73. (d) 74. (a) 75. (a) 76. (d) 77. (c) 78. (a) 79. (d) 80. (a)
81. (c) 82. (d) 83. (d) 84. (d) 85. (d) 86. (c) 87. (b) 88. (c) 89. (a) 90. (a)
91. (a) 92. (d) 93. (a) 94. (a) 95. (c) 96. (b) 97. (c) 98. (d) 99. (a) 100. (a)
101. (b) 102. (c) 103. (d) 104. (d) 105. (d) 106. (d) 107. (d) 108. (c) 109. (a) 110. (b)
111. (d) 112. (b) 113. (d) 114. (a) 115. (d) 116. (b) 117. (b) 118. (b) 119. (d) 120. (b)
121. (a) 122. (d) 123. (a) 124. (d) 125. (b) 126. (c) 127. (a) 128. (b) 129. (a) 130. (a)
131. (d) 132. (d) 133. (a) 134. (b) 135. (d) 136. (b) 137. (a) 138. (a) 139. (d) 140. (a)
141. (d) 142. (c) 143. (b) 144. (b) 145. (a) 146. (c) 147. (d) 148. (c) 149. (b) 150. (c)
151. (d) 152. (d) 153. (b) 154. (a) 155. (d) 156. (d) 157. (a) 158. (b) 159. (a) 160. (a)
161. (b) 162. (b) 163. (c) 164. (b)

SOME CONFUSING WORDS
(Look Alike – Sound Alike)

In the English language, no two words are exactly similar. Even the most similar words have some subtle shade of difference. One particular word may be the most appropriate at one particular place and a similar word used in its place may completely change the sense and meaning and this often leads to error. For instance, the words 'old' and 'ancient' seem to be quite similar. We may say:

'My grandfather is an old man.'

And it shall be quite correct. But it shall be simply absurd and incorrect to say:

'My grandfather is an ancient man.'

Words similar in sound, form and meaning often create confusion. They are often confused and misused. Sometimes we mean one thing, but our words convey a totally different sense. In order to convey the idea that great men never die, it may be said:

'Great men are immortal'.

But if the word immortal is confused with immoral, the sentence will become ridiculous:

'Great men are immoral'.

So in order to be exact and correct in our expression, we must use the right word at the right place. A careful study of the following sets of words, used in illustrative sentences, will help the students in using them correctly.

1.	**(a)**	**Abject (miserable, mean):** People live in abject poverty in many parts of India.
	(b)	**Object (aim, goal):** You must work hard to achieve your object.
	(c)	**Object (to oppose):** No one objected to my proposal.
2.	**(a)**	**Aboard (on the ship):** There were five hundred passengers aboard the ship.
	(b)	**Abroad (out of the country: to foreign countries):** Jawaharlal Nehru was sent abroad for higher education.
3.	**(a)**	**Accept (to take):** An honest man will not accept a bribe.
	(b)	**Except (without):** All the students except Ravi were present in the class.
4.	**(a)**	**Accomplice (helper or companion in wrongdoing):** The murderer and his three accomplices have been arrested.
	(b)	**Accomplish (to achieve: to complete):** The task was accomplished well in time.
5.	**(a)**	**(Access) (approach):** He has access to every minister.
	(b)	**Excess (too much):** Excess of everything is bad.
6.	**(a)**	**Accede (to agree):** She will certainly accede to your request.
	(b)	**Exceed (to be more):** Your expenditure should never exceed your income.
7.	**(a)**	**Advice (Noun):** My parents gave me good advice.
	(b)	**Advise (Verb):** He advised me to work hard.
8.	**(a)**	**Adapt (to adjust):** Old people cannot easily adapt themselves to new ways of life.
	(b)	**Adopt (to own; to take up):** Which profession will you like to adopt?
	(c)	**Adept (expert):** She is adept in painting and music.
9.	**(a)**	**Abstain (to avoid an action):** He abstains from drinks and drugs of all kinds.
	(b)	**Refrain (to avoid an action):** It needs a great effort to refrain from anger.
10.	**(a)**	**Affect (to produce a result):** Overwork affected his health.
	(b)	**Effect (result):** My advice had no effect on him.
	(c)	**Effect (to accomplish):** The prisoner effected his escape from the prison.

11.	(a)	**Ability (capability):** Tagore was a man of great ability as a poet and musician.
	(b)	**Capacity (power to contain):** This hall has a seating capacity of five hundred persons.
12.	(a)	**Able (intelligent):** He is a very able administrator.
	(b)	**Capable (fit to do something):** He is a capable man for this post.
13.	(a)	**Accident (mishap):** Rash-driving is the main cause of accidents.
	(b)	**Incident (happening; event):** There are many interesting incidents in the life of every man.
	(c)	**Event (important happening):** The partition of India was an important event which gave a new turn to history.
14.	(a)	**Altar (place for worship or sacrifice):** The lover sacrificed his life at the altar of love.
	(b)	**Alter (to change):** Why do you go on altering your plans?
15.	(a)	**Affection (love):** Mothers have great affection for their children.
	(b)	**Affectation (pretence):** Her tears on the death of her third husband were a mere affectation.
16.	(a)	**Application (a written request):** Write an application to the principal for full fee concession.
	(b)	**Implication (importance; significance):** The words of the prime minister have very deep implication.
17.	(a)	**Alternate (of things of two kinds by turns, first the one and then the other):** Many farmers alternate crops.
	(b)	**Alternative (choice between two things):** We have no other alternative but to go.
18.	(a)	**Amiable (lovable):** His amiable manners have made him popular.
	(b)	**Amicable (friendly):** We are ready to settle all disputes with Pakistan in an amicable manner.
19.	(a)	**Apposite (suitable, right for the purpose or occasion):** His apposite remark was appreciated by all.
	(b)	**Opposite (facing; front to front or back to back):** Our house is situated on the opposite side of the bank.
20.	(a)	**Ascent (going up):** The ascent of the mountain is very difficult.
	(b)	**Assent (consent, approval):** The president gave his assent to the bill and it became a law.
21.	(a)	**Admit (to accept something):** You must admit your fault.
	(b)	**Confess (to accept one's fault or crime):** The husband confessed that he had killed his wife in a fit of anger.
22.	(a)	**Allude (refer):** In his speech, he alluded to the nefarious designs of Pakistan.
	(b)	**Elude (evade; escape):** Philosophy eludes my grasp.
23.	(a)	**Allusion (reference):** In his speech, there was a direct allusion to the nefarious designs of Pakistan.
	(b)	**Illusion (deception; false perception):** If you take a rope for a snake, it is an illusion.
24.	(a)	**Angel (heavenly creature):** Angels are made of light. They can fly in the air.
	(b)	**Angle (space between two lines):** Every triangle has three angles.
25.	(a)	**Award (to give strictly according to justice):** The judge awarded him death sentence.
	(b)	**Reward (to give the fruit of):** Your efforts will be rewarded with success.
26.	(a)	**Answer (respond to a question):** I have answered every question.
	(b)	**Reply (respond to a letter etc.):** I wrote several letters, but she did not reply.
27.	(a)	**Artful (clever, cunning):** Beware of the artful ways of women.
	(b)	**Artistic (beautiful):** It is really a very artistic picture painted by Sobha Singh.
28.	(a)	**Aspire (to desire):** She aspires to be a top class film heroine.
	(b)	**Expire (to die or end):** The old man expired after a long illness.
29.	(a)	**Avenge (to take vengeance for):** He decided to avenge his father's death upon the murderer.
	(b)	**Revenge (to inflict injury in return for injury):** He revenged himself upon the enemy for the murder of his father.

30.	**(a)**	**Bail (surety or security):** The prisoner was released on bail.
	(b)	**Bale (bundle):** Ten bales of cotton can be loaded on this truck.
	(c)	**Vale (Valley):** Clouds were floating over vales and hills.
31.	**(a)**	**Bare (uncovered):** Do not walk barefooted on the grass.
	(b)	**Bear (to tolerate):** I cannot bear this insult.
32.	**(a)**	**Beside (by the side of):** She is sitting beside her husband.
	(b)	**Besides (in addition to):** Besides this scooter he has a car.
33.	**(a)**	**Beach (sea-shore):** The poet stood at the beach and looked at the waves of the sea.
	(b)	**Beech (a kind of tree):** There is no beech tree in this garden.
34.	**(a)**	**Birth (being born):** No woman will like to tell you her correct age and date of birth.
	(b)	**Berth (seat):** He was lying on the upper berth in the train.
35.	**(a)**	**Brake (device to check speed):** Life without discipline is like a car without brakes.
	(b)	**Break (to shatter):** The lock was broken with a hammer.
36.	**(a)**	**Bridal (relating to marriage):** This is my bridal ring.
	(b)	**Bridle (rein of a horse):** Pull the bridle and the horse will stop.
37.	**(a)**	**Born (given birth):** I was born in the month of January.
	(b)	**Borne (carried):** The wounded man was borne to the hospital.
38.	**(a)**	**Beneficent (kind):** Only a beneficent man can do good to others.
	(b)	**Beneficial (useful):** Morning walk is certainly very beneficial to health.
39.	**(a)**	**Bring (to carry while coming):** Please bring your bedding with you.
	(b)	**Fetch (to go and bring something):** They have to fetch water from a long distance.
40.	**(a)**	**Cast (to give or throw):** I went to the polling station to cast my vote.
	(b)	**Caste (community):** We are Brahmins by caste.
	(c)	**Cost (price):** This watch will cost you more than a thousand rupees.
41.	**(a)**	**Canvas (strong cloth):** I wear canvas shoes when I go out for a walk in the morning.
	(b)	**Canvass (to ask for; to try to gain):** They are canvassing for votes from door to door.
42.	**(a)**	**Casual (occasional, from time to time):** We have two spare beds for casual guests.
	(b)	**Causal (of cause and effect):** There is causal connection between trees and rain.
43.	**(a)**	**Check (control):** She keeps no check on her children.
	(b)	**Cheque (order for withdrawing money from the bank):** A cheque for fifty thousand rupees was presented to the Prime Minister.
44.	**(a)**	**Childish (foolish like a child; used in a bad sense):** I do not like your childish ways.
	(b)	**Childlike (innocent like a child; used in a good sense):** Mahatma Gandhi had child- like simplicity.
45.	**(a)**	**Career (life, course of life):** He had a brilliant career as a student.
	(b)	**Carrier (that which carries):** Flies are the carriers of germs and germs are the carriers of diseases.
46.	**(a)**	**Cannon (a big gun):** Guns and cannons made a loud noise in the battlefield.
	(b)	**Canon (rule or standard):** We should follow the canons of good conduct.
47.	**(a)**	**Cease (to stop):** I am waiting for the rain to cease.
	(b)	**Seize (to catch):** I seized the pick-pocket by the wrist.
48.	**(a)**	**Cemetery (graveyard):** The Christians bury their dead in the cemetery.
	(b)	**Symmetry (balance or harmony):** A scar on her left check has spoilt the symmetry of her face.

49.	(a)	**Carat (measure of the purity of gold), pure gold being 24 carat):** I gave her a gold ring of 24 carat.
	(b)	**Carrot (a vegetable):** Timur and Changez Khan used to cut men like carrots.
50.	(a)	**Cell (a small room in prison, etc.):** Prisoners are kept in cells.
	(b)	**Sell (to put on sale):** This book is selling like hot cakes.
51.	(a)	**Clean (free from dirt):** She keeps her house neat and clean.
	(b)	**Clear (easy to see, hear or understand):** The water of the tank is so clear that you can see your reflection in it.
52.	(a)	**Ceiling (inner side of the roof):** The fan is hanging from the ceiling.
	(b)	**Sealing (closing):** Send this letter by registered post after sealing it properly.
53.	(a)	**Complement (to complete; something that completes):** Man and woman complement each other.
	(b)	**Compliment (to admire; greetings):** Everybody complimented him on his success.
54.	(a)	**Continual (continuing with breaks):** A continual guest loses respect.
	(b)	**Continuous (at a stretch):** There has been a continuous strike for three weeks.
55.	(a)	**Conscious (aware):** Women are not conscious of their rights.
	(b)	**Conscientious (honest):** Everyone respects a conscientious worker.
56.	(a)	**Council (a group of minister, etc.):** Kings used to have a council of ministers to advise them.
	(b)	**Counsel (advice):** He gave me good counsel and I was successful.
57.	(a)	**Confess (to admit crime, etc.):** The husband confessed that he had murdered his wife.
	(b)	**Admit (to accept or acknowledge one's mistake, etc.):** She will never admit her and sellers in the market.
58.	(a)	**Crime (a legal offence punished by law):** Law will punish you for the crime of stealing.
	(b)	**Sin (a religious offence):** God will punish you for the sin of killing a cow.
	(c)	**Vice (a moral offence):** He was ruined by the vice of drinking.
59.	(a)	**Credible (believable):** Your cock and bull story is not at all credible.
	(b)	**Credulous (believing others easily):** My mother is so credulous that she believes everything told by others.
	(c)	**Creditable (worthy of praise and honour):** First position in the university is a creditable achievement.
60.	(a)	**Cool (pleasant):** Let us sit in the cool shade of the tree.
	(b)	**Cold (unpleasant):** It is very cold in winter.
61.	(a)	**Core (innermost corner):** I love my mother from the core of my heart.
	(b)	**Corps (a branch of military):** He is a captain in the National Cadet Corps (N.C.C.).
	(c)	**Corpse (dead body):** The criminal was hanged and his corpse was handed over to his relatives.
62.	(a)	**Considerable (sufficient):** He gets considerable money from his father every month.
	(b)	**Considerate (sympathetic):** She is very kind and considerate to her servants.
63.	(a)	**Cattle (animals like cows and buffaloes):** Cattle are grazing in the fields.
	(b)	**Kettle (a utensil):** The water is boiling in the kettle.
64.	(a)	**Custom (a social practice):** Dowry system is an abominable custom.
	(b)	**Habit (individual practice):** It is my habit to get up early in the morning.
65.	(a)	**Coarse (rough):** Khaddar is a coarse type of cloth.
	(b)	**Course (path; line of action):** This river changes its course every year.

66.	(a)	**Confident (sure):** He is confident of his success in the examination.
	(b)	**Confidant (one who is trusted with private affairs and secrets):** Only the confidant of the minister knows all his plans and programmes.
67.	(a)	**Cue (hint):** He took a cue from his father and spoke very politely to the guests.
	(b)	**Queue (a line of persons waiting for their turn):** Please stand in the queue and wait for your turn.
68.	(a)	**Cloth (unstitched cloth):** My father deals in cloth.
	(b)	**Clothe (stitched dress):** I wear clean clothes every morning.
69.	(a)	**Colonel (a military officer):** His father is a colonel in the army.
	(b)	**Kernel (soft seed):** Nuts have sweet kernels inside.
70.	(a)	**Cite (quote; to give as an example):** He has cited many examples from holy books.
	(b)	**Sight (scene; eyesight):** The daffodils presented a beautiful sight.
	(c)	**Site (a spot):** This is a good site for a hotel.
71.	(a)	**Dear (beloved):** My mother is very dear to me.
	(b)	**Deer (a wild animal):** The hunter killed a deer with a gun.
72.	(a)	**Dairy (a milk booth):** You can get milk and butter from this dairy.
	(b)	**Diary (a note-book):** She noted my name and address in her diary.
73.	(a)	**Deny (to declare as false):** Politicians make a statement and then deny it the next day.
	(b)	**Refuse (to say 'no'):** The principal refused to admit him.
74.	(a)	**Die (to pass away):** Mrs. Indira Gandhi died in 1984.
	(b)	**Dye (to colour):** She looks young when she dyes her hair.

75.	(a)	**Dying (passing away):** She blamed her husband in her dying statement.
	(b)	**Dyeing (the act of colouring):** He is so expert in dyeing the hair that you cannot judge whether it is natural or artificial.
76.	(a)	**Dew (drops of water on grass, etc.):** Dew drops on the grass look like pearls.
	(b)	**Due (right):** Give me my due share.
77.	(a)	**Desert (a sandy tract):** The camel is the ship of the desert.
	(b)	**Deserts (what one deserves):** The dishonest officer got his deserts when he was dismissed.
	(c)	**Dessert (a course of fruit, etc.):** After dinner you will get a dessert of dry fruit.
78.	(a)	**Device (Noun: plan or method):** He has invented a new device for killing rats.
	(b)	**Devise (Verb: to plan):** Students devise new ways to use unfair means in the examination.
79.	(a)	**Defective (faulty):** Our system of examination is very defective.
	(b)	**Deficient (weak):** He cannot make progress in studies because he is deficient in intelligence.
80.	(a)	**Decent (fine):** Decent men have decent habits.
	(b)	**Descent (downward movement):** The aeroplane developed some engine trouble and made a fast descent towards the ground.
81.	(a)	**Discover (to find out):** Columbus discovered America.
	(b)	**Invent (to make something new):** Marconi invented the wireless.
82.	(a)	**Defy (to challenge; oppose):** Good citizens do not defy the law.
	(b)	**Deify (to treat or worship as a god):** Great men are deified by the people.
83.	(a)	**Decidedly (certainly):** A horse is decidedly better than a donkey.
	(b)	**Decisively (firmly or finally):** She has decisively refused to marry him.

84.	(a)	**Disinterested (impartial):** Only a disinterested person is fit to be a judge.
	(b)	**Uninterested (taking no interest):** I hate politicians and I am uninterested in politics.
85.	(a)	**Dearness (high prices):** In these days of dearness, it is difficult to make both ends meet.
	(b)	**Dearth (shortage):** There is great dearth of honesty in our country.
86.	(a)	**Decease (death):** The decease of the beloved leader plunged the nation in grief.
	(b)	**Disease (illness):** Cancer is an incurable disease.
87.	(a)	**Disclose (to tell):** She did not disclose the name of her lover.
	(b)	**Expose (to uncover):** We must expose dis- honest and corrupt politicians.
88.	(a)	**Draught (act of drinking):** He drank a glass of milk in one draught.
	(b)	**Drought (lack of rain):** The crops failed because there was a drought.
89.	(a)	**Dose (a part of medicine, etc.):** Three doses of this medicine will cure you.
	(b)	**Doze (to feel sleepy):** Students who take a heavy breakfast doze in the class.
90.	(a)	**Drown (for living beings):** A young boy was drowned in the swimming pool.
	(b)	**Sink (for lifeless things):** The ship sank and many people were drowned.
91.	(a)	**Dual (double; meant for two):** Two students can sit on this dual desk.
	(b)	**Duel (a fight between two persons):** In a duel, either of the two fighters loses his life.
92.	(a)	**Deference (respect):** Deference for the law is the first principle of a good citizen.
	(b)	**Difference (distinction):** There is a hell of difference between saying and doing.
93.	(a)	**Dependent (one who depends):** He is a dependent on his parents.
	(b)	**Dependence (state of depending):** Too much dependence on parents makes the children weak and helpless.

94.	(a)	**Deprecate (to disapprove):** Everyone deprecated his rude behaviour.
	(b)	**Depreciate (to lower the value of):** Don't depreciate his efforts to help you.
95.	(a)	**Economic (financial):** The economic condition of farmers is much better now.
	(b)	**Economical (frugal):** Only economical people can save some money for a rainy day.
96.	(a)	**Efficient (capable):** The clerk is very efficient in his work.
	(b)	**Efficacious (effective):** The medicine was so efficacious that it cured me in no time.
97.	(a)	**Eligible (fit to be chosen):** Only graduates are eligible for this post.
	(b)	**Illegible (that which cannot be read):** Illegible handwriting creates a poor impression.
98.	(a)	**Error (mistake):** Your essay is full of errors.
	(b)	**Fault (defect):** He is always finding fault with me.
99.	(a)	**Eminent (famous):** Newton was an eminent scientist.
	(b)	**Imminent (likely to happen soon):** There are dark clouds in the sky and rain is imminent.
100.	(a)	**Empty (without things):** Children are playing with empty match boxes.
	(b)	**Vacant (without persons):** No seat is vacant in the hall.
101.	(a)	**Envious (jealous):** My friends are envious of my success.
	(b)	**Enviable (admirable; fit to be followed):** Mahatma Gandhi had enviable qualities of character.
102.	(a)	**Envy (in a good sense):** Your courage arouses my envy.
	(b)	**Jealousy (in a bad sense):** His heart is burning with jealousy at my success.
103.	(a)	**Excuse (for a small thing):** Please excuse me for the delay.
	(b)	**Pardon (for serious thing):** Even God will not pardon you for such a heartless murder.

104.	**(a)**	**Excite (arouse):** Success excited in us a feeling of joy.
	(b)	**Incite (to instigate for evil):** He incited the students to go on strike.
105.	**(a)**	**Expenditure (money spent):** Your expenditure should not exceed your income.
	(b)	**Expenses (cost):** I shall bear the expenses of your travelling.
106.	**(a)**	**Expedient (useful; helpful):** A light exercise in the morning is very expedient for health.
	(b)	**Expeditious (quick):** You will not get an expeditious reply from a government office.
107.	**(a)**	**Elect (to choose by voting):** People elect their representatives.
	(b)	**Select (by choice):** She took a long time to select a saree.
108.	**(a)**	**Elder (senior relative):** She is my elder sister.
	(b)	**Older (only age factor):** The clerk is older than the officer.
109.	**(a)**	**Exercise (physical practice):** A little exercise in the morning will keep you fit.
	(b)	**Exorcise (to drive out an evil spirit by magic or prayers):** A magician was called to exorcise the evil spirit.
110.	**(a)**	**Envelop (to surround):** The baby was enveloped in a shawl.
	(b)	**Envelope (cover of a letter, etc.):** He opened the envelope and read the letter.
111.	**(a)**	**Elicit (to draw out):** You cannot elicit any information from him.
	(b)	**Illicit (unlawful; forbidden):** Her husband killed her because she had illicit relations with some other man.
112.	**(a)**	**Ensure (to make sure):** This book will ensure your success in the examination.
	(b)	**Insure (to enter into contract for payment of damages):** My car has been insured against theft and accident.
113.	**(a)**	**Fair (just; beautiful):** A fair face attracts every eye.
	(b)	**Fare (money charged for a journey; to get on; food):** I paid the fare and got the ticket.
114.	**(a)**	**Farther (more in distance):** From Chandigarh, Delhi is farther than Ambala.
	(b)	**Further (more):** He failed twice and made no further attempt.
115.	**(a)**	**Fatal (deadly; causing death):** Many people were killed in that fatal accident.
	(b)	**Fatalist (one who believes in fate):** Fatalists curse their fate when they fail.
	(c)	**Fateful (important):** Marriage is a fateful event in the life of a person.
116.	**(a)**	**Facile (easy):** Our team won a facile victory because the other team was very weak.
	(b)	**Facial (of the face):** She removes her facial hair with a razor.
117.	**(a)**	**Facility (comfort):** You will get every facility in the college hostel.
	(b)	**Felicity (happiness):** Our parents wish and pray for our felicity.
	(c)	**Faculty (power):** The aim of education is to develop all our faculties.
118.	**(a)**	**Feat (trick):** People were amused to see the feats of the magician.
	(b)	**Feet (plural of 'foot'):** He touched the feet of his father to get his blessings.
119.	**(a)**	**Floor (lower surface of a room, etc.):** Take this chair; do not sit on the floor.
	(b)	**Flour (corn powder):** Bread is made from wheat flour.
120.	**(a)**	**Forceful (powerful):** He made a forceful speech.
	(b)	**Forcible (done by force):** Robbers made a forcible entry into the house.
121.	**(a)**	**Foul (unfair):** He has made a lot of money by foul means.
	(b)	**Fowl (a bird):** Man learnt to kill fowls for his food.
122.	**(a)**	**Forego (to go before):** It was a foregone conclusion that he would fail.
	(b)	**Forgo (to go without):** Late comers will forgo their lunch.
123.	**(a)**	**Flee (to run away):** Cowards flee from the battlefield.
	(b)	**Fly (to soar):** Birds fly in the air.

124.	(a)	**Formally (as a matter of form or ceremony):** The function was formally declared open by the chief guest.
	(b)	**Formerly (earlier):** Formerly people used to travel on horseback.
125.	(a)	**Forth (forward):** He has come forth for the interview.
	(b)	**Fourth (number after third):** April is the fourth month of the year.
126.	(a)	**Flair (taste; aptitude):** She has a flair for dance and music.
	(b)	**Flare (to burst into a flame or rage):** She flared up with rage to see her husband in the arms of another woman.
127.	(a)	**Ferment (to undergo chemical changes):** Fruit juices ferment if they are kept for a long time.
	(b)	**Foment (to increase disorder or discontent):** The leader of the factory workers is out to foment trouble.
128.	(a)	**Gait (manner of walking):** She has got a charming gait.
	(b)	**Gate (main door):** This is the main gate of the college.
129.	(a)	**Gaol (jail; prison):** There are many prisoners in this gaol.
	(b)	**Goal (aim or score):** Our football team scored two goals.
130.	(a)	**Gamble (to play with stakes):** People drink and gamble in clubs.
	(b)	**Gambol (to jump or dance):** The goat was gambolling in the field.
131.	(a)	**Gentle (kind):** Kind and gentle words win every heart.
	(b)	**Genteel (belonging to upper classes of society):** Genteel people are fond of fashions.
132.	(a)	**Graceful (charming):** She looks very graceful in the new dress.
	(b)	**Gracious (kind, merciful):** God is gracious to one and all.
133.	(a)	**Grate (fire place):** Fire is burning in the grate.
	(b)	**Great (big):** Lives of great men inspire us to be great.

134.	(a)	**Guess (imagine):** Can you guess who is coming today?
	(b)	**Suppose (believe):** I suppose. it will rain today.
135.	(a)	**Hail (great; welcome):** People hailed the prime minister with shouts of joy.
	(b)	**Hale (healthy):** The mother and the baby are hale and hearty.
136.	(a)	**Hair:** She has long and curly hair.
	(b)	**Hare (rabbit):** A hare and a tortoise ran a race.
	(c)	**Heir (successor):** The adopted child will be his heir.
137.	(a)	**Heal (to cure):** This wound will heal in a few days.
	(b)	**Heel (back part of the foot or shoe):** Short women wear shoes with high heels.
138.	(a)	**Heard (listened):** I heard a loud noise in the street.
	(b)	**Herd (group of cattle):** We saw a herd of elephants in the forest.
139.	(a)	**Hanged (killed with a rope round the neck):** He was hanged for murder.
	(b)	**Hung (suspended):** The new calendar will be hung on the wall.
140.	(a)	**Honorary (without any salary):** An honorary job carries no salary.
	(b)	**Honourable (worthy of honour; respectable):** I appeal to the honourable judges of this court.
141.	(a)	**Hangar (building in which aircraft are housed):** The new aircraft are kept in this hangar.
	(b)	**Hanger (for holding clothes):** Your shirt is on the hanger.
142.	(a)	**Historic (important):** The Shimla Agreement was a historic decision.
	(b)	**Historical (connected with history):** Delhi is a historical city.
143.	(a)	**Hoard (to amass):** The misers hoard money.
	(b)	**Horde (a gang or group):** Hordes of people from Bangladesh came to India after 1971 Indo-Pak war.

144.	**(a)**	**House (building to live in):** They have built a new house in Model Town.
	(b)	**Home (place for living):** Even birds return home in the evening.
145.	**(a)**	**Human (concerning man):** To err is human, to forgive divine.
	(b)	**Humane (kind):** Women are humane by nature.
146.	**(a)**	**Humiliation (insult; disgrace):** Defeat will bring shame and humiliation.
	(b)	**Humility (modesty):** Out of humility, he touched the feet of his teacher.
147.	**(a)**	**Haunt (to trouble or visit like a ghost):** Your sins will haunt your mind.
	(b)	**Hunt (to go after wild animals):** There was a time when man hunted wild animals for food.
148.	**(a)**	**Hear (natural hearing):** The deaf cannot hear.
	(b)	**Listen (to hear attentively):** Listen to what the teacher says.
149.	**(a)**	**Hamlet (a small village):** It is a hamlet of half a dozen houses.
	(b)	**Helmet (protective head-covering of metal worn by drivers, soldiers and fire- men):** In cities like Chandigarh, you are not allowed to drive a scooter or motorcycle without a helmet on your head.
150.	**(a)**	**Ideal (model; perfect):** Chandigarh is an ideal city.
	(b)	**Idle (without work):** An idle mind is a devil's workshop.
	(c)	**Idol (image of God):** Idols are worshipped in India.
151.	**(a)**	**Imaginary (unreal):** A mountain of butter is an imaginary idea.
	(b)	**Imaginative (full of imagination):** The mind of a poet is highly imaginative.
152.	**(a)**	**Impassable (which cannot be crossed or passed):** The thick forest is impassable.
	(b)	**Impossible (not possible):** It is impossible to live without food and air.

153.	**(a)**	**Industrial (concerning industries):** There are many factories in the industrial area of the city.
	(b)	**Industrious (hard-working):** Industrious people never sit idle.
154.	**(a)**	**Intolerable (unbearable):** My father's insult is intolerable to me.
	(b)	**Intolerant (not liberal; not tolerating the views and opinions of others):** Blind followers of religion are often intolerant.
155.	**(a)**	**Inflammatory (which sets something on fire; exciting):** He was arrested for making inflammatory speeches.
	(b)	**Inflammable (that which catches fire easily; excitable):** Petrol is highly inflammable.
156.	**(a)**	**Ingenious (skilful):** An ingenious mechanic can earn a lot of money.
	(b)	**Ingenuous (frank and innocent):** Children are ingenuous by nature.
157.	**(a)**	**Implicit (hinted; indirectly expressed):** There is an implicit threat in the speeches of the Pakistani prime minister.
	(b)	**Explicit (clear):** It is explicit that Pakistan is helping the militants.
158.	**(a)**	**Immunity (freedom from disease or taxation):** Vaccination gives us immunity from smallpox.
	(b)	**Impunity (without the fear of punishment):** Politicians indulge in crimes with impunity.
159.	**(a)**	**Ill (down with fever):** He has been ill for a week.
	(b)	**Sick (unwell):** He was feeling sick because he ate too much.
160.	**(a)**	**Jealous (having ill will):** We should not be jealous of others.
	(b)	**Zealous (enthusiastic):** A zealous worker never sits idle.
161.	**(a)**	**Judicial (of judge or court of justice):** A village panchayat has some judicial powers.
	(b)	**Judicious (wise):** One should be judicious in the choice of friends.

162.	(a)	**Kindle (to burn):** Her beauty kindled the flame of love in every heart.
	(b)	**Candle (a stick of wax):** You cannot read in the dim light of the candle.
163.	(a)	**Knotty (difficult):** There are many knotty problems before the country.
	(b)	**Naughty (mischievous):** The naughty boy is teasing his mother.
164.	(a)	**Knead (to make flour and water into firm paste):** She was kneading the flour to make chapattis.
	(b)	**Need (necessity):** A friend in need is a friend indeed.
165.	(a)	**Knave (rogue):** Only a knave will cheat his own father.
	(b)	**Naïve (natural and innocent in speech and behaviour):** The naïve girl told me everything about her life.
166.	(a)	**Last (final and no more):** He is the first to come and the last to go.
	(b)	**Latest (fresh):** Have you heard the latest news?
167.	(a)	**Lessen (to reduce):** A dose of medicine will lessen the pain.
	(b)	**Lesson (moral):** What lesson do you learn from this story?
168.	(a)	**Later (more late):** Mohan came later than Sohan.
	(b)	**Latter (the second of the two):** Of tea and milk, the latter is better.
169.	(a)	**Legislation (making laws):** There is no legislation against drinking.
	(b)	**Legislature (a law-making body):** Legislature is concerned with the making of laws.
170.	(a)	**Lightening (reducing the weight or burden):** Friends help us in lightening the burden of our heart.
	(b)	**Lightning (electric discharge in the sky):** It started raining soon after a flash of lightning.
171.	(a)	**Lion (a big tiger):** The lion is the king of the jungle.
	(b)	**Loin (lower part of the back):** The wrestler was wearing a loin cloth.
172.	(a)	**Literal (word for word):** Translation should not be literal.
	(b)	**Literary (concerning literature):** This poem is of great literary value.
	(c)	**Literate (educated):** He is literate enough to write a letter.
173.	(a)	**Live (to have life):** We cannot live without food and air.
	(b)	**Exist (to be):** Ghosts do not exist anywhere.
174.	(a)	**Limit (end):** Greed has no limit.
	(b)	**Limitation (inability):** It is his limitation that he cannot speak in public.
175.	(a)	**Loath (unwilling):** She was loath to sit beside me in the car.
	(b)	**Loathe (to hate):** I loathe the very sight of drunkard.
176.	(a)	**Lose (to suffer a loss):** The more you gamble, the more you lose.
	(b)	**Loose (too big):** My father's coat is too loose for me.
	(c)	**Loss (Noun from 'lose'):** He has suffered a loss in business.
177.	(a)	**Lonely (sad, friendless):** If you feel lonely, get married at once.
	(b)	**Solitary (single):** I love a solitary walk in the morning.
178.	(a)	**Lovable (fit to be loved):** Honesty is a lovable quality.
	(b)	**Lovely (beautiful):** She looks very lovely in a blue saree.
179.	(a)	**Luxury (costly pleasure):** Only the rich can enjoy the luxury of a car.
	(b)	**Comfort (ease):** Fans give us comfort in summer.
180.	(a)	**Luxuriant (rich in growth):** Bengali women have luxuriant hair.
	(b)	**Luxurious (full of luxuries):** The rich lead a luxurious life.
181.	(a)	**Mail (dock):** The postman has delivered the mail.
	(b)	**Male (masculine):** Sweets are distributed when a male child is born.

182.	(a)	**Main (chief):** This is the main gate of the college.
	(b)	**Mane (hair on the neck of a horse):** I have cut off the mane of my horse.
183.	(a)	**Marry (to wed):** She will not like to marry a clerk.
	(b)	**Merry (gay, cheerful):** Let us eat, drink and be merry.
184.	(a)	**Meat (flesh):** Vegetarians do not eat meat.
	(b)	**Meet (to see a person):** I am very glad to meet you.
	(c)	**Mete (to give):** Full justice will be meted out to you.
185.	(a)	**Metal (gold, silver, iron, etc.):** Gold is a precious metal.
	(b)	**Mettle (courage):** Hardships test the mettle of man.
186.	(a)	**Medal (a token of honour):** He has won many prizes and medals in games.
	(b)	**Meddle (to interfere):** Men should not meddle with the affairs of women.
187.	(a)	**Memorable (fit to be remembered):** Marriage is a memorable affair of women.
	(b)	**Memorial (a token of memory):** The Taj is a memorial built by Shah Jahan in the memory of Mumtaz Mahal.
188.	(a)	**Miner (a worker in a mine):** Two hundred miners work in this mine.
	(b)	**Minor (small; petty):** We can overlook this minor mistake.
189.	(a)	**Mantel (shelf above the fire place):** The picture of the grandfather is on the mantel.
	(b)	**Mental (of the mind):** He is suffering from mental trouble.
190.	(a)	**Mayor (head of a municipal corporation):** He is the mayor of Delhi Municipal Corporation.
	(b)	**Mare (female horse):** The horse is running after the mare.
191.	(a)	**Maize (a kind of corn; makki):** The maize crop has been damaged by rain.
	(b)	**Maze (confusing network of lines or paths):** I was lost in the maze of narrow lanes and streets.

192.	(a)	**Moral (concerning good conduct):** Politicians have no moral principles.
	(b)	**Morale (high spirit):** The morale of our players is very high.
193.	(a)	**Mortal (perishable):** The body is mortal but the soul is immortal.
	(b)	**Mortar (mixture of sand and cement, etc.):** We need bricks and mortar to build a house.
194.	(a)	**Momentary (lasting for a moment; short-lived; temporary):** Wine gives a momentary pleasure.
	(b)	**Momentous (important):** Prince Siddhartha took a momentous decision and left the pleasures of the palace.
195.	(a)	**Mysterious (secret, unknown):** Mysterious are the ways of God.
	(b)	**Mystical (spiritual):** Blake is a mystical poet.
196.	(a)	**Meter (an instrument for measurement):** Our electric meter is out of order.
	(b)	**Metre (measure of length):** Cloth is measured by metres.
197.	(a)	**Magnet (lodestone):** Magnet attracts iron.
	(b)	**Magnate (wealthy leading man of business or industry):** Big business magnates were present at the meeting.
198.	(a)	**Negligent (careless):** He is so negligent in his work that he makes several mistakes every day.
	(b)	**Negligible (of no importance):** A negligible amount of ten rupees can please a beggar.
199.	(a)	**Necessaries (basic needs):** Food, clothing and shelter are the necessaries of life.
	(b)	**Necessities (urgent needs):** School and colleges are modern necessities.
200.	(a)	**Notable (important):** Many notable people were present at the function.
	(b)	**Noticeable (visible; which can be seen):** The movement of the minute hand of the watch is hardly noticeable.

201.	(a)	**Notorious (infamous; well known in a bad sense):** He is a notorious smuggler.
	(b)	**Famous (well known in a good sense):** Rabindranath Tagore is a famous poet of India.
202.	(a)	**Official (concerned with office):** My official duty is over at 5 p.m.
	(b)	**Officious (too eager to help or offer services):** He was so officious that he went on pressing me to eat fish against my wishes.
203.	(a)	**Observance (performance of rites, etc.):** She is very careful in the observance of her religious duties.
	(b)	**Observation (seeing carefully):** Writers are interested in the observation of life.
204.	(a)	**Ordinance (authoritative order):** The president has the power to issue an ordinance.
	(b)	**Ordnance (military supplies like guns, shells, bombs):** There is an ordnance factory at Kanpur.
205.	(a)	**Ostensible (apparent; outward):** Business is his ostensible profession, but actually he is a smuggler.
	(b)	**Ostentatious (showy):** Rich people make an ostentatious display of wealth at marriages.
206.	(a)	**Pain (trouble):** Pain and pleasure go hand in hand in life.
	(b)	**Pane (a window glass):** Angry people broke the window panes.
207.	(a)	**Pall (cover, cloak, dark cloud):** There was a pall of gloom after the death of the head of the family.
	(b)	**Pale (yellow):** She turned pale with fear.
208.	(a)	**Pair (a set of two things): I have bought a** new pair of shoes.
	(b)	**Pare (to cut):** I pare my nails every Sunday.
	(c)	**Couple (a husband and a wife):** Ram and Sita were an ideal couple.
209.	(a)	**Patrol (to guard; to go round):** Policemen patrol the streets at night.
	(b)	**Petrol (motor oil):** The car ran short of petrol and stopped.

210.	(a)	**Perpetrate (commit):** Many crimes are perpetrated in the name of religion.
	(b)	**Perpetuate (to make permanent or long lasting):** Noble work perpetuates the memory of a man.
211.	(a)	**Personal (of a person):** My personal needs are very few.
	(b)	**Personnel (staff):** This canteen is meant for military personnel.
212.	(a)	**Persecute (to oppress):** Aurangzeb persecuted the Hindus.
	(b)	**Prosecute (to take legal action; to continue):** Trespassers will be prosecuted.
213.	(a)	**Peal (loud sound):** I heard a peal of thunder.
	(b)	**Peel (to remove the skin):** Peel the banana before eating it.
214.	(a)	**Personate (to play the part of another person):** The person who personated him in the examination hall was arrested.
	(b)	**Personify (to give human qualities to a thing):** Poets personify the objects of nature.
215.	(a)	**Pray (to worship):** We should pray to God for help.
	(b)	**Prey (victim):** The lion is a beast of prey.
216.	(a)	**Pitiable (deserving pity):** The condition of the dying old man was pitiable.
	(b)	**Pitiful (kind, merciful):** We should be pitiful to the animals.
217.	(a)	**Persuade (to bring round):** My mother is persuading me to get married.
	(b)	**Pursued (chased):** The hunter pursued the deer.
218.	(a)	**Prescribe (to recommend):** My doctor has prescribed this medicine.
	(b)	**Proscribe (to ban):** This book has been proscribed in Pakistan.
219.	(a)	**Precedent (example for others):** Teachers who smoke set a bad precedent for their students.
	(b)	**President (highest man):** The President of India has vast powers, but he never exercises them.

220.	(a)	**Precede (to go before):** Rajiv Gandhi preceded P.V. Narasimha Rao as prime minister.
	(b)	**Proceed (to go ahead):** Let us proceed to the next topic.
221.	(a)	**Primary (basic):** Food, clothing and shelter are our primary needs.
	(b)	**Primitive (ancient):** Primitive people lived in forests and hunted animals for food.
222.	(a)	**Prophecy (act of foretelling; Noun):** Your prophecy proved true and she got a son.
	(b)	**Prophesy (to foretell; verb):** You prophesied that she would get a son.
223.	(a)	**Popular (loved by all):** A good teacher is very popular with his students.
	(b)	**Populous (thickly populated):** Calcutta is the most populous city of India.
224.	(a)	**Pour (to put):** She poured tea into my cup.
	(b)	**Pore (a small hole in the skin):** Sweat comes out of the pores of our body.
225.	(a)	**Practice (practical work):** Practice makes a man perfect.
	(b)	**Practise (to work; Verb):** It is easy to preach but difficult to practise.
226.	(a)	**Practical (concerning practice):** Practical work is the secret of success and progress.
	(b)	**Practicable (workable):** Your plan was rejected because it was not practicable.
227.	(a)	**Principal (head of a school or college):** The new principal has given a new shape to our college.
	(b)	**Principle (rule):** Politicians have no principles.
228.	(a)	**Punctual (regular about time):** Only a punctual teacher can make his students punctual.
	(b)	**Punctilious (very careful):** He is very punctilious about his dress and manners.
229.	(a)	**Possible (less likely):** It is not possible for us to fly in the air.
	(b)	**Probable (very likely):** It is probable that the train may be late.
230.	(a)	**Profit (gain):** Every trader works for profit.
	(b)	**Prophet (a divine messenger):** The Buddha was a prophet of peace.
231.	(a)	**Paddle (to walk in water):** Children were paddling in rain water.
	(b)	**Peddle (to sell from door to door):** He peddles bread and eggs from door to door.
	(c)	**Pedal (part of a cycle, etc, worked by foot):** Work the pedals and the bicycle will run.
232.	(a)	**Pole (a long stick or post; of the North):** The flag is flying on the pole.
	(b)	**Poll (to vote):** Five hundred votes were polled at this polling station.
233.	(a)	**Plain (level area of the earth; simple):** In summer, it is very hot in the plains.
	(b)	**Plan (scheme):** I am making a plan to go abroad.
	(c)	**Plane (a carpenter's tool; level; aeroplane):** The carpenter is working with his plane. Soon the plane will land at the airport.
234.	(a)	**Peace (a state of calm):** The rich have no peace of mind.
	(b)	**Piece (part):** The quarrel is all about a piece of land.
235.	(a)	**Perspective (relation between different aspects of a problem):** Try to see things in their right perspective.
	(b)	**Prospective (hoped for):** Every girl wishes to see her prospective husband in a dream.
236.	(a)	**Quiet (silent):** She will not keep quiet for a single minute.
	(b)	**Quit (to leave):** At last, the British had to quit India.
	(c)	**Quite (completely):** She is quite happy after her marriage.
237.	(a)	**Rain (water falling from the clouds):** Thunder was followed by rain.
	(b)	**Rein (rule):** There was peace during the reign of the queen.

238.	(a)	**Raise (to lift):** I raised my hand to stop the car.
	(b)	**Raze (to pull down; to demolish):** In the earthquake, many buildings were razed to the ground.
239.	(a)	**Recollect (to callback to mind):** I could not recollect his name.
	(b)	**Remember (to keep in memory):** The world will remember Gandhi and Nehru.
240.	(a)	**Respectable (worthy of respect):** I belong to a very respectable family.
	(b)	**Respectful (showing respect):** Students should be respectful to their teachers.
	(c)	**Respective (particular):** Students went to their respective classes.
241.	(a)	**Regret (feeling sorry):** I regret my inability to come.
	(b)	**Remorse (repentance):** The heart of the sinner is full of remorse.
242.	(a)	**Right (privilege):** Rights and duties go hand in hand.
	(b)	**Rite (ceremony):** His eldest son performed his last rites.
243.	(a)	**Ring (to toll):** The peon will ring the bell.
	(b)	**Wring (to squeeze):** Wring the clothes and spread them on the line to dry.
244.	(a)	**Road (way or street):** Hard work is the real road to success.
	(b)	**Rod (stick):** Spare the rod and spoil the child.
	(c)	**Rode (ride, rode, ridden):** He jumped on his horse and rode away.
245.	(a)	**Role (part):** Money plays an important role in life.
	(b)	**Roll (register):** He slipped away when the teacher was calling the roll.
246.	(a)	**Root (of a tree or plant):** The roots of this tree have gone very deep.
	(b)	**Rout (to defeat):** We routed the opponents and won the trophy.
	(c)	**Route (way):** We shall go by the shortest route.

247.	(a)	**Recourse (turning for help):** He failed in love and had recourse to wine.
	(b)	**Resource (means):** India is rich in natural resources.
248.	(a)	**Sail (to move on water):** Boats were sailing on the lake.
	(b)	**Sale (act of selling):** This car is for sale.
249.	(a)	**Sensible (having good sense):** Sensible neighbours never quarrel.
	(b)	**Sensitive (easily hurt):** Sensitive people are easily upset.
250.	(a)	**Shade (opposite of light):** Trees provide cool shade in summer.
	(b)	**Shadow (dark shape):** The police was following him like a shadow.
251.	(a)	**Sight (seeing):** He fell in love with her at first sight.
	(b)	**Site (place, spot):** It is a good site for hotel.
252.	(a)	**Sole (only; lower surface of a shoe):** He is the sole owner of his father's property.
	(b)	**Soul (spirit):** Man is mortal, but his soul is immortal.
253.	(a)	**Soar (to fly):** Birds can soar in the sky.
	(b)	**Sore (paining):** Smoking gives a sore throat.
254.	(a)	**Sour (not sweet):** The fox said, 'Grapes are sour.
	(b)	**Sure (certain):** He is sure to pass.
255.	(a)	**Social (of society):** Man is a social animal.
	(b)	**Sociable (fond of mixing in society):** A sociable person can easily win friends.
256.	(a)	**Stair (one of the fixed steps):** He ran down the stairs to catch the thief.
	(b)	**Stare (to look):** Young boys often stare at young girls.
257.	(a)	**Stationary (not moving):** The earth moves but the sun is stationary.
	(b)	**Stationery (writing material):** Students need books and stationery.

258.	(a)	**Stay (to put up):** You must stay with us for a week.
	(b)	**Stop (to halt):** The train stops here only for two minutes.
259.	(a)	**Story (a tale):** He told us many funny stories.
	(b)	**Storey (floor of a house):** This building has five storeys.
260.	(a)	**Suit (a set of clothes; a law case; to fit):** A woollen suit will cost two thousand rupees.
	(b)	**Suite (as set of rooms with bed room, bath room, etc.):** I want a good suite in a hotel.
261.	(a)	**Sweet (tasting like sugar):** Honey is very sweet.
	(b)	**Sweat (perspiration):** The rickshaw-puller was covered with sweat.
262.	(a)	**Son (male child):** He was blessed with a son.
	(b)	**Sun (ball of light):** The earth moves round the sun.
263.	(a)	**Tail (part of the body of a bird or animal):** The cow has a long tail.
	(b)	**Tale (story):** This story looks like a fairy tale.
264.	(a)	**Team (a set of players etc.):** I am a member of the hockey team of the college.
	(b)	**Teem (to be full of):** The pond was teeming with fishes.
265.	(a)	**Temporary (for a short time):** He has got a temporary job for six months.
	(b)	**Temporal (earthly):** A crown is the symbol of temporal power.
266.	(a)	**Throne (the seat of a king):** A pure heart is throne of God.
	(b)	**Thrown (throw, threw, thrown):** He has thrown dust into my eyes.
267.	(a)	**Throw (to cast):** Those who lie in glass houses should not throw stones at others.
	(b)	**Through (from end to end):** The train to Shimla passes through many tunnels.
268.	(a)	**Tamper (to interfere):** It is a crime to tamper with the marks in a university certificate.
	(b)	**Temper (state of mind):** A teacher should never lose temper in the classroom.
269.	(a)	**Unqualified (not properly trained and educated):** I never go to an unqualified doctor.
	(b)	**Disqualified (debarred; punished):** If you use unfair means, you will be disqualified by the university.
270.	(a)	**Vacation (holidays):** We get summer vacation from May to July.
	(b)	**Vocation (profession):** I like the vocation of a teacher.
271.	(a)	**Vain (proud):** She is vain of her beauty.
	(b)	**Vein (blood vessels in the body):** I have noble blood in my veins.
272.	(a)	**Virtual (in practice, not in theory):** A woman is a virtual prisoner in the house.
	(b)	**Virtuous (noble):** The virtuous find virtue everywhere.
273.	(a)	**Waste (to spend uselessly):** Time is money; do no waste it.
	(b)	**Waist (part of the body):** I wear a belt round my waist.
274.	(a)	**Weak (infirm):** He is too weak to walk.
	(b)	**Week (a period of seven days):** There are seven days in a week.
275.	(a)	**Weather (atmosphere):** Rain has made the weather pleasant.
	(b)	**Whether (if):** Tell me whether you are my friend or enemy.
	(c)	**Season (a particular part of the year):** Spring is the season of flowers and fragrance.
276.	(a)	**Wander (move about aimlessly):** Loafers wander about in the streets.
	(b)	**Wonder (to be surprised):** I wonder how he has passed.

277.	(a)	**Wilful (obstinate):** Women are wilful by nature.
	(b)	**Willing (ready):** She is not willing to marry a clerk.
278.	(a)	**Womanish (like a woman, in bad sense):** A man in tears looks womanish.
	(b)	**Womanly (like a woman, in good sense):** Sita had all the womanly qualities.
279.	(a)	**Wait (to look forward to; to expect):** We are waiting for the train.
	(b)	**Weight (burden):** You must reduce your weight.
280.	(a)	**Way (method):** That is not the way to talk of your elders.
	(b)	**Weigh (to measure weight):** This shop-keeper weighs short measures.
281.	(a)	**Yarn (thread for weaving):** This sweater is made of pure woollen yarn.
	(b)	**Yearn (to have a keen desire):** In a foreign land, you will yearn for home.
282.	(a)	**Yoke (frame for two oxen; slavery):** We have thrown off the yoke of slavery.
	(b)	**Yolk (the yellow part of an egg):** The yolk of an egg is full of vitamins.

CONFUSING WORDS (Practice Tests)

Complete the sentences in the given practice tests by inserting the correct words from the brackets. Cross check your answers with the answer key given at the end of the chapter.

TEST – 1

1. All came ________ Tom. (accept, except)
2. We did not follow her ________ (advise, advice)
3. Have you considered all ________ of the question? (angels, angles)
4. We were asked to write an ________ (essay, assay)
5. Try to ________ naturally. (breath, breathe)
6. We shall ________ a chairman. (chose, choose)
7. Only linen ________ were used for the table. (cloths, clothes)
8. They were ________ of victory. (confidant, confident)
9. He was not ________ of his error. (conscience, conscious)
10. The horses were led into the ________ (coral, corral)

TEST – 2

1. He is a member of the U.S. Marine ________ (corpse, corps)
2. It is their ________ to dine at seven. (custom, costume)
3. Good advice is good ________ (consul, counsel)
4. A daily recording of one's personal experiences is a ________ (diary, dairy)
5. Legal heirs of the ________ were notified. (diseased, deceased)
6. The ______ was hazardous). (decent, desecent)
7. To object is to ________ (demure, demur)
8. What have we for lunch ____? (desert, dessert)
9. He constructed a safety ______ (device, devise)
10. The fog will soon ________ the town. (envelope, envelop)

TEST – 3

1. A distinctive period of time in history is an ________ (epoch, epic)
2. Costly and ________ are synonyms. (expensive, expansive)
3. Her ________ words were soothing. (gentle, gentile)
4. He is ________ unaware of his predicament. (holy, wholly)
5. Cruelty to animals is not ________ (human, humane)
6. She arrived ________ than usual. (later, latter)
7. There must be some means of ________ the work. (lightning, lightening)
8. Dialect adds ________ color. (locale, local)
9. Do not ________ your patience. (lose, loose)
10. He walked with a ________ stride. (martial, marital)

TEST – 4

1. He was in a jovial ________ (mood, mode)
2. If one conforms to a standard of what is right, one is ________ (moral, morale)
3. Let us not become ________ in our remarks. (personal, personnel)
4. ________ with your plans. (Proceed, Precede)

5. I ________ your rapid rise to success. (prophesy, prophecy)
6. What is the ________ of this inquiry? (purpose, propose)
7. How ________ the room is! (quiet, quite)
8. I ________ that remark. (recent, resent)
9. The young folks accepted the older man's counsel ________ (respectively, respectfully)
10. A ________ was reserved at the hotel. (suite, suit)

TEST – 5

1. ________ unfortunate for him. (It's, its)
2. ________ turns is it? Who's, Whose)
3. Was ________ no mail today? (there, their)
4. How late are you ________ to stay? (aloud, allowed)
5. ________ going with you? (Who's, Whose)
6. ________ are your papers. (Here, Hear)
7. We were ________ late to ________ the opening number. (to, too, two (here, hear)
8. I need more ________ to complete my letter. (stationary, stationery)
9. We were ________ along narrow paths. (lead, led)
10. No one is ________ bad. (altogether, all together)

TEST – 6

1. Have you ________ Tom your new car? (shone, shown)
2. ________ go my good friends. (They're, Their, There)
3. ________ entering the building. (They're, Their, There)
4. Have you finished, ________? (too, to, two)
5. Let us whistle ________ (altogether, all together)
6. The kitten lost ________ ball. (it's, its)
7. We were ________ through the museum. (shone, shown)
8. The freshly polished silver ________ brightly. (shone, shown)
9. Never board a train that is not ________ (stationery, stationary)
10. ________ not too late to turn back. (Its, It's)

TEST – 7

1. Use the center ________ (aisle, isle).
2. He has ________ gone. (already, all ready)
3. We need to ________ our plans. (altar, alter)
4. He is ________ on time. (always, all ways)
5. The ________ is steep. (ascent, assent)
6. A large ________ is expected. (attendants, attendance)
7. We lolled on the sandy ________ (beech, beach)
8. The present ________ rate is high. (birth, berth)
9. Cars must have good ________ (breaks, brakes)
10. Our horses followed the ________ path. (bridle, bridal)

TEST – 8

1. A house to house ________ was made. (canvas, canvass)
2. Each state has a ________ city. (capital, capitol)
3. The ________ of the play is small. (cast, caste)
4. The story ran as a ________ (cereal, serial)
5. It was necessary for the committee to have a long ________ (session, cession)
6. They have a beautiful ________ beside a lake for their new home. (site, cite)
7. I consider his remark a ________, not an insult. (complement, compliment)
8. The village ________ met to elect new officers. (council, counsel)

9. The capsized boat disappeared in the swift ________ (current, currant)
10. The ________ in this material is not fast. (dye, die)

TEST – 9

1. He has a ________ personality. (duel, dual)
2. A ________ is a mythological character. (faun, fawn)
3. The learning of the entire selection was a ________ of memory. (feet, feat)
4. A distress ________ was noticed. (flair, flare)
5. We went ________ with our plans. (foreword, forward)
6. ________ air is unhealthful. (Foul, Fowl)
7. See the colts ________ in the pasture. (gambol, gamble)
8. Rembrandt was a ________ artist. (grate, great)
9. Although old, he is still ________ (hale, hail)
10. One adversity often comes upon the ________ of another. (heal, heel)

TEST – 10

1. We discussed the ________ matter. (whole, hole)
2. Do not make money your ________ (idle, idol, idyll)
3. ________ years brought hardships. (Lean, Lien)
4. He has a dignified ________ (mean, mien)
5. He excelled at the tennis ________. (meet, mete, meat)
6. A youth under twenty-one is a ________. (minor, miner)
7. She is still ________ her loss. (mourning, morning)
8. Do not live in the ________. (passed, past)
9. ________ has its reward. (Patients, Patience)
10. We walked to the edge of the ________ (peer, pier)

TEST – 11

1. Her clothes are ________ but in good taste. (plain, plane)
2. Every good citizen goes to the ________. (polls, poles)
3. The chairman requested the ________ of every member. (presents, presence)
4. The ________ of the high school addressed the students. (principle, principal)
5. The King's ________ was of short duration. (rain, rein, reign)
6. The old building will be ________ a new one will be built in its place. (razed, raised)
7. Parcels for mailing must be ________ carefully. (rapt, wrapped, rapped)
8. The ________ of this area petitioned for bus service. (residence, residents)
9. A benefit ________ was staged by the students. (review, revue)
10. The bell has a harsh ________. (wring, ring)

TEST – 12

1. ________ yourself for bad news. (Steel, Steal)
2. Come ________ to the point. (strait, straight)
3. It was hard to ________ ourselves away from the exciting discussion. (tare, tear)
4. We have no more room; ________ we must enlarge the building. (therefore, therefor)
5. He ________ away every opportunity. (threw, through)
6. The theatrical ________ traveled in trailers. (troop, troupe)
7. There is a ________ of sarcasm in his remarks. (vein, vane, vain)
8. He ________ all rights. (waived, waved)
9. You ________ blue well. (ware, wear)
10. I am ________ out. (warn, worn)

TEST – 13

1. Have you ________ the invitation? (excepted, accepted)
2. Please ________ me on the matter. (advice, advise)
3. This is easier ________ I thought. (than, then)
4. Are you ________ sure? (quite, quiet)
5. You must ________ between the two. (chose, choose)
6. ________ no time. (Lose, Loose)
7. I am not ________ to blame. (holy, wholly)
8. He spoke ________ to his elders. (respectfully, respectively)
9. After discussing every ________ of the problem, we arrived at no solution. (angle, angel)
10. The actors were attired in colourful ________ (customs, costumes)

TEST – 14

1. Have you decided on a ________ for your story? (local, locale)
2. His ________ of living was different from ours. (mood, mode)
3. He is ________ that he will be chosen. (confident, confidant)
4. What do you ________ that we do? (purpose, propose)
5. A ________ supplies us with milk. (diary, dairy)
6. Let your ________ be your guide. (conscious, conscience)
7. Do not ________ from the path. (wander, wonder)
8. After ________ the load, we proceeded. (lightning, lightening)
9. The ________ of the dejected man was restored by encouraging words. (moral, morale)
10. Mirages are often seen on ________. (deserts, desserts).

TEST – 15

1. ________ are ________ many errors ________. (There, Their, They're) (too, to, two) (here, hear)
2. ________ themes were read ________? (Who's, Whose) (allowed, aloud)
3. ________ personality ________ ________ late. (Its, It's) (all together, altogether) (to, two, too)
4. As we were ________ through the park, we were ________ unusual trees. (lead, led) (shone, shown)
5. ________ not to leave the car until it is ________. (Their, They're, There) (stationery, stationary)
6. He walked slowly ________ the room. (through, threw)
7. Their ________ was recently vacated. (residents, residence)
8. He is a man of high ________. (principals, principles)
9. Have you ________ the test? (passed, past)
10. Many ________ were waiting for the doctor. (patience, patients)

TEST – 16

1. His explanations were ________. (plane, plain)
2. He will ________ for votes. (canvas, canvass)
3. Paris is the ________ of France. (capital, capitol)
4. The two colors are ________. (compliments, complements)
5. ________ jelly is delicious. (Current, Currant)
6. The ________ of a book is in the introductory section. (forward, foreword)
7. ________ seated the audience. (Attendance, Attendants)
8. He looked ________ from overwork. (warn, worn)
9. The building was ________ by fire. (raised, razed)
10. He refused ________ from his elders. (council, counsel)

TEST – 17

1. The coal ________ struck the higher wages. (minors, miners)
2. The police could not ________ a confession from her. (ring, wring)
3. I was asked to play a ________ role. (duel, dual)
4. I attended a court ________ today. (cession, session)
5. Do not ________ the dish. (brake, break)
6. Can you ________ the lines? (cite, site)
7. With ________ attention the children gazed at him. (wrapped, rapped, rapt)
8. She ________ her inheritance. (waved, waived)
9. She has a ________ for dramatics. (flair, flare)
10. They were ________ when I arrived. (all ready, already)

ANSWERS

	TEST – 1	TEST – 2	TEST – 3	TEST – 4	TEST – 5	TEST – 6
1.	except	corps	epoch	mood	it's	shown
2.	advice	custom	expensive	moral	whose	there
3.	angles	counsel	gentle	personal	there	they're
4.	essay	diary	wholly	proceed	allowed	too
5.	breathe	deceased	humane	prophesy	who's	all together
6.	choose	descent	later	purpose	here	its
7.	cloths	demur	lightening	quiet	too, hear	shown
8.	confident	dessert	local	resent	stationery	shone
9.	conscious	device	lose	respectfully	led	stationary
10.	corral	envelop	martial	suite	altogether	it's

ANSWERS

	TEST – 7	TEST – 8	TEST – 9	TEST – 10	TEST – 11	TEST – 12
1.	aisle	canvass	dual	whole	plain	steel
2.	already	capital	faun	idol	polls	straight
3.	alter	cast	feat	lean	presence	tear
4.	always	serial	flare	mien	principal	therefore
5.	ascent	session	forward	meet	reign	threw
6.	attendance	site	foul	minor	razed	troupe
7.	beach	compliment	gambol	mourning	wrapped	Vein
8.	birth	council	great	past	residents	waived
9.	brakes	current	hale	patience	revue	wear
10.	bridle	dye	heel	pier	ring	worn

ANSWERS					
	TEST – 13	TEST – 14	TEST – 15	TEST – 16	TEST – 17
1.	accepted	locale	There, too, here	plain	miners
2.	advise	mode	Whose, were, aloud	canvass	wring
3.	than	confident	It's, altogether, too	capital	dual
4.	quite	propose	led, shown	complements	session
5.	choose	dairy	They're, stationary	currant	break
6.	lose	conscience	through	foreword	cite
7.	wholly	wander	residence	attendants	rapt
8.	respectfully	lightening	principles	worn	waived
9.	angle	morale	passed	razed	flair
10.	costumes	deserts	patients	counsel	all ready

SPELLING OF WORDS (Words Commonly Misspelt)

SET – 1

Abbreviate
Apparently
Commission
Accidentally
Appetite
Committee
Acclaim
Argument
Commodity
Accommodate
Arrangement
Communism
Accompanied
Athlete
Comparative
Accompanying
Athletics
Competitive
Accuse
Attitude
Compulsory
Achievement
Auxiliary
Conceive
Acknowledge
Awkward
Conceivable
Acquaintance
Beginning
Condemn
Acquitted

Breathe
Conscious
Address
Brilliant
Continually
Adolescent
Bulletin
Convenience
Affluent
Bureau
Corner
Affirm
Bureaucracy
Correspond
Affright
Buried
Corrode
Aggravate
Business
Corrupt
Aggression
Cafeteria
Course
Allegory
Campaign
Curiosity
Allure
Casually
Courteous
Allusive
Career

Believed
Conquer
Across
Benefited
Conscientious
Additionally
Curriculum
Amateur
Ceiling
Decision
Amiss
Cemetery
Definitely
Amount
Changeable
Definition

Criticism
Although
Carrying
Criticize
Altogether
Category
Characteristic
Demurrage
Annals
Chosen
Dependent
Annual
Colleague
Describe
Apostle
Colloquial

SET – 2

Despair
Disappeared
Dissolute
Destroy
Disappointment
Divide
Develop
Disastrous
Division
Diagram
Discipline
Eccentric
Dictionary
Dissatisfied

Especially
Generally
Eliminate
Essence
Genius
Elocution
Etiquette
Geography
Eloquence
Evolution
Government
Embarrass
Excellence
Grammar

Ecclesiastic
Different
Dissect
Efficiency
Dilapidated
Dissertation
Effusion
Dining
Dissipate
Egotism
Disease
Dissipation
Eight
Elsewhere
Handle
Enthusiastic
Experience
Height
Environment
Explanation
Hindrance
Epidemic
Extraordinary
Hitherto
Epitaph
Familiar
Humorous
Epitome
Fascinating
Hurriedly
Epoch
February
Imaginary
Equalled

Emissary
Exceptionally
Grievance
Emphasize
Excitement
Guarantee
Encyclopaedia
Exhausted
Guard
Ennoble
Exhilaration
Guidance
Enormous
Existence
Financial
Imagination
Equipment
Foreign
Immediately
Equipped
Formerly
Impromptu
Equivalent
Forty
Inaccessible
Erosion
Fourth
Inadequate
Errand
Friend
Inapplicable
Erroneous
Gauge
Inauspicious

SET – 3

Incidentally
Irrelevant
Mathematics
Incredible

Lieutenant
Nevertheless
Intellectual
Lightning

Knack
Medicine
Indefinitely
Knight
Minute
Independent
Knot
Mischievous
Inexorable
Knowledge
Morale
Influential
Laboratory
Mysterious
Inimical
Legitimate
Naïve
Inimitable
Leisure
Naturally
Innocuous
Librarian
Necessary
Innuendo
Physician
Occurred
Pamphlet
Pleasant
Occurrence
Parallel
Propelled
Offspring
Parliament
Propeller
Omission
Particularly
Quitting
Otherwise
Persuade
Quiz

Niece
Intelligence
Livelihood
Ninety
Intentionally
Loneliness
Ninth
Interfere
Manoeuvre
Noisily
Interpreted
Marriage
Notwithstanding
Interrupted
Marvellous
Nowadays
Obstacle
Outburst
Phenomenon
Occasion
Outcast
Physically
Occasionally
Outright
Operate
Perseverance
Quantity
Opportunity
Personnel
Questionnaire
Optimistic
Persistent
Quite
Original
Perspiration
Psychology
Omitted
Partner
Pursue

SET – 4

Realize
Soliloquy
Undoubtedly
Really
Source
Unnecessary
Recognize
Souvenir
Unparalleled
Recommend
Specifically
Until
Recurring
Specimen
Usual
Referred
Speech
Usually
Regrettable
Stopped
Valley
Reign
Strenuously
Valuable
Relieved
Stretched
Varieties
Religious
Subtle
Vein
Remembrance
Succeed
Tomorrow
Worrying
Secretary
Transferred
Writing
Seize

Vengeance
Renaissance
Successful
View
Resource
Superintendent
Vigorous
Restaurant
Supersede
Village
Rhythm
Surgeon
Villain
Rhythmical
Susceptible
Warring
Ridiculous
Synonym
Weird
Running
Technique
Wholly
Sacrifice
Temperament
Wield
Satisfactorily
Temperature
Wolf
Scarcely
Theatre
Woman
Schedule
Yawn
Severely
Twelfth
Yield
Sincerely
Tyranny

Transferring
Written
Sergeant
Tremendous

Yonder
Simultaneous
Unanimous

SET – 5

Compound words with hyphens

Birth-rate
Home-made
Self-regard
Boarding-house
Kick-off
Self-respect
By-product
Old-fashioned
Semi-independent
Copy-book
Pre-existence
Semi-invalid
Dog-tired
Pocket-knife

Stumbling-block
Ex-president
Printing-house
Tongue-tied
Fellow-player
Quarter-mile
Vice-president
Football-player
Re-echo
Well-being
Half-dozen
Self-made
Working-man

SET – 6

Compound words without hyphens

Afterwards
Gatekeeper
Posthumous
Almost
Handwriting
Postman
Already
Herewith
Riverside
Anybody
Householder
Schoolboy
Anyhow
However
Shoemaker

Into
Somehow
Anywhere
Lifetime
Someone
Birthday
Lighthouse
Something
Cannot
Meanwhile
Sometimes
Childlike
Midnight
Somewhat
Copyright

Anyone
Indoors
Somebody
Anything
Throughout
Downstairs
Newspaper
Together
Everybody
Nobody
Tomorrow
Everyone
Nonessential
Welcome
Everything
Otherwise
Whatever

Moonlight
Threadbare
Downfall
Moreover
Everywhere
Ourselves
Whenever
Extraordinary
Outside
Wherever
Fellowship
Playwright
Within
Football
Postgraduate
Without

SET – 7

Words to be written separately

All right
Do not
Up to
All round
No one
Well done!

At least
Per cent
Young man
At once
Some time

SET – 8

Words ending with –ate

Accelerate
Assimilate
Emancipate
Accumulate
Associate
Emulate
Accurate
Collaborate
Enunciate
Adulterate

Exaggerate
Alleviate
Desperate
Initiate
Ameliorate
Disseminate
Inundate
Annihilate
Effeminate
Literate

Collegiate
Eradicate
Affiliate
Commemorate
Evaporate
Aggregate
Corroborate

Appreciate
Elaborate
Meditate
Appropriate
Elucidate
Separate

SET – 9

Words ending with –tion

Accusation
Conviction
Institution
Affection
Perfection
Collection
Detention
Prevention
Combination
Dilution
Promotion
Commotion
Evaluation
Proportion
Compensation
Expectation
Proposition
Conception

Description
Intention
Assimilation
Detection
Fascination
Repetition
Constitution
Frustration
Reputation
Contention
Imagination
Resurrection
Convention
Inclination
Situation
Conversation
Inflation
Vindication

SET – 10

Words ending with –sion

Allusion
Decision
Precision
Apprehension
Dimension
Pretension
Collision
Dissension

Profusion
Comprehension
Inclusion
Provision
Conversion
Inversion
Tension

SET – 11

Words ending with –ous

Anonymous
Generous
Monstrous
Boisterous
Heinous
Poisonous
Callous
Jealous
Ridiculous
Credulous
Miraculous
Synonymous
Disastrous
Momentous
Treacherous
Fabulous
Monotonous
Venomous

SET – 12

Words ending with -ious

Ambitious
Ceremonious
Curious
Audacious
Contagious
Delicious
Auspicious
Pugnacious
Furious
Judicious
Superstitious
Infectious
Copious
Delirious
Dubious
Injurious
Precarious
Envious
Illustrious
Luxurious
Suspicious
Ingenious
Pernicious
Victorious

SET – 13

Words ending with –uous

Arduous
Impetuous
Sumptuous
Conspicuous
Presumptuous
Superfluous
Contemptuous
Strenuous
Tempestuous

SET – 14

Words ending with –eous

Courageous
Gorgeous
Simultaneous
Erroneous
Outrageous
Courteous
Hideous
Miscellaneous
Spontaneous

SET – 15

Words ending with -ise

Advertise
Demise
Exercise
Advise
Despise
Franchise
Apprise
Devise
Merchandise
Chastise
Disguise
Supervise
Compromise
Enterprise
Surprise

SET – 16

Words ending with –ar

Altar
Molecular
Secular
Beggar
Muscular
Scholar
Burglar
Particular
Similar
Calendar
Peculiar
Singular
Circular
Pedlar
Solar
Collar
Popular
Vicar
Grammar
Regular
Vulgar

SET – 17

Words ending with –er

Adviser
Leather
Premier
Alter
Lecturer
Prisoner
Barrister
Manner
Defender
Meter
Tiger
Diameter
Miner
Traveller
Examiner
Minister

Robber
Character
Manufacturer
Soldier
Debater
Messenger
Summer
Villager
Farmer
Partner
Writer
Interpreter
Plotter

SET – 18

Words ending with –or

Actor
Dictator
Orator
Ancestor
Director
Professor
Auditor
Doctor
Protector
Author
Emperor
Superior
Bachelor
Executor
Suitor
Benefactor
Governor
Surveyor
Censor
Inspector
Survivor
Chancellor
Inventor
Tailor
Conqueror
Investigator
Traitor
Contributor
Liquor
Tutor
Creditor
Manipulator
Visitor
Debtor
Minor

SET – 19

Words ending with –ance

Abundance
Brilliance
Nuisance
Acceptance
Defiance
Predominance
Accordance
Elegance
Radiance
Acquaintance
Endurance
Relevance
Allegiance
Exuberance
Reliance
Alliance
Guidance
Remittance
Allowance
Insurance
Repentance
Appearance
Irrelevance
Resistance
Arrogance
Maintenance
Resonance

SET – 20

Words ending with –ence

Audience
Diffidence
Patience
Circumference
Excellence
Preference
Coherence
Evidence
Prudence
Coincidence
Indolence
Residence
Concurrence
Inference
Resilience
Conference
Influence
Reticence
Conscience
Innocence
Reverence
Convenience
Insistence
Violence
Correspondence
Obedience

SET – 21

Words ending with –able

Acceptable
Avoidable
Fashionable
Admirable
Charitable
Formidable
Adorable
Comfortable
Implacable
Advisable
Commendable
Improbable
Agreeable
Comparable
Incurable
Marriageable
Suitable
Inseparable
Noticeable
Thinkable
Interminable
Objectionable
Transferable
Intolerable
Palatable
Unconquerable
Justifiable
Perishable
Unmistakable
Laudable

Amendable
Dependable
Indispensable
Applicable
Desirable
Inevitable
Available
Detestable
Inflammable
Innumerable
Practicable
Unthinkable
Liable
Profitable
Vulnerable
Lovable
Recognizable
Manageable
Respectable

SET – 22

Words ending with –ible

Accessible
Forcible
Perceptible
Admissible
Repressible
Permissible
Contemptible
Responsible
Plausible
Divisible
Horrible
Sensible
Eligible
Incorrigible
Tangible
Feasible
Invincible
Terrible
Flexible
Irresistible
Visible

SET – 23

Words ending with –al

Annual
Jackal
Menial
Canal
Literal
Metal
Cannibal
Material
Pedal
Gradual
Medal
Total

SET – 24

Words ending with –el

Channel
Level
Parcel
Jewel
Nickel
Rebel
Label
Panel
Satchel

SET – 25

Words ending with –ie

Ankle
Muscle
Principle
Cycle
Noble
Single
Fickle
Obstacle
Title
Mettle
Paddle
Uncle
Middle
Particle
Vehicle

SET – 26

Words ending with –ure

Agriculture
Literature
Nature
Enclosure
Manufacture
Signature
Leisure
Miniature
Venture

SET – 27

Words ending with –ur

Argur
Murmur
sulphur

RULES GOVERNING CERTAIN WORDS

RULE I

Words ending in silent *e* usually drops the silent *e* before adding vowel suffix (e.g., -ing, -able, -ary, -ous).

Exceptions

1. The *e* is retained when a suffix beginning with a consonant letter (e.g., -ment, -ful) is added.
2. After *c* or *g*, if the suffix begins with *a* or *0*, the *e* is retained to indicate the soft sound of *c* or *g*. (e.g., -ous, -able).

Examples:

Drop-e

admire + able = admirable
admire + ation = admiration
allure + ing = alluring

arrange + ing = arranging
arrive + ing = arriving
become + ing = becoming
care + ing = caring
come + ing = coming
compare + able = comparable
deplore + able = deplorable
desire + ous = desirous
dine + ing = dining
divide + ing = dividing
explore + ation = exploration
fame + ous = famous
give + ing = giving
hope + ing = hoping
imagine + ary = imaginary
live + ing = living
lose + ing = losing
love + able = lovable
move + able = movable
name + ing = naming
note + ed = noted

retain-e

arrange + ment = arrangement
care + ful = careful
extreme + ly = extremely
force + ful = forceful
hate + ful = hateful
like + ness = likeness
lone + ly = lonely
move + ment = movement

retain-e

advantage + ous = advantageous
change + able = changeable
courage + ous = courageous
manage + able = manageable
notice + able = noticeable
outrage + ous = outrageous
peace + able = peaceable
service + able = serviceable
trace + able = traceable

RULE 2

Words ending in *ee* or *oo* add suffixes without change.

Examples:

agree + able = agreeable
coo + ing = cooing
flee + ing = fleeing
glee + ful = gleeful
see + ing = seeing
woo + ing = wooing

RULE 3

Words ending in a consonant preceded by two vowels do not double the final consonant before a suffix beginning with a vowel

Examples:

boor + ish = boorish
cook + ing = cooking
cool + ing = cooling
look + ing = looking
meet + ing = meeting
repeat + able = repeatable
shout + ed = shouted
teem +ing = teeming

RULE 4

When a suffix that begins with a consonant is added to a word that ends in silent, *e*, the *e* is, with few exceptions, retained; as–

1. When the suffix -ly is added to an adjec-tive that ends in silent *e*, the *e* is usually retained.
2. Exceptions to the retention of *e* when -ly is added:
3. If the adjective ends in -le, the -le is dropped when the suffix -ly is added.
4. The -le is also dropped from adjectives end-ing in -able and ible when the suffix -ly is added.
5. When the suffix -tion is used to form a noun from a verb ending in silent *e* after *t*, the let-ters *te* are dropped.
6. When the suffix *y* is added to a noun end-ing in silent *e* to make an adjective, the *e* is dropped.
7. When the suffixes -ful, -hood, -less and -ment are added, the *e* is retained.

Examples:

entire + ly = entirely
fine + ly = finely
nice + ly = nicely
safe + ly = safely
false + ly = falsely
late + ly = lately
polite + ly = politely
sure + ly = surely

true + ly = truly
gentle + ly = gently
noble + ly = nobly
whole + ly = wholly
idle + ly = idly

comfortable + ly = comfortably
fashionable + ly = fashionably
forcible + ly = forcibly
honourable + ly = honourably
pleasurable + ly = pleasurably
sensible + ly = sensibly

associate + tion = association
celebrate + tion = celebration
communicate + ion = communication
complete + ion = completion
create + tion = creation
dictate + tion = dictation
frustrate + tion = frustration
pollute + tion = pollution

bone + y = bony
ice + y = icy
smoke + y = smoky
stone + y = stony
ease + y = easy
noise + y = noisy
snake + y = snaky
taste + y = tasty

advertise + ment = advertisement
amaze + ment = amazement
announce + ment = announcement
care + less = careless
excite + ment = excitement
false + hood = falsehood
home + less = homeless
hope + ful = hopeful
hope + less = hopeless
tire + less = tireless
use + ful = useful
use + less = useless
wire + less = wireless

Note: When -ment is added to judge, acknowledge and abridge, two spellings are generally accepted;

judge + ment = judgment, or judgement
acknowledge + ment = acknowledgment or acknowledgement
abridge + ment = abridgment or abridgement

RULE 5

Words ending in two or more consonants usually remain unchanged when a suffix is added.

Examples:

call + ed = called
pull + ed = pulled
roll + ing = rolling
shell + ed = shelled
thrill + ing = thrilling
till + ed = tilled
toll + ing = tolling
will + ed = willed

RULE 6

When a word of one syllable ends in a single vowel and a single consonant, the consonant is usually doubled when a suffix with a vowel is added.

1. The suffix -er, means 'person or thing that does something'.
2. The suffix -ing, present participle and gerund.
3. The suffix -ed, past tense and past participle.
4. The suffix -y, change a noun to adjective.

Examples:

big	bigger	biggest
sad	sadder	saddest
hot	hotter	hottest
thin	thinner	thinnest

cut + er = cutter
hit + er = hitter
rub + er = rubber
run + er = runner
sin + er = sinner
swim + er = swimmer

bid	bidding
brag	bragging
cram	cramming
cut	cutting
dig	digging
din	dinning
drag	dragging
get	getting
plan	planning
run	running
sin	sinning
sit	sitting
beg	begged

drag	dragged
drop	dropped
fit	fitted
hop	hopped
map	mapped
rag	ragged
rub	rubbed
sin	sinned
strap	strapped
fog	foggy
fun	funny
mud	muddy
sun	sunny

RULE 7

In a word of one syllable, the final consonant is not doubled before a suffix beginning with a consonant.

Examples:

fat	fatness
man	manhood
fit	fitful
sad	sadness
glad	gladness
sin	

RULE 8

1. Words of more than one syllable, ending in a single consonant preceded by a single vowel, if accented on the last syllable, usu-ally double the final consonant before add-ing a vowel suffix.
2. When adding a suffix in words of more than one syllable, the accent is shifted to a pre-ceding syllable, the foregoing rule does not apply.
3. In words of more than one syllable, the final consonant is not doubled before a suffix beginning with a consonant.
4. The final consonant is not doubled if the stress is on the first syllable and if the verb ends in -en or -er.
5. The final consonant is doubled if the stress is on the first syllable of the verb and if it ends in -al, -el or -il.
6. If the stress is on the first syllable, and if the verb ends in -ap or -ip, the final consonant is doubled.

Examples:

admit	admitted	admitting	admittance
control	controlled	controlling	controller
regret	regretted	regretting	regrettable
forbid	forbidden	forbidding	
forget	forgotten	forgetting	
prefer	preferred	preferring	
infer	inferred	inferring	

Exception:

excel	excelled	excelling
equip	-equipment	
profit	-profitless	
regret	-regretful	
unfit	-unfitness	
happen	happened	happening
listen	listened	listening
open	opened	opener
offer	offered	offering
cancel	cancelled	cancellation
equal	equaled	equalling
level	leveled	leveller
pedal	pedaled	pedalling
travel	travelled	traveller

Exception:

parallel	paralleled	
kidnap	kidnapped	kidnapper
worship	worshipped	worshipper

RULE 9

Words of more than one syllable, ending in a single consonant preceded by a single vowel, if not accented one the last syllable, usually do not double the final consonant before a suffix begin-ning with a vowel.

Examples:

bigot	bigoted	despot	despotic
redden	reddened	rivet	riveted

Exceptions:

There are words having two syllables almost equally accented.

In such a situation this rule is not applied; as–

handicap	handicapped	outfit	outfitted

RULE 10

When a verb ends in *y* with a consonant preceding it, they become *I* before the suffixes -es and -ed. The *y* remains unchanged before the suffix -ing.

Examples:

bury	buries	buried	burying
carry	carries	carried	carrying
copy	copies	copied	copying
defydefies	defied	defying	
deny	denies	denied	denying
hurry	hurries	hurried	hurrying
marry	marries	married	marrying
multiply	multiplies	multiplied	multiplying
pity	pities	pitied	pitying
rely	relies	relied	relying
reply	replies	replied	replying
satisfy	satisfies	satisfied	satisfying
study	studies	studied	studying
try	tries	tried	trying

RULE 11

If a verb ends with *y* with a vowel preceding, the *y* generally remains unchanged before the ending -s, -ed and -ing.

Examples:

annoy	annoys	annoyed	annoying
destroy	destroys	destroyed	destroying
enjoy	enjoys	enjoyed	enjoying
obey	obeys	obeyed	obeying
play	plays	played	playing
pray	prays	prayed	praying
stay	stays	stayed	staying

Exceptions:

lay	lays	laid	laying
pay	pays	paid	paying
say	says	said	saying

RULE 12

If the suffix -ing is added to verbs ending with *ie,* the *I* becomes *y* and the *e* is omitted.

Examples:

die	dies	died	dying
lie	lies	lied	lying
tie	ties	tied	tying

RULE 13

When a noun or adjective ends in *y* with a consonant preceding, the *y* usually become *I* when a suffix is added.

Examples:

dry, drier, dries, drily;

happy, happier, happiest, happily, happiness;

pity, pitiful, pitiless; plenty, plentiful;

tidy, tidier, tidiest, tidily, tidiness; twenty, twentieth

RULE 14

Words ending with *y* preceded by a consonant use *I* instead of *y* before additions other than those beginning with *I*.

Examples:

beauty	beautiful	happy	happiness
deny	denial	justify	justifies
fly	flier	study	studious

RULE 15

Words ending in *no* do not drop the *n* before add-ing the suffix -ness.

Examples:

clean	cleanness	green	greenness

RULE 16

If the adjective ends in *I*, the adverb formed by adding *ly* will contain two *I*'s immediately before the *y*.

Examples:

cool	coolly	final	finally
formal	formally	hopeful	hopefully
real	really	useful	usefully

RULE 17

If the adjective does not end in *I*, the adverb formed by adding *ly* will contain only one *I* immediately before the *y*.

Examples:

evident	evidently	grim	grimly
fluent	fluently	quick	quickly

RULE 18

Word ending in *ii* usually drop one *I* when compounded.

Examples:

all + most = almost

all + ready = already

all + though = although

all + together = altogether

all + ways = always

dis + till = distil

doubt + full =doubtful

use + full = useful

un + till = until

well + come = welcome

RULE 19

In words with *ie* or *ei* when the sound is long *ee*, use *I* before *e* except after *c*.

Examples:

achieve	chief	niece	shield
belief	cashier	piece	shriek
believe	field	pierce	siege
brief	fierce	priest	thief
besiege	grief	relieve	wield

But: Ceiling, conceive, conceit, deceit, deceive, perceive, receipt, receive.

Exceptions:

Either, financier, leisure; neither; seize; species

CHECK SPELLINGS OF 700 WORDS (28 – Practice Tests)

This chapter consists of practice exercises to check your proficiency in Spellings of Words. Each word entry has four options with a little variation in their spellings. You have to find the correct option with the correct spelling and cross check with the answers provided at the end of the chapter.

TEST – 1

1. (a) Abbreviate (b) Abbriveate (c) Abbrevaite (d) Abbrevitea
2. (a) Apperantly (b) Apparntley (c) Apparently (d) Apparentily
3. (a) Affarm (b) Afform (c) Affirm (d) Affrom
4. (a) Commission (b) Comission (c) Commision (d) Commition
5. (a) Acidentally (b) Accidentally (c) Accidentaly (d) Accidentley
6. (a) Apetite (b) Apeetite (c) Appetete (d) Appetite
7. (a) Committee (b) Comittee (c) Commitee (d) Committe
8. (a) Aclaim (b) Aklaim (c) Acclaim (d) Aclame
9. (a) Arguoment (b) Argoument (c) Argument (d) Argumeant
10. (a) Commodity (b) Comodity (c) Coommodity (d) Comoodity
11. (a) Accommodate (b) Acommodate (c) Accomodate (d) Acomodate
12. (a) Arangement (b) Arrangement (c) Arrangment (d) Arrangemant
13. (a) Comunism (b) Communism (c) Communnism (d) Commuonism
14. (a) Acompanied (b) Acoompanied (c) Accompanied (d) Acompenied
15. (a) Atlete (b) Athlate (c) Athlete (d) Athelete
16. (a) Comparitive (b) Comparative (c) Compartive (d) Comperative
17. (a) Accompanying (b) Acompanying (c) Acoompanying (d) Accompnaying
18. (a) Bureacracy (b) Buraucracy (c) Bureaucracy (d) Bureaucrasy
19. (a) Athlitics (b) Atheletics (c) Athletics (d) Atheletecs
20. (a) Compititive (b) Competetive (c) Competitive (d) Competiteve
21. (a) Accuse (b) Acuse (c) Accuce (d) Acsuse
22. (a) Atitude (b) Attitode (c) Attitude (d) Attitute
23. (a) Compulsery (b) Compelsory (c) Compulsory (d) Cempulsory
24. (a) Acheivement (b) Achievement (c) Achievament (d) Achievemant
25. (a) Auxeliary (b) Auxilary (c) Auxilery (d) Auxiliary

TEST – 2

1. (a) Concieve (b) Conceeve (c) Concevie (d) Conceive
2. (a) Acknowladge (b) Acknowledge (c) Acknowldege (d) Acknowaledge

3. (a) Awkard (b) Awkward
(c) Awkoward (d) Awokward

4. (a) Conceivable (b) Concievable
(c) Conceivible (d) Conciveable

5. (a) Acquaintence (b) Acquiantance
(c) Acqaintuance (d) Acquaintance

6. (a) Beginning (b) Begining
(c) Beggining (d) Beginnning

7. (a) Condmen (b) Condumn
(c) Condemn (d) Cundemn

8. (a) Acquited (b) Acquitted
(c) Accquitted (d) Acquetted

9. (a) Beleived (b) Bilieved
(c) Believed (d) Believid

10. (a) Conquer (b) Concuer
(c) Concuuer (d) Conquuer

11. (a) Acrose (b) Across
(c) Acros (d) Accross

12. (a) Benefited (b) Benifitted
(c) Bennefited (d) Beneffited

13. (a) Conscintious (b) Conscientious
(c) Consciientious (d) Conscentious

14. (a) Aditionally (b) Additionaly
(c) Additionaley (d) Additionally

15. (a) Breethe (b) Breathe
(c) Breathe (d) Brathe

16. (a) Conscious (b) Concsious
(c) Cunscious (d) Consicous

17. (a) Addres (b) Address
(c) Addrress (d) Addrees

18. (a) Brilliant (b) Briliant
(c) Brillient (d) Brelliant

19. (a) Continualy (b) Continualey
(c) Continually (d) Contenually

20. (a) Adolescent (b) Adolecsent
(c) Adolescant (d) Adolascent

21. (a) Buletin (b) Bulletin
(c) Bullettin (d) Bulliten

22. (a) Conveniance (b) Convenience
(c) Convinience (d) Conveniense

23. (a) Afluent (b) Aflluent
(c) Affluant (d) Affluent

24. (a) Buraeu (b) Bureau
(c) Burreau (d) Burriau

25. (a) Cornar (b) Corrner
(c) Corner (d) Cornor

TEST – 3

1. (a) Bureaucracy (b) Buraeucracy
(c) Bureuacracy (d) Bureaucrasy

2. (a) Corespond (b) Coresspond
(c) Correspond (d) Coreespond

3. (a) Afright (b) Affright
(c) Affrihgt (d) Affrieht

4. (a) Buried (b) Bureed
(c) Bureid (d) Burried

5. (a) Corrode (b) Corode
(c) Coorode (d) Corrodde

6. (a) Aggravate (b) Agravate
(c) Agrravate (d) Aggrevate

7. (a) Busines (b) Bussines
(c) Businuss (d) Business

8. (a) Corupt (b) Coruppt
(c) Coorupt (d) Corrupt

9. (a) Agression (b) Aggresion
(c) Aggression (d) Aggretion

10. (a) Cafetiria (b) Cafateria
(c) Cafeteria (d) Cafeterea

11. (a) Cource (b) Course
(c) Cuorse (d) Corsee

12. (a) Alegory (b) Allegory
(c) Alegorry (d) Alleggory

13. (a) Campaing (b) Campeign
(c) Campein (d) Campaign

14. (a) Curiocity (b) Curoisity
(c) Curiosety (d) Curiosity
15. (a) Alure (b) Allurre
(c) Allure (d) Allore
16. (a) Casualy (b) Casually
(c) Casullay (d) Causally
17. (a) Courteous (b) Courtious
(c) Courtous (d) Courceous
18. (a) Alusive (b) Allusive
(c) Allucive (d) Alluseve
19. (a) Career (b) Carreer
(c) Carier (d) Carrer
20. (a) Critzism (b) Criticism
(c) Criticizm (d) Creticism
21. (a) Although (b) Althugh
(c) Althuogh (d) Alhtough
22. (a) Carying (b) Carring
(c) Carrying (d) Carryeng
23. (a) Criticise (b) Critisize
(c) Criticize (d) Critecize
24. (a) Altogethar (b) Altogether
(c) Altogather (d) Altogeter
25. (a) Categorry (b) Category
(c) Catogory (d) Cattegory

TEST – 4

1. (a) Curiculum (b) Curricculum
(c) Curriculum (d) Curricullum
2. (a) Amateur (b) Amatuer
(c) Amatur (d) Ameteur
3. (a) Ceiling (b) Cieling
(c) Ceileng (d) Celing
4. (a) Decicion (b) Decision
(c) Desision (d) Decition
5. (a) Amiss (b) Amis
(c) Ammis (d) Amess
6. (a) Cemetry (b) Cemetery
(c) Cemitery (d) Cemetary
7. (a) Definately (b) Definitley
(c) Defenitely (d) Definitely
8. (a) Amout (b) Amunt
(c) Amount (d) Amuont
9. (a) Changable (b) Changeable
(c) Changeabel (d) Chanegable
10. (a) Definition (b) Defination
(c) Definicion (d) Defenition
11. (a) Analyse (b) Analyze
(c) Analyaze (d) Analize
12. (a) Characteristic (b) Characterestic
(c) Characteristec (d) Characterisetic
13. (a) Demurrage (b) Demurage
(c) Demmurrage (d) Demurragge
14. (a) Anals (b) Annlas
(c) Annals (d) Annalls
15. (a) Chocen (b) Chossen
(c) Chosen (d) Choosen
16. (a) Dependant (b) Dependent
(c) Depandent (d) Depandant
17. (a) Anual (b) Annual
(c) Annaul (d) Anuall
18. (a) Colleageu (b) Colligue
(c) Colleage (d) Colleague
19. (a) Descrebe (b) Desecribe
(c) Desceribe (d) Describe
20. (a) Apostel (b) Apostle
(c) Aposotle (d) Appostle
21. (a) Colloquial (b) Colliquial
(c) Colloquail (d) Coloquial
22. (a) Despair (b) Dispair
(c) Despare (d) Desepair
23. (a) Disappered (b) Disapeared
(c) Disappeared (d) Disappared
24. (a) Disolute (b) Dissolute
(c) Dissolte (d) Dessolute
25. (a) Destroy (b) Distroy
(c) Destrey (d) Desteroy

TEST – 5

1. (a) Disappointment (b) Disapointment (c) Desappointment (d) Disappointmant
2. (a) Devide (b) Divede (c) Divide (d) Dividee
3. (a) Devolop (b) Develop (c) Develope (d) Divelope
4. (a) Disastruos (b) Disestrous (c) Disasterous (d) Disastrous
5. (a) Divicion (b) Division (c) Devision (d) Divesion
6. (a) Diagraam (b) Diagram (c) Diageram (d) Daigram
7. (a) Discipline (b) Dicsipline (c) Disciplene (d) Discepline
8. (a) Eccentric (b) Ecentric (c) Eccentris (d) Ecenteric
9. (a) Dictionery (b) Dictionary (c) Dictionare (d) Dictionari
10. (a) Disatisfied (b) Dissatisfiyed (c) Dessatisfied (d) Dissatisfied
11. (a) Ecclesiastic (b) Eclesiastic (c) Ecclesaistic (d) Ecclisiastic
12. (a) Diferent (b) Different (c) Differant (d) Defferent
13. (a) Disect (b) Dissect (c) Dessect (d) Dissact
14. (a) Efficiency (b) Eficiency (c) Efficeincy (d) Efficiencey
15. (a) Dilapedated (b) Delapidated (c) Dilapidated (d) Dilapideated
16. (a) Dissertation (b) Disertation (c) Discertation (d) Dissertasion
17. (a) Efusion (b) Effusion (c) Effution (d) Effussion
18. (a) Dineng (b) Dening (c) Dinining (d) Dining
19. (a) Disipate (b) Dissepate (c) Dissipate (d) Discipate
20. (a) Egoetism (b) Egoitism (c) Egotism (d) Egoteism
21. (a) Disese (b) Disease (c) Disase (d) Discease
22. (a) Dissipation (b) Disipation (c) Discipation (d) Dissepation
23. (a) Eigth (b) Eighet (c) Eight (d) Eieght
24. (a) Elsewehre (b) Eleswhere (c) Elsewhere (d) Elsewhare
25. (a) Especialy (b) Especillay (c) Espacially (d) Especially

TEST – 6

1. (a) Generaly (b) Generally (c) Generalay (d) Genirally
2. (a) Elimenate (b) Eleminate (c) Elemenate (d) Eliminate
3. (a) Esence (b) Essence (c) Escence (d) Essense
4. (a) Genius (b) Geneius (c) Genieus (d) Gineius
5. (a) Elocusion (b) Elocution (c) Elocotion (d) Elecution
6. (a) Etiqucte (b) Etiquette (c) Ettiquette (d) Etiquatte
7. (a) Geography (b) Goegraphy (c) Geographe (d) Geografy
8. (a) Eloquense (b) Elequence (c) Eloquence (d) Eloquance
9. (a) Evolusion (b) Evolotion (c) Evolution (d) Evolucion
10. (a) Goverment (b) Government (c) Governmant (d) Gobernment
11. (a) Embarass (b) Embarrass (c) Embarras (d) Embarress
12. (a) Excellance (b) Excellense (c) Excellence (d) Excillence

13. (a) Grammar (b) Gramar
(c) Grammer (d) Gremmar
14. (a) Emissary (b) Emisary
(c) Emiscary (d) Emiccary
15. (a) Exceptionaly (b) Exceptionally
(c) Excepsionally (d) Excepcionally
16. (a) Grievance (b) Grievence
(c) Griavence (d) Grievanse
17. (a) Emphasice (b) Emphasize
(c) Emphesize (d) Amphasize
18. (a) Excitement (b) Excitemant
(c) Execitement (d) Excitemenet
19. (a) Guarante (b) Guarrantee
(c) Guarantee (d) Guarantey
20. (a) Encyclopeadia (b) Encyclopaedia
(c) Encyclopaedea (d) Encyclepaedia
21. (a) Exhaustid (b) Exhaustad
(c) Exhausted (d) Exhauzted
22. (a) Guard (b) Guaard
(c) Guared (d) Guerd
23. (a) Ennoble (b) Enoble
(c) Ennobale (d) Ennobal
24. (a) Exhilaracion (b) Exhilaration
(c) Exhilarasion (d) Exhileration
25. (a) Guidancee (b) Guidance
(c) Guidance (d) Guidance

TEST – 7

1. (a) Enormuos (b) Enormous
(c) Enormeus (d) Enorrmous
2. (a) Existance (b) Existence
(c) Exestence (d) Existense
3. (a) Handel (b) Handal
(c) Handlee (d) Handle
4. (a) Enthusiastis (b) Enthuseastic
(c) Enthuziastic (d) Enthusiastic
5. (a) Experience (b) Experance
(c) Exparience (d) Experiense
6. (a) Hieght (b) Heigth
(c) Height (d) Heght
7. (a) Enviroment (b) Environmant
(c) Environment (d) Envirenment
8. (a) Explanation (b) Explanasion
(c) Explanacion (d) Explenation
9. (a) Hindrance (b) Hindrence
(c) Hindranse (d) Hendrance
10. (a) Epidemec (b) Epedemic
(c) Epidemic (d) Epidimic
11. (a) Extraordinary (b) Extrordinary
(c) Extraordinaray (d) Extraordenary
12. (a) Hithrto (b) Hetherto
(c) Hitherrto (d) Hitherto
13. (a) Epitah (b) Epitaph
(c) Epetaph (d) Epitaf
14. (a) Familar (b) Familair
(c) Fameliar (d) Familiar
15. (a) Humorous (b) Humoruos
(c) Humorus (d) Humuoros
16. (a) Epitom (b) Epetome
(c) Epitome (d) Epitoma
17. (a) Fascinating (b) Fasinating
(c) Facinating (d) Fascenating
18. (a) Huriedly (b) Hurriedlay
(c) Hurriedly (d) Hurridely
19. (a) Epoh (b) Epoch
(c) Eposh (d) Epech
20. (a) Febraury (b) February
(c) Feberuary (d) Februery
21. (a) Imaginary (b) Imaginary
(c) Imagenary (d) Imaginery
22. (a) Equaled (b) Equalled
(c) Equalad (d) Equeled

23. (a) Financial (b) Finansial
(c) Financeal (d) Financsial

24. (a) Imaginasion (b) Imagination
(c) Imaginacion (d) Imajination

25. (a) Equipmant (b) Equipment
(c) Eqiupment (d) Equipement

TEST – 8

1. (a) Forein (b) Foreing
(c) Foriegn (d) Foreign

2. (a) Immediately (b) Immidiately
(c) Immediataly (d) Immediatelay

3. (a) Equiped (b) Eqquiped
(c) Equipped (d) Ecuipped

4. (a) Formarly (b) Formerly
(c) Formurly (d) Formeraly

5. (a) Imprompt (b) Impromptu
(c) Impromptо (d) Imprompetu

6. (a) Equivalent (b) Equivalant
(c) Equivaelent (d) Equibalent

7. (a) Forti (b) Forty
(c) Fourty (d) Fortey

8. (a) Inacessible (b) Inaccessible
(c) Inaccesible (d) Inaccissible

9. (a) Erotion (b) Erocion
(c) Erosion (d) Eroscion

10. (a) Forth (b) Furth
(c) Fourth (d) Foureth

11. (a) Inadiquate (b) Inadequate
(c) Inadequete (d) Inadecuate

12. (a) Erand (b) Errand
(c) Eraand (d) Erraned

13. (a) Freind (b) Fraend
(c) Frienad (d) Friend

14. (a) Inapplicable (b) Inaplicable
(c) Inapplikable (d) Inaplicabel

15. (a) Eroneous (b) Errouneous
(c) Erroneous (d) Erronious

16. (a) Guage (b) Gauge
(c) Gaugi (d) Gauje

17. (a) Inauspicious (b) Inauspecious
(c) Inauspiciuos (d) Inauspeceous

18. (a) Incidentally (b) Incidentaly
(c) Incidantelly (d) Incidentaley

19. (a) Irelevant (b) Irrelivant
(c) Irrelevant (d) Irrelevent

20. (a) Mathemetics (b) Mathematics
(c) Mathimatics (d) Mathematecs

21. (a) Incredeble (b) Incridible
(c) Incredibel (d) Incredible

22. (a) Knac (b) Knack
(c) Knak (d) Knacek

23. (a) Medicine (b) Midicine
(c) Medecine (d) Medicene

24. (a) Indefinitaly (b) Indefinately
(c) Indefinitely (d) Indefenately

25. (a) Knight (b) Knigh
(c) Knigth (d) Knigth

TEST – 9

1. (a) Minute (b) Mineute
(c) Minuute (d) Minutee

2. (a) Indipendent (b) Independant
(c) Independent (d) Indepandent

3. (a) Knnot (b) Knot
(c) Knoot (d) Knott

4. (a) Meschievous (b) Mischievous
(c) Mischeivous (d) Mischevious

5. (a) Indexorable (b) Indexorblae
(c) Indexorabele (d) Indexorabale

6. (a) Knowladge (b) Knowlege
(c) Knowledge (d) Knowldage

7. (a) Influencial (b) Infleuntial
(c) Influential (d) Influential

8. (a) Laboratery (b) Laboratory
(c) Laboratoray (d) Laboratori
9. (a) Mysteriuos (b) Myesterious
(c) Mysterious (d) Misterious
10. (a) Inimiccal (b) Inemical
(c) Inimical (d) Inimecal
11. (a) Legitemate (b) Legetimate
(c) Ligitimate (d) Legitimate
12. (a) Naiv (b) Niave
(c) Naivve (d) Naive
13. (a) Inimitable (b) Inemitable
(c) Inimetable (d) Inimitabel
14. (a) Leisure (b) Liesure
(c) Leicure (d) Leiscure
15. (a) Naturally (b) Naturaly
(c) Naturallay (d) Nachurally
16. (a) Innocous (b) Innocuous
(c) Innocuos (d) Inocuous
17. (a) Librarain (b) Librarian
(c) Librarean (d) Librerian
18. (a) Necesary (b) Necessry
(c) Necessary (d) Necessare
19. (a) Inuendo (b) Innueendo
(c) Innuendu (d) Innuendo
20. (a) Lieutenent (b) Lieutenant
(c) Leiutenant (d) Lieutenent
21. (a) Neverthless (b) Neverthaless
(c) Nevertheless (d) Nevertheles
22. (a) Intellectaul (b) Intelectual
(c) Intellectual (d) Intellektual
23. (a) Lightnig (b) Lightening
(c) Lightning (d) Ligthning
24. (a) Neice (b) Niece
(c) Niecie (d) Neece
25. (a) Inteligence (b) Intelligence
(c) Intellegence (d) Intelligance

TEST – 10

1. (a) Livelehood (b) Levelihood
(c) Livelihood (d) Livelihud
2. (a) Ninetey (b) Nineti
(c) Ninety (d) Ninaty
3. (a) Intentionaly (b) Intentionelly
(c) Intensionally (d) Intentionally
4. (a) Loneleness (b) Loneliness
(c) Lonelines (d) Loniliness
5. (a) Nineth (b) Ninth
(c) Nienth (d) Neinth
6. (a) Interfere (b) Interefere
(c) Interfare (d) Interefare
7. (a) Maneuver (b) Manuever
(c) Maneuvere (d) Manouver
8. (a) Noisily (b) Noisly
(c) Noisiley (d) Noisely
9. (a) Interpretted (b) Interprated
(c) Interpreted (d) Interppreted
10. (a) Mariage (b) Marriage
(c) Marraige (d) Marrige
11. (a) Notwitstanding (b) Notwithstanding
(c) Notwithstading (d) Notwistanding
12. (a) Interrupted (b) Interupted
(c) Interrupated (d) Interruptad
13. (a) Marvelous (b) Marevelous
(c) Marveluos (d) Marvilous
14. (a) Nowdays (b) Nowedays
(c) Nowadays (d) Noadays
15. (a) Obstakle (b) Obstacle
(c) Obsetacle (d) Obstecle
16. (a) Outburt (b) Outburst
(c) Outsburt (d) Outtburst
17. (a) Phenomanon (b) Phenomena
(c) Phenomenon (d) Phenemenon
18. (a) Ocasion (b) Occassion
(c) Occasion (d) Occation

19. (a) Outcast (b) Outcas
(c) Oucast (d) Outacast
20. (a) Physicaly (b) Physically
(c) Physicalley (d) Physecally
21. (a) Ocasionally (b) Occasionaly
(c) Ocasionaly (d) Occasionally
22. (a) Ouright (b) Outright
(c) Outrigth (d) Outreight
23. (a) Physician (b) Physisian
(c) Physecian (d) Physicean
24. (a) Occurred (b) Ocurred
(c) Occured (d) Ocured
25. (a) Pamphlat (b) Pamphlet
(c) Pamphlete (d) Pamphlate

TEST – 11

1. (a) Pleasent (b) Plesant
(c) Pleasant (d) Plaesant
2. (a) Ocurrence (b) Occurrence
(c) Occurence (d) Ocurence
3. (a) Paralel (b) Parallal
(c) Parellel (d) Parallel
4. (a) Propelled (b) Propeled
(c) Propellad (d) Propalled
5. (a) Offspring (b) Ofspring
(c) Offspreng (d) Offsepring
6. (a) Parlaiment (b) Parliament
(c) Parliamant (d) Perliament
7. (a) Propeler (b) Propellar
(c) Propaller (d) Propeller
8. (a) Omision (b) Omition
(c) Omission (d) Ommission
9. (a) Particulary (b) Particulerly
(c) Particularley (d) Partecularly
10. (a) Pcsychology (b) Psychology
(c) Psychologe (d) Psykology
11. (a) Omitted (b) Omited
(c) Ommitted (d) Ometted
12. (a) Partener (b) Partner
(c) Pertner (d) Partnar
13. (a) Purseu (b) Pursue
(c) Purseue (d) Puresue
14. (a) Operate (b) Operete
(c) Oparate (d) Oparata
15. (a) Perseverence (b) Perseveranse
(c) Persaverance (d) Perseverance
16. (a) Quantety (b) Quantitey
(c) Quantity (d) Quantiti
17. (a) Opportunity (b) Oportunity
(c) Opporttunity (d) Opportunitty
18. (a) Personel (b) Personnel
(c) Personnal (d) Parsonnel
19. (a) Questionaire (b) Questionniare
(c) Questionnaire (d) Questionnair
20. (a) Optimistic (b) Optemistic
(c) Optimystic (d) Optimistec
21. (a) Persistant (b) Persistent
(c) Persestent (d) Parsistent
22. (a) Quit (b) Qiute
(c) Quiti (d) Quite
23. (a) Originel (b) Origenal
(c) Original (d) Oreginal
24. (a) Perspiration (b) Perspirasion
(c) Persperation (d) Parspiration
25. (a) Quiting (b) Quitteng
(c) Quitting (d) Quetting

TEST – 12

1. (a) Otherwis (b) Otherwise
(c) Otherwize (d) Otherwice
2. (a) Persude (b) Persuade
(c) Persaude (d) Parsuade
3. (a) Quez (b) Quizz
(c) Quuiz (d) Quiz
4. (a) Realise (b) Realize
(c) Realeze (d) Raelize

5. (a) Soliloqy (b) Soliloquy
(c) Solilouquy (d) Soleloquy
6. (a) Undoubtedly (b) Undoubtedley
(c) Undoubtedely (d) Undoubetedly
7. (a) Realy (b) Reallay
(c) Really (d) Raelly
8. (a) Sourse (b) Source
(c) Suorce (d) Sourece
9. (a) Unnecessary (b) Unecessary
(c) Unnecesary (d) Unecesary
10. (a) Recognize (b) Recognise
(c) Recognice (d) Recoganize
11. (a) Souvenir (b) Suovenir
(c) Souveneir (d) Souvaneir
12. (a) Unparalleled (b) Unparaleled
(c) Unparelleled (d) Unpparalleled
13. (a) Recomend (b) Reccommend
(c) Recommend (d) Reccomend
14. (a) Specificaly (b) Specifically
(c) Specifecally (d) Specefically
15. (a) Untill (b) Untel
(c) Unitil (d) Until
16. (a) Reccurring (b) Recuring
(c) Recurring (d) Recuurring
17. (a) Speciman (b) Specimane
(c) Specimen (d) Specemen
18. (a) Usaul (b) Usual
(c) Usuall (d) Uzual
19. (a) Refered (b) Refarred
(c) Referred (d) Referaed
20. (a) Spech (b) Speec
(c) Speech (d) Spich
21. (a) Usualy (b) Usually
(c) Usaully (d) Usualley
22. (a) Regretable (b) Regrettable
(c) Regrattable (d) Rigrettable
23. (a) Stoped (b) Stopped
(c) Stoppad (d) Stoppod
24. (a) Valley (b) Valliy
(c) Valey (d) Velley
25. (a) Reing (b) Reign
(c) Rein (d) Riegn

TEST – 13

1. (a) Streneuously (b) Strenously
(c) Strenuously (d) Strenuosley
2. (a) Valuabal (b) Valuabale
(c) Valauble (d) Valuable
3. (a) Relievede (b) Relieved
(c) Releived (d) Releved
4. (a) Streched (b) Stretched
(c) Stretchad (d) Stratched
5. (a) Varieties (b) Vareities
(c) Varietes (d) Varietis
6. (a) Religious (b) Religoius
(c) Religeous (d) Relegious
7. (a) Subtle (b) Subtel
(c) Subtale (d) Subtele
8. (a) Vein (b) Vien
(c) Vaine (d) Veine
9. (a) Remembrence (b) Remambrance
(c) Remembrance (d) Remembranse
10. (a) Succeed (b) Suceed
(c) Suuceed (d) Succed
11. (a) Vengaence (b) Vengeance
(c) Vengeanse (d) Vengeansce
12. (a) Sucessful (b) Succesful
(c) Successfull (d) Successful
13. (a) Resuorce (b) Resource
(c) Recource (d) Recuorce
14. (a) Superintandant (b) Superintendent
(c) Superentendent (d) Superintandent
15. (a) Vigorous (b) Vigoruos
(c) Vigoros (d) Vigerous
16. (a) Restaurant (b) Restaurent
(c) Restuarant (d) Rastaurant

17. (a) Supercede (b) Superscede
(c) Supersede (d) Superseede

18. (a) Rhyhm (b) Rhythm
(c) Rhethm (d) Rhythem

19. (a) Surgoen (b) Surgon
(c) Surgen (d) Surgeon

20. (a) Villian (b) Villin
(c) Villan (d) Villain

21. (a) Rhythmical (b) Rhythmikal
(c) Rhythemical (d) Rhythmecal

22. (a) Susceptible (b) Sucseptible
(c) Suceptible (d) Suscepteble

23. (a) Waring (b) Warrinng
(c) Warring (d) Werring

24. (a) Ridiculuos (b) Rideculous
(c) Ridiculous (d) Rediculous

25. (a) Synonm (b) Synonym
(c) Sinonym (d) Synonim

TEST – 14

1. (a) Wierd (b) Weired
(c) Weirid (d) Weird

2. (a) Technique (b) Technicue
(c) Techneque (d) Techenique

3. (a) Sacrifise (b) Sacrefice
(c) Sacrifice (d) Sacrifyce

4. (a) Temperamant (b) Tamperament
(c) Temparament (d) Temperament

5. (a) Weild (b) Wieled
(c) Weiled (d) Wield

6. (a) Satisfactorily (b) Satisfactorili
(c) Satisfactorely (d) Satesfactorily

7. (a) Scarceley (b) Scarcily
(c) Scarcely (d) Scarecely

8. (a) Theatar (b) Theater
(c) Theatere (d) Thaeter

9. (a) Scheduele (b) Schedule
(c) Scehedule (d) Scedule

10. (a) Tomorow (b) Tomorrow
(c) Tommorrow (d) Tomoroww

11. (a) Worrying (b) Worying
(c) Worryeng (d) Worreying

12. (a) Secretery (b) Sacretary
(c) Secretary (d) Sacretery

13. (a) Transfered (b) Transfferred
(c) Transferred (d) Transfarred

14. (a) Sieze (b) Seize
(c) Seise (d) Seeze

15. (a) Transfering (b) Transfferring
(c) Transferang (d) Transferring

16. (a) Sergant (b) Sargeant
(c) Surgeant (d) Sergeant

17. (a) Tremendous (b) Tremenduos
(c) Tremandous (d) Tramendous

18. (a) Severely (b) Saverely
(c) Sevarely (d) Severaly

19. (a) Twelefth (b) Twelfth
(c) Tewelfth (d) Twelfeth

20. (a) Sinceraly (b) Sincerely
(c) Sincereley (d) Sincarely

21. (a) Tyranny (b) Tyrany
(c) Tyrenny (d) Tiranny

22. (a) Yonder (b) Yondar
(c) Yonnder (d) Yoonder

23. (a) Simultaneuos (b) Simultaneous
(c) Simultanous (d) Simeltaneous

24. (a) Unanimuos (b) Unanimous
(c) Unenimous (d) Unnanimous

25. (a) Gatekeper (b) Gatekeepeer
(c) Gatekeeper (d) Getekeeper

TEST – 15

1. (a) Posthumuos (b) Poshumous
(c) Posthumous (d) Posthoumous

2. (a) Threadbare (b) Threadbere
(c) Thraedbare (d) Threadebare

3. (a) Nonesential (b) Nonessential
(c) Nonessentail (d) Nonessencial
4. (a) Extrordinary (b) Extraordinary
(c) Extrardinary (d) Extraordenary
5. (a) Acelerate (b) Accelerate
(c) Accelerete (d) Accalerate
6. (a) Assimilate (b) Asimilate
(c) Asimmilate (d) Assimillate
7. (a) Emancepate (b) Emancipate
(c) Emancipete (d) Emencipate
8. (a) Acumulate (b) Accummulate
(c) Accumulete (d) Accumulate
9. (a) Asociate (b) Assocciate
(c) Associate (d) Associete
10. (a) Emulete (b) Emulate
(c) Emmulate (d) Emuelate
11. (a) Acurate (b) Accuratee
(c) Accurate (d) Accurrate
12. (a) Colaborate (b) Collabborate
(c) Collaboreate (d) Collaborate
13. (a) Enunsiate (b) Enunciate
(c) Enunceate (d) Ennunciate
14. (a) Adulterate (b) Aduleterate
(c) Adulterete (d) Adultarate
15. (a) Collegeate (b) Collegiate
(c) Colligiate (d) Collegiete
16. (a) Eradicete (b) Eradicate
(c) Eradecate (d) Eradikate
17. (a) Afiliate (b) Affeliate
(c) Affiliate (d) Affileate
18. (a) Comemorate (b) Commemerate
(c) Commemorate (d) Commamorate
19. (a) Agregate (b) Aggrigate
(c) Agreggate (d) Aggregate
20. (a) Coroborate (b) Corrobborate
(c) Corrobarate (d) Corroborate
21. (a) Exagerate (b) Excaggerate
(c) Exaggerate (d) Excagerate
22. (a) Aleviate (b) Alleveate
(c) Alleviate (d) Alliviate
23. (a) Desperete (b) Desparate
(c) Desperate (d) Dasperate
24. (a) Initiete (b) Inichiate
(c) Initeate (d) Initiate
25. (a) Ameliorete (b) Ameliorate
(c) Ameleorate (d) Amiliorate

TEST – 16

1. (a) Diseminate (b) Disseminete
(c) Disseminate (d) Disceminate
2. (a) Inundete (b) Inondate
(c) Inundate (d) Innundate
3. (a) Anihilate (b) Annihilate
(c) Annihhilate (d) Annihelate
4. (a) Efeminate (b) Effeminate
(c) Effemenate (d) Effiminate
5. (a) Appreciate (b) Apreciate
(c) Appriciate (d) Appreceate
6. (a) Meditate (b) Meditete
(c) Maditate (d) Miditate
7. (a) Apropriate (b) Appropriate
(c) Appropreate (d) Aproppriate
8. (a) Elucedate (b) Elucidete
(c) Elocidate (d) Elucidate
9. (a) Seperate (b) Separete
(c) Separate (d) Saparate
10. (a) Accusation (b) Accusation
(c) Accusation (d) Accusation
11. (a) Convicsion (b) Conviccion
(c) Conviktion (d) Conviction
12. (a) Institusion (b) Institution
(c) Institucion (d) Instetution
13. (a) Affection (b) Afection
(c) Affecsion (d) Affecion
14. (a) Discription (b) Descreption
(c) Description (d) Descripsion

15. (a) Intension (b) Intencion
(c) Intention (d) Intantion

16. (a) Asimilation (b) Assimilation
(c) Assimmilation (d) Assimelation

17. (a) Detection (b) Detaction
(c) Detecsion (d) Detektion

18. (a) Perfection (b) Perfaction
(c) Prefection (d) Perfektion

19. (a) Colection (b) Collection
(c) Colecction (d) Collecsion

20. (a) Detantion (b) Detension
(c) Detention (d) Detencion

21. (a) Prevantion (b) Prevension
(c) Prevencion (d) Prevention

22. (a) Combenation (b) Combination
(c) Combinacion (d) Combinasion

23. (a) Dilusion (b) Dilution
(c) Dilucion (d) Delution

24. (a) Promotion (b) Promocion
(c) Promoshion (d) Promosion

25. (a) Comotion (b) Commotion
(c) Comootion (d) Commosion

TEST – 17

1. (a) Evaluasion (b) Evaluetion
(c) Evaluacion (d) Evaluation

2. (a) Proprotion (b) Proporsion
(c) Proportion (d) Proporcion

3. (a) Compencation (b) Compansation
(c) Compenseation (d) Compensation

4. (a) Expectasion (b) Expactation
(c) Expectacion (d) Expectation

5. (a) Proposetion (b) Proposision
(c) Proposition (d) Proposicion

6. (a) Concepsion (b) Concepcion
(c) Conception (d) Concaption

7. (a) Fascenation (b) Fascination
(c) Fascinacion (d) Fascinasion

8. (a) Repeticion (b) Repetition
(c) Repetision (d) Repetetion

9. (a) Constetution (b) Constitution
(c) Constitusion (d) Constitucion

10. (a) Frustrasion (b) Frustration
(c) Frustracion (d) Frusteration

11. (a) Reputation (b) Reputasion
(c) Reputeation (d) Reputacion

12. (a) Contention (b) Contension
(c) Contencion (d) Contenscion

13. (a) Resurection (b) Ressurrection
(c) Resurrection (d) Resurreaction

14. (a) Convension (b) Convention
(c) Convencion (d) Conventean

15. (a) Inclenation (b) Inclination
(c) Inclineation (d) Inclinasion

16. (a) Convercation (b) Conversation
(c) Converseation (d) Converrsation

17. (a) Inflasion (b) Inflacion
(c) Inflation (d) Inflascion

18. (a) Vindicacion (b) Vindicasion
(c) Vindication (d) Vindecation

19. (a) Alusion (b) Allusion
(c) Allucion (d) Allution

20. (a) Decicion (b) Decision
(c) Decition (d) Decesion

21. (a) Precesion (b) Precition
(c) Precision (d) Precicion

22. (a) Aprehension (b) Apprihension
(c) Apprehension (d) Apprehention

23. (a) Dimention (b) Dimension
(c) Dimencion (d) Demension

24. (a) Pretantion (b) Pretension
(c) Pretencion (d) Pretenscion

25. (a) Colision (b) Collission
(c) Colission (d) Collision

TEST – 18

1. (a) Disension (b) Dissension (c) Dissencion (d) Dissantion
2. (a) Profusion (b) Profucion (c) Profution (d) Profesion
3. (a) Comprehansion (b) prehension (c) Comprihension (d) Compreehension
4. (a) Inclution (b) Inclusion (c) Inclucion (d) Inclusean
5. (a) Provesion (b) Provicion (c) Provisean (d) Provision
6. (a) Conversion (b) Convercion (c) Convearsion (d) Converseon
7. (a) Invercion (b) Inversion (c) Invertion (d) Inversean
8. (a) Tencion (b) Tansion (c) Tention (d) Tension
9. (a) Anonymos (b) Anonymuos (c) Anonimous (d) Anonymous
10. (a) Generous (b) Genarous (c) Generuos (d) Generus
11. (a) Monstrus (b) Monstruos (c) Monstrous (d) Monsterous
12. (a) Boistrous (b) Boisterus (c) Boisterous (d) Boisteruos
13. (a) Heinus (b) Heinuos (c) Heineus (d) Heinous
14. (a) Poisonus (b) Poisonuos (c) Poisenous (d) Poisonous
15. (a) Calous (b) Callous (c) Calluss (d) Cellous
16. (a) Jealous (b) Jelous (c) Jealus (d) Jealuos
17. (a) Ridiculous (b) Ridiculus (c) Ridiculuos (d) Rideculous
18. (a) Credulous (b) Credulus (c) Creduluos (d) Credelous
19. (a) Miraculus (b) Miraculous (c) Miraculuos (d) Meraculous
20. (a) Synonymos (b) Synonymous (c) Synonymuos (d) Synonimous
21. (a) Disasterous (b) Disastrus (c) Disastruos (d) Disastrous
22. (a) Momentus (b) Momentuos (c) Momentous (d) Momantous
23. (a) Treacharous (b) Treacherus (c) Treacherous (d) Treachereus
24. (a) Fabuluos (b) Fabulous (c) Fabulus (d) Fabulas
25. (a) Monotonous (b) Monotonuos (c) Monotonos (d) Monotenous

TEST – 19

1. (a) Venomous (b) Venemous (c) Venomuos (d) Venomus
2. (a) Ambicious (b) Ambitious (c) Ambitsous (d) Ambetious
3. (a) Ceremoneous (b) Ceremonious (c) Ceremoniuos (d) Cerimonious
4. (a) Curiuos (b) Cureous (c) Curious (d) Currious
5. (a) Audasious (b) Audecious (c) Audacious (d) Audaciuos
6. (a) Contageous (b) Contagiuos (c) Contegious (d) Contagious
7. (a) Delisious (b) Deliciuos (c) Delecious (d) Delicious
8. (a) Auspecious (b) Auspicious (c) Auspiceous (d) Auspeceous
9. (a) Copious (b) Copous (c) Copiuos (d) Copeous
10. (a) Delireous (b) Deliriuos (c) Delirious (d) Delerious
11. (a) Dubiuos (b) Dubeous (c) Dubious (d) Dubaous

12. (a) Injureous (b) Injurious
(c) Injuriuos (d) Injurieus

13. (a) Precarcious (b) Precareous
(c) Precariuos (d) Precarious

14. (a) Enviuos (b) Envious
(c) Enveous (d) Envaous

15. (a) Illustriuos (b) Illustrious
(c) Illustreous (d) Illustarious

16. (a) Pugnacious (b) Pugnacsious
(c) Pugnascious (d) Pugnaceous

17. (a) Furiuos (b) Furious
(c) Fureous (d) Furicous

18. (a) Judiciuos (b) Judicious
(c) Judecious (d) Judiceous

19. (a) Superstitious (b) Superstitiuos
(c) Superstetious (d) Superstiteous

20. (a) Infectious (b) Infectiuos
(c) Infectius (d) Infecsious

21. (a) Luxuriuos (b) Luxurious
(c) Luxureous (d) Luxarious

22. (a) Suspiciuos (b) Suspicious
(c) Suspecious (d) Suspiceous

23. (a) Ingeneous (b) Ingenious
(c) Ingenaous (d) Ingeniuos

24. (a) Perniceous (b) Pernicious
(c) Perniciuos (d) Pernecious

25. (a) Victoriuos (b) Victoreous
(c) Victoriaus (d) Victorious

TEST – 20

1. (a) Arduuos (b) Arduous
(c) Ardous (d) Ardus

2. (a) Impetuous (b) Impetuuos
(c) Impetous (d) Impechuous

3. (a) Sumptuous (b) Sumptous
(c) Sumptus (d) Sumpteous

4. (a) Conspicous (b) Conspecuous
(c) Conspicuous (d) Conspiceous

5. (a) Presumptous (b) Presumptus
(c) Presumptuous (d) Presumpteous

6. (a) Superfluos (b) Superflous
(c) Superfleus (d) Superfluous

7. (a) Contemptuos (b) Contemptuous
(c) Contemptous (d) Contempteous

8. (a) Strenuous (b) Strenuos
(c) Strenus (d) Strenous

9. (a) Tempestuos (b) Tempestuous
(c) Tempestous (d) Tempestus

10. (a) Courageos (b) Courageous
(c) Courageus (d) Couragious

11. (a) Gorgeos (b) Gorgeus
(c) Gorgeous (d) Gorgious

12. (a) Outrageous (b) Outragous
(c) Outrageus (d) Outragious

13. (a) Courteus (b) Courtieus
(c) Courteous (d) Courteos

14. (a) Hideus (b) Hideous
(c) Hideos (d) Hedeous

15. (a) Simultaneus (b) Simultaneous
(c) Simultaneos (d) Simulteneous

16. (a) Erroneos (b) Erroneus
(c) Erroneous (d) Erronious

17. (a) Miscellaneus (b) Miscellaneos
(c) Miscellaneous (d) Miscelaneous

18. (a) Spontaneos (b) Spontaneus
(c) Spontaneous (d) Spontanaous

19. (a) Advertize (b) Advertise
(c) Advertese (d) Advartise

20. (a) Demize (b) Demise
(c) Dimise (d) Demisee

21. (a) Exercize (b) Exercise
(c) Exercase (d) Exercisee

22. (a) Advisse (b) Advise
(c) Advize (d) Edvise

23. (a) Despize (b) Despisee
(c) Despise (d) Despiese

24. (a) Franchize (b) Franchisse
(c) Franchise (d) Franchiese

25. (a) Apprise (b) Apprizse
(c) Apprice (d) Appriese

TEST – 21

1. (a) Devisce (b) Devise
(c) Devicse (d) Devize

2. (a) Merchandizse (b) Merchandise
(c) Merchandice (d) Merchandiese

3. (a) Chastise (b) Chastize
(c) Chastice (d) Chastiese

4. (a) Disguise (b) Disgiuse
(c) Disguase (d) Disguice

5. (a) Supervise (b) Supervize
(c) Supervice (d) Superviese

6. (a) Compromiese (b) Compromise
(c) Compromize (d) Compromice

7. (a) Enterprize (b) Enterprice
(c) Enterpriese (d) Enterprise

8. (a) Altra (b) Altar
(c) Aletar (d) Altaar

9. (a) Moleculer (b) Molicular
(c) Moleculear (d) Molecular

10. (a) Secular (b) Seculear
(c) Seculaar (d) Secolar

11. (a) Beggar (b) Begar
(c) Beggaar (d) Begger

12. (a) Musculear (b) Muscular
(c) Mucsular (d) Mascular

13. (a) Scholer (b) Scholar
(c) Sccholar (d) Skolar

14. (a) Burgler (b) Burglar
(c) Buraglar (d) Bureglar

15. (a) Particuler (b) Particolar
(c) Particular (d) Partecular

16. (a) Calender (b) Calandar
(c) Calendar (d) Celandar

17. (a) Peculear (b) Peculiar
(c) Pecular (d) Pekuliar

18. (a) Circuler (b) Circcular
(c) Circullar (d) Circular

19. (a) Peddlar (b) Pedular
(c) Pedlar (d) Pedllar

20. (a) Colar (b) Collar
(c) Collear (d) Colaar

21. (a) Populer (b) Popullar
(c) Popular (d) Popularr

22. (a) Visar (b) Vicsar
(c) Vicar (d) Vizar

23. (a) Grammer (b) Grammar
(c) Gramar (d) Gerammar

24. (a) Regulare (b) Regular
(c) Rigular (d) Regualar

25. (a) Vulger (b) Vulgar
(c) Vulgare (d) Voulgar

TEST – 22

1. (a) Advizer (b) Advicer
(c) Adviser (d) Advissor

2. (a) Laether (b) Leadher
(c) Leather (d) Leathear

3. (a) Premeir (b) Premier
(c) Primier (d) Primeir

4. (a) Altre (b) Alteer
(c) Altere (d) Alter

5. (a) Lecturear (b) Lecturaer
(c) Lecturer (d) Lekchurer

6. (a) Prisoneer (b) Prissoner
(c) Prisonar (d) Prisoner

7. (a) Barrister (b) Barister
(c) Barrisster (d) Barristor

8. (a) Manufactureer (b) Manufacturear
(c) Manufacturer (d) Manufacturaer

9. (a) Soldire (b) Soldiar
(c) Soldiere (d) Soldier

10. (a) Debater (b) Debator
(c) Debeter (d) Dabater

11. (a) Messengere (b) Messenger
(c) Messengar (d) Messanger

12. (a) Defendere (b) Defendar
(c) Defender (d) Defander

13. (a) Diametere (b) Diameter
(c) Diameeter (d) Diameteer

14. (a) Minere (b) Miner
(c) Mener (d) Mineer

15. (a) Traveller (b) Travelor
(c) Traveler (d) Traviler

16. (a) Examinor (b) Examiner
(c) Examinere (d) Examenear

17. (a) Ministre (b) Minister
(c) Ministor (d) Minester

18. (a) Ancestre (b) Ancester
(c) Ancestor (d) Ansestor

19. (a) Executor (b) Executer
(c) Executore (d) Exekutor

20. (a) Suiter (b) Suitor
(c) Suitore (d) Suetor

21. (a) Benefactor (b) Banefactor
(c) Benifactor (d) Banifactor

22. (a) Surveyor (b) Surveyur
(c) Surveor (d) Survayor

23. (a) Censsor (b) Censor
(c) Censore (d) Cencor

24. (a) Survibor (b) Survivore
(c) Surviver (d) Survivor

25. (a) Chanceller (b) Chancoller
(c) Chancellor (d) Chancelor

TEST – 23

1. (a) Conquerer (b) Conquoror
(c) Conqeror (d) Conqueror

2. (a) Investigetor (b) Investigator
(c) Investigater (d) Investegator

3. (a) Liquor (b) Liqor
(c) Liqour (d) Liqeor

4. (a) Creditor (b) Crediter
(c) Creditur (d) Credetor

5. (a) Manipulator (b) Manipulater
(c) Manepulator (d) Manipolator

6. (a) Abundancee (b) Abundance
(c) Abundonce (d) Abandunce

7. (a) Brilliance (b) Brillianse
(c) Brilleance (d) Brelliance

8. (a) Nuisanse (b) Nuiseance
(c) Nuisance (d) Nuesance

9. (a) Acceptence (b) Acceptanse
(c) Aceptance (d) Acceptance

10. (a) Defeance (b) Defianse
(c) Defiance (d) Defance

11. (a) Predominanse (b) Predomenance
(c) Predominance (d) Predominace

12. (a) Accordance (b) Acordance
(c) Accordanse (d) Accordence

13. (a) Radianse (b) Radiance
(c) Radeance (d) Rediance

14. (a) Acquaintanse (b) Acquaintance
(c) Acquainteance (d) Acquantance

15. (a) Endurance (b) Endurence
(c) Enduranse (d) Endureance

16. (a) Relevance (b) Relevanse
(c) Relevence (d) Relivance

17. (a) Allegiance (b) Allegianse
(c) Allegeance (d) Allegance

18. (a) Exuberanse (b) Exuberence
(c) Exubirance (d) Exuberance

19. (a) Relianse (b) Reliance
(c) Releance (d) Relince

20. (a) Aliance (b) Alliance
(c) Alleance (d) Allianse

21. (a) Guidance (b) Guidanse
(c) Guidence (d) Guideanc

22. (a) Remittance (b) Remitance
(c) Remittence (d) Remettance

23. (a) Allowanse (b) Allowence
(c) Allowance (d) Alowance

24. (a) Insuranse (b) Insurance
(c) Insurence (d) Insuerance

25. (a) Repentanse (b) Repentance
(c) Repantance (d) Repentence

TEST – 24

1. (a) Appearanse (b) Appearence
(c) Appearance (d) Apearance

2. (a) Irelevance (b) Irrelevance
(c) Irrelevanse (d) Irrelivance

3. (a) Resistanse (b) Resistence
(c) Resestance (d) Resistance

4. (a) Arroganse (b) Arogance
(c) Arrogence (d) Arrogance

5. (a) Maintenance (b) Maintenence
(c) Maintinance (d) Maintenanse

6. (a) Resonance (b) Resonanse
(c) Resonace (d) Risonance

7. (a) Audiense (b) Audience
(c) Audiance (d) Audeance

8. (a) Difidence (b) Diffidence
(c) Diffidense (d) Diffedence

9. (a) Patience (b) Patiense
(c) Patiance (d) Pateance

10. (a) Circumferense (b) Circumferance
(c) Circumference (d) Circumfarence

11. (a) Excelence (b) Excellence
(c) Excellense (d) Excillence

12. (a) Preferense (b) Preference
(c) Preferance (d) Prefarence

13. (a) Coherense (b) Coherance
(c) Coharence (d) Coherence

14. (a) Evidense (b) Evidance
(c) Evidence (d) Evedence

15. (a) Prudence (b) Prudense
(c) Prudance (d) Prudeance

16. (a) Coincidense (b) Coincidence
(c) Coincidance (d) Coincedence

17. (a) Indolense (b) Indolence
(c) Indolance (d) Indulence

18. (a) Residense (b) Residence
(c) Resedence (d) Residance

19. (a) Concurrence (b) Concurence
(c) Conccurence (d) Concurrance

20. (a) Inference (b) Inferance
(c) Inferense (d) Infirence

21. (a) Resiliense (b) Resilience
(c) Resilince (d) Resilence

22. (a) Conferense (b) Conference
(c) Conferance (d) Confearence

23. (a) Influance (b) Influence
(c) Inflence (d) Influnce

24. (a) Reticence (b) Reticense
(c) Retecence (d) Retisence

25. (a) Conscience (b) Consciense
(c) Concience (d) Consience

TEST – 25

1. (a) Inocence (b) Innocence
(c) Innocense (d) Innocance

2. (a) Reverense (b) Reverence
(c) Reverance (d) Revarence

3. (a) Convenience (b) Conveniense
(c) Conveniance (d) Convinience

4. (a) Insistence (b) Insistance
(c) Insistense (d) Insestence

5. (a) Correspondense (b) Correspondence
(c) Corespondence (d) Correspondance

6. (a) Obediense (b) Obedience
(c) Obedince (d) Obidience

7. (a) Acceptable (b) Aceptable
(c) Acceptabel (d) Aceptabel

8. (a) Avoidabel (b) Avoidable
(c) Avoidible (d) Aviodable

9. (a) Fashionabel (b) Fashionable
(c) Feshionable (d) Fashionbale

10. (a) Admirabel (b) Admireble
(c) Admerable (d) Admirable

11. (a) Charitable (b) Charitabel
(c) Charetable (d) Cheritable

12. (a) Formidabel (b) Formedable
(c) Formidable (d) Formidabel

13. (a) Adorabel (b) Adoreble
(c) Adorable (d) Adurable

14. (a) Comfortabel (b) Comfortable
(c) Comforteble (d) Comfertable

15. (a) Implacabel (b) Implacable
(c) Implecable (d) Implasable

16. (a) Advisabel (b) Advisable
(c) Advizable (d) Advisabale

17. (a) Commendable (b) Comendable
(c) Commendabel (d) Commendible

18. (a) Improbable (b) Improbabal
(c) Impribable (d) Improbible

19. (a) Agreeable (b) Agreable
(c) Agreeabel (d) Agreeabele

20. (a) Comparabale (b) Comparabele
(c) Comparible (d) Comparable

21. (a) Incurrable (b) Inccurable
(c) Incurable (d) Incurabal

22. (a) Amendible (b) Amendabel
(c) Amendeble (d) Amendable

23. (a) Dependeble (b) Dependabel
(c) Dipendable (d) Dependable

24. (a) Indispensabel (b) Indispansable
(c) Indespensable (d) Indispensable

25. (a) Applicable (b) Aplicable
(c) Applicabel (d) Applecable

TEST – 26

1. (a) Desirable (b) Desireble
(c) Desirabal (d) Deserable

2. (a) Inevetable (b) Inevitable
(c) Inevitabel (d) Inevetable

3. (a) Available (b) Availabel
(c) Avaelable (d) Availabel

4. (a) Detestable (b) Detestabel
(c) Detesteble (d) Ditestable

5. (a) Inflamable (b) Inflammabel
(c) Inflammeble (d) Inflammable

6. (a) Inumerable (b) Innumerabel
(c) Innumereble (d) Innumerable

7. (a) Mariageable (b) Marreageable
(c) Marriageable (d) Marriagable

8. (a) Suitabel (b) Suetable
(c) Suitable (d) Suiteble

9. (a) Inseparabel (b) Insepareble
(c) Inseparable (d) Inseperable

10. (a) Noticeabel (b) Noticable
(c) Notiseable (d) Noticeable

11. (a) Thinkabel (b) Thinkeble
(c) Thinkable (d) Thenkable

12. (a) Interminabel (b) Intermenable
(c) Intermineble (d) Interminable

13. (a) Objectionabal (b) Objectioshnable
(c) Objectionable (d) Objecsionable

14. (a) Transferabel (b) Transfereble
(c) Transferable (d) Transfarable

15. (a) Intolerabel (b) Intolirable
(c) Intolerable (d) Intoelerable

16. (a) Palatabel (b) Palatable
(c) Palateble (d) Paletabele

17. (a) Unconquerable (b) Unconquerabel
(c) Unconquereble (d) Unconquarable

18. (a) Justifiable (b) Justifiabel
(c) Justifeable (d) Justefiable

19. (a) Perishabel (b) Perishable
(c) Perisheble (d) Parishable

20. (a) Unmistakabel (b) Unmistakable
(c) Unmistekable (d) Unmistakeble

21. (a) Laudable (b) Laudabel
(c) Laudible (d) Laudbele

22. (a) Practicabel (b) Practisable
(c) Practicable (d) Practecable

23. (a) Unthinkabal (b) Unthinkeble
(c) Unthinkable (d) Unthenkable

24. (a) Liable (b) Liabel
(c) Liabile (d) Leabale

25. (a) Profitabal (b) Profitable
(c) Profitabale (d) Profetable

TEST – 27

1. (a) Vulnerable (b) Vulnerabel
(c) Vulnereble (d) Vulnarable

2. (a) Recognizabel (b) Recognizable
(c) Recognezable (d) Recognisable

3. (a) Manageabel (b) Manageable
(c) Managible (d) Managable

4. (a) Respectable (b) Respectabel
(c) Respecteble (d) Respactable

5. (a) Accessible (b) Acessible
(c) Accesible (d) Accesseble

6. (a) Forcible (b) Forcibel
(c) Forcibal (d) Forceble

7. (a) Perceptibal (b) Perceptible
(c) Perceptable (d) Perseptible

8. (a) Admissible (b) Admisible
(c) Admissibel (d) Admissable

9. (a) Represible (b) Repressible
(c) Repressibal (d) Repressable

10. (a) Permisible (b) Permissible
(c) Permissibel (d) Permissable

11. (a) Contemptibel (b) Contemptible
(c) Contemptable (d) Contempteble

12. (a) Responsible (b) Responsibel
(c) Responsable (d) Responseble

13. (a) Plauseble (b) Plausible
(c) Plausibel (d) Plausable

14. (a) Divisibel (b) Divisible
(c) Divisibal (d) Diviseble

15. (a) Horrible (b) Horible
(c) Horribal (d) Horribel

16. (a) Sensible (b) Sensibal
(c) Sensibel (d) Sensibele

17. (a) Eligible (b) Eligibal
(c) Eligeble (d) Elegible

18. (a) Incorigible (b) Incorrigible
(c) Incorrigibal (d) Incorrigeble

19. (a) Tangibal (b) Tangeble
(c) Tangibel (d) Tangible

20. (a) Feasibel (b) Feasibal
(c) Feaseble (d) Feasible

21. (a) Invincible (b) Invincibal
(c) Invinceble (d) Invincibel

22. (a) Terible (b) Terribal
(c) Terrible (d) Terribel

23. (a) Flexibel (b) Flexibal
(c) Flexible (d) Flexeble

24. (a) Irresistible (b) Iresistible
(c) Irresestible (d) Irresisteble

25. (a) Menail (b) Menial
(c) Meenial (d) Meneal

TEST – 28

1. (a) Metle (b) Metal
(c) Metel (d) Matal

2. (a) Canibal (b) Cannibal
(c) Cannibel (d) Cannebal

3. (a) Pedal (b) Padal
(c) Pedel (d) Pedle

4. (a) Gradaul (b) Gradual
(c) Gragual (d) Gredual

5. (a) Nickle (b) Nickel
(c) Nickal (d) Neckel

6. (a) Reble (b) Rebal
(c) Rebel (d) Rabel

7. (a) Satchal (b) Setchel
(c) Satchel (d) Saschel

8. (a) Ankel (b) Ankal
(c) Ankle (d) Anekle

9. (a) Principel (b) Principle
(c) Principale (d) Princeple

10. (a) Fickle (b) Fickel
(c) Fickal (d) Feckle

11. (a) Obstacel (b) Obstacle
(c) Obstacele (d) Obastacle

12. (a) Metle (b) Mettle
(c) Mettel (d) Mettele

13. (a) Paddle (b) Padle
(c) Paddel (d) Peddle

14. (a) Particle (b) Particel
(c) Partical (d) Partecle

15. (a) Agriculture (b) Agricultuer
(c) Agricultare (d) Agreculture

16. (a) Literaturee (b) Literature
(c) Literrature (d) Literachure

17. (a) Enclosur (b) Enclosure
(c) Enclesure (d) Enclosere

18. (a) Manufacture (b) Manufactuar
(c) Manufecture (d) Manufacsure

19. (a) Signatura (b) Signature
(c) Signatur (d) Signeture

20. (a) Leisur (b) Leisure
(c) Leisuer (d) Liesure

21. (a) Miniature (b) Miniatur
(c) Miniaturre (d) Mineature

22. (a) Venture (b) Venturre
(c) Venchure (d) Vanture

23. (a) Augur (b) Agur
(c) Augr (d) Augor

24. (a) Murmmur (b) Murmur
(c) Murrmur (d) Murmer

25. (a) Sulphar (b) Sulphur
(c) Sulphor (d) Selphur

ANSWERS

	TEST – 1	TEST – 2	TEST – 3	TEST – 4	TEST – 5	TEST – 6	TEST – 7
1.	a	d	a	c	a	b	b
2.	c	b	c	a	c	d	b
3.	c	b	b	a	b	b	b
4.	a	a	a	b	d	a	d
5.	b	d	a	a	b	b	a
6.	d	a	a	b	b	b	c
7.	a	c	d	d	a	a	c
8.	c	b	d	c	a	c	a
9.	c	c	c	b	b	c	a
10.	a	a	c	a	d	b	c
11.	a	b	b	b	a	b	a
12.	b	a	b	a	b	c	d
13.	b	b	d	a	b	a	b
14.	c	d	d	c	a	a	d
15.	c	b	c	c	c	b	a
16.	b	a	b	b	a	a	c
17.	a	b	a	b	b	b	a
18.	c	a	b	d	d	a	c
19.	c	c	a	d	c	c	b
20.	c	a	b	b	c	b	b
21.	a	b	a	a	b	c	b
22.	c	b	c	a	a	a	a
23.	c	d	c	c	c	a	a
24.	b	b	b	b	c	b	b
25.	d	c	b	a	d	b	b

	TEST – 8	TEST – 9	TEST – 10	TEST – 11	TEST – 12	TEST – 13	TEST – 14
1.	d	a	c	c	b	c	d
2.	a	c	c	b	b	d	a
3.	c	b	d	d	d	b	c
4.	b	b	b	a	b	b	d
5.	b	a	b	a	b	a	d
6.	a	c	a	b	a	a	a
7.	b	c	a	d	c	a	c
8.	b	b	a	c	b	a	b
9.	c	c	c	a	a	c	b
10.	c	c	b	b	a	a	b
11.	b	d	b	a	a	b	a
12.	b	d	a	b	a	d	c
13.	d	a	a	b	c	b	c
14.	a	a	c	a	b	b	b
15.	c	a	b	d	d	a	d
16.	b	b	b	c	c	a	d
17.	a	b	c	a	c	c	a
18.	a	c	c	b	b	b	a
19.	c	d	a	c	c	d	b
20.	b	b	b	a	c	d	b
21.	d	c	d	b	b	a	a
22.	b	c	b	d	b	a	a
23.	a	c	a	c	b	c	b
24.	c	b	a	a	a	c	b
25.	a	b	b	c	b	b	c

	TEST – 15	TEST – 16	TEST – 17	TEST – 18	TEST – 19	TEST – 20	TEST – 21
1.	c	c	d	b	a	b	b
2.	a	c	c	a	b	a	b
3.	b	b	d	b	b	a	a
4.	b	b	d	b	c	c	a
5.	b	a	c	d	c	c	a
6.	a	a	c	a	d	d	b
7.	b	b	b	b	d	b	d
8.	d	d	b	d	b	a	b
9.	c	c	b	d	a	b	d
10.	b	c	b	a	c	b	a
11.	c	d	a	c	c	c	a
12.	d	b	a	c	b	a	b
13.	b	a	c	d	d	c	b
14.	a	c	b	d	b	b	b
15.	b	c	b	b	b	b	c
16.	b	b	b	a	a	c	c
17.	c	a	c	a	b	c	b
18.	c	a	c	a	b	c	d
19.	d	b	b	b	a	b	c
20.	d	c	b	b	a	b	b
21.	c	d	c	d	b	b	c
22.	c	b	c	c	b	b	c
23.	c	b	b	c	b	c	b
24.	d	a	b	b	b	c	b
25.	b	b	d	a	d	a	b

	TEST – 22	TEST – 23	TEST – 24	TEST – 25	TEST – 26	TEST – 27	TEST – 28
1.	c	d	c	b	a	a	b
2.	c	b	b	b	b	b	b
3.	b	a	d	a	a	b	a
4.	d	a	d	a	a	a	b
5.	c	a	a	b	d	a	b
6.	d	b	a	b	d	a	c
7.	a	a	b	a	c	b	c
8.	c	c	b	b	c	a	c
9.	d	d	a	b	c	b	b
10.	a	c	c	d	d	b	a
11.	b	c	b	a	c	b	b
12.	c	a	b	c	d	a	b
13.	b	b	d	c	c	b	a
14.	b	b	c	b	c	b	a
15.	c	a	a	b	c	a	a
16.	b	a	b	b	b	a	b
17.	b	a	b	a	a	a	b
18.	c	d	b	a	a	b	a
19.	a	b	a	a	b	d	b
20.	b	b	a	d	b	d	b
21.	a	a	b	c	a	a	a
22.	a	a	b	d	c	c	a
23.	b	c	b	d	c	c	a
24.	d	b	a	d	a	a	b
25.	c	b	a	a	b	b	b

PLAY WITH THE WORDS (30 – Practice Tests)

This Chapter titled 'PLAY WITH THE WORDS' is an entirely and altogether novel and innovative experiment to check the students' 'grasp and grip' over words. The exercises have been framed in the form of completing synonyms, antonyms, one word substitution, fill in the blanks and such other forms with given hints . Solving such diversified types of exercises will help students to evaluate themselves and identify their strong and weak areas. It will equip them to solve any vocabulary related question in any competitive examination.

TEST – 1

Complete the synonyms given with hints on the right hand side

1. Forsake - Aba______
2. late - Abh______
3. Miserable - Abj______
4. Renounce - Abju______
5. Denial - Abne______
6. Disgusting - Abom______
7. Unsuccessful - Abor______
8. Flee from law - Absco______
9. Difficult to understand - Abst______
10. Applaud - Acc______
11. Companion in wrong doing - Accom______
12. Agreement - Accor______
13. Pile up - Accr______
14. Unyielding - Ada______
15. Zenith - Ac______
16. Follower - Aco______
17. Skilful - Adr______
18. Friendly - Amia______
19. Pretend - Aff______
20. Affection - Affi______
21. Promptness - Alac______

TEST – 2

Give the opposite word of the given hints on the right hand side.

1. Ambiguous - Un______
2. Amity - En______
3. Ameliorate - Deteri______
4. Amenable - Unyi______
5. Amiable - Unfr______
6. Anguish - Jo______
7. Antediluvian - Mo______
8. Aplomb - Diffi______
9. Apogee - Nad______
10. Appease - Alien______
11. Applaud - Depre______
12. Apposite - Inappro______
13. Approbation - Cen______
14. Articulate - In______
15. Artless - Art______
16. Assail - Appl______
17. Assent - Diss______
18. Assiduous - Incon______
19. Austere - Luxu______
20. Abortive - Succ______

TEST – 3

Complete the sentence with hints given in the following sentences.

1. I abh______ bad company.
2. The rebellion proved abor______.
3. The match came to an abru______ end.
4. The court absol______ him of the charge of murder.
5. The two parties have reached an acco______.

6. The rich are surrounded by acol_______.
7. The teacher adju_______ us to shun mischief.
8. The AIDS pandemic has aff_______ large parts of Africa.
9. We must help the poor to allev_____ their misery.
10. He is not a party animal and keeps alo_______.
11. From alter_______, they came to blows.
12. A husband and wife should be each other's altere_____.
13. There is no al_______ to hardwork.
14. The ama_______ thrashed her husband.
15. Politicians are good at giving ambi_____ replies.
16. Health, education and hygiene are chief ame _____ of life.
17. You must find out her antece_____ before proposing to her.
18. Benevolence wins us the appro_____ of others.
19. He is an arra_______ rascal.
20. People assa_______ him for his wrong acts.

TEST – 4

Complete the synonym of the given hints on the right hand side

1. Confuse - Baff_______
2. Surround - Beleage_______
3. Disparage - Belitt_______
4. A great poet - Ba_______
5. Great joy - Beati_______
6. Call - Beck_______
7. Make wet and dirty - Bedrag_______
8. Fall to one's lot - Bef_______
9. Make friends - Bef_______
10. Resent - Begr_______
11. Cheat - Beg_______
12. Grateful - Behol_______
13. Fail to come up to expectations - Bel_______
14. Aggressive - Belli_______
15. Blessing - Bened_______
16. A good deed - Benef_______
17. Kind helper - Benefa_______
18. One who receives help - Benefi_______
19. Kind - Ben_______
20. Beg - Besee_______

TEST – 5

Complete the following opposite words given with the hints on the right hand side.

1. Broadminded - Big_______
2. Moral - Bohem_______
3. Disciplined - Boist_______
4. Lack of understanding - Bonho_______
5. Pleasant - Boo_______
6. A narrow road - Boule_______
7. Meagre and measly - Boun_______
8. Add - Bowd_______
9. Well built - Britt_______
10. Praise - Condem_______
11. Polished, Urbane - Brus_______
12. A simple, honest man - Bucca_______
13. Unpromising - Budd_______
14. A weak point - Bul_______
15. Cheerless - Buoy_______
16. Decrease - Burg_______
17. Quietness - Bust_______
18. Full of meaning - Balder_______
19. Encourage - Belitt_______
20. Civilized - Barb_______

TEST – 6

Fill in the blanks completing the given hints in following sentences.

1. You can move better in bagg_______ trousers.
2. I do not relish baw_______ jokes.
3. The beleag_______ king died fighting.
4. I love to go for a walk on balm_______ days.

5. Shakespeare was a great b_______.
6. The little saint was full of beati_______.
7. I wonder what fate befa_______ me.
8. We love to bef_______ cheerful people.
9. You begrud_______ my riches.
10. I am behold_______ to you for help.
11. It does not beho_______ to be nasty.
12. He failed and bel_______ our hopes.
13. The Pathans are a bellic_______ tribe.
14. The hapless youth bemo_______ his fate.
15. Grandmother showered bened_______ on me.
16. The saints are great benefac_______ of mankind.
17. The beni____ old lady looked after the orphans.
18. The lout is bere_______ of all good sense.

TEST – 7

Complete the word on the right hand side.

1. A hidden store - Cach_______
2. Mark of excellence - Cache_______
3. Noise - Cacopho_______
4. Coax - Cajol_______
5. Art of writing - Calligraph_______
6. Inexperienced - Callo_______
7. Disgrace - Calum_______
8. Bonhomie - Cama_______
9. Hide - Camou_______
10. Frank - Can_______
11. One who eats human flesh - Cann_______
12. Shrewd - Cann_______
13. Ill tempered - Cantank_______
14. Yield - Capitu_______
15. Whim - Cap_______
16. Peevish - Capt_______
17. Charm - Captiv_______
18. Slaughter - Car_______
19. Festival - Carni_______
20. Find fault - Car_______

TEST – 8

Give the opposite word. Take the clue.

1. Matrimony - Celiba_______
2. Parochialism - Catholi_______
3. Holding back emotions - Cathar_______
4. Narrowminded - Catho_______
5. Artless - Catti_______
6. Careful, Attentive - Cava_______
7. Accept patiently - Cavi_______
8. Claim, Demand - Ced_______
9. Lack of promptness - Cele_______
10. Divisive - Centri_______
11. Terrestrial - Celes_______
12. Orderly - Chao_______
13. Honest - Charl_______
14. Impure - Chas_______
15. Honesty - Chicane_______
16. Applaud - Chi_______
17. Polite - Chur_______
18. Precision - Circum_______
19. Careless - Circums_______
20. Cruelty - Clemen_______

TEST – 9

Fill in the blanks and complete the sentence

1. Jain monks observe celi_______.
2. The Maharani of Jaipur had a unique charis_______ about her.
3. Politicians are demagogues and charl_______.
4. I am char_______ of bad company.
5. The charw_____ came and cleaned the utensils.
6. The teacher chas_______ the truants.
7. German Chauvin_____ led to two world wars.
8. The chiv_______ young man rescued the damsel in distress.
9. Homoeopathy claims to extirpate chro_______ ailments.

10. His chur____ ways didn't endear him to anyone.
11. The job was a cin_______ and I did it easily.
12. A sense of claustro_____ seized me in Calcutta.
13. The king showed no clem_______ and hanged the rebel.
14. The wife coa_______ the husband into buying a new car.
15. The old man was not cohere_______ and mumbled a few words.
16. The police didn't take any cogniz_______ of my complaint.
17. The boss coer_____ me into doing the dirty job.

TEST – 10

Fill in the blanks with help of given hints and complete the sentences

1. The little girl looked dain_______ with her ribbons.
2. The speaker stood behind the dai_______ and fulminated.
3. Damn_______ awaits the sinners.
4. There was a dead_______ and no progress was made.
5. Our team suffered a debac_______ and we lost the match.
6. The heat in May and June debili_______.
7. The hero looked debo_______.
8. The abandoned baby was found in a heap of deb_______.
9. The debut_______ stole the show.
10. Greed leads to moral deca_______.
11. He was found dere_______ in his duties.
12. The young deri_______ the ways of the old.
13. Lack of love desec_______ a marriage.
14. Guru Nanak reformed Sajjan the cheat, a desper_______.
15. Forsaking one's parents in their old age is a despi_______ act.
16. He felt despon_______ at his defeat.
17. Hitler was a desp_______.
18. Mother Teresa devoted her life to the service of the desti_______.
19. Difficulties must not det_______ us.
20. Smoking is detri_______ to health.

TEST – 11

Complete the word on the right hand side.

1. Treat like a god - Deif_______
2. Condescend - Dei_______
3. According to law - De_______
4. Harmful - Delete_______
5. Salvation - Deli_______
6. Swindle - Del_______
7. Rabble rouser - Demag_______
8. A political procedure - Demar_______
9. Deportment - Demean_______
10. An evil spirit - Dem_______
11. Hesitate - Demu_______
12. Shy - Demur_______
13. Bellitle - Denig_______
14. Climax - Denoue_______
15. Censure - Denou_______
16. Dwindle - Deple_______
17. One who deposes - Depo_______
18. Banish - Depor_______
19. Moral decline - Depra_______
20. Disapprove - Depre_______

TEST – 12

Complete the word on the right hand side.

1. Dashing - Ebull_______
2. Enthusiasm and skill - Ecl_______
3. Great joy - Ecs_______
4. Ordinance - Edi_______
5. Weird - Eer_______
6. Rub off - Eff_______

7. Lively - Effer_______
8. Enfeebled - Eff_______
9. Effective - Effica_______
10. Impudence - Effron_______
11. Glowing - Efful_______
12. Inclined to talk - Effu_______
13. Equalitarian - Egali_______
14. Very wicked - Egreg_______
15. Joy and confidence - El_______
16. Land of opportunity - El D_______
17. Exalt - Ele_______
18. Set free - Emanci_______
19. Difficult to find - Elusi_______
20. Weaken - Emascu_______

TEST – 13

Fill in the blanks with help of given hints and complete the sentences

1. The accountant embezz_______ funds.
2. Pratibha Patil is the embl_______ of women's empowerment.
3. Let us emul_______ the noble and not be jealous of them.
4. Manmohan Singh embod_______ intelligence and integrity.
5. The fans were enamo_______ of the starlet's beauty and talent.
6. Usain Bolt won encom_______ for his world record in 100 metres race.
7. India is encum_______ by her teeming millions.
8. The malarial fever is end_______ to tropics.
9. The June heat ener_______.
10. A viral attack enfeeb_______.
11. In many countries women are yet to be enfran _______.
12. The curse of apart_______ has been lifted from S. Africa.
13. The scholar was engro_______ in his studies.
14. The court enjoi_______ him not to leave the country.
15. A good teacher enkind_______ in us a thirst for knowledge.
16. The saint enligh_______ us on the mysteries of life.
17. He has enlis_______ himself as a sepoy in the army.
18. She enliv_______ the party with her beautiful songs.
19. The modern man is enmes_______ in materialistic values.
20. You must keep busy or face enn_______.

TEST – 14

Give the opposite word. Follow the given hints on the right hand side.

1. Infallible - Fall_______
2. Unfaithfulness - Fea_______
3. Infertile - Fecu_______
4. Unlikely - Feasi_______
5. Unhappy - Fest_______
6. Fresh - Feti_______
7. Constant - Fick_______
8. Unfaithfulness - Fide_______
9. Beginning - Fina_______
10. Firm - Flacc_______
11. Dull - Flam_______
12. Respectful - Flipp_______
13. Wise and careful - Foolh_______
14. Hindsight - Fore_______
15. Cheerful - Forl_______
16. Strong - Fra_______
17. Spendthrift - Fru_______
18. Claim - Fore_______
19. Lack of skill - Fine_______

TEST – 15

Complete the Noun forms of the following words given with hints on the right side

1. Fabricate - Fabricati______
2. Fallacious - Fallac______
3. Fallible - Fallibili______
4. Fatal - Fatalit______
5. Fatuous - Fatuousne______
6. Feasible - Feasibili______
7. Feckless - Fecklessne______
8. Fecund - Fecundi______
9. Feeble - Feeblene______
10. Felicitous - Felicit______
11. Felon - Felon______
12. Fervid - Fervou______
13. Festive - Festivi______
14. Fickle - Ficklene______
15. Fiddle - Fiddli______
16. Flaccid - Flaccidne______
17. Flamboyant - Flamboyanc______
18. Flawless - Flawlessne______
19. Flippant - Flippan______
20. Forbode - Forebodin______
21. Foreclose - Foreclosu______

TEST – 16

Give the equivalents of the following. Follow the hints.

1. Abode - Habi______
2. Habitual frequenter - Habitu______
3. Greet - Ha______
4. In good health - Hale and hear___
5. Unlucky - Hap______
6. Pride - Hau______
7. Time to act - Hi______ti______
8. Disorder - Helter___
9. Nonsense - Hocus______
10. A pile - Hudd______
11. Noise and ado - Hurly______
12. Exaggeration - Hyper______
13. Corruption - Gra______
14. Gist - Esse______
15. Laugh in a silly way - Gi______
16. Bend on knees - Genu______
17. Nonsense - Gibber______

TEST – 17

Give the Adjectives of the following. Follow the clues provided on the right side.

1. Icon - Incon______
2. Inadvertence - Inadverten______
3. Idiosyncrasy - Idiosyncrat______
4. Inanity - Inan______
5. Ignominy - Ignominiou______
6. Incisiveness - Incisiv______
7. Impetuosity - Impetuo______
8. Inclemency - Inclemen______
9. Impiety - Impiou______
10. Incongruity - Incongru______
11. Implore - Implori______
12. Incontinence - Incontinen______
13. Importune - Importunat______
14. Impose - Imposi______
15. Impropriety - Imprope______
16. Improvidence - Improvide______
17. Impudence - Impude______
18. Impulse - Impulsi______
19. Incriminate - Incrimina______
20. Indifference - Indiffere______

TEST – 18

Give one word for the following. Follow the clues.

1. One who does not tire - Inde______
2. That which cannot be erased - Indel______
3. One who breaks idols - Icono______

4. The Eskimo home - Ig_______
5. Before recorded time - Imme_______
6. Go and settle abroad - Emi_______
7. About to happen - Immi_______
8. Put in danger - En_______
9. That which cannot be destroyed - Imperi_______
10. Difficult to please - Impac_______
11. Render weak or poor - Impover_______
12. That which cannot be conquered - Invin_______
13. Difficult to reach - Inacce_______
14. Not legally valid - Inva_______

TEST – 19

Fill in the blanks. Follow the given clues.

1. A jam_______ of Boy Scouts.
2. The jan_______ looks after the mansion.
3. He won kud_______ for his feat.
4. Kashmir was a knott_______ problem.
5. The politicians love to be surrounded with lack_______.
6. Their talks made no lee_______.
7. Dilip Kumar is a leg_______ in film acting.
8. People do not approve of fresh lev_______ by the govt.
9. A lexi_______ is a dictionary.
10. The fans lion_______ the hero.
11. He claims a royal line_______ for his family.
12. She is a live_______ young lass.
13. Exercise renders our bodies lith_______.
14. The boss was liv_______ with anger.
15. The sky was lumi_______ with stars.
16. In rainy season the vegetation is luxu_______.
17. The rich lead a luxu_______ life.
18. It was a lusci_______ piece of mango.
19. Lazy people are loa_______ to work hard.
20. Longe_______ is a fall out of good living.

TEST – 20

Give the opposite word. Take the help of given clues.

1. Fresh - Ja_______
2. Unbiased - Jaun_______
3. Cheerless - Jovi_______
4. Simple and easy - Knott_______
5. Censure - Kudo_______
6. Lazy - Labor_______
7. Exciting - Lackadaisi_______
8. Leader - Lagg_______
9. Interference - Laissez fai_______
10. Energetic - Languish_______
11. Energy - Lassi_______
12. Rigorous - La_______
13. Seriousness - Levi_______
14. Illicit - Lici_______
15. Energetic - List_______
16. Rigid - Lith_______
17. Taciturn - Loqua_______
18. Darksome - Lumi_______

TEST – 21

Give the meanings. No hints.

1. Nadir
2. Naïve
3. Novice
4. Nefarious
5. Nemesis
6. Nettle
7. Noxious
8. Oaf
9. Obeisance
10. Obfuscate
11. Nostalgia

TEST – 22

Give one word for the following.

1. Coming generations - Post_______
2. A great ruler - Poten_______
3. One who precedes - Precur_______
4. One who is graceful - Present_______

5. To hide truth - Prevari______
6. Leading woman singer - Prima______
7. Very ancient - Primev______
8. Force open - Pri______
9. Be in the know of - Pri______
10. A young genius - Prodi______
11. A sequence of events - Prog______
12. Introduction to a book - Prolo______
13. One who changes one's belief - Apos______
14. Divine power - Provi______
15. Human soul or spirit - Psy______
16. Mental disorder - Psycho______
17. Extremely careful - Puncti______
18. Surrounding areas - Purli______
19. A spot with pus - Pust______
20. Fireworks - Pyrotech______

TEST – 23

Give the opposite word for the following words.

1. A genuine doctor - Qua______
2. Dull and ordinary - Quain______
3. Accept - Qua______
4. At ease - Quea______
5. Answer - Quer______
6. Give a direct answer - Quibb______
7. Steadfast - Quicksil______
8. Moving - Quies______
9. Noise; ado - Qui______
10. Patriot - Quisl______
11. Careless - Qui vi______
12. Easy to understand - Quix______
13. Dull - Radia______
14. Controlled - Ramp______
15. In good shape - Ramsh______
16. Lack of greed - Rapa______
17. Joylessness - Rapt______
18. Disagreement - Rapproch______
19. Quiet and peaceful - Razzmata______

TEST – 24

Substitute with one word on the right hand side with help of given hints

1. One who is disobedient - Recalci______
2. Repeat the main points - Recapi______
3. Contraction in business - Rece______
4. One who relapses into crime - Recidi______
5. One who lives in reclusion - Reclu______
6. Detailed survey - Reconnai______
7. Becoming a king - Reg______
8. Rules for food and exercise - Regi______
9. Be born again - Reincar______
10. Repeat again - Reite______
11. Give new life - Rejuve______
12. Beyond repair - Irrepara______
13. Quick and sharp reply - Repar______
14. Send some body back to one's native country - Repatri______
15. Well supplied - Reple______
16. Official admonishment - Repri______
17. Prayer for the dead - Requie______
18. Brief account - Resum______
19. Come back to life - Resurr______

TEST – 25

Give one word for the following on the right hand side with help of given hints.

1. A very small amount - Scinti______
2. A young member of a noble family - Sci______
3. A holy book - Scrip______
4. Breaking away from the mother country - Secess______
5. Accustomed to sit or rest - Seden______

6. Rebellion against the govt. - Sedi______
7. A place for religious instruction - Semi______
8. Withdraw to a quiet place - Sequest______
9. Pleasant coincidence - Serend______
10. Afternoon nap - Sies______
11. A job with lots of money but very little work - Sinec______
12. Mean and dishonest practices - Skulldugg______
13. Contemptible person - Skun______
14. Untidy woman - Slatt______
15. Superficial knowledge - Smatter______
16. A combination of smoke and fog - Smo______
17. Burn without flame - Smoul______
18. Drench thoroughly - Soa______
19. Very wet - Sogg______
20. A short stay - Sojo______
21. Ungrammatical usage - Soleci______

TEST – 26

Give the opposite word of the following on the right hand side.

1. Said in so many words - Taci______
2. Talkative - Taci______
3. Bring credit - Tarn______
4. Politeness - Teme______
5. Unworldly - Tempo______
6. Be decisive - Tempo______
7. Unsustainable - Tenab______
8. Without a bias - Tenden______
9. Final - Tenta______
10. Solid and stable - Tenu______
11. Warm and enthusiastic - Tepi______
12. Celestial - Terres______
13. Longwinded - Ter______
14. Intestate - Tes______
15. Extravagant - Thrif______
16. Ecstasy - Thro______
17. Encourage - Thwa______
18. Fearless - Timo______
19. De facto - Titu______
20. Energetic - Tor______
21. Industry - Tor______
22. Straight - Toru______
23. Extol - Tradu______
24. Lead - Tra______

TEST – 27

Give one word for the following.

1. Copy a speech in writing - Trans______
2. Inject blood - Trans______
3. Go beyond limits - Trans______
4. Short lived - Trans______
5. Writing the same words in a new script - Transl______
6. To be reborn after death - Trans______
7. Bring about a great change - Trans______
8. Pangs of child birth - Trav______
9. Wearisome routine - Tread______
10. A large written document - Trea______
11. Insignificant things - Trif______
12. Base conduct - Turpi______
13. A newspaper with pictures - Tabl______
14. Social restriction - Tab______
15. That which can be felt - Tangi______
16. Be equal to - Tanta______
17. Neither hot nor cold - Temper______
18. Be indecisive - Tempo______
19. Private conversation - Tete-a-te______
20. Violent storm - Tor______

TEST – 28

Give the Adjectives of the following.

1. Taciturnity - Tacitu______
2. Tedium - Tedio______
3. Tempest - Tempestu______
4. Tenacity - Tenaci______
5. Tepidness - Tepi______
6. Therapy - Therapeu______
7. Thriftiness - Thrif______
8. Thwart - Thwarte______
9. Tilt - Tilte______
10. Toil - Toilso______
11. Torment - Tormente______
12. Torpor - Torpi______
13. Traduce - Traduce______
14. Tranquility - Tranqu______
15. Transact - Transacte______
16. Transcend - Transcenden______
17. Transcribe - Transcrib______
18. Transfix - Transf______
19. Transience - Transien______
20. Transmute - Transm______
21. Treachery - Trea______
22. Trifle - Trivi______

TEST – 29

Give one word on the right side for the following words given on the left side.

1. Found everywhere - Ubiqui______
2. In vain - Unavail______
3. Excessively pious - Unctu______
4. Quote a lower price - Under______
5. An oppressed person - Under______
6. Rising and falling - Undul______
7. Dig out - Unear______
8. Difficult to know - Unfathom______
9. Without basis - Unfound______
10. Remove a priest - Unfr______
11. Let loose - Unleas______
12. Poor in quality - Unprofe______
13. Bring to light - Unr______
14. Ill mannered - Unseem______
15. Take by force - Usur______
16. Difficult to carry - Unwiel______
17. Great disturbance - Uphe______
18. Greedy money lender - Usure______
19. Excessive greed - Usur______
20. A dream land - Ut______
21. Devoted to one's wife - Uxorio______

TEST – 30

Give the noun forms of the following words.

1. Vicious - Vicisousne______
2. Vigil - Vigilan______
3. Vindicate - Vindicati______
4. Virile - Virili______
5. Virulent - Virulen______
6. Vital - Vitali______
7. Vitiate - Vitiati______
8. Vituperative - Vitupera______
9. Vivacious - Vivaci______
10. Vivid - Vividne______
11. Vivisect - Vivisecti______
12. Vociferous - Vociferousne______
13. Volatile - Volatili______
14. Voracious - Voraci______
15. Vulnerable - Vulnerabi______
16. Waive - Waive______
17. Wanton - Wantonne______
18. Weird - Weirdne______
19. Whine - Whini______
20. Wily - Wil______
21. Willful - Wilfulne______
22. Yearn - Yearnin______
23. Yell - Yellin______
24. Zestful - Zestfu______

ANSWERS

TEST – 1

1.	Abandon	2.	Abhorrence	3.	Abject
4.	Abjure	5.	Abnegation	6.	Abominable
7.	Abortive	8.	Abscond	9.	Abstruse
10.	Acclaim	11.	Accomplice	12.	Accord
13.	Accrue	14.	Adamant	15.	Acme
16.	Acolyte	17.	Adroit	18.	Amiable
19.	Affect	20.	Affinity	21.	Alacrity

TEST – 2

1.	Unequivocal	2.	Enmity	3.	Deteriorate
4.	Unyielding	5.	Unfriendly	6.	Joy
7.	Modern	8.	Diffidence	9.	Nadir
10.	Alienate	11.	Deprecate	12.	Inapposite
13.	Censure	14.	Inarticulate	15.	Artful
16.	Applaud	17.	Dissent	18.	Inconstant
19.	Luxurious	20.	Successful		

TEST – 3

1.	Abhor	2.	Abortive	3.	Abrupt
4.	Absolved	5.	Accord	6.	Acolytes
7.	Adjured	8.	Afflicted	9.	Alleviate
10.	Aloof	11.	Altercation	12.	Alter ego
13.	Alternative	14.	Amazon	15.	Ambiguous
16.	Amenities	17.	Antecedents	18.	Approbation
19.	Arrant	20.	Assailed		

TEST – 4

1.	Baffle	2.	Beleaguer	3.	Belittle
4.	Bard	5.	Beatitude	6.	Beckon
7.	Bedraggle	8.	Befall	9.	Befriend
10.	Begrudge	11.	Beguile	12.	Beholden
13.	Belie	14.	Bellicose	15.	Benediction
16.	Benefaction	17.	Benefactor	18.	Beneficiary
19.	Benign	20.	Beseech		

TEST – 5

1.	Bigot	2.	Bohemian	3.	Boisterous
4.	Bonhomie	5.	Boorish	6.	Boulevard
7.	Bountiful	8.	Bowdlerize	9.	Brittle
10.	Condemnation	11.	Brusque	12.	Buccaneer
13.	Budding	14.	Bulwark	15.	Buoyant
16.	Burgeon	17.	Bustle	18.	Balderdash
19.	Belittle	20.	Barbarous		

TEST – 6

1.	Baggy	2.	Bawdy	3.	Beleaguered
4.	Balmy	5.	Bard	6.	Beautitude
7.	Befalls	8.	Befriend	9.	Begrudge
10.	Beholden	11.	Behove	12.	Belied
13.	Bellicose	14.	Bemoaned	15.	Benedictions
16.	Benefactors	17.	Benign	18.	Bereft

TEST – 7

1.	Cache	2.	Cachet	3.	Cacophony
4.	Cajole	5.	Calligraphy	6.	Callow
7.	Calumny	8.	Camaraderie	9.	Camouflage
10.	Candid	11.	Cannibal	12.	Canny
13.	Cantankerous	14.	Capitulate	15.	Caprice
16.	Captious	17.	Captivate	18.	Carnage
19.	Carnival	20.	Carp		

TEST – 8

1.	Celibacy	2.	Catholicism	3.	Catharsis
4.	Catholic	5.	Cattish	6.	Cavalier
7.	Cavil	8.	Cede	9.	Celerity
10.	Centripetal	11.	Celestial	12.	Chaotic
13.	Charlatan	14.	Chaste	15.	Chicanery
16.	Chide	17.	Churlish	18.	Circumlocution
19.	Circumspect	20.	Clemency		

TEST – 9

1.	Celibacy	2.	Charisma	3.	Charlatans
4.	Chary	5.	Charwoman	6.	Chastised
7.	Chauvinism	8.	Chivalrous	9.	Chronic
10.	Churlish	11.	Cinch	12.	claustrophobia
13.	Clemency	14.	Coaxed	15.	Coherent
16.	Cognizance	17.	Coerced		

TEST – 10

1.	Dainty	2.	Dais	3.	Damnation
4.	Deadlock	5.	Debacle	6.	Debilitates
7.	Debonair	8.	Debris	9.	Debutante
10.	Decadence	11.	Derelict	12.	Deride
13.	Desecrates	14.	Desperado	15.	Despicable
16.	Despondent	17.	Despot	18.	Destitute
19.	Deter	20.	Detrimental		

TEST – 11

1.	Deify	2.	Deign	3.	De Jure
4.	Deleterious	5.	Deliverance	6.	Delude
7.	Demagogue	8.	Demarche	9.	Demeanour
10.	Demon	11.	Demur	12.	Demure
13.	Denigrate	14.	Denouement	15.	Denounce
16.	Deplete	17.	Deponent	18.	Deport
19.	Depravity	20.	Deprecate		

TEST – 12

1.	Ebullient	2.	Éclat	3.	Ecstasy
4.	Edict	5.	Eerie	6.	Efface
7.	Effervescent	8.	Effete	9.	Efficacious
10.	Effrontery	11.	Effulgent	12.	Effusive
13.	Egalitarian	14.	Egregious	15.	Elan
16.	El Dorado	17.	Elevate	18.	Emancipate
19.	Elusive	20.	Emasculate		

TEST – 13

1.	Embezzled	2.	Emblem	3.	Emulate
4.	Embodies	5.	Enamoured	6.	Encomiums
7.	Encumbered	8.	Endemic	9.	Enervates
10.	Enfeebles	11.	Enfranchised	12.	Apartheid
13.	Engrossed	14.	Enjoined	15.	Enkindles
16.	Enlightened	17.	Enlisted	18.	Enlivened
19.	Enmeshed	20.	Ennui		

TEST – 14

1.	Fallible	2.	Fealty	3.	Fecund
4.	Feasible	5.	Festive	6.	Fetid
7.	Fickle	8.	Fidelity	9.	Finale
10.	Flaccid	11.	Flamboyant	12.	Flippant
13.	Foolhardy	14.	Foresight	15.	Forlorn
16.	Fragile	17.	Frugal	18.	Forego
		19.	Finesse		

TEST – 15

1.	Fabrication	2.	Fallacy	3.	Fallibility
4.	Fatality	5.	Fatuousness	6.	Feasibility
7.	Fecklessness	8.	Fecundity	9.	Feebleness
10.	Felicity	11.	Felony	12.	Fervor
13.	Festivity	14.	Fickleness	15.	Fiddling
16.	Flaccidness	17.	Flamboyance	18.	Flawlessness
19.	Flippancy	20.	Foreboding	21.	Foreclosure

TEST – 16

1.	Habitat	2.	Habitué	3.	Hail
4.	Hale and hearty	5.	Hapless	6.	Hauteur
7.	High time	8.	Helter-Skelter	9.	Hocus pocus
10.	Huddle	11.	Hurly burly	12.	Hyperbole
13.	Graft	14.	Essence	15.	Giggle
16.	Genuflect	17.	Gibberish		

TEST – 17

1.	Iconic	2.	Inadvertent	3.	Idiosyncratic
4.	Inane	5.	Ignominious	6.	Incisive
7.	Impetuous	8.	Inclement	9.	Impious
10.	Incongruous	11.	Imploring	12.	Incontinent
13.	Importunate	14.	Imposing	15.	Improper
16.	Improvident	17.	Impudent	18.	Impulsive
19.	Incriminating	20.	Indifferent		

TEST – 18

1.	Indefatigable	2.	Indelible	3.	Iconoclast
4.	Igloo	5.	Immemorial	6.	Emigrate
7.	Imminent	8.	Endanger	9.	Imperishable
10.	Implacable	11.	Impoverish	12.	Invincible
13.	Inaccessible	14.	Invalid		

TEST – 19

1.	Jamboree	2.	Janitor	3.	Kudos
4.	Knotty	5.	Lackeys	6.	Leeway
7.	Legend	8.	Levies	9.	Lexicon
10.	Lionize	11.	Lineage	12.	Lively
13.	Lithe	14.	Livid	15.	Luminous
16.	Luxuriant	17.	Luxurious	18.	Luscious
19.	Loathsome	20.	Longevity		

TEST – 20

1.	Jaded	2.	Jaundiced	3.	Jovial
4.	Knotty	5.	Kudos	6.	Laborious
7.	Lackadaisical	8.	Laggard	9.	Laissez faire
10.	Languishing	11.	Lassitude	12.	Lax
13.	Levity	14.	Licit	15.	Listless
16.	Lithe	17.	Loquacious	18.	Luminous

TEST – 21

1.	Lowest point	2.	Inexperienced	3.	Beginner
4.	Wicked	5.	Revenge	6.	Annoy
7.	Harmful	8.	Lout	9.	Respect
10.	Confuse	11.	Home sickness		

TEST – 22

1.	Posterity	2.	Potentate	3.	Precursor
4.	Presentable	5.	Prevaricate	6.	Prime Donna
7.	Primeval	8.	Prise	9.	Privy
10.	Prodigy	11.	Progression	12.	Prologue
13.	Apostate	14.	Providence	15.	Psyche
16.	Psychosis	17.	Punctilious	18.	Purlieus
19.	Pustule	20.	Pyrotechnics		

TEST – 23

1.	Quack	2.	Quaint	3.	Quash
4.	Queasy	5.	Query	6.	Quibble
7.	Quicksilver	8.	Quiescent	9.	Quiet
10.	Quisling	11.	Qui vive	12.	Quixotic
13.	Radiant	14.	Rampant	15.	Ramshackle
16.	Rapacity	17.	Rapture	18.	Rapprochement
19.	Razzmatazz				

TEST – 24

1.	Recalcitrant	2.	Recapitulate	3.	Recession
4.	Recidivist	5.	Recluse	6.	Reconnaissance
7.	Regal	8.	Regimen	9.	Reincarnate
10.	Reiterate	11.	Rejuvenate	12.	Irreparable
13.	Repartee	14.	Repatriate	15.	Replete
16.	Reprimand	17.	Requiem	18.	Resume
19.	Resurrect				

TEST – 25

1.	Scintilla	2.	Scion	3.	Scripture
4.	Secession	5.	Sedentary	6.	Sedition
7.	Seminary	8.	Sequester	9.	Serendipity
10.	Siesta	11.	Sinecure	12.	Skullduggery
13.	Skunk	14.	Slattern	15.	Smattering
16.	Smog	17.	Smoulder	18.	Soak
19.	Soggy	20.	Sojourn	21.	Solecism

TEST – 26

1.	Tacit	2.	Taciturn	3.	Tarnish
4.	Temerity	5.	Temporal	6.	Temporize
7.	Tenable	8.	Tendentious	9.	Tentative
10.	Tenuous	11.	Tepid	12.	Terrestrial
13.	Terse	14.	Testate	15.	Thrifty
16.	Throes	17.	Thwart	18.	Timorous
19.	Titular	20.	Torpid	21.	Torpor
22.	Tortuous	23.	Traduce	24.	Trail

TEST – 27

1.	Transcribe	2.	Transfuse	3.	Transcend
4.	Transient	5.	Transliterate	6.	Transmigrate
7.	Transform	8.	Travails	9.	Treadmill
10.	Treatise	11.	Trifles	12.	Turpitude
13.	Tabloid	14.	Taboo	15.	Tangible
16.	Tantamount	17.	Temperate	18.	Temporize
19.	Tete-a-tete	20.	Tornado		

TEST – 28

1.	Taciturn	2.	Tedious	3.	Tempestuous
4.	Tenacious	5.	Tepid	6.	Therapeutic
7.	Thrifty	8.	Thwarted	9.	Tilted
10.	Toilsome	11.	Tormented	12.	Torpid
13.	Traduced	14.	Tranquil	15.	Transacted
16.	Transcendent	17.	Transcribed	18.	Transfixed
19.	Transient	20.	Transmuted	21.	Treacherous
22.	Trivial				

TEST – 29

1.	Ubiquitous	2.	Unavailing	3.	Unctuous
4.	Underbid	5.	Underdog	6.	Undulating
7.	Unearth	8.	Unfathomable	9.	Unfounded
10.	Unfrock	11.	Unleash	12.	Unprofessional
13.	Unravel	14.	Unseemly	15.	Usurp
16.	Unwieldy	17.	Upheaval	18.	Usurer
19.	Usury	20.	Utopia	21.	Uxorious

TEST – 30

1.	Viciousness	2.	Vigilance	3.	Vindication
4.	Virility	5.	Virulence	6.	Vitality
7.	Vitiation	8.	Vituperation	9.	Vivacity
10.	Vividness	11.	Vivisection	12.	Vociferousness
13.	Volatility	14.	Voracity	15.	Vulnerability
16.	Waiver	17.	Wantonness	18.	Weirdness
19.	Whining	20.	Wile	21.	Willfulness
22.	Yearning	23.	Yelling	24.	Zestfulness

PART – B

ELEMENTS OF GRAMMAR AND THEIR USAGE

PARTS OF SPEECH AND FORMATION OF WORDS

INTRODUCING THE VARIOUS FORMS OF WORDS

When we talk, we use sentences. These sentences are made up of words. Words are divided into eight parts of speech according to their use in a sentence.

(i) Noun	*(ii)* Pronoun
(iii) Adjective	*(iv)* Verb
(v) Adverb	*(vi)* Preposition
(vii) Conjunction	*(viii)* Interjection

Do you know the Forms of Words

1. ***A Noun is the name of a person, place or thing.***
2. ***Words used in the place of 'Nouns' are called 'Pronouns' as" I, we, you, he, she, it, they etc.***
3. ***Words used to quality Nouns are called 'Adjectives'. An 'Adjective' is a word that adds something to the meaning of a noun or a pronoun.***
4. ***Words used for indicating 'doing' or 'saying' are called 'Verbs'. They indicate something done or said about a subject.***
5. ***Words which add to the meaning of some verb, adjective or another adverb are called 'Adverb'.***
6. ***A Preposition is a word which is placed before a noun or pronoun. It show its relation with something else.***
7. ***Words used to join words or groups of words are called Conjunctions.***
8. ***An Interjection is an exclamatory word which expresses a sudden feeling or emotion. Like Alas! Lo! Hurrah!***

A Noun is the name of a person, place or thing.

(i) **Delhi** is the **capital** of **India.**

(ii) **Calcutta** is the biggest **city** in **India.**

(iii) The boy plays **hockey.**

(iv) **People** worship Lord **Ram** as a **god.**

(v) **Kalidas** was a great **poet** of **India.**

(vi) My **brother** lives in **Bombay.**

(vii) **Shyam** has many **books.**

In these sentences all words in bold are Nouns. Delhi, Calcutta Bombay, India, city, capital are names of places (or country) and Kalidas and Shyam are names of persons. Similarly other bold words are "name". They are all "Nouns".

Words used in the place of 'Nouns' are called 'Pronouns' as" I, we, you, he, she, it, they etc.

'Ram went to his village with his friend. He carried some gifts with him'.

'He', his', and 'him', have been used here in place of 'Nouns'. Such words are called **Pronouns.**

Without the use of Pronouns, the sentences given here would have been as given below:

Ram went to Ram's village with Ram's friend. Ram carried some gifts with Ram.

Other examples are:

(i) Sukhwant said to Balbir, "**I** shall lend **you my** books."

(ii) The teacher liked Balvinder because he was very hard working and intelligent.

(iii) **We** should obey **our** parents.

An 'Adjective' is a word that adds something to the meaning of a noun or a pronoun.

Words used to qualify Nouns are called 'Adjectives'.

(i) He is an **able** teacher.

(ii) The dog is a **faithful** animal.

(iii) That shopkeeper sells **delicious** sweets.

(iv) Mohan is an **intelligent** student.

In the above sentences, 'able, faithful, delicious, intelligent' are all 'Adjectives'.

They add something to the meanings of the Nouns that come after them.

Words used for indicating 'doing' or 'saying' are called 'Verbs'.

They indicate something done or said about a subject.

(i) I go to the market. (what do I do? – go to the market)

(ii) They helped the flood victims. (something done)

An Adverb is a word which adds to or modifies the meaning of a verb, an adjective or another adverb.

(i) He walked **slowly.**

(ii) She spoke softly.

(iii) She is **extremely** beautiful.

(iv) He is very handsome.

In these sentences 'slowly, softly, extremely, very, are all adverbs.

Words which express the relation between things denoted by 'Nouns' are called prepositions: as,

A Preposition is a word which is placed before a noun or pronoun. It show its relation with something else.

(i) The book is lying **on** the table.

(ii) Hari writes **with** a pen.

(iii) The boys sat **in** the garden.

(iv) My father returns home **at** 5 o'clock.

In these sentences 'on, with, in, at' are all Prepositions.

Words used to join words or groups of words are called Conjunctions.

(i) Mohan **and** Sohan were quarreling.

(ii) **Either** Mohan **or** Sohan is at fault.

(iii) You can pass **if** you work hard.

(iv) Although he is poor, **yet** he is honest.

In these sentences 'and, either, or, if, although, yet', are all Conjunctions.

A Conjunction is a word which joins together words.

Words which are used to express some sudden feeling or emotion are called 'Interjection': as,

An Interjection is an exclamatory word which expresses a sudden feeling or emotion. Like Alas! Lo! Hurrah!

(i) Alas ! the old man is no more (sorrow)

(ii) Hurrah ! we have won the match. (joy)

(iii) Lo ! he has arrived. (wonder)

KEEP REGURGITATING TO LEARN THE FRAMING OF WORDS

(i) A noun is used for naming a thing.

(ii) A pronoun is used as a substitute for a noun.

(iii) An adjective is used for qualifying a noun or pronoun.

(iv) A verb is a doing or saying word.

(v) A preposition is used for showing relation.

(vi) A conjunction is used for joining words or sentences.

(vii) An adverb adds to the meaning of a verb, an adjective or another adverb.

(viii) An interjection expresses joy, sorrow or surprise etc.

SET – 1

I. FORM NOUNS FROM THE FOLLOWING VERBS

	A	B	C	D
1.	Abet	Bathe	Carry	Deceive
2.	Abhor	Believe	Civilize	Decide
3.	Abide	Behave	Close	Define
4.	Abound	Belong	Compare	Destroy
5.	Achieve	Beautify	Choose	Deny
6.	Accomplish	Betray	Compel	Determine
7.	Acknowledge	Bind	Complete	Defend
8.	Admit	Bear	Convert	Deliver
9.	Allot	Bless	Conceal	Die
10.	Amuse	Break	Contain	Differ
11.	Arrange	Bury	Consume	Direct
12.	Acquaint	Breathe	Consider	Discover
13.	Appoint	Bleed	Create	Disturb
14.	Arrive		Criticize	Drink
15.	Approve		Collect	Digest
16.	Ascend		Confine	Dig
17.	Assure		Consider	Descend
18.	Aspire		Commence	Depend
19.	Apply		Commit	Do
20.	Attend		Complain	Defy
21.	Advise		Comply	

	E	F	G	H	I
1.	Earn	Fall	Give	Hate	Imagine
2.	Educate	Fly	Go	Heal	Inquire
3.	Eject	Forgive	Grieve		Inherit
4.	Enjoy	Flow	Govern		Inscribe
5.	Endure	Float	Grow		Inspect
6.	Enter	Feed	Guide		Investigate
7.	Erect	Furnish			Increase
8.	Enclose	Free			Irrigate
9.	Envelop				Introduce
10.	Examine				Illustrate
11.	Explain				Imitate
12.	Exempt				Infer
13.	Extend				Inform
14.	Express				Injure
15.	Expel				Inspire
16.	Exceed				Insure
17.	Expire				Intend
18.	Expect				Interfere
19.	Expand				Invite
20.	Exist				
21.	Except				
22.	Entreat				
23.	Err				

	J	K	L	M	N
1.	Judge	Know	Laugh	Marry	Narrate
2.	Join		Learn	Master	
3.	Justify		Lend	Meditate	
4.			Live	Mix	
5.			Lose	Move	
6.				Mean	

	O	P	Q	R
1.	Obey	Pay	Qualify	Rebel
2.	Object	Pass	Quote	Receive
3.	Oblige	Perform		Recollect
4.	Offend	Pursue		Recommend
5.	Omit	Please		Reflect
6.	Oppose	Pray		Refuse
7.	Organize	Prefer		Refresh
8.		Prepare		Reform
9.		Preserve		Relieve
10.		Press		Rely
11.		Pretend		Respond
12.		Proceed		Recover
13.		Proclaim		Resist
14.		Prohibit		Resolve
15.		Propose		Remain
16.		Prosper		Remove
17.		Prove		Revive
18.		Provide		Revolt
19.		Permit		Recite
20.		Produce		Refer
21.				Repent
22.				Revolve

	S	T	U	V	W
1.	Salute	Tell	Unite	Verify	Wed
2.	Satisfy	Think		Vary	Withdraw
3.	See	Trace		Vacate	Write
4.	Secure	Translate			Wake
5.	Seize	Treat			Weigh
6.	Sell	Try			Waste
7.	Separate	Thieve			Weave
8.	Serve				
9.	Shake				
10.	Sing				
11.	Sit				
12.	Slay				
13.	Solve				
14.	Sow				
15.	Speak				
16.	Steal				
17.	Stick				
18.	Strive				
19.	Subtract				
20.	Succeed				

SET – 2

II. FORM NOUNS FROM THE FOLLOWING ADJECTIVES

	A	B	C	D	E
1.	Able	Brave	Calm	Dear	Exemplary
2.	Active	Brilliant	Certain	Decent	Energetic
3.	Absent	Busy	Chaste	Deaf	Empty
4.	Accurate	Broad	Civil	Dark	Efficient
5.	Abundant	Brief	Clean	Deep	Equal
6.	Adequate	Bitter	Clear	Dense	Excellent
7.	Attractive	Bankrupt	Complete	Delicate	
8.	Anxious	Bold	Constant	Different	
9.		Bright		Difficult	
10.				Diligent	
11.				Dry	

	F	G	H	I	J
1.	Fertile	Gallant	Happy	Ill	Jealous
2.	Frail	Gay	Holy	Idle	Junior
3.	Fragrant	Generous	Hard	Innocent	Just
4.	Free	Grand	High	Inferior	
5.	Faithful	Grave	Honest	Important	
6.	Frugal	Great	Hospitable	Immense	
7.	Funny	Gloomy	Hot	Insane	
8.	Furious	Greedy	Human	Intelligent	
9.	Favourable	Guilty	Humble	Intense	
10.	Fast		Healthy	Infant	
11.	Foolish		Hilly		
12.	Faulty		Hungry		
13.	Floral		Hopeful		

	K	L	M	N	O
1.	Kind	Lazy	Merry	Necessary	Obedient
2.	Knotty	Legal	Moist	Nobel	Obscure
3.		Laborious	Moral		Obstinate
4.		Literary	Mean		Original
5.		Loyal	Magnificent		One
6.		Local	Miserable		
7.		Lousy			
8.		Lucky			

	P	Q	R	S	T
1.	Popular	Quick	Real	Safe	Timid
2.	Perfect		Rich	Scarce	True
3.	Pious		Rigid	Secret	Terrific
4.	Poor		Rival	Severe	Thoughtful
5.	Pure		Round	Silent	Trustworthy
6.	Private		Red	Simple	Thirsty
7.	Prudent		Rapid	Splendid	
8.	Patient		Royal	Special	
9.	Prior			Stable	
10.	Proud			Stupid	
11.				Sure	
12.				Satisfactory	
13.				Short	
14.				Sick	
15.				Social	
16.				Soft	

	U	V	W	Y
1.	Urgent	Vacant	Warm	Young
2.		Vain	Weak	
3.		Various	Wise	
4.		Vaporous	Worthy	
5.			Wide	

SET – 3

III. FORM ABSTRACT NOUNS OF THE FOLLOWING

1.	Act	18.	Father	35.	Patron
2.	Author	19.	Friend	36.	Patriot
3.	Agent	20.	Gentle	37.	Painter
4.	Beggar	21.	Hero	38.	Partner
5.	Boy	22.	Hermit	39.	Person
6.	Brother	23.	Hindu	40.	Poet
7.	Bond	24.	Infant	41.	Relate
8.	Brave	25.	Inspect	42.	Scholar
9.	Cook	26.	King	43.	Serve
10.	Chemist	27.	Lord	44.	Stationer
11.	Child	28.	Mother	45.	Speaker
12.	Christ	29.	Monarch	46.	Superintendent
13.	Coin	30.	Man	47.	Thief
14.	Creator	31.	Member	48.	Widow
15.	Examine	32.	Neighbor	49.	Woman
16.	Earl	33.	Owner		
17.	Enemy	34.	Orphan		

SET – 4

IV. FORM ADJECTIVES OF THE FOLLOWING NOUNS

	A	B	C	D
1.	Ability	Black	Calmness	Danger
2.	Activity	Blindness	Coolness	Dew
3.	Attention	Book	Care	Dearth
4.	Accident	Blood	Crime	Darkness
5.	Art	Boy	College	Drama
6.	Adventure	Bravery	Class	Democracy
7.	Atmosphere	Bush	Capability	Deafness
8.	Abuse	Brother	Comfort	Difference
9.	Absence	Brass	Child	Decency
10.	Anger	Business	Cleanliness	Destruction
11.	Air	Brilliance	Circle	Depth
12.	Anxiety	Brevity	Clerk	Discipline
13.	Angel		Condition	Delicacy
14.	Awe		Character	Duty
15.	Attraction			Death
16.	Age			

	E	F	G	H
1.	Ease	Fault	Gaiety	Happiness
2.	Editor	Favour	Grass	Health
3.	Economy	Father	Grammar	Humility
4.	Excellence	Flower	Gloom	Honesty
5.	Efficiency	Fastness	Geometry	Hand
6.	East	Freedom	Greed	Harm
7.	Expense	Fashion	Guilt	Home
8.	Empire	Fish	Gold	Hill
9.	Example	Face	Geography	Humanity
10.	Energy	Fun	Girl	Height
11.	Emptiness	Fool	Glory	Heat
12.		Friend	Greatness	Habit
13.		Falsehood	Goodness	Heart
14.		Faith		Hair
15.		Fragrance		Hunger
16.				Heaven
17.				Hero
18.				Horror
19.				Hope

	I	J	K	L
1.	Influence	Justice	Kindness	Labour
2.	India	Joy	Knot	Luck
3.	Ice	Jealousy		Logic
4.	Illness	Judge		Leather
5.	Inferiority			Length
6.	Industry			Locality
7.	Intelligence			Love
8.	Ignorance			Law
9.	Innocence			Luxury
10.	Idiom			Loyalty
11.	Idleness			Life
12.	Italy			

	M	N	O	P
1.	Man	Nature	Opening	Popularity
2.	Marriage	Newness	Objection	Propriety
3.	Milk	Notice	Office	Play
4.	Memory	Name	Order	Peace
5.	Morality	Number	Occasion	Poetry
6.	Master	Need	Obedience	President
7.	Mother	Nearness	Oil	Price
8.	Mud	Noise	Origin	Passion
9.	Month	Nobility		Population
10.	Machine	Navy		Poverty
11.	Might	Nation		Possibility
12.	Metal			Publicity
13.	Miracle			Person
14.				Pain
15.				Profit
16.				Patriot
17.				Prince
18.				Progress
19.				Pride
20.				Power
21.				Privacy

	Q	R	S	T
1.	Quickness	Reason	Seed	Truth
2.	Queen	Religion	Slave	Table
3.	Question	Residence	Section	Terror
4.	Quarrel	Redness	Silk	Type
5.		Rust	Stone	Thirst
6.		Reality	Season	Trouble
7.		Royalty	Silver	Time
8.		Roundness	Service	Talk
9.		Rain	Sentiment	Telegraph
10.		Risk	Soap	Tutor
11.		Ruin	Sport	Telephone
12.		Rose	Surgeon	Taste
13.		Right	Station	
14.		Richness	Sleep	
15.		Room	Strength	
16.			Speciality	
17.			Selfishness	

	U	V	W	Y	Z
1.	Universe	Value	Water	Year	Zeal
2.	Use	Vice	Wool	Youth	
3.		Voice	World		
4.		Virtue	Week		
5.		Victory	Wood		
6.		Verb	Wind		

SET – 5

V. FORM ADJECTIVES OF THE FOLLOWING VERBS

1.	Advise	6.	Collect	11.	Differ	16.	Move
2.	Agree	7.	Change	12.	Eat	17.	Save
3.	Avail	8.	Doubt	13.	Glorify	18.	Talk
4.	Boast	9.	Drink	14.	Laugh	19.	Tire
5.	Cease	10.	Divide	15.	Lower		

SET – 6

VI. FORM VERBS OF THE FOLLOWING NOUNS

	A	B	C
1.	Abolition	Bath	Calculation
2.	Abundance	Brood	Centre
3.	Acceptance	Breath	Class
4.	Accommodation	Bond	Collection
5.	Admiration	Burial	Completion
6.	Admission	Beginning	Camp
7.	Arrival	Body	Cancellation
8.	Application	Belief	Custom
9.	Agreement	Bribery	Choice
10.	Attendance	Building	Carriage
11.	Authority	Black	Creation
12.	Absorption	Blood	Critic
13.	Action	Brass	Colony
14.	Achievement	Beggar	Encourage
15.	Advice	Beauty	Company
16.	Addition	Birth	Civilization
17.	Apology		Cultivation
18.	Assistance		Cloth
19.	Approval		Character
20.	Appointment		Chain
21.	Association		Crime
22.	Appearance		Conclusion

	D	E	F	G
1.	Danger	Election	Fright	Game
2.	Drop	Electricity	Friend	Glass
3.	Deed	Enjoyment	Fruit	Glory
4.	Drawing	Extension	Flight	Grief
5.	Dictation	Error	Furniture	Gait
6.	Delivery	Example	Food	Gold
7.	Drama	Entry	Flower	Grass
8.	Departure	Edition, Editor	Force	Guardian
9.	Description	Economy	Fort	Growth
10.	Dinner		Fool	
11.	Death		Fleet	
12.	Discovery			

	H	I	J	K
1.	Hatred	Instruction	Judgment	Knee
2.	Horror	Idol	Joy	Knot
3.	Harmony	Intoxication	Junction	Knowledge
4.	Heart	Interference	Justice	
5.	Half	Introduction		
6.	Health			
7.	Height			
8.	Hand			
9.	Habit			

	L	M	N	O
1.	Laughter	Monopoly	Name	Office
2.	Loan	Meeting	Nature	Origin
3.	Learning	Multiplication	Nation	Organization
4.	Loss	Memory	Notice	Occupation
5.	Life	Movement	Number	
6.	Light	Mixture		
7.	List			
8.	Luster			

	P	Q	R
1.	Painting	Quotation	Removal
2.	Permission	Qualification	Right
3.	Prosperity	Quickness	Relation
4.	Provision		Race
5.	President		Requirement
6.	Preference		Revision
7.	Performance		Remembrance

	P	Q	R
8.	Publication		Resolution
9.	Power		Residence
10.	Pleasure		
11.	Product		
12.	Population		
13.	Payment		
14.	Pressure		
15.	Practice		
16.	Prison		

	S	T	V	W
1.	Sale	Table	Voice	Web
2.	Spark	Term	Vacation	Witch
3.	Stroke	Terror	Verse	Writing
4.	Submission	Translation	Vice	Weakness
5.	Success	Tale	Vacancy	West
6.	Satisfaction	Thought	Victim	
7.	Spelling	Thief	Vibration	
8.	Settlement			
9.	System			
10.	Service			
11.	Speech			
12.	Sympathy			

SET – 7

VII. FORM VERBS OF THE FOLLOWING ADJECTIVES

	A	B	C	D
1.	Able	Broad	Calm	Divisible
2.	Abundant	Black	Civil	Doubtful
3.	Agreeable	Bold	Clear	Dark
4.	Admirable	Bitter	Certain	Different
5.	Available	Boastful	Comfortable	Double
6.	Answerable	Base	Collective	Dreadful
7.			Cheap	Dear
8.			Clean	Deep
9.			Chargeable	
10.			Complete	
11.			Conclusive	

	E	F	G	H
1.	Equal	Fine	Glad	Heedful
2.	Extensive	False	Grave	Humble
3.	Eatable	Full	Glorious	Helpless
4.	Exchangeable	Fond	General	Hard
5.		Fresh		Hale
6.		Fate		
7.		Flat		

	J	L	M	N	P	R
1.	Just	Little	Mean	Noble	Pure	Red
2.		Low	Mad	Natural	Poor	Real
3.		Light		New	Public	Rich
4.		Long				Right

	S	T	V	W
1.	Short	Thick	Vacant	White
2.	Safe	Tight	Various	Worshipful
3.	Sick			Wide
4.	Solid			Workable
5.	Sympathetic			
6.	Sharp			
7.	Soft			
8.	Sweet			
9.	Special			
10.	Simple			
11.	Suitable			

SET – 8

VIII. ADVERBS FROM ADJECTIVES

1.	Able	21.	Possible	41.	Moral
2.	Active	22.	Painful	42.	Near
3.	Brave	23.	Popular	43.	Necessary
4.	Bitter	24.	Practical	44.	Noble
5.	Bold	25.	Punctual	45.	Obedient
6.	Broad	26.	Real	46.	Short
7.	Brief	27.	Right	47.	Strong
8.	Capable	28.	Safe	48.	Stupid
9.	Careful	29.	False	49.	Successful
10.	Careless	30.	Gay	50.	Timid
11.	Certain	31.	Generous	51.	Urgent
12.	Cruel	32.	Greedy	52.	Useful
13.	Close	33.	High	53.	Vague
14.	Curious	34.	Honest	54.	Vain
15.	Dense	35.	Intense	55.	Wide
16.	Double	36.	Just	56.	Wise
17.	Easy	37.	Kind		
18.	Patient	38.	Loyal		
19.	Proud	39.	Mean		
20.	Perfect	40.	Merry		

ANSWERS

SET – 1

I. FORM NOUNS FROM THE FOLLOWING VERBS

	A	B	C
1.	Abetment	Bath	Carriage or Carrier
2.	Abhorrence	Belief	Civilization
3.	Abode	Behaviour	Closure
4.	Abundance	Belonging	Comparison
5.	Achievement	Beauty	Choice
6.	Acknowledgement	Betrayal	Compulsion
7.	Accomplishment	Bound	Completion
8.	Admission	Birth	Conversion
9.	Allotment	Bliss	Concealment
10.	Amusement	Breach	Contents
11.	Arrangement	Burial	Consumption
12.	Acquaintance	Breath	Consideration
13.	Appointment	Blood	Creation
14.	Arrival		Criticism
15.	Approval		Collection
16.	Ascent		Confinement
17.	Assurance		Consideration
18.	Aspiration		Commencement
19.	Application		Commitment
20.	Attendance		Complaint
21.	Advice		Compliance

	D	E	F
1.	Deceit or Deception	Earning	Failure
2.	Decision	Education	Flight
3.	Definition	Ejectment	Forgiveness
4.	Destruction	Enjoyment	Flood
5.	Denial	Endurance	Fleet
6.	Determination	Entry	Food
7.	Defence	Erection	Furniture
8.	Delivery or Deliverance	Enclosure	Freedom
9.	Death	Envelope	
10.	Difference	Examination	
11.	Direction	Explanation	
12.	Discovery	Exemption	
13.	Disturbance	Extension	
14.	Draught	Expression	
15.	Digestion	Expulsion	
16.	Ditch	Excess	
17.	Descent	Expiry	
18.	Dependence	Expectation	
19.	Deed	Expansion	
20.	Defiance	Existence	
21.		Exception	
22.		Entreaty	
23.		Error	

	G	H	I	J
1.	Gift	Hatred	Imagination	Judgment
2.	Gait	Health	Inquiry	Joint
3.	Grief		Inheritance	Justification
4.	Government		Inscription	
5.	Growth		Inspection	
6.	Guidance		Investigation	
7.			Increment	
8.			Irrigation	
9.			Introduction	
10.			Illustration	
11.			Imitation	
12.			Inference	
13.			Information	
14.			Injury	
15.			Inspiration	
16.			Insurance	
17.			Intention	
18.			Interference	
19.			Invitation	

	K	L	M	N
1.	Knowledge	Laughter	Marriage	Narration
2.		Learning	Mastery	
3.		Loan	Meditation	
4.		Life Living	Mixture	
5.		Loss	Motion	
6.		Loser	Movement	
7.			Meaning	

	O	P	Q
1.	Obedience	Payment	Qualification
2.	Objection	Passage	Quotation
3.	Obligation	Performance	
4.	Offence	Pursuit	
5.	Omission	Pleasure	
6.	Opposition	Prayer	
7.	Organization	Preference	
8.		Preparation	
9.		Preservation	
10.		Pressure	
11.		Pretension	
12.		Procedure	
13.		Proclamation	
14.		Prohibition	
15.		Proposal	
16.		Prosperity	
17.		Proof	
18.		Provision	
19.		Permission	
20.		Production	

	R	S	T
1.	Rebellion	Salutation	Tale
2.	Reception or Receipt	Satisfaction	Thought
3.	Recollection	Sight	Track
4.	Recommendation	Security	Translation
5.	Reflection	Seizure	Treatment
6.	Refusal	Sale	Trial
7.	Refreshment	Separation	Theft
8.	Reformation	Service	
9.	Relief	Shock	
10.	Reliance	Song, Singer	
11.	Response	Seat	
12.	Recovery	Slaughter	
13.	Resistance	Solution	
14.	Resolution	Seed	
15.	Remainder	Speech	
16.	Removal	Stealth	
17.	Revival	Stroke	
18.	Revolution	Strife	
19.	Recitation	Subtraction	
20.	Reference	Success	
21.	Repentance		
22.	Revolution		

	U	V	W
1.	Unity or Union	Verification	Wedding
2.		Variety	Withdrawal
3.		Vacation	Writer or Writ or Writing
4.		Vacancy	Watch
5.			Weight
6.			Wastage
7.			Web

SET – 2

II. FORM NOUNS FROM THE FOLLOWING ADJECTIVES

	A	B	C	D
1.	Ability	Bravery	Calmness	Dearness
2.	Activity	Brilliance	Certainty	Decency
3.	Absence	Business	Chastity	Deafness
4.	Accuracy	Breadth	Civility	Darkness
5.	Abundance	Brevity	Cleanliness	Depth
6.	Adequacy	Bitterness	Clarity	Density
7.	Attraction	Bankruptcy	Completion	Delicacy
8.	Anxiety	Boldness	Constancy	Difference
9.		Brightness		Difficulty
10.				Diligence
11.				Dryness or Drought

	E	F	G	H
1.	Example	Fertility	Gallantry	Happiness
2.	Energy	Frailty	Gaiety	Holiness
3.	Emptiness	Fragrance	Generosity	Hardship or Hardness
4.	Efficiency	Freedom	Grandeur	Height
5.	Equality	Faith, Faithfulness	Gravity	Honesty
6.	Excellence	Frugality	Greatness	Hospitality
7.		Fun	Gloom	Heat
8.		Fury	Greed	Humanity or Humane
9.		Favour	Guilt	Humility
10.		Fastness		Health
11.		Folly		Hill
12.		Fault		Hunger
13.		Flower		Hope

	I	J	K	L
1.	Illness	Jealousy	Kindness	Laziness
2.	Idleness	Juniority	Knot	Law
3.	Innocence	Justice		Labour
4.	Inferiority			Literature
5.	Importance			Loyalty
6.	Immensity			Locality, Locale
7.	Insanity			Louse
8.	Intelligence			Luck
9.	Intensity			
10.	Infancy			

	M	N	O	P
1.	Merriment	Necessity	Obedience	Popularity
2.	Moisture	Nobility	Obscurity	Perfection
3.	Morality		Obstinacy	Piety
4.	Meanness		Originality	Poverty
5.	Magnificence		Oneness	Purity
6.	Misery			Privacy
7.				Prudence
8.				Patience
9.				Priority
10.				Pride

	Q	R	S	T
1.	Quickness	Reality	Safety	Timidity
2.		Richness	Scarcity	Truth
3.		Rigidity	Secrecy	Terror
4.		Rivalry	Severity	Thought or Thoughtless
5.		Roundness	Silence	Trust
6.		Redness	Simplicity	Thirst
7.		Rapidity	Splendour	
8.		Royalty	Speciality	
9.			Stability	
10.			Stupidity	
11.			Surety	
12.			Satisfaction	
13.			Shortage	
14.			Sickness	
15.			Society	
16.			Softness	

	U	V	W	Y
1.	Urgency	Vacancy	Warmth	Youth
2.		Vanity	Weakness	
3.		Variety	Wisdom	
4.		Vapour	Worth	
5.			Width	

SET – 3

III. FORM ABSTRACT NOUNS OF THE FOLLOWING

1.	Action	26.	Kingship
2.	Authorship	27.	Lordship
3.	Agency	28.	Motherhood
4.	Beggary	29.	Monarchy
5.	Boyhood	30.	Manhood
6.	Brotherhood	31.	Membership
7.	Bondage	32.	Neighborhood
8.	Bravery	33.	Ownership
9.	Cookery	34.	Orphanage
10.	Chemistry	35.	Patronage
11.	Childhood	36.	Patriotism
12.	Christianity	37.	Painting
13.	Coinage	38.	Partnership
14.	Creation	39.	Personality
15.	Examination	40.	Poetry
16.	Earldom	41.	Relation
17.	Enmity	42.	Scholarship
18.	Fatherhood	43.	Service
19.	Friendship	44.	Stationery
20.	Gentleness	45.	Speech
21.	Heroism	46.	Superintendentship
22.	Hermitage	47.	Theft
23.	Hinduism	48.	Widowhood
24.	Infancy	49.	Womanhood
25.	Inspection		

SET – 4

IV. FORM ADJECTIVES OF THE FOLLOWING NOUNS

	A	B	C
1.	Able	Blackish	Calm
2.	Active	Blind	Cool
3.	Attentive	Bookish	Careful
4.	Accidental	Bloody	Criminal
5.	Artistic	Boyish	Collegiate
6.	Adventurous	Brave	Classic, Classical
7.	Atmospheric	Bushy	Capable
8.	Abusive	Brotherly	Comfortable
9.	Absent	Brassy	Childish
10.	Angry	Busy	Clean
11.	Airy	Brilliant	Circular
12.	Aerial	Brief	Clerical
13.	Anxious		Conditional
14.	Angelic		Characteristic
15.	Awful		
16.	Attractive		
17.	Aged		

	D	E	F
1.	Dangerous	Easy	Faulty
2.	Dewy	Editorial	Favourable or Favourite
3.	Dear	Economical	Fatherly
4.	Dark	Excellent	Floral, Flowery
5.	Dramatic	Efficient	Fast
6.	Democratic	Eastern	Free
7.	Deaf	Expensive	Fashionable
8.	Different	Emperial	Fishy
9.	Decent	Exemplary	Facial
10.	Destructive	Energetic	Funny
11.	Deep	Empty	Foolish
12.	Disciplinary		Friendly
13.	Delicate		False
14.	Dutiful		Faithful
15.	Dead		Fragrant

	G	H	I
1.	Gay	Happy	Influential
2.	Grassy	Healthy	Indian
3.	Grammatical	Humble	Icy
4.	Gloomy	Honest	Ill
5.	Geometrical	Handy	Inferior
6.	Greedy	Harmful	Industrious or industrial
7.	Guilty	Homely	Intelligent
8.	Golden	Hilly	Ignorant
9.	Geographical	Human	Innocent
10.	Girlish	Humanitarian	Idiomatic
11.	Glorious	High	Idle
12.	Great	Hot	Italian
13.	Good	Habitual	
14.		Hearty	
15.		Hairy	
16.		Hungry	
17.		Heavenly	
18.		Heroic	
19.		Horrible	
20.		Hopeful	

	J	K	L	M
1.	Just	Kind	Laborious	Manly
2.	Joyful	Knotty	Lucky	Marriageable
3.	Jealous		Logical	Milky
4.	Judicial		Leathery	Memorable
5.			Long	Moral
6.			Local	Masterly
7.			Lovely	Motherly
8.			Legal	Muddy
9.			Luxurious	Monthly
10.			Loyal	Mechanical
11.			Life-like	Mighty
12.			Lively	Metallic
13.				Miraculous

	N	O	P
1.	Natural	Open	Popular
2.	New	Objectionable	Proper
3.	Noticeable	Official	Playful
4.	Nominal	Officious	Peaceful
5.	Numeral	Orderly	Poetical
6.	Needful	Occasional	Presidential
7.	Needy	Obedient	Precious
8.	Near	Oily	Passionate
9.	Noisy	Original	Populous
10.	Noble		Poor
11.	Naval		Possible
12.	National		Public
13.			Personal
14.			Painful
15.			Profitable
16.			Patriotic
17.			Princely
18.			Progressive
19.			Proud
20.			Powerful
21.			Private

	Q	R	S
1.	Quick	Reasonable	Seedy
2.	Queenly	Religious	Slavish
3.	Questionable	Residential	Sectional
4.	Quarrelsome	Reddish	Silky
5.		Rusty	Stony
6.		Real	Seasonal
7.		Royal	Silvery
8.		Round	Serviceable
9.		Rainy	Sentimental
10.		Risky	Soapy
11.		Ruinous	Sporting
12.		Rosy	Surgical
13.		Righteous	Stationary
14.		Rich	Sleepy
15.		Roomy	Strong
16.			Special
17.			Selfish

	T	U	V
1.	Truthful	Universal	Valuable
2.	True	Useful	Vicious
3.	Tabular	Useless	Vocal
4.	Terrible		Virtuous
5.	Typical		Victorious
6.	Thirsty		Verbal
7.	Troublesome		
8.	Timely		
9.	Talkative		
10.	Telegraphic		
11.	Tutorial		
12.	Telephonic		
13.	Tasty		

	W	Y	Z
1.	Watery	Yearly	Zealous
2.	Woollen	Youthful or Young	
3.	Worldly		
4.	Weekly		
5.	Wooden		
6.	Windy		

SET – 5

V. FORM ADJECTIVES OF THE FOLLOWING VERBS

1.	Advisable	11.	Difference
2.	Agreeable	12.	Eatable
3.	Available	13.	Glorious
4.	Boastful	14.	Laughable
5.	Ceaseless	15.	Low
6.	Collective	16.	Movable
7.	Changeable	17.	Safe
8.	Doubtful	18.	Talkative
9.	Drinkable	19.	Tiresome or Tiring
10.	Divisible		

SET – 6

VI. FORM VERBS OF THE FOLLOWING NOUNS

	A	B	C	D
1.	Abolish	Bathe	Calculate	Endanger
2.	Abound	Breed	Centralise	Drip
3.	Accept	Breathe	Classify	Do
4.	Accommodate	Bind	Collect	Draw
5.	Admire	Bury	Complete	Dictate
6.	Admit	Begin	Encamp	Deliver
7.	Arrive	Embody	Cancel	Dramatize
8.	Apply	Believe	Accustom	Depart
9.	Agree	Bribe	Choose	Describe
10.	Attend	Build	Carry	Dine
11.	Authorise	Blacken	Create	Die
12.	Absorb	Bleed	Criticise	Discover
13.	Act	Braze	Colonise	
14.	Achieve	Beg	Encourage	
15.	Advise	Beautify	Accompany	
16.	Add	Bear	Civilize	
17.	Apologise		Cultivate	
18.	Assist		Clothe	
19.	Approve		Characterise	
20.	Appoint		Enchain	
21.	Associate		Criminalize	
22.	Appear		Conclude	

	E	F	G	H
1.	Elect	Frighten	Gamble	Hate
2.	Electrify	Befriend	Glaze	Horrify
3.	Enjoy	Fructify	Glorify	Harmonize
4.	Extend	Fly	Grieve	Hearten
5.	Err	Furnish	Go	Halve
6.	Exemplify	Feed	Gild	Heal
7.	Enter	Flourish	Graze	Heighten
8.	Edit	Enforce	Guard	Handle
9.	Economise	Fortify	Grow	Habituate
10.		Befool		
11.		Float		

	I	J	K	L	M
1.	Instruct	Judge	Kneel	Laugh	Monopolize
2.	Idolize	Enjoy	Knit	Lend	Meet
3.	Intoxicate	Join	Know	Learn	Multiply
4.	Interfere	Justify		Lose	Memorize
5.	Introduce			Live	Move
6.				Lighten	Mix
7.				Enlist	
8.				Illustrate	

	N	O	P	Q
1.	Nominate	Officiate	Paint	Quote
2.	Naturalize	Originate	Permit	Qualify
3.	Nationalize	Organize	Prosper	Quicken
4.	Notify	Occupy	Provide	
5.	Enumerate		Preside	
6.			Prefer	
7.			Perform	
8.			Publish	
9.			Empower	
10.			Please	
11.			Produce	
12.			Populate	
13.			Pay	
14.			Press	
15.			Practise	
16.			Imprison	

	R	S	T
1.	Remove	Sell	Tabulate
2.	Rectify	Sparkle	Terminate
3.	Relate	Strike	Terrify
4.	Run	Submit	Translate
5.	Require	Succeed	Tell
6.	Revise	Satisfy	Think
7.	Remember	Spell	Thieve
8.	Resolve	Settle	
9.	Reside	Systematize	
10.		Serve	
11.		Speak	
12.		Sympathise	

	V	W
1.	Vociferate	Weave
2.	Vacate	Bewitch
3.	Versify	Write
4.	Vitiate	Weaken
5.	Vacate	Westernize
6.	Victimize	
7.	Vibrate	
8.		
9.		
10.		
11.		
12.		

SET – 7

VII. FORM VERBS OF THE FOLLOWING ADJECTIVES

	A	B	C	D
1.	Enable	Broaden	Becalm	Divide
2.	Abound	Blacken	Civilize	Doubt
3.	Agree	Embolden	Clarify	Darken
4.	Admire	Embitter	Certify	Differ
5.	Avail	Boast	Comfort	Duplicate
6.	Answer	Debase	Collect	Dread
7.			Cheapen	Endear
8.			Cleanse	Deepen
9.			Charge	
10.			Accomplish	
11.			Conclude	

	E	F	G	H	J
1.	Equalise	Refine	Gladden	Heed	Justify
2.	Extend	Falsify	Engrave	Humiliate	
3.	Eat	Fill	Glorify	Help	
4.	Exchange	Fondle	Generalize	Harden	
5.		Refresh		Heal	
6.		Fatten			
7.		Flatten			

	L	M	N	P
1.	Belittle	Demean	Ennoble	Purify
2.	Lower	Madden	Naturalize	Impoverish
3.	Lighten		Renew	Publish
4.	Lengthen			

	R	S	T	V	W
1.	Redden	Shorten	Thicken	Vacate	Whiten
2.	Realise	Save	Tighten	Vary	Worship
3.	Enrich	Sicken			Widen
4.	Rectify	Consolidate or Solidify			Work
5.		Sympathize			
6.		Sharpen			
7.		Soften			
8.		Sweeten			
9.		Specialize			
10.		Simplify			
11.		Suit			

SET – 8

VIII. ADVERBS FROM ADJECTIVES

1.	Ably	20.	Perfectly	39.	Meanly
2.	Actively	21.	Possibly	40.	Merrily
3.	Bravely	22.	Painfully	41.	Morally
4.	Bitterly	23.	Popularly	42.	Nearly
5.	Boldly	24.	Practically	43.	Necessarily
6.	Broadly	25.	Punctually	44.	Nobly
7.	Briefly	26.	Really	45.	Obediently
8.	Capably	27.	Rightly	46.	Shortly
9.	Carefully	28.	Safely	47.	Strongly
10.	Carelessly	29.	Falsely	48.	Stupidly
11.	Certainly	30.	Gaily	49.	Successfully
12.	Cruelly	31.	Generously	50.	Timidly
13.	Closely	32.	Greedily	51.	Urgently
14.	Curiously	33.	Highly	52.	Usefully
15.	Densely	34.	Honestly	53.	Vaguely
16.	Doubly	35.	Intensely	54.	Vainly
17.	Easily	36.	Justly	55.	Widely
18.	Patiently	37.	Kindly	56.	Wisely
19.	Proudly	38.	Loyally		

PRACTICE EXERCISES

I. FORM NOUNS OF THE FOLLOWING VERBS.

SET – 9

	TEST – 1	TEST – 2	TEST – 3	TEST – 4
1.	Abandon	Survive	Bribe	Resolve
2.	Abdicate	Testify	Challenge	Propose
3.	Vary	Confront	Deliver	Provoke
4.	Vindicate	Consecrate	Eager	Qualify
5.	Destroy	Abduct	Accept	Respond
6.	Disturb	Insist	Hypnotize	Advance
7.	Impede	Interfere	Ignite	Depreciate
8.	Impress	Invent	Accuse	Deliberate
9.	Improvise	Absorb	Acquaint	Advise
10.	Quote	Accelerate	Separate	Affirm
11.	Realise	Deceive	Serve	Aggravate
12.	Receive	Delude	Settle	Align
13.	Break	Fluctuate	Adapt	Allege
14.	Bleed	Forfeit	Overdraw	Allocate
15.	Embezzle	Guide	Paralyse	Anticipate
16.	Embroider	Hang	Adequate	Think
17.	Exorcise	Happen	Culminate	Tolerate
18.	Explode	Shoot	Consult	Eradicate
19.	Extradite	Signify	Adopt	Erupt
20.	Modify	Speak	Adulterate	Escalate

	TEST – 5	TEST – 6	TEST – 7	TEST – 8
1.	Applaud	Notify	Indulge	Define
2.	Maintain	Observe	Collide	Divine
3.	Mean	Obstruct	Commend	Declare
4.	Appreciate	Busy	Grieve	Earn
5.	Argue	Bewilder	Hate	Edify
6.	Mean	Persuade	Hinder	Elaborate
7.	Attend	Plant	Commit	Emigrate
8.	Avoid	Possess	Converse	Encroach
9.	Bitter	Brave	Justify	Enlighten
10.	Believe	Perform	Know	Eulogize
11.	Seclude	Permit	Laugh	Excavate
12.	Secure	Bathe	Counsel	Exult
13.	Beautify	Behave	Conceive	Fabricate
14.	Revive	Banish	Clear	Correct
15.	Satisfy	Begin	Determine	Confuse
16.	Scandalize	Bless	Decide	Fascinate
17.	Press	Chasten	Recover	Feel
18.	Prevent	Cogitate	Reflect	Find
19.	Proceed	Carry	Depart	Frequent
20.	Limit	Indicate	Demarcate	Frustrate

	TEST – 9	TEST – 10	TEST – 11
1.	Glide	Move	Remove
2.	Defend	Narrate	Require
3.	Develop	Ascend	Reside
4.	Dissipate	Assert	Retire
5.	Devote	Assure	Revert
6.	Govern	Neglect	Scrutinize
7.	Grade	Nominate	Seize
8.	Greet	Occupy	Select
9.	Humiliate	Operate	Sell
10.	Ignore	Oppose	Elect
11.	Illuminate	Organise	Embellish
12.	Incite	Pay	Stabilize
13.	Inhibit	Peddle	Substitute
14.	Investigate	Penetrate	Succeed
15.	Involve	Practise	Suggest
16.	Like	Predict	Treat
17.	Lose	Prepare	Unify
18.	Magnify	Reform	Unite
19.	Meditate	Elevate	Waste
20.	Migrate	Eliminate	Guard

II. FORM VERBS FROM THE FOLLOWING NOUNS

SET – 10

	TEST – 1	TEST – 2	TEST – 3
1.	Isolation	Composition	Exemption
2.	Judgement	Concentration	Horror
3.	Joy	Product	Humble
4.	Knee	Pleasure	Head
5.	Leader	Pursuit	High
6.	Occupation	Race	Coincidence
7.	Organisation	Reaction	Colony
8.	Peril	Alliance	Combination
9.	Pure	Confession	Compulsion
10.	Poor	Confidence	Notice
11.	Peace	Habit	Nation
12.	Inspiration	Hard	Narrative
13.	Institution	Hatred	Negligence
14.	Invasion	Equation	Reduction
15.	Liberty	Excitement	Reference

	TEST – 4	TEST – 5	TEST – 6
1.	Resolution	Emancipation	Television
2.	Rich	Roll	Termination
3.	Glory	Trust	Retention
4.	Glad	Complication	Revision
5.	Gait	Conquest	Strong
6.	Disruption	Induction	Migrant
7.	Division	Solution	Mixture
8.	Education	Suspicion	Modern
9.	Emphasis	Success	Simple
10.	Abstinence	Conspiracy	Analysis
11.	Adherence	Contribution	Apology
12.	Admission	Teacher	Bequest
13.	Sympathy	Theory	Breath
14.	Song	Relation	Calculation
15.	Speech	Residence	Carriage

	TEST – 7	TEST – 8	TEST – 9	TEST – 10
1.	Cessation	Dedication	Motive	Incarnation
2.	Light	Defence	Memory	Infiltration
3.	Large	Dependence	Following	Loose
4.	Channel	Endurance	Unit	Low
5.	Choice	Enthusiasm	Urgency	Location
6.	Citation	Entry	Furniture	Long
7.	Civilization	Exhibition	Gold	Maturity
8.	Solemn	Terror	Graduation	Meeting
9.	Closure	Thought	Slaughter	Sweet
10.	Cloth	Threat	Tale	Sight
11.	athering	Extension	Training	Strife
12.	Generation	Familiarity	Trifle	Safe
13.	Conviction	Food	Greeting	Sale
14.	Creation	Finality	Growth	Tuition
15.	Death	Flattery	Health	Utilization

III FORM ADJECTIVES FROM THE FOLLOWING WORDS

SET – 11

	TEST – 1	TEST – 2	TEST – 3	TEST – 4
1.	Type	Spirit	Moment	Tide
2.	Wood	Storm	Music	Tire
3.	Wool	Talk	Nation	Joke
4.	Attract	Angel	Adventure	Kind
5.	Fool	Autumn	Art	Land
6.	Force	Education	Ambition	Learn
7.	Father	Emphasis	Ancestor	Benefit
8.	Quality	Exclude	Crime	Blood
9.	Respect	Accident	Comfort	Book
10.	Race	Athlete	Comic	Child
11.	Rain	Pity	Answer	Continue
12.	Reason	Prosper	Anxiety	Courage
13.	Study	Poet	Assert	Season
14.	Social	Man	Awe	Sever
15.	Space	Mean	Base	Sleep

	TEST – 5	TEST – 6	TEST – 7	TEST – 8
1.	Caution	Corrupt	Palace	Fallacy
2.	Custom	Disaster	Plenty	Festival
3.	Chaos	Decide	Extend	Abyss
4.	Horror	Ideal	Energy	Allure
5.	Magic	Introduce	Thunder	Alternate
6.	Nature	Legend	Time	Glory
7.	Notice	Length	Wit	Gold
8.	Occasion	Defend	Enthusiasm	Heart
9.	Office	Refine	Essence	Honour
10.	Parish	Religion	Favour	Luxury
11.	Humility	Rest	Greed	Providence
12.	Imagine	Reward	Grieve	People
13.	Instant	Scene	Hazard	Prime
14.	Clerk	Danger	Fortune	Punish
15.	Collect	Oppress	Fury	Parents
16.				Quarrel
17.				Science
18.				Tempt
19.				Winter
20.				War

IV FORM ADVERBS FROM THE FOLLOWING WORDS

SET – 12

	TEST – 1	TEST – 2	TEST – 3	TEST – 4
1.	Annual	Critic	Ready	Light
2.	Able	Equal	Honour	Loose
3.	Abrupt	Free	Hope	Physical
4.	Deep	Form	Ideal	Poor
5.	Dim	Force	Incredible	Quarter
6.	Accident	Gallant	Individual	Quiet
7.	Accord	Physical	Infinite	Logic
8.	Adverse	Poor	Rude	Menace
9.	Dead	Quarter	Separate	Mad
10.	Divined	Quiet	Joint	Main
11.	Easy	Gentle	Know	Narrow
12.	Effect	Glad	Lavish	Near
13.	Affection	Happy	Amicable	New
14.	Awe	History	Ample	Faith
15.	Bad	Part	Anxious	Firm
16.	Blunt	Patience	Legal	Open
17.	Bold	Person	Calm	Office
18.	Brute	Radical	Casual	Order
19.	Clear	Rare	Certain	Repeat
20.	Comfortable	Rash	Leisure	Sharp
21.				Smooth
22.				Steal
23.				Tender
24.				Thin

ANSWERS

I. NOUNS

SET – 9

	TEST – 1	TEST – 2	TEST – 3
1.	Abandonment	(Survival)	(Bribery)
2.	Abdication	(Testimonial)	(Challenger)
3.	Variation	(Confrontation)	(Deliverance)
4.	Vindication	(Consecration)	(Eagerness)
5.	Destruction	(Abduction)	(Acceptance)
6.	(Disturbance)	(Insistence)	(Hypnotism)
7.	(Impediment)	(Interference)	(Ignition)
8.	(Impression)	(Invention)	(Accusation)
9.	(Improvisation)	(Absorption)	(Acquaintance)
10.	(Quotation)	(Acceleration)	(Separation)
11.	(Realization)	(Deceit)	(Service)
12.	(Receipt)	(Delusion)	(Settlement)
13.	(Breakage)	(Fluctuation)	(Adaptation)
14.	(Blood)	(Forfeiture)	(Overdraft)
15.	(Embezzlement)	(Guidance)	(Paralysis)
16.	(Embroidery)	(Hanger)	(Adequacy)
17.	(Exorcism)	(Happening)	(Culmination)
18.	(Explosion)	(Shot)	(Consultation)
19.	(Extradition)	(Significance)	(Adoption)
20.	(Modification)	(Speech)	(Adulteration)

	TEST – 4	TEST – 5	TEST – 6
1.	(Resolution)	Applause	Notification
2.	(Proposal)	Maintenance	Observation
3.	(Provocation)	Meanness	Obstruction
4.	Qualification	Appreciation	Business
5.	Response	Argument	Bewilderment
6.	Advancement	Meaning	Persuasion
7.	Depreciation	Attendance/ Attention	Plantation
8.	Deliberation	Avoidance	Possession
9.	Advice/Advise	Bitterness	Bravery
10.	Affirmation	Belief	Performance
11.	Aggravation	Seclusion	Permission
12.	Alignment	Security	Bath
13.	Allegation	Beauty	Behaviour
14.	Allocation	Revival	Banishment
15.	Anticipation	Satisfaction	Beginning
16.	Thought	Scandal	Blessing
17.	Toleration or Tolerance	Pressure	Chastity
18.	Eradication	Prevention	Cogitation
19.	Eruption	Procedure	Carriage/ Career
20.	Escalation	Limitation	Indication

	TEST – 7	TEST – 8	TEST – 9
1.	Indulgence	Definition	Glider
2.	Collision	Divinity	Defence
3.	Commendation	Declaration	Development
4.	Grievance	Earnings	Dissipation
5.	Hatred	Edification	Devotion
6.	Hindrance	Elaboration	Government
7.	Commitment	Emigration	Gradation
8.	Conversion or Conversation	Encroachment	Greeting
9.	Justification	Enlightenment	Humiliation
10.	Knowledge	Eulogy	Ignorance
11.	Laughter	Excavation	Illumination
12.	Counsellor or Counsel	Exultation	Incitement
13.	Conception or Concept	Fabrication	Inhibition
14.	Clarity	Correction	Investigation
15.	Determination	Confusion	Involvement
16.	Decision	Fascination	Likelihood
17.	Recovery	Feeling	Loss
18.	Reflection	Finding	Magnification
19.	Departure	Frequency	Meditation
20.	Demarcation	Frustration	Migration

	TEST – 10	TEST – 11
1.	Movement	Removal
2.	Narration	Requirement
3.	Ascent	Residence
4.	Assertion	Retirement
5.	Assurance	Reversion
6.	Negligence	Scrutiny
7.	Nomination	Seizure
8.	Occupancy/ Occupation	Selection
9.	Operation	Sale
10.	Opposition	Election
11.	Organization	Embellishment
12.	Payment	Stability or Stabilizer
13.	Pedlar	Substitution
14.	Penetration	Success
15.	Practice	Suggestion
16.	Prediction	Treatment
17.	Preparation	Unification
18.	Reformation or Reform	Union
19.	Elevation	Wastage
20.	Elimination	Guardian

II. VERBS FROM NOUNS

SET – 10

	TEST – 1	TEST – 2	TEST – 3	TEST – 4
1.	Isolate	Compose	Exempt	Resolve
2.	Judge	Concentrate	Horrify	Enrich
3.	Enjoy	Produce	Humiliate	Glorify
4.	Kneel	Please	Behead	Gladden
5.	Lead	Pursue	Heighten	Go
6.	Occupy	Run	Coincide	Disrupt
7.	Organise	React	Colonise	Divide
8.	Imperil	Ally	Combine	Educate
9.	Purify	Confess	Compel	Emphasise
10.	Impoverish	Confide	Notify	Abstain
11.	Pacify	Habituate	Nationalise	Adhere
12.	Inspire	Harden	Narrate	Admit
13.	Institute	Hate	Neglect	Sympathise
14.	Invade	Equate	Reduce	Sing
15.	Liberate	Excite	Refer	Speak

	TEST – 5	TEST – 6	TEST – 7
1.	Emancipate	Televise	Cease
2.	Enroll	Terminate	Lighten
3.	Entrust	Retain	Enlarge
4.	Complicate	Revise	Channelise
5.	Conquer	Strengthen	Choose
6.	Induct	Migrate	Cite
7.	Solve	Mix	Civilize
8.	Suspect	Modernise	Solemnise
9.	Succeed	Simplify	Close
10.	Conspire	Analyse	Clothe
11.	Contribute	Apologize	Gather
12.	Teach	Bequeath	Generate
13.	Theorise	Breathe	Convict
14.	Relate	Calculate	Create
15.	Reside	Carry	Die

	TEST – 8	TEST – 9	TEST – 10
1.	Dedicate	Motivate	Incarnate
2.	Defend	Memorise	Infiltrate
3.	Depend	Follow	Loosen
4.	Endure	Unite	Lower
5.	Enthuse	Urge	Locate
6.	Enter	Furnish	Lengthen
7.	Exhibit	Gild	Mature
8.	Terrify	Graduate	Meet
9.	Think	Slay	Sweeten
10.	Threaten	Tell	See
11.	Extend	Train	Strive
12.	Familiarize	Trivialise	Save
13.	Feed	Greet	Sell
14.	Finalize	Grow	Tutor
15.	Flatter	Heal	Utilize

III. ADJECTIVES

SET – 11

	TEST – 1	TEST – 2	TEST – 3
1.	Typical	Spirited	Momentary
2.	Wooden	Stormy	Musical
3.	Woollen	Talkative	National
4.	Attractive	Angelic	Adventurous
5.	Foolish	Autumnal	Artful
6.	Forceful	Educational	Ambitious
7.	Fatherly	Emphatic	Ancestral
8.	Qualitative	Exclusive	Criminal
9.	Respectable	Accidental	Comfortable
10.	Racial	Athletic	Comical
11.	Rainy	Pitiable	Answerable
12.	Reasonable	Prosperous	Anxious
13.	Studious	Poetical	Assertive
14.	Sociable	Manly	Awesome
15.	Spacious	Meaningful	Basic

	TEST – 4	TEST – 5	TEST – 6
1.	Tidal	Cautious	Corruptible
2.	Tiresome	Customary	Disastrous
3.	Jolly	Chaotic	Decisive
4.	Kingly	Horrible	Idealistic
5.	Landed	Magical	Introductory
6.	Learned	Natural	Legendary
7.	Beneficial	Noticeable	Long
8.	Bloody	Occasional	Defensive
9.	Bookish	Official	Refined
10.	Childish	Parochial	Religious
11.	Continuous	Humble	Restive
12.	Courageous	Imaginary	Rewarding
13.	Seasonal	Instantaneous	Scenic
14.	Several or Severe	Clerical	Dangerous
15.	Sleepy	Collective	Oppressive

	TEST – 7	TEST – 8
1.	Palatial	Fallacious
2.	Plentiful	Festive
3.	Extensive	Abysmal
4.	Energetic	Alluring
5.	Thunderous	Alternative
6.	Timely	Glorious
7.	Witty	Golden
8.	Enthusiastic	Hearty
9.	Essential	Honourable
10.	Favourable	Luxurious
11.	Greedy	Providential
12.	Grievous	Populous
13.	Hazardous	Primitive
14.	Fortunate	Punitive
15.	Furious	Parental
16.		Quarrelsome
17.		Scientific
18.		Tempting
19.		Wintry
20.		Warlike

IV. ADVERBS

SET – 12

	TEST – 1	TEST – 2
1.	Annually	Critically
2.	Ably	Equally
3.	Abruptly	Freely
4.	Deeply	Formally
5.	Dimly	Forcibly
6.	Accidentally	Gallantly
7.	Accordingly	Physically
8.	Adversely	Poorly
9.	Deadly	Quarterly
10.	Divinely	Quietly
11.	Easily	Gently
12.	Effectively	Gladly
13.	Affectionately	Happily
14.	Awfully	Historically
15.	Badly	Partly
16.	Bluntly	Patiently
17.	Boldly	Personally
18.	Brutally	Radically
19.	Clearly	Rarely
20.	Comfortably	Rashly

	TEST – 3	TEST – 4
1.	Readily	Lightly
2.	Honourably	Loosely
3.	Hopefully	Physically
4.	Ideally	Poorly
5.	Incredibly	Quarterly
6.	Individually	Quietly
7.	Infinitely	Logically
8.	Rudely	Menacingly
9.	Separately	Madly
10.	Jointly	Mainly
11.	Knowingly	Narrowly
12.	Lavishly	Nearly
13.	Amicably	Newly
14.	Amply	Faithfully
15.	Anxiously	Firmly
16.	Legally	Openly
17.	Calmly	Officially
18.	Casually	Orderly
19.	Certainly	Repeatedly
20.	Leisurely	Sharply
21.		Smoothly
22.		Stealthily
23.		Tenderly
24.		Thinly

USE OF PRONOUNS

Read the following sentences:

Ram Lal is my neighbour.

He is a teacher.

He teaches in Govt.High School, Mohali.

His friends respect him because he is kind- hearted.

In the above sentences, the words **he**, **his** and **him** have been used for the noun Ram Lal. Such words are called 'Pronouns'.

A Pronoun is a word which is used in place of a noun.

KINDS OF PRONOUNS:

Personal Pronouns

(a) 1. **I** am a mason.

2. **I** work with **my** tool.
3. These tools are **mine.**
4. People like **me** for **my** good work.
5. **We** study in a school.
6. **Our** school is the best in the city.
7. **Our** headmaster teaches **us** English.

(b) 1. **You** ought to serve **your** parents.

2. This is **your** book.
3. Ram sent **you** a book.
4. **Thou** are a slave to fate.
5. May God bless **thee.**
6. **Thy** need is really great.
7. My love for the country is greater than **thine.**

(c) 1. **He** is weeping because he has lost **his** purse.

2. Let **him** finish **his** work.
3. **She** does not respect **her** mother-in-law.
4. **She** is teaching. Please listen to **her.**
5. **They** are playing in **their** room.
6. This is his cycle and that is **here.**
7. **It** is a black cat. **It** is playing with its kittens.

In the above sentences, the words in bold letters are personal pronouns. They stand for names of persons.

THREE PERSONS:

The pronouns I, my, me, we, our, us, mine and ours in (a) represent the person or persons speaking. They are called Pronouns of the **First Person.**

The Pronouns you, your, yours, thou, thee, thy and thine, in (b) represent the person or persons spoken to. They are called Pronouns of the **Second Person.**

The pronouns he, she, it, his, her, him, its, they, their, them, hers, and theirs in (c) above represent the persons or things spoken of. They are called Pronouns of the **Third Person.**

CASES:

There are three cases of Personas. They are given below:

1. **Nominative Case:** The pronouns I, we, you, thou, he, she, it and they are subjects. They are in the Nominative Case.
2. **Objective Case:** The pronouns me, us, you, thee, him, her, it, and them are objects. They are in the Objective Case.
3. **Possessive Case:** The pronouns my, mine, our, ours, your, yours, thy, thine, his, her, hers, their, theirs and its show possession. They are in the Possessive Case.

The following table shows the different forms of personal pronouns in the three cases:

Case	First Person		Second Person		Third Person		Remarks
Nominative	*Singular*	*Plural*	*Singular*	*Plural*	*Singular*	*Plural*	
Objective	Me	Us	You thee	You	Him, her	They	Stands as object of verbs or prepositions in sentences
Possessive	My mine	Our Ours	Yours Thy Thine yours	Yours Yours	His Her Its Hers	Their Theirs	Used to denote possession.

Notes: 1. Thou, thee, thy and thine are used in poetry and prayers.
2. My, our, your, thy, his, her, its and there are called Possessive Adjective or Determiners.

USE OF PERSONAL PRONOUNS:

1. ***If pronouns of different persons come together in one sentence, they are used in the following order:***
Second person, Third Person, First Person.
You, he and I are members of the Rose club.

2. ***However, while confessing a fault, the pronouns are used in the following order:***
First Person, Second Person, Third Person.
I, you, and he stole Ram's books.

3. ***When a pronoun is used as an object of a verb or preposition the objective form alone should be used.***
Let me and him (not I and he) got out for a walk.
This depends upon me and him (not I and he).

4. ***When a pronoun is the complement of the verb 'to be', it must be in the nominative case.***
If I were, he (not him), I would go abroad.

5. ***The pronoun is singular when two or more singular nouns are joined by "or" "either-or", "neither-nor".***
Either Ram or Sham will lend me his book.
Neither Suman nor her sister has done her work.

6. ***When a pronoun refers to more than one noun or pronoun of different persons. It must be of the first-person plural in preference to the second person, and of the second person plural in preference to the third person.***
You and I have finished our work in time.
You and Sohan have wasted your time.

7. ***When two singular nouns, preceded by 'each' and 'every' are joined by 'and' the pronoun must be singular.***
Every girl and every woman should serve her country.

8. ***When a pronoun stands for a collective noun regarded as a whole, it is in the singular number.***
The team was proud of its captain.
The use of "It"
"It" is used:

(a) ***For lifeless thing, animals, and young children.***
(i) It is a book.
(ii) It is an earthworm, not a snake.

(b) ***The emphasize some noun or pronoun, e.g.:***
(i) It is I who saved the drowning child.
(ii) It was he who attacked my brother.

(c) ***For a word, phrase or clause going before or after.***
(i) To take a walk daily is very good; it makes one healthy.
(ii) It is wrong to tell a lie.

(d) ***In interrogative sentences:***
Who is it?

(e) ***In exclamatory sentences:***
What a fine weather 'it is!

(f) ***In sentences denoting time or weather:***
(i) It is raining.
(ii) It is 5 o'clock.

REFLEXIVE PRONOUNS:

Read the following sentences:

1. She saw the picture.
2. She saw herself in the mirror.
3. We help ourselves.
4. We help them.

It is to be noticed that in sentences (i) and (4) the action goes from one person/thing to another but in sentences (2) and (3), the same person forms the subject and the object. The action comes back to the doer. 'Herself' and 'ourselves' which are objects in (2) and (3) are called Reflexive Pronouns. Here is the complete list of Reflexive Pronouns.

Person	***Singular***	***Plural***
First Person	Myself	Ourselves
Second person	Yourself	Yourselves
Third person	Himself, herself	Themselves

USE OF REFLEXIVE PRONOUNS:

Reflexive Pronoun is used: -

(I) As object of some verb.

They enjoyed themselves.

Suman overworked herself.

(II) An object of preposition.

You are annoyed with yourself.

He told us many interesting stories about himself.

EMPHATIC PRONOUNS:

Read the following sentences:

1. You **yourself** should go to see him.
2. She **herself** decided to go with me.
3. You have to do it **yourself.**
4. The thief **himself** confessed his crime.

In these sentences the subject and the object are not the same person. The pronouns yourself, herself, himself lend emphasis to what is said. They are called **Emphatic Pronouns.**

INTERROGATIVE PRONOUNS:

Interrogative pronouns are used in asking questions. Interrogative pronouns are:

Who, whose, what, which, whom etc.

1. Who made that painting? (Subject to a verb)
2. Of whom are you talking? (Object to a preposition)
3. What did you say? (Object to a verb)
4. Whose pen is this? (possessive)
5. Which of these boys is the captain of team? (Selective)

USE OF INTERROGATIVE PRONOUNS:

1. 'Who, whom and whose' are used for persons only.
   (i) Who is knocking at the door?
   (ii) Whom do you want to see?
   (iii) Whose pen is this?
2. "What' is used for things, professions etc:
   (i) What did you give to the beggar?
   (ii) What is your elder brother?
3. 'Which' is used for things, 'persons and animals:
   (i) Which is your bicycle?
   (ii) Which of these boys will win the medal?

DEMONSTRATIVE PRONOUNS:

Read the following sentences carefully.

1. **This** is my house and **that** is yours.
2. **These** are our best friends.
3. The climate of Shimla is better than **that** of Delhi.
4. **Such** are his tastes.
5. **That** is our old house.
6. **Those** are our fields.

In the above sentences, the pronouns in bold are used to point out the objects to which they refer. They are called Demonstrative Pronouns.

Most of the Demonstrative Pronouns become Demonstrative Adjective when they are followed by nouns.

Demonstrative Pronouns		***Demonstrative Adjectives***	
1.	This is a beautiful pen.	1.	This pen is beautiful.
2.	That is an old book.	2.	That book is old.
3.	Those are rich persons.	3.	Those persons are rich
4.	These are expensive clothes.	4.	These clothes are expensive.

INDEFINITE PRONONS:

Read the sentences given below.

1. **One** should do **one's** duty.
2. **Everybody** likes to be loved.
3. **Somebody** has stolen my pen.
4. **All** are busy in their work.
5. **None** of these books is interesting.
6. **Some** are born with a silver spoon in their mouth.
7. **Many** of them are poor in mathematics.
8. **Few** lived to tell the story of their misfortune.

In the above sentences, the pronouns in bold letters do not refer to any particular person or thing. They refer to persons or things in a general way. They called Indefinite Pronouns.

The Indefinite Pronouns are:

All, any, anybody, anyone, anything, each, both, one, either none, other, some, several, somebody, something, nothing.

USE OF INDEFINITE PRONOUNS:

1. 'One' is used:
   (i) To represent people in general, as,
   One should do one's duty.
   One cannot shut one's eyes to facts.
   (ii) In place of a noun to avoid repetition:
   Give me another apple; this is not a good one.
2. 'Noun' is used in the singular or in the plural according to context:
   Is there any milk in the pot? There is none.
   None but the brave deserves the fair.
   None of these books is mine.
3. The Pronouns: he, his, her etc. are used for everybody, anybody, everyone etc. according to their context; as anybody, everyone etc. according to their context; as.
   Every one of these girls has paid her fees.
   Each of these boys has done his work.

DISTRIBUTIVE PRONOUNS:

Read the following sentences:

1. **Each** of these children has fine clothes.
2. **Neither** of the two sisters attended the meeting.
3. Anaadi and Kamakshi are fond of **each** other.
4. **Either** of two books will do.

In the above sentences, pronouns in bold letters show this persons or things are taken singly or in separate groups. They are distributive Pronouns. They are always singular and take a singular verb.

(a) 'Each' mean two or more persons or things taken one by one; as,
Each of these children has fine clothes.

(b) 'Either' means 'one or the other of two or both'; as
Either of the two books will do.
There are shady trees on either side of the road.

(c) 'Neither' is the negative of 'either' and means 'not the one and not the other of two'; as,
Neither of the two boys is willing to work in factory.

(d) 'Each other' and 'one another' are called Reciprocal Pronouns.
'Each other is used while speaking of two persons while 'one another' for more than two persons; as,
Vikas and Surjit like each other.
All the five sisters love one another.

USE OF PRONOUNS

EXERCISE – 1

Use pronouns in place of the nouns in bold letters in the following sentences:

1. The teacher is teaching the boys. **The** boys are listening to **the teacher.**
2. Gopal is a student of 9th class. **Gopal's father** loves **Gopal.**
3. Suraj invited Sharmila to dinner. **Sharmila** accepted **Suraj's** invitation.
4. Delhi is a very big city. **Delhi** is the capital of India.
5. Sohan Singh met Suman in the market. **Suman** told **Sohan Singh** a story. **Thestory** was very interesting.

EXERCISE – 2

Write the following sentences in two ways as in the examples:

(i) This is my house. (ii) This house is mine.

1. That village is hers.
2. This is your bicycle.
3. He owns this scooter.
4. That is her car.
5. They own that factory.

EXERCISE – 3

Fill in the blanks with suitable reflexive pronouns:

1. He threw ____________ before a running train.
2. She killed ____________ with a knife.
3. He dressed ____________ in fine clothes.
4. Help ____________.
5. She should blame ____________ for her failure.
6. The child found ____________ abandoned.
7. The deer found ____________ caught in a trap.
8. They enjoyed ____________ thoroughly well.
9. Bimal hurt ____________ while running the race.
10. The child hid ____________ under the bed.

EXERCISE – 4

1. He ____________ told me the story of his life.
2. We ____________ have to wash our clothes.
3. She ____________ swept the floor of her bedroom.
4. They ____________ are responsible for their misfortune.
5. We should ____________ solve our problems.
6. The bird ____________ makes its nest.
7. The teacher ____________ dusted the blackboard.
8. I ____________ cooked my food.
9. You ____________ will not like it.
10. He ____________ chose the profession of doctor.

EXERCISE – 5

Fill in the blank with interrogative pronouns:

1. ____________ won the race?
2. ____________ of these pens is yours?
3. ____________ book is this?
4. ____________ do you want?
5. ____________ do you like?

EXERCISE – 6

Fill in the blanks, choosing the correct word from the words given in brackets:

1. The mother and the son loved ____________. (one another, each other, either)
2. The stepmother and the stepdaughter dislike ____________.(each other, one another, neither)
3. The four brothers quarreled with ____________. (one another, each other)
4. People stood on ____________ side of the road.(either both, every)
5. ____________ of the four books will serve the purpose.(neither, either none)
6. ____________ knows where she has gone. (none, each, either)
7. She knows ____________ about the past. (nothing, none, some)
8. ____________ should serve the motherland (none, everyone, each)

ANSWERS

USE OF PRONOUNS

	EXERCISE-1	EXERCISE-2	EXERCISE-3	EXERCISE-4	EXERCISE-5	EXERCISE-6
1.	They, him	This village is hers.	himself	himself	Who	each other
2.	He, him	This bicycle is yours.	herself	ourselves	which	each other
3.	She, his	This is his scooter.	himself	herself	whose	one another
4.	It	That is his car.	yourself	themselves	What	either
5.	She, him, it	That is their factory.	herself	ourselves	What	none
6.			itself	itself		none
7.			itself	herself		nothing
8.			themselves	myself		everyone
9.			himself	yourself		
10.			itself	himself		

USE OF ADJECTIVES

An Adjective is a word that qualifies a noun or a pronoun. It may be used just before the noun or pronoun or may come after it in the predicate:

A clever boy does his work well.

This boy is **clever.**

But some adjectives cannot be used before the noun or pronoun they qualify, e.g., asleep, alive, ill, awake, afraid, fool, none.

We cannot say **'awake man'** as we say 'clever man'

KINDS OF ADJECTIVES:

Adjectives are of the following types.

1. **Adjective of Quality:** These show the kind or quality; as,

   White, nice, beautiful, kind

   They answer the question 'What kind of?'

   1. Ram Singh is a **rich** man.
   2. The forest is **green.**
   3. It is an **interesting** story.
   4. He is an **intelligent** student.
   5. Tagore was a **great** poet.

   The adjectives rich, green, interesting, intelligent and great are adjectives of quality because they denote the quality of nouns-man, forest, story, student and poet respectively.

2. **Adjectives of Quantity:** These show how much of a thing is meant; as – Some, little, enough, no, much

   They answer the question – 'How much of it?'

   1. He gave me **some** money.
   2. There is **no** sugar in the pot.
   3. He has put **alittle** milk in the cup.
   4. He has already wasted **much** time.
   5. There is **enough** food in the kitchen.

   The adjectives some, no, little, much and enough are adjectives of quantity or amount because they denote quantity of nouns-money, sugar, milk, time and food respectively.

3. **Adjectives of Number:** These indicate how many, e.g., three, fourth

   They answer the question – "How many?"

   (i) I was the first boy to receive the prize.

   (ii) There are twelve oranges in the basket.

   (iii) He got the second position in the class.

   The adjectives 'first, twelve and second' are adjectives of number because they denote the number of nouns – boy, oranges and position, respectively.

4. **Demonstrative Adjectives:** These indicate persons, things or places we are speaking of; as

   (i) **This** book is difficult to read.

   (ii) I like **this** shirt.

   (iii) **That** man has stolen my purse.

   (iv) These pictures are beautiful.

   The adjectives 'this, that, these and those,' are demonstrative adjectives because they point out the person or thing they qualify.

5. **Emphasizing Adjectives:** They emphasize the noun or pronoun to which they belong; as,

   (i) This is my **own** house.

   (ii) I hate his **very** sight.

   (iii) Who does not love his **own** country?

6. **Interrogative Adjectives:** These are used with nouns to ask questions; as,

   (i) **Whose** scooter is this?

   (ii) Which house is yours?

   (iii) **What** plans do you have after passing theMatriculation examination?

7. **Possessive Adjectives:** when 'my, your, our, his, her, their' are used as adjectives, they are called possessive adjectives; as,

(i) **His** shoes have been stolen.

(ii) **Our** school is closed today.

8. **Exclamatory Adjectives:** The word **'what'** in the following sentences is called an exclamatory adjective.

(i) **What** a beautiful flower!

(ii) **What** a pity!

COMPARISON OF ADJECTIVES:

Degrees of Comparison

There are three degrees to comparison: positive Comparative and Superlative.

(i) Positive: My table is big.

(ii) Comparative : My table is bigger than that table.

(iii) Superlative: My table is the biggest of all.

In sentence (i) one thing is described and the Simplest form of the adjective 'big' is used. This form is called the Positive Degree.

In sentence (ii), the adjective 'bigger' compares the size of two tables. This form is called the Comparative Degree. The comparative degree is generally followed by 'than'. But when selection is meant, the adjective in the comparative degree is followed by the preposition 'of' and 'the' is placed before 'it' as.

Suman is the taller of the two sisters.

In sentence (iii), 'biggest' compares the 'table' with all other tables. This form is called the Superlative Degree. It is generally followed by the preposition of and preceded by article 'the'; as,

Suman is the tallest of all the three sisters.

The superlative degree is used to denote the highest or lowest degree of quality possessed by a person or thing. It is used to compare more than two persons or things.

Formation of Comparative and superlative Degrees.

The Comparative and Superlative Degrees are formed

(i) ***By adding "–er" and " –est" to the Positive : as,***

Positive	*Comparative*	*Superlative*
Black	blacker	blackest
Bold	bolder	boldest
Bright	brighter	brightest
Broad	broader	broadest
Calm	calmer	calmest
Cheap	cheaper	cheapest
Clever	cleverer	cleverest
Cold	colder	coldest
Deep	deeper	deepest
Fair	fairer	fairest
High	higher	highest
Kind	kinder	kindest
Long	longer	longest
Mean	meaner	meanest
Old	older	oldest
Poor	poorer	poorest
Rich	richer	richest
Shallow	shallower	shallowest
Small	smaller	smallest
Sweet	sweeter	sweetest
Tall	taller	tallest
Thick	thicker	thickest
Weak	weaker	weakest
Young	younger	youngest

(ii) ***by adding only "r" and 'st' if the positive ends in 'e' as,***

Able	abler	ablest
Brave	braver	bravest
Blue	bluer	bluest
Fine	finer	finest
Late	later	latest
Large	larger	largest
Noble	nobler	noblest
Pure	purer	purest
Simple	simpler	simplest
True	truer	truest
Wise	wiser	wisest
Wide	wider	widest

(iii) ***by changing 'y' into 'I' before 'er' and 'est', if the positive ends by y, preceded by a consonant : as,***

Busy	busier	busiest
Dry	drier	driest
Easy	easier	easiest
Funny	funnier	funniest
Happy	happier	happiest
Heavy	heavier	heaviest
Holy	holier	holiest
Merry	merrier	merriest
Wealthy	wealthier	wealthiest
Healthy	healthier	healthiest
Pretty	Prettier	prettiest

(iv) ***By adding " –er" and " – est" without changing 'y' if the positive ends in 'y' preceded by a vowel: as,***

Gay	gayer	gayest
Coy	coyer	coyest
Grey	greyer	greyest

(v) ***Sometimes the final consonant is doubled and sometimes It s not doubled: as,***

Hot	hotter	hottest
Red	redder	reddest
Big	bigger	biggest
Fat	fatter	fattest
Thick	thicker	thickest
Low	lower	lowest

(vi) ***Positive of two or more than two syllables form the so comparative and superlative by prefixing more and most: as***

Awful	more awful	most awful
Beautiful	more beautiful	most beautiful
Difficult	more difficult	most difficult
Careful	more careful	most careful
Fertile	more fertile	most fertile
Intelligent	more intelligent	most intelligent
Splendid	more splendid	most splendid

Note : "Less" and "Least" are used with the Comparative and superlative of inferiority.

(vii) ***Irregular comparisons. Some adjectives are compared in an irregular fashion: as,***

Bad	worse	worst
Good	better	best
Far	farther	farthest
Fore	former	foremost, first
Fore	further	furthest
Hinder	hinder	hinder
In	inner	innest
Ill	worse	worst
Late (order)	latter	last
Much (quantity)	more	most
Many (number)	more	most
Near	nearer	nearest
		Next
Old	older (of community)	oldest
		Eldest
Out	outer (of blood)	outmost
	Utter	utmost
		Outermost
Up	upper	uppermost

USE OF SOME IMPORTANT ADJECTIVES:

1. Some, any

Some is used in affirmative sentences: as,

He has got some money.

We never say, 'He has got any money.'

'Any' is used in negative sentences; as,

He has not got any money.

'Some' and 'any' can both be used in interrogative; but the use of 'any' in such sentences is preferable: as,

Has he got some money?

Has he got any money?

2. Little, a little, the little

'Little' is used in the negative sense. It means 'not much' or almost nothing' as,

There is little butter left in the tin.

It means, "There is not much butter left in the tin."

'A little' is used in the positive sense and mean: as least some; as,

"There is a little butter left in the tin."

"There is at least some butter left in the tin."

'The little' implies both the negative and the positive sense and means, not much, but the whole of it, as,

"He spent the little money he had."

It means he had not much money, but he spent the whole of what he had.

3. **Few, a few, the few**

'Few' is negative, meaning not many, almost none; as,

'Few men are free from faults.'

It **means** not many men (almost none) are free from faults.

'A few' is used in the affirmative sense. It means some at least; as,

I have read a few books.

It means I have read some books at least, though the number is small.

'The few' implies both the negative and the affirmative; as,

I have read the few books I have.'

It means I have read some books though not many, but I have read all thc books I have.

4. **Many a, a many**

'Many', is followed by singular nouns, and 'a many' by plural nouns; as,

(i) The enemy killed many soldiers.

(ii) The enemy killed a good many soldier.

The meaning in both cases is many soldiers.

5. **Each other, one another**

The former is used when two persons, things or groups are concerned: as,

These two boys love each other.

'One another' is used when more than two persons, things or groups are concerned; as,

The three sisters love one another.

6. **Each, every**

'Each' is used when the number is limited and 'every' is used when the number is not limited; as,

(i) Each of these two boys got a prize.

(ii) Everyone loves his country.

7. **Much, many**

'Much' shows quantity, and many numbers; as,

(i) I eat much fruit.

(ii) I ate many apples.

8. **All, whole**

The first denotes number, the second quantity; as,

(i) All the brothers were 'punished'.

(ii) They spoiled the whole milk.

9. **Older, elder**

'Other' is used generally; as,

(i) He is older than I.

(ii) This is the older building of the two.

'Elder' is used for human beings, and chiefly with reference to members of the same family; as,

He is my elder brother.

My sister is elder to me.

'Elder' is not followed by 'than'

'Elder' is used as a noun to mean one who is elder; as,

You are my elder brother.

'Elders' means 'superiors', as,

Respect your elders.

'Oldest' is used generally to denote time, and 'eldest' is applicable to a human family; as,

He is the oldest man in the village.

He is my eldest brother.

Elder and eldest are used only for persons.

Older and oldest are used not only for persons, but also for things as,

This is the oldest building in the town.

10. Common, mutual

'Common' means belonging to or shared by more than one; mutual means reciprocal: as,

The meeting was held at the house of common friend.

There is mutual friendship between India and Russia.

11. Later, latter, latest, last

'Later' refers to time; as,

I want the later edition of the book.

'Latter' refers to order; as,

The latter part of the novel is interesting.

'Latest' refers to time; as,

What is the latest news?

'Last' refers to order. As.

The last chapter of the book is dull.

12. Farther, further.

'Farther' means more distance: as,

Delhi is farther from Amritsar than Chandigarh.

'Further' means additional; as,

I am waiting for further orders from my officer.

13. Nearest, next

'Nearest' refers to distance; as,

This is the nearest police post from our village.

'Next' refers to order or position; as,

He is next to me in order of merit.

14. Less, fewer

'Less' refers to quantity, and 'fewer' to number: as,

I bought no less than five kilograms of apples.

Our School library has no fewer than ten thousand books.

15. First, foremost

'First' refers to position; as,

Dr. Bakshi was the first Principal of our college.

'Foremost' means the most important; as,

Madhuri Dixit is the foremost heroine of today.

EXERCISE – 1

Fill in the blanks with comparative or superlative degree of the adjectives given in brackets:

(i) Sheela is the ________ girl of her class. (tall)

(ii) Hardwar is one of the __________ places for the Hindus (holy)

(iii) The Taj is ______ than any other building. (beautiful)

(iv) The climate of Shimla is _____ than that of Delhi. (good)

(v) Suman is _____ girl in her class. (honest)

(vi) This is the _____ book I have ever read. (bad)

(vii) This shirt is _____ than his brother's. (costly)

(viii) Sham has ______ sense than his brother. (little)

(ix) Ram is ______ than his brother. (intelligent)

(x) Calcutta is _____ than any other city in India. (large)

EXERCISE – 2

Fill in the blanks by choosing the correct adjectives from those given in brackets:

(i) He lent me __________ books he had. (many, few, the few, some)

(ii) ________ people are fond of reading novels. (many, many a)

(iii) He does not want to study any ________. (farther, further)

(iv) Pt. Ravi Shankar is the __________ musician of India. (first, foremost)

(v) He reported the matter at the ________ police station. (nearest, next)

(vi) No _________ than ten boys were present in the class. (less, few, fewer)

(vii) I can lend you __________ money. (some, few, any)

(viii) He bought the ________ edition of the book. (latest, last)

(ix) He is our _________ enemy. (mutual, common)

(x) He is the __________ member of the family (older, oldest, elder, eldest)

ANSWERS

USE OF ADJECTIVES

	EXERCISE – 1	EXERCISE - 2
1.	tallest	few
2.	holiest	many
3.	more beautiful	further
4.	better	foremost
5.	the most honest	nearest
6.	worst	less
7.	costlier	some
8.	less	latest
9.	more intelligent	common
10.	larger	eldest

USE OF ADVERBS

An **Adverb** adds to the meaning of a verb as,

He walks slowly.

The horse runs fast.

'Slowly' and 'fast' modify the verbs 'walks' and 'runs' respectively.

But some adverbs 'modify not verbs, but an adjective and another adverb. In that case they show degree or quality or quantity of the adjective or adverb they modify; as,

He is very **honest**.

He walks very **quickly**.

She drives quite **fast**.

KINDS OF ADVERBS:

Adverb are of three broad classes:

I Simple Adverb

II Interrogative Adverbs

III Relative Adverbs

I. **Simple Adverbs** are of five kinds:

(i) **Adverbs of Time** modify verbs indicating time of an action; as,

You should go **at once.**

I met him **yesterday.**

He is going at 5 p.m. **today.**

Yesterday I met an old friend.

Note :

But 'yet' and 'still' used as adverbs of time, have slightly different rules.

'Yet' should be placed at the end of a sentence and 'still' should be placed before the verb (doing verb only), though after the verb 'to be' (is, am, was, were etc.)

She has not come **yet.**

They **still** live in their old house.

Though old, you are **still** handsome.

(ii) **Adverbs of place** indicate where an action is performed; as,

He sat there.

She sat **down.**

He is not **there.**

They will come **here.**

(iii) **Adverbs of Manner** indicate the manner of an action; as,

The hare ran **swiftly.**

He works **carefully.**

She speaks **beautifully.**

Pranav learnt English **properly.**

(iv) **Adverbs of Number** indicate how often as action is performed; as,

Come **again.**

I meet him **twice** a week.

Pranav**seldom** comes to me.

(v) **Adverbs of Degree** or **Quantity** indicate extent of degree and modify an adjective; as,

He is **quite** careful about his health, whereas you are **rather** careless.

He is too weak to walk.

Kinds of Adverbs

1. ***Adverbs of Time:*** 'Now, then, before, after, when, soon, immediately, presently, instantly, early, late, today, tomorrow, yet, still, etc', are some of the 'adverbs of time'. They are generally placed at the end of a clause or sentence. They can also be placed at the very beginning.
2. ***Adverbs of Place:*** Here, there, hither, thither, then, within, without, above, somewhere, away, below, inside, outside etc', are some of the adverb of place.

3. ***Adverbs of Manner:*** 'Well, ill, slowly, quickly, happily, badly, etc, are some of the adverbs of manner. These adverbs answer the question "how" They are generally placed after the direct object, if there is one.
4. ***Adverbs of Number:*** Once, twice, thrice, often, seldom, again, firstly etc' are some of the adverbs of number. These adverbs answer the question "how often?" or "in what order?"
5. ***Adverbs of Degree or Quantity:*** 'Very, quite, rather, too, almost, enough, partly, wholly, much, more, most, little, less etc.',are some of the adverbs of degree or quantity.
6. ***Interrogative Adverb:*** As, why, when, where, how, how many.

II. ***Interrogative Adverbs are used for asking questions; as, why, when, where, how, how many.***

Why are you weeping? (asking reason)

When will you see your friend? (asking time)

Where will you be staying? (asking place)

How many students were present? (asking number)

How ill is he? (asking degree)

How much milk do you take daily? (asking quantity)

III. Relative Adverbs join two sentences (like a conjunction). They refer back to an antecedent (like a pronoun). These are all interrogative adverbs, but do not ask questions.

Relative adverbs also modify some verb.

He took me to the place **(where)** – he intended to build his house.

'Where' joins two sentences and refers to a place. The antecedent is expressed.

But in the following sentence, the antecedent in understood.

This is where he intends to build his house

Some other examples:

I can't explain **why** he failed. (antecedent understood)

I can't explain the reasons **why** he is sad? (antecedent expressed)

Do you know **why** he is sad? (antecedent understood)

Do you know the reason **why** he is sad? (antecedent expressed

FORMATION OF ADVERBS

(a) ***Adverbs are generally formed by adding 'ly.' But some adverbs are formed differently. In some cases the form is identical with the adjective form***

The **early** bird catches the worm.(adjective)

Rise **early**(adverb)

He is the **only** son of his parents.(adjective)

I **only** want your books.(adverb)

Some times 'ly' is added to the adjective form (also used as adverb) but the two forms of adverbs are differently used.Some times they differ in meaning too, as, late, lately; quick, direct, directly; free, freely.

They work **hard.** (diligently)

They **hardly** work. (scarcely)

She came home **direct.** (straight)

Directly the bell went, she ran home. (at once)

Price lists are given **free.** (without cost)

He spent his money **freely.** (liberally)

(b) ***Adverbs are also formed by adding 'ly' to nouns; as, monthly, weekly, daily, for-nightly***

(c) ***Some adverbs are formed by adding suffixes to nouns, adjectives and adverbs; as, aside, away, besides, afloat, above, behind, below, hereby, therein, midnight, sometimes etc.***

USE OF SOME ADVERBS:

1. Quite, very

'Quite' conveys the sense of wholly. 'Very' conveys the sense of high degree.

He is **quite** all-right.

She is **very** clever.

2. **Very, much**

'Very' modifies adjectives or adverbs in positive degree while 'much' modifies those in the comparative degree'.

He is a **very nice man.**

He was **much nicer than your friend.**

Similarly 'very' modifies a Present Participle, while 'much' modifies a Past Participle.

This is a very interesting story.

He was much interested in the story.

'Very' sometimes modifies the adverb 'much' as,

He was very much pleased with me.

3. **Since, ago, before**

'Since' refers to a previous time till now: as,

The rain has **since** stopped.

He has **since** arrived.

'Ago' is used to suggest a span of time ending in the past, as,

His father died a year **ago**.

'Before' is used to suggest formerly; as,

I had never seen him **before.**

4. **Too much, much too**

'Too much' is used before a noun, while 'much too' is used before an adjective; as,

He is **much too** clever for me.

Too much of anything is **bad**

5. **However and rather**

'However' means 'as much as can be'

However hard you may try, you cannot succeed.

'Rather' means 'somewhat':

He behaved **rather** nicely.

EXERCISE – 1

Fill in the blanks with suitable adverbs out of the list given below:

Thrice, once, enough, always, seldom, quick, clearly, yesterday, gently, here, there, eagerly, soundly, day before yesterday, never, extremely, highly, nicely.

1. She can speak ____________.
2. He went there ________________.
3. She talks ____________________.
4. Please sit ___________________.
5. Go ________________.
6. I met him___________.
7. He is sleeping ____________.
8. ____________ I saw a tiger.
9. He is ____________ late.
10. He ______________ speaks the truth.
11. She is ______________ absent.
12. They are ____________ rich.
13. She is rich ____________ to buy a car.
14. I shall teach you ______________ aweek.
15. I have met him ____________.

EXERCISE – 2

Fill in the blanks with suitable interrogative adverbs.

1. ___________ are you wasting time?
2. ___________ will he go to Delhi?
3. ___________ will you learn manners?
4. ___________ did you fare in the examination?
5. ___________ do you blame me?
6. ___________ boys were present in the hall?
7. ___________ noble your mother is?
8. ___________ big your house is?
9. ___________ tall the building is?
10. ___________ brothers are you?

EXERCISE – 3

Fill in the blanks with suitable relative adverbs.

1. He told me _____ the accident had taken place.
2. He does not know _____ the guests will arrive.
3. This is the time _____ you should pay attention to studies.
4. This is the shop _____ sports items are available.
5. He took me _____ the examination was held.

Fill in the blanks (Exercise 4 & 5) by choosing adverbs from the list given below:

Too, often, very, much, since, too much, ago, rather, however, quite, already, seldom, never, always, extremely, now, earlier

EXERCISE – 4

1. He was ________ tired.
2. His services are ________ in demand.
3. They are ________ quick.
4. She is ________ good to cheat anyone.
5. I meet him ________.
6. The novels were________ interesting.
7. He is a ________ nice man.
8. ________ quick your action, they aren't impressed.
9. You should ________ tell a lie.
10. We should ________ speak the truth.

EXERCISE – 5

1. Barking dogs ________ bite.
2. My officer is ________ satisfied with my performance.
3. I have ________ finished my work.
4. I am ________ sorry at your failure in the examination.
5. He is ________ happy in his new house.
6. It is a ________ lonely place.
7. The patient is ________ better.
8. I have not met you ________.
9. He is ________ weak to walk.
10. She is ________ innocent to understand the ways of the world.

EXERCISE – 6

Fill in the blanks with suitable degrees of the adverbs given in the brackets:

1. They behaved ________ than their neighbours. (kindly)
2. He talked to me ________ than his brother. (rudely)
3. She speaks ________ than her sister. (sweetly)
4. He gets up ________ than his wife does. (early)
5. He talks ________ than his father does. (loudly)
6. He treats his servants ________ than we do. (badly)
7. My father feels ________ today. (well)
8. The Prime Minister's house is ______ guarded. (heavily)
9. My mother treats me ________ than my father. (lovingly)
10. Of all the runners,Milkha Singh ran ___. (fast)

ANSWERS

USE OF ADVERBS

	EXERCISE-1	EXERCISE-2	EXERCISE-3	EXERCISE-4	EXERCISE-5	EXERCISE-6
1.	Clearly	Why	Where	Too	Seldom	More kindly
2.	Once	When	When	Very much	Quite	More rudely
3.	Gently	When	When	Too much	Already	More sweetly
4.	Here	How	Where	Too	Extremely	Earlier
5.	There	Why	Where	Ago	Very	More loudly
6.	Yesterday	How many		Quite	Quite	Worst
7.	Sunday	How		Very	Now	Better
8.	Day before yesterday	How		However	Earlier	The most heavily
9.	Always	How		Never	Too	More lovingly
10.	Seldom	How many		always	Too	The fastest
11.	Never					
12.	Highly					
13.	Enough					
14.	Thrice					
15.	Once					

USE OF DETERMINERS

DETERMINERS

are the words that determines fix, restrict or define the name coming after them.

Look at the sentences given below carefully:

1. You take *an* apple every day.
2. I have *little* money to help you.
3. Our team *won* the match.
4. *Each* boy got a packet of sweets.
5. I do not see *any* sense in going there now.

In all these sentences, the words in italics determine the position of a noun. Such words are called Determiners.

KINDS OF DETERMINERS:

Determiners

1	Article: a, an, the
2	Demonstratives:this, that, these those
3	Possessives: My, her, his, him, our their etc.
4	Numerical:One, two, first, both, none, few, a, few, each, every, either, neither
5	Quantitative: Some, any, much, more, less, little, a little, the little
6	Wh-Words:What (ever) which (ever) whosoever, whose

ARTICLES

The Use of Articles

A, an andthe are called Articles. They are in fact, demonstrative adjective which point out to the noun that comes after them.

Functionally, Articles are Determiners because they determine, fix, restrict or define the noun coming after them.

1. Rahul wrote *a* letter to his sister.
2. *The* book is lying on the table.
3. Take *an* umbrella with you as it is raining.

In sentence 1 the article *a* modifies the noun letter by referring to it in a general way.

In sentence 2 *the* used before the noun book makes it a particular or specific book. The second *the* in this sentence modifies the noun table and makes it a particular or specific table.

In sentence 3 the article *an* refers, in a general way, to the noun after it: umbrella. In all these sentences, the articles are used to determine, fix or specify the nouns coming after them.

An article can also be used before an adjective if this adjective is followed by a noun. Consider the following examples.

4. Shivani is *a* beautiful girl.
5. Rahul is *an* intelligent boy.
6. *The* scenery of Shimla is *a* charming one.

In sentence 4 the article *a* comes before the adjective beautiful.

So do the articles *an* in sentences 5, and *a* in sentence 6.

But these articles are because of the nouns and not because of the adjective. This fact can be easily verified by removing the intervening adjectives.

Conversely, we can rewrite these sentences without using the adjectives and the nouns modified by them, but then we shall have to remove the articles also.

4 *(a)* Shivani *is* beautiful.

5 *(a)* Rahul *is* intelligent.

6 *(a)* The scenery of Shimla *is* charming.

Secondly, if an adverb comes before an adjective which is followed by a noun, the article is placed before the adverb:

4 *(b)* Shivani is a very beautiful girl.

5 *(b)* Rahul is a very intelligent boy.

6 *(b)* The scenery of Shimla is an extremely charming one.

In these examples too, though the articles come before adverbs, they are there because of the nouns and not because of the adverbs.

POSSESSIVE DETERMINER

Possessive determiners are personal pronouns in their possessive case. They show relationship or possession of the noun which they are used. Possessive determiners are the following:

my	our	your
his	her	its
their	everybody's	nobody's
of which	whose	someone's
everyone's	somebody's	

Note: How the possessive determiners (given in italic type in the following examples are used before nouns. Remember that a possessive determiner is a pronoun. As such, its antecedent (the noun which it replaces) must be quite clear.

1. ***My*** name is Pranav Chopra.
2. ***His*** parents live in the USA.
3. I do not know ***which*** book he will pick up.
4. ***Your*** name is difficult to pronounce.
5. ***Her*** house is just across this garden.
6. ***Their*** names have been struck off the rolls.
7. ***Its*** price is five hundred rupees.
8. ***One*** should always remember one's duty.
9. ***His*** conduct has displeased his parents.
10. ***Our*** sole purpose is to help you.

NUMERAL DETERMINERS

Numeral determiners are primarily Adjectives of Number. They tell the number of persons, places, or things before which they are used. They also denote the order or degree in which a person, place or thing stands in relation to another.

1. She has given me ***many*** favours.
2. You have not seen her for ***several*** days.
3. I borrowed ***a hundred*** rupees from him.
4. Only ***a few*** people attended the poet's funeral.
5. All men desire happiness but ***very few*** get it.

Numeral determiners are of three kinds: (1) Definite, (2) Indefinite, and (3) distributive.

Definite Five, ten twenty, etc. Fifth, tenth, last etc.
Indefinite Many, several, a few, most, any, some, all, etc.
Distributive Each, every, either, neither, etc.

DEFINITE NUMRAL DETERMINERS

A definite numeral determiner refers to a definite or exact number such as one, two five,

1. She has ***five*** hundred rupees in her purse.
2. There are ***fifty*** students in this class.
3. He has stood ***first*** in the university.
4. Her house is the ***last*** in this row.
5. Your name figures ***next*** in the last.

Definite numeral determiners belong to two categories		
	Cardinals	***Ordinals***
	A cardinal numeral points how many persons, places or things are meant.	***Ordinal Numeral Determiners point out the order, rank or position of a person, place or thing before which they are used.***
1.	I have deposited one thousand rupees in the bank.	She was the last person to enter the hall.
2.	Simmi has two brothers and three sisters.	I have secured the first division in my M.A.
3.	We walked for five kilometers.	He has stood second in his class.

INDEFINITE NUMERAL DETERMINERS

Indefinite numeral determiners refer to indefinite or vague numbers such as many, several, any, and some.

1. I have only ***a few*** good friends.
2. ***Some*** girls are sitting in the common room.
3. Are there ***any*** boys, too?
4. She spent ***several*** weeks in Switzerland.
5. We have bought ***many*** books for the library.

DISTRUBUTIVE NUMERALS

Distributive numerals refer to each one of a group of persons, places or things, such as each, either, neither, and every.

1. ***Each*** girl has to sing a song here.
2. ***Every*** guest must be well looked after.
3. ***Neither*** of the party is happy with compromise.
4. ***Either*** book will serve my purpose equally well.
5. ***Every*** word that I have uttered is true.

QUANTITATIVE DETERMINERS

A quantitative determiners is like a quantitative adjective. It refers to the quantity of a thing which cannot be otherwise counted. It answers the question "How much?" Examples of Quantitative Determiners are the following.

Some	any	little
a little	a good/great deal of	
The little	no	enough
much	a lot of	

Examples:

1. There is ***enough*** money in the house.
2. I would love to have ***some*** coffee.
3. The ***little*** milk there was in the house has turned sour.
4. Not ***much*** effort was needed.
5. Can you give me ***a little*** help in this matter?
6. Is there ***any*** tea in the kettle?
7. Dr. A.P.J Abdul Kalam enjoys ***a lot*** of good will.
8. ***A great deal of*** discussion took place in the conference hall.

Some of the determiners which serve as numerals can also serve as quantitative determiners when used to refer to quantity or mass of a thing. Study the following table for examples and the difference between the two.

Numeral Determiners

1. Some girls are absent today.
2. He gifted all his books.
3. There are not enough seats.
4. He has no friends in this city.
5. Have you any supporters in this constituency?

Quantitative Determiners

1. There is some milk in the jug.
2. He has gifted all his money.
3. There is not enough money.
4. She has no money left with her.
5. He does not have any money in the bank.

The Simple method to decide whether a determiner or numeral or quantitative is this: a Numeral Determiner is used before a countable form (pen, pencil, man, woman, girl, etc); a Quantitative Determiner is used before an uncountable noun referring to mass or weight.

DEMONSTRATIVE DETERMINERS

Demonstrative determines are, as pointed out earlier, demonstrative adjectives. They point out to the persons, places or thing before which they are used; e.g. this, that, these, and those.

1. Have you read this book?
2. I did not like that picture.
3. We bought these oranges in the market.
4. Those days really belonged to us.
5. No one is happy in this world.
6. She did not like that sari.
7. These girls are just waiting for their marriage.

It is to be remembered that only demonstrative adjectives are determiners, while demonstrative pronouns are not. The difference between a demonstrative adjective (determiner) and demonstrative pronoun is this: whereas a demonstrative determiner or adjective must be followed by a noun, a demonstrative pronoun can stand on its won and is therefore not followed by a noun. Study the following table carefully.

Demonstrative Adjective

1. This pen is mine.
2. There girls are beautiful.
3. That book on history is interesting.
4. This book deals with writing.
5. These toys are for the children.

Demonstrative Pronoun

1. This is my pen.
2. These are girls who discuss us boys.
3. That is an interesting book on history.
4. This is a book about writing.
5. These are children's toys.

PRACTICE EXERCISES

EXERCISE – 1

Fill in the blanks in the following sentences with suitable possessive determiners.

1. ……………. house is just across this park.
2. ……………. beauty is the talk of the town.
3. ……………. business is nobody's business.
4. This is ………… pen ……… price is Rs. 35/-.
5. I don't know ……….. book this is.
6. What you do is none of ………… business.
7. ……………. brother is now past thirty.
8. Maya did not like ……………. husband's brothers and sisters.
9. He says that ……. girlfriend has betrayed him.
10. Our brave soldiers know …………… duty to the motherland.

EXERCISE – 2

Fill in the blanks with suitable numeral determiners.

1. I have only……………… friends. But they are all reliable.
2. ………. words the old man spoke were true.
3. How ………. books did he borrow from you?
4. Are there …………….. boys who were absent yesterday?
5. There are only ……………… girls in this class.
6. Anil and Pankaj are friends ………………. of them is reliable.
7. There are trees on ……….. side of the road.
8. I gave him ………… rupees that I had in my pocket.
9. He is very intelligent. He stood ……………. in the university.
10. You must account for ……………. Rupee that I have given you.

EXERCISE – 3

Fill in the blank spaces with suitable quantitative determiners.

1. There is ………………. Sense in what he says.
2. He drank the ……………… Milk that was there in the jug.
3. ………….. work and …………… play makes Jack a dull boy.
4. Does he have ………… Sense of shame left?
5. He offered a lot but actually gave ………. help.
6. ……… money was spent on the marriage of his daughter.
7. I have given him only ……………… help.
8. There is not ………… Money in your account.
9. There is not …………… truth in what she says.
10. Could you give me ………. Money as loan?

EXERCISE – 4

Fill in the blank spaces with "this," "that," "these" or "those," whichever may be suitable.

1. Look at …… Boy! He is running after the bus.
2. ………….. picture is selling like hot cake.
3. …………… boys will never mend themselves.
4. ………… days prices were not so high.
5. She is going to visit …….. place in a few days.
6. ………… boys are hardworking.
7. ……………… book is interesting to read.
8. Do you see ……… cloud shaped like a camel?
9. ………….days girls used to wear tight dresses.
10. …………… pen does not write well.

EXERCISE – 5

In the following sentences supply "a" or "an" (whichever is suitable) in each of the spaces left blank.

1. Urvashi is ……………… untidy girl.
2. Iron is ……………… useful metal.
3. ……… University is …… temple of learning.
4. ……….. apple a day keeps the doctor away.
5. Sushma is ………… honour to her school.
6. Set the clock back. It is ……….. hour too fast.
7. Brutus was ……………honorable man.
8. The river has ………… iron bridge over it.
9. ……..… honest man is the greatest work or God.

EXERCISE – 6

Fill in the blanks with suitable determiners.

1. The camel is …………….. ship of the desert.
2. Nasir is ……………..honourable man.

3. Anita resembles ……………brother.
4. I don't expect …………… reward.
5. Neil Armstrong was………….. first man to land on the moon.
6. Yesterday ……….. European visitor came to our school.
7. ……………..salt gives a taste to the soup.
8. In ………….. words he expressed his gratitude to his friend.
9. Don't eat …………..more of that ice-cream, leave ……………. of it for your sister.
10. ………….. ever thought of such a thing.

EXERCISE – 7

1. There are ……… Beautiful flowers in the park.
2. …………….. door of the garage is broken.
3. Is there …………… sugar in the pot?
4. ………. island is a piece of land surrounded by water on all sides.
5. Will you please lend me : …………….. money?
6. This pen is mine but that is ……………… here.
7. There is ……….. milk in the jug. You can make a cup of tea.
8. You must reward ………. boy who helped you.
9. I gave him …………….. story books to read.
10. There isn't ……………… Ink in the inkpot.

EXERCISE – 8

1. ……… boys are sitting in the class.
2. I don't think there is ………. oil in the lamp.
3. ……..of the land he owns is agricultural land.
4. How ………….. milk do you drink?
5. ………. Houses were damaged by the cyclone.
6. He did not make …….. mistake in his essay.
7. I would like ……………… more tea.
8. Would you lend me ……………….. money?
9. How ……… stories does this book contain?
10. The ration-shop did not have …………….. sugar, so I came back without it.

EXERCISE – 9

1. How …………… money do you need?
2. All the boys went to beach, but only ……….. could swim.
3. Do you have ……………… plan to go abroad?
4. Please give me …………… rice.
5. There is ……………… tea in the pot.
6. After the serious bomb-blast………….. person were found uninjured.
7. There is …………… sugar in this shop so we will have to buy it from some other shop.
8. These mangoes are raw, but ………. are ripe.
9. You will get one mark for …….. correct answer.
10. …….. flag on top of the school is the tri-colour.

EXERCISE – 10

1. I asked my mother for …………… money to buy my ticket.
2. …………blue car belongs to my uncle.
3. Don't you have ……………… friends in the other section?
4. I shall not buy ……………… mangoes.
5. Read the letter again to see if there are ……… mistakes.
6. There isn't ……….. boot polish in this tin.
7. Please give me ………………. More toffees.
8. …………….. car is ready now.
9. There are only …………toffees left in the tin.
10. Is there …………… use of my advising you?

EXERCISE – 11

1. …………… New book-shop has been opened near my home.
2. She collected a large number of mosquitoes. She dissected ……………
3. She cares only for …………… And not for others.
4. Some boys have come to college without……… knowledge of English.
5. How ……… milk will be needed for breakfast?
6. Her father was ……………..eminent artist.
7. ………. boys who called on the Prime Minister are here.
8. …………….. body wants freedom.
9. The classroom is empty. Where have ……………………the students gone?
10. This book is mine, but ………………. Is yours.

EXERCISE – 12

1. .... boys had to carry their own bags on the trek.
2. The cow is ....animal sacred to the Hindus.
3. The Ganges is .... holy river.
4. I shall not buy .... book.
5. How ....trees are there in the garden?
6. French is .... easy language.
7. Varanasi is .... holy city.
8. There are still .... flowers in the garden.
9. I want .... sugar for tea.
10. How .... land does a man need.

EXERCISE – 13

1. I have spent .... rupees I had.
2. He made ....mistake in his answer.
3. How .... money do you need?
4. I brought .... ice-cream for children.
5. He can play on .... flute.
6. Do you play ....game at home?
7. All ....boys ran away.
8. I have bought .... umbrella.
9. I have read .... book I bought last week.
10. Are there .... books in the box?

ANSWERS

USE OF DETERMINERS

	EXERCISE 1	EXERCISE 2	EXERCISE 3	EXERCISE 4	EXERCISE 5	EXERCISE 6	EXERCISE 7
1.	His	few	no	that	an	the	many
2.	Her	The	whole	This	a	an	The
3.	His	many	Only, no	Those	A, a	her	any
4.	the, it's	any	any	Those	an	any	An
5.	whose	a few	no	that	an	the	some
6.	My	both	A lot of	These	an	a	very much
7.	My	either	some	This	an	The	some
8.	her	few	any	that	an	a few	the
9.	his	first	any	Those	an	any	some
10.	their	a	some	This		some	any

	EXERCISE 8	EXERCISE 9	EXERCISE 10	EXERCISE 11	EXERCISE 12	EXERCISE 13
1.	The	much	some	A	The	few
2.	an	a few	that	them	an	a
3.	Most	any	any	some	the	much
4.	much	some	any	any	any	an
5.	Many	no	some	much	many	a
6.	any	a few	any	an	an	any
7.	some	little	a few	The	the	the
8.	some	a few	That	The	many	an
9.	many	each	a few	the	some	the
10.	any	The	any	which	much	any

USE OF VERBS

A **verb** is a word which says what the subject is or does. No sentence can be constructed without a verb.

HELPING VERBS AND MAIN VERBS:

Read the following sentences:

1. She is writing a poem.
2. He has painted a picture.

In these sentences, the verb is in two parts. In sentence 1, is, is the Helping verb and writing is the main verb. In sentence 2, has is the helping verbs and painted is the Main verb. 'Is', has' etc, are called Helping verbs and painted is the Main verb. 'Is', 'has' etc. are called Helping verb because they help the main verb. Take another sentence:

The roads are being repaired.

In this sentence, the verb is in three parts. 'Are being' is the helping verb and 'repaired' is the main verb.

1. Suman is an intelligent girl.
2. She was a good teacher.
3. They are good workers.

OBJECT OF A SENTENCE:

Read the following:

1. He obeyed.
2. Parents love.

These groups of words do not make complete sense. We want to know, "Whom does he obey?" "Whom do parents love"!

So we say:

1. He obeys his teachers.
2. Parents love their children.

'His teachers' is the object of verb 'obeys'. 'Their children' is the object of the verb 'love'.

Thus, the object is a noun or pronoun to whom the action of the verb is directed.

TRANSITIVE AND INTRANSITIVE VERBS:

Read the following sentences:

1. The hunter ***killed a deer.***
2. Ram ***broke my*** slate.
3. The servant ***broke the cups.***

The words in bold letters are called Transitive verbs. They are followed by objects. A Transitive verb is one which requires an object to complete its sense. The action passes on to the object.

Read the following sentences:

1. Ram goes to school daily.
2. The child cries.
3. He sat in an arm chair.
4. The old woman sleeps soundly.

No objects are generally placed after such verbs as go, cry, sit, come, sleep etc. They are called Intransitive verbs. In an intransitive verb the action stops with the subject. It does not pass on to an object.

A. ***Some Transitive verbs can be used intransitively:***

	Transitive	*Intransitive*
1.	He boiled rice.	Water boils at 100° C.
2.	He wrote an essay	She writes legibly.
3.	He ran a race.	He ran fast.
4.	He is flying a kite.	Birds fly in the sky.
5.	I stopped the machine	Suddenly the machine stopped.
6.	He moved heaven and earth.	The earth moves round the sun.

B. ***Similarly, some Intransitive verbs can be used transitively.***

	Intransitive	*Transitive*
1.	He laughed heartily.	He laughed a hearty laugh.

2.	He fought bravely.	He fought a worthy fight.
3.	Suddenly the door opened.	Ram opened the door.
4.	She failed in the examination.	Courage failed him.
5.	He fell down.	The woodcutter is felling the trees.

TRANSITIVE VERBS WITH TWO OBJECTS:

Some transitive verbs have two objects. (i) The direct and (ii) the Indirect object. The direct object refers to a thing, while the indirect object generally refers to a person.

I. Mr. Kapoor teaches us English.

II. He lent me his books.

(Mr. Kapoor teaches English to us.)

(He lent his books to me.)

Note:

When the direct and the indirect objects change places (as suggested in the sentences within brackets above) the indirect object takes a preposition (to/for) in front of it.

OBJECT COMPLEMENTS.

Read the following sentences:

1. We ***elected*** him our leader.
2. We ***found*** the house in flames.
3. I have ***painted*** my car green.

The words in bold letters in the above sentences help to complete what is said about the objects. They are called object complements.

AUXILIARY VERBS:

Auxiliary verbs are of two kinds:

1. Primary Auxiliaries.
2. Modal Auxiliaries

Primary Auxiliaries help to form tense, questions, negative sentences, passive voice etc. They are also called helping verbs. There are three Primary Auxiliaries: be, have and do. Their forms are given below:

Forms of Be:	Be, is, am, are, was, were, been, being
Forms of Have:	Have, has, had, having
Forms of Do:	Do, does, did, done, doing

These auxiliaries change their form according to the person and number of the subject.

Modal Auxiliaries express the mode or manner of the actions denoted by the verbs. They express ideas such as ability, possibility, probability, advisability, permission, expectation, certainty, intention, promises, obligation or duty etc.

The following is the list of modal auxiliaries:

Can, could, may, might, shall, should, will, would, must, ought to, need and dare.

A modal Auxiliary is different from a Primary Auxiliary. Unlike the latter, it does not change according to number, person, tense and voice.

Primary Auxiliary	***Modal Auxiliary***
He is singing.	He can sing.
I am singing.	Change in auxiliary
I can sing.	No change in auxiliary.
They are singing.	They can sing.

AGREEMENT OF THE VERB WITH THE SUBJECT:

1.	The verb agrees with the subject in number and person. Two or more singular subjects joined by 'and' take a verb in the plural; as, Mohan and Sohan are sitting on the same bench.
2.	If two singular nouns refer to the same person, thing or idea, the verb used is in the singular form: as, The poet and scholar is dead. Bread and butter is my favourite food.
3.	If the singular subjects are preceded by each or the verb is in the singular form; as, 'Every', boy and girl was working hard. 'Each' day and each hour bring new responsibilities.

4.	Two or more singular subjects joined ***by or not, either – or, neither – nor*** take a singular verb; as, Neither Ram nor his sister was present. Either you or he is in the wrong. No man or woman was able to understand his lecture.
5.	When the subjects joined by or, nor, neither – nor, either – or are of different numbers, the verb used must be plural, and the plural subject must be placed near the verb; as, Sheela or her sisters have done this mischief.
6.	When the subjects joined by or, nor neither-nor, either-or are of different persons, the verbs must agree with the subject placed near it; as, Neither you nor he is at fault.
7.	A collective noun takes singular or plural verb according to its sense. If it expresses the idea of oneness, it takes a singular verb. If it expresses individuals who form it, it takes a plural verb; as, The jury is of one opinion. The jury are divided in their opinions.
8.	Either, neither each, everyone, many a, must be followed by a singular verb; as, Either of the two brothers is guilty. Neither of the two brothers is at fault. Each of the three sister sings sweetly. Every one of us is prepared to defend the motherland. Many a boy is absent today.
9.	When some specific amount or quantity is considered to be one whole, the plural generally takes a singular verb: as, Fifty rupees is not a big sum. Five miles is not a long distance.

PRACTICE EXERCISE

EXERCISE – 1

Pick out the direct and indirect objects in the following sentences:

1. The teacher gave us a test.
2. I gave him some money.
3. My mother gave me good food.
4. I offered him a drink.
5. My father told me a story.

EXERCISE – 2

Fill in the blanks with the correct verb:

1. Our only guide ____________ the teacher. (is, are)
2. Suman as well as her brothers _________ present in the function. (was, were)
3. A large number of students ______________ absent. (was, were)
4. Neither you nor he _________ to blame. (is, are)
5. Neither of the two sisters nor their brother ___________ eligible (are, is)
6. Not only his brothers but also he __________ absent.(was, were)
7. (vii) Either you or I _____________ responsible for this. (is am, are)
8. Each member of the family _____________ hand-working and honest. (is, are)
9. The minister together with his wife and daughter _______ killed in a road accident. (was, were)
10. Forty miles ____________ not a long distance. (is, are)

EXERCISE – 3

1. Five thousand rupees ____________ a big sum. (is, are)
2. Suman, as well as Anu and Diya ____________ mangoes. (like, likes)
3. Either Suraj or his brother _________ bought the house. (has, have)

4. Neither the driver not the passengers ____________ hurt in accident. (was, were)

5. A number of books ____________ been bought for the library. (has, have)

6. Not only she but also her parents ______________ gone to England. (has, have)

7. The first innings ____________ come to a close. (has, have)

8. The cattle ____________ grazing. (is, are)

9. The wages of sin ____________ death. (is, are)

10. Many a man ____________ killed in the earthquake.(was, were)

ANSWERS

EXERCISE – 1

1. The teacher gave a test to us.
2. I gave some money to him.
3. My mother gave good food to me.
4. I offered a drink to him.
5. My father told a story to me.

EXERCISE – 2

1. is	2. was	3. were
4. is	5. is	6. was
7. am	8. is	9. was
10. is		

EXERCISE – 3

1. is	2. likes	3. has
4. were	5. have	6. have
7. has	8. are	9. is/ are
10. was		

USE OF TENSES

What is Tense?

Tense is a form that a verb takes to show the time of action or a state expressed by the verb.

1.	The Present Tense :	I sing a song.
2.	The Past Tense :	I sang a song yesterday.
3.	The Future Tense :	I shall sing a song tomorrow.

Read the Following sentences:

1. I call
2. I am calling
3. I have called
4. I have been calling

All these refer to the present time, and therefore, all are in the Present Tense. But there is a distinction in the way in which the action is regarded.

In sentence 1, the action is mentioned simply. There is no reference to the completeness of the action. The ***verb call*** in the sentence is, therefore, said to be in the **Simple Present Tense.**

In sentence 2, the action is mentioned as incomplete, that is, as still going on. Hence ***the verb am calling*** is said to be in the **Present Continuous Tense.**

In sentence 3, the action is mentioned as finished, complete or perfect. Hence ***the verb have called*** is said to be in the **Present Perfect Tense.**

In sentence 4, the action is mentioned as having been going on continuously but not completed at the present moment. Hence ***the verb have been calling*** is said to be in the **Present Perfect Continuous Tense.**

So the Present Tense has four forms:

1. Simple Present (also called **Present Indefinite**)
2. Present Continuous
3. Present Perfect
4. Present Perfect Continuous

Just as the Present Tense has four forms, the Past Tense also has the following four forms:

1.	I called	(Simple Past or Past Indefinite)
2.	I was calling	(Past Continuous)
3.	I had called.	(Past Perfect)
4.	I had been calling.	(Past Perfect Continuous)

Similarly, the Future Tense has the following four forms:

1.	I shall call	(Simple Future or Future Indefinite)
2.	I shall be calling.	(Future Continuous)
3.	I shall have called.	(Future Perfect)
4.	I shall have been calling.	(Future Perfect continuous)

Brief Introduction in Tabular Form – Read it, Chew it, Digest it.

1. Present Indefinite (simple)	2. Past Indefinite (simple)	3. Future Indefinite (simple)
Continuous	Continuous	Continuous
Perfect	Perfect	Perfect
Perfect Continuous	Perfect Continuous	Perfect Continuous

TENSE	SIMPLE	CONTINUOUS	PERFECT	PERFECT CONTINUOUS
Present				
Active	Calls (s/es)	is/am/are calling	has/have called	has/have been calling
Passive	is/am/are	is/am/are	has/have been called	No passive
Past				
Active	called	Was/were calling	had called	had been calling
Passive	was/were Called	Was/were being called	had been called	No passive
Future				
Active	Will/shall	Will/shall calling	Will/shall have called	Will/shall have been calling
Passive	be called	No Passive	Will/shall have been called	No passive

Use of Tenses:

PRESENT INDEFINITE TENSE (SIMPLE)

(i) **Affirmative Sentences –**

I read my book.

He loves his school.

You help the poor.

They love their country.

(ii) **Negative Sentence –**

I do not read my book.

He does not love his school.

You do not help the poor.

They do not love their country.

(iii) **Interrogative Sentences:**

Affirmative –

Do I read my book?

Does he love his school?

Do you help the poor?

(iv) **Interrogative Sentences:**

Negative –

Do I not read my book?

Do you not help the poor?

Where does he not go?

RULES: LEARN THEM BY HEART

Rule 1.

In Affirmative Sentences, I, We You, They and Plural noun use ***first form of verb like love, read, help, etc.***

He, She, It and Singular noun use ***first Form of Verb in s, es or ies, like loves, reads, helps.***

Rule 2.

In Negative Sentences, I, We, You, They and Plural noun ***use Verb first form before do not***.

He, She, It and Singular noun use ***Verb first Form before does not***.

Rule 3.

Two type of Interrogative Sentences. First type of Sentences start according to Subject ***Do or Does*** and after Subject first form of Verb.

Second types of Sentences start with ***who, what, where, how*** and ***use of Verb first form and question mark***.

Rule 4.

Interrogative Sentences Negative,Use Verb before not.

PRESENT CONTINUOUS TENSE

(i) **Affirmative Sentences –**

I am reading my book.

He is going to school.

They are playing football.

You are going.

(ii) **Negative Sentences –**

I am not reading my book.

He is not going to school.

You are not going.

(iii) **Interrogative Sentences:**

Affirmative –

Am I reading my book?

Is he going to School?

Are you going?

Where are you going?

(iv) **Interrogative Sentences:**

Negative –

Am I not reading my book?

Is he not going to school?

Are you not going?

Where are you not going?

RULES: LEARN THEM BY HEART

Rule 1.

In Affirmative sentences, I, with Am and You, They, We and Plural Noun use are.

He, She, It and Singular Noun use is and Verb first form with ing.

Rule 2.

In Negative sentences, Is, Am or Are used and "not" is used after that.

Rule 3.

Interrogative sentences start with auxiliary verb Is, Am or Are.

If sentences start with What, Who, How, then use auxiliary verb Is, Am, Are just after that.

Rule 4.

Interrogative Negative sentences main Verb before not.

PRESENT PERFECT TENSE

Rule

(i) **Affirmative Sentences –**

I have read my book.

You have finished your work.

He has gone to Calcutta.

They have left Agra.

(ii) **Negative Sentences –**

I have not read my book.

You have not finished your work.

He has not gone to Calcutta.

They have not left Agra.

(iii) **Interrogative Sentences:**

Affirmative –

Have I read my book?

Have you finished your work?

Has he gone to Calcutta?

Have they left Agra?

(iv) **Interrogative Sentences:**

Negative –

Have I not read my book?

Have you not finished your work?

Has he not gone to Calcutta?

Have they not left Agra?

RULES: LEARN THEM BY HEART

Rule 1.

Affirmative sentences– I, You, They, We and Plural Noun use ***"have"*** with Verb third form.

He, She, It and Singular Noun ***use "has" and Verb third form***.

Rule 2.

Negative sentences–Have or Has after not.

Rule 3.

Interrogative sentences start with auxiliary verb ***Have or Has and Verb third form***.

If sentences start with ***What, Who, How and Where*** after that same use of Has, Have and 3rd form of verb...

Rule 4.

Interrogative Negative sentences main Verb is used before ***"not"*** is used.

PRESENT PERFECT CONTINUOUS TENSE

(i) Affirmative Sentences –

I have been working for four hours.

He has been sleeping since 6 O'clock.

You have been living since July.

(ii) Negative Sentences –

I have not been working for four hours.

He has not been sleeping since 6 O'clock.

You have not been living since July.

(iii) Interrogative Sentences: Affirmative –

Have I been working for four hours?

Has he been sleeping since 6 O'clock?

Why has the child been weeping for two hours?

(iv) Interrogative Sentences: Negative –

Have I not been working for four hours?

Has he not been sleeping since 6 O'clock?

Why have you not been reading since the morning?

RULES:

Rule 1.

Present Perfect Continuous Tense, if starting time of point is given, ***"since"*** is used; for example; since July; since 4 O'clock; since Monday; since 1964 etc.

Rule 2.

If number of hours, days, month, years, etc. given, then ***"for"*** is used, e.g. for 4 hours, for 2 days, for 2 months, for 3 years.

SIMPLE PRESENT TENSE OR PRESENT INDEFINITE TENSE (In Tabular Form)

Verb "work"

AFFIRMATIVE	NEGATIVE	INTERROGATIVE	INTERROGATIVE NEGATIVE
(Plural Number) I / We / You / They] work	(Plural Number) I / We / You / They] do not work	(Plural Number) Do [I / We / You / They] work?	(Plural Number) Do [I / We / You / They] not work?
(Singular Number) He / She / It] s or / es or / ies] work	(Singular number) He / She / It] does not work	(Singular Number) Does [He / She / It] work?	(Singular Number) Does [He / She / It] not work?

PRESENT CONTINUOUS TENSE (In Tabular Form)

Verb "work"

AFFIRMATIVE	NEGATIVE	INTERROGATIVE	INTERROGATIVE NEGATIVE
(Plural Number) I] am We / You / They] are (Singular Number) working He / She / It] is	I] am not We / You / They] are not He / She / It] is not] working	Am [I Are [We / You / They working? Is [He / She / It]	Am [I Are [We / You / They not working? Is [He / She / It]

PRESENT PERFECT TENSE (In Tabular Form)

Verb "work"

AFFIRMATIVE	NEGATIVE	INTERROGATIVE	INTERROGATIVE NEGATIVE
(Plural Number) I / We / You / They — have (Singular Number) He / She / It — has	I / We / You / They — have not He / She / It — has not worked	Have — I / We / You / They worked? Has — He / She / It	Have — I / We / You / They not worked? Has — He / She / It

PRESENT PERFECT CONTINUOUS TENSE (In Tabular Form)

Verb "work"

AFFIRMATIVE	NEGATIVE	INTERROGATIVE	INTERROGATIVE NEGATIVE
(Plural Number) I / We / You / They — have been (Singular Number) He / She / It — has been working (for two weeks)	I / We / You / They — have not been He / She / It — has not been working (for two weeks)	Have — I / We / You / They Has — He / She / It been working (for two weeks)	Have — I / We / You / They Has — He / She / It not been working (for two weeks)?

PRESENT TENSE – PRACTICE SETS

SET – 1

Supply the correct form (Present Indefinite Tense) of the verb in brackets:

1. Who (swim) in the pond everyday?
2. We (burn) fuel to get heat.
3. Here (come) the bride.
4. The sum (rise) in the east.
5. They (come) to school by bus.
6. I (go) for a walk every day.
7. Raindrop (fall) from the clouds.
8. You always (speak) the truth.
9. Father asked me, "How (be) you?"
10. I (not object) to this proposal,
11. He (not like) mangoes.
12. When ___________ the train (leave)?
13. The boys (know) the answer.

SET – 2

Fill the blanks with Present Continuous form of the verbs given in brackets:

1. What _________ you _________ now? (do)
2. They _________ to London next week. (go)
3. Deepika ________ to see me tomorrow. (come)

4. We ____________ football. (play)
5. I ____________ notes. (not take)
6. Why ________ He _________ at me? (laugh)
7. Rajan ____________ a book. (write)
8. The boys ____________ in the river. (not swim)
9. The workers ____________ the walls. (paint)
10. Why _______ he _______ his clothes? (change)
11. She ____________ the candles. (blow out)
12. The old man ____________ with cold. (shiver)

SET – 3

Use the correct form of the Verb given in brackets:

(Present Simple or Present Progressive)

1. He ____________ (know) several persons here.
2. Leela __________ (do) her homework. Don't disturb her.
3. I __________ (believe) what you say.
4. Run fast! The Train __________ (whistle)
5. He ________ (resemble) his father.
6. Look! Smoke __________ (come) out of that window.
7. He always __________ (take) his coffee without sugar.
8. The Ganga __________ (rise) in the Himalayas and _________ (flow) into thc Bay of Bengal.
9. Our School __________ (begin) with prayer every day.
10. A brave man __________ (not lose) heart.
11. She hardly ever __________ (play) on her veena these days.
12. A gentleman __________ (not laugh) at others.
13. Madhu __________ (keep) awake till midnight these days.
14. Lions _______ (not live) on fruit and vegetables.
15. Irregular work _________ (not bring) success.
16. This parcel _________ (contain) a gift for you.
17. My friends often ____________ (send) me presents.

SET – 4

Rewrite the following sentences using the Present Perfect Tense of the verb in brackets:

1. We (know) each other for the past ten years.
2. The appointed day (come)
3. Do you know what (happen) to his leg?
4. I (finish) my work.
5. I (never deceive) you.
6. The train _________ just _________ (arrive)
7. I shall go there after he (finish) his homework.
8. Why_________ they_________ there? (go)
9. _________ she _________ her meals? (have)
10. I (never see) the Taj.

SET – 5

Complete the following sentences using the Present Perfect Continuous Tense:

1. We ____________ for you for two hours. (wait)
2. It ____________ since morning. (rain)
3. Who _____ at the door for ten minutes? (knock)
4. They ___________ here since 1997. (live)
5. The girls ____________ for two hours. (sing)
6. __________ he __________ from fever since Monday? (not suffer)
7. You __________ this book since January. (write)
8. __________ the tap __________ for two hours? (not run)
9. Why __________ you __________ since yesterday?(fight)
10. Why __________ he __________ to school for three days? (not come)

SET – 6

Fill in the blanks with correct Tense form Tense form of the verb given in brackets:

(Past Simple or Present Perfect)

1. He __________ (be) a teacher since 1984.
2. I don't know him because I __________ (never meet) him.

3. I __________ (come) to this town in 1980.
4. Two convicts __________ (escape) from prison last night.
5. He __________ (already entertain) the guests for two hours.
6. He __________ (get) a new car now.
7. He __________ (buy) it last month.
8. I __________ (already see) this film.
9. I __________ (see) it in Mumbai last month.
10. Your officer will be angry with you because you __________ (not work) properly.
11. He __________ (tour) India for a month last year.
12. No he __________ (write) a book about it.
13. Here is your note-book. I __________ (correct) it.
14. He __________ (leave) his house some days ago.
15. He __________ (not come) back yet.

PRESENT TENSE – ANSWERS/HINTS

	SET – 1	SET – 2	SET – 3	SET – 4	SET – 5	SET – 6
1.	swims	are, doing	knows	have known	have been waiting	has been
2.	burn	are going	is doing	has come	has been raining	have never met
3.	comes	is coming	believe	has happened	has been knocking	has come
4.	rises	are playing	is whistling	have finished	have been living	have escaped
5.	comes	am not taking	resembles	have never deceived	have been singing	has already entertained
6.	go	is, laughing	is coming	has, arrived	has, been not suffering	has got
7.	fall	is writing	takes	he has finished	have been writing	has bought
8.	speak	are not swimming	rises, flows	have, gone	has, been running	have seen already
9.	are	are painting	Begins	has, had	have, been fighting	have seen
10.	do not object	is, changing	doesn't lose	have never seen	has, not been coming	have not worked
11.	does not like	is blowing out	plays			has toured
12.	does leave	is shivering	doesn't laugh			has written
13.	know		keeps			have corrected
14.			do not live			has left
15.			doesn't bring			has not come
16.			contains			
17.			send			

PAST TENSE

Read the following sentences carefully –

PAST INDEFINITE TENSE (SIMPLE PAST)

(*i*) Affirmative Sentences –

I helped my friend.

You loved your school.

He wrote a book.

(*ii*) Negative Sentences –

I did not help my friend.

You did not love your school.

He did not write a book.

(*iii*) Interrogative Sentences:

Affirmative –

Did I help my friend?

Did you love your school?

Did you write a book?

Where did you go?

(*iv*) Interrogative Sentences:

Negative –

Did I not help my friend?

Did you not love your school?

Where did you not go?

RULES

This tense is used for following purposes:

(*a*) To express a single act or even that happened in the past, e.g.

1. He broke this table.
2. They were in the garden.
3. She was absent yesterday.

(*b*) To express a habitual action or custom in the past, e.g.

1. She got up at 4 a. m. every day.
2. Our ancestors were honest and hard working.

(*c*) As a substitute for the Past Continuous Tense, e.g.

1. While they played, we took tea.
2. While we talked, they slept.

PAST CONTNUOUS TENSE

(*i*) Affirmative Sentences –

I was reading my book.

He was going to school.

They were playing foot ball.

You were going.

(*ii*) Negative sentences –

I was not reading my book.

He was not going to school.

You were not going.

(*iii*) Interrogative Sentences:

Affirmative –

Was I reading my book?

Was he going to school?

Were you going?

Where were you going?

(*iv*) Interrogative Sentences:

Negative –

Was I not reading my book?

Was he not going to school?

Were you not going?

Where were you not going?

RULES

This tense is used to denote an action that was going on at some time in the past, e.g.

1. They were playing hockey.
2. She was singing a song.

PAST PERFECT TENSE

(*i*) Affirmative Sentences –

He had left India before independence.

He had already gone.

I had taken my dinner before sunset.

He had gone before you reached there.

The patient had died before the doctor reached.

Mohan came after Ram had left.

(ii) Negative Sentences –

I did not take my dinner after the sun had set.

He had not gone before you reached there.

The patient had not died before the doctor reached.

(iii) Interrogative Sentence:

Affirmative –

Did I take my dinner after the sun had set?

Had he gone before you reached there?

Had he gone before you reached there?

Why had you gone before he came?

(iv) Interrogative Sentences:

Negative –

Had I not taken my dinner before the sun set?

Had he not gone before you reached there?

Had the patient not died before the doctor reached?

Why had you not gone before he came?

RULES

This tense is used to denote an action which had been completed before another action began in the past. It is most often used in a Complex sentence, e.g.

1. When I reached there, she had finished her work.
2. The doctor arrived after the patient had died.

Rule 1:

(i) The Past Perfect cannot be used to denote an isolated action in the past. For that, Past Indefinite should be used.

(ii) Rarely, however, when the Past Perfect is used by itself in Simple sentence, it implies another action which followed, e.g. He had already finished his paper.

Rule 2:

In order to express two related action completed in the past –

(1) The past Perfect (had + V_3) is used for the action that took place first.

The Past Simple (V_2) is used for the action that took place later.

PAST PERFECT CONTINUOUS TENSE

(i) Affirmative Sentences –

I had been working for four hours.

He had been sleeping since 6 O'clock.

We had been living in Delhi since 1980.

(ii) Negative Sentences –

I had not been working for four hours.

He had not been sleeping since 6 O'clock.

We had not been living in Delhi since 1960.

(iii) Interrogative Sentences:

Affirmative –

Had he been working for four hours?

Had he been sleeping since 6 O'clock?

Had we been living in Delhi since 1980?

Why had the child been weeping for two hours?

(iv) Interrogative Sentences:

Negative –

Had I not been working for four hours?

Had he not been sleeping since 6 O'clock?

Had we not been living in Delhi since 1980?

Why had you not been reading since morning?

RULES

This tense is used to denote an action that had been going on at or before some point of time in the past, e.g.

1. He had been living in this locality for two years before he became my friend.
2. She had been meeting her boy-friend regularly before it came to the notice of her parents.

SIMPLE PAST OR PAST INDEFINITE TENSE (In Tabular Form)

Verb "work"

AFFIRMATIVE	NEGATIVE	INTERROGATIVE	INTERROGATIVE NEGATIVE
I We You He She It They Any noun — worked	I We You He She It They Any noun — did not worked	Did — I We you He She It They Any noun — work?	Did — I We you He She It They Any noun — not work?

PAST CONTINUOUS TENSE (In Tabular Form)

Verb "work"

AFFIRMATIVE	NEGATIVE	INTERROGATIVE	INTERROGATIVE NEGATIVE
Singular Number I He She It — was Plural Number — working We You They — were	I He She It — was not We You They — was not — working	Was — I He She It Were — We You They — working?	Was — I He She It Were — We You They — not working?

PAST PERFECT TENSE (In Tabular Form)

Verb "work"

AFFIRMATIVE	NEGATIVE	INTERROGATIVE	INTERROGATIVE NEGATIVE
I We you He She It They Any noun — had worked	I We you He She It They Any noun — had not worked	Had — I We you He She It They Any noun — worked?	Had — I We you He She It They Any noun — not worked?

PAST PERFECT CONTINUOUS TENSE (In Tabular Form)

Verb "work"

AFFIRMATIVE	NEGATIVE	INTERROGATIVE	INTERROGATIVE NEGATIVE
I We You He She It They Any noun had been working (for two weeks)	I We You He She It They Any noun had been working (for two weeks)	Had I We You He She It They Any noun been working? (for two weeks)	Had I We You He She It They Any noun not been working? (for two weeks)

PAST TENSE – PRACTICE SETS

SET – 7

Fill in the blanks with the Past Indefinite form of the verbs given in brackets:

1. Meera ________ (turn) and ________ (move) to the door.
2. We ________ (see) a lion in the jungle.
3. I ________ (meet) him yesterday.
4. While the girls ________ (sing) we ________ (dance).
5. He ________ (go) out for ten minutes.
6. Who ________ (break) the window yesterday?
7. She ________ (send) him a letter last month.
8. They ________ (know) the answer.
9. We ________ (copy) from the blackboard.
10. The dog ________ (bites) the postman.
11. The birds ________ (fly) away.
12. The little girl ________ (cry) bitterly.

SET – 8

Fill in the blanks with the correct Tense form of the verb given in brackets:

1. Last Saturday I ________ (stay) at home.
2. Who ________ (play) the hero in that film?
3. She was sick; so she ________ (not come) to party.
4. We ________ (eat) dinner at ten last night.
5. She ________ (walk) to college yesterday morning.
6. He often ________ (write) to his daughter when she ________ (be) away to England.
7. Radha ________ (buy) a new saree last month.
8. He ________ (not go) to his office on Saturday. He had fever.
9. We ________ (drink) coffee for breakfast yesterday.
10. It ________ (not rain) heavily last summer.
11. The Sun ________ (rise) yesterday at five o/ clock.
12. The brave Rajput women ________ (prefer) death to dishonour.
13. I ________ (have) work and ________ (not go) out for lunch.
14. When he was unmarried, he often ________ (arrive) home late and his father ________ (be) angry with him.

SET – 9

Fill in the blanks with correct Tense form (Past Simple or Past Progressive) of the verbs given in brackets:

Note:

(1) For an action begun and continuing in past time, use the Past Continuous.

(2) For an action completed in the past, use the Past Simple.

1. I __________ (read) a novel when my friend came.
2. I __________ (go) to bed early last night.
3. At midnight I __________ (lie) awake in my bed.
4. As I __________ (go) to my school, I met an old friend of mine.
5. He jumped off the train while It __________ (move).
6. I did not see that the teacher __________ (stand) behind me.
7. It __________ (begin) to rain just as we moved out.
8. I heard that the child __________ (cry).
9. He looked out of the window to see what __________ (happen) in the street.
10. I saw that two policemen __________ (chase) a thief.
11. I __________ (have) my lunch when the postman came.
12. When I __________ (see) him last he was quite healthy.
13. A thief__________ (break) into our house last night.
14. I __________ (sleep) on the roof when it __________ (start) raining.
15. Ashoka __________ (decide) to give up war and became a Buddhist.

SET – 10

Fill in the blanks with suitable form (Past Perfect Tense) of the verbs:

1. He ______ just ______ his breakfast when I arrived. (Finish)
2. The Nawab ______ (die) years before his son took over.
3. The train ______ (leave) before he reached the station.
4. The patient ______ (die) before the doctor arrived.
5. The ship ______ (sink) before help could reach.
6. Suraj ______ (complete) his work when Kiran came.
7. Why ______ you ______ home till then? (not reach)
8. I ______ (never expect) it to come this way.
9. ______ they ______ (buy) the tickets before the train arrived?
10. Mother ______ (tell) him not go there.
11. We ______ often ______ such messages. (receive)

SET – 11

Fill in the blanks with the right Tense form (Past Simple or Past Perfect) of the verbs given in brackets:

1. He said that he __________ (write) the letter.
2. Mohan __________ (reach) home before it started raining.
3. She said that she __________ (win) the first prize.
4. We __________ (understand) the poem after the teacher had explained it to us.
5. He had broken the lock before I __________ (bring) the key.
6. The boys said that they __________ finish their work.
7. We __________ (reach) the ground before the match started.
8. He __________ (not put) on his clothes when the bell rang.
9. We __________ (have) our dinner before she left.
10. The officer was glad to find that the clerk __________ (type) all the letters.
11. I __________(close) the book after I had read it.
12. The patient __________ (die) before the doctor came.
13. The teacher said that the boys __________ (go) for a picnic.
14. He __________ (not see) me before that.
15. He __________ (not recognize) me when I went to meet him.

SET – 12

Fill in the blanks with the Past Perfect Continuous Tense of the verbs given in brackets:

1. We _______ (wait) for you for ten hours when you come.
2. He said that he _______ (live) here for ten years before they met him.
3. She told me that she _______ (work) for the last four hours before the light went off.
4. She _______ (knit) a sweater for a month before she fell ill.
5. It _______ (rain) for two days.
6. The farmer _______ (milk) the cows for an hour before the bell rang.
7. She _______ (teach) us English since 200 *2.*
8. The police _______ (look for) this thief for the last five years.
9. The boys _______ (learn) their lessons for two hours before the test started.

PAST TENSE – ANSWERS/HINTS

	SET – 7	SET – 8	SET – 9	SET – 10	SET – 11	SET – 12
1.	turned, moved	stayed	was reading	had, finished	had written	had been waiting
2.	saw	played	went	had died	had reached	had been living
3.	met	did not come	lay	had left	had won	had been working
4.	sang, danced	ate	was going	had died	had understood	had been knitting
5.	went	walked	was moving	had sunk	had brought	had been raining
6.	broke	wrote, was	was standing	had completed	had finished	had been milking
7.	sent	bought	began	had, not reached	had reached	had been teaching
8.	knew	did not go	was crying	had never expected	had not put	had been looking
9.	copied	drank	was happening	had, bought	had, had	had been learning
10.	bit	did not rain	were chasing	had told	had typed	
11.	flew	rose	was having	had, received	closed	
12.	cried	preferred	saw		had died	
13.		had, did not go	broke		had gone	
14.		arrived, was	was sleeping, started		had not seen	
15.			decided		had not recognized	

FUTURE TENSE

Read the following sentences carefully –

FUTURE INDEFINITE (SIMPLE FUTURE)

(*i*) Affirmative Sentences –

I shall help you.

He will come to-day.

You will do your work.

They will go to Kanpur.

(*ii*) Negative Sentences –

I shall not help you.

He will not come to-day.

You will not do your work.

They will not go to Kanpur.

(*iii*) Interrogative Sentences:

Affirmative –

Shall I help you?

Will he come to-day?

Will you do your work?

Will they go to Kanpur?

Where will they go?

(*iv*) Interrogative Sentences:

Negative –

Shall I not help you?

Will he not come to-day?

Will you not do your work?

Will they not go to Kanpur?

Where will they not go?

RULES: LEARN THEM BY HEART

This tense is used to denote a single action in the future, e.g.

1. I shall go to see my friend.
2. He will help me.
3. They will come here tomorrow.

FUTURE CONTINUOUS

(*i*) Affirmative Sentences –

I shall be helping you.

You will be going to Kanpur.

He will be coming to-day.

(*ii*) Negative Sentences –

I shall not be helping your.

You will not be going to Kanpur.

He will not be coming to-day.

(*iii*) Interrogative Sentences:

Affirmative –

Shall I be helping you?

Will you be going to Kanpur?

Will he be coming to-day?

Where will you be going?

(*iv*) Interrogative Sentence:

Negative –

Shall I not be helping you?

Will you not be going to Kanpur?

Will he not becoming to-day?

Where will you not be going?

RULES: LEARN THEM BY HEART

The Future Continuous is used to express an action going on at some point in future time; as,

1. I shall be reading the paper then.
2. They will be playing a match at that time.

This tense is also used to indicate some future plan; as,

1. We shall be staying there for a week.
2. I shall be visiting this place regularly.

Note:

(1) The Future Indefinite Tense (Simple Future) indicates some point of time in the future.

(2) The Future Continuous Tense (Future Progressive) indicates some period of time in the future.

(3) In the following sentences, the use of Future Indefinite seems to be as appropriate as the use of Future Continuous:

1. I shall do this work at 7 a. m. tomorrow.

(Future Indefinite)

2. I shall be doing this work at 7 a.m. tomorrow. (Future Continuous)

But note the difference in the meanings of the sentences:

1. I shall do this work at 7 a.m. tomorrow.
   (and I shall not start earlier than that)
2. I shall be doing this work at 7a.m. tomorrow. (I shall start before 7 a.m. and shall continue working even after 7 a.m.)

The Future indefinite show that the action begins at the started future moment. The Future Continuous shows that the action began before the stated moment in the future.

FUTURE PERFECT TENSE

(i) Affirmative Sentences –

I shall have finished my work.

You will have gone before he comes.

He will have reached the station before the train leaves.

(ii) Negative Sentences –

I shall not have finished my work.

You will not have gone before he comes.

He will not have reached the station before the train leaves.

(iii) Interrogative Sentences:

Affirmative –

Shall I have finished my work?

Will You have gone before he comes?

Will he have reached the station before the train leaves?

Why will he have gone before you reach?

(iv) Interrogative Sentences:

Negative –

Shall I not have finished my work?

Will you not have gone before he comes?

Will he not have reached the station before she leaves?

Why will he not have gone before you reach?

RULES: LEARN THEM BY HEART

The Future Perfect is used to indicate the completion of an action by a certain future time; as,

1. I shall have finished my homework by evening.
2. She will have cleaned the room before you reach there.

FUTURE PERFECT CONTINUOUS TENSE

LEARN THEM BY HEART

(i) Affirmative Sentences –

I shall have been reading for four hours.

He will have been living in Delhi since 1980.

You will have been waiting for him for two hours.

(ii) Negative Sentence -

I shall not have been reading for four hours.

He will not have been living in Delhi since 1980.

You will not have been waiting for him for two hours.

(iii) Interrogative Sentences:

Affirmative -

Shall I have been reading for four hours?

Will he have been living in Delhi since 1980?

Why will he have been waking for four hours?

(iv) Interrogative Sentence:

Negative -

Shall I have not been reading for four hours?

Will he not have been living in Delhi since 1980?

Why will he not have been waiting for us since the morning?

RULES:

This tense denotes an action that will have been going on at or before some point of time in the future e.g.

1. She will have been dancing for two hours before we reach there.
2. I shall have been working for seven days before my employer comes back.

SIMPLE FUTURE OR INDEFINITE TENSE (In Tabular Form)

Verb "work"

AFFIRMATIVE	NEGATIVE	INTERROGATIVE	INTERROGATIVE NEGATIVE
I / We — shall work You / He / She / It / They / Any noun — will work	I / We — shall not work You / He / She / It / They / Any noun — will not work	Shall — I / We — work? Will — You / He / She / It / They / Any noun — work?	Shall — I / We — not work? Will — You / He / She / It / They / Any noun — not work?

FUTURE CONTINUOUS TENSE (In Tabular Form)

Verb "work"

AFFIRMATIVE	NEGATIVE	INTERROGATIVE	INTERROGATIVE NEGATIVE
I / We — shall be working You / He / She / It / They / Any noun — will be working	I / We — shall not be working You / He / She / It / They / Any noun — will not be working	Shall — I / We — be working? Will — You / He / She / It / They / Any noun — be working?	Shall — I / We — not be working? Will — You / He / She / It / They / Any noun — not be working?

FUTURE PERFECT TENSE (In Tabular Form)

Verb "work"

AFFIRMATIVE	NEGATIVE	INTERROGATIVE	INTERROGATIVE NEGATIVE
I / We — shall have worked You / He / She / It / They / Any noun — will have worked	I / We — shall not have worked You / He / She / It / They / Any noun — will not have worked	Shall — I / We — have worked? Will — You / He / She / It / They / Any noun — have worked?	Shall — I / We — not have worked? Will — You / He / She / It / They / Any noun — not have worked?

FUTURE PERECT CONTINUOUS TENSE (In Tabular Form)

Verb "work"

AFFIRMATIVE	NEGATIVE	INTERROGATIVE	INTERROGATIVE NEGATIVE
I We shall have been You He She It been They Any noun will have been working (for two weeks)	I We shall not have been You He She It They Any noun will have been working (for two weeks)	Shall I We Shel will You He It They Any noun have been working? (for two weeks)	Shall I We Shel will You He It They Any noun not have been working? (for two weeks)

FUTURE TENSE – PRACTICE SETS

SET – 13

Fill in the blanks with correct Tense form (Future Simple or Future Progressive) of the verbs given in brackets:

1. I ____________ (reach) there at five o'clock.
2. We __________ (wait) for you when you come back.
3. He __________ (lie) in bed when you go to his room.
4. I _________ (finish) this work by tomorrow evening.
5. He _________ (live) in London at this time next year.
6. The sky is dark. I think it _________ rain.
7. It _________ (rain) by the time you get ready to leave.
8. The Principal __________ (talk) to the students about this problem.
9. I __________ (see) what I can do for you.
10. Don't come next week, I __________ (prepare) for my examination.
11. __________ you (please return) my money just now?
12. He ______ (pass) through a forest at this time.
13. They ________ (live) in their new house by next year.
14. When you come, I _________ (sit) in the school library.
15. Bill always has to work on Sundays: so he will say, "I _________ (work) as usual."

SET – 14

Fill in the blanks with the correct Tense form of the verbs given in brackets:

(Present Perfect, Past Perfect or Future Perfect)

1. I __________ (finish) my work just now.
2. I _________ (finish) my work before he came.
3. I __________ (finish) my work by the time you come back in the evening.
4. The train ________ (come). Try to find a seat for me.
5. The train ________ (come) when I reached the station.
6. The train ________ (come) before you reach the station.
7. I __________ (read) the book which you gave me.
8. I __________ (already read) the book which you gave me.
9. I __________ (read) the whole book before you come back.
10. We __________ (do) all these exercises by the time the teacher comes.
11. They _______ (not yet return) from the market.
12. The clock _________ (just strike) twelve.
13. He ________ (eat) all the food by the time we return.
14. She __________ (discuss) the matter with her parents by next Tuesday.

FUTURE TENSE – ANSWERS/HINTS

	SET – 13	SET – 14
1.	shall reach	have finished
2.	shall be waiting	had finished
3.	will be lying	will have finished
4.	will finish	has come
5.	will be living	had come
6.	will rain	will have come
7.	will be raining	have read
8.	will talk	had already read
9.	shall see	will have read
10.	shall be preparing	will have done
11.	will you please return	have not yet returned
12.	will be passing	has just struck
13.	will be living	will have eaten
14.	will be sitting	will had discussed
15.	shall be working	

Rules of tenses – A chromosome – Read them, re–read them, re–read them and read them – No other way out.

SIMPLE PRESENT TENSE OR PRESENT INDEFINITE TENSE (In Tabular Form)

Verb "work"

AFFIRMATIVE	NEGATIVE	INTERROGATIVE	INTERROGATIVE NEGATIVE
(Plural Number) I / We / You / They] work	(Plural Number) I / We / You / They] do not work	(Plural Number) Do [I / We / You / They] work?	(Plural Number) Do [I / We / You / They] not work?
(Singular Number) He / She / It] [s or es or ies] work	(Singular Number) He / She / It] does not work	(Singular Number) Does [He / She / It] work?	(Singular Number) Does [He / She / It] not work?

PRESENT CONTINUOUS TENSE (In Tabular Form)

Verb "work"

AFFIRMATIVE	NEGATIVE	INTERROGATIVE	INTERROGATIVE NEGATIVE
(Plural Number) I am We / You / They are working (Singular Number) He / She / It is	(Plural Number) I am not We / You / They are not working (Singular Number) He / She / It is not	Are I Are We / You / They working? Is He / She / It	Are I Are We / You / They not working? Is He / She / It

PRESENT PERFECT TENSE (In Tabular Form)

Verb "work"

AFFIRMATIVE	NEGATIVE	INTERROGATIVE	INTERROGATIVE NEGATIVE
(Plural Number) I / We / You / They have worked (Singular Number) He / She / It has	I / We / You / They have not worked He / She / It has not	Have I / We / You / They worked? Has He / She / It	Have I / We / You / They not worked? Has He / She / It

PRESENT PERFECT CONTINUOUS TENSE (In Tabular Form)

Verb "work"

AFFIRMATIVE	NEGATIVE	INTERROGATIVE	INTERROGATIVE NEGATIVE
(Plural Number) I / We / You / They have been working (for two weeks) (Singular Number) He / She / It has been	I / We / You / They have not been working (for two weeks) He / She / It has not been	Have I / We / You / They been working two weeks? Has He / She / It	Have I / We / You / They not been working (for two weeks)? Has He / She / It

USE OF TENSES IN NUTSHELL – ***Keep them regurgitating.***

SIMPLE PRESENT INDEFINITE

Affirmative	Negative
I play	I do not play
We play	We do not play
You play	You do not play
He/she/it plays	He/she/it does not play
They play	They do not play
Ravi plays	Ravi does not play
Boys play	Boys do not play

Interrogative	Negative Interrogative
Do I play?	Do I not play?
Do we play?	Do we not play?
Do you play?	Do you not play?
Does he/she/it play?	Does he/she/it not play?
Do they play?	Do they not play?
Does Ravi play?	Does Ravi not play?
Do boys play?	Do boys not play?

PRESENT CONTINUOUS

Interrogative	Negative interrogative
Am I playing?	Am I not playing?
Are we playing?	Are we not playing?
Are you playing?	Are you not playing?
Is he/she/it playing?	Is he/she/it not playing?
Are they playing?	Are they not playing?
Is Ravi playing?	Is Ravi not playing?
Are boys playing?	Are boys not playing?

Affirmative	Negative
I am playing	I am not playing
We are playing	We are not playing
You are playing	You are not playing
He/she/it is playing	He/she/it is not playing
They are playing	They are not playing
Ravi is playing	Ravi is not playing
Boys are playing	Boys are not playing

PRESENT PERFECT

Interrogative	Negative interrogative
Have I played?	Have I not played?
Have we played?	Have we not played?
Have you played?	Have you not played?
Has he/she/it played?	Has he/she/it not played?
Have they played?	Have they not played?
Has Ravi played?	Has Ravi not played?
Have boys played?	Have boys not played?

Affirmative	Negative
I have played.	I have not played
We have played.	We have not played
You have played.	You have not played
He/she/it has played.	He/she/it has not played
They have played.	They have not played
Ravi has played.	Ravi has not played
Boys have played	Boys have not played

PRESENT PERFECT CONTINUOUS

Affirmative
I (we, you, they) have been playing since noon
We have been playing since morning
You have been playing for the last two hours
He (she/it) has been playing
They have been playing
Ravi has been playing
Boys have been playing
Negative
I (we, you, they) have not been playing
We have been not playing
You have not been playing
He/she/it has not been playing
They have not been playing
Ravi has not been playing
Boys have not been playing
Interrogative
Have I (we, you, they) been playing?
Have we been playing?
Have you been playing?.
Has he/she/it been playing?
Have they been playing?
Has Ravi been playing?
Have Boys been playing?

SIMPLE PAST OR PAST INDEFINITE TENSE (In Tabular Form)

Verb "work"

AFFIRMATIVE	NEGATIVE	INTERROGATIVE	INTERROGATIVE NEGATIVE
I We You He She It They Any noun work	I We You He She It They Any noun did not work	Did I We You He She It They Any noun work?	Did I We You He She It They Any noun not work?

PAST CONTINUOUS TENSE (In Tabular Form)

Verb "work"

AFFIRMATIVE	NEGATIVE	INTERROGATIVE	INTERROGATIVE NEGATIVE
Singular Number I He She It was Plural Number We You They were working	I He She It was not We You They were not working	Was I He She It Were We You They working?	Was I He She It Were We You They not working

PAST PERFECT TENSE (In Tabular Form)

Verb "work"

AFFIRMATIVE	NEGATIVE	INTERROGATIVE	INTERROGATIVE NEGATIVE
Singular Number I He She It had Plural Number We You They had worked	I He She It had not We You They had not worked	Had I He She It Had We You They worked	Had I He She It Had We You They not worked?

PAST PERFECT CONTINUOUS TENSE (In Tabular Form)

Verb "work"

AFFIRMATIVE		NEGATIVE		INTERROGATIVE			INTERROGATIVE NEGATIVE		
I We You He She It They Any noun	had been working (for two weeks?	I We You He She It They Any noun	had not been working (for two weeks?	Had	I We You He She It They Any noun	been working? (for two weeks)	Had	I We You He She It They Any noun	been working? (for two weeks)

PAST INDEFINITE

Affirmative	Negative
I played.	I did not play
We played.	We did not play
You played.	You did not play.
He/she/it played.	He/she/it did not play.
They played.	They did not play.
Ravi played.	Ravi did not play.
Boys played.	Boys did not play.

Interrogative	Negative interrogative
Did I play?	Did I not play?
Did we play?	Did we not play?
Did you play?	Did you not play?
Did he/she/it play?	Did he/she/it not play?
Did they play?	Did they not play?
Did Ravi play?	Did Ravi not play?
Did boys play?	Did boys not play?

PAST CONTINUOUS

Affirmative	Negative
I was playing	I was not playing
We were playing.	We were not playing.
You were playing.	You were not playing.
He/she/it was playing.	He/she/it was not playing.
They were playing	They were not playing
Ravi was playing	Ravi was not playing
Boys were playing	Boys were not playing

Interrogative	Negative Interrogative
Was I playing?	Was I not playing?
Were we playing?	Were we not playing?
Were you playing?	Were you not playing?
Was he/she/it playing?	Was he/she/it not playing?
Were they playing?	Were they not playing?
Was Ravi playing?	Was Ravi not playing?
Were boys playing?	Were boys not playing?

PAST PERFECT

Affirmative	Negative
I had played.	I had not played.
We had played.	We had not played.
You had played.	You had not played.
He/she/it had played.	He/she/it had not played.
They had played.	They had not played.
Ravi had played.	Ravi had not played.
Boys had played.	Boys had not played.

Interrogative	Negative interrogative
Had I played?	Had I not played?
Had we played?	Had we not played?
Had you played?	Had you not played?
Had he/she/it played?	Had he/she/it not played?
Had they played?	Had they not played?
Had Ravi played?	Had Ravi not played?
Had boys played?	Had boys not played?

PAST PERFECT CONTINUOUS

Affirmative	Negative
I had been playing since morning	I had not been playing since morning
We had been playing since 1980	We had not been playing since 1980
You had been playing since evening	You had not been playing since evening
He/she/it had been playing since 5'o clock.	He/she/it had not been playing since 5'o clock
They had been playing for the last 2 hours.	They had not been playing for the last two hours
Ravi had been playing since morning.	Ravi had not been playing since morning
Boys had been playing for two hours.	Boys had not been playing for two hours

Interrogative	Negative interrogative
Had I been playing since afternoon?	Had I not been playing since afternoon?
Had we been playing since morning?	Had we not been playing since morning?
Had you been playing since afternoon?	Had you not been playing since afternoon?
Had he/she/it been playing since 5'o clock?	Had he/she/it not been playing since 5'o clock?
Had they been playing since evening?	Had they not been playing since evening?
Had Ravi been playing for the last two hours?	Had Ravi not been playing for the last two hours?
Had boys been playing since morning?	Had boys not been playing since morning?

SIMPLE FUTURE OR INDEFINITE TENSE (In Tabular Form)

Verb "work"

AFFIRMATIVE	NEGATIVE	INTERROGATIVE	INTERROGATIVE NEGATIVE
[I, We] shall [You, He, She, It, They, Any noun] will work	[I, We] shall not [You, He, She, It, They, Any noun] will not work	Shall [I, We] Will [You, He, She, It, They, Any noun] work?	Shall [I, We] Will [You, He, She, It, They, Any noun] not work?

FUTURE CONTINUOUS TENSE (In Tabular Form)

Verb "work"

AFFIRMATIVE	NEGATIVE	INTERROGATIVE	INTERROGATIVE NEGATIVE
[I, We] shall be [You, He, She, It, They, Any noun] will be working	[I, We] shall not be [You, He, She, It, They, Any noun] will not be working	Shall [I, We] Will [You, He, She, It, They, Any noun] be working?	Shall [I, We] Will [You, He, She, It, They, Any noun] not be working?

FUTURE PERFECT TENSE (In Tabular Form)

Verb "work"

AFFIRMATIVE	NEGATIVE	INTERROGATIVE	INTERROGATIVE NEGATIVE
I / We — shall have; You / He / She / It / They / Any noun — will have; working (for two weeks)	I / We — shall not have been; You / He / She / It / They / Any noun — will have been; working (for two weeks)	Shall — I / We; Will — You / He / She / It / They / Any noun; have worked?	Shall — I / We; Will — You / He / She / It / They / Any noun; not have worked?

FUTURE PERECT CONTINUOUS TENSE (In Tabular Form)

Verb "work"

AFFIRMATIVE	NEGATIVE	INTERROGATIVE	INTERROGATIVE NEGATIVE
I / We — shall have been; You / He / She / It been / They / Any noun — will have; working (for two weeks)	I / We — shall not have been; You / He / She / It been / They / Any noun — will have been; working (for two weeks)	Shall — I / We; Will — You / He / She / It / They / Any noun; have been working? (for two weeks)	Shall — I / We; Will — You / He / She / It / They / Any noun; not have been working? (for two weeks)

FUTURE INDEFINITE

Affirmative	Negative	Affirmative	Negative
He will play	He will not play	Will he play?	Will he not play?
She will play	She will not play	Will she play?	Will she not play?
I shall play	I shall not play	Shall I play?	Shall I not play?
They will play	They will not play	Will they play?	Will they not play?
You will play	You will not play	Will you play?	Will you not play?
We shall play	We shall not play	Shall we play?	Shall we not play?
Ravi will play	Ravi will not play	Will Ravi play?	Will Ravi not play?
Girls will play	Girls will not play	Will girls play?	Will girls not play?

FUTURE CONTINUOUS

Affirmative	Negative	Interrogative	Negative Interrogative
He will be playing	He will not be playing	Will he be playing?	Will he not be playing?
She will be playing	She will not be playing	Will she be playing?	Will she not be playing?
I shall be playing	I shall not be playing	Shall I be playing?	Shall I not be playing?
They will be playing	They will not be playing	Will they be playing?	Will they not be playing?
You will be playing	You will not be playing	Will you be playing?	Will you not be playing?
We shall be playing	We shall not be playing	Shall we be playing?	Shall we not be playing?
Ravi will be playing	Ravi will not be playing	Will Ravi be playing?	Will Ravi not be playing?
Girls will be playing	Girls will not be playing	Will girls be playing?	Will girls not be playing?

FUTURE PERFECT

Affirmative	Negative	Interrogative	Negative Interrogative
He will have played	He will not have played	Will he have played?	Will he not have played?
She will have played	She will not have played	Will she have played?	Will she not have played?
I shall have played	I shall not have played	Shall I have played?	Shall I not have played?
They will have played	They will not have played	Will they have played?	Will they not have played?
You will have played	You will not have played	Will you have played?	Will you not have played?
We shall have played	We shall not have played	Shall we have played?	Shall we not have played?
Ravi will have played	Ravi will not have played	Will Ravi have played?	Will Ravi not have played?
Girls will have played	Girls will not have played	Will girls have played?	Will girls not have played?

FUTURE PERFECT CONTINUOUS

Affirmative	Negative	Interrogative	Negative Interrogative
He will have been playing	He will not have been playing	Will he have been playing since morning?	Will he not have been playing since morning?
She will have been playing	She will not have been playing	Will she have been playing since evening?	Will she not have been playing since evening?
I shall have been playing	I shall not have been playing	Shall I have been playing since noon?	Shall I not have been playing since noon?
They will have been playing	They will not have been playing	Will they have been playing for the last two hours?	Will they not have been playing for the last two hours?
You will have been playing	You will not have been playing	Will you have been playing for the last seven days?	Will you not have been playing for the last seven days?
We shall have been playing	We shall not have been playing	Shall we have been playing since Monday?	Shall we not have been playing since Monday?
Ravi will have been playing	Ravi will not have been playing	Will Ravi have been playing since 1985?	Will Ravi not have been playing since 1985?
Girls will have been playing	Girls will not have been playing	Will girls have been playing for the last three days?	Will girls not have been playing for the last three days?

TENSES : PRACTICE SETS

Fill in the blanks using the correct form of the words given in brackets:

SET – 15

The Sun comes up in the east and ………(1)……. (go) down in the west. When the sun ……..(2)……… (rise), it is morning. When the sun ……..(3)……. (set), it is evening. When does the sun shine? The sun ……..(4)……. (shine) during the day. The moon and the stars ……(5)…… (shine) during the night. Does the sun rise in the east or in the west? It …… (6)…….. (rise) in the east. Where does the sun set? It ……(7)……. (set) in the west. In winter the sun ……(8)….. (rise) at about seven o'clock and …… (9)……… (set) at about five o'clock. In summer the sun ……(10)……. (rise) at about five o'clock and ……(11)……. (set) at about seven o'clock.

SET – 16

When evening ……(1)…….. (come) it ……(2)…… (get) dark. What do we do when it ……(3)…… (get) dark? We ……(4)…… (turn) the lights on. If we have electric light in our houses, there are switches. The switch is usually near the door. When it …… (5)…….. (get) dark, we ……(6)…….. (turn) the light on. We ……(7)……. (push) the switch. When we ……(8)…… (go) dark, we ……(9)…….. (turn) the light on. We ……(10)….. (turn) the light off. We ……(11)…… (push) the switch again. What do you do when you …..(12)……. (want) to listen to the radio ? You ……(13)……. (switch) the set on. There are usually three or four controls on a radio set. When you ……(14)…….. (turn) this control to the left, you ……(15)……… (switch) the set off.

SET – 17

When Rita wants to make tea, she ……(1)……. (go) into the kitchen and ………(2)….. (take) the kettle to the water tap. She …….(3)………. (take) the lid off the kettle, ……..(4)……… (hold) the kettle under the tap, ……(5)…….. (turn) the water on, and ……(6)……… (fill) the kettle. Then she …… (7)…….. (turn) the water off, ……(8)……. (put) the lid back on the kettle, and ……(9)…….. (put) the kettle on the gas stove. Next, Rita wants to make tea, she ……(10)……… (strike) a match and ……... (11)……. (light) the gas. As soon as the water …… (12)……… (boil), she ………(13)……… (empty) this water out and then ……(14)……… (put) some tea–leaves in the pot. Then she ……(15)…….. (fill) the teapot with boiling water. In two or three minutes the tea is ready to pour out.

SET – 18

When Aslam wants to get on his bicycle, he …… (1)……. (take) hold of the handlebars with both hands. He ……(2)…… (put) his left foot on the left pedal. He ………(3)……… (push) himself forward with his right foot. When the bicycle …… (4)….. (move) forward, he ……(5)…… (raise) his right leg over the saddle. He ……(6)…… (put) his right foot on the right pedal, ……(7)…… (push) the pedal down, and ……(8)….. (lower) himself on to the saddle.

SET –19

Mrs. Soni gets up at half past six every morning and ……(1)…….. (go) to the bathroom. She …… (2)……. (wash), ……(3)…… (clean) her teeth and ……(4)……… (comb) her hair. Then she …… (5)…… (prepare) breakfast for her husband. Her husband ………(6)………… (go) to work and after that she ……(7)…… (wake) Ashok and Pinkie up. Pinkie is only three years old. Mrs. Soni …… (8)…….. (wash) And ……(9)……. (dress) Pinkie. She ……(10)…… (cook) breakfast of the children and then she ……(11)……… (wash) the dishes. She ……(12)…… (do) all her housework. After that she ……(13)……. (go) for shopping. She……. (14)………. (take) Pinkie with her.

SET – 20

The Sun shines during the day. It …..(1)……. (not shine) at night. The moon and the stars ……(2)….. (shine) at night. They ……(3)…… (not shine) during the day. Sometimes there are clouds in the sky. Then the sun ……(4)…… (not shine). It ……(5)……. (go) behind the clouds,. The stars also ……(6)…….. (not twinkle) when there are clouds. The clouds …… (7)……. (cover) the moon and the stars. The moon

……(8)……. (revolve) round the earth. The earth ……(9)…….. (not revolve) round the moon. It …… (10)…….. (revolve) round the sun. The sun ……… (11)………… (not revolve) round the earth. Other planets like Mars and Venus also ……(12)……. (revolve) round the Sun.

SET – 21

A dog was crossing a stream. He ……(1)……. (have) a bone in his mouth. He ……(2)……. (see) his shadow in the water. He ……(3)……… (think) it was another dog with a bigger piece of meat. The dog ……(4)…….. (open) his mouth to attack the shadow. The piece of meat ……(5)…… (fall) from his mouth. He ……(6)……. (lose) the meat.

SET – 22

A mouse ran across the nose of a sleeping lion. The mouse ……(1)……. (wake) the lion. The lion …… (2)……. (be) going to kill the mouse. The mouse ……(3)…….. (beg) for its life. The lion …… (4)……. (give) it its wish. Some time later the lion ……(5)……… (fall) into a trap. He ………(6)……. (cannot) escape from it. The mouse ……(7)……. (hear) the roars of the lion. It ……(8)……. (go) to the trap. It ……(9)…… (bite) through the ropes, and thus the lion ……(10)……… (get) his freedom again.

SET – 23

Amrit ……(1)…….. (buy) a camera from his friend. Deepak last month. Deepak ……(2)…... (sell) the camera to him for two hundred rupees. Amrit …… (3)……. (pay) at that time. Deepak ………(4)…….. (give) Amrit a book with complete directions.Amrit ……(5)……. (read) all the directions carefully. He ……(6)…… (keep) the camera in a leather case for protection. Then Amrit ………(7)……… (take) photos of all his friends.

SET –24

One day Mohandas ……(1)….. (steal) a piece of gold. Stealing was a great sin. He ……(2)…… (know) that he had committed a great crime. He …… (3)……… (decide) never to steal again in his life. He ……(4)……. (write) a confession of his crime and ……(5)……. (read) the confession. He ……(6)…… (tear) up the paper without saying a word. The pieces of paper ……(7)……. (fall) to the floor. He …… (8)……… (sink) back on his bed. Mohandas …… (9)……… (leave) the room with tears in his eyes.

SET – 25

Mrs. Toofat always seemed to be ill and unhappy. She often ……(1)….. (have) painful headaches Medicines ……(2)….. (not seem) to make her any better. So at last her husband ……(3)……. (take) her to an elderly doctor. The doctor ……(4)……. (examine) her carefully and ………(5)……. (ask) her a lot of questions. Then he suddenly ……(6)……. (put) his arms around her and ……(7)……. (give) her a big kiss. Mrs. Toofat at once ….….(8)……… (look) better and happier. "You see?" ……(9)……. (say) the doctor to her husband, "that is all she needs. I suggest that she ……(10)……. (have) the same thing every Tuesday, Thursday and Saturday," and he ……(11)…….. (smile).

SET –26

A dog ……(1)……. (be) the only animal that …… (2)….. (not have) to work for a living. A hen …… (3)…… (have) to lay eggs and a cow ……(4)…… (have) to give milk. But a dog ……(5)….. (make) its living by giving you nothing but love.

SET –27

I just ……(1)…… (receive) a letter from my old friend Shindie. He ……(2)…… (say) that he …… (3)…… (go) to England next year. He ……(4)….. (live) in London with his uncle. Shindie …… (5)……. (join) the University of London. His uncle ……(6)….. (pay) for his education. After a few years, he ……(7)….. (return) to India as a Bachelor of Arts. But I ……(8)…. (think) he ……(9)…… (not be) a real bachelor. Most probably he ……(10)….. (bring) back a British girl as his wife.

SET –28

Phool Singh was cutting a branch off a tree in his field. While he …….(1)……. (saw) it, a man …… (2)…….. (pass) by the field. He stopped and said, "Excuse me, but if you continue to saw that branch like that, you ……(3)…. (fall) down with it." He said this because PhoolSingh ……. (4)……. (sit) on the branch and ……(5)….. (cut) it at a place between himself and the trunk of the tree. Phool Sing said nothing. He thought: "This is a foolish person who ......(6)...... (have) no work to do. He ......(7)..... (go) about telling other people what not to do." The man ....(8).......... (continue) on his way. Of course, after a few minutes, the branch fell and Phool Singh fell down with it.

SET –29

When night came, Hamlet ......(1)..... (join) the soldiers who ......(2)..... (guard) the walls. He ...... (3)....... (meet) them at the place where the ghost ......(4)....... (appear) the previous night. It ...... (5)..... (be) very cold there, but they ......(6)..... (can) hear voices of laughing and singing inside the castle.

SET – 30

There ......(1)...... (be) a great rush at the counter yesterday. I ....(2)...... (want) to get a ticket for the movie. It ....(3)..... (be) the first day of its release. The manager suddenly ......(4)...... (appear) on the scene and ......(5)........ (announce) that the show ......(6)...... (cancel) for reasons beyond control.

SET – 31

Yesterday a Blue Line bus ....(1)....... (run) over a school boy who ....(2)........ (cross) the road. The boy ......(3)...... (injure) seriously and .... (4).......... (rush) to the hospital. The passengers ...... (5)......... (catch) of the driver and ......(6)...... (hand) him over to the police.

SET – 32

The wedding procession ......(1)......... (already start) when we ......(2)....... (reach) Mohan's house. While we ....(3)...... (be) on way to the place, we ......(4)....... (decide) not to dance at all but the scene ......(5)........ (prove) so attractive, that we ......(6)...... (draw) into it.

SET – 33

Once there was king. He ......(1)..... (know) for his benevolence. Every day he ......(2)...... (feed) the hungry and ......(3)....... (give) clothes to the poor before he ......(4)......... (take) his food He ...... (5)...... (do) so for many years. He ......(6)........ (love) by his subjects.

TENSES : ANSWERS

	SET – 15	SET – 16	SET – 17	SET – 18	SET – 19	SET – 20	SET – 21	SET – 22
1.	goes	comes	goes	takes	goes	does not shine	had	woke
2.	rises	gets	takes	puts	washes	shine	saw	was
3.	sets	gets	takes	pushes	cleans	do not shine	thought	begged
4.	shines	turn	holds	is moving	combs	does not shine	opened	gave
5.	shine	gets	turn	raises	prepares	goes	fell	fell
6.	rises	turn	fills	puts	goes	do not twinkle	lost	couldn't
7.	sets	push	turns	pushes	wakes	cover		heard
8.	rises	go	puts	lowers	washes	revolves		went
9.	sets	turn	puts		dresses	does not revolve		bit
10.	rises	turn	strikes		cooks	revolves		got

11.	sets	push	lights		washes	does not revolve		
12.		want	boils		does	revolve		
13.		switch	empties		goes			
14.		turn	puts		takes			
15.		switch	fills					

	SET – 23	SET – 24	SET – 25	SET – 26	SET – 27	SET – 28	SET – 29
1.	bought	stole	had	is	just received	was sawing	joined
2.	sold	knew	did not seem	doesn't have	says	passed	were guarding
3.	paid	decide	took	has	is going	will fall	met
4.	gave	wrote	examined	has	will live	was sitting	had appeared
5.	read	read	asked	makes	will join	cutting	was
6.	kept	tore	put		will pay	has	could
7.	took	fell	gave		will return	goes (is going)	
8.		sank	looked		think	continued	
9.		left	said		won't be		
10.			has		will bring		
11.			smiled				

	SET – 30	SET – 31	SET – 32	SET – 33
1.	was	ran	had already started	was known
2.	wanted	was crossing	reached	fed
3.	was	was injured	were	gave
4.	appeared	was rushed	decided	took
5.	announced	caught	proved	did
6.	had been cancelled	handed	were drawn	was loved

CHANGE OF VOICE

A thorough acquaintance with `change of voice'.

Voice is that form of the verb which shows the relation of the subject of the verb to the action expressed by it. It shows whether the subject of the verb acts or is acted upon.

A transitive verb has two voices: active and passive.

In active voice the subject names the actor that is, the subject is the performer of the action expressed by the verb. In other words, we can say that the person or thing denoted by the subject does something that is, it is the doer of the action; as –

Raju kills a tiger.

(Here the person denoted by the subject, namely Raju, does something to a tiger).

In passive voice the subject names the object or receiver of the action. In other words, it means that something is done to the person or thing denoted by the subject; as –

A tiger is killed by Raju.

(Here the thing denoted by the subject, namely a tiger, suffers something from Raju).

The active voice is used when the doer of the action (that is, agent) is to be made prominent. The passive voice is used when the person or thing acted upon is to be made prominent. The passive voice is generally used when the doer of the action is not known, is not important, or is not to be mentioned.

To change sentences from active to passive voice, the following points must be taken note of:

1. ***The object of the active sentence becomes the subject of the passive sentence***
2. ***The subject of the active sentences becomes the object of the passive sentence.***
3. ***The past participle of the main verb is used.***
4. ***The past participle of the main verb is preceded by the appropriate form of the verb 'to be' (am, is, are, was, were, be, been, being), keeping in mind the number of the subject and the tense of the verb.***
5. ***By precedes the agent of the passive voice, if it is necessary.***

Note : We can, use another word in place of 'by' especially when the verbs express 'states' rather than 'actions' done by the agent; as–

	Active	Passive
1.	The result surprised me.	I was surprised at the result.
2.	The news shocked me.	I was shocked at the news.
3.	His manners pleased me.	I was pleased with his manners.

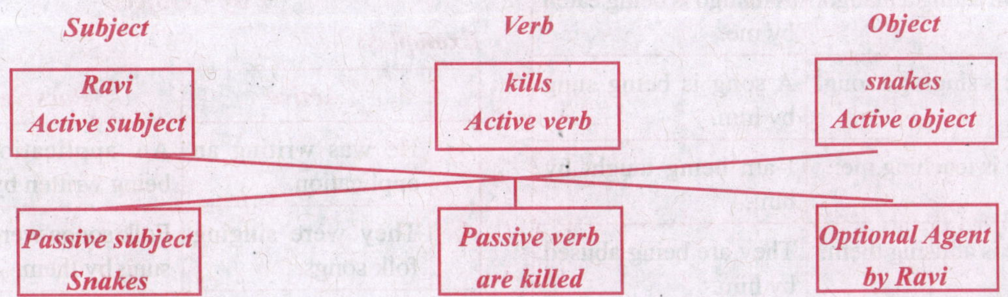

The passive of an active tense is formed by putting the verb 'to be' into the same tense as the active verb and adding the past participle of the active verb. You would do well to look at the table of active tenses and their passive equivalents.

Tense / Verb form	Active Voice	Passive Voice
Present indefinite	*keep / keeps*	*am / is / are kept*
Present continuous	*am / is / are keeping*	*am / is / are being kept*
Past indefinite	*kept*	*was / were kept*
Past continuous	*was / were keeping*	*was / were being kept*
Present perfect	*has / have kept*	*has / have been kept*
Past perfect	*had kept*	*had been kept*
Modal verb	*may keep*	*may be kept*

You have different formulas for conversion of the verb of active sentences into passive form. Here they are:

1. Present Indefinite Tense

Subject + am / is / are + V_3 + by / Preposition + Object

Examples:

	Active	*Passive*
1.	I sip tea.	Tea is sipped by me.
2.	I help the poor.	The poor are helped by me.
3.	He helps me.	I am helped by him.

2. Present Continuous Tense

Subject + am / is / are + being + V_3 + by + Object

Examples:

	Active	*Passive*
1.	I am eating a mango.	A mango is being eaten by me.
2.	He is singing a song.	A song is being sung by him.
3.	He is teaching me.	I am being taught by him.
4.	He is abusing them.	They are being abused by him.

3. Present perfect tense.

Subject + has / have + been + V_3 + by + Object

Examples:

	Active	*Passive*
1.	He has done this work.	This work has been done by him.
2.	She has helped them.	They have been helped by her.

4. Past Indefinite Tense

Subject + was / were + V_3 + Object

Examples:

	Active	*Passive*
1.	He wrote an essay.	An essay was written by him.
2.	He wrote several novels.	Several novels were written by him.

5. Past Continuous Tense

Subject + was / were + being + V_3 + by + Object

Examples:

	Active	*Passive*
1.	He was writing an application.	An application was being written by him.
2.	They were singing folk songs.	Folk songs were being sung by them.

6. Past Perfect Tense

Subject + had been + V_3 + by + Object

Examples:

	Active	Passive
1.	I had purchased a scooter.	A scooter had been purchased by me.
2.	They had invited me.	I had been invited by them.

7. Future Indefinite Tense

Subject + shall / will + be + V_3 + by + Object

Examples:

	Active	Passive
1.	I shall help Ravi.	Ravi will be helped by me.
2.	He will feed me.	I shall be fed by him.

8. Future Perfect Tense

Subject + shall / will + have been + V_3 + by + Object

Examples:

	Active	Passive
1.	I shall have helped him.	He will have been helped by me.
2.	He will have taught me.	I shall have been taught by him.

9. Verb 'to be'

Subject + Aux. Verb (is / am / are / was / were etc.) + to be + V_3 + by + Object

Examples:

	Active	Passive
1.	He is to invite me	. I am to be invited by him
2.	There is nothing to do.	There is nothing to be done.
3.	They are to sell the house.	The house is to be sold by them.
4.	They were to play the match.	The match was to be played by them.

10. Verb 'to have'

Subject + has / have / had + to be + V_3 + by + Object

Examples:

	Active	Passive
1.	You have to teach him.	He has to be taught by you.
2.	He has to feed the beggars.	The beggars have to be fed by him.
3.	She had to help me.	I had to be helped by her.

11. Sentences having may / can / could / should / must / etc. + Verb

Subject + may / can / could + be + V_3 + by + Object

Examples:

	Active	Passive
1.	He can teach you.	You can be taught (by him).
2.	She may win the match.	The match may be won (by her).
3.	He could fry fish.	Fish could be fried (by him).
4.	I must help her.	She must be helped (by me).
5.	I should please her.	She should be pleased (by me)

12. Sentences having Verb + Preposition + Object

Subject + Aux. Verb + V_3 + Preposition + by + Object

Examples:

	Active	Passive
1.	I will look after you well.	You will be well–looked after.
2.	She looks after the child.	The child is looked after by her.
3.	The police enquired into this case.	This case was enquired into.

13. Passive of Infinitives

If the active sentence contains infinitive (to + verb), its passive will be: Subject + to be + V_3

Examples:

	Active	Passive
1.	There is nothing to read.	There is nothing to be read.
2.	He is a man to rely on.	He is a man to be relied on.
3.	We have nothing to worry about.	We have nothing to be worried about.

14. Dummy "it"

If the active sentence starts with 'People think / acknowledge / know / consider / understand / believe / find / say / report / claim .... that he is', it can be changed into passive form in two different ways.

(i) Use the dummy subject "it".

It was thought ...... It was written ....

It was said .... It was declared ....

(ii) The subject of the noun clause in the active sentence is used as the subject of the passive form. Besides this to is used.

(iii) People say is replaced by It is saidd.

Examples:

1.	People say that he is miser.	*(a)*	It is said that he is miser.
		(b)	He is said to be miser.
2.	People thought that Mr. Ravi was	*(a)*	It was thought that Mr. Ravi was honest to a pie.
		(b)	Mr. Ravi was thought to be honest to a pie.

15. Verbs with two Objects

If the active sentence contains two objects (one direct object and the other, indirect) we can change it into the passive form by making either of the two objects the subject, considering which of the two objects is to be given prominence. Usually the indirect object of the active sentence is made the subject of the passive sentence.

Examples:

	Active		Passive
1.	He handed her a book.	*(a)*	A book was handed to her.
		(b)	She was handed a book.
2.	Our grandmother told us stories.	*(a)*	We were told stories by our grandmother.
		(b)	Stories were told us by our grandmother.
3.	The examiner will award you good marks	*(a)*	You will be awarded good marks by the examiner.
		(b)	Good marks will be awarded to you by the examiner.
4.	The bodyguard refused him admittance.	*(a)*	Admittance was refused him by the bodyguard.
		(b)	He was refused admittance by the bodyguard.

16. Passive of Commands

If the active sentence is imperative, it can be changed into passive form in three ways:

(i) If the imperative sentence denotes command, the passive form will start with Let.

Let + Subject + be + V_3

Examples:

	Active	Passive
1.	Open the door.	Let the door be opened.
2.	Switch off the light.	Let the light be switched off.
3.	Close the window.	Let the window be closed.
4.	Call the waiter on duty.	Let the waiter on duty be called.

(ii) If the imperative sentence denotes advice, its passive form will be like this:

Subject + should + be + V_3

Examples:

	Active	Passive
1.	Speak the truth.	Truth should be spoken.
2.	Love the children.	The children should be loved.
3.	Help the needy.	The needy should be helped.

(iii) If the active sentence contains Please / Kindly, its passive form will start with You are requested to. 'Please' and 'Kindly' should be dropped.

Examples:

	Active	Passive
1.	Kindly read this news item.	You are requested to read this news item.
2.	Please lend me rupees five hundred.	You are requested to lend me rupees five hundred.
3.	Please sit down.	You are requested to sit down.
4.	Come in, please.	You are requested to come in

17. Passive Of Yes – No Questions

The questions beginning with Do / Does / Did / Am / Is / Are / Was / Were / Has / Have / Had are called yes–no questions. If the active sentences contains yes – no question, we can change it into the passive form in the ways noted below:

(i) If the active sentence starts with Do / Does / Did, the form of passive sentence will be:

Am / Is / Are / Was / Were + V_3

Examples:

	Active	Passive
1.	Does he play tennis?	Is tennis played by him?
2.	Do they feed the poor?	Are the poor fed by them?
3.	Did you abuse him?	Was he abused by you?

(ii) If the question in the active sentence begins with Has / Have / Had, its passive form will be like this:

Has / Have / Had + been + V_3

Examples:

	Active	Passive
1.	Has Dick beaten you?	Have you been beaten by Dick?
2.	Have they won the match?	Has the match been won by them?
3.	Had he scored the winning goal?	Had the winning goal been scored by him?

18. Passive of Questions With Modal Verbs

If the question in the active sentence starts with modal verbs such as, Can / Could / Shall / Should / May / Might / Will / Would / Must / Ought etc., its passive form will be like this:

Modal Auxiliaries + be + V_3

Examples:

	Active	Passive
1.	Can we climb Mount Everest?	Can Mount Everest be climbed by us?
2.	Will they help you?	Will you be helped by them?
3.	Should he take the examination?	Should the examination be taken by him?
4.	Must you heckle him?	Must he be heckled by you?

19. Passive of wh – questions?

If the question in the active sentence begins with a question word (What, When, Where, How, They, Who, Which) the following steps be taken:

(i) Change the wh – question into yes – no question.

(ii) The passive question should be placed first.

Example:

Where did Suman buy the doll? (Active)

Where was the doll bought by Suman? (Passive)

Did Suman buy the doll? (Active)

Was the doll bought by Suman? (Passive)

Examples:

	Active	Passive
1.	When do they convene a meeting?	When is a meeting convened by them?
2.	Why do they shout slogans?	Why are slogans shouted by them?
3.	How did he win the prize?	How was the prize won by him?
4.	What did he teach you?	What were you taught by him?
5.	Who wrote 'Macbeth'?	Who was 'Macbeth' written by? OR By whom was 'Macbeth' written?

KEEP REGURGITATING

VARIEGATED EXAMPLES FINALIZED FOR UNDERSTANDING

	ACTIVE		PASSIVE
1.	One should keep one's promises	1.	Promises should be kept
2.	They made him the Vice-chancellor of this University	2.	He was made the Vice-chancellor of this University
3.	Nelson defeated the French fleet	3.	The French fleet was defeated by Nelson
4.	Srikant scored a breezy century	4.	A breeze century was scored by Srikant
5.	Somebody has switched the light off	5.	The light has been switched off
6.	Do not oppress the poor	6.	The poor should not be oppressed
7.	The girls were decorating the room	7.	The room was being decorated by the girls
8.	Where did Ramu sow those seeds?	8.	Where were those seeds sown by Ramu?
9.	People say that some ministers are involved in Bofors deal	9.	It is said that some Ministers are involved in Bofors deal
10.	They should not doubt my sincerity	10.	My sincerity should not be doubted
11.	There was no time to lose	11.	There was no time to be lost
12.	Why did he pass such a filthy remark?	12.	Why was such a filthy remark passed by him?
13.	Please pull that man out of trying situation	13.	You are requested to pull that man out of a trying situation
14.	Someone has picked my pocket	14.	My pocket has been picked
15.	It is time to take tea	15.	It is time for tea to be taken
16.	You cannot pump the ocean dry	16.	The ocean cannot be pumped dry
17.	We need sufficient money to complete this project	17.	Sufficient money is needed to complete this project
18.	What caused this accident?	18.	What was the accident caused by?
19.	We must obey our elders	19.	Our elders must be obeyed
20.	A truck ran over an old man	20.	An old man was run over by a truck
21.	He taught me how to dance	21.	I was taught how to dance

22.	We hope that they will succeed in their mission	22.	It is hoped that they will succeed in their mission
23.	The news of his success pleased.	23.	I was pleased with the news of his success
24.	How do they roast meat?	24.	How is meat roasted?
25.	He made them work hard	25.	They were made to work hard
26.	We saw them go out	26.	They were seen to go out
27.	I remember my father taking me to the salarjung Museum	27.	I remember being taken to the SalarjungMuseum by my father
28.	They called him a traitor	28.	He was called a traitor
29.	There is a lot of work to do	29.	There is a lot of work to be done
30.	Nobody can solve it	30.	It cannot be solved
31.	Do it now or never	31.	Let it be done now or never
32.	Who wrote "Gulliver's Travels"?	32.	By Whom was 'Gulliver's Travels written?
33.	Listen to me.	33.	I should be listened to.

VOICE IN DETAIL WITH ILLUSTRATIONS

1. PRESENT INDEFINITE TENSE

Passive Voice:- Is/am/are + 3rd Form.

Assertive Sentences

	Active Voice	*Passive Voice*
	[Ist form + s/es]	*[is/am/are + 3rd form]*
1.	He loves me	I am loved by him
2.	She lights the candle	The candle is lighted by her
3.	I do my duty	My duty is done by me
4.	They expect good news	Good news is expected by them
5.	We help the poor	The poor are helped by us

Negative Sentences

	Active Voice	*Passive Voice*
	[do not/does not + Ist form]	*[is/am/are + not + 3rd form]*
1.	The boys do not make a noise.	A noise is not made by the boys.
2.	She does not abuse you.	You are not abused by her.

Interrogative Sentences

	Active Voice	*Passive Voice*
	[do/does ← Subject → Ist form.]	**[Is/am/are ← Subject→ 3rd form.]**
1.	Do you eat meat?	Is meat eaten by you?
2.	Does she pluck flowers?	Are flowers plucked by her.
Note: If When/Where/Why/How before use helping verb before.		
3.	When do you eat your breakfast	When is your breakfast eaten by you?
4.	Why does he tell lies?	Why are lies told by him?
5.	How do you prepare tea?	How is tea prepare by you?
6.	Where does she keep her money?	Where is her money kept by her?
7.	What do you see?	What is seen by you?
8.	Which pen do you like?	Which peon is liked by you?
9.	Who abuse you?	By whom are you abused?
10.	Whom do you want?	Who is wanted by you?

EXERCISE – 1

Change the Voice:

1. My father helps me.
2. She gathers flowers.
3. He helps the poor.
4. You do not keep your word.
5. This officer does not punish his juniors.
6. I expect good news.
7. Children like toys and dolls.
8. She speaks English fluently.
9. Where do you keep your books?
10. How do you wash your clothes?
11. Who teaches you?
12. Whom do you like?
13. A lesson is learnt by me.
14. Letters are delivered by the postman.
15. Is this proposal liked by him?

2. PRESENT CONTINUOUS TENSE

Passive Voice :- is/am/are + being + 3rd form.

	Active Voice	*Passive Voice*
	[Is/am/are + Ist form + ing]	[is/am/are + being + 3rd form]
	[Is/am/are + not Ist form + ing]	[Is/am/are + not + being 3rd form]
	[Is/am/are ← Subject → Ist form + ing]	[Is/am/are ← Subject → being 3rd form]
1.	He is driving a car.	A car is being driven by him.
2.	She is watering the plants.	The plants are being watered.
3.	I am not running a race.	A race is not being run by me.
4.	Why are you abusing him?	Why is he being abused by you?
5.	What are they doing?	What is being done by them?

EXERCISE – 2

Change the voice:

1. He is plucking flowers.
2. I am making a kite.
3. They are watching the sports.
4. Are you helping the poor?
5. The farmers are not ploughing the field.
6. Why are you not given a test?
7. Who is feeding the baby?
8. He is speaking not a word.
9. She is not doing anything.
10. A meeting is being held.
11. She is being abused by them.
12. The prize are being given away by the Principal.

3. PRESENT PERFECT TENSE

Passive Voice: has/have + been + 3rd form.

	Active Voice	*Passive Voice*
	[has/have + 3rd form]	[has/have + been + 3rd form]
	[has/have + not + 3rd form]	[has/have + not + been 3rd form]
	[has/have + ← Subject → 3rd form]	[has/have + ← Subject → been + 3rd form]
1.	I have kept my promise.	My promise has been kept by me.
2.	She has not stolen my book.	My book has not been stolen by her.
3.	Have you taken medicine?	Has medicine been taken by you?
4.	Why have you wound the watch?	Why was the watch been wound by you?
5.	Who has torn this letter?	By whom has this letter been torn?
6.	What have you done?	What has been done by you?

EXERCISE – 3

Rewrite the following sentences in the Passive Voices:

1. She has confessed her fault.
2. He has misspelt the word.
3. I have received my transfer orders.
4. Have you spent all you money?
5. Has Mamata spoiled your clothes?
6. Who has broken the window–pane?
7. Why have you torn the letter?
8. He has cleared the account.
9. He has read a number of books?
10. How has he solved this sum?

4. PAST INDEFINITE TENSE

Passive Voice:- was/were + 3rd form.

	Active Voice	*Passive Voice*
	[2nd form did not Ist form]	[was/were + 3rd form]
		[was/were + not + 3rd form]
1.	Edison invented the first gramophone	The first gramophone was invented by Edison.
2.	The cat drank all the milk.	All the milk was drunk by the cat
3.	They did not expect me.	I was not expected by them.
4.	Did you make a noise?	Was a noise made by you?
5.	When did he do his home–task?	When was his home–task done by him?
6.	Where did you find the diary?	Where was the diary found by you?
7.	Which picture did you see last night?	Which picture was seen by you last night?

EXERCISE – 4

Change the voice of the following sentences:

1. Sohrab threw the ball.
2. He employed two hundred workmen.
3. They took no notice of me.
4. Pardeep flew a kite all day long.
5. She never disturbed me.
6. Why did you eat my share of sweets?
7. Who abused me yesterday?
8. No news was expected by us.
9. They were not beaten by the teacher.
10. Was a noise made by them.

5. PAST CONTINUOUS TENSE

Passive Voice:- was/were + being + 3rd form.

	Active Voice	*Passive Voice*
	[was/were + Ist form + ing]	[was/were + being + 3rd form]
	[was/were + not + Ist form + ing]	[was/were + not + being + 3rd form]
1.	The teacher was calling the rolls.	The rolls were being called by the teacher.
2.	The masons were not building the house.	The house was not being built by the masons.
3.	Was he revising his books?	Were his books being revised by him?
4.	Why were you wasting you time?	Why was your time being wasted by you?
5.	What was Veena doing?	What was being done by Veena?
6.	Whom were you abusing?	Who was being abused by you?

EXERCISE – 5

Change the voice of the verb in the following sentences:

1. She was ironing her clothes.
2. They were playing a game.
3. He was not plucking the flowers.
4. You were not writing a story-book.

5. Was Reena teasing the baby?
6. Why was the peon not posting the letters?
7. Whom were you abusing?
8. She was being abused by you.
9. His old parents were being served by him.
10. Not a word was being spoken by her.

6. PAST PERFECT TENSE

Passive Voice:- had + been + 3rd form.

	Active Voice	Passive Voice
	[had 3rd form]	[had +been + 3rd form]
	[had + not 3rd form]	[had + not been + 3rd form]
1.	They had bribed the clerk.	The clerk had been bribed by them.
2.	She had already taken the medicine.	The medicine had already been taken by her.
3.	I had not tasted this dish before.	This dish had not been tasted by me before.
4.	Had she posted the letter?	Had the letter been posted by her?
5.	Why had you disturbed him?	Why had he been disturbed by her?

EXERCISE – 6

Rewrite the following sentences in the Passive Voice:

1. The servant had posted the letter.
2. I had solved all the sums before ten.
3. He had already heard the news.
4. She had not written such a letter.
5. Had you ever seen the Taj before.
6. Why had he sold his books?

7. FUTURE INDEFINITE TENSE

Passive Voice:- will/shall + be + 3rd form.

	Active Voice	Passive Voice
	[will/shall + Ist form]	[will/shall + be + 3rd form]
	[will/shall + not + Ist form]	[will/shall + not + be + 3rd form]
1.	This little boy will post my letter.	My letter will be posted by this little boy.
2.	She will not sign these papers.	These papers will not be signed by her.
3.	I shall not speak a word to you.	Not a word will be spoken to you by me.
4.	Will you spend thirty rupees?	Will thirty rupees be spent?
5.	Why will she pay the bill?	Why this bill will be paid by her?
6.	What will you have for breakfast?	What will be had for breakfast by you?

EXERCISE – 7

Change the voice of the following sentences:

1. My uncle will pay my tuition fee.
2. She will help me with money.
3. Everbody will blame you.
4. He will not do any work.
5. I shall never forget.
6. Shall I ever forget those happy days?
7. When will the teacher give a test?
8. The toy will be broken by the baby.
9. I shall not be rebuked by the teacher.

8. FUTURE PERFECT TENSE

Passive Voicc: - will have + shall have + been + 3rd form.

	Active Voice	Passive Voice
	[will/shall have + 3rd form]	[will/shall have + been + 3rd]
1.	The patient will have taken medicine.	Medicine will have been taken by the patient.
2.	We shall have done our home–task.	Our home–task will have been done by us.
3.	He will not have abused me.	I shall not have been abused by him.
4.	Will you have revised your course by then.	Will your course have been revised by you by then?
5.	Who will have broken the chair?	By whom will the chair have been broken?

EXERCISE – 8

Change the voice of the following sentences:

1. He will have milked the cow.
2. She will have taken the test.
3. The peon will not have rung the bell as yet.
4. The farmer will not have watered the fields.
5. Who will not have spoken the truth?
6. Lunch will not have been eaten by her.
7. The letters will have been posted by him.
8. All the sums will have been solved by them.

9. VERBS FOLLOWED BY MODALS

(can, may, could, should, would, must etc.)

Passive Voice:- modal and 3rd form of verb.

	Active Voice	Passive Voic
1.	I can do this work.	This work can be done by me.
2.	He could not help us.	We could not be helped by him.
3.	You should obey your parents.	Your parents should be obeyed by you.
4.	Would you take a cup of tea?	Would a cup of tea be taken by you?
5.	May I help you?	May you be helped by me?
6.	Who will shut the door?	By whom will the door be shut?

EXERCISE – 9

Change the voice of the verbs in the following sentences:

1. We should respect our parents.
2. I can solve these sums.
3. You may use my pen.
4. She would not help you.
5. May I use your umbrella?
6. Where can we find such a leader?
7. What should she do now?
8. This lesson must be finished by you today.
9. Such a mistake cannot be committed by him.

10. IMPERATIVE SENTENCES

1. Let + new object + be/not be + 3rd form.
2. You are requested to/advised to/ordered to

Note: please/kindly remove.

	Active Voice	Passive Voice
1.	Shut the door.	Let the door be shut.
2.	Post the letter at once.	Let the letter be posted at once.
3.	Do not starve the cow.	Let the cow not be starved.
4.	Speak the truth.	Let the truth always be spoken.
5.	Please do me a favour.	You are requested to do me a favour.
6.	Kindly do not lose your patience.	You are requested not to lose your patience.
7.	Let him help his brother.	Let his brother be helped by him.

EXERCISE – 10

Chang the voice of the verbs in the following sentences:

1. Do it.
2. Ask him to come in.
3. Open the window.
4. Do not tell a lie.
5. Always help the weak and the needy.
6. Kindly grant me a leave.
7. Bring a cup of tea for me.
8. Love your country.
9. Please do this much for me.
10. Go to the market.
11. Let it not be touched.
12. Let us pluck flowers.

11. CHANGE OF VIOCE IN THE INFINITIVE VERBS

Infinitives to be verb 3rd form.

	Active Voice	Passive Voice
	to + Ist form	to + be + 3rd form
1.	We ought to respect our elders.	Our elders ought to be respected by us.
2.	There is no shop to let.	There is no shop to be let.
3.	I expect to finish the work in time.	I expect the work to be finished in time.
4.	I expect her to finish the work in time.	I expect the work to be finished by her in time.
5.	It is time to pay the fee.	It is time for the fee to be paid.
6.	It is time to pay the fee.	It is time for the fee to be paid.
7.	I am to do this work.	This work is to be done by me.

EXERCISE – 11

Change the voice of the verbs in the following sentences:

1. You ought to do your duty.
2. The peon has to post the letters every day.
3. she will have to do it.
4. It is time to say our prayers.
5. It is time to close the shops.
6. I expect you to forget this episode.
7. He was to drive the car.
8. We are to play a match in the evening.
9. It is necessary to write this essay.
10. It is time to register the names.

12. TWO OBJECTS OF THE VERB

Object Verb Object Subject

	Active Voice	Passive Voice
1.	He teaches us English.	We are taught English by him.
2.	We refused them admission.	They were refused admission by us.
3.	She has given me a message.	I have been given a message by her.
4.	I shall give her ten rupees.	She will be given ten rupees by me.

EXERCISE – 12

Change the voice of verbs in the following sentences:

1. She told me a wonderful story.
2. The teacher will give us a test.
3. Bring me a cup of tea.
4. Who teaches you English?
5. The booking clerk issued me a ticket.
6. I asked him a question.
7. She offered me a chair.
8. The hawker gave the wares a fancy name.
9. Some body gave her a box of chocolates on her birthday.
10. My uncle sent me a birthday present.

13. PREPOSITIONAL SENTENCES

Active voice verb Preposition Passive voice Preposition 3rd form of verb.

	Active Voice	Passive Voice
1.	They laughed at the blind man.	The blind man was laughed at by them.
2.	We thought over the problem.	The problem was thought over by us.
3.	He will look into the matter.	The matter will be looked into by him.
4.	She acceded to my request.	My request was acceded to by her.
5.	A car ran over a child.	A child was run over by a car.

EXERCISE – 13

Change the voice of the verbs in the following sentences:

1. We long for peace.
2. I am listening to you.
3. She objected to my proposal.
4. The hunter aimed at the bird.

5. She did not speak to me.
6. He acted upon my advice.
7. She agreed to my request.
8. Call in the doctor.
9. He is knocking at the door.
10. Beware of the pick–pockets.

14. WHERE 'BY' IS NOT USED

Learn by heart:

(i) alarmed at
(ii) annoyed at
(iii) contained in
(iv) disgusted with
(v) displeased with a person at behavior
(vi) lined with
(vii) married with a girl/to a boy
(viii) satisfied with
(ix) pleased with a person at behavior
(x) surprised at
(xi) offended with a person at behaviors

	Active Voice	*Passive Voice*
1.	She knows me.	I am known to her.
2.	Mohan married Rita.	Rita was married to Mohan.
3.	The news alarmed him.	He was alarmed at the news.
4.	His success surprised us.	We were surprised at his success.
5.	This bottle contains ink.	Ink is contained in this bottle.

EXERCISE – 14

Change the Voice of the Verbs in the following sentences:

1. This tumbler contains milk.
2. I know the reason of his success.
3. His victory surprised us.
4. This news will alarm you.
5. My work satisfied the teacher.
6. Flower–pots lined the whole path.
7. My behaviour offended him.
8. I am satisfied with your progress.

MISCELLANEOUS SENTENCES

	Active Voice	*Passive Voice*
1.	Sit down.	Be seated.
2.	One should keep one's promise.	Promise should be kept.
3.	She kept us waiting.	We were kept waiting by her.
4.	Some one has stolen my purse.	My purse has been stolen.
5.	A bridge was building.	A bridge was being built.
6.	They say honesty is the best policy.	It is said that honest is the best policy.
7.	The rose smells sweet.	The rose is sweet when smelt
8.	The students should respect their teachers.	The teacher should be respected.

RULES GOVERNING THE VOICE IN NUTSHELL AND THEIR USES

KEEP THESE RULES READY ON YOUR FINGER TIPS

1. PRESENT INDEFINITE TENSE

Assertive Sentences – A

	Active Voice	*Passive Voice*
	I Form of verb	Is, am, are + III form of verb
1.	She sings a song.	A song is sun by her.
2.	I love my parents.	My parents are loved by me.

Negative Sentences – B

	Active Voice	*Passive Voice*
	Do/does + not + I Form of verb	Is, am, are + not + III form of verb

1.	He does not obey his teachers.	The teachers are not obeyed by him.
2.	I do not cheat any one.	None is cheated by me

Interrogative Sentences – C

	Active Voice	*Passive Voic*
	Do/does + Subject +I Form of verb	Is, am, are + Subject + III form of verb
1.	Do you learn your lesson daily?	Is your lesson leant by your daily?
2.	Do he respect his parents?	Are his parents respected by him?

2. PRESENT CONTINUOUS TENSE

Assertive Sentences – A

	Active Voice	*Passive Voice*
	Is/am/are+(I form of verb)	Is, am, are + being +III form of verb
1.	He is reading a book.	A book is being read by him.
2.	She is cooking food.	Food is being cooked.

Negative Sentences – B

	Active Voice	*Passive Voice*
	Is/am/are + not + (I form of verb + ing)	Is, am, are + not + being +III form of verb
3.	I am not writing a letter.	A letter is not being written by me.
4.	He is not killing a snake.	A snake is not being killed by him.

Interrogative Sentences – C

	Active Voice	*Passive Voice*
	Is/am/are + subject (I form of verb + ing)	Is, am, are + subject + being +III form of verb
5.	Is the peon ringing the bell?	Is the bell being rung by the peon?
6.	Who is knocking at the door?	By whom is the door being knocked at?
7.	What is she reading?	What is being read by her?

3. PRESENT PERFECT TENSE

Assertive Sentences – A

	Active Voice	*Passive Voice*
	Has/have + III form of verb	Has/have + been + III form of verb
1.	He has killed a bird.	A bird has been killed.
2.	She has broken my slate	My slate has been broken by her.

Negative sentences – B

	Active Voice	*Passive Voice*
	Has/have + not + III form of verb	Has/have + not + been + III form of verb
3.	I have not broken your slate.	Your slate has not been broken by me.
4.	She has not washed the clothes	The clothes have not been washed by her.

Interrogative Sentences – C

	Active Voice	*Passive Voice*
	Has/have + subject + III form of verb	Has/have + subject + been + III form of verb
5.	Have you finished your homework?	Has your home work been finished by you?
6.	Has he told a lie?	Has a lie been told by him?
7.	Who has stolen my book?	By whom has my book been stolen?

4. PAST INDEFINTE TENSE

Assertive Sentences – A

	Active Voice	*Passive Voice*
	II form of verb	Was/were + III form of verb
1.	He flew a kite.	A kite was flown by him.

2.	She knitted a sweater.	A sweater was knitted by her.
3.	I slapped him.	He was slapped by me.

Negative Sentences – B

	Did + not + I form of verb	Was/were + not + III form of verb
4.	I did not like him.	He was not liked by me.
5.	She did not help me.	I was not helped by her.

Interrogative Sentences – C

	Did + Subject + not + I form of verb	Was/were + subject + III form of verb
6.	Did he meet you?	Were you met by him?
7.	Who killed the tiger?	By whom was the tiger killed?
8.	Whom did you help?	Who was helped by you?

5. PAST CONTINUOUS TENSE

Assertive Sentences – A

	Active Voice	*Passive Voice*
	Was/were + I form of verb + ing	Was/were + being + III form of verb
1.	She was reading a book.	A book was being read by her.
2.	I was doing my work.	My work was being done my me.

Negative Sentences– B

	Active Voice	*Passive Voice*
	Was/were + not + I form of verb + ing	Was/were + not + being + III form of verb
3.	He was not laughing.	She was not being laughed at by him.
4.	They were not obeying the teacher.	The teacher was not being boyed by him.

Interrogative Sentences– C

	Active Voice	*Passive Voice*
	Was/were + Subject + I form of verb + ing	Was/were + Subject + being + III form of verb
5.	Was she cooking food?	Was food being cooked by her?
6.	Who was watering the plants?	By whom were the plants being watered?
7.	What was she doing?	What was being done by her?

6. PAST PERFECT TENSE

Assertive Sentences – A

	Active Voice	*Passive Voice*
	Had + III form of verb	Had + been + III form of verb
1.	He had cheated me.	I had been cheated by him.
2.	She had borrowed my book.	My book had been borrowed by her.
3.	They had opened a shop	A shop had been opened by them.

Negative Sentences – B

	Active Voice	*Passive Voice*
	Had + not + III form of verb	Had + not + been + III form of verb
4.	She had not taken her.	Her breakfast had not been taken by her.
5.	We had not won the match.	The match had not been won by us.

Interrogative Sentences – C

	Active Voice	*Passive Voice*
	Had + Subject + III form of verb	Had + Subject + been + III form of verb
6/	Had he done his home–work?	Had his home work been done by him?
7.	Who had stolen my pen?	By whom had my pen been stolen?
8.	What had she done?	What had been done by her?

7. FUTURE INDEFINITE

Assertive Sentences – A

	Active Voice	Passive Voice
	Will/shall + I form of verb	Will/Shall + be + III form of verb
1.	I shall marry her.	She will be married by me.
2.	They will win the match.	The match will be won by them.

Negative Sentences – B

	Active Voice	Passive Voice
	Will/shall + Not + I form of verb	Will/Shall + not + be + III form of verb
3.	I will surely not help you.	You shall surely not be helped by me.
4.	She will write an essay.	An essay will not be written by her.

Interrogative Sentences – C

	Active Voice	Passive Voice
	Will/shall + Subject + I form of verb	Will/Shall + Subject + be + III form of verb
5.	Will he write a novel?	Will a novel be written by him?
6.	Shall I read your letter?	Will your letter be read by me?
7.	Who will open the door?	By whom will the door be opened?

8. FUTURE PERFECT TENSE

Assertive Sentences – A

	Active Voice	Passive Voice
	Will/shall + have + III form of verb	Will/shall + have + been + III form of verb
1.	I shall have helped you with money.	You will have been helped with money by me.
2.	He will have painted a picture.	A picture will have been painted by him.

Negative Sentences– B

	Active Voice	Passive Voice
	Will/shall + have + not + III form of verb	Will/shall + have + not + been + III form of verb
3.	He will not have sung a song.	A song will not have been sung by him.
4.	They will not have whitewashed the house.	The house will not have been white-washed by them.

Interrogative Sentences – C

	Active Voice	Passive Voice
	Will/shall + subject + have + III form of verb	Will/shall + subject + have + been + III form of verb
5.	Who will have done such a mischief?	By whom will such a mischief have been done?
6.	Will she have liked your brother?	Will your brother have been liked by her?

9. PASSIVE VOICE WITH MODAL AUXILIARIES

(can, could, may, might, would, should, must, ought to etc.)

	Active Voice	Passive Voice
	Modal Auxiliary + I form of Verb	Model Auxiliary + be + III form of verb
1.	I can help you.	You can be helped by me.
2.	May I use your pen?	May your pen be used by me?
3.	We could not catch the thief.	The thief could not be caught by us.
4.	You ought to obey your parents.	Your parents ought to be obeyed by you.
5.	He must obey me.	I must be obeyed by him.
6.	You should have rung the bell.	The bell should have been rung by you.
7.	I must look after my brother.	My brother must be looked after by me.

10. IMPERATIVE SENTENCES

(i) Imperative sentences are changed into Passive Voice by using 'Let' in the beginning of the sentence.

'Let' is followed by the object, 'be' and 3rd form of verb.

(ii) When an imperative sentence begins with 'Please' or 'Kindly, the sentence in the Passive Voice begins with 'You are requested' by the active infinitive.

(iii) 'You are ordered', 'You are advised' or 'You are forbidden' may be used in sentences having no object.

(iv) Sometimes 'Let' is retained in the Passive Voice.

	Active Voice	*Passive Voice*
1.	Shut the door.	Let the door be shut.
2.	Bring a glass of water	Let a glass of water be brought.
3.	Do not cheat any-body.	You are advised not cheat any body.
4.	Please lend me your book.	You are requested to lend me your book.
5.	Let us help the poor.	Let the poor be helped by us.
6.	Let Sheela marry him.	Let him be married to Sheela.
7.	Keep to the left.	You are advised to keep to the left.

11. PASSIVE VOICE OF SENTENCES WITH TWO OBJECTS

When a transitive verb has to objects either of them can be made the subject of the sentence in the Passive.

	Active Voice	*Passive Voice*
1.	He teaches me math-ematics.	I am taught mathe-matics by him Or Mathematics is taught me by him.
2.	He lent me books.	I am lent books by him. Or Books were lent to me by him.

12. VERBS FOLLOWED BY PREPOSITIONS

Rule: If a verb in the Active Voice is followed by a preposition, the preposition is retained in the Passive Voice. In addition, 'by' is used before the 'doer'.

	Active Voice	*Passive Voice*
1.	They laughed at the beggar.	The beggar was laughed by them.
2.	He agreed to my proposal.	My proposal was agreed to by him.
3.	Were the boys listen-ing to the teacher?	Was the teacher being listened to by the boys.
4.	Who called on you yesterday?	By whom were you called on yesterday?

13. VERBS IN PASSIVE FOLLOWED BY PREPOSITIONS OTHER THAN 'BY'

Rule: In some verb, a preposition other 'by' is used in Passive Voice.

	Active Voice	*Passive Voice*
1.	He knows me.	I am known to him.
2.	This box contains clothes.	Clothes are contained in this box.
3.	His sudden death shocked everyone.	Everyone was shocked at his sud-den death.

14. SENTENCES WHERE OBJECT IS MISSING

Rule: Where the object is missing one should supply a suitable object and then change the Voice.

	Active Voice	*Passive Voice*
1.	They say that God is omnipresent.	It is said that God is omnipresent.
2.	We believe that he is innocent.	It is believed that he is innocent.

15. ACTIVE INEFINITIVE AND PASSIVE INFINITIVE ACTIVE GERUND AND PASSIVE GERUND

	Active Voice	*Passive Voice*
	To + I form of verb	To be + be III form of verb
1.	It is time to reap the crops.	It is time for the crops to be reaped.

2.	He wants to buy a car.	He wants a car to be bought.
3.	He expects me to help.	He expects to be helped by me.

Gerund:

	Active Voice	*Passive Voice*
	I form of Verb + ing	Being + III form of Verb

1.	I remember your helping me in difficult.	I remember being helped by you in difficulty.
2.	I value your consulting me.	I value being consulted by you.

PRACTICE EXERCISE

EXERCISE – 15

Change into Passive Voice:

1. She sings sweet songs.
2. He helps his mother.
3. Who does not love his country?
4. Does she obey her parents?
5. He is building a house.
6. Why are you beating your brother?
7. Are the boys laughing at the beggar?
8. Are you writing a story?
9. He has written a novel.
10. I have bought a scooter.
11. Have you painted this picture?
12. The teacher has marked my answer book.

EXERCISE – 16

Change into Passive Voice:

1. They did not sell their house.
2. Did he lend you money?
3. I did not like his behaviour.
4. Was he selling oranges?
5. Who ate my apple?
6. Who was making the speech?
7. She was stitching a shirt.
8. He was waiting for you.
9. They had told a lie.
10. Had he followed your advice?
11. We had built a new house.
12. They had opposed me.

EXERCISE – 17

Change into Passive Voice:

1. I shall have finished this letter.
2. He will have written a story.
3. She will have cooked food.
4. I shall have lent you my books.
5. Will she have polished her shoes?
6. Will they have cheated their own friend?
7. The President will address the nation.
8. She will deliver a speech.
9. Who will solve your problem?
10. Will she wash your clothes?
11. I shall buy a new shirt.
12. She will stitch a frock.

EXERCISE – 18

Change the Voice:

1. I can cook food.
2. She must obey her husband.
3. We should serve our country.
4. He may lend you books.
5. They might help us.
6. We may win the match.
7. The hunters may kill the tiger.
8. Can this sum be solved by you?
9. The game may be won by him.
10. You do not cheat any body.

EXERCISE – 19

Change the Voice:

1. Never tell a lie.
2. Obey your teachers.
3. Enter by the left door.
4. Please help me.
5. Always respect your elders.
6. Let him teach her.
7. You are requested to sit in the front row.
8. You are ordered to stand on the bench.
9. Let them be looked after by their children.

EXERCISE – 20

Change the Voice:

1. I am amazed at his learning.
2. She looks after her brother.
3. He glanced at me.
4. The police is looking into the matter.
5. I congratulated my friend.
6. Who is knocking at the door?
7. The light was switched off by the servant.
8. Why are you mocking at your friend?
9. He was accused of murder by the police.
10. Why do you depend on your parents?

EXERCISE – 21

Change the Voice:

1. What is contained in this can?
2. What surprises you?
3. Her success amazed everyone.
4. Your failure in the examination has astonished everyone.
5. Your behaviour displease me.
6. His work satisfied his boss.
7. His remarks offended the teacher.
8. We were alarmed at the news.
9. Death of dear ones shocks everybody.

ANSWERS

EXERCISE – 1

1. I am helped by my father.
2. Flowers are gathered by her.
3. The poor are helped by him.
4. Your word is not kept by you.
5. His juniors are not punished by this officer.
6. Good news is expected by me.
7. Dolls and toys are liked by children.
8. English is spoken fluently by her.
9. Where are your books kept by you?
10. How your clothes are washed by you?
11. By whom are you taught?
12. By whom are you liked?
13. I learn a lesson.
14. Postman delivers the letters.
15. Do you like this proposal?

EXERCISE – 2

1. I am helped by my father.
2. A kite is being made by me.
3. The sports are being watched by them.
4. Are the poor being helped by you?
5. The field is not be ploughed by the farmer.
6. Why the test is not being given by you?
7. By whom is the baby being fed?
8. A word is not being spoken by him.
9. Anything is not being done by her.
10. The teachers are holding a meeting.
11. They are abusing her.
12. The principal is giving away the prizes.

EXERCISE – 3

1. Her fault has been confessed by her.
2. The word has been mis spelt by him.

3. My transfer orders have been received by me.
4. Has all your money been spent by you.
5. Have your clothes been spoilt by Mamta.
6. By whom has the window pane been broken?
7. Why the letter has been torn by you?
8. The account has been cleared by him.
9. A number of books have been read by him.
10. How this sum has been solved by you?

EXERCISE – 4

1. The ball was thrown by Sohrab.
2. Two hundred workmen were employed by him
3. No notice was taken of me by them.
4. A kite was flown by Pradeepall the day long.
5. I was never disturbed by her.
6. Why my share of sweets were eaten by you?
7. By whom was i abused yesterday?
8. We expected no news.
9. The teacher did not beat them.
10. Is they make a noise?

EXERCISE – 5

1. Her clothes were being ironed by her.
2. A game was being played by them.
3. The flowers were not being plucked by them
4. A story book was not being written by you.
5. Was the baby being teased by Reema?
6. Why were not the letters being posted by the peon?
7. Who was being abused by you?
8. You were abusing her.
9. He was serving his parents.
10. She did not speak a word.

EXERCISE – 6

1. The letter had been posted by the servant.
2. All the sums had been solved by me before ten.
3. The news had already been heard by him.
4. Such a letter had not been written by her.
5. Had the Tajbeen seen by you before?
6. Why his books had been sold by him?

EXERCISE – 7

1. My tuition fee will be paid by my uncle.
2. I will be helped with money by her.
3. I will be blamed by everyone.
4. Any work will not be done by him.
5. It will not be forgotten by me.
6. Will those happy days be ever forgotten by me?
7. When will the test be given by the teacher?
8. The baby will break the toys.
9. The teacher will not rebuke me.

EXERCISE – 8

1. The cow will have been milked by him.
2. The test will have been taken by her.
3. The bell will not have been rung by the peon as yet.
4. The fields will not have been watered by the farmer.
5. By whom the truth will not have been spoken.
6. She will not have eaten her lunch.
7. He will have posted the letter.
8. They will have solved all the sums.

EXERCISE – 9

1. Our parents should be respected by us.
2. These sums can be solved by me.
3. My pen maybe used by you.
4. You would not be helped by her.
5. May your umbrella be used by me?
6. Where such a leader can be found by us
7. What should be done now by her?
8. You must finish this lesson today.
9. He can commit such a mistake.

EXERCISE – 10

1. It should be done.
2. He should be asked to come in.
3. The window should be opened.
4. A lie must not be told

5. The weak and the needy should always be helped.
6. It is requested to grant me a leave.
7. You are requested to bring a cup of tea for me.
8. Your country must be loved.
9. You are requested to do this much for me.
10. You are ordered to go to the market.
11. Do not touch it.
12. Let the flowers be plucked by us.

EXERCISE – 11

1. Your duty ought to be done by you.
2. The letters have to be posted by the peon everyday.
3. It will have to be done by her.
4. It is time for our prayers to be said
5. It is time for the shops to be closed.
6. It is expected of you to forget this episode.
7. The car was to be driven by him.
8. A match is to be played by us in the evening.
9. This essay is necessarily to be written by someone.
10. It is a time for the names to be registered.

EXERCISE – 12

1. A wonderful story was told to me by her.
2. A test will be given to us by a teacher.
3. A cup of tea must be brought by someone for me.
4. By whom are you taught English?
5. A ticket was issued to me by a booking clerk.
6. A question was asked to him by me.
7. A chair was ordered to me by her.
8. The wares were given a fancy name by the hawker.
9. A box of chocolates was given to her on her birthday.
10. A birthday present was sent to me by my uncle.

EXERCISE – 13

1. Peace is longed for by us.
2. You are being listened to by me.
3. My proposal was objected to by her.
4. The bird was aimed at by the hunter.
5. I was not spoken to by her.
6. My advice was acted upon by him.
7. My request was agreed to by her.
8. The doctor should be called in.
9. The door is being knocked at by him.
10. We must be beware of the big pocketers.

EXERCISE – 14

1. Milk is contained in this tumbler.
2. The reason of his success is known to me.
3. We were surprised at his victory.
4. You will be alarmed at this news.
5. The teacher was satisfied with my work.
6. The whole path was lined with flowerpots.
7. He was offended at my behaviour.

EXERCISE – 15

1. Sweet songs are sung by her.
2. His mother is helped by him.
3. By whom is not his country loved?
4. Are her parents obeyed by her?
5. A house is being built by him.
6. Why is your brother being beaten by you?
7. Is the beggar being laughed at by the boys?
8. Is a story being written by you?
9. A novel has been written by him.
10. A scooter has been bought by me.
11. Has this picture been painted by you?
12. My answer book has been marked by the teacher.

EXERCISE – 16

1. Their house was not sold by them.
2. Was money lent to you by him?
3. His behavior was not liked by me.
4. Were the oranges being sold by him?
5. By whom was my apple eaten?

6. By whom was the speech made?
7. A shirt was being stitched by him.
8. You were being waited for by him.
9. A lie had been told by them.
10. Had your advice been followed by him?
11. A new home had been built by us.
12. I had been opposed by them.

EXERCISE – 17

1. This letter will have been finalized by me.
2. A story will have been written by him.
3. Food will have been cooked by me.
4. My books will have been lent to you be me.
5. Will her shoes have been polished by her?
6. Will their own friends have been cheated by them?
7. The nation will be addressed by the President.
8. A speech will be delivered by her.
9. By whom your problems will be solved?
10. Will your clothes be washed by her?
11. A new shirt will be bought by me.
12. A frock will be stitched by her.

EXERCISE – 18

1. Food cannot be cooked by me.
2. Her husband must be obeyed by him.
3. Our country should be served by us.
4. Your books may be lent by him.
5. We might be helped by them.
6. The match may be won by us.
7. The tiger may be killed by the hunter.
8. Can you solve this sum?
9. He may win the game.
10. Anybody should not be cheated by you.

EXERCISE – 19

1. A lie should never be told.
2. Your teacher must be obeyed.
3. You are advised to enter by the left door.
4. You are requested to help me.
5. Your elder should always be respected.
6. He should be allowed to teach her.
7. Please sit in the front row.
8. Stand on the bench.

EXERCISE – 20

1. His learning amazed me.
2. Her brother is looked after by her.
3. I was glanced at by him.
4. The matter is being looked into by the police.
5. My friend was congratulated by me.
6. By whom is the door knocked at?
7. The servant switched off the lights.
8. Why is your friend being mocked at by you?
9. The police accused him a murderer.
10. Why are your parents being depended on by you?

EXERCISE – 21

1. What does this can contain?
2. By what are your surprised at?
3. Everyone was amazed at his success.
4. Everyone has been astonished at your failure.
5. I am displeased at you behaviour.
6. His boss was satisfied with his work.
7. The teacher was offended by his remarks.
8. The news alarmed us.
9. Everybody is shocked at the death of dear ones.

CHANGE OF NARRATION (DIRECT & INDIRECT SPEECH)

Definitions. There are two ways of narrating something-

Let us take the following examples:

1. Satish said, "I am going to punish him."

2. Satish said that he was going to punish him.

In the first sentence, the exact words of Satish have been reproduced. This is called the Direct form of Narration.

In the second sentence the substance of what Satish said has been reproduced in the words of the narrator. This is called Indirect form of Narration.

Reported Speech. ***The exact words of the speaker which are put within the inverted commas are called the Reported Speech.***

Reporting Verb. ***The Verb that introduces the Reported speech is called the Reporting Verb.***

Rules of change of Narration from Direct to Indirect form

A. If the reporting verb is in the present tense (e.g., says, is saying, am/are saying or telling, has/have said, has/have been saying) or in the future tense (e.g., will/shall say, will be/shall be saying, will have/shall have said, will have been/shall have been saying), ***no change takes place in verb of reported speech.***

Examples:

1. Direct : He says, "I like coffee."

Indirect : He says that he likes coffee.

2. Direct : Shila will say, "life has been very hard."

Indirect : Shila will say that life has been very hard.

3. Direct : Ram has said, "This law does not hold good in this case."

Indirect : Ram has said that law does not hold good in the case.

4. Direct : Sheila has always been saying, "He is a big rogue."

Indirect : Sheila has always been saying that he is a big rogue.

5. Direct : Your mother will say, "the lure of lottery ruined his life."

Indirect : Your mother will say that the lure of lottery ruined his life.

B. ***When the reporting verb is in the past tense (e.g., said, was saying, were saying had been saying, used to say, etc.) the following changes take place in the reported speech:***

(i) Present Indefinite Tense

changes to

Past Indefinite tense.

(ii) Present Continuous Tense

changes into

Past Continuous Tense.

(iii) Present Perfect Tense

changes into

Past Perfect Tense.

(iv) Present Continuous Tense

changes into

Past Perfect Tense.

(v) Past indefinite Tense

changes into

Past Perfect continuous tense.

(vi) Past Continuous Tense

changes into

Past Perfect Continuous Tense.

(vii) Past perfect and Past Perfect Continuous Tenses do not change.

(viii) First form / + s, es

changes into

Second form.

Do / Does 1st form (Interrogative)

changes into

Second form.

Do/Does first form

changes into

did + first form

Assertive or Negative

Second form

changes into

had + third form

Is /am /are

changes into

was, were

Was / were

changes into

had been

Did + first form

changes into

had + third form

Will / shall

changes into

would / should

May / can

changes into

might / could

(ix) **Might, would, should, had to, ought to, had better,** used to remain unchanged.

(x) Words denoting nearness of time or position are replaced by corresponding words denoting remoteness or distance.

this	*is changed into*	***that***
here	*is changed into*	***there***
now	*is changed into*	***then***
ago	*is changed into*	***before***
last	*is changed into*	***the previous***
next	*is changed into*	***the following***
today	*is changed into*	***that day***
tonight	*is changed into*	***that night***
yesterday	*is changed into*	***the previous day***
tomorrow	*is changed into*	***the next day***

(xi) Reporting verb generally changes from "said to" into "told".

Examples:

1. Direct : He said, "Radha is coming for lunch today."

Indirect : He said that Radha was coming for lunch that day.

2. Direct : Rajesh said to him, "If the strike continues, the factory will have to be closed."

Indirect : Rajesh told to him that if the strike continued, the factory would have to be closed down.

3. Direct : He said, "The Principal was out of station yesterday but would come back today or tomorrow."

Indirect : He said that the Principal had been out of station the previous day but would come back that day or the next day.

4. Direct : She said, "If the students are treated leniently, they think they can befool teachers."

Indirect : She said that if the students were treated leniently, they thought they could befool teachers.

5. Direct : The tourist said, "The foreigners want to come to India, but they do not like the red tapism in the offices here."

Indirect : The tourist said that the foreigners wanted to come to

India, but they did not like the red tapism in the offices there.

6. Direct : He said, "Accidents have been happening very often on this narrow bridge, but the authorities are quite careless."

Indirect : He said that accidents had been happening very often on the narrow bridge, but the authorities were quite careless.

7. Direct : The secretary declared, "I cannot make any announcement because no decision has yet been made."

Indirect : The secretary declared that he could not make any announcement because no decision had yet been made.

8. Direct : The Principal said, "The authorities are trying their best to improve things."

Indirect : The Principal said that the authorities were trying their best to improve things.

9. Direct : Sheetal said to Subhash, "Things have improved a lot, but a lot more was expected."

Indirect : Sheetal said to Subhash that things had improved a lot, but a lot more had been expected.

10. Direct : He said, "The boss dismissed the sweeper because he did not like his work."

Indirect : He said that the boss had dismissed the sweeper because he had not liked his work.

Rules for the Change of Pronouns

Change of Pronouns of the First Person

Study the following examples carefully:

1. Direct : I said, "I have my own likes and dislikes."

Indirect : I said that I had my own likes and dislikes.

2. Direct : You said, "I have my own likes and dislikes."

Indirect : You said that you had your own likes and dislikes.

3. Direct : He said, "I have my own likes and dislikes."

Indirect : He said that he had his own likes and dislikes.

Now, a careful study of the above sentences reveals that pronouns of the first person are changed into the pronouns of the same person as the person of the subject of the reporting verb.

Change of Pronouns of the Second Person

Study the following examples carefully:

1. Direct : He said to me, "You should respect your elders."

Indirect : He told me that I should respect my elders.

2. Direct : He said to you, "You should respect your elders."

Indirect : He told you that you should respect t your elders.

3. Direct : He said to him, "You should respect your elders."

Indirect : He told him that he should respect his elders.

A careful study of the above sentences reveals that the pronouns of the second person are changed into the pronouns of the same person as the persons of the object of the reporting verb.

Change of Pronouns of the Third Person

Pronouns of the third person generally remain unchanged.

Examples:

1. Direct : He said to me, "He disobeys his father."

Indirect : He told me that he disobeyed his father.

2. Direct : Ram said, "Sita loves her friends."

Indirect : Ram told that Sita loved her friends.

3. Direct : I said to you, "His behaviour irritated his officers."

Indirect : I told you that his behaviour had irritated his officers.

So Remember:

First Person changes according to the subject.

Second Person changes according to the object.

Third Person does not change.

You can remember this easily if you keep in mind the following:

Aid to Memory: $\frac{\text{SON}}{123}$

Sentences having a Universal Truth.

If the reported speech expresses some universal truth or a habitual fact, its tense remains unchanged when the sentence is changed from Direct into the Indirect form of Narration.

Narration:

1. Direct : The teacher said, "Honesty is the best policy."

Indirect : The teacher said that honesty is the best policy.

2. Direct : Shesaid,"Twoandtwomakefour."

Indirect : Shesaidthattwoandtwomakefour.

3. Direct : Rita said. "Boys are usually stronger than girls."

Indirect : Rita said that boys are usually stronger that girls.

INTERROGATIVE SENTENCES

There are two types of Interrogative sentences:

(a) Sentences beginning with a word like 'What, When, Why, Where, etc.'

(b) Sentences formed by changing the position of the helping verb like 'Do, Does, Is, Am, Are, Was, Were, Has, Have, Had, Can, Could, May, Might, etc.'

Now here are the rules to be followed while changing these sentences into the indirect form of narration:

1. Change the reporting verb 'say' into 'ask', 'enquire' or 'demand' etc.
2. Change the question form into assertive form and remove the sign of interrogation (?).
3. Do not use any conjunction to introduce the reported speech in sentences belonging ***"to type (a) above" mentioned above.***
4. ***Use 'if' or 'whether',*** as conjunction to introduce the reported speech in sentences ***belonging to type (b) mentioned above.***
5. The conjunction 'that' is not to be used to introduce the reported speech.

Examples:

Direct to Indirect

1. Direct : He said, "Where are the boys ?"

Indirect : He asked where the boys were.

2. Direct : I said to him, "Where are you going ?"

Indirect : I asked him where he was going.

3. Direct : He asked, "Will you serve me faithfully ?"

Indirect : He enquired whether he would serve him faithfully.

4. Direct : Rattan said to me, ' Are you going to Shimla ?"

Indirect : Rattan asked me whether I was going to Shimla.

5. Direct : The mother said to her daughter, "Did you prepare the lunch ?"

Indirect : The mother asked her daughter if she had prepared the lunch.

Indirect to Direct

1. Indirect : He asked me whether I was successful in my attempt.

Direct : He said to me, "Are you successful in your attempt ?"

2. Indirect : I enquired of her what the matter was.

Direct : I said to her, "What is the matter?"

3. Indirect : I demanded of her if she wished to sit for the competition.

Direct : I said to her, "Do you wish to sit for the competition ?"

4. Indirect : The boy asked the principal if the college would remain closed the next day.

Direct : The boy said to the principal, "Will the college remain closed tomorrow ?"

5. Indirect : The commander-in-chief enquired if he would serve the country faithfully.

Direct : The commander-in-chief asked, "Will you serve the country faithfully ?"

IMPERATIVE SENTENCES

In order to change imperative sentences into the Indirect speech, proceed as follows:

1. Change the reporting verb into a verb denoting request or advice, etc., as the case is.
2. Change the verb of the reported speech into Infinitive mood.
3. In the case of negative sentences, place the negative 'not' before the infinitive.

Examples:

Direct to Indirect

1. Direct : My friend said to me, "Please accept this invitation."

Indirect : My friend requested me to accept that invitation.

2. Direct : The doctor said to the patient, "Give up smoking."

Indirect : The doctor advised the patient to give up smoking.

3. Direct : The young man said to his father, "Pardon me, sir."

Indirect : The young man begged his father to pardon him.

4. Direct : He said to me, "Wait there till I come back."

Indirect : He ordered me to wait there till he came back.

5. Direct : I said to him, "Don't worry about me."

Indirect : I told him not to worry about me.

6. Direct : The mother said, "Run away, children. Do not disturb me."

Indirect : The mother ordered the children to run away and forbade them to disturb her.

Indirect to Direct

1. Indirect : The mother ordered the servant to go and call the doctor.

Direct : The mother ordered the servant, "Go and call the doctor."

2. Indirect : He requested the visitor to take a seat.

Direct : She said to the visitor, "Take a seat, please."

3. Indirect : He ordered the servant to let the man come in.

Direct : He said to the servant, " Let the man come in."

4. Indirect : She advised me not to trust such a man.

Direct : She said to me, "Do not trust such a man."

5. Indirect : The mother ordered the children to get away.

Direct : The mother said, "Get away, children."

USE OF 'LET'

'Let' is used to make a proposal, to grant permission or to express some concession or contrast. Sentences involving 'let' are changed as follows:

1. Direct : He said to his friends, "Let us go out for a picnic."

Indirect : He proposed (or suggested) to his friends that they should go out for a picnic.

2. Direct : She said to Ruchika, "Let the servant come in."

Indirect : She ordered Ruchika to let the servant come in.

OR

She said to Ruchika that the servant might be allowed to come in.

3. Direct : He said to Rajiv, "Let me go on with my work, please."

Indirect : He requested Rajiv to let him go on with his work.

4. Direct : Ajay said, "Let her work ever so hard, she will not win a scholarship."

Indirect : Ajay said that she might work ever so hard she would not win a scholarship.

Conversion of Optative and Exclamatory Sentences

1. The optative and exclamatory form is changed into an assertive and dealt with accordingly.
2. The Reporting Verb is changed into some such verb or expression as 'wish', 'bless', 'pray', 'exclaim', 'declare', 'confess', 'disapprove', 'say in astonishment' etc., with such phrases, as 'with regard', 'with delight or joy', 'with sorrow' where necessary.
3. All interjections and interjectional phrases are omitted and a new word or phrase in the principal clause to express their meaning is supplied.
4. The conjunction 'that' is used to introduce the 'Reported speech'.
5. All other rules of change of pronouns and tenses are observed.

Remember:

(a)

Ho ! Hurrah! Hu! etc.	express	joy
What ! Oh! etc.	express	surprise
Bravo! Hear! etc.	express	approval
Alas! etc.	express	grief or pain
Hark ! Hush! Lo Behold! etc.	express	attention
Pooh ! Pshaw! etc.	express	contempt

(b) We wish Good morning, Good evening, Good night etc. and bid welcome, farewell, goodbye, etc.

Examples:

Direct to Indirect

1. Direct : She said, "What a lovely scene !"

Indirect : She exclaimed that it was a lovely scene.

2. Direct : The children said, "Long live our Grand Pa !"

Indirect : The children wished that their Grand Pa might live long.

3. Direct : She said, "Alas! I shall never be able to see him again."

Indirect : She exclaimed with sorrow that she would never be able to see him again.

4. Direct : The players said, "Hurrah ! We have won the match"

Indirect : The players exclaimed with joy that they had won the match.

5. Direct : "What a pity, you have been wasting opportunities !" he said.

Indirect : He regretted that I had been wasting opportunities.

6. Direct : She said to her friend, "Good morning! How do you do?"

Indirect : She wished her friend good morning and asked her how she was.

7. Direct : "So help me God !" the thief cried, "I will never steal again."

Indirect : The thief called upon God to witness and resolved that he would never steal again.

Indirect to Direct

1. Indirect : He exclaimed with joy that he had topped again.
   Direct : "Hurrah ! I have topped again," he said.
2. Indirect : She wished her friend good morning and asked her how she was.
   Direct : She said to her friend, "Good morning! How are you ?"
3. Indirect : The general exclaimed that it was shameful for a soldier to be afraid of fighting.
   Direct : "Fie ! A soldier and afraid of fighting !" said the general
4. Indirect : The old woman exclaimed with sorrow that she was ruined.
   Direct : The old woman cried out, "Alas! I am ruined."
5. Indirect : He expressed a strong desire for a glass of water.
   Direct : "O for a glass of water !" said he.

PRACTICE EXERCISE

EXERCISE – 1

Change the Narration:

1. The teacher says, "I am on leave."
2. Sunita says, "I am doing my home-work."
3. He will say, "I do not know you."
4. Your father will say, "Life was very hard during the war."
5. She said," India won freedom in 1947".
6. Rekha said," The First Battle of Panipat was fought in 1526."
7. You said," I am going home."
8. They said," We love our country."
9. Sanjay said to him," You have displeased your teacher."
10. I said to them, "You should take exercise regularly."

EXERCISE – 2

Change the Narration:

1. The small boy said to his tutor, "I had a German lesson this afternoon. So, I could not do my home-work."
2. Ram said to Sita, "You have never been in the forest. Life here is so hard that you will not be able to bear it."
3. He said, "We opened a branch of our firm here two years ago."
4. He said to his father, "You will be glad to hear that I have got through the examination.
5. "We have moved into our new flat, but we don't like it nearly so much as our last one," said my aunt.
6. I called my idle brother and said, "You must decide what you want to do."
7. The police alleged that Pritam had committed the murder.
8. The mother told her daughter that her father would be angry if she persisted in her ways.
9. He told the king that he had got the rarest gift for the princess and deserved to marry her.
10. The old man said to his son that man is mortal.

EXERCISE – 3

Change the Narration

1. "What can be done ?" said my father.
2. "Where is my book ?" said Ramesh.
3. I said, "Where shall I send the car ?"
4. He said, "Where do you want to go ?"
5. I said to my teacher, "Is this fair ?"

6. I enquired of the poor boy why he had wished he had been a king's son.
7. He asked me whether he promised to do as he was instructed.
8. I asked her whether she promised to help me.
9. The teacher enquired of the boy why he had forgotten that God helps those who help themselves.
10. I asked my mother if she had told me all that she wanted to tell.

EXERCISE – 4

Change the Narration

1. The father said to his son, "Go and post this letter."
2. The officer said to the peon, "Send the visitor in."
3. The widow said, "Please save me from ruin."
4. My elder brother said, "Let me finish my work today."
5. She said to them, "Let us go to see the fair."
6. They said to him, "Do not go about torturing others."
7. She said to me, "Let us go out for a picnic today."
8. I ordered my servant not to disturb me when I was busy.
9. The doctor advised the students to take exercise daily and to sleep with the windows open.
10. The prisoner begged the jailor to let him have a glass of water as he was feeling very thirsty.

EXERCISE – 5

Change the narration in the following sentences

1. He said, "O for a cup of tea !"
2. He said, "I wish I were a king !"
3. She said to me, "How charming Dalhousie is !"
4. "What a stupid fellow I have to put up with !" said Ito my room-mate.
5. The captain said, "Hurrah! My team has won the championship."
6. The children said, "May our teacher live long!"
7. The boy said, "Alas ! My mother has died."
8. The General applauded them saying that they had done wonders.
9. He confessed with regret that he had been very Simple.
10. The old lady prayed to God that she might live long.

ANSWERS

EXERCISE – 1

1. The teachers says that he is on leave.
2. Sunita says that she is doing her home work.
3. He will say that he doesn't know him.
4. Your father will say that life was very hard during the war.
5. She said that India won freedom in 1947.
6. Rekha said that the First Battle of Panipat was fought in 1526.
7. You said that you were going home.
8. They said that they loved their country.
9. Sanjay told him that he had displeased his teacher.
10. I told him that they should take exercise regularly.

EXERCISE – 2

1. The small boy told his tutor that he had a German class so he could not do his work.
2. Ram told Sita that she had never been in the forest. Life there was hard that she would not be able to bear that.
3. He told that they opened a branch of their firm there few years ago.
4. He told his father that he would be glad to hear this he had got through examination.
5. My aunt said that they had moved into their new flat, but they didn't like that nearly so much as that last one.
6. I advised my idle brother that he must decide what he wants to do.
7. The police said, "Pritam has committed murder."
8. The mother said to her daughter, "Your father will be angry if your persist in your ways."
9. He said to king, "I have got the rarest gift for the princess and deserve to marry her.
10. The old man said to his son, "Man is mortal."

EXERCISE – 3

1. My father asked what could be done.
2. Ramesh asked where was his book.
3. I asked where should I send the car.
4. He asked where did he want to go.
5. I asked the teacher if that was fair.
6. I asked poor boy, "Why has he wished, he has been a King's son".
7. He said to me, "Do I promise to do as I am instructed."
8. I said to him, "Does she promise to help me."
9. The teacher said to the boy, "Why he forgot that God helps those who help themselves.
10. I said to my mother, "Have you told me all that you want to tell."

EXERCISE – 4

1. The father ordered the son to go and post that letter.
2. The officer ordered the peon to send the visitor in.
3. The widow requested to save her from ruin.
4. My elder brother wished to let him finish his work that day.
5. She proposed that they should go to see the fair.
6. They advised him to not to go about torturing others.
7. She proposed to me that we should go out for a picture that day.
8. I said to my servant, "Do not disturb me when I am busy."
9. The doctor said to students, "Take exercise daily and sleep with windows open."
10. The prisoner said to Jailor, "Please give me a glass of water, as I am feeling thirsty."

EXERCISE – 5

1. He wished a cup of tea.
2. He expressed his wish if he had been a King.
3. She exclaimed with wonder that Dalhousie was charming.
4. I expressed with contempt that I had to put up with a stupid fellow.
5. The captain exclaimed with joy that his team had won the championship.
6. The children wished that their teacher lived long.
7. The boy expressed with sorrow that his mother had died.
8. The General said, "Bravo! You have done wonder."
9. He said, "Sorry! I have been very simple."
10. The old lady said to God, "May she live long."

24

CHAPTER

USE OF ARTICLES

THE USE OF ARTICLES

A, *an*, and *the* are called Articles. They are in fact, demonstrative adjective which point out to the noun that comes after them.

Functionally, they are Determiners because they determine, fix, restrict or define the noun coming after them.

1. Rahul wrote *a* letter to his sister.
2. *The* book is lying on the table.
3. Take *an* umbrella with you as it is raining.

In sentence 1, the article *a* modifies the noun letter by referring to it in a general way.

In sentence 2, *the* used before the noun book makes it a particular or specific book. The second *'the'* in this sentence modifies the noun table and makes it a particular or specific table.

In sentence 3, the article *an* refers, in a general way, to the noun after it: *umbrella*. In all these sentences, the articles are used to determine, fix or specify the nouns coming after them.

An article can also be used before an adjective if this adjective is followed by a noun. Consider the following examples.

4. Shivani is *a* beautiful girl.
5. Rahul is *an* intelligent boy.
6. *The* scenery of Shimla is *a* charming one.

In sentence 4 the article *a* comes before the adjective beautiful.

So do the articles *an* in sentences 5, and *a* in sentence 6.

But these articles are because of the nouns and not because of the adjective. This fact can be easily verified by removing the intervening adjectives.

Conversely, we can rewrite these sentences without using the adjectives and the nouns modified by them, but then we shall have to remove the articles also.

4 (*a*) Shivani *is* beautiful.

5 (*a*) Rahul *is* intelligent.

6 (*a*) The scenery of Shimla *is* charming.

Secondly, if an adverb comes before an adjective which is followed by a noun, the article is placed before the adverb:

4 (*b*) Shivani is a very beautiful girl.

5 (*b*) Rahul is a very intelligent boy.

6 (*b*) The scenery of Shimla is an extremely charming one.

In these examples too, though the articles come before adverbs, they are there because of the nouns and not because of the adverbs.

THE INDEFINTE AND THE DEFINITE ARTICLES

Articles are of two kinds: ***Definite and Indefinite.***

A and *an* are called Indefinite Articles because they refer in a general and indefinite way to the nouns that come after them.

1. A man was sitting in the shade of a tree.
2. An umbrella was lying on a bench in the park.
3. Give me an inkpot.

In sentences 1-3, the articles *'a* and *an'* refer to singular nouns in a general way. That is to say, all that the article *'a'* tells about man in sentence 1 is that ***this man is only one.*** Apart from this, there is nothing specific about this man. This is also true of a tree in this sentence. ***It is one tree,*** but we do not know if there is anything specific about it.

In sentence 2 the noun umbrella is proceeded by ***'an'***, ***which suggests one umbrella.*** Here again, there is nothing specific about this umbrella. Any umbrella will do. Again, in sentence 3 ***an inkpot*** virtually ***means any one inkpot.***

4. Where is the present that he brought for me?
5. What happened to the book I gave you?
6. The girl in blue jeans is my fiancés.

You note that the article *'the'* in sentence 4 refers to a particular present – ***the one that he brought for me.*** It is not any or every present.

In sentence 5, *'the'* refers to a ***specific book – the book I gave you.***

Again, in sentence 6 *'the'* refers to a specific girl and not any or every girl: she is my fiancée.

The second thing to note about the definite article is that it can be used with both the singular and the plural nouns, while a and an can be used only with singular nouns. Compare the following sentences.

7. Where is the pen that I gave you?
8. Where are the pens that we bought from the market yesterday?
9. I am thankful to you for the gift you have brought.
10. I am thankful to you all for the gifts that you have brought.

THE USE OF "A" AND "AN

As already mentioned, ***a*** and ***an*** are indefinite articles. They are used before singular nouns and they refer to these nouns in a general way. The choice between ***a / an*** is determined by the initial sound of the noun before which the indefinite article is used.

When the initial sound of a noun is a vowel sound (a, e, i, o and u are all vowels), we use an.

The indefinite article* a *is used when the initial sound is that of a consonant (all sounds except those created by a, e, i, o, u are consonant sounds).

THE USE OF THE INDEFINITE ARTICLE "AN"

Rule 1. As mentioned above, *'an'* is used before a noun beginning with a vowel sound (a, e, i, o, u or any variant of their sounds).

1. She gave me an umbrella as it was raining.
2. An egg a day is good for health.
3. I have bought an inkpot from the store.
4. Suman is an accomplished woman.

Note: If the noun requiring an article is preceded by an adjective or an adverb and adjective, the choice of ***'a or an'*** is made on the basis of the initial sound of that adjective or adverb.

1. He has bought an elegant car.
2. Rohit is an extremely hardworking boy.
3. Sudha is an unreliable woman.

Rule 2. If a noun requiring an article begins with a consonant but that initial consonant is either silent or unstressed, we use *'an'* before it.

1. Abhay is an honest worker. (Honest is pronounced as (onest.)
2. He was late by an hour. (Hour is pronounced as our.)
3. The rich old man is looking for an heir. (Heir is pronounced as air.)

THE USE OF THE INDEFINITE ARTICLE "A"

Rule 1. The indefinite article *a* is used before nouns which begin with a consonant sound (All letters except a, e, i, o, u are consonants and have consonant sounds if the initial consonant is silent or unstressed).

1. I found a novel lying on the table of his bedroom.
2. A bird in hand is worth two in the bush.
3. There was a woman behind the whole episode.

Note: If a noun taking an indefinite article is preceded by an adjective or an adverb + adjective, the article is used according to the initial sound of that adjective or adverb and not that of the noun. In case of a, the adjective or the adverb + adjective combination must begin with a consonant sound.

1. This is a costly inkpot
2. Prakash gave him a spoiled egg.
3. Ravi is a very honest man.

If the above sentences did not have adjectives/ adverbs before them, all of them would take *an* and not *a:*

1. This is an inkpot.
2. Prakash gave him an egg.
3. Ravi is an honest man.

Rule 2. If a noun begins with a vowel but the sound of that vowel is that of a consonant, we use a before it.

1. A university is a place of higher learning (University is pronounced as ***y university***).

2. A one-eyed man was staring at Shalini. (One-eyed is pronounced as *won-eyed*).
3. This may prove to a be a useful plan. (Useful is pronounced as *youseful*).

THE USE OF THE DEFINITE ARTICLE "THE"

The definite article the, unlike the indefinite articles a and an can be used before both singular and plural nouns. The main consideration is that there must be something specific about the noun which follows the, *the* definite article.

Rule 1. To refer to specific persons, places and things:

1. Put the book on the table. (*A specific book and a specific table; not any book and any table*)
2. The girl in blue jeans is my fiancée. (*one specific girl, the one in blue jeans*)
3. The boys who are sitting in the lawn have been detained. (Not all boys *but only those sitting in the lawn,* which is also a specific lawn.

Rule 2. To refer to a single noun when it is meant to represent the whole class:

1. The rose smells sweet. (*All roses smell sweet.*)
2. The cow is a very useful animal. (*All cows are useful animals.*)
3. The whale yields huge quantities of oil. (*All whales do so.*)
4. Child is the father of man.

Rule 3. Before a common noun which is unique, i.e., one of its own kind:

The sun, the moon, the earth, the universe, etc.

Rule 4. With names of rivers, canals, gulfs, straits, seas, oceans, groups of islands, deserts, bays, etc.

1. *The* Ganga, *The* Nile, *The* Godavari (all rivers)
2. *The* Persian Gulf, *The* Palk Straits, *The* Bay of Bengal (gulfs, bays, and straits)
3. *The* Arabian Sea, *The* Red Sea, *The* Indian Ocean, *The* Atlantic Ocean, etc. (all seas and oceans)
4. *The* Andamans, *The* Maldives, *The* Nicobars (all islands)
5. *The* Suez Canal, *The* Sirhind Canal, *The* Upper Bari Doab Canal (all canals)
6. *The* Thar Desert, *The* Kalahari Desert, *The* Sahara Desert (all deserts)
7. *The* Himalayas, *The* Vindhyas, *The* Alps (all mountain ranges)

Rule 5. With places which derive their names from geographical, historical, or political factors:

1. *The* Punjab, *The* Deccan Plateau, *The* USA, *The* United Kingdom, etc.

Rule 6. Before the names of epics and religious books:

1. *The* Iliad, *The* Mahabharata, *The* Ramayana (all epics)
2. *The* Bible, *The* Quran, *The* Gita, *The* Vedas (all holy books)

Note: But when the name of the author precedes such a book, an epic or a holy book, no article is used:

1. Valmiki's Ramayana, Jerome's Bible
2. Homer's Iliad, Milton's Paradise Lost

Rule 7. Before the names of newspapers, Journals, magazines, weeklies etc.:

1. *The* Times of India, *The* Tribune, *The* Statesman, etc.
2. *The* Readers' Digest, *The* Eve's Weekly, *The* Punjab Journal of History, *The* Quest, etc.

Rule 8. Before adjectives in their superlative degree:

1. This is *the best* book on history I have got.
2. Manish is *the most* intelligent boy in this class.
3. Suman is *the rarest* of the rarest blend of beauty and brain.

Rule 9. Before adjectives in the Comparative Degree when used in the following kind of constructions:

1. *The* more, *the* merrier.
2. *The* higher you go, *the* cooler it is.
3. *The* more he earns, *the* more his wife spends.

Rule 10. Before adjectives in their comparative degree when one of the two is referred to:

1. Suman is more beautiful of *the* two Godara sisters.
2. Rohit is better of *the* two students.
3. Karina is the more charming of *the* two actresses.

Rule 11. Before an adjective, that is used as a plural noun and stands for a class, section, or group.

1. *The* educated should help *the* illiterate.
2. *The* rich often detest *the* poor.
3. We should think of *the* welfare of *the* handicapped.

Rule 12. Before a proper noun when it is used as a common noun to indicate some special quantity associated with that proper noun:

1. Kalidas is said to be *the* Shakespeare of India (the greatest dramatist)
2. He boasts to *the* Sachin Tendulkar of his club.
3. Martin Luther king was described as *the* Gandhi of America.

Rule 13, Before a material noun when it is used as a common noun:

1. *The* wheat of the Punjab is superior to that of Haryana.
2. *The* milk of this cow is richer in quality than that of the black one.
3. *The* gold mine in India is very expensive.

Rule 14. Before a proper noun if it is modified by an adjective:

1. *The* great Gavaskar
2. *The* match-winning Tendulkar
3. *The* mercurial Sehwag
4. *The* sober Suman
5. *The* sweet Ruchika
6. *The* innocent Navjot
7. *The* stylish Kanni
8. *The* pure Anvi Singh

Rule 15. Before an abstract noun when it is used as a common noun:

1. *The* beauty of Kashmir cannot be compared with the beauty of any other valley.
2. *The* performance of Kapil Dev as a world-class bowler remains still unbeaten.
3. *The* integrity of Suman is just like the integrity of Caesar's wife.

Rule 16. Before numbers indicating order or position:

1. He was ***the last*** man in the queue.
2. You are ***the first*** person to call me dishonest.
3. You will find this information in ***the ninth*** chapter of this book.

Rule 17. Before a noun to give it the force or emphasis of a superlative:

1. Philosophy is ***the subject*** to study.
2. Sushmita is ***the beautiful*** woman in this city.

Rule 18. Before the names of a community, nation, or race:

1. ***The Jews*** are a well-knit race no matter where they live.
2. ***The Hindus***, like the Greeks, believe in many gods and goddesses.
3. ***The Rajputs*** consider themselves a martial race.

Rule 19. Before a common noun to give it the sense of an abstract noun:

1. ***The best*** in him enjoyed the sight.
2. ***The mother*** in her was moved to tears on the sight of the orphan.
3. ***The soldier*** in him could not remain a silent spectator to foul play.

OMISSION OF THE ARTICLE

It is very important to know the use of articles. But it is no less important to know when or where articles are not used. There are, in fact, many words which do not take any article before them.

Rule 1. No article is used before a proper, material, and abstract noun when such a noun is used in its own form and not as a common noun:

1. Mohit was hurt in an accident (No article before "Mohit" which is a proper noun.)
2. Beauty is said to be nine days wonder. (No articles before "beauty" which is an abstract noun "health" is an abstract noun.)

Rule 2. No article is used before the names of subjects, languages, arts, and sciences:

1. Physics, chemistry, philosophy, mathematics, economics, political science, etc. (*All subjects*)
2. English, Punjabi, Hindi, Sanskrit, Greek, Latin, Persian, etc (*All languages*)
3. Music, sculpture, painting, poetry etc. (*All arts*)

Rule 3. No article is used before the names of relations:

Mother, father, brother, sister, cousin, wife, husband, etc.

Rule 4. No article is used before 'school," "college," "hospital," "bed," "church," "prison/ jail/gas etc. when they are used or visited for the purpose for which they are meant:

1. She is still lying-in bed.
2. The patient has been taken to hospital.
3. I go to church every Sunday.

Note: But when these places/things are used for other purposes, they take an article:

1. I went to the school to deposit my son's fee.
2. He went to the prison to see his brother, who is a jailer there.
3. The mason went to the church to repair its damaged parts.

Rule 5. No article is used before plural nouns if there is nothing specific about them:

1. Women who drink make bad mothers.
2. Scientists believe in rational thinking.
3. Men, women, and children were passing through the streets.

Rule 6. No article is used before certain nouns which figure in certain propositional phrases:

At home, at night, by day, by train, by bus, at sunset, on earth, in jest, on horseback, underground, in debt, by day and night, etc.

Rule 7. No article is used before certain singular nouns when they form a part of phrase or consists of a transitive verb:

To set foot, to bring word, to lay siege, to set sail, to lose heart, to take offence, etc.

Rule 8. No articles is used before "man"," woman" and "child" even when they refer to the whole class.

1. Man is the maker of his own destiny.
2. Woman belongs to the fairer but the weaker sex.
3. Child is the father of man.

Rule 9. No article is used before nouns acting as subject complements when they denote a position held by only one man at time:

1. Dr. A.P.J. Abdul Kalam was elected President.
2. Rohit became principal of this school two years ago.

CATEGORY – 1

Fill in the blanks with appropriate articles, ***'a', 'an' & 'the', wherein none fits then write NOTA.*** (***NOTA means none of the given answers***)

SET – 1

1. ______ team of three brave climbed ______ Mt. Everest, ______ highest peak in ______ world.
2. I had not seen Anish for ______ long time and it was ______ surprise when I saw him at ______ doorsteps of my house.
3. At Brisbane, I stayed with ______ old friend and we had ______ great fun together.
4. ______ word to ______ wise is sufficient.
5. It is ______ pity that ______ opposition parties have not been able to forge ______ unity.
6. We will be travelling to Shimla by ______ road.
7. Nelson went to ______ sea at ______ early age.
8. ______ producer and ______ director of this movie has been honoured.
9. It was such ______ funny sight that we burst into ______ laughter.
10. It's ______ time for ______ school bell to ring. ______ children are getting impatient to go home.

SET – 2

Choose the correct alternative from those given below:

1. A. Man is social being.
   B. The man is social being.
   C. A man is a social being.
   D. Man is a social being.
2. A. Oranges are sold by the dozen.
   B. The oranges are sold by the dozen.
   C. Oranges are sold by dozen.
   D. The oranges are sold by dozen.
3. A. The Sri Lanka is to the south of India.
   B. Sri Lanka is to the south of India.
   C. Sri Lanka is to south of India.
   D. The Sri Lanka is to south of India.
4. A. Older the wine, stronger it is.
   B. The older the wine, stronger it is.
   C. The older a wine, the stronger it is.
   D. The older the wine, the stronger it is.
5. A. The day before yesterday he went to the Europe by air.
   B. The day before yesterday he went to Europe by air.
   C. Day before yesterday he went to Europe by air.
   D. The day before yesterday he went to Europe by the air.
6. A. The leader of the party walked out, and his followers followed suit.
   B. Leader of the party walked out, and his followers followed suit.
   C. Leader of the party walked out, and his followers followed a suit.
   D. The leader of the party walked out, and his followers follows a suit.
7. A. The whole system is corroded with the corruption from the top to the bottom.
   B. The whole system is corroded with corruption from top to bottom.
   C. Whole system is corroded with the corruption from the top to the bottom.
   D. Whole system is corroded with corruption from top to bottom.
8. A. Great many students who are at home in other subjects fail because of their poor performance in the English.
   B. A great many students who are at home in other subjects fail because of their poor performance in the English.
   C. The great many students who are at home in other subjects fail because of their poor performance in the English.
   D. A great many students who are at home in other subjects fail because of their poor performance in English.
9. A. The desire for wealth often tempts man to do evil.
   B. Desire for wealth often tempts a man to do evil.
   C. The desire for wealth often tempts a man to do evil.
   D. The desire for the wealth often tempts a man to do an evil.
10. A. He displayed wisdom and patience that would have done credit to Solomon.
    B. He displayed wisdom and patience that would have done a credit to a Solomon.
    C. He displayed wisdom and patience that would have done a credit to Solomon.
    D. He displayed that wisdom and patience that would have done credit to a Solomon.

SET – 3

Study the following pairs of sentences and write 'R' against the correct one.

1. A. What kind of a programme is this?
   B. What kind of programme is this?
2. A. This was only mistake he made.
   B. This was the only mistake he made.
3. A. You must be careful in future.
   B. You must be careful in the future.
4. A. I have more than a thousand rupee.
   B. I have more than thousand rupees.
5. A. He could not get work in spite of his best efforts.
   B. He could not get work in spite of his best efforts.

6. A. I invited him to dinner.
   B. I invited him to the dinner.
7. A. They made him a king.
   B. They made him king.
8. A. He went to hospital to meet an ailing friend.
   B. He went to the hospital to meet an ailing friend.
9. A. The man is mortal.
   B. Man is mortal.
10. A. English are a disciplined nation.
    B. The English are a disciplined nation.

CATEGORY – 2

SET – 1

Fill in the blanks with suitable articles in all the following sets.

1. I saw _______ snake in _______ grass.
   (*a*) in, the (*b*) the, in
   (*c*) a, the (*d*) a, in
2. _______ boy ran across _______ street.
   (*a*) the, to (*b*) the, at
   (*c*) a, to (*d*) a, the
3. I have waited for _______ hour.
   (*a*) an (*b*) to
   (*c*) in (*d*) none of these
4. It is _______ old house.
   (*a*) an (*b*) to
   (*c*) in (*d*) at
5. _______ moon is shining in sky.
   (*a*) a (*b*) the
   (*c*) an (*d*) none of these
6. I need _______ book of verse.
   (*a*) the (*b*) a
   (*c*) few (*d*) to
7. There is _______ big tree in front of _______ house.
   (*a*) an, the (*b*) the, an
   (*c*) to, an (*d*) a, the
8. Delhi is _______ capital of India.
   (*a*) the (*b*) a
   (*c*) an (*d*) none of these
9. It is _______ airy room.
   (*a*) a (*b*) an
   (*c*) the (*d*) none of these
10. _______ book on _______ table is new.
    (*a*) the, a (*b*) a, the
    (*c*) an, the (*d*) the, an
11. _______ old horse stumbles and nods.
    (*a*) an (*b*) a
    (*c*) the (*d*) none of these
12. Here I am _______ old man being read to by _______ boy.
    (*a*) an, the (*b*) the, an
    (*c*) an, a (*d*) a, an
13. _______ old man is like _______ tattered coat upon _______ stick.
    (*a*) an, the, the (*b*) on, an, the
    (*c*) an, on, the (*d*) the, on, with
14. _______ shepherd in _______ field is playing on _______ pipe.
    (*a*) a, the, the (*b*) on, the, an
    (*c*) an, on, the (*d*) the, on, the
15. He gave me _______ guava and _______ orange.
    (*a*) a, a (*b*) an, an
    (*c*) an, the (*d*) the, an

SET – 2

1. _______ Asia is a big continent.
   (*a*) the (*b*) a
   (*c*) an (*d*) none of these
2. _______ Deccan is in the South of India.
   (*a*) the (*b*) an
   (*c*) a (*d*) none of these
3. _______ Punjab is _______ land of five rivers.
   (*a*) the, the (*b*) a, a
   (*c*) the, a (*d*) none of these

4. _______ Times has _______ high reputation forreliable news.
(a) the, the (b) the, a
(c) a, the (d) none of these

5. _______ Narmada and _______ Tapti flow into_______ Arabian Sea.
(a) the, the, a (b) the, a, the
(c) a, the, a (d) the, the, the

6. _______ Vindhyas separate _______ Gangetic plain from _______ Deccan.
(a) a, the, the (b) the, a, the
(c) the, the, a (d) the, the, the

7. _______ Ravi left Singapore.
(a) the (b) a
(c) an (d) none of these

8. They started at _______ Pacific from _______ top of _______ Mountain.
(a) the, the, the (b) the, a, the
(c) an, an, the (d) none of these

9. _______ West Wind wakens _______ Mediterranean from its summer dream.
(a) the, an (b) the, the
(c) a, the (d) none of these

10. Do you read _______ Times of India?
(a) the (b) a
(c) an (d) none of these

SET – 3

1. If _______ gold rusts, what will _______ iron do?
(a) the, the (b) the, a
(c) an, the (d) a, an

2. She has _______ endurance _______ foresight_______ strength and _______ skill.
(a) the, an, a, the (b) the, a, an, the
(c) an, a, the, a (d) the, the, the, the

3. Keats tried to be _______ Milton of _______ Romantic age.
(a) the, the (b) a, an
(c) a, the (d) the, a

4. _______ tiger is _______ wild animal.
(a) the, the (b) a, the
(c) the, a (d) the, an

5. _______ milk in that bottle has become sour.
(a) an (b) the
(c) a (d) none of these

6. _______ coal of Jharia belt is very rich.
(a) the (b) a
(c) an (d) none of these

7. Beware of _______ fury of _______ patient man.
(a) the, the (b) a, an
(c) the, a (d) the, an

8. You should come here by _______ shortest route.
(a) the (b) a
(c) an (d) none

9. _______ donkeys are _______ stupid animals.
(a) the, the (b) the, a
(c) a, the (d) the, an

10. _______ girls do not often wear _______ hats.
(a) the, the (b) an, the
(c) the, an (d) none of these

11. _______ few students who read for _______ knowledge do not care for _______ results.
(a) a, the, the (b) the, the, the
(c) the, an, the (d) a, an, the

12. Only _______ few books should be chewed and digested.
(a) a (b) the
(c) little (d) none of these

13. _______ memory is _______ fond deceiver.
(a) the, the (b) a, the
(c) the, a (d) a, a

14. This is _______ finest song I have ever heard.
(a) the (b) a
(c) an (d) none of these

15. _______ happiness is _______ inner state of mind.
(a) the, the (b) a, the
(c) the, a (d) none of these

SET – 4

1. _______ young man was sent to _______ prison for hitting _______ old man on _______ head.
   (*a*) a, the, the, a (*b*) a, the, a, the
   (*c*) the, the, a, a (*d*) a, the, an, the
2. _______ youngest brother went to _______ school in _______ morning. I will go to _______ school now to fetch him home.
   (*a*) a, the, a, the (*b*) the, a, the, a
   (*c*) a, an, the, a (*d*) the, the, the, the
3. If _______ rich grow richer and _______ poor poorer, the country will go to _______ dogs.
   (*a*) the, the, the (*b*) a, an, the
   (*c*) the, a, an (*d*) the, an, a
4. _______ ship has come to _______ port _______ port has been recently repaired.
   (*a*) a, an, the, the (*b*) the, the, a, a
   (*c*) a, an, the, the (*d*) a, the, the
5. Not always is _______ race to _______ swift or _______ battle to _______ strong.
   (*a*) a, an, the, a (*b*) the, a, an, the
   (*c*) the, an, the, a (*d*) a, the, a, the
6. My mother went to _______ market and bought _______ pound of _______ sugar.
   (*a*) the, the, a (*b*) a, the, the
   (*c*) the, a, the (*d*) none of these
7. We should help _______ needy and not _______ affluent.
   (*a*) the, the (*b*) a, a
   (*c*) a, the (*d*) the, a
8. You should take _______ umbrella when you go _______ office because it may rain today.
   (*a*) the, a (*b*) a, the
   (*c*) an, the (*d*) the, a
9. _______ young and _______ old rejoiced at his success.
   (*a*) the, the (*b*) a, a
   (*c*) a, the (*d*) the, a
10. _______ crack troops went into _______ battle.
   (*a*) a, a (*b*) the, a
   (*c*) a, the (*d*) none of these

SET – 5

1. There is _______ garden behind _______ house.
   (*a*) a, an (*b*) a, the
   (*c*) an, the (*d*) the, an
2. _______ dog ran across _______ street.
   (*a*) the, the (*b*) the, a
   (*c*) a, the (*d*) a, a
3. We choose _______ knave or _______ eunuch to rule over us.
   (*a*) a, the (*b*) the, a
   (*c*) the, the (*d*) a, a
4. April is _______ cruellest month.
   (*a*) the (*b*) a
   (*c*) an (*d*) none of these
5. _______ eye for _______ eye and _______ tooth for _______ tooth, that was _______ old law.
   (*a*) the, the, a, an, the (*b*) the, the, an, an, a
   (*c*) the, an, an, a, the (*d*) an, an, a, a, an
6. Have you seen _______ Pope?
   (*a*) a (*b*) the
   (*c*) an (*d*) none of these
7. _______ people of _______ Deccan are hardy.
   (*a*) the, the (*b*) a, the
   (*c*) the, a (*d*) none of these
8. The cavalry rode into _______ battle.
   (*a*) a (*b*) the
   (*c*) an (*d*) none of these
9. I am going _______ market to buy _______ book.
   (*a*) a, an (*b*) the, a
   (*c*) a, a (*d*) none of these
10. I shall visit _______ prison to see _______ prisoner.
   (*a*) a, an (*b*) the, the
   (*c*) the, an (*d*) the, a

11. Life is ______ tale told by ______ idiot.
(*a*) a, the (*b*) the, a
(*c*) a, an (*d*) none of these

12. ______ sun rises in ______ east and sets in ______ west.
(*a*) the, the, the (*b*) a, a, a
(*c*) a, the, the (*d*) the, the, a

13. You should be kind to ______ old and ______ sick.
(*a*) the, the (*b*) the, a
(*c*) a, the (*d*) an, the

14. Drink ______ plenty of ______ water.
(*a*) the, the (*b*) a, a
(*c*) the, a (*d*) none of these

15. ______ water of ______ Caspian Sea is blackish.
(*a*) the, a (*b*) a, the
(*c*) a, a (*d*) the, the

16. How is ______ circle different from ______ ellipse?
(*a*) the, a (*b*) a, the
(*c*) the, the (*d*) a, an

17. We were on board ______ Maharajah.
(*a*) a (*b*) an
(*c*) the (*d*) none of these

18. Read ______ Times of India regularly.
(*a*) the (*b*) an
(*c*) a (*d*) none of these

19. I travelled in ______ third-class carriage in ______ company of some Americans who could peak ______ French.
(*a*) a, the, the (*b*) the, the, a
(*c*) the, a, the (*d*) a, the, a

20. ______ clouds over ______ sea are lovely in ______ morning.
(*a*) a, the, the (*b*) the, the, the
(*c*) the, a, the (*d*) a, the, a

21. At ______ dawn he got up and prayed to ______ God for help.
(*a*) a, the (*b*) the, a
(*c*) a, an (*d*) the, the

22. ______ honest man hates ______ liar.
(*a*) the, the (*b*) a, a
(*c*) the, a (*d*) an, the

23. ______ love is and was my lord king.
(*a*) the (*b*) a
(*c*) an (*d*) none of these

24. ______ earth has not anything to show more fair.
(*a*) the (*b*) a
(*c*) an (*d*) none of these

25. There is ______ fly in ______ ointment.
(*a*) a, an (*b*) a, the
(*c*) the, a (*d*) an, the

26. ______ poverty is ______ curse.
(*a*) a, an (*b*) an, a
(*c*) the, a (*d*) the, the

27. Blessed are ______ poor for they shall see God.
(*a*) the (*b*) a
(*c*) an (*d*) none of these

28. ______ camel is an ugly animal.
(*a*) the (*b*) a
(*c*) an (*d*) none of these

29. Have you come on ______ foot or by ______ bus?
(*a*) the, the (*b*) a, the
(*c*) the, a (*d*) an, the

30. If you go out in ______ rain without ______ raincoat on, you will catch ______ cold.
(*a*) the, a, the (*b*) the, the, the
(*c*) a, a, the (*d*) none of these

ANSWERS

CATEGORY – 1

	SET – 1	SET – 2	SET – 3
1.	A, NOTA, THE, THE	D	B-R
2.	A, A, THE	A	B-R
3.	AN, NOTA	B	A-R
4.	A, THE	D	A-R
5.	A, THE, NOTA	B	A-R
6.	NOTA	A	A-R
7.	NOTA, AN	B	B-R
8.	THE, NOTA	D	B-R
9.	A, NOTA	C	B-R
10.	NOTA, THE, THE	A	B-R

CATEGORY – 2

SET – 1		SET – 2		SET – 3		SET – 4		SET – 5			
1.	(c)	1.	(a)	1.	(a)	1.	(d)	1.	(b)	16.	(d)
2.	(d)	2.	(a)	2.	(d)	2.	(d)	2.	(c)	17.	(c)
3.	(a)	3.	(a)	3.	(a)	3.	(a)	3.	(d)	18.	(a)
4.	(a)	4.	(a)	4.	(c)	4.	(d)	4.	(a)	19.	(a)
5.	(b)	5.	(d)	5.	(b)	5.	(d)	5.	(d)	20.	(b)
6.	(b)	6.	(d)	6.	(a)	6.	(c)	6.	(b)	21.	(d)
7.	(d)	7.	(a)	7.	(c)	7.	(a)	7.	(a)	22.	(d)
8.	(a)	8.	(a)	8.	(a)	8.	(c)	8.	(a)	23.	(a)
9.	(b)	9.	(b)	9.	(a)	9.	(a)	9.	(b)	24.	(a)
10.	(a)	10.	(a)	10.	(a)	10.	(b)	10.	(d)	25.	(b)
11.	(a)			11.	(a)			11.	(c)	26.	(c)
12.	(a)			12.	(a)			12.	(a)	27.	(a)
13.	(a)			13.	(c)			13.	(d)	28.	(a)
14.	(a)			14.	(a)			14.	(d)	29.	(c)
15.	(a)			15.	(a)			15.	(d)	30.	(a)

PREPOSITIONS

INTRODUCTION

Preposition is a part of speech that governs a noun, pronouns, phrase or clause.

It has its position (pre-position) before a noun, pronoun or phrase. For example:

1. Ram came into my room.
2. The dog jumped upon the table.
3. I went to college.
4. He acted under compulsion.
5. A bridge was built across the river.
6. She sat beside me.
7. In compliance with his orders, schools were closed immediately.
8. Come to my home at seven o'clock.
9. He could not go to England on account of his marriage in September.
10. Leaves fell from the tree.

But sometimes, a preposition is placed after the word it governs. For example:

1. I need a house to live in.
2. Who are you talking about?
3. What is he aiming at?

PREPOSITION OF TIME

A number of prepositions may be used to denote time:

1. **from** Monday
2. **till** tomorrow
3. **after** my return
4. a quarter **to** ten
5. **during** the night
6. **before** 5 p.m.

I. At, on, in

1. **At** usually denotes a ***definite point of time*** but can also be used for ***indefinite periods***:

at 7 p.m., **at** this moment	definite points of time
at midnight	
at the end of the class	
at night; **at** dawn	indefinite periods
at Durga Puja;	
at Diwali	

2. **On** is used with ***days*** and ***dates***:

   on Monday;

   on 1st May;

   on the annual day;

   on a May afternoon.

3. **In** is used with ***parts of the day***, and with ***months, years, seasons***:

   in the morning;

   in September;

   in 2015;

   in winter

4. **In** is also used with the ***future tense*** to show the period in which an action will happen:

   in a week;

   in four hours

5. **In** and **within:**

   ➤ **In** = ***at the end of***

   ➤ **Within** = ***before the end of***

   I shall be back **in** a week. (when the week is over)

   I shall be back **within** a week. (before a week is over)

II. By

6. **By** refers to ***a point of future time*** and denotes the ***latest time*** at which ***an action will be over***:

The competition will be over ***by*** 6 p.m.

(It should be over before it is 6 p.m., but the latest time at which it can be over is 6 p.m.)

They will have declared the result ***by*** tomorrow evening.

III.For

7. **For** is used with ***periods of time*** to show the ***duration of an action***. It is mostly used with ***perfect continuous tenses*** though it may be found with other tenses as well:

   The discussion has been going to **for** two hours.

   I have worked in this office **for** two years.

   For may sometimes be omitted also:

   I have been busy the whole morning. (***for*** the whole morning).

IV.Since

8. **Since** marks ***the points of time at which an action began.*** It is used only if the action has continued till the time of speaking; hence it is found with ***perfect continuous tenses***. Unlike ***for***, it can never be omitted:

   She has been teaching in this college ***since*** 2015.

   A cool breeze has been blowing ***since*** morning.

V.From

9. **From** denotes the starting point of an action. It is used in all cases except invariably used with **to** or **till**:

   The examination will be held **from** 8 a.m. to 11 a.m.

   He was the Chief Minister of the state **from** 2009 to 2014.

PREPOSITIONS OF POSITION

Many prepositions may be used to define the position of one object in relation to another:

- **at** the table
- **in** the bed
- **on/ in** the chair
- **behind** the curtain
- **below** the surface
- **beside** the wall
- **under** the table
- **across** the field
- **near** Delhi
- **within** the house
- **along** the border
- **among** the bushes

Most important and easily confused among these are discussed below.

I.At, in

1. **At** has the idea of ***an exact point***. It used with ***houses, villages, small towns***. ***In*** has the idea of ***a larger area*** and is used while speaking of ***bigger towns, states, countries***, etc.

   at Karol Bagh;

   at Ambala;

   at the end;

   in New Delhi

   in England;

   in the middle.

2. **At** conveys the idea of a ***general neighbourhood***; **In** conveys the idea of ***something contained***:

   We sat **at** the table to take our lunch.

   Please wait for me **at** the Waves PVR.

   Turn left **at** the next crossing.

   There are two Pepsi bottles **in** the refrigerator.

   You will find the stapler **in** the drawer.

II.Between, among

3. **Between** means ***in the middle of two***; it may be two persons or things, or any two items from a larger group:

   A small table was lying ***between*** the two almirahs.

   He walked in the garden ***between*** the flowerbeds.

   Notice the use of ***between*** in:

   Between you and me, he is rather unreliable.

4. **Among** is used with ***more than two persons or things***:

The restaurant lay hidden **among** a group of high rising buildings.

Distribute the question paper **among** the candidates.

III. On, upon

5. On is used while speaking of things at rest; upon is used with things in motion:

The file is on the table.

The dog sprang upon the table.

IV. Above, over

6. Both **above** and **over** mean ***higher than***. Sometimes we can use either of them:

The flags waved **over** our heads.

The flags waved **above** our heads.

7. **Over** can also mean ***covering***, or ***vertically above***:

My father put a blanket **over** me.

There is a fan exactly **over** the table.

V. Below, under

8. Both **below** and **under** mean ***lower than***. Sometimes we can use either of them. **Under** can also mean ***vertically below***. It also has the idea of ***contact***:

There was a beautiful lake **below** us in the valley.

His shoes were lying **under** the table.

She put the keys of the wardrobe **under** her pillow.

VI. Above, over, below, under can all be used figuratively:

9. Above

His expenditure is **above** his income.

He is **above** partiality.

His name was **above** mine in the list.

10. Over

He is **over** forty years old.

I have no power **over** him.

I have no influence **over** him.

11. Below

He is **below** me in the office.

The number was **below** ten.

It is **below** your dignity to mix with such people.

12. Under

The road is **under** repair.

The people present in the meeting were definitely **under** five hundred.

Fifty persons work **under** him.

13. Beneath

Beneath also means ***in a lower position*** but is mostly used ***figuratively*** only:

She married **beneath** her status.

His actions are **beneath** contempt.

PREPOSITIONS OF DIRECTION

Prepositions of direction towards

These prepositions are: **to, towards, into, at, for, against.**

1. To, towards

To has the sense of ***destination***, **towards** of ***direction***:

He came **to** me to seek advice on a certain matter.

We went **towards** the site of the accident, but the police did not allow us to go very close.

2. Into

Into denotes ***movement towards the interior of something***:

He quietly walked **into** the conference hall.

One stream flows **into** another.

Figuratively: we have entered **into** an agreement to export handicrafts to some European countries.

3. At

At has usually the idea of ***aim***:

He threw a stone **at** the dog. (He wanted to hit the dog with a stone).

Compare:

(a) He threw a ball **to** the child. (The ball reached the child)

(b) He threw a ball **towards** the child. (He threw a ball in the direction in which the child was standing. The ball may or may not have reached the child).

(*c*) He threw the ball **at** the child. (He wanted to hit the child with the ball).

At is also sued with the following verbs figuratively: aim at, point at, smile at, throw at, laugh at, look at, jeer at.

4. **For**

For is used to denote ***direction*** when the verb shows the beginning of a movement:

The child leaves **for** the school at 7 A.m.

We shall soon set off **for** Mumbai.

5. **Against**

Against shows ***pressure*** or ***contact***:

He threw the goods ***against*** the wall.

We shall now discuss the relations expressed by some other prepositions. In some cases, they also include the relations of time, position and direction not covered earlier.

1.	**About** shows ***nearness of some kind:*** The bell is **about** to go. I was **about** to go to bed when he called on me. It also means ***concerning:*** He told us **about** his past experiences.
2.	**Across** means ***from one side to the opposite***, or ***on the opposite side of***: He swam **across** the river. There is a beautiful orchard **across** the fields.
3.	**After** denotes ***some kind of sequence***: I shall enter **after** you. The policeman ran **after** the robber. **After** all you have told me, I am convinced of the truth of your statement. The younger sister takes **after** the elder.
4.	**Against** shows ***opposition of some kind:*** Following this course of action will be **against** the rules. We must be adequately equipped ***against*** all foreign aggression.
5.	**Along** means ***in the same lien with***: There are several decent hotels ***along*** the mall road.
6.	**At** denotes ***proximity with actual*** or ***intended contact***: The cat rushed **at** the rat. Tomatoes are being sold **at** Rs.60 a kilo. We were **at** the dinner then. He is **at** the top of the class.
7.	**Before** means ***in front of***: The culprit was brought **before** the judge. It also denotes priority: Death **before** dishonor!
8.	**Behind** means ***at the back of***; it is the opposite of ***before***: They hid ***behind*** the curtain. The dog ran **behind** its master.
9.	**Beside** means ***by the side of***: His emptied purse was lying **beside** the door. It also shows ***irrelevance.*** All this discussion is **beside** the point.
10.	**Besides** means ***in addition to***: **Besides** these textbooks, I shall be needing a few reference books also.
11.	**Beyond** means ***out of, on the farther side of***: This is **beyond** my understanding. Our new college building is **beyond** the market.
12.	**By** shows ***nearness of some kind***: Let us sit **by** the seaside. **By** also denotes ***agency, manner, measure***: He was given this information **by** me. I caught hold of the chain snatcher **by** the neck. He is senior to me **by** a year.
13.	**Down** denotes ***descent***: Very cautiously we climbed **down** the hill.
14.	**For** denotes the following relations: ***Purpose:*** Walking is good **for** health. ***Reason:*** He was punished **for** theft. ***Extent:*** I had to walk **for** two kilometres to reach your place. ***On behalf of:*** I shall willingly fight **for** you. ***Exchange:*** He sold all his belongings **for** a petty sum. ***In spite of:*** **For** all his defects, I love him.

15.	**From** denotes ***source, inference and motive***: I borrowed a few rupees **from** my cousin. I can safely conclude **from** your account that he is quite reliable. He committed this murder **from** jealousy.
16.	**In** denotes ***rest in the interior of anything***: He is **in** a cheerful mood. He spent the whole of his life **in** poverty.
17.	**Of** means ***proceeding from, pertaining to, belonging to***: He died **of** heart attack. He often talks **of** you. One leg **of** this chair is broken. It also shows ***quality and comparison***: He is a man **of** noble character. The elder brother is more intelligent **of** the two.
18.	**On** or **upon** denotes ***rest on the upper surface of a thing***: I put my books **on** the table. He wrote an essay **on** the food problem of India. I depend **on** my father.
19.	**Than** denotes ***comparison or difference***: It is hotter in Delhi **than** at Shimla. None other **than** a qualified chartered accountant is eligible for this post.
20.	**Through** means ***across the interior of anything***: Bore a hole **through** this board. He has passed **through** many difficulties. I could seed **through** his trick. It also denotes ***motive:*** All this was done **through** jealousy.
21.	**To** shows ***proportion, limit, effect***, in addition to showing ***motion towards anything***: The chances are two **to** one. They fought **to** the last man. **To** their disappointment he failed.
22.	**Up** denotes ***motion to a higher place***: We climbed **up** the mountain.
23.	**With** mainly shows ***association, instrumentality***: He came back **with** his whole family. This stain can be removed **with** spirit. It also shows ***cause, manner, agreement***: He is confined to bed **with** fever. She treats her juniors **with** contempt. His views do not accord **with** mine.

PRACTICE SETS

CATEGORY – I

Fill in the blanks with suitable prepositions from SET – 1 to SET - 8

SET – 1

1. I shall be going to Musoorie _______ about a week's time for my training.
2. This annual function of the college will be held _______ Friday, the 23rd March _______ 4 p.m.
3. I have been having a tough time _______ the day I joined this office.
4. I shall wait for you _______ 5 p.m. _______ 6 p.m. _______ Sunday; I hope you will come.
5. He has been the Principal of this College _______ the last six years.
6. This term ends _______ 24th December, and _______ 21st all assignments should be completed.
7. A meeting of the review committee is held _______ the last day of the month.
8. I am always at home _______ a Sunday morning.
9. The second term begins _______ 16th July and ends _______ 24th December.
10. I have been looking after the welfare department _______ the day I became deputy manager.

SET – 2

1. It appears we have not met _______ ages. Have you been doing well?
2. He has been in the hospital _______ January.
3. He was in the hospital _______ January _______ March.

4. _______ the time the fire brigade arrived, the shop had been reduced to ashes.
5. Our shop has announced a clearance sale _______ Durga Puja.
6. The irritated manager shouted _______ the assistant.
7. Her face was so sweet that I could not keep my eyes _______ it.
8. Leaning _______ me, he told me a few startling secrets.
9. They ran _______ the scene of the crash to see what they could do for the wounded passengers.
10. Keep your dog _______ the flower beds. It might damage the flowers.

SET – 3

1. We have decided to hold our next meeting _______ my house _______ Model Town.
2. Can you distinguish _______ these two words?
3. The sound of the engine changes when a train passes _______ a bridge.
4. She does not like mixing with people _______ her.
5. _______ others, I have invited Sushil also.
6. His name was _______ mine in the list, so he was preferred for the job.
7. Two vehicles collided _______ the middle of the road.
8. Children often quarrel _______ a trifle but almost immediately patch up.
9. A person sitting _______ the back of the class tried to disrupt the lecture.
10. I was made to sign the letter _______ pressure.

SET – 4

1. The members of his family are always quarreling _______ themselves.
2. Allahabad is _______ Varanasi on the Ganga.
3. You are not entitled to vote as you are _______ age.
4. He is courteous, polite, gentle, but _______ all, he is very noble.
5. There are only a couple of pine trees _______ the top of the hill but many _______ the valley.
6. Understanding _______ the partners is very essential for a happy married life.
7. You should sign neither _______ nor _______ the stamp but _______ it.
8. We can make no progress if we continue working _______ these conditions.
9. The patient has been _______ treatment for _______ a week, but he has shown no signs of improvement.
10. I have always been _______ the impression that he was _______ this sort of meanness.

SET – 5

1. The Prime Minister is leaving _______ Washington D.C. tomorrow in the morning.
2. The crowd pressed _______ the fence.
3. He fell _______ his bike and got a nasty cut in the leg.
4. The two neighbouring countries seem to be moving _______ war.
5. The brave youth immediately jumped _______ the river to save the drowning child.
6. Be cautious, you aren't still _______ danger.
7. He threw a stone _______ the dog to scare it away.
8. Taking a knife _______ his pocket, he pounced _______ his enemy.
9. I have borrowed this book _______ one of my friends.
10. He shouted _______ him to come.

SET – 6

1. This novel is _______ a cancer patient who uses his positivity to cure himself.
2. I want to be active _______ the last breath _______ my life.
3. Climbing _______ a mountain is actually more difficult than climbing up.
4. There is a beautiful orchard _______ trees _______ the valley.

5. None other _______ you knows the truth.

6. He hid _______ the cupboard and recorded the whole conversation.

7. Above all, he is your friend, and instead _______ jeering _______ him, you ought to sympathise _______ him.

8. The child needs a lot of love _______ nutritious food.

9. He was _______ himself _______ rage when his friends teased him.

10. The school is far _______ the house and it is difficult _______ this little child to go there daily _______ foot.

SET – 7

1. Come and sit _______ me.

2. He married _______ money.

3. You ought to have been patients _______ the child.

4. Does he have much difficulty _______ his school work?

5. _______ all that has happened, I wash my hands _______ you.

6. We now expect improvement _______ the relationship _______ the police and the general public.

7. You can pay _______ cheque or _______ cash. Which one will you prefer?

8. _______ my opinion, too many advertisements are shown _______ the screening of a movie _______ television.

9. She was dressed _______ white _______ head _______ foot.

10. The police fired _______ the dacoit who was armed _______ the teeth.

SET – 8

1. He sat _______ the table to write a letter. (at, on)

2. We rested _______ a tree. (below, under)

3. She stared _______ me in anger. (at, on)

4. They have troubled us _______ the beginning. (from, since)

5. Throw the ball _______ your little brother. (at, to)

6. These articles are free _______ sales tax. (of, from)

7. I am tried _______ walking; I need some rest. (of, from)

8. I have never believed _______ his tall talk. (on, in)

9. I feel I should warn you _______ keeping an unlicensed gun. (for, against)

10. It is very rude to point _______ the point. (at, to)

CATE

Fill in the blanks with appropriate prepositions from the options given against each sentence in all the sets.

SET – 1

1. The point you spoke of will be attended _______. But if you ever touch _______ it again, I hope you will speak _______ length on the wider question _______ which that points hinges.

(*a*) to, at, on, upon (*b*) to, upon, at, on
(*c*) at, on, upon, to (*d*) upon, to, at, on

2. This is an exception _______ the usual rule. I hope, therefore, you make an exception _______ of my son's case and show some forbearance _______ his inexperience.

(*a*) to, of, for
(*b*) of, for, to
(*c*) for, to, of
(*d*) to, for, of

3. Live amenably _______ reason, and independently _______ other man's help.

(*a*) of, to (*b*) to, at
(*c*) to, of (*d*) at, of

4. It is better even to be blind _______ an eye, than to be blind _______ one's own fault.

(*a*) to, of (*b*) of, to
(*c*) at, of (*d*) of, at

5. He is committed _______ a policy which he now dislike and is not certain _______ success.
(a) to, at (b) at, to
(c) to, of (d) at, of

6. He is blessed _______ good health.
(a) at (b) the
(c) to (d) with

7. This ship is bound _______ India and is bound by contract to arrive at Calcutta _______ the 18th of July.
(a) for, on (b) at, for
(c) on, for (d) for, at

8. He is accountable to his master _______ the money.
(a) at (b) for
(c) on (d) with

9. I do no concur _______ you _______ that opinion.
(a) in, with (b) in, at
(c) with, in (d) at, with

10. The decision of the dispute is left _______ me; but I have not yet given my decision _______ the matter.
(a) on, to (b) at, to
(c) to, at (d) to, on

SET – 2

1. I was born _______ India _______ Delhi.
(a) in, at (b) in, to
(c) at, in (d) to, in

2. The moon rose _______ twelve o'clock _______ the night.
(a) in, at (b) at, to
(c) at, in (d) to, in

3. We knew him _______ a glance as soon as he came _______ sight.
(a) at, in
(b) to, in
(c) in, at
(d) at, to

4. He lives _______ Naddish _______ the province _______ Bengal.
(a) in, at, of (b) in, of, at
(c) at, in, of (d) at, of in

5. The boat was tied _______ the shore _______ a sailor _______ a rope.
(a) to, by, with (b) with, to, by
(c) to, with, by (d) by, with, to

6. The field was ploughed _______ a peasant _______ a pair of oxen.
(a) with, by (b) by, with
(c) by, to (d) to, with

7. The work must be done _______ twelve o'clock.
(a) at (b) to
(c) in (d) by

8. You must be back _______ a week _______ the present time.
(a) from, within (b) at, within
(c) within, from (d) to, from

9. No one has seen him _______ Thursday last.
(a) for (b) since
(c) to (d) at

10. I have not seen him _______ his last birthday.
(a) for (b) at
(c) to (d) since

SET – 3

1. He will not get home _______ sunset.
(a) before (b) by
(c) at (d) to

2. I shall be ready to start _______ two or three hours.
(a) at (b) to
(c) by (d) within

3. Take care _______ be back by midday.
(a) to (b) by
(c) in (d) at

4. I shall not be back ______ the end of the week.
(a) to (b) in
(c) at (d) by

5. He has been absent ______ home ______ Friday last and I do not think he will return ______ the 30th next month.
(a) since, by, from (b) from, by, since
(c) from, since, by (d) by, since, from

6. Let me see you again ______ an hour's time.
(a) at (b) in
(c) by (d) to

7. I shall have completed my task ______ tomorrow evening.
(a) by (b) at
(c) in (d) to

8. The train will start ______ forty minutes from now.
(a) to (b) the
(c) in (d) within

9. I have lived in Allahabad ______ 1st March.
(a) on (b) since
(c) by (d) to

10. I do not expect that he will be here ______ a week and I am certain that he will not be here ______ sunset today.
(a) before, within (b) before, to
(c) within, before (d) since, within

SET – 4

1. I was born ______ India ______ Mumbai.
(a) at, in (b) in, at
(c) in, to (d) to, at

2. I shall expect you ______ be here ______ four o'clock or at least ______ three hours from the present time.
(a) to, within, by
(b) to, by, within
(c) by, within, to
(d) within, to, by

3. He shot this bird ______ a gun.
(a) with (b) to
(c) in (d) the

4. He fell ______ a violent rage.
(a) with (b) in
(c) into (d) at

5. Come ______ my private room.
(a) at (b) with
(c) in (d) into

6. I have not seen him ______ the last three day.
(a) at (b) for
(c) to (d) in

7. You need not get up ______ 8 A.M., but you go to bed ______ nine P. M. at the latest.
(a) at, before (b) at, in
(c) before, at (d) before, in

8. He has been hard ______ work ______ sunrise.
(a) since, at (b) at, with
(c) with, at (d) at, since

9. He slept soundly ______ three hours running.
(a) in (b) for
(c) to (d) at

10. It rained ______ seven to twelve o'clock
(a) from (b) at
(c) with (d) in

SET – 5

1. You have not visited me ______ a long time past.
(a) at (b) in
(c) for (d) with

2. I have not heard ______ you ______ the last week.
(a) since, of (b) of, since
(c) at, in (d) in, since

3. I shall start ______ two hours.
(a) at (b) within
(c) into (d) with

4. I have lived _______ Calcutta for a year.
(*a*) at (*b*) with
(*c*) to (*d*) in

5. Call _______ me _______ an hour.
(*a*) in, on (*b*) on, in
(*c*) on, at (*d*) at, in

6. I live _______ London _______ No. 16, Trafalgar Squire.
(*a*) in, at (*b*) at, by
(*c*) at, in (*d*) by, in

7. I have had no rest _______ the last one hour.
(*a*) by (*b*) for
(*c*) at (*d*) in

8. He has been a lucky person _______ the day _______ which be began business, and I believe he will be lucky _______ the rest of his life.
(*a*) since, for, on (*b*) on, for, since
(*c*) since, on, for (*d*) for, on, since

9. Thirty men applied for help, but there was only a small sum to be divided _______ them.
(*a*) between (*b*) with
(*c*) into (*d*) among

10. Perfect confidence ought _______ exist _______ two such friends as we are.
(*a*) between, to (*b*) to, them
(*c*) to, between (*d*) to, by

SET – 6

1. The dog is lying _______ the floor, _______ the table.
(*a*) under, on (*b*) on, at
(*c*) on, under (*d*) by, to

2. There are some boats _______ the lake.
(*a*) at (*b*) in
(*c*) on (*d*) by

3. Tom is _______ the garden. He is looking _______ an aeroplane _______ the sky.
(*a*) in, at, in (*b*) at, in, in
(*c*) in, in, at (*d*) at, by, in

4. Mr Dick is sitting _______ an arm chair _______ the window.
(*a*) near, in (*b*) near, on
(*c*) on, by (*d*) in, near

5. The lottery is _______ x and z.
(*a*) between (*b*) to
(*c*) with (*d*) among

6. There is a cup on the plate. There is a knife _______ the side on the plate.
(*a*) to (*b*) at
(*c*) by (*d*) in

7. Mr Singh is standing _______ the board.
(*a*) with (*b*) by
(*c*) to (*d*) in front of

8. There are two apples _______ the basket.
(*a*) at (*b*) in
(*c*) by (*d*) to

9. There are sixty-minutes _______ an hour.
(*a*) by (*b*) at
(*c*) to (*d*) in

10. It is half _______ twelve.
(*a*) with (*b*) to
(*c*) past (*d*) by

SET – 7

1. I am going to put the tin _______ the oven.
(*a*) in (*b*) at
(*c*) to (*d*) by

2. Mr West is _______ the door.
(*a*) to (*b*) at
(*c*) by (*d*) in

3. She is _______ the kitchen.
(*a*) by (*b*) at
(*c*) to (*d*) in

4. She is cutting the cake _______ pieces.
(*a*) into (*b*) to
(*c*) with (*d*) by

5. The mirror is _______ the wash basin.
(a) in (b) above
(c) on (d) by

6. There is a row _______ book _______ the wall.
(a) of, on (b) on, of
(c) at, by (d) by, at

7. We are going _______ listen _______ the news.
(a) to, in (b) in, with
(c) to, to (d) to, with

8. Each horse has a number _______ its side.
(a) by (b) to
(c) in (d) on

9. I don't know anything _______ this book.
(a) with (b) about
(c) of (d) in

10. What are the names _______ the other horses _______ the race?
(a) of, in (b) of, to
(c) in, of (d) to, by

SET – 8

1. The horses are not _______ grand stand.
(a) with (b) in
(c) in front of the (d) on

2. Mr Bose is sitting _______ the table _______ his wife and his sons.
(a) between, at (b) at, by
(c) at, between (d) by, between

3. Do you go to work _______ bus?
(a) at (b) by
(c) in (d) with

4. Has the train arrived _______ the station?
(a) at (b) to
(c) in (d) with

5. I am putting the letter _______ the envelope?
(a) to (b) into
(c) in (d) by

6. Frank's plane crashed into the sea. Did he escape _______ the plane? The helicopter will reach Frank _______ few minutes. Frank was _______ the water for several minutes. He had to answer question _______ or _______ the crash.
(a) from, about, on, in, in
(b) about, in, on, from, in
(c) from, in, in, about, on
(d) in, from, about, in, on

7. He washed his hands in the stream _______ the side of the road.
(a) at (b) in
(c) by (d) with

8. This is a photograph _______ a girl who stayed _______ a hotel in London.
(a) of, in (b) at, of
(c) of, by (d) of, at

9. I am fond _______ reading. I have time _______ reading.
(a) for, of (b) for, at
(c) of, for (d) by, in

10. Ram put the spare wheel _______ then he put the tools _______ in the car.
(a) away, on (b) on, away
(c) away, in (d) in, on

SET – 9

1. Sometimes she turns _______ the radio and listens _______ BBC programmes _______ Spanish.
(a) to, in, on (b) in, on, to
(c) on, to, in (d) on, in, to

2. Everyone pus food _______ for the birds when there is snow _______ the ground.
(a) on, away (b) on, to
(c) to, away (d) away, on

3. The answers are given _______ the end of the book.
(a) in (b) at
(c) to (d) by

4. Let us go _______ a walk _______ the country side.
(*a*) for, in (*b*) in, for
(*c*) at, for (*d*) for, at

5. He likes problems that are _______ the form of short stories.
(*a*) at (*b*) by
(*c*) in (*d*) to

6. You can find the answer _______ this problem _______ several ways.
(*a*) in, to (*b*) to, in
(*c*) to, at (*d*) at, in

7. I read this book _______ beginning to end _______ three hours.
(*a*) from, in (*b*) in, from
(*c*) in, to (*d*) from, to

8. Who's going to pay _______ the records? How much do you spend _______ records?
(*a*) on, for (*b*) for, on
(*c*) for, at (*d*) at, on

9. They looked _______ the motor cars as they walked _______ the street.
(*a*) in, at (*b*) at, to
(*c*) at, in (*d*) by, in

10. Burglars break _______ houses at night, while the people _______ them are asleep.
(*a*) into, in (*b*) in, into
(*c*) at, in (*d*) into, at

SET – 10

1. The Times has a high reputation _______ reliable news.
(*a*) at (*b*) by
(*c*) for (*d*) on

2. The evening reports are _______ sale.
(*a*) at (*b*) on
(*c*) by (*d*) in

3. Newspapers can be bought _______ many street corners.
(*a*) in (*b*) on
(*c*) at (*d*) with

4. Do you bet _______ horse races.
(*a*) on (*b*) at
(*c*) in (*d*) by

5. This shop has no connection _______ the shop next door.
(*a*) on (*b*) with
(*c*) in (*d*) at

6. This cannot be sold _______ a profit without the money received from advertisement.
(*a*) to (*b*) at
(*c*) in (*d*) the

7. This article is _______ the latest fashions in clothes.
(*a*) for (*b*) By
(*c*) at (*d*) about

8. Do you prefer entertainment _______ information?
(*a*) to (*b*) in
(*c*) by (*d*) at

9. In addition _______ the London papers, there are many provincial papers.
(*a*) to (*b*) with
(*c*) in (*d*) by

10. These sell in competition _______ the London papers.
(*a*) in (*b*) to
(*c*) at (*d*) with

SET – 11

1. Help yourself _______ anything you want.
(*a*) to (*b*) by
(*c*) in (*d*) at

2. The sun keeps us warm _______ summer.
(*a*) at (*b*) with
(*c*) through (*d*) in

3. Open your mouth wide so that I may look _______ it.
(*a*) at (*b*) into
(*c*) in (*d*) by

4. The cold weather turned the leaves dry _______ trees.
(a) in (b) at
(c) on (d) by

5. Shall we paint the doors and windows green _______ show.
(a) for (b) in
(c) by (d) the

6. You've made your shoes dirty _______ the mud.
(a) in (b) with
(c) the (d) at

7. I have been looking _______ you.
(a) by (b) in
(c) to (d) for

8. Do you approve _______ lipstick?
(a) at (b) in
(c) of (d) by

9. How much does your firm spend _______ advertisements?
(a) in (b) on
(c) at (d) by

10. Shall we try selling it _______ a higher price?
(a) in (b) by
(c) to (d) at

SET – 12

1. Do the advertisements interfere _______ the programmes?
(a) with (b) by
(c) at (d) in

2. What kind of books are you interested _______?
(a) to (b) by
(c) in (d) at

3. Do you try to keep up _______ your neighbours?
(a) with
(b) to
(c) in
(d) at

4. That is a question you must decide _______ yourself.
(a) at (b) by
(c) for (d) in

5. What's the French word _______ wrist?
(a) at (b) for
(c) to (d) by

6. Do you ever walk _______ your sleep?
(a) at (b) to
(c) by (d) in

7. Dover is _______ the south coast.
(a) on (b) in
(c) with (d) at

8. The pilot flies _______ silence.
(a) to (b) in
(c) the (d) at

9. Are you making good progress _______ your study of English?
(a) to (b) by
(c) in (d) at

10. I am trying to catch _______ with my letter-writing.
(a) up (b) to
(c) by (d) at

SET – 13

1. I like to keep books _______ which I find enjoyment.
(a) at (b) in
(c) by (d) to

2. What is the increase in the cost _______ living since 1939.
(a) in (b) at
(c) of (d) by

3. Please, do not blame the accident _______ me.
(a) on
(b) in
(c) by
(d) at

4. Why do you blame me _______ what has happened?
(*a*) at (*b*) for
(*c*) in (*d*) by

5. Her employer finds fault _______ her.
(*a*) at (*b*) for
(*c*) with (*d*) in

6. How old must a child be _______ it is legally responsible _______ what it does?
(*a*) before, for (*b*) for, before
(*c*) at, for (*d*) at, before

7. _______ whom is the prime minister chosen and of whom is he responsible?
(*a*) in (*b*) at
(*c*) by (*d*) to

8. No one familiar _______ the facts will doubt.
(*a*) to (*b*) with
(*c*) at (*d*) in

9. The name is familiar _______ me.
(*a*) with (*b*) to
(*c*) in (*d*) at

10. The city of London is _______ one square mile in area.
(*a*) about (*b*) on
(*c*) with (*d*) by

SET – 14

1. Have you ever been _______ love?
(*a*) by (*b*) at
(*c*) in (*d*) to

2. My Greek Friends reads English books _______ ease, but has some difficulty _______ understanding broadcast talk in English.
(*a*) with, in (*b*) in, with
(*c*) at, in (*d*) with, at

3. The part of the Thames called pool is _______ London Bridge.
(*a*) over (*b*) under
(*c*) in (*d*) on

4. Mr Green has left London _______ Paris.
(*a*) in (*b*) at
(*c*) to (*d*) for

5. Trams disappeared _______ the streets of London several years ago.
(*a*) to (*b*) on
(*c*) from (*d*) for

6. He is in some way or other connected _______ journalism.
(*a*) with (*b*) to
(*c*) by (*d*) in

7. The boat trains _______ London to Dover run in connection _______ the steamers from Dover to Calais.
(*a*) with, from (*b*) from, to
(*c*) from, with (*d*) to, with

8. Scotland is to the north of England. Glasgow is _______ the river Clyde.
(*a*) in (*b*) on
(*c*) at (*d*) by

9. I have much experience _______ sickness, but none _______ curing them. He guesses _______ his answers: for he has genius for mathematics; in fact, he is not a genius _______ anything.
(*a*) of, at, in, to (*b*) of, at, in, in
(*c*) of, in, at, in (*d*) in, at, of, in

10. In old times an incursion was made _______ England _______ the Danes who at first were more than a match _______ the Saxon.
(*a*) by, for, into
(*b*) into, for, by
(*c*) for, into, by
(*d*) into, by for

SET – 15

1. Abstain _______ alcohol. It's dangerous _______ you in your condition.
(*a*) from, to (*b*) to, from
(*c*) to, with (*d*) to, by

2. I suggest we adjourn to billiard room _______ further discussion on subjects _______ considerations.

(*a*) under, for (*b*) for, to

(*c*) for, under (*d*) for, with

3. Our newspaper aims _______ having million readers by next year.

(*a*) with (*b*) in

(*c*) at (*d*) for

4. I appeal to you _______ mercy _______ the prisoner.

(*a*) on, for (*b*) for, on

(*c*) on, at (*d*) for, by

5. Thanks are also due _______ all those working _______ the scene for their kind cooperation _______ the show.

(*a*) behind, during, to (*b*) during, to, behind

(*c*) to, behind, during (*d*) to, during, behind

6. You cannot blame me _______ the mistakes _______ others in this affair.

(*a*) of, for (*b*) for, to

(*c*) to, of (*d*) for, of

7. For speaking rudely _______ the judge, my sentence was increased _______ fifteen days for contempt of court.

(*a*) to, to

(*b*) of, by

(*c*) to, of

(*d*) by, to

8. I am tired _______ depending _______ the tram service for getting up to town and back.

(*a*) on, of (*b*) of, to

(*c*) of, on (*d*) to, with

9. I have been looking _______ hearing from you by letter for ages.

(*a*) with (*b*) to

(*c*) forward to (*d*) at

10. I must congratulate him _______ his success _______ examination.

(*a*) on, in

(*b*) on, in the

(*c*) in, with

(*d*) on, to

ANSWERS

CATEGORY – 1

	SET – 1	SET – 2	SET – 3	SET – 4
1.	in	for	at; in	among
2.	on; at	since	between	above
3.	since	from; to	over	under
4.	from; to; on	by	below/beneath/above	above
5.	for	at	among	at; in
6.	on; by	at	above	between
7.	on	off	in	above;below; on
8.	on	towards	over	under
9.	on; on	to	at	under; over
10.	since	off	under	under; above

	SET – 5	SET – 6	SET – 7	SET – 8
1.	for	about	by/ beside	at
2.	against	till; of	for	under
3.	off	down	with	at
4.	towards	of; in	with	from
5.	into	than	After; off	to
6.	out of	behind	in; between	from
7.	at	of; at; with	by; in	from
8.	out of; at	besides	in; during; on	in
9.	from	besides; with	in; from; to	against
10.	to	from; for; on	at; to	at

CATEGORY – 2

	SET – 1	*SET – 2*	*SET – 3*	*SET – 4*	*SET – 5*	*SET – 6*	*SET – 7*	*SET – 8*
1.	*(b)*	*(a)*	*(a)*	*(b)*	*(c)*	*(c)*	*(a)*	*(c)*
2.	*(a)*	*(c)*	*(c)*	*(b)*	*(b)*	*(b)*	*(b)*	*(c)*
3.	*(c)*	*(a)*	*(a)*	*(a)*	*(b)*	*(a)*	*(d)*	*(b)*
4.	*(b)*	*(c)*	*(d)*	*(c)*	*(d)*	*(d)*	*(a)*	*(a)*
5.	*(c)*	*(a)*	*(c)*	*(d)*	*(b)*	*(a)*	*(d)*	*(b)*
6.	*(d)*	*(b)*	*(b)*	*(b)*	*(a)*	*(c)*	*(a)*	*(c)*
7.	*(a)*	*(d)*	*(a)*	*(c)*	*(b)*	*(d)*	*(c)*	*(c)*
8.	*(b)*	*(c)*	*(d)*	*(d)*	*(c)*	*(b)*	*(d)*	*(d)*
9.	*(c)*	*(b)*	*(b)*	*(b)*	*(d)*	*(d)*	*(b)*	*(c)*
10.	*(d)*	*(d)*	*(c)*	*(a)*	*(c)*	*(c)*	*(a)*	*(b)*

	SET – 9	*SET – 10*	*SET – 11*	*SET – 12*	*SET – 13*	*SET – 14*	*SET – 15*
1.	*(c)*	*(c)*	*(a)*	*(a)*	*(b)*	*(c)*	*(a)*
2.	*(d)*	*(b)*	*(c)*	*(c)*	*(c)*	*(a)*	*(c)*
3.	*(b)*	*(c)*	*(b)*	*(a)*	*(a)*	*(b)*	*(a)*
4.	*(a)*	*(a)*	*(c)*	*(c)*	*(b)*	*(d)*	*(b)*
5.	*(c)*	*(b)*	*(a)*	*(b)*	*(c)*	*(c)*	*(c)*
6.	*(b)*	*(b)*	*(a)*	*(d)*	*(a)*	*(a)*	*(d)*
7.	*(a)*	*(d)*	*(d)*	*(a)*	*(c)*	*(c)*	*(a)*
8.	*(b)*	*(a)*	*(c)*	*(b)*	*(b)*	*(b)*	*(c)*
9.	*(c)*	*(a)*	*(b)*	*(c)*	*(b)*	*(c)*	*(c)*
10.	*(a)*	*(d)*	*(d)*	*(a)*	*(a)*	*(d)*	*(b)*

CONJUNCTIONS

Below is a list of common conjunctions.

and	whenever	wherever	so that
or	while	because	that
but	after	as	though
yet	before	since	although
so	till	if	even though
either … or	until	unless	even if
neither … nor	as soon as	in case	as if
when	where	than	as though

A few conjunctions (like **and, but, or**) join words or groups of words. Other conjunctions always join groups of words.

We use **and** to connect two similar ideas.

I had bread **and** coffee for breakfast.

She has two daughters **and** a son.

He sold his motorbike **and** bought a car.

We use **or** to talk about alternatives.

Would you like tea **or** coffee?

I will see him this evening **or** tomorrow morning.

Shall we walk **or** take a bus?

Note the use of **either … or** and **neither … nor**:

I don't like **either** tea **or** coffee.

I like **neither** tea **nor** coffee.

We also use **or** to mean "if not".

Hurry up **or** you will be late for school.

Wear a sweater **or** you will catch cold.

We use **but** to join two different or opposite ideas.

He was ill **but** cheerful.

We invited Usha **but** she didn't come.

I tried to phone him **but** his number was engaged.

We use **yet** to mean "in spite of that".

He worked hard, **yet** he didn't pass the exam.

We started late, **yet** we arrived on time.

We use **so** to talk about result.

I got up late, **so** I missed the first bus.

He didn't study hard, **so** he failed the exam.

We also use **so … that** to talk about result. **That** is often left out in spoken English.

I was **so** tired (that) I fell asleep in the chair.

The film was **so** good that we went to see it again.

He spoke **so** fast that I couldn't understand him.

The following conjunctions are used to talk about time relationships: **when, while, whenever, as, before, after, as soon as, till, until, since**, etc.

The crowd cheered loudly **when** the Prime Minister arrived.

The phone range **while** I was having a shower.

Please come to my house **whenever** you are free.

She waved to me **as** the train left the station.

The train had left **before** they arrived at the station.

Ring me up **as soon as** you arrive.

We waited **till** it stopped raining.

It is nearby two years **since** we saw him.

We use **where** and **wherever** to talk about a position or place.

Put it back **where** you found it.

You may sit **wherever** you like.

We use **so that** to talk about purpose. In spoken English, people often just say so (without **that**).

I'll give you a map **so** (**that**) you can get there easily.

My uncle lifted me onto his shoulders **so** (**that**) I could see over the other people's heads.

We can also use **in order that**, but today it is not used except in a very formal style.

To talk about reason we use **because, as, since**, etc.

She phoned the police **because** she lost her handbag.

He didn't go to the party **as** he was ill.

Since I had a lot of work to do at home, I didn't have time to come.

We use **in case** to talk about doing something because something else might happen later. In case means "because … might".

Take an umbrella **in case** it rains. (= because it might rain later)

I'll leave you my phone number **in case** you want to contact me. (= because you might want to contact me later)

If is used to say that one thing will or might happen, depending on another thing happening. We can also use **unless** (= **if … not**).

If it rains, we will postpone our trip.

We will be late if we don't hurry.

We will be late unless we hurry.

Don't wake me up unless it is really necessary.

As if and **as though** answer the question "How"?

Do **as** I tell you.

He looked **as if/ as though** he hadn't slept well.

She felt **as if/ as though** she had fever.

When we want to contrast two statements, we use **though, although, even though** and **even if**. **Even though** is stronger than **though/ although**. **Even if** means "whether or not".

They went out **though** it was raining.

Although it is hard work, I enjoy the job.

Even though I didn't know anybody at the party, I had a nice time.

Even if you take a taxi, you will still miss your train.

We use **as** and **than** to talk about comparison or degree.

She is not **as** clever **as** she appears to be.

The hotel was not **as** good **as** we expected.

He is older **than** I thought.

As you must have seen, some conjunctions (e.g. **as, since**) can be used in more than one sense.

EXERCISE

Underline the correct conjunction.

1. The watch is cheap, (or/ yet) it works very well.
2. We stayed at home (and/ but) watched a video.
3. I saw him (but/ or) he didn't see me.
4. Walk fast (but/ or) you will miss the bus.
5. He is very old, (yet/ so) he can walk fast.
6. It is a long time (when/ since) we met.
7. (Though/ As) they are rich, they live very simply.
8. She behaves (even though/ as though) she owns the place.
9. He is not as old (as/ than) I thought.
10. He dressed so quickly (that/ as) he put his shoes on the wrong feet.
11. Be careful (since/ when) you cross the road.
12. The train suddenly started moving (till/ as) I was getting on.
13. He gave up his seat on the bus (so that/ because) a woman with a baby could sit down.
14. It was his birthday (because/ so) we decided to buy him a present.
15. I will write down the address (so that/ in case) I, forget it.
16. The bag was so heavy (that/ as) I couldn't carry it.
17. I did (so/ as) he told me.
18. I will get there, (if/ even if) I have to talk.
19. They went out for a walk (even though/ in case) the weather was bad.
20. They have put broken glass on top of the walls (because/ so that) thieves won't get in.

ANSWERS

EXERCISE – 1

1. The watch is cheap, yet it works very well.
2. We stayed at home and watched a video.
3. I saw him but he didn't see me.
4. Walk fast or you will miss the bus.
5. He is very old, yet he can walk fast.
6. It is a long time since we met.
7. Though they are rich, they live very simply.
8. She behaves as though she owns the place.
9. He is not as old as I thought.
10. He dressed so quickly that he put his shoes on the wrong feet.
11. Be careful when you cross the road.
12. The train suddenly started moving as I was getting on.
13. He gave up his seat on the bus so that a woman with a baby could sit down.
14. It was his birthday so we decided to buy him a present.
15. I will write down the address in case I, forget it.
16. The bag was so heavy that I couldn't carry it.
17. I did as he told me.
18. I will get there, even if I have to talk.
19. They went out for a walk even though the weather was bad.
20. They have put broken glass on top of the walls so that thieves won't get in.

WORDS CONNECTORS

This chapter deals with the type of words which link two main clauses or sentences. Such connectors can be classified as follows:

1. words meaning "**and**":
   and, **besides, in addition, moreover, both** _____ **and, not only** _____ **but also**, etc.
2. words meaning "**or**":
   or, either _____ **or, neither** _____ **nor**
3. words meaning "**but**":
   but, yet, still, however, nevertheless, etc.
4. words meaning "**so**":
   so, therefore, as a result, consequently, etc.

Study the examples below carefully so as to learn how to use these connectors.

Words meaning "**and**"

Gopi talked **and** the others listened.

She **not only** watered the plants **but also** washed the dishes.

She **both** watered the plants **and** washed the dishes.

The rent is too high. **Besides/ Moreover**, the house isn't in a suitable condition.

Words meaning "**or**"

I'll sweep the floor **or** dust the furniture.

Either sweep the floor **or** dust the furniture.

She **neither** swept the floor **nor** dusted the furniture.

Word meaning "**but**"

We started rather late, **but** we arrived on time.

The doctor told him to rest. **Yet** we went on working.

Mr. Jain is a strict headmaster; **still** the pupils like him.

She drove very fast to the airport. **However**, she missed the plane.

Words meaning "**so**"

He had fever, **so** he didn't go to school.

We have a growing population and **therefore** we need more food.

He didn't work hard. **As a result**/**Consequently**, he failed his exam.

(We can also use **as a result** and **consequently** in a clause with **and**: "He didn't work hard and **as a result**/ **consequently** ...")

EXERCISE – 1

Choose the correct connective to fill in each space.

1. He tried very hard, __________ he couldn't force the door open.
   (a) and (b) or (c) but
2. He didn't understand, __________ he asked the teacher to explain.
   (a) so (b) but (c) or
3. We do only saw the exhibition __________ went to the zoo.
   (a) and (b) but also (c) besides
4. The children finished their homework __________ went out to play.
   (a) but (b) or (c) and
5. They stole the jewels. __________ they murdered the woman.
   (a) Therefore (b) But (c) Besides
6. The colour didn't suit her and __________ she decided not to buy the sari.
   (a) yet (b) therefore (c) still
7. You can buy a computer __________ go on holiday. Not both!
   (a) and (b) or (c) but
8. The sun is shining __________ it's hot outside.
   (a) but (b) or (c) and

9. He had overslept. __________ he was late for work.

(a) However (b) As a result (c) or

10. He neither smokes __________ drinks.

(a) or (b) nor (c) but

EXERCISE – 2

Join the following pairs of sentences, using **and, or, but, so, therefore, not only .... but also** or another connector.

Example:

He was very hungry. He ate a lot.

He was very hungry, so he ate a lot.

1. The party wasn't good. I left early.
2. It was raining. I didn't go out.
3. This year's harvest was very poor. The price of wheat has gone up.
4. I have often invited him here. He has never come.
5. He scolded the girl. He also beat her.
6. She finished her work. She went out shopping.
7. I was very tired. I went to bed early.
8. She was very busy. She was able to help me.
9. We searched everywhere. The watch was not to be found.
10. He never learnt to swim. He tried hard.

ANSWERS

Exercise - 1

1. (*c*) 2. (*a*) 3. (*b*) 4. (*c*) 5. (*c*) 6. (*c*) 7. (*b*) 8. (*c*) 9. (*b*) 10. (*b*)

Exercise – 2

1. The party wasn't good so I left early.
2. It was raining so I didn't go out.
3. This year's harvest was very poor therefore the price of wheat has gone up.
4. I have often invited him here but he has never come.
5. He scolded the girl and he also beat her.
6. She finished her work and she went out shopping.
7. I was very tired so I went to bed early.
8. She was very busy still she was able to help me.
9. We searched everywhere but the watch was not to be found.
10. He never learnt to swim though he tried hard.

PART – C

COMMON ERRORS

28

CHAPTER

COMMON ERRORS

Identifying common errors in a given set of sentences or a passage is one of the most important topics in almost all the competitive examinations. However, it is a ticklish and taxing task indeed that requires a comprehensive knowledge of English language.

The clarity of the basics of grammar such as use of parts of speech, articles, determiners, tenses etc. is not only an inevitable, but also one of the most indispensable imperatives to get expertise in finding errors. In addition to it, the proper understanding of words with their meanings and usage is an obvious and apparent requirement in the context of marking common errors.

To enable the students to identify common errors, concepts of grammar and basic vocabulary have been outlined and explained extensively and comprehensively in Part A and Part B of the book. Having mastered Part A and Part B, students will find themselves in a comfortable position while attempting the questions related to common errors.

In this chapter on **COMMON ERRORS**, all possible efforts have been made to provide sufficient sentences, wherein errors are most frequently and repetitively committed. The prominent areas in which errors are predominantly committed have been segregated and provided under topics as errors in the prepositions, nouns, pronouns, verbs, adverbs, adjectives etc. Having gone through the chapter on **COMMON ERRORS**, the students will be able to notice errors in the given sentences or passages quite easily and comfortably.

ERRORS IN PREPOSITIONS

A preposition is a word used with a noun or noun equivalent to show its relation with some other word in the sentence:

as, in, into, at, on, upon, for, with etc.

	Incorrect Sentences	Correct Sentences
1.	Mohan has ordered for a cup of tea.	Mohan has ordered a cup of tea.
2.	Renu resembles with her mother.	Renu resembles her mother.
3.	I have joined in the army.	I have joined the army.
4.	He reached at the station late	He reached the station late.
5.	India does not lack in patriots.	India does not lack patriots.
6.	The thief attacked on me with a staff.	The thief attacked me with a staff.
7.	You can accompany with me to Delhi.	You can accompany me to Delhi.
8.	Will you recommend for me to your boss?	Will you recommend me to your boss?
9.	We should not violate against the rules.	We should not violate the rules.
10.	The committee comprises of five members.	The committee comprises five members.
To remember : *Do not use any preposition after order, resemble, join, reach, lack, attack, invade, accompany, recommend, violate, comprise, assist, combat, afford, regret, marry, shirk, etc.*		
11.	They live in Ramgarh (a village).	They live at Ramgarh.
12.	We live at Bombay.	We live in Bombay.
13.	She came to see me at the evening.	She came to see me in the evening.

14.	I saw him into his bedroom.	I saw him in his bedroom.
15.	I saw him going in his bedroom.	I saw him going into his bedroom.
16.	Distribute these books between all these boys.	Distribute these books among all those boys.
17.	Distribute these sweets among these two girls.	Distribute these sweets between these two girls.
18.	Besides the students, many teachers also attended the meeting.	Besides the students, many teachers also attended the meeting.
19.	He sat besides his wife.	He sat beside his wife.
20.	You should be ashamed at your behaviour.	You should be ashamed of your behaviour.
21.	Rajesh is suffering with fever.	Rajesh is suffering from fever.
22.	He was convicted with the charge of theft.	He was convicted of the charge of theft.
23.	He is jealous with his friend.	He is jealous of his friend.
24.	He was accused with murder.	He was accused of murder.
25.	She is always boasting about her riches.	She is always boasting of her riches.
26.	Wait your friend to go to movie.	Wait for your friend to go to movie.
27.	They invited us for dinner.	They invited us to dinner.
28.	We had to walk five miles by foot.	We had to walk five miles on foot.
29.	Have you any interest for painting?	Have you any interest in painting?
30.	He is fond for music.	He is fond of music.
31.	I prevented her to go there.	I prevented her from going there.
32.	You should not interfere in her work.	You should not interfere with her work.
33.	He is in the habit of quarrelling on trifles.	He is in the habit of quarrelling over trifles.
34.	I want to get rid from him.	I want to get rid of him.
35.	I knocked the door twice.	I knocked at the door twice.
36.	I sympathized him in his loss.	I sympathized with him in his loss.
37.	I objected his remarks.	I objected to his remarks.
38.	This book has been translated in many languages.	This book has been translated into many languages.
39.	My brother was angry with my behaviour.	My brother was angry at my behaviour.
40.	I am tired from him.	I am tired of him.
41.	All of us rejoiced on his brilliant success.	All of us rejoiced at his brilliant success.
42.	Are you afraid from your wife?	Are you afraid of your wife?
43.	He burst in tears.	He burst into tears.
44.	She is not capable for doing this job.	She is not capable of doing this job.
45.	Is he satisfied by my work?	Is he satisfied with my work?
46.	Describe about the scene in two hundred words.	Describe the scene in two hundred words.
47.	He has only added my worries.	He has only added to my worries.
48.	Have faith for God.	Have faith in God.
49.	Neglect in duty can have serious consequences.	Neglect of duty can have serious consequences.
50.	We lodged complaint for the arrogant peon.	We lodged a complaint against the arrogant peon.
51.	The complaint was lodged to the manager.	The complaint was lodged with the manager.
52.	All should contribute for this fund.	All should contribute to this fund.

53.	I caught her from the arm.	I caught her by the arm.
54.	You should guard yourself from bad habits.	You should guard yourself against bad habits.
55.	The officer did not accede on my request.	The officer did not accede to my request.
56.	I insisted to do this.	I insisted on doing this.
57.	The Prime Minister called for a meeting of the cabinet.	The Prime Minister called a meeting of the cabinet.
58.	She is proud at her beauty.	She is proud of her beauty.
59.	She takes pride of her beauty.	She takes pride in her beauty.
60.	She met me in the way.	She met me on the way.
61.	We congratulated him for his success.	We congratulated him on his success.
62.	Please attend your lesson.	Please attend your lesson.
63.	I have no pencil to write.	I have no pencil to write with.
64.	His right arm has been operated.	His right arm has been operated upon.
65.	You will have to regret for the delay.	You will have to regret the delay.
66.	Rajesh married with Babita.	Rajesh married Babita.
67.	I am not accustomed with this type of work.	I am not accustomed to this type of work.
68.	This glass is full with water.	This glass is full of water.
69.	The old man died from cholera.	The old man died of cholera.
70.	Do you agree with my proposal?	Do you agree to my proposal?
71.	Is she related with you?	Is she related to you?
72.	Our examination begins from Monday.	Our examination begins on Monday.

73.	We were surprised by his failure.	We were surprised at his failure.
74.	Mr. Verma has resigned his post.	Mr. Verma has resigned from his post.
75.	He is slow in accounts.	He is slow at accounts.
76.	We cannot buy this house for such a price.	We cannot buy this house at such a price.
77.	They arrived to the conclusion.	They arrived at the conclusion.
78.	She rejoiced on my success.	She rejoiced at my success.
79.	I advised him much but of no purpose.	I advised him much but to no purpose.
80.	He died of over work.	He died from over work.
81.	You are late in the meeting	You are late for the meeting.
82.	Fear is natural for man.	Fear is natural to man.
83.	Aeroplanes carry out passengers from place to place.	Aeroplanes carry passengers from one place to another.
84.	I want to enquire about his health.	I want to inquire after his health.
85.	There is another side of this question.	There is another side to this question.
86.	This is a saying in the Hindu.	This is a saying among the Hindus.
87.	She does not desire for a change.	She does not desire a change.
88.	I could not prevail her.	I could not prevail upon her.
89.	The father has no influence on his son.	The father has no influence over his son.
90.	I have no prejudice for you.	I have no prejudice against you.
91.	I shall partake the dinner.	I shall partake of the dinner.

92.	His name precedes before mine.	His name precedes mine.
93.	Please send this letter on this address.	Please post this letter at this address.
94.	You should sign on this paper.	You should sign this paper.
95.	This old lady is blind to one eye.	This old lady is blind of one eye.
96.	This pen is different to that.	This pen is different from that.
97.	You will have to agree to me.	You will have to agree with me.
98.	The dead body was covered by piece of cloth.	The dead body was covered with a piece of cloth.
99.	We searched his lost pen.	We searched for his lost pen.
100.	Ram has met an accident.	Ram has met with an accident.
101.	The police inquired about this matter.	The police enquired into the matter.
102.	Have you some acquaintance to the Minister?	Have you some acquaintance with the Minister?
103.	Those who shirk from duty never succeed in life.	Those who shirk duty never succeed in life.
104.	Let us discuss about this problem	Let us discuss this problem.
105.	Ran comes off a rich and respectable family.	Raj comes from a rich and respectable family.
106.	Please write with ink.	Please write in ink.
107.	His father stopped him to go there.	His father stopped him from going there.
108.	She has passed in the examination.	She has passed the examination.
109.	This is a house for letting.	This is a house to let.
110.	I travel in the first class.	I travel first class.

111.	We sat under the shade of a tree.	We sat in the shade of a tree.
112.	What is the time on your watch?	What is the time by your watch?
113.	He got down his bicycle.	He got off his bicycle.
114.	She fell in the hands of ruffians.	She fell into the hands of ruffians.
115.	He took the business into his hand.	He took the business in his hand.
116.	I bow down to your order.	I bow to your order.
117.	Pity upon the poor.	Pity the poor.
118.	He encroached my land.	He encroached upon my land.
119.	I subscribe for this magazine.	I subscribe to this magazine.
120.	Conversation was carried into whispers.	Conversation was carried in whispers.
121.	I am awaiting for him.	I am waiting for him.
122.	Sobha Singh is an authority over painting.	Sobha Singh is an authority on painting.
123.	He is debarred to contest.	He is debarred from contesting.
124.	I shall return in two hours.	I shall return within two hours.
125.	You have not claim to this post.	You have no claim for this post.
126.	What is your comment for this unrest?	What are your comments on this unrest?
127.	He has a great capacity to work.	He has a great capacity for work.
128.	She turned a deaf ear for my advice.	She turned a deaf ear to my advice.
129.	He sat under the feet of his teachers.	He sat at the feet of his teachers.
130.	A deputation will wait at the Prime Minister.	A deputation will wait on (or upon) the Prime Minister.

131.	Do not be indifferent about your health.	Do not be indifferent to your health.
132.	We should pray God daily.	We should pray to God daily.
133.	The soldier saluted to the officer.	The soldier saluted the officer.
134.	She is very anxious for the health of her children.	She is very anxious about the health of her children.
135.	He failed as he lacks in common sense.	He failed as he lacks common sense.
136.	They are leaving to America tomorrow.	They are leaving for America tomorrow.
137.	She always rides on a car.	She always rides in a car.
138.	The cat pounced at the mouse.	The cat pounced on (or upon) the mouse.
139.	My child is precious for me.	My child is precious to me.
140.	The publisher ran out a thousand copies of his book.	The publisher ran off a thousand copies of his book.

ERRORS IN THE USE OF NOUNS

A Noun is the name of a person or a place or a thing. For example:-

Kapil, Agra, college, match, honesty, lion, class, gold, India, bench, the Ganges etc.

	Incorrect Sentences	Correct Sentences
1.	The sceneries of Kashmir are charming.	The scenery of Kashmir is charming.
2.	He gave me many advices.	He gave me many pieces of advice
3.	Arvind loves the poetries of Wordsworth.	Arvind loves the poetry (or poems) of Wordsworth.
4.	She gave us no informations.	She gave us no information.
5.	Kapil has many works to do.	Kapil has much work to do.
6.	I have sold my old furnitures.	I have sold my old furniture.
7.	She has packed her luggages.	She has packed her luggage.
8.	You did many mischiefs yesterday.	You did many acts of mischief yesterday.
9.	Mohan gave the beggar two breads.	Mohan gave the beggar two loaves (or pieces) of bread.
10.	Radha has no issues.	Radha has no issue.
11.	India is importing new machineries.	India is importing new machinery.
12.	We shall spend our summer vacations at Shimla.	We shall spend our summer vacation at Shimla.
13.	You must help the poors and the blinds.	You must help the poor and the blind.
14.	The naughty boy does not avoid bad companies.	The naughty boy does not avoid bad company.
15.	Good boys do not move in bad companies.	Good boys do not move in bad company.
16.	He is a man of words.	He is a man of words.
17.	His hairs are grey.	His hair is grey.

Remember: *Certain nouns such as scenery, furniture, hair advice, stationery, machinery, luggage, information, expenditure, abuse, business, damage, poetry, issue, vacation etc. are used in the singular form and carry the singular verb.*

18.	I have purchased a new scissor.	I have purchased a new pair of scissors.
19.	Punam does not like vegetable.	Punam does not like vegetables.
20.	Tell me the content of his letter.	Tell me the contents of his letter.
21.	He old woman always wears a spectacle.	The old woman always wears spectacles.
22.	We must give alm to the beggar.	We must give alms to the beggar.
23.	Your trouser is dirty.	Your trousers are dirty.
24.	He is weak in study.	He is weak in studies.

25.	I am feeling out of sort.	I am feeling out of sorts.
26.	Riches has turned his head.	Riches have turned his head.

Remember: *Some nouns like thanks, contents, trousers, circumstances, alms, ashes, scissors, spectacles, vegetables, annals, remains tongs, proceeds, meals, orders, sorts, means, riches, wages etc. are used in the plural.*

27.	In this circumstance I cannot help you.	In these circumstances I cannot help you.
28.	His thank is due to me.	His thanks are due to me.
29.	These are happy news.	This is happy news.
30.	Politics are a dirty game.	Politics is a dirty game.
31.	Mathematics are my favourite subject.	Mathematics is my favourite subject.
32.	Gallows have been erected.	Gallows has been erected.
33.	The wages of sin are death.	The wages of sin is death.

Remember: *Some nouns as politics, news, Economics, Mathematics, innings, gallows, summons, etc. are plural in form but singular in content.*

34.	There are twenty fishes in this tank.	There are twenty fish in this tank.
35.	I saw a flock of sheeps.	I saw a flock of sheep.
36.	He killed some deers.	He killed some deer.
37.	She gave five cent to the beggar.	She gave five cents to the beggar.
38.	The farmer has four yokes of oxen.	The farmer has four yoke of oxen.

Remember: *Some nouns like fish, sheep, deer, pice, yoke etc. have the same form in both singular and plural.*

39.	She bought this bicycle for five hundreds rupees.	They bought four dozen eggs.
40.	I bought this bicycle for five hundreds rupees.	I bought this bicycle for five hundred rupees.
41.	He lent me a fifty rupees note.	He lent me a fifty rupee note.
42.	They had a four hours talk.	They had a four-hour talk.
43.	He joined the three years B.Com Course.	He joined the three-year B.Com. Course.
44.	Sahil ran a two miles race.	Sahil ran a two-mile race.
45.	Thousand of men and women attended the meeting.	Thousands of men and women attended the meeting.

Remember: *Some nouns as dozen, score, hundred, thousand, pound etc. (Signifying exact number or measure) are used in the singular when they come after numerical, otherwise in the plural as in sentence no. 45.*

46.	The cattles are grazing.	The cattle are grazing.
47.	Gentry of the town was present at the function.	Gentry of the town were present at the function.
48.	The village folk is simple.	The village folk are simple.
49.	All the peoples laughed at her song.	All the people laughed at her song.
50.	The police deserves credit for this.	The police deserve credit for this.
51.	Vermin causes disease.	Vermin causes disease.
52.	The peasantry is hard hit by the land ceiling.	The peasantry are hard hit by the land ceiling.
53.	I do not know the alphabets of Urdu.	I do not know the alphabet of Urdu.

Remember: *Gentry, folk, cattle, people, poultry, public, peasantry, police, vermin, alphabet are some of the collective nouns. They are singular in form but plural in meaning. They require a plural verb.*

54.	My house is built of brick and stones.	My house is built of bricks and stone.

55.	The Taj is built of white marbles.	The Taj is built of white marble.

Remember: *When material nouns are used to denote a mass of matter, they are used as singular.*

56.	I shall dine at my uncle's house today.	I shall dine at my uncle's today.

Remember: *The words 'house, church, 'chool, shop', are often omitted after a possessive case.*

57.	It is a girl's hostel.	It is a girls' hostel.
58.	I shall wait for you in the teacher's staff room.	I shall wait for you in the teachers' staff room.
59.	I am a member of the women club.	I am a member of the women's club.
60.	It is a childrens playground.	It is a children's playground.

Remember: *In case of plural form ending in 's' indicate the possessive case by adding an apostrophe after 's' (See sentences 57 and 58). But when the plural noun does not end in 's', indicate the possessive by adding 's' (see sentences 59, 60).*

61.	His shirt's colour is blue.	The colour of his shirt is blue.
62.	His pen's ink is red.	The ink of his pen is red.

Remember: *As a rule 's' is used for indicating persons, living beings and personified objects.*

MORE COMMON ERRORS IN THE USE OF NOUNS AND NOUN PHRASES

	Incorrect Sentences	Correct Sentences
1.	There was no place on the bench for you.	There was no room on the bench for you.
2.	She is my cousin sister.	She is my cousin.
3.	We saw a theatre.	We saw a play.
4.	I want to buy a copy.	I want to buy a copy book (or note book or exercise book).
5.	Please put your sign here.	Please put your signatures here.
6.	They like the play of cricket.	They like the game of cricket.
7.	Good night sir, I have come to consult you.	Good evening sir, I have come to consult you.
8.	A hundred miles are a long distance.	A hundred miles is a long distance.
9.	There were many females in the compartment.	There were many women in the compartment.
10.	Renu stays in the boarding.	Renu stays in the boarding house.
11.	Ashu failed by five numbers.	Ashu failed by five marks.
12.	My family members have gone to Delhi.	The members of my family have gone to Delhi.
13.	They weather of Dalhousie is very pleasant.	The climate of Dalhousie is very pleasant.
14.	Please give me some blotting.	Please give me some blotting paper.
15.	The teachers needed a chalk.	The teacher needed a piece of chalk.
16.	I have got an employment in this office.	I have got a job in this office.
17.	Mohan and Sohan are not on talking terms with each other.	Mohan and Sohan are not on speaking terms with each other.
18.	I have an urgent work with you.	I have an urgent piece of work with you.
19.	You have a big number of money.	You have a big amount of money.
20.	Arun is one of my fast friend.	Arun is one of my fast friends.
21.	Mr. D.K. Sharma is our English professor.	Mr. D.K. Sharma is our professor of English.
22.	I have read a quantity of novels.	I have read a number of novels.
23.	Ravi will buy a new home.	Ravi will buy a new house.
24.	Anjana and Neelam are sitting under the shadow of a tree.	Anjana and Neelam are sitting under the shade of a tree.

25.	Anu saw her shade in the river.	Anu saw her shadow in the river.
26.	Fifty B.A. and ten M.A. applied for the job.	Fifty B.A.'s and ten M.A.'s applied for the job.
27.	Entry to the cinema hall will be by tickets.	Entry to the cinema hall will be by ticket.
28.	The chair's leg is broken.	The leg of the chair is broken.
29.	The English invaded the French.	The English attacked the French.
30.	Pakistan may attack India.	Pakistan may invade India.
31.	Ravi will go by 4.30 o'clock train.	Ravi will go by the 4.30 train.
32.	Sneh has no rupees to spend.	Sneh has no money to spend.
33.	The French have strange habits.	The French have strange customs.
34.	Stealing is a bad custom.	Stealing is a bad habit.
35.	All my relations are rich.	All my relatives are rich.
36.	The dacoit was set at freedom.	The dacoit was set free.
37.	Tell me the cost of this box.	Tell me the price of this box.
38.	My uncle's secretary's wife is very charming.	The wife of my uncle's secretary is very charming.
39.	Collegiates are fond of fashions.	Collegians are fond of fashion.
40.	Cities after cities were attacked.	City after city was attacked.
41.	Vijay took insult at my remark.	Vijay took offence (or felt insulted) at my remark.
42.	I love to read the poetry of Byron.	I love to read Byron's poetry.
43.	Kamal enjoys a freeship in the college.	Kamal enjoys a free studentship in the college.
44.	We have read two-third of this novel.	We have read two-thirds of this novel.

45.	You gave false witness.	You gave false evidence.
46.	She was standing in the centre of the room.	She was standing in the middle of the room.
47.	We should show respect to the fair sex.	We should show respect to women.
48.	I live in the boarding.	I live in the boarding house (or hostel).
49.	He invited all his son-in-laws to the party.	He invited all his sons-in-law to the party.
50.	Crowds after crowds went to welcome the Prime Minister.	Crowd after crowd went to welcome the Prime Minister.
51.	A five men deputation met the Governor.	A five man deputation met the Governor.
52.	Woods are used for making chairs.	Wood is used for making chairs.
53.	She sent me a verbal message.	She sent me an oral message.
54.	People must study the story of the Indians.	People must study the history of the Indians.
55.	Your brother is a drunkard.	Your brother is a drunkard.
56.	We saw a joker at the circus.	We saw a clown at the circus.
57.	She got passing marks in English.	She got pass marks in English.
58.	Kindly grant me one day's leave.	Kindly grant me leave for one day.
59.	Ram's house is different from Sham.	Ram's house is different from Sham's
60.	I do not know my date of birth.	I do not know the date of my birth.
61.	The roads of our town are very narrow.	The streets of our town are very narrow.
62.	Which street leads to your village?	Which road leads to your village?

63.	Describe the reason of an earthquake.	Describe the causes of an earthquake.
64.	We won a running cup.	We won a challenge cup.

ERRORS IN THE USE OF PRONOUNS

A pronoun is a word used in place of a Noun. For example: I, we, you, your, he, him, she, her, it etc.

1.	I and you are class-fellows.	You and I are class-fellows.
2.	He and you must go out for a walk.	You and he must go out for a walk.
3.	I, he and you are playing a match.	You, he and I are playing a match.
4.	You and we must work together.	We and you must work together.
5.	They and you can play now.	You and they can play now.

Remember: *While referring to persons, it is customary to place pronoun like this – II person, III person, Ist Person (II, III, I) But in case of plural pronouns, 'we' comes before 'you' and 'you' before 'they'*

6.	Each of the boys must bring their own books.	Each of the boys must bring his own books.
7.	Every boy was in their must attend their class.	Everyone of these boys must attend his class.
8.	Everyone of these girls must attend their class.	Everyone of these girls must attend her class.
9.	Either of these two boys are your friend.	Either of these two boys is your friend.
10.	Either Ram or Mohan forgot to bring their books.	Either Ram or Mohan forgot to bring his books.
11.	Neither Kapil nor Sahil attended their class.	Neither Kapil nor Sahil attended his class.

Remember: *'Each, every, everyone, everybody, anyone, either, neither, none' are followed by verbs and pronouns in the singular.*

12.	None are allowed to miss their class.	None is allowed to miss his class.
13.	The two sisters love one another.	The two sisters love each other.
14.	Mohan, Sohan and Ram help each other.	Mohan, Sohan and Ram help one another.

Remember: *'Each other' is used for two persons or things, 'one another' for more than two persons of things.*

15.	Distribute these mangoes among two boys.	Distribute these mangoes between two boys.
16.	Distribute sweets between four girls.	Distribute sweets among four girls.

Remember: *'Between' is used for two persons or things, 'among' for more than two persons or things.*

17.	Who did you beat yesterday?	Whom did you beat yesterday?
18.	Whom do you think will win the prize?	Who do you think will win the prize?

Remember: *'Who' denotes subject and 'Whom' stands for object.*

19.	One must do his duty.	One must do one's duty.
20.	It is one of the best book that has been written by Arvind.	It is one of the best books that have been written by Arvind.
21.	He is one of those persons who never shirks work.	He is one of those persons who never shirk work.

Remember: A *relative pronoun always agrees with its antecedent in gender, number and person.*

22.	Let you and I play here.	Let you and me play here.
23.	Between you and I she is a lazy girl.	Between you and me she is a lazy girl.
24.	These toys are for he and I.	These toys are for him and me.

Remember: *When a pronoun appears as the object of a verb or of a preposition, it should be used in the objective case.*

25.	Any of these two umbrellas will serve my purpose.	Either of these two umbrellas will serve my purpose.

26.	You can take either of the four books.	You can take any of the four books.
27.	None of these two boys are sincere.	Neither of these two boys is sincere.
28.	Neither of my ten friends have helped me.	None of my ten friends has helped me.

Remember: *Either and neither should be used for two persons or things, anyone and none for more than two persons or things. The verb in each case will be in the Singular.*

29.	This is the chair whose leg is broken.	This is the chair the leg of which is broken.
30.	You are the boy which is wanted by me.	You are the boy who is wanted by me.

Remember: *Pronouns like who, whose, whom are used for persons while 'which' is used for animals and things. But 'which' is also used for animate objects when there is a mention of two such objects as in sentence no. 32.*

31.	Whom do you think is the best actor?	Who do you think is the best actor?
32.	Who do you think is your sister between Seema and Savita?	Which is your sister between Seema and Savita?
33.	You must avail of this chance.	You must avail yourself of the chance.
34.	Radha absented from the class.	Radha absented herself from the class.
35.	We should go out and enjoy ourselves.	We should go out and enjoy ourselves.
36.	I am amused by reading a enjoy.	I amused myself by reading a novel.
37.	We should resign to the will of God.	We should resign ourselves to the Will of God.

Remember: *The reflexive pronoun is used after such verbs as enjoy, avail, absent, amuse, resign, apply, oversleep, revenge, distinguish, over reach, exert etc.*

38.	I kept myself away from the class.	I kept away from the class.
39.	She qualified herself for this post.	She qualified for this post.
40.	The boy hid himself behind a bush.	The boy hid behind a bush.

Remember: *No reflexive pronoun is used after such verbs as keep, qualify, hide, rest, break, enlist, bath, dash, open, spread, turn, steal, stop, repent, gather, burst, feed etc.*

41.	It was him who stole your pen.	It was he who stole your pen.
42.	It is me.	It is I.
43.	If I were her, I would not disobey my teacher.	If I were she, I would not disobey my teacher.

Remember: *The complement of the verb 'to be', when it is expressed by a pronoun, should be in the nominative form.*

44.	You are clever than me.	You are cleverer than I.
45.	She is viser than him.	She is wiser than he.
46.	I am senior to he.	I am senior to him.
47.	She considers herself to be superior to I.	Who considers herself superior to me.
48.	May I take you cycle?	May I take your bicycle?
49.	You are as good a student as me.	You are as good a student as I.
50.	Have you any good camera? No. I have not.	Do you have any good cameras? No, I have none.

MORE ERRORS IN THE USE OF PRONOUNS

1.	Being a fine day, we went out for a picnic.	It being a fine day, we went out for a picnic.
2.	Being blind, I showed him the way.	He being blind, so I showed him the way.
3.	Suffice to say, you are at fault.	Suffice it to say, you are at fault.

4.	I was glad at my mother coming.	I was glad when my mother came.
5.	HE made your mention.	He made mention of you.
6.	I have read Shelley's poetry who was a romantic poet.	I have read the poetry of Shelley who was a romantic poet.
7.	The climate of Madras is hotter than Shimla.	The climate of Madras is hotter than that of Shimla.
8.	The population of China is large than India.	The population of China is larger than that of India.
9.	My pen is superior to Mohan.	My pen is superior to Mohan's (pen).
10.	Your need is greater than me.	Your need is greater than mine.
11.	Will you mind me smoking here?	Will you mind my smoking here?
12.	Please excuse me for being late.	Please excuse my being late.
13.	He objected to me going out.	He objected to my going out.
14.	The cup is hot, is it?	The cup is hot, isn't it?
15.	They have not failed, haven't they?	They have not failed, have they?
16.	All but him had passed.	All but he had passed.
17.	Except he, all failed.	Except him, all failed.
18.	This is my new cap.	This cap of mine is new.
19.	He and me went to Srinagar.	He and I went to Srinagar.
20.	Her brother and herself are fond of mangoes.	Her brother and she are fond of mangoes.
21.	I am your faithful servant.	I am your faithful servant.
22.	I take you leave now.	I take leave of you now.
23.	She cannot bear my separation.	She cannot bear separation from me.

24.	At my sight she started weeping.	At the sight of mine, she started weeping.
25.	Who is able-Ram or Sham?	Who is abler-Ram or Sham?
26.	I hope to receive your good news.	I hope to receive good news of you (or from you).
27.	We want your reply at once.	We want a reply from you at once.
28.	Both did not go there.	Neither went there.
29.	We all did not attend the function.	None of us attended the function.
30.	It was them who helped us.	It was they who helped me.
31.	Your's sincerely.	Yours sincerely.
32.	I told my story to whom-so-ever I met.	I told my story to who-so-ever I met.
33.	The carpet cost me five hundred rupees on which you sat.	The carpet on which you sat cost me five hundred rupees.
34.	The man is my friend who met you yesterday.	The man who met you yesterday is my friend.
35.	His teaching is like Buddha.	His teaching is like that of the Buddha.
36.	The greatest name in modern India is Gandhi.	The greatest name in modern India is that of Gandhi.
37.	This is the book whose cover is red.	This is the book the cover of which is red.
38.	This is the tree in whose shade we slept.	This is the tree in the shade of which we slept.
39.	She came here without anyone knowledge.	She came here without anyone's knowledge.
40.	Arvind is a neighbour of us.	Arvind is a neighbour of ours.
41.	You can eat as many apples that you like.	You can eat as many apples as you like.

42.	I sang the same way that you did.	I sang the same way as you did.
43.	Varsha called at mine last evening.	Varsha called at my house last evening.
44.	The boy was punished by the teacher who misbehaved.	The boy who misbehaved was punished by the teacher.
45.	Wanted a stool for a lady with three legs.	Wanted a stool with three legs for a lady.

ERRORS IN THE USE OF VERBS

1.	Every boy and girl were present.	Every boy and girl was present.
2.	Everyone of them are coming.	Everyone of them is coming.
3.	Each one of these girls are my friend.	Each one of these girls is my friend.
4.	Everyday and each hour bring new news.	Everyday and each hour brings new news.
5.	None of the four books are yours.	None of the four books is yours.
6.	Neither of the two boys are good players.	Neither of the two boys is a good player.

Remember: *Each, every, neither, either, nobody, anyone, anybody, none, are followed by verbs in the singular.*

7.	Either you or your brother have done it.	Either you or your brother has done it.
8.	Neither you nor I are guilty.	Neither you nor I am guilty.
9.	Sita a Gita are at fault.	Sita or Gita is at fault.
10.	Either he or his sister have broken my slate.	Either he or his sister has broken my slate.
11.	Neither the king nor the ministers desires it.	Neither the king nor the ministers desire it.

Remember: *Two or more singular nouns or pronouns connected by the conjunctions 'either' – 'or', 'neither – nor' require a singular verb. If the subjects differ in number or in person, the verb agrees with the number or person which stands nearest to it.*

12.	Slow and steady with the race.	Slow and steady wins the race.
13.	Law and order are to be maintained at all costs.	Law and order is to be maintained at all costs.
14.	Rice and curry are my favorite food.	Rice and curry is my favorite food.

Remember: *When two different nouns combine to form one idea or are treated as a unity, the verb* **is singular.**

15.	Fifty rupees are a big sum.	Fifty rupees is a big sum.
16.	Five miles are not a long distance.	Five miles is not a long distance.
17.	Ten thousand rupees are not a small sum.	Ten thousand rupees is not a small sum.

Remember: *When a plural noun is considered collectively, the verb is a singular.*

18.	'The Tale of Two Cities' are an interesting novel.	'The Tale of Two Cities' is an interesting novel.
19.	'The United States' have a big navy.	'The United States' has a big navy.

Remember: *When a plural noun is a proper name for some collective unit or some single objector denotes some specific quality or amount, the verb is in the singular.*

20.	The teacher to together with his students were there.	The teacher together with his students was there.
21.	Mohan alongwith his sisters were present there.	Mohan along with his sisters was present there.
22.	The leader besides his followers were arrested.	The leader beside his followers was arrested.
23.	Arvind, like Kapil are a good singer.	Arvind, like Kapil, is a good singer.
24.	A table in addition to two chairs are all that he has.	A table in addition to two chairs is all that he has.
25.	Kamal and not his brothers are to blame.	Kamal, and not his brother, is to blame.

26.	The commander with all his soldiers were in the battle-field.	The commander, with all his soldiers, was in the battle-field.

Remember: *Two nouns or pronouns connected by and – not, with, in addition to, like, besides, together, as well as, not only – but also, are followed by a verb in the singular when the former of the two nouns or pronouns is in the singular.*

27.	I have seen him yesterday.	I saw him yesterday.
28.	She has passed the examination last year.	She passed the examination last year.
29.	The patient died before the doctor came.	The patient had died before the doctor came.
30.	The bell went when I reached the college.	The bell had gone when I reached the college.

Remember: *When two actions or events take place in the past, the action or event taking place first is shown in the Past Perfect Tense, the other one in the Past Indefinite Tense.*

31.	I shall help you if you will speak the truth.	I shall help you if you speak the truth.
32.	She will repent if she will wastes her time.	She will repent if she waste her time.

Remember: *Don't use two future tenses together. The sentence beginning with when or if should be in the Present Indefinite Tense.*

33.	Many a girls were playing.	Many girls were playing (or Many girls were playing).
34.	Many a boys have left the class.	Many boys have left the class.

Remember: *'Many a' should be followed by a singular noun and a singular verb.*

35.	I knew that she will disobey me.	I knew that she would disobey me.
36.	You told us that honesty was the best policy.	You told us that honesty is the best policy.

Remember: *If the Principal Clause is in the Past Tense, the Subordinate Clause must be in the Past Tense unless it has a universal truth or a historical truth or a habitual truth.*

37.	This is one of the best novels that has been published.	This is one of the best novels that have been published.
38.	He is one of the greatest leaders who has served India.	He is one of the greatest leaders who have served India.

Remember: *The plural antecedents of the relative pronoun should have a plural verb.*

39.	I do not know where is he going.	I do not know where he is going.
40.	Can you tell when will she come back?	Can you tell when she will come back?
41.	Tell me how are you now.	Tell me how you are now.

Remember: *If there are two clauses in a sentence, the Subordinate Clause should not be in the question form.*

42.	You behave as if you are a prince.	You behave as if you were a prince.
43.	She weeps as though she is in despair.	She weeps as though she were in despair.
44.	I wish I was a child again.	I wish I were a child again.
45.	He walked as if he were lame.	He walked as he had been lame.

Remember: *Expression like 'as if', 'as though', or expression of a wish should be followed by a Past Tense and in the plural form. But if the Principal clause is in the Past Indefinite tense, it should be followed by Perfect Tense.*

46.	Walking on the road he met an old man.	While (or when) he was walking on the road he met an old man.
47.	Entering the office, I heard the telephone ring.	As I was entering the office, I heard the telephone ring.
48.	Waiting for the bus, an old friend came there.	When I was waiting for the bus, an old friend came there.

Remember: *The participle should not be left without proper agreement. It must be attached with a noun or a pronoun to which it refers.*

49.	The difficulty of getting house in big cities are great.	The difficulty of getting houses in big cities is great.
50.	Your choice of friends are not good.	Your choice of friends is not good.

Remember: *When the subject is in the singular form, it must have a singular verb.*

51.	The poet and the novelist is dead.	The poet and the novelist are dead. (Two persons).
52.	The white and black now are grazing.	The white and black cow is grazing. (one)

Remember: *When two or more persons refers to one person or thing, the verb is singular. But when the article is respected before every person the verb should be in the plural form.*

53.	I have never and will never disobey you.	I have never disobeyed and will never disobey you.
54.	She has never and will never tell a lie.	She has never told & will never tell a lie.

Remember: *Use 3rd form of the verb after have and has.*

55.	Our only guide were that stars.	Our only guide was the stars.
56.	The stars was our only guide.	The stars were our only guide.

Remember: *A verb should agree with its subject and not with the complement.*

57.	A large number of students was present today.	A large number of students were present today.
58.	None but the brave deserve the fair.	None but the brave deserves the fair.
59.	The rest of the students was on leave.	The rest of the students were on leave.

Remember: *Some nouns like number, plenty, rest, variety, army etc. are plural in meaning though they are singular in form, so the verb is in plural.*

60.	Not riches but education ensure success.	Not riches but education ensures success.
61.	Not wealth but health count in life.	Not wealth but health counts in life.
62.	The committee have issued its report.	The committee has issued its report.
63.	The jury have given its verdict.	The jury has given its verdict.

Remember: *When a collective noun like committee, crowds, army, fleet is thought of as a whole, acting together as one unit, it is used in the singular sense.*

64.	The ministry is divided on the language issue.	The ministries are divided on the language issue.

Remember: *When a collective noun is not acting as a unit, it takes a plural verb.*

65.	My brother prevented me to go to bazaar.	My brother prevented me from going to the bazaar.
66.	She insisted to marry an actor.	She insisted on marrying an actor.
67.	My father checked me to smoke.	My father checked me from smoking.
68.	Sahil persisted to attend the meeting.	Sahil persisted in attending the meeting.
69.	I did not hinder him to do his duty.	I did not hinder him from doing his duty.
70.	Pooja succeeded to reach her goal.	Pooja succeeded in reaching her goal.

Remember: *Verbs like succeed, insist, persist, prevent, check, desist, avoid, restrain, addict, hinder, bent, prohibit etc. are followed by a gerund (i.e. a verbal noun).*

71.	You had better not to go there.	You had better not go there.
72.	None can dare to touch me.	None can dare touch me.
73.	The teacher made the boy to do it.	The teacher made the boy do it.
74.	You need not to go there.	You need not go there.

Remember: *No infinitive (i.e. 'to') is used after the phrase – Had better, had rather and after some verbs like dare, need make, let.*

75.	My brother as well as I am playing.	My brother as well as I are playing.
76.	She as well as her friends are reading.	She as well as her friends is reading.

Remember: *When two subjects, not of the same person, are joined by as well as, the verb agrees with the first subject.*

77.	Neither she went there nor I did.	Neither did she go there, nor did I.
78.	You did not do so, nor he did.	You did not do so, nor did he.
79.	No sooner he reached the station than the train steamed off.	No sooner did he reach the station than the train steamed off.
80.	Hardly I had stepped out when it started raining.	Hardly had I stepped out, when it started raining.

Remember: *The verb comes before its subject when it is introduced by neither or nor or hardly or no sooner.*

81.	She did not see you for two months.	She has not seen you for two months.
82.	I am working in this office for 1980.	I have been working in this office since 1980.

Remember: *Use Perfect Continuous Tense where time is given.*

MORE ERRORS IN THE USE OF VERBS

1.	Two and two makes four.	Two and two make four.
2.	A company to two hundred soldiers were crossing the bridge.	A company of two hundred soldiers was crossing the bridge.
3.	Five times five are twenty five.	Five times five is twenty five.
4.	She did nothing but wept.	She did nothing but weep.
5.	The teacher asked me where was I going.	The teacher asked me where I was going.
6.	He hanged his coat on a peg.	He hung his coat on a peg.
7.	The murderer was hung yesterday.	The murderer was hanged yesterday.
8.	She laid in her bed.	She lay in her bed.
9.	Let me lay here.	Let me lie here.
10.	The hen lay an egg.	The hen laid an egg.
11.	He felled on the ground.	He fell on the ground.
12.	The woodcutter is falling the tree.	The woodcutter is felling the tree.
13.	Babar fund the Mughal Empire.	Babar founded the Mughal Empire.
14.	She founded a ten-paisa coin.	She found a ten-paisa coin.
15.	This news was broadcasted over the radio.	This news was broadcast over the radio.
16.	We shall give a test in English to-morrow.	We shall take a test in English to-marrow.
17.	Our teacher will take a test in English to-morrow.	Our teacher will give us a test in English to-morrow.
18.	Is not she your sister?	Is she not your sister?
19.	Can I come in, Sir?	May I come in, sir?
20.	This river has overflown its banks.	The river has overflowed its banks.
21.	He went there with a view to see me.	He went there with a view to seeing me.
22.	We shall look forward to see you.	We shall look forward to seeing you.
23.	I know to play hockey?	I know how to play hockey?
24.	She enjoys to walk.	She enjoys walking.
25.	Mohan could not help to laugh.	Mohan could not help laughing.
26.	This book is worth to buy.	This book is worth buying.
27.	It is no good to visit him.	It is no good visiting him.

28.	This ship was drowned and its crew sank into sea.	This ship sank and its crew drowned into the sea.
29.	Do not cut stale jokes in the class.	Do not crack stale jokes in the class.
30.	She never met me today.	She did not meet me today.
31.	He struck a blow on my face.	He struck (or hit) me in the face.
32.	Please borrow me some money.	Please lend me some money.
33.	Let me to play.	Let me play.
34.	He informed the matter to the police.	He reported the matter to the police.
35.	How are you going on with your work?	How are you getting on with your work?
36.	He offered to hire his house.	He offered to let his house.
37.	The Prime Minister gave a speech.	The Prime Minister made (or delivered) a speech.
38.	When do you sleep?	When do you go to bed?
39.	My tooth is paining.	My tooth is aching.
40.	The thief has robbed all his money.	The thief has stolen all his money.
41.	I saw a car stopping.	I saw a car stop.
42.	She closed the tap.	She turned off the tap.
43.	Arun opened the tap.	Arun turned on the tap.
44.	She used to wake up early in the morning.	She wakes up early in the morning.
45.	I prefer to walk than to ride.	I prefer walking to riding.
46.	The general was killed and the soldiers taken prisoner.	The general was killed and the soldiers were taken prisoner.
47.	Please mend my pencil.	Please sharpen my pencil.
48.	The teacher is seeing my answer book.	The teacher is looking over my answer book.

49.	I shall mark these answer books.	I shall evaluate these answer books.
50.	Do not speak nonsense.	Do not talk nonsense.
51.	Keep it on the table.	Put it on the table.
52.	We won our opponents.	We beat our opponents.
53.	Hear my advice.	Listen to my advice.
54.	We made two goals.	We scored two goals.
55.	I have done no fault.	I have committed no fault.
56.	I avenged myself for the injustice done to my brother.	I avenged myself for the injustice done to my brother.
57.	He revenged his father's murder.	He avenged his father's murder.
58.	He is opening the knot.	He is untying the knot.
59.	Shut the light.	Switch off the light.
60.	Burn the lamp.	Light the lamp.
61.	See this word in the dictionary.	Look up this word in the dictionary.
62.	He put off his hat.	He took off his hat.
63.	I do not afraid of a dog.	I am not afraid of a dog. (or do not fear).
64.	You will have to leave your rights.	You will have to abandon (or relin-quish) your rights.
65.	An old begger was over run by a truck.	An old beggar was run over by a truck.
66.	He said his friend good-bye.	He bade his friend good-bye.
67.	Kindly see my testimonials.	Kindly look at (or examine) my testimonials.
68.	Tell me not such a dreadful story.	Do not tell me such a dreadful story.
69.	I filled water in the bucket.	I filled the bucket with water.
70.	She cannot live without a car.	She cannot do without a car.
71.	A snake cut him yesterday.	A snake bit him yesterday.

72.	A pick-pocket cut my pocket.	A pick-pocket picked my pocket.
73.	The doctor saw my pulse.	The doctor felt my pulse.
74.	Rajni has left photography.	Rajni has given up photography.
75.	Leave my arm, please.	Let off my arm, please.
76.	I felt pity on the beggar.	I took pity on the beggar.
77.	She gave no answer.	She made no answer.
78.	I had a mind to join a college.	I intended to join a college.
79.	She has thrown milk on the floor.	She has spilt milk on the floor.
80.	This shop was put on fire.	The shop was set on fire.
81.	This word is wrong, cut it.	This word is wrong, erase it (or rub it or scratch it or cross it).
82.	I hope he will fail.	I fear he will fail.
83.	He said me a liar.	He called me a liar.
84.	She has forgotten to fetch her camera.	She has forgotten to bring her camera.
85.	Please bring my cycle from my office.	Please fetch my bicycle from my office.
86.	She is fail in English.	She fails (or has failed) in English.
87.	I refused his invitation.	I declined his invitation.
88.	He denied to help me.	He refused to help me.
89.	The thief refused having broken the door.	The thief denied having broken the door.
90.	She ate her meals.	She had (or took) her meals.
91.	He needs not wait for me.	He need not wait for me.
92.	I think I shall pass.	I think I will pass.
93.	Shall Mohan or will Sohan attend the meeting?	Will Mohan or Sohan attend the meeting?
94.	I cannot find my book nowhere.	I cannot find my book anywhere. Or I can find my book nowhere.
95.	You cannot pass unless you do not work hard.	You cannot pass unless you work hard. Or You cannot pass if you do not work hard.
96.	Work hard lest you may fail.	Work hard lest you should fail.
97.	She forbade her son not to go there.	She forbade her son to go there.
98.	Wait for me until I do not come back.	Wait for me until I come back.
99.	I don't hardly think that you will pass.	I hardly think that you will pass.
100.	The train stayed here for five minutes.	The train stopped here for five minutes.
101.	I shall stop with you for two days.	I shall stay with you for two days.
102.	I have eaten my meals.	I have taken my meals.
103.	Later on he knew his mistake.	Later on he realized his mistake.
104.	I believe you are better now.	I hope you are better now.
105.	Should you mind opening the window?	Would you mind opening the window?
106.	It can rain today.	It may rain today.
107.	A number of writers has arrived here.	A number of writers have arrived here.
108.	It is no good to visit him now.	It is no good visiting him now.
109.	I requested him to not disturb me.	I requested him not to disturb me.
110.	He talks English well.	He speaks English well.

ERRORS IN THE USE OF ADJECTIVES

An 'Adjective' is a word used to modify or qualify a Noun or a pronoun as :-

black, small, happy, proud, thin etc.

1.	I prefer English than Hindi.	I prefer English to Hindi.
2.	She is senior than I by two years.	She is senior to me by two years.
3.	Health is more preferable than wealth.	Health is preferable to wealth.
4.	Your pen is more superior than me.	Your pen is superior to mine.
5.	My hat is more inferior than you.	My hat is inferior to yours.
6.	Mohan is junior than I.	Mohan is junior to me.
7.	I met her prior from her departure.	I met her prior to her departure.

Remember: *Use 'to' after, 'prefer, senior, junior, preferable, superior, inferior.' Don't use 'more' before these words.*

8.	You are wise than I.	You are wiser than I.
9.	She is beautiful than her sister.	She is more beautiful than her sister.

Remember: *Use comparative degrees when there is a comparison between two persons or two things.*

10.	He is more happier than I.	He is happier than I.
11.	I am more cleverer than you.	I am cleverer than you.

Remember: *Double comparatives should be avoided.*

12.	Mohan is taller in his four brothers.	Mohan is the tallest of his four brothers.
13.	She is more intelligent of all her class-fellows.	She is the most intelligent of her class-fellows.

Remember: *Superlative Degree should be used when there is a comparison among more than two persons or things.*

14.	Radha is the most happiest girl.	Radha is the happiest girl.
15.	You are the most smartest boy.	You are the smartest boy.

Remember: *Double superlatives should be avoided.*

16.	Raj is better than any player in the team.	Raj is better than any other player in the team.
17.	Amitabh is more famous than any actor of Hindi films.	Amitabh is more famous than any other actor in Hindi films.

Remember: *In a comparative degree, use, than any 'other'*

18.	You are the richest of all other friends.	You are the richest of all the friends.
19.	She is the most charming of all other girls.	She is the most charming of all the girls.

Remember: *In a superlative degree, don't use 'other' or 'any other'. Definite article 'the' should be used before the superlative degree.*

20.	Madhu is comparatively weaker in English.	Mohan is comparatively weak in English.

Remember: *Don't use comparative degree with 'comparatively'*

21.	She is cleverer than industrious.	She is more clever than industrious.

Remember: *When two qualities in the same person are compared we should use 'more' before the positive degree.*

22.	You are the most ideal teacher.	You are an ideal teacher.
23.	Her beauty is the most unique.	Her beauty is unique.
24.	It is the most impossible to cross this river.	It is impossible to cross this river.
25.	Nehru was the most perfect gentleman.	Nehru was a perfect gentleman.
26.	Your performance is the most excellent.	Your performance is excellent.

Remember: *Certain adjectives like ideal, unique, impossible, extreme, perfect, excellent, complete, entire, chief etc, do not admit of any comparison.*

27.	She is my oldest daughter.	She is my eldest daughter.
28.	You are the eldest player in the team.	You are the oldest player in the team.
29.	My house is older than your.	My house is older than yours.
30.	She is elder than her sister.	She is older than her sister.

Remember: *'Older' or 'oldest' is used when comparative age is in question 'Elder' or 'eldest' is used when comparative age of the members of the same family is un question. Moreover, 'older' and 'oldest' may be used both for persons and things but 'elder' and 'eldest' are used only for persons.*

31.	Few boys are present in the class.	A few boys are present in the class.
32.	A poor man has a few friends.	A poor man has few friends.
33.	Few friends I have are sincere.	The few friends I have are sincere.

Remember: *'Few' is negative and means practically none. 'A few' is positive and means 'some'. 'The few' conveys negative as well positive idea. I mean 'some but all'.*

34.	Little knowledge is a dangerous thing.	A little knowledge is a dangerous thing.
35.	There is little hope of success.	There is a little hope of success.
36.	I have spent little money I had.	I have spent the little money I had.

Remember: *'Little' is negative and means 'not much'. 'A little' means 'some'. 'The little' implies both negative and positive meanings i.e. 'not much' and 'all the money'.*

37.	No less than twenty students were present.	No fewer than twenty students were present.
38.	She needs no fewer than four kilos of sugar.	She needs no less than four kilos of sugar.

Remember: *'Fewer' denotes number and 'less' refers to quality.*

39.	I have much friends.	I have many friends.
40.	You have many works to do.	You have much work to do.
41.	Renu bought as many as four kilos of sugar.	Renu bought as much as four kilos of sugar.
42.	Kusum needs as much as fifty rupees.	Kusum needs as many as fifty rupees.

Remember: *'Many' and 'as many as' refer to numbers while 'much' and 'as much as' denote quantity.*

43.	Mohan came latter than Sohan.	Mohan came later than Sohan.
44.	Of these two friends the later is more intelligent.	Of these two friends, the latter is more intelligent.
45.	What is the last news?	What is the latest news?
46.	The latest chapter of this book is very interesting.	The last chapter of this book is very interesting.

Remember: *'Later' and 'latest' are used to show time. 'Latter' and 'last' are used to show position.*

47.	Radha is the ablest and intelligent of all the girls.	Radha is the ablest and the most intelligent of all the girls.
48.	Mango is the best and sweet fruit.	Mango is the best and the sweetest fruit.

Remember: *When adjectives are used for the same subject, and one of them is superlative, the other one must also be superlative.*

49.	I shall not buy some sweets.	I shall not buy any sweets.
50.	The teacher gave her any books.	The teacher gave her some books.

Remember: *'Any' is used in the negative sentence while 'some' is used in a positive one. Both can be used in the Interrogative also.*

51.	He knows both girls.	He knows both the girls.

52.	Ramesh lost both hands.	Ramesh lost both of his hands.
53.	I shall attend both meetings.	I shall attend both the meetings.

Remember: *Use article 'the' after 'both' when it is used as an adjective. It is placed before the noun or possessive pronoun.*

54.	Bombay is further from Delhi than Madras.	Bombay is farther from Delhi than Madras.
55.	The P.M. made no farther remarks.	The P.M. made no further remarks.

Remember: *'Farther' refers to distance while 'further' means more or additional.*

56.	Suman is rather richer than her friends.	Suman is richer than her friends.
57.	I am rather happier than you.	I am happier than you.

Remember : *'Rather' has a force of comparison. Avoid the use of double comparatives.*

58.	The climate of Srinagar is cooler than Shimla.	The climate of Srinagar is cooler than that of Shimla.
59.	My books are superior to you.	My books are superior to those of you (or yours).

Remember : *Comparison is always made between things of the same kind.*

60.	The whole India loved Nehru and Gandhi.	The whole of India loved Nehru and Gandhi.
61.	She ate whole mango.	She ate the whole mango.
62.	His all friends were insincere.	All of his friends were insincere.
63.	I worked all day.	I worked all day.

Remember: *When 'whole' is used as an adjective it is preceded by 'the' and followed by 'of'. 'All' is placed before the noun or possessive noun.*

64.	She is two years smaller than I.	She is two years younger than I.
65.	You are three inches younger than he.	You are three inches smaller than he.

Remember: *'Young' or 'old' show age while 'big' or 'small' show size.*

66.	Sugar tastes sweetly.	Sugar tastes sweet.
67.	Quinine taste bitterly.	Quinine tastes bitter.
68.	Please run fastly.	Please run fast.

Remember: *Use an adjective (not an adverb) after such verb as look, feel, taste, smell etc.*

69.	I do not these kinds of books.	I do not like this kind of book.
70.	These sort of pictures are not liked by me.	These sorts of pictures are not liked by me.

Remember: *'Kind' and 'sort' should be used in the singular.*

71.	Rich should help poor.	The rich should help the poor.
72.	Only brave deserve the fair.	Only the brave deserve the fair.

Remember: *If we place 'the' before an adjective, it becomes plural noun.*

MORE ERRORS IN THE USE OF ADJECTIVES

1.	It is much hot today.	It is very hot today.
2.	He sat nearest to her.	He sat next to her.
3.	Cinema has proved much harmful than useful.	Cinema has proved more harmful than useful.
4.	Her camera is superior and deserve more praise than yours.	Her camera is superior to yours and deserves more praise.
5.	Mohan is wise for his age.	Mohan is wiser for his age.
6.	No leader was great as Nehru.	No other leader was as great as Nehru.
7.	You are sick in appearance.	You are sick in appearance.
8.	He is miser man.	He is a miserly man.
9.	I am better now.	I am much better now.
10.	Open your book at seven page.	Open your book at page seven.
11.	She is becoming clever day by day.	She is becoming cleverer day by day.

12.	My brother considers it a great luck.	My brother considers it a good luck.
13.	I got nearly cent per cent marks in Sanskrit.	I got nearly full marks in Sanskrit.
14.	This statement sounds strangely.	This statement sounds strange.
15.	Arvind is in six class.	Arvind is in sixth class.
16.	Ravi gets a less salary.	Ravi gets a small salary.
17.	I am on leave of four days.	I am on leave for four days (or four days' leave).
18.	I have never seen a so beautiful girl.	I have never seen such a beautiful girl.
19.	Yours sincere friend.	Yours sincerely or Your sincere friend.
20.	He is a coward man.	He is a cowardly man.
21.	These all books are worth reading.	All these books are worth reading.
22.	Any one cannot cross Tiber by swimming.	None can cross the Tiber by swimming.
23.	I have no other friend except Sahil.	I have no other friend than Sahil.
24.	This book cost me rupees six.	This book cost me six rupees.
25.	A few number of student have passed.	A few students have passed.
26.	Anil Grover is our mutual friend.	Anil Grover is our common friend.
27.	I gave him my fullest co-operation.	I gave him my full cooperation.
28.	Both men have not come back.	Neither man has come back.
29.	My economical condition is not good.	My economic condition is not good.
30.	Science has proved much harmful than useful.	Science has proved more harmful than useful.
31.	Stop this non-sense talk.	Stop this nonsensical talk.
32.	Rains were plenty last year.	Rains were plentiful last year.
33.	Tribune has the largest circulation than any newspaper.	The Tribune has larger circulation than any other newspaper. Or The Tribune has the largest circulation of all the newspapers.
34.	The last half of the picture is interesting.	The second half of the picture is interesting.
35.	The five last pages of this book are torn.	The last five pages of this book are torn.
36.	I gave my son one and a half rupees.	I gave my son one rupee and a half.
37.	Jagga was a noted robber.	Jagga was a notorious robber.
38.	Of these two pens. I shall buy the least costly.	Of these two pens, I shall buy the less costly one.
39.	My father brought much sweet and oranges.	My father brought a lot of sweets and many oranges.
40.	Mohan and Sohan are brothers, the first is wiser than the second.	Mohan and Sohan are brothers, the former is wiser than the latter.
41.	Car, scooter or bicycle, either will do.	Car, scooter or bicycle, any will do.
42.	The best team won the final match.	The better team won the final match.
43.	He behaved friendly when I met him.	He behaved in a friendly manner when I met him.
44.	Cinema is terrible harmful for eyes.	Cinema is terribly harmful for eyes.
45.	I have strong headache.	I have a severe headache.
46.	He is my fast enemy.	He is my sworn enemy.

47.	He has money enough to support you.	He has enough money to support you.
48.	This room is too much small for me.	This room is much too small for me.
49.	She is suffering from severe cold.	She is suffering from a bad cold.

ERRORS IN THE USE OF ADVERBS

An Adverb is a word that modified a verb, an adjective or another adverb as :- *always, enough, seldom, much, sometimes, extremely etc.*

1.	It is too cold today.	It is very cold today.
2.	You are too busy.	You are very busy.

Remember: *'Too' should not be used in the sense of 'very' or 'much' 'Too' means some kind of excess or more than enough.*

3.	He is enough rich to help you.	He is rich enough to help you.
4.	I am enough tired to go farther.	I am tired enough to go farther.

Remember: *The Adverb 'enough' is generally used after the word it modifies.*

5.	I visit his house often.	I often visit his house.
6.	Mohan smokes seldom.	Mohan seldom smokes.
7.	You should speak the truth always.	You should always speak the truth.
8.	He takes tea sometimes.	He sometimes takes tea.
9.	We visit this temple frequently.	We frequently visit this temple.

Remember: *The adverbs of time : seldom, often, sometimes, frequently, never, ever, always etc, are generally used before the verbs they modify.*

10.	It is nothing else than pride.	It is nothing else but pride.
11.	You can call him anything else than a fool.	You can call him anything but a fool.

Remember: *'Else' should be followed by 'but' any not by 'than'.*

12.	She is wonderful beautiful.	She is wonderfully beautiful.
13.	You are regular irregular.	You are regularly irregular.

Remember: *'Wonderful' and 'regular' are adjectives. Use the correct adverbs here.*

14.	He was compelled to at once leave the place.	He was compelled to leave the place at once.
15.	She tried to hurriedly reach there.	She tried to reach there hurriedly.

Remember: *An adverb should not be used before an infinitive.*

16.	Ramesh will tomorrow call on you.	Rames will call on you tomorrow.
17.	I last night visited the circus.	I visited the circus last night.

Remember: *Adverb or adverbial phrases of definite time like 'yesterday, tomorrow, last night, today, four month ago' are usually placed at the end of the sentences.*

18.	It is very hot to go out.	It is too hot to go out.
19.	Ram is very poor to help you.	Ram is too poor to help you.
20.	You are too proud.	You are very pround.

Remember: *'Too' means 'more than enough' while 'very' is used simply to make the adjective or adverb stronger.*

21.	I only spent five rupees.	I spent only five rupees.
22.	I only worked two sums.	I worked only two sums.

Remember: *'Only' should be placed immediately before the word it qualifies.*

23.	He does carefully his work.	He does his work carefully.
24.	You have almost reached at your goal.	You have almost reached your goal.
25.	I fluently spoke.	I spoke fluently.

Remember: *With a 'transitive verb' the adverb generally comes after the object. But when the verb is intransitive, the adverb or adverbial phrase is placed after the verb.*

26.	I fortunately passed the test.	Fortunately I passed the test.
27.	We reached our goal at length.	At length we reached our goal.

Remember: *An adverb should be placed at the beginning of a sentence when it is intended to qualify not any word in particular, but the sentence as a whole.*

28.	You are speaking much fluently.	You are speaking very fluently.
29.	Mohini is very wiser than Lalita.	Mohini is much wiser than Lalita.

Remember: *'Very' modifies adjectives or adverbs in a positive degree and 'much' in the comparative degree.*

30.	I shall come back just now.	I shall come back right now.
31.	My friend has met me presently.	My friend has met me just now.

Remember: *'Presently' should be used for near future while 'just now' refers to present or past time.*

32.	She is so nice.	She is very nice.
33.	Radha is very proud as sita.	Radha is as proud as Sita.
34.	I work quicker than he.	I work more quickly than him.
35.	You should know to respect others.	You should know how to respect others.

Remember: *'Adjectives' should not be used as 'Adverbs'.*

36.	We seldom or ever tell a lie.	We seldom or never tell a lie.
37.	Firstly you should be obedient and secondly dutiful.	First you should be obedient and secondly, dutiful.

Remember: *'First' is an adverb. Therefore, in an enumeration, use first, secondly, thirdly etc.*

38.	She *never* remembers having sent me a letter.	She does not remember having sent me a letter.
39.	I *never* saw him today.	I did not see him today.

Remember: *Here 'never' is incorrectly used for 'not'. Never means 'not ever'.*

40.	Are you an obedient boy? Yes, you see not an obedient boy.	Are you an obedient boy? Yes, you are an obedient (or No, you are not an obedient boy).

Remember: *If the answer to a question is yes, the verb following must be in the affirmative. But if the answer is no, the verb following must be in the negative.*

MORE ERRORS IN THE USE OF ADVERBS

1.	You are somewhat tall for your age.	You are rather tall for your age.
2.	The train reached rather lately.	The train arrived rather late.
3.	They found me lying senselessly.	They found me lying senseless.
4.	I recovered my health by and by.	I gradually recovered my health.
5.	The guests went away by and by.	The guests went away one by one.
6.	She is named as Rani.	She is named Rani.
7.	The box is too much heavy for me.	The box is much too heavy for me.
8.	Ranjit ran quicker than I thought.	Ranjit ran more quickly than I had thought.
9.	Indira Gandhi was respected greatly everywhere.	Indira Gandhi was greatly respected everywhere.
10.	My heart is much full for words.	My heart is too full for words.
11.	I saw you long before.	I saw you long ago.
12.	Her statement is somewhat true.	Her statement is partially true.
13.	We should face cheerfully our miseries.	We should face our miseries cheerfully.
14.	To-day it is bitter cold.	To-day it is bitterly cold.
15.	They came at once there.	They came there at once.

16.	I shall tell you about it little by little.	I shall tell you about it by and by.
17.	The cuckoo sang beautiful.	The cuckoo sang beautifully.
18.	The doctor gives me the medicine freely.	This doctor gives me the medicine for free.
19.	Go home directly.	Go home directly.
20.	Some students cannot even write correct English.	Some students cannot even write correct English.
21.	My house needs repairs badly.	My house badly needs repairs.
22.	I care a fig for him.	I do not care a fig for him.
23.	You care a straw for your boss.	You do not care about a straw for your boss.
24.	My brother is presently in Lebanon.	My brother is at present in Lebanon.
25.	I have only finished two novels.	I have finished only two novels.
26.	Your father is very miser.	Your father is very miserly.
27.	The widow feels sadly.	The widow feels sad.
28.	She hurriedly reached there.	She reached there hurriedly.
29.	Radha speaks very hasty.	Radha speaks very hastily.
30.	Please carry carefully my luggage.	Please carry my luggage carefully.
31.	Firstly you should be regular and secondly hard working.	First you should be regular and secondly, hard working.
32.	Luggage is too much heavy for me.	The luggage is much too heavy for me.
33.	My grandmother peacefully died.	My grandmother died peacefully.
34.	She exactly came in time.	She came exactly in time.
35.	You must come at 5 p.m. sharply.	You must come at 5 p.m. sharp.

ERRORS IN THE USE OF CONJUNCTIONS

A conjunction is a part of speech that connects words, clauses or sentences, or shows relations between sentences as :- and, but, as–as, either-or, as well as, unless etc.

1.	Though he is poor but he is honest.	Though he is poor, yet he is honest.
2.	I like such boys who are industrious.	I like such boys who are industrious.
3.	Work hard lest you may not fail.	Work hard lest you should fail.
4.	No sooner the sun rose, the mist disappeared.	No sooner did the sun rise than the mist disappeared.
5.	Hardly had we reached the ground, than the match started.	Hardly had we reached the ground when the match started.
6.	We had scarcely come out then it started raining.	We had scarcely come out when it started raining.
7.	She met no other woman but her aunt.	She met no other woman than her aunt.
8.	He is not only wise but hard working.	He is not only wise but hard working also.
9.	I am so happy like you are.	I am so happy as you are.
10.	The hare runs as fast like the dog.	The hare runs as fast as the dog.

Remember: *The following points should be kept in mind.*

(1) Though or although ***is followed by*** *yet*
(2) Such " " " as
(3) Lest " " " should
(4) No sooner " " " than
(5) Hardly or Scarcely " " " when or before
(6) No other " " " than
(7) Not only " " " but also
(8) So " " " as
(9) As " " " as

11.	Unless you do not speak the truth, I shall not forgive you.	Unless you speak the truth, I shall not forgive you.
Remember: *Unless is already negative. It means 'If not'.*		
12.	Wait here until I do not return.	Wait here until I return.
Remember: *'Until' is already negative. Don't use 'do not' with it.*		
13.	The choice is between glorious death or shameful life.	The choice is between glorious death and shameful life.
Remember: *Function of 'or' is to express alternative or choice but 'and' denotes addition.*		
14.	College life is charming and school life is dull.	College life is charming but school life is dull.
15.	You are very rich but you help the poor.	You are very rich and you help the poor.
Remember: *'And' joins two words or clauses of the same nature while 'but' is to join two antithetical clauses.*		
16.	Lions are both found in Asia and Africa.	Lions are found both in Asia and Africa.
17.	Both Mohan as well as Sohan are lazy.	Both Mohan and Sohan are lazy.
Remember: *'Both' should be followed but 'and', and not by 'as well as'. Moreover, it should be used immediately before the words to which it refers.*		
18.	Both Rajesh and Parveen are not cloth merchants.	Neither Rajesh nor Parveen is a cloth merchant.
Remember: *'Both' is used in the positive sense. In the negative sense, we should use 'neither-nor'.*		
19.	Neither did she attend the class nor he attended.	Neither she nor he attended the class.
20.	Neither did Mohan finish the work nor his brother finished.	Neither did Mohan finish the work nor did his brother finish.
Remember: *If neither is followed by an auxiliary verb, nor should also be followed by the same auxiliary verb.*		
21.	My pen is as good if not better than yours.	My pen is as good as if not better than yours.
22.	She is as noble or even nobler than he.	She is as noble as or even nobler than he.
Remember: *Use, as-as.*		
23.	Because she is dull, therefore she cannot pass.	She is dull, therefore, cannot pass. Or Because she is dull, she cannot pass.
Remember: *Don't use 'because' and 'therefore' in the same sentence.*		
24.	Supposing if you miss the bus where will you go?	Supposing (or if) you miss the bus where will you go?
25.	When you abuse no then I shall punish you.	When you abuse me, I shall punish you.
Remember: *'Supposing' and 'if' and 'when' and 'then' should not be used together.*		
26.	As I am busy so I cannot so out.	As I am busy, I cannot go out.
27.	I was appointed as the secretary of the club.	I was appointed the secretary of the club.
28.	She considers me as her brother.	She considers me her brother.
29.	I regard her my sister.	I regard her as my sister.
30.	My teacher doubts that I shall pass.	My teacher doubts whether (or if) I shall pass.
31.	I am not sure if I shall succeed.	I am not sure that I shall succeed.
32.	He neither speaks Hindi nor Punjabi.	He speaks neither Hindi nor Punjabi.
33.	Either your stand was right or wrong.	Your stand was either right or wrong.

34.	You should do like I.	You should do like I do.
35.	She asked me that what I was doing.	She asked me what I was doing.
36.	Two years have passed since I have seen my brother.	Two years have passed since I saw my brother.
37.	This is the first time when you have behaved well.	This is the first time that you have behaved well.
38.	The reason why he is angry is because he is hungry.	The reason why he is angry is that he is hungry.
39.	I am equally clever as my friend.	I am as clever as my friend.
40.	His behaviour is different that what it used to be.	His behaviour is different from what it used to be.
41.	In case if you fail what will you do?	In case (or if) you fail what will you do?
42.	If you are regular you will be dismissed.	Unless you are regular you will be dismissed.
43.	He is the fastest runner and he came last.	He is the faster runner but he came last.

29

CHAPTER

COMMON ERRORS
20 Practice Tests

Directions: *Here are 20 practice tests for finding "common errors' in the given sentences of each practice test. On the basis of understanding developed through common errors outlined and explained with rules given in Chapter 28, the readers will be able to identify and figure out errors in the given practice tests easily. These practice tests intend to serve the twin purposes of checking the level of understanding regarding common errors and proficiency in marking common errors. These practice tests are indicators to the level of language proficiency acquired by the learners and identify their grey areas.*

TEST – 1

1. When a baby my grandfather gave me a toy.
2. His father uses to go out for a walk daily.
3. The cattle is grazing in the ground.
4. One of his remarks were insulting.
5. If he will come here I shall give him a book.
6. He is the most strongest boy in the class.
7. You are sitting on a chair whose leg is broken.
8. He did not like me going there.
9. The thief with his companion have been arrested.
10. There is not nobody in the room.

TEST – 2

1. Have you brought some mangoes?
2. The Ganga is the sacred river.
3. I and Chetan did all the work.
4. He said it himself.
5. Blessed is he that has found a job.
6. He is much ill to do any work.
7. One of the boy was absent for a week.
8. Gopal came home lately.
9. She was sitting besides him.
10. Our hoard is small and our hearts are large.

TEST – 3

1. The manager was angry upon the employee.
2. One of the answer was wrong.
3. You should buy new furnitures for your house.
4. They pitched the tent besides the lake.
5. The wood-cutter was falling the trees in the forest.
6. The hens had stopped lying eggs.
7. The mother sings until the child does not go to sleep.
8. There was no one to look at the children in the hostel.
9. The reply is awaited for.
10. The chairman flew the flag.

TEST – 4

1. The doctor saw my pulse.
2. We walked for the end of the street.
3. I differ along with you on this question.
4. He turned a blind ear to his son's fault.
5. I prevailed under him to join our union.
6. I saw him felling a big tree off with an axe.
7. He is devoted to gambling.
8. We should not dabble with policies.
9. He is my fast enemy.
10. The prime minister gave a speech.

TEST – 5

1. He died with fever.
2. Ram acted with my proposal.
3. She quarreled against me over the property issue.
4. Be careful for your mother's health.
5. A Sikh, tall than any of his comrades, rushed forward.
6. They cheated each another.

7. Old father looks to his children.
8. Many a man have been ruined by speculation.
9. Let him and I go together.
10. The priest was very kind for all of us.

TEST – 6

1. The older the wine, better it tastes.
2. You cannot cross the bridge until you do not come to it.
3. He asked me what was my profession.
4. Give me a pencil to write.
5. Netaji is one of the bravest patriot of the country.
6. I met an one-eyed beggar in the street.
7. The traders dealing with garments are jittery about the impact of GST.
8. His efficiency soon made him the boss's blue-eyes boy.
9. She does not know cooking doesn't she?
10. No sooner the bell rang than the children rushed out of their classrooms.

TEST – 7

1. I request your favour to grant me leave.
2. He lived there for a day.
3. He is the fastest runner and he came last.
4. They know each other since January.
5. All the patients have been admitted and received attention.
6. They didn't see any movies since March.
7. We shall go on a tour as soon as the schools will close.
8. Each of the answers was not correct.
9. If we had had money we would go shopping.
10. I wanted that he should get leave.

TEST – 8

1. He enjoyed during the holidays.
2. Whoever works hard he will win.
3. The man who knocked at the door was stranger.
4. I asked my colleague when was he going to his home town.
5. Besides clothes, the shopkeeper deals with cosmetics too.
6. He is desirous for joining the army.
7. The judge said that the truth always triumphed.
8. One should help his friend in difficulty.
9. Sachin Tendulkar is the best batsman India has produced, isn't it?
10. More you read less you understand.

TEST – 9

1. School is very near my home.
2. They never fail who die in great cause.
3. It rained an hour before.
4. He wrote a most complete account of his travels.
5. Either of these three answers is incorrect.
6. You will be late until you hurry.
7. He is seldom or ever absent from school.
8. The colours so passed off one another that she could not distinguish them.
9. The general as well as his soldiers were killed in the battle.
10. The boat was drowned.

TEST – 10

1. One must do what he thinks best.
2. He will surely not do that, did he?
3. Can I leave the room now, Sir?
4. My neighbour, along with two friends, was pushing his car which is stalled.
5. I thought to help him, but he did not welcome my suggestion.
6. When I was a child, I enjoyed to eat ice cream in the bench.
7. The Principal, along with the teachers, are planning to apply for a leave.
8. Do you have an idea who is that man?
9. Unemployment as well as poverty influence the votes.
10. When I woke up, the man already disappeared after committing murder in the running train.

TEST – 11

1. The vehicular pollution causes serious harm to human beings.
2. Both Ashish and Smita came late to college today.

3. There is many problems relating to this matter.
4. Not only David passed but got a distinction.
5. We'd like some informations about the types of cars available.
6. I prefer to pay by cash.
7. My uncle has proposed me a job in his company.
8. All of a sudden she burst in tears.
9. I enjoy this type of music still now.
10. The teacher said me to submit the assignment the next day.

TEST – 12

1. Saints desire nothing to the society.
2. I regret at the delay in doing this.
3. I congratulate you for your success.
4. Ram as well as Mohan have gone.
5. He has passed order on my application.
6. He is more intelligent than any boy.
7. What will be ensued on this?
8. This is high time that we should change the bike.
9. I did nothing but laughed.
10. I informed him, "Leave the room."

TEST – 13

1. I live half of a mile from here.
2. "Do you like music?" "I like"
3. Do you like some more coffee?
4. He worked like a waiter for two years.
5. Like what does she look?
6. I know him since 1960.
7. I wasn't used to drive a big car.
8. He suggested me to try the main car park.
9. I have never met so nice person.
10. Too many Mathematics is usually taught in schools.

TEST – 14

1. We reached at home at seven o'clock.
2. I am knowing him for many years.
3. Vishal has watched this movie yesterday.
4. Where you have parked the car?
5. She will visit Chennai next month isn't it?
6. She knows when will Sushma reach Kolkata.
7. Mukta's teaching made his disciple to think again.
8. Neither Lakshmi and her father have met the Director.
9. I am seeing a man outside the door.
10. If I were a Minister, I would have appointed you the Principal of this school.

TEST – 15

1. The Greeks were brave peoples.
2. His hat was blown off by the strong air.
3. I am the one who am to blame.
4. We should sympathies with blind.
5. I'd rather play cricket and not swim.
6. Walking through the front door a wasp stung him.
7. Two plus nine are eleven.
8. I have built the house in 1960.
9. Their wedding has not been a very happy one.
10. Choose only such friends whom you can trust.

TEST – 16

1. Neither percept nor discipline are so forceful as example.W
2. Do you know if there is a house for letting in the neighbourhood?
3. Who you said was coming to see me in the morning?
4. He was finding it increasingly difficult to make his two ends meet.
5. The poor people of the village buy neither vegetables nor grow them.
6. On entering the hall, the number of visitors surprised me.
7. The short story should not exceed more than two hundred words.
8. Before giving the mixture to the child, shake it thoroughly.
9. Nothing has or could be more tragic than his death.
10. The reason that the students these days are so undisciplined is that they do not get any guidance from their parents.

TEST – 17

1. Too great a variety of studies destruct the mind.
2. The whole fleet of their ships were captured.
3. Each of these students have done their work.
4. None but fools has ever believed it.
5. He is one of cleverest boy that has passed through the school.
6. My friend, philosopher and guide have come.
7. The majority are opposed to this proposal.
8. He told me that he saw his father last month.
9. If he would have worked hard, he would have passed the examination.
10. Unless he will be more careful, he will not recover.

TEST – 18

1. The rain was accompanied by hail and storm.
2. I cannot help but to think that he is a fool.
3. I have never seen a clever man at engineering than him.
4. It is all the more better if he marries your daughter.
5. Objection to this proposal can be stated as thus.
6. He travelled from one corner of India to the other.
7. She could not make up the mind.
8. They tried to wipe out the poor widow's tears.
9. It is the best ideal each person may aspire for.
10. You are not entitled for admission.

TEST – 19

1. Each of the scholars, belonging to various countries have spoken about it.
2. All were present except he and his sister.
3. I wonder if ten thousand rupees are large sum.
4. She lay the table an hour ago.
5. He was absented from class for no reason.
6. He is untidy boy.
7. All his plans fell out for lack of help.
8. Of milk, coke and coffee, the latter is my favorites.
9. All this happened prior 1971 war.
10. Scarcely had she gone that he arrived.

TEST – 20

1. He boasts his achievements now and then.
2. She is living in this flat since 1995.
3. The Principal was angry upon the boys.
4. Character is more preferable than intelligence.
5. Krishna hanged all the pictures on the wall.
6. The sceneries of Kashmir move me most.
7. Cattle is grazing in the field.
8. Hari is going foreign next month.
9. She knew that I am leaving the place.
10. His elder brother gave him many good advices.

ANSWERS

TEST – 1

1. When I was a baby, my grandfather gave me a toy.
2. His father used to go out for a walk daily.
3. The cattle are grazing in the ground.
4. One of his remarks was insulting.
5. If he comes here, I shall give him a book.
6. He is tWWhe strongest boy in the class.
7. You are sitting on a chair of which a leg is broken.
8. He did not like my going there.
9. The thief and his companion have been arrested.
10. There is nobody in the room.

TEST – 2

1. Have you brought any mangoes?
2. The Ganga is a sacred river.
3. Chetan and I did all the work.
4. He said it to himself.
5. Blessed is he who has found a job.
6. He is too ill to do any work.
7. One of the boys was absent for a week.
8. Gopal came home late.
9. She was sitting beside him.
10. Our hoard is little and our hearts are large.

TEST – 3

1. The manager was angry with the employee.
2. One of the answers was wrong.
3. You should buy new furniture for your house.
4. They pitched the tent beside the lake.
5. The wood-cutter was felling the trees in the forest.
6. The hens had stopped laying eggs.
7. The mother sings until the child goes to sleep.
8. There was no one to look after the children in the hostel.
9. The reply is awaited.
10. The chairman unfurled the flag.

TEST – 4

1. The doctor felt my pulse.
2. We walked till the end of the street.
3. I differ with you on this question.
4. He turned a blind eye to his son's fault.
5. I prevailed upon him to join our union.
6. I saw him felling a big tree with an axe.
7. He is addicted to gambling.
8. We should not dabble in politics.
9. He is my sworn enemy.
10. The prime minister delivered a speech.

TEST – 5

1. He died of fever.
2. Ram acted on my proposal.
3. She quarreled with me over the property issue.
4. Be careful about your mother's health.
5. A Sikh, taller than any of his comrades, rushed forward.
6. They cheated each other.
7. Anold father looks to his children.
8. Many men have been ruined by speculation
9. Let him and me go together.
10. The priest was very kind to all of us.

TEST – 6

1. The older the wine, the better it tastes.
2. You cannot cross the bridge until you come to it.
3. He asked me what my profession was.
4. Give me a pencil to write with.
5. Netaji is one of the bravest patriots of the country.
6. I met a one-eyed beggar in the street.
7. The traders dealing with garments are feeling jittery about the impact of GST.
8. His efficiency soon made him the boss's blue-eyed boy
9. She does not know how to cook, does she?
10. No sooner did the bell ring than the children rushed out of their classrooms.

TEST – 7

1. I request you to grant me leave.
2. He lived there for one day.
3. He is the fastest runner but he came last.
4. They have known each other since January.
5. All the patients were admitted and received attention.
6. They haven't seen any movies since March.
7. We shall go on a tour as soon as the schools close.
8. Every answer was not correct.
9. If we had money we would go shopping.
10. I wanted him to get leave.

TEST – 8

1. He enjoyed himself during the holidays.
2. Whoever works hard will win.
3. The man who knocked at the door was a stranger.
4. I asked my colleague when he was going to his home town.
5. Besides clothes, the shopkeeper deals in cosmetics too.
6. He is desirous of joining the army.
7. The judge said that the truth always triumphs.
8. One should help one's friend in difficulty.
9. Sachin Tendulkar is the best batsman India has produced, isn't he?
10. The more you read, the less you understand.

TEST – 9

1. School is very near to my home.
2. They never fail who die for a great cause.
3. It has rained an hour before.
4. He wrote a complete account of his travels.
5. Anyone of these three answers is incorrect.
6. You will be late unless you hurry.
7. He is seldom or never absent from school.
8. The colours so matched that she could not distinguish them.
9. The general as well as his solders was killed in the battle.
10. The boat was sunk.

TEST – 10

1. One must do what one thinks is best.
2. He will surely not do that, will he?
3. May I leave the room now, Sir?
4. My neighbour, along with two friends, was pushing his car which was stalled.
5. I thought of helping him, but he did not welcome my suggestion.
6. When I was a child, I enjoyed eating ice cream in the bench.
7. The Principal, along with the teachers, is planning to apply for a leave.
8. Do you have an idea who that man is?
9. Unemployment as well as poverty influences the votes.
10. When I woke up, the man had already disappeared after committing the murder in the running train.

TEST – 11

1. Vehicular pollution causes serious harm to human beings.
2. Today, both Ashish and Smita came to college late.
3. There are many problems relating to this matter.
4. David not only passed but also got a distinction.
5. We'd like some information about the types of cars available.
6. I prefer to pay in cash.
7. My uncle has proposed to me a job in his company.
8. All of sudden she burst into tears.
9. I enjoy this type of music even now.
10. The teacher said to me to submit the assignment the next day.

TEST – 12

1. Saints desire nothing from the society.
2. I regret the delay in doing this.
3. I congratulate you on your success.
4. Ram as well as Mohan has gone.
5. He has passed order against my application.
6. He is more intelligent than any other boy.

7. What will be ensued after this?
8. It is high time that we should change the bike.
9. I did nothing but laugh.
10. I told him to leave the room.

TEST – 13

1. I live half a mile from here.
2. "Do you like music?" "I do."
3. Would you like some more coffee?
4. He worked as a waiter for two years.
5. What does she look like?
6. I have known him since 1960.
7. I wasn't used to driving a big car.
8. He suggested me to try the main car park.
9. I have never met such a nice person.
10. Too much mathematics is usually taught in schools.

TEST – 14

1. We reached home at seven o'clock.
2. I know him for many years.
3. Vishal watched this movie yesterday.
4. Where have you parked the car?
5. She will visit Chennai next month. Won't she?
6. She knows when Sushma will reach Kolkata.
7. Mukta's teaching made his disciple think again.
8. Neither Lakshmi nor her father has met the Director.
9. I am watching a man outside the door.
10. If I were a Minister, I would have appointed you the Principal of the school.

TEST – 15

1. The Greeks were brave people.
2. His hat was blown off by the strong wind.
3. I am the one who is to be blamed.
4. We must sympathise with the visually impaired.
5. I'd rather play cricket than swim.
6. While walking through the front door he was stung by a wasp.
7. Two plus nine equals eleven.
8. I had built this house in 1960.
9. Their wedding has not been a very happy one.
10. Choose only such friends who are trustworthy.

TEST – 16

1. Neither percept nor discipline is as forceful as an example.
2. Do you know if there is a house for to-let in the neighbourhood?
3. Whom did you mention was coming to see me in the morning?
4. He was finding it increasingly difficult to make both ends meet.
5. The poor villagers neither buy vegetables nor grow them.
6. I was surprised to see the number of visitors after I entered the hall.
7. The short story should not exceed the limit of 200 words.
8. Shake the mixture thoroughly before giving it to the child.
9. Nothing can or could be more tragic than his death.
10. The lack of discipline in students is due to the lack of guidance from their parents.

TEST – 17

1. Too much diversity in studies destructs the mind.
2. The whole fleet of ships was captured.
3. Each of these students has done his work
4. Only fools have believed it.
5. He is one of the most intelligent students to have passed out of this school.
6. Here comes my friend, philosopher and guide.
7. This proposal has been opposed by a majority of the members.
8. He informed me that he had seen his father last month.
9. He would have passed the examination only if he had worked hard.
10. He would not recover unless he becomes more careful.

TEST – 18

1. Hail and storm accompanied the rain.
2. I cannot help but think he is a fool.
3. I have never seen a clever man in engineering than him.
4. It is best if he marries your daughter.
5. Objections to this proposal can be stated as follows.
6. He travelled in India from one corner to the other.
7. She could not make up her mind.
8. They tried to wipe away the poor widow's tears.
9. It is the best ideal for which every person may aspire for.
10. You are not entitled to admission.

TEST – 19

1. Each of the scholars belonging to different countries has spoken about it.
2. All were present except his sister and himself.
3. I wonder if ten thousand rupees is a large sum.
4. She laid the table an hour ago.
5. He was absent from the class for no reason.
6. He is an untidy boy.
7. All his plans failed due to lack of help.
8. Between milk, coke and coffee, the latter is my favorite.
9. All this happened prior to the 1971 war.
10. Scarcely had she gone, than he arrived.

TEST – 20

1. He boasts of his achievements now and then.
2. She lives in this apartment since 1995.
3. The Principal was angry with the boys.
4. Character is preferred to intelligence.
5. Krishna put up all the pictures on the wall.
6. The sceneries of Kashmir allure me most.
7. Cattle are grazing in the field.
8. Hari is be going abroad next month.
9. She knew that I would be leaving the place.
10. His elder brother gave him many a good advice.

PART – D

COMPREHENSION

COMPREHENSION

INTRODUCTION

What is Comprehension?

COMPREHENSION means 'understanding'. Not a superficial understanding but an understanding in depth with all the ramifications of thoughts (both expressed and implied). Sometimes thoughts are so embedded in the cobweb of words that it becomes rather difficult to follow, at first glance, the drift of thought. An average student may read the passage and yet fail to grasp the main ideas. Mere skimming over the surface is not of much help. For language is the art of concealing thought. A proper understanding of the given passage, therefore, requires, among other things, a fairly good command over English, a keen power of observation, a quick understanding of the central idea, a knack to detect error in logic, a quick reading habit, a sufficient stock of words and a little bit of imagination.

Methods of Comprehension

- Read the given passage with purpose and imagination. A careful reading will help you enter into the spirit of the passage.
- Read the passage once again, concentrating on the drift of thought. Notice the key words and see how the passage is developed.
- Read with an open mind, with purposeful concentrated attention even if the topic is new or not to your liking.
- Read all the questions carefully lest you should miss the spirit of any question.

When you have read all the questions, you should read through the passage again bearing in mind the questions. Answer the questions methodically, one by one. If you are bogged down by a particular question, don't waste your time over it. Switch over to another question, leaving the space for questions unanswered. Sometimes the question that appears tricky at first attempt becomes easier as you answer other questions.

Keep in mind the qualifying words such as all, none, never, always, sometimes, wholly, forever, least while selecting the right answers.

Follow the instruction in letter and spirit. Write the answer in as many words or lines as you are asked to do.

Check the questions asked and the answer given. Avoid verbosity and repetition. Your answers should be precise and to the point.

CATEGORY – 1

COMPREHENSION – 1

FROM "PACKING"

My tooth-brush is a thing that haunts me when I'm travelling, and makes my life a misery. I dream that I haven't packed it, and wake up in a cold perspiration and get out of bed, and hunt for it. and, in the morning, I pack it before I have used it, and have to unpack again to get it, and it is always the last thing I turn out of the bag, and then repack and forget it, and have to rush upstairs for it the last moment and carry it to the railway station, wrapped up in my pocket-handkerchief.

(Jerome K. Jerome)

Now answer the following questions:

1. How does the writer's tooth-brush make his life a misery?
2. What happens in the morning?
3. What happens at the last moment?
4. How does Jerome K. Jerome carry the tooth-brush to the railway station?
5. Frame the following words into sentences:

   Haunts; misery; in a cold perspiration; to hunt for; to turn out of; rush: upstairs; to wrap up

COMPREHENSION – 2

FROM "TELEPHONICS"

Telephony, it is clear, both from one's own experience and not from reading the letters on the papers, is not yet an exact science. Not, that is in real life; although on the stage and in American detective novels it seems to be perfect. The actor lifts the receiver, mentions the number, and begins instantly to talk. If he is on the film his lips move like burning rubber and his mouth becomes a shifting cavern. Do the rank and file of us, I wonder, when telephoning, thus grimace? I must fix up a mirror and see.

(E.V. Lucas)

Now answer the following questions:

1. How do you know that telephony is not an exact science?
2. What is telephony?
3. Where does it seem to be perfect?
4. How does the writer criticize the film?
5. Frame sentences of the following words:
   Receiver; cavern; rank and file; grimace; mirror

COMPREHENSION – 3

FROM "A FOOTBALL MATCH"

A crash of human thunder smote the air. Arms, umbrellas, hats, caps, and programmes flew up in a flurry of gesticulation all round the ground, while the shouting rosc wave upon wave to a crescendo that seemed to go on forever. The villa centre-half raced back to his own end of the field, partly carrying and partly carried by half a dozen of his team-mates.

(John Drinkwater)

Now answer the following questions:

1. What do you understand by human thunder?
2. How did the sound rise?
3. How did the Villa centre-half return to his end of the field?
4. How did the people express their joy besides shouting?
5. Frame sentences of the following words:
   Crash, smote, flurry, gesticulation, crescendo

COMPREHENSION – 4

FROM "CRICKET"

The laws of cricket tell of the English love of compromise between a particular freedom and a general orderliness, or legality. Macdonald's best break-bak is rendered null and void if he should let his right foot stray merely an inch over the crease as he wheels his arm. Law and order are represented at cricket the umpires in their magisterial coats (in England it is to be hoped these coats will never be worn as short as umpires wear them in Australia, much to the loss of that dignity which should always invest dispensers of justice). And in England umpires are seldom mobbed or treated with the contumely which is the lot of the football referee. If everything else in this nation of ours were lost

but cricket-her Constitution and the Laws of England of Lord Halsbury – it would be possible to reconstruct from the theory and the practice of cricket all the eternal Englishness which has gone to the establishment of that Constitution and the laws aforesaid.

Neville Cardus

Now answer the following questions:

1. What do the laws of cricket reveal?
2. By whom are law and order represented?
3. How is an umpire treated?
4. What does the writer say about the theory and the practice of cricket?
5. Frame sentences of the following words:
   Compromise, null and void, magisterial, mobbed, contumely, reconstruct, eternal

COMPREHENSION – 5

FROM "A CALL TO YOUTH"

I have been a teacher for nearly all my adult life, for over forty years. I have lived with students and it hurts me very deeply when I find that the precious years during which a student has to live in the university are wasted by some of them. I do not say by all of them. Teachers and students form a family and in a family you cannot have the spirit of the trade union. Such a thing should be inconceivable in a university. University life is a co-operative enterprise between teachers and students and I do hope that the students will not do a disservice to themselves by resorting to activities which are anti-social in character.

S. Radhakrishnan

Now answer the following questions:

1. What does the writer say about himself?
2. What does the writer say about University life?
3. What does the writer hope?
4. What do you understand by "the spirit of the trade union" and 'a co-operative enterprise'?
5. Frame sentences of the following words:

   Adult, precious, inconceivable, enterprise, disservice, resort

COMPREHENSION – 6

Happiness, after all, is an inner state of mind. It is little dependent on outside environment. Happiness has very little to do, for instance with whether you are rich or not rich. Some of the most miserable person I have come across in my life are the rich people. It is true that poverty makes one miserable in a very acute way. But my points is that it is no wealth but co-ordination of one's thought and action which remove inner conflicts. It is in that way that integration of personality is achieved.

Jawaharlal Nehru

Now answer the following questions:

1. What is Nehru's conception of happiness?
2. What has wealth or poverty to do with happiness?
3. What are inner conflicts? How can they be removed?
4. Frame sentences of the following words:

   Environment, miserable, acute, co-ordination, conflicts, integration

COMPREHENSION – 7

FROM "OPPORTUNITY FOR YOUTH"

If you think about the Five-year plans, you will find what a vital part the engineer plays in them. We shall require tens of thousands of engineers and hundreds of thousands of overseers, mechanics, and other technicians for our plans. The whole word is becoming more and more a world of trained people. They need to be trained in-two ways. They must be trained in mind and have some vision and understanding of the world picture. Then they must be trained in particular jobs which they can do well, whether it be science or engineering or medicine or education. Such are the skills which will build India.

(Jawaharlal Nehru)

Now answer the following questions:

1. What part does the engineer play in Five Year Plans?
2. What are the two kinds of training?
3. What are the skills which will build India?
4. Frame sentences of the following words:

   Vital, mechanics, technicians, vision, jobs, skills

COMPREHENSION – 8

FROM "THE MAN OF THE HOUSE"

In the afternoon my mother wanted me to play but I wouldn't go far. I remembered my own weakness. I knew if once I went a certain distance from the house I should drift towards the Glen, with the barrack drill-field perched on a chalky cliff above; the rifle-range below it, and below that again, the mill-pond and mill-stream running through a wooded gorge-the Rockies, the Himalayas or Highlands according to your mood. Concentration, that was what I had to practice.

(Frank O'Connor)

Now answer the following questions:

1. What was the writer's weakness?
2. What did the wooded gorge seem to be?
3. What had he to practise and why?
4. Frame sentences of the following words:

   drift, barrack, perched, gorge, mood, concentration

COMPREHENSION – 9

FROM "TELEPHONIES"

There are many good telephone stories. The best that I know is told of a journalist with a somewhat hypertrophied bump of reverence for worldly success, whose employer is a peer. We will call the employer Lord Forthestait and the journalist Mr. Blank. A number of the staff were talking together, in one of the rooms of the newspaper, when the telephone rang.

'You're wanted at the phone, Mr. Blank', said the clerk.

Blank who was just going out to lunch, came back impatiently and snatched at the instrument.

'Yes, what is it?' he snapped out.

'Is the Blank?' came the reply, lord Forthestait speaking'

'Yes, my lord,'' said Blank, with the meekest deference, removing his hat.

L.V. Lucas

Now Answer the following questions:

1. What was Mr. Blank?
2. Who was his employer?
3. What did Mr. Blank do?
4. What do you think of him?
5. Use the following words in sentences of your own:

   Journalist, employer, peer, staff, deference, hypertrophied, bump, reverence, snatch at, snap out

COMPREHENSION – 10

FROM "ON TRAVEL BY TRAIN"

Seafaring men make good companions on a railway journey. They are always ready for a pipe and a crack with any man, and there is usually some entertaining matter in their talk. But they are not often met with away from the coast towns. Nor do we often come across the confidential stranger in an English railway carriage, though his company is inevitable on the Continent, and, I believe, in America. When the confidential stranger does make an appearance here, he is usually a very dull dog, who compels us to yawn through the interminable story of his life, and rides some wretched old hobby-horse to death.

(J.B. Priestley)

Now answer the following questions:

1. Who are seafaring men? Why do they make good companions on a railway journey?
2. Who is the confidential stranger? Where does he appear most often?
3. How does the confidential stranger appear in England?
4. Frame sentences of the following words:

   Crack, confidential, yawn, interminable

ANSWERS

COMPREHENSION – 1

1. The writer has to travel. His tooth-brush makes his life a misery. In his sleep he dreams that he has not packed it. He gets up in a cold sweat to search for it.
2. In the morning the writer packs his tooth-brush before using it. So he has to open his bag and scatter everything to find it. Usually it is at the bottom and so all the things have to be taken out.
3. At the last moment he has not packed his tooth-brush. He has to go upstairs to find it.
4. Jerome K. Jerome has to wrap his tooth-brush in his pocket-handkerchief and carry it to the station in that way.
5. haunts – A ghost haunts this house

misery – The life of a poor man is full of misery.

in a cold perspiration – When I do not find a thing, I am always in a cold perspiration.

to hunt for – In the morning we hunted for a tea-shop.

to turn out of – The wicked boy was turned out of the class-room.

rush – The policeman rushed to the spot.

upstairs – I went upstairs to speak to my father.

to wrap up – The book was wrapped up in a piece of paper.

COMPREHENSION – 2

1. Our personal experiences and letters published in the newspapers make it clear that the telephony is not a perfect science.
2. By telephony we mean the art of communication by telephone.
3. Telephony seems to be perfect in the theatre and the American crime stories. There one does not have to wait.
4. In the film the actor telephones. He moves his lips. His mouth looks like a cave whose shape changes every second. According to the writer the common man does not make such facial expressions while telephoning. The writer wants to say that the film actor overdoes everything.
5. Receiver – I took up the receiver and heard his voice.

Cavern – The sage lives in a cavern.

Rank and file – The rank and file do not care for things of luxury.

Grimace – We laughed at the grimaces of the monkey.

Mirror – I saw my image in a mirror.

COMPREHENSION – 3

1. By 'human thunder' we understand the roar of the people.
2. The sound rose in waves to a crescendo which seemed to go on for ever.
3. The Villa centre-half was partly carried by half a dozen to his end of the field.
4. The people threw arms, umbrellas, hats, caps and programmes into the air.
5. Crash – The plane crashed near Cairo.

Smote – The soldier smote the man with his sword.

Flurry – He rushed out in a flurry to see what the matter was.

Gesticulation – We laughed at the orator's gesticulation.

Crescendo – His voice rose in a crescendo.

COMPREHENSION – 4

1. The laws of cricket reveal the Englishman's love of the freedom of the individual and general orderliness.
2. In cricket law and order are represented by the umpire.
3. An umpire is treated with respect. No umpire is mobbed or abused like a football referee.

4. The writer says that the theory and the practice of cricket present the essence of the British Constitution and the laws of the land. The same English spirit is noticed in cricket and government.

5. Compromise – When two persons quarrel, there must be a compromise between them.

Null and void – This rule is now null and void.

Magisterial – He was dressed in his magisterial coat.

Mobbed – The referee was mobbed and beaten.

Contumely – He was turned out because he used contumely.

Reconstruct – Can you reconstruct the broken wall?

Eternal – Truth is eternal.

COMPREHENSION – 5

1. The writer says that he has been a teacher for forty years. It pains him to see that some students waste their time at the University.
2. University life is like a family life. Teachers and students form one family. There should be co-operation between them. The atmosphere of a factory should not prevail in University life. The relation between the employers and the employed is not the relation between the teachers and the taught.
3. The writer hopes that the students will not harm themselves by adopting the attitude of the workers and having the spirit of the trade union.
4. The spirit of the trade union is the attitude of the workers towards their employers. The students should not have the spirit because the University is not a factory.

   In university life there should be co-operation between the teachers and the students. The students can derive the maximum amount of benefit from University education if they co-operate with their teachers.

5. Adult – This film is meant for adults only.

Precious – Time is precious.

Inconceivable – Such cruelty is inconceivable.

Enterprise – No enterprise can fail if you are sincere.

Disservice – He did a great disservice to me.

Resort – Students should not resort to violence.

COMPREHENSION – 6

1. According to Nehru happiness is the absence of conflicts man's thought and his action must be in harmony. Then his personality will not be divided. He will then be happy.
2. Wealth and poverty have very little to do with the integration of personality. So they have no direct bearing on happiness.
3. When a man thinks of doing one thing but is forced to do another thing, he develops an inner conflict. When he wants to do something but cannot do it, he has an inner conflict. The co-ordination between thought and action can remove these inner conflicts.
4. Environment – Our teacher is moulded by our environment.

Miserable – He was miserable because he could not buy the book he loved.

Acute – He is feeling an acute pain.

Co-ordination – There must be co-ordination among players.

Conflicts – Conflicts lead to unhappiness.

Integration – The integration of states was achieved by Sardar Patel.

COMPREHENSION – 7

1. The engineering plays a very important part in Five Year Plans.
2. The two kinds of training are the training of the mind and the training for jobs.
3. The skills which will build India are the skills in engineering, science, medicine and education.
4. Vital – Industries are of vital importance to us.

Mechanics – Motor mechanics earn a lot of money.

Technicians – A modern factory needs many technicians.

Vision – We see the vision of a great country.

Jobs – Many graduates need jobs.

Skills – Men without skills cannot prosper.

COMPREHENSION – 8

1. The writer's weakness was his rambling habit. He could not control himself. Once he went out to play, he would go to the cliff with the barrack, the mill, the stream and the gorge.
2. According to his mood he considered the wooded gorge to be the Rockies of America, the Himalayas of India or the Highlands of Scotland.
3. He had to practise concentration. He had to control his mind because he strayed if once he started.
4. Drift – He was a democrat but he drifted slowly towards Communism.

   Barrack – There are many soldiers in the barrack.

   Perched – The boy was perched on the top of a heap of things.

   Gorge – A stream flows through the gorge.

   Mood – When he is in a happy mood, he talks much.

   Concentration – If you lack concentration, you cannot do well in studies.

COMPREHENSION – 9

1. Mr. Blank was a journalist. He worked for a newspaper.
2. His employer was a peer named Lord Forthestait.
3. Mr. Blank went to the telephone. When he learnt that his employer was speaking, he removed his hat out of respect.
4. Mr. Blank had a turgid respect for successful men.
5. Journalist – A journalist works for a newspaper.

   Employer – The worker has a kind employer.

   Peer – A peer is a man of rank and power.

   Staff – All the members of the staff were present.

   Deference – He stood up out of deference, (respect)

   Hypertrophied– He has a hypertrophied dislike for sweets.

   Bump – I heard the sound of a bump, (knock)

   Reverence – I have no reverence for the foolish rich.

   Snatch at – A man snatched at her bag.

   Snap out – She snapped out that she would not go. (said irritably)

COMPREHENSION – 10

1. Seafaring men are sailors. They make excellent companions because they like smoking and a chat and because they can be entertaining.
2. The confidential stranger is a man who will tell anybody the secrets of his life. He appears most in Europe and America.
3. The confidential stranger seems to be a boring person in England.
4. Crack – I like your crack.

   Confidential – He is a confidential clerk.

   Yawn – When a man is bored, he yawns.

   Interminable – The argument was interminable.

CATEGORY – 2

COMPREHENSION – 1

When Tolstoy led a party composed of his family and visitors to harvest a field for a widow, he was doing two things. In part, he was saying that everyone ought to do his share of what he called "bread labour", and earn his keep by the sweat of his brow. At the same time, he was affirming that each of us should help our less fortunate neighbours. Mahatma Gandhi agreed whole-heartedly with both these principles, but he linked them more closely than Tolstoy with what he saw as the decadence of industrial life that takes people away from the home and village crafts, which are varied and rewarding, to the soul-destroying monotony of machines. Even before either of these great men had given their philosophy to the world, an American author named Thoreau, had built himself a hut in the woods to prove that he could support himself by the simples manual work; and in Britain, Ruskin had led his students out from Oxford to build a raised footpath across the water meadows to a village to demonstrate the dignity of labour. The path remains of this day, almost one hundred and fifty years later, lined with tall poplars, as a memorial to a fine ideal.

One could trace the history of such ideas still further back, to the writings of Jean-Jacques Rousseau, who preached the dignity and equality of man and the educational value of Nature and manual work, from the Swiss city of Geneva in the eighteenth century. It was however, a Swiss called Pierre Ceresole, a contemporary of Gandhiji, who took these basic principles and used them to promote international reconciliation.

Pierre was no ordinary Swiss, for it is rare for ordinary people to have the courage to dream and attempt to put them into practice. Pierre's father's family originated in Italy, his mother's family came from France, he had a German grandmother and had relations in England. He used to point out the stupidity of frontiers.

Pierre described how, at the age of seventeen, he was walking in the woods and experienced "something which seemed to me like a solemn dedication to truth ... in which the first necessity was to recognize one's own faults. In a blinding fashion there came to me the Vision of Truth amid Nature's mysteries and solitude." He had the habit of keeping a pencil and a notebook with him for entering his stray thoughts, and from these notebooks, of which there are more than a hundred, it is seen that he fretted over the many failures of the Western way of life and yet was generous about the people he met. Despite being an engineer, Pierre, in order to work his way, took a job on a poultry farm and later in an oil-field. While he was in Honolulu, Hawaii, he earned his living by teaching French, but this resulted in his being paid more than he needed for his keep; he gave all his savings away to charity.

From Hawalli he moved on to Japan, experiencing there an entirely new way of life which helped him to see more clearly the virtues and follies of European culture. Returning home at the outbreak of the war, in 1914, he gave all the money inherited from his father to the State, saying, "I believe that the teachings of Christ are superior to good business sense." Later he wrote, "Two thousand years ago there came a radiant light, full of peace and loving kindness – and we immediately crucified it."

Pierre had been impressed with the sacrifice and heroism in war and wanted something equally positive mobilized in the cause of peace. He organised the first international work-camp at a war-devastated village in France. The idea was that people of different nationalities, including those whose countries had recently been enemies of one another, should be joined side by side in honest work to rebuild not only the concrete things but also the feelings of brotherhood that are shattered by war. The number of volunteers and the number of camps began to grow rapidly, and what had been the Swiss Service Civil became the Service Civil International (SCI). Pierre died in 1945 after World War II.

Pierre Ceresole had the satisfaction of doing what he believed to be right. Each year a growing number of volunteers go to work-camps and there is scarcely a country that has not heard of them. Anyone can become a work-camper, and for many this is the place to start – planting young trees and crossing the frontiers.

(*a*) What were the principles of Tolstoy with which Mahatma Gandhi agreed?

(*b*) How are Thoreau and Ruskin linked to Gandhi and Tolstoy in the passage?

(*c*) What was Pierre's philosophy of life?

(*d*) What is SCI and how did it come into existence?

(*e*) How is Pierre's work different from the work of those mentioned in the passage?

COMPREHENSION – 2

History has a great variety of definitions and applications. In the broadest sense, it considers every action and every thought that man has had since his first appearance and records every significant advance or recession. It attempts to evaluate all the developments in science, in art, in literature, in philosophy, in architecture, in sociology, in politics, in war, in religion, and in law. It sketches as complete a picture as possible of everything that has influenced man directly or indirectly.

History, more than any other subject, has been enslaved and distorted for selfish purposes. Members of the clergy have used it to glorify and to promote the interests of the church, statesmen have utilized it to sway masses, and writers have distorted facts to substantiate their conclusions. War spirit has been kindled through undue emphasis upon facts, if not falsification of them. The historian is likely to exaggerate the history of his own country – sometimes unintentionally – because of his environment and sometimes in order to facilitate the sale of his book. In all countries, there are zealots in responsible positions who cannot bear to have their fatherhood criticized. Truth is frequently sacrificed at the altar of patriotism. Henry C. Lea, an outstanding American historian, declared that history should be "a serious attempt to ascertain the severest truth as to the past and set it forth without fear or favour." Michelet, a famous French historian, believed that "sacrilege and the mocking of false goods are the historian's first duty, his indispensable instrument for re-establishing the truth."

The slight progress that we have made in the direction indicated by Lea and Michelet is rather discouraging, but there is a trend toward a broader and more inclusive point of view in the writing and teaching of history. World history, correctly interpreted, puts the individual state in the proper perspective and lessens the dangers of excessive nationalism. History has become more than war and politics. To make the story complete, the historian of the new school makes use of the work of the ethnologist, the anthropologist, the geographer, and archaeologist, the geologist, the psychologist, the astronomer, the zoologist, the biologist, the chemist, the sociologist and the economist. He is concerned with man's cultural advances and his society, as well as with charters, constitutions, and wars.

There are dangers, as well as virtues, in the vast scope of the "new history". Overpopularization and underspecialization tend to cheapen history and to destroy some of its qualities as a basic and sober study. There are decided advantages in the comprehension of the broad scope of history, but, in addition, the student should be able to appreciate the depth of the subject. Years of research have been spent and volumes have been written on a single topic. Without these specialized works, surveys would be of no particular value. However, some of the historians of the "new history" have sacrificed important fundamental facts in order to make a chronicle of heroic persons and romantic occurrence. They have overstepped the point where history and fiction should meet. The historian should make his description of the past lifelike hence, he should include grim realities as well as romantic incidents.

One of the important aspects of the "new history" is the emphasize upon man's cultural developments, popularly termed civilization. Civilization is difficult to define and evaluate. Just where it began and where man's actions and thoughts became human is impossible to determine. Man, like animals, has senses but some are less acutely developed; man has emotions, most of which are present, but latent, in animals. Comfort seems to be the chief goal of the lower forms of animal life, but man pushes beyond that towards something that he has difficulty in defining. This intangible something maybe called civilization. Professor Lynn Thorndike believes that civilization "is the product of our higher qualities as exercised first by original and superior individuals and then accepted or followed by a sufficient number of human beings to make it a social fact." Buckle held that moral and intellectual progress is the basis of civilization. Emerson believed that civilization is a progress and Bertrand Russell, a modern philosopher, thinks that it is the progress and predominance of science. Perhaps we can agree that acknowledge of nature, progress in art, an ethical code, a government, and a degree of material prosperity are essential in any form of civilized society. Civilization became possible when chaos and insecurity were minimized. Curiosity and constructiveness were encouraged when fear was overcome and man turned his attention toward the understanding and embellishment of life.

(*a*) Why does the author consider history an all-inclusive area of study?

(*b*) According to the author, how has history suffered distortions and why?

(*c*) How does the author describe the new school of historians?

(*d*) What are the dangers associated with "new history"?

(*e*) Why is it difficult to define and evaluate civilization?

COMPREHENSION – 3

It is often said that the Ghaznavid and Ghurid soldiers regarded death in a war against infidels a martyrdom in the cause of Islam. But it is more likely that the real draw was the attraction of plunder, the likes of which they had not seen in campaigns in more arid lands. For Indian commanders, apart from plunder, battles incorporated the niceties of a sport with its own rules of play. Immortalizing the heroism of kings in battle, the poets and bards empathized the rules of war and chivalry. To apply the chivalric code in minor campaigns may have relieved the tedium of war, but the campaigns against the Ghurids were of an entirely different nature and this may not have been realized initially. Notions of honour and devotion were often placed above expediency, and gradually the astrologically determined auspicious moment for attach took precedence over strategy and tactics. Inflated claims to valour, such as the hero who could defeat a thousand warriors simultaneously, began to enter the rhetoric of courtly literature.

The organization of Indian armies added to their weakness. Each army had as its permanent core the standing army, but many of the soldiers were local levies or soldiers supplied by Samantas where this was part of the latter's obligation to the suzerain. In addition, mercenaries were a visible section of the armies of these times. Such a collection of soldiers had not always been trained to fight as a consolidated army. It was possibly also the dispersed of the army that gave it a license to plunder indiscriminately. Villagers were harassed and looted by armies on the march, particularly if the campaign coincided with the harvesting of the crop, as it often did. For peasants and merchants, war was a nightmare that disrupted the routine of earning a livelihood. Laying waste vast tracts of inhabited and cultivated land, merely because it was part of the enemy's territory, was a proud boast attributed to Prithviraj Chauhan on defeating the Chandela ruler.

Historians have sometimes commented, perhaps more from hindsight, on why Indian rulers did not make a conjoint effort through the centuries to defend the North-Western passes. Time and again invaders came through these passes, yet little was done to prevent this, the defence of the region lying arbitrarily in the hands of the local rulers. It appears the construction of a series of fortification along the passes was not thought feasible. Perhaps the need for defence was not given priority, the area being viewed as a natural frontier. Alternatively, given the mountainous terrain, the only routes for pastoralists and caravan were through the passes and it was therefore thought better to leave them open. The local kings and chief who controlled the passes derived an income from this trade. There would have been familiarity too with those coming across the passes and therefore a slow recognition that sometimes friendliness had turned into hostility. The effectiveness of mountains as a frontier was also thwarted by the many occasions when the Punjab was conquered from across the borders or was involved in the politicos of Afghanistan and Central Asia. This closeness militated against a properly focused perspective on political developments across the borderlands and in Central Asia.

Invasions by outsiders are known in many parts of the world: the Huns attacking Rome, the Arabs invading Spain or the Spanish and Portuguese conquering Latin America. The potentialities of invasions were recognised only in Hindsight. These invasions were mounted by alien peoples who were little known, if at all, to the societies they invaded. But the Turks had been a contiguous people, familiar from trade in horses and other commodities and from the Turkish mercenaries employed in some Indian Armies. However, the historical scene in Central Asia and West Asia had now changed, with new political ambitions after the rise of Islam. For the rulers of Northern India, to recognize this would have required an understanding of a wider range of politics beyond the areas enclosed by the immediate frontiers. This does not appear to have been an Indian concern. Indians who travelled to different parts of Asia on a variety of assignments wrote little about what they observed, remaining silent on the politics of other lands. It was almost as if the exterior landscape was irrelevant. Political interests therefore tended to be parochial. This marks a striking contrast to the world of the Chinese and the Arabs, both made aware of distant places through the detailed accounts of travelers and traders. The Arabs had a fascination for the geography of other lands and the Chinese were wary of happenings in their neighbourhood in Central Asia.

Alberuni, in the opening chapter of this book, suggests other reasons for this lack of recording observations concerning the wider perception of the world, which one may or may not agree with: "The Hindus believe that there is no country but theirs, or nation like theirs, no king like theirs, no religion like theirs, no science like theirs ...... They are by nature niggardly in communicating what they know, and they take the greatest possible care to withhold it from men of another caste from among their own people, still more of course from any foreigner".

(*a*) What was then nature of campaigns against Ghurids?

(*b*) According to the passage "the Indian rulers did not find it necessary to fortify the North-Western Pass". Why?

(*c*) Explain the statement "The potentialities of invasions were recognised only in hindsight".

(*d*) Give your critical observations on Alberuni's comments on Hindus.

(*e*) Enumerate the major view points of the given passage.

COMPREHENSION – 4

Man, since antiquity, has been an inveterate traveller. Only the motivations for travel have changed. In ancient times, the main motivations for travel were trade, pilgrimage and conquest. It is not often realised how extensive were the contacts among the peoples several thousand years ago. For instance, there was considerable interchange of ideas and knowledge between India and West Asia and the Graeco-Roman civilization.

Travel became the means of acquiring culture in Europe. The tradition of the Grand Tour which started in the 17th century was more firmly established in the 18th and the 19th centuries by the emergence of an affluent mercantile class. After the Second World War, Europe lay in ruins. The Marshall Plan which was introduced by the United States for the revival of the economies of European countries made tourism as one of its planks. It provided large amount of money for the reconstruction of hotels and tourism infrastructure of Western Europe. What was more significant was that for the first time tourism was viewed as an engine for economic development. This made the Governments start assuming responsibility for the promotion of tourism.

Three technological inventions have fuelled the growth of travel on a large scale in successive periods. First, the steam engine which made travel by rail and steamship possible before 1914; then the internal combustion engine which popularise travel by automobile in the inter-War years and lastly, the jet propulsion engine which has led to the international tourist explosion of the post-War era.

The Government of India also took note of the new phenomenon of tourism and its economic implications. In 1947, the private sector consisted of a number of hotels and travel agencies in the main cities mainly owned and operated by foreign interests. As it happened in other industries after Independence, the control of many of these hotels passed into the hands of Indian entrepreneurs. At the same time, a number of new indigenously owned and operated travel agencies and hotels started being set up. In the last 50 years, the Indian travel industry has shown remarkable enterprise. Some of the leading Indian hotel groups and travel agencies have branched out overseas and their performance is highly regarded in the international tourism remarks.

The tourism revolution which started in full measure 50 years ago has not run its course. There are several reasons for taking a long-term optimistic view of tourism. First, the increase in leisure time in industrialised societies; paid holidays which were introduced as a social welfare measure have now become an accepted feature not only in industrialised countries but also in many developing countries. The length of paid holidays has increased. The working week, both in public and private sectors, has come down to 40 hours spread over 5 days. Evidently Governments will have to concern themselves with the quality of use of leisure. Tourism has become a preeminent form of recreation for the younger people. This is reflected in the increase in travel in the age group of 18 to 25 years. Second, the rise in literacy and educational standards. Third, better healthcare has made it possible for retired persons, above 60 years, to undertake travel for pleasure. Fourth, the increase in discretionary incomes in real terms in the last twenty years, partly due to income elasticity. Many research studies have established that increase in income level in real terms resulted in increase in propensity for travel. And lastly, taking a vacation, generally twice a year, has become a way of life in modern societies.

(*a*) What, according to the author, were the main motivations for travel in ancient times?

(*b*) What was the state of tourism in Europe and the United States?

(*c*) What part did technology play in the growth of tourism?

(*d*) How does the author describe the state of tourism in the post-Independence India?

(*e*) Why does the author think that there is a bright future for tourism in modern societies?

COMPREHENSION – 5

The thought of Young Bengal (Pearychand Mitra, one of the circle, called it in 1877 'Young Calcutta') flowed through the fourth decade of the 19th century, arising in the late twenties and ebbing away after the mid-forties. Its inspirer was Derozio (1809-31), competent scholar, gifted writer, radical thinker, and the most famous of our teachers in the new education. It will be unusual to link with Young Bengal a second name, that of David Hare (1775-1841) who seems so different from Derozio in so many ways. Hare was indeed no professional instructor or intellectual, no man of letters or of academic learning. He had neither the brilliance nor the waywardness of his contemporary; unlike him he had become in diet and habits almost a half-Hindu. Yet between the two may be detected an underlying resemblance which furnishes a key to a proper estimation of Young Bengal.

Common to both was the passionate conviction that for India nothing was more essential than "a dissemination of European learning and science among her people." Both encouraged freedom of thinking and discussion and inspired a courage and personal integrity in their followers "to throw off the fetters of that antiquated bigotry which still clung to their countrymen." And unlike other leaders around them, both were 'godless' secularists with little faith in denominations or religious instruction, and yet staunch idealists. Nor can one forget that in the hour of trial, Hare tried to stand by Derozio and his maligned pupils about whom he declared – "your countrymen look upon you as – their reformers and instructors"' while the Derozians were the first to honour Hare publicly, and after his death they were in the forefront in the endeavour to perpetuate his memory, in the unique First of June anniversaries for 25 years without a break.

Henry Louis Vivian Derozio was a Calcutta Eurasian of Portuguese-Indian ancestry, the son of an officer in an English mercantile firm. (in the Hindu College Records of 1831, the name is occasionally spelt as De Rozio; Max Muller wrote D. Rozario). He was educated in one of the pioneer English-teaching private schools of the early 19th century, run by the Scotsman Drummond in the Dharmatala area. Drummond was a scholar-poet, and as a notorious free-thinker an exile from his native land. It may safely be conjectured that Derozio derived from Durmmond his taste in literature and philosophy, his love of Burns, his faith in the French Revolution and English Radicalism.

Derozio's youthful critique on Kant was considered as something which "would not disgrace even gifted philosophers"; his translation of a French essay on Moral Philosophy was printed posthumously. The fame already won secured him an appointment as teacher to the senior classes in the Hindu College before he had ended his 'teens'.

Derozio's personality brought "a new era in the annals of the College", the youthful teacher drawing the senior boys "like a magnet" round him. According to his biographer "neither before, nor since his day has any teacher, within the walls of any native educational establishment in India, ever exercised such an influence over his pupils." Not alone in the classrooms, but outside the hours as well, he strove with success "to broaden and deepen the knowledge of his pupils" in Western thought and literature, the new fountain which emancipated and intoxicated. The College students clustered round him and very many of them carried down to their last days the deep impress stamped on them by their Master. This was the cementing link which held together the Young Bengal group, the memory which made a close-knit fellowship of affection and friendship even in later life.

Unlike most teachers, Derozio encouraged his students to debate freely and question authority. He urged them to think for themselves, "to be in no way influenced by any of the idols mentioned by Bacon-to live and die for truth". One of his pupils, Radhanath Sikdar, said of him: "he has been the cause and the sole cause of the spirit of enquiry after truth, and that contempt of vice – which cannot but be beneficial to India." Another, Ramgopal Ghosh, held up the motto: "He who will not reason is a bigot; he who cannot is a fool, and he how does not is a slave."

(*a*) Which of the period when the thought of Young Bengal, the youthful band of reformers flourished in Bengal? Who were the two main teachers of the new education and in what ways were they different from each other?

(*b*) What was common to both these teachers? How did they support each other?

(*c*) Comment on the education of Derozio. Did Drummond have any influence on him? Justify your answer.

(*d*) What kind of influence did Derozio have on his pupils i.e., the Young Bengal Group?

(*e*) 'He has been the cause and the sole cause of the spirit of enquiry after truth'. Explain the significance of the statement by Radhanath Sikdar.

COMPREHENSION – 6

A desert is a barren area of land where little precipitation occurs and consequently living conditions are threatening for plant and animal life. The lack of vegetation exposes the vulnerable surface of the ground to the processes of denudation. About one-third of the land surface of the world is arid or semi-arid. Deserts are usually hot and barren places; yet they are also beautiful. A few plants, rocks and dusty red-brown soil make up the ingredients of most North American deserts where there is sufficient food and water for certain animals to survive. Deserts cover more than one-fifth of the Earth's land and they are found on every continent. A place that receives less than 10 inches of rain per year is normally considered a desert. They are part of a wider classification of regions called "dry land". These areas exist under a moisture deficit, which means they repeatedly lose more moisture through evaporation than they receive from annual precipitation.

Deserts are biologically rich habitats with a vast array of animals and plants that have adapted to harsh conditions there. Some deserts are among the planet's last remaining areas of total wilderness. Yet more than one billion people, one-sixth of the Earth's population, actually live in the desert regions.

Despite the common notion of deserts as dry and hot, there are cold deserts as well. One famous dry and hot place in the world with no visible rock or plant and barely any water is the Sahara desert. It is the largest hot desert in the world that reaches temperatures of up to 122 degrees Fahrenheit during the day. Some deserts are very cold, like the Gobi desert in Asia and the desert on the continent of

Antarctica. Only about 10 percent of deserts are covered by sand dunes. The driest deserts get less than half an inch of precipitation each year and that is from condensed fog.

Desert animals have adapted ways to help them keep cool when the going gets tough. Camels also have thick hair in their ears for keeping out sand; they also sport closable nostrils, an eye membrane, and wide feet that act like snow-shoes in the land. Desert plants may have to go without fresh water for years at a time. Some plants have adapted to the arid climate by growing long roots that tap water from deep underground. Other plants, such as cacti, have special means of storing and conserving water. Many desert plants can live to be hundreds of years old.

Some of the world's semi-arid regions are turning into deserts at an alarming rate. This process, known as "desertification", is not caused by drought, but usually arises from the demands of human population that settles on the semi-arid lands to grow crops and graze animals. The pounding of the soil by the hooves of livestock may degrade the soil and encourage erosion by wind and water. Global warming also threatens to change the ecology of deserts. Higher temperature may produce an increasing number of wildfires that alter desert landscape by eliminating slow-growing trees and shrubs and replacing them with fast-growing grasses.

(*a*) Explain what you understand by 'barren and dry land'.

(*b*) What do you understand by rich habitats?

(*c*) How have desert animals and plants in arid climate adapted themselves to the use of less water?

(*d*) Describe the process of desertification.

(*e*) What are the camel's two most visible features that make it perfect for deserts?

COMPREHENSION – 7

A complete reading programme, therefore, should include four factors: at least one good book each week, a newspaper or news magazine, magazines of comment and interpretation, and book reviews. If your keep feeding your intelligence with these four foods, you can be sure that your brain cells will be properly nourished. To this must be added the digestive process that comes from your own thinking and from discussion with individuals or groups.

It is often desirable to make books that you own personally, part of your mind by underlining or by marking in the margin the more important statements. This will help you to understand the book as you first read it, because out of the mass of details you must have selected the essential ideas. It will help you to remember better the gist of the book, since the physical act of underlining, with your eyes on the page, tends to put the thought more firmly into your brain cells. It will save time whenever you need to refer to the book.

Above all, never forget that creative intelligence is correlation of facts and ideas, not mere memorising. What counts is what you can do with your knowledge, by linking it with other things you have studied or observed. If you read Plutarch's life of Julius Caesar, think how his rise to political power paralleled the technique of Adolf Hitler, or that of your local political boss. If you read a play by Shakespeare, think how his portrayal of the characters helps you to understand someone you know. In everything you read, keep at the back of your mind what it means to your life here and now, how it supports or challenges the things you were taught in school, in church and at home, and how the wisdom you get from books can guide you in your thinking, in your career, in your voting as a citizen and in your personal morals.

(*a*) What are the four things required for a complete reading programme and why?

(*b*) What else is required to feed your intelligence?

(*c*) Why does the writer recommend underlining or marking in the margin the more important statements?

(*d*) What use can you put your knowledge to?

(*e*) How can what you learn from books help you in your life?

COMPREHENSION – 8

In barely one generation, we've moved from exulting in the time – saving devices that have so expanded our lives, to trying to get away from them – often, in order to make more time. The more ways we have to connect, the more of us seem desperate to unplug. Like a teenager, we appear to have gone from knowing nothing about the world to knowing too much, all but overnight.

The average person spends at least eight and a half hours a day in front of the screen. The average teenager spends or receives 75 text messages a day. Since luxury, as any economist will tell you, is a function of scarcity, the children of tomorrow will crave nothing more than freedom, if only for a short while, from all the blinking machines, streaming videos and scrolling headlines that leave them feeling empty, and too full all at once. The urgency of slowing down – to find the time and space to think – is nothing new, of course, and wiser souls have always reminded us that the more attention we pay to the moment, the less time and energy we have to place it in some larger context. Even half a century ago, Marshall McLuhan warned, "When things come to you very fast, naturally you lose touch with yourself".

Yet few of those voices can be heard these days, precisely because 'breaking news' is coming through perpetually on the news channels, and Meena is posting images of her summer vacation and the phone is ringing. We barely have enough time to see how little time we have. And the more that floods in on us, the less of ourselves we have to give to every snippet.

We have more and more ways to communicate, as Thoreau noted, but less and less to say. Partly because we are so busy communicating, and as he might also have said – we are rushing to meet so many deadlines that we hardly register that what we need most are lifelines. So what to do? The central paradox of the machines that have made our lives so much brighter, quicker, longer and healthier is that they cannot teach us how to make the best use of them; the information revolution came without an instruction manual. All the data in the world cannot teach us how to sift through data; images don't show us how to process images. The only way to do justice to our onscreen lives is by summoning exactly the emotional and moral clarity that cannot be found on any screen.

Maybe that is why more and more people, even if they have no religious commitment, seem to be turning to yoga or meditation, or tai chi; these are not New Age fads so much as ways to connect with that what could be called the wisdom of old age. A series of tests in recent years has shown that after spending time in a quiet rural setting, subjects "exhibit greater attentiveness, stronger memory and generally improved cognition. Their brains become both calmer and sharper." More than that, empathy, as well as deep thought, depends on neural processes that are "inherently slow". The very ones our high-speed lives have little time for.

(*a*) According to the author, what is likely to become a scarcity in the future?

(*b*) What ability have people lost thanks to the constant inflow of data?

(*c*) Why does the author say, "We have more and more ways to communicate, but less and less to say"?

(*d*) Why are people taking an active interest in old-age fads?

(*e*) Why is modern man unable to empathise with others?

COMPREHENSION – 9

Oratory demands enthusiasm, which can spring only in an earnest soul; and neither beauty of composition nor graceful delivery can compensate for want of passion. To be able to interest people without tiring them is a prime test of oratory. It is a gift that may draw valuable aid from such natural advantages as a noble figure, handsome countenance, and pleasant voice. But there has been no lack of eminent orators of ungainly men at any time. Few have equaled Sir Robert Peel in skillful management of the House of Commons, but he often assumed very undignified postures standing with his hands behind his coat tails, or thumbs buried in the pockets of his waistcoat, and threw one leg over the other in attitudes of nonchalance. The composition of his speeches was slovenly and they were noted for the disorder of their contents. Oliver Cromwell was one of the most influential speakers of his day, but he rarely wore clean linen and his voice was "harsh and untuneable."

The indispensable requisite of oratory is a mind well-stored with knowledge and information, sound reasoning, wit and humour, vehemence, fire, and imaginative insight all conducive to enhance the power of eloquence; but the same speakers are not able to make the same impression in all places, nor secure the same effect at all times. The pinnacle of triumph of oratory is reached when a speaker is able to magnetise his hearers into thinking as he thinks, and feeling as he feels. When Sheridan had concluded his famous speech in Parliament on the "Begum Charge", so great was the excitement caused by it that the Minister concerned besought the House to adjourn the decision of the question, "as being incapacitated from forming a just judgment under the influence of such powerful eloquence."

It is clear that there is a rivalry between the orator and the occasion and the dazzling effect of the moment does not always endure through later cool reflection. The world moves in continual cycles of action and reaction, and the homage paid to speakers is followed by tests in the course of which there is unrelenting research as to what extent precept and example tally. When there is no wide gulf between the two, further speeches are listened to with increased respect.

(*a*) What are the most important qualities required for becoming a good orator?

(*b*) What was the effect created by Sheridan's speech?

(*c*) How can one judge the true effect of a good oration?

(*d*) What research does the audience do when they listen to speakers?

(*e*) Which speeches are not taken seriously by an audience?

COMPREHENSION – 10

Water is the basis of all life. Every animal and every plant contains a substantial proportion of free or combined water in its body, and no kind of physiological activity is possible in which the fluid does not play an essential part. Water is, of course, necessary for animal life, while moisture in the soil is equally imperative for the life and growth of plants and trees, though the quantity necessary varies enormously with the species. The conservation and utilisation of water is thus fundamental for human welfare. Apart from artesian water, the ultimate source in all cases is rain or snowfall. Much of Indian agriculture depends on seasonal rainfall and is therefore very sensitive to any failure or irregularity of the same. It is clear that the adoption of techniques preventing soil erosion would also help to conserve and keep the water where it is wanted. In other words, on and in the soil, such techniques therefore serve a double purpose. It is evident however that in a country having only a seasonal rainfall, an immense quantity of rain-water must be necessarily run off the ground. The collection and utilisation of water is therefore of vital importance. Much of it flows down into the streams and rivers and ultimately finds its way to the sea. The harnessing of our rivers, the waters of which now mostly run to waste, is a great national problem which must be considered and dealt with on national lines. Closely connected with the conservation of water supplies is the problem of afforestation. The systematic planting of suitable trees in every possible or even in impossible areas and the development of what one can call civilized forests as distinguished from wild and untamed jungle is one the most urgent needs of India. Such plantation would directly and indirectly prove a source of untold wealth to the country. They would check soil erosion and conserve the rainfall of the country from flowing away to waste and would provide the necessary supplies of cheap fuel and thus stop unnecessary waste of farmyard manure.

(*a*) Where does the world get water from?

(*b*) What is the national problem relating to our rivers?

(*c*) What are the benefits of afforestation?

(*d*) What is fundamental for human welfare?

(*e*) What are the advantages of preventing soil erosion?

ANSWERS

COMPREHENSION – 1

(*a*) Tolstoy gave two principles with which Mahatma Gandhi agreed. One was that everyone ought to do his share of what he called "bread labour", and earn his keep by the sweat of his brow. The other was that each of us should help our less fortunate neighbours.

(*b*) Thoreau and Ruskin were linked to Gandhi and Tolstoy in their simple ways of thinking and living. Thoreau proved that he could support himself by simple manual work and Ruskin demonstrated the dignity of labour.

(*c*) Pierre believed in the vision of truth and nature's mysteries and solitude. He fretted over the failure of western ways of life. He earned his living by teaching and gave away his savings to charity.

(*d*) SCI is Service Civil International. It came into existence with the efforts of Pierre. Pierre had been impressed with the sacrifice and heroism in war and wanted something equally positive mobilized in the cause of peace. He organised the first international work-camp at a war-devastated village in France. The idea was that people of different nationalities, including those whose countries had recently been enemies of one another, should be joined side by side in honest work to rebuild not only the concrete things but also the feelings of brotherhood that are shattered by war. The number of volunteers and the number of camps began to grow rapidly, and what had been the Swiss Service Civil became the Service Civil International (SCI).

(*e*) Pierre's work is different from those mentioned in the passage in a way that he translated his beliefs into action and put his theories in the practice. He used the principles and preaching of his contemporaries and predecessors to promote international reconciliation. He organized an international work camp to bring together people of different nationalities devastated by war to rebuild the feelings of brotherhood shattered by war. So, he was a man of action.

COMPREHENSION – 2

(*a*) The author considers history an all-inclusive area of study because it considers every action and every thought that man has had since his first appearance and records every significant advance or recession. It also attempts to evaluate all the developments in science, in art, in literature, in philosophy, in architecture, in sociology, in politics, in war, in religion, and in law. It attempts to sketch as complete a picture as possible of everything that has influenced man directly or indirectly.

(*b*) History has been enslaved and distorted for selfish purposes. Members of the clergy have used it to glorify and to promote the interests of the church, statesmen have utilized it to sway masses, and writers have distorted facts to substantiate their conclusions. War spirit has been kindled through undue emphasis upon facts, if not falsification of them. The historian is likely to exaggerate the history of his own country – sometimes unintentionally – because of his environment and sometimes in order to facilitate the sale of his book. In all countries, there are zealots in responsible positions who cannot bear to have their fatherhood criticized. Truth is frequently sacrificed at the altar of patriotism.

(*c*) The historian of the new school makes use of the work of the ethnologist, the anthropologist, the geographer, and archaeologist, the geologist, the psychologist, the astronomer, the zoologist, the biologist, the chemist, the sociologist and the economist. He is concerned with man's cultural advances and his society, as well as with charters, constitutions, and wars.

(*d*) There are dangers, as well as virtues, in the vast scope of the "new history". Overpopularization and underspecialization tend to cheapen history and to destroy some of its qualities as a basic and sober study.

(*e*) Civilization is difficult to determine and define. Just where it began and where man's actions and thoughts became human is impossible to determine. The comfort seems to be the chief goal of the lower forms of animal life, but man pushes beyond that towards something that he has difficulty in defining. This intangible something may be called civilization and this intangible makes civilization indefinable and indeterminable.

COMPREHENSION – 3

(*a*) The campaigns against the Ghurids were of an entirely different nature. Notions of honour and devotion were often placed above expediency, and gradually the astrologically determined auspicious moment for attack took precedence over strategy and tactics. Indeed, claims to valour, such as the hero who could defeat a thousand warriors simultaneously, began to enter the rhetoric of courtly literature.

(*b*) The Indian rulers didn't find it necessary to fortify the north western pass as they thought that fortifications along the passes are not feasible. Moreover, passes were considered as a natural frontier.

(*c*) The statement means that the repercussions and complications were realised by the invaded societies and rulers after they suffered invasion. They had no forethought of the consequences of war in advance.

(*d*) Alberuni believed that the Hindus suffered from superiority complex with regard to their nation and rulers. There were no exchanges taking place between the intercaste people, and almost none with foreigners. These remarks/ observations about Hindus seem prejudiced and demeaning too.

(*e*) The key ideas/ view points of the given passage is about the invasions that this country and its people suffered from in the past. The passage also highlights the divisive tendencies and closed mindedness of Indian rulers who, in view of their petty interests compromised with the safety and security of the nation.

COMPREHENSION – 4

(*a*) In ancient times, the main motivations for travel were trade, pilgrimage and conquest.

(*b*) Travel was the means of acquiring culture in Europe. The tradition of the Grand Tour which started in the 17th century was more firmly established in the 18th and the 19th centuries by the emergence of an affluent mercantile class. After the Second World War, Europe lay in ruins. The Marshall Plan which was introduced by the United States for the revival of the economies of European countries made tourism as one of its planks. It provided large amount of money for the reconstruction of hotels and tourism infrastructure of Western Europe. What was more significant was that for the first time tourism was viewed as an engine for economic development. This made the Governments start assuming responsibility for the promotion of tourism.

(*c*) Three technological inventions have fuelled the growth of travel on a large scale in successive periods. First, the steam engine which made travel by rail and steamship possible before 1914; then the internal combustion engine which popularised travel by automobile in the inter-War years and lastly, the jet propulsion engine which has led to the international tourist explosion of the post-War era.

(*d*) In 1947, the private sector operated a number of hotels and travel agencies in the main cities. These were mainly owned and operated by foreigners. As it happened in other industries, after Independence the control of many of these hotels passed into the hands of Indian entrepreneurs. At the same time, a number of new indigenously owned and operated travel agencies and hotels started coming up. In the last 50 years, the Indian travel industry has shown remarkable enterprise. Some of the leading Indian hotel groups and travel agencies have branched out overseas and their performance is highly regarded in the international tourism rankings.

(*e*) The author thinks that tourism has a very bright future because of rapidly rising income levels. The author says income elasticity and tourism are directly proportional. Moreover, rising literacy and education level giving stimulus to standard of living and taking regular vacation and going out on tourist places is becoming a way of life in modern societies. Tourism is one of the fastest growing industries worldwide and governments are taking full responsibility for promotion of this industry and are becoming one of the biggest resources of revenue generation. Health facilities enabling the aged and retired people to enjoy once they are free from their personal and professional responsibility is also adding to the growth of tourist industry. So, there is no doubt that the tourism industry has a very bright future.

COMPREHENSION – 5

(*a*) The period for "The Thought of Young Bengal," when the youthful brand of reformers flourished in Bengal was roughly the second quarter of the 19th Century. The two main teachers, competent scholars and radical educationists were Derozio (1809-1831) and David Hare (1775-1841). The two seem to be different from each other as unlike Derozio, David Hare was neither a professional instructor or intellectual, nor a man of letters. David Hare had neither the brilliance nor the waywardness of Derozio: unlike Derozio, Hare had become in diet and habits almost a half-Hindu.

(*b*) Despite the differences between Derozio and Hare there were certain underlying commonalities between them. Both had a passionate conviction for dissemination of European learning and study of science among Indian people. Both encouraged free thinking, courage, personal integrity in their fellow beings to throw of the fetters of antiquated bigotry. Both were secularists and staunch idealist. They supported each other and try to stand by each other on the issues of reforms and the renaissance that Bengal was to undergo.

(*c*) Derozio was a Calcutta Eurasian of Portuguese Indian ancestry and the son of an officer in an English mercantile firm. He was educated in a pioneer English teaching private school, run by the Scotsman Drummond in the Dharmatala area of Calcutta. Drummond had heavily influenced Derozio in his taste in literature and philosophy, his love of Burns, his faith in the French Revolution and English Radicalism.

(*d*) Derozio had tremendous influence on his pupils i.e. the Young Bengal Group. His personality brought a new era in the annals of the college. Derozio tried with success to broaden and deepen the knowledge of his pupils in western thought and literature, and this new wave emancipated and intoxicated his students.

(*e*) Radhanath Sikdar's statement about Derozio that "He has been the cause and the sole cause of the spirit of enquiry after truth," underscores the point that students must debate freely and question authority and not to be influenced by any of the idols. Only the spirit of inquiry can be beneficial to India.

COMPREHENSION – 6

(*a*) A barren and dry land is the land where little precipitation occurs and which doesn't provide living conditions for plant and animal life.

(*b*) Rich habitat is an area with vast array of animals and plants that have adapted to harsh conditions.

(*c*) Desert animals have adapted ways to help them keep cool when the going gets tough. Desert plants may have to go without fresh water for years at a time. Some plants have adapted to the arid climate by growing long roots that tap water from deep underground. Other plants, such as cacti, have special means of storing and conserving water. Many desert plants can live to be hundreds of years old.

(*d*) Some of the world's semi-arid regions are turning into deserts at an alarming rate. This process, known as "desertification", is not caused by drought, but usually arises from the demands of human population that settles on the semi-arid lands to grow crops and graze animals.

(*e*) Camels also have thick hair in their ears for keeping out sand; they also sport closable nostrils, an eye membrane, and wide feet that act like snow-shoes in the land.

COMPREHENSION – 7

(*a*) Reading of a good book each week, a newspaper, magazines and book-reviews go into making a complete reading programme. This is so because these reading activities give food for thought and thus contribute to the growth of our psyche and intelligence.

(*b*) To feed our intelligence, critical thinking and constructive discussion with individuals and groups are indispensable.

(*c*) While engaged with reading, underlining or marking in the margin is important as it is quite helpful in remembering the core message of the book. It also saves time whenever the book is referred to in future.

(*d*) Knowledge acquired though the act of memorisation is not of much significance. It matters when it is linked with the things we study or observe. In other words, the knowledge should give a better understanding of life and the society in which we live.

(*e*) Knowledge that we acquire through books must help us in conducting and organising ourselves in better terms, than those who are ignorant and unknowledgeable. It should help us in facing head on the challenges of our life.

COMPREHENSION – 8

(*a*) According to the author, on account of excessive dependence on machines, the scarcity would be to get freedom from all sorts of gadgets and machinery.

(*b*) People have lost the capacity to think, thanks to the constant flow of data.

(*c*) The author says that we have more and more ways to communicate but less and less to say because we are highly busy with communicating through various medium, but not able to articulate our thoughts and express them.

(*d*) People are taking active interest in old-age fads as the latter give ways to people to get connected with the wisdom of the age.

(*e*) The very high-speed lives or life-styles leave little time for empathy as the latter requires a deep emotional connect.

COMPREHENSION – 9

(*a*) Good oratory requires enthusiasm, passion, knowledge, reasoning, wit and humour, vehemence, fire and imaginative insights.

(*b*) The effect of Sheridan's speech caused excitement which dumbed the nerves of the concerned Minister to form a just judgment.

(*c*) One can judge the true effect of a good oration when a speaker is able to mesmerize his listeners to think as he thinks, and feel as he feels.

(*d*) There is unrelenting research as to what extent precept and example tally.

(*e*) The speeches which exhibit shallowness and hollowness are not taken seriously.

COMPREHENSION – 10

(*a*) The world gets its water mainly from rainfall, snowfall and artesian wells.

(*b*) The harnessing of our rivers is a great national problem. The waters of many rivers now are mostly wasted. The problem must be dealt on national lines.

(*c*) Afforestation would check soil erosion and. conserve the rainfall of the country from flowing away and would provide the necessary supplies of cheap fuel and thus stop unnecessary waste of farmyard manure.

(*d*) The conservation and utilisation of water is fundamental for human welfare. The moisture in the soil is equally imperative for the life and growth of plants and trees as well.

(*e*) The adoption of techniques preventing soil erosion would help to conserve and keep the water where it is wanted. In other words, such techniques serve a double purpose collection and utilization of water.

PART – E

ASSESS YOUR ACTUAL LEVEL & PROFICIENCY OF ENGLISH LANGUAGE

ASSESS YOUR ACTUAL LEVEL & PROFICIENCY OF ENGLISH LANGUAGE

The Part E 'ASSESS YOUR LEVEL & PROFICIENCY OF ENGLISH LANGUAGE' has been framed with multiple purposes of assessing the level of understanding of words, their meanings, usage and proficiency in English language. The different chapters with different titles have been designed to check the mastery over usage from various angles. The tests of synonyms, antonyms, cloze tests, sentence completion, sentence sequencing or reordering of jumbled sentences and completing the paragraphs with appropriate words, are some of the prominent topics adapted herein under different chapters.

PART A of the book provides MCQs to check the retention of words and their variants. PART B, C & D of the book are prepared with a view to build a strong foundation in grammar, common errors and comprehension and check the same at the same time through various practice exercises. PART E, being the final part of the book has been designed to check and enhance an overall and in depth understanding of the students. As the title suggests; 'English Wizard' – 'Descriptive & Objective,' the book seeks to be a facilitator.

Honest and sincere efforts have been made to make it a perfect TWO-IN-ONE, providing extensive and intensive coverage of the subject matter along with thousands of questions for practice. Over and above all, 'PART E' sums up the sum and substance of the whole Book through various types of practice tests. Having gone through this part, the students will be able to assess their actual level of understanding, usage, and proficiency regarding English language. With improved proficiency of finding errors, conceptual clarity of grammar, learning the subtle nuances of language and at the top of all, the refined and rich diction and proper usage will rejig the confidence of students. The students will be able to crack any English language component in an examination quite comfortably.

The breadth and depth of coverage, clarity and simplicity of usage, multiplicity and variety of practice exercises are some of the most prominent features of this book. The book has been made a concise, compact, complete, and comprehensive manual to act as a wizard for the students. Hence titled ENGLISH WIZARD!

USE OF WORDS – SYNONYMS

Directions: *In the following sentences given below, a word or phrase is written in the bold italicized letter. For each bold italicized word four words/phrases are listed below each sentence. Choose the word nearest in meaning to the italicized word.*

TEST – 1

1. He had a ***penchant*** for fine phrases.
   (*a*) bias (*b*) liking
   (*c*) training (*d*) desire
2. The parade route was down the main ***boulevard***.
   (*a*) alley (*b*) high way
   (*c*) avenue (*d*) drive way
3. Your master will like you if you are ***diligent***.
   (*a*) conscientious (*b*) obedient
   (*c*) meticulous (*d*) hard working
4. ***Incensed*** by his rude behaviour the manager suspended the work.
   (*a*) enthused (*b*) enraged
   (*c*) inflamed (*d*) excited
5. In the existing circumstances her success is ***out of the question.***
   (*a*) impossible (*b*) possible
   (*c*) unquestionable (*d*) certain
6. The five experiments gave ***disparate*** results.
   (*a*) similar (*b*) encouraging
   (*c*) strange (*d*) different
7. Though he is a teacher, his speed lacks ***distinctness***.
   (*a*) clarity (*b*) precision
   (*c*) distinction (*d*) fluency
8. On account of the ***paucity*** of the funds plan remained incomplete.
   (*a*) lack (*b*) scarcity
   (*c*) abundance (*d*) excess
9. We walked down a ***precipitous*** slope.
   (*a*) precarious (*b*) steep
   (*c*) precise (*d*) gradual
10. The ***indiscriminate*** demand for mass consumption goods is deplorable.
    (*a*) desperate (*b*) undifferentiated
    (*c*) discreet (*d*) insensitive
11. ***Malice*** is a feeling that we should always avoid.
    (*a*) Ill–will (*b*) Spite
    (*c*) Cruelty (*d*) Every
12. It is discouraging to find educated people being *taken in* ***easily*** by the lies of religious charlatans.
    (*a*) creditable (*b*) credulous
    (*c*) credible (*d*) creative
13. Outside I am nothing but a ***frolicsome*** little goat who is broken loose.
    (*a*) happy (*b*) playful
    (*c*) gay (*d*) delightful
14. Due to the long ***lapse*** of time, I could not recognize my old friend.
    (*a*) delay (*b*) passage
    (*c*) duration (*d*) movement
15. How I ***envy*** the man who can always produce his reading glasses at a moment's notice.
    (*a*) begrudge (*b*) desire
    (*c*) crave (*d*) covet
16. The communal politics has done ***imponderable*** loss to the unity of India.
    (*a*) incalculable
    (*b*) invaluable
    (*c*) irreparable
    (*d*) invulnerable

17. Wealth acquired through ***dishonourable*** means lead to moral downfall.
(*a*) incredulous (*b*) discreditable
(*c*) incredible (*d*) disgraceful

18. Some satirists are known of their ***trenchant*** style.
(*a*) sharp (*b*) critical
(*c*) aggressive (*d*) incisive

19. I am filled with ***remorse*** for my failure to help the young man.
(*a*) despair (*b*) regret
(*c*) anger (*d*) hatred

20. ***Sanguine*** as he is in his attitude to life and its problems, he cannot but be noticed wherever he goes.
(*a*) optimistic (*b*) enthusiastic
(*c*) realistic (*d*) dispassionate

21. Our Prime Minister is young and ***dynamic***.
(*a*) belligerent (*b*) explosive
(*c*) energetic (*d*) intelligent

22. Quite ***unabashed***, he began his scholarly lecture on what was obvious to every one
(*a*) unashamed (*b*) unimpressed
(*c*) unnerved (*d*) unchecked

23. He ***hardly*** works.
(*a*) arduously (*b*) mostly
(*c*) scarcely (*d*) strenuously

24. The maid servant left the police station ***contrite***.
(*a*) penitent (*b*) sore
(*c*) angry (*d*) remorseless

25. Would you please ***rectify*** the mistake?
(*a*) correct (*b*) clarify
(*c*) condone (*d*) regularize

TEST – 2

1. He had ***insidiously*** wormed his way into her affections.
(*a*) in a polite manner (*b*) in a secret manner
(*c*) in ugly way (*d*) in a forceful manner

2. His close friends, who was senior to him in the office, did not hesitate to ***reprimand*** him when he misplaced one important file.
(*a*) demote (*b*) rebuke
(*c*) suspend (*d*) penalise

3. One must not be ***callous*** to womenfolk.
(*a*) kind (*b*) hard hearted
(*c*) arrogant (*d*) proud

4. Last fortnight the rains came to the parched soils of India after the merciless drought that had already ***sapped*** the vitality and livelihood of millions of peasants.
(*a*) decreased (*b*) demolished
(*c*) destroyed (*d*) drained away

5. That young man is quite ***sanguine*** about the result of his competitive examination.
(*a*) optimistic (*b*) anxious
(*c*) depressed (*d*) pessimistic

6. He tried to ***cajole*** her, but it was in vain.
(*a*) rejoice (*b*) inspire
(*c*) enjoin (*d*) coax

7. The new government decided to ***rescind*** most of the decisions of its predecessor
(*a*) re-consider (*b*) impose
(*c*) modify (*d*) repeal

8. He had the ***nerve*** to suggest that I was cheating
(*a*) strength (*b*) capacity
(*c*) audacity (*d*) courage

9. Even today many people are guided by ***abstruse*** moral values.
(*a*) dangerous (*b*) impracticable
(*c*) obscure (*d*) irrational

10. Millionaires become ***eccentric*** in their old age.
(*a*) miserly (*b*) dull
(*c*) peculiar (*d*) irritable

11. The performance of the candidates was ***deplorable***.
(*a*) horrible (*b*) contentious
(*c*) laughable (*d*) lamentable

12. Indian economy has always shown enough ***resilience*** in crisis.
(*a*) diversity (*b*) strength
(*c*) elasticity (*d*) adjustment

13. Whatever the ***verdict*** of history may be, Chaplin will occupy a unique place in its pages.
(*a*) prediction (*b*) outcome
(*c*) judgement (*d*) voice

14. Poonam is ever ready to ***lend a hand.***
(*a*) assist (*b*) obstruct
(*c*) praise (*d*) hand over

15. She is very ***discreet***.
(*a*) mannered (*b*) mild
(*c*) proud (*d*) prudent

16. The judge asked the contending parties to state their position ***unequivocally***.
(*a*) adequately (*b*) completely
(*c*) effectively (*d*) plainly

17. If a leader wants to be popular he should master the art of being ***civil*** to everyone.
(*a*) polite (*b*) civilized
(*c*) friendly (*d*) obedient

18. We have witnessed an ***inexorable*** march of progress by the organization.
(*a*) inexhaustible (*b*) relentless
(*c*) comprehensive (*d*) sluggish

19. Indian cricketers were ***brimming*** over with confidence after their English tour.
(*a*) overflow (*b*) blow over
(*c*) flow over (*d*) overspill

20. His ***adulatory*** remarks surprised us.
(*a*) discreet (*b*) insulting
(*c*) flattering (*d*) funny

21. The great dancer impressed the appreciative crowd by her ***nimble*** movements.
(*a*) subtle
(*b*) clear
(*c*) quickening
(*d*) arrhythmic

22. He whirled round in a ***trice*** with a revolver in his hand.
(*a*) a trifle (*b*) a triangle
(*c*) an instant (*d*) a circle

23. He used to ***regale*** us with anecdotes
(*a*) flatter (*b*) bore
(*c*) tire (*d*) entertain

24. Many of his acquaintances avoid him because he is so ***garrulous***
(*a*) unreasonable (*b*) quarrelsome
(*c*) talkative (*d*) proud

25. He spent his whole life caught up in ***mundane*** matters.
(*a*) inconsequential (*b*) foolish
(*c*) criminal (*d*) worldly

TEST – 3

1. It is the Prime Minister's ***prerogative*** to appoint or dismiss a Minister.
(*a*) monopoly (*b*) authority
(*c*) mastery (*d*) privilege

2. Some people are extremely ***fastidious*** in their choice of dress
(*a*) careless (*b*) pompous
(*c*) careful (*d*) discriminating

3. A ***posthumous*** award was given to the poet
(*a*) postal (*b*) after death
(*c*) creditable (*d*) literary

4. The ***antidote*** to these problems is hard to find.
(*a*) result of (*b*) cause for
(*c*) consequence of (*d*) remedy for

5. Before I could ***expostulate*** he had spoken again.
(*a*) explain (*b*) disclose
(*c*) protest (*d*) postulate

6. Ramnath is such a ***sham*** that it is difficult to get along with him.
(*a*) pretender (*b*) unnatural
(*c*) blunt (*d*) unfair

7. Whatever opinion he gives is ***sane***.
(*a*) arrogant (*b*) wild
(*c*) obscure (*d*) rational

8. The early monsoon have brought ***respite*** to the people.
(*a*) despite (*b*) inspite of
(*c*) interval of relief (*d*) rest

9. Such conduct deserves ***reprimand***.
(*a*) praise (*b*) punishment
(*c*) rebuke (*d*) reward

10. Businessmen who lack ***acumen*** cannot be expected to be very successful.
(*a*) smartness (*b*) sharpness
(*c*) keenness (*d*) cleverness

11. The journey to Siliguri is quite ***tedious***.
(*a*) diverting (*b*) wearisome
(*c*) lively (*d*) resolute

12. The navy gave ***tactical*** support to the marines.
(*a*) sensitive (*b*) strategic
(*c*) expedient (*d*) expert

13. The poets are known to ***fly*** in their thoughts more than a practical man.
(*a*) sore (*b*) soar
(*c*) sour (*d*) soare

14. The ***facade*** of our school building got a face lift recently.
(*a*) basement (*b*) floor
(*c*) top (*d*) front

15. Peace keeping for the United Nations is, at best of times an ***arduous*** task.
(*a*) laborious (*b*) inconvenient
(*c*) difficult (*d*) delicate

16. Before I could ***make out anything*** he had spoken again.
(*a*) find out (*b*) apprehend
(*c*) explain (*d*) reveal

17. I won't go out of my way to ***placate*** him.
(*a*) please (*b*) pacify
(*c*) serve (*d*) satisfy

18. He has traveled all over the continent by ***hitchhiking*** most the time.
(*a*) free ride (*b*) ride
(*c*) drive (*d*) drive freely

19. He is notorious for his ***voracious*** appetite
(*a*) acute (*b*) haughty
(*c*) gluttonous (*d*) strong

20. He kept his eyes peeled and his ears pricked for some important ***clue***
(*a*) point (*b*) inkling
(*c*) intimation (*d*) signal

21. I wrote to him as ***lately*** as last week.
(*a*) immediately (*b*) early
(*c*) recently (*d*) late

22. Timely first aid ***resuscitated*** the patient.
(*a*) soothed (*b*) rescued
(*c*) revived (*d*) cured

23. The eyewitness testimony was ***incontrovertible***.
(*a*) debatable (*b*) unquestionable
(*c*) unacceptable (*d*) disputable

24. A careful ***preservation*** of wild life is the need of the hour.
(*a*) conservation (*b*) management
(*c*) promotion (*d*) enhancement

25. She is not seen even smiling these days; she is rather ***pensive***.
(*a*) sad (*b*) thoughtful
(*c*) gloomy (*d*) black

TEST – 4

1. He displayed a distinct tendency to ***long–winded*** speeches when asked how he was.
(*a*) boring (*b*) repetitive
(*c*) circumlocutory (*d*) hyperbolic

2. The man lives long through his ***good deeds*** after he had died.
(*a*) beneficial (*b*) benevolent
(*c*) beneficient (*d*) benediction

3. In *exasperation* she railed at the shopkeeper.
(a) irritation (b) fear
(c) astonishment (d) disappointment

4. The prisoner has been *languishing* in the jail for the last many years.
(a) enjoying (b) avoiding
(c) suffering (d) convicted

5. Buoyed by these visions of the future of his son, the artist *soldiered* on.
(a) continued bravely (b) stopped further
(c) struggled hard (d) fought on

6. He did not succeed in his *endeavour*.
(a) enterprise (b) effort
(c) trick (d) plan

7. He does not know how to *husband* his resources.
(a) manage (b) govern
(c) rule (d) watch

8. The number of *aboriginal* inhabitants in Australia is considerable
(a) unoriginal (b) irrational
(c) primitive (d) ancient

9. The guests were offended with his *uncouth* manners
(a) wasteful
(b) uncultured
(c) undesirable
(d) ungracious

10. He does *unpaid* work for the Red Cross.
(a) honourable (b) honorary
(c) honest (d) honorific

11. We did not expect such a *judicious* remark from him.
(a) legal (b) shrewd
(c) rational (d) sagacious

12. It was pure fabrication with an *eye* for a sensation.
(a) observation (b) wish
(c) desire (d) aim

13. His *judicious* handling of the matter saved the situation from going out of control.
(a) sensible (b) nervous
(c) cautious (d) helpful

14. *Furtive* glances were exchanged between the lovers at the feast.
(a) unknown (b) secret
(c) unsuspecting (d) clandestine

15. She purchased *gimcrack* ornaments from the market.
(a) expensive (b) worthless
(c) rare (d) smuggled

16. The villagers offered us an excellent *repast*.
(a) pass time (b) a good meal
(c) entertainment (d) fate

17. The *unlawful* activities of the terrorists need to be dealt with iron hand.
(a) lugubrious (b) salubrious
(c) nefarious (d) deleterious

18. We will carry out the enquiry as *expeditiously* as possible.
(a) fairly (b) speedily
(c) timely (d) justifiably

19. Don't entertain any *misgivings* about his conduct.
(a) distrust (b) doubt
(c) suspicion (d) impression

20. He could rise to this stature because of his *invincible* courage.
(a) inviolable (b) unmanageable
(c) unbeatable (d) immeasurable

21. Many educationists think that the classroom instruction should be made more *vigorous*.
(a) serious (b) brisk
(c) lively (d) active

22. What meaning have you *drawn* from her tongue in cheek remarks.
(a) deduced (b) induced
(c) conduced (d) deducted

23. The Collector has yet not ***relinquished*** his charge.
(*a*) give up (*b*) abdicate
(*c*) leave (*d*) renounce

24. Even though Akshay does not study hard, he always ***comes*** first in his class.
(*a*) scores (*b*) stands
(*c*) arrives (*d*) completes

25. We should abstain from ***bullying*** our colleagues.
(*a*) silly jokes (*b*) frightening
(*c*) passing remarks (*d*) compliments

TEST – 5

1. His ***trite*** remarks failed to cut any ice with the audience.
(*a*) hackneyed (*b*) sharp
(*c*) illogical (*d*) bitter

2. The prince fell in love with a ***comely*** young maiden.
(*a*) elegant (*b*) homely
(*c*) pretty (*d*) delightful

3. My philosophy lecturer is unfailingly ***bombastic***.
(*a*) sensitive in the use of words (*b*) impressionistic
(*c*) impressive (*d*) pompous

4. Inspite of their efforts, the team of scientists could not make much ***headway*** to solve the problem.
(*a*) results (*b*) start
(*c*) efforts (*d*) progress

5. John Milton wrote 'Paradise Lost' to ***vindicate*** the ways of God to man.
(*a*) explain (*b*) support
(*c*) justify (*d*) criticise

6. Some satirists are known for their ***trenchant*** style.
(*a*) critical (*b*) sharp
(*c*) aggressive (*d*) incisive

7. The newspapers are ***clamouring*** against the injustice to the landless labourers.
(*a*) protesting (*b*) noising
(*c*) complaining (*d*) demonstrating

8. The ***inexorable*** demands of the workers brought the company to a closure.
(*a*) unreasonable (*b*) relentless
(*c*) monetary (*d*) violent

9. It is ***exasperating*** to listen to the suggestions of the minister about the educational reforms of which he knows nothing.
(*a*) irritating (*b*) amusing
(*c*) disappointing (*d*) boring

10. The ***surreptitious*** movements of a long figure among the dunes filled the villagers with curiosity and awe.
(*a*) invisible (*b*) nocturnal
(*c*) secret (*d*) concealed

11. ***Forthrightness*** in speech may not always be a desirable quality.
(*a*) outspokenness (*b*) obliqueness
(*c*) mendacity (*d*) equivocation

12. The courage shown by the soldiers at this moment of crisis is ***exemplary***.
(*a*) admirable (*b*) clear
(*c*) elementary (*d*) suitable

13. During the short stay in India, he had quite a few ***frustrating*** experiences.
(*a*) repulsive
(*b*) humiliating
(*c*) disappointing
(*d*) disenchanting

14. His ***lascivious*** habits brought him nothing but bad name.
(*a*) vicious (*b*) lustful
(*c*) erotic (*d*) treacherous

15. Some army units were ***decimated*** during the surprise attack
(*a*) defamed (*b*) captured
(*c*) destroyed (*d*) denounced

16. The travel agent will ***confirm*** my reservation for next week flight to London
(*a*) approve (*b*) obtain
(*c*) verify (*d*) ratify

17. Everybody laughed at the ***puerility*** of his statement
(*a*) insincerity (*b*) falsehood
(*c*) childishness (*d*) inaccuracy

18. Reading of poetry is not ***congenial*** to his taste.
(*a*) preferable (*b*) helpful
(*c*) beneficial (*d*) suited

19. The committee did not find him ***fit*** for the job.
(*a*) genuine (*b*) correct
(*c*) suitable (*d*) selected

20. The novel was so interesting that I was ***oblivious*** of my surroundings.
(*a*) indifferent (*b*) watchful
(*c*) unmindful (*d*) precarious

21. He is very much interested in the ***study of mankind***.
(*a*) anthropology (*b*) philology
(*c*) physiology (*d*) pathology

22. The five day week in Government Offices is bound to benefit the ***jaded*** office goers.
(*a*) refreshed (*b*) routine
(*c*) fatigued (*d*) vigorous

23. He is a good looking but ***insipid*** young man.
(*a*) arrogant
(*b*) unscrupulous
(*c*) sick
(*d*) lacking in spirit

24. A genius tends to ***deviate*** from the routine way of thinking.
(*a*) dispute (*b*) differ
(*c*) disagree (*d*) distinguish

25. Her evidence totally ***refuted*** the charges.
(*a*) refused (*b*) denied
(*c*) disproved (*d*) repelled

TEST – 6

1. Honest officers find it difficult to ***attune*** themselves to corrupt bureaucracy.
(*a*) tune (*b*) adapt
(*c*) harmony (*d*) accusation

2. He mentioned in the ***postscript*** that he might need some money, soon.
(*a*) end of the letter after signature
(*b*) manuscript
(*c*) after the address
(*d*) post diction

3. When youngsters do not have good role-models to ***emulate*** they start searching for them among sportsmen or filmstars.
(*a*) inhabit (*b*) imitate
(*c*) mollify (*d*) modify

4. A ***rupture*** in the relationship of the two brothers is quite apparent.
(*a*) gap (*b*) damage
(*c*) break (*d*) breach

5. ***Defection*** is quite common in our present day political life.
(*a*) desertion (*b*) disobedience
(*c*) disloyalty (*d*) indiscipline

6. His conscience ***pricked*** him.
(*a*) soothed (*b*) cut
(*c*) hurt (*d*) pinched

7. A person unrestrained by the rules of morality or tradition is called a ***licentious*** person.
(*a*) libertine (*b*) loafer type
(*c*) criminal (*d*) freelance

8. I don't see why he should be so ***obsequious*** to his brother just because the latter is rich.
(*a*) unfriendly
(*b*) unusually kind
(*c*) offensive
(*d*) excessively respectful

9. He was ***admonished*** for the delay
(*a*) admired (*b*) warned
(*c*) censured (*d*) dismissed

10. ***Hybrid*** variety of plants generally yield better crops
(*a*) combined (*b*) transplanted
(*c*) complex (*d*) mixed

11. The people welcomed the budget as there was ***judicious*** allocation of funds to all the sectors.
(*a*) legal (*b*) indiscriminate
(*c*) generous (*d*) sensible

12. The poem is written in a very ***lucid*** style.
(*a*) intricate (*b*) noble
(*c*) elaborate (*d*) clear

13. All the characters in the novel are ***fictitious***.
(*a*) unreliable (*b*) unbelievable
(*c*) unreal (*d*) imaginative

14. Elsie is seventy years old and a ***fanatical*** gardener.
(*a*) crazy
(*b*) fantastic
(*c*) excessively enthusiastic
(*d*) obsessed

15. It is so ***gratifying*** to know that there are not many cases of small pox these days.
(*a*) pleasing (*b*) surprising
(*c*) satisfying (*d*) happy

16. India has not yet been able to ***harness*** her domestic resources in full.
(*a*) complete (*b*) utilize
(*c*) produce (*d*) bridle

17. She ***upbraided*** the little girl who got frightened.
(*a*) make tails (*b*) make up
(*c*) scolded (*d*) handed

18. The two opposing parties have reached a ***stalemate***.
(*a*) dilemma (*b*) deadlock
(*c*) exhaustion (*d*) settlement

19. Rich people often have ***sycophants*** around them
(*a*) pilots (*b*) sadists
(*c*) flatterers (*d*) servants

20. The obstacles seem to be ***insurmountable***, but no one should doubt what this fearless woman can accomplish
(*a*) too tall and too high
(*b*) too trivial to attract attention
(*c*) too easy to achieve
(*d*) too difficult to overcome

21. Everybody in the assembly shouted and there was ***pandemonium*** in the hall.
(*a*) disorderly scene (*b*) noise
(*c*) laughter (*d*) crowd

22. She looked ***gorgeous*** in her new dress.
(*a*) great (*b*) fantastic
(*c*) silly (*d*) splendid

23. The ***aberration*** in the Indian Economy can be attributed to short sightedness of its political masters.
(*a*) deviation (*b*) steadfastness
(*c*) privilege (*d*) procrastination

24. Sunlight and shadow made the landscape a ***Kaleidoscope*** of colour.
(*a*) tube containing mirrors and loose pieces of coloured glass
(*b*) frequently changing pattern of bright scenes
(*c*) a mixture of black and white
(*d*) resembling the seven coloours of rainbow

25. My neighbours is an ***extravagant*** person
(*a*) pompous (*b*) reckless
(*c*) unreasonable (*d*) wasteful

TEST – 7

1. He is so ***garrulous*** that all sober persons avoid his company.
(*a*) quarrelsome (*b*) talkative
(*c*) domineering (*d*) foolish

2. Mumbai is the ***terminus*** of the Western Railways.
(*a*) last stop (*b*) termination
(*c*) junction (*d*) tenure

3. Our fates seemed ***intertwined***.
(*a*) complicated (*b*) destined
(*c*) complex (*d*) linked

4. The Prime Minister delivered an ***impromptu*** speech to the students.
(*a*) important (*b*) impressive
(*c*) inspiring (*d*) extempore

5. The *honesty* of the king's minister was ***above board*** and the king was fond of him.
(*a*) propinquity (*b*) polarity
(*c*) beyond suspicion (*d*) posterity

6. The treaty was later ***ratified***.
(*a*) charged (*b*) confirmed
(*c*) reformed (*d*) updated

7. The District Collector made it clear that the Government cannot ***sustain*** for long the support for such a scheme.
(*a*) pay (*b*) succeed
(*c*) manage (*d*) continue

8. The invasion forces had no artillery and were completely ***annihilated***.
(*a*) reduced (*b*) destroyed
(*c*) dismembered (*d*) split

9. Our talks with the foreign delegation were really ***productive***.
(*a*) growing (*b*) efficient
(*c*) fruitful (*d*) lengthy

10. Dr. S. Radha Krishnan has written an ***erudite*** commentary on the Bhagwad Gita.
(*a*) scholarly (*b*) inspiring
(*c*) effective (*d*) perfect

11. Scientific knowledge is an intoxicating ***draught***, and it may be one which the human race is unable to sustain.
(*a*) process (*b*) product
(*c*) drink (*d*) disease

12. The story is ***embellished*** with amusing put perhaps undue details.
(*a*) adorned (*b*) balanced
(*c*) sprinkled (*d*) filled

13. In so far as his research is concerned, he is very ***meticulous***.
(*a*) alert to improve technique
(*b*) slovenly and inexact
(*c*) about to start
(*d*) stupendous

14. ***Weird*** noises came from the haunted houses
(*a*) beastly (*b*) unpleasant
(*c*) frightening (*d*) unnatural

15. Something should be done about the ***insanitary*** conditions of our parks.
(*a*) poor (*b*) dingy
(*c*) ugly (*d*) unhygienic

16. He had to ***curtail*** his leave as a lot of work was pending in his office.
(*a*) cancel (*b*) extend
(*c*) shorten (*d*) postpone

17. True religion does not require one to ***proselytise*** through guile or force.
(*a*) convert (*b*) attack
(*c*) hypnotize (*d*) translate

18. We should always try to maintain and promote communal ***amity***.
(*a*) understanding (*b*) bondage
(*c*) friendship (*d*) contention

19. He displayed a distinct tendency to ***long winded*** speeches when asked how he was.
(*a*) circumlocutory (*b*) hyperbolic
(*c*) repetitive (*d*) boring

20. English conversation means the learning of many ***catchy*** phrases.
(*a*) easily remembered (*b*) easily spoken
(*c*) easily understood (*d*) lucid

21. This is a ***lucrative*** business.
(*a*) profitable (*b*) dangerous
(*c*) challenging (*d*) questionable

22. We are happy that the two countries are trying to find an ***amicable*** solution to their disputes.
(*a*) a just (*b*) an appropriate
(*c*) a durable (*d*) a friendly

23. A man of unsound mind, he was ***exonerated*** from all responsibility for his actions.

(*a*) exculpated (*b*) prevented

(*c*) excused (*d*) liberated

24. The coach followed a ***devious*** course to its destination.

(*a*) difficult (*b*) short–cut

(*c*) straight (*d*) winding

25. The millions of the poor ***hapless*** Indians' future does not hold any promise.

(*a*) unhappy (*b*) unfortunate

(*c*) helpless (*d*) adverse

TEST – 8

1. He tried to ***alleviate*** the sufferings of his neighbours.

(*a*) abate (*b*) dissipate

(*c*) remove (*d*) relieve

2. The ***disgruntled*** members of a party are constant source of tension to the party leader.

(*a*) disloyal (*b*) dishonest

(*c*) discontented (*d*) dispirited

3. The young girl appeared ***self-possessed*** in front of TV cameras.

(*a*) shy (*b*) confident

(*c*) introvert (*d*) extrovert

4. He ended his speech on a ***supercilious*** note which was quite unexpected of a person of balanced and stable temperament.

(*a*) defamatory (*b*) contemptuous

(*c*) superfluous (*d*) irrelevant

5. Factory workers are ***restive*** as the company has not declared any bonus this year.

(*a*) restful (*b*) restless

(*c*) resting (*d*) satisfied

6. She cannot tolerate ***exceptionable*** remarks about her parents.

(*a*) exceptional (*b*) objectionable

(*c*) exception (*d*) humility

7. His ***forthright*** behaviour shows that he is honest but he seems rude to some people.

(*a*) courteous (*b*) correct

(*c*) straightforward (*d*) tactful

8. It is amazing how such a ***motley*** group could get along so well.

(*a*) heterogeneous (*b*) assorted

(*c*) promiscuous (*d*) confused

9. She leaned back, feeling ***enervated***.

(*a*) disheartened (*b*) confused

(*c*) saddened (*d*) weakened

10. He was accused of ***graft***.

(*a*) corruption (*b*) inefficiency

(*c*) favouritism (*d*) negligence

11. We didn't believe in his statement but ***subsequent*** events proved that he was right.

(*a*) latter (*b*) many

(*c*) few (*d*) conclusive

12. He has been able to ***unearth*** a secret.

(*a*) suppress (*b*) discover

(*c*) disclose (*d*) decade

13. It is difficult to ***authenticate*** these old manuscripts.

(*a*) elucidate (*b*) illustrate

(*c*) establish genuineness (*d*) edit properly

14. Corruption ***stalks*** every sphere of national life

(*a*) pervades (*b*) poisons

(*c*) pollutes (*d*) penetrates

15. The rebels returned home under an ***amnesty***

(*a*) general pardon

(*b*) financial assistance

(*c*) police security

(*d*) literary

16. He is being treated for his ***somnolence***

(*a*) sleepiness

(*b*) weakness

(*c*) intoxication

(*d*) severe pain in the joints

17. The recent acts of ***vandalism*** in the country cannot be ignored.
(*a*) disturbance (*b*) ravage
(*c*) provocation (*d*) violence

18. A bone got stuck in his ***gullet***.
(*a*) throat (*b*) chest
(*c*) molars (*d*) stomach

19. For quick promotion, he hit on a plan to ***propitiate*** the Manager.
(*a*) evict (*b*) incite
(*c*) praise (*d*) conciliate

20. He tried to ***mollify*** my hurt feelings.
(*a*) arouse (*b*) ignore
(*c*) soften (*d*) suppress

21. The boy gave a ***vivid*** description of all that happened.
(*a*) brilliant (*b*) fresh
(*c*) explanatory (*d*) picturesque

22. A ***conscientious*** worker is always admired by his employers.
(*a*) obedient (*b*) sinecure
(*c*) skilful (*d*) carefull

23. Few teachers have been spared the problem of an ***obstreperous*** pupil in the class.
(*a*) awkward (*b*) lazy
(*c*) unruly (*d*) sullen

24. The ***deployment*** of para–military forces in Punjab has helped the provincial government a lot.
(*a*) activated (*b*) employment
(*c*) use (*d*) spreading out

25. His boss's criticism left him feeling rather ***abashed***.
(*a*) annoyed (*b*) arrogant
(*c*) embarrassed (*d*) awakened

TEST – 9

1. Leaders of some political parties make ***fiery*** speeches.
(*a*) fantastic (*b*) inflammatory
(*c*) passionate (*d*) eloquent

2. It was an ***astute*** move to sell the property at that stage.
(*a*) shrewd (*b*) unwise
(*c*) dishonest (*d*) inexplicable

3. There is a ***tacit*** agreement between the superpowers not to engage themselves in armed conflict.
(*a*) unspoken (*b*) speechless
(*c*) silent (*d*) introvert

4. No one expects a ***facile*** solution to the Punjab Problem.
(*a*) satisfactory (*b*) easy
(*c*) satisfying (*d*) difficult

5. When I visited him he was in a ***retrospective*** mood.
(*a*) thoughtful (*b*) thinking of past
(*c*) pensive (*d*) introspective

6. Plants that grow and exist in deserts have highly specialized means of adapting themselves to the ***arid*** environment.
(*a*) reproductive (*b*) useless
(*c*) withering (*d*) dry

7. The arguments of the lawyer of the accused were so ***persuasive*** that the judge acquitted him.
(*a*) convincing (*b*) clever
(*c*) eloquent (*d*) logical

8. He was sad that his seniority had been ***overlooked***.
(*a*) rejected (*b*) neglected
(*c*) confused (*d*) sidestepped

9. He delivered a lengthy speech in which he committed several ***ludicrous*** mistakes.
(*a*) glaring (*b*) funny
(*c*) absurd (*d*) serious

10. ***Eventually*** vision is affected and the patient is able to see only if light is present.
(*a*) primarily (*b*) initially
(*c*) gradually (*d*) ultimately

11. It is ***futile*** to argue with a person who does not want to understand.
(*a*) unnecessary (*b*) useless
(*c*) dangerous (*d*) infuriating

12. People of different ***persuasions*** have met on the same platform
(*a*) taste (*b*) personalities
(*c*) convictions (*d*) qualifications

13. He is believed to be a very ***industrious*** worker
(*a*) successful (*b*) punctual
(*c*) sensible (*d*) diligent

14. He found it an ***arduous*** task to perform.
(*a*) boring (*b*) ardent
(*c*) ordinary (*d*) difficult

15. Lack of occupation is not necessarily revealed by ***manifest*** idleness.
(*a*) easily perceived (*b*) easily acquired
(*c*) easily infected (*d*) easily deflected

16. He did his job with ***scrupulous*** care.
(*a*) exact (*b*) marvelous
(*c*) great (*d*) inattentive

17. She is really a ***fantastic*** girl.
(*a*) wonderful (*b*) charming
(*c*) beautiful (*d*) intelligent

18. He ***corroborated*** the statement of his brother.
(*a*) condemned (*b*) confirmed
(*c*) seconded (*d*) disproved

19. There must be lively discussion of Indian authors if we are to ***foster*** *our* knowledge.
(*a*) promote (*b*) cherish
(*c*) nourish (*d*) nurture

20. He wrote a ***scathing*** review of the prize–winning novel.
(*a*) biased (*b*) scornful
(*c*) unbalanced (*d*) subjective

21. The library was built with donations from the ***munificent*** citizens of this city.
(*a*) generous (*b*) respectable
(*c*) learned (*d*) well–to–do

22. As a speaker he was an ***utter*** failure.
(*a*) total (*b*) partial
(*c*) completely (*d*) relative

23. Mohinder Amarnath had ***penchant*** for hook shots.
(*a*) art (*b*) inclination
(*c*) strength (*d*) desire

24. After he came back from his evening walk, he felt ***famished***.
(*a*) exhausted (*b*) hungry
(*c*) peevish (*d*) relaxed

25. Medical science is yet to come out with a ***panacea*** for cancer.
(*a*) remedy (*b*) medicine
(*c*) treatment (*d*) drug

TEST – 10

1. The new volume provides substantial critical ***excerpts*** and biographical information on eight to ten major poets from all eras.
(*a*) sources (*b*) explanation
(*c*) extracts (*d*) substances

2. The chairman conducted the meeting with ***aplomb***.
(*a*) arrogance (*b*) annoyance
(*c*) poise (*d*) authority

3. Even the most careful researcher cannot predict the possible future ***ramifications*** of his findings.
(*a*) uses (*b*) developments
(*c*) consequences (*d*) conclusions

4. There was no ***ostensible*** reason for her being angry at her husband's remarks.
(*a*) hidden (*b*) covert
(*c*) apparent (*d*) secret

5. Ritui asked Rashmi not to ***meddle*** in her affairs.
(*a*) intercede
(*b*) impose
(*c*) cross
(*d*) interfere

6. A pervading sense of ***ennui*** grips Gaurav.
(*a*) anger (*b*) anxiety
(*c*) weariness (*d*) melancholy

7. We don't know how we are to ***recompense*** you for the trouble you have taken.
(*a*) reward (*b*) help
(*c*) praise (*d*) thank

8. Most of the politicians these days have a large number of ***toadies*** around them.
(*a*) followers
(*b*) professional assistants
(*c*) servants
(*d*) sycophants

9. The small boy was able to give a ***graphic*** description of the thief.
(*a*) vague (*b*) vivid
(*c*) drawing (*d*) picture

10. The secret of good style is to avoid ***redundant*** words.
(*a*) repetitive (*b*) unwilling
(*c*) wrong (*d*) retarded

11. Dowry is a ***pernicious*** social practice.
(*a*) traditional
(*b*) prevalent
(*c*) painful
(*d*) injurious

12. I ***stood up for him*** when everyone else was criticizing him
(*a*) tolerated him
(*b*) opposed him insistently
(*c*) supported him energetically
(*d*) faced him boldly

13. He is quite ***parsimonious*** by nature
(*a*) cruel (*b*) haughty
(*c*) prodigal (*d*) miserly

14. ***Sporadic*** rise in his temperature caused us much worry.
(*a*) scattered (*b*) occasional
(*c*) irksome (*d*) frequent

15. I gave a shout when I sighted an ***oasis*** in the desert.
(*a*) waterfall
(*b*) a patch of grass
(*c*) a place with water and trees
(*d*) waterway

16. He was warned at the ***outset*** of his career.
(*a*) end (*b*) beginning
(*c*) middle (*d*) entrance

17. On scrutiny the police officer found out that the documents provided by the landlord were totally ***fabricated***.
(*a*) historical (*b*) genuine
(*c*) forged (*d*) prepared

18. Most of the staff is ***restive*** under the new manager's rule.
(*a*) relaxed (*b*) friendly
(*c*) obstinate (*d*) discontented

19. Grandfather has been getting ***feeble*** of late.
(*a*) tall (*b*) weak
(*c*) diseased (*d*) small

20. His visit to foreign countries brought about a ***sea change*** in his outlook and his attitude to the people.
(*a*) favourable change
(*b*) complete change
(*c*) unfavourable change
(*d*) partial change

21. Being a sociable bird she was ***conspicuous*** by her absence in the club last evening.
(*a*) important (*b*) prominent
(*c*) ignorant (*d*) apparent

22. There seems to be ***perpetual*** war going on between the rich and the poor.
(*a*) never ending (*b*) regular
(*c*) always (*d*) intermittent

23. The flat has been ***refurbished*** recently.
(*a*) white–washed (*b*) painted
(*c*) renovated (*d*) repaired

24. The officer gave a ***lucid*** explanation of the company's course of action

(*a*) vague (*b*) unconvincing
(*c*) long (*d*) clear

25. ***Temperance*** in eating is conducive to health.

(*a*) discipline (*b*) caution
(*c*) moderation (*d*) care

TEST – 11

1. One's ***remonstration*** against social ills has to be consistent to be fruitful.

(*a*) outrage (*b*) demonstration
(*c*) protest (*d*) criticism

2. It would be ***impertinent*** to suggest that he was generally wrong.

(*a*) fair (*b*) correct
(*c*) rude (*d*) impartial

3. The opposition criticised the ruling party for the ***deteriorating*** law and order situation in the state.

(*a*) disrupting (*b*) worsening
(*c*) crumbling (*d*) eroding

4. One of the ***salient*** features of your proposal is a stress on self employment.

(*a*) prominent (*b*) silent
(*c*) loud (*d*) important

5. Man has to ***encounter*** many hardships in life.

(*a*) solve (*b*) face
(*c*) bear (*d*) overcome

6. After the ***dismal*** performance of the team in the series concluded yesterday the captain offered his resignation to the President of the club.

(*a*) poor (*b*) miserly
(*c*) short (*d*) sorrowful

7. Some of the discoveries of modern science are simply ***marvellous***.

(*a*) praiseworthy (*b*) commendable
(*c*) amazing (*d*) admirable

8. The scheme failed for want of ***adequate*** funds.

(*a*) required (*b*) recommended
(*c*) sufficient (*d*) necessary

9. The Border Security Force ***intercepted*** yesterday a truck carrying arms and ammunition.

(*a*) found (*b*) stopped
(*c*) met (*d*) interrupted

10. Because of a family ***feud***, he never spoke to his wife parents.

(*a*) trouble (*b*) crisis
(*c*) quarrel (*d*) problem

11. Everyone turned to stare at the visitor and his ***preposterous*** dress.

(*a*) strange (*b*) vague
(*c*) pompous (*d*) absurd

12. Mulberry plantation is a prerequisite for ***sericulture***.

(*a*) growing softgrass (*b*) breeding silk worms
(*c*) growing trees for timber (*d*) breeding shrimps

13. I found his crude manners ***abominable***.

(*a*) detestable (*b*) flattering
(*c*) attractive (*d*) sloppy

14. The international community may begin to doubt the ***credentials*** of the largest democracy in the world.

(*a*) principles
(*b*) credibility
(*c*) capacity to return loans
(*d*) trustworthiness

15. It is a ***scandal*** that the murderer was declared innocent.

(*a*) rum our (*b*) silly notion
(*c*) talk (*d*) disgraceful action

16. The prisoner made an ***abortive*** attempt to escape from the jail.

(*a*) courageous (*b*) futile
(*c*) illegal (*d*) furtive

17. A million cinemas a year bring the same stale ***balderdash***.

(*a*) adventure (*b*) nonsense
(*c*) thriller (*d*) romance

18. His speech was nothing but a string of ***platitudes***.

(*a*) grand statements
(*b*) stereo–typed statements
(*c*) noble sentiments
(*d*) humorous anecdotes

19. The opposition made a ***strident*** demand for putting the bill to vote.

(*a*) courageous (*b*) brave
(*c*) vociferous (*d*) powerful

20. He soon got fed up with his ***sedentary*** job.

(*a*) involving much sitting
(*b*) routine
(*c*) roving
(*d*) drab

21. Though long, your essay is ***vague*** on the point.

(*a*) doubtful (*b*) eloquent
(*c*) indistinct (*d*) lucid

22. The field was ***even*** enough for the joggers to have their practice.

(*a*) plane (*b*) plain
(*c*) plan (*d*) plaine

23. On public occasions, she was very ***punctilious*** about forms and manners.

(*a*) serious (*b*) careful
(*c*) artificial (*d*) casual

24. This library was built with donations from the ***munificent*** citizens of the city.

(*a*) well-to-do (*b*) generous
(*c*) respectable (*d*) learned

25. The ***perspicuity*** of the lawyer's arguments was remarkable.

(*a*) logic (*b*) precision
(*c*) lucidity (*d*) profundity

TEST – 12

1. The import of technology as an alternative to ***indigenous*** technology has not been discussed fully

(*a*) aboriginal (*b*) indigent
(*c*) terrestrial (*d*) native

2. The ***ascending*** temperature in many parts of the world confirms global warming which is an environmental hazard.

(*a*) mounting (*b*) shooting
(*c*) falling (*d*) rising

3. Reading fiction is an ***absorbing***, creative and entertaining hobby.

(*a*) a concentrating (*b*) an engrossing
(*c*) a fascinating (*d*) an enriching

4. The data is ***misleading***.

(*a*) illusory (*b*) deceptive
(*c*) misplaced (*d*) misinformative

5. Graduation day is a ***momentous*** day for most students.

(*a*) memorable (*b*) melancholy
(*c*) important (*d*) hectic

6. There was a major ***split*** in the Congress party in 1969.

(*a*) breach (*b*) division
(*c*) break (*d*) unity

7. Her views are not *in* ***consonance*** with her husband's.

(*a*) in disagreement (*b*) in conflict
(*c*) in agreement (*d*) contradictory

8. The claims of students look hollow when they ***attribute*** their poor performance to difficulty of examination.

(*a*) inundate (*b*) inhere
(*c*) impute (*d*) infer

9. It is ***compulsory*** for all the students to join this tour.

(*a*) regular (*b*) necessary
(*c*) dutiful (*d*) obligatory

10. The old man shows no sign of ***infirmity*** even though he is eighty years old.

(*a*) indolence (*b*) fickleness
(*c*) feebleness (*d*) lack of firmness

11. The defendant was grateful for the judge's ***clemency***.

(*a*) patience (*b*) mercy
(*c*) relaxed attitude (*d*) politeness

12. Pakistan has been vigorously pursuing a ***clandestine*** nuclear weapons programme.
(*a*) secretive (*b*) systematic
(*c*) progressive (*d*) nefariou

13. He likes his friend inspite of his little ***frailties***.
(*a*) frenzy (*b*) timidness
(*c*) oddities (*d*) weakness

14. I doubt the ***veracity*** of your statement
(*a*) tenacity (*b*) wisdom
(*c*) truthfulness (*d*) reliability

15. We should abstain from ***casting aspersions*** on the character of our colleagues
(*a*) passing critical remarks
(*b*) paying left handed compliments
(*c*) cracking silly jokes
(d) passing slanderous remarks

16. We should encourage ***indigenous*** industries.
(*a*) foreign (*b*) cottage
(*c*) big (*d*) native

17. The number of ***aboriginal*** inhabitants in Australia is considerable.
(*a*) primitive (*b*) ancient
(*c*) unoriginal (*d*) irrational

18. The leader's ***charisma*** attracted many followers.
(*a*) humility (*b*) power
(c) magnetic appeal (*d*) **candour**

19. The teacher felt that the student lacked ***discrimination*** in the study of his data.
(*a*) imagination (*b*) good taste
(*c*) objectivity (*d*) good judgement

20. The ***intrepid*** mountaineers who scaled the peak in winter should be specially congratulated.
(*a*) bold (*b*) courageous
(*c*) vigorous (*d*) brave

21. The inspector was a ***vigilant*** young man.
(*a*) smart (*b*) watchful
(*c*) ambitious (*d*) intelligent

22. The resignation of the Chief Minister is ***intriguing***.
(*a*) gripping (*b*) interesting
(*c*) secret (*d*) diplomatic

23. India has made ***spectacular*** progress in Science and technology.
(*a*) remarkable (*b*) great
(*c*) formidable (*d*) super

24. The ***acerbic*** remarks of the manager were unwarranted.
(*a*) bitter (*b*) furious
(*c*) arrogant (*d*) childish

25. In modern hospitals, computers ***check*** the patients before they see the doctor.
(*a*) stop (*b*) protect
(*c*) cover (*d*) screen

ANSWERS

TEST – 1

1. liking
2. drive way
3. hard working
4. enraged
5. unquestionable
6. different
7. distinction
8. scarcity
9. steep
10. undifferentiated
11. Ill–will
12. credulous
13. delightful
14. passage
15. covet
16. incalculable
17. disgraceful
18. critical
19. regret
20. optimistic
21. energetic
22. unashamed
23. scarcely
24. penitent
25. correct

TEST – 2

1. in ugly way
2. rebuke
3. hard hearted
4. destroyed
5. optimistic
6. coax
7. repeal
8. courage
9. obscure
10. peculiar
11. lamentable
12. elasticity
13. judgement
14. assist
15. proud
16. completely
17. polite
18. relentless
19. overflow
20. flattering
21. clear
22. a circle
23. entertain
24. talkative
25. worldly

TEST – 3

1. privilege
2. careful
3. after death
4. remedy for
5. explain
6. pretender
7. rational
8. interval of relief
9. rebuke
10. sharpness
11. wearisome
12. strategic
13. soar
14. front
15. difficult
16. find out
17. pacify
18. free ride
19. gluttonous
20. inkling
21. recently
22. revived
23. unquestionable
24. conservation
25. thoughtful

TEST – 4

1. circumlocutory
2. benevolent
3. irritation
4. convicted
5. struggled hard
6. effort
7. manage
8. primitive
9. ungracious
10. honorary
11. sagacious
12. aim
13. cautious
14. secret
15. rare
16. pass time
17. nefarious
18. speedily
19. suspicion
20. unbeatable
21. lively
22. deducted
23. abdicate
24. stands
25. frightening

TEST – 5

1. hackneyed
2. pretty
3. impressive
4. progress
5. justify
6. critical
7. noising
8. relentless
9. irritating
10. secret
11. outspokenness
12. admirable
13. disappointing
14. lustful
15. destroyed
16. verify
17. childishness
18. suited
19. suitable
20. unmindful
21. anthropology
22. fatigued
23. lacking in spirit
24. differ
25. denied

TEST – 6

1. adapt
2. end of the letter after signature
3. imitate
4. break
5. desertion
6. pinched
7. libertine
8. excessively respectful
9. warned
10. mixed
11. sensible
12. clear
13. imaginative
14. obsessed
15. pleasing
16. utilize
17. scolded
18. deadlock
19. flatterers
20. too difficult to overcome
21. disorderly scene
22. splendid
23. deviation
24. frequently changing pattern of bright scenes
25. wasteful

TEST – 7

1. talkative
2. junction
3. linked
4. extempore
5. beyond suspicion
6. confirmed
7. continue
8. destroyed
9. fruitful
10. scholarly
11. disease
12. adorned
13. stupendous
14. beastly
15. unhygienic
16. shorten
17. convert
18. friendship
19. circumlocutory
20. easily remembered
21. profitable
22. a friendly
23. exculpated
24. winding
25. unfortunate

TEST – 8

1. abate
2. discontented
3. confident
4. defamatory
5. restful
6. objectionable
7. straightforward
8. heterogeneous
9. weakened
10. corruption
11. latter
12. discover
13. establish genuinence
14. pervades
15. general pardon
16. sleepiness
17. ravage
18. stomach
19. conciliate
20. soften
21. brilliant
22. careful
23. sullen
24. employment
25. embarrassed

TEST – 9

1. inflammatory
2. shrewd
3. silent
4. easy
5. pensive
6. dry
7. convincing
8. neglected
9. absurd
10. ultimately
11. useless
12. convictions
13. diligent
14. difficult
15. easily perceived
16. great
17. wonderful
18. confirmed
19. nourish
20. scornful
21. generous
22. total
23. inclination
24. exhausted
25. remedy

TEST – 10

1. extracts
2. poise
3. consequences
4. apparent
5. interfere
6. weariness
7. help
8. sycophants
9. drawing
10. repetitive
11. injurious
12. supported him energetically
13. miserly
14. occasional
15. a place with water and trees
16. beginning
17. forged
18. discontented
19. weak
20. complete change
21. apparent
22. never ending
23. renovated
24. clear
25. moderation

TEST – 11

1. outrage
2. rude
3. worsening
4. important
5. face
6. poor
7. amazing
8. sufficient
9. interrupted
10. problem
11. absurd
12. breeding silk worms
13. detestable
14. credibility
15. disgraceful action
16. futile
17. nonsense
18. stereo–typed statements
19. vociferous
20. involving much sitting
21. doubtful
22. plain
23. artificial
24. generous
25. precision

TEST – 12

1. native
2. rising
3. an engrossing
4. misplaced
5. memorable
6. division
7. in agreement
8. impute
9. obligatory
10. feebleness
11. mercy
12. secretive
13. weakness
14. truthfulness
15. passing slanderous remarks
16. native
17. primitive
18. magnetic appeal
19. objectivity
20. bold
21. watchful
22. gripping
23. remarkable
24. bitter
25. screen

32 CHAPTER

USE OF WORDS – ANTONYMS

Directions: The following sentences consist of a word or a phrase which is written in bold italicized letter. Each of them is followed by four words or phrases. Select the word or the phrase which is closest to the opposite in meaning of the italicised word or phrase.

TEST – 1

1. India will have to cultivate all her ***barren*** land to meet with her food requirements.
   (*a*) arid (*b*) simple
   (*c*) sterile (*d*) productive

2. The members of the opposition made ***derogatory*** remarks about the policies of government.
   (*a*) praise worthy (*b*) laudatory
   (*c*) respectable (*d*) admirable

3. The area is known of its ***plentiful*** rain.
   (*a*) poor (*b*) impoverished
   (*c*) scarce (*d*) miserly

4. We were surprised by the ***hostile*** attitude of the villagers.
   (*a*) gentle (*b*) friendly
   (*c*) self (*d*) forgiving

5. Old people are usually more ***conservative*** than young people.
   (*a*) modern (*b*) old fashioned
   (*c*) dynamic (*d*) liberal

6. Lucy is a ***smart*** girl.
   (*a*) lazy (*b*) active
   (*c*) indecent (*d*) casual

7. Of all the companions of our joyous ***ascent***, there were only the two of us left.
   (*a*) descant (*b*) descendant
   (*c*) descent (*d*) decent

8. I was deeply affected by his ***urbane*** behavior.
   (*a*) rural (*b*) indifferent
   (*c*) rude (*d*) unsympathetic

9. We went to the first floor through the ***rickety*** wooden stairs.
   (*a*) stable (*b*) old
   (*c*) narrow (*d*) uncomfortable

10. Those in ***distress*** should not be laughed at because they deserve our sympathy.
    (*a*) trouble (*b*) prosperity
    (*c*) affluence (*d*) adversity

11. His face bore ***a blank*** look all the time while I was telling him about that exciting incident.
    (*a*) a passive (*b*) an expressive
    (*c*) a passionate (*d*) a mysterious

12. ***Counterfeit*** coins are in circulation because of negligence on the part of police authorities.
    (*a*) spurious (*b*) genuine
    (*c*) truthful (*d*) fake

13. Though generous and ***benevolent***, he did not meet with success in his career.
    (*a*) beneficent (*b*) malevolent
    (*c*) goodwill (*d*) liberal

14. The town has been experiencing ***incessant*** rains since 4 o' clock.
    (*a*) continual (*b*) continuous
    (*c*) uninterrupted (*d*) irregular

15. Many snakes are ***innocuous***.
    (*a*) poisonous (*b*) harmless
    (*c*) deadly (*d*) ferocious

16. It was universally characterized as ***progressive*** measure.
    (*a*) regressive (*b*) obstructive
    (*c*) retrograde (*d*) abhorent

17. His business ***acumen*** led him to the zenith of his career.
(*a*) imbecility (*b*) mental alertness
(*c*) enterprise (*d*) shrewdness

18. The mountains present a ***bleak*** sight at night.
(*a*) warm (*b*) desolate
(*c*) dense (*d*) deserted

19. The speaker has a ***superficial*** knowledge of the subject.
(*a*) artificial (*b*) deep
(*c*) fictitious (*d*) overt

20. They made a ***profligate*** use of scarce resources.
(*a*) proper (*b*) extravagant
(*c*) effective (*d*) thrifty

21. The outgoing Chairman has a number of ***laudable*** achievements to his credit.
(*a*) noble (*b*) disreputable
(*c*) glorious (*d*) praiseworthy

22. His ***meanness*** is proverbial.
(*a*) generosity (*b*) pragamatism
(*c*) timidity (*d*) kindness

23. Her dress was too ***slovenly*** for that kind of interview.
(*a*) gaudy (*b*) tidy
(*c*) formal (*d*) old–fashioned

24. He was in a ***dejected*** mood.
(*a*) jubilant (*b*) rejected
(*c*) irritable (*d*) romantic

25. Have you seen that ***timid*** child.
(*a*) tender (*b*) tall
(*c*) brave (*d*) big

TEST – 2

1. He glanced through the letter ***perfunctorily***.
(*a*) nicely (*b*) ceremoniously
(*c*) carefully (*d*) particularly

2. She paid special attention to those women who had ***succumbed*** to adversity.
(*a*) surrendered (*b*) given up
(*c*) overcome (*d*) demanded

3. Throughout the evening, Rahul looked very ***doleful***.
(*a*) aggressive (*b*) cheerful
(*c*) tired (*d*) involved

4. ***Genuine*** jewellery is available only in this shop.
(*a*) false (*b*) cheap
(*c*) imitation (*d*) duplicate

5. An honest person need not ***hesitate*** to take bold steps.
(*a*) shirk (*b*) demur
(*c*) act willingly (*d*) malinger

6. Nothing has been organised properly and confusion seems ***inevitable***.
(*a*) uncertain (*b*) ineligible
(*c*) inevident (*d*) inefficient

7. There is something ***repulsive*** about the way he handles people's complaints.
(*a*) lovely (*b*) delightful
(*c*) attractive (*d*) distinctive

8. His ***vindictive*** nature often came up for comment among his friends.
(*a*) timid (*b*) obedient
(*c*) forgiving (*d*) forgetful

9. ***Misogynists*** are not applauded in society.
(*a*) Philanthropists (*b*) Philogists
(*c*) Philogynists (*d*) Philanderers

10. Every self–respecting circus needs at least one ***dwarf***.
(*a*) pigmy (*b*) undersized
(*c*) giant (*d*) human

11. The new government has ***abolished*** the gold control act.
(*a*) removed (*b*) approved
(*c*) passed (*d*) restored

12. It was a very ***dreary*** day.
(*a*) drab (*b*) dangerous
(*c*) beautiful (*d*) bright

13. He appears to be a ***phony*** person.
(*a*) beautiful (*b*) unread
(*c*) genuine (*d*) ugly

14. The revised pay scale is ***uniform***.
(*a*) equal (*b*) opposite
(*c*) varied (*d*) different

15. We had a ***delectable*** meal yesterday.
(*a*) heavy (*b*) unsavoury
(*c*) tasty (*d*) nice

16. The two friends were ***distinct*** in everything, dress, manners, hair–style and food habits.
(*a*) similar (*b*) uniform
(*c*) opposite (*d*) different

17. The last show of the concert at the Ritz theatre was ***fiasco***.
(*a*) triumph (*b*) victory
(*c*) fruitful (*d*) success

18. Everybody called it a ***lavish*** party.
(*a*) expensive (*b*) frugal
(*c*) wasteful (*d*) big

19. Her ***adamant*** attitude brought her on the verge of divorce.
(*a*) flexible (*b*) inflexible
(*c*) hard (*d*) abrasive

20. Even a ***lunatic*** person sometimes talk intelligently.
(*a*) sane (*b*) insane
(*c*) insensible (*d*) mad

21. He is ***zealous*** only in the initial stages of a project.
(*a*) absent–minded (*b*) distraught
(*c*) inattentive (*d*) indifferent

22. The politician was ***flummoxed*** by the questions put to him.
(*a*) comfortable (*b*) annoyed
(*c*) delighted (*d*) disconcerted

23. The state government for its part can identify ***vulnerable*** villages where these forces can be stationed.
(*a*) important (*b*) famous
(*c*) remote (*d*) invincible

24. In facing adverse situations, he was very ***stoical***.
(*a*) tactless (*b*) flinching
(*c*) awkward (*d*) assured

25. Professors are generally ***serious*** about what they say.
(*a*) jolly (*b*) thoughtful
(*c*) smug (*d*) insincere

TEST – 3

1. There was ***dismal*** atmosphere in the dressing room of the defeated team.
(*a*) cheerful (*b*) dreadful
(*c*) gloomy (*d*) jovial

2. What he tells me ***confirms*** my ideas.
(*a*) verifies (*b*) contradicts
(*c*) opposes (*d*) strengthens

3. There are no permanent ***adversaries*** in politics.
(*a*) associates (*b*) allies
(*c*) collaborators (*d*) partners

4. There is not a trace of ***vanity*** in her behavior.
(*a*) humility (*b*) selflessness
(*c*) modesty (*d*) dignity

5. All the employees of this organization want to have an officer who is ***lenient***.
(*a*) capable (*b*) strict
(*c*) strong (*d*) conservative

6. A ***fortuitous*** combination of circumstances led to the discovery of his lineage.
(*a*) unfortunate (*b*) accidental
(*c*) planned (*d*) ludicrous

7. He made several attempts to ***placate*** his opponents.
(*a*) infuriate (*b*) defeat
(*c*) discourage (*d*) deceive

8. The ***feebleness*** of mind is the greatest hurdle to success in life.
(*a*) sound (*b*) infirm
(*c*) imbecility (*d*) strength

9. ***Formidable*** obstacles have to be overcome before success is achieved.

(*a*) indomitable (*b*) facile
(*c*) dangerous (*d*) invincible

10. He has been accorded ***lukewarm*** welcome.

(*a*) cordial (*b*) trepid
(*c*) stately (*d*) grand

11. He liked the ***pungent*** sauce prepared by his mother.

(*a*) gentle (*b*) mild
(*c*) insipid (*d*) unsavoury

12. The deliberate ***suavity*** of Dev's behavior made the emotions of the audience volatile.

(*a*) politeness (*b*) impetuosity
(*c*) stupidity (*d*) pleasant

13. We should not ***belittle*** other's achievement.

(*a*) recommend (*b*) praise
(*c*) encourage (*d*) inspire

14. Every thing about him especially his talkative nature proclaims his ***effeminacy***.

(*a*) aggressiveness (*b*) attractiveness
(*c*) manliness (*d*) boorishness

15. He has a weakness for ***foreign*** goods.

(*a*) exported (*b*) indigenous
(*c*) fashionable (*d*) exotic

16. Everybody was astonished when he used such a ***profane*** language.

(*a*) high (*b*) pure
(*c*) profound (*d*) sacred

17. I liked the poem for its ***literal*** meaning.

(*a*) deep (*b*) complex
(*c*) fictitious (*d*) figurative

18. I like his ***friendly*** attitude.

(*a*) jealous (*b*) envious
(*c*) hostile (*d*) vicious

19. She handled the machine with ***deft*** fingers.

(*a*) delicate (*b*) sturdy
(*c*) quick (*d*) clumsy

20. At the beginning of the novel we see the hero in all the fresh ***vivid*** detail in which he would appear to be a curios stranger from Spain.

(*a*) obscure (*b*) unintelligible
(*c*) hazy (*d*) inanimate

21. ***Genuine*** drugs are available in most of the medical shops.

(*a*) spurious (*b*) dubious
(*c*) wrong (*d*) harmful

22. Her ***impetuous*** behavior was attributed to her upbringing.

(*a*) poised (*b*) hash
(*c*) quiet and gentle (*d*) sluggish

23. The committee set about making ***provisional*** arrangements for the annual conference.

(*a*) unconditional (*b*) abiding
(*c*) permanent (*d*) lasting

24. I thought about her a lot during the ***following*** months.

(*a*) receding
(*b*) preceding
(*c*) proceeding
(*d*) succeeding

25. His failure in this venture may be attributed to his ***lackadaisical*** approach.

(*a*) enthusiastic (*b*) insufficient
(*c*) indifferent (*d*) reckless

TEST – 4

1. The Board of Directors showered ***encomium*** on the Chairman for his liberal policies.

(*a*) denunciation (*b*) generosity
(*c*) tribute (*d*) praise

2. The minister was accused of indulging in ***nepotism***.

(*a*) impartiality (*b*) hatred (*b*) condemnation (*d*) indifference

3. Their arrival ***defiled*** the atmosphere.

(*a*) purified (*b*) polluted
(*c*) disturbed (*d*) glorified

4. He has translated the play into English with *fidelity*.
(*a*) difficulty (*b*) insincerity
(*c*) carelessness (*d*) inaccuracy

5. The consultant analysed the proposal carefully before he decided to *jettison* it.
(*a*) abandon (*b*) strengthen
(*c*) accept (*d*) modify

6. I am in a rather *precarious* position in my place of work.
(*a*) comfortable (*b*) senior
(*c*) privileged (*d*) secure

7. How dare you *desecrate* an idol of this temple.
(*a*) defile (*b*) pollute
(*c*) deify (*d*) impious

8. *Bereft* of his support he died poor.
(*a*) deprived (*b*) invested
(*c*) enjoying (*d*) disinvested

9. He was *dejected* when he heard the news.
(*a*) elated (*b*) impressed
(*c*) hilarious (*d*) gleeful

10. He proved utterly *capricious* in his dealings with his friends.
(*a*) helpful (*b*) steadfast
(*c*) understanding (*d*) obstinate

11. The General Manager is quite *tactful* and handles the workers' union very effectively.
(*a*) relaxed (*b*) strict
(*c*) naïve (*d*) disciplined

12. His style was *smooth*, but there was no mistaking his determination.
(*a*) hard (*b*) dense
(*c*) harsh (*d*) rough

13. His family has *accumulated* wealth over the years.
(*a*) amassed
(*b*) collected
(*c*) drained
(*d*) squandered

14. Her *debonair* manners were noticed by everyone present in the party.
(*a*) pleasant (*b*) courteous
(*c*) cheerless (*d*) stiff

15. We received a *cordial* welcome from our host.
(*a*) indifferent (*b*) distrustful
(*c*) cold (*d*) official

16. Silence in this place is *mandatory*.
(*a*) optional (*b*) compulsory
(*c*) imperative (*d*) irritating

17. India is a *heterogeneous* country.
(*a*) strange (*b*) homogeneous
(*c*) complex (*d*) vast

18. She used to *disparage* her neighbours every now and then.
(*a*) please (*b*) praise
(*c*) belittle (*d*) denigrate

19. In ancient days a *fragile* glass jar was considered to be more valuable than a human slave.
(*a*) broad (*b*) tall
(*c*) strong (*d*) heavy

20. Sanjay's point of view was correct but his behaviour with his father was quite *impertinent*.
(*a*) impressive (*b*) smooth
(*c*) healthy (*d*) respectful

21. Water scarcity is a *perennial* problem in that village
(*a*) transitory
(*b*) ephemeral
(*c*) momentary
(*d*) temporary

22. Why do you *disparage* him all the time?
(*a*) abuse (*b*) criticise
(*c*) encourage (*d*) glorify

23. He stood gazing at the *serene* expanse of the sea.
(*a*) scenic (*b*) clear
(*c*) tranquil (*d*) ruffled

24. The timely action ***foiled*** his evil designs.
(*a*) checked (*b*) opposed
(*c*) succeeded (*d*) avert

25. The ***fetters*** of slavery are hard to shake off.
(*a*) bondage (*b*) shackles
(*c*) freedom (*d*) irons

TEST – 5

1. Born in ***squalid*** surroundings of the slums she rose to stardom overnight.
(*a*) dirty (*b*) clean
(*c*) disorderly (*d*) mean

2. ***Modesty*** is a virtue but it must not be allowed to be exploited.
(*a*) reserve (*b*) boldness
(*c*) mildness (*d*) humility

3. The speaker recalled the deceased leader's ***benevolent*** deeds.
(*a*) unpopular (*b*) unkind
(*c*) unbecoming (*d*) unplanned

4. He walked in ***ungainly*** strides.
(*a*) quick (*b*) short
(*c*) awkward (*d*) graceful

5. Some of the needs of a modern man are surely ***dispensable***.
(*a*) desirable (*b*) acceptable
(*c*) relevant (*d*) essential

6. It was ***fortuitous*** that I met her in that party.
(*a*) unlucky (*b*) bad
(*c*) distressing (*d*) abominable

7. After a day's toil he was feeling ***fatigue***.
(*a*) energy
(*b*) listlessness
(*c*) exertion
(*d*) tiredness

8. Manuscripts of Shakespeare's plays are still ***extant*** in the British Museum.
(*a*) existing (*b*) extinct
(*c*) present (*d*) alive

9. Drink proved to be the ***bane*** of his otherwise spotless career.
(*a*) evil (*b*) boon
(*c*) joy (*d*) stigma

10. Overeating can often be ***detrimental*** to health.
(*a*) beneficial (*b*) injurious
(*c*) useful (*d*) destructive

11. ***Feasibility*** of the project is under study.
(*a*) unsuitability (*b*) impracticability
(*c*) impropriety (*d*) cheapness

12. In all places, and at all times, there is a ***profusion*** of talents.
(*a*) plenty (*b*) scarcity
(*c*) aversion (*d*) generosity

13. He has been ***acquitted*** of the charge of theft.
(*a*) convicted (*b*) exonerated
(*c*) released (*d*) punished

14. We have no doubt about the ***veracity*** of his statement.
(*a*) truthfulness (*b*) propriety
(*c*) falsity (*d*) morality

15. The criminal was ***detained*** by the police.
(*a*) deterred (*b*) released
(*c*) dismissed (*d*) protected

16. He made an ***exhaustive*** list of the items his secretary should attend to.
(*a*) short (*b*) incomplete
(*c*) interesting (*d*) meticulous

17. That man is known for his ***elegance***.
(*a*) awkwardness (*b*) indelicacy
(*c*) clumsiness (*d*) savagery

18. Sherlock Holmes is ***fictitious*** character.
(*a*) foreign (*b*) imaginative
(*c*) fancy (*d*) real

19. His was ***sulky*** disposition.
(*a*) kind (*b*) loving
(*c*) cheerful (*d*) mild

20. That was a ***dauntless*** action.

(*a*) cowardly (*b*) secret
(*c*) subtle (*d*) devious

21. Under the circumstances, such ***pejorative*** comments should have been avoided.

(*a*) soothing (*b*) sporting
(*c*) appreciative (*d*) critical

22. His partners felt that it was a ***viable*** business proposition.

(*a*) impracticable (*b*) inviolable
(*c*) unavailable (*d*) enviable

23. She used to ***deprecate*** her neighbour's conduct every now and then.

(*a*) denigrate (*b*) disparage
(*c*) praise (*d*) please

24. He was asked to ***accelerate*** the pace of work.

(*a*) check (*b*) control
(*c*) slacken (*d*) supervise

25. He ***endeavoured*** hard to reach the top of his career.

(*a*) shirked (*b*) strove
(*c*) undertake (*d*) laboured

TEST – 6

1. Like poverty, ***affluence*** can sometimes create its own problems.

(*a*) sorrow (*b*) indigence
(*c*) exuberance (*d*) opulence

2. There is an ***obscure*** cave on the other side of the hill.

(*a*) admired (*b*) notorious
(*c*) infamous (*d*) well known

3. The visit of the Vice Chancellor has been ***deferred*** indefinitely.

(*a*) expedited (*b*) dissolved
(*c*) postponed (*d*) put off

4. Sometimes it is necessary to ***retreat*** in a battle.

(*a*) retrograde (*b*) march
(*c*) advance (*d*) go back

5. However hard you may try to ***mitigate*** his problems, you will not succeed.

(*a*) augment (*b*) increase
(*c*) expand (*d*) enlarge

6. The forwards of their football team made ***sporadic*** raids into the opponent's territory.

(*a*) rare (*b*) frequent
(*c*) sharp (*d*) coordinated

7. The officer had issued ***explicit*** instructions to his staff.

(*a*) inadequate (*b*) elusive
(*c*) ambiguous (*d*) queer

8. Some people always drive their cars ***recklessly***.

(*a*) slowly (*b*) regularly
(*c*) carefully (*d*) patiently

9. Some have the habit of ***disparaging*** the success of their friend because of jealously.

(*a*) belittling (*b*) esteeming
(*c*) lauding (*d*) castigating

10. You will have to learn to gloss over the ***trivial*** mistakes of the youngsters.

(*a*) important (*b*) pardonable
(*c*) insignificant (*d*) futile

11. There has always been a feeling of ***rancour*** between the two families.

(*a*) rivalry
(*b*) competition
(*c*) friendliness
(*d*) suspicious

12. ***Adversity*** teaches man to be humble and self reliant.

(*a*) prosperity (*b*) curiosity
(*c*) animosity (*d*) sincerity

13. We ***solicit*** your co–operation.

(*a*) acknowledge (*b*) reject
(*c*) refute (*d*) cherish

14. He is a very ***timid*** person.

(*a*) chivalrous (*b*) bold
(*c*) outgoing (*d*) dashing

15. They took note of the ***humility*** of the visiting dignitary.
(*a*) grandeur (*b*) arrogance
(*c*) friendliness (*d*) decency

16. He is quite ***industrious***.
(*a*) indisposed (*b*) hard working
(*c*) indifferent (*d*) lazy

17. It is ***obligatory*** for a common citizen to follow the rules.
(*a*) advisable (*b*) unnecessary
(*c*) superfluous (*d*) optional

18. The principal hardly managed to give the papers a ***cursory*** glance.
(*a*) curious (*b*) thorough
(*c*) through (*d*) superficial

19. It was ***voluntary*** gesture.
(*a*) valuable (*b*) violent
(*c*) compulsory (*d*) deliberate

20. Your term is full of ***delinquent*** children.
(*a*) law abiding (*b*) uncivil
(*c*) quarrelsome (*d*) jealous

21. Unlike the other candidates, his manner was entirely ***languid***.
(*a*) energetic (*b*) lazy
(*c*) liquid (*d*) slow

22. The two girls are always together. There is a great ***affinity*** between them.
(*a*) apathy (*b*) empathy
(*c*) antipathy (*d*) sympathy

23. His principles are ***flexible***.
(*a*) accurate (*b*) rigid
(*c*) distinct (*d*) strict

24. Every move I make seems to affect him ***adversely***.
(*a*) deeply (*b*) favourably
(*c*) badly (*d*) internally

25. The actor is well known both for his ***humility*** and courage.
(*a*) gentleness (*b*) honesty
(*c*) determination (*d*) pride

TEST – 7

1. Many an ***abortive*** attempts to scale the mountains disappointed him.
(*a*) fruitless (*b*) successful
(*c*) futile (*d*) useless

2. ***Hectic*** arrangements are on for the coming visit of the Minister.
(*a*) unhurried (*b*) unhindered
(*c*) feverish (*d*) fast

3. ***Reunion*** was overwhelming as he returned home after long time.
(*a*) meeting (*b*) parting
(*c*) division (*d*) home coming

4. He produced ***cogent*** reasons for the change of policy.
(*a*) flimsy (*b*) unconvincing
(*c*) improper (*d*) simple

5. The booking–clerk looked very ***grumpy***.
(*a*) surly (*b*) pleasant
(*c*) efficient (*d*) honest

6. Some democratic countries believe in racial ***segregation***.
(*a*) subordination (*b*) integration
(*c*) inferiority (*d*) domination

7. Though aware of his crimes, he remained ***impenitent*** throughout.
(*a*) repentant (*b*) sorrowful
(*c*) hot–headed (*d*) pertinent

8. The facts of the case were ***obscured*** by the speech of the defence counsel.
(*a*) reflected (*b*) illustrated
(*c*) clarified (*d*) exhibited

9. None but his ***sycophants*** were impressed by his haughtiness.
(*a*) detractors (*b*) flatterers
(*c*) benefactors (*d*) officious

10. Twenty point programme is aimed at ***alleviating*** the sufferings of the poor.
(*a*) aggravating (*b*) mitigating
(*c*) eradicating (*d*) appeasing

11. The leader was ***pragmatic*** in his approach to the problems facing the country.
(*a*) optimistic (*b*) idealistic
(*c*) indefinite (*d*) vague

12. The influence of political broadcasts on elections is ***considerable***.
(*a*) immense (*b*) influential
(*c*) negligible (*d*) insignificant

13. ***Recession*** causes unemployment.
(*a*) poverty (*b*) computerisation
(*c*) education (*d*) inflation

14. They have not been eating ***nourishing*** food.
(*a*) unhygienic (*b*) undercooked
(*c*) poor (*d*) heavy

15. Nothing has been organized properly and confusion seems ***inevitable***.
(*a*) inevident (*b*) inefficient
(*c*) ineligible (*d*) uncertain

16. That police officer is known to be ***humane*** in his approach.
(*a*) uncivilised (*b*) uncultured
(*c*) unsympathetic (*d*) uncompromising

17. The decision was ***delayed*** because of him.
(*a*) expedited (*b*) advanced
(*c*) released (*d*) triggered

18. There was a marked ***deterioration*** in his condition
(*a*) improvement (*b*) revision
(*c*) reformation (*d*) amendment

19. He has a passion for ***indigenous*** goods.
(*a*) native (*b*) foreign
(*c*) silly (*d*) cheap

20. His ***frivolous*** remarks provoked no comments.
(*a*) fanciful (*b*) frantic
(*c*) momentous (*d*) serious

21. His friends liked everything about him except his ***frugality***.
(*a*) punctuality (*b*) shabbiness
(*c*) extravagance (*d*) short temper

22. People who are actually running the system often take a ***myopic*** view of the situation.
(*a*) farsighted (*b*) visionary
(*c*) blind (*d*) glassy

23. The students ***assembled*** in the meeting hall.
(*a*) removed (*b*) diffused
(*c*) dispersed (*d*) eliminated

24. The minster gave a public speech on the controversial subject to ***precipitate*** the matter.
(*a*) pull (*b*) push
(*c*) defer (*d*) create

25. The usual ***adulation*** of the officers must end.
(*a*) back–biting (*b*) flattery
(*c*) condemnation (*d*) praise

TEST – 8

1. His health has been ***deteriorating*** since he returned from trekking expedition.
(*a*) ameliorating (*b*) amending
(*c*) undertaking (*d*) worsening

2. You are advised to show ***clemency*** to the defeated enemy.
(*a*) callousness (*b*) mercy
(*c*) leniency (*d*) kindness

3. Guerillas ***infiltrated*** into the region during the severe winter of 1997.
(*a*) entered (*b*) expelled
(*c*) penetrated (*d*) filtered

4. While facing that situation he turned out to be ***dauntless***.
(*a*) tactful (*b*) stoical
(*c*) bashful (*d*) cowardly

5. The judge thought that the offence was ***deliberate***.
(*a*) negligible (*b*) casual
(*c*) unintentional (*d*) legitimate

6. He gave the reply written in a ***terse*** style.
(*a*) pleasant (*b*) verbose
(*c*) rude (*d*) concise

7. The professor had to share a hotel room with a ***garrulous*** tax collector.
(*a*) dumb (*b*) speechless
(*c*) tongue–tied (*d*) silent

8. A lady of a few words she is given to ***laconic*** answers.
(*a*) copious (*b*) lingering
(*c*) terse (*d*) brief

9. She is known for her ***frugality*** in household expenditure.
(*a*) economy (*b*) extravagance
(*c*) miserliness (*d*) niggardliness

10. ***Ambivalence*** on his part caused the ruin of all his aspirations.
(*a*) firmness (*b*) clarity of thoughts
(*c*) confusion (*d*) ambiguity

11. His ***amiable*** nature has won him many admirers.
(*a*) surly (*b*) pleasing
(*c*) amicable (*d*) complaisant

12. It was a ***revolting*** sight.
(*a*) comfortable (*b*) pleasant
(*c*) delicious (*d*) remarkable

13. He was the most ***eccentric*** and difficult patron.
(*a*) normal (*b*) sober
(*c*) genial (*d*) sociable

14. The momentum of the movement ***slackened*** in course of time.
(*a*) stopped (*b*) quickened
(*c*) multiplied (*d*) recovered

15. He is well known for coming up with ***impracticable*** solutions.
(*a*) easy (*b*) possible
(*c*) feasible (*d*) alternate

16. There is a great deal of ***spurious*** family affection.
(*a*) genuine (*b*) obvious
(*c*) fictitious (*d*) authentic

17. His ***servility*** makes him detestable.
(*a*) slavery (*b*) insolence
(*c*) prudence (*d*) bravery

18. Philosophers say that the world is an ***illusion***.
(*a*) a fact (*b*) a reality
(*c*) an actuality (*d*) a truth

19. The drug will have ***pernicious*** effect on your health.
(*a*) pornographic (*b*) ruinous
(*c*) prolonged (*d*) beneficial

20. There is only the most ***tenuous*** evidence for it.
(*a*) enough (*b*) reasonable
(*c*) less (*d*) abundant

21. Mala was often teased as ***corpulent*** by her friends.
(*a*) fat (*b*) belligerent
(*c*) garrulous (*d*) gaunt

22. Let us not ***aggravate*** the sufferings of the poor.
(*a*) advocate (*b*) appreciate
(*c*) alleviate (*d*) abbreviate

23. The principal ***deprecated*** the attitude of some student leaders.
(*a*) appreciated (*b*) tolerated
(*c*) derided (*d*) ignored

24. He directed a couple of ***mediocre*** films.
(*a*) noble (*b*) successful
(*c*) outstanding (*d*) famous

25. The director had a ***derisive*** attitude towards some of the members of the committee.
(*a*) enthusiastic (*b*) respectful
(*c*) deprecatory (*d*) encouraging

TEST – 9

1. The climate in the north of Europe is really ***dreadful***.
(*a*) pleasant (*b*) amiable
(*c*) comfortable (*d*) gratifying

2. There are many anecdotes about his sister who is an ***imperious*** personality.
(*a*) characterless (*b*) pious
(*c*) arrogant (*d*) submissive

3. Arrangements were made to handle the ***mammoth*** gathering tactfully.
(*a*) quiet (*b*) significant
(*c*) huge (*d*) small

4. He is showing signs of ***senility***.
(*a*) virility (*b*) laziness
(*c*) maturity (*d*) exhaustion

5. The young business executive was very ***perspicacious***.
(*a*) banal (*b*) clever
(*c*) humble (*d*) unreliable

6. The task assigned to him was ***arduous***.
(*a*) absorbing (*b*) good
(*c*) plain (*d*) easy

7. His speech was full of frequent ***facetious*** remarks.
(*a*) stupid (*b*) grave
(*c*) dull (*d*) sarcastic

8. A character without a ***blemish*** is a virtue of a leader.
(*a*) stigma (*b*) adornment
(*c*) strength (*d*) blot

9. ***Apathy*** for the poor is common to officials of every cadre.
(*a*) indifference (*b*) sympathy
(*c*) eagerness (*d*) antipathy

10. She is ***exquisite*** in figure.
(*a*) strong (*b*) well–built
(*c*) clumsy (*d*) slim

11. All these measures will ***augment*** employment opportunities.
(*a*) constrain (*b*) restrain
(*c*) diminish (*d*) circumscribe

12. After meeting the holy man his nagging mood of ***diffidence*** suddenly changed.
(*a*) confusion
(*b*) self assurance
(*c*) contentment
(*d*) consternation

13. It is surprising to find ***condoning*** such an act.
(*a*) disparaging (*b*) condemning
(*c*) disliking (*d*) forbidding

14. Many of the incidents in the autobiography appear to be ***fictitious***.
(*a*) imaginary (*b*) real
(*c*) creative (*d*) boring

15. Many people try to ***resist*** reforms in the society.
(*a*) repel (*b*) welcome
(*c*) accept (*d*) fight

16. The leader was ***pragmatic*** in his approach to the problems facing the country.
(*a*) indefinite (*b*) vague
(*c*) idealistic (*d*) optimistic

17. The new officer is a ***brash*** young man.
(*a*) handsome (*b*) arrogant
(*c*) kind (*d*) polite

18. His ***timidity*** proved to be costly.
(*a*) self confidence (*b*) self assertion
(*c*) arrogance (*d*) boldness

19. It used to be said that travel ***broadens*** ones outlook.
(*a*) narrows (*b*) shrinks
(*c*) contracts (*d*) restricts

20. She is ***slender*** in figure.
(*a*) slim (*b*) stout
(*c*) well built (*d*) strong

21. Unsettled conditions in the land led to the ***exodus*** of hundreds of its citizens.
(*a*) invasion (*b*) intrusion
(*c*) immigration (*d*) expulsion

22. Her ***vivacity*** attracted everybody.
(*a*) lethargy (*b*) truthfulness
(*c*) beauty (*d*) apathy

23. The author has ***perspicuity*** in his style.
(*a*) frankness (*b*) bluntness
(*c*) obstruseness (*d*) vivacity

24. The club meets on the last Thursday of every month in a ***dilapidated*** palace.
(*a*) furnished (*b*) renovated
(*c*) neglected (*d*) regenerated

25. His books are well known for their ***progressive*** ideas
(*a*) useless (*b*) old–fashioned
(*c*) complex (*d*) reactionary

TEST – 10

1. The research showed that the drug has ***pernicious*** effect on the health of patients.
(*a*) fair (*b*) advantageous
(*c*) beneficial (*d*) satisfactory

2. At his success in the examination he felt ***elated***.
(*a*) exultant (*b*) dejected
(*c*) resting (*d*) jubilant

3. Mrs. Nisha made ***fervent*** appeal to the members of the club to maintain unity.
(*a*) active (*b*) impassive
(*c*) cold (*d*) passionate

4. He was charged with ***abetting*** the murder of an innocent child.
(*a*) baffle (*b*) instigate
(*c*) promote (*d*) support

5. The ***indignation*** of the retreating troops resulted in large scale killings.
(*a*) displeasure (*b*) happiness
(*c*) orderliness (*d*) anger

6. His ***servility*** makes him detestable.
(*a*) bravery (*b*) prudence
(*c*) insolence (*d*) slavery

7. She had nothing but ***scorn*** for my ideas.
(*a*) admiration (*b*) encouragement
(*c*) appreciation (*d*) agreement

8. The hall was packed with people, who came to hear the ***celebrated*** author.
(*a*) obscure (*b*) well-known
(*c*) ordinary (*d*) up-coming

9. The chairman ***initiated*** the proceedings with a brief speech.
(*a*) complicated (*b*) started
(*c*) closed (*d*) confused

10. The plantation workers were on ***collision*** course before the labour officer intervened.
(*a*) retaliatory (*b*) perfunctory
(*c*) conciliatory (*d*) circuitous

11. Athletes tend to ***conceal*** their disappointment when they lose.
(*a*) hide (*b*) show
(*c*) ignore (*d*) accept

12. He was a most ***fanatic*** person.
(*a*) tolerable (*b*) genial
(*c*) sober (*d*) tolerant

13. The government empowered itself to ***attach*** the assets of all the scam suspects.
(*a*) release (*b*) return
(*c*) donate (*d*) detach

14. His ***appointment*** was confirmed last month.
(*a*) disappointment (*b*) suspension
(*c*) dismissal (*d*) discharge

15. The room was filled with a ***delicious*** odour.
(*a*) bitter (*b*) repulsive
(*c*) strange (*d*) unpalatable

16. He tried to ***conceal*** the secret that they were already married.
(*a*) announce (*b*) reveal
(*c*) declare (*d*) state

17. She was ***sceptical*** about the safety of the new drug.
(*a*) doubtful (*b*) certain
(*c*) hopeful (*d*) sanguine

18. It was ***altercation*** throughout and there was no discussion.
(*a*) consonance (*b*) alternative
(*c*) inconsistency (*d*) resonance

19. She is beautiful as well as ***frivolous***.
(*a*) indecent (*b*) serious
(*c*) insane (*d*) rude

20. ***Miscellaneous*** items were discussed at the meeting.
(*a*) minor (*b*) unrelated
(*c*) mixed (*d*) classified

21. High School students generally take pleasure in asking ***puerile*** questions.
(*a*) sensible (*b*) pleasing
(*c*) sure (*d*) familiar

22. The ***tranquil*** surroundings of Shimla are healthful.
(*a*) noisy (*b*) peaceful
(*c*) healthy (*d*) congenial

23. A crowd ***gathered*** quickly when the police came.
(*a*) collected (*b*) dispersed
(*c*) spread (*d*) disappeared

24. Though ***novice*** in art he shows great promise.
(*a*) tyro (*b*) inexperienced
(*c*) veteran (*d*) green horn

25. I was ***disgusted*** at the manner he was flattering the party leader.
(*a*) revolting (*b*) pleased
(*c*) sickening (*d*) irritated

TEST – 11

1. At least some students are in the habit of doing their exercises in a ***slovenly*** manner.
(*a*) neat (*b*) proper
(*c*) decent (*d*) correct

2. The error in the newspaper article is ***accidental***.
(*a*) permissible (*b*) usual
(*c*) conventional (*d*) intentional

3. He is a man of ***mellow*** temper.
(*a*) fickle (*b*) hot
(*c*) irrational (*d*) excitable

4. ***Crestfallen*** he returned as he had never faced such humiliation in the whole of his life.
(*a*) vainglorious (*b*) indignant
(*c*) triumphant (*d*) disturbed

5. The explosion and the plane's take off occurred ***simultaneously***.
(*a*) cotemporary (*b*) coincident
(*c*) separately (*d*) momentarily

6. She was surprised by his ***amiability***.
(*a*) petulance (*b*) sincerity
(*c*) prudence (*d*) pessimism

7. We should not ***belittle*** the value of small things.
(*a*) extol (*b*) praise
(*c*) inflate (*d*) expand

8. Self reliance has been ***adopted*** as an important objective of economic planning in modern India.
(*a*) refused (*b*) forsaken
(*c*) denied (*d*) discarded

9. The leader might have had some ***covert*** reason for the change of his political affiliations.
(*a*) unjustifiable (*b*) obvious
(*c*) inexplicable (*d*) flimsy

10. Thousands of people died of ***spurious*** liquor in Baroda this year.
(*a*) diluted (*b*) genuine
(*c*) poisonous (*d*) illicit

11. There is a ***dearth*** of dedicated workers in our party.
(*a*) scarcity (*b*) affluence
(*c*) prosperity (*d*) abundance

12. Our knowledge of the past is still largely a matter of ***conjecture***.
(*a*) certainty (*b*) guess
(*c*) position (*d*) form

13. The commission took two years to go through the ***massive*** collection of files and documents before preparing its reports
(*a*) ugly (*b*) short
(*c*) light (*d*) meagre

14. He is known for his ***arrogance***.
(*a*) honesty (*b*) cheerfulness
(*c*) generosity (*d*) humility

15. James had the habit of ***running down*** his colleagues.
(*a*) deriding (*b*) pushing down
(*c*) praising (*d*) supporting

16. He is quite ***industrious***.
(*a*) hard working (*b*) indifferent
(*c*) lazy (*d*) indisposed

17. The children are playing in the ***nearby*** park.
(*a*) different (*b*) close
(*c*) separate (*d*) distant

18. The plane lay burnt in ***fragments***.
(*a*) whole (*b*) parts
(*c*) scraps (*d*) pieces

19. Their family ***feud*** has taken ugly turn lately.
(*a*) brotherhood (*b*) dispute
(*c*) fraternal (*d*) quarrel

20. You are advised not to ***dissipate*** your energy on impracticable schemes.
(*a*) conserve (*b*) reform
(*c*) waste (*d*) utilise

21. He has always been ***fastidious*** while examining answer scripts.
(*a*) amiable
(*b*) discriminating
(*c*) critical
(*d*) judicious

22. The speaker made some very ***cogent*** remarks.
(*a*) flattering (*b*) unconvincing
(*c*) superfluous (*d*) vociferous

23. He ***despises*** classical music.
(*a*) appreciates (*b*) respects
(*c*) comprehends (*d*) endures

24. His ***magnanimous*** gesture came to his employees as a surprise.
(*a*) small (*b*) cruel
(*c*) thoughtless (*d*) mean

25. His ***urbane*** attitude won him many friends.
(*a*) indifferent (*b*) violent
(*c*) rustic (*d*) rude

TEST – 12

1. This offer has come as a great ***boon*** to me.
(*a*) curse (*b*) blemish
(*c*) trouble (*d*) misfortune

2. The treaty was ***ratified*** by the Heads of states.
(*a*) annulled (*b*) destroyed
(*c*) unsettled (*d*) set aside

3. The painting is full of ***radiant*** colours.
(*a*) rare (*b*) bright
(*c*) dull (*d*) delicate

4. In the interest of one's reputation one should avoid ***ostentation*** while entertaining friends.
(*a*) miserliness (*b*) simplicity
(*c*) purity (*d*) innocence

5. His was a ***delicate*** constitution.
(*a*) fit (*b*) strong
(*c*) rugged (*d*) ungainly

6. The inhabitants of the island were ***barbarians***.
(*a*) bad (*b*) uncivilsed
(*c*) cruel (*d*) civilised

7. They had an ***insipid*** conversation.
(*a*) curious (*b*) loud
(*c*) argumentative (*d*) lively

8. The minister is ***optimistic*** about the new project just launched.
(*a*) stoical (*b*) dubious
(*c*) pessimistic (*d*) cynical

9. The principal is popular with students for his ***benign*** attitude.
(*a*) malignant (*b*) kindly
(*c*) generous (*d*) liberal

10. It is ***Herculean*** task for me.
(*a*) indecent (*b*) puny
(*c*) ponderous (*d*) big

11. Her ***candid*** confession of the crime earned her reprieve.
(*a*) frank (*b*) crafty
(*c*) simple (*d*) ambiguous

12. Indian economy is basically dependent on ***fickle*** monsoons.
(*a*) unsteady (*b*) benign
(*c*) stable (*d*) capricious

13. You must put up the facts ***straight*** before me and don't try to befool me.
(*a*) distort (*b*) candid
(*c*) soften (*d*) direct

14. He is very ***fastidious*** about his choice of food.
(*a*) sloppy (*b*) thoughtless
(*c*) careless (*d*) indiscreet

15. The Prime Minister's radio broadcast ***galvanized*** the people's spirit.
(*a*) frightened (*b*) pacified
(*c*) dampened (*d*) distracted

16. They approached the stranger ***warily***.
(*a*) suspiciously (*b*) cautiously
(*c*) carefully (*d*) carelessly

17. He received the news ***coldly***.
(*a*) angrily (*b*) enthusiastically
(*c*) gratefully (*d*) bravely

18. He is showing signs of ***senility***.
(*a*) virility (*b*) laziness
(*c*) maturity (*d*) exhaustion

19. This officer is noted for his ***zeal***.
(*a*) intolerance (*b*) inefficiency
(*c*) insensibility (*d*) indifference

20. Due to his excessive ***craftiness*** he achieved success but lost friends.
(*a*) simplicity (*b*) sincerity
(*c*) straight forwardness(*d*) innocence

21. One usually feels ***languid*** on summer noons.
(*a*) brisk (*b*) fussy
(*c*) drowsy (*d*) listless

22. There exists ***rancour*** between the two brothers.
(*a*) animosity (*b*) harmony
(*c*) devotion (*d*) enmity

23. We must realise the ***futility*** of wars.
(*a*) urgency (*b*) usefulness
(*c*) value (*d*) importance

24. In such difficult times it ***behoves*** all of us to remain united.
(*a*) becomes (*b*) discredits
(*c*) suits (*d*) creditable

25. The police tried to find out the ***rightful*** owner of the ornaments left in the train.
(*a*) indefinite (*b*) mistaken
(*c*) unlawful (*d*) claimant

ANSWERS

TEST – 1

1. productive
2. admirable
3. scarce
4. friendly
5. liberal
6. indecent
7. descent
8. rude
9. stable
10. prosperity
11. an expressive
12. genuine
13. malevolent
14. irregular
15. ferocious
16. regressive
17. imbecility
18. dense
19. deep
20. thrifty
21. disreputable
22. generosity
23. tidy
24. jubilant
25. brave

TEST – 2

1. ceremoniously
2. overcome
3. cheerful
4. duplicate
5. act willingly
6. uncertain
7. delightful
8. forgiving
9. Philogynists
10. giant
11. restored
12. bright
13. genuine
14. varied
15. unsavoury
16. uniform
17. victory
18. frugal
19. flexible
20. sane
21. indifferent
22. comfortable
23. invincible
24. awkward
25. insincere

TEST – 3

1. cheerful
2. contradicts
3. partners
4. humility
5. strict
6. ludicrous
7. infuriate
8. strength
9. facile
10. grand
11. mild
12. impetuosity
13. encourage
14. manliness
15. indigenous
16. sacred
17. figurative
18. hoWstile
19. clumsy
20. obscure
21. spurious
22. poised
23. permanent
24. preceding
25. enthusiastic

TEST – 4

1. denunciation
2. indifference
3. purified
4. insincerity
5. strengthen
6. secure
7. deify
8. invested
9. hilarious
10. helpful
11. naïve
12. rough
13. squandered
14. cheerless
15. indifferent
16. optional
17. homogeneous
18. praise
19. strong
20. respectful
21. temporary
22. glorify
23. ruffled
24. succeeded
25. freedom

TEST – 5

1. clean
2. boldness
3. unkind
4. graceful
5. essential
6. unlucky
7. energy
8. extinct
9. boon
10. beneficial
11. impracticability
12. scarcity
13. convicted
14. falsity
15. released
16. short
17. awkwardness
18. real
19. cheerful
20. cowardly
21. appreciative
22. enviable
23. praise
24. slacken
25. shirked

TEST – 6

1. indigence
2. well known
3. expedited
4. advance
5. augment
6. frequent
7. ambiguous
8. carefully
9. esteeming
10. important
11. friendliness
12. prosperity
13. reject
14. chivalrous
15. grandeur
16. lazy
17. optional
18. thorough
19. compulsory
20. law abiding
21. energetic
22. antipathy
23. rigid
24. favourably
25. pride

TEST – 7

1. successful
2. unhurried
3. parting
4. unconvincing
5. pleasant
6. integration
7. repentant
8. illustrated
9. detractors
10. aggravating
11. idealistic
12. insignificant
13. inflation
14. poor
15. uncertain
16. unsympathetic
17. advanced
18. improvement
19. foreign
20. serious
21. extravagance
22. farsighted
23. dispersed
24. defer
25. condemnation

TEST – 8

1. ameliorating
2. callousness
3. expelled
4. tactful
5. unintentional
6. verbose
7. tongue–tied
8. copious
9. extravagance
10. clarity of thoughts
11. surly
12. pleasant
13. normal
14. quickened
15. feasible
16. genuine
17. bravery
18. a reality
19. beneficial
20. reasonable
21. gaunt
22. alleviate
23. appreciated
24. outstanding
25. respectful

TEST – 9

1. gratifying
2. pious
3. small
4. maturity
5. humble
6. easy
7. dull
8. adornment
9. eagerness
10. clumsy
11. diminish
12. self assurance
13. condemning
14. real
15. accept
16. idealistic
17. kind
18. boldness
19. narrows
20. well built
21. intrusion
22. lethargy
23. bluntness
24. renovated
25. old–fashioned

TEST – 10

1. beneficial
2. dejected
3. impassive
4. baffle
5. happiness
6. bravery
7. admiration
8. ordinary
9. closed
10. conciliatory
11. show
12. tolerant
13. release
14. dismissal
15. unpalatable
16. reveal
17. sanguine
18. consonance
19. serious
20. classified
21. sensible
22. noisy
23. dispersed
24. veteran
25. pleased

TEST – 11

1. decent
2. intentional
3. hot
4. triumphant
5. separately
6. petulance
7. extol
8. denied
9. obvious
10. genuine
11. affluence
12. certainty
13. meagre
14. humility
15. supporting
16. lazy
17. distant
18. whole
19. brotherhood
20. conserve
21. discriminating
22. unconvincing
23. appreciates
24. mean
25. rustic

TEST – 12

1. misfortune
2. annulled
3. dull
4. simplicity
5. ungainly
6. civilised
7. lively
8. pessimistic
9. malignant
10. puny
11. crafty
12. stable
13. distort
14. careless
15. dampened
16. cautiously
17. enthusiastically
18. maturity
19. inefficiency
20. simplicity
21. brisk
22. harmony
23. usefulness
24. discredits
25. unlawful

33

CHAPTER

CLOZE TEST

Innumerable Questions have been provided throughout the book to test vocabulary along with other aspects of language proficiency. Cloze Test is one of them. Here, a passage is taken and words are deleted at intervals. These could be words of a particular class, like nouns, verbs, adjectives, adverbs or prepositions. Four or five words are generally given. You have thus a number of options, only one of which is correct (the answer), the others (the detractors) being wrong. You have to supply the missing words to fill in the blanks by choosing them from the words listed.

Directions: *In the following passage there are blanks, each of which has been numbered. These numbers are printed below the passage and against each, four or five words are suggested, one of which fits the blank appropriately. Find out the appropriate words.*

CLOZE TEST – 1

Jawaharlal Nehru was probably the first important public leader to realize that if India were to (*1*) _________ its problems, it would have to (*2*) _________ the age of science. The (*3*) _________ the Government has attached to science is also clear (*4*) _________ the fact that the portfolio of science and technology has always been (*5*) _________ by the Prime Minister himself.

1. (*a*) usher (*b*) work (*c*) solve (*d*) face (*e*) raise
2. (*a*) enter (*b*) come (*c*) continue (*d*) direct (*e*) evolve
3. (*a*) depth (*b*) weight (*c*) budget (*d*) policy (*e*) importance
4. (*a*) for (*b*) when (*c*) above (*d*) from (*e*) to
5. (*a*) offered (*b*) held (*c*) charged (*d*) appointed (*e*) regarded

CLOZE TEST – 2

Human nature has an extraordinary power of (*1*) _________ Social and political institutions are (*2*) _________ to the same laws of (*3*) _________ to which all other things in the world are subject. If we have (*4*) _________ in the (*5*) _________ of human nature, the healing power of time, the (*6*) _________ of social and political institutions and above all the (*7*) _________ of the people, the problems which divide us so (*8*) _________ today may appear to be purely (*9*) _________ after some time.

1. (*a*) resistance (*b*) resilience (*c*) patience (*d*) toleration
2. (*a*) set (*b*) tuned (*c*) subject (*d*) equal
3. (*a*) gravitation (*b*) mutation (*c*) acceleration (*d*) change
4. (*a*) confidence (*b*) belief (*c*) trust (*d*) faith
5. (*a*) resilience (*b*) patience (*c*) perseverance (*d*) toleration
6. (*a*) working (*b*) mutability (*c*) flexibility (*d*) dynamics
7. (*a*) generosity (*b*) magnanimity (*c*) goodwill (*d*) sincerity
8. (*a*) foolishly (*b*) fiercely (*c*) acutely (*d*) powerfully
9. (*a*) academic (*b*) intellectual (*c*) unproductive (*d*) inane

CLOZE TEST – 3

Perhaps, we Americans do not yet fully understand the great (*1*) __________ that India has to teach in thus (*2*) __________ her freedom (*3*) __________ her mighty triumph of a (*4*) __________ revolution our War of Independence (*5*) __________ in size and concept. India has taught humanity a lesson, and it is (*6*) __________ our peril if we do not learn it. The lesson? That war and killing (*7*) __________ nothing (*8*) __________ loss, and that a noble end is assured only if the (*9*) __________ to attain it are of a (*10*) __________ with it and also noble.

1. (*a*) message (*b*) lesson (*c*) moral (*d*) instruction
2. (*a*) attaining (*b*) obtaining (*c*) getting (*d*) winning
3. (*a*) Beside (*b*) Besides (*c*) Despite (*d*) Notwithstanding
4. (*a*) bloody (*b*) blood-free (*c*) bloodless (*d*) non-violent
5. (*a*) pales (*b*) shrinks (*c*) squeezes (*d*) reduces
6. (*a*) to (*b*) for (*c*) in (*d*) on
7. (*a*) bring (*b*) get (*c*) achieve (*d*) secure
8. (*a*) except (*b*) beside (*c*) besides (*d*) but
9. (*a*) measures (*b*) means (*c*) technique (*d*) method
10. (*a*) piece (*b*) peace (*c*) harmony (*d*) conformity

CLOZE TEST – 4

Within the (*1*) __________ we are more friendly to each other than are many (*2*) __________ of animals but in our attitude towards those outside the herd, inspite of all that has been done by moralists and (*3*) __________ teachers, our emotions are as (*4*) __________ as those of any animal, and our (*5*) __________ enables us to give them a scope which is (*6*) __________ to even the most savage beast.

1. (*a*) society (*b*) caste (*c*) herd (*d*) institution
2. (*a*) species (*b*) kinds (*c*) types (*d*) specimens
3. (*a*) college (*b*) school (*c*) religious (*d*) social
4. (*a*) uncontrolled (*b*) hostile (*c*) wild (*d*) ferocious
5. (*a*) intellect (*b*) intelligence (*c*) knowledge (*d*) exuberance
6. (*a*) relegated (*b*) denial (*c*) denied (*d*) conceded

CLOZE TEST – 5

Science (*1*) __________ the average man and woman in two ways already. He or she benefits by its (*2*) __________, driving in a motor-car or omnibus instead of a horse-drawn (*3*) __________, being treated for disease by a doctor or surgeon rather than a priest or a (*4*) __________, being (*5*) __________ with an automatic pistol or a shell in (*6*) __________ of a danger or battle-axe. It also affects is or her opinions. Almost everyone believes that the earth is (*7*) __________, and the heavens nearly (*8*) __________, instead of solid. And we are beginning to believe in our animal (*9*) __________ and the possibility of vast improvements in (*10*) __________ nature by biological methods.

1. (*a*) effects (*b*) affects (*c*) helps (*d*) alienate
2. (*a*) implication (*b*) applications (*c*) use (*d*) admission
3. (*a*) automobile (*b*) carriage (*c*) vehicle (*d*) cart
4. (*a*) quack (*b*) magician (*c*) swindler (*d*) witch
5. (*a*) hacked (*b*) killed (*c*) murdered (*d*) gagged
6. (*a*) lieu (*b*) spite (*c*) place (*d*) want
7. (*a*) flat (*b*) oval (*c*) opaque (*d*) round

8. (a) hollow (b) empty
(c) vacant (d) fallow
9. (a) ancestry (b) progeny
(c) lineage (d) association
10. (a) humane (b) human
(c) animal (d) basic

CLOZE TEST – 6

Every society depends on energy (1) __________ from one source or another to supply its needs. In the past the energy of beasts and water power from water-mills was used to (2) __________ what man could not do alone. Modern society (3) __________ above all on heat-based energy. This produces electricity, cooks food and (4) __________ motor cars, ships and planes. The (5) __________ is oil. Without it industry would (6) __________, standard of living would drop. Oil is no longer so cheap and (7) __________ as it was. Existing supplies will not last (8) __________. Yet world energy demand goes (9) __________ increasing.

1. (a) got (b) obtained
(c) generated (d) derived
2. (a) compliment (b) complement
(c) supplement (d) augment
3. (a) draws (b) bases
(c) depends (d) stands
4. (a) moves (b) drives
(c) propels (d) pushes
5. (a) principal (b) principle
(c) only (d) main
6. (a) ruin (b) collapse
(c) wreck (d) perish
7. (a) available (b) aplenty
(c) plentiful (d) luxuriant
8. (a) infinitely (b) indefinitely
(c) eternally (d) always
9. (a) by
(b) from
(c) on
(d) none of these

CLOZE TEST – 7

Human society is a (1) __________ growth, an unfoldment in terms of (2) __________. If so, it must be based on ever-increasing restraint upon the demands of the (3) __________. Thus marriage must be considered to be a (4) __________ imposing discipline upon the (5) __________, restricting them to the physical (6) __________ only among themselves and for the purpose only of (7) __________ when both the partners desire and are prepared (8) __________ it.

1. (a) perennial (b) continual
(c) ceaseless (d) continuing
2. (a) spirit (b) spiritual
(c) spirittuous (d) spirituality
3. (a) body (b) flesh
(c) sex (d) ego
4. (a) sacrament (b) contract
(c) contact (d) union
5. (a) couples (b) partners
(c) set (d) duo
6. (a) union (b) contact
(c) penetration (d) rapport
7. (a) creation (b) procreation
(c) multiplication (d) adjustment
8. (a) in (b) about
(c) for (d) no word

CLOZE TEST – 8

Books introduce to us the best (1) __________; they bring us (2) __________ the presence of the greatest (3) __________ that have ever live. We hear what they said and did; we see them as if they were (4) __________ alive; we share their (5) __________, we sympathize with them, (6) __________ with them in the scenes which they describe. The great and the good do not (7) __________ even in this world.

1. (a) social (b) society
(c) company (d) atmosphere
2. (a) before (b) in
(c) into (d) through

3. (a) man (b) minds
(c) intellect (d) scholars
4. (a) actually (b) really
(c) decidedly (d) indeed
5. (a) thoughts (b) ideas
(c) feelings (d) observations
6. (a) enjoy (b) grieve
(c) exult (d) sorrow
7. (a) die (b) dye
(c) disappear (d) eclipse

CLOZE TEST – 9

India is (1) __________ the move and the old order passes. Too long have we been (2) __________ spectators of events and the (3) __________ of others. The (4) __________ comes to our people now and we shall make the history of our (5) __________. Let us all join in this mighty (6) __________ and make India, the (7) __________ of our heart, great among nations, foremost in the arts of peace and progress. The door is open and destiny (8) __________ to all. There is no question of who wins and who (9) __________, for we have to go forward and together as comrades and either all of us win or we all (10) __________ together.

1. (a) for (b) on
(c) in (d) at
2. (a) passive (b) silent
(c) detached (d) impartial
3. (a) toys (b) hireling
(c) playthings (d) subordinates
4. (a) initiative (b) charge
(c) opportunity (d) offer
5. (a) desire (b) need
(c) dream (d) choice
6. (a) work (b) venture
(c) task (d) project
7. (a) heaven (b) pride
(c) cynosure (d) seat
8. (a) calls (b) beckons
(c) summons (d) reiterates
9. (a) loses (b) falls
(c) fails (d) stumbles
10. (a) fall down
(b) lie down
(c) perish
(d) go down

CLOZE TEST – 10

Put all your knowledge, learning and (1) __________ in one scale and truth and (2) __________ in the other and the (3) __________ will by far (4) __________ the former. The (5) __________ of moral impurity has today spread among our school-going children and like a hidden (6) __________ is causing (7) __________ among them. I, therefore, appeal to you, boys and girls, to keep your minds and bodies (8) __________. All your scholarship, all your study of the (9) __________ will be in vain if you fail to translate their teachings (10) __________ your daily life.

1. (a) showmanship
(b) thoughts
(c) scholarship
(d) experiences
2. (a) honesty (b) purity
(c) sincerity (d) falsehood
3. (a) later (b) latter
(c) least (d) last
4. (a) outweigh (b) outsmart
(c) outsource (d) outshine
5. (a) evil (b) filth
(c) virus (d) stink
6. (a) epidemic (b) disease
(c) cancer (d) pestilence
7. (a) harm (b) vengeance
(c) havoc (d) discord
8. (a) free (b) pious
(c) pure (d) healthy
9. (a) Bible (b) Ramayan
(c) arts (d) scriptures
10. (a) in (b) into
(c) on (d) for

CLOZE TEST – 11

In (1) _________ life there is always a feeling of want. It is this which makes man (2) _________. Man (3) _________ for things which he cannot get and feels sad looking (4) _________ upon the past, and looking forward (5) _________ future. This (6) _________ with the past and future does not allow man to live (7) _________ in the present. Thus, there is always a pain in man's (8) _________ always a sense of (9) _________ in the moment of enjoyments. That is why the best poetry of man is the poetry of (10) _________. 'Our sweetest songs are those that tell of (11) _________ thoughts', has been rightly said.

1. (a) man's (b) our (c) human (d) humane
2. (a) sad (b) disappointed (c) unhappy (d) mundane
3. (a) looks (b) pines (c) hankers (d) aspires
4. (a) on (b) for (c) back (d) No word
5. (a) into (b) to (c) the (d) for
6. (a) preoccupation (b) engagement (c) connection (d) relation
7. (a) carelessly (b) blissfully (c) happily (d) honourably
8. (a) laugh (b) smile (c) laughter (d) heart
9. (a) want (b) loss (c) fulfilment (d) scarcity
10. (a) pain (b) dejection (c) sorrow (d) joy
11. (a) saddest (b) loftiest (c) happiest (d) sorrowful

CLOZE TEST – 12

In life there are no (1) _________ without pains. Life indeed would be (2) _________ if there (3) _________ no difficulties. Games lose their (4) _________ if there is no real (5) _________, if the result is a (6) _________ conclusion. Both (7) _________ and loser enjoy a game most if it is closely (8) _________ to the last. No victory is a real triumph unless the (9) _________ is worthy of the (10) _________. Whether we like it or not, life is one (11) _________ competitive examination.

1. (a) earning (b) profit (c) gains (d) relief
2. (a) dull (b) stale (c) colourless (d) cheerful
3. (a) is (b) are (c) was (d) were
4. (a) zest (b) enthusiasm (c) charm (d) attraction
5. (a) fight (b) contest (c) struggle (d) obstacle
6. (a) known (b) foregone (c) expected (d) predictable
7. (a) victor (b) victorious (c) winner (d) gainer
8. (a) fought (b) contested (c) watched (d) balanced
9. (a) rival (b) adversary (c) foe (d) enemy
10. (a) prize (b) steal (c) steel (d) contest
11. (a) regular (b) continuous (c) continual (d) severe

CLOZE TEST – 13

It is not good for man that his life should be all joy and (1) _________. The lands which only know sunshine and never rain become (2) _________. The most beautiful countries are those which are (3) _________ visited by both sunshine and rain. It is in these lands that (4) _________ and fruits grow and sweet birds sing. There is nothing more beautiful than a (5) _________. If life is to be rounded and many-coloured (6) _________ the rainbow, both joy and sorrow must come to it. Those who have never known (7) _________ but prosperity and pleasure become hard and (8) _________ but those whose prosperity has been mixed with (*9*) ________ become kind and (*10*) ________.

1. (*a*) adversity (*b*) pain (*c*) prosperity (*d*) sorrow
2. (*a*) deserts (*b*) garbage (*c*) marshy (*d*) fallow
3. (*a*) regularly (*b*) interminably (*c*) occasionally (*d*) fairly
4. (*a*) flowers (*b*) hedges (*c*) vegetables (*d*) bowers
5. (*a*) sky (*b*) flower (*c*) rainbow (*d*) rain
6. (*a*) like (*b*) so (*c*) as (*d*) by
7. (*a*) nothing (*b*) something (*c*) anything (*d*) no word
8. (*a*) cruel (*b*) harsh (*c*) shallow (*d*) stern
9. (*a*) adversity (*b*) hardship (*c*) poverty (*d*) tragedy
10. (*a*) gracious (*b*) meek (*c*) gentle (*d*) generous

CLOZE TEST – 14

Civilization, like (*1*) ________, fall, not so much because of the (*2*) ________ of the enemy outside, as through the weaknesses and (*3*) ________ within. Rome fell not because of the (*4*) ________; they merely knocked (*5*) ________ something that was already dead. The heart of Rome had (*6*) ________ beating when the arms and legs were cut (*7*) ________. We see something of this (*8*) ________ in India and China and in the case of the Arabs. The (*9*) ________ of Arabian Civilization was sudden even as their rise had been. In India and China the process is long-drawn (*10*) ________ and it is not easy to (*11*) ________ it.

1. (*a*) states (*b*) kingdom (*c*) empires (*d*) buildings
2. (*a*) weakness (*b*) strength (*c*) power (*d*) tenacity
3. (*a*) disease (*b*) decease (*c*) decay (*d*) fortitude
4. (*a*) barbarity (*b*) barbarous (*c*) barbarians (*d*) Romans
5. (*a*) off (*b*) on (*c*) down (*d*) no word
6. (*a*) seized (*b*) rotated (*c*) ceased (*d*) started
7. (*a*) down (*b*) off (*c*) up (*d*) no word
8. (*a*) process (*b*) procedure (*c*) spectacle (*d*) scene
9. (*a*) downfall (*b*) death (*c*) collapse (*d*) dismemberment
10. (*a*) out (*b*) up (*c*) upon (*d*) no word
11. (*a*) find (*b*) single (*c*) spot (*d*) pick

CLOZE TEST – 15

It is not luck but (*1*) ________ that makes men. Luck, says an American writer, is ever waiting for something to turn (*2*) ________; labour with keen eye and strong (*3*) ________ always turns up something. Luck lies in bed and wishes the postman would bring him news of a (*4*) ________; labour turns out at six and with busy pen and (*5*) ________ hammer lays the foundation of a (*6*) ________. Luck relies on chance; labour on (*7*) ________. Luck slips downwards to (*8*) ________ labour (*9*) ________ upwards and aspires (*10*) ________ independence. The conviction, therefore, is extending that diligence is the (*11*) ________ of good luck; in other words, that a man's success in life will be (*12*) ________ to his efforts, to his industry, to his attention to small things.

1. (*a*) work (*b*) diligence (*c*) labour (*d*) experience
2. (*a*) on (*b*) up (*c*) down (*d*) off
3. (*a*) will (*b*) power (*c*) resourcefulness (*d*) grit
4. (*a*) windfall (*b*) treasure (*c*) legacy (*d*) wealth

5. (*a*) swinging (*b*) ringing
(*c*) moving (*d*) powerful

6. (*a*) competence (*b*) knowledge
(*c*) skill (*d*) learning

7. (*a*) work-culture (*b*) character
(*c*) honesty (*d*) integrity

8. (*a*) self-indulgence (*b*) self-effacement
(*c*) selfishness (*d*) self-gratification

9. (*a*) jumps (*b*) strides
(*c*) climbs (*d*) ascends

10. (*a*) after (*b*) for
(*c*) to (*d*) on

11. (*a*) progeny (*b*) father
(*c*) offspring (*d*) mother

12. (*a*) equal (*b*) proportionate
(*c*) subject (*d*) match

ANSWERS

TEST – 1

1. solve
2. enter
3. importance
4. from
5. held
6. (none)
7. achieve
8. but
9. means
10. peace

TEST – 2

1. resilience
2. subject
3. mutation
4. faith
5. resilience
6. mutability
7. goodwill
8. fiercely
9. inane

TEST – 3

1. lesson
2. winning
3. Beside
4. bloodless
5. pales
6. to

TEST – 4

1. herd
2. species
3. religious
4. ferocious
5. intelligence
6. denied

TEST – 5

1. affects
2. applications
3. vehicle
4. witch
5. killed
6. place
7. round
8. hollow
9. ancestry
10. animal

TEST – 6

1. derived
2. supplement
3. depends
4. propels
5. principal
6. collapse
7. plentiful
8. indefinitely
9. on

TEST – 7

1. ceaseless
2. spirituality
3. A body
4. sacrament
5. partners
6. contact
7. procreation
8. for

TEST – 8

1. society
2. into
3. minds
4. rally
5. thoughts
6. grieve
7. die

TEST – 9

1. on
2. passive
3. playthings
4. opportunity
5. choice
6. task
7. pride
8. beckons
9. loses
10. go down

TEST – 10

1. scholarship
2. purity
3. latter
4. outweigh
5. virus
6. epidemic
7. havoc
8. pure
9. scriptures
10. into

TEST – 11

1. human
2. unhappy
3. pines
4. back
5. into
6. engagement
7. happily
8. heart
9. want
10. sorrow
11. saddest

TEST – 12

1. gains
2. dull
3. were
4. charm
5. contest
6. predictable
7. winner
8. contested
9. adversary
10. steel
11. continuous

TEST – 13

1. prosperity
2. deserts
3. regularly
4. flowers
5. rainbow
6. like
7. anything
8. shallow
9. adversity
10. gracious

TEST – 14

1. empires
2. strength
3. decay
4. barbarians
5. down
6. ceased
7. off
8. process
9. collapse
10. out
11. spot

TEST – 15

1. labour
2. up
3. will
4. windfall
5. powerful
6. competence
7. character
8. self-indulgence
9. strides
10. for
11. mother
12. proportionate

SENTENCE SEQUENCING OR REORDERING OF JUMBLED SENTENCES

Sentence Sequencing or Reordering of Jumbled sentences is a very tough exercise. It requires to flex muscles to read the sentences carefully and fetch the central idea and correlation between different sentences. Reordering of jumbled sentences requires you to read the sentences, re-read them and re-read them before making sense out of it.

Directions for Question 1 to 8: *In each questions a set of six sentences of a continuous paragraph are provided. The sentence numbered 1 starts the paragraph and the sentence numbered 6 ends it. Arrange statements A, B, C, D between 1 and 6 to form a coherent paragraph.*

1. ***1. What does the state do in a country where tax morality is very low?***

(A) It ties to spy upon the tax payers.

(B) It investigates income sources and spending patterns.

(C) Exactly what the tax authority tries to do now, even if inconsistently.

(D) It could also encourage people to denounce to the tax authorities any conspicuously prosperous neighbours who may be suspected of not paying their taxes properly.

6. The ultimate solution would be an Orewellian system

(*a*) BACD (*b*) DBAC
(*c*) ABCD (*d*) DCBA

2. ***1. The fragile Yugoslav state has an uncertain future.***

(A) Thus, there will surely be chaos and uncertainty if the people fail to settle their differences.

(B) Sharp ideological differences already exist in the country.

(C) Ethnic, regional, linguistic and material disparities are profound.

(D) The country will also lose the excellent reputation it enjoyed in the international arena.

6. At worst, it will once more become vulnerable to international conspiracy and intrigue.

(*a*) BCAD (*b*) ADCB
(*c*) ACBD (*d*) DBCA

3. ***1. India's experience of industrialization is characteristic of the difficulties faced by a newly independent developing country.***

(A) In 1947, India was undoubtedly an under-developed country with one of the lowest per capita incomes in the world.

(B) Indian industrialization was the result of a conscious deliberate policy of growth by an indigenous political elite.

(C) Today India ranks fifth in the international community of nations if measured in terms of purchasing power.

(D) Even today, however, the benefits of Indian industrialization since independence have not reached the masses.

6. Industrialization in India have thus been a limited success: One more example of growth without development.

(*a*) CDAB (*b*) DCBA
(*c*) CABD (*d*) BACD

4. ***1. The New Economic Policy comprises the various policy measures and changes introduced since July 1991.***

(A) There is a common thread running through all these measures.

(B) The objective is simple – to improve the efficiency of the system.

(C) The regulatory mechanism involving multitude of controls has fragmented the capacity and reduced competition even in the private sector.

(D) The thrust of the new policy is towards creating a more competitive environment as a means to improving the productivity and efficiency of the economy.

6. This is to be achieved by removing the barriers and restrictions on the entry and growth of firms.

(*a*) DCAB (*b*) ABCD

(c) BDAC (*d*) CDBA

5. 1. ***It is significant that one of the most common objections to competition is that it is blind.***

(A) This is important because in a system of free enterprise based on private property, chances are not equal and there is indeed a strong case for reducing that inequality of opportunity.

(B) Rather it is a choice between a system where it is the will of a few persons that decides who is to get what and one where it depends at least partly, on the ability and the enterprise of the people concerned.

(C) Although competition and justice may have little else in common, it is as much as commendation of competition as of justice that it is no respecter of persons.

(D) The choice today is not between a system in which everybody will get what he deserves according to some universal standard and one where individual shares are determined by chance or goodwill.

6. The fact that opportunities open to the door in a competitive society are much more restricted than those open to the rich, does not make it less true that in such a society, the poor are more free than a person commanding much greater material comfort in a different type of society.

(*a*) CDBA (*b*) DCBA

(*c*) ABCD (*d*) BADC

6. 1. ***The necessity for regional integration in South Asia is underlined by the very history of the last 45 years since the liquidation of the British Empire in this part of the world.***

(A) After the partition of the Indian subcontinent, Pakistan was formed in that very area which the imperial powers had always marked out as the potential base for operations against the Russian power in Central Asia.

(B) Because of the disunity and ill-will among the South Asian neighbours, particularly India and Pakistan, great powers from outside the area could meddle into their affairs and thereby keep neighbours apart.

(C) It needs to be added that it was the bountiful supply of sophisticated arms that emboldened Pakistan to go for warlike bellicosity toward India.

(D) As part of the cold war strategy of the US, Pakisan was sucked into Washington's military alliance spreading over the years.

6. Internally too, it was the massive induction of American arms into Pakistan which empowered the military junta of that country to snuff out the civilian government and destroy democracy in Pakistan.

(*a*) ACBD (*b*) ABDC

(*c*) CBAD (*d*) DCAB

7. 1. ***Commercial energy consumption shows an increasing trend and poses the major challenge for the future.***

(A) The demand, for petroleum, during 1996-97 and 2006-07 is anticipated to be 81 million tonnes and 125 million tonnes respectively.

(B) According to the projections of the 14th Power Survey Committee Report, the electricity generation requirements from utilities will be about 416 billion units by 1996-97 and 824 billion units by 2006-07.

(C) The production of coal should reach 303 million tonnes by 1996-97 to achieve Plan targets and 460 million tonnes by 2006-07.

(D) The demand for petroleum products has already rapidly outstripped indigenous production.

6. Electricity is going to play a major role in the development of infrastructural facilities.

(*a*) DACB (*b*) CADB
(*c*) BADC (*d*) ABCD

8. *1. The success of any unit in a competitive environment depends on prudent management of resources.*

(A) In this context, it would have been more appropriate if the concept of accelerated depreciation, together with additional incentives towards capital allowances for recouping a portion of the cost of replacements out of the current generations had been accepted.

(B) Added to this are the negligible retention of profits because of inadequate capital allowances and artificial disallowances of genuine outflows.

(C) One significant cause for the poor generation of surpluses is the high cost of capital and its servicing cost.

(D) The lack of mechanism in Indian tax laws for quick recovery of capital costs has not received its due attention.

6. While this may apparently look costly from the point of view of the exchequer, the ultimate cost to the Government and the community in the form of losses suffered through poor viability will be prohibitive.

(*a*) ADBC (*b*) BCDA
(*c*) CBDA (*d*) DBAC

Directions for Question 9 to 14: *A number of sentences are given below which, when properly sequenced form a coherent paragraph. Each sentence is labeled with a letter. Choose the most logical order of sentences from among the four given choices to construct a coherent paragraph.*

9. (A) Realists believe that there is an object reality out there independent of ourselves.

(B) This reality exists solely by virtue of how the world is, and it is in principle discoverable by application of the methods of science.

(C) They believe in the possibility of determining whether or not a theory is indeed really true or false.

(D) I think it is fair to say that this is the position to which most working scientists subscribe.

(*a*) ABCD (*b*) CDBA
(*c*) DCBA (*d*) BCAD

10. (A) There is a strong manufacturing base for a variety of products.

(B) India has come a long way on the technology front.

(C) But the technology adopted has been largely of foreign origin.

(D) There are, however, areas such as atomic energy, space, agriculture and defence where significant strides have been made in evolving relevant technologies within the country.

(*a*) ADCB (*b*) DBAC
(*c*) BACD (*d*) CBAD

11. (A) In emission trading, the government fixes the total amount of pollution that is acceptable to maintain a desired label to air quality.

(B) Economists argue that this approach makes air pollution control more cost effective than the current practice of fixing air pollution standards and expecting all companies to pollute below these standards.

(C) USA uses emission trading to control air pollution.

(D) It then distributes emission permits to all companies in the region, which add up to the overall acceptable level of emission.

(*a*) BADC
(*b*) ACBD
(*c*) CBAD
(*d*) DBAC

12. **(A)** The individual companies vary in size, from the corner grocery to the industrial giant.

(B) Policies and management methods within firms range from formal, well-planned organizations and controls to slipshod day-to-day operations.

(C) Various industries offer a wide array of products or services through millions of firms largely independent of each other.

(D) Variation in the form of ownership contributes to diversity in capital investment, volume of business, and financial structure.

(*a*) DBCA (*b*) CADB
(*c*) BADC (*d*) ADCB

13. **(A)** All levels of demand, whether individual, aggregate, local, national, or international are subject to change.

(B) At the same time, science and technology add new dimensions to products, their uses and the methods used to market them.

(C) Aggregate demand fluctuates with changes in the level of business activity, GNP, and national income.

(D) The demand of individuals tend to vary with changing need and rising income.

(*a*) CBDA (*b*) DCAB
(*c*) BCAD (*d*) ADCB

14. **(A)** Secret persons shall strike with weapons, fire or poison.

(B) Clans, mutually supporting each other, shall be made to strike at the weak points.

(C) He shall destroy their caravans, herds, forests and troop reinforcements.

(D) The conqueror shall cause enemy kingdom to be destroyed by neighbouring kings, jungle tribes, pretenders or unjustly treated princes.

(*a*) DCBA
(*b*) ABCD
(*c*) ABDC
(*d*) ADCB

Directions for Questions 15 to 17: *Arrange the sentences A, B, C and D to form a logical sequence between sentences 1 and 6.*

15. **1.** ***That was the day that Walter Alva made the boldest decision of his career.***

(A) He had believed that somehow the situation would resolve itself.

(B) First, he apologized to his teammates for putting them in danger.

(C) He now encouraged anyone who wished to leave to do so without delay.

(D) Until recently, he explained, his fascination with the tomb had blinded him to the peril of their position.

6. ***None did.***

(*a*) BACD (*b*) DBAC
(*c*) BDAC (*d*) DABC

16. **1.** ***During this summer, I spent blissfully long days with my friend.***

(A) In the afternoons, we would retire to the cottage, and she would talk about her husband – what a fine man he'd been.

(B) I discovered she made the finest shortbread (a kind of biscuit) in the universe.

(C) Once or twice she seemed about to cry and left the room quickly to make more tea.

(D) We could explore Bear Wood, munching happily and discussing the books she had lent me.

6. ***But she always came back smiling.***

(*a*) BCAD (*b*) ADCB
(*c*) ACBD (*d*) DABC

17. **1.** ***The chainsaw howled as I finished cutting through the branch.***

(A) The branch crashed to the ground, taking my spectacles with it.

(B) I almost dropped the saw as I shielded my face from the twigs that brushed by.

(C) Howard retrieved my glasses and handed them up to me.

(D) I pulled the saw away, and my husband tugged against the other end of the rope that I had tied just above the cut.

6. Are you okay? He asked.

(*a*) BCAD (*b*) DBAC
(*c*) DCAB (*d*) BDAC

Directions for Questions 18 to 19: *Sentences given in each question, when properly sequenced form a coherent paragraph. Each sentence is labeled with a letter. Choose the most logical order of sentences from among the four given choices to construct a coherent paragraph.*

18. (A) One reason can be that the total investment allocated to power was deficient.

(B) However, it may also be that the demand for power was based on incorrect information.

(C) The question arises as to why the planning of the power sector in Indian plans turned out to be faulty, as widely alleged.

(D) In that case, obviously the plan was bad even on paper

(*a*) DABC (*b*) CBAD
(*c*) CADB (*d*) DBAC

19. (A) Children need to be loved, and in a sense they cannot have too much of it.

(B) She herself doesn't want to grow up and attempts to make time stand still.

(C) Fortunately, she cannot succeed.

(D) But it is not because of love that a mother prevents her child from growing up.

(*a*) ACDB (*b*) DABC
(*c*) CADB (*d*) ADBC

Directions for Questions 20 to 22: *Arrange the sentences A, B, C and D to form a logical sequence between sentences 1 and 6.*

20. 1. *The market mechanism is the natural coordinator of private sector activities.*

(A) It is also linked to the centrality of the notion of a free contract for both the operation of the market mechanism and the safeguarding of private property.

(B) This is linked to the autonomy of the decision maker under the market mechanism.

(C) It is futile to expect the State unit to behave as if it were privately owned.

(D) It is time to get rid of this vain hope once and for all.

6. There is no reason to be astonished by the fact that the State ownership permanently recreates the bureaucracy because it is but an organic part of the bureaucratic hierarchy.

(*a*) BADC (*b*) ACDB
(*c*) DCBA (*d*) BACD

21. 1. *A manager is faced with innumerable situations in which he has to make a choice.*

(A) These are not the only kind of decisions that managers take.

(B) As a seller, he has to decide what to sell.

(C) As a producer, he has to decide what to produce, how to produce, how much to produce and where to produce.

(D) As a buyer, he has to decide what to buy.

6. They generally face a wide range of situations involving choice.

(*a*) ABCD (*b*) DCBA
(*c*) CDBA (*d*) BDAC

22. 1. *Operating a small motel, I tried to avoid answering the doorbell before 6:30 a.m.*

(A) One morning at about 5'O clock, the doorbell rang.

(B) So I had a box put up next to the door and placed a sign on it saying, Deposit keys here.

(C) But some guests continued to summer me as early as 4: 30 a.m.

(D) Customers were told me to leave their keys in the rooms when checking out.

6. When I opened the office door, a smiling guest greeted me with: I just wanted you to know, I put my key in the box.

(*a*) DCBA (*b*) DACB
(*c*) BADC (*d*) ABDC

Directions for Questions 23 to 27: *Sentences given in each question, when properly sequenced form a coherent paragraph. Each sentences is labeled with a letter: Choose the most logical order of sentences from among the four given to construct a coherent paragraph.*

23. **(A)** Widely publicized tables of income levels of all countries indicate that when incomes are higher, the greater is the contribution made by the manufacturing industry.

(B) Countries which have little or no industry are almost invariably poor.

(C) The lesson is clear: to overcome poverty and backwardness, a country must industrialize.

(D) Industrialization is seen as the key to growth and a prerequisite for development.

(*a*) CBAD (*b*) DCBA
(*c*) DABC (*d*) CABD

24. **(A)** A wife may not be sure that what her husband is saying means the end.

(B) She has found that people's voices often get higher or shriller when they lie, and they are more likely to stumble over words.

(C) According to De Paulo, changes in voices can be significant.

(D) She should listen closely, not only to what he says, but how he says it.

(*a*) ADCB (*b*) ACDB
(*c*) ADBC (*d*) ABCD

25. **(A)** He pulled popcorn dipped in ketchup out of her mouth with a pair of pliers.

(B) Soon Steven was making horror pictures, using his sisters as victims.

(C) A few years later, Steven borrowed hid dad's eight-millimeter movie camera to film 'The Last Train Wreck' using his own electric train set.

(D) In one, he played a dentist, with his sister Ann as the patient.

(*a*) CBAD (*b*) DACB
(*c*) DABC (*d*) CBDA

26. **(A)** In bulk processing, a set of standard prices typically emerge.

(B) Competing therefore means keeping products flowing, trying to improve quality, getting costs down.

(C) Let us look at the two cultures of competition.

(D) Production tends to be repetitive – much the same from day to day or even from year to year.

(*a*) CDBA (*b*) ABDC
(*c*) CADB (*d*) DCBA

27. **(A)** A moment later, my prospective fiancée reappeared and shoved a ticket to Jiuquan through the hatch.

(B) The queue gazed at me dumbstruck, then broke into a little ripple of applause.

(C) The station master and clerk retreated into the back room.

(D) I lifted it like a trophy.

(*a*) CABD (*b*) ACDB
(*c*) ACBD (*d*) CADB

Directions for Questions 28 to 30: *Arrange the sentences A, B, C and D to form a logical sequence between sentences 1 and 6.*

28. **1.** ***So now, let's sum it up.***

(A) We can call this the. material of knowledge.

(B) According to Kant, there are two elements that contribute to man's knowledge of the world.

(C) The other is the internal conditions in man himself.

(D) One is the external conditions that we cannot know of before we have perceived them though the sense.

6. ***We can call this the form of knowledge.***

(*a*) BDAC
(*b*) BADC
(*c*) CADB
(*d*) CBDA

29. 1. ***I may have a strong desire for a fresh ripe peach, but no peaches may be available.***

(A) I am about to take a bite when news arrives of an accident injuring someone dear to me.

(B) The hay fever passes.

(C) One the other hand, I buy some preaches but a sudden track of hay fever prevents me from enjoying their fragrance or taste.

(D) My interest in the peach vanished.

6. ***I no longer have any appetite.***

(*a*) DCBA (*b*) CBAD
(*c*) ABCD (*d*) ACBD

30. 1. ***A national like an individual, has many personalities and many approaches to life.***

(A) If there is a strong organic bond between different possibilities, it is well.

(B) Otherwise, this could lead to disintegration and trouble.

(C) Normally, some kind of equilibrium is eventually established.

(D) If normal development is arrested, then conflict arises between different personalities.

6. ***In the mind and spirit of India, there has been this fundamental conflict due to a long period of arrested growth.***

(*a*) ABCD (*b*) BDCA
(*c*) CABD (*d*) DBCA

Directions for Questions 31 to 33: *Sentences given in each question, when properly sequenced form a coherent paragraph. Each sentence is labeled with a letter. Choose the most logical order of sentences from among the four given choices to construct a coherent paragraph.*

31. (A) Because negotiations had been delayed until the last moment, he was at a tremendous disadvantage.

(B) Only then did the truth dawn on him.

(C) He broke off talks and returned home.

(D) My friend was under intense pressure to make concessions.

(*a*) DBAC (*b*) ACBD
(*c*) ABCD (*d*) DBCA

32. (A) "Son, why are you reading this sissy magazine?" he asked.

(B) 'There's an article that tells women where to meet men" I responded; pointing to the magazine's cover.

(C) "I need to know where I'm supposed to be."

(D) When I was a teenager, my father caught me reading one of my older sister's magazines.

(*a*) DCAB (*b*) ADCB
(*c*) DABC (*d*) DACB

33. (A) "Actually," Ronnie replied, "I asked my wife."

(B) One day, a man named Ronnie answered a difficult one correctly to put the men in front.

(C) Impressed, the host kept Ronnie on the line and asked how he knew the answer to such a tough question.

(D) Occasionally, a local radio station airs "Battle of the sexes," in which listeners phone in to answer trivial questions.

(*a*) BCAD (*b*) ACDB
(*c*) CABD (*d*) DBCA

Directions for Questions 34 to 36: *Arrange the sentences A, B, C and D to form a logical sequence between sentences 1 and 6.*

34. 1. ***Why are horses the same?***

(A) It may be old and lame, and in time, it will die.

(B) A particular horse 'flows', naturally.

(C) But there is something all horses have in common.

(D) You probably don't think they are at all.

6. ***But the 'form' of the horse is eternal and immutable.***

(*a*) DCAB (*b*) CABD
(*c*) CBDA (*d*) DCBA

35. 1. ***Buddhism is a way to salvation.***

(A) But Buddhism is more severely analytical.

(B) In the Christian tradition, there is also a concern for the fate of human society conceived as a whole, rather than merely as a sum or network of individuals.

(C) Salvation is a property, or achievement, of individuals.

(D) Not only does it dissolve society into individuals; the individual in turn is dissolved into component parts and instants, a stream of events.

6. ***In modern terminology, Buddhist doctrine is reductionism.***

(*a*) BCAD (*b*) ADBC
(*c*) CBAD (*d*) CDAB

36. 1. ***Matrilineal systems of land inheritance advantaged women in many respects, especially in granting them economic and social security.***

(A) Women, in particular; were profoundly affected by these changes.

(B) The large joint family estates came to be partitioned; there was an increasing penetration of market forces and patriarchal ideologies spread in influence.

(C) These systems, however, did not remain fixed over time.

(D) Interventions by the colonial and post-colonial states, and the processes of social change which these set in motion, eroded customary practices.

6. ***At the same time, their customary exclusion from major authority in public bodies meant that they were unlikely to be the ones directing the changes.***

(*a*) BDCA (*b*) CDBA
(*c*) CDAB (*d*) CADB

Directions for Questions 37 to 39: *Sentences given in each question, when properly sequenced form a coherent paragraph, each sentences is labeled with a letter. Choose the most logical order of sentences from among the four given choices to construct a coherent paragraph.*

37. (A) However, the real challenge today is unlearning, which is much harder.

(B) But the new world of business behaves differently from the world in which we grew up.

(C) Learning is important for both people and organizations.

(D) Each of us has a 'mental model' that we've used over the years to make sense.

(*a*) DBCA (*b*) CADB
(*c*) DACB (*d*) CBDA

38. (A) A large number of intellectuals believe that the North is using its military and economic powers to force unequal contracts on the South.

(B) The make-believe ethical issue of the sanctity of law camouflages the unethicality of the entire transaction, which is a travesty of the ethical concept of the greatest good for the greatest number.

(C) Once these contracts are made, the North uses the façade of legality and ethics to pin down the South.

(D) Thus, it suffers from the flaw that the flaw – one of the useful means to implement ethics – has fouled the ethicality of the ends.

(*a*) DACB (*b*) CBDA
(*c*) ACBD (*d*) BDAC

39. (A) The fact that he could find absolutely nothing to substantiate their wild claims made no difference.

(B) We always gave the poor man a cup of tea, and he grew quite fond of some of the animals.

(C) The neighbours, now thoroughly indignant, kept bombarding the local health authorities.

(D) On an average, twice a week, the poor inspector was forced to come up to the house.

(*a*) DBAC (*b*) CDAB
(*c*) ADBC (*d*) CADB

Directions for Questions 40 to 44: *Sentences given in each question, when properly sequenced form a coherent paragraph. Each sentence is labeled with a letter. Choose the most logical order of sentences from among the four given choices to construct a coherent paragraph.*

40. **(A)** In rejecting the functionalism in positivist organization theory, either wholly or partially, there is often a move towards a political model of organization theory.

(B) Thus the analysis would shift to the power resources possessed by different groups in the organization and the way they use these resources in actual power plays to shape the organizational structure.

(C) At the extreme, in one set of writings, the growth of administration in the organization is held to be completely unrelated to the work to be done and to be caused totally by the political pursuit of self-interest.

(D) The political model holds that individual interests are pursued in organizational life through the exercise of power and influence.

(*a*) ADBC (*b*) CBAD
(*c*) DBCA (*d*) ABDC

41. **(A)** Group decision making, however, does not necessarily fully guard against arbitrariness and anarchy, for individual capriciousness can get substituted by collusion of group members.

(B) Nature itself is an intricate system of checks and balances, meant to preserve the delicate balance between various environmental factors that affect our ecology.

(C) In institution also, there is a need to have in place a system of checks and balances which inhibits the concentration of power in only some individuals.

(D) When human interventions alter this delicate balance, the outcome have been seen to be disastrous.

(*a*) CDAB (*b*) BCAD
(*c*) CABD (*d*) BDCA

42. **(A)** He was bone-wary and soul-weary, and found himself muttering, "either I can't manage this place, or it's unmanageable".

(B) To his horror; he realized that he had become the victim of an amorphous, unwitting, unconscious conspiracy to immerse him in routine work that had no significance.

(C) It was one of those nights in the office when the office clerk was moving towards four in the morning and Bennis was still not through with the incredible mass of paper stacked before him.

(D) He reached for his calendar and ran his eyes down each hour, half-hour, and quarter hour, to see where his time had gone that day, the day before, the month before.

(*a*) ABCD (*b*) CADB
(*c*) BDCA (*d*) DCBA

43. **(A)** With that I swallowed the shampoo, and obtained most realistic results almost on the spot.

(B) The man shuffled away into the back regions to make up a prescription, and after a moment, I got through on the shop-telephone to the Consulate, intimating my location.

(C) Then, while the pharmacist was wrapping up a six-ounce bottle of the mixture, I groaned and inquired whether he could give me something for acute gastric cramp.

(D) I intended to stage a sharp gastric attack, and entering an old-fashioned pharmacy, I asked for a popular shampoo mixture, consisting of olive oil and flaked soap.

(*a*) DCBA (*b*) DACB
(*c*) BDAC (*d*) BCDA

44. **(A)** Since then, intelligence tests have been mostly used to separate dull children in school from average or bright children, so that special education can be provided to the dull.

(B) In other words, intelligence tests give us a norm for each age.

(C) Intelligence is expressed as intelligence quotient, and tests are developed to indicate what an average child of a certain age can do – what a 5-year old can answer, but a 4-year old cannot, for instance.

(D) Binet developed the first set of such tests in the early 1900s to find out which children in school needed special attention.

(E) Intelligence can be measured by tests.

(*a*) CDABE (*b*) DECAB
(*c*) EDACB (*d*) CBADE

Directions for Questions 45 to 49: *Sentences given in each question, when properly sequenced form a coherent paragraph. The first and last sentences are 1 and 6, and the four in between are labeled A, B, C and D. Choose the most logical order of these four sentences from among the four given choices to construct a coherent paragraph from sentences 1 to 6.*

45. 1. ***Security inks exploit the same principle that causes the vivid and constantly changing colours of a film of oil on water.***

(A) When two rays of light meet each other after being reflected from these difference surfaces, they have each traveled slightly different distances.

(B) The key is that the light is bouncing off two surfaces, that of the oil and that of the water layer below it.

(C) The distance the two rays travel determines which wavelengths, and hence colours, interface constructively and look bright.

(D) Because light is an electromagnetic wave, the peaks and troughs of each ray then interface either constructively, to appear bright, or destructively, to appear dim.

6. ***Since the distance the rays travel changes with the angle as you look at the surface, different colours look bright from different viewing angles.***

(*a*) ABCD (*b*) BADC
(*c*) BDAC (*d*) DACB

46. 1. ***Commercially reared chicken can be unusually aggressive, and are often kept in darkened sheds to prevent them pecking at each other:***

(A) The birds spent far more of their time – up to a third – pecking at the inanimate objects in the pens, in contrast to birds in other pens which spent a lot of time attacking others.

(B) In low light conditions, they behave less belligerently, but are more prone to ophthalmic disorders and respiratory problems.

(C) In an experiment, aggressive head pecking was all but eliminated among birds in the enriched environment.

(D) Altering the bird's environment, by adding bales of wood – shavings to their pens, can work wonders.

6. ***Bales could diminish aggressiveness and reduce injuries; they might even improve productivity, since a happy chicken is a productive chicken.***

(*a*) DCAB (*b*) CDBA
(*c*) DBAC (*d*) BDCA

47. 1. ***The concept of a 'nation-state' assumes a complete correspondence between the boundaries of the nation and the boundaries of those who live in a specific state.***

(A) Then there are members of national collectivities who live in other countries, making a mockery of the concept.

(B) There are always people living in particular states who are not considered to be (and often do not consider themselves to be) members of the hegemonic nation.

(C) Even worse, there are nations which never had a state or which are divided across several states.

(D) This, of course, has been subject to severe criticism and is virtually everywhere, a fiction.

6. ***However, the fiction has been, and continues to be, at the basis of nationalist ideologies.***

(*a*) DBAC (*b*) ABCD
(*c*) BACD (*d*) DACB

48. 1. ***In the sciences, even questionable examples of research fraud are harshly punished.***

(A) But no such mechanism exists in the humanities – much of what humanities researchers call research does not lead to results that are replicable by other scholars.

(B) Given the importance of interpretation in historical and literary scholarship, humanities researchers are in a position where they can explain away deliberate and even systematic distortion.

(C) Mere suspicion is enough for funding to be cut off, publicity guarantees that careers can be effectively ended.

(D) Forgeries, which take the form of practices in which the forger intersperses fake and real parts can be defended as mere mistakes or aberrant misreading.

6. ***Scientists fudging data have no such defenses.***

(*a*) BDCA (*b*) ABDC
(*c*) CABD (*d*) CDBA

49. 1. ***Horses and communism were, on the whole, a poor match.***

(A) Fine horses bespoke the nobility the party was supposed to despise.

(B) Communist leaders, when they visited villages, preferred to see cows and pigs.

(C) Although a working horse was just about tolerable, the communists were right to be wary.

(D) Peasants from Poland to the Hungarian Pustza preferred their horses to party dogma.

6. ***'A farmer's pride is his horse, his cow may be thin but his horse must be fat,' went a Slovak saying.***

(*a*) ACDB (*b*) DBCA
(*c*) ABCD (*d*) DCBA

Directions for Questions 50 to 54: *The sentences given in each questions, when properly sequenced form a coherent paragraph. Each sentence is labeled with a letter. Choose the most logical order of sentences from among the four given choices to construct a coherent paragraph.*

50. **(A)** If caught in the act, they were punished, not for the crime, but for allowing themselves to be caught, with another lash of the whip.

(B) The bellicose Spartans sacrificed all the finer things in life military expertise.

(C) Those fortunate enough to survive babyhood were taken away from their mothers at the age of seven to undergo rigorous military training.

(D) This consisted mainly of beatings and deprivations of all kinds like going around barefoot in winter, and worse, starvation so that they would be forced to steal food to survive.

(E) Male children were examined at birth by the city council and those deemed too weak to become soldiers were left to die of exposure.

(*a*) BECDA (*b*) ECADB
(*c*) BCDAE (*d*) ECDAB

51. **(A)** This very insatiability of the photographing eye changes the terms of confinement in the cave, our world.

(B) Humankind lingers unregenerately in Plato's cave, still reveling, its age-old habit, in mere image of truth.

(C) But being educated by photographs is not like being educated by older images drawn by hand; for one thing, there are a great many more images around, claiming our attention.

(D) The inventory started in 1839 and since then, just about everything has been photographed, or so it seems.

(E) In teaching us a new visual code, photographs alter and enlarge our notions of what is worth looking at and what we have a right to observe.

(*a*) EABCE (*b*) BDEAC
(*c*) BCDAE (*d*) ECDAB

52. (A) To be culturally literate is to possess the basic information needed to thrive in the modern world.

(B) Nor is it confined to one social class; quite the contrary.

(C) It is by no means confined to "culture", narrowly understood as an acquaintance with the arts.

(D) Cultural literacy constitutes the only sure avenue of opportunity for disadvantaged children, the only reliable way of combating the social determinism that now condemns them.

(E) The breadth of that information is great, extending over the major domains of human activity from sports to science.

(*a*) AECBD (*b*) DECBA

(*c*) ACBED (*d*) DBCAE

53. (A) Both parties use capital and labour in the struggle to secure property rights.

(B) The thief spends time and money in his attempt to steal (he buys wire cutters) and the legitimate property owner expends resources to prevent the theft (he buys locks).

(C) A social cost of theft is that both the thief and the potential victim use resources to gain or maintain control over property.

(D) These costs may escalate as a type of technological arms race unfolds.

(E) A bank may purchase more and more complicated and sophisticated safes, forcing safecrackers to invest further in safecracking equipment.

(*a*) ABCDE (*b*) CABDE

(*c*) ACBED (*d*) CBEDA

54. (A) The likelihood of an accident is determined by how carefully the motorist drives and how carefully the pedestrian crosses the street.

(B) An accident involving a motorist and a pedestrian is such a case.

(C) Each must decide how much care to exercise without knowing how careful the other is.

(D) The simplest strategic problem arises when two individuals interact with each other and each must decide what to do without knowing what the other is doing.

(*a*) ABCD (*b*) ADCB

(*c*) DBCA (*d*) DBAC

Directions for Questions 55 to 59: *Arrange sentences A, B, C and D to form a logical sequence between sentences 1 to 6.*

55. 1. ***Making people laugh is tricky.***

(A) At times, the intended humour may simply not come off.

(B) Making people laugh while trying to sell them something is a tougher challenge, since the commercial can fell flat on two grounds.

(C) There are many advertisements which do amuse, but do not even begin to set the cash tills ringing.

(D) Again, it is rarely sufficient for an advertiser simply to amuse the target audience in order to reap the sales benefit.

6. ***There are indications that in substituting the hard sell for a more entertaining approach, some agencies have rather thrown out the baby with the bath water.***

(*a*) CDBA (*b*) ABCD

(*c*) BADC (*d*) DCBA

56. 1. ***Picture a termite colony, occupying a tall mud hump on an African Plain.***

(A) Hungry predators often invade the colony and unsettle the balance

(B) The colony flourishes only if the proportion of soldiers to workers remains roughly the same, so that the queen and workers can be protected by the soldiers, and the queen and soldiers can be serviced by the workers.

(C) Bit its fortunes are presently restored, because the immobile queen, walled in well below ground level, lays eggs not only in large enough numbers, but also in the varying proportions required.

(D) The hump is alive with worker termites and soldier termites going about their distinct kinds of business.

6. ***How can we account for her mysterious ability to respond like this to events on the distant surface?***

(*a*) BADC (*b*) DBAC
(*c*) ADCB (*d*) BDCA

57. 1. ***According to recent research, the critical period of developing language skills is between the ages of three and five and a half hears.***

(A) The read-to child already has a large vocabulary and a sense of grammar and sentence structure.

(B) Children who are read to in these years have a far better chance of reading well in school, indeed, of doing well in all their subjects.

(C) And the reason is actually quite simple.

(D) This correlation is far and away the highest yet found between home influences and school success.

6. ***Her comprehension of language is therefore very high.***

(*a*) DACB (*b*) ADCB
(*c*) ABCD (*d*) BDCA

58. 1. ***High-powered outboard motors were considered to be one of the major threats to the survival of the Beluga whales.***

(A) With these, hunters could approach Belugas within hunting range and profit from its inner skin and blubber.

(B) To escape an approaching motor, Belugas have learned to dive to the ocean bottom and stay there for up to 20 minutes, by which time the confused predator has left.

(C) Today, however; even with much powerful engines, it is difficult to come close, because the whales seem to disappear suddenly just when you thought you had them in your sights.

(D) When the first outboard engines arrived in the early 1930s, one came across 4 and 8 HP motors.

6. ***Belugas seem to have used their well-known sensitivity to noise to evolve an 'avoidance' strategy to outsmart hunters and their powerful technologies.***

(*a*) DACB (*b*) CDAB
(*c*) ADBC (*d*) BDAC

59. 1. ***The reconstruction of history by post-revolutionary science texts involves more than a multiplication of historical misconstructions.***

(A) Because they aim quickly to acquaint the student with what the contemporary scientific community thinks it knows, textbooks treat the various experiments, concepts, law and theories of the current normal science as separately and as nearly seriatim as possible.

(B) Those misconstructions render revolutions invisible; the arrangement of the still visible material in science texts implies a process that, if it existed, would deny revolutions a function.

(C) But when combined with the generally unhistorical air of science writing and with the occasional systematic misconstruction, one impression is likely to follow.

(D) As pedagogy, this technique of presentation is unexceptionable.

6. ***Science has reached its present state by a series of individual discoveries and inventions that, when gathered together, constitute the modern body of technical knowledge.***

(*a*) BADC (*b*) ADCB
(*c*) DACB (*d*) CBDA

Directions for Questions 60 to 64: *The sentences given in each question, when properly sequenced form a coherent paragraph. Each sentence is labeled with a letter: Choose the most logical order of sentences from among the given choices to construct a coherent paragraph.*

60. **(A)** Although there are large regional variations, it is not infrequent to find a large number of people sitting here and there and doing nothing.

(B) Once in office, they receive friends and relatives who feel free to call any time without prior appointment.

(C) While working, one is struck by the slow and clumsy actions and reactions, indifferent attitudes, procedure rather than outcome orientation, and the lack of consideration for others.

(D) Even those who are employed often come late to the office and leave early, unless they are forced to be punctual.

(E) Work is not intrinsically values in India.

(F) Quite often, people visit ailing friends and relatives or go out of their way to help them in their personal matters even during office hours.

(*a*) ECADBF (*b*) EADCFB

(*c*) EADBFC (*d*) ABFCBE

61. **(A)** But in the industrial era, destroying the enemy's productive capacity means bombing the factories which are located in the cities.

(B) So in the agrarian era, if you need to destroy the enemy's productive capacity, what you want to do is burn his fields, or if you're really vicious, salt them.

(C) Now in the information era, destroying the enemy's productive capacity means destroying the information infrastructure.

(D) How do you battle with your enemy?

(E) The idea is to destroy the enemy's productive capacity, and depending upon the economic foundation, that productive capacity is different in each case.

(F) With regard to defence, the purpose of the military is to defend the nation and be prepared to do battle with its enemy.

(*a*) FDEBAC (*b*) FACBED

(*c*) DEBACF (*d*) DFEBAC

62. **(A)** Michael Hofman, a poet and translator, accepts this sorry fact without approval or complaint.

(B) But thanklessness and impossibility do not daunt him.

(C) He acknowledges too – in fact he returns to the point often that best translators of poetry always fail at some level.

(D) Hofman feels passionately about his work, and this is clear from his writings.

(E) In terms of the gap between worth and rewards, translators come somewhere near nurses and street-cleaners.

(*a*) EACDB (*b*) ADEBC

(*c*) EACBD (*d*) DCEAB

63. **(A)** Passivity is not, of course, universal.

(B) In areas where there are no lords or laws, or in frontier zones where all men go armed, the attitude of the peasantry may well be different.

(C) So indeed, it may be on the fringe of the unsubmissive.

(D) However, for most of the soil-bound peasants, the problem is not whether to be normally passive or active, but when to pass from one state to another.

(E) This depends on an assessment of the political situation.

(*a*) BEDAC (*b*) CDABE

(*c*) EDBAC (*d*) ABCDE

64. **(A)** The situation in which violence occurs and the nature of that violence tends to be clearly defined at least in theory, as in the proverbial Irishman's question: "Is this a private fight or can anyone join in?"

(B) So the actual risk to outsiders, though no doubt higher than our societies, is calculable.

(C) Probably the only uncontrolled applications of force are those of social superiors to social inferiors and even here, there are probably some rules.

(D) However, binding the obligation to kill, members of feuding families engaged in mutual massacre will be genuinely appalled if by some mischance, a bystander or outsiders is killed.

(*a*) DABC (*b*) ACDB
(*c*) CBAD (*d*) DBAC

Directions for Questions 65 to 72: *The sentences given in each questions, when properly sequenced form a coherent paragraph. Each sentence is labeled with a letter. Choose the most logical order of sentences from among the given choices to construct a coherent paragraph.*

65. (A) The wall does not simply divide Israel from a putative Palestinian state on the basis of the 1967 borders.

(B) A chilling omission from the road map is the gigantic 'separation wall' now being built in the West Bank by Israel.

(C) It is surrounded by trenches, electric wire and moats; there are watchtowers at regular intervals.

(D) It actually takes in new tracts of Palestinian land, sometimes five or six kilometers at a stretch.

(E) Almost a decade after the end of South African apartheid, this ghastly racist wall is going up with scarcely a peep from Israel's American allies, who are going to pay for most of it.

(*a*) EBCAD (*b*) BADCE
(*c*) AEDCB (*d*) ECADB

66. (A) Luckily, the tide of battle moved elsewhere after the American victory at Midway and an Australian victory over Japan at Milne Bay.

(B) It could have been no more than a delaying tactic.

(C) The Australian military, knowing the position was homeless, planned to fall back to the south-east in the hope of defending the main cities.

(D) They had captured most of the Solomon Islands and much of New Guinea, and seemed poised for an invasion.

(E) Not many people outside Australia realize how close the Japanese got.

(*a*) EDCBA (*b*) ECDAB
(*c*) ADCBE (*d*) CDBAE

67. (A) Call it the third wave sweeping the Indian media.

(B) Now, they are starring in a new role, as suave dealmakers who are in a hurry to strike alliances and agreements.

(C) Look around and you will find a host of deals that have been inked or are ready to be finalized.

(D) Then the media barons wrested back control from their editors, and turned marketing warriors with the brand as their missile.

(E) The first came with those magnificent men in their mahogany chambers who took on the world with their mighty fountain pens.

(*a*) ACBED (*b*) CEBDA
(*c*) CAEBD (*d*) AEDBC

68. (A) The celebrations of economic recovery in Washington may be as premature as that "Mission Accomplished" banner hung on the USS Abraham Lincoln to hail the end of the Iraq war.

(B) Meanwhile, in the real world, the struggles of families and communities continue unabated.

(C) Washington responded to the favourable turn in economic news with enthusiasm.

(D) The celebrations and high-fives up and down Pennsylvania Avenue are not to be found beyond the Beltway.

(E) When the third quarter GDP showed growth of 7.2% and the monthly unemployment rate dipped to 6%, euphoria gripped the US capital.

(*a*) ACEDB
(*b*) CEDAB
(*c*) ECABD
(*d*) ECBDA

69. (A) To much of the Labour movement, it symbolizes the brutality of the upper classes.

(B) And to everybody watching, the current mess over fox hunting symbolizes the government's weakness.

(C) To fox hunting's supporters, Labour's 1991 manifesto commitment to ban it, symbolizes the party's metropolitan roots and hostility to the countryside.

(D) Small issues sometimes have large symbolic power.

(E) To those who enjoy thundering across the countryside in red coats after foxes, foxhunting symbolizes the ancient roots of rural lives.

(*a*) DEACB (*b*) ECDBA
(*c*) CEADB (*d*) DBAEC

70. (A) In the case of King Merolchazzar's courtship of the Princess of the Outer Isles, there occurs a regrettable hitch.

(B) She acknowledges the gifts, but no word of a meeting date follows.

(C) The monarch, hearing good reports of a neighbouring princess, dispatches messengers with gifts to her court, beseeching an interview.

(D) The princess names a date, and a formal meeting takes place; after that everything buzzes along pretty smoothly.

(E) Royal love affairs in olden days were conducted on the correspondence method.

(*a*) ACBDE (*b*) ABCDE
(*c*) ECDAB (*d*) ECBAD

71. (A) Who can trace to its first beginnings, the love of Damon for Pythias, of David for Jonathan, of Swan for Edgar?

(B) Similarly with men.

(C) There is about great friendships between man and man a certain inevitability that can only be compared with the age-old association of ham and eggs.

(D) One simply feels that it is one of the things that must be so.

(E) No one can say what was the mutual magnetism that brought the deathless partnership of these wholesome and palatable foodstuffs about.

(*a*) ACBED (*b*) CEDBA
(*c*) ACEBD (*d*) CEABD

72. (A) Events intervened, and in the late 1930s and 1940s, Germany suffered from "over-branding".

(B) The British used to be fascinated by the home of Romanticism.

(C) But reunification and the federal government's move to Berlin have prompted Germany to think again about its image.

(D) The first foreign package holiday was a tour of Germany organized by Thomas Cook in 1855.

(E) Since then, Germany has been understandably nervous about promoting itself abroad.

(*a*) ACEBD (*b*) DECAB
(*c*) BDAEC (*d*) DBAEC

Directions for Questions 73 to 77: *The sentences given in each question, when properly sequenced form a coherent paragraph. Each sentence is labeled with a letter. Choose the most logical order of sentences from among the given choices to construct a coherent paragraph.*

73. (A) He felt justified in bypassing Congress altogether, on a variety of moves.

(B) At times, he was fighting the entire Congress.

(C) Bush felt he had a mission to restore power to the presidency.

(D) Bush was not fighting just the democrats.

(E) Representative democracy is a messy business, and a CEO of the White House does not like a legislature of second guessers and time wasters.

(*a*) CAEDB

(*b*) DBAEC

(*c*) CEADB

(*d*) ECDBA

74. **(A)** The two neighbours never fought each other.

(B) Fights involving three male fiddler crabs have been recorded, but the status of the participants was unknown.

(C) They pushed or grappled only with the intruder.

(D) We recorded 17 cases in which a resident that was fighting an intruder, was joined by an immediate neighbor, an ally.

(E) We therefore tracked 268 intruder males until we saw them fighting a resident male.

(*a*) BEDAC (*b*) DEBAC

(*c*) BDCAE (*d*) BCEDA

75. **(A)** In the west, Allied Forces had fought their way through southern Italy as far as Rome.

(B) In June 1944, Germany's military position in World War Two appeared hopeless.

(C) In Britain, the task of amassing the men and materials for the liberation of northern Europe had been completed.

(D) The Red Army was poised to drive the Nazis back through Poland.

(E) The situation on the eastern front was catastrophic.

(*a*) EDACB (*b*) BEDAC

(*c*) BDECA (*d*) CEDAB

76. **(A)** But this does not mean that death was the Egyptians' only preoccupation.

(B) Even papyri come mainly from pyramid temples.

(C) Most of our traditional sources of information about the Old Kingdom are monuments of the rich like pyramids and tombs.

(D) Houses in which ordinary Egyptians lived have not been preserved, and when most people died, they were buried in simple graves.

(E) We know infinitely more about the wealthy people of Egypt that we do about the ordinary people, as most monuments were made for the rich.

(*a*) CDBEA (*b*) ECDAB

(*c*) EDCBA (*d*) DECAB

77. **(A)** Experts such as Larry Burns, head of research at GM, reckon that only such a full hearted leap will allow the world to cope with the mass motorization that will one day come to China or India.

(B) But once hydrogen is being produced from biomass or extracted from underground coal or made from water, using nuclear or renewable electricity, the way will be open for a huge reduction in carbon emissions from the whole system.

(C) In theory, once all the bugs have been sorted out, fuel cells should deliver better total fuel economy than any existing engines.

(D) That is twice as good as the internal combustion engine, but only five percentage points better than a diesel hybrid.

(E) Allowing for the resources needed to extract hydrogen from hydrocarbon, oil, coal or gas, the fuel cells has an efficiency of 30%.

(*a*) CEDBA (*b*) CEBDA

(*c*) AEDBC (*d*) ACEBD

ANSWERS

1. (*c*)	**2.** (*a*)	**3.** (*d*)	**4.** (*c*)	**5.** (*a*)	**6.** (*b*)	**7.** (*a*)	**8.** (*d*)	**9.** (*a*)	**10.** (*c*)
11. (*c*)	**12.** (*d*)	**13.** (*d*)	**14.** (*c*)	**15.** (*c*)	**16.** (*d*)	**17.** (*b*)	**18.** (*a*)	**19.** (*d*)	**20.** (*a*)
21. (*c*)	**22.** (*c*)	**23.** (*b*)	**24.** (*d*)	**25.** (*d*)	**26.** (*c*)	**27.** (*c*)	**28.** (*a*)	**29.** (*d*)	**30.** (*a*)
31. (*b*)	**32.** (*d*)	**33.** (*d*)	**34.** (*d*)	**35.** (*c*)	**36.** (*b*)	**37.** (*a*)	**38.** (*c*)	**39.** (*b*)	**40.** (*a*)
41. (*d*)	**42.** (*b*)	**43.** (*a*)	**44.** (*c*)	**45.** (*b*)	**46.** (*d*)	**47.** (*a*)	**48.** (*c*)	**49.** (*c*)	**50.** (*a*)
51. (*d*)	**52.** (*a*)	**53.** (*b*)	**54.** (*d*)	**55.** (*c*)	**56.** (*b*)	**57.** (*d*)	**58.** (*a*)	**59.** (*a*)	**60.** (*c*)
61. (*d*)	**62.** (*c*)	**63.** (*d*)	**64.** (*b*)	**65.** (*b*)	**66.** (*a*)	**67.** (*d*)	**68.** (*d*)	**69.** (*a*)	**70.** (*c*)
71. (*b*)	**72.** (*c*)	**73.** (*d*)	**74.** (*a*)	**75.** (*b*)	**76.** (*b*)	**77.** (*a*)			

ASSESS YOUR LEVEL OF UNDERSTANDING OF ENGLISH LANGUAGE

Directions: *These paragraphs are basically meant to check your level of understanding of English language, your word power and its usage. Fill in the blanks with appropriate words, prepositions, determiners, modals and other options given in the answers.*

Passage 1

This … (*1*) … balance of payment situation must be seen along with an equally … (*2*) … problem of deficits in the government's own budget. A growing … (*3*)… exists between the government's total … (*4*) …. And the sum of its current revenue and capital receipts. This gap, which has to be met through either external assistance or .. (*5*) … deficit finance, has grown over the years. The government … (*6*) … cannot resort to indefinitely growing volumes of external assistance of finance deficit to meet the increasing gap between its total … (*7*) … and total receipts. … (*8*)…. under these conditions, there has been strong pressure on government to … (*9*) … various development programmes. The … (*10*)… of these programmes may be reduced in real terms or their rate of expansion at least brought down.

1. (*a*) expanding (*b*) increasing (*c*) yawning (*d*) deteriorating
2. (*a*) ignored (*b*) posed (*c*) understood (*d*) significant
3. (*a*) disparity (*b*) bond (*c*) gap (*d*) awareness
4. (*a*) resources (*b*) budget (*c*) outlay (*d*) planning
5. (*a*) zero (*b*) planning (*c*) budget (*d*) domestic
6. (*a*) perhaps (*b*) probably (*c*) willingly (*d*) obviously
7. (*a*) outlay (*b*) services (*c*) planning (*d*) expenditure
8. (*a*) Taking (*b*) From (*c*) Under (*d*) Above
9. (*a*) curtail (*b*) stop (*c*) reject (*d*) promote
10. (*a*) services (*b*) outlay (*c*) scope (*d*) effect

Passage 2

Broadly speaking letters may be said to …. (*1*) …. into two classes: the formal and ….. (*2*) ….. Formal letters ….. (*3*) …… of official or business matters and are …. (*4*) ….. to an employer, officials of a department or institutions. Letters to the …. (*5*) … of a newspaper also belong to this class. In fact all …. (*6*) …. using formal pattern is of this category. The …. (*7*) … has to be precisely stated. It must be … (*8*) …. In style and quite …. (*9*) ….. No ….. (*10*) ….. has any place in it.

1. (*a*) describe (*b*) fall (*c*) escape (*d*) rise
2. (*a*) affectionate (*b*) abusive (*c*) personal (*d*) flattering
3. (*a*) consist (*b*) apprise (*c*) contain (*d*) comprise
4. (*a*) addressed (*b*) prayed (*c*) respected (*d*) typed
5. (*a*) editor (*b*) publisher (*c*) salesman (*d*) typed
6. (*a*) writings (*b*) columns (*c*) correspondence (*d*) letters
7. (*a*) language (*b*) content (*c*) criticism (*d*) objection
8. (*a*) lucid (*b*) florid (*c*) high (*d*) descriptive

9. (*a*) creative (*b*) objective
   (*c*) critical (*d*) subjective
10. (*a*) unifying (*b*) divisive
   (*c*) malice (*d*) personal

Passage 3

Dhritrashtra, the elder brother of the Pandu, was blind by birth. When he grew young, he was married to Gandhari. She loved him so …. (*1*) …. That she …. (*2*) …. up her own eyes with a cloth. A hundred sons were born to Dhritrashtra and Gandhari.. They were called Kaurvas. Duryodhana was the …. (*3*) ….. son of Dhritrashtra, who was quite obstinate by nature. When Kunti …. (*4*) ….. to Hastinapur with her five sons, Duryodhana did not …. (*5*) …. it. He wanted that the Pandavas should live in the forest with their mother, Kunti. In fact he wanted to rule … (*6*) Hastinapur without any interference in his affairs, although outwardly he made a …. (*7*) … of happiness. His mother Gandhari consoled Kunti but her son Duryodhana did not like this at all. Pandavas were so good and …. (*8*) ….. that every one who saw them … (*9*) ….. them greater … (*10*) …. to the Pandavas than to the Kauravas

1. (*a*) closely (*b*) deeply
   (*c*) keenly (*d*) excessively
2. (*a*) closed (*b*) folded
   (*c*) bound (*d*) blinded
3. (*a*) eldest (*b*) greatest
   (*c*) dearest (*d*) loveliest
4. (*a*) refreated (*b*) retracted
   (*c*) receded (*d*) returned
5. (*a*) concede (*b*) approve
   (*c*) understand (*d*) like
6. (*a*) on (*b*) over
   (*c*) upon (*d*) from
7. (*a*) show (*b*) pretention
   (*c*) face (*d*) pretext
8. (*a*) feeble (*b*) attractive
   (*c*) innocent (*d*) noble
9. (*a*) glorified (*b*) praised
   (*c*) respected (*d*) applauded
10. (*a*) importance (*b*) praise
   (*c*) consideration (*d*) admiration

Passage 4

I want to avoid violence. Non-violence also … (*1*) … the first article of my faith. It is also the … (*2*) ….. article of my creed. But I had to …. (*3*) …. my choice. I had either to submit … (*4*) ….. a system which I considered …. (*5*) …. done irreparable harm to my country … (*6*) …… incur the risk of the mad fury ….. (*7*) …. my people bursting forth, when they …. (*8*) …. The truth from my lips. I ….. (*9*) …. that my people have sometimes …. (*10*) ….. mad. I am deeply sorry for it.

1. (*a*) was (*b*) be
   (*c*) is (*d*) being
2. (*a*) last (*b*) common
   (*c*) simple (*d*) unique
3. (*a*) make (*b*) select
   (*c*) prepare (*d*) do
4. (*a*) over (*b*) in
   (*c*) against (*d*) to
5. (*a*) is (*b*) was
   (*c*) had (*d*) has
6. (*a*) nor (*b*) but
   (*c*) but (*d*) and
7. (*a*) with (*b*) by
   (*c*) in (*d*) of
8. (*a*) listen (*b*) get
   (*c*) understood (*d*) understand
9. (*a*) know (*b*) knows
   (*c*) knew (*d*) known
10. (*a*) going (*b*) gone
   (*c*) goes (*d*) went

Passage 5

New industries supported by foreign interests … (*1*) …. offer …. (*2*) …. salaries to their employees at all levels of responsibility than … (*3*) …. locally owned industries. They need …. (*4*) …. People and are …. (*5*) ….. to pay high wages to …. (*6*) ….. them. Local industries often … (*7*) …. the high salaries offered by foreign supported industries, arguing that this will .... (8) ..... raise all wages to an excessive level. Workers in local industries, seeing the sharp ... (9) .... In job-pay will agitate for an improvement in their salaries. This eventually will drain the resources and ... (10) ... their profitability.

1. (a) seldom (b) hardly (c) never (d) usually
2. (a) better (b) comparable (c) unreasonable (d) proportionate
3. (a) did (b) do (c) their (d) does
4. (a) less (b) talented (c) more (d) several
5. (a) bound (b) willing (c) forced (d) reluctant
6. (a) hire (b) bribe (c) retain (d) enrich
7. (a) accept (b) pay (c) protest (d) uphold
8. (a) not (b) unreasonably (c) artificially (d) considerably
9. (a) hike (b) cut (c) decrease (d) difference
10. (a) check (b) lower (c) fulfil (d) enhance

Passage 6

It is not proper to damn a system without understanding it. The Indian bureaucracy may be as bad after all, as it is made out to be. Times without number, it has been ... (1) that our bureaucrat is a ... (2) ..... creature who has the habit of sitting .... (3) .... the files and also happens to sleep .... (4) .... The remainders. What is worse is ..... (5) ..... his own word. He turns a .... (6) .... Ear to the visitor's request and binds his hands and feet with ... (7) .... tape. However, in all fairness .... (8) .... The bureaucracy, it is necessary to note that a major reason for its ..... (9) ..... to discharge its functions ....(10)..... throughout has been the concentration of power in the hands of the politicians. The bureaucrat may be a devil, but because he has his own share of difficulties, we would not deny him his due.

1. (a) declared (b) proclaimed (c) said (d) pronounced
2. (a) strange (b) sober (c) sophisticated (d) solid
3. (a) on (b) at (c) by (d) with
4. (a) off (b) by (c) away (d) over
5. (a) minces (b) eats (c) minds (d) shuffles
6. (a) busy (b) cold (c) deaf (d) callous
7. (a) brown (b) blue (c) red (d) green
8. (a) fox (b) to (c) with (d) of
9. (a) adequacy (b) efficacy (c) position (d) inability
10. (a) effectively (b) elegantly. (c) evenly (d) equitably

Passage 7

Some people believe that marriages are made in heaven. One cannot say ... (1) ... this is true or not. However, in America now many ... (2) ....who get married seek to evolve a fool proof ... (3) ... to ensure that the marriage survives. However, the idea of married persons ... (4) ... the burden of domestic chores, instead of all the dirty work being dumped on the woman has ... (5)... been propagated by the feminist ... (6) .... And it has gradually, if grudgingly, been ... (7).... This arrangement may work on a temporary basis but taking ... (8) ... of a particular domestic work on a permanent basis will pose problems of its own. For instance, taking out the rubbish may ... (9) .... Make a refreshing change from washing baby's nappies. However, a contract is a contract and must be ... (10) ... You may not like it but this is what life coming out to be in the most modern of the countries in the world.

1. (a) whether (b) still (c) however (d) that

2. (*a*) pairs (*b*) men
   (*c*) couples (*d*) women
3. (*a*) method (*b*) project
   (*c*) plans (*d*) system
4. (*a*) executing (*b*) dividing
   (*c*) undertaking (*d*) sharing
5. (*a*) long (*b*) sometimes
   (*c*) always (*d*) occasionally
6. (*a*) groups (*b*) lobby
   (*c*) section (*d*) faction
7. (*a*) affirmed (*b*) approved
   (*c*) accepted (*d*) favoured
8. (*a*) control (*b*) care
   (*c*) charge (*d*) duty
9. (*a*) occasionally (*b*) often
   (*c*) intermittently (*d*) rarely
10. (*a*) respected (*b*) executed
    (*c*) maintained (*d*) obeyed

Passage 8

We will be crushed if civil … (*1*) …. is started. It will be a … (*2*) … to the clock. The technique of … (*3*) … against it has been … (*4*) … We may have to wait … (*5*) … a year or more, for a suitable … (*6*) … to be created. Any hasty … (*7*) … may result in complete … (*8*) … Labour troubles will … (*9*) … to violence and there will be … (*10*) … discord.

1. (*a*) riot (*b*) disturbance
   (*c*) war (*d*) disobedience
2. (*a*) damage (*b*) reversal
   (*c*) setback (*d*) rewinding
3. (*a*) defence (*b*) protection
   (*c*) fighting (*d*) guarding
4. (*a*) learnt (*b*) practised
   (*c*) rehearsed (*d*) perfect
5. (*a*) at least (*b*) minimum
   (*c*) for (*d*) approximately
6. (*a*) condition (*b*) climate
   (*c*) atmosphere (*d*) weather
7. (*a*) decision (*b*) work
   (*c*) deed (*d*) action
8. (*a*) demoralization (*b*) doom
   (*c*) disobedience (*d*) disaster
9. (*a*) draw (*b*) take
   (*c*) lead (*d*) grow
10. (*a*) labour (*b*) communal
    (*c*) religious (*d*) community

Passage 9

It looks like the trail that leads to a magical land. The path climbs out of the forest …. (*1*) …. White and yellow butterflies flutter …. (*2*) …. the hanging creepers. It emerges on a … (*3*) ….. meadow basking in the sun …. (*4*) …. this is no fairy-tale country. The …. (*5*) …. Inhabitants of the meadows …. (*6*) …. Barely living human skeletons, with sunken, fevered …. (*7*) …. and clothed in filthy and … (*8*) …. rags. They are there refugees who have been …(*9*)…. to flee deeper into Thailand, and have … (*10*) ….. instead to stay close to their Cambodian homeland, inspite of all the dangers and hardships they face everyday.

1. (*a*) that (*b*) when
   (*c*) where (*d*) which
2. (*a*) among (*b*) at
   (*c*) on (*d*) in
3. (*a*) stony (*b*) beautiful
   (*c*) gaudy (*d*) dry
4. (*a*) As (*b*) And
   (*c*) But (*d*) So
5. (*a*) happy (*b*) only
   (*c*) erstwhile (*d*) cheerful
6. (*a*) were (*b*) are
   (*c*) have (*d*) being
7. (*a*) eyes (*b*) ears
   (*c*) feet (*d*) hands
8. (*a*) fluttered (*b*) cluttered
   (*c*) tattered (*d*) battered
9. (*a*) denied (*b*) asked
   (*c*) wanted (*d*) refused
10. (*a*) wondered (*b*) refused
    (*c*) chosen (*d*) needed

Passage 10

After an absence of thirty years, I decided to visit my old school again. I had …. (*1*)…. to find changes but not a … (*2*)… different building. As I walked up …. (*3*) …. school driven, I wondered for a …. (*4*) …. if I had come to the …. (*5*) …. address. The grimy, red-brick fortress with … (*6*) …. tall windows that had looked down …. (*7*) …. on the playground and playing fields …. (*8*) …. been swept away. In its place …. (*9*) …. a bright, modern block raised from …. (*10*) …. ground on great concrete stilts.

1. (*a*) known (*b*) expected (*c*) hoped (*d*) imagined
2. (*a*) entirely (*b*) barely (*c*) completely (*d*) very
3. (*a*) our (*b*) my (*c*) the (*d*) a
4. (*a*) moment (*b*) while (*c*) instance (*d*) period
5. (*a*) school (*b*) actual (*c*) right (*d*) exact
6. (*a*) her (*b*) its (*c*) the (*d*) some
7. (*a*) pleasantly (*b*) seriously (*c*) grimly (*d*) sorrowfully
8. (*a*) did (*b*) has (*c*) have (*d*) had
9. (*a*) stood (*b*) was (*c*) appeared (*d*) rose
10. (*a*) solid (*b*) a (*c*) the (*d*) low

Passage 11

Most experts agree that even people who think they are sleeping enough would … (*1*) …. be better off with more …. (*2*) …. as evidence of a general sleep deficit, they …. (*3*) …. the use of the bedside alarm clock used by people to …. (*4*) …. their waking hours. The most relentless robbery of …. (*5*) …. Is the complexity of every day life. Whenever pressures from work, family and community …. (*6*) …. many people …. (*7*) …. with sleep. another …. (*8*) …. of sleep is the shift work. the …. (*9*) ….. of round-the-clock entertainment, especially all-night television, also takes its … (*10*)….

1. (*a*) mainly (*b*) probably (*c*) suddenly (*d*) attentively (*e*) meaningfully
2. (*a*) rest (*b*) work (*c*) time (*d*) energy (*e*) freedom
3. (*a*) prove (*b*) cite (*c*) ignore (*d*) explain (*e*) overlook
4. (*a*) widen (*b*) disturb (*c*) prolong (*d*) improve (*e*) minimise
5. (*a*) stress (*b*) sleep (*c*) leisure (*d*) pleasure (*e*) motivation
6. (*a*) mount (*b*) unite (*c*) happen (*d*) diminish (*e*) disappear
7. (*a*) depend (*b*) desist (*c*) detach (*d*) deprive (*e*) dispense
8. (*a*) study (*b*) product (*c*) thief (*d*) drawback (*e*) contributor
9. (*a*) telecast (*b*) viewing (*c*) deficiency (*d*) requirement (*e*) availability
10. (*a*) toll (*b*) credit (*c*) risk (*d*) pressure (*e*) enjoyment

Passage 12

The feeling of insecurity among the people has increased even though there is … (*1*) …. use of the para-military and the military. The excesses …. (*2*) …. by the two forces, particularly by the first, do not …. (*3*) …. the type of anger it should because they are seen …. (*4*) …. those who are trying to disintegrate the country. Even a …. (*5*) …. for more say in the administration is shouted down. Human rights organizations and Civil liberty activists are considered a …. (6) …., if not unpatriotic. Even the …. (7) …. cases of cruelty are not pursued by the government …. (8) ….. the inquiry should …. (9) ….. the forces and …. (10) ….. the instrument on which it has come to depend.

1. (*a*) free (*b*) reduced (*c*) little (*d*) liberal
2. (*a*) cleared (*b*) committed (*c*) condoned (*d*) displayed
3. (*a*) resist (*b*) evoke (*c*) convey (*d*) suppress
4. (*a*) obeying (*b*) ignoring (*c*) supporting (*d*) fighting
5. (*a*) demand (*b*) desire (*c*) prayer (*d*) plea
6. (*a*) nuisance (*b*) help (*c*) threat (*d*) boon
7. (*a*) minor (*b*) blatant (*c*) new (*d*) concealed
8. (*a*) because (*b*) for (*c*) till (*d*) lest
9. (*a*) disperse (*b*) derail (*c*) demoralise (*d*) degrade
10. (*a*) blunt (*b*) raise (*c*) change (*d*) lose

Passage 13

A university stands for humanism, reason and the adventure of ideas. It stands for the onward … (1) …. of the human race … (2) …. higher objectives. If the universities …. (3) … their duty adequately, then it …. (4) …. well with the nation and … (5) …. people. But if the temple of learning itself becomes a home of narrow bigotry and petty objectives… (6) …. will the nation prosper?

1. (*a*) motion (*b*) march (*c*) progress
2. (*a*) towards (*b*) on (*c*) for
3. (*a*) finish (*b*) obey (*c*) discharge
4. (*a*) was (*b*) will be (*c*) is
5. (*a*) the (*b*) her (*c*) their
6. (*a*) when (*b*) why (*c*) how

Passage 14

Children are loved by all human beings. But … (1) …. this world of human … (2) … there is no …. (3) …. nuisance than a boy …. (4) …. the age of fourteen. He is neither ornamental … (5) …. useful It is impossible to …. (6) …. Affection on him as on a …. (7) … boy and he is always getting …. (8) ….. the ways. If he talks with a childish lips he is called a baby, and if he answers in a grown up way he is called impertinent. Then he is …. (9) …. the unattractive, growing age. He grows out … (10) ….. his clothes, with indecent haste. His voice begins to break and loses its childish charm.

1. (*a*) of (*b*) on (*c*) for (*d*) in
2. (*a*) affairs (*b*) life (*c*) beings (*d*) world
3. (*a*) worst (*b*) bad (*c*) worse (*d*) better
4. (*a*) at (*b*) of (*c*) on (*d*) in
5. (*a*) and (*b*) or (*c*) nor (*d*) so
6. (*a*) show (*b*) shower (*c*) repose (*d*) showering
7. (*a*) tiny (*b*) big (*c*) small (*d*) little
8. (*a*) through (*b*) in (*c*) on (*d*) off
9. (*a*) with (*b*) on (*c*) of (*d*) at
10. (*a*) of (*b*) from (*c*) beyond (*d*) through

Passage 15

Decisions may be … (1) …. at either through initiative or through inertia. Many misfortunes in the world come across the bridge of indecision. Power corrupts but weakness also corrupts. The fruits of weakness like fear, bitterness and suspicion can … (2) …. in a paralysis of decision. Inner division can produce indecision, and indecision is results of weakness of character.

An occasional wrong decision may be sometimes … (*3*) …. to indecision. The … (*4*) …. man is often self-centred. He fears making a …. (*5*) …. and the fear paralyses him. When indecision grips a nation, free men feel the need for an … (*6*) …. ruler and they are prepared to … (*7*) …. democracy overboard. In certain large democracies, the governments rule with a …. (*8*) …. majority. They often know what decisions would be beneficial in the long run, but they …. (*9*) ….. to take them lest they be unpopular. Their … (*10*) …. to carry the opposition and to rally people to a larger purpose makes them ineffective rulers.

1. (*a*) aimed (*b*) looked (*c*) arrived (*d*) deferred (*e*) formulated
2. (*a*) drown (*b*) result (*c*) exist (*d*) indulge (*e*) entangle
3. (*a*) useful (*b*) preferable (*c*) acceptable (*d*) susceptible (*e*) questionable
4. (*a*) dishonest (*b*) common (*c*) selfish (*d*) indecisive (*e*) trustworthy
5. (*a*) decision (*b*) query (*c*) mistake (*d*) presentation (*e*) submission
6. (*a*) indecisive (*b*) energetic (*c*) eccentric (*d*) optimistic (*e*) autocratic
7. (*a*) regard (*b*) accept (*c*) throw (*d*) cultivate (*e*) sacrifice
8. (*a*) derisive (*b*) slender (*c*) vast (*d*) winning (*e*) substantial
9. (*a*) like (*b*) fail (*c*) prefer (*d*) decide (*e*) hesitate
10. (*a*) desire (*b*) skill (*c*) apathy (*d*) inability (*e*) indifference

Passage 16

'Quit India' came not from the lips but the aching heart of millions. In this open rebellion, the Indian … (*1*) … reached its climax. The British were not only … (*2*) … by it, but also were obliged to quite unilaterally. The importance of Quit India can be … (*3*) … from Lord Linlithgow's statement, "I am engaged here, in meeting by far the most … (*4*) … rebellion since that of 1857, the gravity and extent of which we have so far … (*5*) … from the world for reasons of military security". Still more significant was Churchill's gloomy disclosure to the King Emperor that "the idea of .. (*6*) … of power had become an admitted … (*7*) … in the minds of British party leaders" although his public statements were diametrically opposite. The… (*8*) … created by Quit India made the British … (*9*) … that they could no longer keep India in … (*10*)…

1. (*a*) patriotism (*b*) freedom (*c*) liberation (*d*) revolution (*e*) leadership
2. (*a*) attacked (*b*) inspired (*c*) enfeebled (*d*) threatened (*e*) impressed
3. (*a*) established (*b*) diffused (*c*) gauged (*d*) determined (*e*) invigorated
4. (*a*) trivial (*b*) serious (*c*) auspicious (*d*) praiseworthy (*e*) magnificent
5. (*a*) elicited (*b*) excluded (*c*) abstained (*d*) concealed (*e*) prevented
6. (*a*) transfer (*b*) seizure (*c*) grabbing (*d*) retainment (*e*) enhancement
7. (*a*) fantasy (*b*) tactics (*c*) occurrence (*d*) inevitability (*e*) disillusionment

8. (a) anarchy (b) violence
(c) taboos (d) exigencies
(e) vengeance

9. (a) anxious (b) realise
(c) imagine (d) pretend
(e) apprehend

10. (a) exile (b) power
(c) bondage (d) suspense
(e) obeyance

Passage 17

Why is it that the CRP, BSF and the Army give a better account of themselves than the state police? It is the structure of the state police that needs to be looked … (1) …. In a district or city, where there is a separate police force, a majority of the policemen are …. (2) …. in police stations. The police station staff is often over-extended and no …. (3) …. Is available at that level. It is the state force that has to be called …. (4) ….. But it takes time to … (5)…. forces. If the law and order situation … (6) …. Simultaneously at many places, there is manpower …. (7) ….. Thus once rioting breaks …. (8) …. it takes time to bring it under control so that there is a time …. (9) …. Between the first incident and the appearance of the adequate force to … (10) …. The situation. The public hue and cry about the delayed arrival of the police force is not unjustified.

1. (a) through (b) on
(c) into (d) at

2. (a) detained (b) deployed
(c) deputed (d) employed

3. (a) reserve (b) force
(c) company (d) squad

4. (a) upon (b) up
(c) at (d) on

5. (a) move (b) arrange
(c) mobilise (d) prepare

6. (a) worsens (b) proliferates
(c) degenerates (d) aggravates

7. (a) default (b) shortage
(c) shortcoming (d) failure

8. (a) away (b) in
(c) off (d) out

9. (a) lag (b) interval
(c) delay (d) difference

10. (a) control (b) restrain
(c) step (d) prevent

To change the hearts of the …. (1) …. in such a way as to make it …. (2)…. for them to indulge in these …. (3) …. Without changing the …. (4) …. Of the governments that rule over …. (5) …. is an impossibility. When …. (6) ….. reaches that point it will …. (7) …. To be human; it will become an …. (8) … of supermen of gods and it will no …. (9) … need the guidance of …. (10) …. of the type of Mahatma Gandhi.

1. (a) crowd (b) groups
(c) men (d) mobs

2. (a) impossible (b) likely
(c) unlikely (d) possible

3. (a) cruelties (b) misdeeds
(c) brutalities (d) actions

4. (a) stands (b) hearts
(c) minds (d) decisions

5. (a) you (b) us
(c) them (d) people

6. (a) life (b) nature
(c) humanity (d) behaviour

7. (a) continue (b) cease
(c) start (d) begin

8. (a) committee (b) government
(c) organisation (d) body

9. (a) less (b) further
(c) more (d) longer

10. (a) men (b) man
(c) god (d) gods

ANSWERS

Test – 1

1. deteriorating
2. significant
3. gap
4. resources
5. budget
6. obviously
7. expenditure
8. Under
9. curtail
10. scope

Test – 2

1. fall
2. personal
3. consist
4. addressed
5. editor
6. writings
7. content
8. lucid
9. objective
10. malice

Test – 3

1. deeply
2. blinded
3. eldest
4. retracted
5. like
6. over
7. pretention
8. attractive
9. glorified
10. importance

Test – 4

1. is
2. last
3. make
4. to
5. had
6. but
7. of
8. listen
9. know
10. gone

Test – 5

1. usually
2. better
3. do
4. talented
5. willing
6. hire
7. protest
8. unreasonably
9. hike
10. lower

Test – 6

1. declared
2. strange
3. at
4. over
5. eats
6. deaf
7. red
8. to
9. efficacy
10. effectively

Test – 7

1. whether
2. couples
3. method
4. undertaking
5. always
6. groups
7. approved
8. care
9. occasionally
10. executed

Test – 8

1. war
2. setback
3. defence
4. learnt
5. for
6. atmosphere
7. decision
8. disaster
9. grow
10. community

Test – 9

1. where
2. at
3. beautiful
4. As
5. happy
6. were
7. eyes
8. tattered
9. denied
10. chosen

Test – 10

1. expected
2. completely
3. my
4. moment
5. right
6. its
7. pleasantly
8. had
9. stood
10. solid

Test – 11

1. probably
2. rest
3. ignore
4. prolong
5. sleep
6. mount
7. desist
8. thief
9. viewing
10. toll

Test – 12

1. reduced
2. committed
3. evoke
4. fighting
5. demand
6. boon
7. blatant
8. because
9. demoralise
10. blunt

Test – 13

1. progress
2. towards
3. discharge
4. will be
5. their
6. how

Test – 14

1. in
2. beings
3. bad
4. of
5. nor
6. shower
7. little
8. through
9. on
10. of

Test – 15

1. arrived
2. result
3. preferable
4. selfish
5. decision
6. autocratic
7. sacrifice
8. substantial

9. **hesitate**
10. **inability**

Test – 16

1. **patriotism**
2. **threatened**
3. **gauged**
4. **serious**
5. **elicited**
6. **transfer**
7. **inevitability**
8. **anarchy**
9. **realise**
10. **bondage**

Test – 17

1. **into**
2. **deployed**
3. **reserve**
4. **upon**
5. **mobilise**
6. **worsens**
7. **shortage**
8. **out**
9. **lag**
10. **control**

Test – 18

1. **men**
2. **possible**
3. **actions**
4. **stands**
5. **them**
6. **humanity**
7. **cease**
8. **organisation**
9. **longer**
10. **men**

CHAPTER 36 SENTENCE COMPLETION

Sentence Completion demands precise understanding of the words and their usage. It is possible only and only if one is well-versed with copious vocabulary, its understanding and usage as various forms of speech.

Choose the correct option:

TEST – 1

1. George Bernard Shaw said that the contemporary social values could be flippant and ________ at some times
   (*a*) important (*b*) profound
   (*c*) inane (*d*) riveting
   (*e*) absurd
2. ________ the general had been told by the field staff that continuing warfare would be ________ to his soldiers, he insisted on deploying more battle tanks
   (*a*) Although ….. detrimental
   (*b*) Because ….. instrumental
   (*c*) Although ….. formidable
   (*d*) Because ….. immediate
   (*e*) Because ….. incremental
3. The Senate warned the Prime Minister that if he did not accept their advice, the differences between the Legislative and the Executive arms of the Government would be ________
   (*a*) eliminated (*b*) eroded
   (*c*) exacerbated (*d*) exemplified
   (*e*) exasperated
4. Most journalistic writing could do with ________ of paragraphs to make the prose more ________
   (*a*) suppression ….. legible
   (*b*) removal ….. argumentative
   (*c*) simplification ….. abstruse
   (*d*) deletion ….. succinct
   (*e*) exemplification ….. incoherent
5. Varun has been accused of murdering his wife, and though he was never ________, he never recovered from the shame and the scandal
   (*a*) charged (*b*) booked
   (*c*) indicted (*d*) acquitted
6. The earthquake warning and the fragility of our houses make us certain that disaster is ________
   (*a*) available (*b*) imminent
   (*c*) forthcoming (*d*) catastrophic
7. The television serials are characterized by an ________ story line and ________ plots and sub-plots
   (*a*) unending ….. convoluted
   (*b*) infantile ….. simple
   (*c*) uniform ….. emotional
   (*d*) extempore ….. routine
   (*e*) erratic ….. forthcoming
8. The ________ transformation of the former Soviet Union of Russia as it was popularly known, remains one of the biggest stories of the decade
   (*a*) smooth (*b*) singular
   (*c*) tumultuous (*d*) prophetic
   (*e*) traumatic
9. If mankind has to survive for long, it must ________ and deliberately renounce the fruits of ________ and whirling technology
   (*a*) willfully ….. wild
   (*b*) honestly ….. responsible
   (*c*) sincerely ….. labor
   (*d*) effectively ….. sliding
   (*e*) knowingly ….. impending

10. Although similar to moth in many ways, butterflies may be __________ moths by the beauty of their wings

(*a*) akin to (*b*) in comparison with

(*c*) listed as (*d*) distinguished from

(*e*) equal to the

11. Renu saw no __________ in the exercises that had been set for her and worked at them in a __________ manner

(*a*) reason ….. organized

(*b*) point ….. desultory

(*c*) strength ….. careless

(*d*) meaning ….. doubtful

(*e*) sense ….. painful

12. Mother Teresa was __________ about her achievements and unwilling to __________ them before anyone

(*a*) modest ….. discuss

(*b*) proud ….. promote

(*c*) unsure ….. reveal

(*d*) ignorant ….. eulogise

(*e*) immodest ….. play

13. Martin Luther strived for justice and fought against attempts to __________ ignorant peasants in the medieval ages

(*a*) influence

(*b*) change

(*c*) exploit

(*d*) corrupt

(*e*) discharge

14. The instruction manual that came with the computer is not masterpiece of __________ prose because its instructions are so __________ that we still do not know how to set up the computer

(*a*) clear ….. garbled

(*b*) valuable ….. intelligent

(*c*) worthless …. clear

(*d*) confused ….. varied

(*e*) worth ….. muffled

15. The strike will not end because both the management and the workers are __________

(*a*) insipid (*b*) intransigent

(*c*) intricate (*d*) inexplicable

(*e*) saddened

TEST – 2

1. Book lovers who think of Gone With The Wind as a Southern romance miss its underlying __________ important

(*a*) democratic (*b*) novelistic

(*c*) thematic (*d*) exceptional

(*e*) argumentative

2. The professors at Lucknow University have a permanent __________ on their positions and do not have to look for more secure __________ in

(*a*) fixture ….. jobs

(*b*) tenure ….. employment

(*c*) security ….. means

(*d*) right ….. employees

(*e*) eye ….. seats

3. It is very difficult to overcome the __________ of habits such as smoking and taking drugs

(*a*) stupidity (*b*) tenacity

(*c*) insecurity (*d*) insistence

4. The __________ and __________ happenings in many talk shows annoy many viewers

(*a*) aggravating ….. irritating

(*b*) trite ….. predictable

(*c*) happy ….. playful

(*d*) dramatic ….. eventful

(*e*) ranting ….. jocular

5. Slander and libel laws stand as a protection of a person's reputation against the __________ dissemination of falsehood

(*a*) inferential (*b*) inevitable

(*c*) incontestable (*d*) irresponsible

(*e*) semblance

6. Most of the settlements that grew up near the logging camps were __________ affairs, thrown together in a hurry because people needed to live on the job
(*a*) nomadic (*b*) protracted
(*c*) unobtrusive (*d*) rickety
(*e*) uncouth

7. Pipes are not a safer __________ to cigarettes because, though pipe smokers do not inhale, they are still __________ higher rates of lung and mouth cancers than nonsmokers
(*a*) preference ….. free from
(*b*) answer ….. responsible for
(*c*) alternative ….. subject to
(*d*) rejoinder ….. involved in
(*e*) offer ….. involved with

8. Author Anjali Agarwal was a rare phenomenon, a single woman who maintained and even __________ a respectable reputation while earning a living by her pen
(*a*) impaired (*b*) decimated
(*c*) avoided (*d*) enhanced
(*e*) evacuated

9. Because Sherry is so __________, we can never predict what he will do at any moment
(*a*) old (*b*) immature
(*c*) capricious (*d*) lazy
(*e*) dormant

10. Paper money is merely a representation of wealth; therefore unlike gold or any other precious metal, it has no __________ value
(*a*) financial (*b*) fiscal
(*c*) inveterate (*d*) intrinsic

11. The law cannot and should not pardon such __________ act of violence
(*a*) a flagrant (*b*) a lavish
(*c*) a cautious (*d*) a dull
(*e*) condemn

12. As many students know, a / (an) __________ response, if skillfully worded, can imply at least a superficial __________ of knowledge about the subject
(*a*) ambiguous ….. veneer (*b*) garbled ….. ignorance
(*c*) inarticulate ….. piece (*d*) elegant ….. lack
(*e*) wrong ….. lack

13. There are too many __________ and not enough serious students
(*a*) dilettantes (*b*) hunky dory
(*c*) lay-men (*d*) novices
(*e*) nascent

14. Her parents were __________ when, despite losing the first three games, Sandy __________ to win the set by a 6 – 3 score
(*a*) surprised ….. failed
(*b*) relieved ….. came back
(*c*) puzzled ….. refused
(*d*) alarmed ….. attempted
(*e*) shocked ….. failed

15. The reviews of Deepak Chopra's latest literary work were enjoyed by many of his readers, but the subjects dreaded Mr. Chopra's comments; he was scathing, bitter, irritating and never __________
(*a*) logical (*b*) constructive
(*c*) uncharitable (*d*) controversial
(*e*) acidic

TEST – 3

1. In poor and under developed countries, trucks are the only means of getting about town, the public transportation being virtually __________
(*a*) indecipherable (*b*) ubiquitous
(*c*) inadequate (*d*) nonexistent
(*e*) negligent

2. Given the __________ state of published evidence, we cannot conclude here that exposure to low-level microwave energy is either hazardous or safe
(*a*) inconclusive (*b*) indulging
(*c*) descriptive (*d*) immaculate
(*e*) descriptive

3. The clothes Nafees, the famous designer, designs for men are conservative, but her fashions for women are more __________

(a) subtle (b) flamboyant

(c) tasteful (d) expensive

(e) open

4. The equipments that were being used in the survey were __________, and because of the below-zero temperature, it was feared they would freeze and __________

(a) icy ..... capsize

(b) frosty ..... shide

(c) fragile ..... shatter

(d) frozen ..... dehydrate

(e) useless ..... capsize

5. Because of its tendency to __________, most Indian art is __________ Japanese art, where symbols have been minimized and meaning has been conveyed by using the method of the merest suggestion

(a) imitate ..... superior to

(b) understate ..... reminiscent of

(c) overdraw ..... similar to

(d) sentimentalise ..... supportive of

(e) synergise ..... half

6. Irony can sometimes become a mode of escape; to laugh at the terrors of life is, in a way, to __________ them

(a) bolster (b) approve

(c) evade (d) foster

(e) avail

7. The negotiations for the deal were often surprisingly __________, deteriorating at times into a volley of accusations and counter-accusations

(a) insouciant

(b) sedate

(c) acrimonious

(d) propitious

(e) adequate

8. A __________ student is unlikely to gain admission to a top level institution

(a) mediocre (b) putative

(c) mendacious (d) vicarious

(e) commerce

9. Either Japanese dishes are __________, or the one I had was a poor example

(a) delicious (b) overrated

(c) underestimated (d) unpopular

10. A person who is __________ is slow to adapt to a new way of life

(a) intractable (b) furious

(c) insolent (d) valiant

(e) constructive

11. Amit, who refrained from excesses in his personal life, differed markedly from Nirmal, who __________ notorious drinking bouts with his buddies

(a) minimised (b) indulged in

(c) shunned (d) compensated for

(e) specialised

12. The library incharge proposed a new schedule of fines for overdue books with the __________, if not the outright encouragement, of the faculty library committee

(a) cynosure (b) acquiescence

(c) scorn (d) applause

(e) management

13. Maya's remarks were so __________ that Arun could not decide which possible meaning was correct

(a) congruent (b) impalpable

(c) ambiguous (d) facetious

(e) incorrigible

14. By nature, Rahul was __________, given to striking up casual conversation with strangers he encountered at bus stops or check-out stands

(a) gregarious (b) reticent

(c) casual (d) diffident

(e) indulgent

15. In the absence of native predators, to stop the spread of their population, the imported goats __________ to such an inordinate degree that over grazed the country side and __________ the native vegetation

(*a*) propagated ..... cultivated

(*b*) suffered ..... abandoned

(*c*) thrived ..... threatened

(*d*) dwindled ..... eliminated

(*e*) outnumbered ..... cultivated

TEST – 4

1. Jayashree was habitually so docile and __________ that her friends could not understand her sudden __________ her employers

(*a*) accommodating ..... outburst against

(*b*) erratic ..... envy of

(*c*) truculent ..... virulence toward

(*d*) hasty ..... annoyance toward

(*e*) apologetic ..... hostile

2. That Amitabh's newest film is No. 1 at the box office this week is a testament to the star's __________ power and not the reviews, which were __________ at best

(*a*) increasing ..... matchless

(*b*) ongoing ..... glowing

(*c*) drawing ..... modest

(*d*) waning ..... indifferent

(*e*) super ..... dismal

3. The __________ background music hinted of the dangers threatening the movie's protagonist

(*a*) loud (*b*) sardonic

(*c*) ebullient (*d*) portentous

(*e*) icy

4. In order to ensure that she passed the exam, Asha __________ outlined every chapter of her course book, painstakingly noting the most obscure points

(*a*) carefully (*b*) playfully

(*c*) jokingly (*d*) superficially

(*e*) cursory

5. Mr. Murty hastily __________ all the warnings of his friends. And now, he finds it difficult to complete the task within its time and budget __________

(*a*) accepted ..... amounts

(*b*) ignored ..... amounts

(*c*) listened to ..... problems

(*d*) disregarded ..... constraints

(*e*) acknowledged ...... schedule

6. Lacking confidence in his skills in English, Pervez was __________ when called on to speak in class

(*a*) horrified (*b*) reticent

(*c*) impolite (*d*) sartorial

(*e*) shocked

7. The castle has been __________, we cannot even be sure exactly where it stood

(*a*) obliterated

(*b*) burned down

(*c*) ruined

(*d*) debilitated

(*e*) spoilt

8. Being a bit hesitant about __________ the man as the complete fraud he suspected him to be, Bill close to attack the weaker points of his theory, __________ them one by one

(*a*) denouncing ..... debunking

(*b*) ridiculing ..... proving

(*c*) castigating ..... strengthening

(*d*) mocking ..... destroying

(*e*) mistrusting ..... telling

9. The analysis of the coach's report was anything but __________, but those of us who have learned to discount such dismal __________ are optimistic

(*a*) pessimistic ..... confusion

(*b*) sanguinary ..... traps

(*c*) malicious ..... benefits

(*d*) pleasant ..... prognostications

(*e*) sugary ..... performances

10. Angered by the bureaucrat's ________ comments, the reporter insisted for a more ________ response

(a) redundant ….. repetitive

(b) tactless ….. immediate

(c) phlegmatic ….. lackadaisical

(d) circumlocutions ….. direct

(e) sarcastic ….. beneficial

11. Raman's ________ record collection included everything from Bach to rock

(a) effusive (b) rhapsodic

(c) eclectic (d) inherent

(e) refulgent

12. My grandparents were such ________ followers of the soap opera that they taped every episode

(a) avid (b) skillful

(c) flagrant (d) retentive

(e) hopeless

13. ________ the finger points of etiquette in high society, Devesh simply watched his host and followed his actions

(a) Arguing for (b) Unaware

(c) Ignorant of (d) Saddened by

(e) Looking at

14. This book of Covey creates a mood of ________, a (n) ________ of tranquility and calm

(a) somberness ….. atmosphere

(b) serenity ….. ambience

(c) melancholy ….. oasis

(d) formality ….. feeling

(e) tranquility ….. sea

15. Although they seem amateurish, primitive art has become more sophisticated as its creator becomes increasingly ________

(a) infamous

(b) aged

(c) jaded

(d) impotent

(e) ignorant

TEST – 5

1. Though a ________ of four campaigns, Bush had never seen such demonstrations

(a) watchman (b) veteran

(c) volunteer (d) witness

(e) follower

2. Carried away by the ________ effects of the experimental medication, the patients ________ his desire to continue as a subject for as long as he could

(a) supplementary ….. announced

(b) noxious ….. proclaimed

(c) frantic ….. repeated

(d) salutary ….. reiterated

(e) painful ….. undermined

3. Confused and ________, Hogwart fumbled to make sense of seemingly inconsistent statements, ________ the impatience of his listeners

(a) prostrate ….. listening to

(b) muddled ….. aware of

(c) philosophical ….. overlooking

(d) incoherent ….. oblivious to

(e) agitated ….. following

4. One of the most productive research ________ in contemporary neuroscience is devoted to ________ maps of human consciousness

(a) trajectories ….. reconnoitering

(b) designs ….. enunciating

(c) paradigms ….. elucidating

(d) declensions ….. obfuscating

(e) terminologies ….. newal

5. Today computers can ________ information from a number of sources, then automatically create a picture of their data manipulations

(a) collate (b) inculcate

(c) extrapolate (d) adjudicate

(e) execute

6. Just as a highway automobile accident leaves lasting marks of spilled coolant, __________ and oil, the smashing together of gigantic land masses releases and redirects fluids that flow, heat, __________ and deposit, leaving an enduring record of their presence

(*a*) petrol ..... disappear (*b*) fuel ..... evaporate
(*c*) paint ..... mark (*d*) anti-freeze ..... drip
(*e*) gases ..... electric

7. Although publicity has been __________ the film itself is intelligent, well-acted, handsomely produced and altogether __________

(*a*) tasteless ..... respectable
(*b*) extensive ..... moderate
(*c*) sophisticated ..... amateur
(*d*) perfect ..... spectacular
(*e*) useless ..... extraneous

8. Ironically, his normally __________ speaker became shy and __________ when confronted with the approbatory stares of her eager audience

(*a*) quiet ..... passionate
(*b*) garrulous ..... reticent
(*c*) dispassionate ..... passionate
(*d*) humble ..... supercilious
(*e*) soft ..... remorseful

9. Although the whole team acted in unison, each member was __________ for a (n) __________ of the production process

(*a*) reliable ..... source (*b*) responsible ..... element
(*c*) appointed ..... article (*d*) agreeable ..... felony
(*e*) agreeable ..... amount

10. The studies of the children were __________ and __________ was the result of it

(*a*) neglected ..... ignorance
(*b*) interrupted ..... incongruence
(*c*) off tracked ..... alienation
(*d*) instructed ..... genius
(*e*) ignored ..... negligence

11. The US has shown little __________ to go after the terrorist or help India get him

(*a*) inclination (*b*) urgency
(*c*) importance (*d*) alacrity
(*e*) endeavour

12. Most young children are highly conformist and will __________ a classmate whose appearance or manners are __________

(*a*) ostracise ..... conventional
(*b*) emulate ..... different
(*c*) shun ..... unusual
(*d*) deride ..... ordinary
(*e*) choose ..... deriding

13. The royal astrologers had to determine the most __________ date for the coronation ceremony

(*a*) propitious (*b*) sacred
(*c*) approximate (*d*) resplendent
(*e*) expected

14. A satirical poem is often venom-filled, __________ with scorn

(*a*) contained (*b*) filled up
(*c*) dripping (*d*) sardonic
(*e*) acidic

15. The __________ rites in the Black Magic cult were kept secret by the members and were never __________ to outsiders

(*a*) eclectic ..... delegated
(*b*) esoteric ..... divulged
(*c*) inscrutable ..... introduced
(*d*) elusive ..... prescribed
(*e*) exclusive ..... delegated

TEST – 6

1. Mr. Sharma, the critic was __________ enough to praise an author he detested

(*a*) magnanimous
(*b*) loquacious
(*c*) parsimonious
(*d*) surreptitious
(*e*) verbose

2. The goodwill of its clients is a genuine __________ asset for any business

(a) redolent (b) dismissive
(c) intangible (d) vigilant
(e) indolent

3. Though the law's __________ purpose is to curtail false advertising, its actual result is to __________ free speech

(a) erroneous ….. eschew
(b) ostensible ….. characterise
(c) illicit ….. reconcile
(d) recalcitrant ….. repress
(e) elusive ….. contain

4. __________ by her children, Radha Devi ultimately agreed to sell the house

(a) Decimated (b) Importuned
(c) Interpolated (d) Designated
(e) Apportioned

5. There was a __________ all about the palace, and the __________ concerned the security guards

(a) gift ….. distribution (b) silence ….. quiet
(c) tranquil ….. temper (d) feast ….. circulation
(e) commotion ….. quiet

6. Guilliano Benetton __________ a small neighbourhood business into a worldwide chain of stores

(a) renovated (b) infused
(c) parlayed (d) blessed
(e) decimated

7. The football team was once __________ by injuries; of 11 members, only 5 were fit to play

(a) decimated (b) isolated
(c) boycotted (d) heckled
(e) ambushed

8. Displeased with the __________ of the novel, the writer abandoned the idea of a film to be made on his writings

(a) adaptation (b) transfer
(c) transfusion (d) resurgence
(e) imagination

9. Because of his indecisive nature, Mr. Bhushan has a reputation for __________

(a) impartiality (b) tenacity
(c) prevarication (d) vacillation
(e) wandering

10. The conspirators met __________ in order to plot a (n) __________ against the oppressive governance of Julius Ceaser

(a) clandestinely ….. revolt
(b) wickedly ….. invocation
(c) craftily ….. referendum
(d) wittily ….. ban
(e) aggressively ….. crime

11. Vinay is much too __________ in his writings: he writes a paragraph when a sentence should suffice

(a) benevolent (b) skilled
(c) verbose (d) lucid
(e) crafted

12. With one __________ motion, Rakesh disarmed his assailant

(a) swift (b) ponderous
(c) superficial (d) boisterous
(e) levitations

13. The patient put up with the pain __________, neither wincing, nor whimpering when the surgeon made an incision to drain the pus of his abscess

(a) surprisingly (b) miserably
(c) logically (d) stoically
(e) enduringly

14. In relation to the interrelationships among a number of the Indo-Pakistani stalwarts treated in this compilation there is surely a certain amount of __________ in some of the essays presented here

(a) overlap
(b) indulgence
(c) exaggeration
(d) subjectivity
(e) complacency

15. Being an advocate of consumer rights, Sharad has spent much of his career trying to__________ the fraudulent claims of the businessmen of his home-town Patna

(*a*) reprove (*b*) debunk
(*c*) immortalise (*d*) import
(*e*) improve

TEST – 7

1. The report was __________ since the information on which it was based was erroneous, but it was brilliantly presented

(*a*) intelligent (*b*) wonderful
(*c*) worthless (*d*) verbose
(*e*) elegant

2. Pretending not to notice the toys in the shop, Aryan the small boy, acted in a __________ manner

(*a*) doleful (*b*) nonchalant
(*c*) convincing (*d*) ordinary
(*e*) indulgent

3. As several shops have __________ across the street, the old directory is__________

(*a*) relocated ….. obsolete
(*b*) reversed ….. enticing
(*c*) transferred ….. dismantled
(*d*) vanished ….. beautiful
(*e*) transferred ….. upto date

4. The __________ room in this apartment has not been used for a long time

(*a*) derelict (*b*) contractual
(*c*) bereaved (*d*) crowded
(*e*) interpolated

5. Salman the superstar, felt that certain incidents in his life were too __________ to be divulged

(*a*) intriguing
(*b*) derivative
(*c*) private
(*d*) rudimentary
(*e*) incremental

6. Distressed at an increasing __________ for books, Amrita, the famous novelist has turned to painting

(*a*) disregard (*b*) imagination
(*c*) panacea (*d*) prominence
(*e*) derelict

7. The bank is negotiating with Group 4 security to devise a system to provide __________ security to account holders

(*a*) accurate (*b*) prompt
(*c*) reliable (*d*) tough
(*e*) proactive

8. As the rate of life expectancy has increased due to tremendous progress in medical science, the over-population problem has__________

(*a*) aggravated (*b*) minimised
(*c*) distorted (*d*) encouraged
(*e*) unfazed

9. The story of the novel, *The Deranged*, is very __________. It shows how a man cut off from the world for a long time because a mad man

(*a*) absorbing (*b*) irritating
(*c*) controversial (*d*) useless
(*e*) derived

10. Although Agatha is arguably as good a mystery writer as Grundy, she is clearly far less __________ than Grundy, having written only six books in comparison to Grundy's sixty

(*a*) prolific (*b*) equivocal
(*c*) verbose (*d*) gripping
(*e*) astronomical

11. Being cynical, Ashish was reluctant to __________ the __________ of any kind act until he had ruled out all possible secret, uncharitable motives

(*a*) acknowledge ….. wisdom
(*b*) accept ….. unselfishness
(*c*) endure ….. loss
(*d*) witness ….. outcome
(*e*) uncover ….. outcome

12. A golden rule which should always be followed by an investor is that: never invest on sentiment or on a tip; look for stocks with promising __________ potential for growth

(*a*) fast (*b*) long-term
(*c*) higher (*d*) quick
(*e*) string

13. At the world's finest educational institutes, only students with the __________ to succeed are selected

(*a*) luck (*b*) drive
(*c*) resources (*d*) experience
(*e*) reliable

14. Jamshedji Tata, the founder of the Tata Group in India, knew that only dedication and __________ could ensure that the customer gets the very best

(*a*) commitment (*b*) money
(*c*) perception (*d*) supervision
(*e*) perception

15. Parveen fascinated the world with her beauty and her charm, and her life mixed public spectacle with private anguish; her tragic death __________ a flood of grief on every continent

(*a*) brought (*b*) prompted
(*c*) called (*d*) managed
(*e*) revoked

TEST – 8

1. As Shyam __________ retirement, he became more intelligent and active

(*a*) awarded (*b*) withdrew
(*c*) derived (*d*) neared
(*e*) recollected

2. As a steadfast __________ of our right to liberty time, Mishra had few __________

(*a*) defender ….. equals (*b*) opponent ….. enemies
(*c*) follower ….. enemies (*d*) advocate ….. defenders
(*e*) leader ….. unequals

3. A careful __________ of the premises revealed some useful clues

(*a*) autospy (*b*) incarceration
(*c*) examination (*d*) incineration
(*e*) emphases

4. Almost everyone was __________ by the cheerful, lively sound of the dance music

(*a*) revived (*b*) tired
(*c*) fired (*d*) bored
(*e*) withdrawn

5. The __________ of the air crash could have been avoided if more safety __________ had been taken

(*a*) sad event ….. preservers
(*b*) disasters ….. reservations
(*c*) scientist ….. measures
(*d*) tragedy ….. precautions
(*e*) aftermath ….. steps

6. They were disappointed to see the armed guards. It __________ them from doing anything disruptive

(*a*) inspired (*b*) prevented
(*c*) encouraged (*d*) irritated

7. The __________ politicians thought that all bureaucrats should be polite to him

(*a*) insolent (*b*) merciless
(*c*) civilised (*d*) docile
(*e*) amateur

8. The newspapers accused the politician of __________ for making promises he knew he could not __________

(*a*) revulsion ….. condone
(*b*) liability ….. improve
(*c*) impunity ….. reprise
(*d*) hypocrisy ….. fulfill
(*e*) forgery ….. overcome

9. Paula was __________ as a child, accepting without a question, everything she was told

(*a*) reticent (*b*) taciturn
(*c*) recalcitrant (*d*) credulous
(*e*) impatient

10. Cautioned by an anonymous phone call that an explosion was ________, the anti bomb police squad ________ the building immediately

(*a*) expected ….. filled

(*b*) ubiquitous ….. purged

(*c*) imminent ….. evacuated

(*d*) eminent ….. checked

(*e*) eminent ….. entered

11. The route between the two cities has always been known to wind its ________ way through steep mountain passes and coarse terrain

(*a*) easy (*b*) smooth

(*c*) elusive (*d*) tortuous

(*e*) trajectory

12. As there were not enough seats to ________ so many people at the venue of the address, they had to put up a big tent outside

(*a*) entertain (*b*) ascertain

(*c*) welcome (*d*) accommodate

13. This ________ old stone farmhouse has been a landmark since before the Independence

(*a*) fragile (*b*) sturdy

(*c*) ramshackle (*d*) flimsy

(*e*) rickety

14. The Chief Minister was ________ in his commitment to ________ the rise of crime and unemployment among his constituents

(*a*) uncertain ….. staunch (*b*) headstrong ….. stem

(*c*) faltering ….. identity (*d*) firm ….. uphold

(*e*) sturdy ….. counter

15. Sahil's clear ________ of the situation kept the meeting from breaking up into ________

(*a*) idea ….. humor

(*b*) notion ….. anarchy

(*c*) understanding ….. chaos

(*d*) wit …… tumult

(*e*) report ….. tumult

TEST – 9

1. In the past, the coach had always viewed Kapil's ideas with ________, but today he surprised the team by enthusiastically ________ his proposal

(*a*) disdain ….. rejecting

(*b*) empathy ….. considering

(*c*) objectivity ….. forgetting

(*d*) skepticism ….. adopting

(*e*) temerity ….. dissuading

2. The embarrassed host felt that the uninvited guest's rude comments and offensive jokes were ________

(*a*) steadfast (*b*) reactionary

(*c*) intolerable (*d*) partisan

(*e*) alarming

3. The celebrated trainer's ________ for helping his trainees to learn and achieve their goals was highly ________

(*a*) propensity ….. commendable

(*b*) distinction ….. enigmatic

(*c*) predilection ….. reprehensible

(*d*) derision ….. admissible

(*e*) decisiveness ….. desired

4. A few decades ago, ________ about gender roles made it somewhat difficult for a woman to study veterinary science, but today, female veterinarians are quite ________

(*a*) diatribes ….. affluent

(*b*) preconception ….. prevalent

(*c*) mindsets ….. poor

(*d*) lectures ….. negligent

(*e*) analysis ….. prominent

5. Greg Chappell was impressed by the ________ of the youthful Railways team

(*a*) ardor

(*b*) corpulence

(*c*) languor

(*d*) impertinence

(*e*) turbulence

6. In the plots of most Bollywood movies, there is/are a character/s with ________ intentions, whose primary role is to try to ________ the handsome hero in his noble mission

(*a*) furtive ….. abet

(*b*) malevolent ….. thwart

(*c*) unsavory ….. depict

(*d*) inappropriate ….. derail

(*e*) benevolent ….. obstruct

7. After a natural spring was discovered in the arid region, the family's old, abandoned farm was quickly ________ into a profitable private business, centered around a state-of-the-art well that ________ valuable water

(*a*) turned ….. expiates

(*b*) configured ….. manipulates

(*c*) transformed ….. emanates

(*d*) expropriated ….. eradicates

(*e*) transpired ….. exhaled

8. The young boy's ________ attempts to explain to his girlfriend why he had failed to show for their movie date did little to ease her ________ feelings

(*a*) impassioned ….. disconsolate

(*b*) veracious ….. vacuous

(*c*) unbelievable ….. gluttonous

(*d*) chronic ….. vicarious

(*e*) immeasurable ….. vacuous

9. For some politicians, charm is a mere ________ adopted to get votes and ________ criticism

(*a*) prerequisite ….. distort

(*b*) affectation ….. alleviate

(*c*) tool ….. inflict

(*d*) ruse ….. condone

(*e*) contender ….. earn

10. Although the food in the hostel mess was barely ________, after six months, the residents of the hostel had become ________ to it

(*a*) edible ….. immune

(*b*) edible ….. inured

(*c*) palatable ….. immune

(*d*) palatable ….. inured

(*e*) affordable ….. attuned

11. During childhood and adolescence, individuals acquire habits that are ________ to good health: which include having a sedentary lifestyle, frequently eating fatty and fast foods, and developing poor sleep patterns

(*a*) dangerous (*b*) harmful

(*c*) inimical (*d*) unsuitable

(*e*) despicable

12. Divyansh's disciplined and ________ study habits resulted in his earning numerous honors and awards which also included an academic scholarship

(*a*) painstaking (*b*) sedulous

(*c*) unhealthy (*d*) taciturn

(*e*) pecuniary

13. The old miser's ________ did him little good when he died without heir or friend, and all his precious money was ________ to the state

(*a*) frugality ….. escheated

(*b*) miserliness ….. ordained

(*c*) exemplariness ….. given

(*d*) frugality ….. ordained

(*e*) indulgence ….. willed

14. To most modern day readers, the language in Shakespeare's plays seems obscure and inaccessible, lacking the ________ of modern day authors

(*a*) elegance (*b*) impertinence

(*c*) perspicuity (*d*) perceptibility

(*e*) diligence

15. Unlike the other photojournalists, Rochelle despised the ________ nature of the newspaper business because she craved ________

(*a*) permutable ….. habitude

(*b*) flexible …. chaos

(*c*) permutable ….. chaos

(*d*) flexible ….. stable

(*e*) heinous ….. posterity

ANSWERS

TEST – 1

1. inane
2. Although ….. detrimental
3. exacerbated
4. deletion ….. succinct
5. indicted
6. imminent
7. unending ….. convoluted
8. tumultuous
9. willfully ….. wild
10. equal to the
11. point ….. desultory
12. modest ….. discuss
13. exploit
14. clear ….. garbled
15. intransigent

TEST –2

1. thematic
2. tenure ….. employment
3. tenacity
4. trite ….. predictable
5. irresponsible
6. rickety
7. alternative ….. subject to
8. enhanced
9. capricious
10. intrinsic
11. a flagrant
12. ambiguous ….. veneer
13. dilettantes
14. relieved ….. came back
15. constructive

TEST –3

1. nonexistent
2. inconclusive
3. flamboyant
4. fragile ….. shatter
5. understate ….. reminiscent of
6. evade
7. acrimonious
8. mediocre
9. overrated
10. intractable
11. indulged in
12. acquiescence
13. ambiguous
14. gregarious
15. thrived ….. threatened

TEST –4

1. accommodating ….. outburst against
2. drawing ….. modest
3. portentous
4. carefully
5. disregarded ….. constraints
6. horrified
7. obliterated
8. denouncing ….. debunking
9. pleasant ….. prognostications
10. circumlocutions ….. direct
11. effusive
12. avid
13. Ignorant of
14. sombreness…atmosphere
15. jaded

TEST –5

1. veteran
2. salutary ….. reiterated
3. incoherent ….. oblivious to
4. paradigms ….. elucidating
5. collate
6. fuel ….. evaporate
7. extensive…moderate
8. garrulous ….. reticent
9. responsible ….. element

10. neglected ….. ignorance
11. inclination
12. shun ….. unusual
13. propitious
14. dripping
15. esoteric ….. divulged

TEST – 6

1. magnanimous
2. intangible
3. recalcitrant ….. repress
4. Importuned
5. silence ….. quiet
6. parlayed
7. decimated
8. adaptation
9. vacillation
10. clandestinely ….. revolt
11. verbose
12. swift
13. stoically
14. overlap
15. debunk

TEST –7

1. worthless
2. nonchalant
3. relocated ….. obsolete
4. derelict
5. private
6. disregard
7. reliable
8. aggravated
9. absorbing
10. prolific
11. accept ….. unselfishness
12. long-term
13. drive
14. commitment
15. prompted

TEST –8

1. neared
2. defender ….. equals
3. examination
4. revived
5. tragedy ….. precautions
6. prevented
7. insolent
8. hypocrisy ….. fulfill
9. credulous
10. imminent ….. evacuated
11. tortuous
12. accommodate
13. sturdy
14. headstrong ….. stem
15. understanding ….. chaos

TEST – 9

1. skepticism ….. adopting
2. intolerable
3. propensity ….. commendable
4. preconception ….. prevalent
5. ardor
6. malevolent ….. thwart
7. transformed ….. emanates
8. impassioned ….. disconsolate
9. affectation ….. alleviate
10. palatable ….. inured
11. inimical
12. sedulous
13. frugality ….. escheated
14. perspicuity
15. permutable ….. habitude